Sixth Canadian Edition

Lifespan Development

Denise Boyd | Paul Johnson | Helen Bee

Houston Community
College System

 Pearson

EDITOR-IN CHIEF: Claudine O'Donnell
ACQUISITIONS EDITOR: Darcey Pepper
MARKETING MANAGER: Leigh-Anne Graham
PROGRAM MANAGER: Madhu Ranadive
PROJECT MANAGER: Andrea Falkenberg
DEVELOPMENTAL EDITOR: Patti Sayle
MEDIA DEVELOPER: Shalin Banjara
PRODUCTION SERVICES: Sonam Arora, Cenveo® Publisher Services

PERMISSIONS PROJECT MANAGER: Kathryn O'Handley
PHOTO PERMISSIONS RESEARCH: Integra Publishing Services, Inc.
TEXT PERMISSIONS RESEARCH: Integra Publishing Services, Inc.
COVER DESIGNER: Cenveo Publisher Services
COVER IMAGE: Debbie Margetts - Max Topchii/Shutterstock
VICE-PRESIDENT, CROSS MEDIA AND PUBLISHING SERVICES: Gary Bennett

Pearson Canada Inc., 26 Prince Andrew Place, Don Mills, Ontario M3C 2T8.

978-0-13-443131-4

4   18

Library and Archives Canada Cataloguing in Publication

Boyd, Denise Roberts, author
    Lifespan development / Denise Boyd, Paul Johnson, Helen
Bee. — Sixth Canadian edition.

Includes bibliographical references and index.
ISBN 978-0-13-443131-4 (hardback)

    1. Developmental psychology—Textbooks. I. Johnson,
Paul A., author II. Bee, Helen L., 1939-, author III. Title.

BF713.B437 2017   155   C2016-906290-2

This book is dedicated to my husband, Jerry Boyd, in appreciation for the help and support he provided to me while I was preparing the seventh US edition of *Lifespan Development*.

Denise Boyd

To my best friend, my wife, Bonnie Johnson, and the newest member of the family, our grandson, Merritt.

Paul Johnson

Brief Contents

List of Features

Contents

Preface

Welcome to the sixth Canadian edition of *Lifespan Development*. Since the first edition was published in 2003, we have seen some fairly dramatic shifts both in Canadian demographics and in the developmental sciences. For one, our population is aging. As well, our young adults are increasingly well educated and culturally diverse. They are also more likely to be single or living in common-law relationships than prior generations, and of those who are having children, most are having fewer. On the scientific front, current research is yielding a clearer understanding of the importance of prenatal and early childhood experiences on later development and, at the other end of the lifespan, new insights into the intricacies of the aging process and longevity.

Therefore, to help you prepare for the study of human development from the Canadian perspective, it is important to reflect for a moment on what an incredibly fascinating, complex, and indispensable field of study it is. To convey this richness, *Lifespan Development* includes teaching and learning features to help you manage and sort out all this information in an engaging and meaningful manner, whether in the context of a standard one- or two-semester course or a course offered via an alternate delivery format.

New Content Highlights

The sixth Canadian edition of *Lifespan Development* has been thoroughly revised and updated to reflect the latest research in the field of human development. Notably, one of the recognized strengths of this textbook continues to be its breadth of current Canadian content. To provide you with a brief overview, we offer some chapter-by-chapter highlights:

Chapter 1: Basic Concepts and Methods

- Renewed emphasis on the terms "human development," "developmentalists," and "developmental researchers/scientists"
- Revised discussions of the sections on "toys: more than just playthings," "the lifespan perspective," and "continuity and discontinuity in development"
- **NEW** updated section on "longitudinal designs" including reference to the Research Unit on Children's Psychosocial Maladjustment - Québec Study of Newborn Twins (QSNT), the Quebec Longitudinal Study of Kindergarten Children (QLSKC), and the Quebec Longitudinal Study of Child Development (QLSCD)

Chapter 2: Theories of Development

- Revised coverage of multifactorial inheritance
- **NEW** information on epigenome mapping, behavioural epigenetics, and human epigenomics
- Revised discussion of Erikson's psychosocial theory
- **NEW** Critical Thinking question on the implications of children growing up in refugee camps and their resettlement in destination countries, such as Canada

Chapter 3: Prenatal Development and Birth

- Updated research and revisions to assisted human reproduction, sex differences, teratogens, and epimutagenic teratogens
- **NEW** coverage of paternal influences on preconceptual and prenatal development
- Revised coverage of fetal assessment and treatment and drugs during labour and delivery

Chapter 4: Physical, Sensory, and Perceptual Development in Infancy

- Updated revision of behavioural states and sleep facts
- **NEW** research and discussion of colic
- Updated research and discussion of motor skills development
- Major update and revision on nutrition
- **NEW** information on the critical role of gut microbiota
- **NEW** discussion on circumcision
- **NEW** Critical Thinking question on considerations surrounding female and male circumcision
- Revised section on discriminating speech sounds

Chapter 5: Cognitive Development in Infancy

- **NEW** update and revision on measuring intelligence in infancy
- **NEW** update and revision on the effects of environmental risks on intelligence with an emphasis on water fluoridation
- Updated Canadian research on late talking

Chapter 6: Social and Personality Development in Infancy

- Major update and revision on adoption and development
- **NEW** discussion of Reactive Attachment Disorder (RAD)

- Major update and revision on the parents' attachment to the infant with an emphasis on fathers and attachment
- Updated research and discussion of attachment and mental health including Autism Spectrum Disorders
- Revised section on the long-term stability of temperament

Chapter 7: Physical and Cognitive Development in Early Childhood

- Updated research on the brain and nervous system
- Major update and revision on Adverse Childhood Experiences (ACEs)
- **NEW** Critical Thinking question on environmental adversity and outcomes
- Revised coverage of Theory of Mind
- **NEW** research and discussion of modern intelligence tests and intelligence

Chapter 8: Social and Personality Development in Early Childhood

- **NEW** update and revision of Canadian parenting styles
- Major update and revision of Canadian parenting and child discipline
- Major update and revision of ethnicity, socioeconomic status, and parenting styles
- Revised coverage of Canadian family structures
- Revised discussions of play, aggression, temperament, self-concept, and sex-typed behaviour
- Updated and revised coverage of the effects of childhood poverty in Canada

Chapter 9: Physical and Cognitive Development in Middle Childhood

- Major update and revision on the brain and nervous system
- **NEW** research and discussion of the human connectome
- Revised coverage of unintentional injuries in Canada
- Major update and discussion on healthy bodies and weights
- Revised discussion on the effects of video games
- Updated and revised coverage of schooling, literacy, and achievement
- Updated and revised discussion of Attention-Deficit/ Hyperactivity Disorder

Chapter 10: Social and Personality Development in Middle Childhood

- **NEW** updated and revised coverage of self-esteem and meaningfulness
- Updated and revised coverage of friendships
- Revised discussion of patterns of aggression and bullies and victims
- Revised discussion of after-school care in Canada
- Major update and discussion of media influences

Chapter 11: Physical and Cognitive Development in Adolescence

- Revised discussions of sexual development, body weight and fitness, sexual behaviour, and STIs
- Major update and discussion of sex education
- Revised discussion of teen pregnancy
- Updated and revised coverage of gay, lesbian, and bisexual adolescents
- Updated and revised coverage of sensation-seeking, substance use, and eating disorders in Canada
- Revised discussion of the First Nations youth suicide crisis in Canada
- **NEW** update and discussion of suicide
- Major update and revision of early school leavers in Canada

Chapter 12: Social and Personality Development in Adolescence

- **NEW** update and revision of moral development and conduct disorder
- **NEW** updates and revised discussion of youth criminal justice in Canada
- Revised discussions of friendships and peer groups
- Major update and discussion on gambling among Canadian youth

Chapter 13: Physical and Cognitive Development in Early Adulthood

- Revised discussions of primary and secondary aging, immune system functioning, STIs, and mental health
- **NEW** updates and revision of schizophrenia
- Major update and revision of alcohol and substance use disorders in Canada
- Major update and revision of post-secondary education in Canada
- **NEW** Critical Thinking question on why so many new graduates are overqualified and underemployed

Chapter 14: Social and Personality Development in Early Adulthood

- Revised discussions of emerging adulthood and theories of mate selection
- Updates and revised coverage of cohabiting heterosexual couples and gay and lesbian couples
- Major update and revision of parenthood
- Updates and revised coverage of the role of worker
- **NEW** update and revision of job satisfaction
- Major update and revision of strategies for coping with conflict between work and family life

Chapter 15: Physical and Cognitive Development in Middle Adulthood

- Revised discussions of the brain and nervous system, menopause and hormone therapy
- **NEW** update and revision of sexual activity
- Updates and revised coverage of cancer, cardiovascular disease, and alcohol use disorders
- Updates and revised discussion of health and cognitive functioning
- Revised discussions of memory function, memory types, and creativity

Chapter 16: Social and Personality Development in Middle Adulthood

- **NEW** updates and revised discussion of generativity
- Revised overview of Vaillant's revision of Erikson's theory and a life events approach to aging
- Revised discussion of the sandwich generation
- Updates and revised discussion of emptying the nest, failure-to-launch, and the revolving door
- Revised discussion of grandparenting in Canada
- Updates and revised discussion of continuity and change in personality
- Updates and revised discussion career changers and preparing for retirement
- Major update and revision on Canada's position on stem cell research

Chapter 17: Physical and Cognitive Development in Late Adulthood

- Updates and revised discussion of life expectancy and longevity, aging, and health
- **NEW** updates and revised overview of hearing and tinnitus
- Updates and revised discussion of sleeping and eating patterns

- Updates and revised discussion of sexual activity
- Updates and revised discussion of Alzheimer's disease and other dementias
- Major update and revision on institutionalization among Canadian seniors
- Updates and revised overview of depression prevention and interventions
- Updates and revised discussion of memory, wisdom, and creativity

Chapter 18: Social and Personality Development in Late Adulthood

- **NEW** updates and revision of Erikson's discussions on reminiscence and generativity
- Updates and revised discussion of retaining cognitive abilities
- **NEW** updates and revision of social engagement and age-friendly cities and communities
- **NEW** Critical Thinking question on the associations between religious faith and physical and mental health
- Updates and revised overview of social relationships
- Updates and revised discussion of elder abuse in Canada
- Updates and revised discussion of retirement in Canada

Chapter 19: Death, Dying, and Bereavement

- **NEW** updates and revised discussion of brain death
- **NEW** updates and revised overview of caregiver support
- Revised discussions of the meaning of death across the lifespan
- Revised discussion of Kübler-Ross's stages of dying
- Updates and revised overview of widowhood, mental health and pathological grief
- **NEW** update and revision of exercising one's right to die and medical assistance in dying considerations

Retained Learning Features

Learning Objectives. Numbered learning objectives remain a prominent feature in the sixth edition. These objectives are listed in the chapter opener, called out in the margin next to their corresponding sections, and repeated in the chapter summary to facilitate learner review. In addition, the Instructor's Resources correspond to these learning objectives, allowing the instructor to assess learners' knowledge of key educational objectives.

Test Yourself Before Going On. The end of each section contains brief quizzes with matching, true/false, fill-in-the-blank, and critical thinking questions for learners to test their knowledge before moving on to the next section. The answers to these questions are provided in the Instructor's Manual.

Chapter Outlines. Before you read each chapter, read over the outline at its beginning. More information will stick in your mind if you have an idea of what to expect.

Running Glossary. Key terms are defined when they are first used in the text.

Critical Thinking Boxes. These personalized questions encourage you to relate material in the book to your own experiences. They can also help you remember the information in the text, because linking new information to things you already know is a highly effective memory strategy.

Development in the Real World. Development in the Real World essays help you understand the complexities involved in trying to apply developmental theories and research to real-life problems. They offer practical advice on parenting, teaching, caregiving, and other aspects of daily life to which developmental psychology is relevant.

Policy Questions. Discussions of Canadian social policy issues relevant to human development appear at the end of each unit. These discussions will provide you with insight into how the findings of developmental research may be used to influence policy changes in the real world. They may also serve as starting points for group discussions and research projects.

Chapter Summaries. Looking over each chapter summary can help you assess how much of the information you remember.

Supplements for the Learner

REVEL™

Designed for the way today's students read, think, and learn, REVEL is a ground-breaking immersive learning experience. It's based on a simple premise: When students are engaged deeply, they learn more and get better results.

Built in collaboration with educators and students, REVEL brings course content to life with rich media and assessments—integrated directly within the authors' narrative—that provide opportunities for students to read, learn, and practise in one environment.

Learn more about REVEL

http://www.pearsonhighered.com/revel/

MyVirtualLife is an interactive resource with two simulations in one. The first simulation allows students to raise a child from birth to age 18 and to monitor the effects of their parenting decisions over time. The second simulation encourages students to make first-person decisions and to see the impact of those decisions on their simulated future selves over time. At each age, students are given feedback about the various milestones their child has attained; key stages of the child's development will include personalized feedback. As in real life, certain "unplanned" events might occur randomly. Students take a personality test at the beginning of the program, the results of which will have an impact on the temperament of their child or simulated future selves. Observational videos are included throughout the program to help illustrate key concepts. Critical thinking questions within the program help students to apply to their own virtual person what they are learning in class and in their textbook. These questions can be assigned or used as the basis for in-class discussion.

Supplements For The Instructor

Instructor Supplements. The following supplements are available for download from a password protected section of Pearson Canada's online catalogue (**http://catalogue .pearsoned.ca/**):

- *Instructor's Manual.* Each chapter includes the following sections:
  - Chapter Preview
  - Learning Goals
  - Extensive Teaching Notes, which include the Learning Objectives
  - Lecture Enhancement Notes
- *PowerPoint Presentations.* These slide presentations pair key points covered in the chapters with figures from the textbook to provoke effective classroom discussion.
- *Test Bank.* This test bank in Microsoft Word format includes almost 2000 questions, in multiple-choice, true/false, short answer, and essay formats, each with an answer justification, page references, difficulty rating, and type designation. This test bank is also available as a computerized testbank (see below).
- *Image Library.* The image library provides you with chapter figures and tables for insertion into PowerPoint presentations.

Computerized Test Bank. Pearson's computerized test banks allow instructors to filter and select questions to create quizzes, tests, or homework. Instructors can revise questions or add their own, and may be able to choose print or online options. These questions are also available in Microsoft Word format.

Learning Solutions Managers. Pearson's Learning Solutions Managers work with faculty and campus course designers to ensure that Pearson technology products, assessment tools, and online course materials are tailored to meet your specific needs. This highly qualified team is dedicated to helping schools take full advantage of a wide range of educational resources by assisting in the integration of a variety of instructional materials and media formats. Your local Pearson Canada sales representative can provide you with more details on this service program.

Acknowledgments

Preparing this sixth Canadian edition of *Lifespan Development* was made possible only with the considerable coordinated efforts of many people who each played a vital role in the process.

I am especially grateful to Bonnie Johnson for her feedback on the preliminary drafts.

I have also had the extra good fortune to be able to collaborate with the good-spirited people on the Pearson Canada team. As always, they continue to demonstrate the epitome of professionalism. In particular, I wish to express my fondest gratitude to Darcey Pepper, Acquisitions Editor; Madhu Ranadive, Program Manager; Patti Sayle, Developmental Editor, whose expert coordination kept us all moving forward with ease; Andrea Falkenberg, Project Manager; Lila Campbell, Copy Editor, whose exquisite editing has once again added a fine finish to the manuscript; and Lisa Gillis and Leigh-Anne Graham, Marketing Managers. Thank you all—you are a remarkable team to work with.

Paul Johnson

Chapter 1
Basic Concepts and Methods

Wayne R Bilenduke/The Image Bank/Getty Images

 Learning Objectives

THE SCIENTIFIC STUDY OF HUMAN DEVELOPMENT

1.1 Explain each of the philosophies that are important to the study of human development.

1.2 Describe the contributions of the early developmental scientists.

1.3 Describe the contributions made by Canadian developmental psychologists during the field's formative years.

CONTEMPORARY HUMAN DEVELOPMENT

1.4 Explain the importance of the lifespan perspective.

1.5 List and describe the three major domains of development.

1.6 Describe the interactionist model of development.

1.7 Explain developmental changes in terms of continuity and discontinuity.

RESEARCH DESIGNS AND METHODS

1.8 List and describe the research goals of scientists who study human development.

1.9 Describe how cross-sectional, longitudinal, and sequential research designs differ.

1.10 State the advantages and disadvantages of the research methods used in identifying relationships among variables.

1.11 Describe the importance of cross-cultural research to the study of human development.

1.12 Identify five ethical standards that developmental researchers must follow.

The last time you saw a relative or friend whom you hadn't seen for a while, perhaps you remarked on how much or how little the person had changed. About a child, you may have said: "Nella's grown so much since the last time I saw her." About an older person: "Uncle Orland looks much frailer than he did at Grandpa's birthday party." Such comments suggest that we humans are natural observers of the ways in which we change with age. But we also notice characteristics that seem to stay the same over time. We might say, "Nella's always been such a sweet child," or "Uncle Orland's mind is as sharp as ever." And our powers of observation don't stop with simple descriptions. We also come up with theories to explain our observations. Perhaps you've said something like, "Nella's parents are great role models. That's probably why she's so well behaved," or "Grandpa and Uncle Orland are both pretty sharp for their age. I guess they have good genes." As these observations suggest, the developmental pathway that each person follows results from the person's own characteristics, the choices that others make for her in childhood, and the decisions that she makes for herself in adulthood. These interactive effects are the driving theme behind *MyVirtualLife*, an online simulation that allows you to raise a child to adulthood and then adopt a first-person perspective to make decisions in adulthood.

In this introductory chapter, you will learn how the science of human development came into being. You will also learn about the key issues in the scientific study of development. When you finish reading the chapter, you will be acquainted with the research designs and methods used by developmentalists.

The Scientific Study of Human Development

human development

the scientific study of age-related changes in our bodies, behaviour, thinking, emotions, social relationships, and personalities

The field of **human development** is the scientific study of age-related changes in our bodies, behaviour, thinking, emotions, social relationships, and personalities. Long before the scientific method was used to study development, though, philosophers offered a variety of explanations for differences they observed in individuals of different ages. Their ideas continue to influence the field today, and many Western beliefs about human development are based on them.

Philosophical Roots

Learning Objective 1.1

Explain each of the philosophies that are important to the study of human development.

Early philosophers based their ideas about development on spiritual authorities, deductive logic, and general philosophical orientations. Typically, philosophers' inquiries into the nature of development focused on why babies, who appear to be quite similar, grow up to vary widely (see **Table 1.1**).

Table 1.1 Philosophical Approaches to Development

Historical Philosophical Perspective	Child's Inherent Predisposition	Parental Responsibility
Original Sin	Sinful	Intervene to correct
The Blank Slate	Neutral	Shape behaviours
Innate Goodness	Good	Nurture and protect

ORIGINAL SIN   For centuries, the Christian doctrine of *original sin*, often attributed to the 4th-century North African philosopher Augustine of Hippo, taught that all humans are born with a selfish and stubborn nature. To reduce the influence of this inborn tendency toward sinfulness, Augustine taught, humans must seek redemption by leading a disciplined life. Thus, from this perspective, parents facilitate the child's struggle to overcome an inborn tendency to act immorally by restraining and correcting the child's immoral tendencies.

THE BLANK SLATE   By contrast, the 17th-century English philosopher John Locke drew on a broad philosophical approach known as *empiricism* when he claimed that the mind of a child is a *blank slate*. Empiricism is the view that humans possess no innate tendencies and that all differences among humans are attributable to experience. As such, the blank slate view suggests that adults can mould children into whatever they want them to be. Therefore, differences among adults can be explained in terms of the differences in their childhood environments rather than as a result of a struggle to overcome their inborn tendencies, as the original sin view proposed.

INNATE GOODNESS   Different still was the *innate goodness* view proposed by the 18th-century Swiss philosopher Jean-Jacques Rousseau. He claimed that all human beings are naturally good and seek out experiences that help them grow (Ozmon, 2012). Rousseau believed that children need only nurturing and protection to reach their full potential. Good developmental outcomes happen when a child's environment refrains from interfering in her attempts to nurture her own development. In contrast, poor outcomes occur when a child experiences frustration in her efforts to express the innate goodness with which she was born.

The Study of Human Development Becomes a Science

The 19th century saw an explosion of interest in how scientific methods might be applied to questions that previously had been thought to belong within the domain of philosophy. In particular, by 1930, the field of psychology played a major role in establishing the foundations of modern human development and had begun to influence everyday child-rearing practices (see **Development in the Real World**).

DARWIN   Charles Darwin and other evolutionists believed they could understand the development of the human species by studying child development. Many, including Darwin, kept detailed records of their own children's early development (called *baby biographies*) in the hope of finding evidence to support the theory of evolution (Charlesworth, 1992; Dewsbury, 2009). These were the first organized studies of human development.

Darwin's theory of evolution is the source of many important ideas in modern human development. For example, the concept of developmental stages comes from evolutionary theory. However, critics of baby biographies claimed that studying children for the purpose of proving a theory might cause observers to misinterpret or ignore important information.

Critical Thinking

Other cultures and religions have different ways of viewing the process of development. How do the original sin, blank slate, and innate goodness views compare with your own beliefs? How do you think your own culture and religion have contributed to these beliefs?

Learning Objective 1.2

Describe the contributions of the early developmental scientists.

Development in the Real World

Toys: More Than Just Playthings

Today, a vital element of children's development is centred on playing with toys: "If play is the child's work, then toys are the child's tools" (Cuffaro et al., 2013, p. 138), and appropriately designed tools can help the child do their work well. Accordingly, it is important to design toys that promote the development of the child (Auerback, 2014). With this in mind, toy designers now create many toys to promote children's:

- *physical development*—improve muscle control and strength, and eye–hand coordination
- *cognitive development*—strengthen language and numeracy development; and foster imagination and reasoning ability through creative expression and problem-solving
- *emotional development*—act out inner thoughts, feelings, and fantasies in a safe manner; and learn persistence and mastery
- *social development*—learn to share and cooperate with others; and practise social-cultural values and rules through make-believe

The Developmental Science Behind Toys

In Canada, the Canadian Toy Testing Council (CTTC) (2016) is a non-profit, volunteer organization that has been conducting ongoing research since 1952 to ensure the value and appropriateness of toys. *Age-appropriate* means that a toy not only matches a child's capabilities, but also captures a child's interest. "No matter how promising, if a toy is not fun, it will gather dust" (CTTC, n.d.). While toy-testing research helps to identify what parents and children want in toys, it also considers safety, performance, appeal, usefulness, durability, age-appropriateness, and potential improvements.

At each stage of development a child faces new challenges and different risks (Canadian Child Care Federation [CCCF], 2009). The Canadian and international toy industries have developed age-appropriate recommendations so that toys challenge and stimulate based on a child's chronological age, as well as physical size, skill level, temperament, and maturity. Toys that are beneath or beyond a child's capabilities may discourage the child from developing further interests.

The research that goes into toy design and manufacture is represented by the information contained on toy product labels. The label provides important guidelines for parents when making toy selections (Health Canada, 2015a). For instance, babies tend to put things into their mouths and are therefore at high risk for choking on small toys or toy parts; riding toys for toddlers pose a risk because children at this age do not have well-developed coordination and this can result in a child running into objects or falling down stairs; and projectile toys, although appealing to young children, can cause a variety of injuries, especially eye injuries (CCCF, 2009). As a result, toys are labelled with suitable age ranges—for example, "recommended for children from 18 months to 3 years." In many instances, toy labels may also carry a safety warning—for example, "Choking hazard: This toy contains small parts and is not intended for children under the age of 3." At any age, parental supervision is important, and toys meant for older children should be kept away from smaller children (CCCF, 2009).

(Photo: James Shaffer/PhotoEdit, Inc.)

LEGO means "play well." The "automatic building brick," invented by a Danish carpenter in 1949, can be considered an ideal toy in that it fosters development in the four key areas of growth: physical, cognitive, emotional, and social (Froberg Mortensen, 2012; Pisani, 2006; Toy Retailers Association, n.d.).

HALL G. Stanley Hall of Clark University wanted to find more objective ways to study development. He used questionnaires and interviews to study large numbers of children. His 1891 article titled "The Contents of Children's Minds on Entering School" represented the first scientific study of child development (White, 1992). Hall agreed with Darwin that the milestones of childhood were similar to those that had taken place in the development of the human species. He thought that developmentalists should identify **norms**, or average ages at which developmental milestones are reached. Norms, Hall said, could be used to learn about the evolution of the species as well as to track the development of individual children.

GESELL   Arnold Gesell's research suggested the existence of a genetically programmed sequential pattern of change (Gesell, 1925; Thelen & Adolph, 1992). Gesell used the term **maturation** to describe such a pattern of change. He thought that maturationally determined development occurred regardless of practice, training, or effort (Crain, 2011). For example, infants don't have to be taught how to walk—they begin to do so on their own once they reach a certain age. Because of his strong belief that maturation determines many important developmental changes, Gesell spent decades studying children and developing norms. He pioneered the use of movie cameras and one-way observation devices to study children's behaviour. His findings became the basis for many **norm-referenced tests** that are used today to determine whether individual children are developing at a rate that is similar to that of other children of the same age. Such tests help early educators find ways of helping young children whose development differs significantly from that of their peers.

PIAGET   One of the most influential theories in the history of human development is that of Swiss developmentalist Jean Piaget (Thomas, 2005). At the age of 10, Piaget published his first scientific article, on sparrows. By the time he was 21, he had published more than 20 scientific articles and had received a Ph.D. in natural science from the University of Geneva. In 1918, he went to Paris to work with Theodore Simon, the co-author of the Binet-Simon IQ test, at the school that Alfred Binet started. Piaget married his colleague and student Valentine Châtenay in 1923, and two years later Châtenay gave birth to their first child, Jacqueline. Piaget and Châtenay made detailed notes about Jacqueline's and their two other children's intellectual and language development.

Piaget became a professor at the University of Geneva in 1921 and spent the next six decades studying the development of logical thinking in children, until his death in 1980. His studies convinced him that logical thinking develops in four stages between birth and adolescence. At first, infants explore the world by using their senses and motor abilities. Through their actions, they develop basic concepts of time and space. Next, young children develop the ability to use symbols (primarily words) to think and communicate. Once they become proficient in the use of symbols, around age 6 or 7, children are ready to develop the skills needed for logical thinking. They spend the next five to six years using these skills to solve problems in the everyday world. Finally, in the teenage years, individuals develop the capacity to apply logic to both abstract and hypothetical problems.

The stages Piaget described and the theory he proposed to explain them became the foundation of modern cognitive-developmental psychology. Consequently, you will be reading a great deal more about them in later chapters.

A Brief History of the Roots of Developmental Psychology in Canada

The first psychology course in Canada was taught at Dalhousie University in 1838. Later, in the 1850s, prescientific psychology courses were offered at McGill University in Montreal and the University of Toronto. In these early years, psychology was not considered a distinct discipline but rather a branch of mental and moral philosophy (Wright & Myers, 1982, p. 86). It wasn't until 1889 that modern scientific psychology came to Canada. James M. Baldwin began lecturing in the fall of that year at the University of Toronto and set up a small psychophysical laboratory (Hoff, 1992).

norms

average ages at which developmental milestones are reached

maturation

the gradual unfolding of a genetically programmed sequential pattern of change

norm-referenced tests

standardized tests that compare an individual's score to the average score of same-aged peers

Learning Objective 1.3

Describe the contributions made by Canadian developmental psychologists during the field's formative years.

In the 1920s, funding became available for child-related and family research and, in 1925, William Blatz opened the St. George's School for Child Study in Toronto. Blatz is regarded as "the founder and leader of child study in Canada" (Wright & Myers, 1982, p. 86). St. George's was later renamed the Institute of Child Study and is now incorporated into the Ontario Institute for Studies in Education (OISE). Blatz is also known for his three years of work with the Dionne quintuplets, beginning in 1935.

Prior to World War II, there was no formal organization of practising psychologists in Canada. The impetus for creating a psychological organization came from the threat of war in Europe. In June 1938, psychologists were deliberating how they could provide their services for the war effort. From these discussions, E.A. Bott of the University of Toronto, George Humphrey of Queen's University, and Roy Liddy of the University of Western Ontario founded the Canadian Psychological Association (CPA) in 1939. Also present during these early discussions were Mary Wright and Mary Salter (later Ainsworth). Mary Wright, an assistant to Mary Salter Ainsworth, became the first woman president of the CPA in 1969 (Wright, 1993). Mary Salter Ainsworth, whose work on infant attachment you will encounter in the chapter Social and Personality Development in Infancy, established the theoretical and empirical framework through which developmentalists continue to view infant–caregiver relations.

(Photo: Courtesy of the Estate of Mary Salter Ainsworth)

In the early days of psychology, female psychologists seldom received credit for their accomplishments because of societal attitudes toward women. Mary Salter Ainsworth was one of the earliest female psychologists to be recognized in Canada; she was part of a group of psychologists actively involved in the creation of the Canadian Psychological Association.

Canadian psychologists were very active during World War II, especially in Britain, where they focused on personnel selection, recruitment and training methods, morale issues, and all aspects of public opinion. Important strides in early education came about at that time because of the major evacuation of children in Britain away from urban centres. Canadian psychologists were empowered to generate solutions to the ensuing child-care problems. William Blatz was called on to establish a nursery school teachers' training school in Birmingham (Ferguson, 1993). The school was staffed by Canadian child psychologists.

In 1981, the Developmental Section of the CPA was established. Its goal is to facilitate communication among developmental psychologists in terms of research, teaching, and practice. At present, the Developmental Section provides a forum for collaboration and the sharing of expertise for hundreds of members. It has recently added the Elinor Ames Award for the best student presentation in the Developmental Section at the annual CPA convention.

Test Yourself before going on

1. Write the name of the philosopher who is associated with each view of development.
   a. original sin _____
   b. blank slate _____
   c. innate goodness _____

2. What did each of these early researchers do?
   a. Charles Darwin _____
   b. G. Stanley Hall _____
   c. Arnold Gesell _____

3. Early in Canada, the discipline of psychology was originally studied as a branch of _____ and _____.

Critical Thinking

4. What are the child-rearing implications of the original sin, blank slate, and innate goodness views of development?

Contemporary Human Development

The study of human development has changed considerably since the early days. For one thing, the term *development* now encompasses the entire human lifespan rather than just childhood and adolescence. For another, developmentalists have come to understand that inborn characteristics interact with environmental factors in complex ways. Finally, the pioneers thought of change almost exclusively in terms of norms, whereas today's developmentalists view norms as representing only one way to measure change.

Learning Objective 1.4
Explain the importance of the lifespan perspective.

The Lifespan Perspective

Developmentalists once thought of adulthood as a long period of stability followed by a short span of unstable years immediately preceding death. This view has changed because, for one thing, it has become common for adults to go through major life changes, such as divorce and career shifts. There has also been a significant increase in life expectancy in the developed countries of the world. The life expectancy of a Canadian born in 1921 was 59 years for a male and 61 years for a female; a Canadian male born today can expect to live beyond age 80 and a female to 84 (Statistics Canada, 2012a; World Health Organization [WHO], 2015a). As a result, older adults now constitute a larger proportion of the population than ever before. In fact, adults over the age of 100 are one of the most rapidly growing age groups in Canada, and their numbers are expected to increase tenfold over the next 50 years (Statistics Canada, 2015a).

The changes outlined above have led to the adoption of a **lifespan perspective**, the idea that important changes occur during every period of development and that these changes must be interpreted in terms of the culture and context in which they occur (Baltes, Lindenberger, & Staudinger, 2006; Baltes, Reese, & Lipsitt, 1980). Thus, understanding change in adulthood has become just as important as understanding change in childhood, and input from many disciplines is necessary to fully explain human development.

lifespan perspective
the current view of developmentalists that changes happen throughout the entire human lifespan and that changes must be interpreted in light of the culture and context in which they occur; thus, interdisciplinary research is critical to understanding human development

Paul Baltes (1939–2006) of the Max Planck Institute in Germany was one of the early leaders in the development of a comprehensive theory of lifespan human development (Lerner, 2008). Baltes proposed that the capacity for positive change, or *plasticity*, in response to environmental demands is possible throughout the entire lifespan. One such area of positive adult development is the area of personal goals—older adults pursue their goals more intensely than younger adults (Riediger, Freund, & Baltes, 2005). Consequently, one of Baltes's most important contributions to the study of human development was his emphasis on the positive aspects of advanced age. He emphasized that, as human beings age, they adopt strategies that help them maximize gains and compensate for losses. For instance, one of Baltes's most often quoted examples is that of concert pianist Arthur Rubinstein, who was able to outperform much younger musicians well into his 80s (Cavanaugh & Whitbourne, 1999). Rubinstein reported that he maintained his performance capacity by carefully choosing pieces that he knew very well (maximizing gain) and by practising these pieces more frequently than he had at earlier ages (compensating for the physical losses associated with age). You will read more about Baltes's theories and his research later, in the chapters devoted to late adulthood.

The Domains of Development

Scientists who study age-related changes across the lifespan often use three broad categories, called *domains of development*, to classify these changes. The **physical domain** includes changes in the size, shape, and characteristics of the body. For example, developmentalists study the physiological processes associated with puberty. Also included in this domain are changes in how individuals sense and perceive the physical world, such as the gradual development of depth perception over the first year of life.

Learning Objective 1.5
List and describe the three major domains of development.

physical domain
changes in the size, shape, and characteristics of the body

cognitive domain

changes in thinking, memory, problem-solving, and other intellectual skills

social domain

changes in variables that are associated with the relationship of an individual to others

Changes in thinking, memory, problem-solving, and other intellectual skills are included in the **cognitive domain**. Researchers working in the cognitive domain study topics as diverse as how children learn to read and why some memory functions deteriorate in old age. They also examine the ways in which individual differences among children and adults, such as intelligence test scores, are related to other variables within this domain.

The **social domain** includes changes in variables that are associated with the relationship of an individual to others. For instance, studies of children's social skills fall into the social domain, as does research on individual differences in personality. Individuals' beliefs about themselves are also usually classified within the social domain.

Using domain classifications helps to organize discussions of human development. We need to remember, however, that the three domains do not function independently. For instance, when a girl goes through puberty, a change in the physical domain, her ability to think abstractly (cognitive domain) and her feelings about potential romantic partners (social domain) change as well. Likewise, older adults who suffer from Alzheimer's disease demonstrate obvious changes in the cognitive domain. But these changes both result from and lead to others in the remaining two domains. Physical changes in the brain are the most likely cause of Alzheimer's disease. The experience of living with the disease may cause a sufferer to be unable to maintain a regular eating and exercise schedule, thus leading to deterioration in physical health. Moreover, individuals who have such severe memory impairments often forget important things about the people with whom they associate, such as their names and relationships. As a result, social relationships are disrupted or may even be impossible.

Learning Objective 1.6

Describe the interactionist model of development.

interactionist model

the theory that development results from complex reciprocal interactions between multiple personal and environmental factors

The Interactionist Model of Development

Some early developmentalists thought of change as resulting from *either* forces outside the person *or* forces inside the person. The debate about the relative contributions of biological processes and experiential factors was known as the *nature–nurture controversy*. In struggling with this important issue, developmentalists have moved away from either/or toward more subtle ways of looking at both types of influences. Today, many theorists have adopted an **interactionist model** that considers development to be the result of complex reciprocal interactions between multiple personal and environmental factors.

A good example of research that exemplifies the interactionist model is implicit in the ideas of *vulnerability* and *resilience* (Willms, 2002a). According to this view, each child is born with certain vulnerabilities, such as a tendency toward emotional irritability or alcoholism, a physical abnormality, or an allergy. Each child is also born with some protective factors, such as high intelligence, good physical coordination, an easy temperament, or a lovely smile, that tend to make her more resilient in the face of stress. These vulnerabilities and protective factors then interact with the child's environment so that the same environment can have quite different effects, depending on the qualities the child brings to the interaction.

Studies of Canadian children have shown that a combination of a highly vulnerable child and a disadvantaged/unsupportive environment produces by far the most negative outcome (Schonert-Reichl, 1999; Willms, 2002b). Either of these two negative conditions alone—a vulnerable child or an adverse environment—can be overcome. A resilient child in a poor environment may do quite well, since she can find and take advantage of all the stimulation and opportunities available; similarly, a vulnerable child may do quite well in a highly supportive environment in which parents help the child overcome or cope with her vulnerabilities.

Continuity and Discontinuity in Development

Another key issue in the study of human development is the *continuity–discontinuity* issue. The question is whether age-related change is primarily a matter of amount or degree (the *continuity* side of the debate) or of changes in type or kind (the *discontinuity* side). For example, generally speaking, do you have more or fewer friends than you did when you were in elementary school? If you're like most other people, you have fewer. But do age differences in the number of friends people have really capture the difference between friendship in childhood and adulthood? Isn't it also true that friendship itself is different in childhood and adulthood? For example, mutual trust is a characteristic of adult and teen friendships but is not a feature of friendship prior to age 10 or so. Thus, the continuous aspect of friendship is that people of all ages have peer relationships, and the discontinuous aspect of friendship is that the characteristics of friendship itself vary by age.

Another way of approaching the continuity–discontinuity question is to think of it in terms of *quantitative* and *qualitative* change. A **quantitative change** is a change in amount. For instance, children get taller as they get older. Their heights increase, but the variable of height itself never changes. In other words, height changes continuously; it has continuity from one age to the next. Alternatively, a **qualitative change** is a change in characteristic, kind, or type. For example, puberty is a qualitative change. Prior to puberty, humans are incapable of reproduction. After puberty, they can reproduce. Therefore, postpubescent humans possess a characteristic that prepubescent humans do not: the capacity to reproduce. In other words, postpubescent and prepubescent humans are qualitatively different, and changes in the capacity to reproduce are discontinuous in nature. Later in life, another qualitative change in reproductive capacity occurs when women go through menopause and lose the capacity for reproduction.

Of particular significance is the idea that, if development consists only of additions (quantitative change), then the concept of **stages**, qualitatively distinct periods of development, is not needed to explain it. However, if development involves reorganization or the emergence of wholly new strategies, qualities, or skills (qualitative change), then the concept of stages may be useful. As you'll learn in the chapter Theories of Development, one of the important differences among theories of development is whether they assume development occurs in stages or is primarily continuous in nature. Nevertheless, most human development theorists and researchers would agree that age-related changes can be classified by using three categories: *universal changes*, *group-specific changes*, and *individual differences*.

UNIVERSAL CHANGES *Universal changes* are common to every individual in a species and are linked to specific ages. Some universal changes happen because we are all biological organisms subject to a genetically programmed maturing process. The infant who shifts from crawling to walking and the older adult whose skin becomes progressively more wrinkled are following a plan that is an intrinsic part of the physical body, most likely something in the genetic code itself.

However, some changes are universal because of shared experiences. A social clock also shapes all (or most) lives into shared patterns of change (Helson, Mitchell, & Moane, 1984). In each culture, the **social clock**, or a set of *age norms*, defines a sequence of normal life experiences, such as the right time to start school, the appropriate timing of marriage and child-bearing, and the expected time of retirement.

Age norms can lead to **ageism**—a set of prejudicial attitudes about older adults, analogous to sexism or racism. In Canadian society, for example, conventional wisdom states that job performance will decline in older adults. As a result, many older adults are denied opportunities to work because employers believe that they are less capable of carrying out required job functions than younger adults. Thus, social expectations about the appropriate age for retirement work together with ageism to

Learning Objective 1.7
Explain developmental changes in terms of continuity and discontinuity.

quantitative change
a change in amount

qualitative change
a change in kind or type

stages
qualitatively distinct periods of development

social clock
a set of age norms that defines a sequence of life experiences that is considered normal in a given culture and that all individuals in that culture are expected to follow

ageism
a prejudicial view of older adults that characterizes them in negative ways

The biological clock obviously constrains the social clock to some extent at least. Virtually every culture emphasizes family formation in early adulthood because that is, in fact, the optimal biological time for child-bearing.

shape individual lives, resulting in a pattern in which most people retire or significantly reduce their working hours in later adulthood.

GROUP-SPECIFIC CHANGES   *Group-specific changes* are shared by all individuals who grow up together in a particular group. One of the most important groups to which we all belong is our culture (Iverson, Larsen, & Solem, 2009). The term *culture* has no commonly agreed-on definition, but in essence it describes some system of meanings and customs, including values, attitudes, goals, laws, beliefs, moral guidelines, and physical artifacts of various kinds, such as tools, forms of dwellings, and the like. Culture shapes not only the development of individuals, but also our ideas about what normal development is.

For example, researchers interested in middle and late adulthood often study retirement: why people retire, how retirement affects their health, and so on. But their findings do not apply to older adults in developing nations, where adults gradually shift from one kind of work to another as they get older rather than giving up work altogether and entering a new phase of life called *retirement*. Consequently, developmentalists must be aware that retirement-related phenomena do not constitute universal changes. Instead, they represent developmental experiences that are culturally specific.

Equally important as a source of variation in life experience are historical forces, which affect each generation somewhat differently. Social scientists use the word **cohort** to describe a group of individuals who are born within some fairly narrow span of years and thus share the same historical experiences at the same time in their lives. Within any given culture, successive cohorts may have quite different life experiences.

cohort

a group of individuals who share the same historical experiences at the same times in their lives

INDIVIDUAL DIFFERENCES   *Individual differences* are changes resulting from unique, unshared events. One clearly unshared event in each person's life is conception; the combination of genes each individual receives at conception is unique. Thus, genetic differences—including physical characteristics, such as body type and hair colour, as well as genetic disorders—represent one category of individual differences. Characteristics influenced by both heredity and environment, such as intelligence and personality, constitute another class of individual differences.

Other individual differences are the result of the timing of a developmental event. Child development theorists have adopted the concept of a **critical period**. The idea is that there may be specific periods in development when an organism is especially sensitive to the presence (or absence) of some particular kind of experience.

critical period

a specific period in development when an organism is especially sensitive to the presence (or absence) of some particular kind of experience

Most knowledge about critical periods comes from animal research. For baby ducks, for instance, the first 15 hours or so after hatching is a critical period for the development of a following response. Newly hatched ducklings will follow any duck or any other moving object that happens to be around them at that critical time. If nothing is moving at that critical point, they don't develop any following response at all (Hess, 1972).

The broader concept of a sensitive period is more common in the study of human development. A **sensitive period** is a span of months or years during which a child may be particularly responsive to specific forms of experience or particularly influenced by their absence. For example, the period from 6 to 12 months of age may be a sensitive period for the formation of parent–infant attachment. The presence or absence of specific environmental factors during critical and sensitive periods early in life can produce changes, for better or worse, that last a lifetime (Tzschentke & Plagemann, 2006). This important concept will be further examined when we discuss *epigenetics* in later chapters.

In studies of adults, one important concept related to timing has been the idea of *on-time* and *off-time* events (Neugarten, 1979). The idea is that experiences occurring at the expected times for an individual's culture or cohort (on-time events) will pose fewer difficulties for her than will off-time experiences. Thus, being widowed at 30 is more likely to produce serious life disruption or forms of pathology, such as depression, than would being widowed at 70.

Atypical development is another kind of individual change. **Atypical development** refers to deviation from a typical, or "normal," developmental pathway. Examples of atypical development include exceptionalities, developmental delay, psychological disorders, and behavioural problems, such as extreme aggressiveness in children and compulsive gambling in adults.

Critical Thinking

From birth onward your cohort has encountered and will continue to encounter the same social events, moods, and trends at similar ages. What momentous historical events and shifts in society-wide attitudes and trends make your cohort group truly unique? How does your cohort react toward families, sex roles, marriage, careers, religion, social justice, and personal responsibility?

sensitive period

a span of months or years during which a child may be particularly responsive to specific forms of experience or particularly influenced by their absence

atypical development

development that deviates from the typical developmental pathway

Test Yourself before going on

1. The view that human development from conception to death should be studied from multiple disciplinary perspectives is known as the _____ _____.

2. Give an example from the text of development in each domain.

Domain	Example
Physical	
Cognitive	
Social	

3. How does the interactionist theory of development explain the nature–nurture controversy?

4. Developmental stages are often a feature in the theories of developmentalists who emphasize _____ changes.

5. Evidence of both continuity and discontinuity in development is based in _____ and _____ changes and individual differences resulting from the unique personal experiences.

Critical Thinking

6. How do your culture's behavioural expectations for 20-year-olds, 40-year-olds, and 60-year-olds differ?

Research Designs and Methods

The easiest way to understand research methods is to look at a specific question and the alternative ways we might answer it. For example, older adults frequently complain that they have more trouble remembering people's names than they did when they were younger. Suppose we wanted to find out whether memory really declines with age. How would we go about answering this question?

Learning Objective 1.8

List and describe the research goals of scientists who study human development.

Relating Goals to Methods

Developmental researchers use the scientific method to achieve four goals: to *describe*, *explain*, *predict*, and *influence* human development from conception to death.

DESCRIBE   To describe development is simply to state what happens. In attempting to describe human development, for example, we might make a descriptive statement such as "Older adults make more memory errors than young and middle-aged adults." To test whether this statement meets its descriptive goal, we could simply measure memory function in adults of various ages.

EXPLAIN   Explaining development involves telling why a particular event occurs. To generate explanations, developmentalists rely on *theories*—sets of statements that propose general principles of development. Students often say that they hate reading about theories; what they want are the facts. However, theories are important because they help us look at facts from different perspectives. For example, "Older adults make more memory mistakes because of changes in the brain that happen as people get older" is a statement that attempts to explain the fact of age-related memory decline from a biological perspective. Alternatively, we could explain memory decline from an experiential perspective and hypothesize that memory function declines with age because older adults don't get as much memory practice as younger adults do.

PREDICT   Useful theories produce predictions, or *hypotheses*, that researchers can test, such as "If changes in the brain cause declines in memory function, then elderly adults whose brains show the most change should also make the greatest number of memory errors." To test this hypothesis about changes in the brain and memory, we would have to measure some aspects of brain structure or function as well as memory function. Then we would have to find a way to relate one to the other. Alternatively, we could test the experiential explanation by comparing the memories of older adults who presumably get the most memory practice, such as those who are still working, with the memories of those who get less practice. If the working adults do better on tests of memory, the experiential perspective gains support. It is in this way that theories add tremendous depth to researchers' understanding of the facts of human development and provide them with information they can use to influence development.

INFLUENCE   Let's say, for example, that an older adult is diagnosed with a condition that can affect the brain, such as high blood pressure. If we know that brain function and memory are related, we can use tests of memory to make judgments about how much the person's medical condition may have already influenced his brain. At the same time, because we know that experience affects memory as well, we may be able to provide him with training that will help prevent memory problems from developing or worsening.

cross-sectional design

a research design in which groups of different ages are compared

longitudinal design

a research design in which people in a single group are studied at different times in their lives

Learning Objective 1.9

Describe how cross-sectional, longitudinal, and sequential research designs differ.

sequential design

a research design that combines cross-sectional and longitudinal examinations of development

Studying Age-Related Changes

When a researcher sets out to study age-related change, she has basically three choices: (1) Study different groups of people of different ages, using what is called a **cross-sectional design**; (2) study the same people over a period of time, using a **longitudinal design**; (3) combine cross-sectional and longitudinal designs in some fashion, in a **sequential design** (see **Table 1.2**).

CROSS-SECTIONAL DESIGNS   **Figure 1.1** is a good example of a cross-sectional study in which researchers examined age differences in people's ability to recognize facial expressions. As you can see, younger adults outperformed those who were older in identifying anger. If these findings fit the researchers' hypothesis, they might be tempted to conclude that the ability to identify anger in facial expressions declines with age. But we cannot say this conclusively based on the cross-sectional

Table 1.2 Research Designs

Design	Description	Advantages	Limitations
Cross-sectional	Participants of different ages studied at one time	Quick access to data about age differences	Ignores individual differences; cohort effects
Longitudinal	Participants in one group studied several times	Track developmental changes in individuals and groups	Time-consuming; findings may apply only to the group that is studied
Sequential	Study that combines both longitudinal and cross-sectional components	Cross-sectional and longitudinal data relevant to the same hypothesis	Time-consuming; different attrition rates across groups

Figure 1.1 In this cross-sectional study, researchers compared the ability to recognize various kinds of facial expressions across young adult, middle-aged adult, and older adult groups. This study is cross-sectional because it measured the same variable at the same time in people of different ages.

(**SOURCE:** "Age Differences in Recognition of Emotion in Lexical Stimuli and Facial Expressions," by Derek M. Isaacowitz et al., 2007, from *Psychology and Aging*, Vol. 22 (1), pp. 147–159, Mar. 2007, American Psychological Association. Reprinted by permission.)

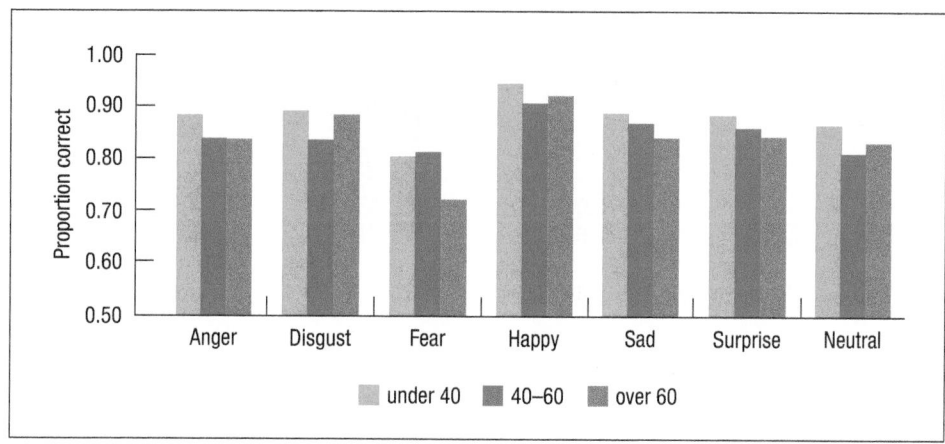

data, because these adults differ in both age and cohort. Thus, the age differences in this study might reflect, for example, differences in education and not changes linked to age or development. Influences of this kind lead to cohort effects, findings that are the result of historical factors to which one age group in a cross-sectional study has been exposed.

Furthermore, cross-sectional studies cannot tell us anything about sequences of change with age or about the consistency of individual behaviour over time, because each participant is tested only once. Still, cross-sectional research is very useful because it can be done relatively quickly and can reveal possible age differences or age changes.

LONGITUDINAL DESIGNS Longitudinal designs seem to solve the problems presented by cross-sectional designs, because they follow the same individuals over a period of time. Such studies allow researchers to look at sequences of change and at individual consistency or inconsistency over time. And because longitudinal studies compare performance by the same people at different ages, they get around some aspects of the cohort problem.

Some well-known Canadian longitudinal studies have been following groups of children into adulthood. One study is the ongoing Concordia Longitudinal Risk Project (CLRP) initiated by Alex Schwartzman (Professor Emeritus, Concordia University) and Jane Ledingham (formerly Concordia University, now University

Figure 1.2 These Concordia Longitudinal Risk Project data illustrate the "adverse birth circumstances" associated with mothers who had a history of aggression and withdrawal during their adolescence and early adulthood.

(**SOURCE:** Adapted from Serbin et al., 1998, from Table 1, p. 1251. Copyright © 1998 by the American Psychological Association. Adapted with permission.)

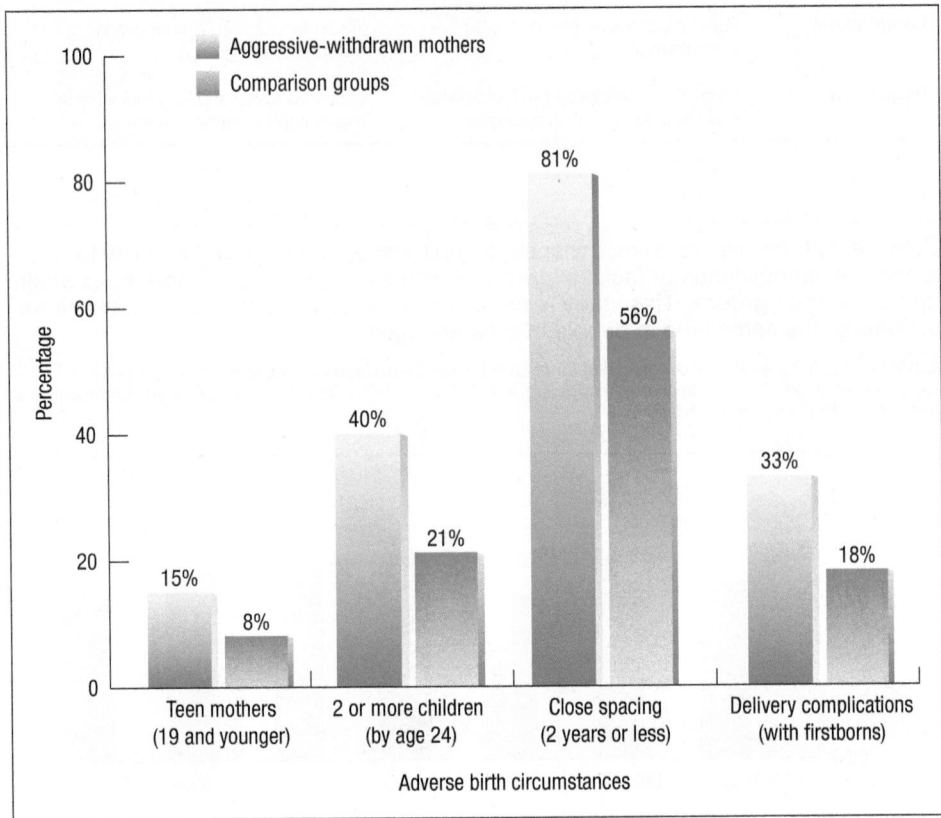

of Ottawa) in 1976. The CLRP researchers began studying children living in low-income, inner-city neighbourhoods who are currently in their 50s and are still part of the study that now includes their offspring (see **Figure 1.2**). More recent longitudinal studies fall under the purview of the Research Unit on Children's Psychosocial Maladjustment (GRIP) which is comprised of multidisciplinary, inter-university (Université de Montréal, Laval University, McGill University) researchers. The longitudinal studies in this cluster of research projects includes the Quebec Study of Newborn Twins (QSNT), the Quebec Longitudinal Study of Kindergarten Children (QLSKC), and the Quebec Longitudinal Study of Child Development (QLSCD). Such projects are extremely important in the study of human development, and you'll be reading more about them in later chapters.

Despite their importance, longitudinal designs have several drawbacks and limitations. They can be time-consuming, and it can be difficult to maintain contact with subjects over a long period of time. Some participants drop out; others die or move away.

Some longitudinal studies involve giving each participant the same tests over and over again. Over time, people learn how to take the tests. Such *practice effects* may distort the measurement of any underlying developmental changes. As a general rule, the healthiest and best educated are most likely to stick it out, and that fact biases the results, particularly if the study covers the final decades of life. Each succeeding set of test results comes from proportionately more and more healthy adults, which may make it look as if there is less change, or less decline, than actually exists.

Longitudinal studies don't completely get around the cohort problem either. Longitudinal studies that were conducted decades ago may offer useful information, but

Figure 1.3 This grid represents a design for a sequential study of memory function.

		Age at testing point 1	Age at testing point 2	Age at testing point 3
Group	A	30 to 35	35 to 40	40 to 45
	B	25 to 30	30 to 35	35 to 40

they may be contaminated by factors that are unique to that group of subjects at that particular time. Each generation experiences unique cultural, social, economic, and historical conditions that may not apply to subjects living at other times.

SEQUENTIAL DESIGNS   One way to avoid the shortcomings of both cross-sectional and longitudinal designs is to use a sequential design. To study our memory hypothesis using a sequential design, we would begin with at least two age groups. One group might include 25- to 30-year-olds, and the other 30- to 35-year-olds. We would then test each group several times over a number of years, as illustrated in **Figure 1.3**. In a sequential study, each testing point beyond the initial one allows researchers to make two types of comparisons. Age-group comparisons provide them with the same kind of information as a cross-sectional study. Comparison of each group with itself at an earlier testing point allows the researchers to collect longitudinal evidence at the same time.

Sequential designs also allow for comparisons of cohorts. For example, notice in Figure 1.3 that Group A is 30 to 35 years old at testing point 1, and Group B is 30 to 35 years old at testing point 2. Likewise, Group A is 35 to 40 at point 2, and their counterparts in Group B are this age at point 3. If same-age comparisons of the two groups reveal that their memory performance is different, researchers have evidence that, for some reason, the two cohorts differ. Conversely, if the groups perform similarly, investigators can conclude that their respective performances represent developmental characteristics rather than cohort effects. Moreover, if both groups demonstrate similar age-related patterns of change over time, researchers can conclude that the developmental pattern is not specific to any particular cohort. Finding the same developmental pattern in two cohorts provides researchers with stronger evidence than either cross-sectional or longitudinal data alone.

In 1994, Human Resources Development Canada (HRDC, 1996) embarked on an ambitious sequential design study: the National Longitudinal Survey of Children and Youth (NLSCY). The NLSCY measured how social and environmental factors influence a child's physical, social, intellectual, emotional, and behavioural development. Beginning with an initial base of almost 23 000 children aged 0 to 11 years, the NLSCY was designed to collect data every two years (one cycle) until the youngest of this cohort reaches age 25 in 2018. A new sample of newborns and 1-year-old children was added at each subsequent two-year cycle. The NLSCY had surveyed nearly 36 000 Canadians from birth to 25 years of age before it was halted after the eighth cycle in 2010 (Statistics Canada, 2008a; 2010a). Ongoing research results from this study will be examined in later chapters.

Identifying Relationships Between Variables

A researcher interested in age and memory ability must decide how to go about finding relationships between *variables*. To developmentalists, variables are characteristics that vary from person to person, such as physical size, intelligence, and personality. When two or more variables vary together, there is some kind of relationship between

Learning Objective 1.10

State the advantages and disadvantages of the research methods used in identifying relationships among variables.

them. The hypothesis that memory declines with age involves two variables, memory and age, and suggests a relationship between them. There are several ways of identifying such relationships.

case study

an in-depth examination of a single individual

naturalistic observation

the process of studying people in their normal environments

DESCRIPTIVE METHODS **Case studies** are in-depth examinations of single individuals. To test the hypothesis about memory and age, we could use a case study comparing one individual's scores on tests of memory in early and late adulthood. Such a study might tell us a great deal about the stability or instability of memory in the individual studied, but we wouldn't know if our findings applied to others.

Still, case studies are extremely useful in making decisions about individuals. For example, to find out whether a child is intellectually delayed, a psychologist would conduct an extensive case study involving tests, interviews of the child's parents, behavioural observations, and so on. Case studies are also frequently the basis of important hypotheses about unusual developmental events, such as head injuries and strokes.

When psychologists use **naturalistic observation** as a research method, they observe people in their normal environments. For instance, to find out more about memory in older adults, a researcher could observe them in their homes or workplaces. Such studies provide developmentalists with information about psychological processes in everyday contexts.

(Photo: ©Michael Doolittle/The Image Works)

Naturalistic observation refers to the research method used by psychologists who observe and study people in their natural, everyday environments.

The weakness of naturalistic observation, however, is *observer bias*. For example, if the researcher who is observing older adults is convinced that most of them have poor memories, he is likely to ignore any behaviour that goes against this view. Because of observer bias, naturalistic observation studies often use "blind" observers who don't know what the research is about. In most cases, for the sake of accuracy, researchers use two or more observers so that the observations of each observer can be checked against those of the other(s).

Like case studies, naturalistic observation studies are limited in the extent to which the results can be generalized. In addition, naturalistic observation studies are very time-consuming. They must be repeated in a variety of settings so that researchers can be sure people's behaviour reflects development and not the influences of a specific environment.

Have you ever been questioned about health practices, such as sun exposure, alcohol use, or sexual activity, or for whom you plan to vote in the next election? If so, then you have participated in a **survey**, a study in which researchers use interviews and/or questionnaires to collect data about attitudes, interests, values, and various kinds of behaviours. Surveys allow researchers to quickly gather information. They can also be used to track changes over time.

survey

a data collection method in which participants respond to questions

correlation

a relationship between two variables that can be expressed as a number ranging from –1.00 to +1.00

CORRELATIONS A **correlation** is a relationship between two variables that can be expressed as a number ranging from –1.00 to +1.00. A zero correlation indicates that there is no relationship between those variables. A positive correlation means that high scores on one variable are usually accompanied by high scores on the other. The closer a positive correlation is to +1.00, the stronger the relationship between the variables. Two variables that change in opposite directions result in a negative correlation, and the nearer the correlation is to –1.00, the more strongly the two variables are connected.

To understand positive and negative correlations, think about the relationship between temperature and the use of air conditioners and heaters here in Canada. Temperature and air conditioner use are positively correlated. As the temperature climbs, the number of air conditioners in use goes up. Conversely, temperature and heater use are negatively correlated. As the temperature decreases, the number of heaters in use goes up.

If we wanted to know whether age is related to memory, we could use a correlational study. All that would be necessary would be to administer memory tests to adults of varying ages and calculate the numerical correlation between test scores and ages. If there is a positive correlation between age and the number of memory errors people make—if older people make more errors—then we could say that our hypothesis has been supported. Conversely, if there is a negative correlation—if older people make fewer errors—then we would conclude that our hypothesis has not been supported.

Useful as they are, though, correlations have a major limitation: They do not indicate *causal* relationships. For example, even a high positive correlation between memory errors and age would tell us only that memory performance and age are connected in some way. It wouldn't tell us what caused the connection. It might be that younger adults understand the test instructions better. In order to identify a cause, we have to carry out experiments.

EXPERIMENTS   An **experiment** is a study that tests a causal hypothesis. Suppose, for example, that we think age differences in memory are caused by older adults' failure to use memory techniques, such as repeating a list mentally to remember it. We could test this hypothesis by providing memory technique training to one group of older adults and no training to another group. If the trained adults got higher scores on memory tests than they did before training and the no-training group showed no change, then we could claim support for our hypothesis.

A key feature of an experiment is that participants are assigned *randomly* to one of two or more groups. In other words, chance determines which group each participant is placed in. When participants are randomly assigned to groups, the groups have equal amounts of variation with respect to characteristics such as intelligence, personality traits, height, weight, health status, and so on. Consequently, none of these variables can affect the outcome of the experiment.

Participants in the **experimental group** receive the treatment the experimenter thinks will produce a particular effect, while those in the **control group** receive either no special treatment or a neutral treatment. The presumed causal element in the experiment is called the **independent variable**, and the characteristic or behaviour that the independent variable is expected to affect is called the **dependent variable**.

In a memory technique training experiment like the one suggested above, the group that receives the memory training is the experimental group, and the one that receives no instruction is the control group. Memory-technique training is the variable that we, the experimenters, think will cause differences in memory function, so it is the independent variable. Performance on memory tests is the variable we are using to measure the effect of the memory technique training. Thus, performance on memory tests is the dependent variable.

Experiments are essential for understanding many aspects of development. But two special problems in studying child or adult development limit the use of experiments. First, many of the questions researchers want to answer have to do with the effects of particular unpleasant or stressful experiences on individuals—abuse, prenatal influences of alcohol or tobacco, low birth weight, poverty, unemployment, widowhood. For obvious ethical reasons, researchers cannot manipulate these variables—they cannot ask one set of pregnant women to have two alcoholic drinks a day and others to have none. To study the effects of such experiences, they must rely on nonexperimental methods, such as correlations.

Second, the independent variable that developmentalists are often most interested in is age itself, and researchers cannot assign participants randomly to age groups. They can compare 4-year-olds and 6-year-olds in their approach to some particular task, such as searching for a lost object, but the children differ in a host

experiment
a study that tests a causal hypothesis

experimental group
the group in an experiment that receives the treatment the experimenter thinks will produce a particular effect

control group
the group in an experiment that receives either no special treatment or a neutral treatment

independent variable
the presumed causal element in an experiment

dependent variable
the characteristic or behaviour that is expected to be affected by the independent variable

of ways other than their ages. Older children have had more and different experiences. Thus, unlike psychologists studying other aspects of behaviour, developmental psychologists cannot systematically manipulate many of the variables they are most interested in.

To get around this problem, researchers can use any one of a series of strategies, sometimes called *quasi-experiments*, in which they compare groups without assigning the participants randomly. Cross-sectional studies are a form of quasi-experiment. So are studies in which researchers compare members of naturally occurring groups that differ in some dimension of interest, such as children whose parents choose to place them in daycare programs and children whose parents keep them at home. Such comparisons have built-in problems, because groups that differ in one way are likely to differ in other ways as well. Parents who send their children to private schools may be wealthier and have different social values compared with parents who keep their children in public schools. If researchers find that the two groups of children differ on a specific academic measure, is it because they have spent their school days in different environments or because of other differences in their families? Researchers can make such comparisons a bit easier if they select comparison groups that are matched on those variables the researchers think might matter, such as income, marital status, or religion. But a quasi-experiment, by its very nature, will always yield more ambiguous results than will a fully controlled experiment.

Learning Objective 1.11

Describe the importance of cross-cultural research to the study of human development.

ethnography

a detailed description of a single culture or context

Cross-Cultural Research

Increasingly common in human development are studies comparing cultures or contexts, a task that researchers approach in several ways. For example, an **ethnography** is a detailed description of a single culture or context based on extensive observation. Often the observer lives in the culture or context for a period of time, perhaps as long as several years. Each ethnographic study is intended to stand alone, although it is sometimes possible to combine information from several different studies to see whether similar developmental patterns exist in the various cultures or contexts.

Alternatively, investigators may attempt to compare two or more cultures directly, by testing children or adults in each of the cultures with the same or comparable measures. Sometimes this involves comparing groups from different countries. Sometimes the comparisons are between subcultures within the same country; for example, increasingly common in Canada is research involving comparisons of children or adults living in different ethnic groups or communities, such as First Nations, South Asian, Caribbean, and European Canadians (Statistics Canada, 2016a). This is important in Canada because in 1971 our nation was the first in the world to make multiculturalism an official policy; the *Canadian Multicultural Act* was passed in 1988 (Canadian Heritage, 2001).

Cross-cultural research is important to developmental psychology for two reasons. First, developmentalists want to identify universal changes, that is, predictable events or processes experienced by individuals in all cultures. Developmentalists don't want to make a general statement about development—such as "Memory declines with age"—if the phenomenon in question happens only in certain cultures. Without cross-cultural research, it is impossible to know whether studies involving North Americans and Europeans apply to people in other parts of the world.

Second, one of the goals of developmentalists is to produce findings that can be used to improve people's lives. Cross-cultural research is critical to this goal as well. For example, developmentalists know that children in cultures that emphasize the community more than the individual are more cooperative than children in more individualistic cultures. However, to use this information to help all children learn to cooperate, they need to know exactly how adults in such cultures teach their children to be cooperative. Cross-cultural research helps developmentalists identify specific variables that explain cultural differences.

Research Ethics

Research ethics are the guidelines researchers follow to protect the rights of animals used in research and humans who participate in studies. Ethical guidelines are published by professional organizations such as the CPA. Universities, private foundations, and government agencies have review committees that make sure all research sponsored by their institutions is ethical. Guidelines for animal research include the requirement that animals be protected from unnecessary pain and suffering. Further, researchers must demonstrate that the potential benefits of their studies to either human or animal populations will be greater than any potential harm to animal subjects.

The CPA (2000, 2015) has published ethical standards for practitioners, researchers, and scientists that include the following principles: respect for the dignity of persons, responsible caring, integrity in relationships, and responsibility to society. These ethical standards address the following major concerns.

PROTECTION FROM HARM It is unethical to do research that may cause participants permanent physical or psychological harm. Moreover, if the possibility of temporary harm exists, then researchers must provide participants with some way of repairing the damage. For example, if the study will remind subjects of unpleasant experiences, such as rape, then researchers must provide them with counselling.

INFORMED CONSENT Researchers must inform participants of any possible harm and have them sign a consent form stating that they are aware of the risks of participating. In order for children to participate in studies, their parents must give permission after the researcher has informed them of possible risks. Children older than 7 must also give their own consent. If the research takes place in a school or daycare centre, an administrator representing the institution must consent. In addition, both children and adults have the right to discontinue participation in a study at any time. Researchers are obligated to explain this right to children in language they can understand.

CONFIDENTIALITY Participants have the right to confidentiality. Researchers must keep the identities of participants confidential and must report their data in such a way that no particular piece of information can be associated with any specific participant. The exception to confidentiality is when children reveal to researchers that they have been abused in any way by an adult. In Canada, citizens are required to report suspected cases of child abuse.

KNOWLEDGE OF RESULTS Participants, their parents, and the administrators of institutions in which research takes place have a right to a written summary of a study's results.

DECEPTION In some cases, deception is deemed necessary in situations where a participant's expectations of the outcomes can influence how they behave in a research study, thus biasing the results. If deception is a necessary part of a study, it must not cause participants distress and they have the right to be informed about the deception as soon as the study is over.

Learning Objective 1.12
Identify five ethical standards that developmental researchers must follow.

research ethics
the guidelines researchers follow to protect the rights of animals used in research and humans who participate in studies

Test Yourself before going on

1. The goals of developmental science are to _____, _____, _____, and _____ age-related changes.

2. Match each research method with its definition.

   _____ (a) Manipulated independent variable

   _____ (b) Behaviour observed in controlled settings

   _____ (c) In-depth study of a single individual

   _____ (d) Behaviour observed in typical settings

   _____ (e) Mathematical relationship between two variables

      (i) Correlation

      (ii) Case study

      (iii) Experiment

      (iv) Laboratory observation

      (v) Naturalistic observation

3. List the advantages and disadvantages of each method of studying age-related changes.

Method	Advantages	Disadvantages
Cross-sectional		
Longitudinal		
Sequential		

4. What are two reasons for the importance of cross-cultural research?

   (a) _____

   (b) _____

5. Explain what researchers must do to meet ethical standards in each area listed in the table.

Issue	What Researchers Must Do
Protection from Harm	
Informed Consent	
Confidentiality	
Knowledge of Results	
Deception	

Summary

The Scientific Study of Human Development

1.1 **Explain each of the philosophies that are important to the study of human development.**

- The philosophical concepts of original sin, the blank slate, and innate goodness have influenced Western ideas about human development.

1.2 **Describe the contributions of the early developmental scientists.**

- Darwin studied child development to gain insight into evolution. Hall published the first scientific study of children and introduced the concept of norms. Gesell studied the maturational milestones of development. Piaget identified stages of cognitive development.

1.3 **Describe the contributions made by Canadian developmental psychologists during the field's formative years.**

- William Blatz founded a school for child studies in the 1920s. Mary Salter (Ainsworth) became a leading authority on attachment behaviour. Canadian psychologists helped solve child-care problems in Britain during WWII.

Contemporary Human Development

1.4 **Explain the importance of the lifespan perspective.**

- Information from a variety of disciplines is needed to understand development. Today's developmentalists recognize that change happens throughout life, development occurs in multiple contexts, and plasticity exists throughout the lifespan.

1.5 List and describe the three major domains of development.

- Theorists and researchers group age-related changes into three broad categories: the physical, cognitive, and social domains.

1.6 Describe the interactionist model of development.

- Developmentalists believe that every developmental change is a product of both nature and nurture.

1.7 Explain developmental changes in terms of continuity and discontinuity.

- Development is a matter of changes both in degree (continuity) and kind (discontinuity). Contemporary developmental psychologists study three kinds of changes: universal, group-specific, and individual.

Research Designs and Methods

1.8 List and describe the research goals of scientists who study human development.

- Developmental psychologists use scientific methods to describe, explain, predict, and influence (when appropriate) age-related changes and individual differences.

1.9 Describe how cross-sectional, longitudinal, and sequential research designs differ.

- In cross-sectional studies, separate age groups are each tested once. In longitudinal designs, the same individuals are tested repeatedly over time. Sequential designs combine cross-sectional and longitudinal comparisons.

1.10 State the advantages and disadvantages of the research methods used in identifying relationships among variables.

- Case studies and naturalistic observation provide a great deal of important information about individuals, but it usually isn't generalizable to other individuals or groups. Correlational studies measure relationships between variables and can be done quickly. The information they yield is more generalizable than that from case studies or naturalistic observation. To test causal hypotheses, it is necessary to use experimental designs in which participants are assigned randomly to experimental or control groups.

1.11 Describe the importance of cross-cultural research to the study of human development.

- Cross-cultural research helps developmentalists identify universal factors and cultural variables that affect development.

1.12 Identify five ethical standards that developmental researchers must follow.

- Ethical principles governing psychological research include protection from harm, informed consent, confidentiality, knowledge of results, and protection from deception.

Chapter 2
Theories of Development

Pavel L Photo and Video/Shutterstock

 Learning Objectives

BIOLOGY AND EVOLUTIONARY THEORIES

2.1 Describe the structure and function of genes.

2.2 Describe the ways genes influence development.

2.3 Describe how epigenetic mechanisms regulate genes and development.

2.4 Describe how evolutionary theories explain individual differences.

2.5 Describe how biology and evolutionary theories contribute to our understanding of disease processes and interventions.

PSYCHOANALYTIC THEORIES

2.6 Summarize the main ideas of Freud's psychosexual theory.

2.7 Identify the conflict associated with each of Erikson's psychosocial stages.

2.8 Describe the basic concepts of humanistic theory.

LEARNING THEORIES

2.9 Explain how classical conditioning occurs.

2.10 Explain the process of operant conditioning.

COGNITIVE THEORIES

2.11 Describe how cognitive development progresses, according to Piaget.

2.12 Describe information-processing theory processes.

2.13 Describe how Vygotsky's concepts of scaffolding and zone of proximal development influence cognitive development.

2.14 Describe Bandura's concepts of modelling, reciprocal determinism, and self-efficacy.

SYSTEMS THEORY

2.15 Describe how contexts influence development from Bronfenbrenner's bioecological perspective.

2.16 Explain why ecobiodevelopmentalists endorse early intervention strategies.

COMPARING THEORIES

2.17 Determine the distinguishing characteristics of human development theories.

Every parent knows it's a constant struggle to keep babies from putting everything in their mouths. Whether it's an attractive toy or a dead insect they encounter while crawling across the living room floor, infants seem to be driven to use their mouths to explore. Have you ever wondered why? An inborn drive to explore the environment may be responsible, or babies may find the physical sensation of mouthing an object highly pleasurable. Perhaps babies use their mouths more than toddlers and preschoolers do because they don't yet have the ability to fully control other parts of their bodies. Clearly, there are many possible explanations.

As you learned in the chapter on Basic Concepts and Methods, developmental psychologists use theories to formulate *hypotheses*, or testable answers, to such "why" questions. For this reason, you'll be reading about theories in every chapter of this book. To help you make sense of all these theories, this chapter will introduce you to five influential families of theories that have quite different ways of answering questions about development—the biological and evolutionary theories; the three "families" of psychological theories; and systems theory, which aims to integrate multiple theoretical perspectives into a comprehensive theory of human development.

Biology and Evolutionary Theories

A knowledge of biological processes is an important foundation for understanding evolutionary theories of development. Both *genetic* and *epigenetic* factors interact with environmental variables to shape our level of health and well-being across the lifespan. We are just beginning to understand how epigenetic processes integrate nature and nurture—*epigenetics* is positioned to profoundly change the way we think of human development.

Learning Objective 2.1

Describe the structure and function of genes.

chromosomes

strings of genetic material in
the nuclei of cells

deoxyribonucleic acid (DNA)

a chemical material that makes
up chromosomes and genes

genes

complex chemical units
of a chromosome that
control or influence
inherited traits

Evolutionary theories propose that the genetic and physiological processes that underlie human behaviour changed gradually over time through genetic mutation and natural selection. Evolution is used to explain cognitive and, by extension, social and cultural behaviour.

Genetics

Our body cells' nuclei contain 23 pairs of **chromosomes** that are made up of an astounding almost 2.0 metres of finely coiled **deoxyribonucleic acid (DNA)** molecules (see **Figure 2.1**). Each chromosome contains segments, called **genes**, each of which

Figure 2.1 Four essential organic compounds, A – adenine, T – thymine, C – cytosine, and G – guanine, are organized into base pairs that form the double helix structure of DNA. The human genome—the DNA contained in the nuclei of our body cells—comprises 23 pairs of chromosomes containing strands of genes. DNA is wound around histones (a protein material) to form what resembles beads on a string, called the *nucleosomes*. Deposited along the nucleosomes are epigenetic markers, which, collectively, make up the epigenome. Epigenetic markers control gene expression by either opening up or tightly packing nucleosome clusters (chromatin). When chromatin is loosely spaced, gene expression is possible, but when chromatin is tightly packed, genes are silenced. Thus, when epigenetic markers signal chromatin to open, genes (segments of DNA base pairs) are ready to be transcribed and translated into proteins.

(**SOURCE:** Nevid, J.S., Greene, B., Johnson, P.A, & Taylor, S. (2009), *Essentials of Abnormal Psychology*, 2nd Canadian Edition. Toronto, ON: Pearson Education Canada. Figure 2.1. Artwork copyright © Alexandra Enns. Printed with permission.)

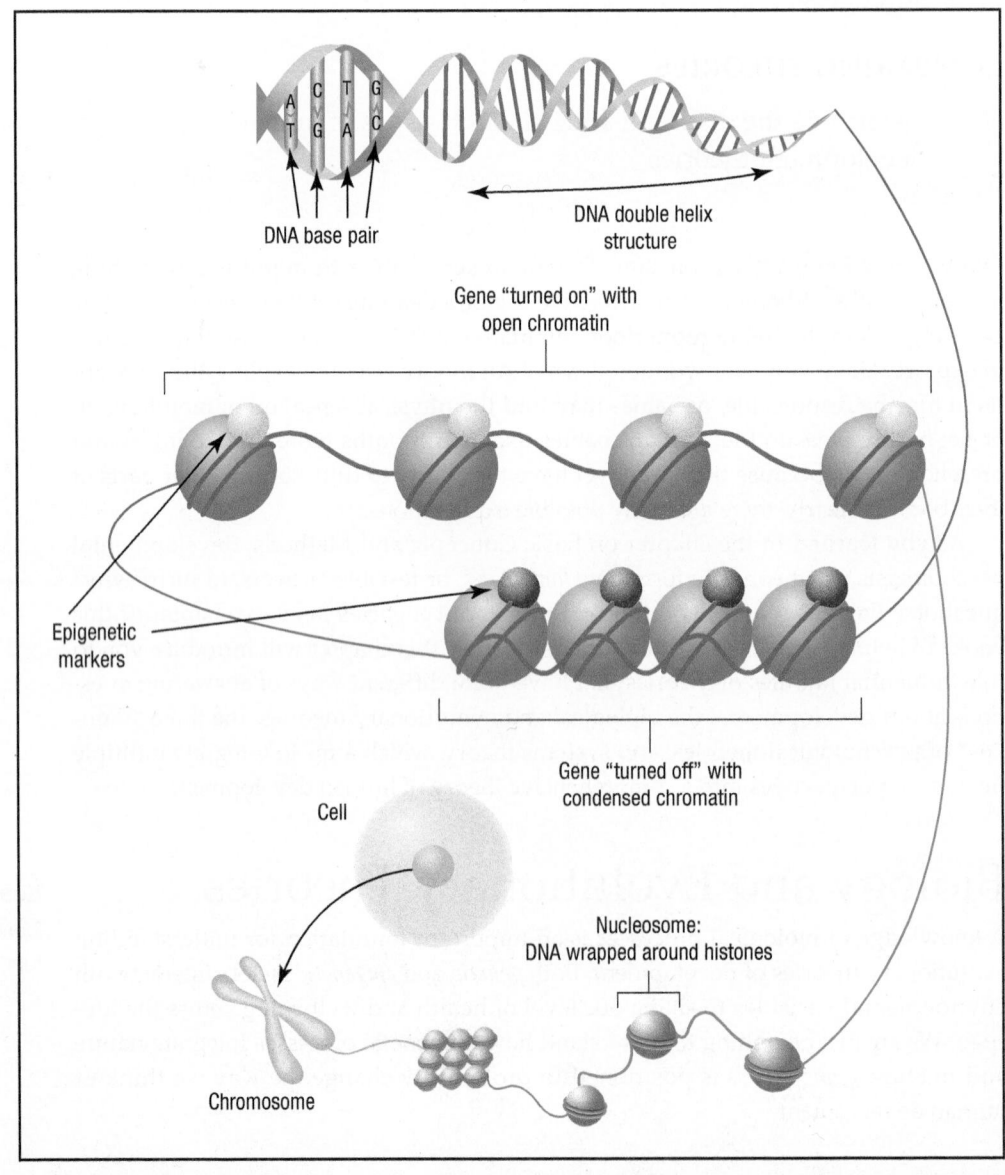

influences a particular trait or developmental pattern. A gene controlling a specific characteristic always appears in the same place (the *locus*) on the same chromosome in every individual of the same species. For example, the locus of the gene that determines whether a person's blood is type A, B, or O is on chromosome 9. A **genome** is all the DNA an organism possesses. To appreciate the complexity of the genome, consider that, in humans, each of our 46 chromosomes contains anywhere from a few dozen to a couple of thousand genes. In all, each human body cell nucleus possesses an estimated 20 000 **protein-coding genes** (Uhlén et al., 2015).

An essential function of genes is to instruct body cells to combine 20 standard amino acids to build the *proteins* that our bodies need to function properly. **Proteins** are organic compounds that form the structures of the body and regulate its maintenance. Basic structural elements of our bodies—for example, muscle, brain, and bone—are made up of different proteins. Proteins also control all biological processes ranging from metabolic and immune functions to intercellular communications.

Genotypes, Phenotypes, and Patterns of Inheritance

The **genotype** is the actual DNA material that determines each person's unique genetic blueprint. The **phenotype** is the individual's whole set of observable characteristics. One way to remember the distinction is that the phenotype can be identified by directly observing the individual. For example, you can easily see that a woman has brown eyes, which are part of her phenotype. Her genotype, though, can't be so easily determined. In many cases, you would have to know the eye colour of her parents and offspring to determine whether she carries genes for another eye colour, because complex rules govern the way genotypes influence phenotypes. Three principles of genetic transmission explain such patterns of inheritance.

DOMINANT AND RECESSIVE GENES The simplest genetic rule is the **dominant-recessive pattern**, in which a single dominant gene strongly influences phenotype. (**Table 2.1** lists several normal phenotypical traits and indicates whether they arise from dominant or recessive genes.) People whose chromosomes carry either two dominant or two recessive genes are referred to as *homozygous*. Those with one dominant and one recessive gene are said to be *heterozygous*.

If a child receives a single dominant gene for a trait from one parent, the child's phenotype will include the trait determined by that gene. In contrast, a child's phenotype will include a recessive trait only if she inherits a recessive gene from both parents. For example, geneticists have found that the curliness of hair is controlled by

genome
all the DNA that an organism possesses

protein-coding genes
genes that direct the production of proteins

proteins
organic compounds, consisting of amino acids, that perform most life functions and make up the majority of cellular structures

Learning Objective 2.2
Describe the ways genes influence development.

genotype
an individual's unique genetic blueprint

phenotype
an individual's whole set of observable characteristics

dominant-recessive pattern
a pattern of inheritance in which a single dominant gene influences a person's phenotype but two recessive genes are necessary to produce an associated trait

Table 2.1 Genetic Sources of Normal Traits

Dominant Genes	Recessive Genes	Polygenic (many genes)
Broad lips	Thin lips	Height
Nearsightedness	Flat feet	Eye colour
Coarse hair	Fine hair	Body type
Curly hair	Straight hair	Skin colour
Dark hair	Blond hair	Personality
Types A and B blood	Type O blood	
Rh-positive blood	Rh-negative blood	
Freckles	Red hair	
Dimples		

(**SOURCE:** Data from Tortora, G., & Grabowski, S. (1993). *Principles of anatomy and physiology*. New York, NY: HarperCollins.)

a single pair of genes (see **Figure 2.2**). The gene for curly hair is dominant; therefore, if a man has curly hair, his genotype includes at least one gene for curly hair and at least half of his sperm carry this gene. Conversely, straight hair is recessive, so a straight-haired man's genotype must include two straight-hair genes for his phenotype to include straight hair. Geneticists also know that the only kind of hair type a straight-haired father can pass on to his children is straight hair, because all his sperm carry recessive, straight-hair genes.

Critical Thinking

Think about your hair type and that of your siblings. What does your hair suggest about your parents' genotypes?

In addition, human geneticists have learned that both dominant and recessive genes differ in *expressivity*, meaning that the degree to which any gene influences phenotypes varies from person to person. For example, all individuals who have the gene for curly hair don't have equally curly hair. So, even when a child receives a dominant gene for curly hair from her father, the amount and type of curl in her hair probably won't be exactly the same as his.

Blood type is also determined by a dominant-recessive pattern of inheritance. Because a person must have two recessive genes to have type O blood, the genotype of every person who has this type is clear. However, the genotype of people with type A or B blood is not obvious because types A and B are dominant. Thus, when a person's phenotype includes either type A or type B blood, one of the person's blood type genes must be for that type, but the other could be for some other type. However, if a type A father and a type B mother produce a child with type O, each of them carries a gene for type O, because the child must receive one such gene from each parent to have the type O phenotype.

Figure 2.2 Examples of how the recessive gene for straight hair passes from parents to children.

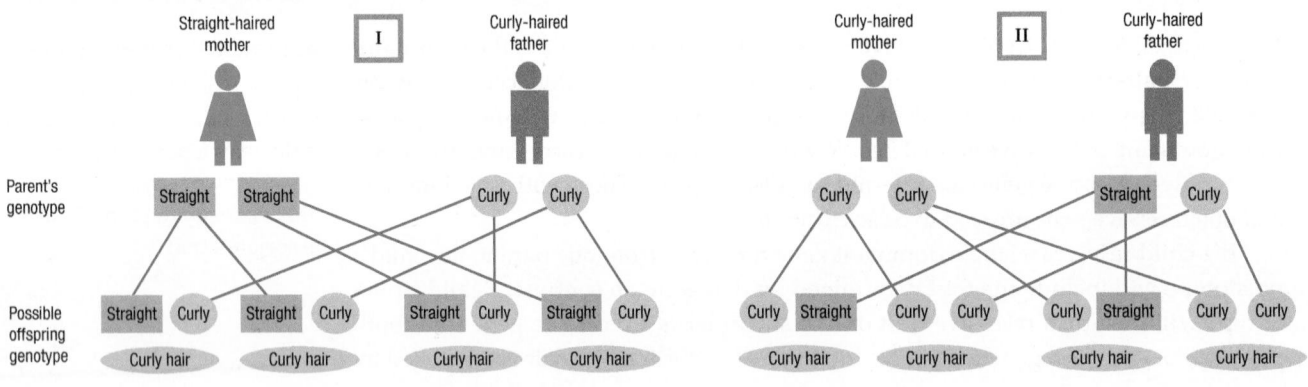

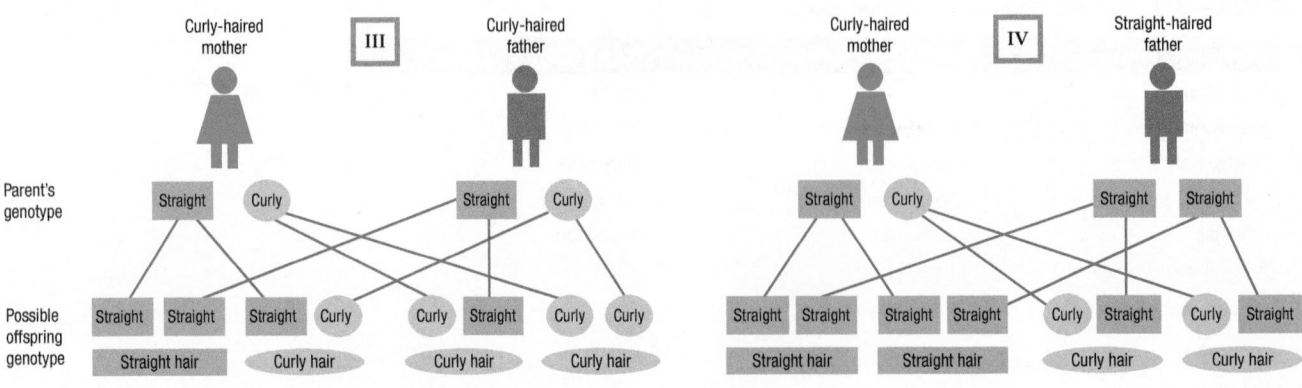

POLYGENIC AND MULTIFACTORIAL INHERITANCE With **polygenic inheritance**, many genes influence the phenotype. There are many polygenic traits in which the dominant-recessive pattern is also at work. For example, geneticists believe that children get three genes for skin colour from each parent (Barsh, 2003). Dark skin is dominant over light skin, but the skin colours also blend together. Thus, when one parent is dark-skinned and the other is fair-skinned, the child will have skin that is somewhere between the two. The dark-skinned parent's dominant genes will ensure that the child will be darker than the fair parent, but the fair-skinned parent's genes will prevent the child from having skin as dark as that of the dark-skinned parent.

Eye colour is another polygenic trait with a dominant-recessive pattern (Liu et al., 2010). Scientists don't know for sure how many genes influence eye colour. They do know, however, that these genes don't cause specific colours. Instead, they cause the coloured part of the eye to be dark or light. Dark colours (black, brown, hazel, and green) are dominant over light colours (blue and grey). However, blended colours are also possible. People whose chromosomes carry a combination of genes for green, blue, and grey eyes can have blue-grey, green-blue, or blue-green eyes. Likewise, genes that cause different shades of brown can combine their effects to make children's eye colour phenotypes different from those of their brown-eyed parents.

Many physical traits are influenced by both genes and environment, a pattern known as **multifactorial inheritance**. Height is one example. Many genes contribute to a child's height and rate of growth. However, if he is ill, poorly nourished, or emotionally neglected, a child may be smaller than others his age even though he carries genes that should result in his being as tall as his peers. Thus, when a child is shorter than 97% of his agemates, doctors may try to determine whether he is short because of his genes or because something is causing him to grow poorly (Jospe, 2015; Tanner, 1990).

Psychological traits, such as intelligence and personality, are also influenced by both heredity and environment. Similarly, many neurodevelopmental disorders, a group of conditions in which children's neurological development follows an atypical pattern, often result from multifactorial inheritance (Zeidán-Chuliá et al., 2013). Neurodevelopmental disorders include conditions such as intellectual disabilities, communication disorders, autism spectrum disorders, and attention-deficit/hyperactivity disorder (American Psychiatric Association, 2013)—disorders you will read more about in the chapter on Physical and Cognitive Development in Middle Childhood.

MITOCHONDRIAL INHERITANCE Scientists have discovered some additional principles of genetic inheritance involving genetic material that is found in the mitochondria, rather than the nucleus, of a woman's eggs. In **mitochondrial inheritance**, children inherit genes that are carried in structures called *mitochondria*, which are found in the fluid that surrounds the nucleus of the ovum before it is fertilized. Consequently, mitochondrial genes are passed only from mother to child. Geneticists have learned that several serious disorders, including some types of blindness, are transmitted in this way (Levy & Marion, 2015). In most such cases, the mother herself is unaffected by the harmful genes.

Epigenetics

Current genetics research has revealed that our genome accounts for only one aspect of heredity influences. In particular, one question has remained unanswered until now—if each of our cells carries essentially the same genome, how is it that the cells of our body can be so different? Put another way, how can cells that have the same genotype differentiate into specialized cells (phenotype), such as liver, heart, or brain tissue? The answer comes to us from the discovery of molecular biological compounds that overlay our DNA, known collectively as the **epigenome** (Callinan & Feinberg, 2006) (see Figure 2.1). Just as the human genome was mapped, efforts, such as the International Human Epigenome Consortium (IHEC) of which Canada is a participant, are under way to map the human epigenome and locate specific epigenetic markings and

polygenic inheritance

a pattern of inheritance in which many genes influence a trait

multifactorial inheritance

a pattern of inheritance affected by both genes and the environment

mitochondrial inheritance

a pattern of inheritance in which a cell's mitochondrial DNA (mtDNA) is inherited from the mother's egg and not the father's sperm

Learning Objective 2.3

Describe how epigenetic mechanisms regulate genes and development.

epigenome

the sum total of inherited and acquired molecular modifications to the genome that leads to changes in gene regulation without changing the DNA sequence of the genome

sites associated with, for example, gene regulation, cell differentiation, and human health and disease across the lifespan (IHEC, n.d.)

Possessing the gene for a specific trait does not guarantee that it will be *expressed*. Although each cell in our body contains the same genetic code (the same genotype), our unique set of epigenetic markers regulate *gene expression* (our phenotype). Epigenetic markers work by signalling some genes to "turn on" (**gene expression**) and others to "turn off" (**gene silencing**). For example, soon after conception, epigenetic markers "tell" "brain genes" to be active in brain tissue but inactive in liver tissue. Epigenetic structures also control ongoing cellular functioning in a similar way. They signal a gene or polygene to turn on (e.g., when a cell needs to produce a specific protein) or turn off (e.g., when protein production needs to stop until further notice). In this way, epigenetic mechanisms regulate normal bodily processes, such as regulating blood sugar levels, activating immune functions, or controlling brain cell activity.

Moshe Szyf and Michael Meaney, two McGill University pioneers in the emerging field of **epigenetics**, and their Dalhousie University colleague, Ian Weaver, have found that **epigenetic factors** play a pivotal role in development across the lifespan. Through animal studies, they were the first researchers to demonstrate that maternal care can physically alter molecular epigenetic structures in offspring. For example, a mother rat's increased postnatal levels of feeding and grooming of her pups resulted in calmer rat pups by actually altering the molecular epigenetic structures in the rat pups (Weaver et al., 2004; Weaver et al., 2007; Weaver, Meaney, & Szyf, 2006). In follow-up studies, they found that although these early-life epigenetic changes persist into adulthood, they could be reversed experimentally (Weaver et al., 2005).

Although epigenetic modifications acquired during the lifetime of the parent are typically expunged during the earliest stages of prenatal development of subsequent generations (Kimmins & Sassone-Corsi, 2005), recent studies have shown that some acquired epigenetic modifications can be passed on. For example, animal studies have shown that epigenetic changes to liver, heart, and brain proteins in mice and endocrine, reproductive, and behavioural changes in rats acquired during the lifetime of the parent can be transmitted to the offspring (Anway, Cupp, Uzumca, & Skinner, 2005; Roemer, Reik, Dean, & Klose, 1997). Even epigenetic changes caused by changes to maternal diet, as well as paternal stress have been shown to transfer across generations in mice populations (Cropley, Suter, Beckman, & Martin, 2006; Wu et al., 2016). Preliminary research suggests that acquired epigenetic traits linked to chromosome structure alterations can also be transferred across generations in humans (Jablonka & Lamb, 2015; Wei, Schatten, & Sun, 2015; Whitelaw & Whitelaw, 2006).

A decade on, and we have seen an ever-growing interest in epigenetics (Lester, Conradt, & Marsit, 2016). And, in addition to studying the relationship between epigenetic changes and health and disease, the field is now branching out into other specialized research areas, such as **behavioural epigenetics**—for example, the study of the epigenetic changes related to the development of the brain, behaviour, and psychological processes in relation to environmental factors. Some of the main areas of research include the study of parenting styles, cognition (learning and memory), neurological and mental disorders, stress, substance use, and suicidal behaviour (Champagne & Rissman, 2011; Heller et al., 2014; Isles, 2015; Jensen, 2015; Kaminsky et al, 2015; Keverne, Pfaff, & Tabansky, 2015; McGowan & Roth, 2015; Moore, 2013, 2015; Pal et al., 2016)—we'll look at these areas in more detail in this and later chapters.

Evolutionary Theories

Evolutionary theories attempt to explain our differences as individuals and our commonalities as a species. These theories often focus on the genetic and environmental mechanisms that underlie development throughout the lifespan and across generations.

---

gene expression

when a gene sequence is activated ("turned on") and ready to be translated into gene products—proteins, for the most part

gene silencing

when a gene sequence is made inactive ("turned off") and is prevented from being translated into gene products—proteins, for the most part

epigenetics

the study of the gene regulation patterns that alter gene function (phenotype) without changing gene structure (genotype)

epigenetic factors

inheritable and acquired gene regulation patterns that alter gene function (phenotype) without changing gene structure (genotype)

behavioural epigenetics

the study of how the environment and personal behaviour can cause epigenetic changes that affect gene expression resulting in changes to behaviour and psychological processes over the course of a life and across generations

Learning Objective 2.4

Describe how evolutionary theories explain individual differences.

ETHOLOGY **Ethology** emphasizes genetically determined survival behaviours that are assumed to have evolved through natural selection. For example, nests are necessary for the survival of young birds. Therefore, ethologists say, evolution has equipped birds with nest-building genes.

Similarly, ethologists believe that emotional relationships are necessary to the survival of human infants (Bowlby, 1969, 1980). They claim that evolution has produced genes that cause humans to form these relationships. For example, most people feel irritated when they hear a newborn crying. Ethologists say the baby

(Photo: Bryan Creely/Fotolia)

is genetically programmed to cry in a certain way, and adults are genetically programmed to get irritated when they hear it. The caretaker responds to a crying baby's needs to remove the irritating stimulus of the noise. As the caretaker and infant interact, an emotional bond is created between them. Thus, genes for crying in an irritating manner increase infants' chances of survival.

BEHAVIOUR GENETICS A related area of study, **behaviour genetics**, focuses on the effect of heredity on individual differences. Traits or behaviours are believed to be influenced by genes when those of related people, such as children and their parents, are more similar than those of unrelated people. Behaviour geneticists have shown that heredity affects a broad range of traits and behaviours, such as intelligence, altruism, substance use and abuse, and hyperactivity (Plomin, DeFries, Knopik, & Neiderhiser, 2016).

EVOLUTIONARY PSYCHOLOGY Evolutionary psychology is a unifying approach to explain human behaviour that involves all branches of psychology and life sciences. In particular, **evolutionary psychology** looks at how genetically inherited cognitive and social traits have evolved through natural selection. Accordingly, the adaptation of neuro networks that support cognitive abilities that underlie social relations and interactions are a major focus (Cosmides & Tooby, 2013; Tooby & Cosmides, 2016).

Montreal-born Harvard psychologist Steven Pinker (1997, 2002) has been a leading advocate of evolutionary psychology. His basic premise is that, through a process of biological evolution, the mind, like the body, has been shaped by natural selection to serve adaptive functions and promote survival. Moreover, Pinker (2002, 2013) contends that we have hard-wired inherited patterns of thinking and feeling shaped over time by the demands made on the species for survival. Today, this "human nature," as he calls it, affects every aspect of our lives, from child-rearing practices to the formation of our political views to our taste in art and music.

EVOLUTIONARY DEVELOPMENTAL PSYCHOLOGY The proponents of this view say that, contrary to what philosopher John Locke thought about infants, a newborn's mind is not a blank slate. Rather, the mind has been genetically programmed with a predisposition to learn and develop in certain ways—for instance, it has a readiness to learn language and recognize human faces (Bjorklund & Pellegrini, 2002; Tooby, Cosmides & Barrett, 2005).

Evolutionary developmental psychology theorists agree that nature (genes) and nurture (environment) interact in determining individual intelligence, personality, and

Ethologists assert that the first two years of life are a critical period for the establishment of relationships between infants and caregivers.

ethology
a perspective on development that emphasizes genetically determined survival behaviours presumed to have evolved through natural selection

behaviour genetics
the study of the role of heredity in individual differences

evolutionary psychology
the view that genetically inherited cognitive and social traits have evolved through natural selection

evolutionary developmental psychology
the view that genetically inherited cognitive and social characteristics that promote survival and adaptation appear at different times across the lifespan

social behaviour (Bjorklund & Ellis, 2014; Bjorklund & Pellegrini, 2002). But they also suggest that we need the ability to display different forms of behaviour at different times over the course of our lives. For example, the cognitive and emotional abilities that help infants and children adapt and survive are qualitatively different from those that adults require to adapt and survive. Specifically, infants need to form attachments while adults must contend with mating and, once children arrive, parenting and, later, grandparenting (Buss, 1999, 2016). From this perspective, then, evolutionary forces have contributed to the development of age-dependent traits that promote survival and adaptation across the lifespan (Bjorklund, Hernández Blasi, & Ellis, 2016).

EVOLUTIONARY PRENATAL PROGRAMMING AND ADULT HEALTH AND DISEASE Changing one's lifestyle habits later in life to reduce the risk of disease may be a case of "too little, too late." In addition to genetic and lifestyle factors, the risk of developing non-communicable diseases such as heart disease, diabetes, and obesity may have its roots in very early life influences. This is the case according to evolutionary theorists Peter Gluckman of the University of Auckland, NZ, and Mark Hanson of the University of Southampton, UK, and their colleagues, who have proposed some intriguing ideas (Gluckman & Hanson, 2006a, 2006b, 2007; Gluckman et al., 2009; Gluckman, Hanson, & Beedle, 2007; Gluckman, Hanson, & Spencer, 2005). They suggest that the *prenate* (i.e., the fetus) picks up cues about existing environmental conditions from its mother and is thereby able to predict what kind of environment it can expect to live in after birth. In response, the fetus undergoes epigenetic changes that ensure the best chance for survival in the anticipated future environment. These so-called **predictive-adaptive responses** are adaptive only if the forecast is correct. Where there is a mismatch between the early (prenatal) and later (postnatal) environment, physiological adaptations may be ill-suited to the postnatal environment and thus contribute to lifestyle-related diseases in adulthood—the greater the mismatch, the greater the risk. **Figure 2.3** depicts an example of how these mismatches predict metabolic disease.

Some responses of the embryo or the fetus to its environment may, however, be developmentally disruptive with no adaptive value—for example, a response to an environmental toxic agent that goes beyond the organism's ability to adapt (Gluckman & Hanson, 2004a; Heindel & Lawler, 2006) (you'll read about these *teratogens* in the chapter on Prenatal Development and Birth). Epigenetic changes to the DNA made prenatally can persist throughout the lifespan and the response made to the predicted future environmental conditions in one generation may also extend over several generations (Gluckman, Hanson, & Spencer, 2005; Waterman, 2006). The **Research Report** illustrates how a gene variation, which may have aided adaptation for generations, can suddenly give rise to an epidemic when lifestyle behaviours are altered.

Applying Biology and Evolutionary Theories

Biological principles that underlie genetics and epigenetics are expanding our understanding of disease processes. Scientists are discovering the complex role that inheritance plays in human health and the related importance of early intervention.

DISEASE CONTROL Advances in **human genomics** will play a vital role in predicting and preventing diseases. Some scientists claim that developments in relatively rare single-gene diseases, such as *hemophilia, Huntington's disease,* and *sickle-cell disease,* will have a limited impact on overall national health care (Hall, Morley, & Lucke, 2004; Holtzman & Marteau, 2000). In total, these types of genetic diseases account for only about 5% of all human disease in developed countries (Khoury, 2003). Still, other scientists predict that the greatest impact of advances in human genomics will likely be seen in the treatment of *multifactoral diseases,* such as heart disease and cancer. In these cases, having a genome-wide perspective will be an advantage (Hall, Morley, &

predictive-adaptive responses
the prenate's ability to use information about the current environment to adjust its physiology in anticipation that it will match future environmental conditions and optimize the chances to survive and reproduce in adulthood

Learning Objective 2.5
Describe how biology and evolutionary theories contribute to our understanding of disease processes and interventions.

human genomics
the study of the human genome including the location of genes, their function, and their role in human physical and mental health

Figure 2.3 The developing organism senses maternally transmitted environmental cues, such as undernutrition, during prenatal and early postnatal life. Developmental flexibility in response to these cues modifies the default trajectory defined by the inherited fetal genome and epigenome according to whether the environment is perceived as adequate (dark background) or deprived (light background), resulting in metabolic adjustments. If the eventual mature environment, whether adequate or deprived, matches the prediction, then the risk of metabolic disease in later life is low. If there is a mismatch between the predicted and actual mature environments, particularly if the mature environment is richer than anticipated, then the risk of metabolic disease is enhanced.

(**SOURCE:** Gluckman, P.D., Hanson, M.A., & Beedle, A.S. (2007). *American Journal of Human Biology, 19* (1), 1–19 (p. 8). Reprinted with permission of Wiley–Liss, Inc., a subsidiary of John Wiley & Sons, Inc.)

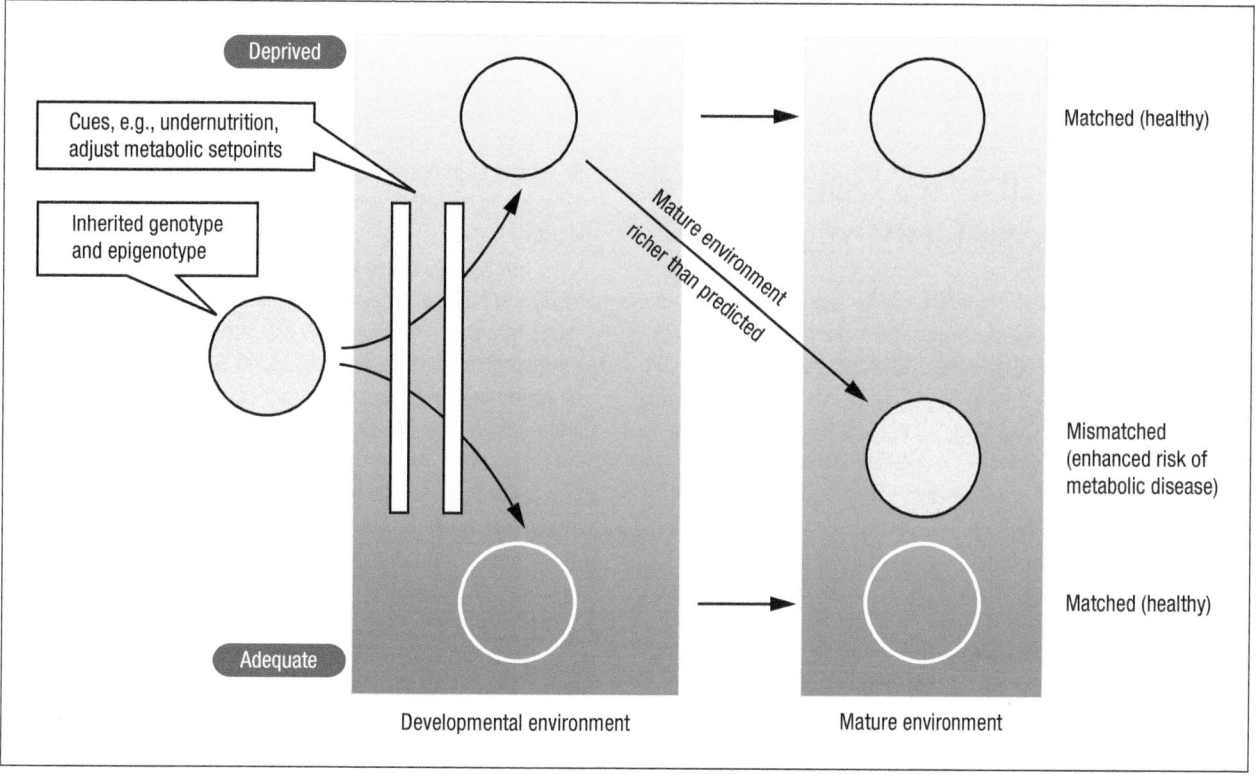

Lucke, 2004). For example, the British Columbia Cancer Agency research team headed by Samuel Aparicio recently decoded the 3 billion letters in the DNA sequence of a type of breast cancer that accounts for 10% of all breast cancers (Shah et al., 2009). Shortly after this discovery, Canadian scientists joined an international partnership that intends to decode the genomes and epigenomes of some 25 000 cancer samples, with the aim of developing new strategies for early detection and prevention (International Cancer Genome Consortium, 2010).

In addition to genomics, *epigenomics* is rapidly contributing to our understanding, diagnosis, and treatment of human diseases and disorders (Chen & Li, 2016; IHEC, n.d.; Meaney & Szyf, 2005; Ramsay, 2015; Wong, Gottesman, & Petronis, 2005). **Human epigenomics** looks at how epigenetic changes alter gene expression, which can increase the risk for developing both physical and psychological disorders (Keshavan, Nasrallah, & Tandon, 2011; Petronis, 2003, 2004, 2006; Szyf, 2006). Epigenetic markings on DNA are continually modified throughout the lifespan (Heyn et al., 2012; Martin, 2005) and any acquired epigenetic traits and/or predispositions may be passed onto the next generation (Jablonka & Lamb, 2005, 2015; Lahiri et al., 2016). Indeed, newly discovered epigenetic factors may prove to be the proverbial "missing link" that helps us explain how nurture interacts with nature.

human epigenomics

the study of the human epigenome including the location of all acquired and inherited epigenetic markers, their function, and their role in human physical and mental health

EARLY INTERVENTION Evolutionary theory and research are making scientists more aware of the relative importance of early-life events on altering susceptibility to chronic, non-communicable diseases in later life (Godfrey, Costello, & Lillycrop, 2015; Hanson & Gluckman, 2014, 2015). This growing awareness has focused attention on the need to promote early intervention strategies during prenatal development (e.g., supporting good health and nutrition in females of reproductive age) versus strategies instituted later in life. This early intervention has the potential to prevent chronic diseases in future generations (Gluckman & Hanson, 2004a, 2004b, 2006b; Hanson & Gluckman, 2015)—a concept we'll look at in more detail in this and later chapters.

Research Report

Type 2 Diabetes Epidemic in a Remote Community

Prior to the middle of the last century, type 2 diabetes was rare among Indigenous populations (Hackett, Abonyi, & Dyck, 2016). By the 1970s, however, research suggested that an epidemic might be emerging; two decades later, this was confirmed (Young, Reading, Elias, & O'Neil, 2000). Today, in Canada, type 2 diabetes is three times as prevalent (and the incidence rate is escalating) in First Nations Peoples as in the general population. An estimated 20% of all First Nations Peoples currently live with the disease (Picard, 2010).

Type 2 diabetes generally occurs later in life and carries with it serious health and social ramifications. It leads to conditions such as heart disease, blindness, kidney failure, and gangrene (Park & Peters, 2014) and is a leading cause of death and disability among First Nations Peoples (Park, Tjepkema, Goedhuis, & Pennock, 2015).

Robert Hegele and his research team at the John P. Robarts Research Institute in London, Ontario, discovered a strong genetic effect related to a single gene variant. This genetic mutation was discovered in the Oji-Cree, who reside on the Sandy Lake Reserve in Northern Ontario. The adults of the community were found to have a high incidence of the G319S mutation, which affects the structure of a specific liver protein. The incidence of type 2 diabetes was found to be five times higher than it is in the general Canadian population. This rate is the third highest in the world (Hegele, Cao, Harris, Hanley, & Zinman, 1999).

The type 2 diabetes epidemic demonstrates how we can study the interaction between genes and behaviour and suggests that a genetic susceptibility interacts with multiple environmental factors. The sudden increase in the incidence of the disease may be related to a significant change in lifestyle. For instance, the Oji-Cree's traditional low-carbohydrate diet has been replaced by a "junk food" and high "fatty" content diet and is coupled with a more sedentary level of physical activity. This modern lifestyle encourages obesity of the midbody area in Oji-Cree who have the G319S mutation, and this is connected to a higher risk of diabetes (Hegele et al., 1999; Park & Peters, 2014).

This new understanding of the interplay between genetics and environment has led to a complex health care initiative. Community-wide prevention and health education programs that actively involve Oji-Cree residents and demonstrate an appreciation for their language and cultural concerns begin in Grade 3. The focus is on healthy lifestyle practices that include a balanced diet and physical exercise. Moreover, a screening program for detecting diabetes and a lifestyle support program for those who are living with the disease were both established to decrease the severity of its effects (Health Canada, 2010; John P. Robarts Research Institute, 2000).

Test Yourself before going on

1. Match each term with its definition.
   _____ (a) chromosomes
   _____ (b) heterozygous
   _____ (c) epigenetic factors
   _____ (d) phenotype
   _____ (e) proteins
   _____ (f) genes
   _____ (g) gene expression
   _____ (h) polygenic inheritance

   _____ (i) mitochondria
   _____ (j) genotype
   (i) organic compounds, consisting of amino acids, that perform most life functions and make up the majority of cellular structures
   (ii) strings of genetic material
   (iii) pieces of genetic material that control or influence traits

(iv) when a gene sequence is activated ("turned on") and ready to be translated into gene products, such as proteins

(v) a pattern of inheritance in which many genes influence a trait

(vi) DNA-bearing structures outside the nucleus of the ovum

(vii) an individual's particular set of observed characteristics

(viii) inheritable and acquired gene regulation patterns that alter gene function without changing gene structure

(ix) individuals whose chromosomes carry one dominant and one recessive gene for a given trait

(x) the unique genetic blueprint of each individual

2. Match each theoretical approach to its emphasis.
_____ (a) evolutionary developmental psychology
_____ (b) behaviour genetics
_____ (c) ethology
_____ (d) predictive-adaptive response

(i) relative effects of heredity on individual differences

(ii) genetically determined survival behaviours

(iii) genetically inherited age-dependent cognitive and social traits that promote survival and adaptation

(iv) the prenate picks up on environmental cues to adjust its physiology in anticipation that it will match future environmental conditions

Psychoanalytic Theories

One theoretical approach to explaining babies' fascination with mouthing objects might suggest that infants derive more physical pleasure from mouthing objects than from manipulating them with other parts of their bodies. Such an approach would most likely belong to the family of **psychoanalytic theories**, a school of thought that originated with Sigmund Freud (1856–1939). Psychoanalytic theorists believe that developmental change happens because internal drives and emotions influence behaviour.

Freud's Psychosexual Theory

Although much of Freud's formal theory remains contentious, his ideas still influence our understanding of personality development. One of Freud's most distinctive concepts is the idea that behaviour is governed by both conscious and unconscious processes. The most basic of these unconscious processes is an internal drive for physical pleasure that Freud called the **libido**. He believed the libido to be the motivating force behind most behaviour.

PERSONALITY DEVELOPMENT Many of Freud's patients had memories of sexual feelings and behaviour in childhood. This led Freud to believe that sexual feelings are important to personality development. Based on his patients' childhood memories, Freud also argued that personality has three parts. The **id** contains the libido and operates at an unconscious level; the id is a person's basic sexual and aggressive impulses, which are present at birth. The **ego**, the conscious, thinking part of the personality, develops in the first two to three years of life. One of the ego's jobs is to keep the needs of the id satisfied. For instance, when a person is hungry, it is the id that demands food immediately, and the ego is supposed to find a way to obtain it. The **superego**, the portion of the personality that acts as a moral judge, contains the rules of society and develops near the end of early childhood, at about age 6. Once the superego develops, the ego's task becomes more complex. It must satisfy the id without violating the superego's rules.

The ego is responsible for keeping the three components of personality in balance. According to Freud, a person experiences tension when any of the three components is in conflict with another. For example, if a person is hungry, the id may motivate her to do anything to find food, but the ego—her conscious self—may be unable to find any. Alternatively, food may be available, but the ego may have to violate one of the superego's moral rules to get it. In such cases, the ego may generate

psychoanalytic theories
theories proposing that developmental change happens because of the influence of internal drives and emotions on behaviour

Learning Objective 2.6
Summarize the main ideas of Freud's psychosexual theory.

libido
in Freud's theory, an instinctual drive for physical pleasure present at birth that forms the motivating force behind virtually all human behaviour

id
in Freud's theory, the part of the personality that comprises a person's basic sexual and aggressive impulses; it contains the libido and motivates a person to seek pleasure and avoid pain

ego
according to Freud, the thinking element of personality

superego
Freud's term for the part of personality that is the moral judge

defence mechanisms

strategies for reducing anxiety, such as repression, denial, or projection, proposed by Freud

psychosexual stages

Freud's five stages of personality development through which children move in a fixed sequence determined by maturation; the libido is centred on a different body part in each stage

defence mechanisms—ways of thinking about a situation that reduce anxiety. Without defence mechanisms, Freud thought, the degree of tension within the personality would become intolerable, leading to mental illness or suicide.

FIVE PSYCHOSEXUAL STAGES   Freud proposed a series of **psychosexual stages** through which a child moves in a fixed sequence determined by maturation. In each stage, the libido is centred on a different part of the body. In the infant, the mouth is the focus of the drive for physical pleasure; the stage is therefore called the *oral stage.* As maturation progresses, the libido becomes focused on the anus (hence, the *anal stage*), and later on the genitals (the *phallic stage* and, after a period of dormancy called the *latency stage*, the *genital stage*).

Optimum development, according to Freud, requires an environment that will satisfy the unique needs of each period. For example, the infant needs sufficient opportunity for oral stimulation. An inadequate early environment will result in *fixation*, characterized by behaviours that reflect unresolved problems and unmet needs. Thus, emphasis on the formative role of early experiences is a hallmark of psychoanalytic theories.

Erikson's Psychosocial Theory

Learning Objective 2.7

Identify the conflict associated with each of Erikson's psychosocial stages.

Apart from Freud, Erik Erikson (1902–1994) is the psychoanalytic theorist who has had the greatest influence on the study of development (Erikson, 1950, 1959, 1980b, 1982; Erikson, Erikson, & Kivnick, 1986). Erikson, like many of Freud's other early followers, accepted many of Freud's ideas but later went on to expand on them. For instance, Erikson claimed that development results from the interaction between internal drives and cultural demands; thus, his theory refers to **psychosocial stages** rather than to psycho*sexual* ones. Furthermore, Erikson thought that development continued through the entire lifespan.

psychosocial stages

Erikson's eight stages, or crises, of personality development in which inner instincts interact with outer cultural and social demands to shape personality

EIGHT PSYCHOSOCIAL CRISES TO RESOLVE   In Erikson's view, to achieve a healthy personality, an individual must successfully resolve a psychosocial crisis at each of the eight stages of development, as summarized in **Table 2.2**. The key idea

Critical Thinking

In which of Erikson's psychosocial stages would you place yourself? Does Erikson's description of this stage correspond to the challenges and concerns you are confronting?

Table 2.2 Erikson's Psychosocial Stages

Approximate Ages	Stage	Positive Characteristics Gained and Typical Activities
Birth to 1 year	Trust versus mistrust	Hope; trust in primary caregiver and in one's own ability to make things happen (secure attachment to caregiver is key)
1 to 3	Autonomy versus shame and doubt	Will; new physical skills lead to demand for more choices, most often seen as saying "no" to caregivers; child learns self-care skills, such as toileting
3 to 6	Initiative versus guilt	Purpose; ability to organize activities around some goal; more assertiveness and aggressiveness (harsh parental criticism may lead to guilt)
6 to 12	Industry versus inferiority	Competence; cultural skills and norms, including school skills and tool use (failure to master these leads to sense of inferiority)
12 to 18	Identity versus role confusion	Fidelity; a unified and consistent sense of self that integrates pubertal changes into a mature sexual identity, assumes adult social and occupational roles, and establishes personal values and attitudes
18 to 30	Intimacy versus isolation	Love; person develops intimate relationships beyond adolescent love; many become parents
30 to old age	Generativity versus stagnation	Care; people rear children, focus on occupational achievement or creativity, and train the next generation; turn outward from the self toward others
Old age	Integrity versus despair	Wisdom; person conducts a life review, integrates earlier stages, and comes to terms with basic identity; develops self-acceptance

underlying Erikson's theory is that each new crisis is thrust on the developing person because of changes in social demands that accompany changes in age. Moreover, each crisis is defined by a pair of opposing possibilities. Successful resolution of a crisis results in the development of the characteristic on the positive side of the dichotomy. A healthy resolution, however, does not mean moving totally to the positive side. For example, an infant needs to have experienced some mistrust in order to learn to identify people who are not trustworthy. But healthy development requires a favourable ratio of positive to negative.

According to Erikson, the four childhood stages form the foundation of adult personality. The outcome of the first stage, *trust versus mistrust* (birth to 1 year), depends on the reliability of the care and affection infants receive from their primary caregiver. During the second stage, *autonomy versus shame and doubt*, children aged 1 to 3 express their independence. To help children resolve this crisis, caregivers must encourage them to function independently with regard to self-care skills, such as dressing themselves. In the third stage, *initiative versus guilt*, 3- to 6-year-olds begin to develop a sense of social initiative. In order to do so, a child needs opportunities to interact with peers during this stage. During the fourth stage, *industry versus inferiority*, children ages 6 to 12 focus on acquiring culturally valued skills. In order to emerge from this stage with a sense of industry, children need support and encouragement from adults.

Erikson's description of the transition from childhood to adulthood, the *identity versus role confusion* stage, has been particularly influential. He argued that, in order to arrive at a mature sexual and occupational identity, every adolescent must examine his identity and the roles he must occupy. He must achieve an integrated sense of self, of what he wants to do and be, and of his appropriate sexual role. The risk is that the adolescent will suffer from confusion arising from the profusion of roles opening up to him at this age.

Erikson's adulthood stages are not strongly tied to age. In the first, the young adult builds on the identity established in adolescence to confront the crisis of *intimacy versus isolation*. Erikson hypothesized that an individual's capacity for intimacy is dependent upon a positive resolution of the identity crisis (Erikson, 1963). Many young people, Erikson thought, make the mistake of thinking they will find their identity in a relationship, but in his view, it is only those who have already formed (or are well on the way to forming) a clear identity who can successfully enter this fusion of identities that he called *intimacy*. Young adults whose identities are weak or unformed will remain in shallow relationships and will experience a sense of isolation or loneliness.

The middle and late adulthood crises are shaped by the realization that death is inevitable. Middle-aged adults confront the crisis of *generativity versus stagnation*, which is "primarily the concern in establishing and guiding the next generation" (Erikson, 1963, p. 267). The rearing of children is the most obvious way to achieve a sense of generativity. Doing creative work, giving service to an organization or to society, or serving as a mentor to younger colleagues can help a mid-life adult achieve a sense of generativity. Failing that, a self-absorbed, nongenerative adult may feel a sense of stagnation. Finally, older adults experience ego *integrity versus despair*. The goal of this stage is an acceptance of one's life in preparation for facing death in order to avoid a sense of despair.

The Humanistic Alternative

In addition to criticizing the fuzziness of some psychoanalytic concepts, psychologists have taken issue with the psychoanalytic emphasis on atypical development. Some have proposed alternative theories that focus on the positive aspects of development while accepting the psychoanalytic assumption that behaviour is motivated by internal drives and emotions. These *humanistic theories* share Jean-Jacques Rousseau's basic premise of *innate goodness*, and they begin with the optimistic assumption that the

Learning Objective 2.8
Describe the basic concepts of humanistic theory.

self-actualization

the process of fulfilling one's unique personal potential

motives

internal factors or conditions that tend to initiate, direct, or sustain behaviour

esteem needs

the need for a person to have a sense of value and acceptance based, in part, on their experience of respect and admiration from others and on their perceived self-confidence and self-worth

most important internal drive is each individual's motivation to achieve his or her full potential. A key figure in the humanistic tradition is Abraham Maslow (1908–1970), who used the term **self-actualization** to describe this ultimate goal of human life (Maslow, 1968, 1970).

MOTIVES Maslow's greatest interest was in the development of **motives**, or needs, which he divided into two subsets: deficiency motives and being motives. *Deficiency motives* involve drives to maintain physical or emotional homeostasis (inner balance), such as the drive to get enough to eat or drink, the sexual drive, or even the drive to obtain sufficient love or respect from others. *Being motives* involve the desire to understand, to give to others, and to grow—that is, to achieve *self-actualization*. In general, the satisfaction of deficiency motives prevents or cures illness or re-creates homeostasis. In contrast, the satisfaction of being motives produces a general sense of well-being. The distinction is like the "difference between fending off threat or attack and positive triumph and achievement" (Maslow, 1968, p. 32).

Maslow described these various needs or motives in his famous needs hierarchy, shown in **Figure 2.4**. He argued that the various needs must be met in order, from the bottom of the pyramid up. For example, only when physiological needs are met do safety needs come to the fore; only when love and esteem needs are met can the need for self-actualization become dominant. For that reason, Maslow thought that being motives were likely to be significant only in adulthood, and only in those individuals who had found stable ways to satisfy both love and **esteem needs**. In this sense, Maslow's theory sounds very similar to Erikson's stages of intimacy and generativity.

PERSONAL GROWTH Another prominent humanistic psychologist, Carl Rogers (1902–1987), talked about the capacity of each individual to become a "fully

Figure 2.4 In Maslow's view, needs operate from the bottom up in this needs hierarchy. Until physiological needs are met, no other need will be prominent; until love needs are met, esteem needs will not emerge; and so on. Similarly, there is a developmental aspect: A baby is primarily dominated by physiological needs, a toddler by safety needs, and so forth. Only in adulthood may the need for self-actualization become central.

(**SOURCE:** Maslow, Abraham H., Frager, Robert D., and Fadiman, James. *Motivation and Personality*, 3rd Edition, © 1997. Adapted by permission of Pearson Education, Inc., Upper Saddle, NJ.)

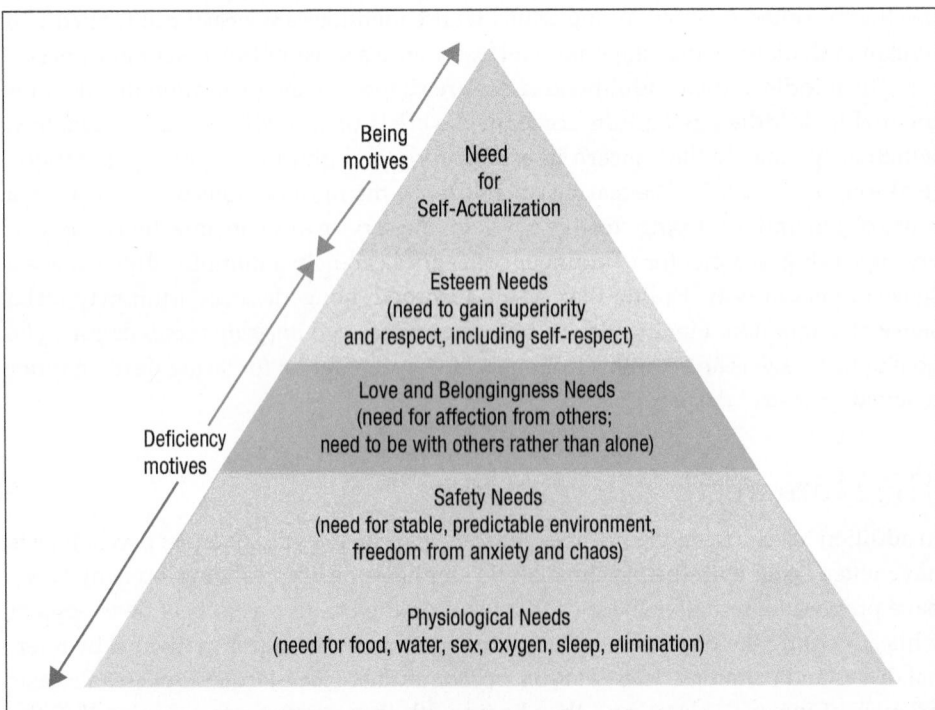

functioning person," without undue guilt or seriously distorting defences (Rogers, 1961). Early experience with caregivers whose acceptance of the child is conditional on the child behaving in an approved manner can diminish the child's sense of self-worth. The child begins to think of himself as worthwhile only when he behaves in approved ways. In Carl Rogers's view, it is never too late to overcome early conditioning or the residue of unresolved dilemmas. He believed people have the potential and motivation to try to do just that—a concept known as *personal growth*.

Test Yourself before going on

1. Psychoanalytic theories share the belief that _____ and _____ shape development.

2. Write "F" for each concept or term that belongs to Freud's theory, and "E" for each concept that belongs to Erikson's theory.
   _____ (a) psychosocial
   _____ (b) psychosexual
   _____ (c) id, ego, superego
   _____ (d) eight stages from birth to death
   _____ (e) five stages from birth to adolescence
   _____ (f) libido is driving force behind development
   _____ (g) development consists of a series of crises
   _____ (h) defence mechanisms
   _____ (i) interaction between internal drives and cultural demands

3. Match each humanistic concept to its emphasis.
   _____ (a) self-actualization
   _____ (b) deficiency motives
   _____ (c) self-esteem
   _____ (d) personal growth
       (i) the drive to maintain physical or emotional homeostasis
       (ii) a sense of value and acceptance
       (iii) the potential and motivation to become a "fully functioning person"
       (iv) the process of fulfilling one's unique personal potential

---

Learning Theories

In general, **learning theories** assert that development results from an accumulation of experiences. Learning theories are aligned with the philosophy of John Locke who said that children are born with neither good nor bad tendencies, but their behaviour is shaped, for better or worse, by their environment. Thus, in contrast to psychoanalytic and humanistic views, learning theorists would say that infants repeat the behaviour of putting objects in their mouths because they find the sensations it produces rewarding. Alternatively, when they put something in their mouths that tastes bad, infants learn not to mouth such an object again.

A central learning theory, known as **behaviourism**, views development in terms of behaviour changes caused by environmental influences—a process called *conditioning*. As you will see, there are two ways that conditioning changes our behaviour.

learning theories

theories that assert that development results from an accumulation of experiences

behaviourism

the view that defines development in terms of behaviour changes caused by environmental influences

Pavlov's Classical Conditioning

Russian physiologist and Nobel prize winner, Ivan Pavlov (1849–1936), discovered that organisms can acquire new signals for existing responses (behaviours). The term **classical conditioning** refers to this principle. Each incidence of learning begins with a biologically programmed stimulus–response connection, or *reflex*. For example, salivation happens naturally when you put food in your mouth. In classical conditioning terms, the food is the *unconditioned (unlearned, natural) stimulus*; salivating is an *unconditioned (unlearned, natural) response*.

Learning Objective 2.9

Explain how classical conditioning occurs.

classical conditioning

learning that results from the association of stimuli

THE CONDITIONING PROCESS Stimuli presented just before or at the same time as the unconditioned stimulus are those that are likely to be associated with it. For example, most foods have odours, and, to get to your mouth, food has to pass near your nose. Thus, you usually smell food before you taste it. Food odours eventually become *conditioned (learned) stimuli* that elicit salivation. In effect, they act as a signal to your salivary glands that food is coming. Once the connection between food odours and salivation is established, smelling food triggers the salivation response even when you do not actually eat the food. When a response occurs reliably in connection with a conditioned stimulus in this way, it is known as a *conditioned (learned) response.*

EARLY CONDITIONING   Classical conditioning is of interest in the study of development because of the role it plays in the acquisition of emotional responses. For example, things or people that are present when you feel good will become conditioned stimuli for pleasant feelings, while those associated with uncomfortable feelings may become conditioned stimuli for a sense of unease. Classical conditioning is especially important in infancy. Because a child's mother or father is present so often when nice things happen, such as when the child feels warm, comfortable, and cuddled, the mother and father usually serve as conditioned stimuli for pleasant feelings, a fact that makes it possible for the parents' presence to comfort a child.

Learning Objective 2.10

Explain the process of operant conditioning.

operant conditioning

learning to repeat or stop behaviours because of their consequences

reinforcement

any immediate consequence that follows a behaviour and increases the likelihood that the behaviour will be repeated

punishment

any immediate consequence that follows a behaviour and decreases the likelihood that the behaviour will be repeated

Skinner's Operant Conditioning

Another type of learning is **operant conditioning**, a term coined by B.F. Skinner (1904–1990), the most famous proponent of this theory (Skinner, 1953, 1980). Operant conditioning involves learning to repeat or stop behaviours because of the consequences they bring about. **Reinforcement** is any immediate consequence that follows a behaviour that increases the likelihood that the behaviour will be repeated. **Punishment** is any immediate consequence that follows a behaviour that decreases the likelihood that the behaviour will be repeated.

REINFORCEMENT   *Positive reinforcement* entails adding a consequence (usually something pleasant) that follows a behaviour and increases the chances that the behaviour will occur again. Some kinds of pleasant consequences, such as attention, serve as reinforcers for most people most of the time. But, strictly speaking, reinforcement is defined by its effect; we don't know something is reinforcing unless we see that its presence increases the probability of some behaviour.

Negative reinforcement entails taking away a condition (usually something unpleasant) following a behaviour and increases the chances that the behaviour will occur again. For example, coughing is an unpleasant experience for most of us, and taking a dose of cough medicine usually stops it. As a result, the next time we begin to cough, we reach for the cough syrup because the behaviour of consuming a spoonful of cough syrup is reinforced by the cessation of coughing. In other words, we make the unpleasant experience of coughing go away when we engage in the behaviour of swallowing cough syrup. Thus, the behaviour of taking cough syrup is learned through negative reinforcement.

Definitions and simple examples of positive and negative reinforcement may be misleading when it comes to understanding how the two operate in real-life contexts. For example, most people understand that paying attention to a preschooler's whining is likely to increase it. This case shows positive reinforcement—a child's whining is reinforced whenever a parent shows attention. At the same time, however, a parent learns to attend

Laboratory research involving animals was important in the development of Skinner's operant conditioning theory.

(Photo: Sam Falk/Photo Researchers, Inc./Science Source)

to a whining preschooler because whining is irritating, and responding to it usually makes it stop. As a result, the parent's behaviour of responding to whining is negatively reinforced by its consequence—namely, that the child *stops* whining. In this case of negative reinforcement, parental attention is reinforced when the child stops whining.

PUNISHMENT   There are two general forms of punishment but, in contrast to both kinds of reinforcement, both forms of punishment stop a behaviour. Sometimes punishments involve eliminating nice things, for example, taking away TV privileges. This is referred to as *negative punishment* and entails taking away a condition (usually something pleasant) that follows a behaviour and decreases the chances that the behaviour will occur again. Negative punishment can be considered a type of **extinction**, which is the gradual elimination of a behaviour through repeated nonreinforcement. If a teacher succeeds in eliminating a student's undesirable behaviour by ignoring it, the behaviour is said to have been *extinguished*.

extinction
the gradual elimination of a behaviour through repeated nonreinforcement

However, punishment may also involve unpleasant things such as scolding. A *positive punishment* entails adding a consequence (usually something unpleasant) that follows a behaviour and decreases the chances that the behaviour will occur again. Like reinforcement, however, punishment is defined by its effect. Consequences that do not stop behaviour can't be properly called punishments.

CHANGING BEHAVIOUR   Such examples illustrate the complex manner in which reinforcements and punishments operate in the real world. In laboratory settings, operant conditioning researchers usually work with only one participant or animal subject at a time; they needn't worry about the social consequences of behaviours or consequences. They can also control the situation so that a particular behaviour is reinforced every time it occurs. In the real world, *partial reinforcement*—reinforcement of a behaviour on some occasions but not others—is more common (see **Development in the Real World**). Studies of partial reinforcement show that people take longer to learn a new behaviour under partial reinforcement conditions; once established, however, such behaviours are very resistant to extinction.

Critical Thinking

Describe instances in your everyday life when your behaviour is affected by classical or operant conditioning, or when you use these principles to affect others' behaviour.

Shaping is the reinforcement of intermediate steps until an individual learns a complex behaviour. For example, you wouldn't start learning to play tennis by challenging a skilled player to a match. Instead, you would first learn to hold the racquet properly. Next, you would learn the basic strokes and practise hitting balls hit or thrown to you by an instructor. Next, you would learn to serve. Finally, you would put all your skills together and play an actual match. All along the way, you would be encouraged by the sense of satisfaction gained from accomplishing each step toward the goal.

shaping
the reinforcement of intermediate steps until an individual learns a complex behaviour

Development in the Real World

Learning Principles in Real Life

Let's consider how principles of learning work in some common real-life situations. For example, suppose your 3-year-old daughter repeatedly demands your attention while you are fixing dinner. Because you don't want to reinforce this behaviour, you ignore her the first six or eight times she calls you or tugs at your clothes. But after the ninth or tenth repetition, with her voice getting whinier each time, you can't stand it any longer and finally say something like "All right! What do you want?"

Since you have ignored most of her demands, you might think you have not been reinforcing them. But what you have actually done is create a partial reinforcement schedule. By responding to every ninth or tenth demand, you have, in essence, taught her that persistent whining will eventually be rewarded with attention. This intermittent pattern of reinforcement helps create behaviour that is very hard to extinguish. So your daughter may continue to be overly demanding for a very long time.

Another thing we know about reinforcement is that, when two people interact, they mutually shape each other's behaviour—for better or for worse. For example, if a child begins to holler at his mother to fetch his school lunch bag before he goes out the door, and the mother complies, two things happen. First, the mother has just strengthened the child's hollering behaviour through positive reinforcement by giving him what he wanted when he hollered; in this case, the school lunch bag. Second, the child has just strengthened the mother's obliging behaviour through negative reinforcement by taking away something the mother finds distressing; in this case, hollering.

We would predict that the next time the boy wants something from his mother, he is more likely to holler and, unfortunately, his mother is more likely to comply if the boy stops hollering once his mother gets him what he wants. As you can see, we can easily and inadvertently set up reciprocal patterns of reinforcement and expectations that can benefit one person, but disadvantage the other. Moreover, once such a pattern of reciprocal parent–child interaction is established, it can be very difficult to break, especially if you are not aware of the reinforcing sequence of events.

If such situations are all too familiar to you, then it may pay to keep careful records for a while, noting each incident and your response. Then see whether you can figure out which principles are really at work and how you might change the pattern.

Test Yourself before going on

1. Choose the correct options to complete the following sentence:
   Pavlov's experiments addressed (classical/operant) conditioning; Skinner's dealt with (classical/operant) conditioning.

2. A consequence that causes a behaviour to be repeated is a _____; one that stops a behaviour is a _____.

cognitive theories

theories that emphasize mental processes in development, such as logic and memory

scheme

in Piaget's theory, an internal cognitive structure that provides an individual with a procedure to follow in a specific circumstance

Learning Objective 2.11

Describe how cognitive development progresses, according to Piaget.

Cognitive Theories

The group of theories known as **cognitive theories** emphasize mental aspects of development, such as logic and memory. A cognitive theorist might propose that babies use their senses, including the sense of taste, to build mental pictures of the world around them. Thus, infants mouth everything in their environment until they have learned all they can from this behaviour, and then they move on to a more mature way of interacting with the world.

Piaget's Cognitive-Developmental Theory

For Jean Piaget (1896–1980) the central question of interest in developmental psychology was "How does thinking develop?" (Piaget, 1952, 1970, 1977; Piaget & Inhelder, 1969). He was struck by the fact that all children seem to go through the same sequence of discoveries about their world, making the same mistakes and arriving at the same solutions. For example, all 3- and 4-year-olds seem to think that if water is poured from a short, wide glass into a taller, narrower one, there is then more water, because the water level is higher in the narrow glass than it was in the wide glass. In contrast, most 7-year-olds realize that the amount of water has not changed. To explain such age differences, Piaget proposed several concepts that continue to guide developmental research.

SCHEMES A pivotal idea in Piaget's model is that of a **scheme**, an internal cognitive structure that provides an individual with a procedure to follow in a specific circumstance. For example, when you pick up a ball, you use your

(Photo: © Bill Anderson/Photo Researchers, Inc./Science Source)

Piaget based many of his ideas on naturalistic observations of children of different ages on playgrounds and in schools.

picking-up scheme. To throw the ball to someone, you use your looking scheme, your aiming scheme, and your throwing scheme. Piaget proposed that each of us begins life with a small repertoire of sensory and motor schemes, such as looking, tasting, touching, hearing, and reaching. As we use each scheme, it becomes better adapted to the world; in other words, it works better. During childhood and adolescence, mental schemes allow us to use symbols and think logically. Piaget proposed three processes to explain how children get from built-in schemes such as looking and touching to the complex mental schemes used in childhood, adolescence, and adulthood.

Assimilation is the process of using schemes to make sense of events or experiences. Piaget would say that a baby who grasps a toy is *assimilating* it to his grasping scheme. The complementary process is **accommodation**, which involves changing the scheme as a result of some new information acquired through assimilation. When the baby grasps a square object for the first time, he will accommodate his grasping scheme; so the next time he reaches for a square object, his hand will be more appropriately bent to grasp it. Thus, the process of accommodation is the key to developmental change. Through accommodation, we improve our skills and reorganize our ways of thinking.

Equilibration is the process of balancing assimilation and accommodation to create schemes that fit the environment. To illustrate, think about infants' tendency to put things in their mouths. In Piaget's terms, they assimilate objects to their mouthing scheme. As they mouth each object, their mouthing scheme changes to include the instructions "*Do* mouth this" or "*Don't* mouth this." The accommodation is based on mouthing experiences. A pacifier feels good in the mouth, but a dead insect has an unpleasant texture. So, eventually, the mouthing scheme says it's okay to put a pacifier in the mouth, but it's not okay to mouth a dead insect. In this way, an infant's mouthing scheme attains a better fit with the real world.

STAGES Piaget's research suggested to him that logical thinking evolves in four stages. During the *sensorimotor stage,* from birth to 18 months, infants use their sensory and motor schemes to act on the world around them. In the *preoperational stage,* from 18 months to about age 6, youngsters acquire symbolic schemes, such as language and fantasy, that they use in thinking and communicating. Next comes the *concrete operational stage,* during which 6- to 12-year-olds begin to think logically and become capable of solving problems, such as the one illustrated in **Figure 2.5**. The last phase is the *formal operational stage,* in which adolescents learn to think logically about abstract ideas and hypothetical situations.

Table 2.3 describes these stages more fully; you will read about each of them in detail later in the book. For now, it is important to understand that, in Piaget's view, each stage grows out of the one that precedes it, and each involves a major restructuring of the child's way of thinking. It's also important to know that research has confirmed Piaget's belief that the sequence of the stages is fixed. However, children progress through them at different rates. In addition, some individuals do not attain the formal operational stage in adolescence or even in adulthood. Consequently, the ages associated with the stages are approximations.

assimilation

the process of using schemes to make sense of events or experiences

accommodation

changing a scheme as a result of some new information

Critical Thinking

Describe three or four examples of assimilation and accommodation in your everyday life.

equilibration

the process of balancing assimilation and accommodation to create schemes that fit the environment

(Photo: Victoria Blackie/Dorling Kindersley, Ltd)

Using Piaget's terminology, we would say this infant is assimilating the object to his grasping scheme. What scheme is being accommodated at the same time as he adapts his grasping scheme?

information-processing theory

theoretical perspectives that use the computer as a model to explain how the mind manages information

Information-Processing Theory

The goal of **information-processing theory** is to explain how the mind manages information (Munakata, 2006). Information-processing theorists use the computer as a

Learning Objective 2.12

Describe information-processing theory processes.

Figure 2.5 In one of the problems Piaget devised, a child is shown two clay balls of equal size and asked if they both contain the same amount of clay. Next, the researcher rolls one ball into a sausage shape and asks the child if the two shapes still contain the same amount of clay. A preoperational child will say that one now contains more clay than the other and will base his answer on their appearance: "The sausage has more because it's longer now." A concrete operational thinker will say that the two still contain the same amount of material because no clay was added or taken away from either.

(Photo: © Tom Lindfors, www.lindforsphoto.com)

model of human thinking. Consequently, they focus on what happens to information as it enters the mind (*input*), is transformed by mental programs (*throughput*), and is used to perform actions (*output*).

MEMORY PROCESSES   Theorizing about and studying memory processes are central to information-processing theory. This theory breaks memory down into the subprocesses of encoding, storage, and retrieval. *Encoding* is organizing information to be stored in memory. For example, you may be encoding the information in this chapter

Table 2.3 Piaget's Cognitive-Developmental Stages

Approximate Ages	Stage	Description
Birth to 18 months	Sensorimotor	The baby understands the world through her senses and her motor actions; she begins to use simple symbols, such as single words and pretend play, near the end of this period.
18 months to 6 years	Preoperational	By age 2, the child can use symbols both to think and to communicate; he develops the abilities to take others' points of view, classify objects, and use simple logic by the end of this stage.
6 years to 12 years	Concrete operational	The child's logic takes a great leap forward with the development of new internal operations, such as conservation and class inclusion, but is still tied to the known world; by the end of the period, he can reason about simple "what if" questions.
12+ years	Formal operational	The child begins to manipulate ideas as well as objects; she thinks hypothetically and, by adulthood, can easily manage a variety of "what if" questions; she greatly improves her ability to organize ideas and objects mentally.

Figure 2.6 Information-processing research on memory is based on the assumption that information moves into, out of, and through the sensory, short-term, and long-term memories in an organized way.

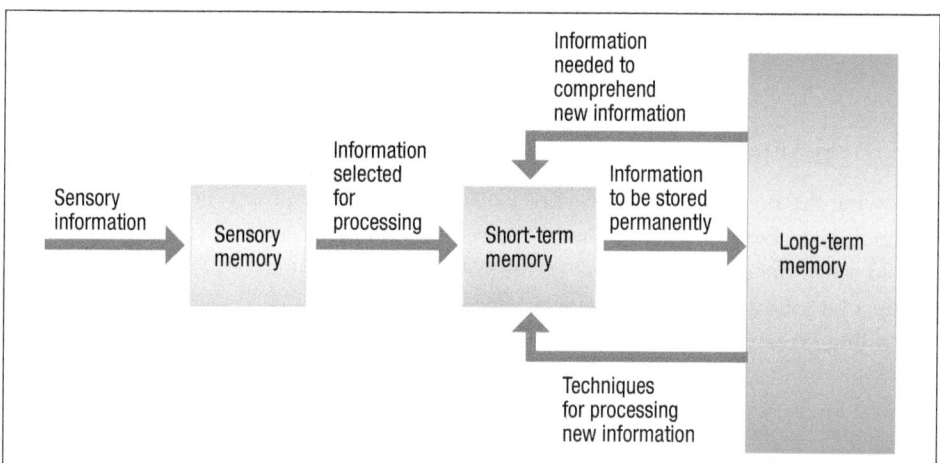

by relating it to your own childhood. *Storage* is keeping information, and *retrieval* is getting information out of memory. As information flows through these memory processes, we use mental strategies to manipulate information so that we can complete mental operations, solve everyday problems, and learn new tasks.

MEMORY COMPONENTS   Most memory research assumes that the human memory is made up of multiple components. The idea is that information moves through these components in an organized way (see **Figure 2.6**). The process of understanding a spoken word serves as a good example.

First, you hear the word when the sounds enter your *sensory memory*. Your experiences with language allow you to recognize the pattern of sounds as a word. Next, the word moves into your *short-term memory*, the component of the memory system where all information is processed. Thus, short-term memory is often called *working memory*. Knowledge of the word's meaning is then called up out of *long-term memory*, the component of the system where information is permanently stored, and placed in short-term memory, where it is linked to the word's sounds to enable you to understand the word.

Each memory component manages information differently. Information flows through the sensory memory in a constant stream, and bits of information that are not attended to drop out quickly. The short-term memory is extremely limited in capacity—it can contain only about seven items at a time. However, information can be retained in short-term memory as long as it is processed in some way—as you do when you repeat your grocery list to yourself on the way to the store.

Long-term memory is unlimited in capacity, and information is often organized and stored in terms of meaningful associations. For example, suppose you read a sentence such as "Bill wrote a letter to his brother." When you think about the sentence later, you might mistakenly recall that it contained the word *pen*. This happens because information about the process of writing and the tools used to do it are stored together in long-term memory.

York University psychologist Juan Pascual-Leone (1987) established **neo-Piagetian theories** by using information-processing theory to explain Piaget's stages. As fellow Canadian theorist Robbie Case (1944–2000) put it, neo-Piagetian theories expand on Piaget's theory rather than contradict it (Case, 1985, 1997). According to neo-Piagetians, older children and adults can solve complex problems such as those in Piaget's research because they can hold more pieces of information in their short-term memories at the same time than younger children can. To solve the problem described in

neo-Piagetian theory
an approach that uses information-processing principles to explain the developmental stages identified by Piaget

Figure 2.5, for example, a child must be able to think about the appearance of the two balls of clay before one was rolled into a sausage shape and their appearance afterward in her working memory at the same time. She must also think about how the transformation was carried out. Neo-Piagetians maintain that children are incapable of performing all this mental work in short-term memory until after age 6 or 7 (Case, 1985, 1997).

Vygotsky's Sociocultural Theory

Learning Objective 2.13

Describe how Vygotsky's concepts of scaffolding and zone of proximal development influence cognitive development.

sociocultural theory

Vygotsky's view that complex forms of thinking have their origins in social interactions rather than in an individual's private explorations

scaffolding

a process in which the learning of new cognitive skills is guided by someone who is more skilled

zone of proximal development

signifies tasks that are too hard for a child to do alone but that can be managed with guidance

Following the Bolshevik revolution of 1917, the new Soviet government hired Russian psychologist Lev Vygotsky (1896–1934), among others, to create a school system that would serve the ends of the new communist regime (Vygotsky, 1978). The historical events that followed his death—World War II and the Cold War—resulted in his work remaining largely unknown outside the former Soviet Union for decades. Since then, however, developmentalists have become interested in his views on the influence of cultural forces on individual development (Thomas, 2005).

SOCIAL INTERACTIONS BUILD COGNITIVE SKILLS   Vygotsky's **sociocultural theory** asserts that complex forms of thinking have their origins in social interactions rather than in the child's private explorations, as Piaget thought. According to Vygotsky, children's learning of new cognitive skills is guided by an adult (or a more skilled child, such as an older sibling), who structures the child's learning experience—a process Vygotsky called **scaffolding**. To create an appropriate scaffold, the adult must gain and keep the child's attention, model the best strategy, and adapt the whole process to the child's developmental level, or **zone of proximal development** (Landry, Garner, Swank, & Baldwin, 1996; Rogoff, 1990). Vygotsky used this term to signify tasks that are too hard for the child to do alone but that the child can manage with guidance. For example, parents of a beginning reader provide a scaffold when they help him sound out new words.

Vygotsky's ideas have important educational applications. Like Piaget's, Vygotsky's theory suggests the importance of opportunities for active exploration. But assisted discovery would play a greater role in a Vygotskian than in a Piagetian classroom; the teacher would provide the scaffolding for children's discovery, through questions, demonstrations, and explanations (Tharp & Gallimore, 1988). To be effective, the assisted discovery processes would have to be within the zone of proximal development of each child.

(Photo: inarik/Fotolia)

Developmental psychologist Lev Vygotsky hypothesized that social interactions among children are critical to both cognitive and social development.

Bandura's Social-Cognitive Theory

Learning theorist Albert Bandura was born and raised in Alberta and graduated with a bachelor's degree in psychology from the University of British Columbia in 1949 and a Ph.D. from the University of Iowa in 1952. His early theory emphasized the importance of psychological *modelling* in shaping our thoughts, emotions, and behaviour. Later, he describes how we exert influence over the events that affect our lives.

Learning Objective 2.14

Describe Bandura's concepts of modelling, reciprocal determinism, and self-efficacy.

LEARNING BY OBSERVING   Bandura's ideas emphasize the roles of thinking (cognition) and of learning by observation (modelling) in human behaviour (Bandura, 2001; Pajares, 2004; Zimmerman & Schunk, 2002). For example, Bandura's social-cognitive theory suggests that phobias may be learned *vicariously*, by watching

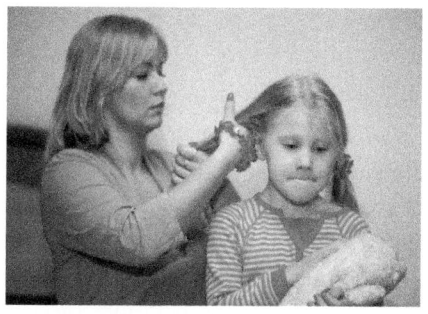

(*Photos*: left, Raisa Kanareva/Shutterstock; right, IAN HOOTON/Getty Images)

Modelling is an important source of learning for both children and adults. What behaviours have you learned by watching and copying others?

someone else perform some action and experience reinforcement or punishment. Learning of this type, called **observational learning, or modelling**, is involved in a wide range of behaviours. Children learn to hit by watching other people in real life and on television. Adults learn job skills by observing or being shown them by others. Bandura's ideas are more influential among developmental psychologists than those of the conditioning theorists, as he contends that learning does not always require reinforcement (Bandura, 1977a, 1982, 1989, 2001).

Furthermore, what a person learns from observing others is influenced by processes such as attention and memory. Maturation is important as well: A 4-year-old probably won't learn geometry from watching his high-school-age sister do her homework. Bandura also suggests that what an observer learns from a particular model is influenced by his own goals, expectations about what kinds of consequences are likely if he adopts the model's behaviour, and judgments of his own performance.

RECIPROCAL DETERMINISM   Bandura (1977a, 1986, 2001, 2006) later put forth the idea of **reciprocal determinism**, a process of human development based on the interaction of three factors: *personal* (cognitive abilities, physical characteristics, beliefs, attitudes, and expectations), *behavioural* (physical-motor and verbal actions), and *environmental* (other people and physical surroundings). Bandura's *reciprocal determinism model* forms a triangle of bidirectional influence (*modes of agency*) as depicted in **Figure 2.7**. From this perspective, we are not only affected by our circumstances, but we are also able to exert influence over our situation, which in turn affects our expectations

observational learning, or modelling

learning that results from seeing a model reinforced or punished for a behaviour

reciprocal determinism

a process of human development based on the interaction of personal, behavioural, and environmental factors

Figure 2.7 Bandura's social-cognitive model of human behaviour emphasizes the interaction of personal, behavioural, and environmental factors.

(**SOURCE:** Adapted from A. Bandura, 1977a, *Social Learning Theory* (1st ed.). Upper Saddle River, NJ: Prentice-Hall. © 1977. Reprinted by permission of Pearson Education Inc., Upper Saddle River, NJ.)

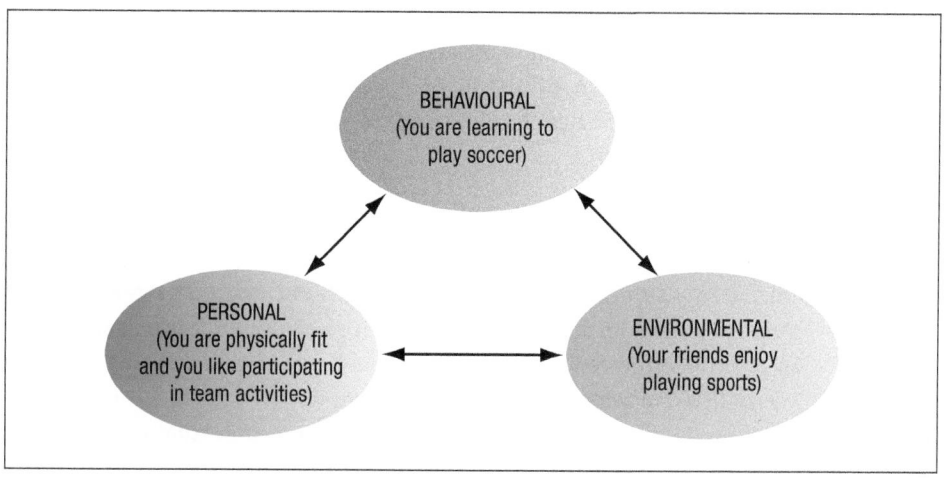

about how much influence we have over future events (a process of *coevolution*). In the case of children, they are actively involved in shaping the very environments that influence their behaviour and personality development.

self-efficacy

the belief in one's own capacity to cause an intended event to occur or to perform a task

SELF-EFFICACY With respect to personal factors, Bandura (1997a, 1997b) has placed particular emphasis on a concept he called **self-efficacy**—the belief in one's own capacity to cause an intended event to occur (a topic we will cover in later chapters). People who have a strong sense of self-efficacy have higher expectations for success and will put forth more effort and persistence when faced with a challenge. Conversely, a person with low self-efficacy has a lower expectation for success, which is associated with acquiescence or avoidance when confronted with a difficult task.

Test Yourself before going on

1. Piaget defined _____ as cognitive structures that provide a procedure to follow in a specific situation.
2. Match each term with its definition.
   _____ (a) assimilation
   _____ (b) accommodation
   _____ (c) equilibration
      (i) changing a scheme in response to new information
      (ii) adapting schemes to the real world
      (iii) incorporating new information into an existing scheme

3. Choose the correct option to complete the following sentence:
   Information-processing theorists (expand on/contradict) Piaget's ideas about cognitive development.
4. According to Vygotsky, a child's _____ includes tasks that the child cannot do alone but can accomplish with the help of an adult or older child.
5. Learning by watching someone else perform some action and receive either reinforcement or punishment is called _____ .
6. According to Bandura, the process of development based on the interaction of personal, behavioural, and environmental factors is called _____ .

systems approach

the view that personal factors together with external factors form a dynamic integrated system

holism

the view that the whole is greater than the sum of its parts

wellness

a measure of optimal holistic health

bioecological systems theory

Bronfenbrenner's theory that explains development in terms of the relationships among individuals and their environments, or interconnected contexts

Learning Objective 2.15

Describe how contexts influence development from Bronfenbrenner's bioecological perspective.

Systems Theory

The **systems approach** to human development takes into consideration the ever-changing (dynamic) interaction of personal factors with external factors. Personal factors may include biophysical, spiritual, intellectual, emotional, behavioural, and interpersonal aspects of functioning. External factors typically include the physical environment and social and cultural influences. A basic tenet of systems theory is that of *holism*. **Holism** maintains that the "whole" is primary and is greater than the sum of its parts. By way of example, consider that a loaf of bread is more than the sum of its ingredients: wheat flour, yeast, and water. A person develops in relation to changes in any part of the whole dynamic system. From this perspective, growth is the result of a reorganization of the system as it adjusts to change. When adjustment is adaptive, it promotes a high level of holistic health called **wellness**; when it is maladaptive, it can lead to disorder or dysfunction.

Bronfenbrenner's Bioecological Systems Theory

One prominent systems approach is Bronfenbrenner's **bioecological systems theory**. It explains development in terms of the relationships among individuals and their environments, or interconnected *contexts* (as Bronfenbrenner called them), over the passage of time, called the *chronosystem* (Bronfenbrenner, 1979, 2005). Urie Bronfenbrenner (1917–2005) attempted to classify the individual and contextual variables that affect development and to specify how they interact.

Figure 2.8 Bronfenbrenner's bioecological theory proposes that people are exposed to interconnected contexts that interact in complex ways over time to influence development.

(**SOURCE:** Artwork copyright © Alexandra Johnson. Printed with permission.)

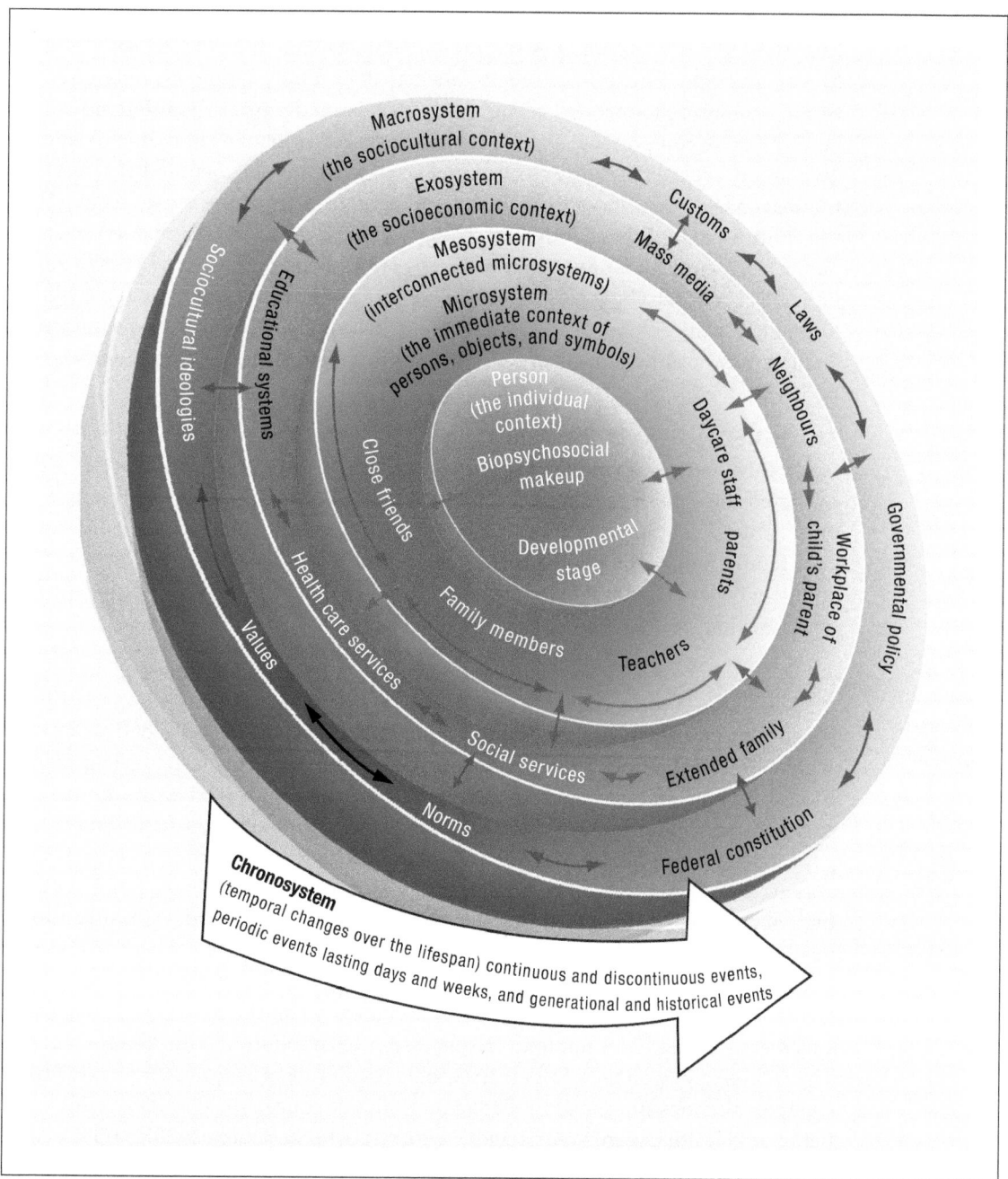

MACROSYSTEM According to Bronfenbrenner's theory, the contexts of development are like spheres within spheres (see **Figure 2.8**). The outermost sphere, the *macrosystem* (the sociocultural context), is the manifestation of the overarching sociocultural ideologies, values, and beliefs, and organization of the social systems and public policy through macroinstitutions, such as the federal government, in which a child is growing up. For example, Canadians' beliefs about the importance of education exist in the cultural context.

EXOSYSTEM The next level, the *exosystem* (the socioeconomic context), includes the institutions of the culture that affect children's development indirectly (e.g., the workplace of a child's parent, the social services, and the health care and educational systems). For example, funding for education exists in the socioeconomic context. The citizens of a specific nation may strongly believe that all children should be educated (sociocultural context), but their ability to provide universal education may be limited by the country's wealth (socioeconomic context).

MICROSYSTEM The *microsystem* (the immediate context) includes those variables to which people are exposed directly, such as their families, schools, religious institutions, and neighbourhoods. The *mesosystem* is made up of the interconnections between these components. For example, the specific school a child attends and her own family are part of the microsystem. Her parents' involvement in her school and the response of the school to their involvement are part of the mesosystem. Thus, the culture a child is born into may strongly value quality education. Moreover, her nation's economy may provide ample funds for schooling. However, her own education will be more strongly affected by the particular school she attends and the connections, or lack thereof, between her school and her family. Thus, the child's immediate context may be either consistent with the cultural and socioeconomic contexts or at odds with them.

THE PERSON Finally, the child's genetic makeup and developmental stage—her *individual context*—also influence her development. For example, a student who hasn't mastered the skill of reading isn't likely to benefit from an enriched literature program. Thus, her culture, the socioeconomic situation, the school she attends, and her own family may all be geared toward providing a quality education; however, her ability to benefit from it will be determined by the degree to which her education fits her individual needs.

Learning Objective 2.16

Explain why ecobiodevelopmentalists endorse early intervention strategies.

Ecobiodevelopmental Theory

Recent conceptualizations are building upon earlier systems theories of development such as Bronfenbrenner's bioecological model. Harvard University developmentalist Jack P. Shonkoff and others are helping the systems approach become more mainstream by encouraging stakeholders, ranging from policy makers to practitioners and parents to embrace a more interdisciplinary approach to human development (Garner, Forkey, & Szilagyi, 2015; Shonkoff & Garner, 2012; Thiele & Anderson, 2016). Notably, their efforts were influential in the American Academy of Pediatrics' (AAP) endorsement of an interdisciplinary, science-based approach toward national early childhood policy and practice. Accordingly, the AAP now supports an *ecobiodevelopmental* (EBD) framework for designing, testing, and refining early childhood interventions aimed specifically at health promotion and disease prevention (Shonkoff & Garner, 2012). The AAP is calling on its members to become leaders and advocates for national social change—a sentiment echoed by Canadian health organizations (Hertzman, 2013) and the World Health Organization's global efforts (Garner & Shonkoff, 2012; WHO, 2012).

This new EBD framework for research, policy, and programs is informed by a growing body of evidence that indicates that the foundations of healthy development, and the origins of many impairments and susceptibilities to diseases and metal disorders, can be biologically embedded through epigenetic–environment interactions beginning prior to conception and continuing throughout the early years of life (Lomanowska, Boivin, Hertzman, & Fleming, 2015; Pembrey, Saffery, & Bygren, 2014; Shonkoff, 2010; Vaiserman, 2015a, 2015b). The implication is that the most cost-effective way to bring about improvements in health, both nationally and globally, is to focus efforts on, and intervene prior to and during, the prenatal and early childhood periods of development (Nagle & Usry, 2016; Shonkoff & Garner, 2012). These efforts may include the formation and implementation of policies and strategies that reduce the disruptive effects of prolonged and intense adversity in early childhood

Critical Thinking

Many of the children growing up in refugee camps experience traumatic events, inadequate food and shelter, and many are not enrolled in school. What implications does this hold for these children's futures and for their resettlement in destination countries, such as Canada?

(what scientists now call *toxic stress*) ranging from nutritional deficiencies to maltreatment (read more about toxic stress in the chapter on Physical and Cognitive Development in Early Childhood).

Comparing Theories

Overview of Human Development Theories

After learning about theories, students usually want to know which one is right. However, developmentalists don't think of theories in terms of right or wrong but instead compare theories on the basis of their assumptions and how useful they are in promoting understanding of development. Today's developmentalists often don't adhere to a single theory but take an approach that is more integrated and taps the strengths of each of the major theoretical perspectives (see **Table 2.4**). Although theories provide a framework for understanding human development, they are dynamic and always changing. As new discoveries are made, theories are modified and adapted to account for new information.

Learning Objective 2.17
Determine the distinguishing characteristics of human development theories.

Table 2.4 Overview of Human Development Theories

Theory	Main Idea	Evaluation Strengths	Weaknesses
Biological	**Biological and physiological processes (e.g., those involving genes, hormones, and neurotransmitters) influence traits and behaviours.**	**Biological principles that underlie genetics and epigenetics are expanding our understanding of human health and disease processes; discovering the complex role that inheritance plays in human health and the related importance of early intervention.**	**Biological approaches may neglect the impact of psychological factors, sociocultural factors, and family conditions on development.**
Genetic	Emphasizes the genetic origins of human behaviour.	Relevant to many fields, ranging from molecular medicine to a better understanding of human evolution; has contributed to advances in medicine and biotechnology.	Ethical issues around gene patents, genetic testing, discrimination, privacy, genetic modification; our genetic makeup accounts for only a portion of human traits.
Epigenetic	The environment and life experiences have immediate and long-term influences on gene expression, the genetic code, and, by extension, human behaviour and health.	Contributes to our understanding of the inheritance factors involved in vulnerability and resilience to disease and disorder; focuses attention on the need to promote early interventional strategies during prenatal and early childhood development.	The precise, underlying mechanisms by which the environment and life experiences can alter epigenetic markings remain largely unknown.
Evolutionary	The genetic makeup of populations changes over generations by favouring traits that enable individuals to survive and reproduce.	Focuses attention on the importance of early-life influences on later behaviour and health outcomes.	Underestimates the impact of the environment and places too much emphasis on heredity; the theories are difficult to prove.

(Continued)

Table 2.4 Overview of Human Development Theories (*Continued*)

Theory	Main Idea	Evaluation Strengths	Weaknesses
Psychoanalytic	**Adult behaviour and feelings, including psychological problems, stem from our childhood experiences.**	**Highlights the important role parenting has on early childhood experiences; proposes that the child's needs change with age, so that parents and other caregivers must constantly adapt to the changing child.**	**Many psychoanalytic concepts were derived from individual case studies and cannot be readily applied universally; the concepts are difficult to test empirically (e.g., how do we objectively measure internal drives and emotions?).**
Freud's Psychosexual Theory	Personality develops in five stages from birth to adolescence; in each stage, the need for physical pleasure is focused on a different part of the body.	Emphasizes importance of experiences in infancy and early childhood; provides psychological explanations for mental illness; has given psychologists a number of helpful concepts, such as the unconscious, the ego, and defence mechanisms.	Sexual feelings are not as important in personality development as Freud claimed; concepts, such as libido and psychosexual, are more descriptive than scientific in nature.
Erikson's Psychosocial Theory	Personality develops through eight life crises across the entire lifespan; a person finishes each crisis with either a good or a poor resolution.	Helps explain the role of culture in personality development; important in lifespan psychology; useful description of personality development at different ages.	Describing each period in terms of a single crisis is probably an oversimplification.
Humanistic	**Emphasized the basic goodness of human beings; each individual has a unique potential and has an inborn drive for personal growth and achieving self-actualization.**	**Shifted the focus of development on to individual choices more so than emotional, biological, or societal forces; inherently optimistic and gives people more credit in controlling and determining their well-being.**	**The concepts are difficult to test empirically because the propositions are not stated clearly enough (e.g., how do we objectively measure self-actualization?).**
Maslow's Theory of Motivation	One is motivated to satisfy a range of physical, social, and psychological needs; the ultimate goal in life is to achieve self-actualization.	Focused attention on healthy development.	The terms and hierarchical ranking of Maslow's list of needs are unproven.
Rogers's Theory of the Self	Emphasized the individual's responsibility for, and the active role one plays in, furthering one's personal growth.	The individual can effect change toward personal growth.	Tends to discount the importance of past events.
Behavioural	**Behaviour is determined by the environment through conditioning; behaviourism is primarily concerned with observable behaviour, as opposed to internal mental events like thinking; empirical data is collected through careful and controlled observation and measurement.**	**Learning theories can explain both consistency and changes in behaviour; optimistic about the possibility of change—behaviour can change if the reinforcement system changes, so, problem behaviours can be modified; provide an accurate picture of the way in which many behaviours are learned.**	**The traditional learning theorists' approach is not developmental; it doesn't tell us much about change over a lifespan, in either childhood or adulthood.**
Pavlov's Classical Conditioning	Learning happens when neutral stimuli become so strongly associated with natural stimuli that they elicit the same response.	Useful in explaining how emotional responses, such as phobias, are learned.	Explanation of behavioural change is too limited to serve as a comprehensive theory of human development.
Skinner's Operant Conditioning Theory	Development involves behaviour changes that are shaped by reinforcement and punishment.	Basis of many useful strategies for managing and changing human behaviour.	Humans are not as passive as Skinner claimed; the theory ignores hereditary, cognitive, emotional, and social factors in development.
Cognitive	**Behaviour can be largely explained in terms of how the mind operates, e.g., memory, thinking, and problem-solving processes occur between stimulus and response.**	**The science of cognitive psychology is based mainly on laboratory experiments; has contributed to many effective therapeutic interventions.**	**Much research involves artificial laboratory tasks, such as learning lists of words, and therefore, it doesn't always fully describe how the mind works in the real world.**
Piaget's Theory of Cognitive Development	Reasoning develops in four universal stages from birth through adolescence; in each stage, the child builds a different kind of scheme.	Helps explain how children of different ages think about and act on the world.	Piaget was inexact about some of the ages at which children develop particular skills; the stage concept may cause adults to underestimate children's reasoning abilities; there may be additional stages in adulthood.

Information-Processing Theory	Human cognitive functioning; encoding, storage, and retrieval processes change with brain maturation and practice, causing changes in cognitive functioning.	Helps explain how much information people of different ages can manage at one time and how they process it; provides a useful framework for studying individual differences in people of the same age.	Human information-processing is much more complex than that of a computer; the theory doesn't provide an overall picture of development.
Vygotsky's Sociocultural Theory	Cognitive development is strengthened through social interactions that involve speaking during guided problem-solving tasks.	Stresses the importance of sociocultural interaction for cognitive development.	Verbal instructions may not benefit cognitive development in some cultures.
Bandura's Social-Cognitive Theory	People learn from models and what is learned depends on how they interpret the situation; a child's level of cognitive development affects his or her impressions and reactions to circumstances; we both shape and are shaped by our environment.	Helps explain how models influence behaviour; adds further to our understanding of human development by integrating cognitive, emotional, social, and environmental factors.	Does not provide an overall picture of development—biological influences are underemphasized.
Systems	**Provides an interdisciplinary perspective to the study of human development; both humans and their environments are active in the developmental process.**	**Captures the complexity of individual and contextual variables and the interactions among these variables.**	**It is hard to form generalizations and predictions because of the complexity of interactions among variables.**
Bronfenbrenner's Bioecological Theory	Human development is a product of individual and contextual variables interacting over time.	Highlights the need for research examining the complex interactions among individual and contextual variables.	Underplays physical environmental influences (ranging from pollution to poor nutrition or disease).
Shonkoff's Ecobiodevelopmental Theory	There is a need for a science-based approach toward creating early childhood policies, practices, and interventions aimed specifically at health promotion and disease prevention.	Promotes advocacy across all levels of the socioeconomic and political spectrums with health care professionals taking on a lead role.	Determining causal links among developmental variables raises research methodological and ethical challenges.

Test Yourself before going on

1. Identify whether the following theoretical trends in human development are True or False.
_____ (a) nowadays developmentalists generally adhere to a single theory
_____ (b) theories provide a framework for understanding human development
_____ (c) theories are modified and adapted to account for new information

Critical Thinking

2. Which of the many theories in this chapter do you find to be most useful to your own efforts to understand development? What are the theory's assumptions that you may find helpful as a caregiver?

Summary

Biology and Evolutionary Theories

2.1 **Describe the structure and function of genes.**
- Biological theories focus on the contribution of hereditary genetic mechanisms in development.

2.2 **Describe the ways genes influence development.**
- Geneticists distinguish between the genotype (the pattern of inherited genes) and the phenotype (the individual's observable characteristics).

2.3 **Describe how epigenetic mechanisms regulate genes and development.**
- Inherited and acquired epigenetic mechanisms regulate gene expression.

2.4 **Describe how evolutionary theories explain individual differences.**
- Evolutionary theories take the view that, through a process of biological evolution, the body, mind, and social behaviours have been

shaped by natural selection to serve adaptive functions and promote survival.

2.5 Describe how biology and evolutionary theories contribute to our understanding of disease processes and interventions.

- After conception, both external and personal factors act to modify epigenetic regulators. These factors can alter patterns of gene expression and suppression and play a role in disease processes. Epigenetic changes can influence the health of future generations.

Psychoanalytic Theories

2.6 Summarize the main ideas of Freud's psychosexual theory.

- Freud emphasized that behaviour is governed by both conscious and unconscious motives and that the personality develops in steps: The id is present at birth; the ego and the superego develop in childhood. Freud proposed psychosexual stages: the oral, anal, phallic, latency, and genital stages.

2.7 Identify the conflict associated with each of Erikson's psychosocial stages.

- Erikson emphasized social forces more than unconscious drives as motives for development. He proposed that personality develops in eight psychosocial stages over the course of the lifespan: trust versus mistrust; autonomy versus shame and doubt; initiative versus guilt; industry versus inferiority; identity versus role confusion; intimacy versus isolation; generativity versus stagnation; and integrity versus despair.

2.8 Describe the basic concepts of humanistic theory.

- Humanistic theorist Abraham Maslow suggested that individuals are motivated to fulfill inner needs in order to ultimately attain self-actualization.

- Carl Rogers maintained that parents influence a child's developing sense of self-worth, which in turn affects his personal growth.

Learning Theories

2.9 Explain how classical conditioning occurs.

- Classical conditioning—learning through association of stimuli—helps explain the acquisition of emotional responses.

2.10 Explain the process of operant conditioning.

- Operant conditioning involves learning to repeat or stop behaviours because of their consequences.

Cognitive Theories

2.11 Describe how cognitive development progresses, according to Piaget.

- Piaget focused on the development of logical thinking. He discovered that such thinking develops across four childhood and adolescent stages: the sensorimotor, preoperational, concrete operational, and formal operational. He proposed that movement from one stage to another is the result of changes in mental frameworks called schemes.

2.12 Describe information-processing theory processes.

- Information-processing theory uses the computer as a model to explain intellectual processes such as memory and problem-solving. It suggests that there are both age differences and individual differences in the efficiency with which humans use their information-processing systems.

2.13 Describe how Vygotsky's concepts of scaffolding and zone of proximal development influence cognitive development.

- Vygotsky's sociocultural theory has become important to developmentalists' attempts to explain how culture affects development.

2.14 Describe Bandura's concepts of modelling, reciprocal determinism, and self-efficacy.

- Bandura's social-cognitive theory assumes reciprocal interactions among persons and behavioural factors and the environment.

Systems Theory

2.15 Describe how contexts influence development from Bronfenbrenner's bioecological perspective.

- Bronfenbrenner's bioecological systems theory has helped developmental psychologists categorize environmental factors and think about the ways in which they influence individuals.

2.16 Explain why ecobiodevelopmentalists endorse early intervention strategies.

- Policy makers and caregivers are encouraged to embrace an interdisciplinary approach to human development because the origins of many impairments can be biologically embedded through gene–environment interactions beginning at conception and continuing throughout the early years of life.

Comparing Theories

2.17 Determine the distinguishing characteristics of human development theories.

- Developmentalists take an integrated approach that taps into the strengths of each of the major theoretical perspectives. Although theories provide a framework for understanding human development, they are revised by new discoveries.

Chapter 3
Prenatal Development and Birth

Andersen Ross/Blend Images/Corbis

 Learning Objectives

CONCEPTION

3.1 Explain the process of reproduction.

PREGNANCY AND PRENATAL DEVELOPMENT

3.2 Describe the mother's experience during the three trimesters of pregnancy.

3.3 Outline the milestones of the three stages of prenatal development.

3.4 List some of the ways male and female fetuses differ.

3.5 Describe some of the behaviours scientists have observed in fetuses.

ISSUES IN PRENATAL DEVELOPMENT

3.6 Identify the effects of the major dominant, recessive, and sex-linked disorders.

3.7 Identify common trisomy errors and sex-chromosome anomalies that can affect development.

3.8 Identify the risks associated with teratogenic maternal diseases.

3.9 Describe the potential adverse effects of drugs on prenatal development.

3.10 Describe other maternal factors that can adversely influence prenatal development.

3.11 Describe how mutagenic, environmental, and epigenetic teratogens adversely affect prenatal development.

3.12 Describe how preconceptual and prenatal paternal factors can adversely influence development.

3.13 Identify preconceptual and prenatal assessment and diagnostic procedures.

BIRTH AND THE NEONATE

3.14 Summarize the birth choices available to expectant parents.

3.15 Describe what happens in each of the three stages of labour.

3.16 Identify what assessment tools are used to assess the health of a newborn.

3.17 Describe the risks associated with low birth weight in infants.

Today, news of an impending birth is cause for celebration, but it hasn't always been that way. In years past, high rates of maternal and infant mortality caused people in most cultures to delay celebrations and even the naming of the child until long after her birth. Thankfully, most mothers and babies survive and flourish these days, and, as a result, pregnancies and births are seen as important decision points in both parents' and children's lives. "What should I eat?" the mother-to-be wonders. Family and friends ask her, "What do you think about midwives?" and "Will the baby be born in a birthing centre or a hospital?" and "Are you planning a medication-free delivery?" It helps to know what long-term consequences the child may experience as a result of the prenatal and birth choices that her parents make.

The technological advances that have reduced maternal and fetal mortality rates have transformed the subjective and social experience of pregnancy from one of fear and dread to one of joy and anticipation. These advances have also been accompanied by innovations that have allowed researchers and parents-to-be to gain insight into prenatal developmental processes that were shrouded in mystery just a few decades ago. As you explore this chapter, you will become acquainted with some of these insights and, we hope, gain a greater appreciation for the amazing process of prenatal development.

Conception

The first step in the development of an individual human being happens at conception, when each of us receives a combination of genes that will shape our experiences throughout the rest of our lives.

Learning Objective 3.1

Explain the process of reproduction.

The Process of Conception

Ordinarily, a woman produces one *ovum* (egg cell) per month from one of her two ovaries, roughly midway between menstrual periods. If the ovum is not fertilized, it travels from the ovary down the *fallopian tube* toward the *uterus*, where it gradually disintegrates and is expelled as part of the menstrual fluid. However, if a couple has intercourse during the crucial few days when the ovum is in the fallopian tube, one of the millions of sperm ejaculated as part of each male orgasm may travel the full distance through the woman's vagina, cervix, uterus, and fallopian tube and penetrate the wall of the ovum.

gametes

cells that unite at conception (ova in females; sperm in males)

zygote

a single cell created when sperm and ovum unite

CONCEPTION Every cell in the human body contains 23 pairs of chromosomes, or strings of genetic material. However, sperm and ovum, collectively called **gametes**, contain 23 single (unpaired) chromosomes.

At conception, chromosomes in the ovum and the sperm combine to form 23 pairs in an entirely new cell called a **zygote**. Twenty-two of these pairs of chromosomes, called *autosomes*, contain most of the genetic information for the new individual. The 23rd pair, the *sex chromosomes*, determines the sex. One of the two sex chromosomes, the *X chromosome*, is one of the largest chromosomes in the body and carries a large number of genes. The other, the *Y chromosome*, is quite small and contains only a few genes. Zygotes containing two X chromosomes develop into females, and those containing one X and one Y chromosome develop into males. Since the cells in a woman's body contain only X chromosomes, all her ova carry X chromosomes. Half of a man's sperm contain X chromosomes; the other half contain Y chromosomes. Consequently, the sex of the new individual is determined by the sex chromosome in the sperm.

MULTIPLE BIRTHS In most cases, human infants are conceived and born one at a time. However, in about 3.2 out of every 100 births in Canada, more than one baby is born, usually twins (Statistics Canada, 2016b). Roughly two-thirds of twins are *fraternal twins*, or twins that come from two sets of ova and sperm. Such twins, also called *dizygotic twins* (meaning that they originate from two zygotes), are no more alike genetically than any other pair of siblings and need not even be of the same sex. The remaining one-third of twins are *identical twins* (*monozygotic*, or arising from one zygote). Identical twins result when a single zygote, for unknown reasons, separates into two parts, each of which develops into a separate individual. Because identical twins develop from the same zygote, they have identical genes. Research involving identical twins is one of the major investigative strategies in the field of behaviour genetics (see the **Research Report**).

Over the past three decades, the annual number of multiple births has tripled in Canada (Bushnik & Garner, 2008; Statistics Canada, 2016a). Furthermore, births of triplets, quadruplets, and quintuplets have increased even more dramatically—over 230% since the mid-1990s (Public Health Agency of Canada [PHAC], 2008a). One reason for the increase is that the number of women over age 35 giving birth for the first time has grown. Two factors underlie the association between multiple births and maternal age. First, for reasons that researchers don't yet understand, women are far more likely to naturally conceive twins and other multiples after age 35. Second, women over age 35 are more likely than younger women to experience difficulty becoming pregnant and thus are more likely to be treated with *assisted human reproduction* procedures—including ovulation stimulation drugs (Johnson & Tough, 2012; Sultana, Chen, Lee, & Hader, 2011). Women of all ages who use these procedures are more likely to deliver multiples than women who conceive naturally.

assisted human reproduction (AHR)

"any activity undertaken for the purpose of facilitating human reproduction" (Health Canada, 2001a)

ASSISTED HUMAN REPRODUCTION Assisted human reproduction (AHR) and related research is now regulated in Canada. The legislation, introduced as Bill C-6, protects the health and safety of Canadians undergoing AHR treatment and the children born from such procedures (Communication Canada, 2004).

Research Report

Twins in Genetic and Epigenetic Research

Researchers interested in the role of heredity in human development have been comparing identical and fraternal twins since the earliest days of developmental psychology. The logic is this: If identical twins (whose genes are exactly the same) who are raised apart are more similar than fraternal twins or non-twin siblings (whose genes are similar, but not identical) who are raised together, heredity must play a role in the trait being studied. For example, the numbers below are correlations based on several studies of twins' intelligence test scores (Eliot, 1999). The closer to +1.00 a correlation is, the stronger the relationship.

Identical twins reared together	0.86
Identical twins reared apart	0.72
Fraternal twins reared together	0.60
Non-twin siblings reared apart	0.24

As you can see, intelligence test scores are more strongly correlated in identical twins than in fraternal twins or non-twin siblings, even when the identical twins are raised in different families. Such findings are taken to be evidence for the heritability of intelligence.

Canadian researchers from the University of Western Ontario and the University of British Columbia have also studied the heritability of other human traits, such as attitudes. They surveyed 195 pairs of identical and 141 pairs of fraternal adult twins and found that about 35% of the difference in attitudes could be attributed to genetic factors. Measures of how strongly twins favoured various issues, activities, and social settings revealed that twins' attitudes about, for example, abortion on demand, roller-coaster rides, playing organized sports, and the death penalty for murder yielded a high genetic influence (Olson, Vernon, Aitken Harris, & Jang, 2001).

Taken together, the findings of these studies point to strong genetic components in both intelligence and attitudes.

However, what these studies reveal about environment may be even more significant. If psychological characteristics such as intelligence and attitudes were determined solely by heredity, identical twins would be exactly alike, and researchers would find correlations of +1.00. The correlations that twin researchers have found are less than +1.00, even for identical twins who grow up in the same home. Moreover, the correlations for identical twins raised apart are lower than those for identical twins raised together.

To help explain these puzzling facts, scientists are now looking closely at a third component, epigenetic variables, to help explain phenotypic differences (Fraga, 2009; Gordon et al., 2012; Haque, Gottesman, & Wong, 2009; Hochberg et al., 2011; Rutter, 2007)—especially in cases of complex non-Mendelian conditions, such as Alzheimer's, breast cancer, or psychotic disorders (Guintivano, & Kaminsky, 2016; Kaminsky et al., 2009). A landmark study of 80 pairs of monozygotic (Mz) twins, conducted by Fraga et al. (2005), helps to illustrate the point that discordance in behaviour and disease observed in pairs of identical twins is linked to epigenetic variables. Researchers in the study found that younger pairs of Mz twins had indistinguishable epigenetic patterns and physical traits. In comparison, middle-aged pairs of Mz twins showed sizeable differences in their epigenetic patterns and phenotypic characteristics and, in these pairs, twins who lived dissimilar lifestyles and spent less time together during their lifetimes had even greater epigenetic differences. The researchers suggest that, over the course of a lifetime, environmental variables (e.g., differences in diet, smoking, fitness levels) bring about changes in epigenetic markers in genetically identical pairs of twins, which, in turn, produce phenotypic changes, including the frequency and onset of disease.

To date, genetic twin studies have proved useful, although not altogether complete. Epigenetic analysis of twins will likely spur on the next wave of heritability research. As Canadian epigeneticist, Arturas Petronis (2006, p. 349), contends, "epigenetics could emerge as a unifying concept for the large variety of non-Mendelian features in complex traits."

The use of fertility drugs (e.g., hormones that stimulate gamete production) is one of many AHR procedures available to couples who have trouble conceiving. Another is *in vitro fertilization* (IVF), popularly known as the "test-tube baby" method (*in vitro* is Latin for "in glass"). This technique involves uniting an ovum and a sperm in a laboratory dish and implanting the resulting embryo in a woman's uterus. The egg can come from the woman who will carry the child or from a donor. Likewise, sperm can be from the woman's partner or a donor.

Typically, IVF laboratories create numerous embryos, which are then frozen, or *cryopreserved*, prior to being implanted. Newer **cryopreservation** protocols involve immersing embryos in *cryoprotectants* (antifreeze-like liquid that permeates the

cryopreservation

preserving cells or tissues through a freezing process that stops all biological activity

vitrification

the use of cryoprotectants along with rapid cooling to prevent the fluid in biological tissues (e.g., eggs, semen, embryos) from forming ice crystals (that act like glass shards on cell structures) and from dehydrating; the tissue becomes an intact, non-crystalline, glass-like solid that can be preserved for years

embryo) and then plunging them into super-cooled liquid nitrogen (–210 °C), which freezes the embryos almost instantly (Huang et al., 2005). This **vitrification** protocol significantly improves the survival rate of embryos during the thawing process, implantation, and pregnancy (Kim, Laufer, & Wook Hong, 2010; Liebermann, 2009, 2015). This newer protocol reduces the need to transfer multiple fertilized embryos to a woman's womb, which lowers the potential risk of multiple gestations.

Several studies have addressed concerns about the possible side effects of cryopreservation on children's development. In fact, one recent large-scale Australian study did not find any significant side effects of the procedure (Davies et al., 2012). However, IVF is not a highly successful procedure. For one thing, the older a woman is, the lower the probability that she will be able to achieve a successful IVF pregnancy following a frozen embryo transfer. Roughly 31% of Canadian women under age 35 undergoing IVF achieve a live birth, but only about 15% of IVF procedures involving women aged 40 and over are successful (Canadian Fertility and Andrology Society, 2015). And, even though younger Canadian women who wish to delay motherhood until a later age can harvest, freeze, and store their "younger" eggs (gametes) for many years, there is no guarantee that using "youthful" eggs will increase the odds of successful fertilization of those eggs when these women are older (Roberts, 2007).

Multiple births are more frequent among women who become pregnant by using IVF because doctors typically transfer several embryos at once to increase the likelihood of at least one live birth, but multiple births place both mother and babies at risk. This increased risk has contributed to an ongoing debate in Canada and across the globe as to what constitutes a relevant standard of success in reproductive technology. Some argue that successful AHR outcomes should be defined as a single, term-gestation, live baby per fertility cycle (e.g., Min, Breheny, MacLachlan, & Healy, 2004). Others emphasize that once couples who are undergoing AHR are made aware of the maternal and neonatal mortality rates and they accept the risk associated with the possibility of having more than one baby, then having either one or more could be considered an AHR success (e.g., Buckett & Tan, 2004). All the same, *single embryo transfer* (SET) will likely become the international norm in IVF treatment. Nordic countries, for example, have high rates of SET (~70%) and a consistent pregnancy rate of ~30% per embryo transfer (Nygren, 2007). To reduce the chance of multiple births following IVF, Canadian guidelines now recommend that women under the age of 35 years should receive no more than two embryos per fertility cycle and women over 39 years of age should be transferred no more than four, unless there are exceptional circumstances when a woman with a poor conception prognosis has a history of multiple failed IVF attempts (Min, Claman, & Hughes, 2006).

Another technique, *artificial insemination*, is more successful and less likely to result in multiple births. In artificial insemination, sperm are injected directly into a woman's uterus, usually during the part of her menstrual cycle when she is most likely to conceive. The procedure can employ the sperm of a woman's partner or that of a donor. This method is most often used by couples in which the male partner has a low sperm count or by fertile women who want to conceive without a male partner. However, as in any invasive medical procedure, artificial insemination carries some risk of infection.

Assisted human reproductive techniques have been somewhat controversial. For example, if ova and sperm are provided by anonymous donors, it is impossible to determine the genetic heritage of children conceived through these donations. Canada's *Assisted Human Reproduction Act* has addressed this concern by legislating the maintenance of a personal health information registry that contains nonidentifying medical information about the sperm and egg donors (Clement, 2006). This registry will allow children of donated sperm and ova to have access to their medical histories.

Test Yourself before going on

1. Match each term with its definition.
_____ (a) gametes
_____ (b) zygote
_____ (c) dizygotic

(i) sperm and ovum unite to form 23 pairs of chromosomes in this entirely new cell
(ii) cells that unite at conception
(iii) describes twins that develop from two fertilized ova

2. Match the AHR technique with its description.
_____ (a) fertility drug injections
_____ (b) in vitro fertilization
_____ (c) artificial insemination

(i) hormones are used to stimulate gamete production
(ii) sperm are injected directly into a woman's uterus
(iii) ovum and a sperm unite in a laboratory dish before implanting the resulting embryo in a woman's uterus

Pregnancy and Prenatal Development

Pregnancy is a physical condition in which a woman's body is nurturing a developing embryo or fetus. *Prenatal development*, or *gestation*, is the process that transforms a zygote into a newborn. Thus, the process that ends with the birth of a baby involves two sets of experiences: those of the pregnant woman, and those of the developing zygote, embryo, and fetus.

The Mother's Experience

Pregnancy is customarily divided into *trimesters*, three periods of three months each (see **Table 3.1**).

FIRST TRIMESTER Pregnancy begins when the zygote implants itself in the lining of the woman's uterus (also called the *womb*). The zygote then sends out chemical messages that cause the woman's menstrual periods to stop. Some of these chemicals are excreted in her urine, making it possible to diagnose pregnancy within a few days after conception. Other chemicals cause physical changes, such as breast enlargement.

Learning Objective 3.2

Describe the mother's experience during the three trimesters of pregnancy.

Table 3.1 Pregnancy Summary

Trimester	Events	Prenatal Care	Serious Problems
First trimester: From first day of last menstrual period (LMP) to 12 weeks after LMP	Missed period Breast enlargement Abdominal thickening	Confirmation of pregnancy Calculation of due date Blood and urine tests (and other tests, if needed) Monthly doctor visits to monitor vital functions, uterine growth, weight gain, and sugar and protein in urine	Ectopic pregnancy Abnormal urine or blood tests Increased blood pressure Malnutrition Bleeding Miscarriage
Second trimester: From 12 weeks after LMP to 24 weeks after LMP	Weight gain "Showing" Fetal movements felt Increased appetite	Monthly doctor visits continue Ultrasound to measure fetal growth and locate placenta	Gestational diabetes Excessive weight gain Increased blood pressure Rh incompatibility of mother and fetus Miscarriage 13 to 20 weeks Premature labour 21+ weeks
Third trimester: From 25 weeks after LMP to beginning of labour	Weight gain Breast discharge	Weekly visits beginning at 32nd week Ultrasound to assess position of fetus, if needed Treatment of Rh incompatibility, if needed Pelvic exams to check for cervical dilation	Increased blood pressure Bleeding Premature labour Bladder infection

The *cervix* (the narrow, lower portion of the uterus, which extends into the vagina) thickens and secretes mucus that serves as a barrier to protect the developing embryo from harmful organisms that might enter the womb through the vagina. The uterus begins to shift position and put pressure on the woman's bladder, causing her to urinate more often. This and other symptoms, such as fatigue and breast tenderness, may interfere with sleep. Another common early symptom of pregnancy is *morning sickness*—feelings of nausea, often accompanied by vomiting, that usually occur in the morning but can occur at any time of the day or the night.

Prenatal care during the first trimester is critical to prevent congenital anomalies, because all of the baby's organs form during the first eight weeks. Early prenatal care can identify maternal conditions, such as sexually transmitted infections (STIs), that may threaten prenatal development. Health professionals can also urge women to abstain from drugs and alcohol early in prenatal development, when such behaviour changes may prevent congenital anomalies.

Early prenatal care can also be important to the pregnant woman's health. For example, in a small number of cases, a zygote implants in one of the fallopian tubes instead of in the uterus, a condition called *ectopic pregnancy*. Early surgical removal of the zygote is critical to the woman's future ability to have children.

About 15% of pregnancies end in miscarriage, or *spontaneous abortion*. From the woman's point of view, an early-term miscarriage is similar to a menstrual period, although feelings of discomfort and blood loss are usually greater. Medical care is always necessary after a late-term miscarriage because the woman's body may fail to completely expel the embryo.

SECOND TRIMESTER   During the second trimester of pregnancy, from the end of week 12 through week 24, morning sickness usually disappears, resulting in increased appetite. The pregnant woman gains weight, and the uterus expands to accommodate a rapidly growing fetus. Consequently, the woman begins to "show" sometime during the second trimester. She also begins to feel the fetus's movements, usually at some point between the 16th and 18th weeks.

At monthly prenatal checkups, the doctor or midwife monitors both the mother's and the baby's vital functions and keeps track of the growth of the baby in the womb. Ultrasound tests are usually performed, and the sex of the baby can be determined

During the second trimester of pregnancy, an ultrasound test allows for the diagnosis of fetal deformities and growth problems, the fetus's position in the uterus, and the position of the placenta. As well, sometimes it is possible to identify the sex of the fetus.

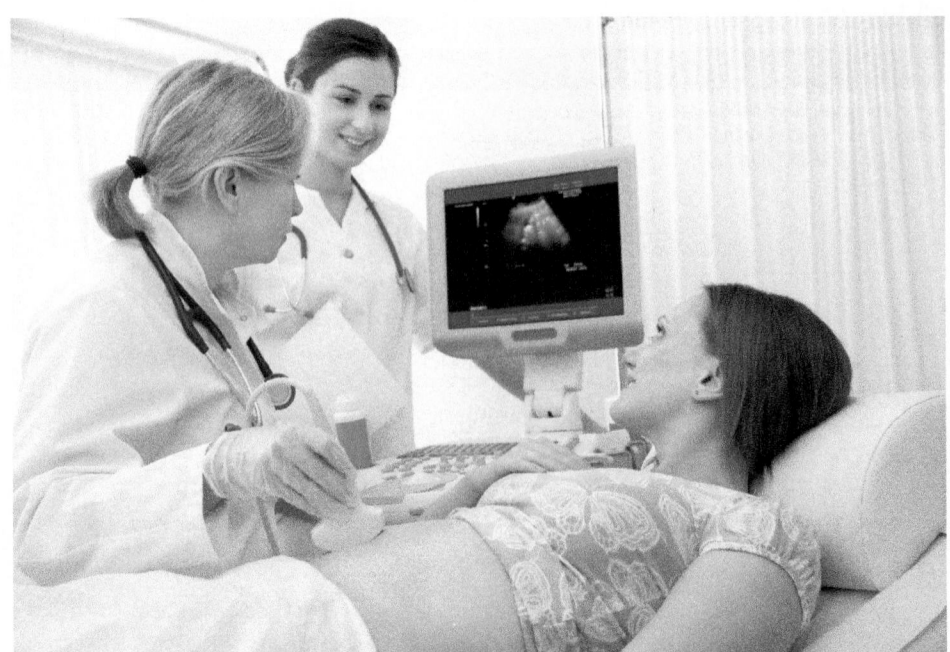

(Photo: Alexander Raths/Fotolia)

after about the 13th week. Monthly urine tests check for *gestational diabetes*, a kind of diabetes that happens only during pregnancy. A woman who has any kind of diabetes, including gestational diabetes, has to be carefully monitored during the second trimester because her baby may grow too rapidly, leading to premature labour or a baby that is too large for vaginal delivery.

The risk of miscarriage drops in the second trimester. However, a few fetuses die between the 13th and 20th weeks of pregnancy. In addition, premature labour after the 21st week can result in delivery of a living but extremely small baby. A small percentage of such infants survive, but most have significant health problems.

(Photo: bikeriderlondon/Shutterstock)

Supportive partners, friends, and relatives can help third-trimester mothers-to-be maintain positive attitudes and balance negative emotions that often accompany their feelings of physical awkwardness against the anticipated joy of birth.

THIRD TRIMESTER   At 25 weeks, the pregnant woman enters her third trimester. Weight gain and abdominal enlargement are the main experiences of this period. In addition, the woman's breasts may begin to secrete a substance called *colostrum* in preparation for nursing.

Most women begin to feel more emotionally connected to the fetus during the third trimester (DiPietro, 2010). Individual differences in fetal behaviour, such as hiccupping or thumb-sucking, sometimes become obvious during the last weeks of pregnancy. In addition, most women notice that the fetus has regular periods of activity and rest.

Monthly prenatal checkups continue in the third trimester until week 32, when most women begin visiting their doctor or midwife once a week. Monitoring of blood pressure is especially important, as some women develop a life-threatening condition called *toxemia of pregnancy* during the third trimester. This condition is signalled by a sudden increase in blood pressure and can cause a pregnant woman to have a stroke.

Prenatal Development

In contrast to the trimesters of pregnancy, the three stages of prenatal development are defined by specific developmental milestones and are not of equal length. Moreover, the entire process follows two developmental patterns that you can see at work in the photographs in **Table 3.2**. With the **cephalocaudal pattern**, development proceeds from the head downward. For example, the brain is formed before the reproductive organs. With the **proximodistal pattern**, development happens in an orderly way from the centre of the body outward to the extremities. In other words, structures closer to the centre of the body, such as the rib cage, develop before the fingers and toes.

THE GERMINAL STAGE   The first two weeks of gestation, from conception to *implantation*, constitute the **germinal stage**. During this stage, cells specialize into those that will become the fetus's body and those that will become the structures needed to support its development. Cell division happens rapidly, and by the fourth day, the zygote contains dozens of cells.

On day 5, the cells become a hollow, fluid-filled ball called a *blastocyst*. Inside the blastocyst, cells that will eventually become the embryo begin to clump together. On day 6 or 7, the blastocyst comes into contact with the uterine wall, and by the 12th day, it is completely buried in the uterine tissue, a process called **implantation**. Some cells from the blastocyst's outer wall combine with cells of the uterine lining to begin creating the **placenta**, an organ that allows oxygen, nutrients, and other substances to be transferred between the mother's and baby's blood. The placenta's specialized structures bring the mother's and baby's blood close to one another without allowing them to mix.

cephalocaudal pattern

growth that proceeds from the head downward

Learning Objective 3.3

Outline the milestones of the three stages of prenatal development.

proximodistal pattern

growth that proceeds from the middle of the body outward

germinal stage

the first stage of prenatal development, beginning at conception and ending at implantation (approximately two weeks)

implantation

attachment of the blastocyst to the uterine wall

placenta

specialized organ that allows substances to be transferred from mother to embryo and from embryo to mother without their blood mixing

Table 3.2 Milestones in Prenatal Development

Stage/Timeframe	Milestones
Germinal Stage Day 1: Conception	Sperm and ovum unite, forming a zygote containing genetic instructions for the development of a new and unique human being.

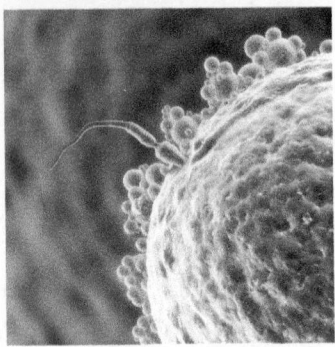

(*Photo:* Zygote Media Group/Dorling Kindersley, Ltd)

Days 10 to 14: Implantation	The zygote burrows into the lining of the uterus. Specialized cells that will become the placenta, umbilical cord, and embryo are already formed.

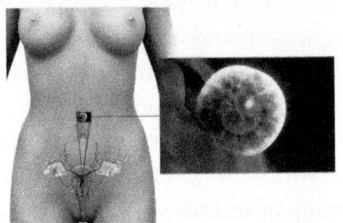

(*Photo:* 3D4Medical/Photo Researchers, Inc./Science Source)

Embryonic Stage Weeks 3 to 8: Organogenesis	All the embryo's organ systems form during the six-week period following implantation.

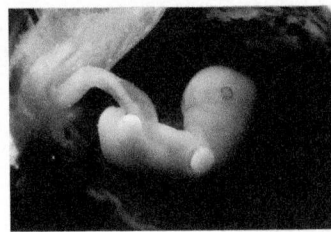

(*Photo:* Dopamine/Photo Researchers, Inc./Science Source)

Fetal Stage Weeks 9 to 38: Growth and Organ Refinement	The fetus grows from 2.5 cm and 7 g to a length of about 51 cm and a weight of 3.2 kg. By week 12, most fetuses can be identified as male or female. Changes in the brain and lungs make viability possible by week 24; optimum development requires an additional 14 to 16 weeks in the womb. Most neurons form by week 28, and connections among them begin to develop shortly thereafter. In the last eight weeks, the fetus can hear and smell, is sensitive to touch, and responds to light. Learning is also possible.

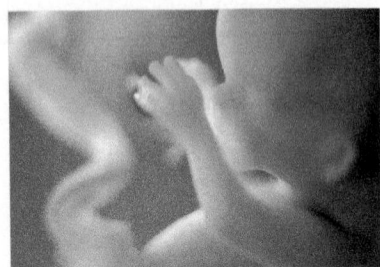

(*Photo:* Dopamine/Photo Researchers, Inc./Science Source)

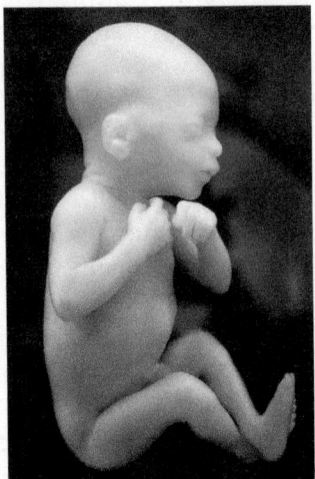

(*Photo:* ninjaMonkeyStudio/E+/Getty Images)

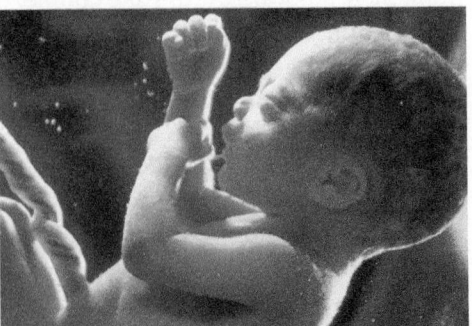

(*Photo:* Petit Format/Photo Researchers, Inc./Science Source)

(**SOURCES:** Kliegman, 1998; Tortora & Grabowski, 1993).

Like the zygote, the placenta secretes chemical messages (hormones) that stop the mother's menstrual periods and keep the placenta connected to the uterus. Other placental hormones allow the bones of the woman's pelvis to become more flexible, induce breast changes, and increase the mother's metabolic rate. At the same time, the blastocyst's inner cells begin to specialize. One group of cells will become the **umbilical cord**, the organ that connects the embryo to the placenta. Vessels in the umbilical cord carry blood from the baby to the mother and back again. Other cells will form the *yolk sac*, a structure that produces blood cells until the embryo's blood-cell-producing organs are formed. Still others will become the **amnion**, a fluid-filled sac in which the baby floats until just before it is born. By the 12th day, the cells that will become the embryo's body are also formed.

THE EMBRYONIC STAGE   The **embryonic stage** begins at implantation, approximately two weeks after conception, and continues until the end of week 8. By the time many women first suspect a pregnancy, usually three weeks after conception, the embryo's cells are starting to specialize and come together to form the foundations of all the body's organs. For example, the cells of the nervous system, the **neurons**, form a structure called the *neural tube*, from which the brain and spinal cord will develop. A primitive heart and the forerunners of the kidneys also develop during week 3, along with three sacs that will become the digestive system.

In week 4, the end of the embryo's neural tube swells to form the brain. Spots that will become the eyes appear on the embryo's head, and its heart begins to beat. The backbone and ribs become visible as bone and muscle cells move into place. The face starts to take shape, and the endocrine system begins to develop.

By week 5, the embryo is about 6.5 millimetres long, 10 000 times larger than the zygote. Its arms and legs are developing rapidly. Five fingers are visible on each hand. Its eyes have corneas and lenses, and its lungs are beginning to develop.

In week 6, the embryo's brain begins to produce patterns of electrical activity. It moves in response to stimuli, and the **gonads**, or sex glands (ovaries in females and testes in males), develop. Development of the gonads depends upon the presence or absence of *androgens* (male sex hormones, such as testosterone). Androgens cause the gonads to become testes, but in the absence of androgens, the gonads develop into ovaries.

During week 7, embryos begin to move spontaneously (Joseph, 2000). They have visible skeletons and fully developed limbs. The bones are beginning to harden and the muscles are maturing; by this point, the embryo can maintain a semi-upright posture. The eyelids seal shut to protect the developing eyes. The ears are completely formed, and X-rays can detect tooth buds in the jawbones.

During the last week of the embryonic stage, week 8, the liver and spleen begin to function. These organs allow the embryo to make and filter its own blood cells. Its heart is well developed and efficiently pumps blood to every part of the body. The embryo's movements increase as the electrical activity in its brain becomes more organized. Connections between the brain and the rest of the body are also well established. The embryo's digestive and urinary systems are functioning. By the end of week 8, **organogenesis**, the technical term for organ development, is complete.

THE FETAL STAGE   The final phase is the **fetal stage**, beginning at the end of week 8 and continuing until birth. The fetus grows from a weight of about 2 grams and a length of 2.5 centimetres to a baby born around 38 weeks weighing about 3.2 kilograms and having a length of about 50 centimetres. In addition, this stage involves refinements of the organ systems—especially the lungs and brain—that are essential to life outside the womb (see **Table 3.3**).

A few babies born as early as week 20 or 21 survive. By the end of week 22, 20 to 33% of babies have attained **viability**, the ability to live outside the womb (Kyser, Morriss, Bell, Klein, & Dagle, 2012). Remaining in the womb just one week longer,

umbilical cord

organ that connects the embryo to the placenta

amnion

fluid-filled sac in which the fetus floats until just before it is born

embryonic stage

the second stage of prenatal development, from week 2 through week 8, during which the embryo's organ systems form

neurons

specialized cells of the nervous system

gonads

sex glands (ovaries in females; testes in males)

organogenesis

process of organ development

fetal stage

the third stage of prenatal development, from week 9 to birth, during which growth and organ refinement take place

viability

ability of the fetus to survive outside the womb

Table 3.3 Milestones of the Fetal Stage

Period	What Develops
Weeks 9–12	Fingerprints; grasping reflex; facial expressions; swallowing and rhythmic "breathing" of amniotic fluid; urination; genitalia appear; alternating periods of physical activity and rest
Weeks 13–16	Hair follicles; responses to mother's voice and loud noises; 8 to 12 centimetres long, crown to rump; weighs 25 to 100 g
Weeks 17–20	Fetal movements felt by mother; heartbeat detectable with stethoscope; lanugo (hair) covers body; eyes respond to light introduced into the womb; eyebrows; fingernails; 13–17 cm long, crown to rump; weighs 140–300 g
Weeks 21–24	Vernix (oily substance) protects skin; lungs produce surfactant (vital to respiratory function); viability becomes possible, although most born now do not survive
Weeks 25–28	Recognition of mother's voice; regular periods of rest and activity; 35–38 cm long, crown to heel; weighs 660–1000 g; good chance of survival if born now
Weeks 29–32	Very rapid growth; antibodies acquired from mother; fat deposited under skin; 39–43 cm long, crown to heel; weighs 1.2–1.7 kg; excellent chance of survival if born now
Weeks 33–36	Movement to head-down position for birth; lungs mature; approximately 44–48 cm long, crown to heel; weighs about 1.9–2.6 kg; virtually 100% chance of survival if born now
Weeks 37+	Full-term status; about 49 cm long, crown to heel; weighs about 3 kg

until the end of week 23, increases a baby's chances of survival to 38 to 58%. By the end of week 24, 58 to 87% survive. The extra weeks probably allow time for lung function to become more efficient. In addition, most premature babies today are treated with drugs that accelerate lung development. As a result, survival rates of even the earliest-born preemies have greatly increased since the turn of the 21st century (Kyser et al., 2012).

THE FETAL BRAIN   As you learned earlier, the foundational structures of all the body's organ systems are formed during the embryonic stage. Yet most of the formation and fine-tuning of the brain takes place during the fetal stage. Recall that neurons, the specialized cells of the nervous system, begin developing during the embryonic stage in week 3. But the pace of neural formation picks up dramatically between the 10th and 18th weeks, a process known as *neuronal proliferation*.

Between the 13th and 21st weeks, the newly formed neurons migrate to the parts of the brain where they will reside for the rest of the individual's life (Johnson, 2011). While migrating, neurons consist only of **cell bodies**, the part of the cell that contains the nucleus and in which all the cell's vital functions are carried out (see **Figure 3.1**). Once they have reached their final destinations in the fetal brain, the neurons begin to develop connections. These connections are called **synapses**, tiny spaces between neurons across which neural impulses travel from one neuron to the next. Several changes in fetal behaviour signal that the process of synapse formation is underway. For instance, the fetus exhibits alternating periods of activity and rest and begins to yawn (Walusinski, Kurjak, Andonotopo, & Azumendi, 2005). When observed, these changes tell physicians that fetal brain development is proceeding normally.

Synapse formation requires the growth of two neuronal structures. **Axons** are tail-like extensions that range in length from 1 to 200 millimetres within the brain, but they can grow to be more than a metre long (e.g., between the spinal cord and the body's extremities). **Dendrites** are tentacle-like branches that extend out from the cell body (see Figure 3.1). Dendrite development is thought to be highly sensitive to adverse environmental influences such as maternal malnutrition and defects in placental functioning (Dieni & Rees, 2003).

cell bodies

the part of a neuron that contains the nucleus and is the site of vital cell functions

synapses

tiny spaces across which neural impulses flow from one neuron to the next

axons

tail-like extensions of neurons

dendrites

branch-like protrusions from the cell bodies of neurons

Figure 3.1 The structure of a single developed neuron. The cell bodies are the first to be developed, primarily between weeks 12 and 24. Axons and dendrites develop later, especially during the final 12 weeks, and continue to increase in size and complexity for several years after birth.

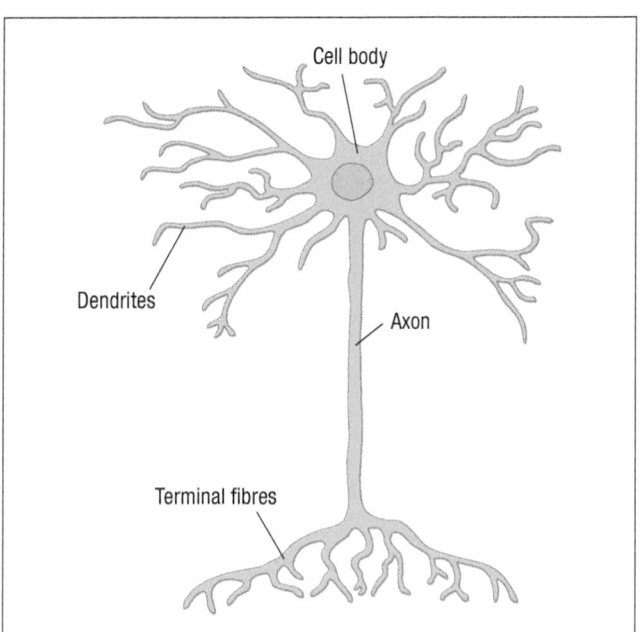

Simultaneously with neuronal migration, **glial cells** begin to develop. These cells are the "glue" that hold the neurons together to give shape to the brain's major structures. The brain now begins to assume a more mature appearance, one that can be observed using *magnetic resonance imaging* (MRI) and other modern technologies that you will read more about later in the chapter (see **Figure 3.2**).

glial cells

specialized cells in the brain that support neurons

Figure 3.2 This image shows a normal third-trimester fetal brain. Glial cells that develop during the last few months of prenatal development hold neurons together and give form and structure to the fetal brain.

(**PHOTO:** Courtesy of Michael and Alexandra Enns)

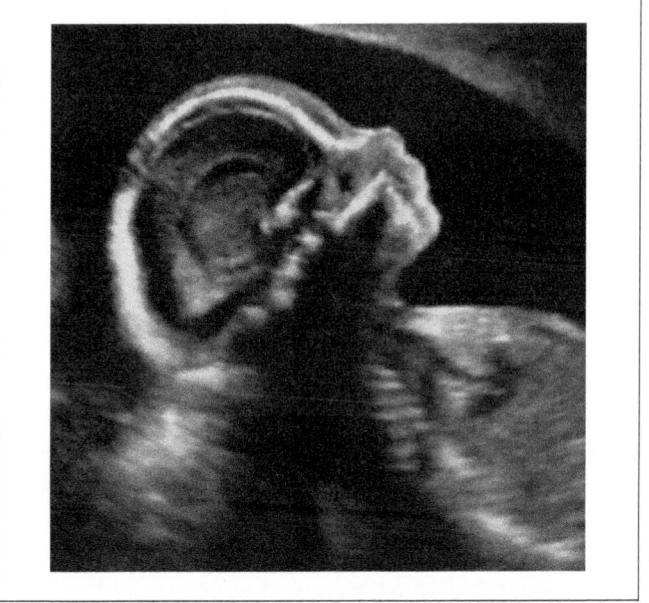

Sex Differences

Sometime between four and eight weeks following conception, the *SRY gene* on the Y chromosome signals the male embryo's body to begin secreting hormones called androgens. As mentioned earlier, development of the gonads—testes in males and ovaries in females—depends upon the presence or absence of androgens. These hormones also cause male genitals to develop. If androgens are not present, female genitals develop no matter what the embryo's chromosomal status is. Likewise, female embryos that are exposed to androgens, either via medications that the mother is taking or a genetic disorder called *congenital adrenal hyperplasia*, can develop male-appearing external genitalia.

Prenatal androgens also influence the developing brain, although any sex differences in the brain do not necessarily translate into sex differences in behaviour (McCarthy, 2016). Still, there are some structural differences in the developing prenatal brain wherein some brain regions are larger (e.g., due to more numerous and densely packed neurons) while other regions are smaller, so that some areas of the brain can be more masculine in males and more feminine in females (McCarthy, 2015). This may play a role in the development of sex differences in areas of cognitive functioning, spatial ability, verbal ability, physical aggression, communication skills, and the development of sexual orientation later in life (Auyeung, Lombardo, & Baron-Cohen, 2013; Hines, Constantinescu, & Spencer, 2015), as well as in certain neuropsychiatric disorders such as major depressive disorder in females and autism spectrum disorders in males (McCarthy, 2015). It also is becoming apparent that all body organs are sexually differentiated to some extent and this may help to explain sex differences in disease patterns later in life (De Vries, & Forger, 2015). (We will explore these topics in greater detail in later chapters.)

Before birth, boys and girls show some differences in growth patterns in the second and third trimesters. Females tend to grow more slowly, which is determined by some standard measures such as head width and circumference, femur length, weight, and overall length (Melamed et al., 2013). Another finding is that male fetuses are more responsive to touch, while female fetuses appear to be more responsive to sounds (Arabin, 2009; Groome et al., 1999). Female infants are about one to two weeks ahead in bone development at birth, even though newborn boys are typically longer and heavier. Female superiority in skeletal development persists through childhood and early adolescence, causing girls to acquire many coordinated movements and motor skills, especially those involving the hands and wrists, earlier than boys. The gap between the sexes gets wider every year until the mid-teens, when boys catch up and surpass girls in general physical coordination (Tanner, 1990).

Prenatal Behaviour

Centuries before scientists began to study prenatal development, pregnant women noticed fetal responses to music and other sounds. In recent years, techniques such as ultrasound imaging have provided researchers with a great deal more information about fetal behaviour. Some researchers suggest that establishing norms for fetal behaviour would help health care providers better assess fetal health and predict postnatal problems (DiPietro et al., 2010; Nijhuis, 2003). Thus, in recent years, the number of research studies examining fetal behaviour has increased significantly. These studies have revealed some rather remarkable findings.

For one thing, researchers have discovered that the fetus can distinguish between familiar and novel stimuli by the 32nd or 33rd week (Sandman, Wadhwa, Hetrick, Porto, & Peeke, 1997). Evidence for fetal learning comes from studies in which newborns appear to remember stimuli to which they were exposed prenatally: their mother's heartbeats, the odour of the amniotic fluid, and the stories or pieces of music they heard in the womb (Righetti, 1996; Schaal, Marlier, & Soussignan, 1998). For example, in a classic study of prenatal learning, pregnant women read Dr. Seuss's children's story *The Cat in the Hat* out loud each day for the final six weeks of their pregnancies. After the infants were born, they were allowed to suck on special pacifiers that turned a variety of sounds off and on. Each kind of sound required a special type of sucking. Researchers found that the babies quickly adapted their sucking patterns in order to listen to the familiar story, but did not increase their sucking in order to listen to an unfamiliar story (DeCasper & Spence, 1986). In other words, babies preferred the sound of the story they had heard *in utero* (in the womb).

In another study, researchers from Queen's University and Zhejiang University in China exposed full-term fetuses to either their mother's voice or to the voice of a female stranger via loudspeaker. In both cases the same poem was read to each fetus. The fetuses demonstrated a significantly different heart-rate pattern in response to the poem read by their mother (heart rate increase) than to that read by a stranger (heart rate decrease), suggesting that fetuses can remember and recognize their mother's voice (Kisilevsky et al., 2003).

Stable individual differences in behaviour are also identifiable in fetuses. Longitudinal studies have shown that very active fetuses, both males and females, tend to become children who are very active (DiPietro, Ghera, & Costigan, 2008). Moreover, these children are more likely to be labelled "hyperactive" by parents and teachers. In contrast, fetuses who are less active than average are more likely to be intellectually delayed (Accardo et al., 1997).

Test Yourself before going on

1. Label each item on the list as characteristic of the first, second, or third trimester of pregnancy.
   _____ (a) ectopic pregnancy
   _____ (b) fetal movement felt
   _____ (c) breast enlargement
   _____ (d) colostrum production may begin
   _____ (e) ultrasound to locate placenta
2. In which stage, germinal, embryonic, or fetal, does each of these milestones of prenatal brain development occur?
   _____ (a) migration of neurons to lifelong positions in the brain
   _____ (b) brain begins to produce patterns of electrical activity
   _____ (c) neural tube swells to form the brain
   _____ (d) synapses between neurons form
3. Prenatal differences in _____ _____ may be a factor in the development of male/female differences in physical, cognitive, and social development.
4. Why do some researchers believe that it is important to establish norms for prenatal behaviour?

Critical Thinking

5. Why do you think most expectant mothers become emotionally attached to the fetus during the third trimester?

Issues in Prenatal Development

Prenatal development is not immune to outside influences, as you'll see in this section. Keep in mind that most of the problems you'll read about are very rare, many are preventable, and many need not have permanent consequences for the child. In Canada, ~4% of babies are born with a **congenital anomaly**—an abnormal structure, function, or body metabolism present at birth that results in physical or mental disability or death (PHAC, 2012a).

congenital anomaly
an abnormality present at birth

Genetic Disorders

Many disorders appear to be transmitted through the operation of dominant and recessive genes (see **Table 3.4**). *Autosomal disorders* are caused by genes located on the autosomes (chromosomes other than sex chromosomes). The genes that cause *sex-linked* disorders are found on the X chromosome.

Learning Objective 3.6
Identify the effects of the major dominant, recessive, and sex-linked disorders.

Table 3.4 Some Genetic Disorders

Autosomal Dominant Disorders	Autosomal Recessive Disorders	Sex-Linked Recessive Disorders
Huntington's disease	Phenylketonuria	Hemophilia
High blood pressure	Sickle-cell disease	Fragile-X syndrome
Extra fingers	Cystic fibrosis	Red–green colour blindness
Migraine headaches	Tay-Sachs disease	Missing front teeth
Schizophrenia	Kidney cysts in infants	Night blindness
	Albinism	Some types of muscular dystrophy
		Some types of diabetes

(**SOURCES:** Amato, 1998; Tortora & Grabowski, 1993.)

AUTOSOMAL DISORDERS   Most disorders caused by recessive genes are diagnosed in infancy or early childhood. For example, a recessive gene causes a baby to have problems digesting the amino acid phenylalanine. Toxins build up in the baby's brain and cause developmental delay. This condition, called *phenylketonuria (PKU)*, is found in about 1 in every 12 000 to 17 000 babies (Levy & Marion, 2015). If a baby consumes no foods containing phenylalanine, however, he will not become intellectually delayed. Milk is one of the foods PKU babies can't have, so early diagnosis is critical. For this reason, there is universal screening for PKU soon after birth in all Canadian provinces.

Like many recessive disorders, PKU is associated with ethnicity. Caucasian babies are more likely to have the disorder than infants in other groups. Similarly, West African and African American infants are more likely to suffer from *sickle-cell disease*, a recessive disorder that causes red blood cell deformities (Raj & Bertolone, 2010). In sickle-cell disease, the blood can't carry enough oxygen to keep the body's tissues healthy. However, with early diagnosis and antibiotic treatment, more than 90% of children diagnosed with the disease survive to adulthood (Maakaron, 2013).

About 1 in every 3000 babies born to couples of Eastern European Jewish ancestry suffers from another recessive disorder, *Tay-Sachs disease*. Another group that is at risk for the disease is French Canadians in the Gaspé region of Quebec; they carry the gene for a severe form of Tay-Sachs disease at a rate 10 times that of the general population (Myerowitz & Hogikyan, 1987; Triggs-Raine, Richard, Wasel, Prence, & Natowicz, 1995). A baby with Tay-Sachs is likely to be severely intellectually delayed and blind. Very few survive past the age of 3 (Ierardi-Curto, 2013).

Disorders caused by dominant genes, such as *Huntington's disease*, are usually not diagnosed until adulthood (Levy & Marion, 2015). This disorder causes the brain to deteriorate and affects both psychological and motor functions. The risk of Huntington's in Canada is 1 in 10 000, and the child of a parent with Huntington's has a 50% chance of developing the disease (Huntington Society of Canada, 2013). A blood test can now identify the Huntington's gene. Thus, people who have a parent with this disease can now make better decisions about their own child-bearing, as well as prepare themselves to live with a serious disorder when they get older.

SEX-LINKED DISORDERS   Most sex-linked disorders are caused by recessive genes. One fairly common sex-linked recessive disorder is *red–green colour blindness*. People with this disorder have difficulty distinguishing between the colours red and green when these colours are adjacent. About 7 to 8% of men and 0.5% of women have this disorder. Most learn ways of compensating for the disorder and thus live perfectly normal lives.

A more serious sex-linked recessive disorder is *hemophilia*. The blood of people with hemophilia lacks the chemical components that cause blood to clot. Thus, when a person with hemophilia bleeds, the bleeding doesn't stop naturally. Approximately 1 in 5000 baby boys is born with this disorder, which is almost unknown in girls (Zaiden, 2016).

About 1 in every 4000 males and 1 in every 8000 females has a sex-linked disorder called *fragile-X syndrome* (Jewell, 2009). A person with this disorder has an X chromosome with a "fragile," or damaged, spot. Fragile-X syndrome can cause developmental delay that becomes progressively worse as a child gets older (Jewell, 2009).

Chromosomal Errors

Learning Objective 3.7

Identify common trisomy errors and sex-chromosome anomalies that can affect development.

A variety of problems can be caused by a child having too many or too few chromosomes, a condition referred to as a *chromosomal error* or *chromosomal anomaly*. Like genetic disorders, these are distinguished by whether they involve autosomes or sex chromosomes.

TRISOMIES   A *trisomy* is a condition in which a child has three copies of a specific autosome. The most common is *trisomy 21*, or *Down syndrome*, in which the child has three copies of chromosome 21. The number of infants born with this anomaly has remained fairly constant in Canada, averaging one in 800 births (Mamayson, 2009). These children are intellectually delayed and have distinctive facial features and often other health concerns such as hypothyroidism, hearing loss, or heart anomalies (Chen, 2010).

The risk of bearing a child with trisomy 21 is greatest for mothers over 35. Among Canadian women aged 35 to 39, the rate of Down syndrome is about 1 in 350 births. Among women 40 to 45, it climbs to 1 in 150 births and for women above age 45, Down syndrome is present in almost one-quarter of all births (Health Canada, 2002a). These figures underestimate the true rates by 15 to 24% because they exclude spontaneous abortions and terminated pregnancies (Benn & Egan, 2000).

Scientists have identified children with trisomies in the 13th and 18th pairs of chromosomes as well (Best & Gregg, 2009; Chen, 2009). These disorders have more severe effects than trisomy 21. Few trisomy 13 or trisomy 18 children live past the age of 1 year. As with trisomy 21, the chances of having a child with one of these disorders increase with a woman's age.

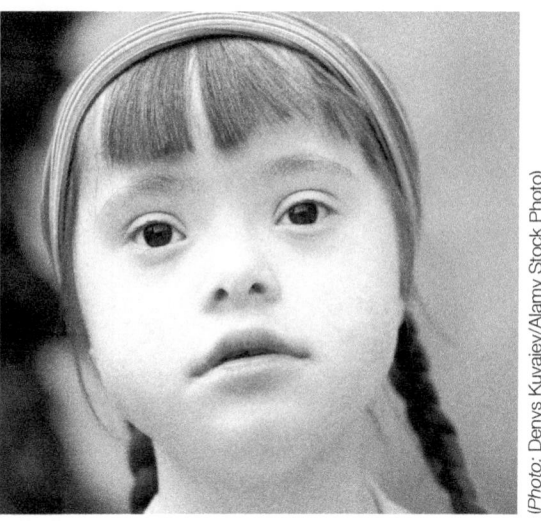

This child shows the distinctive facial features of a child with Down syndrome.

SEX-CHROMOSOME ANOMALIES   A second class of anomalies is associated with the sex chromosomes. The most common is an XXY pattern, called *Klinefelter's syndrome,* which occurs in 1 or 2 out of every 1000 males (Levy & Marion, 2015). Affected boys usually look normal but have underdeveloped testes and, as adults, very low sperm production. Most are not intellectually delayed, but many have language and learning disabilities. At puberty, these boys experience both male and female changes. For example, their penises enlarge and their breasts develop.

A single-X pattern (XO), called *Turner's syndrome*, may also occur. Individuals with Turner's syndrome are anatomically female but show stunted growth. They are also at higher risk than others of having malformations of internal organs such as the heart and kidneys (Levy & Marion, 2015). Without hormone therapy, most individuals with Turner's syndrome do not menstruate or develop breasts at puberty. Nevertheless, about 10% experience normal puberty and have little or no difficulty conceiving children and carrying them to term (Levy & Marion, 2015). Many others can achieve successful pregnancies with the aid of donor ova.

Teratogens: Maternal Diseases

teratogens

substances such as viruses and drugs that can cause congenital anomalies

Learning Objective 3.8

Identify the risks associated with teratogenic maternal diseases.

Deviations in prenatal development can result from exposure to **teratogens**, agents that cause damage to an embryo or a fetus. The general rule is that each organ system is most vulnerable to harm when it is developing most rapidly (Moore, Persaud,

& Torchia, 2011). Because most organ systems develop most rapidly during the first eight weeks of gestation, this is the period when exposure to teratogens carries the greatest risk (see **Figure 3.3**). Moreover, maternal lifestyle factors, such as smoking, physical activity, and diet, can also have an *indirect* effect on prenatal development by modifying the genetic expression, and thus the functioning, of the placenta (Day et al., 2015; Grandjean et al., 2015). Because of space limitations, we will discuss only a few of the most significant teratogens.

Several viruses pass through the placental filters and attack the embryo or fetus directly. For example, *rubella*, or *German measles*, causes a short-lived mild reaction in adults but may be deadly to a fetus. Most infants exposed to rubella during the embryonic stage show some degree of hearing impairment, visual impairment, and/or heart anomalies (Gowen, 2011).

Figure 3.3 The timing of teratogen exposure.

(**SOURCE:** Based on Moore, C., Barresi, J., & Thompson, C. (1998). The cognitive basis of future-oriented prosocial behavior. *Social Development*, Vol 7, 198 -218.)

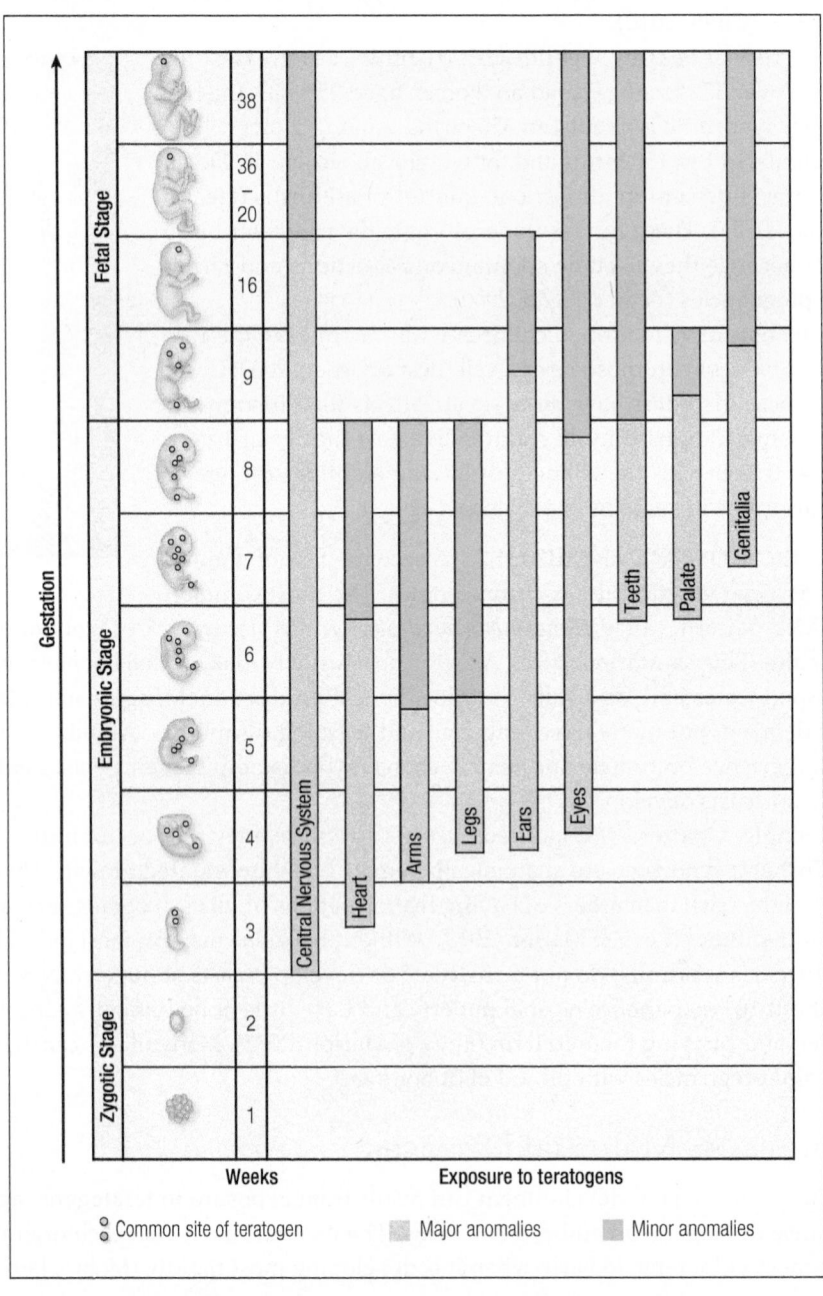

A much less well-known viral infection is *cytomegalovirus (CMV)*. CMV is in the herpes group and is transmitted through contact with body fluids, including saliva, breast milk, vaginal fluids, semen, urine, and stool. As many as 60% of all women carry CMV, but most have no recognizable symptoms. A recent Canadian study found that 0.2 to 2.4% of babies whose mothers are infected with CMV become infected prenatally (Vaudry, Lee, Rosychuk, & Pelletier, 2009). The highest risk for the fetus is when the mother is infected or has a reactivation of the infection during pregnancy. About 10% of infected newborns display serious symptoms of CMV and have a variety of serious problems, including deafness, central nervous system damage, and intellectual delay (Ontario Hospital Association, 2009; Vaudry et al., 2009). Another 5 to 17% of infected newborns who don't initially show symptoms later develop varying degrees of abnormality.

HIV, the virus that causes AIDS, is one of many sexually transmitted organisms that can be passed directly from mother to fetus. The virus can cross the placenta and enter the fetus's bloodstream, the infant may contract the virus in the birth canal during delivery, or the virus can be passed through the breast milk after delivery (PHAC, 2012b). The rate of HIV infection among pregnant women in Canada's provinces is estimated to be about 2 per 1000 (Society of Obstetricians and Gynaecologists of Canada [SOGC], 2011). Moreover, one Canadian study found that 6 in 10 women who are infected with HIV intend to become pregnant in the future (Loutfy et al., 2009). Fortunately, Canadian researchers have demonstrated that HIV-positive pregnant women who take anti-HIV drugs in combination with Caesarean section birth and formula feeding have a markedly lower risk of transmitting the disease to their children (Loutfy et al., 2012; Walmsley, 2003).

Infants who acquire HIV from their mothers typically become ill within the first two years of life (Springer, 2010). The virus weakens children's immune systems, allowing a host of other infectious agents, such as the bacteria that cause pneumonia and meningitis, to attack their bodies. Even children who remain symptom-free must restrict their exposure to viruses and bacteria. For example, HIV-positive children cannot be immunized with vaccines that utilize live viruses, such as the polio vaccine (Rivera & Frye, 2010).

Other STIs, including *syphilis, genital herpes*, and *gonorrhea*, cause a variety of congenital anomalies. Unlike most teratogens, the bacterium that causes syphilis is most harmful during the last 26 weeks of prenatal development and causes eye, ear, and brain anomalies. Genital herpes is usually passed from mother to infant during birth. One-third of infected babies die, and another 25 to 30% suffer blindness or brain damage. Thus, doctors usually advise surgical delivery for the babies of women who have herpes. Gonorrhea, which can cause the infant to be blind, is also usually transmitted during birth. For this reason, the eyes of newborns are usually treated with a special ointment that prevents damage from gonorrhea.

Teratogens: Drugs

Any drug, including many whose safety we take for granted (e.g., antibiotics), can be *teratogenic*. That is why doctors always ask women of child-bearing age whether they might be pregnant before prescribing medication for them. Unless a drug is absolutely necessary to a woman's health, doctors recommend avoiding drugs of any kind during pregnancy. However, sorting out the effects of drugs (prescription and nonprescription, legal and illegal) on prenatal development has proven to be an immensely challenging task because many pregnant women take multiple drugs. Other factors, such as maternal stress, lack of social support, or poverty and poor prenatal care, also often accompany illegal drug use (Best Start, n.d.). Nevertheless, several drugs seem to affect infant development, independent of other variables.

Learning Objective 3.9

Describe the potential adverse effects of drugs on prenatal development.

PRESCRIPTION AND OVER-THE-COUNTER DRUGS You may have heard about the thalidomide tragedy that occurred in the 1960s. The drug involved was a mild tranquilizer that doctors prescribed to pregnant women who were experiencing severe symptoms of morning sickness. Sadly, the drug caused serious malformations of the limbs in thousands of fetuses that were exposed to it (Vogin, 2005).

Even relatively common prescription drugs used in the treatment of anxiety and depression have been found to have teratogenic effects (Calderon-Margalit, Qiu, Ornoy, Siscovick, & Williams, 2009). For example, benzodiazepine tranquilizers taken during pregnancy have been associated with an increased risk of preterm delivery, low birth weight, low Apgar score (see **Table 3.5**, later in this chapter), neonatal intensive-care-unit admissions, and respiratory distress syndrome. As well, selective serotonin reuptake inhibitors (SSRIs) have been associated with preterm deliveries among women who started treatment after the first trimester.

In general, doctors advise against taking any unnecessary medicines during pregnancy. Nevertheless, some pregnant women must take drugs to treat health conditions that may be threatening to their own and their unborn child's life. For instance, pregnant women with epilepsy must take anti-seizure medication because the seizures themselves are potentially harmful to their unborn children. Other drugs that pregnant women may have to risk taking, even though they can be harmful, include medications that treat heart conditions and diabetes, those that control asthma symptoms, and some kinds of psychiatric drugs. In all such cases, physicians weigh the benefits of medication against potential teratogenic effects and look for a combination of drug and dosage that will effectively treat the mother's health condition while placing her unborn child at minimal risk.

In contrast to prescription drugs, most people, pregnant or otherwise, take over-the-counter medicines on a casual, as-needed basis without consulting a doctor. Many of these drugs, such as acetaminophen, are safe for pregnant women unless taken to excess (Organization of Teratology Information Specialists [OTIS], 2005). However, experts advise pregnant women to discuss the medicines they usually take with physicians at the outset of their pregnancies. These discussions should deal both with drugs and with any vitamins or supplements that the pregnant woman usually takes. Their doctors will advise them as to which of the substances are safe and which are risky. Often, too, physicians can suggest safer alternatives. Typically, most look to older drugs that have been thoroughly tested (Vogin, 2005).

TOBACCO Infants of mothers who smoke are, on average, about 150 grams lighter at birth than infants of nonsmoking mothers, and lower birth weight has a variety of potential negative short- and long-term risks. For instance, pregnant women who smoke have higher rates of miscarriage, stillborn babies, premature birth, neonatal death, low-birth-weight babies, and **neurobehavioural disorders** (Grandjean & Landrigan, 2014; Ivorra et al., 2015). Overall, rates of smoking during pregnancy are on the decline in Canada; however, younger women (33%) are more likely to smoke during pregnancy than women over 30 (13%). Even among nonsmoking women, reportedly 36% of younger women and 13% of older women are regularly exposed to second-hand smoke during their pregnancy (Millar & Hill, 2004). Moreover, roughly twice as many Indigenous as non-Indigenous women in Canada smoked throughout their pregnancy (Heaman & Chalmers, 2005). In comparison, immigrant mothers had, by far, the lowest rates of smoking during pregnancy—just 2% smoked (Millar & Hill, 2004).

ALCOHOL Researchers have also documented the effects of alcohol on prenatal development. In fact, recent studies show that alcohol can even adversely affect an ovum prior to ovulation or during its journey down the fallopian tube to the uterus. Likewise, a zygote can be affected by alcohol even before it has been implanted in the uterine lining (Dharan & Parviainen, 2009).

neurobehavioural disorders cognitive and behavioural disorders that are associated with brain dysfunction, such as autism spectrum disorder, ADHD, and dyslexia

Mothers who are heavy drinkers or alcoholics are at significant risk of delivering infants with *fetal alcohol syndrome (FAS)*. These children are generally smaller than normal, with smaller-than-typical brains. They frequently have heart anomalies and hearing losses, and their faces are distinctive, with smallish-looking, wide-set eyes, a somewhat flattened nose, a thin upper lip, and often a long, flattened space between the nose and mouth (Levy & Marion, 2015). As children, adolescents, and adults, they are shorter than normal and have smaller heads, and their intelligence test scores indicate mild developmental delay. Children with FAS who are not intellectually delayed often have learning and behavioural difficulties (Bertrand et al., 2004; Chudley, 2006).

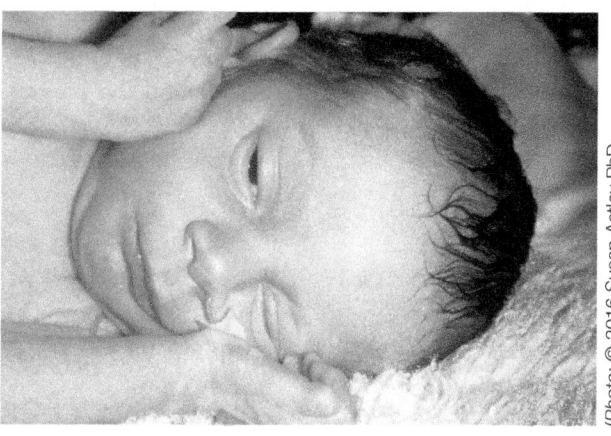

Children with fetal alcohol syndrome have distinctive features.

(Photo: © 2016 Susan Astley PhD, University of Washington)

The term *Fetal Alcohol Spectrum Disorder (FASD)*[1] has often been used to encompass a continuum of effects caused by the consumption of alcohol while pregnant. At one end, FASD includes FAS; at the other, it includes *fetal alcohol effects (FAE)*, which characterizes the milder or partial adverse effects of ethanol. For example, a child with FAE may not exhibit the physical characteristics of FAS, but the secondary disabilities, such as mental health problems or behavioural and learning difficulties, become apparent during childhood (Wedding et al., 2007).

The overall alcohol consumption rate during pregnancy is coming down in Canada; roughly 14% of women reported consuming alcohol at some point during their pregnancy and 5% admitted to drinking throughout their pregnancy (Dell & Roberts, 2006). Both younger (under 21) and older (over 30) Canadian women are more likely to consume alcohol during pregnancy than women 21 to 30 years of age (Dell & Roberts, 2006). Unfortunately, even moderate drinking by a pregnant woman may cause her child to have learning and behavioural difficulties in childhood and adolescence (Chudley, 2006). In the face of this evidence, the safest course for pregnant women is to drink no alcohol at all. In addition, women who are trying to become pregnant should abstain while they are trying to conceive, as women who do not discover their pregnancy immediately may inadvertently continue to drink well into their first trimester. One concerning finding is that Canadian women who smoked during pregnancy were also more likely to consume alcohol—a circumstance that magnifies the detrimental risks associated with both substances on the developing prenate (Lange, Probst, Quere, Rehm, & Popova, 2015).

PSYCHOTROPIC DRUGS   Both heroin and methadone, a drug often used in treating heroin addiction, can cause miscarriage, premature labour, and early death (Brockington, 1996). Further, 60 to 80% of babies born to heroin-addicted women are addicted to heroin as well. Addicted babies have high-pitched cries and suffer from withdrawal symptoms, such as irritability, uncontrollable tremors, vomiting, convulsions, and sleep problems. These symptoms may last as long as four months. Use of cocaine by pregnant women, in either powder or "crack" form, is linked to many kinds of developmental problems in their children (Gowen, 2011). However, most cocaine-using pregnant women are poor and abuse multiple substances, making it difficult to separate the effects of cocaine from those of poverty and other drugs. Some studies suggest that cocaine alone has no long-term effects on cognitive or social development (Dharan & Parviainen, 2009). Still, cocaine can lead to pregnancy complications, such as disruption of placental function and premature labour, that may adversely affect the developing fetus (Gowen, 2011).

---

[1]Neurobehavioral Disorder Associated With Prenatal Alcohol Exposure (ND-PAE) is a new term proposed in the DSM-5 to encompass the full range of developmental anomalies associated with exposure to alcohol before birth (APA, 2013).

Studies of the effects of marijuana use during pregnancy have yielded mixed results. Some studies have found a small reduction in birth weight (Centre for Addiction and Mental Health [CAMH], 2010). To date, chemicals found in marijuana (i.e., THC) have not been implicated as a human teratogen. However, exposure to second-hand smoke should be taken into consideration both pre- and postnatally. As well, cannabis is excreted in moderate amounts in breast milk.

Learning Objective 3.10

Describe other maternal factors that can adversely influence prenatal development.

Teratogens: Other Harmful Influences on Prenatal Development

Other factors that can adversely affect prenatal development include the mother's diet, her age, and her physical and mental health.

DIET Some specific nutrients are vital to prenatal development (Christian & Stewart, 2010). One is folic acid, a B vitamin found in beans, spinach, and other foods. Inadequate amounts of this nutrient are linked to neural tube anomalies, such as *spina bifida* (Lewis, 2011). The potential negative effects of insufficient folic acid occur in the very earliest weeks of pregnancy, before a woman may know she is pregnant. So it is important for women who plan to become pregnant to obtain at least 400 micrograms of this vitamin daily, the minimum required level.

It is also important for a pregnant woman to take in sufficient overall calories and protein to prevent malnutrition. A woman who experiences malnutrition during pregnancy, particularly during the final three months, has an increased risk of delivering a low-birth-weight infant (under 2500 grams) who will have intellectual difficulties in childhood (Mutch, Leyland, & McGee, 1993). In addition, researchers have recently identified prenatal malnutrition, along with a variety of obstetrical complications, as an important risk factor in the development of mental illnesses in adulthood (Xu et al., 2009).

The impact of maternal malnutrition appears to be greatest on the developing nervous system—a pattern found in studies of both humans and other mammals. For example, rats whose protein intake has been substantially restricted during the fetal and early postnatal periods show a pattern of reduced brain weight and capacity for learning (Wang & Xu, 2007). In human studies of cases in which prenatal malnutrition has been severe enough to cause the death of the fetus or newborn, effects similar to those seen in the rat studies have been observed. That is, these infants had smaller brains and fewer and smaller brain cells (Georgieff, 1994). Moreover, studies of adults whose mothers were malnourished during pregnancy suggest that the detrimental effects of prenatal malnutrition can persist throughout the lifespan (Susser, St. Clair, & He, 2008).

body mass index (BMI)

a ratio of weight to height that estimates healthy and unhealthy body composition

Canadian weight-gain guidelines suggest that a woman with a normal weight based on the **body mass index (BMI)** (BMI is a ratio of weight to height) should gain 11.5 to 16.0 kilograms during a *singleton* pregnancy. Women who are underweight should gain more weight than those who are overweight or obese (Health Canada, 2009). Generally, if a woman follows the *Eating Well with Canada's Food Guide* (Health Canada, 2011) recommendations for pregnant women from early in her pregnancy, she will likely maintain the necessary degree of weight gain.

AGE One intriguing trend in Canada over the past 20 years is that increasingly more women postpone their *first* pregnancy until their 30s—this accounts for more than 41% of firstborns. Furthermore, more than half of women giving birth in Canada are now aged 30 and older and ~20% of women giving birth are aged 35 and older (Statistics Canada, 2016c).

In most cases, older mothers have uncomplicated pregnancies and deliver healthy babies, but the risks associated with pregnancy do increase somewhat as women age (Johnson & Tough, 2012; Vézina & Turcotte, 2009). Their babies are also at greater risk of weighing less than 2.5 kilograms at birth, a finding that is partly explained by the greater incidence of multiple births among older mothers. Still, infants born to women over the age of 35, whether single or multiple birth, are at higher risk of having problems such as heart malformations and chromosomal disorders.

At the other end of the age continuum, higher rates of congenital anomalies are seen in teenage mothers compared with mothers in their 20s (Chen, Wen, Fleming, Yang, & Walker, 2007; Evans & Fortier, 2006). For example, teenage pregnancy is associated with a higher risk for non-chromosomal congenital anomalies such as neural tube and central nervous system anomalies, gastrointestinal system and female genitalia anomalies, and musculoskeletal/integumental (e.g., cleft lip/palate and club foot) anomalies. However, Canadian teenage mothers are also less likely to receive adequate prenatal care, have a healthy diet and sufficient multivitamin and folic acid intake, and avoid exposure to smoke, alcohol, and drugs; they are more likely to experience mood disorders, STIs, and partner abuse (Fleming et al., 2015). This makes it hard to sort out the causal factors, but it does point to the need for improved preventative measures where lifestyle factors contribute to negative outcomes for mother and baby (Fleming et al., 2015; Langille, 2007).

CHRONIC ILLNESSES Conditions such as heart disease, diabetes, lupus, hormone imbalances, and epilepsy can also affect prenatal development negatively (Ross & Mansano, 2010). Thus, one of the most important goals of the new specialty of *fetal-maternal medicine* is to manage the pregnancies of women who have such conditions in ways that will support the health of both mother and fetus. For example, pregnancy often makes it impossible for a diabetic woman to keep her blood sugar levels under control. In turn, erratic blood sugar levels may damage the fetus's nervous system or cause it to grow too rapidly (Gowen, 2011). To prevent such complications, a fetal-maternal specialist must find a diet, a medication, or a combination of the two that will stabilize the mother's blood sugar but will not harm the fetus. Similarly, fetal-maternal specialists help women who have epilepsy balance their own need for antiepileptic medication against possible harm to the fetus. Interestingly, Canadian researchers have found that recent immigrants experience fewer chronic health problems (the so-called "immigrant effect"), which is related to significantly lower prenatal complications, such as common placental disorders, in comparison to original residents (Ray et al., 2007).

MATERNAL MENTAL HEALTH Some psychologists have suggested that maternal emotions can affect prenatal development. One fairly consistent finding is that the fetuses of severely distressed mothers are more likely to have emotional or cognitive disorders later in childhood (Talge, Neal, & Glover, 2007). Their rationale is that stressful psychological states such as anxiety and depression lead to changes in body chemistry. In a pregnant woman, these changes result in both qualitative and quantitative differences in the hormones and other chemicals that may affect the fetus. Some studies have shown an association between maternal stress hormones and reduced rates of fetal growth (e.g., Kivlighan, DiPietro, Costigan, & Laudenslager, 2008).

Similarly, the fetuses of mothers who have depression tend to grow more slowly than those of women who do not (Yonkers et al., 2009). Developmentalists do not really know whether this effect results directly from emotion-related hormones or is an indirect effect of the mother's emotional state. A stressed or depressed mother may eat less, or her weakened immune system may limit her ability to fight off viruses and bacteria—either of these situations may retard fetal growth. Consequently, providing stressed and at-risk pregnant women with social support and counselling during home visits by nurses can lead to improvements in prenatal and infant health and development, especially within high-risk families (Olds, Sadler, & Kitzman, 2007).

Learning Objective 3.11

Describe how mutagenic, environmental, and epigenetic teratogens adversely affect prenatal development.

mutagens

agents that cause changes (mutations) in genomic DNA

cell proliferation

the increase in cell numbers by means of cell growth and cell division

cell migration

the movement of cells to their genetically predetermined destinations in the body

epimutagens

agents that cause abnormal gene silencing or expression without changing the genomic DNA

Teratogens: Mutagenic, Environmental, and Epimutagenic

Current research suggests that teratogens fall within three broad categories: mutagenic, environmental, and unknown (Brent, 2004a). Researchers suspect that much of the unknown category is composed of epigenetic factors and that a single teratogen may fit more than one category.

MUTAGENIC TERATOGENS One group of teratogens is composed of **mutagens**, agents that cause alterations (mutations) to *genomic* DNA. Exposure to mutagens, such as radiation and biological or chemical toxins, can cause *germinal mutations* that interfere with both conception and the normal development of the embryo and the fetus. For example, if gametes are exposed to high levels of X-rays, then infertility can result, but if conception does occur, then the resulting genetic mutation can lead to a failure to implant or a miscarriage (Brent, 2004b; Edwards, n.d.; Kalter, 2003). In other instances, embryos that are exposed to mutagens may develop *somatic mutations*—chromosomal or genetic errors that can cause congenital anomalies that can be transmitted to future generations (Prasad, Cole, & Hasse, 2004).

ENVIRONMENTAL TERATOGENS Environmental agents can have direct, nonheritable effects on prenatal development by damaging cells or disrupting normal cell development (Brent, 2004b; Finnell, Waes, Eudy, & Rosenquist, 2002; Kalter, 2003). These agents may interfere with normal **cell proliferation** in the embryo (the formation of specific body tissues, such as neurons, muscles, and bones) or with **cell migration** (the movement of differentiated cells to their genetically predetermined location; for example, when neural cells migrate along the threads of glial cells to their proper location in the brain). They can also cause cellular *structural* and *functional abnormalities* (the destruction or degeneration of cells; for example, when damaged neurons disrupt neural networks in the brain).

EPIMUTAGENIC TERATOGENS Mutagens account for about 15 to 25% of congenital anomalies, and environmental factors account for another 10% (Brent, 2004a). That leaves around two-thirds unaccounted for, but scientists suspect that a large proportion of these "unknown" factors may turn out to be epigenetic in nature (Horsthemke, 2006; Martin, Ward, & Suter, 2005; Pembrey, Saffery, & Bygren, 2014; Szyf, 2009). **Epimutagens** are agents that cause alterations (epimutations) to the epigenome without changing the genomic DNA. In most cases, any *teratogenic* damage is limited to an individual in only one generation because any acquired epimutations are usually reset following conception. In other instances, however, some acquired epimutations can be passed on to the next generation and sometimes beyond (Eaton et al., 2015; Feil, 2006, 2008; Fraga, 2009; Lahiri et al., 2016). As one example, a grandparent's diet can produce enduring changes on successive generations independent of later changes in diet of the offspring (Pembrey, Saffery, Bygren, & Network in Epigenetic Epidemiology, 2014). This means there is now good reason to believe that our current dietary habits may, by means of *epimutagenic* processes, have an impact on "grandchildren who will be born decades from now, independent of the diets that their parents consume" (Cropley, Suter, Beckman, & Martin, 2006, p. 17311).

Learning Objective 3.12

Describe how preconceptual and prenatal paternal factors can adversely influence development.

Paternal Influences: Preconceptual and Prenatal

Lately, scientists have been paying more attention to the father's role in reproductive risk and found that, on average, fathers pass on roughly 55 genetic mutations to their children compared to a mother's 14 mutations (Kong et al., 2012). Research shows how the production, abnormalities, or performance of sperm contribute to conditions such as infertility, decreased fertility, and miscarriage. As well, DNA damage to sperm has been shown to contribute to conditions such as congenital anomalies, childhood cancer, and neurobehavioural disorders in offspring (Paul & Robaire, 2015; OTIS, 2010; Sartorius & Nieschlag, 2010).

Genetic effects (gene mutation and chromosomal errors) and epigenetic effects (altered gene expression) have the greatest impact during the first two trimesters of pregnancy. The means of contaminating the mother and prenate during this time-frame may involve toxins in seminal fluids that can be transmitted during intercourse or indirect exposure by way of toxic agents transmitted from work clothes, shoes, and equipment that are brought into the home (Trasler & Doerksen, 1999). Epidemiological studies have shown that there is a higher reproductive risk associated with men working in specific occupations, such as janitors, painters, printers, firefighters, and woodworkers, as well as occupations related to agriculture, such as farmers, gardeners, and butchers, and the art and textile industries (Chia & Shi, 2002; Fear, Hey, Vincent, & Murphy, 2007; Regidor, Ronda, Garcia, & Dominguez, 2004; Trasler & Doerksen, 1999). It is suspected that male-mediated teratogenic and mutagenic risk is related to paternal exposure to toxic substances, including heavy metals (e.g., lead and mercury), solvents, wood preservatives, pesticides, hydrocarbons, and radiation (Chia & Shi, 2002; OTIS, 2010). Notably, sperm adversely affected up to two to three months before conception can impact the prenate.

Concerns have also been raised regarding the impact of the father's age. For example, evidence links adverse birth outcomes and congenital anomalies with both teenage fathers (Chen et al., 2008; Forster et al., 2015; Yang et al., 2007) and fathers who are in their 40s or older (Green et al., 2010; Kovac et al., 2013; Sartorius & Nieschlag, 2010; Sharma et al., 2015; Yang et al., 2007). Of increased concern, perhaps, is with older fathers—the average age of Canadian fathers at the time of the birth of their first biological child has risen to ~28 years of age (Statistics Canada, 2015b). A recent study of Icelandic families revealed that fathers pass on exponentially more mutations with advancing age—the number of mutations a father will pass on to his child doubles every 16.5 years from the time the father reaches puberty, whereas a mother's contribution of mutations remains relatively constant regardless of her age (Kong et al., 2012). Notably, advancing paternal age is associated with increases in offspring that are later diagnosed with disorders such as autism and schizophrenia (Frans, MacCabe, & Reichenberg, 2015).

Physical abuse of the mother during pregnancy is another serious threat to maternal and child health. It can lead to premature labour, a premature breaking away of the placenta from the uterine wall, and/or low birth weight (Murphy, Schei, Myhr, & Du Mont, 2001). Canadian researchers have reported that the prevalence of physical abuse increases during pregnancy, affecting roughly 6% of pregnant Canadian women (Cox et al., 2004; Muhajarine & D'Arcy, 1999; Murphy et al., 2001). One Canadian study found that almost two-thirds of the violence was perpetrated by a pregnant woman's husband, boyfriend, or ex-husband (Muhajarine & D'Arcy, 1999). Abuse during pregnancy is preventable, and perhaps the place to start intervening would be to screen newly pregnant women or women planning to conceive for potential abuse along with other preventable lifestyle risk factors such as lack of paternal care and support, exposure to second-hand smoke, and unhealthy nutrition during pregnancy (Braun & Champagne, 2014; Fleming et al., 2015; Sarkar, 2008).

Fetal Assessment and Treatment

Learning Objective 3.13

Identify preconceptual and prenatal assessment and diagnostic procedures.

A woman faces some legitimate concerns regarding genetic testing. For one, there are medical risks involved with genetic testing for both the mother and the prenate. There can also be intense emotional and social effects on the mother and other family members as they consider the consequences of the course of action they take based on the test results. As well, there can be privacy and confidentiality concerns with regard to how genetic test results can impact insurability, employment, and other forms of social and cultural interaction. In Canada, for instance, there is no law governing how test results can be used—it is hoped that legislation such as Bill S-201 (the *Genetic Non-Discrimination Act*) will take care of the concerns of discrimination based on genetic information. Genetic counsellors help women who are at risk of bearing a child with a congenital anomaly to understand potential outcomes and choices (Canadian Association of Genetic Counsellors, n.d.). Preconception and first-trimester screening procedures assess the potential for developmental complications and determine if prenatal diagnostic testing is warranted or even desired. If diagnostic tests are performed and they detect abnormal results, then a genetics counsellor can help the mother and her family make informed decisions about her options.

Ultrasonography has become a routine part of prenatal care in Canada because of its usefulness in monitoring fetal growth (ultrasound images are produced by the echoes that result from bouncing sound waves off of internal tissues). Other tests, including *chorionic villus sampling (CVS)* and *amniocentesis*, can be used to identify chromosomal errors and many genetic disorders prior to birth (see **Figure 3.4**). With CVS, cells are extracted from the placenta and used in a variety of laboratory tests during the early weeks of prenatal development. With amniocentesis, which is done between weeks 14 and 16 of a woman's pregnancy, a needle is used to extract amniotic fluid containing fetal cells. Fetal cells filtered out of the fluid are then tested in a variety of ways to diagnose chromosomal and genetic disorders. CVS is used most often when a medical condition in the mother necessitates early diagnosis of fetal abnormalities (Springer, 2010). In general, amniocentesis carries a lower risk of miscarriage and fetal injury than CVS does. Thus, it is usually the preferred prenatal diagnostic technique and is routinely recommended as a screening tool for Down syndrome and other chromosomal disorders in pregnant women over age 35.

In addition, many laboratory tests use maternal blood, urine, and/or samples of amniotic fluid to help health care providers monitor fetal development. For example, the presence of a substance called *alpha-fetoprotein* in a pregnant woman's blood is associated with a number of prenatal anomalies, including abnormalities in the brain

Figure 3.4 Chorionic villus sampling (left) and amniocentesis (right).

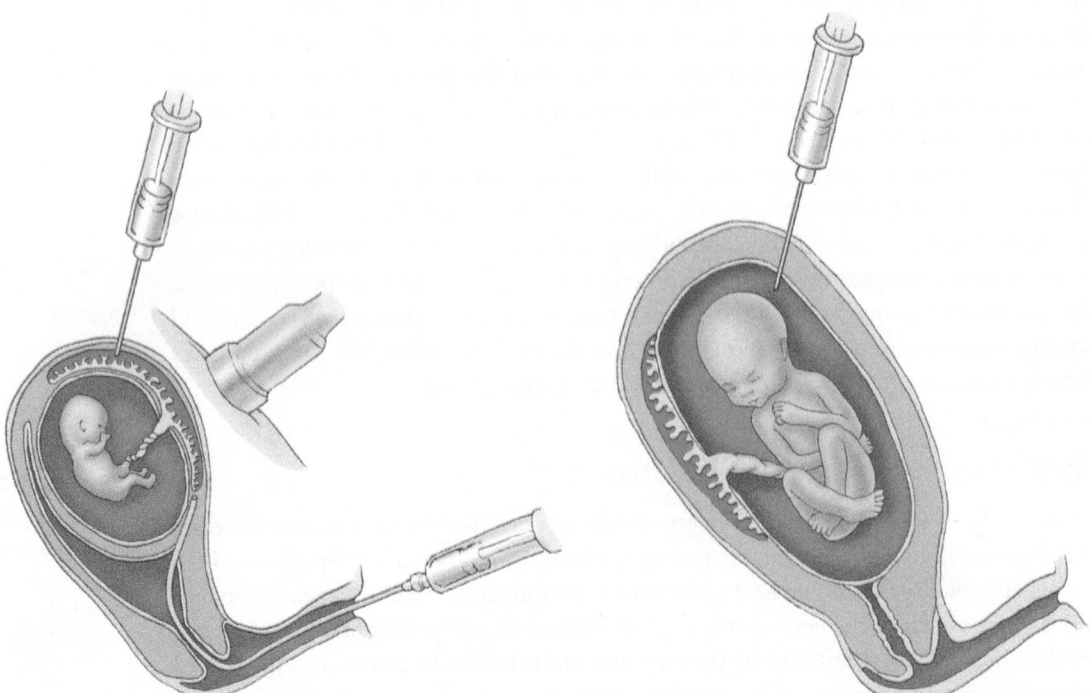

and the spinal cord. Doctors can also use a laboratory test to assess the maturity of fetal lungs (Springer, 2010). This test is critical when doctors advise early delivery of a baby because of the mother's health.

Fetoscopy involves insertion of a tiny camera into the womb to directly observe fetal development. Fetoscopy makes it possible for doctors to correct some kinds of anomalies surgically (Springer, 2010). Likewise, fetoscopy has made techniques such as fetal blood transfusions and bone marrow transplants possible. Specialists also use fetoscopy to take samples of blood from the umbilical cord. Laboratory tests performed on fetal blood samples can assess fetal organ function, diagnose genetic and chromosomal disorders, and detect fetal infections (Springer, 2010). For example, fetal blood tests can help doctors identify a bacterial infection that is causing a fetus to grow too slowly. Once diagnosed, the infection can be treated by injecting antibiotics into the amniotic fluid (so that they will be swallowed by the fetus) or into the umbilical cord (Springer, 2010).

Test Yourself before going on

1. Select the correct answers in the following sentence:

   Most autosomal recessive disorders are diagnosed in (childhood/adulthood), while most autosomal dominant disorders are diagnosed in (childhood/adulthood).

2. Red–green colour blindness is a(n) _____ disorder that is _____ common in males than in females.

3. In most cases, teratogens are most harmful during the _____ period of prenatal development.

4. Match each disease and maternal factor with its potentially harmful effect(s) on prenatal development. (Diseases can have more than one harmful effect.)

   _____ (a) cytomegalovirus
   _____ (b) rubella
   _____ (c) HIV
   _____ (d) syphilis
   _____ (e) genital herpes
      (i)   visual impairment/blindness
      (ii) AIDS
      (iii) death
      (iv) heart anomalies
      (v)   brain anomalies
      (vi) hearing impairment/deafness
      (vii) intellectual delay

5. Describe the potentially harmful effects of each substance in the table on prenatal development.

Drug	Effects
Thalidomide	
Tobacco	
Alcohol	
Heroin	

6. Mutagenic teratogens cause alterations to _____.

7. A father's _____ and _____ increase reproductive risk.

8. Select the correct answers in the following sentence:

   (CVS/amniocentesis) is done during the first trimester; (CVS/amniocentesis) is done during the second trimester.

Critical Thinking

9. With the advent of antiretroviral drugs, the rate of mother-to-fetus transmission of HIV has been greatly reduced. Do you think that these findings justify mandatory testing and treatment of pregnant women who are at high risk of having HIV/AIDS?

Birth and the Neonate

Once gestation is complete, the fetus must be born—an event that holds some pain for the mother as well as a good deal of joy for most parents.

Birth Choices

In most places around the world, tradition dictates how babies are delivered. However, in developed countries, especially in Canada, hospital deliveries became routine in the second half of the 20th century. Today, though, parents have several

Learning Objective 3.14

Summarize the birth choices available to expectant parents.

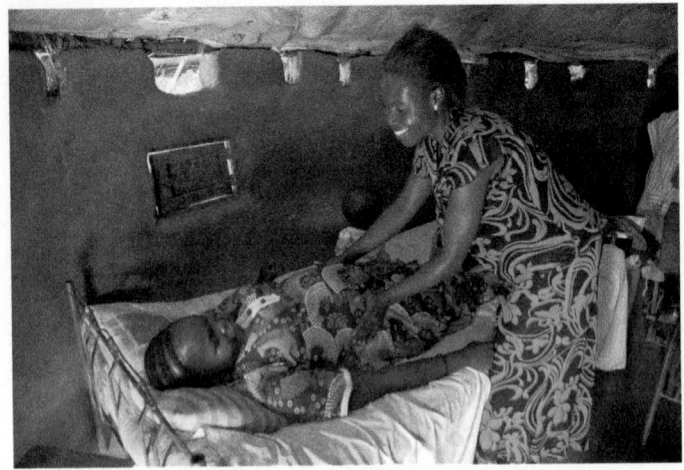
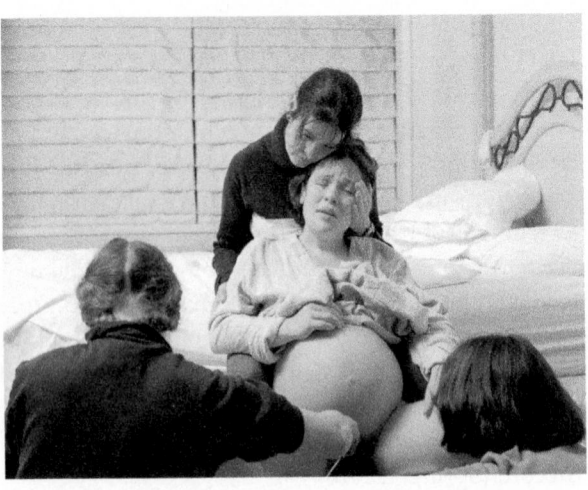

In the developing world, tradition determines where a baby is born and who attends its birth. Hospital deliveries are common in Canada, but many hospitals offer parents the option of delivering their babies in nonsurgical settings such as the birthing room pictured on the right.

choices as to who will attend their baby's birth, whether medication will be used to manage the physical discomforts of labour and delivery, and where the birth will take place.

MIDWIVES Midwifery is a regulated health care profession in most provinces and territories in Canada. Midwife practice involves assessing, supervising, and caring for women prior to and during pregnancy, labour, and the postpartum period. A midwife is licensed to conduct deliveries and to care for the newborn infant. To become a midwife in Canada, one must graduate from a midwifery education program at a recognized institution.

DRUGS DURING LABOUR AND DELIVERY One key decision for expectant mothers concerns whether to use drugs during labour and delivery. *Analgesics* may be given during labour to reduce pain. *Sedatives* or *tranquillizers* can be administered to reduce anxiety. *Anaesthesia*, when used, is usually given later in labour to block pain, either totally (general anaesthesia) or in certain portions of the body (local anaesthesia, such as an epidural).

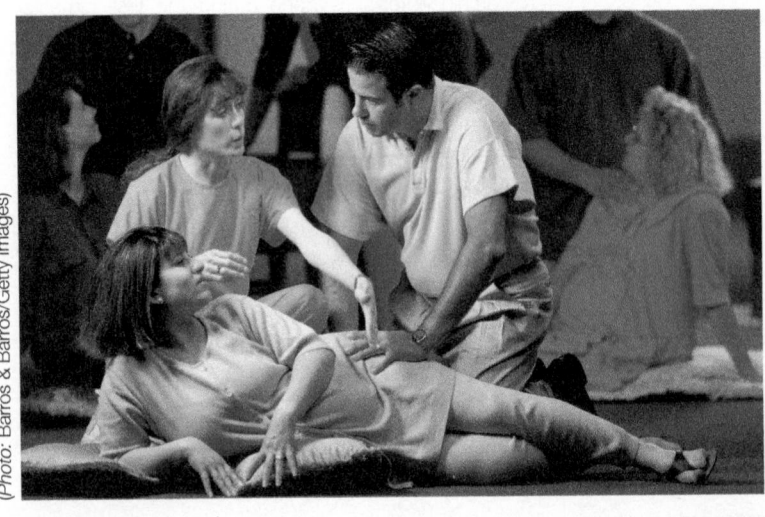

Many fathers take prenatal classes like this one so that they can provide support to their partners during labour.

Studying the causal links between drug use during labour and delivery and the baby's later behaviour or development has proven to be difficult. First, it's clear that nearly all drugs given during labour pass through the placenta, enter the fetal bloodstream, and may remain there for several days. Not surprisingly, then, infants whose mothers have received any type of drug are typically slightly more sluggish, gain a little less weight, and spend more time sleeping in the first few weeks than do infants of mothers who do not receive anesthetics during labour and delivery (Gowen, 2011).

Second, there are no consistently observed effects from analgesics and tranquillizers beyond the first few days, and only a few studies hint at the long-term effects of anaesthesia (Rosenblith, 1992). Given such inconclusive findings, only one specific piece of advice seems warranted: If you are a new mother who receives medication during childbirth, bear in mind that your baby is also drugged, and that this will affect her behaviour in the first few days. If you allow for this effect and realize that it will wear off, your long-term relationship with your child is likely to be unaffected.

Nevertheless, many women choose to avoid drugs altogether. The term *natural childbirth* is commonly used to refer to this particular choice—the *Lamaze method* being a common technique in Canada. Natural childbirth involves several components. First, a woman selects someone, typically the baby's father or another supportive person, to serve as a labour coach. Then they attend *childbirth classes* that psychologically prepare the woman and her labour coach for the experience of labour and delivery. For example, they learn to use the term *contraction* instead of *pain*. Believing that her baby will benefit from natural childbirth provides the woman with the motivation she needs to endure labour without the aid of pain-relieving medication. Further, relaxation and breathing techniques provide her with behavioural responses that serve to replace the negative emotions that typically result from the physical discomfort of contractions.

THE LOCATION OF BIRTH   Another choice parents must make is where the baby is to be born. In most of the developed world, women deliver their babies in specialized maternity clinics. However, in Canada, there are four alternatives in most communities

- a traditional hospital maternity unit
- a birth centre or birthing room located within a hospital, which provides a more homelike setting for labour and delivery and often allows family members to be present throughout the birth
- a free-standing birth centre, like a hospital birth centre except that it is located apart from the hospital, with delivery typically attended by a midwife rather than (or in addition to) a physician
- the mother's home

Most babies in Canada are born in hospitals (~98.5%) (Statistics Canada, 2012b). Home deliveries are appropriate for uncomplicated pregnancies during which the woman has received good prenatal care. When these conditions are met, with a trained birth attendant present at delivery, the rate of home delivery complications or infant problems in Canada is no higher than for hospital deliveries (Janssen et al., 2009).

The Physical Process of Birth

Labour is typically divided into three stages (see **Figure 3.5**). Stage 1 covers the period during which two important processes occur: dilation and effacement. The cervix (the opening at the bottom of the uterus) must open up like the lens of a camera (*dilation*) and also flatten out (*effacement*). At the time of actual delivery, the cervix must normally be dilated to about 10 centimetres.

Customarily, stage 1 is itself divided into phases. In the *early* (or *latent*) phase, contractions are relatively far apart and typically not too uncomfortable. In the *active* phase, which begins when the cervix is 3 to 4 centimetres dilated and continues until dilation has reached 8 centimetres, contractions are closer together and more intense. The last two centimetres of dilation are achieved during a phase usually called *transition*. It is this phase, when contractions are closely spaced and strong, that women typically find the most painful. Fortunately, transition is also ordinarily the shortest phase.

Learning Objective 3.15

Describe what happens in each of the three stages of labour.

Figure 3.5 The sequence of steps during delivery is shown clearly in these drawings.

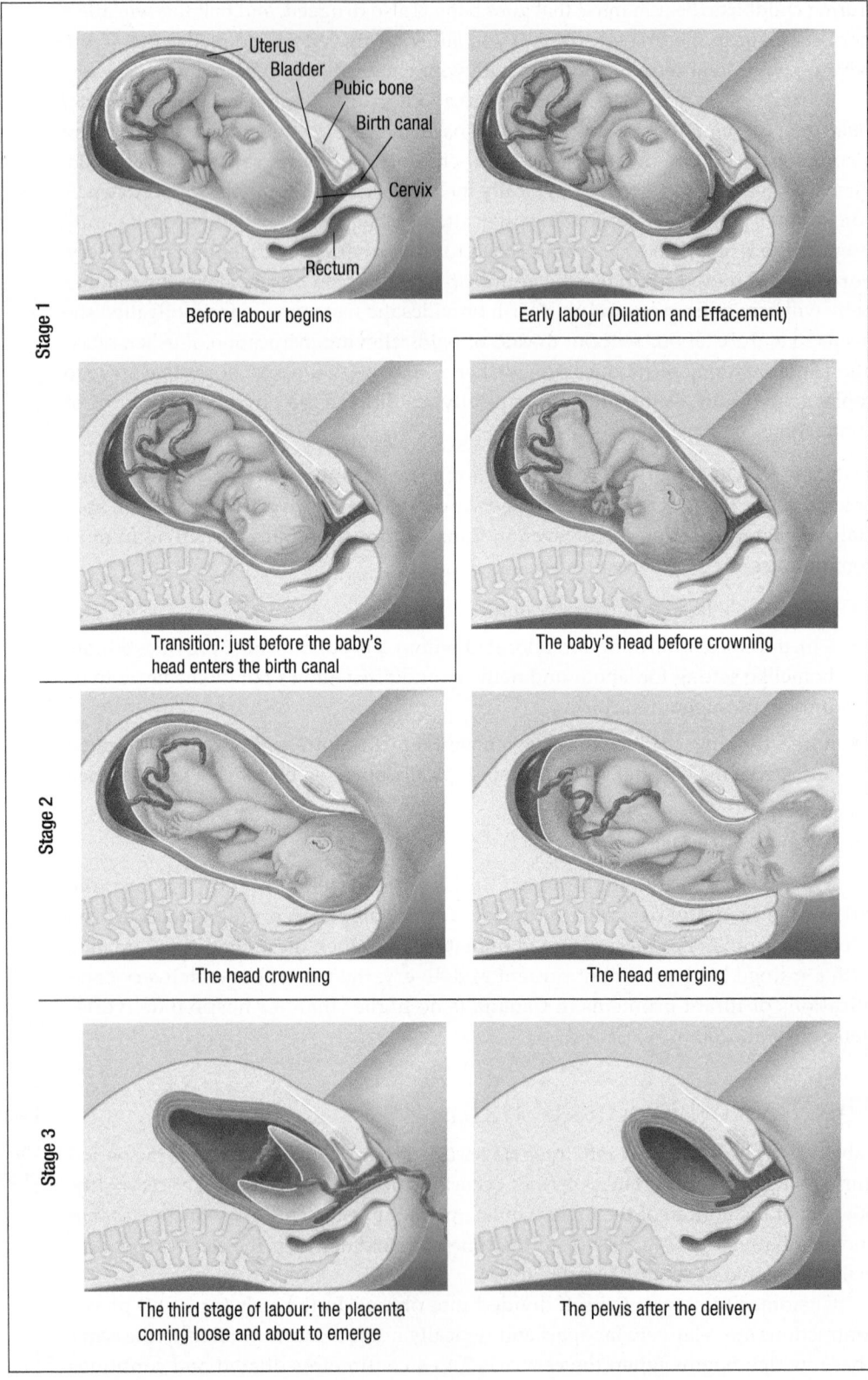

Figure 3.6 shows the typical length of these various phases of labour for first births and later births. What the figure does not convey is the wide individual variability that exists. Among women delivering a first child, stage 1 may last as few as 3 hours or as many as 20 (Biswas & Craigo, 1994; Kilpatrick & Laros, 1989).

Figure 3.6 Typical pattern of the stages of labour for first births and subsequent births.

(**SOURCE:** Based on Biswas & Craigo, 1994, from Figures 10–16, p. 216 and 10–17, p. 217.)

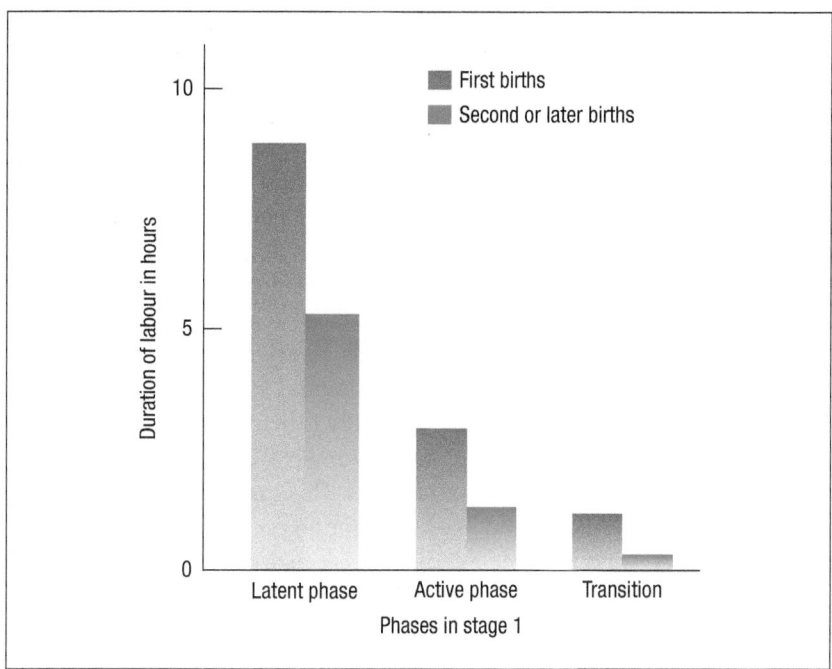

At the end of the transition phase, the mother will normally have the urge to help the infant emerge by "pushing." When the birth attendant (physician or midwife) is sure the cervix is fully dilated, she or he will encourage this pushing, and stage 2 of labour, the actual delivery, begins. The baby's head moves past the stretched cervix, into the birth canal, and finally out of the mother's body. Most women find this part of labour markedly less distressing than the transition phase because at this point they can assist the delivery process by pushing. Stage 2 typically lasts less than an hour and rarely takes longer than two hours. Stage 3, also typically quite brief, is the delivery of the placenta (also called the *afterbirth*) and other material from the uterus.

CAESAREAN DELIVERIES   Most infants are delivered head first, facing toward the mother's spine; 3 to 4%, however, are oriented differently, either feet first or bottom first (called *breech* presentations) (Brown, Karrison, & Cibils, 1994). In Canada today, infants in breech positions are nearly all delivered through an abdominal incision (a **Caesarean section or C-section**) rather than vaginally. Other factors that call for the procedure include fetal distress during labour, labour that fails to progress in a reasonable amount of time, a fetus that is too large to be delivered vaginally, and maternal health conditions that may be aggravated by vaginal delivery (e.g., cardiovascular disease, spinal injury) or may be dangerous to a vaginally delivered fetus (e.g., herpes). Thus, in many situations, Caesarean sections prevent maternal and fetal complications and, no doubt, save lives.

Though most physicians agree that in certain cases a Caesarean delivery is warranted, the procedure itself is somewhat controversial. Critics argue that the operation is often performed unnecessarily. There are concerns about possible increased risk due to complications (e.g., increased risk of excessive blood loss/blood clots and infection) and the increased health care cost arising from unnecessary C-sections. In the late 1960s, only about 5% of babies in Canada were delivered by C-section. By 2001, the frequency of surgical delivery had risen above 21% (Health Canada, 2003a), among the highest in the world. The Society of Obstetricians and Gynaecologists of Canada does not promote C-section on demand and recommends that the decision to have an

Caesarean section (C-section)

delivery of an infant through incisions in the abdominal and uterine walls

elective Caesarean delivery be based on an informed discussion about risks and benefits between a woman and her doctor (SOGC, 2004).

BIRTH COMPLICATIONS   During the process of birth, some babies go into *fetal distress*, signalled by a sudden change in heart rate. In most cases, doctors don't know why a baby experiences fetal distress. However, one cause of distress is pressure on the umbilical cord. For example, if the cord becomes lodged between the baby's head and the cervix, each contraction will push the baby's head against the cord. The collapsed blood vessels can no longer carry blood to and from the baby. When this happens, the baby experiences **anoxia**, or oxygen deprivation. Anoxia can result in death or brain damage, but doctors can prevent long-term effects by acting quickly to surgically deliver infants who experience distress (Gowen, 2011).

Infants may also dislocate their shoulders or hips during birth. Some experience fractures, and in others, nerves that control facial muscles are compressed, causing temporary paralysis on one side of the face. Such complications are usually not serious and resolve themselves with little or no treatment.

If a labouring woman's blood pressure suddenly increases or decreases, a Caesarean delivery may be indicated. In addition, some women's labour progresses so slowly that they remain in stage 1 for more than 24 hours. This can happen if the infant's head is in a position that prevents it from exerting enough pressure on the cervix to force it open. In such cases, surgery is often indicated because continuing labour can cause permanent damage to the mother's body.

After giving birth, most women require a period of a month or so to recover. During this time, the mother's body experiences a variety of hormonal changes, including those required for nursing and for returning to the normal menstrual cycle. A few women experience a period of depression after giving birth (a potential problem that you will read more about in the chapters on early adulthood). However, most recover quickly, both physically and emotionally, from the ordeal of pregnancy and birth.

anoxia

oxygen deprivation experienced by a fetus during labour and/or delivery

Assessing the Neonate

Learning Objective 3.16

Identify what assessment tools are used to assess the health of a newborn.

neonate

baby between birth and 1 month of age

During the first month of life a baby is referred to as a **neonate**. The health of babies born in hospitals and birthing centres, as well as most who are delivered at home by professional midwives, is usually assessed with the *Apgar scale* (Apgar, 1953). The baby receives a score of 0, 1, or 2 on each of five criteria, listed in **Table 3.5**. A maximum score of 10 is fairly unusual immediately after birth, because most infants are still somewhat blue in the fingers and toes at that stage. At a second assessment, usually five minutes after birth, however, 85 to 90% of infants score 9 or 10. Any score of 7 or better indicates that the baby is in no danger. A score of 4, 5, or 6 usually means that the baby needs help establishing normal breathing patterns; a score of 3 or below indicates a baby in critical condition.

Table 3.5 The Apgar Scale

Aspect Observed	Score Assigned		
	0	1	2
Heart rate	Absent	< 100 beats per minute	> 100 beats per minute
Respiratory rate	No breathing	Weak cry and shallow breathing	Good cry and regular breathing
Muscle tone	Flaccid	Some flexion of extremities	Well-flexed extremities
Response to stimulation of feet	None	Some motion	Crying
Colour	Blue, pale	Body pink, extremities blue	Completely pink

(**SOURCE:** Based on Francis, P.L., Self, P.A., & Horowitz, F.D. (1987). The behavioral assessment of the neonate: An overview. In J.D. Osofsky (Ed.), *Handbook of Infant Development* (2nd ed., pp. 723 – 779). New York, NY: Wiley-Interscience.)

Standard screening procedures across Canada have been expanded to include the detection of rare metabolic disorders in newborns (Dyack, 2004). New *tandem mass spectrometry* technology is capable of running multiple tests at the same time in an efficient and cost-effective way. This test means that inborn metabolic anomalies can now be detected presymptomatically, which allows for early treatment measures and better outcomes for infants and their families.

Health professionals often use the *Brazelton Neonatal Behavioral Assessment Scale* to track a newborn's development over the first two weeks or so following birth (Brazelton & Nugent, 1995). A health professional examines the neonate's responses to stimuli, reflexes, muscle tone, alertness, cuddliness, and ability to quiet or soothe himself after being upset. Scores on this test can be helpful in identifying children who may have significant neurological problems.

Low Birth Weight

Classification of a neonate's weight is another important factor in assessment. All neonates below 2500 grams are classified as having **low birth weight (LBW)**. The proportion of LBW infants has been rising slightly over the past few decades in Canada, and accounts for ~6.2% of newborns; furthermore, hospitalization rates are higher for LBW infants and the incidence of illness and mortality is also elevated (Canadian Institute of Child Health, n.d.; Statistics Canada, 2012c).

Most LBW infants are *preterm*, or born before the 38th week of gestation. However, it is possible for an infant to have completed 38 weeks or more of gestation and still be an LBW baby. In addition, some preterm babies weigh the right amount for their gestational age, while others are smaller than expected. These *small-for-date* neonates appear to have suffered from retarded fetal growth and, as a group, have poorer prognoses than do infants who weigh an appropriate amount for their gestational age.

LBW infants display markedly lower levels of responsiveness at birth and in the early months of life. Those born more than six weeks early also often suffer from *respiratory distress syndrome* (also referred to as *hyaline membrane disease*). Their poorly developed lungs cause serious breathing difficulties. In 1990, physicians began treating this problem by administering surfactant (the chemical that makes it possible for the lungs to exchange oxygen and carbon dioxide in the blood) to preterm neonates, a therapy that has reduced the rate of death among very-low-birth-weight infants by about 30% (Corbet, Long, Schumacher, Gerdes, & Cotton, 1995; Schwartz, Anastasia, Scanlon, & Kellogg, 1994).

The majority of LBW babies who weigh more than 1500 grams and who are not small-for-date catch up to their normal peers within the first few years of life, although they do so at widely varying rates (Hill, Brooks-Gunn, & Waldfogel, 2003). But those below 1500 grams remain smaller than normal and have significantly higher rates of neonatal and long-term health problems, and *neurodevelopmental* outcomes, such as motor and sensory impairment, lower intelligence test scores, and more problems in school (Breslau, Johnson, & Lucia, 2001; Behrmann & Butler, 2007b; Weindrich, Jennen-Steinmetz, Laucht, & Schmidt, 2003).

Boys are more likely than girls to show long-term effects of low birth weight. A study involving more than 700 6-year-olds found a higher rate of learning disabilities and other problems in LBW boys than among their normal-birth-weight (NBW) peers (Johnson & Breslau, 2000). By contrast, LBW girls did not differ at all from their NBW counterparts. The difference between LBW and NBW boys persisted when they were examined again at age 11.

Learning Objective 3.17

Describe the risks associated with low birth weight in infants.

low birth weight (LBW)
newborn weight below 2500 grams

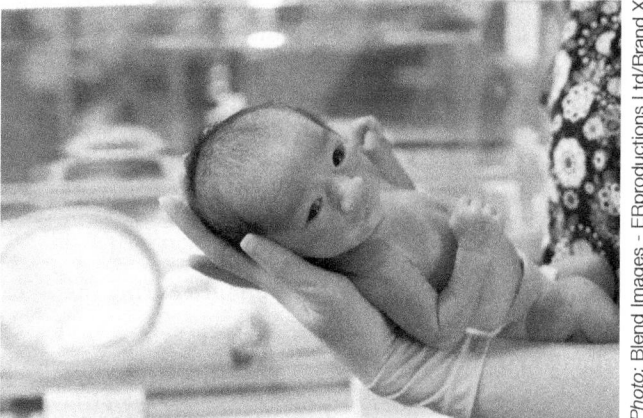

(Photo: Blend Images - ERproductions Ltd/Brand X Pictures/Getty Images)

LBW infants' chances of survival are better when they receive care in a neonatal intensive care unit.

Critical Thinking

What three pieces of advice would you give a pregnant friend after reading this chapter?

Test Yourself before going on

1. Which of the drugs that women take during the birth process enter the fetus's body?

2. Number these events in the order in which they occur during the birth process.
   _____ (a) delivery of the placenta
   _____ (b) flattening out of the cervix
   _____ (c) cervix dilated to about 10 centimetres
   _____ (d) contractions are far apart
   _____ (e) woman has the urge to push
   _____ (f) the newborn's entire body emerges from the womb

3. Immediately after birth, health care professionals use the _____ _____ to assess the newborn's condition.

4. Most low-birth-weight newborns who weigh more than _____ and are not _____ catch up to their peers during the first few years of life.

Summary

Conception

3.1 Explain the process of reproduction.

- At conception, the 23 chromosomes from the sperm join with the 23 chromosomes from the ovum to make up the set of 46 that will be reproduced in each cell of the new individual. Fertility drugs, in vitro fertilization, and artificial insemination are used for assisted human reproduction.

Pregnancy and Prenatal Development

3.2 Describe the mother's experience during the three trimesters of pregnancy.

- During the first trimester, a woman experiences morning sickness, breast enlargement, and fatigue. As the woman's abdomen enlarges during the second trimester, her pregnancy becomes noticeable. She feels fetal movements for the first time and experiences an increase in her appetite. During the third trimester, the woman gains weight and may experience breast discharge in preparation for nursing.

3.3 Outline the milestones of the three stages of prenatal development.

- During the germinal phase, from conception to the end of week 2, the zygote travels down the fallopian tube to the uterus and implants itself in the uterine wall. During the embryonic phase, from week 3 through week 8, organogenesis occurs. From week 9 through the end of pregnancy, the fetal stage, the fetus grows larger, and the structure and functioning of the various organs is refined.

3.4 List some of the ways male and female fetuses differ.

- Prenatal androgens influence gonad, genital, and brain development. Female fetuses develop more slowly than male fetuses, but show superiority in skeletal development.

3.5 Describe some of the behaviours scientists have observed in fetuses.

- The fetus is responsive to stimuli and appears to learn in the womb. Prenatal temperamental differences (for example, activity level) persist into infancy and childhood, and some aspects of the prenatal sensory environment may be important to future development.

Issues in Prenatal Development

3.6 Identify the effects of the major dominant, recessive, and sex-linked disorders.

- Dominant disorders are usually manifested in adulthood. Huntington's disease, a fatal affliction of the nervous system, is one such disorder. Recessive disorders affect individuals earlier in life, often leading to intellectual disability and/or early death. These disorders include phenylketonuria, Tay-Sachs disease, cystic fibrosis, and sickle-cell disease. Hemophilia and fragile-X syndrome are serious sex-linked disorders that affect males far more often than females; fragile-X syndrome can cause progressive intellectual disability.

3.7 Identify common trisomy errors and sex-chromosome anomalies that can affect development.

- Abnormal numbers of chromosomes and damage to chromosomes cause a number of serious disorders, including Down syndrome. Sex-chromosome anomalies may affect sexual development and certain aspects of intellectual functioning.

3.8 Identify the risks associated with teratogenic maternal diseases.

- Some diseases contracted by the mother may cause abnormalities or disease in the child. These include rubella, CMV, HIV, syphilis, genital herpes, and gonorrhea.

3.9 Describe the potential adverse effects of drugs on prenatal development.

- Drugs such as alcohol and tobacco appear to have harmful effects on the developing fetus, often resulting in lower birth weights and learning and behavioural difficulties. The effects of drugs depend on the timing of exposure, the dosage, and the quality of the postnatal environment.

3.10 Describe other maternal factors that can adversely influence prenatal development.

- If the mother has poor nutrition, her fetus faces increased risks of stillbirth, low birth weight, and death during the first year of life. Older mothers and very young mothers run increased risks, as do their infants. Long-term, severe depression or chronic physical illnesses in the mother may also increase the risk of complications of pregnancy or difficulties in the infant.

3.11 Describe how mutagenic, environmental, and epigenetic teratogens adversely affect prenatal development.

- Mutagens cause changes to DNA, environmental agents can damage cells and disrupt normal cell development, and epimutagens cause alterations to epigenetic structures without changes to DNA.

3.12 Describe how preconceptual and prenatal paternal factors can adversely influence development.

- The father's role in reproductive risk indicates his occupation, age, and/or physical abuse of the mother during pregnancy have been shown to contribute to congenital anomalies.

3.13 Identify preconceptual and prenatal assessment and diagnostic procedures.

- Techniques such as fetoscopy, ultrasonography, chorionic villus sampling, and amniocentesis are used to diagnose chromosomal and genetic disorders, and, along with laboratory tests, identify problems in fetal development. A few such problems can be treated prior to birth with surgery and/or medication.

Birth and the Neonate

3.14 Summarize the birth choices available to expectant parents.

- Most babies in Canada are delivered by physicians; however, midwifery care is becoming more available. In uncomplicated, low-risk pregnancies, delivery at home or in a birthing centre is as safe as hospital delivery.

3.15 Describe what happens in each of the three stages of labour.

- The normal birth process has three parts: dilation and effacement, delivery, and placental delivery. Most drugs given to the mother during delivery pass through to the infant's bloodstream and have short-term effects on infant responsiveness and feeding patterns.

3.16 Identify what assessment tools are used to assess the health of a newborn.

- Doctors, nurses, and midwives use the Apgar scale to assess a neonate's health immediately after birth and the Brazelton Neonatal Behavioral Assessment Scale to track a newborn's development over the first two weeks of life.

3.17 Describe the risks associated with low birth weight in infants.

- Neonates weighing less than 2500 grams are designated as having low birth weight. The lower the weight, the greater the risk of significant lasting problems, such as low intelligence test scores or learning disabilities.

Policy Question

What Legal Protection Exists for the Pregnant Mother and Her Fetus?

Society has developed laws to protect a person's rights while prescribing consequences for those who violate those rights. In the case of a pregnant woman and her fetus, society wants to act in the best interests of both. However, because of the integral relationship between mother and fetus, we are sometimes faced with a legal dilemma when their respective needs conflict. The relationship between mother and fetus from a physical point of view seems obvious, but when we try to define the relationship in legal terms we are faced with an imperfect description of that relationship.

We can look to the history of Canadian law for guidance regarding what behaviour constitutes a criminal act. The Canadian *Criminal Code* specifies what acts against a human being are criminal acts, but it does not recognize the fetus as a human being and therefore we do not have laws that recognize the killing of a fetus as homicide or infanticide. This state of affairs has a long tradition that is based in the common law, which did not recognize a fetus as a person until it was born alive. This line of thinking was incorporated into the first Canadian *Criminal Code* of 1892 and persists to this day. There have been laws against procuring a miscarriage (an abortion), and, in 1969, Section 287 of the *Criminal Code* made abortions illegal. However, doctors were exempted from prosecution if a hospital ethical review committee deemed that the mother's health or life was endangered if she carried the fetus to full term. In 1982, the *Canadian Charter of Rights and Freedoms* stated in Section 7 that "everyone has the right to life, liberty and security of the person and the right not to be deprived thereof...." At about the same time, Henry Morgentaler was testing the "lawfulness" of the abortion law of the day by setting up nonhospital abortion clinics. In 1988, his case went before the Supreme Court of Canada, which ruled that the abortion law violated Section 7 of the *Charter* in that the law interfered with a woman's body and liberty. As a result, the abortion law, Section 287 (Department of Justice Canada, 2001a), was modified. This essentially decriminalized abortions, and by implication a fetus is not protected under the *Charter*. Henceforth, abortions, at any stage of pregnancy, have not been prohibited in Canada.

At the end of the 20th century, this turn of events led to some challenging legal questions with regard to the rights of a pregnant woman versus the status and well-being of her fetus. Three court challenges in particular exemplify the difficulty we have in deciding what to do when a fetus, and subsequently a child that has been born, are at risk of harm.

What is the legal status of the pregnant mother and her fetus in Canada? The three court cases supply clues.

The first case involved the Winnipeg Child Family Services and a woman who was five months pregnant. The agency wanted to detain her in a health centre for treatment of her glue-sniffing addiction until her child was born because glue sniffing can produce permanent nervous-system damage in the developing fetus. Two of the woman's three children had already been made wards of the state at birth because they had been born with brain damage associated with glue sniffing. The intention of the social agency was to protect the health of the fetus until it was born, but in doing so it was judged to be in violation of the mother's rights and freedom.

The case made its way to the Supreme Court of Canada, which, in 1997, ruled that the mother's rights prevail over those of the fetus. The decision was based on the *Charter of Rights and Freedoms*, which in its present form applies only to human beings (not to fetuses). Therefore, in this instance, protecting the fetus by detaining the mother for treatment violated the liberties of the mother. Moreover, it was noted that if this mother could be detained for sniffing glue, then the ruling could be extended and applied to all pregnant women. It would set a precedent that would allow pregnant women to be scrutinized and incarcerated for lifestyle choices that allegedly cause harm to the fetus. This leads to questions about who would set the standard for appropriate maternal behaviour. The judgment in this case reaffirmed that a fetus has no legal rights (although a fetus does retain a moral right to be treated well).

The second case, *Dobson v. Dobson*, involved a New Brunswick woman who was 27 weeks pregnant. She had been driving on a snow-covered road when she lost control and collided with a pickup truck. The child, a boy, was later delivered by Caesarean section and has permanent mental and physical problems attributable to the accident. The mother's father was suing her for negligence on behalf of the boy. There was already a legal precedent that permits legal action to be taken by a child born alive against a third party for injuries that the child incurred while in the womb. For example, children of mothers who took thalidomide for morning sickness in the 1950s were able to receive compensation from the manufacturer of the drug. The drug caused congenital anomalies such as missing or deformed limbs, which limited the children's ability to have a full life. The courts were asked to decide if the mother in *Dobson v. Dobson* could be sued as if she were a third party to the case. The New Brunswick Courts ruled that the boy was indeed entitled to compensation. An appeal of this ruling was sent to the Supreme Court in 1999 and was overturned on several grounds. It was noted that the relationship between a mother and her fetus is unlike any other.

Mother and fetus are essentially one until birth. Therefore, no analogy can be made between the role of the mother and that of a third party in terms of any damage committed upon the fetus. Furthermore, there is no practical way to determine what standard of care a pregnant mother should have to live up to in caring for her fetus that wouldn't violate her privacy and autonomy.

The third case concerned Brenda Drummond, an Ontario woman who was charged with attempted murder and failing to provide the necessities of life. The woman apparently kept her pregnancy hidden from co-workers and her husband, and late in her pregnancy she fired a pellet through her vagina into the head of her full-term fetus. The boy was born two days later and over the following week his health deteriorated to a critical level. A brain scan was taken and revealed a pellet lodged in his skull. An operation removed the pellet and the boy recovered, but the mother didn't explain what had happened until after the operation.

In an Ontario Provincial Court, the judge ruled that at the time of the shooting the fetus could not be legally considered a victim separate from its mother. Thus, because the fetus has no separate rights in law, no crime was committed and the case was dismissed. However, the mother was then charged with the lesser offence of failing to provide the necessities of life for her newborn child when she failed to inform the doctors that she had shot her son, thereby allowing his health to be dangerously compromised. She pleaded guilty to this charge and was given a suspended sentence.

Your Turn

- What do you think the result would be if the outcome of the court decisions were different in each case? For instance, what problems do you foresee if pregnant women could be forced into treatment, or what may happen if children could sue their mothers for damages that were sustained prenatally?
- Describe a hypothetical legal standard of conduct for pregnant women.
- If Canadian laws were changed to protect the fetus from a mother's potentially damaging behaviour, then how do you think the laws should address the following concerns? How would the rights of Canadian mothers be affected? What lifestyle behaviours of the mother would be considered harmful to the fetus? Who would decide how much protection is sufficient? How would you enforce such a law?
- In what ways would forcing a woman to seek treatment do more harm than good?
- To what extent do you think society is at least indirectly responsible for harm to fetuses?

Chapter 4
Physical, Sensory, and Perceptual Development in Infancy

Elena Stepanova/Fotolia

⌄ Learning Objectives

PHYSICAL CHANGES

4.1 Describe what important changes in the brain take place during infancy.

4.2 Describe how infants' reflexes and behavioural states change.

4.3 Outline how infants' bodies change, and the typical pattern of motor skill development in the first two years.

4.4 Discuss the health issues of infants.

4.5 Discuss the developmental issues of preterm and low-birth-weight infants.

4.6 Identify the general outcomes of post-term infants.

4.7 Discuss the issue of infant mortality in Canada.

SENSORY SKILLS

4.8 Describe how infants' visual abilities change across the first months of life.

4.9 Describe how infants' senses of hearing, smell, taste, touch, and motion compare to those of older children and adults.

PERCEPTUAL SKILLS

4.10 Describe how researchers study perceptual development in infants.

4.11 Detail how depth perception and patterns of looking change over the first two years.

4.12 Detail how infants perceive human speech, recognize voices, and recognize sound patterns other than speech.

4.13 Explain the importance of intermodal perception.

4.14 Summarize what arguments nativists and empiricists offer in support of their theories of perceptual development.

One of the most fascinating features of babies' behaviour is their "busyness." They seem to be constantly on the go, manipulating objects with their hands, looking at them, feeling them, tasting them, and making sounds with them. At times, such activities seem purposeless, but they provide just the kind of skill practice and information infants need for both physical and cognitive development. Considering the energy it takes to keep up with infants' level of activity, it's little wonder their parents seem to be exhausted much of the time.

As you study this chapter, you will be become familiar with the processes through which a relatively unskilled newborn becomes a 2-year-old who can move about efficiently, the ways that infants respond to a variety of sensory stimuli, and how perception develops in infants and how they come to perceive the world as older children and adults do. The first topic we will tackle will include changes in infants' bodies and how their health can be maintained. We then move on to an exploration of infants' sensory and perceptual abilities.

Physical Changes

What comes to mind when you think about the first two years of life? If you take the time to reflect on this period, you will realize that, apart from prenatal development, it is the period during which the greatest degree of physical change occurs. Babies grow 25 to 30 centimetres and triple their body weight in the first year of life. By age 2 for girls and about 2½ for boys, toddlers are half as tall as they will be as adults. This means a 2- to 2½-year-old's adult height can be reliably predicted by doubling his current height. But 2-year-olds have proportionately much larger heads than do adults—which they need to hold their nearly full-sized brains.

The Brain and the Nervous System

The body's systems grow and develop at different rates and at different times. The reproductive system, for instance, is completely formed at birth but doesn't grow or change much until puberty. In contrast, the brain and nervous system develop rapidly during the first two years. **Figure 4.1** shows the main structures of the brain. At birth, the midbrain and the medulla are the most fully developed. These two parts, both

Learning Objective 4.1

Describe what important changes in the brain take place during infancy.

Figure 4.1 The medulla and the midbrain are largely developed at birth. In the first two years after birth, it is primarily the cortex that develops, with each neuron going through an enormous growth of dendrites and a vast increase in synapses.

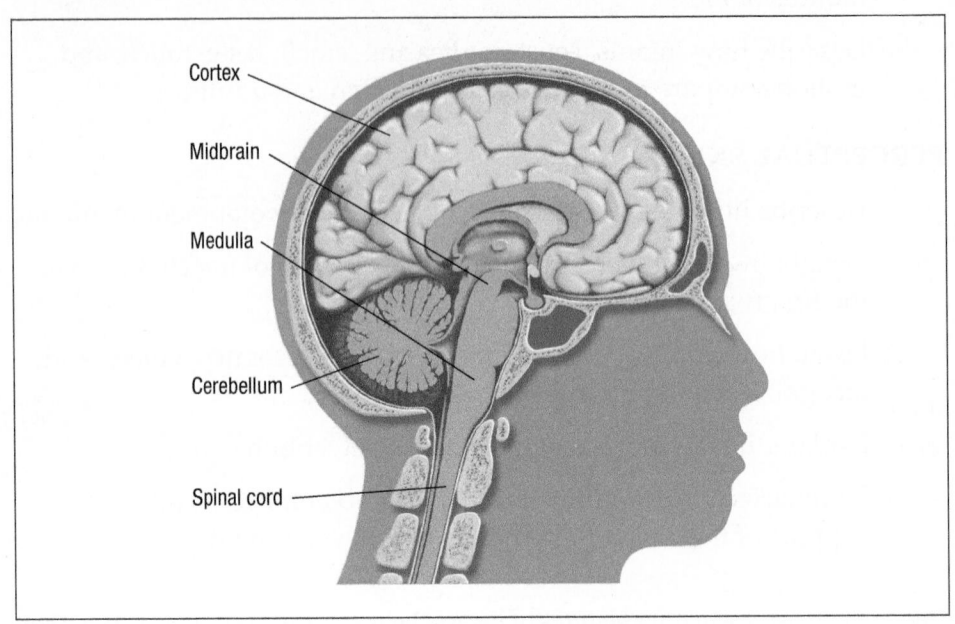

synaptogenesis

the process of synapse development

synaptic pruning

process by which unused or unnecessary neural pathways and connections are eliminated

neuroplasticity

the ability of the brain to reorganize its neural structures and functioning in response to experiences

of which are in the lower part of the skull and connected to the spinal cord, regulate vital functions such as heartbeat and respiration, as well as attention, sleeping, waking, elimination, and movement of the head and the neck—all actions a newborn can perform at least moderately well. The least-developed part of the brain at birth is the cortex, the convoluted grey matter that wraps around the midbrain and is involved in perception, body movement, thinking, and language.

SYNAPTIC DEVELOPMENT All brain structures are composed of two basic types of cells: neurons and glial cells. At birth, millions of these cells are present, and synapses, or connections between neurons, have already begun to form (Johnson, 2011). Synapse development results from growth of both dendrites and axons. **Synaptogenesis**, the creation of synapses, occurs rapidly in the cortex during the first few years after birth, resulting in a quadrupling of the overall weight of the brain by age 4 (Johnson, 2011). However, synaptogenesis is not smooth and continuous. Instead, it happens in spurts.

Typically, each synaptic growth spurt generates many more connections between neurons than the individual actually needs. Thus, each burst of synaptogenesis is followed by a period of **synaptic pruning** in which unnecessary pathways and connections are eliminated (Tau & Peterson, 2010). For example, each muscle cell seems to develop synaptic connections with several motor neurons (nerve cells that carry impulses to muscles) in the spinal cord. As the infant works to gain control over his movements, some of these connections are used repeatedly, while others are ignored. Soon, the unused connections die off, or get "pruned" by the system. Once the pruning process is completed, each muscle fibre is connected to only one motor neuron.

This cycle of synaptogenesis followed by synaptic pruning continues through the lifespan. With each cycle, the brain becomes more efficient. Consequently, a 1-year-old actually has denser dendrites and synapses than an adult does, but the 1-year-old's network operates far less efficiently than that of the adult. However, efficiency comes at a price. Because infants have more unused synapses than adults, they can bounce back from a host of insults to the brain (e.g., malnutrition, head injury) much more easily than an adult. Neuroscientists use the term **neuroplasticity** to refer to the brain's ability to change in response to experience.

Developmentalists draw several important implications from the cyclical synaptogenesis–pruning feature of neurological development. First, it seems clear that brain development follows the old dictum "Use it or lose it." A child growing up in a rich or intellectually challenging environment will retain a more complex network of synapses than one growing up with fewer forms of stimulation. In addition, as mentioned earlier, the brains of infants possess greater neuroplasticity than those of older children and adults. Paradoxically, though, the period of greatest neuroplasticity is also the period in which the child may be most vulnerable to major deficits—just as a fetus is most vulnerable to teratogens during the time of most rapid growth of any body system (Uylings, 2006). Thus, a young infant needs sufficient stimulation and order in his environment to maximize the early period of rapid growth and neuroplasticity (Johnson & de Haan, 2015). A really inadequate diet or a serious lack of stimulation in the early months may thus have subtle but long-range effects on the child's later cognitive progress. Some have even argued that watching too much television in the early months may impede brain development, as discussed in the **Development in the Real World** feature in the chapter on Cognitive Development in Infancy.

Finally, new information about the continuation of synaptogenesis and synaptic pruning throughout the lifespan has forced developmental psychologists to change their ideas about the links between brain development and behaviour. If the brain were almost completely organized by age 2, as most developmentalists believed until recently, then it would seem logical to assume that whatever developments occurred after that age were largely the product of experience. But researchers now know that changes in psychological functioning are linked to physical changes in the brain throughout the entire human lifespan.

MYELINIZATION Another crucial process in the development of neurons is the creation of sheaths, or coverings, around individual axons, which insulate them from one another electrically and improve their conductivity. These sheaths are made of a substance called myelin; the process of developing the sheath is called **myelinization**.

The sequence of myelinization follows both cephalocaudal and proximodistal patterns (these were defined in the chapter on Prenatal Development and Birth). For example, nerves serving muscle cells in the neck and shoulders are myelinized earlier than those serving the abdomen. As a result, babies can control their head movements before they can roll over. Myelinization is most rapid during the first two years after birth, but it continues at a slower pace throughout childhood and adolescence. For example, the parts of the brain that are involved in vision reach maturity by the second birthday (Lippé, Perchet, & Lassonde, 2007). By contrast, those that govern motor movements are not fully myelinized until a child is about 6 years old.

Other structures take even longer to become myelinized. For example, the **reticular formation** is the part of the brain responsible for keeping your attention on what you're doing and for helping you sort out important and unimportant information. Myelinization of the reticular formation begins in infancy but continues in spurts across childhood and adolescence. In fact, the process isn't complete until a person is in her mid-20s (Johnson, 2011). Consequently, during the first two years, infants improve their ability to focus on a task. Likewise, a 12-year-old is much better at concentrating than an infant but is still fairly inefficient when compared to an adult.

Reflexes and Behavioural States

Changes in the brain result in predictable changes in babies' reflexes, sensory capacities, and patterns of waking and sleeping. In fact, such changes, or the absence of such changes, can be important indicators of nervous system health.

REFLEXES Humans are born with many **adaptive reflexes** that help them survive. Some, such as those that aid in obtaining nourishment, e.g., the *rooting reflex* (when a newborn's cheek is touched, it will turn its head to that side) and the *sucking reflex*

myelinization

a process in neuronal development in which sheaths made of a substance called myelin gradually cover individual axons and electrically insulate them from one another to improve the conductivity of the nerve

reticular formation

the part of the brain that regulates attention

Learning Objective 4.2

Describe how infants' reflexes and behavioural states change.

adaptive reflexes

reflexes, such as sucking, that help newborns survive; some adaptive reflexes persist throughout life (newborns automatically begin sucking any object that enters the mouth), disappear in infancy or childhood. Others protect us against harmful stimuli over the whole lifespan. These adaptive reflexes include withdrawal from a painful stimulus and the opening and closing of the pupil of the eye in response to variations in brightness. Some research suggests that stimulation of some reflexes may facilitate later development. For instance, University of Toronto psychologist Philip Zelazo has found that infants who were encouraged to exercise the *stepping reflex* were more likely to spontaneously display the stepping movements and began walking at an earlier age (Zelazo, Zelazo, Cohen, & Zelazo, 1993; Zelazo, Zelazo, & Kolb, 1972). Weak or absent adaptive reflexes in neonates suggest that the brain is not functioning properly and that the baby requires additional assessment.

primitive reflexes

reflexes, controlled by "primitive" parts of the brain, that disappear during the first year of life

The purposes of **primitive reflexes**, so called because they are controlled by the less sophisticated parts of the brain (the medulla and the midbrain), are less clear. For example, if you make a loud noise or startle a baby in some other way, you'll see her throw her arms outward and arch her back, a pattern that is part of the *Moro*, or *startle*, *reflex*. Stroke the bottom of her foot and she will splay out her toes and then curl them in, a reaction called the *Babinski reflex*. By 6 to 8 months of age though, primitive reflexes begin to disappear. If such reflexes persist past this age, the baby may have some kind of neurological problem (Adolph & Berger, 2011).

(Photo: Moroz Elena/Shutterstock)

This 4-week-old baby is using the inborn adaptive reflex of sucking.

states of consciousness

different states of sleep and wakefulness in infants

BEHAVIOURAL STATES   Researchers have described five different states of sleep and wakefulness in neonates, referred to as **states of consciousness**. Most infants move through these states in the same sequence: from deep sleep to lighter sleep and then to alert wakefulness and fussing. After they are fed, they become drowsy and drop back into deep sleep. The cycle repeats itself about every two hours.

Neonates sleep as much as 80% of the time, as much in the daytime as at night (Sola, Rogido, & Partridge, 2002). By 8 weeks of age, the total amount of sleep per day has dropped somewhat and signs of day/night sleep rhythms (called *circadian rhythms*) become evident. Babies of this age begin to sleep through two or three two-hour cycles in sequence without coming to full wakefulness and are thus often said to have started to "sleep through the night." By 6 months, babies are still sleeping around 13 hours per day, but sleep is more regular and predictable. Most have clear nighttime sleep patterns and nap during the day at more predictable times.

Of course, babies' sleeping patterns vary a lot around these averages. Of the 0–2-month-old babies in one meta-analysis study, the average was 14.6 hours of sleep per day with a range of 9.3 to 20 hours per day. By 6 months of age, babies average ~13 hours of sleep per day with the lower limit dropping to just under 9 hours and the upper limit dropping to 17 hours—a pattern that doesn't change much until 2 years of age (Galland, Taylor, Elder, & Herbison, 2012). Night wakings are common in infancy and some babies do not develop a long nighttime sleep period until late in the first year of life. Moreover, cultural beliefs play an important role in parents' responses to infants' sleep patterns (Cole & Packer, 2011). For example, North American parents typically see a newborn's erratic sleep cycle as a behaviour problem that requires "fixing" through parental intervention (Harkness, 1998). As a result, they focus a great deal of attention on trying to force babies to sleep through the night. In contrast, many

European parents are more likely to regard newborns' patterns of sleeping as manifestations of normal development and tend to expect babies to acquire stable sleeping patterns naturally, without parental intervention, during the first two years.

Infants have different cries for pain, anger, or hunger. The basic cry, which often signals hunger, usually has a rhythmical pattern: cry, silence, breath, cry, silence, breath, with a kind of whistling sound often accompanying the in-breath. An anger cry is typically louder and more intense, and the pain cry normally has a very abrupt onset—unlike the other two kinds of cries, which usually begin with whimpering or moaning.

Cross-cultural studies suggest that crying increases in frequency over the first six weeks and then tapers off (Gahagan, 2011). Moreover, parents across a variety of cultures use very similar techniques to soothe crying infants. Most babies stop crying when they are picked up, held, and talked or sung to. Getting a baby to suck on a pacifier also usually helps. Parents sometimes worry that picking up a crying baby will lead to even more crying. But research suggests that prompt attention to a crying baby in the first three months actually leads to less crying later in infancy (Sulkes, 1998).

There is one fairly common exception to the typical pattern of crying, however. An estimated 5–19% of infants suffer from **colic**, a pattern involving intense bouts of crying totalling three or more hours a day, three or more times a week, for more than three weeks, for no immediately apparent reason (such as hunger or a wet diaper) and that nothing will alleviate. Typically, colic appears at about 2 or 3 weeks of age and then disappears on its own at about 3 to 4 months of age. The crying is generally worst in late afternoon or early evening (Gelfand, 2015, 2016). Some suggest colic dissipates naturally as the maturing baby's sleep cycle stabilizes as *melatonin* secretion levels harmonize with the baby's natural *circadian rhythm* (Henderson, France, Blampied, 2011; Weissbluth & Weissbluth, 1992a, 1992b).

Until recently, dietary needs or abdominal discomfort have been thought to be the culprits. However, new research indicates colic is likely a form of migraine. Several studies have shown a connection between colic and migraines in childhood and adolescence (Gelfand, 2016; Gelfand, Goadsby, & Allen, 2015; Romanello et al., 2013; Sillanpää & Saarinen, 2015). As well, mothers who have migraines are twice as likely to have infants who have colic, which suggests a genetic link. Educating parents about sleep cycle and migraine management may be a useful approach to explore for the benefit of both parent and infant (Gelfand, 2015; Qubty & Gelfand, 2016).

Developing Body Systems and Motor Skills

Like behavioural states, the acquisition of motor skills also depends on brain development. Substantial changes in other body systems—bones, muscles, lungs, and heart, for example—are required as well. As you read about them, keep in mind that physical development proceeds from the head downward (cephalocaudal pattern) and from the centre of the body outward (proximodistal pattern).

BONES During infancy, bones change in size, number, and composition. Increases in the lengths of the body's long bones—those in the legs and arms—underlie increases in height (Tanner, 1990). Changes in the number and density of bones in particular parts of the body are responsible for improvements in coordinated movement. For example, at birth, the wrist contains a single mass of cartilage; by 1 year of age, the cartilage has developed into three separate bones. The progressive separation of the wrist bones is one of the factors behind gains in manipulative skills over the first two years. Wrist bones continue to differentiate over the next several years until eventually, in adolescence, the wrist has nine separate bones (Tanner, 1990).

The process of bone hardening, called *ossification*, occurs steadily, beginning in the last weeks of prenatal development and continuing through puberty. Bones in

Critical Thinking

What advice would you give to parents who believe that picking up a baby when he cries will "spoil" him?

colic

an infant behaviour pattern involving intense, inconsolable bouts of crying, totalling three or more hours a day

Learning Objective 4.3

Outline how infants' bodies change, and the typical pattern of motor skill development in the first two years.

different parts of the body harden in a sequence that follows the typical proximodistal and cephalocaudal patterns. Motor development depends on ossification to a large extent. Standing, for example, is impossible if an infant's leg bones are too soft, no matter how well developed the muscles and nervous system are.

MUSCLES   The body's full complement of muscle fibres is present at birth, although the fibres are initially small and have a high ratio of water to muscle (Tanner, 1990). In addition, a newborn's muscles contain a fairly high proportion of fat. By 1 year of age, the water content of an infant's muscles is equal to that of an adult, and the ratio of fat to muscle tissue has begun to decline. Changes in muscle composition lead to increases in strength that enable 1-year-olds to walk, run, jump, climb, and so on.

LUNGS AND HEART   The lungs also grow rapidly and become more efficient during the first two years (Kercsmar, 1998). Improvements in lung efficiency, together with the increasing strength of heart muscles, give a 2-year-old greater *stamina*, or ability to maintain activity, than a newborn. Consequently, by the end of infancy, children are capable of engaging in fairly long periods of sustained motor activity without rest (often exhausting their parents in the process!).

MOTOR SKILLS   Changes in all of the body's systems are responsible for the impressive array of motor skills children acquire in the first two years. Developmentalists typically divide these skills into three groups. *Locomotor skills*, also often called *gross motor skills*, include abilities such as crawling that enable the infant to get around in the environment. *Non-locomotor skills*, such as controlling head movements, improve babies' ability to use their senses and motor skills to interact with the objects and the people around them. Many of these skills are used in play as well. *Manipulative skills*, or *fine motor skills*, involve use of the hands, as when a 1-year-old stacks one block on top of another. **Table 4.1** summarizes developments in each of these three areas over the first 24 months.

Cross-cultural research suggests using caution when referring to standardized milestones for motor development. Through observations made in various, natural cultural settings, recent studies have shown fairly wide variability in the ages at which infants reach **developmental milestones**. For example, infants from some parts of the world are well ahead of average, while in other regions they are delayed (Eaton, 2015; Karasik, Tamis-LeMonda, Adolph, & Bornstein, 2015).

developmental milestones

near-universal, age-related events whose first appearance signals noteworthy change or growth (Eaton, 2015)

Table 4.1 Milestones of Motor Development in the First Two Years

Age (in months)	Locomotor Skills	Non-locomotor Skills	Manipulative Skills
1	Stepping reflex	Lifts head slightly; follows slowly moving objects with eyes	Holds object if placed in hand
2–3		Lifts head up to 90-degree angle when lying on stomach	Begins to swipe at objects in sight
4–6	Rolls over; sits with support; moves on hands and knees ("creeps")	Holds head erect while in sitting position	Reaches for and grasps objects
7–9	Sits without support; crawls		Transfers objects from one hand to the other
10–12	Pulls self up and walks grasping furniture; then walks alone	Squats and stoops; plays patty cake	Shows some signs of hand preference; grasps a spoon across palm but has poor aim when moving food to mouth
13–18	Walks backward, sideways; runs (14–20 mos.)	Rolls ball to adult; claps	Stacks two blocks; puts objects into small container and dumps them out
19–24	Walks up and down stairs, two feet per step	Jumps with both feet off ground	Uses spoon to feed self; stacks 4 to 10 blocks

To help address some of the challenges of determining clear, developmental milestone measures, Canadian and cross-cultural norms are being developed as part of University of Manitoba psychologist Warren Eaton's ongoing infant *Milestone Study*. To date, hundreds of babies have been tracked to determine week-to-week changes as they progress toward motor skills milestones. Although the timing of the first time a baby sits, creeps, crawls, and walks is variable, the researchers have, for example, observed a seasonal trend whereby babies born in the spring reach crawling and walking milestones at a younger age (Eaton, 2003). The project has been expanded to include gestures, words, and personality development up to 24 months of age (Eaton, 2013)—if you're interested in participating, link to http://milestoneshome.org.

As well, a comprehensive Canadian screening tool is now available to assist professionals and parents to identify various aspects of a child's development that may require early intervention. The *Nipissing District Developmental Screen* (NDDS) can be used with children aged 1 month to 6 years to screen for problems in any of the critical areas that you'll read more about in the chapters on infancy—gross motor, fine motor, vision, hearing, speech, language, communication, cognitive, social/emotional, and self-help. This culturally sensitive tool is now being used in many jurisdictions across Canada and internationally and is available in English, French, and numerous other languages. (NDDS webpage: www.ndds.ca.)

GENDER DIFFERENCES Throughout infancy, girls are ahead of boys in some aspects of physical maturity. For example, the separate bones of the wrist appear earlier in girls than in boys (Tanner, 1990). This means that female infants may have a slight advantage in the development of manipulative skills such as self-feeding.

University of Manitoba researchers found that boys are typically more physically active (Campbell & Eaton, 1999). In both human and primate studies, male infants also display a clear preference for rough-and-tumble play, even during the first few months of life (Brown & Dixson, 2000; Humphreys & Smith, 1987). Likewise, differences between boys and girls in physical aggression are already evident near the end of the second year, a finding that has been replicated in studies of many cultures (e.g., Archer, 2004; Hyde, 2005).

EXPLAINING MOTOR SKILL DEVELOPMENT Despite gender differences in the rate of physical development, the sequence of motor skill development is virtually the same for all children, even those with serious physical or mental anomalies. Developmentally delayed children, for example, move through the various motor milestones

The striking improvements in motor development in the early months are easy to illustrate. Between 6 and 12 months of age, babies progress from sitting alone, to creeping and crawling, to walking.

(Photos: Courtesy of Michael and Alexandra Enns)

more slowly than normal children do, but they do so in the same sequence. Further-more, motor skill development follows the cephalocaudal and proximodistal patterns. Whenever developmentalists find such consistencies, maturation of some kind seems an obvious explanation (Thelen, 1995).

However, research involving infants living in normal environments supports the notion that experience influences motor development. For example, the reasons why infants transition from relatively reliable and safe crawling to unsteady and precari-ous walking (think of the number of times a baby falls or bangs into obstacles when he first starts walking), requires some explanation when the immediate rewards may not be obvious. It seems there are costs and benefits to walking with the benefits win-ning out over the course of several weeks that it takes to make the transition—benefits such as having a vaster perspective and seeing more distant objects, exploring further faster, and with their hands free, interacting with those distant objects in new ways, such as sharing with others—all fairly rich incentives to persist with walking. As well, infants typically elicit praise and encouragement from caregivers when they start walking (Adolph & Tamis-LeMonda, 2014). Even though infants' exploratory walking can be goal driven (e.g., a desirable object in the distance), there are also many inter-esting objects, people, or scenes to be discovered merely by walking around—another incentive to keep walking, perhaps (Cole, Robinson, & Adolph, 2016).

Learning Objective 4.4

Discuss the health issues of infants.

Health Promotion and Wellness

Babies depend on adults to help them stay healthy. Specifically, babies need the right foods in the right amounts, and they need regular medical care.

NUTRITION   After several decades of extensive research in many countries, experts agree that, for most infants, breastfeeding is substantially superior nutritionally to bottle-feeding. Health Canada, the Canadian Paediatric Society (CPS), Dieticians of Canada, and Breastfeeding Committee for Canada (Health Canada, 2015b) recom-mend that breastfeeding should be the sole source of infant nutrition for at least the first six months of life. Currently, in Canada, ~90% of mothers *initiate* breastfeed-ing of their babies (Gionet, 2013), up from just 38% in 1963 (McNally, Hendricks, & Horowitz, 1985).

One Canadian study that looked at infant feeding diaries of breastfeeding mothers determined there are three distinct feeding patterns—exclusive, partial, and no breast-feeding. The researchers found the transition from exclusive to partial took a long time for infants 6 months and younger, whereas the shift from partial to no breastfeeding was relatively quick for infants older than 6 months (Bodnarchuk, Eaton, & Martens, 2006).

Although health care experts recommend exclusive breastfeeding for six months or more, only about half of mothers still *exclusively* breastfeed their infants by four, and only one-quarter by six, months of age. Still, there is a wide disparity in exclusive breastfeeding trends across the country. Mothers in the western provinces have the highest rates, while mothers in Quebec and the Maritime provinces have the lowest rates (Gionet, 2013). As well, breastfeeding practices vary among other Canadian sub-groups. Women who are older, are better educated, have higher incomes, and are not single parents are more likely to initiate and maintain breastfeeding (Gionet, 2013). Recent immigrant mothers are more likely to initiate and sustain exclusive breastfeed-ing than Canadian-born mothers—with a median duration of 4.6 months verses 3.9 months, respectively (Woldemicael, 2009). However, this tendency diminishes with length of residency—for those in Canada 10 years or more, these differences in breast-feeding practices disappear.

Breastfeeding is associated with a number of benefits (Wagner, 2009). For one, breast milk contributes to more rapid weight and size gain. On average, breastfed infants are also less likely to suffer from such problems as diarrhea, gastroenteritis, bronchitis, ear infections, and colic, and they are less likely to die in infancy. Breast milk also appears to stimulate better immune system function. For these reasons, physicians strongly recommend breastfeeding if it is at all possible, even if the mother can nurse for only a few weeks after birth or if her breast milk must be supplemented with formula feedings (Krebs & Primak, 2011). (See **Development in the Real World.**)

Surprisingly, though, there are situations in which breast milk is not sufficient to meet babies' nutritional needs. For instance, preterm babies' intestinal tracts are not as mature as those of full-term infants. As a result, preterm babies require special formulas that contain amino acids and fats that full-term infants' bodies can manufacture on their own (Krebs & Primak, 2011). However, these babies also need the immunological benefits of breast milk. Thus, physicians typically recommend feeding preterm babies expressed breast milk that has been fortified with the proteins, fats, vitamins, and minerals their bodies need (O'Connor et al., 2008).

However, Canadian experts caution that breastfeeding is not recommended for all babies (Health Canada, 2015b). For example, drugs are often present in the breast milk of mothers who are substance abusers or who depend on medications to maintain their own health. Many of these drugs can negatively affect infant development. Consequently, doctors recommend that these women avoid breastfeeding. In such cases, babies who are fed high-quality infant formula, prepared according to the manufacturer's instructions and properly sterilized, usually thrive on it.

Up until 6 months, babies need only breast milk or formula accompanied by appropriate supplements (Krebs & Primak, 2011). For example, pediatricians usually recommend iron supplements for most babies over 4 months of age and vitamin B12 supplements for infants whose nursing mothers are vegetarians. Likewise, doctors may recommend supplemental formula feeding for infants who are growing poorly.

Although breastfeeding can continue to beyond 2 years, at 6 months, healthy, full-term infants are ready for the introduction of solid foods, which helps meet the infants' increasing nutritional needs (PHAC, 2009a). The first foods should include iron-fortified infant single-grain cereal, followed by puréed vegetables, fruits, and, lastly, meat or meat substitutes. A gradual introduction of new foods allows for better

gut microbiota
the population of microbes that colonizes the gastrointestinal tract

---

Development in the Real World

The Critical Role of Gut Microbiota

A key health benefit of breastfeeding is ensuring the infant has a full range of the essential nutrients needed for healthy growth and functioning. Breastfeeding also plays a role in strengthening the infant's immune system. But what is it that makes breast milk so advantageous in comparison to formula? The emerging evidence indicates breastfeeding provides health benefits by enhancing the infants **gut microbiota**—the population of microbes that colonizes the gastrointestinal tract.

Canadian researchers are on the forefront of infant gut microbiota research and are finding several key factors influence robust gut microbiota development. It is now recognized that gut microbiota colonization first starts prenatally, and then other early life exposures take over (Koleva, Kim, Scott, & Kozyrskyj, 2015). Differences in postnatal levels of exposure to gut microbiota vary depending on several factors such as vaginal versus C-section delivery, breastfeeding versus formula, antibiotic use by the mother before and during the birth process, antibiotics administered to the neonate, and the location of birth—home versus hospital, just to name a few (Azad et at, 2013; Koleva, et al., 2015; Kozyrskyj & Sloboda, 2016; Persaud, et al., 2015). For instance, recent studies show that, in comparison to scheduled C-section deliveries, babies delivered vaginally develop healthier gut microbiota characterized by greater diversity and abundance. The newborn's gut microbiota is further strengthened through exclusive breastfeeding. Infants that were bottle-fed partially or exclusively showed less microbiota diversity and abundance than did breastfed babies (Azad et al., 2013; Cabrera-Rubio, Mira-Pascual, Mira, & Collado, 2016).

Future research is warranted based on evidence from earlier studies that show a relationship between neonatal gut microbiota and later health issues such as allergies, obesity, and autoimmune diseases (Azad et al., 2013; Koleva, Bridgman, & Kozyrskyj, 2015; Kozyrskyj, 2015; Wallace, Gohir, & Sloboda, 2016).

Eating Well with Canada's Food Guide

guidelines for a balanced and healthy diet based on the four major food groups: vegetables and fruits, grain products, milk and alternatives, and meat and alternatives

macronutrients

large amounts of carbohydrates, fats, and proteins that are needed for energy and for body- and brain-building elements

micronutrients

essential vitamins and minerals that are needed in small amounts to regulate physical and mental processes

identification of possible food allergies. By 1 year of age, the baby should have a wide variety of foods based on **Eating Well with Canada's Food Guide** (Health Canada, 2011).

MALNUTRITION Malnutrition in infancy can seriously impair a baby's brain because the nervous system is the most rapidly developing body system during the first two years of life. **Macronutrient** malnutrition results from a diet that contains too few calories. Macronutrient malnutrition is the world's leading cause of death of children under the age of 5 (Krebs & Primak, 2011).

When the calorie deficit is severe, a disease called *marasmus* results. Infants with marasmus weigh less than 60% of what they should at their age, and many suffer permanent neurological damage from the disease. Most also suffer from parasitic infections that lead to chronic diarrhea. This condition makes it very difficult to treat marasmus by simply increasing an infant's intake of calories. However, a program of dietary supplementation with formula combined with intravenous feedings and treatment for parasites can reverse marasmus (Krebs & Primak, 2011).

Some infants' diets contain almost enough calories but not enough protein. Diets of this type lead to a disease called *kwashiorkor*, which is common in countries where infants are weaned too early to low-protein foods. Kwashiorkor-like symptoms are also seen in children who are chronically ill because of their bodies' inability to use the protein from the foods they eat. Like marasmus, kwashiorkor can lead to a variety of health problems as well as permanent brain damage (Krebs & Primak, 2011).

A small proportion of infants in North America have feeding problems, such as a poorly developed sucking reflex, that place them at risk for macronutrient malnutrition (Wright & Birks, 2000). However, most nutritional problems in developed nations involve **micronutrient** malnutrition, a deficiency of certain vitamins and/or minerals. The exception is Canada, which is a world leader in food fortification. Micronutrients have been added to our food supply for well over 60 years. Specifically, vitamin D has been added to fluid milk since the 1960s, essentially eliminating childhood rickets; iodine is added to table salt, which has eliminated endemic goitre; and vitamin A is added to low-fat milk and butter substitutes, such as margarine (Lofti, 2001). Canada is also a leader in promoting and distributing three essential micronutrients—vitamin A, iodine, and iron—throughout developing countries (CIDA, 2000). As a result, for example, George Beaton, professor emeritus of the University of Toronto and a world-renowned pioneer in the study of human nutrition requirements, found that mortality rates can be reduced by 23% by supplying young children living in at-risk countries with vitamin A (Beaton et al., 1993).

HEALTH CARE AND IMMUNIZATIONS Infants need frequent medical checkups. Much of *well baby care* may seem routine, but it is extremely important to development. For example, during routine visits to the doctor's office or health clinic, babies' motor skills are usually assessed. An infant whose motor development is less advanced than expected for his age may require additional screening for a developmental or intellectual anomaly (Levine, 2011).

One of the most important elements of well baby care is vaccination against a variety of diseases. Although immunizations later in childhood provide good protection, the *Canadian Immunization Guide* recommends that routine immunization should commence at 2 months of age and continue through childhood and adolescence (Public Health Agency of Canada [PHAC], 2015). Still, it is important to be informed of the benefits and possible adverse reactions and risks of vaccines when consenting to immunization services (e.g., answers to parents' questions about vaccine effectiveness, safety, and side effects can be found on the Canadian Paediatric Society's "Caring for Kids" website: www.caringforkids.cps.ca/handouts/immunization-index).

At the beginning of the last century, infectious diseases were a leading cause of childhood death, but they have since been virtually eradicated as the result of mass vaccination programs (Trovato, 1991). Depending on the province or territory, Canadian children typically receive vaccinations starting at 2 months of age for DTaP (diphtheria, tetanus, pertussis [acellular]), IPV (inactivated poliovirus), Hib (haemophilus influenzae type b), Pneu-C-13 (pneumococcal conjugate [13-valent]), Men-C-C (meningococcal conjugate [Strain C]), and Rota (rotavirus). Vaccinations for influenza generally start at age 6 months and vaccinations for MMR (measles, mumps, and rubella), Hep B (hepatitis B), and Var (varicella) are administered around an infant's first birthday (Government of Canada, 2016a).

The public can easily become complacent about immunizations (PHAC, 2015a). For example, failure to be vaccinated against measles led to an outbreak involving nearly 776 confirmed cases of the illness in Quebec in 2011 (Gouvernement du Québec, 2012). Thus, it is important to remember that diseases such as measles will remain rare only as long as parents are diligent in having their children immunized.

Medical checkups and immunizations are essential medical interventions. However, there are medical procedures that some parents choose to have done that aren't *medically necessary*. One such procedure is discussed in **Development in the Real World**.

ILLNESSES IN THE FIRST TWO YEARS   Well over half of infants in Canada have a respiratory illness in the first year of life (James, 2010). Interestingly, research in a number of countries shows that babies in daycare centres have about twice as many infections as those reared entirely at home, with those in small-group daycare falling somewhere in between, presumably because babies cared for in group settings are exposed to a wider range of germs and viruses (Collet et al., 1994; Lau, Uba, & Lehman, 2002). In general, the more people a baby is exposed to, the more often she is likely to be sick.

Neuropsychologists have suggested that the timing of respiratory illnesses that can lead to ear infections is important (Waseem & Aslam, 2010). Many note that infants who have chronic ear infections are more likely than their peers to have learning disabilities, attention disorders, and language deficits during the school years (Asbjornsen et al., 2005). These psychologists hypothesize that, because ear infections temporarily impair hearing, they may compromise the development of brain areas that are essential for language learning during the first two years of life. Thus, most pediatricians emphasize the need for effective hygiene practices in daycare centres, such as periodic disinfection of all toys and prompt treatment of infants' respiratory infections.

Critical Thinking

Should the practice of out-of-country female circumcision be controlled by legal means in Canada? What difficulties might arise? In what other ways could this practice be controlled? Should male circumcision be viewed on the same level as female circumcision and, therefore, deserve the same attention from Canadian authorities? Why or why not?

Development in the Real World

Circumcision

Circumcision is a very emotionally laden topic in Canada and reaching consensus on circumcision is not likely in the foreseeable future. Female circumcision (the removal of some or all of the labia and clitoris) is illegal in Canada. As a result, some parents take their girls out of the country to have it performed—a practice that is not illegal, but contentious. For boys in Canada, circumcision (the partial or complete removal of the foreskin [prepuce]) although legal, is rarely medically indicated and, therefore, not recommended for every newborn male (Sorokan, Finlay, Jefferies, & Canadian Paediatric Society [CPS], 2015).

Although the numbers have dropped, roughly one-third of Canadian male neonates still undergo the procedure (CPS, 2015). Both female circumcision and male circumcision seem to be entrenched practices, primarily for reasons of religion, culture, and/or tradition. Some objectors have raised questions about the practice, arguing there are serious practical, ethical, constitutional, and human rights considerations surrounding non-medically necessary circumcision for either females or males (Bhimji, 2000; Canadian Children's Rights Council, n.d.).

Preterm and Low-Birth-Weight Infants

Infants born live before 37 weeks of gestation are considered preterm. The Canadian preterm rate has steadily increased since the early 1980s before stabilizing at ~8 per 100 live births by the 2010s (PHAC, 2008a; 2013a). Although preterm rates are significantly higher for multiple-birth infants, singleton births still account for about 80% of all preterm births (see **Figure 4.2**) (PHAC, 2008a).

Infants born before 32 weeks of gestation may not have adaptive reflexes that are sufficiently developed to enable them to survive. Sucking and swallowing, for example, are extremely difficult for these tiny infants. Consequently, many preterm infants must be fed intravenously or through a tube inserted into the esophagus or the stomach (Kliegman, 1998). Preterm babies are also at higher risk for neurological impairment, cardiovascular disorders, respiratory difficulties, gastrointestinal complications, immunologic deficiencies which cause a susceptibility to infections, and neonatal infant mortality (Behrman & Butler, 2007a; PHAC, 2008a). Over the long haul, preterm babies are also more likely to experience motor, cognitive, visual, hearing, behavioural, and growth problems.

Most low-birth-weight (LBW—weighing less than 2.5 kilograms at birth) infants are preterm, although it is possible for an infant to have completed 37 weeks or more of gestation and still be a LBW baby. Preterm and LBW babies move more slowly from one developmental milestone to the next because the preterm baby is, in fact, maturationally younger than the full-term baby. If a correction is made for the baby's gestational age, then most (but not all) of the difference in physical development disappears. For example, a 12-month-old who was born two months early would have a corrected age of 10 months. Parents of preterms need to keep this in mind when they compare their babies' progress with that of full-term babies. By age 2 or 3, the physically normal preterm can catch up to his peers, but in the early months he is definitely behind.

Figure 4.2 Preterm birth rates, by single and multiple births, Canada (excluding Ontario*), 2004.

* Ontario is excluded because of data quality concerns.

** Excludes live births with unknown age and gestational age.

(SOURCE: Adapted from PHAC, 2008a, Figure 20.2.)

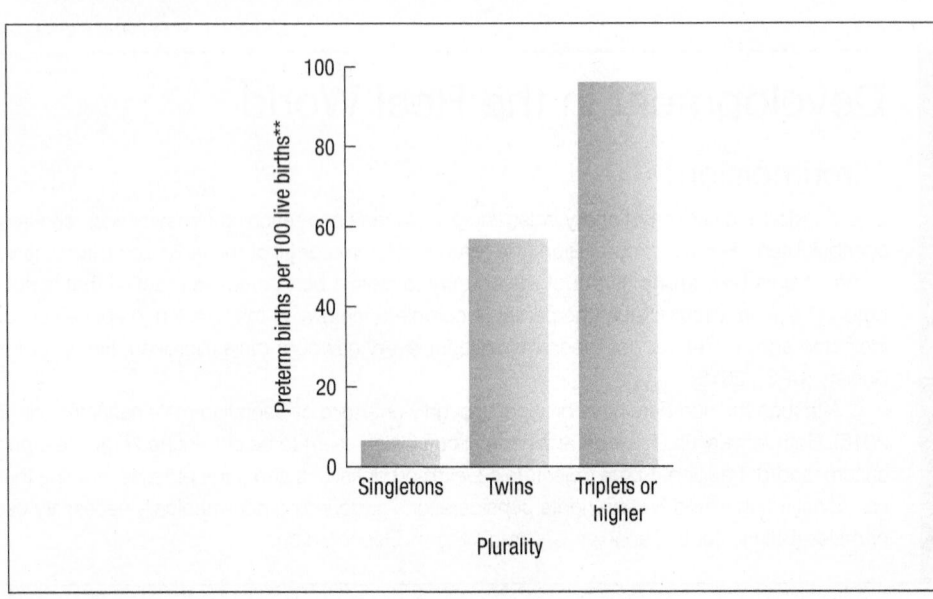

Although experience influences the developmental progress in preterm infants just as it does full-term infants, it is especially important for parents, particularly mothers, to know that their responses to the child contribute to how rapidly she develops (White-Traut et al., 2013; 2002). For example, a relatively recent innovation in the care of preterm newborns is an intervention called *kangaroo care* in which parents are shown how to increase the amount of skin-to-skin contact infants engage in with them. An important part of the intervention involves allowing parents to hold these tiny newborns for very long periods of time. Researchers from Canada and across the globe have found that preterm babies who receive kangaroo care grow and develop more rapidly than preterm infants given conventional neonatal care (Cooper et al., 2007; Moore et al., 2012; Suman, Udani, & Nanavati, 2008; Tessier et al., 2009). McGill University researchers (Johnston et al., 2008, 2014) have also found that kangaroo mother care alleviates the pain response in premature neonates.

Post-Term Infants

Infants born after 42 or more weeks of gestation are referred to as *post-term*. Post-term pregnancies are associated with higher risk for maternal medical complications and with fetal and neonatal mortality (PHAC, 2008a). Fortunately, the rate of post-term deliveries in Canada has decreased substantially from 4.4% in 1991 to a low of 0.8% by the mid-2000s (PHAC, 2008a). This decrease can be attributed in part to the effective use of ultrasound dating and the practice of inducing post-term pregnancies. However, the rates of post-term deliveries vary dramatically among Canada's provinces and territories (see **Figure 4.3**) (PHAC, 2008a).

Learning Objective 4.6

Identify the general outcomes of post-term infants.

Figure 4.3 Post-term birth rates, by province/territory, Canada (excluding Ontario*), 2006–2010.

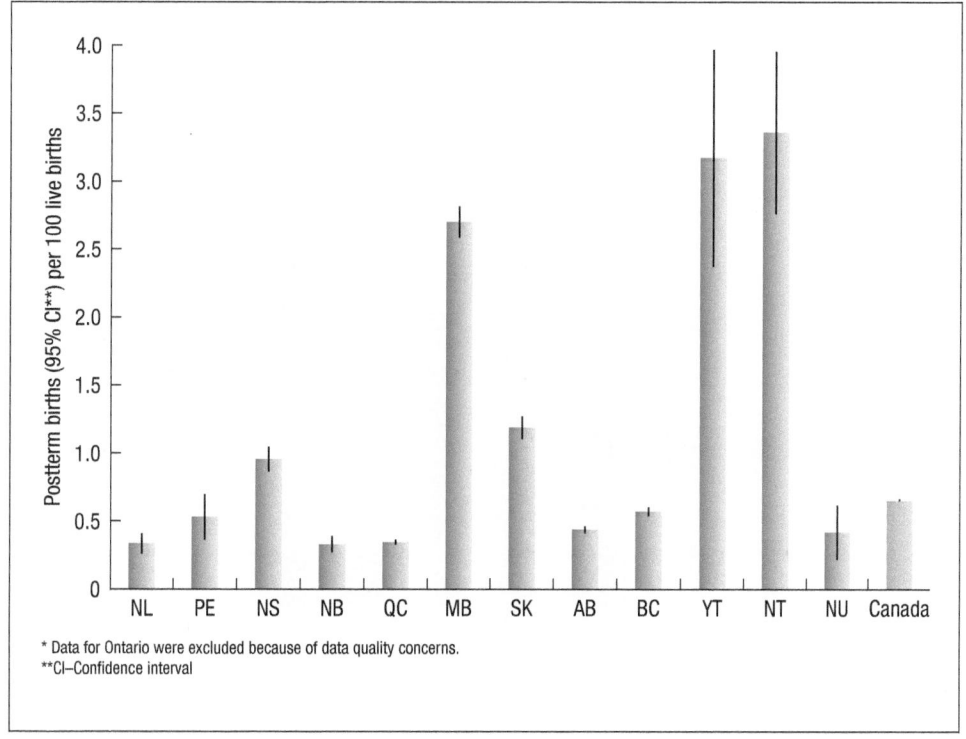

* Data for Ontario were excluded because of data quality concerns.
**CI–Confidence interval

Learning Objective 4.7

Discuss the issue of infant mortality in Canada.

infant mortality

death within the first year of life

Infant Mortality in Canada

About half of infant deaths in Canada occur in the neonate and the rest between 4 weeks and 1 year of age. Over the past century, Canada's rate of **infant mortality** has shown a dramatic rate of decline—from 134 per 1000 live births in 1901 to 27 in the 1960s to just ~5 in 2007 (Conference Board of Canada [CBofC], 2016a; Wilkins, Houle, Berthelot, & Ross, 2000). Still, despite Canada's high calibre of health care, it has made less progress in reducing infant deaths than many other nations: Of 17 peer countries, Canada is now tied with the United Kingdom for the second highest infant mortality rate—only the United States performs worse (CBofC, 2016a).

Even though regional disparities in infant mortality rates across Canada have diminished significantly, income disparity stubbornly remains a problem: Lower-income families experience higher infant mortality rates than middle- and upper-income groups (see **Figure 4.4**). Moreover, infant mortality rates for First Nations and Inuit are two and four times higher, respectively, than the general Canadian population (McShane, Smylie, & Adomako, 2009). Although living closer to an urban setting is associated with lower infant mortality rates for non-First Nations, there is no such difference for First Nations (Luo et al., 2010). The rates of infant mortality for First Nations were the same in rural and urban environments, suggesting a need for improved urban First Nations' infant care in light of increasing urban migration.

sudden infant death syndrome (SIDS)

the term used to describe the sudden and unexpected death of an apparently healthy infant

SUDDEN INFANT DEATH SYNDROME   **Sudden infant death syndrome (SIDS)** is the term associated with the sudden and unexpected death of an apparently healthy infant. The rate of SIDS in Canada has declined quite dramatically from 12 per 1000 in 1980 to 0.3 per 1000 in the 2000s (PHAC, 2008a; Health Canada, 1999a). However, there are significant differences in the incidence of SIDS across Canada, with lower rates in British Columbia, Quebec, and Ontario. Rates for First Nations infants are three times the national average.

Researchers have not yet uncovered the underlying cause(s) of SIDS, but some factors have been shown to reduce risk. Parents and caregivers can provide a safe sleep environment that reduces the risk of SIDS by

- placing the baby on his back when he sleeps (CPS, 2009; Carpenter et al., 2004; Trifunov, 2009)

Figure 4.4 Infant mortality by income quintile, urban Canada, 1996.

(**SOURCE:** Adapted from Statistics Canada, 1999, *Health Reports* 11(3), cited in Wilkins, Houle, Berthelot, & Ross, 2000.)

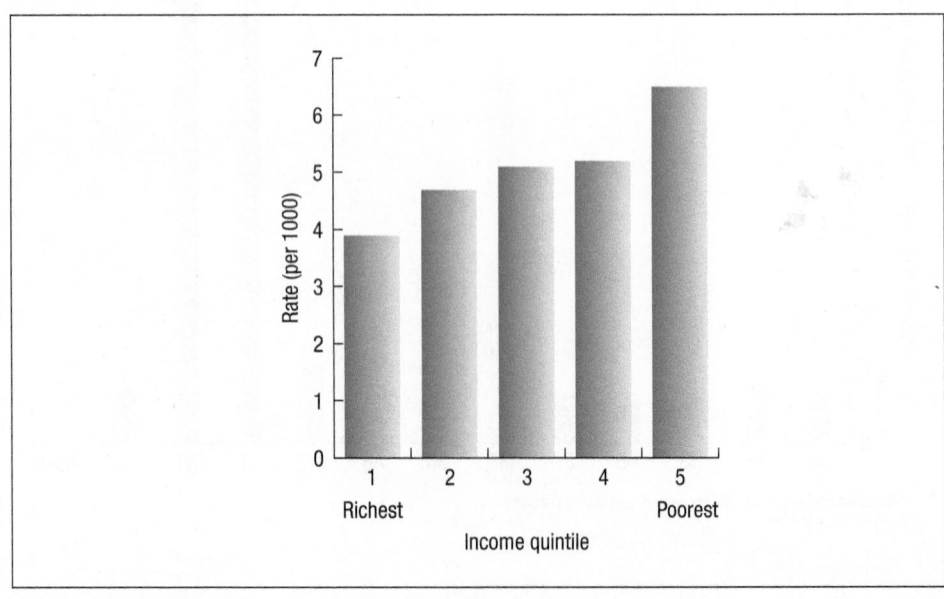

- eliminating quilts, duvets, pillows, soft toys, and crib bumpers that may cover the infant's head: a fitted sheet on a crib mattress that meets current Canadian safety regulations is best (CPS, 2009)

- avoiding laying the baby on soft surfaces or on loose bedding (such as bunched-up blankets or cushions) to sleep or nap, either alone or with someone else (CPS, 2009)

- having the baby sleep in a crib or a cot near to the parent's bed for the first six months (CPS, 2009; McIntosh, Tonkin, & Gunn, 2009)

- avoiding bed sharing or otherwise sleeping or napping with the baby on a sofa, especially if the parents smoke, are more tired than usual, or have consumed alcohol or other substances that promote fatigue (CPS, 2009; Carpenter et al., 2004; Trifunov, 2009)

- providing a smoke-free environment during pregnancy and in the home after the infant's birth (CPS, 2009; Trifunov, 2009)

Test Yourself before going on

1. Match each term with its definition.
   - _____ (a) synaptogenesis
   - _____ (b) pruning
   - _____ (c) neuroplasticity
   - _____ (d) adaptive reflexes
   - _____ (e) primitive reflexes
       - (i) reflexes that disappear during the first year of life
       - (ii) the process of synapse development
       - (iii) the brain's capacity to change in response to experience
       - (iv) reflexes that help infants survive
       - (v) the elimination of unused synapses

2. Infant colic is thought to be a form of _____.

3. Match each term with its definition.
   - _____ (a) stamina
   - _____ (b) locomotor skills
   - _____ (c) non-locomotor skills
   - _____ (d) manipulative skills
       - (i) abilities such as crawling that enable the infant to get around in the environment
       - (i) involve use of the hands or fingers, as when an infant reaches for and grasps objects
       - (iii) improvements in lung efficiency, together with the increasing strength of heart muscles, give a 2-year-old greater ability to maintain activity than a newborn
       - (iv) abilities, such as controlling head movements, that improve babies' ability to use their senses and motor skills to interact and play with the objects and the people around them

4. What are some reasons why breast milk is superior to formula?

5. Label each case of malnutrition as (MAC) macronutrient malnutrition, (MIC) micronutrient malnutrition, (K) kwashiorkor, or (MAR) marasmus.
   - _____ (a) Jerome's diet is deficient in calcium and vitamin C.
   - _____ (b) Because she doesn't get enough to eat, 8-year-old Nala's weight is equivalent to that of an average 4-year-old.
   - _____ (c) George's diet is so low in protein that he is at risk of permanent brain damage.
   - _____ (d) This type of malnutrition is the world's leading cause of death among children under age 5.

6. Why is the statement "Healthy babies don't need to go to the doctor" false?

7. A risk in both preterm and post-term pregnancies is _____.

8. Write Y next to risk factors for SIDS, and write N next to characteristics that are not risk factors for SIDS.
   - _____ (a) sleeping on the stomach
   - _____ (b) summer birth
   - _____ (c) mother smoked during pregnancy
   - _____ (d) exposure to second-hand smoke
   - _____ (e) family history of lung cancer
   - _____ (f) sleeping on a firm mattress with no pillow

Sensory Skills

When we study sensory skills, we are asking just what information the sensory organs receive. Does the structure of the eye permit infants to see colour? Are the structures of the ear and the cortex such that a very young infant can discriminate among different pitches? The common theme running through all of what you will read in this section is that newborns and young infants have far more sensory capacity than physicians or psychologists thought even as recently as a few decades ago.

Vision

Until half a century ago, many medical texts stated that the newborn infant was blind. Now we know that the newborn has poorer visual skills than older children but is quite definitely not blind. Still, an estimated 5 to 10% of babies have some form of visual problem (Amit, Canadian Paediatric Society, 2009; Canadian Ophthalmological Society, n.d.; Castanes, 2003; Walker & Harris, 2012). A visual assessment is recommended at birth and at all routine health checkups, or if there are any changes or complaints with the eyes or vision. The consequences of undetected or untreated visual problems can lead to lifelong visual problems that can interfere with educational achievement and quality of life.

visual acuity

how well one can see details at a distance

VISUAL ACUITY   The usual standard for **visual acuity** in adults is 20/20 vision, which means that you can see and identify something 20 feet (6 metres) away that the average person can also see at 20 feet (6 metres). A person with 20/100 vision, in contrast, has to be as close as 20 feet (6 metres) to see something that the ordinary person can see at 100 feet (30.5 metres). In other words, the higher the second number, the poorer the person's visual acuity. At birth, acuity is in the range of 20/200 to 20/400, but it improves rapidly during the first year as a result of synaptogenesis, synaptic pruning, and myelination in the neurons that serve the eyes' and the brain's vision processing centres. Stated another way, the visual acuity of a newborn is about 40 times worse than that of a normal sighted adult, but, by 6 months of age, vision improves to the point where it is only eight times worse than that of an adult. Gradually, most children reach adult levels of visual acuity at about 7 years of age (Lewis & Maurer, 2005; Maurer, Mondloch, & Lewis, 2007).

The fact that the newborn sees so poorly is not so negative a thing as it might seem at first. Of course, it does mean that a baby doesn't see faraway things clearly; he probably can't see well enough to distinguish two people standing nearby. But he sees quite well close-up, which is all that is necessary for most encounters with the people who care for him or with the objects immediately at hand, such as a breast, a bottle, or a mobile hanging above his crib.

A thorough visual screening is recommended if there is a family history of eye or visual problems or if there is a noticeable change in the eye or in eye movements, e.g., eyes turning in or misalignment.

tracking

the smooth movements of the eye used to follow the track of a moving object

TRACKING OBJECTS IN THE VISUAL FIELD   The process of following a moving object with your eyes is called **tracking**, and you do it every day in a variety of situations. You track the movement of other cars when you are driving; you track as you watch a friend walk toward you across the room; a baseball outfielder tracks the flight of the ball so that he can catch it. Because a newborn infant can't yet move independently, many of her experiences are with objects that move toward her or away from her. If she is to have any success in recognizing objects, she has to be able to keep her eyes on them as they move: she must be able to track. Classic research by Richard Aslin (1987) and others shows that tracking is initially fairly inefficient but improves quite rapidly. Infants younger than 2 months show some tracking for brief periods if the target is moving very slowly, but somewhere around 6 to 10 weeks a shift occurs and babies' tracking becomes skilful rather quickly.

COLOUR VISION   Researchers have established that the types of cells in the eye (cones) necessary for perceiving red and green are clearly present by 1 month (and perhaps present at birth); those required for perceiving blue are probably present by then as well (Bornstein, 1992). Thus, infants can and do see and discriminate among various colours. Indeed, researchers have determined that infants' ability to sense colour, even in the earliest weeks of life, is almost identical to that of adults (Pereverzeva, Hui-Lin Chien, Palmer, & Teller, 2002).

Taken together, these findings certainly do not support the notion that an infant is blind at birth. While it is true that the infant's acuity is initially poor, it improves rapidly, and other visual capacities are remarkably well developed early on. Still, a number of visual skills depend on a specific kind of visual stimulation during sensitive periods of development. For example, the onset of visual deprivation beginning at age 6 months through adolescence can prevent the development of normal *peripheral vision*, whereas sensitivity to the *global direction of motion* (e.g., when an observer sees an identifiable group of dots moving together in a particular direction among dots moving randomly) is affected only by visual deprivation that occurs near birth (Lewis & Maurer, 2005).

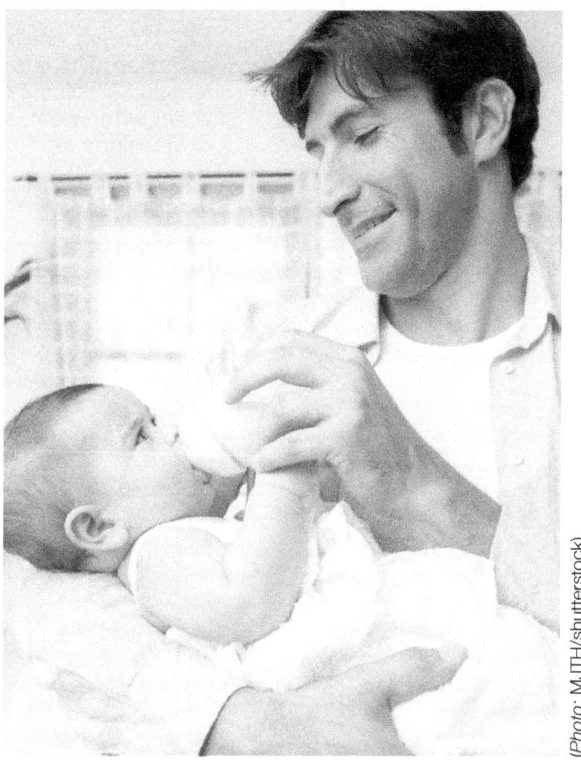

(Photo: MJTH/shutterstock)

Hearing and Other Senses

As you learned in the chapter on Theories of Development, babies can hear long before they are born. However, like vision, hearing improves considerably in the early months of life. The other senses follow a similar course.

AUDITORY ACUITY   Although children's hearing improves up to adolescence, newborns' **auditory acuity** is actually better than their visual acuity. Research evidence suggests that, within the general range of pitch and loudness of the human voice, newborns hear nearly as well as adults do (Ceponiene et al., 2002). Only with high-pitched sounds is their auditory skill less than that of an adult; such a sound needs to be louder to be heard by a newborn than to be heard by older children or adults (Werner & Gillenwater, 1990).

DETECTING LOCATIONS   Another basic auditory skill that exists at birth but improves with age is the ability to determine the location of a sound. Because your two ears are separated from each other, sounds arrive at one ear slightly before the other, which allows you to judge location. Only if a sound comes from a source equidistant from the two ears (the *midline*) does this system fail. In this case, the sound arrives at the same time to both ears and you know only that the sound is somewhere on your midline. We know that newborns can judge at least the general direction from which a sound has come because they will turn their heads in roughly the right direction toward a sound. Finer-grained location of sounds, however, is not well developed at birth. For example, Barbara Morrongiello of the University of Guelph, has observed babies' reactions to sounds played at the midline and then sounds coming from varying degrees away from the midline. Among infants 2 months old, it takes a shift of about 27 degrees off of midline before the baby shows a changed response; among 6-month-olds, only a 12-degree shift is needed; by 18 months, discrimination of a 4-degree shift is possible—nearly the skill level seen in adults (Morrongiello, Fenwick, & Chance, 1990).

SMELLING AND TASTING   The senses of smell and taste have been studied much less than vision and hearing, but we do have some basic knowledge. The two senses

Newborns are quite nearsighted, so they can focus very well at about 25 to 80 centimetres, just the distance between a parent's face and the baby's eyes when the baby is held for feeding.

Learning Objective 4.9

Describe how infants' senses of hearing, smell, taste, touch, and motion compare to those of older children and adults.

auditory acuity

how well one can hear

Figure 4.5 Steiner observed these three newborns in his experiments on taste response. The left-hand column shows the babies' normal expressions; the remaining columns show the change in expression when they were given flavoured water with sweet, sour, and bitter tastes. What is striking is how similar the expressions are for each taste.

(**SOURCE:** Reprinted from Advances in Child Development and Behavior, Vol 13, Jacob E. Steiner, Pages 257–295, Copyright 1979, with permission from Elsevier.)

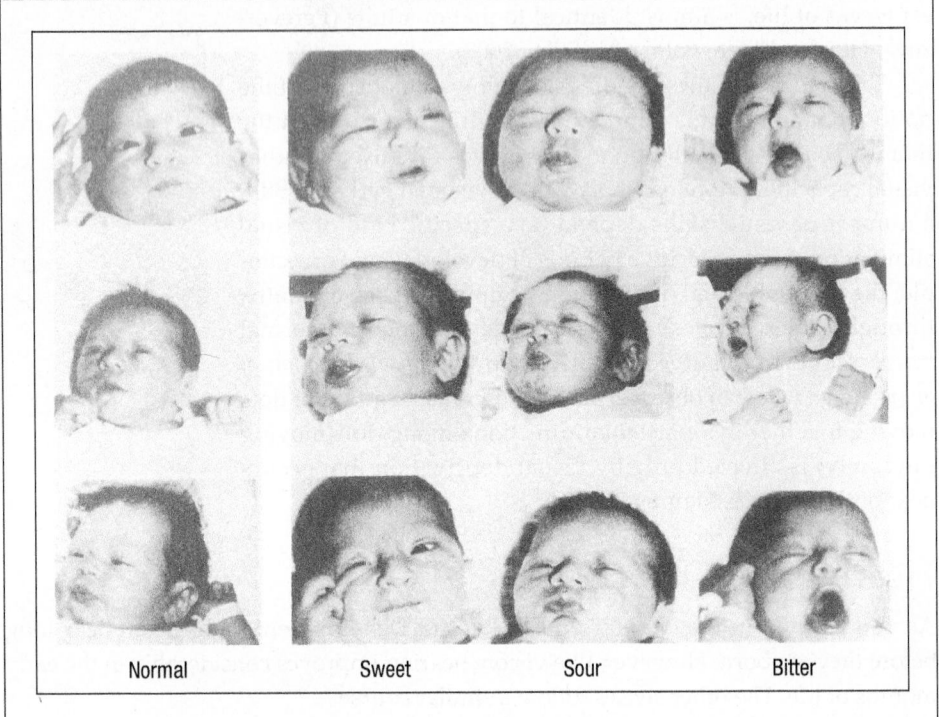

| Normal | Sweet | Sour | Bitter |

are intricately related in infants, just as they are in adults—that is, if you cannot smell for some reason (e.g., because you have a cold), your taste sensitivity is also significantly reduced. Taste is detected by the taste buds on the tongue, which register five basic flavours: sweet, sour, bitter, salty, and umami. Smell is registered in the mucous membranes of the nose and has nearly unlimited variations.

Newborns appear to respond differentially to all five of the basic flavours (Domínguez, 2011). Some of the clearest demonstrations of this come from an elegantly simple set of early studies by Jacob Steiner (Ganchrow, Steiner, & Daher, 1983; Steiner, 1979). Newborn infants who had never been fed were photographed before and after flavoured water was put into their mouths. By varying the flavour, Steiner could determine whether the babies reacted differently to different tastes. As you can see in **Figure 4.5**, babies responded quite differently to sweet, sour, and bitter flavours. Newborns can also taste umami (savoury), the characteristic flavour that comes from adding monosodium glutamate (MSG) to food and which is typical of high-protein foods that are high in glutamates (e.g., meat, cheese). Generally, newborns express pleasure when researchers test them for umami sensitivity (Nicklaus, Boggio, & Issanchou, 2005). Some researchers speculate that newborns' preferences for umami-flavoured and sweet foods explain their attraction to breast milk, a substance that is naturally rich in sugars and glutamates (Schwartz, Chabanet, Laval, Issanchou, & Nicklaus, 2012).

SENSES OF TOUCH AND MOTION The infant's senses of touch and motion may well be the best developed of all. Certainly these senses are sufficiently well developed to get the baby fed. If you think back to the discussion of reflexes earlier in the chapter, then you'll realize that the rooting reflex relies on a touch stimulus to the cheek while the sucking reflex relies on touch in the mouth. Babies appear to be especially sensitive to touches on the mouth, the face, the hands, the soles of the feet, and the abdomen, with less sensitivity in other parts of the body (Reisman, 1987). Likewise, babies display sensitivity to temperature by increasing physical activity in a cold room and to touch by becoming calmer when stroked and showing discomfort with irritants such as a rash or even scratchy clothing.

Test Yourself before going on

1. Select the correct answers in the following sentence: At birth, (visual/auditory) acuity is better than (visual/ auditory) acuity.
2. What taste sensations do newborns prefer, and how do their preferences relate to nutritional needs?

Critical Thinking

3. In what ways do babies' sensory skills contribute to the development of parent–infant relationships?

Perceptual Skills

When we turn to studies of perceptual skills, we are asking what the individual does with sensory information—how it is interpreted or how different information is combined together. Researchers have found that very young infants are able to make remarkably fine discriminations among sounds, sights, and feelings, and they pay attention to and respond to patterns, not just to individual events.

Studying Perceptual Development

Babies can't talk and can't respond to ordinary questions, so how are we to decipher just what they can see, hear, or discriminate? Researchers use three basic methods that allow them to "ask" a baby about what he experiences (Bornstein, Arterberry, & Mash, 2011). In the **preference technique**, devised by Robert Fantz (1956), the baby is simply shown two pictures or two objects, and the researcher keeps track of how long the baby looks at each one. If many infants shown the same pair of pictures consistently look longer at one picture than the other, then this not only tells us that babies see some difference between the two, but also may reveal something about the kinds of objects or pictures that capture babies' attention.

Another strategy takes advantage of the processes of **habituation**, or getting used to a stimulus (characterized by a diminished rate of responding), and its opposite, **dishabituation**, responding to a habituated stimulus as if it were new (characterized by the recurrence of a response to a stimulus following habituation). Researchers first present the baby with a particular sight, sound, or object over and over until he habituates—that is, until he stops looking at it or showing interest in it. Then the researchers present another sight, sound, or object that is novel or slightly different from the original one and watch to see whether the baby shows renewed interest (dishabituation). If the baby does show renewed interest, you know he perceives the slightly changed sight, sound, or object as "different" in some way from the original.

The third option is to use the principles of *operant conditioning*. For example, an infant might be trained to turn her head when she hears a particular sound, with the sight of an interesting moving toy used as a reinforcement. After the learned response is well established, the experimenter can vary the sound in some systematic way to see whether the baby still turns her head.

Learning Objective 4.10

Describe how researchers study perceptual development in infants.

preference technique
a research method in which a researcher keeps track of how long a baby looks at each of two objects shown

habituation
the decline in responding that occurs as a stimulus becomes familiar

dishabituation
recurrence of a response to a stimulus that has undergone habituation

Looking

One important question to ask about visual perception is whether the infant perceives his environment in the same way as older children and adults do. Can he see fine detail clearly or judge how far away an object is by looking at it? Does he visually scan an object in an orderly way? Developmentalists believe that infants' patterns of looking at objects tell us a great deal about what they are trying to gain from visual information.

EARLY VISUAL STIMULATION   Appropriate visual stimulation in infancy is vital to the later development of visual perception. Research supporting this was undertaken by McMaster University psychologists Daphne Maurer, Terri Lewis, and their colleagues who were studying infants born with cataracts on their eyes (infants who have cataracts have clouded vision and can see only light and dark). In a longitudinal study, the researchers examined people aged 9 through 21, who, when they were between 2 and 6 months of age, had had cataracts removed and were then fitted with corrective lenses that gave them normal vision. When these individuals were examined years later, they were found to have subtle visual abnormalities. For example, they did not develop the ability to distinguish the relative position of facial features in the same way that normal-sighted people do (Le Grand, Mondloch, Maurer, & Brent, 2001).

Although early deprivation of visual stimulation does not affect all visual processes, there are critical periods of time in early infancy and beyond when an infant or child needs a specific quality of visual stimulation to develop normal visual perception (Le Grand et al., 2001; Lewis & Maurer, 2005; Maurer et al., 2007). In some instances, early visual input of a type that visually normal newborns cannot yet detect (e.g., mid to high spatial frequency stimuli such as thin-striped patterns) acts to set up the neural foundations that will enable later visual development to proceed normally (Maurer, Ellemberg, & Lewis, 2006). When early experience is lacking, visual capability fails to develop normally many years later. In particular, this so-called *"sleeper effect"* in the development of visual perception is apparent for sensitivity to mid and high narrow-striped images, face processing, and facial identity based on the spacing of internal facial features (the eyes, nose, and mouth) (Maurer et al., 2007).

DEPTH PERCEPTION   One of the perceptual skills that has been most studied is **depth perception**. You need this ability any time you reach for something or decide whether you have room to make a left turn before an oncoming car gets to you. Similarly, an infant needs to judge depth to perform all kinds of simple tasks, including determining how far away an object is so that he can reach for it, how far it is to the floor if he has ideas about crawling off the edge of the couch, or how to aim a spoon toward a bowl of chocolate pudding.

It is possible to judge depth by using any (or all) of three rather different kinds of information. First, *binocular cues* involve both eyes, each of which receives a slightly different visual image of an object; the closer the object is, the more different these two views are. In addition, of course, information from the eye muscles tells you something about how far away an object may be. Second, *pictorial information*, sometimes called *monocular cues*, requires input from only one eye. For example, when one object is partially in front of another one, you know that the partially hidden object is farther away—a cue called *interposition*. The relative sizes of two similar objects, such as two telephone poles or two people you see in the distance, may also indicate that the smaller-appearing one is farther away. *Linear perspective* (e.g., the impression that railroad lines are getting closer together as they get farther away) is another monocular cue. Third, *kinetic cues* come from either your own motion or the motion of some object: If you move your head, objects near you seem to move more than objects farther away (a phenomenon called *motion parallax*). Similarly, if you see objects moving, such as a person walking across a street or a train moving along a track, closer objects

depth perception

ability to judge the relative distances of objects

appear to move over larger distances in a given period of time. With younger babies, researchers have studied kinetic cues by watching babies react to apparently looming objects. Most often, the baby observes a film of an object moving toward him, apparently on a collision course. If the infant has some depth perception, then he should flinch, move to one side, or blink as the object appears to come very close. Such flinching has been observed in 3-month-olds (Yonas & Owsley, 1987).

How early can an infant judge depth, and which of these cues does he use? This is still an active area of research, so the answer is not final. The best conclusion at the moment seems to be that kinetic information is used first, perhaps by about 3 months of age (as noted above); binocular cues are used beginning at about 4 months; and linear perspective and other pictorial (monocular) cues are used last, perhaps at 5 to 7 months (Bornstein, 1992; Yonas, Elieff, & Arterberry, 2002).

WHAT BABIES LOOK AT   In the first two months, a baby's visual attention is guided by a search for meaningful patterns (Bornstein, Arterberry, & Mash, 2011). Babies scan the world around them until they come to a sharp light–dark contrast, which typically signals the edge of some object. Once she finds such an edge, the baby stops searching and moves her eyes back and forth across and around the edge. Motion also captures a baby's attention at this age, so she will look at things that move, as well as things with large light–dark contrast. Between 2 and 3 months, the cortex has developed more fully, and the baby's attention seems to shift from where an object is to what an object is. Babies this age begin to scan rapidly across an entire figure rather than getting stuck on edges. As a result, they spend more time looking for patterns.

One early study that illustrates this point particularly well comes from the work of Albert Caron and Rose Caron (1981), who used stimuli like those in **Figure 4.6** in a habituation procedure. The babies were first shown a series of pictures that shared some particular relationship—for example, a small figure positioned above a larger version of the same figure (small over big). After the baby stopped being interested in these training pictures (i.e., after he habituated), the Carons showed him another figure (the test stimulus) that either followed the same pattern or followed some other pattern. If the baby had really habituated to the pattern of the original pictures (small over big), he should show little interest in stimuli like test stimulus A in **Figure 4.6**

Figure 4.6 In the Carons' study, the researchers first habituated each baby to a set of training stimuli (all "small over large" in this case). Then they showed each baby two test stimuli: one that had the same pattern as the training stimuli (A) and one that had a different pattern (B). Babies aged 3 and 4 months showed renewed interest in stimulus B but not stimulus A, indicating that they were paying attention to the pattern and not just specific stimuli.

(**SOURCE:** Based on Caron, A.J., & Caron, R.F. (1981). Processing of relational information as an index of infant risk. In S. Friedman & M. Sigman (Eds.), *Preterm birth and psychological development* (pp. 219–240). New York, NY: Academic Press.)

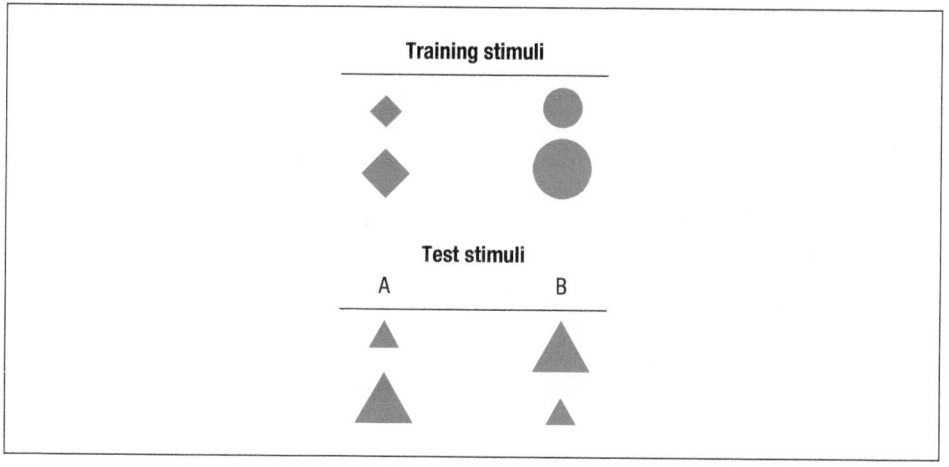

("Ho hum, same old boring small over big thing"), but he should show renewed interest in test stimulus B ("Hey, here's something new!"). Caron and Caron found that 3- and 4-month-old children did precisely that. So even at this early age, babies find and pay attention to patterns, not just specific stimuli.

FACES: AN EXAMPLE OF RESPONDING TO A COMPLEX PATTERN   There is little indication that faces are uniquely interesting to infants; that is, babies do not systematically choose to look at faces rather than other complex pictures. However, among faces, babies clearly prefer some to others. They prefer attractive faces (an intriguing result, discussed in the **Research Report**), and it now looks as if they prefer their mother's face from the earliest hours of life, a finding that has greatly surprised psychologists, although it may not surprise you.

Beyond the issue of preference, we also question what babies look at when they scan a face. Before about 2 months of age, babies seem to look mostly at the outer edges of faces (the hairline and the face shape), an observation buttressed by the finding of Pascalis and his colleagues (1995) that newborns could not discriminate Mom's face from a stranger's if the hairline was covered. After 4 months, however, covering the hairline did not affect the baby's ability to recognize Mom. In general, babies appear to begin to focus on the internal features of a face, particularly the eyes, at about 2 to 3 months.

EFFECTS OF VISUAL DEPRIVATION   Canadian researchers, for example, Daphne Maurer and Sybil Geldart of McMaster University, Richard Le Grand of Kwantlen University College, Catherine Mondloch of Brock University, and Henry Brent of Toronto's Hospital for Sick Children, have looked at the effects of early visual deprivation caused by congenital cataracts (treated in infancy) on the development of face

Research Report

Babies' Preferences for Attractive Faces

Studies on infant perception point toward the conclusion that many perceptual rules are inborn. One such rule seems to be a preference for attractive faces. In the first study in a classic series of experiments, Langlois and her colleagues (1987) tested 2- to 3-month-olds and 6- to 8-month-olds. Each baby was shown colour slides of adult Caucasian women, half rated by adult judges as attractive and half rated as unattractive. On each trial, the baby was shown two slides simultaneously, with each face approximately life-sized, while the experimenter peeked through a hole in the screen to count the number of seconds the baby looked at each picture. Each baby saw some attractive/attractive pairs, some unattractive/unattractive pairs, and some mixed pairs. With mixed pairs, even the 2- and 3-month-old babies consistently looked longer at the attractive faces. Several studies, including some in which pictures of individuals of different races were used, produced similar findings in that infants showed a preference for one face in a pair regardless of race (Langlois, Roggman, & Rieser-Danner, 1990; Langlois et al., 1991). Interestingly, studies have shown that infants prefer to look at images of other infants that have been rated

as attractive by adults than at images of infants who have been deemed unattractive (Quinn, Kelly, Lee, Pascalis, & Slater, 2009).

Just what makes a face attractive? You may be surprised to find out that average faces (as opposed to distinctive featured faces) are rated most attractive (Rhodes et al., 2005). Other aspects of attractiveness include attributes such as facial symmetry and femininity in females and masculinity in males (Rhodes, 2006).

Although experience affects the perception of attractiveness during development and attractiveness is also affected by one's experience with a population of faces (Cooper, Geldart, Mondloch, & Maurer, 2006; Rhodes, 2006; Rhodes et al., 2005), it is hard to imagine what sort of learning experiences could account for such preferences in a 2-month-old. These findings raise the possibility that there is some inborn template for the "correct" or "most desired" face shape and configuration for members of our species, and that we simply prefer those who best match this template. From an evolutionary perspective, those very attributes that signal attractiveness may also signal mate quality. As an example, attractiveness is perceived as an indication of good health (Langlois et al., 2000; Rhodes, 2006; Rhodes et al., 2005; Rhodes et al., 2007).

processing and have reported several key findings. First, early visual input is required for the later development of face-processing expertise in adulthood (Mondloch et al, 2013; Rhodes, Nishimura, de Heering, Jeffery, & Maurer, 2016). Individuals who were deprived of early visual stimulation did not develop the ability to recognize faces in a holistic manner. That is, they failed to readily process faces as a whole (i.e., automatically recognize faces in terms of the relationship or configuration of features such as the eyes, nose, and mouth). Instead, they tended to process faces as a collection of independent facial features seen in isolation (Le Grand, Mondloch, Maurer, & Brent, 2004). A second characteristic of adults deprived of early visual stimulation is their failure to distinguish the relative spacing of facial features in the same way as normal-sighted people did when they viewed sets of faces—as depicted in **Figure 4.7** (e.g., Le Grand, Mondloch, Maurer, & Brent, 2001, 2003). Adults who experienced early visual deprivation also had difficulty identifying faces when head orientation or facial expressions changed (Geldart, Mondloch, Maurer, de Schonen, & Brent, 2002).

Although face recognition increases dramatically between 7 and 11 years of age, adult-like expertise is not achieved before adolescence (Mondloch, Leis, & Maurer, 2006). Distinguishing differences in the spacing among facial features (e.g., the distance between and among the mouth, nose, and eyes) develops much more slowly than distinguishing differences in facial contours (e.g., upright faces have a common external shape along with common internal features—two eyes above a nose and a mouth) (Mondloch, Dobson, Parsons, & Maurer, 2004; Mondloch, Geldart, Maurer, & Le Grand, 2003; Mondloch, Le Grand, & Maurer, 2002; Mondloch, Maurer, & Ahola, 2006). Using fMRI (*functional magnetic resonance imaging* , which will be discussed in greater detail in the chapter on Physical and Cognitive Development in Early Childhood) technology, researchers have confirmed that facial recognition involves distinctively different neural pathways for the processing of facial features than it does for processing the spacing among facial features (Maurer et al., 2007).

Figure 4.7 In studying sensitivity to facial differences, researchers used three types of facial stimuli: all test samples were presented close to life-size and displayed either variations in eye and mouth shape (set a), variations in facial contours (set b), or variations in the spacing of the eyes and the eyes and mouth (set c). Patients who experienced early visual deprivation caused by congenital cataracts (treated in infancy) had trouble discriminating between faces in the spacing set (c).

(**SOURCE:** Reprinted by permission from Macmillan Publishers Ltd. Le Grand, R., Mondloch, C. J., Maurer, D., & Brent, H.P. (2003). Expert face processing requires visual input to the right hemisphere during infancy, *Nature Neuroscience*, 6(10), 1108-1112.)

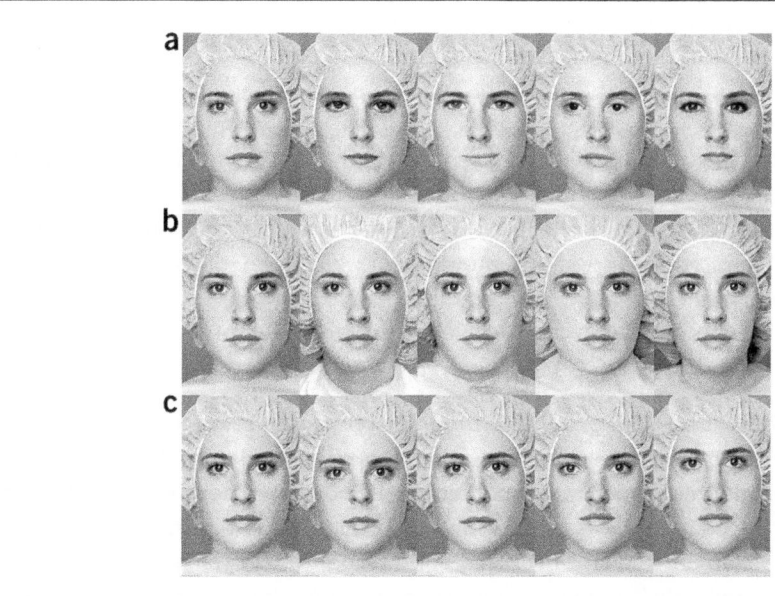

Learning Objective 4.12

Detail how infants perceive human speech, recognize voices, and recognize sound patterns other than speech.

Listening

When we turn from looking to listening, we find similarly intriguing indications that very young infants not only make remarkably fine discriminations among individual sounds, but also pay attention to patterns.

DISCRIMINATING SPEECH SOUNDS   Early studies established that as early as 1 month, babies can discriminate between speech sounds like *pa* and *ba* (Trehub & Rabinovitch, 1972). Studies using conditioned head-turning responses have shown

that by perhaps 6 months of age, babies can discriminate between two-syllable "words" like *bada* and *baga* and can even respond to a syllable that is hidden inside a string of other syllables, like *tibati* or *kobako* (Gerken & Aslin, 2005).

Even more striking is the finding that babies are actually better at discriminating some kinds of speech sounds than adults are. Each language uses only a subset of all possible speech sounds. Japanese, for example, does not use the *l* sound that appears in English; Spanish makes a different distinction between *d* and *t* than occurs in English. It turns out that up to about 6 months of age, babies can accurately discriminate all

Newborns recognize their mother's voice and by 1 month of age can discriminate between syllables such as *ba* and *pa*.

sound contrasts that appear in any language, including sounds they do not hear in the language spoken to them. At about 6 months of age, they begin to lose the ability to distinguish pairs of vowels that do not occur in the language they are hearing; by age 1, the ability to discriminate nonheard consonant contrasts begins to fade (Polka & Werker, 1994) (see how speech perception sets the stage for language in the **Research Report** in the chapter on Cognitive Development in Infancy). These findings are entirely consistent with what we now know about the pattern of rapid, apparently preprogrammed, growth of synapses in the early months of life, followed by synaptic pruning. Many connections are initially created, permitting discriminations along all possible sound continua, but only those pathways that are actually used in the language the child hears are strengthened or retained.

Interestingly, University of British Columbia researchers have demonstrated that accurate speech perception and language development involves more than just hearing—it also involves mouth movements in sound production. By temporarily restricting *oral-motor* (i.e., tongue) movements with teething toys, and thus inhibiting the accurate production of sounds while listening to novel speech sounds, the researchers discovered that speech perception in 6-month olds was impeded (Bruderer, Danielson, Kandhadai, & Werker, 2015). So it seems that sensorimotor experiences, along with hearing are both important for speech perception development and language acquisition.

DISCRIMINATING INDIVIDUAL VOICES   Newborns also seem to be able to discriminate between individual voices. DeCasper and Fifer (1980) found that the newborn can tell the mother's voice from another female voice (but not the father's voice from another male voice) and prefers the mother's voice. Moreover, there is a correlation between gestational age and maternal voice recognition: Premature infants are less likely to recognize their mother's voice than are babies born at term (DeRegnier,

(Photo: Monart Design/Fotolia)

Wewerka, Georgieff, Mattia, & Nelson, 2002). Thus, in utero learning appears to be responsible for newborns' preference for the maternal voice.

DISCRIMINATING OTHER SOUND PATTERNS   As was true with studies of looking, there is also evidence that infants pay attention to, and discriminate among, patterns or sequences of sounds from the very beginning (Gervain, Werker, Black, & Geffen, 2016). For example, University of Toronto psychologist Sandra Trehub and her colleagues (1984, 1985) have found that, as early as 6 months of age, babies listen to melodies and recognize the patterns. Trehub trained 6-month-old babies to turn their heads toward a loudspeaker for a particular six-tone melody and then tested the babies with melodies that varied in a number of ways. Babies continued to turn their head to new melodies if the melodies had the same contour (notes going up and down in the same sequence) and were in approximately the same pitch range. They responded to the melodies as different if the contour changed or if the notes were much higher or much lower. Thus, as is true with patterns of looking, within the first few months of life, babies appear to pay attention to and respond to sound patterns, not just the specific sounds.

Combining Information from Several Senses

If you think about the way you receive and use perceptual information, you'll realize that you rarely have information from only one sense at a time. Psychologists have been interested in knowing how early an infant can integrate such information. Even more complex, how early can a baby learn something via one sense and transfer that information to another sense (for example, recognize solely by feel a toy he has seen but never before felt)? This skill is usually called **intermodal perception**.

Research findings show that intermodal perception is possible as early as 1 month and becomes common by 6 months (Rose & Ruff, 1987). Moreover, research comparing these skills in children born prematurely and those born at term suggests that prenatal maturational processes play an important role in their development (Espy et al., 2002).

Research suggests that intermodal perception is important in infant learning. One group of researchers found that babies who habituated to a combined auditory-visual stimulus were better able to recognize a new stimulus than infants who habituated to either the auditory or the visual stimulus alone (Bahrick & Lickliter, 2000). For example, suppose you played an audiovisual recording of someone singing for one baby, played the same recording without the sound for another, and played an audio recording of the song for a third. Research suggests that the first baby would recognize a change in either the singer (visual stimulus) or the song (auditory stimulus) more quickly than would either of the other two infants.

In older infants, intermodal perception and transfer can be readily demonstrated, not only between touch and sight, but also between other modalities such as sound and sight. For instance, researchers exposed 6- to 8-month-old babies to audio recordings of speech or singing for 30 seconds (Trehub, Plantinga, & Brcic, 2009). Then the infants watched two silent visual recordings, one of which included the previously heard speaker or singer. The babies in this experiment looked significantly longer at the silent recording of the person heard previously. That is, they appeared to have some understanding of the link between the pattern of sound and the pattern of movement—knowledge that demonstrates not only intermodal perception, but also a surprisingly sophisticated use of cross-modal cues to match auditory and visual cues to the identity of unfamiliar persons.

Learning Objective 4.13

Explain the importance of intermodal perception.

intermodal perception
formation of a single perception of a stimulus that is based on information from two or more senses

(Photo: eugenesergeev/Fotolia)

Even though 7-month-old Leslie is not looking at this toy while she chews on it, she is nonetheless learning something about how it ought to look based on how it feels in her mouth and in her hands—an example of cross-modal transfer.

Learning Objective 4.14
Summarize what arguments nativists and empiricists offer in support of their theories of perceptual development.

nativists

theorists who claimed that perceptual abilities are inborn

empiricists

theorists who argued that perceptual abilities are learned

Explaining Perceptual Development

The study of perceptual development was one of the historic battlegrounds for the dispute about the significance of nature versus nurture in development. **Nativists** claimed that most perceptual abilities were inborn, while **empiricists** argued that these skills were learned. Developmentalists are now rethinking the relationship that exists between nature and nurture and how they interact with each other to determine development.

There are strong arguments for a nativist position on perceptual development. As researchers have become more and more clever in devising ways to test infants' perceptual skills, they have found more and more skills already present in newborns or very young infants: Newborns have good auditory acuity, poor but adequate visual acuity, and excellent tactual and taste perception. They have at least some colour vision and at least rudimentary ability to locate the source of sounds around them. More impressive still, they are capable of making quite sophisticated discriminations from the earliest days of life, including identifying their mother by sight, smell, or sound.

On the other side of the ledger, however, we find evidence from research with other species that some minimum level of experience is necessary to support the development of the perceptual systems. For example, animals deprived of light show deterioration of the whole visual system and a consequent decrease in perceptual abilities (Hubel & Weisel, 1963). Likewise, animals deprived of auditory stimuli display delayed or no development of auditory perceptual skills (Dammeijer, Schlundt, Chenault, Manni, & Anteunis, 2002).

We can best understand the development of perceptual skills by thinking of it as the result of an interaction between inborn and experiential factors. A child is able to make visual discriminations between people or among objects within the first few days or weeks of life. The specific discriminations she learns and the number of separate objects she learns to recognize, however, will depend on her experience. A perfect example of this is the newborn's ability to discriminate her mother's face from a very similar woman's face. Such a discrimination must be the result of experience, yet the capacity to make the distinction must be built in. Thus, as is true of virtually all dichotomous theoretical disputes, both sides are correct. Both nature and nurture are involved.

Test Yourself before going on

1. What are three methods used to study perceptual development in infants?
2. Early visual deprivation caused by cataracts interferes with the development of _____.
3. Infants can discriminate among (more/fewer) speech sounds than adults.
4. Intermodal perception is possible as early as _____ month(s).
5. Label these statements as consistent with the (N) nativist or (E) empiricist view of perceptual development.
   _____ (a) Perceptual skills are inborn.
   _____ (b) Perceptual skills are learned.
   _____ (c) The development of perceptual skills depends on experience.
   _____ (d) Newborns can make perceptual discriminations.

Critical Thinking

6. If the empiricists are correct, and much of early perceptual learning depends on experience, what kinds of objects and activities do you think would be helpful in supporting an infant's visual and auditory perceptual development?

Summary

Physical Changes

4.1   Describe what important changes in the brain take place during infancy.

- Changes in the nervous system are extremely rapid in the first two years. In most parts of the brain, development of dendrites and synapses reaches its first peak between 12 and 24 months, after which "pruning" of synapses occurs. Myelinization of nerve fibres also occurs rapidly in the first two years.

4.2   Describe how infants' reflexes and behavioural states change.

- Adaptive reflexes include such essential responses as sucking; primitive reflexes include the Moro (startle) and Babinski reflexes, which disappear within a few months. Neonates sleep much of the time and move through a series of states of consciousness in a cycle that lasts about two hours.

4.3   Outline how infants' bodies change, and the typical pattern of motor skill development in the first two years.

- During infancy, bones increase in number and density, and muscle fibres become larger and contain less water. Stamina improves as the lungs grow and the heart gets stronger. Motor skills improve rapidly in the first two years, as the baby moves from creeping to crawling to walking to running, and becomes able to grasp objects.

4.4   Discuss the health issues of infants.

- The Canadian Paediatric Society recommends breastfeeding, which has been shown to be better for a baby nutritionally than bottle feeding. Babies need regular checkups and a variety of immunizations.

4.5   Discuss the developmental issues of preterm and low-birth-weight infants.

- Infants born before 32 weeks gestation may not have adaptive reflexes, such as sucking and swallowing, that are sufficiently developed to enable them to survive. Infants born preterm or with low birth weight move more slowly through all the developmental milestones. By age 2 or 3, the physically normal preterm baby will catch up with his peers.

4.6   Identify the general outcomes of post-term infants.

- Post-term pregnancies put the mother, fetus, and/or neonate at risk. The incidence of high-risk post-term deliveries has dropped to less than 1% in Canada, in part because of a change in delivery protocols.

4.7   Discuss the issue of infant mortality in Canada.

- The rates of infant mortality and SIDS in Canada have declined significantly in recent decades. Risk factors for SIDS include sleeping on the stomach and/or on soft surfaces and exposure to tobacco smoke before and after birth.

Sensory Skills

4.8   Describe how infants' visual abilities change across the first months of life.

- Colour vision is present at birth, but visual acuity and visual tracking skills are relatively poor at birth and then develop rapidly during the first few months.

4.9   Describe how infants' senses of hearing, smell, taste, touch, and motion compare to those of older children and adults.

- Basic auditory skills are more fully developed at birth; acuity is good for the range of the human voice, and the newborn can locate at least the approximate direction of sounds. The sensory capacities for smelling, tasting, touching, and moving are also well developed at birth.

Perceptual Skills

4.10   Describe how researchers study perceptual development in infants.

- In the preference technique, researchers track how long babies look at each of a pair of stimuli. Habituation involves exposing babies to stimuli until they are no longer interested in them. The purpose is to see whether the babies will then respond to a new stimulus that is only slightly different from the original one (dishabituation). By using operant conditioning, researchers train babies to perform behaviours such as turning their heads in response to specific stimuli. Then the researchers vary the stimulus slightly; if babies do not respond as they have been trained to do, then the researchers know that they can tell the difference between the original and the new stimulus.

4.11 Detail how depth perception and patterns of looking change over the first two years.

- Early visual stimulation is required for later visual perception to develop normally. Depth perception is present in at least rudimentary form by 3 months. Facial recognition begins early in life but isn't complete before adolescence. Babies can discriminate the mother's face from other faces, and the mother's voice from other voices, almost immediately after birth.

4.12 Detail how infants perceive human speech, recognize voices, and recognize sound patterns other than speech.

- Month-old babies appear to attend to and discriminate among speech contrasts present in all possible languages; by 6 months of age, babies also attend to and discriminate among different patterns of sounds, such as melodies or speech. By 1 year of age, the infant makes fine

discriminations only among speech sounds salient in the language he is actually hearing.

4.13 Explain the importance of intermodal perception.

- Studies show that infants can learn something via one sense and transfer it to another sense—a skill known as intermodal perception. The capacity for intermodal perception develops before birth and matures across the first few months of life.

4.14 Summarize what arguments nativists and empiricists offer in support of their theories of perceptual development.

- The study of perceptual development supports the integration of nativism and empiricism. Many basic perceptual abilities, including strategies for examining objects, appear to be built into the system at birth or to develop as the brain develops over the early years. But specific experience is required both to maintain the underlying system and to learn fundamental discriminations and patterns.

Chapter 5
Cognitive Development in Infancy

Evgeny Atamanenko/Shutterstock

 ## Learning Objectives

COGNITIVE CHANGES

5.1 Describe the milestones of Piaget's sensorimotor stage.

5.2 Identify some challenges offered to Piaget's explanation of infant cognitive development.

5.3 Summarize what the research tells us about infants' understanding of objects.

LEARNING, CATEGORIZING, AND REMEMBERING

5.4 Describe the kinds of ways infants can learn.

5.5 Describe how categorical understanding changes over the first two years.

5.6 Describe memory function in the first two years.

5.7 Identify how intelligence is measured in infancy.

THE BEGINNINGS OF LANGUAGE

5.8 Describe how the environment influences language development.

5.9 Trace the pattern of early language development in infants.

5.10 Identify the characteristics of toddlers' first words.

5.11 Identify what kinds of sentences children produce between 18 and 24 months of age.

5.12 Describe individual differences that are evident in language development.

5.13 Describe how language development varies across cultures.

Advertisements for books, videos, and expensive toys often make parents wonder whether they're providing their infant with the stimulation needed for optimum intellectual development. But the influence of experience on cognitive development is most evident in cases in which a rather dramatic disruption in environmental support—malnourishment, child abuse, lead poisoning, and the like—impedes intellectual development. As to what is actually required, anxious parents may rest easy. Research shows that, in order to fulfill their intellectual potential, babies require caretakers who respond to all of their needs and who avoid narrowly focusing on a specific developmental outcome, such as increasing the odds that an infant will be able to get high scores on intelligence tests when she starts school.

When you finish studying the chapter, you will be able to characterize Piaget's explanation of the universal changes in thinking that happen in the first two years of life, as well as how other theorists explain Piaget's research findings; summarize learning, memory, and individual differences in intelligence among infants; and outline the pattern of language development in infants.

Cognitive Changes

The remarkable cognitive advances that happen in infancy are highly consistent across environments. Of course, 2-year-olds are still a long way from cognitive maturity, but some of the most important steps toward that goal are taken in the first two years of life (see **Table 5.1**).

Piaget's View of the First Two Years

Learning Objective 5.1

Describe the milestones of Piaget's sensorimotor stage.

sensorimotor stage

Piaget's first stage of development, in which infants use information from their senses and motor actions to learn about the world

Piaget assumed that a baby *assimilates* incoming information to the limited array of schemes she is born with—looking, listening, sucking, grasping—and *accommodates* those schemes based on her experiences. Piaget called this form of thinking *sensorimotor intelligence*. Thus, the **sensorimotor stage** is the period during which infants develop and refine sensorimotor intelligence.

SENSORIMOTOR STAGE In Piaget's view, the newborn who is in substage 1 (roughly 0–1 months) of the sensorimotor stage is entirely tied to the immediate present, responding to whatever stimuli are available. She forgets events from one encounter to the next and does not appear to plan. Each substage represents a definite advance over the one that came before. Substage 2 (from roughly 1 to 4 months) is marked by the beginning of the coordinations between looking and listening, between reaching and looking, and between reaching and sucking that are such central features of the 2-month-old's means of exploring the world. The technique

Table 5.1 Substages of Piaget's Sensorimotor Stage

Substage	Age (in months)	Primary Technique	Characteristics
1	0–1	Reflexes	Use of built-in schemes or reflexes such as sucking or looking. Primitive schemes begin to change through very small steps of accommodation. Limited imitation, no ability to integrate information from several senses.
2	1–4	Primary circular reactions	Further accommodation of basic schemes, as the baby practises them endlessly—grasping, listening, looking, sucking. Beginning coordination of schemes from different senses, so that the baby now looks toward a sound and sucks on anything he can reach and bring to his mouth. But the baby does not yet link his body actions to results outside of his body.
3	4–8	Secondary circular reactions	The baby becomes much more aware of events outside his own body and makes them happen again in a kind of trial-and-error learning. Scientists are unsure whether babies this young understand the causal links yet; however, Imitation may occur, but only of schemes already in the baby's repertoire. Beginning understanding of the "object concept" can also be detected in this period.
4	8–12	Coordination of secondary schemes	Clear, intentional means–end behaviour. The baby not only goes after what she wants but also may combine two schemes to do so, such as moving a pillow aside to reach a toy. Imitation of novel behaviour occurs, as does transfer of information from one sense to the other (cross-modal perception).
5	12–18	Tertiary circular reactions	"Experimentation" begins, in which the infant tries out new ways of playing with or manipulating objects. Very active, very purposeful trial-and-error exploration.
6	18–24	Beginning of mental representation	Development of use of symbols to represent object or events. The child understands that the symbol is separate from the object. Deferred imitation can occur only after this point because it requires the ability to represent internally the event to be imitated.

that distinguishes substage 2, **primary circular reactions**, refers to the many simple repetitive actions seen at this time, each organized around the infant's own body. For example, the baby may accidentally suck his thumb one day, find it pleasurable, and repeat the action.

In substage 3 (from about 4 to 8 months), the baby repeats some action to trigger a reaction outside her own body, a **secondary circular reaction**. The baby coos and Mom smiles, so the baby coos again to get Mom to smile again. These initial connections between body actions and external consequences seem to be simple, almost mechanical, links between stimuli and responses. However, in substage 4, the 8- to 12-month-old baby shows the beginnings of understanding causal connections, at which point she moves into exploratory high gear. One consequence of this new drive to explore is **means–end behaviour**, or the ability to keep a goal in mind and devise a plan to achieve it. Babies show this kind of behaviour when they move one toy out of the way to gain access to another. The end is the toy they want; the means to the end is moving the other toy.

In substage 5 (from about 12 to 18 months), exploration of the environment becomes more focused, with the emergence of **tertiary circular reactions**. In this pattern, the baby doesn't merely repeat the original behaviour but tries out variations. He may try out many sounds or facial expressions to see if they will trigger Mom's smile, or he may try dropping a toy from several heights to see if it makes different sounds or lands in different places. At this stage, the baby's behaviour has a purposeful, experimental quality. Nonetheless, Piaget thought that the baby still did not have mental symbols to stand for objects in this substage.

The ability to manipulate mental symbols, such as words or images, marks substage 6, which lasts from roughly 18 to 24 months of age. This new capacity allows the infant to generate solutions to problems simply by thinking about them, without the trial-and-error behaviour typical of substage 5. As a result, means–end behaviour becomes far more sophisticated than in earlier stages. For example, a 24-month-old who knows there are cookies in the cookie jar can figure out how to get one. Furthermore, he can find a way to overcome just about any obstacle placed in his path (Bauer, Schwade, Wewerka, & Delaney, 1999). If his parents respond to him climbing

primary circular reactions
Piaget's phrase to describe a baby's simple repetitive actions in substage 2 of the sensorimotor stage; the actions are organized around the baby's own body

secondary circular reactions
Piaget's phrase to describe the repetitive actions in substage 3 of the sensorimotor period; the actions are oriented around external objects

means–end behaviour
purposeful behaviour carried out in pursuit of a specific goal

tertiary circular reactions
deliberate experimentation with variations of previous actions that occurs in substage 5 of the sensorimotor period

Three-month-old Andrea may be showing a secondary circular reaction here, shaking her hand repeatedly to hear the sound of the rattle. A learning theorist would say that the pleasure she experiences from hearing the sound is reinforcing her hand-shaking behaviour.

object permanence

the understanding that objects continue to exist when they can't be seen

deferred imitation

imitation that occurs in the absence of the model who first demonstrated it

on the kitchen counter in pursuit of a cookie by moving the cookie jar to the top of the refrigerator, then the substage 6 toddler's response will likely be to find a way to climb to the top of the refrigerator. Thus, changes in cognition are behind the common impression of parents and other caregivers that 18- to 24-month-olds cannot be left unsupervised, even for very short periods of time.

OBJECT PERMANENCE You know that this book continues to exist even when you are unable to see it—an understanding that Piaget called **object permanence**. In a series of studies, many of which involved his own children, Piaget discovered that babies acquire this understanding gradually during the sensorimotor period. According to his observations, replicated frequently by later researchers, the first sign that a baby is developing object permanence comes at about 2 months of age (in substage 2). Suppose you show a toy to a child of this age and then put a screen in front of the toy and remove the toy. When you then remove the screen, the baby will show some indication of surprise, as if he knows that something should still be there. The child thus seems to have a rudimentary expectation about the permanence of an object. But infants of this age show no signs of searching for a toy that has fallen over the side of the crib or that has disappeared beneath a blanket or behind a screen.

In substage 3 (at about 6 to 8 months), however, babies will look over the edge of the crib for dropped toys or on the floor for food that was spilled. (In fact, babies of this age may drive their parents nuts playing "dropsy" from the high chair.) Infants this age will also search for partially hidden objects. If you put a baby's favourite toy under a cloth but leave part of it sticking out, then the infant will reach for the toy, which indicates that in some sense she "recognizes" that the whole object is there even though she can see only part of it. But if you cover the toy completely with the cloth or put it behind a screen, then the infant will stop looking for it and will not reach for it, even if she has seen you put the cloth over it.

This behaviour changes again between 8 and 12 months (in substage 4). Infants of this age will reach for or search for a toy that has been covered completely by a cloth or hidden by a screen. Thus, by 12 months, most infants appear to grasp the basic fact that objects continue to exist even when they are no longer visible.

IMITATION Piaget also studied infants' ability to imitate the actions of others. He observed that as early as the first few months of life, infants could imitate actions they could see themselves make, such as hand gestures. But he found that they could not imitate other people's facial gestures until substage 4 (8 to 12 months). This second form of imitation seems to require some kind of intermodal perception, combining the visual cues of seeing the other's face with the kinesthetic cues (perceptions of muscle motion) from one's own facial movements. Piaget argued that imitation of any action that wasn't already in the child's repertoire did not occur until about 1 year, and that **deferred imitation**—a child's imitation of some action at a later time—was possible only in substage 6, since deferred imitation requires some kind of internal representation.

Finally, what effect does television viewing have on the child's later behaviour and cognitive progress? Some have argued that television viewing patterns in the early months can adversely influence later social interactions, as well as cognitive and language development, as discussed in **Development in the Real World**.

Development in the Real World

What Do Babies Really Learn from Watching Television?

Infants are exposed to about 5 hours of background television on average per day, most often while they are playing or eating (Lapierre, Piotrowski, & Linebarger, 2012). By the age of 24 months, television is a regular part of 9 out of 10 babies' daily routine (Christakis, 2009) although it has been recommended that children under the age of 2 years should be discouraged from watching television (Canadian Paediatric Society [CPS], 2012a). In one longitudinal study of American infants, researchers assessed both the amount of time infants spent in front of the television and the trajectory of TV viewing over time (Certain & Kahn, 2002). They found that TV viewing of three or more hours a day increased from 7% in infants under 12 months of age to 41% in children between 24 and 35 months. They also found that the amount of time spent watching television at ages 24 to 35 months was associated with how much time 6-year-olds spent watching television. In contrast to children who watched less than three hours of television daily, children who watched three or more hours at age 2 were three times as likely to watch more than three hours of television daily at age 6. Thus, greater TV viewing in early childhood predicted greater viewing at school age.

The effects of viewing so much television during childhood remain uncertain. When asked, parents of babies younger than 2 years say they use television for its educational value, entertainment, and babysitting (Zimmerman, Christakis, & Meltzoff, 2007). A study by University of Winnipeg's Wendy Josephson (1995), for Child & Family Canada found that 3-month-old infants pay minimal attention to television. But, by 10 months of age, infants could imitate what they saw on television and point at familiar characters on shows that they viewed regularly. Parents should be concerned about what infants watch because later TV-viewing patterns are becoming established at this age. For instance, if left unmonitored, toddlers prefer to watch fast-paced programs, such as cartoons, which often have violent content. And, although many studies have indicated that watching TV shows with prosocial themes can have a positive impact in terms of social interactions and altruistic behaviour, viewing television with antisocial themes has been connected with negative outcomes, such as aggression and the development of stereotypes (Mares & Woodard, 2001, 2005).

In fact, studies have shown that TV viewing by children under 3 years of age may be harmful in terms of a child's cognitive and language development in the areas of reading recognition, reading comprehension, and attentional abilities (Christakis, 2009; Zimmerman & Christakis, 2005), as well as delayed speech development, by the time they enter school (Tanimura, Okuma, & Kyoshima, 2007). In contrast, ordinary infant toys, such as rattles and balls, and even common household items such as pots and pans, are just as useful in an infant's attempts to learn about the world as TV programs. Thus, many developmentalists suggest that, at best, the main thing babies learn from watching television is the behaviour of watching television.

Challenges to Piaget's View

Many studies since Piaget's time have suggested that he underestimated the cognitive capacity of infants. For instance, by changing the methods used to measure object permanence, researchers have found that younger infants than Piaget suggested can understand object movements (Thomas, 2005). Additionally, studies have shown that imitation appears at younger ages than Piaget's research implied.

OBJECT PERMANENCE In Piaget's studies of object permanence, infants were judged as having object permanence if they moved a blanket to retrieve a hidden object. However, infants are unable to grasp and move objects in this way until they are 7 to 8 months old. Thus, Piaget's methods made it impossible to tell whether younger infants failed to exhibit object permanence because they were physically unable to perform the task of moving the blanket (Birney & Sternberg, 2011).

Thanks to the advent of computers, researchers have been able to measure infants' understanding of objects in ways that do not depend on motor skill development. In many post-Piagetian studies of object permanence, researchers use computer technology to keep track of how infants' eyes respond when researchers move objects from one place to another. These "looking" studies have demonstrated that babies as young as 4 months show clear signs of object permanence if a visual response rather than a reaching response is used to test it (Baillargeon, 2004). Moreover, many studies have

Critical Thinking

How would you explain an infant's habit of throwing things out of her crib to a parent who viewed it as misbehaviour that needed to be corrected?

Learning Objective 5.2

Identify some challenges offered to Piaget's explanation of infant cognitive development.

examined how infants respond to a moving object that temporarily disappears behind a screen (Hespos & Baillargeon, 2008). In these studies, most 5-month-olds immediately looked to the other side of the screen when the moving object disappeared behind it and were delighted when it reappeared. These findings indicate that infants are holding some kind of representation of the hidden object in mind when it is behind the screen: the essence of object permanence. Nevertheless, such studies typically show that younger infants' understanding of object permanence is tied to the specific experimental situation. By contrast, babies who are nearing or past their first birthday understand object permanence sufficiently to use it across all kinds of situations, such as when they playfully hide objects from themselves and delight in "finding" them.

Piaget assumed that a baby came equipped with a repertoire of sensorimotor schemes, but his most fundamental theoretical proposal was that the child constructed an understanding of the world based on experience. In contrast, recent theorizing suggests that the development of object permanence is more a process of elaboration than one of discovery. Newborns may have considerable awareness of objects as separate entities that follow certain rules (Valenza, Leo, Gava, & Simion, 2006). Certainly, all the research on the perception of patterns suggests that babies pay far more attention to relationships between events than Piaget's model supposed. Still, no one would argue that a baby comes equipped with a full-fledged knowledge of objects or a well-developed ability to experiment with the world.

IMITATION   With respect to imitation, Piaget's proposed sequence has been supported. Imitation of someone else's hand movement or an action with an object seems to improve steadily, starting at 1 or 2 months of age; imitation of two-part actions develops much later, perhaps around 15 to 18 months (Poulson, Nunes, & Warren, 1989). Yet there are two important exceptions to this general confirmation of Piaget's theory: Infants imitate some facial gestures in the first weeks of life, and deferred imitation seems to occur earlier than Piaget proposed.

Several researchers have found that newborn babies will imitate certain facial gestures—particularly tongue protrusion, as shown in **Figure 5.1** (Anisfeld, 2005). This seems to happen only if the model sits with his tongue out looking at the baby for a fairly long period of time, perhaps as long as a minute. But the fact that newborns

Figure 5.1 Although researchers still disagree on just how much newborns will imitate, everyone agrees that they will imitate the gesture of tongue protrusion, demonstrated here by Andrew Meltzoff from the earliest study of this kind.

(**SOURCE:** From Meltzoff & Moore, *Science* 198:75 (1977). Reprinted with permission from AAAS.)

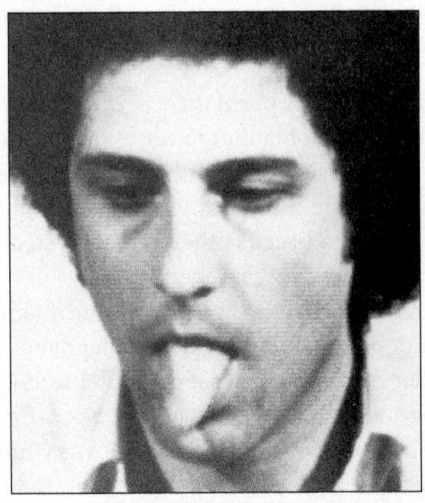
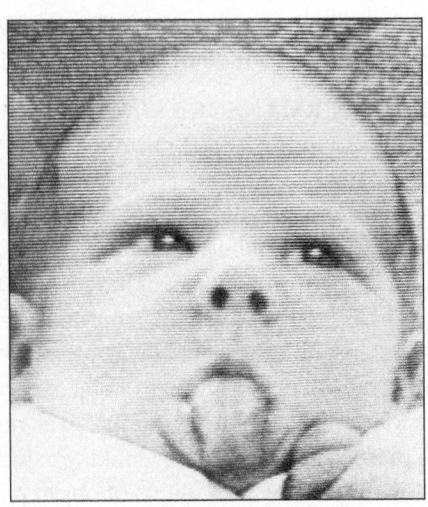

imitate at all is striking—although it is entirely consistent with the observation that quite young babies are capable of tactile-visual intermodal transfer, or perception.

Most studies of deferred imitation also support Piaget's model. However, some research indicates that infants as young as 6 weeks of age can defer imitation for at least a few minutes, and for ~10 minutes or so by 6 months (Bremner, 2002; Goertz et al., 2011). Moreover, studies show that babies as young as 9 months can defer their imitation for as long as 24 hours (Herbert, Gross, & Hayne, 2006). By 14 months, toddlers can recall and imitate someone's actions as many as two days later (Hanna & Meltzoff, 1993).

These findings are significant for several reasons. First, they make it clear that infants can and do learn specific behaviours through modelling, even when they have no chance to imitate the behaviour immediately. In addition, these results suggest that babies may be more skilful than Piaget thought. Clearly, too, more abilities than he suggested may be built in from the beginning and develop continuously, rather than in stages, throughout infancy (Courage & Howe, 2002).

Alternative Approaches

The many challenges to Piaget's characterization of infant thinking discussed above have led some developmental researchers to investigate object permanence within the more general context of infants' understanding of what objects are and how they behave. Researchers use the term **object concept** to refer to this understanding. Elizabeth Spelke and her colleagues (Spelke & Hespos, 2001) have done some very thorough and clever work on the development of the object concept. Spelke believes that babies are born with certain built-in assumptions that guide their interactions with objects. One of these is the assumption that when two surfaces are connected to each other, they belong to the same object; Spelke calls this the *connected surface principle*. For instance, you know that all sides of your textbook are connected together in a single, solid object.

In Spelke's early studies of this phenomenon (e.g., Spelke, 1982), she first habituated some 3-month-old babies to a series of displays of two objects; other babies were habituated to the sight of one-object displays. Then the babies were shown two objects touching each other, such as two square blocks placed next to each other so that they created a rectangle. Under these conditions, the babies who had been habituated to two-object displays showed renewed interest, clearly indicating that they "saw" this display as different (an unexpected outcome), presumably as a single object. Babies who had seen the one-object displays during habituation showed no renewed interest. In later experiments, Spelke (1991) used **violation-of-expectancy**, a research strategy in which an infant is habituated to a display that depicts the movement of an object and then is shown another display in which the object moves in a way that goes against what the infant expects to happen. Babies in this type of experiment were quite uninterested in the consistent condition but showed sharply renewed interest in the inconsistent condition. This suggests that very young infants' understanding of the rules governing relations among objects was more fully developed than Piaget's theory argues.

An important question remains: When does an infant recognize that a particular object seen at one time is actually the *same* object viewed at another time, a process called **object individuation**? University of British Columbia psychologist Fei Xu and her colleagues (Carey & Xu, 2001; Xu, 2003, 2005; Xu & Baker, 2005; Xu & Carey, 1996) have been investigating object individuation by using a *violation-of-expectancy* looking time procedure. Their research suggests that infants use three broad categories to *individuate* objects; the first relies on *spatiotemporal* information (i.e., information about the location and motion of objects), which is active in infants at 4 months of age. The second category, which is apparent in 10-month-old infants, is based on the use of an

Learning Objective 5.3

Summarize what the research tells us about infants' understanding of objects.

object concept

an infant's understanding of the nature of objects and how they behave

violation-of-expectancy

a research strategy in which researchers move an object in one way after having taught an infant to expect it to move in another

object individuation

the process by which an infant differentiates and recognizes distinct objects based on their mental images of objects in the environment

object's *property* information (i.e., the perceptual qualities of an object, such as colour, texture, and size, such that an infant would know that a red ball is a different object from a green ball that is viewed on a separate occasion). The last system to develop involves the awareness of distinct *kinds* of objects (e.g., a duck versus a ball); this adult-like ability first becomes apparent in infants by 9 to 12 months of age.

Test Yourself before going on

1. Number the milestones of the sensorimotor stage in the order in which they occur.
   _____ (a) means–end behaviour
   _____ (b) object permanence
   _____ (c) deferred imitation

2. In contrast to the research strategies that Piaget used, contemporary computerized methods of studying object permanence do not rely on infants' _____ _____ development.

3. _____ argued that babies are born with built-in assumptions about objects.

Critical Thinking

4. Think about children's television shows that you are familiar with. How would any of them benefit or harm the development of infants and toddlers?

Learning, Categorizing, and Remembering

Generally, the term *learning* is used to denote permanent changes in behaviour that result from experience. From the first moments following birth, babies exhibit evidence of learning—that is, environmental forces change their behaviours. However, babies also actively organize their interactions with these forces, as research examining categorization and memory clearly shows. Measures of intelligence help health care professionals identify infants who require special interventions to support cognitive development.

Conditioning and Modelling

Learning Objective 5.4

Describe the kinds of ways infants can learn.

Learning of emotional responses through classical conditioning processes may begin as early as the first week of life. For example, in classic research, pediatrician Mavis Gunther (1955, 1961) found that inexperienced mothers often held nursing newborns in ways that caused the babies' nostrils to be blocked by the breast. Predictably, the babies reflexively turned away from the breast in response to the sensation of smothering. During future nursing sessions, babies who had experienced the smothering sensation while nursing at their mother's right breast refused to nurse on the right side; babies who had associated the smothering sensation with the left breast displayed the opposite pattern of refusal. Gunther hypothesized that classical conditioning was at work in such cases. She developed an intervention based on principles of stimulus-response learning to help babies "unlearn" the response of turning away from the breast they had learned to associate with the sensation of smothering.

Critical Thinking

What other classically conditioned emotional responses might develop in early infancy? How may this affect a child's mental health or behaviour later on?

Newborns also clearly learn by operant conditioning. For example, music therapists have discovered that the use of *pacifier-activated lullaby (PAL)* systems in neonatal intensive care units improves preterm infants' sucking reflexes, which, in turn, causes them to gain weight more rapidly (Cevasco & Grant, 2005; Yildiz & Arikan, 2012). These systems reward infants with music whenever they suck on specially designed pacifiers. At the least, the fact that conditioning of this kind can take place in preterm infants means that whatever neurological wiring is needed for operant learning is present before birth. Results like these also tell developmentalists something about the sorts of reinforcements that are effective with very young children; it is surely highly significant for the whole process of mother-infant interaction that the mother's voice is an effective reinforcer for virtually all babies.

Infants can also learn by watching models. In one study, 10- and 12-month-olds were randomly assigned to two learning groups (Provasi, Dubon, & Bloch, 2001). "Observers" first watched an adult demonstrate how to find a toy by lifting the lids of various containers, and then the observers were allowed to play with the containers. "Actors" played with the containers without first watching an adult engage with them. Researchers found that observers were more proficient at finding the toy than actors in both age groups. However, the proficiency was much more pronounced among the older infants. Moreover, by 14 months, infants distinguish between successful and unsuccessful models and, like older children and adults, are more likely to imitate those who succeed at an attempted task (Zmyj, Buttelmann, Carpenter, & Daum, 2010).

In an interesting variation on modelling, German researchers conducted experiments in which 9- and 11-month-old infants would play with objects (e.g., a toy car or a ribbon) and then watch a video of adults playing with the same object or a different one (Hauf, Aschersleben, & Prinz, 2007). Researchers found that infants were more interested in watching adults engage with the object the infant had previously played with than with a novel one, which suggests infants' prior experience of playing with an object increases their interest in the actions of other people with the same object. This finding suggests a relationship between infants' actions and their perception of other peoples' actions.

Schematic Learning

Schematic learning is the organizing of experiences into expectancies, or "known" combinations. These expectancies, often called *schemas*, are built up over many exposures to particular experiences. Once formed, they help babies distinguish between the familiar and the unfamiliar.

One kind of schematic learning involves categories. Research suggests that by 7 months of age, and perhaps even earlier, infants actively use categories to process information (Elsner, Jeschonek, & Pauen, 2013). For example, a 7-month-old is likely to habituate to a sequence of 10 animal pictures, and, if the next picture is of another animal, then the baby will not show surprise or look at it any longer than he looked at any of the first 10 pictures. If, however, researchers show the baby a picture of a human after 10 animal pictures, then he will look surprised and gaze at the picture longer. The same thing is likely to happen if researchers show an infant several pictures of humans and then switch to an animal picture.

Such findings suggest that infants build and use categories as they take in information. However, categorical organization as a cognitive tool is not well developed in 7-month-olds. For one thing, infants of this age clearly do not understand the difference between lower-level and higher-level categories. "Dogs" and "animals," for example, can both be thought of as categories, but the higher-level one ("animals") includes the lower-level one. Thus, categories such as "animals" are referred to as *superordinates*. Researchers have found that infants respond to superordinate categories before they display reactions to basic-level categories (Pauen, 2002). In other words, 7- or 8-month-olds view "animals" and "furniture" as different categories, but not "dogs" and "birds." By contrast, 12-month-olds appear to understand both types of categories.

Still, 12-month-olds don't yet know that basic-level categories such as "dogs" and "birds" are nested within the superordinate category "animals." The concept

Learning Objective 5.5
Describe how categorical understanding changes over the first two years.

schematic learning
organization of experiences into expectancies, called *schemas*, which enable infants to distinguish between familiar and unfamiliar stimuli

that smaller categories are nested within larger ones, or hierarchical categorization, is demonstrated to some degree by 2-year-olds (Diesendruck & Shatz, 2001). However, full understanding of this kind of categorization is not typical until age 5 or so and is linked to language development and experiences with using words as category labels (Malabonga & Pasnak, 2002; Omiya & Uchida, 2002).

Memory

Learning Objective 5.6

Describe memory function in the first two years.

You have probably heard that it is impossible to form memories while you are sleeping, and so playing audio recordings of your text while you sleep is not likely to help you perform well on your next exam. However, newborns *do* appear to be able to remember auditory stimuli to which they are exposed while sleeping (Cheour et al., 2002). This interesting characteristic of infant memory is one of several.

An ingenious series of studies by Carolyn Rovee-Collier and her colleagues has shown that babies as young as 3 months of age can remember specific objects and their own actions with those objects over periods as long as a week (Rovee-Collier & Cuevas, 2009). A researcher first hangs an attractive mobile over a baby's crib, as shown in **Figure 5.2**, and watches to see how the baby responds, noting how often he kicks his legs while looking at the mobile. After three minutes of this "baseline" observation, a string is used to connect the mobile to the baby's leg, so that each time the baby kicks his leg, the mobile moves. Babies quickly learn to kick repeatedly to make

Figure 5.2 This 3-month-old baby in one of Rovee-Collier's memory experiments will quickly learn to kick her foot to make the mobile move. Several days later, she will remember this connection between kicking and the mobile.

(SOURCE: Carolyn Rovee-Collier, 1993, p. 131.)

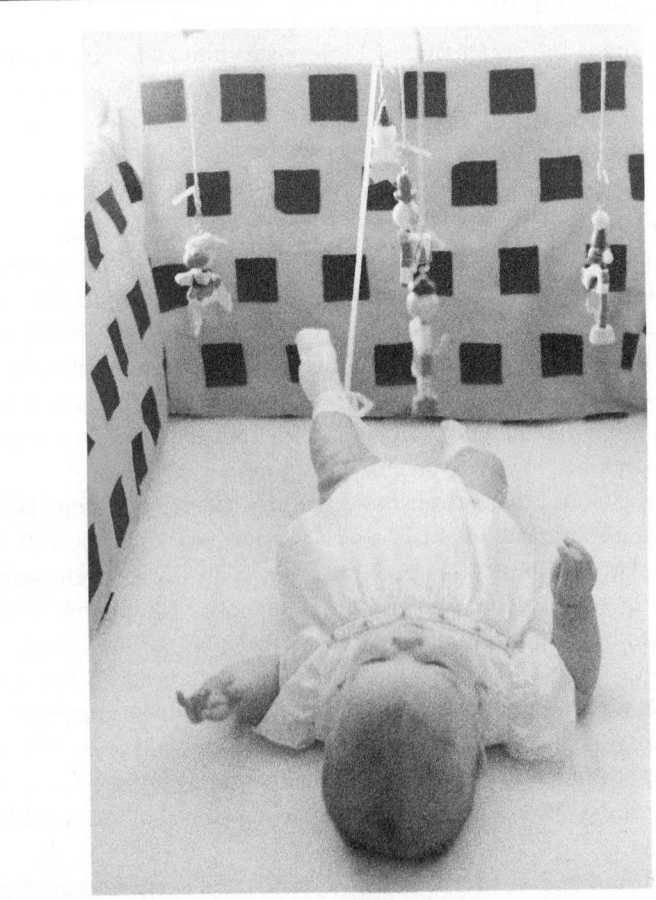

this interesting action occur. Within 3 to 6 minutes, 3-month-olds double or triple their kick rates, clearly showing that learning has occurred. The researcher next tests the baby's memory of this learning by coming back some days later and hanging the same mobile over the crib but not attaching the string to the baby's foot. The crucial issue is whether the baby kicks rapidly at the mere sight of the mobile. If the baby remembers the previous occasion, then he should kick at a higher rate than he did when he first saw the mobile, which is precisely what 3-month-old babies do, even after a delay of as long as a week.

Researchers have discovered that infants as young as 3 months make associations between objects that happen to appear together in their physical surroundings (Campanella & Rovee-Collier, 2005). Further research found that infants as young as 6 months can not only form new associations between objects, but also form new associations with their memories of objects (Cuevas, Rovee-Collier, & Learmouth, 2006). This discovery provides evidence that what infants see when they are just "looking around" can bring to mind things they saw before and they can combine them in new ways. This highlights the important role of early experiences and rich and varied environments on cognitive development.

Such findings demonstrate that the young infant is more cognitively sophisticated than developmentalists (and Piaget) had supposed. At the same time, these studies support Piaget's view that infants show systematic gains in the ability to remember over the months of infancy. Two-month-olds can remember their kicking action for only one day; 3-month-olds can remember it for over a week; and 6-month-olds can remember it longer than two weeks. However, early infant memories are strongly tied to the specific context in which the original experience occurred (Barr, Marrott, & Rovee-Collier, 2003; Patel, Gaylord, & Fagan, 2013). Even 6-month-olds do not recognize or remember the mobile if the context is changed even slightly—for example, by hanging a different cloth around the crib in which the infant is tested. Still, lost infant memories can be "reactivated" with the use of cues that remind the baby of the association between a behaviour, such as kicking, and a stimulus, such as a mobile (Bearce & Rovee-Collier, 2006). Thus, babies do remember more than Piaget believed, but their memories are highly specific. With age, their memories become less and less tied to specific cues or contexts.

Measuring Intelligence in Infancy

As you will learn in the chapter on Physical and Cognitive Development in Early Childhood, psychologists over the years have designed many instruments that measure **intelligence** in children and adults—an ability to take in information and use it to adapt to the environment. However, it is quite difficult to create a test that can effectively measure intelligence in infants. One widely used test, the Bayley Scales of Infant and Toddler Development, measures many aspects of cognitive, language, and motor development (Bayley, 1969, revised 1993, 2006). For example, 3-month-old infants are challenged to reach for a dangling ring; older babies are observed as they attempt to put cubes in a cup (9 months) or build a tower of three cubes (17 months). Some more clearly cognitive items are also included; for example, covering a toy with a cloth while the child observes and then watching to see if the child removes the cloth to reveal the toy is a test item used with 8-month-old infants to measure an aspect of object permanence. The most recent version of the Bayley Scales (Bayley-III) also includes items that address adaptive behaviour and social-emotional skills (Bayley, 2006).

In contrast to earlier editions of the Bayley Scales, the Bayley-III has been found to be a strong predictor of intelligence test scores in preschoolers (Bode, D'Eugenio, Mettelman, & Gross, 2014). Still, a primary role of the Bayley Scales is to help identify infants and toddlers who are in need of early intervention for developmental

Learning Objective 5.7

Identify how intelligence is measured in infancy.

intelligence

the ability to take in information and use it to adapt to the environment

(Photo: Courtesy of Michael and Alexandra Enns)

At 19 months, Merr would clearly pass the 17-month item on the Bayley Scales of Infant Development that calls for the child to build a tower of three cubes.

delays or neurological impairment (Dezoete, MacArthur, & Tuck, 2003; Gardner et al., 2006; Parekh et al., 2016). However, a limitation of the recent version, the Bayley-III, is that it tends to underestimate the severity of impairment in such children. It is therefore recommended that multiple tests and measures be used to assess neurodevelopmental outcomes until new norms for the Bayley-III are developed (Johnson, Moore, & Marlow, 2014; Lefebvre, Gagnon, Luu, Lupien, Dorval, 2016; Picciolini et al., 2015).

Other developmentalists support the notion that utilizing *habituation* tasks (as described in the chapter on Physical, Sensory, and Perceptual Development in Infancy) has high potential as a means of measuring infant intelligence (Birney & Sternberg, 2011; Kavšek & Bornstein, 2010). For example, if a baby is shown an object or a picture over and over, how many exposures does it take before the infant stops showing interest? The speed with which such habituation/recognition takes place may reveal something about the efficiency of the baby's perceptual/cognitive system and its neurological underpinnings. And, if such efficiency lies behind some of the characteristics that psychologists call intelligence, then individual differences in rate of habituation in the early months of life may predict later intelligence-test scores. That is exactly what some of the research examining links between measures of habituation in infants and later intelligence test scores has found (Kavšek, 2004; Rose, Feldman, & Jankowski, 2004).

Psychologist Joseph Fagan has developed a standardized test of *habituation rate* known as the Fagan Test of Infant Intelligence (Fagan & Detterman, 1992). Fagan argues that tests of habituation rate—also known as *novelty preference and visual recognition*—are particularly appropriate for infants who are incapable of responding to conventional tests such as the Bayley Scales (Fagan, 2000). For example, infants who suffer from cerebral palsy can't perform many of the tasks required by the Bayley Scales. However, they are fully capable of viewing visual stimuli and exhibiting habituation to them. Fagan's research and that of others has shown that the Fagan Test is a useful measure of cognitive function among such special populations (Smith, Fagan, & Ulvund, 2002; Gaultney & Gingras, 2005).

One of the conundrums of predicting later IQ based on infant measures is that, although for the most part intelligence is relatively consistent over time, there are multiple factors that can modify intelligence—for better or for worse, intelligence is somewhat malleable, especially under exceptional conditions. For example, early educational interventions can enhance intelligence (Protzko, Aronson, & Blair, 2013; Protzko, 2015, 2016), whereas adverse environmental conditions can limit intelligence. Adverse conditions include socioeconomic disadvantages (Kavšek & Bornstein, 2010; Oulhote & Grandjean, 2016) as well as environmental risks (Grandjean et al., 2015).

Numerous environmental risks involve exposure to neurotoxins, many of which can be naturally occurring elements, such as fluoride. Fluoride, in acceptable concentrations, is commonly added to our water supply for the purpose of reducing cavities and tooth decay in children (Health Canada, 2015c). Yet, fluoride is not a benign substance—in excessive amounts it can contribute to dental or skeletal *fluorosis* (mottled or pitted teeth in children and brittle bones and joint pain later in life) (Gupta, Gupta, & Chhabra, 2016). As well, children reared in communities where exposure to fluoride is high have been found to have lower IQ scores (alas, it remains to be determined what specific exposure levels are linked to adverse cognitive effects) (Choi, Sun, Zhang, & Grandjean, 2012; Fluoride Action Network, 2016). The impact of neurotoxins—including substances ranging from pesticides to industrial chemicals such as arsenic, lead, and methylmercury—on neurological and intellectual development is still in the early stages of study (Júlvez, & Grandjean, 2009). Researchers are calling for a global response to determine the impact of early in life exposure to the 214 or so known neurotoxins on brain and cognitive development (Júlvez et al., 2016; Suk et al., 2016).

Critical Thinking

Consider the known benefits and potential risks of water fluoridation. How might the two be balanced to maximize benefits and minimize harm?

Test Yourself before going on

1. During the second year, infants begin to imitate models they view as _____.

2. Organization of experience into expectancies is called _____ learning.

3. Rovee-Collier's research showed that _____ is important in infant memory.

4. The (Bayley/Fagan) test is used by researchers to study the relationship between habituation rate and intelligence test scores.

5. _____ is added to many municipal water supplies to reduce cavities and tooth decay in children, but at high exposure levels it may adversely affect intellectual development.

The Beginnings of Language

Most of us think of "language" as beginning when a baby uses her first words, at about 12 months of age. But all sorts of important developments precede the first words. Before we look at these developments, though, we'll look briefly at the various theoretical perspectives that try to explain them. The early discussions of language development were steeped in the classic nature–nurture debate (see **Table 5.2**).

Table 5.2 Theoretical Perspectives of Language Development

Theory and Proponent(s)	Main Idea	Example
Behaviourist B.F. Skinner (1957)	Behaviourist theories of language development claim that infants learn language through parental reinforcement of word-like sounds and correct grammar.	While babbling, babies accidentally make sounds that somewhat resemble real words as spoken by their parents. Parents hear the word-like sounds and respond to them with praise and encouragement, which serve as reinforcers. Thus, word-like babbling becomes more frequent, while utterances that do not resemble words gradually disappear from babies' vocalizations.
Nativist Noam Chomsky (1959)	Nativist theories of language development state that an innate language processor called the **language acquisition device (LAD)**, which contains the basic grammatical structure of all human language, guides children's comprehension and production of language.	In effect, the LAD tells infants what characteristics of language to look for in the stream of speech to which they are exposed. Simply put, the LAD tells babies that there are two basic types of sounds—consonants and vowels—and enables them to properly divide the speech they hear into the two categories so that they can analyze and learn the sounds specific to the language they are hearing.
Interactionist Lois Bloom (2000) Melissa Bowerman (1985) Michael Tomasello (1999, 2008) Lev Vygotsky (1962)	**Interactionists** assert that infants are biologically prepared to attend to language and that language development is a subprocess of cognitive development. They believe social interactions are critical to language development.	From the beginning of language, the child's intent is to communicate, to share the ideas and concepts in his head. He does this as best he can with the gestures or words he knows, and he learns new words when they help him communicate his thoughts and feelings.

language acquisition device (LAD)

an innate language processor, theorized by Chomsky, that contains the basic grammatical structure of all human language

interactionists

theorists who argue that language development is a subprocess of general cognitive development and is influenced by both internal and external factors

The child's amazing progress in this domain in the early years of life has been explained from both behaviourist and nativist points of view and as part of the larger process of cognitive development.

Influences on Language Development

Today, developmentalists better understand how the environment influences language development than they did when Skinner and Chomsky began their historic debate in the 1950s. Moreover, the increasing emphasis on the interactionist approach has led researchers to examine the kinds of environmental influences to which children are exposed during different phases of language development. For example, adults and older children speak differently to infants than they do to preschoolers, a way of speaking that researchers call **infant-directed speech (IDS)**. This pattern of speech is characterized by a higher pitch than that which is exhibited by adults and children when they are not speaking to an infant. Moreover, adults speaking to infants and young children also repeat a lot, introducing minor variations ("Where is the ball? Can you see the ball? Where is the ball? There is the ball!"). They may also repeat the child's own sentences but in slightly longer, more grammatically correct forms, a pattern referred to as an *expansion* or a *recasting*. For example, if a child said "Mommy sock," the mother might recast the text as "Yes, this is Mommy's sock," or if a child said "Doggie not eating," the parent might say "The doggie is not eating."

infant-directed speech (IDS)

the simplified, higher-pitched speech that adults use with infants and young children

Developmentalists believe that IDS influences language development to some degree (Cristia, 2013). For one thing, babies as young as a few days old can discriminate between IDS and adult-directed speech and they prefer to listen to IDS, whether it is spoken by a female or a male voice (Cooper & Aslin, 1994; Pegg, Werker, & McLeod, 1992). This preference exists even when the IDS is being spoken in a language other than the one normally spoken to the child. Janet Werker and her colleagues (1994), for example, have found that both English and Chinese infants prefer to listen to IDS, whether it is spoken in English or Cantonese (one of the major languages of China). Other studies by Werker indicate that IDS helps infants identify the sounds in their mothers' speech that are specific to the language they are learning (e.g., the English *schwa*, the Spanish rolled *r*) by emphasizing those sounds more than others (Werker et al., 2007).

Infant-directed speech may also be important to grammar development. Babies appear to find the high-pitched quality of IDS particularly attractive. Once the child's attention is drawn by this special tone, the simplicity and repetitiveness of the adult's speech may help the child to pick out repeating grammatical forms. Children's attention also seems to be drawn to recast sentences. For example, Farrar (1992) found that a 2-year-old was two or three times more likely to imitate a correct grammatical form after he heard his mother recast his own sentences than when the mother used that same correct grammatical form in her normal conversation. Experimental studies confirm this effect of recastings. Children who are deliberately exposed to higher rates of specific types of recast sentences seem to learn the modelled grammatical forms more quickly than do those who hear no recastings (Nelson, 1977). IDS has also been shown to facilitate long-term recognition of words (Singh, Nestor, Parikh, & Yull, 2009).

Developmentalists also know that children whose parents talk to them often, read to them regularly, and use a wide range of words in their speech differ from children whose parents do not. These children begin to talk sooner, develop larger vocabularies, use more complex sentences, and learn to read more readily when they reach school age (MacWhinney, 2011). Thus, the sheer quantity of language a child hears is a significant factor.

Early Milestones of Language Development

Children across cultures tend to follow a common general pattern of language development, whether they are growing up learning one language or two (Gervain, 2015; Werker, Byers-Heinlein, & Fennell, 2009; Werker & Hensch, 2015) (see the **Research Report**). From birth to about 1 month of age, the most common sound an infant makes is a cry, although she also produces other fussing, gurgling, and satisfied sounds. Over the next few months, the number of ways in which a baby can express herself increases tremendously. Although some of these vocalizations may seem to be of little consequence, each of the early milestones of language development makes a unique contribution to the language skills that all healthy children achieve in the first few years of life.

FIRST SOUNDS AND GESTURES   At about 1 or 2 months, the baby begins to make some laughing and **cooing** vowel sounds. Sounds like this are usually signals of pleasure and may show quite a lot of variation in tone, running up and down in volume or pitch. Consonant sounds appear at about 6 or 7 months, frequently combined with vowel sounds to make a kind of syllable. Babies of this age seem to play with these sounds, often repeating the same sound over and over (such as *babababababa* or *dahdahdah*). This sound pattern is called **babbling**, and it makes up about half of babies' noncrying sounds from about 6 to 12 months of age (Mitchell & Kent, 1990).

The left side of the brain controls the right side of the body and, in most people, the left brain is also home to our language capacity (see the chapter on Physical and Cognitive Development in Early Childhood for more details on brain specialization). With these facts in mind, McGill University psychologists studied the mouth movements of 5- to 12-month-olds to see if babies display a right mouth bias when babbling similar to the right mouth asymmetry seen in adults when they talk. Indeed the researchers Holowka & Petitto (2002) found that babies differentially used right mouth openings when babbling, but not when engaging in nonlanguage mouthing activity, such as chewing or crying. This finding suggests that babbling is not just generic oral-motor behaviour but is related to the beginnings of language production.

Any parent can tell you that babbling is a delight to listen to. It also seems to be an important part of the preparation for spoken language. For one thing, infants' babbling gradually acquires some of what linguists call the intonational pattern of the language they are hearing—a process one developmental psychologist refers to as "learning the tune before the words" (Bates, O'Connell, & Shore, 1987). At the very least, infants do seem to develop at least two such "tunes" in their babbling. Babbling with a rising intonation at the end of a string of sounds seems to signal a desire for a response; a falling intonation requires no response.

A second important thing is that when babies first start babbling, they typically babble all kinds of sounds, including some that are not part of the language they are hearing. But at about 9 or 10 months, their sound repertoire gradually begins to narrow to the set of sounds they are listening to, with the nonheard sounds dropping out (Oller, 1981). Such findings do not prove that babbling is necessary for language development, but they certainly make it look as if babbling is part of a connected developmental process that begins at birth.

Another part of that process appears to be a kind of gestural language that develops at around 9 or 10 months. At this age, babies begin "demanding" or "asking" for things by using gestures or combinations of gestures and sound. A 10-month-old baby who apparently wants you to hand her a favourite toy may stretch and reach for it, opening and closing her hand while making whining or whimpering sounds. Interestingly, infants of this age use gestures in this way whether they are

Learning Objective 5.9
Trace the pattern of early language development in infants.

cooing
making repetitive vowel sounds, particularly the *uuu* sound

babbling
the repetitive vocalizing of consonant-vowel combinations by an infant

exposed to spoken language or sign language. At about the same age, babies enter into those gestural games much loved by parents—"patty cake," "soooo big," and "wave bye-bye" (Bates et al., 1987).

WORD RECOGNITION   Research has shown that babies are beginning to store individual words in their memories at around 6 months of age (Tincoff & Jusczyk, 2012). By 9 or 10 months, most understand the meanings of 20 to 30 words; this ability to understand words is known as **receptive language**. In the next few months of the babies' lives, the number of words understood increases dramatically. In one investigation, researchers asked hundreds of mothers about their babies' understanding of various words. Reportedly, 10-month-olds understood an average of

receptive language

comprehension of spoken language

Research Report

Setting the Stage for Language Acquisition and Word Learning

Just as there are developmental milestones in motor development, it is intriguing to consider that there may also be developmental stages in speech perception and language development. Janet Werker and her colleagues at the University of British Columbia Infant Studies Centre have been studying the possibility that humans have a predisposition for language acquisition. They contend that language acquisition has two transitional stages: the first is characterized by a "reorganization of communication sounds" (Werker, 1989, p. 58) and the second by a "reorganization in infants' use of phonetic detail" (Stager & Werker, 1997, p. 381).

To begin with, researchers believe that neonates show a bias for speech that could be innate (Vouloumanos & Werker, 2007a, 2007b). Early in her research, Werker (1995) found that newborns display a special sensitivity to speech sounds and can distinguish between human speech sounds and non-speech sounds, e.g., dogs barking, traffic bustling, cutlery clanging. By 2½ months of age infants show a strong preference for listening to complex speech sounds compared with equally complex nonspeech sounds (Vouloumanos & Werker, 2004). At 4 to 6 months of age, infants are sensitive to all the essential speech sounds that correspond to the universal body of human language sounds (Werker, 1989); therefore, it seems that infants are perceptually ready to make the necessary sound distinctions required to learn any human language. A perceptual transition occurs, however, by 10 to 12 months of age, whereby infants, like adults, can no longer distinguish between the subtle language sounds that lie beyond the range of the dominant language in which they are being raised. This apparent loss of sensitivity to universal speech sounds is related to perceptual filtering and is not a *sensory-neural* loss, because the sensitivity can be recovered under experimental conditions (Werker & Tees, 1984). Additional evidence for a language acquisition timetable comes from a study comparing bilingual (French and English) with monolingual (English only)

infants, where it was found that both sets of infants 6 to 8 months of age responded in a similar manner to both French and English words (Burns, Yoshida, Hill, & Werker, 2007). By 10 to 12 months, however, the infants raised from birth in a bilingual environment were able to distinguish phonetic sounds in two language groups (French and English), whereas the monolingual infants could distinguish phonetic sounds corresponding to only one language (English). Collectively, these studies suggest that, from birth to 12 months of age, there is a shift in perceptual sensitivity away from universal speech sounds. This shift in perceptual attention facilitates the processes of language acquisition and word development (J. Werker, personal communication, July 17, 2001).

Not only are infants sensitive to auditory sounds, but they have also been shown to visually discriminate languages (e.g., French and English) (Sebastián-Gallés, Albareda-Castellot, Weikum, & Werker, 2012). Infants 4 to 6 months of age can detect when a different language is being spoken when shown silent video clips of bilingual speakers. By 8 months, the monolingual infants lost the ability to detect a switch in language, whereas bilingual infants were still able to visually discriminate the two languages. It seems that both auditory and visual speech information play a vital role in the process of tuning an infant's perceptual sensitivities toward their particular language environment.

Stager and Werker (1997) describe a second developmental stage based on the results of a random word–object association task. They designed an experiment in which infants were tested to see if they could notice a change in either the word, the object, or both the word and object. Stager and Werker discovered that, in the random word–object pairing task, 14-month-old infants could readily link a word with an object but were insensitive to the nuances of fine speech sound distortions. In contrast, 8-month-olds could not associate random words with objects but detected fine differences in speech sounds that the older infants failed to detect. The 8-month-olds were at a stage in which they were still developing familiarity with fundamental speech sounds, but they did not yet have the capacity to make meaningful

(*Photo:* Courtesy of Dr. Janet Werker.)

Along with the newborn's perceptual sensitivity to subtle speech sound differences, infants come prepared to differentiate words into two categories: *grammatical* and *lexical*. In infancy, a wide assortment of sound cues makes it possible for infants to distinguish between these two word categories. Specifically, **grammatical words** include those words that are primarily structural, such as articles, prepositions, and auxiliaries, which are generally of short vowel duration and have a simple syllable structure, for example, "its, the, in, and you" (Shi, Werker, & Morgan, 1999, pp. B12–B15).

By contrast, **lexical words** have high meaningfulness, such as nouns, verbs, adjectives, and adverbs. These words tend to be longer, have full vowels, and have more complex syllable structure, for example, "mommy, new, bounced, and great" (Shi & Werker, 2001, pp. 70–71).

Shi and Werker (2001) demonstrated that by 6 months infants show a clear preference for lexical words. This finding may help to explain how infants learn and understand lexical words before grammatical words—that is, an inborn preference for lexical words may serve to focus the infant's attention on those words that carry meaning, which prepares the infant for the acquisition of language (Shi, Werker, & Morgan, 1999). This innate perceptual ability to differentiate words into lexical and grammatical categories may be a critical first step in understanding the formal properties of human languages.

associations between words and objects. This finding signifies an important change in perception, in which infants at 14 months, having mastered the essential sounds of their dominant language, are capable and ready to learn associations between words and corresponding objects. The ability to identify and remember word–object associations that appears at 14 months of age is an important step in the preparation for the accelerated acquisition of language and vocabulary that occurs at around 18 months of age (Werker, Cohen, Lloyd, Casasola, & Stager, 1998).

---

about 30 words; for 13-month-olds, the number was nearly 100 words (Fenson et al., 1994).

But how do babies separate a single word from the constant flow of speech to which they are exposed? Many linguists have proposed that children can cope with the monumentally complex task of word learning only because they apply some built-in biases or constraints (Archibald & Joanisse, 2013; Räsänen, 2012). For example, children may have a built-in assumption that words refer to objects or actions but not both.

Learning a language's patterns of word stress may also help babies identify words. Research suggests that infants discriminate between stressed and unstressed syllables fairly early—around 7 months of age—and use syllable stress as a cue to identify single words (Yu & Ballard, 2007). For example, first-syllable stress, such as in the word *market*, is far more common in English than second-syllable stress, such as in the word *garage*. Thus, when English-learning infants hear a stressed syllable, they may assume that a new word is beginning. This strategy would help them single out a very large number of individual English words.

All this information—the beginning of meaningful gestures, the drift of babbling toward the heard language sounds, imitative gestural games, and the first comprehension of individual words—reveals a whole series of changes that seem to converge by 9 or 10 months of age. It is as if the child now understands something about the process of communication and is intending to communicate to adults.

grammatical words

words that pertain to the rules of language and proper sentence construction, such as articles, prepositions, and auxiliaries

lexical words

words with a high level of meaning, such as nouns, verbs, adjectives, and adverbs

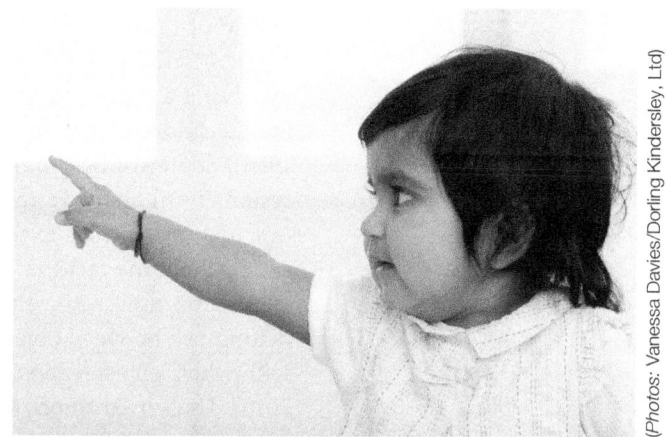

Gestures are just one of several skills in infants' repertoire of communication skills.

(*Photos:* Vanessa Davies/Dorling Kindersley, Ltd)

expressive language

the ability to use sounds, signs, or symbols to communicate meaning

(Photo: Ruth Jenkinson/Dorling Kindersley Ltd.)

These little boys probably haven't yet spoken their first words, but chances are they already understand quite a few. Receptive language usually develops before expressive language.

holophrases

combinations of gestures and single words that convey more meaning than just the word alone

naming explosion

the period when toddlers experience rapid vocabulary growth, typically beginning between 16 and 24 months

The First Words

If you have ever studied another language, then you probably understood the language before you could produce it yourself. Likewise, the 9- to 10-month-old infant understands far more words than he can say. **Expressive language**—the ability to produce, as well as understand and respond to, meaningful words—typically appears at about 12 or 13 months (Levine, 2011). The baby's first word is an event that parents eagerly await, but it's fairly easy to miss. A word, as linguists usually define it, is any sound or set of sounds that is used consistently to refer to some thing, action, or quality. So a child who uses *ba* consistently to refer to her bottle is using a word, even though the sound isn't considered a word in English.

Often, a child's earliest words are used in specific situations and in the presence of many cues. The child may say "bow-wow" or "doggie" only in response to such promptings as "How does the doggie go?" or "What's that?" Typically, this early word learning is very slow, requiring many repetitions for each word. In the first six months of word usage, children may learn as few as 30 words. Most linguists have concluded that this earliest word-use phase involves learning each word as something connected to a set of specific contexts. What the child has apparently not yet grasped is that words are symbolic—they refer to objects or events.

Very young children often combine a single word with a gesture to create a "two-word meaning" before they use two words together in their speech. For example, a child may point to his father's shoe and say "Daddy," as if to convey "Daddy's shoe" (Bates et al., 1987). In such cases, meaning is conveyed by the use of gesture and body language combined with a word. Linguists call these word-and-gesture combinations **holophrases**, and children use them frequently between 12 and 18 months of age.

Between 16 and 24 months, after the early period of very slow word learning, most children begin to add new words rapidly, as if they have figured out that things have names. Developmentalists refer to this period as the **naming explosion**. In this period, children seem to learn new words with very few repetitions, and they generalize these words to many more situations. According to one large cross-sectional study based on mothers' reports, the average 16-month-old has a speaking vocabulary of about 50 words; for a 24-month-old, the total has grown to about 320 words (Fenson et al., 1994).

Most observers agree that the bulk of new words learned during this early period of rapid vocabulary growth are names for things or people: *ball, car, milk, doggie, he.* Action words tend to appear later (Gleitman & Gleitman, 1992). One study involving a large group of children suggested that as many as two-thirds of the words children knew by age 2 were nouns, and only 8.5% were verbs (Fenson et al., 1994). Some studies suggest that infants cannot consistently associate words with actions until about 18 months of age (Casasola & Cohen, 2000). However, studies in which researchers expose infants to languages that they have never heard before suggest that the fact that nouns occur more frequently than verbs in natural speech is an important factor. In such studies, infants demonstrate a remarkable ability to distinguish between object names and other types of words, based on the frequency with which object names occur in a stream of speech (Hochmann, Endress, & Mehler, 2010). Thus, infants may learn nouns before verbs due to a built-in strategy that says something like "Learn the most frequent types of words first and then concentrate on the others."

The First Sentences

Research suggests that sentences appear when a child has reached a threshold vocabulary of around 100 to 200 words (Fenson et al., 1994). For most children, this threshold is crossed at between 18 and 24 months of age.

The first sentences have several distinguishing features: They are short, generally two or three words, and they are simple. Language development researcher Roger Brown coined the term **telegraphic speech** to refer to this pattern (Brown & Bellugi, 1964). Nouns and verbs are usually included, but virtually all grammatical markers (which linguists call **inflections**) are missing. At the beginning, for example, children learning English do not normally use the -*s* ending for plurals or put the -*ed* ending on verbs to make the past tense.

It is also clear that even at this earliest stage children create sentences following rules—not adult rules, to be sure, but rules nonetheless. They focus on certain types of words and put them together in particular orders. They also manage to convey a variety of different meanings with their simple sentences.

For example, young children frequently use a sentence made up of two nouns, such as "Mommy sock" or "sweater chair" (Bloom, 1973). The child who says "Mommy sock" may mean either "This is Mommy's sock" or "Mommy is putting a sock on my foot" (Bloom, 1973). Thus, to understand what a child means by a two-word sentence, it is necessary to know the context in which it occurred.

Individual Differences in Language Development

The sequences of development of language you've read about, and which are shown in **Table 5.3**, are accurate on the average, but the speed with which children acquire language skill varies widely. One factor influencing this rate is the number of languages to which a child has daily exposure (see **Development in the Real World**).

DIFFERENCES IN RATE Some children begin using individual words at 8 months, others not until 18 months; some do not use two-word sentences until 3 years or even later. The majority of children who talk late eventually catch up. One study found that 97% of late-talking infants' language development was within the average range by age 6 (Ellis & Thal, 2008). Those who do not catch up are primarily children who also have poor receptive language development (Ellis & Thal, 2008). This group appears to remain behind in language development and, perhaps, in cognitive development. In practical terms, this means that if your child—or a child you care for—is significantly delayed in understanding as well as speaking language, you should seek professional help to try to diagnose the problem and begin appropriate intervention.

Learning Objective 5.11

Identify what kinds of sentences children produce between 18 and 24 months of age.

telegraphic speech

simple two- or three-word sentences that usually include a noun and a verb

inflections

grammatical markers attached to words to indicate tense, gender, number, and the like, such as the use of the ending -*ed* to mark the past tense of a verb in English

Learning Objective 5.12

Describe individual differences that are evident in language development.

Table 5.3 Language Development in the First Two Years

Age	Milestone
2–3 months	Makes cooing sounds when alone; responds with smiles and cooing when talked to
4–5 months	Makes various vowel and consonant sounds with cooing
6 months	Babbles; utters phonemes of all languages
8–9 months	Focuses on the phonemes, rhythm, and intonation of language spoken in the home; has receptive vocabulary of 20 to 30 words
12 months	Expressive language emerges; says single words
12–18 months	Uses word-gesture combinations combined with variations in intonation (holophrases)
18–20 months	Uses two-word sentences (telegraphic speech); has expressive vocabulary of 100 to 200 words

Development in the Real World

One Language or Two?

Just over 18% of Canadians are fluent in English and French and, because of recent immigration trends, about one in five Canadians speaks one of 200 other languages (Statistics Canada, 2012d, 2016d). Knowing two languages is clearly a social and economic benefit to an adult. However, York University researcher, Ellen Bialystok, suggests there are cognitive advantages and disadvantages to growing up bilingual (Bialystok, 2007; Morales, Calvo, & Bialystok, 2013).

On the positive side are the findings of Elena Nicoladis of the University of Alberta and Fred Genesee of McGill University. They conducted a longitudinal study of infants raised in English/French bilingual homes and found that at about 2 years of age infants would start to speak in the mother's dominant language with the mother and speak the father's dominant language with the father (1996). They also noted that, unlike monolingual children who resist the idea that there can be more than one word for the same object, bilingual children had no difficulty using two translation terms for the same object. As well, in preschool and school-age children, bilingualism is associated with a clear advantage in metalinguistic ability, or the capacity to think about language (Bialystok, Shenfield, & Codd, 2000). Bilingual children also demonstrate better performance on working memory tasks (Morales et al., 2013) and most display greater ability to focus attention on language tasks than do monolingual children (Bialystok & Majumder, 1998). These advantages enable bilingual children to more easily grasp the connection between sounds and symbols in the beginning stages of learning to read (Bialystok, 1997).

On the downside, Nicoladis and Genesee (1997) contend that inconsistent exposure to a second language can lead to both uncertain language patterns and levels of competence. Children who become bilingual do so through exposure to a variety of influences—from parents, grandparents, child-care workers, or peer groups who speak different languages— and these different influences determine a bilingual child's proficiency. Consequently, to avoid incomplete acquisition (i.e., vocabulary only) and develop functional competence (i.e., effective social and grammatical usage) in both languages, bilingual children require abundant and regular exposure to both languages.

Petitto and Holowka (2002) found that the earlier a child is exposed to two languages the better: Early exposure promotes higher levels of language competence and mastery. Moreover, bilingual children who are equally fluent in two languages encounter few, if any, learning problems in school (Vuorenkoski, Kuure, Moilanen, & Peninkilampi, 2000). However, most bilingual children do not attain equal fluency in two languages (Hakansson, Salameh, & Nettelbladt, 2003). As a result, they tend to think more slowly in the language in which they have less fluency (Chincotta & Underwood, 1997). When the language in which they are less fluent is the language in which they are schooled, they are at risk for learning problems (Anderson, 1997; Thorn & Gathercole, 1999). Therefore, parents who choose bilingualism should probably take into account their ability to fully support their children's attainment of fluency in both languages.

The advantages in adulthood of being bilingual are substantial, not the least of which is the finding by Canadian researchers that bilingualism acts as a buffer against the onset of Alzheimer's disease (e.g., Bialystok, Craik, & Luk, 2012; Craik, Bialystok, & Freedman, 2010; Schweizer, Craik, & Bialystok, 2012). Thus, bilingual parents need to balance the various advantages and disadvantages of attaining bilingualism to reach an informed decision about the kind of linguistic environment to provide for their babies.

Researchers from the University of Calgary and their colleagues have been looking into risk and protective factors associated with the ~13% of Canadian toddlers who are late talkers (Collisson et al., 2016). For one, a family history of late talking and/or diagnosed speech language delay was found more frequently in late-talking toddlers than in the general population. As well, boys had speech delays more often than girls. Both findings suggest a biological disposition for delayed speech. They also found that infants who experienced language-based social interactions—such as infants who were read to from an early age, interacted with books daily, engaged in interactive play, and were primarily cared for in child-care centres—were less likely to be late talkers.

Learning Objective 5.13

Describe how language development varies across cultures.

Language Development Across Cultures

Studies in a wide variety of language communities, including Turkish, Serbo-Croatian, Hungarian, Hebrew, Japanese, a New Guinean language called Kaluli, German, and Italian, have revealed important similarities in language development (Maitel, Dromi,

Sagi, & Bornstein, 2000). Babies the world over coo before they babble; all babies understand language before they can speak it; babies in all cultures begin to use their first words at about 12 months.

Moreover, holophrases appear to precede telegraphic speech in every language, with the latter beginning at about 18 months. However, the specific word order that a child uses in early sentences is not the same for all children in all languages. In some languages, a noun/verb sequence is fairly common; in others, a verb/noun sequence may be heard. In addition, particular inflections are learned in highly varying orders from one language to another. Japanese children, for example, begin very early to use a special kind of marker, called a *pragmatic marker*, that indicates feeling or context. In Japanese, the word *yo* is used at the end of a sentence when the speaker is experiencing some resistance from the listener; the word *ne* is used when the speaker expects approval or agreement. Japanese children begin to use these markers very early, much earlier than children whose languages contain other types of inflections.

Most strikingly, there are languages in which there seems to be no simple two-word-sentence stage in which the children use no inflections. Children learning Turkish, for example, use essentially the full set of noun and verb inflections by age 2 and never go through a stage of using uninflected words. Their language is simple, but it is rarely ungrammatical from the adult's point of view (Aksu-Koc & Slobin, 1985; Maratsos, 1998).

Test Yourself before going on

1. (Behaviourists/Nativists) emphasize the role of the environment in language development.

2. _____ _____ _____ is the simplified, higher-pitched speech that adults use with infants and young children.

3. Number these milestones of language development in the order in which they occur.
   _____ (a) holophrases
   _____ (b) cooing
   _____ (c) babbling
   _____ (d) first words
   _____ (e) telegraphic speech
   _____ (f) naming explosion

4. In what ways do children's first sentences vary across cultures?

Summary

Cognitive Changes

5.1 Describe the milestones of Piaget's sensorimotor stage.

- Piaget described the sensorimotor infant as beginning with a small repertoire of basic schemes, from which she moves toward symbolic representation in a series of six substages. The milestones of this stage include primary, secondary, and tertiary circular reactions as well as object permanence, means–end behaviour, and deferred imitation.

5.2 Identify some challenges offered to Piaget's explanation of infant cognitive development.

- More recent research suggests that Piaget underestimated infants' capabilities, as well as the degree to which some concepts may be wired into the brain.

5.3 Summarize what the research tells us about infants' understanding of objects.

- Developmentalists, such as Spelke and Xu, have studied object permanence within the context of infants' global understanding of objects. Their research shows that Piaget underestimated how much younger infants know about objects and their movements.

Learning, Categorizing, and Remembering

5.4   Describe the kinds of ways infants can learn.

- Within the first few weeks of life, babies are able to learn through classical conditioning, operant conditioning, and observing models. By 14 months, they recognize the difference between successful and unsuccessful modelled behaviours and are more likely to imitate models they view as competent.

5.5   Describe how categorical understanding changes over the first two years.

- From an early age, infants use categories to organize information. The sophistication of these categories, and an understanding of how they relate to each other, increases over the first two years of life.

5.6   Describe memory function in the first two years.

- Three- and four-month-old infants show signs of remembering specific experiences over periods of as long as a few days or a week, a sign that they must have some form of internal representation well before Piaget supposed.

5.7   Identify how intelligence is measured in infancy.

- It is a challenge to create a test that can effectively measure intelligence in infants. Measures of basic information-processing skills in infancy, such as rate of habituation at 4 months, is one way to predict later intelligence-test scores. Socioeconomic and environmental factors can limit intelligence.

The Beginnings of Language

5.8   Describe how the environment influences language development.

- High-pitched infant-directed speech (IDS) helps infants learn language by attracting

their attention to the simple, repetitive, and expanded expressions that adults use. The amount of verbal interaction that takes place between infants and mature speakers is another influence. Poverty is associated with language development as well.

5.9   Trace the pattern of early language development in infants.

- Babies' earliest sounds are cries, followed at about 2 months by cooing, and then at about 6 months by babbling. At 9 months, babies typically use meaningful gestures and can understand a small vocabulary of spoken words.

5.10   Identify the characteristics of toddlers' first words.

- The first spoken words, usually names for objects or people, typically occur at about 1 year of age, after which toddlers add words slowly for a few months and then rapidly.

5.11   Identify what kinds of sentences children produce between 18 and 24 months of age.

- Simple two-word sentences appear in children's expressive language at about 18 months.

5.12   Describe individual differences that are evident in language development.

- The rate of language development varies from one child to another. Late talking in toddlers has been linked to both biological and environmental factors.

5.13   Describe how language development varies across cultures.

- Early word learning seems to follow similar patterns in all cultures. However, the word order of a child's telegraphic speech depends on which language he is learning.

Chapter 6
Social and Personality Development in Infancy

Britta Kasholm-Tengve/Vetta/Getty Images

Learning Objectives

THEORIES OF SOCIAL AND PERSONALITY DEVELOPMENT

6.1 Describe how Freud's and Erikson's views of personality development in the first two years differ.

6.2 Describe the main ideas of attachment theory from the ethological perspective.

ATTACHMENT

6.3 Describe how synchrony affects parent–infant relations.

6.4 Identify the four phases of attachment and the behaviours associated with them.

6.5 Identify characteristics of the four attachment patterns discovered by Ainsworth.

6.6 Describe what variables might affect a parent's ability to establish an attachment relationship with an infant.

Infancy is the period during which parents and children experience more physical closeness than at any other time in development. Proximity is pleasurable for both parents and babies, but it is also practical. For one thing, a mother or father usually has to carry out other duties while simultaneously caring for a baby. For another, keeping babies close by helps parents protect babies from harm. Practical considerations aside, proximity contributes to the development of strong emotional bonds between infants and caregivers. Physical closeness provides parents with many opportunities to comfort and show affection for infants. It also allows them to interact by exchanging smiles, frowns, or silly faces.

In the context of frequent physical contact, interactions between infants and the social world around them lay the foundations of development in the social and personality domains that are the topics of this chapter. We will first review the ideas proposed by psychoanalytic theorists about the first two years along with those of theorists who take a different approach. Next, you will read about the process of attachment. The infant's emerging personality and sense of self come next, followed by a discussion of the effects of nonparental care on infants' development.

Theories of Social and Personality Development

Psychologists use all the theoretical perspectives you learned about in the chapter on Theories of Development to formulate hypotheses about infant social and personality development. The two most influential perspectives on these issues are the psychoanalytic and the ethological perspectives.

Learning Objective 6.1

Describe how Freud's and Erikson's views of personality development in the first two years differ.

Psychoanalytic Perspectives

You may recall from the chapter on Theories of Development that Freud proposed a series of psychosexual stages that extend from birth through adolescence, during which individuals attempt to satisfy certain basic drives in different ways. In the oral stage, from birth to age 2, infants derive satisfaction through the mouth. Freud further believed that the weaning process should be managed in such a way that the infant's need to suck is neither frustrated nor overgratified. The consequences of either, Freud claimed, would be fixation at this stage of development. Fixation would manifest itself, in Freud's view, in oral behaviours such as nail-biting and swearing.

Freud also emphasized the *symbiotic* relationship between the mother and young infant, in which the two behave as if they are one. He believed that the infant did not understand herself to be separate from her mother. Thus, another result of a gratifying nursing period followed by a balanced weaning process, Freud thought, was the infant's development of a sense of both attachment to and separation from the mother.

Erikson went beyond Freud's view. Nursing and weaning are important, he conceded, but they are only one aspect of the overall social environment. Erikson claimed that responding to the infant's other needs by talking to him, comforting him, and so on, was just as important. He proposed that during the first two years of life, the infant learns to trust the world around him or becomes cynical about the social environment's ability to meet his needs: the *trust versus mistrust stage.*

One of the best-known studies in developmental psychology demonstrated that Erikson's view of infant development was more accurate than Freud's (Harlow & Zimmerman, 1959). In this study, infant monkeys were separated from their mothers at birth. The experimenters placed two different kinds of surrogate mothers in their cages. The monkeys received all their feedings from a wire mother with a nursing bottle attached. The other mother was covered with soft terrycloth. The researchers found that the monkeys approached the wire mother only when hungry. Most of the time, they cuddled against the cloth mother and ran to it whenever they were frightened or stressed. Subsequent studies with human infants correlating maternal feeding practices with infant adjustment suggested that the infants' social relationships are not based solely on either nursing or weaning practices (Schaffer & Emerson, 1964).

Freud asserted that infant weaning practices were central to the attachment process.

Harlow's ingenious research demonstrated that infant monkeys became attached to a terrycloth covered "mother" and would cling to it rather than to a wire mother that provided them with food.

Ethological Perspectives

The *ethological perspective* claims that all animals, including humans, have innate predispositions that strongly influence their development. Thus, the ethological approach to social and personality development proposes that evolutionary forces have endowed infants with genes that predispose them to form emotional bonds with their caregivers, an approach known as **attachment theory**. Consequently, in contrast to psychoanalysts, ethologists view the infant's capacity for forming social relationships as highly resistant to environmental forces such as variations in the quality of parenting. However, ethologists do claim that the first two years of life constitute a sensitive period for the formation of such relationships. They say that infants who fail to form a close relationship with a caregiver before the age of 2 are at risk for future social and personality problems (see the **Research Report**).

Because ethologists hypothesize that early emotional bonds influence later social and personality development, ethological perspectives have been very influential in the study of development in this domain across the entire lifespan. In John Bowlby's

Learning Objective 6.2

Describe the main ideas of attachment theory from the ethological perspective.

attachment theory

the view that the ability and need to form an attachment relationship early in life are genetic characteristics of all human beings

terminology, infants create different *internal models* of their relationships with parents and other key adults (Bowlby, 1969). These models include such elements as the child's confidence (or lack of it) that the attachment figure will be available or reliable, the child's expectation of rebuff or affection, and the child's sense of assurance that the primary caregiver is really a safe base for exploration. The internal model begins to be formed late in the child's first year of life and becomes increasingly elaborated and better established through the first four or five years. By age 5, most children have a clear internal model of the mother (or other primary caregiver), a self model, and a model of relationships. Once formed, such models shape and explain experiences and affect memory and attention. Children notice and remember experiences that fit their models and miss or forget experiences that don't match. As Piaget might say, a child more readily *assimilates* data that fit the model. More importantly, the model affects the child's behaviour: The child tends to recreate, in each new relationship, the pattern with which he is familiar. This tendency to recreate the parent–infant relationship in each new relationship, say Bowlby and other ethologists, continues into adulthood. For this reason, ethologists believe that, for example, poor communication between adult romantic partners may result from maladaptive communication patterns that developed between one of the individuals and his or her early caregivers.

Research Report

Adoption and Development

Most people who adopt a child assume that if they provide enough love and support, then the child will develop both cognitively and emotionally pretty much the way their biological child would. By now, you should know enough about human development to realize that it just isn't that simple. For one thing, many aspects of temperament and personality are inherited. Therefore, an adopted child is more likely than a biological child to be different from his parents in these traits, which may give rise to problems. For example, if two extremely shy parents adopt a very outgoing child, then the parents may view the child's behaviour as difficult or even "disturbed" in some way, rather than just different from theirs.

Adoptive parents also need to take into account the child's circumstances prior to the adoption in order to form a realistic set of expectations (Brisch, 2015). Children adopted before the age of 6 months who have no history of institutionalization or abuse are generally indistinguishable from nonadopted children in security of attachment, cognitive development, and social adjustment (Rutter et al., 2010). For instance, Simon Fraser University (SFU) psychologists have been studying *Romanian orphans* (RO) who were adopted by Canadian families early in the 1990s. The infants had been raised in Romanian orphanages, where they experienced extreme deprivation, understimulation, malnourishment, and only minimal custodial care. Elinor Ames's (1997) research team found that the infants who had lived in the Romanian orphanages for more than four months before being adopted by British Columbian families tended to have more psychological and motor-behaviour problems than nonadopted children.

Lucy Le Mare of SFU and co-investigator Karyn Audet (Douglas College) have continued the project and last assessed the RO when they were 17 years old on average. Earlier, their team found that there was considerable variability between individuals when the RO were assessed at age 10, although as a group the RO had lower than average IQs and academic achievement, and more difficulties with attention, learning, and peer relationships (Audet & Le Mare, 2011; Le Mare, Fernyhough, & Warford, 2001). However, a later analysis that took place when the RO were adolescents revealed that the RO who had lived in a Romanian orphanage for more than 24 months prior to adoption displayed more serious behavioural difficulties at twice the rate found in the general population and compared to RO children who had spent less than two years in orphanages before adoption (Le Mare & Audet, 2014). Important mediating factors within the adoptive home were associated with positive adolescent-parent attachment relationships and open communication about adoption.

However, parents who adopt high-risk children should keep the following important facts in mind. Children who are adopted later, who have histories of abuse and/or neglect, or who have lived in institutions for long periods tend to have more cognitive, motor, and emotional problems than nonadopted children (Juffer, Finet, Vermeer, van den Dries, 2015; Juffer, van IJzendoorn, & Palacios, 2011; Palacios, Román, Moreno, León, & Peñarrubia, 2014). For example, infants who are institutionalized for many months typically lack opportunities for forming attachments. As a result, they are at risk of developing *reactive attachment disorder*, a condition that seriously impairs an individual's capacity for forming social relationships (American Psychiatric Association, 2013). Children with this disorder are irritable and difficult to comfort. Most rarely show signs of positive emotional states, such as smiling. Many of these children also experience episodes of extreme fear. All the same, adopted children are better off developmentally than their peers who remain institutionalized (Bos et al., 2011).

The task of raising high-risk children can be made more manageable with parent training (Smyke, 2015). Thus, adoptive parents should take advantage of any training offered by the institutions through which an adoption is arranged or look for training elsewhere in their community. Finally, at the first sign of difficulty, adoptive parents should seek help from a social worker or psychologist who specializes in treating children. Therapists can help with everyday tasks such as toilet training and can teach parents strategies for dealing with behaviours, such as self injury, that reflect severe emotional disturbance.

Test Yourself before going on

1. Classify each of the following statements as consistent with (A) Freud's, (B) Erikson's, or (C) the ethological view of infant development.
   _____ (a) Feeding is the basis of attachment.
   _____ (b) Responsive caregivers help the infant develop a sense of trust.
   _____ (c) An infant whose needs are not met may become cynical.
   _____ (d) Infants satisfy their desire for pleasure with their mouths.
   _____ (e) Infants create internal models of social relationships.
   _____ (f) Harlow's infant monkeys preferred cloth mothers to those that had fed them.
   _____ (g) Infants are biologically predisposed to develop emotional bonds with caregivers.

Critical Thinking

2. How would learning theorists' explanations of early social relationships and their influences on later relationships differ from those of psychoanalysts and ethologists?

Attachment

Somehow, in the midst of endless diaper changes, food preparation, baths, and periods of exhaustion that exceed anything they have ever experienced before, the overwhelming majority of parents manage to respond to their infants in ways that foster the development of an **attachment** relationship. An attachment is an emotional bond in which a person's sense of security is bound up in the relationship. As the research discussed in the **Research Report** suggests, a child need not be biologically related to her parents in order to develop such a relationship. In fact, the development of attachment relationships depends on the quantity and quality of the interactions that take place between infants and parents. To understand attachment between parent and infant, it is necessary to look at both sides of the equation—at both the parents' bond to the child and the child's attachment to the parents.

attachment
the emotional tie, experienced by an infant, to a parent from which the child derives security

The Parents' Attachment to the Infant

Contact between mother and infant immediately after birth does not appear to be sufficient for the formation of a stable long-term bond between them (Wong, 1993). What is essential for the formation of that bond is the opportunity for mother and infant to develop a mutual, interlocking pattern of *attachment behaviours*, called **synchrony** (Moore, 2007). Synchrony is like a conversation. The baby signals his needs by crying or smiling; he responds to being held by quieting or snuggling; he looks at the parents when they look at him. The parents, in turn, enter into the interaction with their own repertoire of caregiving behaviours.

The father's bond with the infant, like the mother's, seems to depend more on the development of synchrony than on contact immediately after birth. Aiding the development of such mutuality is the fact that fathers have the same repertoire of attachment behaviours as do mothers. In the early weeks of the baby's life, fathers touch,

Learning Objective 6.3
Describe how synchrony affects parent–infant relations.

synchrony
a mutual, interlocking pattern of attachment behaviours shared by a parent and a child

Fathers engage in physical play with infants more often than mothers do.

talk to, and cuddle their babies in the same ways that mothers do (George, Cummings, & Davies, 2010).

After the first weeks of the baby's life, however, signs of a kind of specialization of parental behaviours begin to emerge. Fathers spend more time playing with the baby, with more physical roughhousing; mothers spend more time in routine caregiving and also talk to and smile at the baby more (Lamb & Lewis, 2011). These differences in parental behaviours may have a neurobiological basis (Abraham et al., 2014; Apter-Levi, Zagoory-Sharon, & Feldman, 2014; Atzil, Hendler, & Feldman, 2014; Feldman, 2016). When mothers observe or interact with their infants, their bodies release *oxytocin*, a hormone that is correlated with empathy, the desire for physical closeness with another person for whom one feels affection, and physical relaxation. By contrast, watching and interacting with babies stimulates *vasopressin* in fathers, a hormone that is linked to stimulatory contact—physical activity and *joint attention* to objects.

By 6 months, infants display distinctive patterns of responding to these mother–father differences (Feldman, 2003). Signs of positive emotional states, such as smiling, appear gradually and subtly when babies are interacting with their mothers. In contrast, babies laugh and wriggle with delight in short, intense bursts in interactions with their fathers. This isn't a matter of babies' preference for one parent or the other. Instead, such results mean that infants recognize the same behavioural differences in mothers and fathers that developmental scientists do when they observe parental behaviour. In fact, some researchers have noted that measures of attachment behaviours based on typical mother–infant interactions may cause researchers to inappropriately conclude that fathers are less involved with babies than mothers and, therefore, less important to infants' development (Lewis & Lamb, 2003). On the contrary, research clearly indicates that babies benefit tremendously when both kinds of interaction are available to them. Moreover, longitudinal research has demonstrated that infants whose fathers do not engage them in typical father–infant play activities in the early months of life are at risk of developing behaviour problems such as excessive aggressiveness later in childhood (Ramchandani et al., 2013).

Recent studies of the father–infant relationship that have been done across global settings indicate that the father's involvement is beneficial to infants' development regardless of cultural context (Adamson, 2016; Gray & Anderson, 2016; Levtov, van der Gaag, Greene, Kaufman, & Barker, 2015). Ongoing, positive, paternal involvement in the lives of their children can take many forms, and it not only benefits the children on a day-to-day and long-term basis in that it provides protection, material resources, direct care, and/or serves as a role model, but it also benefits the fathers in terms of lowered risk-taking and improved physical, mental, and sexual health, as well as a better relationship with the mother. In short, good fathering benefits the overall well-being of families. However, the elements needed for building a strong father–child attachment and continued paternal involvement in the ongoing positive development of the child may be lacking, especially in cases where there are strong cultural traditions that see the father's role as a secondary caregiver or when the development of the father's parenting skills is disrupted for myriad reasons ranging from oppression and violence, to forced separation (e.g., as was the case with Indian Residential Schools in Canada) which, in turn, adversely impact the father's ability to be an involved parent (Adamson, 2016; Ball & Moselle, 2015; Chaudhary, Tuli, & Sharda, 2015). Although paternal involvement has increased across societies over the last several decades, a gap still remains between what's ideal for child development and the current reality of the father's role in childrearing. We still have a way to go before fathers move from a complementary role to a more hands-on caregiver role in ways that enhance child development (Fagan & Palm, 2016).

The Infant's Attachment to the Parents

Like the parents' bond to the baby, the baby's attachment emerges gradually and is based on her ability to discriminate between her parents and other people. As you learned in the chapter on Prenatal Development and Birth, an infant can recognize her mother's voice prior to birth. By the time the baby is a few days old, she recognizes her mother by sight and smell as well (Cernoch & Porter, 1985; Walton, Bower, & Bower, 1992). Thus, the cognitive foundation for attachment is in place within days after birth.

ESTABLISHING ATTACHMENT   Bowlby suggested four phases in the development of the infant's attachment (Bowlby, 1969). Bowlby and other ethologists claim that these phases appear in a fixed sequence over the first 24 to 36 months of life that is strongly influenced by genes that are present in all healthy human infants. The infant exhibits a distinctive set of attachment-related behaviours and interaction patterns in each phase.

- Phase 1: *Nonfocused orienting and signalling (birth to 3 months).* Babies exhibit what Ainsworth (1989) described as "proximity promoting" behaviours: actions that signal their needs and draw the attention of others, such as crying, making eye contact, clinging, cuddling, and responding to caregiving efforts by being soothed. Babies direct these signals to everyone with whom they come into contact.

- Phase 2: *Focus on one or more figures (3 to 6 months).* Babies direct their "come here" signals to fewer people, typically those with whom they spend the most time, and are less responsive to unfamiliar people.

- Phase 3: *Secure base behaviour (6 to 24 months).* True attachment emerges. Babies show what Ainsworth called "proximity seeking" behaviours, such as following and clinging to caregivers whom they regard as "safe bases," especially when they are anxious, injured, or have physical needs, such as hunger. Most babies direct these behaviours to a primary caregiver when that person is available and to others only when the primary caregiver, for some reason, cannot or will not respond to them or is absent (Lamb, 1981). Not all infants have a single attachment figure, even at this stage. Some may show strong attachment to both parents or to a parent and another caregiver, such as a babysitter or a grandparent. But even these babies, when under stress, usually show a preference for one of their favoured persons over the others.

- Phase 4: *Internal model (24 months and beyond).* An internal model of the attachment relationship allows children older than 2 years to imagine how an anticipated action might affect the bonds they share with their caregivers (van IJzendoorn, 2005). The internal model plays a role in later relationships with early caregivers (e.g., adult children and their parents) and in other significant relationships (e.g., romantic partnerships) throughout life.

Learning Objective 6.4

Identify the four phases of attachment and the behaviours associated with them.

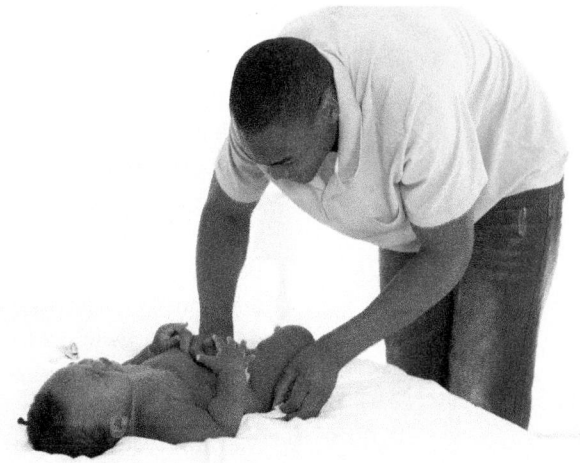

(Photo: michaeljung/Fotolia)

Dads like this one, who get involved with the day-to-day care of their babies, seem to develop stronger attachment relationships with their babies.

(Photo: Christina Kennedy/Alamy Stock Photo)

Whether a child cries when he is separated from his mother is not a helpful indicator of the security of his attachment. Some securely attached infants cry when separated from their mothers; others do not. The same is true of insecurely attached infants.

stranger anxiety

expressions of discomfort, such as clinging to the mother, in the presence of strangers

separation anxiety

expressions of discomfort, such as crying, when separated from an attachment figure

social referencing

infants' use of others' facial expressions as a guide to their own emotions

ATTACHMENT BEHAVIOURS Once the child has developed a clear attachment, at about 6 to 8 months of age, several related behaviours also begin appearing. *Stranger anxiety* and *separation anxiety*, attachment behaviours that are rare before 5 or 6 months, rise in frequency until about 12 to 16 months, and then decline. Infants express **stranger anxiety** with behaviours such as clinging to their mothers when strangers are present. **Separation anxiety** is evident when infants cry or protest being separated from the primary caregiver. The research findings are not altogether consistent, but fear of strangers apparently emerges first. Separation anxiety starts a bit later but continues to be visible for a longer period. Such an increase in fear and anxiety has been observed in children from a number of different cultures, and in both home-reared children and children in daycare.

Another attachment behaviour is **social referencing** (Carver & Cornew, 2009). Infants use cues from the facial expressions and the emotional tone of voice used by their attachment figures to help them figure out what to do in novel situations, such as when they are about to be examined by a health care provider (Flom & Bahrick, 2007; Kim, Walden, & Knieps, 2010). Babies this age will first look at Mom's or Dad's face to check for the adult's emotional expression. If Mom looks pleased or happy, then the baby is likely, for example, to accept a stranger with less fuss. If Mom looks concerned or frightened, then the baby responds to those cues and reacts to the novel situation with equivalent fear or concern.

Social referencing also helps babies learn to regulate their own emotions. For example, an infant who is angry because an enjoyable activity is no longer available may use his caregiver's pleasant, comforting emotional expressions to transition himself into a more pleasant emotional state. By contrast, a baby whose caregiver responds to his anger with more anger may experience an escalation in the level of his own angry feelings. Most developmentalists think that the quality of the emotional give-and-take in interactions between an infant and his caregivers is important to the child's ability to control emotions such as anger and frustration in later years (Cole, Martin, & Dennis, 2004).

Learning Objective 6.5

Identify characteristics of the four attachment patterns discovered by Ainsworth.

Variations in Attachment Quality

Virtually all babies seem to go through the four phases of attachment first identified by Bowlby, but the quality of the attachments they form differs from one infant to the next.

SECURE AND INSECURE ATTACHMENTS Variations in the quality of the first attachment relationship are now almost universally described using Ainsworth's category system (Ainsworth, Blehar, Waters, & Wall, 1978). The Ainsworth system distinguishes between secure attachment and two types of insecure attachment, which psychologists assess by using a procedure called the *Strange Situation*.

The Strange Situation consists of a series of eight episodes played out in a laboratory setting, typically with children between 12 and 18 months of age. The child is observed in each of the following situations:

- With the mother
- With the mother and a stranger
- Alone with the stranger
- Completely alone for a few minutes
- Reunited with the mother
- Alone again
- With the stranger again
- Reunited with the mother

Ainsworth suggested that children's reactions in these situations—particularly to the reunion episodes—showed attachment of one of three types: **secure attachment**, **avoidant attachment**, and **ambivalent attachment**. A fourth type, **disorganized/ disoriented attachment**, includes attachment reactions that do not readily fit into the other two insecure patterns (Main & Solomon, 1990).

Whether a child cries when he is separated from his mother is not a helpful indicator of the security of his attachment. Some securely attached infants cry in this situation, others do not; the same is true of insecurely attached infants. It is the entire pattern of the child's response to the Strange Situation that is critical, not any one response. These attachment types have been observed in studies in many different countries, and secure attachment is the most common pattern in every country.

David Pederson and Greg Moran (1996) of the University of Western Ontario have refined the measurement of attachment. Unlike the Strange Situation, which is laboratory-based, they observed mother–infant interactions in the more natural and convenient surroundings of the home environment. The use of either method revealed that in a secure type of relationship, mothers were more sensitive to their infant's needs and their infant tended to be less fussy and enjoyed physical contact with the mother (Pederson, Gleason, Moran, & Bento, 1998; Pederson & Moran, 1996).

STABILITY OF ATTACHMENT CLASSIFICATION   When a child's family environment or life circumstances are reasonably consistent, the security or insecurity of her attachment also seems to remain consistent, even over many years (Hamilton, 1995; Weinfield & Egeland, 2004). However, when a child's circumstances change in some major way, such as when the parents divorce or the family moves, the security of the child's attachment may change as well, either from secure to insecure, or the reverse. For example, in one important study, developmentalists followed one group of middle-class white children from 1 to 21 years of age (Waters, Treboux, Crowell, Merrick, & Albersheim, 1995). Those whose attachment classification changed over this long interval had nearly all experienced some major upheaval, such as the death of a parent, physical or sexual abuse, or a serious illness. Research on the impact of domestic violence on attachment stability yields similar results. Securely attached infants are at risk of becoming insecurely attached preschoolers if the level of domestic violence in their homes increases across the early years of life (Levendosky, Bogat, Huth-Bocks, Rosenblum, & von Eye, 2011).

The fact that the security of a child's attachment can change over time does not refute the notion of attachment as arising from an internal model. Bowlby suggested that, for the first two or three years, the particular pattern of attachment a child shows is in some sense a property of each specific relationship. For example, studies of toddlers' attachments to mothers and fathers show that some infants are securely attached to one parent and insecurely attached to the other (Minzi, 2010). It is the quality of each relationship that determines the security of the child's attachment to that specific adult. If the relationship changes markedly, the security of attachment may change too. But, Bowlby argued, by age 4 or 5, the internal model becomes more a property of the child and more generalized across relationships, and thus more resistant to change. At that point, the child tends to impose the model on new relationships, including relationships with teachers or peers.

ATTACHMENT AND AUTISM SPECTRUM DISORDERS   Influenced by Bowlby's theory of attachment, developmentalists once believed that **autism spectrum disorders (ASDs)**, disorders that impair an individual's ability to understand and engage in the give-and-take of social relationships, result from a disturbance in the attachment process caused by insensitive parenting. However, despite their difficulties with synchrony, most infants with ASDs are securely attached to their caregivers (Rutgers et al., 2004). Moreover, contemporary research suggests that ASDs have neurological origins (American Psychiatric Association, 2013). Consequently, today's developmental

secure attachment

a pattern of attachment in which an infant readily separates from the parent, seeks proximity when stressed, and uses the parent as a safe base for exploration

avoidant attachment

a pattern of attachment in which an infant avoids contact with the parent and shows no preference for the parent over other people

ambivalent attachment

a pattern of attachment in which the infant shows little exploratory behaviour, is greatly upset when separated from the parent, and is not reassured by the parent's return or efforts to comfort him

disorganized/disoriented attachment

a pattern of attachment in which an infant seems confused or apprehensive and shows contradictory behaviour, such as moving toward the parent while looking away from him or her

autism spectrum disorders (ASDs)

disorders that impair an individual's ability to understand and engage in the give-and-take of social relationships

scientists believe that ASDs are caused by a variety of interactive biological and environmental factors rather than a flawed attachment process. (By the way, there is no evidence that vaccines increase a child's risk of developing autism spectrum disorders [Orenstein, Paulson, Brady, Cooper, Seib, 2012].)

Clinicians use a three-category system to describe the severity of an individual's ASD (American Psychiatric Association, 2013). Children with *Level 1 ASD* have very limited or nonexistent language skills, display *stereotypic behaviours* such as hand-flapping and rocking, and have a severely limited range of interests. Most also have intellectual disabilities. Those with *Level 2 ASD* are capable of some degree of verbal communication and have mild degrees of cognitive impairment. However, most have difficulty looking at situations from other people's perspectives and often utter repetitive words or phrases that are inappropriate for the situations in which they occur. As a result, children with Level 2 ASD have a limited capacity for normal conversations and social interactions. Finally, children with *Level 3 ASD* have age-appropriate language and cognitive skills. As a result, most are not diagnosed with the disorder until later in childhood. In preschool or kindergarten, the unusual behaviours of children with Level 3 ASD set them apart from typically developing children. Some become intensely focused on memorizing things that have little meaning to them, such as bus schedules. Others engage in obsessive-compulsive behaviours, such as counting and recounting the number of squares on a tile floor. By school age, their inability to form friendships like those of other children their age is also quite apparent.

Treatments such as intensive behavioural, social skills, and play/interaction-based training can reduce, although not consistently, the impact of ASD symptoms on children's lives and improve cognitive, language, communication, and adaptive skills. Such treatments are most successful when they are implemented during the early years of life, are intensive (>15 hours per week), and address numerous areas of functioning (Weitlauf et al., 2014). Furthermore, training parents to administer such treatments in the home may improve the symptoms of ASD (Bearss, Johnson, Handen, Smith, & Scahill, 2013).

Caregiver Characteristics and Attachment

Learning Objective 6.6

Describe what variables might affect a parent's ability to establish an attachment relationship with an infant.

Researchers have found that several characteristics of caregivers influence the attachment process. These characteristics include the caregivers' emotional responses to the infant, their marital status, and their mental health.

EMOTIONAL RESPONSIVENESS   Studies of parent–child interactions suggest that one crucial ingredient for secure attachment is *emotional availability* on the part of the primary caregiver (Biringen, 2000). An emotionally available caregiver is one who is able and willing to form an emotional attachment to the infant. For example, economically or emotionally distressed parents may be so distracted by their own problems that they can't invest emotion in the parent–infant relationship (Cassibba, van IJzendoorn, & Coppola, 2012). Such parents may be able to meet the baby's physical needs but unable to respond emotionally.

Contingent responsiveness is another key ingredient of secure attachment (Blehar, Lieberman, & Ainsworth, 1977; Pederson & Moran, 1995; Pederson et al., 1990). Parents who demonstrate **contingent responsiveness** are sensitive to the child's cues and respond appropriately. They smile when the baby smiles, talk to the baby when he vocalizes, pick him up when he cries, and so on (Ainsworth & Marvin, 1995). Infants of parents who display contingent responsiveness in the early months after birth are more likely to be securely attached at 12 months (George et al., 2010). They are also less likely to exhibit behaviour problems and emotional difficulties later in childhood (Marwick et al., 2013; Nuttall, Valentino, & Borkowski, 2012).

A low level of parental responsiveness thus appears to be an ingredient in any type of insecure attachment. However, each of the several subvarieties of insecure

contingent responsiveness

being sensitive to the child's verbal and nonverbal cues and responding appropriately

attachment is affected by additional distinct factors. For example, if the mother rejects the infant or regularly withdraws from contact with her, the baby is more likely to show an avoidant pattern of attachment, although the pattern also seems to occur when the mother is overly intrusive or overly stimulating toward the infant (Isabella, 1995). An ambivalent pattern is more common when the primary caregiver is inconsistently or unreliably available to the child. A disorganized/disoriented pattern seems especially likely when the child has been abused and in families in which either parent had some unresolved trauma in his or her own childhood, such as abuse or a parent's early death (Cassidy & Berlin, 1994; Main & Hesse, 1990).

MARITAL STATUS   Researchers have found that infants whose parents are married are more likely to be securely attached than babies whose parents are either cohabiting or single (e.g., Rosenkrantz, Aronson, & Huston, 2004). However, the effects of marital status may be due to other characteristics of parents who choose to marry, cohabit, or remain single. Married parents typically have more education and are less likely to be poor than parents in the other groups.

Marital conflict poses risks for the development of attachment. Researchers have found that 6-month-olds who are exposed to parental arguments, especially those in which parents are verbally aggressive toward each other, are more likely to display signs of emotional withdrawal than babies who are not so exposed (Crockenberg, Leerkes, & Lekka, 2007). Emotional withdrawal on the part of the infant interferes with synchrony, thereby lessening the chances that he will develop a secure attachment to his primary caregiver.

MENTAL HEALTH   Mental illness, especially depression, is another caregiver characteristic that appears to be related to attachment quality (Murray et al., 1999; Teti, Gelfand, Messinger, & Isabella, 1995). Research suggests that depression diminishes a mother's capacity to interpret and respond to important infant signals such as crying (Quitmann, Krison, Romer, & Ramsauer, 2012). Thus, infants of mothers who have depression are at increased risk of developing insecure attachments as well as later emotional problems (Goodman & Brand, 2009; Quitmann et al., 2012). They are also at higher risk of developing mental illnesses themselves in adulthood (Maki et al., 2004).

Of course, many depressed mothers are just as sensitive and responsive to their babies' needs as mothers who do not suffer from depression. And, as you might expect, infants whose depressed mothers exhibit sensitive parenting behaviours are less likely to display long-term negative effects than babies of less sensitive depressed mothers (Quitmann et al., 2012). In other words, when depressed mothers exhibit the same kinds of parenting behaviours as most nondepressed mothers, their emotional status doesn't appear to have negative effects on their babies' development.

Studies involving mothers with panic disorder have shown that these mothers, like mothers with depression, exhibit behaviours that may interfere with synchrony (Warren et al., 2003).

Long-Term Consequences of Attachment Quality

Learning Objective 6.7

Summarize the research on the long-term consequences of attachment quality.

As we noted earlier, attachment theory proposes that early emotional relationships shape later ones. Thus, researchers have examined the links between Ainsworth's classification system and a wide range of other behaviours in infants, children, adolescents, and adults. Dozens of studies show that children rated as securely attached to their mothers in infancy are later more sociable, more positive in their behaviour toward friends and siblings, less clingy and dependent on teachers, less aggressive and disruptive, more empathetic, and more emotionally mature in their interactions in school and other settings outside the home (Brumariu & Kerns, 2010; Shaver & Mikulincer, 2012).

Adolescents who were rated as securely attached in infancy or who are classed as secure on the basis of interviews in adolescence are also more socially skilled, have more intimate friendships, are more likely to be rated as leaders, and have higher self-esteem and better grades (Kobak, Zajac, & Smith, 2009; Woodhouse, Ramos-Marcuse, Ehrlich, Warner, & Cassidy, 2010). Those with insecure attachments—particularly those with avoidant attachments—not only have less positive and supportive friendships in adolescence, but also are more likely to become sexually active early and to practise riskier sex (Carlson, Sroufe, Egeland, 2004).

Quality of attachment in infancy also predicts sociability and relationship quality in adulthood (Fraley, Roisman, Booth-LaForce, Owen, & Holland, 2013; Thompson, 2008). Developmentalists have also found that an adult's internal model of attachment affects his or her parenting behaviours (Steele, Hodges, Kaniuk, Hillman, & Henderson, 2003). For example, mothers who are themselves securely attached are more responsive and sensitive in their behaviour toward their infants or young children (Hammond, Landry, Swank, & Smith, 2000). In fact, researchers have found marked consistency across three generations of Canadian grandmothers, young mothers, and infants (Benoit & Parker, 1994). Attachment history affects parental attitudes as well. Some studies have shown that parents with a history of insecure attachment are more likely to view their infants negatively (Pesonen, Raikkonnen, Strandberg, Kelitikangas-Jarvinen, & Jarvenpaa, 2004). Such parents may also lack confidence in their ability to perform effectively in the parenting role (Huth-Bocks, Levendosky, Bogat, & von Eye, 2004).

Examinations of the long-term consequences of quality of attachment suggest that both psychoanalysts and ethologists are correct in their assumption that the attachment relationship becomes the foundation for future social relationships. Certainly, it appears to be critical to the relationship most similar to it—the relationship an individual ultimately develops with her or his own child.

Test Yourself before going on

1. Fill in the table below with information about the four phases of attachment proposed by Bowlby.

Phase	Name of Phase	Age	Attachment Behaviours
1			
2			
3			
4			

2. Classify each separation/reunion behaviour pattern below according to Ainsworth's category of attachment that it represents.

_____ (a) upset at separation, but not comforted by mother's return

_____ (b) easily separates and greets mother positively upon return

_____ (c) not upset at separation; avoids mother at reunion

_____ (d) inconsistent pattern of behaviour at separation and reunion

Critical Thinking

3. Look back at the discussion of synchrony at the beginning of this section. How do you think it is manifested in adult relationships, and in what way do you think synchrony, or the lack thereof, influences those relationships?

Personality, Temperament, and Self-Concept

personality
a pattern of responding to people and objects in the environment

temperament
inborn predispositions, such as activity level, that form the foundations of personality

Psychologists typically use the word **personality** to describe patterns in the way children and adults relate to the people and objects in the world around them. Individual differences in personality appear to develop throughout childhood and adolescence, based on a basic set of behavioural and emotional predispositions present at birth (McCrae & Costa, 2013). These predispositions are usually referred to as **temperament** (Rothbart, 2012).

Dimensions of Temperament

Psychologists who study infant temperament have yet to agree on a basic set of temperament dimensions. One influential early theory, proposed by Alexander Thomas (1913–2003) and his wife Stella Chess (1914–2007), the research team who authored one of the best-known longitudinal studies in developmental science, the New York Longitudinal Study, proposed that three temperament classifications apply to about 75% of infants (1977). The remaining 25% of infants exhibit combinations of two or three of the main types of temperament.

- **Easy children (40% of infants).** These children approach new events positively, display predictable sleeping and eating cycles, are generally happy, and adjust easily to change.

- **Difficult children (10% of infants).** Patterns that include irregular sleeping and eating cycles, emotional negativity and irritability, and resistance to change characterize children in this category.

- **Slow-to-warm-up children (15% of infants).** Children in this group display few intense reactions, either positive or negative, and appear nonresponsive to unfamiliar people.

Other researchers have examined temperament from a trait perspective rather than a categorical perspective. These developmentalists view an individual infant's temperament as a function of how much or how little of various characteristics she possesses. For example, an infant in whom a high level of physical activity was combined with emotional irritability would have a different temperamental profile than an infant in whom high activity was combined with a more easygoing nature.

Although temperament researchers have not reached a clear agreement on the key dimensions of temperament (Thompson, Winer, & Goodvin, 2011), over the past decade or so, a consensus has emerged that is reflected in the writings of leading researchers in the field (Caspi & Shiner, 2006; Kagan & Herschkowitz, 2005; Rothbart, 2012). Many theorists are now emphasizing the following five key dimensions of temperament:

- **Activity level.** A tendency to move often and vigorously, rather than to remain passive or immobile.

- **Approach/positive emotionality/sociability.** A tendency to move toward rather than away from new people, situations, or objects, usually accompanied by positive emotion.

- **Inhibition and anxiety.** The flip side of approach is a tendency to respond with fear or to withdraw from new people, situations, or objects.

- **Negative emotionality/irritability/anger.** A tendency to respond with anger, fussiness, loudness, or irritability; a low threshold of frustration. This dimension appears to be what Thomas and Chess are tapping with their concept of the "difficult" child.

- **Effortful control/task persistence.** An ability to stay focused, to manage attention and effort.

Origins and Stability of Temperament

Because temperamental differences appear so early in life, even during the prenatal period, it may seem that genes are entirely responsible for them. However, research suggests that both nature and nurture contribute to individual differences in temperament.

HEREDITY   Studies of twins in many countries show that identical twins are more alike in their temperament than are fraternal twins (Lemery-Chalfant, Kao, Swann, Goldsmith, 2013; Stilberg et al., 2005). For example, one group of researchers studied 100 pairs of identical twins and 100 pairs of fraternal twins at both 14 and 20 months. At

Learning Objective 6.8

Summarize the dimensions of temperament.

Learning Objective 6.9

Describe the roles of heredity, neurological processes, and environment in the formation of temperament.

each age, the children's temperaments were rated by their mothers, and each child's level of behavioural inhibition was measured by observing how the child reacted to strange toys and a strange adult in a special laboratory playroom. Did the child approach the novel toys quickly and eagerly or hang back or seem fearful? Did the child approach the strange adult or remain close to the mother? The correlations between temperament scores on all four of these dimensions were consistently higher for identical than for fraternal twins, indicating a strong genetic effect (Emde et al., 1992; Plomin et al., 1993).

Critical Thinking

How would you describe your own temperament as a child? Is your adult personality similar to the temperament you displayed in childhood?

NEUROLOGICAL PROCESSES   Many temperament theorists take the heredity argument a step further and trace the basic differences in behaviour to variations in underlying physiological patterns (Caspi & Shiner, 2006). For example, studies examining the genes that control the functions of two important neurotransmitters, *dopamine* and *serotonin*, support this hypothesis (Davies, Cicchetti, Hentges, & Sturge-Apple, 2013). These neurotransmitters regulate the brain's responses to new information and unusual situations—precisely the kinds of stimuli that appear to overstimulate shy children in most studies.

Another important neurological variable that has been found to be associated with shyness is *frontal lobe asymmetry* (LoBue, Coan, Thrasher, & DeLoache, 2011). In most people, the left and right hemispheres of the frontal lobes respond similarly to new stimuli; in other words, they exhibit *symmetry*. In shy infants, however, the two hemispheres respond differently—that is, *asymmetrically*—to such stimuli. Specifically, these children exhibit higher levels of arousal in the right hemisphere than in the left (Fox, Henderson, Rubin, Calkins, & Schmidt, 2001; Henderson, Marshall, Fox, & Rubin, 2004). Such findings make it tempting to conclude that temperamental differences are based in neurological processes. Research, however, suggests that it is difficult to say whether neurological differences are a cause or an effect of temperament. Developmentalists have found that shy infants whose temperaments change over the first four years of life—that is, those who become more outgoing—also become less likely to exhibit the asymmetrical pattern of arousal (Fox et al., 2001).

ENVIRONMENT   Critics of neurological studies point out that it is impossible to know whether such findings are causes or effects (Johnson, 2003). They argue that behaviour shapes the brain. Thus, shy children may exhibit different neurological patterns than outgoing children because their exhibition of shy behaviour contributes to the neural networks that developmental processes in the brain, such as pruning, allow to develop and those that are shut down due to lack of use.

Consistent with these critics' claims, researchers have found that temperament–environment interactions tend to strengthen built-in qualities. For one thing, people of all ages choose their experiences, a process Sandra Scarr refers to as **niche-picking** (Scarr & McCartney, 1983). Our choices reflect our temperaments. For example, highly sociable children seek out contact with others; children low on the activity dimension are more likely to choose sedentary activities, such as puzzles or board games, than baseball.

niche-picking

the process of selecting experiences on the basis of temperament

Parents may also be able to either increase or decrease the effects of an infant's inborn temperamental tendencies. In one longitudinal study, researchers recorded play sessions in which Chinese parents interacted with their 4-year-old children (Hou, Chen, & Chen, 2005). When the children were 7 years old, the researchers found that parent behaviour at age 4 predicted behavioural inhibition (shyness) at age 7. Specifically, the more controlling parents were during the play sessions, the more likely their children were to be rated as more behaviourally inhibited at age 7 than they had been at age 4. Such findings suggest that, perhaps contrary to what you might expect, parents who accept an inhibited child's temperament may contribute more to the child's ability to overcome shyness later in life than parents who try to force a child to be more outgoing. Some experts suggest that parental influences may be greatest for children who are at the extremes of a given temperamental continuum. That is, children who are extremely inhibited may be more subject to parental influence than those who are moderately so (Buss & Plomin, 1984).

Developmentalists argue that the **goodness of fit** between children's temperaments and their environments influences how inborn temperamental characteristics are manifested later in life (Thomas & Chess, 1977). For example, if the parents and caregivers of an irritable baby are good at tolerating his irritability and persist in establishing a synchronous relationship with him, then his irritability doesn't lead to the development of an insecure attachment or inhibit social adjustment (Pluess & Belsky, 2010).

LONG-TERM STABILITY   There is convincing evidence that some aspects of temperament are stable across infancy and childhood, through to adulthood (Neppl et al., 2010; Thompson et al., 2011). This may be reassuring news for parents who have toddlers who display temperaments such as *positive affectivity* (positive social responses and emotional expression) and *disinhibition* (assertiveness, activity, low conformity, and general reactivity), which have been shown to predict extroversion in adolescence and both well-being and career success in adulthood (Blatný, Millová, Jelínek, & Osecká, 2015). But for parents with toddlers who display more difficult temperaments, it can be a different story. For example, problems with peers, a behaviour pattern that is moderately stable across infancy and into childhood, is related to temperament traits such as *negative emotionality* (extreme emotional distress, especially when frustrated) and *low sociability* (disinterest in initiating interactions with peers) (Hasenfratz, Benish-Weisman, Steinberg, & Knafo-Noam, 2015). Researchers have also found considerable consistency in *inhibition* at various ages—children who had shown high levels of crying and motor activity in response to a novel situation when they were 4 months old were still classified as highly inhibited at 8 years of age (Kagan, Snidman, & Arcus, 1993). Subsequent studies showed that this trend continued into the children's teen and early adulthood years (Kagan & Herschkowitz, 2005).

Self-Concept

During the same months when a baby is creating an internal model of attachment and expressing her own unique temperament, she is also developing an internal model of self. Freud suggested that the infant needed to develop a sense of separateness from her mother before she could form a sense of self. Piaget emphasized that the infant's understanding of the basic concept of object permanence was a necessary precursor for the child's attaining self-permanence. Both of these aspects of early self-development reappear in current descriptions of the emergence of the sense of self (Lewis, 1990, 1991).

Canadian researchers have demonstrated that an infant's capacity to differentiate objects emerges well before object permanence is achieved. For instance, an infant can begin to discriminate between objects and people by 2 months of age (Legerstee, Pomerleau, Malcuit, & Feider, 1987). An infant can also differentiate between images of herself, other infants, and dolls between 5 and 8 months of age (Legerstee, Anderson, & Schaffer, 1998).

THE SUBJECTIVE SELF   The child's first task is to figure out that he is separate from others and that this separate self endures over time and space. Developmentalists call this aspect of the self-concept the **subjective self**, or sometimes the *existential self*, because the key awareness seems to be "I exist." The roots of this understanding

goodness of fit

the degree to which an infant's temperament is adaptable to his environment, and vice versa

subjective self

an infant's awareness that he is a separate person who endures through time and space and can act on the environment

Learning Objective 6.10

Describe how the subjective self, the objective self, and the emotional self develop during the first two years.

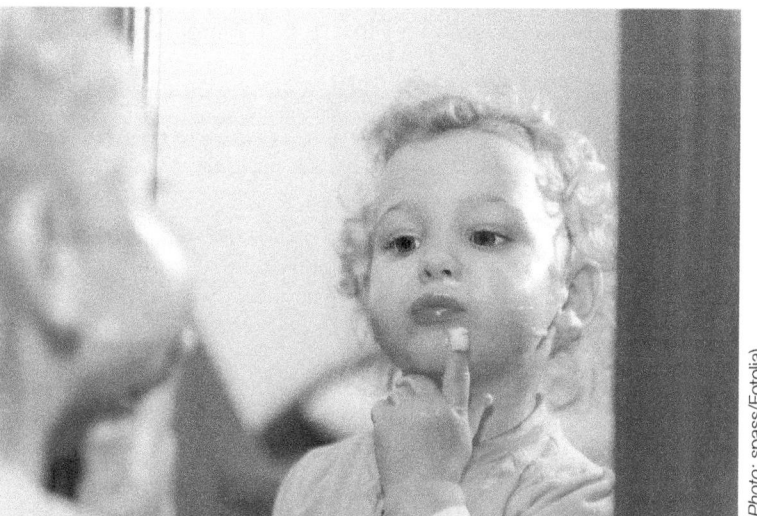
(Photo: spass/Fotolia)

Research that has examined babies' ability to recognize themselves suggests that self-awareness develops in the middle of the second year.

lie in the myriad everyday interactions the baby has with the objects and people in his world that lead him to understand during the first two to three months of life that he can have effects on things (Thompson et al., 2011). For example, when the child touches a mobile, it moves; when he cries, someone responds. Predictably, the *social smile*, a facial expression that is directed at another person in order to elicit a response, appears about this time, although the frequency and duration of social smiles vary greatly from one baby to another (Levine, 2011; Washburn, 1929). Through this process, the baby separates self from everything else and a sense of "I" begins to emerge.

By the time the infant has constructed a fairly complete understanding of object permanence, at about 8 to 12 months, the subjective self has fully emerged. Just as he is figuring out that Mom and Dad continue to exist when they are out of sight, he is figuring out—at least in some preliminary way—that he exists separately and has some permanence.

THE OBJECTIVE SELF The second major task is for the toddler to come to understand that she is also an object in the world (Thompson et al., 2011). Just as a ball has properties—roundness, the ability to roll, a certain feel in the hand—so the "self" also has qualities or properties, such as gender, size, a name, or qualities such as shyness or boldness and coordination or clumsiness. This self-awareness is the hallmark of the second aspect of identity, the **objective self**, sometimes called the **categorical self**, because once the child achieves self-awareness, the process of defining the self involves placing oneself in a whole series of categories.

It has not been easy to determine just when a child has developed the initial self-awareness that delineates the formation of the objective self. The most commonly used procedure involves a mirror. First, the baby is placed in front of a mirror, just to see how she behaves. Most infants between about 9 and 12 months old will look at their own images, make faces, or try to interact with the baby in the mirror in some way. After allowing this free exploration for a time, the experimenter, while pretending to wipe the baby's face with a cloth, puts a spot of rouge on the baby's nose, and then lets the baby look in the mirror again. The crucial test of self-recognition, and thus of awareness of the self, is whether the baby reaches for the spot on her own nose, rather than the nose on the face in the mirror. **Figure 6.1** shows the results of a classic

objective (categorical) self
the toddler's understanding that she is defined by various categories, such as gender, or qualities, such as shyness

---

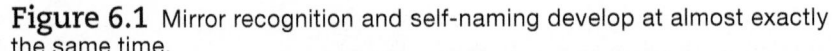

Figure 6.1 Mirror recognition and self-naming develop at almost exactly the same time.

(**SOURCE:** Lewis, M., & Brooks, J. (1978). Self-knowledge and emotional development. In M. Lewis & L.A. Rosenblum (Eds.), *The development of affect* (pp. 205–226). New York, NY: Plenum. With kind permission from Springer Science+Business Media B.V.)

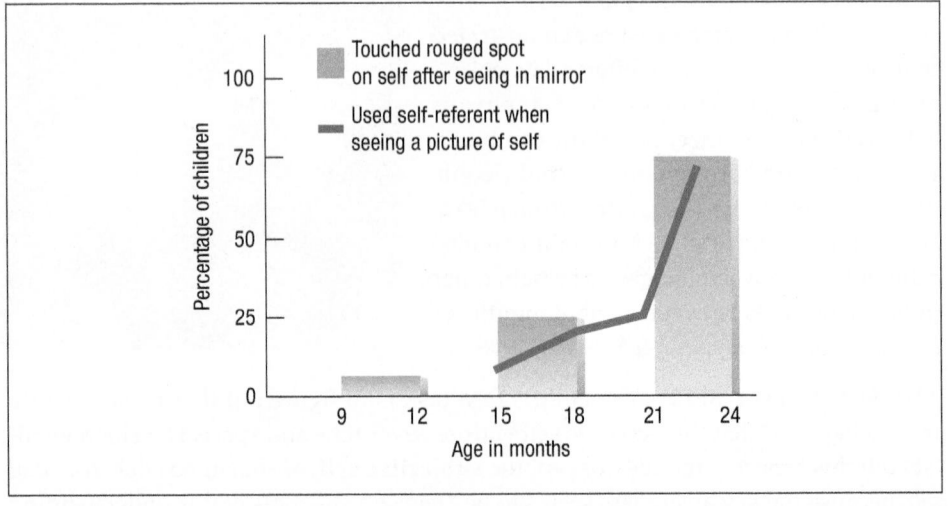

study using this procedure. As you can see, few of the 9- to 12-month-old babies in this study touched their own noses, but three-quarters of the babies aged 21 months showed that level of self-recognition, a result confirmed in a variety of other research studies, including studies in Europe (Asendorpf, Warkentin, & Baudonnière, 1996; Lewis & Brooks, 1978).

As self-awareness develops, toddlers begin to show a newly proprietary attitude ("Mine!") toward toys or other treasured objects. They also begin to refer to themselves by name and, near the end of the second year, to label themselves as boys or girls. In addition, infants recognize that they belong to the "child" category. They also use categorical terms such as "good" and "big" to describe themselves. For example, a girl might say "good girl" when she obeys her parent or "big girl" when she is successful at a task, such as using the toilet (Stipek, Gralinski, & Kopp, 1990).

THE EMOTIONAL SELF   Development of the *emotional self* begins when babies learn to identify changes in emotion expressed in others' faces, at 2 to 3 months of age. Initially, they discriminate emotions best when they receive information on many channels simultaneously—such as when they see a particular facial expression and hear the same emotion expressed in the adult's voice (Walker-Andrews, 1997). Moreover, in these early weeks, infants are much better at discerning the emotional expressions of a familiar face than those of an unfamiliar face (Kahana-Kalman & Walker-Andrews, 2001). By 5 to 7 months, babies begin to "read" one channel at a time, responding to facial expression alone or vocal expression alone, even when the emotions are displayed by a stranger rather than Mom or Dad (Balaban, 1995). They also respond to a much wider variety of emotions than younger infants do and can distinguish among happy, surprised, angry, fearful, interested, and sad faces (Soken & Pick, 1999; Walker-Andrews & Lennon, 1991).

Near the end of the first year, infants' perceptions of others' emotions help them anticipate others' actions and guide their own behaviour (Phillips, Wellman, & Spelke, 2002). For instance, they react to another infant's neutral facial expression by actively trying to elicit an emotional expression from that child (Striano & Rochat, 1999). Just as adults often work at getting a baby to smile at them, babies seem to be following the same sort of script by 8 to 10 months of age.

As the infant's understanding of others' emotions advances, it is matched by parallel progression in expression of emotions. At birth, infants have different facial expressions for interest, pain, and disgust, and an expression that conveys enjoyment develops very quickly. By the time a baby is 2 to 3 months old, adult observers can also distinguish expressions of anger and sadness, with expressions of fear appearing by 6 or 7 months (Izard et al., 1995; Izard & Harris, 1995). At about the same time, infants begin to smile more to human faces than to dolls' faces or other inanimate objects, suggesting that at this early stage babies are already responding to the added social signals available in the human face (Ellsworth, Muir, & Hains, 1993; Legerstee et al., 1987).

Over the next several months, the infant's emotional expressions, and the behaviours that arise from them, become more sophisticated. For example, as you learned earlier in the chapter, infants who have formed an attachment to a caregiver (typically in the last few months of the first year) use the caregiver's emotions to guide their own feelings. Moreover, by this age, babies have learned to calm themselves when their caregivers behave in expected ways (Cole et al., 2004). For example, a baby who is frustrated by hunger will calm down when she sees her caregiver preparing to nurse her or to provide her with some other kind of nourishment. Finally, near the middle of the second

(Photo: Vladimir Costas/Shutterstock)

This baby's emotional reaction is best described as joy or delight rather than pride; her sense of self is not yet well-enough developed that she can feel pride in learning to walk.

year, at about the same time that a child shows self-recognition in the mirror, such self-conscious emotional expressions as embarrassment, pride, and shame emerge (Lewis, Allesandri, & Sullivan, 1992).

AWARENESS OF THE INTENTIONS OF OTHERS Developmentalists have also been interested in when an infant becomes aware that other people have separate intentions or "internal mental states" (D'Entremont, Hains, & Muir, 1997). University of New Brunswick psychologist Barbara D'Entremont began studying this inquiry by observing infants' reactions to an adult's gaze and by studying a child's finger pointing. D'Entremont (2000) contended that, although infants between 3 and 6 months are capable of following the direction of the gaze of another person, following the gaze is more likely a response to an attention-getting cue than true social communication. In another study, finger pointing was used as a measure of an infant's awareness of what another person is paying attention to. It was discovered that 1-year-olds point as a means to heighten "social interaction," whereas 2-year-olds point in an attempt to redirect another person's attention. This implies there is an age-related shift in development whereby, at 2 years, a child has developed the capacity to appreciate that other people are not always paying attention to what she is paying attention to and that she can redirect another person's attention by pointing. This capability to pay attention to both another person's intentions and an object at the same time is a form of **joint attention**, and it is related to later language, intellectual, behavioural, and emotional adjustment (D'Entremont & Hartung, 2003; Moore & D'Entremont, 2001).

Other Canadian theorists, such as Jeremy Carpendale of Simon Fraser University, Timothy Racine of the University of Manitoba, and Ulrich Müller of the University of Victoria (Carpendale & Lewis, 2004; Müller, Carpendale, Bibok, & Racine, 2006; Racine & Carpendale, 2007), proposed that *joint attention* is a good example of the infant's dawning awareness that other people have separate mental states—an understanding that other people have "minds of their own." Joint attention shows that the infant appreciates the import of paying attention to another person's intentions. According to this perspective, an infant begins to construct an understanding of mental states and the social world primarily within the context of her social interactions with others, seemingly from birth onward (Markova & Legerstee, 2008). (We will revisit this idea in the chapter on Physical and Cognitive Development in Early Childhood.) Researchers have linked both joint attention and secure emotional attachment to mother–infant social interactions that occur early in life (D'Entremont & Hartung, 2003).

joint attention

when two people are focusing their attention on an object and each is aware that the other is attending to that same object

Test Yourself before going on

1. Classify each infant behaviour pattern as consistent with (E) easy temperament, (D) difficult temperament, or (S) slow-to-warm-up temperament:
   _____ (a) irregular eating and sleeping
   _____ (b) regular eating and sleeping
   _____ (c) lack of responsiveness to unfamiliar people
   _____ (d) positive responses to new experiences
   _____ (e) irritability
   _____ (f) few intense emotions

2. What behaviours are associated with the development of each component of the self during infancy?

Component of Self	Behaviours
Subjective/existential	
Objective/categorical	
Emotional	

Critical Thinking

3. How do you think your genes and environment interacted to produce the temperamental characteristics and self-concept that you have today?

Effects of Nonparental Care

In virtually every developed country in the world, women have entered the workforce in great numbers over the past several decades. In Canada, the change has been particularly rapid and massive. In 1967, only 17% of Canadian mothers with preschool children were in the labour force; by 2007, roughly 70% of such women were working outside the home (HRDC, 2003; Roy, 2006; Statistics Canada, 2009). As you can see in **Figure 6.2**, employment rates have been increasing for both lone mothers and, even more dramatically, for partnered mothers with children under 3 years of age.

Nearly 70% of Canadian children reside in households where both parents are wage earners, most of whom work full time, and this has led to major changes in child-care services (Uppal, 2015). In 2000, changes to the federal *Employment Insurance Act* that extended the duration of benefit payments for parental leave had an immediate effect in the first year; the length of parental leaves and the number of parents staying home from work to care for their infants rose sharply (Marshall, 2003). The good news for infants is that the trend has had a particularly dramatic effect on fathers: By 2007, 55.2% of fathers took time off from work for the birth or the adoption of a child, up from 37.9% in 2001 (Beaupré & Cloutier, 2007). And when changes were made to Quebec's Parental Insurance Plan in 2006 (which includes higher benefits and no waiting period), the proportion of Quebec fathers' participation in paternal leave jumped to the highest levels of anywhere in Canada and North America (Marshall, 2008; Tremblay, 2010).

Figure 6.2 Trends in employed mothers with a child/children younger than 3 years of age with and without an employed husband or common-law partner present.

(**SOURCE:** Adapted from Statistics Canada (2013a). Labour force survey estimates (LFS), by family type and family age composition, unadjusted for seasonality (Year-to-date (averages) (CANSIM Table 282-0210). This does not constitute an endorsement by Statistics Canada of this product.)

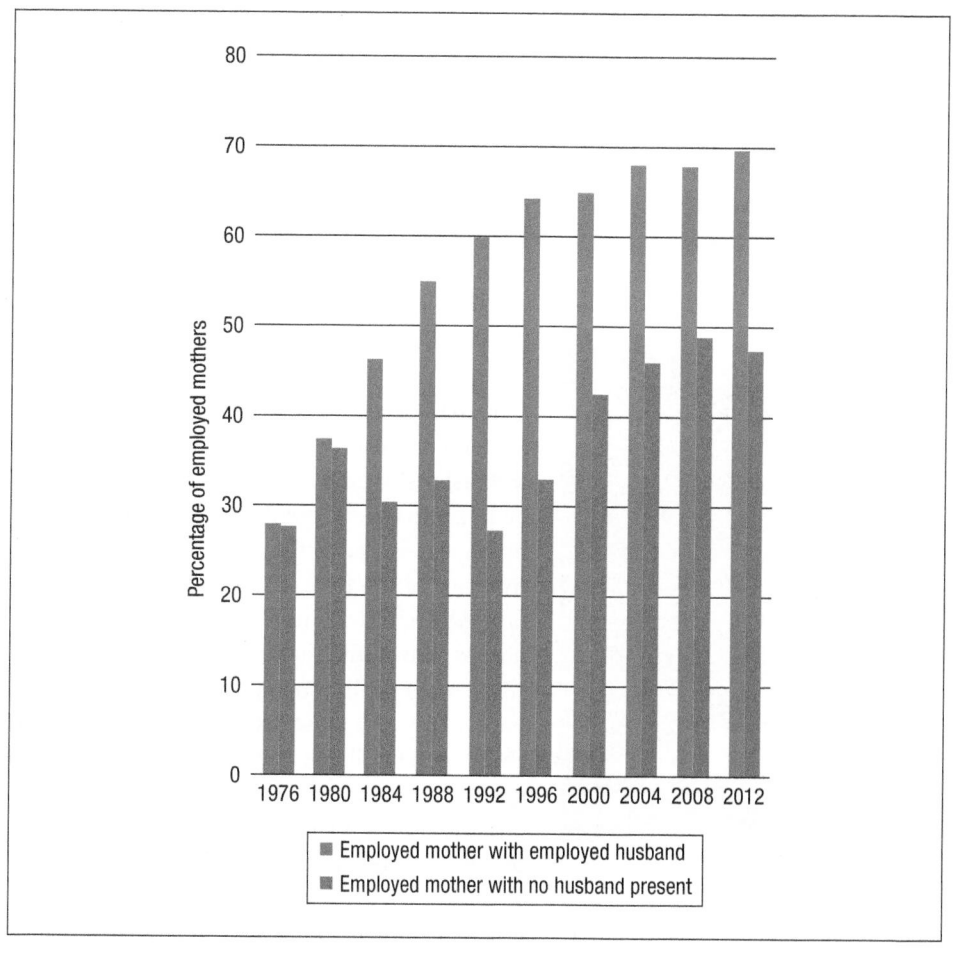

Even with all the additional support, the duration of fathers' leaves has remained far briefer than that of mothers—only about 33% of men took more than a month off before returning to work. In contrast, roughly 50% of mothers remained with the baby for a period of 1 to 2 years (Beaupré & Cloutier, 2007). The evidence suggests a continued preference for Canadian mothers to spend considerable time with their infants and toddlers (Beaujot & Ravanera, 2009).

In addition to contributing to a better work–family balance for both mothers and fathers, better parental leave plans in Canada, and especially in Quebec (Marshall, 2008; Tremblay, 2010), have contributed to one more added benefit. More Canadian mothers have now met the global breastfeeding standard set by public health organizations, including the World Health Organization (Baker & Milligan, 2007). The proportion of mothers who breastfed exclusively for at least six months (28%) increased about 40% after the child-care reforms took effect—an increased health benefit for both infant and mother.

Still, many children have had some form of nonparent care before their first birthday. Moreover, about 54% of Canadian children under age 5 are cared for by someone other than a parent on a regular basis (Bushnik, 2006). The key question for psychologists is as follows: What effect does such nonparental care have on infants and young children?

Difficulties in Studying Nonparental Care

Learning Objective 6.11

Explain why it is difficult to study the effects of nonparental care on development.

It might seem that the effect on infant development of this trend toward nonparental care could easily be determined by comparing babies receiving nonparental care with those cared for by their parents. However, both "nonparental care" and "parental care" are really complex interactions among numerous variables rather than single factors whose effects can be studied independently. Thus, interpretation of research on nonparental care has to take into account a variety of issues.

First, an enormous range of different care arrangements in Canada are all lumped under the general title of "nonparental care." Infants who are cared for by grandparents in their own homes as well as those who are enrolled in daycare centres receive nonparental care. In addition, infants enter these care arrangements at different ages, and they remain in them for varying lengths of time. Some have the same nonparental caregiver over many years; others shift often from one care setting or caregiver to another. Moreover, nonparental care varies widely in quality (Corapci, 2010).

(Photo: Dick Blume/Syracuse Newspapers/The Image works)

The majority of infants in North America now experience at least some nonparental care.

Furthermore, even distinguishing among the various types of care arrangements does not begin to convey the numerous hybrid solutions Canadian parents use to organize alternative care for their children (Cleveland, Forer, Hyatt, Japel, & Krashinsky, 2008). For example, children may be in some type of combined care, such as family daycare some of the time and care by a relative part of the time (in family daycare, people take care of other parents' children in their own homes). Since the majority of researchers have studied only children in daycare centres, it is not known whether these findings will generalize to children in family daycare or to children who are given at-home care by someone other than a parent. Moreover, it's not clear whether the results of these studies apply to non-Western cultures.

Nonparental care of children is now a part of the Canadian way of life. The most common pattern, especially for infants and toddlers, is for a nonrelative to care for the child in a setting outside the child's home (Bushnik, 2006). Nonparental child care is provided about equally (~30% each) either by nonrelatives outside the home or in regulated licensed daycare centres. The remaining 40% of care is either provided outside the home by relatives or within the home by either relatives or nonrelatives. To further complicate matters, families who place their children in nonparental care are different in a whole host of ways from those who care for their children at home. How can researchers be sure that effects attributed to nonparental care are not, instead, the result of these other family differences? Mothers also differ in their attitudes toward the care arrangements they have made (Rose & Elickere, 2010). Some mothers with children in nonparental care would far rather be at home taking care of their children; others are happy to be working. Similarly, some mothers who are at home full time would rather be working, and some are delighted to be at home. Some studies suggest that children show more positive reactions to their situations when the mother is satisfied with her situation, whether she is working or at home. For instance, Canadian researchers have found that when a mother's employment preference and her employment decision agree, she is less depressed and provides her children with more stable care (McKim, Cramer, Stuart, & O'Conner, 1999).

Most of the research on nonparental versus parental care has not taken these complexities into account. Researchers have frequently compared children "in daycare" with those "reared at home" and assumed that any differences between the two groups were attributable to the daycare experience. Thus, clear answers to even the most basic questions about the impact of nonparental care on children's development are still not available. Nonetheless, because the issue is so critical, you need to be aware of what is and is not yet known.

Effects on Cognitive Development, Peer Relations, and Attachment

A good deal of evidence indicates that high-quality, cognitively **enriched daycare** has beneficial effects on many children's overall cognitive and language development (Owen, 2011). This effect is particularly strong for children from socioeconomically disadvantaged families, who show significant and lasting gains in IQ and later school performance after attending enriched daycare throughout infancy and early childhood (Belsky et al., 2007; Burger, 2010; Laurin et al., 2015; Pungello et al., 2010). Moreover, most children, regardless of their social backgrounds, show some cognitive and language benefit when they are in high-quality daycare (Vandell, Belsky, Burchinal, Steinberg, & Vandergrift, 2010) (for a list of characteristics of "high-quality" daycare, see **Development in the Real World**).

According to researchers, the impact of daycare on children's personalities is not entirely rosy. Recent Canadian and American studies link the number of hours spent in daycare with later behaviour problems at school age (Baker, Gruber, & Milligan, 2008; Belsky, 2011; Belsky et al., 2007). However, the association is not a simple one—subsequent findings suggest that the number of hours spent in daycare is more strongly related to *externalizing behaviour* (e.g., heightened aggression with peers and lower compliance with teachers and parents) when children were in low-quality daycare and spent proportionally more time with large groups of peers (McCartney et al, 2010). Of course, a child's level of aggressiveness in elementary school is influenced by a wide variety of things, including temperament and the effectiveness of the parents' disciplinary techniques, but daycare's implication in this equation certainly sounds a cautionary note (Pluess & Belsky, 2010).

Lastly, can an infant or toddler develop secure attachments to her mother and father if she is repeatedly separated from them? This question is still up for debate. Until the mid-1980s, most psychologists believed that infant daycare had no negative effect on attachment. But then developmental psychologist Jay Belsky (1985) sounded an alarm. After decades of research, he concluded that daycare and attachment are

Learning Objective 6.12
Describe the impact of nonparental care on cognitive and social development.

enriched daycare
daycare that provides structured programming to build skills, such as literacy, numeracy, social, art, and physical skills

Development in the Real World

Choosing a Daycare Centre

You may be wondering what criteria a parent can use to identify a high-quality daycare setting. Of course, it's important to realize that the "fit" between an infant and her daycare setting is what really matters. Some babies do well no matter where they are cared for or by whom. Others, perhaps those with more difficult temperaments, seem to have problems adjusting to even the best of settings. Consequently, parents can't really judge the quality of a given setting until their babies have spent some time in it. Nevertheless, a few general characteristics are common to high-quality daycare settings.

Canadian child-care experts suggest that the following characteristics should be considered for both centre- and home-based daycare:

- low child-to-staff ratios
- warm, friendly, patient, capable caregivers who are trained in child development, first aid, and CPR
- stable, committed, experienced caregivers (low turnover rate) who respond to the child's individual needs
- a variety of enjoyable activities that support healthy development (i.e., emotional, physical, motor, social, moral, linguistic, and cognitive development)
- daily routines that are predictable but flexible
- a relaxed, caring, and stimulating environment that is safe, clean, and tidy
- written program policies and plans
- a variety of toys, equipment, and learning materials at the child's level
- space for active and quiet activities, indoor and outdoor play, and rest
- the promotion of good hygiene to prevent the spread of bacteria and adherence to policies for sick children
- nutritious meals and snacks
- cultural sensitivity
- regular communication between parent and caregiver
- compatible child-rearing philosophy and goals (with those of the parents)
- mutual respect and trust
- access to community resources and supports

(**SOURCES:** Centre of Excellence for Early Childhood Development [CEECD], 2009a; CEECD, 2009b; Cleveland et al, 2008; Co-ordinated Access for Child Care, 2009; Ahnert & Lamb, 2011.)

connected, although in a complex way. For example, he participated in an American study that revealed that, when coupled with insensitive mothering, insecure attachment was amplified by any one of three conditions: averaging more than 10 hours per week in any type of care, irrespective of quality; multiple child-care arrangements; or exposure to low-quality daycare (NICHD Early Child Care Research Network, 2005). However, this result was found to be at odds with other national studies—that is, one in Israel (Sagi, Koren-Karie, Gini, Ziv, & Joels, 2002) and another in Australia (Harrison & Ungerer, 2002). Belsky (2009) concluded that there are likely no inevitable effects of daycare on attachment and that the quality of attachment seems dependent on the larger familial, community, societal, and cultural context in which child care occurs.

Interpreting Research on Nonparental Care

Learning Objective 6.13

Identify what variables should be taken into account when interpreting research on nonparental care.

What is it about nonparental care that may predispose infants to become aggressive, disobedient kindergartners? Studies of infants' psychological responses to nonparental care may hold a clue. Researchers have found that levels of the stress hormone *cortisol* increase from morning to afternoon in infants who are enrolled in centre-based care, especially in children under the age of 3 years (Berry et al., 2014; Gunnar, Kryzer, Van Ryzin, & Phillips, 2010; Sumner, Bernard, & Dozier, 2010). By contrast, cortisol levels decrease over the course of the day in home-reared infants. Interestingly, cortisol levels of home-reared and centre-care infants are identical on weekends and holidays. Thus, some developmentalists argue that the higher levels of cortisol experienced by centre-care infants affect their rapidly developing brains in ways that lead to problem behaviours. Research showing associations between individual differences in cortisol responses and problem behaviours in infancy and early childhood supports this view (Bagner, Sheinkopf, Vohr, & Lester, 2010). However, studies also suggest that stress hormones have both positive and negative effects on the young brain (Gunnar et al., 2010; Lyons, Parker, & Schatzberg, 2010). Thus, although research has established that nonparental care increases cortisol levels in infants and young children, developmentalists do not yet have a definitive answer as to how this association affects the developing brain.

Some developmentalists argue that nonparental care arrangements probably vary in the degree to which they induce stress in infants and young children. In other words, they say, quality of care may be just as important as quantity of care (Maccoby & Lewis, 2003; Vandell et al., 2010). For example, some researchers have found that, when infants are cared for in high-quality centres, the amount of time they spend in such care is unrelated to social behaviour (Love et al., 2003). Thus, developmentalists urge parents, especially those who must leave their infants in centre-based care for extended periods of time, to make every effort to ensure that the arrangement they choose has the characteristics discussed in **Development in the Real World**.

Another point to keep in mind is that individual and gender differences have been found to interact with nonparental care. For example, infants who are behaviourally inhibited, in Kagan's terms, may be more sensitive to the stresses associated with centre-based care but may also benefit more from increased opportunities to interact with other children (Bohlin & Hagekull, 2009). Moreover, boys in nonparental care are more likely than girls in similar care settings to be insecurely attached to their caregivers (Crockenberg, 2003). For these reasons, more research that takes both temperament and gender into account is needed before we can say for certain that nonparental care has uniformly negative effects on children's social development (Pluess & Belsky, 2009).

Finally, it is important to understand that, on average, the differences between children in nonparental care and their home-reared peers, both positive and negative, are not large (NICHD Early Child Care Research Network, 2006). Moreover, studies that have attempted to examine all the complex variables associated with parental and nonparental care have shown that parenting quality variables (e.g., warmth, affection, acceptance, and sensitivity) are more important than the type of daycare arrangements a family chooses (Adi-Japha & Klein, 2009; Belsky et al, 2007; Lugo-Gil & Tamis-LeMonda, 2008). The confusion inherent in the mixed findings on nonparental care serves to underline the importance of the quality of child care. We can draw the general conclusion that high-quality care is generally linked with positive or neutral outcomes, while inconsistent or poor-quality care can be actively detrimental to children. Canadian researchers are now turning their focus on the value of integrating the child care and formal education for young children (McMillan, 2010). For instance, in an Ontario program called *Full-Day Learning*, both early childhood educators and kindergarten teachers will see to the care and learning of 4- and 5-year-olds (Government of Ontario, 2010).

Test Yourself before going on

1. Classify each statement as True or False.
   _____ (a) Research results on the effects of nonparental care on cognitive development are mixed.
   _____ (b) Infants whose parents exhibit behaviours associated with insecure attachment, such as poor sensitivity to the child's needs, are more likely to be negatively affected by nonparental care.
   _____ (c) The levels of the stress hormone cortisol decrease from morning to afternoon in infants who are enrolled in centre-based care.
   _____ (d) Family variables are more important than the type of daycare arrangements a family chooses.

Summary

Theories of Social and Personality Development

6.1 Describe how Freud's and Erikson's views of personality development in the first two years differ.

- Freud suggested that individual differences in personality originated in the nursing and weaning practices of infants' mothers. Erikson emphasized the roles of both mothers and fathers, as well as other adults in the infant's environment, in providing for all the infant's needs, thereby instilling a sense of trust concerning the social world.

6.2 Describe the main ideas of attachment theory from the ethological perspective.

- Ethologists hypothesize that early emotional bonds are the foundation of later personality and social development. They further suggest that the first two years of life are a sensitive, or critical, period for the development of attachment.

Attachment

6.3 Describe how synchrony affects parent–infant relations.

- For parents to form a strong attachment relationship with an infant, what is most crucial is the development of synchrony, a set of mutually reinforcing and interlocking behaviours that characterize most interactions between parent and infant. Fathers as well as mothers form strong bonds with their infants, but fathers show more physically playful behaviours with their children than do mothers.

6.4 Identify the four phases of attachment and the behaviours associated with them.

- Bowlby proposed that the child's attachment to a caregiver develops in four phases: (1) indiscriminate aiming of attachment behaviours toward anyone within reach, (2) focus on one or more figures, (3) "secure base behaviour" at about 6 months of age, signalling the presence of a clear attachment, and (4) an internal model of attachment that influences current and future close relationships.

6.5 Identify characteristics of the four attachment patterns discovered by Ainsworth.

- Using a procedure called the Strange Situation, Ainsworth identified four patterns of attachment distinguished by infants' responses to separations from and reunions with their mothers. *Securely attached* infants separate easily and greet mothers positively when they return. Infants with *insecure/avoidant* attachments avoid contact with mothers especially at reunion. Infants with *insecure/ambivalent* attachments are upset at separation but do not greet mothers positively at reunion. Infants with *insecure/disorganized* attachment display confused, contradictory patterns such as moving toward the mother while looking elsewhere.

6.6 Describe what variables might affect a parent's ability to establish an attachment relationship with an infant.

- Caregiver characteristics such as marital status can affect infants' attachment quality. Also, infants whose parents have psychiatric illnesses are more likely to form insecure attachments than babies whose parents do not have these disorders.

6.7 Summarize the research on the long-term consequences of attachment quality.

- The security of the initial attachment is reasonably stable; later in childhood, securely attached children appear to be more socially skilful, more curious and persistent in approaching new tasks, and more mature. The internal model of attachment that individuals develop in infancy affects how they parent their own babies.

Personality, Temperament, and Self-Concept

6.8 Summarize the dimensions of temperament.

- Temperament theorists generally agree on the following basic temperamental dimensions: activity level, approach/positive emotionality, inhibition, negative emotionality, and effortful control/task persistence.

6.9 **Describe the roles of heredity, neurological processes, and environment in the formation of temperament.**

- There is strong evidence that temperamental differences have a genetic component and are at least somewhat stable over infancy and childhood. However, temperament is not totally determined by heredity or neurological processes. The "fit" between children's temperaments and their environments may be more important than temperament itself.

6.10 **Describe how the subjective self, the objective self, and the emotional self develop during the first two years.**

- The infant develops a sense of self, including the awareness of a separate self and the understanding of self-permanence (the subjective self); an awareness of oneself as an object in the world (the objective self); and the ability to make use of information about emotions, such as facial expressions (an emotional self). The infant also develops an awareness that other people have separate thoughts and intentions.

Effects of Nonparental Care

6.11 **Explain why it is difficult to study the effects of nonparental care on development.**

- Comparing parental with nonparental care is difficult because there are so many types of nonparental care arrangements. Families who choose nonparental care also differ from families who care for their children at home.

6.12 **Describe the impact of nonparental care on cognitive and social development.**

- When a child receives more intellectual stimulation in nonparental care than he would at home, there are likely to be positive effects on cognitive development. But when the reverse is true, nonparental care may have neutral or negative effects on cognitive development. The impact of daycare on children's social development is unclear. Some studies show a small difference in security of attachment between children in daycare and those reared at home; others suggest that home-care and daycare children do not differ with respect to attachment. Some studies show children who spend more time in daycare to be more aggressive; others show them to be more socially skilful.

6.13 **Identify what variables should be taken into account when interpreting research on nonparental care.**

- Infants' physiological responses to the stresses associated with nonparental care may underlie its association with developmental outcomes. Individual differences and gender may interact with the quality of a care arrangement, the quantity of outside-the-home care a child receives, or both. Average differences between children who receive nonparental care and those who are cared for entirely in their own home are small. High-quality care is generally linked with positive or neutral outcomes, while inconsistent or low-quality care can be actively detrimental to the child.

Chapter 7
Physical and Cognitive Development in Early Childhood

Ariel Skelley/Blend Images/Getty Images

⌄ Learning Objectives

PHYSICAL CHANGES

7.1 Summarize the major milestones of growth and motor development between 2 and 6.

7.2 Highlight the important changes that happen in the brain during these years.

7.3 Highlight the nutritional and health care needs of young children.

7.4 Describe the factors surrounding adverse childhood experiences, and how traumatic events affect children's development.

COGNITIVE CHANGES

7.5 Summarize the characteristics of children's thought during Piaget's preoperational stage.

7.6 Describe how recent research has challenged Piaget's view of this period.

7.7 Describe theory of mind and how it develops.

7.8 Describe how information-processing and sociocultural theorists explain changes in young children's thinking.

CHANGES IN LANGUAGE

7.9 Describe how fast-mapping helps children learn new words.

7.10 Highlight what happens during the grammar explosion.

7.11 Describe what phonological awareness is, and why it is important.

7.12 Describe the similarities and differences in language and numeracy development.

DIFFERENCES IN INTELLIGENCE

7.13 Describe the strengths and weaknesses of IQ tests.

7.14 Identify what kinds of evidence support the nature and nurture explanations for individual differences in IQ.

Watch a group of 2- to 6-year-olds on a playground and you are likely to be amazed by the pure joy they get from moving their bodies. They climb things, throw things, run, leap, and build elaborate forts out of blocks. When a child first masters any one of these skills, the utter delight and pride on the child's face is a wonder to behold. When a child is working hard on some physical skill—trying to string beads or to build a castle out of blocks—she is likely to have a look of intense concentration. And even when children this age are clearly exhausted, they usually refuse to stop playing.

At other times you may see 2-year-old playing near her mom or dad and you'll notice that she glances at her parent regularly, as if checking to make sure the safe base is still there. Her play is dominated by sensory explorations of objects; she seems motivated to touch and manipulate everything in her environment. In contrast to infants, however, most 2-year-olds have added a new dimension to sensorimotor play—the idea that objects have names. Consequently, almost every object manipulation is accompanied by an important question for nearby adults: "Whazit?" (What is it?) A few years later, by about age 4, sophisticated forms of pretending, such as "dress-up," become the preferred modes of play.

Profound changes in the physical and cognitive domains underlie these shifts in play behaviour. In the years from 2 to 6, the period known as early childhood, the child changes from a dependent toddler, able to communicate only in very primitive ways, to a remarkably competent, communicative, social creature, ready to begin school. In this chapter, you will learn about the subtle physical changes and a number of advances in cognitive and language development that happen during early childhood. Furthermore, after reading the chapter, you should have a better understanding of the issues involved in intelligence testing.

Physical Changes

The chapter on Physical, Sensory, and Perceptual Development in Infancy chronicled the many rapid changes taking place in the infant's developing body. The physical changes between ages 2 and 6 in children are less dramatic, yet these changes are foundational for the cognitive and social leaps that lie ahead of them.

Learning Objective 7.1

Summarize the major milestones of growth and motor development between 2 and 6.

Growth and Motor Development

Changes in height and weight happen far more slowly in the preschool years than in infancy. Each year, the child adds about 5 to 8 centimetres in height and 2.7 kilograms in weight. At the same time, the young child makes steady progress in motor development. The changes are not as dramatic as the child's first steps, but they enable the child to acquire skills that markedly increase his independence and exploratory ability.

By age 3, most preschoolers discover the thrill of running at full stride.

(Photo: Sylvia Melissa Scott and Owen Kenneth Sloan)

University of Manitoba developmentalists, using stringent motor-behaviour assessment techniques, have uncovered some intriguing findings about children's activity levels and behavioural self-control. The researchers discovered that children who exhibited higher motor activity levels demonstrated a significantly better ability to control or inhibit their behaviour, allowing for successful task achievement. They suggest that children's extraneous motor activity is an important form of purposeful, exploratory behaviour, especially in children less than 5½ years of age (Campbell, Eaton, & McKeen, 2002). The researchers also found that children's motor activity levels increase linearly with age and tend to peak between 7 and 9 years of age—later than previously thought (Eaton, 1994; Eaton, McKeen, & Campbell, 2001).

Table 7.1 lists the major motor skills that emerge in these preschool years. What is most striking are the impressive gains the child makes in large-muscle skills. By age 5 or 6, children are running, jumping, hopping, galloping, climbing, and skipping. They can ride a tricycle; some can ride a two-wheeled bike. The degree of confidence with which the 5-year-old uses her body for these movements is impressive, particularly in contrast to the somewhat unsteady movements of the 18-month-old.

Fine motor skills also improve in these years, but not to the same level of confidence. Three-year-olds can indeed pick up Cheerios, and 5-year-olds can thread beads on a string. But even at age 5 or 6, children are not highly skilled at such fine motor tasks as cutting accurately with scissors or using a pencil or crayon. When a young child uses a crayon or a pencil, he uses his whole body—his tongue is moving and his whole arm and back are involved in the writing or drawing motion.

These are important facts for teachers of young children to understand. It is the rare kindergartner who is really skilled at such fine motor tasks as writing letters. Younger pre-schoolers, of course, are even less skilled at these tasks. However, a "wait

Table 7.1 Milestones of Motor Development

Age	Gross Motor Skills	Fine Motor Skills
18–24 months	Runs (20 months); walks well (24 months); climbs stairs with both feet on each step; pushes and pulls boxes or wheeled toys; unscrews lid on a jar	Shows clear hand preference; stacks four to six blocks; turns pages one at a time; picks up things without overbalancing
2–3 years	Runs easily; climbs on furniture unaided; hauls and shoves big toys around obstacles	Picks up small objects; throws small ball while standing
3–4	Walks upstairs one foot per step; skips on two feet; walks on tiptoe; pedals and steers tricycle; walks in any direction pulling large toys	Catches large ball between outstretched arms; cuts paper with scissors; holds pencil between thumb and fingers
4–5	Walks up and down stairs one foot per step; stands, runs, and walks on tiptoe	Strikes ball with bat; kicks and catches ball; threads beads on a string; grasps pencil properly
5–6	Skips on alternate feet; walks on a line; slides, swings	Plays ball games well; threads needle and sews large stitches

(**SOURCES:** Connolly & Dalgleish, 1989; The Diagram Group, 1977; Fagard & Jacquet, 1989; Mathew & Cook, 1990; Thomas, 1990.)

Figure 7.1 Examples of drawings in each category of two object forms.

(SOURCE: Toomela, A. (1999). Drawing development: Stages in the representation of a cube and a cylinder. *Child Development*, 70, 1141–1150.)

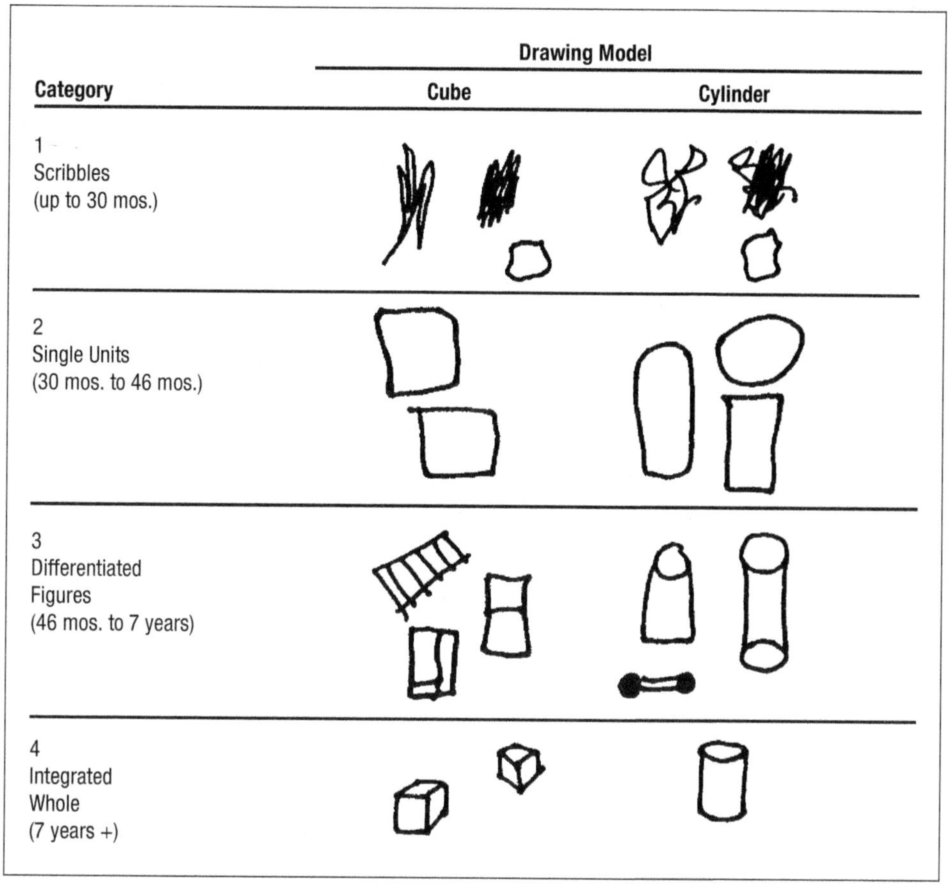

and see" strategy isn't the best approach for helping children learn to write letters and draw simple forms. St. Francis Xavier University psychologist, Tara Callaghan, and colleagues have found that early training, beginning at about age 2½, can accelerate the rate at which young children acquire school-related fine motor skills, such as writing letters (Callaghan & Corbit, 2015; Callaghan, Rochat, & Corbit, 2012).

Training effects are evident in studies of children's drawing as well (Callaghan & Rankin, 2002). Nevertheless, drawing appears to follow the developmental sequence shown in **Figure 7.1**, even when accelerated by training (Toomela, 1999). Moreover, the effectiveness of training seems to depend on how well young children understand the figures that experimenters are attempting to teach them how to draw. That is, a child who has some grasp of what letters are will be more responsive to training in letter-writing (Callaghan & Corbit, 2015). Thus, older preschoolers—those beyond age 3—benefit more from training than younger children. Moreover, learning to write letters appears to help children more fully understand them (Callaghan & Rankin, 2002). Thus, research examining young children's writing demonstrates that, in some cases, physical and cognitive development are interactive processes.

The Brain and Nervous System

Brain growth, synapse formation, and myelinization continue in early childhood, although at a pace slower than in infancy (Stiles & Jernigan, 2010). However, the slower rate of growth should not be taken to mean that brain development is nearly complete. Indeed, a number of important neurological milestones happen between

Learning Objective 7.2

Highlight the important changes that happen in the brain during these years.

Figure 7.2 Brain functions are lateralized, as shown in the figure. Neurologists think that the basic outline of lateralization is genetically determined, whereas the specific timing of the lateralization of each function is determined by an interaction of genes and experiences.

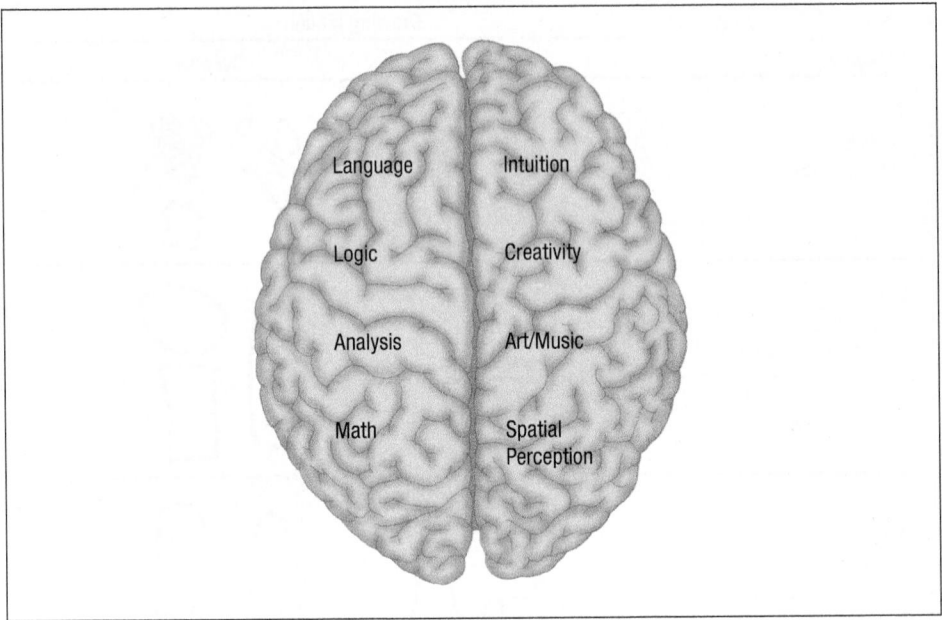

ages 2 and 6. It is likely that these milestones represent the neurological underpinnings of the remarkable advances in thinking and language that occur during this period.

corpus callosum

the structure that connects the right and left hemispheres of the cerebral cortex

lateralization

the process through which brain functions are divided between the two hemispheres of the cerebral cortex

LATERALIZATION The **corpus callosum**, the brain structure through which the left and right sides of the cerebral cortex communicate, grows and matures more during the early childhood years than in any other period of life. The growth of this structure accompanies the functional specialization of the left and right hemispheres of the cerebral cortex. This process is called **lateralization**. **Figure 7.2** shows how brain functions are lateralized in most people.

Neuroscientists suspect that our genes dictate which functions will be lateralized and which will not be. However, experience shapes the pace at which lateralization occurs. For example, in 95% of humans, language functions that enable us to understand the meanings of words and the structure of sentences are carried out in the left hemisphere. Studies of fetal responses to different kinds of sounds (e.g., language and music) show that this pattern is evident even before we are born (de Lacoste, Horvath, & Woodward, 1991). The fact that left-side processing of language appears so early in life suggests that lateralization of these functions is dictated by our genes.

Nevertheless, language functions are not as fully lateralized in fetuses as they are in children and adults. Moreover, research indicates that the degree to which these language functions are relegated to the left side of the brain is linked to individual differences in a number of cognitive functions (Prichard, Propper, & Christman, 2013). For example, preschoolers who display the most advanced language skills in their everyday speech, as well as on standardized tests, show the highest levels of left-side lateralization of these functions (Mills, Coffey-Corina, & Neville, 1994). Of course, we don't know whether children acquire language more rapidly *because* their brains are lateralizing at a faster pace. It seems that the reverse is just as likely to be true—namely, that some children's brains are lateralizing language functions more rapidly because they are learning language faster. But such findings suggest that maturation and experience are both at work in the lateralization process.

THE RETICULAR FORMATION AND THE HIPPOCAMPUS Myelinization of the neurons of the reticular formation, which is the brain structure that regulates attention and concentration, is another important milestone of early childhood brain development. Neurons in other parts of the brain, such as the *hippocampus*, are also myelinated during this period (Tanner, 1990). The **hippocampus** is involved in the transfer of information to long-term memory. Maturation of this brain structure probably accounts for improvements in memory function across the preschool years (Rolls, 2000). Moreover, maturation of the connections between the hippocampus and the cerebral cortex is probably responsible for our inability to remember much about the first three years of life, a phenomenon called *infantile amnesia* (Zola & Squire, 2003). Note that **infantile amnesia** does not involve a complete absence of early memories; thus, some people do have legitimate memories of very early experiences. Typically, though, memories of events that were laid down in the brain prior to age 3 are small in number and fragmentary in character. And, as Piaget's early memory experience suggests, children's early memories are strongly influenced by the verbal recollections of adults that children hear later in their lives, even when those "recollections" turn out to be entirely false.

hippocampus

a brain structure that is essential for the formation of memories

infantile amnesia

the inability of adults and older children to remember more than a few events that took place before they were 3 years of age

HANDEDNESS **Handedness**, the tendency to rely primarily on the right or the left hand, is another neurological milestone that appears very early in life—often before the first birthday—although it doesn't become well established until the preschool years (Stroganova, Posikera, Pushina, & Orekhova, 2003). By examining skeletons, archeologists have determined that the percentages of right- and left-handers were about the same in illiterate ancient populations as modern humans (83% right-handed, 14% left-handed, and 3% ambidextrous) (Steele & Mayes, 1995). These findings suggest that the prevalence of right-handedness is likely to be the result of genetic inheritance (Forrester, Quaresmini, Leavens, Mareschal, & Thomas, 2013). However, the genetic basis of handedness is quite complicated. Several years ago, geneticists identified a dominant gene for right-handedness, which they believe to be so common in the human population that most people receive a copy of it from both parents (Klar, 2003). Moreover, another gene determines the degree to which a right-handed individual is dependent on the dominant hand (Arning et al., 2013). To further complicate the picture, an international team of researchers discovered yet another gene that predisposes children to be left-handed, but only when they receive it from their fathers (Francks et al., 2007).

handedness

a strong preference for using one hand or the other that develops between 3 and 5 years of age

Health Promotion and Wellness

Learning Objective 7.3

Highlight the nutritional and health care needs of young children.

Young children continue to require periodic medical checkups as well as a variety of immunizations. Just as they do with infants, doctors monitor preschoolers' growth and motor development. At the same time, doctors and nurses often serve as parents' first source of help with children who have sensory or developmental disabilities that were not diagnosed in infancy (Levine, 2011).

EATING AND ACTIVITY PATTERNS Because children grow more slowly during the early childhood years, they may seem to eat less than when they were babies. Moreover, food aversions often develop during the preschool years. For example, a child who loved carrots as an infant may refuse to eat them at age 2 or 3. Consequently, conflicts between young children and their parents often focus on eating behaviour (Ramsay, 2013; Wong, 1993).

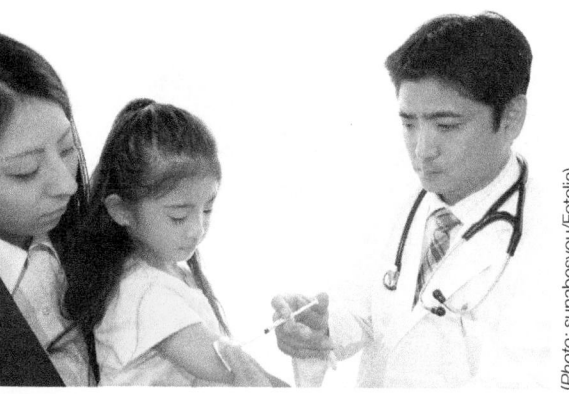

Immunizing young children against a variety of diseases is an important goal of routine health care for this age group.

(Photo: sunabesyou/Fotolia)

Parents should also keep in mind that young children eat only about half as much food as adults, and, unlike adults, many don't consume the majority of their daily calories at regular meals (Wong, 1993). Nutritionists suggest that concerned parents keep a daily record of what their children are actually eating for a week. In most cases, parents will find that children are consuming plenty of food.

In Canada, we have seen an unhealthy rise in weight gain over the last few decades, and roughly 12% of children aged 2 to 5 are now obese (Carroll, Navaneelan, Bryan, & Ogden, 2015). A part of the problem is our increasingly **obesogenic environments**, which foster an overconsumption of high-fat and high-sugar foods (e.g., fast foods and junk-food snacks), inadequate amounts of nutritious foods (e.g., fruits and vegetables), and sedentary lifestyles—even in youngsters. Results from the Québec Longitudinal Study of Child Development (LSCDQ) also found that preschoolers who watched more hours of television than their peers also ate more snacks on a daily basis while watching television (Dubois, Farmer, Girard, & Peterson, 2008). And preschoolers who ate more snacks had higher BMIs than children who never or seldom ate snacks in front of the television.

obesogenic environments
environments in which social influences and context contribute to obesity in individuals or populations

Relatedly, increased hours of television viewing in the early childhood years was found to be strongly associated with poorer explosive leg strength (an indicator of general muscular strength and important for exercise activities and many sports) in Grade 2 and larger waistline measurement in Grade 4—conditions that can carry on into adulthood and are predictive of negative health outcomes (Fitzpatrick, Pagani, & Barnett, 2012). Accordingly, Canadian experts recommend preschoolers be provided with an hour (cumulative) of daily structured physical activities that encourage competence in movement skills, as well as an hour of fun, creative, exploratory, and safe unstructured physical activities (CEECD, 2011). Increasingly fewer Canadian children aged 2–4 (62%) meet the physical activity guidelines and two-thirds exceed the maximum screen-time recommendations (Pujadas Botey, Bayrampour, Carson, Vinturache, & Tough, 2016).

Critical Thinking

Do you know of any young children who fit these facts: Boys are more likely than girls to be injured; more than half of all injuries are likely to happen at home; most injuries occur during the warmer months between April and October; and most injuries happen in the afternoon (Yanchar, Warda, & Fuselli, 2012; Statistics Canada, 1994, 1995)? How would you explain the facts?

Not only is TV viewing associated with obesity and poorer health outcomes, but the messages put forth in the content of what is being watched may also be playing a role in TV-watchers' weight gain. For example, when University of British Columbia researchers analyzed the messages about food and eating portrayed in preschool TV shows, such as *Barney*, *Max & Ruby*, and *The Backyardigans*, they found that references to non-nutritious foods are about as equally common as nutritious foods, but the consumption of snacks is more prevalent and is reinforced more than eating proper meals (Anderson & Anderson, 2010). These researchers, using social cognitive theory, suspect that the prevalence of such eating patterns in children's TV shows may reinforce eating patterns associated with childhood obesity. It's no surprise that Canadian experts now recommend limiting preschoolers' media viewing time to no more than one to two hours a day of quality programming (CEECD, 2011).

Each year, about 0.4% of Canadian children ages 1 to 4 have an unintentional injury that requires hospitalization.

ACCIDENTS   Another concern parents have regarding young children is accidents causing injury and death (Harvey, Towner, Peden, Soori, & Bartolomeos, 2009). Although in any given year ~3 in 1000 children aged 1 to 4 years in Canada have an accident that requires hospitalization, unintentional injuries account for slightly more than one in five of all deaths for children in this age range (PHAC, 2016a). Sadly, an estimated 90% of childhood injuries are preventable (Howard, 2006), and Canadian physicians recommend that caregivers develop ongoing home safety and childproofing measures. These can range, for example, from removing choking hazards from a child's reach, to using child-resistant lids, to lowering household hot water temperature below 50°C, to ensuring that functioning smoke alarms are placed properly in the home (LeBlanc et al., 2006). Urban planners also need to be involved in the design and the construction of safe environments, where, for example, walking and cycling venues can be engineered to reduce injury while promoting healthy activity (Howard, 2010). You can read about other risk factors associated with unintentional injuries in the **Research Report**.

Research Report

Unintentional Injuries in Canadian Preschoolers

Parents shouldn't assume that children can readily recall safety rules. In one study, 4- to 6-year-olds could recite fewer than half of their home safety rules. Nor should parents assume that a child's knowledge of the rules will protect them. Barbara Morrongiello of the University of Guelph found that a child's knowledge of home safety rules was not significantly related to the incidence of injuries. It is more important that parents see their children demonstrate actions that are consistent with the rules. Researchers have found that the children of parents who practised greater levels of protective supervision and children who were more compliant with respect to home safety rules experienced lower rates of injury (Morrongiello, Kane, & Zdzieborski, 2011; Morrongiello, Midgett, & Shields, 2001). Moreover, being within easy reach of the child was the only technique that lowered risk-taking behaviour and resulted in fewer injuries in young children (Morrongiello & House, 2004; Saluja et al., 2004).

Morrongiello and Rennie (1998) examined cognitive factors that may contribute to a higher risk of injury in boys. They found that boys express greater optimism about their ability to perform activities and believe that they are less susceptible to injury than their female peers. This sense of optimism increases with age in both boys and girls. By age 6, boys believe that they will not get hurt and that any injury they may incur will not be severe. Boys attribute injuries to bad luck rather than a dangerous choice of activity. Parents expect that boys are more likely to be injured than girls, yet they are less likely to intervene in their sons' activities with safety precautions. Conversely, parents see girls as more vulnerable than boys and therefore make their daughters more aware of the potential for harm, although their risk of injury is lower than it is for boys. Parents also assume that boys are natural risk takers, which may foster risk-taking behaviour, as boys are allowed to engage in situations that put them at greater risk for injury.

Another aspect of how cognitive factors affect the rates of injury was found in a study that looked at mothers' differing expectations of risk for different clusters of home injuries. Mothers considered burns, cuts, and falls less severe than injuries caused by such accidents as drowning, poisoning, and suffocation/strangulation/choking (Morrongiello & Kiriakou, 2004). Accordingly, mothers in this study were less motivated

to engage in precautionary measures for less severe types of potential injuries. Somewhat ironically, a later study found that even though falls are a leading, yet preventable, cause of hospitalization due to injury, mothers had fewer safety rules for falls than for other types of injuries (Morrongiello, Kane, & Bell, 2011). Although much research has focused on mothers' supervision beliefs and practices, a subsequent study has determined that there were virtually no differences between the supervisory practices of mothers and fathers (Morrongiello, Walpole, & McArthur, 2009).

Morrongiello and Dawber (1999) investigated socialization factors that contribute to higher rates of injury in boys. They discovered that mothers and fathers are similar in their interactions with their children, with both parents treating boys differently than girls. Both parents put more pressure on their sons, beginning as young as age 3, to play independently with less supervision, and they give them more freedom to roam. By contrast, parents will intervene and support their daughters when they are using play equipment, for example. Furthermore, boys receive more encouragement and direct instructions while girls receive more verbal cautions about safety and possible injury. These differences in parental interaction were evident regardless of the fact that their sons and daughters were all equally physically capable of performing various activities.

As children get a little older, their safety practices are influenced by both parental teaching and parental actions (Morrongiello, Corbett, & Bellissimo, 2008). A child's future safety behaviours are best predicted by his parents' actions, which, in turn, have been shown to be modifiable with training. For example, parents who underwent a one-month intervention, the *Supervising for Home Safety* program, that includes a risk/supervision video, followed by discussion and reinforcement of active supervision, improved their supervision practices. When followed up, this positive change was found to have persisted for at least a year (Morrongiello, Sandomierski, Zdzieborski, & McCollam, 2012; Morrongiello, Zdzieborski, Sandomierski, & Munroe, 2013). Lastly, another recent study has shown that young children can show improvement in knowledge and safety behaviour with training. An interactive video game, *The Great Escape*, developed by Thunder Bay, Ontario, firefighters, was shown to significantly improve knowledge and fire safety behaviours in children who played the game (Morrongiello, Schwebel, Bell, Stewart, & Davis, 2012).

Learning Objective 7.4
Describe the factors surrounding adverse childhood experiences, and how traumatic events affect children's development.

adverse childhood experiences (ACEs)

childhood stressors, ranging from day-to-day maltreatment to traumatic events, that increase the risk of wide-ranging, negative health and social consequences over the life course

Adverse Childhood Experiences (ACEs) in Canada

Certain characteristics of both children and their caregivers can have an impact on **adverse childhood experiences (ACEs)**. ACEs have immediate and long-term effects that cross all domains of development. Prevention and protection from harm are important strategies for dealing with childhood adversity.

PATTERNS OF ADVERSITY   A nationwide investigation revealed an annual rate of slightly more than 14 in 1000 substantiated cases of ACEs (i.e., child maltreatment) in Canada (PHAC, 2010a). The most common forms of substantiated cases were *neglect* (34%), which involves a failure to supervise, leading to harm or the risk of harm to a child's safety or development; *exposure to intimate partner violence* (34%), where the child witnessed, overheard, or saw the physical injuries from violence occurring between the caregivers and/or their partners; *physical abuse* (20%), including hitting, shaking, choking, or burning; *emotional maltreatment* (9%), where the child has suffered or is at high risk of suffering from mental, emotional, or developmental problems caused by exposure to family violence, overtly punitive treatment, habitual or extreme verbal abuse, or inadequate affection; and *sexual abuse* (3%), involving a child who has been or is at substantial risk of being sexual molested or sexual exploited. Of all the substantiated cases of child maltreatment, about 18% involved more than one category, with the most prevalent combinations involving a mixture of either neglect, exposure to intimate partner violence, emotional maltreatment, or physical abuse. Biological parents accounted for the largest portion of alleged maltreatment. Mothers (86%), followed by fathers (8%), were implicated most often. A small percentage of cases involved grandparents (2%) or a parent's partner or adoptive parent (1% each). About 1% of alleged maltreatment involved children living with nonrelative caregivers (PHAC, 2010a).

RISK FACTORS   One useful model for explaining ACEs classifies its causes into four broad categories: sociocultural factors, characteristics of the child, characteristics of the abuser, and household stresses (Bittner & Newberger, 1981). The main idea of this model is that episodes of abuse are typically precipitated by everyday interactions between parents and children—for example, when a parent reprimands a young child for spilling a glass of milk. At the time of the episode, several causal factors work together to produce abusive responses in parents. Thus, what differentiates abusive from nonabusive parents, according to this model, is the presence of a number of risk factors that shape how they respond to the ordinary stresses of parenting.

Sociocultural factors include personal or cultural values that regard physical abuse of children as morally acceptable. Parents are more likely to be abusive if they believe that there are few, if any, moral limits on what they can do to their children physically. Sociologists suggest that such beliefs stem from cultural traditions that regard children as property rather than human beings with individual rights (Mooney, Knox, & Schacht, 2010). Moreover, parents who live in communities where others share and act on these beliefs are more likely to be abusive.

Several characteristics of children or parents may set the stage for child maltreatment. For example, children with academic difficulties, mental health and intellectual issues (e.g., depression, anxiety, attention deficit disorders, or developmental delay/ disability), aggressive behaviour, or who have attachment issues are more likely to be abused than others (PHAC, 2010a). Parents who themselves have been victims of abuse, have few social supports, are alcohol or substance abusers, or have mental health issues are at a higher risk to abuse or neglect their children (Christian & Bloom, 2011; PHAC, 2010a). Household stressors include factors linked to living on social assistance/employment insurance, one or more moves in the past year, and

Critical Thinking

How is it that not all children raised in privileged environments do well, and conversely, not all children who experience adversity do poorly, later in life?

Research Report

Traumatic Events and Neurobiological and Functional Changes in the Brain

Bruce Perry, senior consultant to the Alberta Ministry of Children's Services, contends that traumatic experiences from early childhood affect long-term behaviour (Perry, 2002, 2009; Perry & Pollard, 1998). His ideas are supported by neurological studies that have found that severe maltreatment during childhood (physical, sexual, and/or emotional abuse) is related to molecular and neurobiological damage in the emotional and memory areas of the brain that are still growing (Teicher, 2002, 2010; Teicher & Samson, 2016). In particular, brain imaging studies of adults who were traumatized as children have revealed reductions in the size of the hippocampus, where memory processing takes place, and an enhanced response of the **amygdala**, which regulates negative emotions, to threatening situations.

These findings complement the research of Ruth Lanius, of the University of Western Ontario, who has been using a brain-imaging technique called **functional magnetic resonance imaging (fMRI)** to see if people who experience traumatic life events use different regions of the brain when they recall the events. Lanius and others (Daniels et al., 2012; Lanius et al., 2003, 2004) compared the brain functioning of people who developed **post-traumatic stress disorder (PTSD)** with those who did not, in the aftermath of comparably traumatic events. When subjects were prompted to recall their traumatic event (e.g., a horrific auto accident or sexual assault), those with PTSD showed arousal in the right brain areas whereas those who did not develop PTSD experienced heightened activation in the left brain. As you recall from Figure 7.2, the right brain generally deals with nonverbal information, which may help to explain why people who have PTSD react so strongly to memories that are perceptually vivid and visceral in nature. In comparison, the left brain is better at processing verbal information, which may account for why people who do not develop PTSD recall a less emotionally laden, narrative memory of traumatic events. To what extent traumatic life events either cause these disparities in brain functioning or somehow trigger a predisposition to process emotionally charged information in atypical ways remains unclear.

---

household hazards (e.g., the presence of accessible weapons, drugs and drug paraphernalia, and/or insufficient heat or unhygienic conditions). Keep in mind that no single factor necessarily contributes to abuse; more often it's the presence of several of these variables in a particular family setting that significantly increases the chances that the children will experience abuse.

OUTCOMES   It's becoming clear that ACEs have an *exposure effect* whereby the degree of intensity and duration of a stressor is related to the intensity of the response. In its most extreme form, children who endure a **toxic stress response**—persistently elevated physiological arousal caused by strong, recurring, and/or unabated adversity—early in their development experience high levels of stress hormones that can disrupt and alter normal development and functioning of the brain and other body systems (see the **Research Report**). Without the buffering protection afforded by nurturing families and supportive communities, ACEs—whether due to maltreatment, poor/dysfunctional parenting, the accumulated burdens of socioeconomic hardship, discrimination, and/or victimization—can lead to lifelong impairments in intellect and learning, as well as emotional, behavioural, physical, and social problems. There is also an increased risk of disease and mortality in adulthood (Bellis et al., 2015; Campbell, Walker, & Egede, 2016; Coley, Lynch, & Kull, 2015; Cronholm et al., 2015; Garner & Shonkoff, 2012; Hughes, Lowey, Quigg, & Bellis, 2016; Jimenez, Wade, Lin, Morrow, & Reichman, 2016; Shonkoff & Garner, 2012; Wade et al., 2016). Moreover, scientists are now finding ACEs early in life elevate the risk of chronic conditions (ranging from neuropsychiatric disorders to cardiovascular disease) by means of epigenetic modifications (Garner, Forkey, & Szilagyi, 2015; Jawahar, Murgatroyd, Harrison, & Baune, 2015; Suderman et al., 2014; Vaiserman, 2015a, 2015b). And, since epigenetic changes are reversible, epigenetics therapies hold promise of undoing the epigenetic markers that contribute to adverse long-term health outcomes.

amygdala

an almond-shaped brain structure that plays a key role in the regulation of defensive emotions like fear and anger

functional magnetic resonance imaging (fMRI)

a form of magnetic resonance imaging (MRI) that records what regions of the brain are active during specific mental activities

post-traumatic stress disorder (PTSD)

a disorder that involves extreme levels of anxiety, emotional discomfort and/or numbness, flashback memories of episodes of abuse, nightmares, and other sleep disturbances in response to traumatic life events

toxic stress response

persistently elevated physiological arousal caused by recurring and/or unabated adversity that threatens healthy development

PREVENTIVE MEASURES   Preventing abuse begins with education. Informing parents about the potential consequences of some physical acts, such as the link between shaking an infant and brain damage, may help. In addition, parents need to know that injuring children is a crime, even if the intention is to discipline them. Parenting classes, perhaps as a required part of high school curricula, can help inform parents or future parents about principles of child development and appropriate methods of discipline (Mooney et al., 2010).

Another approach to prevention of maltreatment involves identification of families at risk. Health care professionals, social workers, educators, coaches, and others who routinely interact with parents of infants and young children have a particularly important role to play in this kind of prevention (Christian & Bloom, 2011). Parents who seem to have problems attaching to their children can sometimes be identified during home visits or medical office visits. These parents can be referred to parenting classes or to social workers for help. Similarly, parents may ask doctors or nurses how to discipline their children. Such questions provide professionals with opportunities to discuss which practices are appropriate and which are not. Involving parents in intensive, targeted programs designed to prevent child abuse and neglect have been shown to have effective, long-lasting results. One such program is nurse-based home visitations that provide continuing parental support during the child's early years, thereby helping parents make informed decisions about how they want to parent their children (Boivin & Hertzman, 2012).

Finally, children who are abused must be protected from further injury. This can be supported through vigorous enforcement of existing child abuse laws. Health professionals must report suspected abuse; however, ordinary citizens are also bound by mandatory reporting laws in all Canadian provinces and territories. Any person who has reasonable grounds to suspect abuse or neglect of a child or youth has a duty to report the abuse or neglect to the local child protection agency. Once abuse is reported, steps must be taken to protect injured children from suspected abusers.

Test Yourself before going on

1. Select the correct answers in the following sentence:

   At the end of early childhood, children's (gross/fine) motor skills are developed to a higher level of confidence than their (gross/fine) motor skills are.

2. Match each term with its definition.

   _____ (a) lateralization
   _____ (b) reticular formation
   _____ (c) hippocampus
   _____ (d) handedness

   (i) the part of the brain involved in transferring information to long-term memory

   (ii) the division of brain functions between the two hemispheres of the cerebral cortex

   (iii) a strong preference for using one hand or the other that develops between 2 and 6 years

   (iv) the part of the brain that regulates attention and concentration

3. Select the correct answer in the following sentence:

   Preschoolers (consume/do not consume) the majority of their calories at regular meals.

4. What are the four broad categories of risk factors for child abuse?

Critical Thinking

5. Ask your friends and fellow students to estimate the age at which brain development is complete. How do you think people's assumptions about the completeness of brain development affect their attitudes and behaviour toward children?

Cognitive Changes

The changes in thinking that happen during the early childhood years are staggering. At the beginning of this period, children are just beginning to learn how to accomplish goals. By the time they reach age 5 or 6, they are proficient at manipulating symbols and can make accurate judgments about others' thoughts, feelings, and behaviour.

Piaget's Preoperational Stage

According to Piaget, children acquire the **semiotic (symbolic) function** between ages 18 and 24 months. The semiotic function is the understanding that one object or behaviour can represent another—a picture of a chair represents a real chair, a child pretending to feed a doll stands for a parent feeding a baby, and so on. Once this understanding has been achieved, children are in Piaget's **preoperational stage**.

During the preoperational stage, children become proficient at using symbols for thinking and communicating but still have difficulty thinking logically. At age 2 or 3, children begin to pretend in their play (Walker-Andrews & Kahana-Kalman, 1999). A broom may become a horse, or a block may become a train. Cross-cultural research suggests that this kind of object use by 2- to 3-year-olds in pretend play is universal (Barthélémy-Musso, Tartas, & Guidetti, 2013). In fact, observing children at play can provide parents or teachers with a good idea about their levels of cognitive development (see **Table 7.2**). Young children also show signs of increasing proficiency at symbol use in their growing ability to understand models, maps, and graphic symbols, such as letters (Callaghan & Corbit, 2015; DeLoache, 1995).

Although young children are remarkably good at using symbols, their reasoning about the world is often flawed. For example, Piaget described the preoperational child's tendency to look at things entirely from her own point of view, a characteristic Piaget called **egocentrism** (Piaget, 1954). This term does not suggest that the young child is a self-centred egomaniac. It simply means that she assumes that everyone sees the world as she does. For example, while riding in the back seat of a car, a 3- or 4-year-old may suddenly call out "Look at that, Mom!"—not realizing that Mom can't see the object she's talking about. Moreover, the child doesn't realize that the car's motion prevents Mom from ever seeing the object in question. As a result, the youngster may become frustrated in her attempts to communicate with her mother about what she saw.

Learning Objective 7.5

Summarize the characteristics of children's thought during Piaget's preoperational stage.

semiotic (symbolic) function

the understanding that one object or behaviour can represent another

preoperational stage

Piaget's second stage of cognitive development, during which children become proficient in the use of symbols in thinking and communicating but still have difficulty thinking logically

egocentrism

the young child's belief that everyone sees and experiences the world the way she does

Table 7.2 Children's Play and Cognitive Development

Types of Play	Description
Sensorimotor play	A 12-month-old child spends most of her playtime exploring and manipulating objects. She puts things in her mouth, shakes them, and moves them along the floor.
Constructive play	By age 2, children also begin to use objects to build or construct things. Building a tower with blocks, drawing a picture, and digging in sand are typical activities at this stage.
First pretend play	The first instances of such pretending are usually simple, such as pretending to drink from a toy cup. The toy is used for its actual or typical purpose (a cup is for drinking), and the actions are still oriented to the self, but some pretending is involved. Between 15 and 21 months, the recipient of the pretend action becomes another person or a toy. The child is still using objects for their usual purposes, but now he is using the toy cup with a stuffed bear instead of using it himself.
Substitute pretend play	Between 2 and 3 years of age, children begin to use objects to stand for something altogether different. Children this age may use a broom as a horse or make "trucks" out of blocks.
Sociodramatic play	Sometime in the preschool years, children also begin to play parts or take roles. For example, in playing "house," participants fill roles such as "mommy," "daddy," "sister," "brother," and "baby." At first, children simply take up these roles; later, they name the various roles and may give each other explicit instructions about the right way to pretend a particular role. Interestingly, at about the same age, a great many children seem to create imaginary companions (Taylor, Cartwright, & Carlson, 1993).
Rule-governed play	By age 5 or 6, children begin to prefer rule-governed pretending and formal games. For example, children of this age use rules such as "Whoever is smallest has to be the baby" when playing "house" and play simple games such as Red Rover and Red Light, Green Light. Younger children play these games as well, but 5- and 6-year-olds better understand their rules and will follow them for longer periods of time.

Figure 7.3 The experimental situation shown here is similar to one Piaget used to study egocentrism in children. The child is asked to pick out a picture that shows how the mountains look to her, and then to pick out a picture that shows how the mountains look to the doll.

Figure 7.3 illustrates a classic experiment in which most young children demonstrate this kind of egocentrism. The child is shown a three-dimensional scene with mountains of different sizes and colours. From a set of drawings, she picks out the one that shows the scene the way she sees it. Most preschoolers can do this without much difficulty. Then the examiner asks the child to pick out the drawing that shows how someone else sees the scene, such as a doll or the examiner. At this point, most preschoolers choose the drawing that shows their own view of the mountains (Flavell, Everett, Croft, & Flavell, 1981; Gzesh & Surber, 1985).

Piaget also pointed out that the preschool-aged child's thinking is guided by the appearance of objects—a theme that still dominates the research on children of this age. Children may believe, for example, that any moving object is an animal of some kind. This kind of thinking reflects the child's tendency to think of the world in terms of one variable at a time, a type of thought Piaget called **centration**. Because of centration, the child reaches the conclusion that all moving objects are animals through a series of false conclusions. The premise on which these conclusions is based is the fact that it is evident in everyday interactions with the world that all animals move—or, as scientists put it, have the capacity for *locomotion* (self-movement). But the preoperational thinker isn't capable of thinking of objects in terms of both their motion and their capacity for self-movement. Thus, movement, without regard to any other relevant characteristic of objects, becomes the sole criterion for distinguishing between

centration

the young child's tendency to think of the world in terms of one variable at a time

At age 2 to 3, children begin to pretend in their play, using one object to stand in for something else, as the child in the photo on the left is doing. During the preschool years, children will also begin to play parts or take roles. In playing doctor, as the girls in the photo on the right are doing, participants fill roles such as "doctor" and "patient."

(*Photos:* left, Cheryl Casey/Shutterstock; right, Altanaka/Shutterstock)

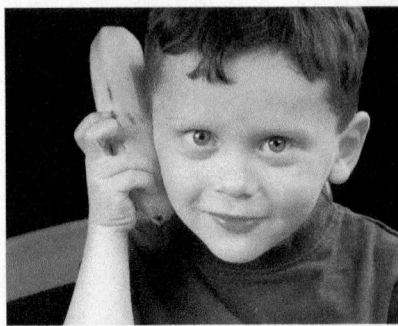

living and nonliving objects. As a result, a child may fear a leaf that blows across the playground because he believes that the leaf is trying to follow him. Piaget used the term *animism* to refer to this particular product of preoperational logic.

Some of Piaget's most famous experiments deal with a cognitive process called **conservation**, the understanding that matter can change in appearance without changing in quantity. Because of centration and irreversibility (i.e., the inability to recognize that changes made to objects can be reversed and returned to their original state), children rarely show any kind of conservation before age 5. When they do begin to understand this concept, they demonstrate their understanding with arguments based on three characteristics of appearance-only transformations of matter. The first of these is *identity*, the knowledge that quantities are constant unless matter is added to or subtracted from them. The second is *compensation*, the understanding that all relevant characteristics of the appearance of a given quantity of matter must be taken into account before reaching a conclusion about whether the quantity has changed. The third is *reversibility*, the awareness that conditions, numbers, or actions can be reversed and returned to their original state. Some of the conservation tasks Piaget used, along with children's typical responses to them, are shown in **Figure 7.4**. As you can see, assessing a child's stage of cognitive development involves finding out how she arrived at her answer to a question, not just evaluating the answer as right or wrong.

conservation

the understanding that matter can change in appearance without changing in quantity

Challenges to Piaget's View

Studies of conservation have generally confirmed Piaget's observations (e.g., Baucal, Arcidiacono, & Budjevac, 2013; Ciancio, Sadovsky, Malabonga, Trueblood, & Pasnak, 1999; Desrochers, 2008). Although younger children can demonstrate some understanding of conservation if the task is made very simple, most children cannot consistently solve conservation and other kinds of logical problems until at least age 5. However, evidence suggests that preschoolers are a great deal more cognitively sophisticated than Piaget thought.

Learning Objective 7.6

Describe how recent research has challenged Piaget's view of this period.

EGOCENTRISM AND PERSPECTIVE TAKING Despite their egocentrism, children as young as 14½ months appear to have at least some ability to understand that another person perceives things or experiences things differently than they do (Song & Baillargeon, 2008). By age 2 or 3, children can adapt their speech or their play to the demands of a companion. They play differently with older and younger playmates and talk differently to a younger child (Brownell, 1990; Guralnik & Paul-Brown, 1984).

However, such understanding is clearly not perfect at this young age. Developmental psychologist John Flavell has proposed two levels of perspective-taking ability. At level 1, the child knows that other people experience things differently. At level 2, the child develops a whole series of complex rules for figuring out precisely what the other person sees or experiences (Flavell, Green, & Flavell, 1990). At 2 and 3 years old, children have level 1 knowledge but not level 2; level 2 knowledge begins to be evident in 4- and 5-year-olds. For example, a child of 4 or 5 understands that another person feels sad if she fails or happy if she succeeds. The

(Photo: Kaesler Media/Fotolia)

This young child is able to adapt his speech to the needs of his younger sibling, one of many indications that preschoolers are less egocentric than Piaget thought.

preschool child also begins to figure out that unpleasant emotions occur in situations in which there is a gap between desire and reality. Sadness, for example, normally occurs when someone loses something that is valued or fails to acquire some desired object (Harris, 1989).

Figure 7.4 Piaget's research involved several kinds of conservation tasks. He classified children's thinking as concrete operational with respect to a particular task if they could correctly solve the problem and provide a concrete operational reason for their answer. For example, if a child said, "The two circles of marbles are the same because you didn't add any or take any away when you moved them," the response was judged to be concrete operational. Conversely, if a child said, "The two circles are the same, but I don't know why," the response was not classified as concrete operational.

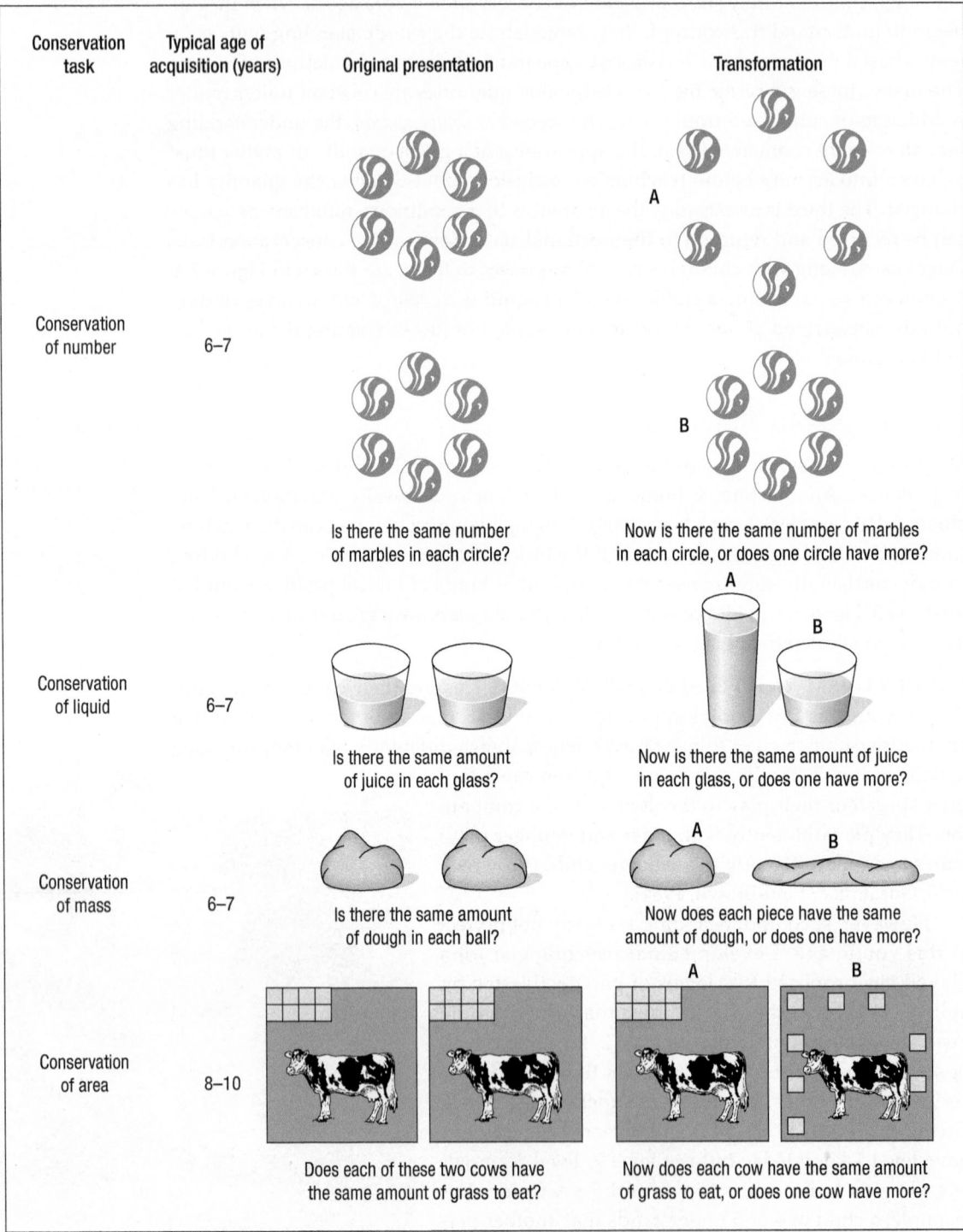

Studies of preschoolers' understanding of emotion have also challenged Piaget's description of the young child's egocentrism. For example, between ages 2 and 6, children learn to regulate or modulate their expressions of emotion to conform to others' expectations (Dunn, 1994). In addition, preschool children use emotional expressions such as crying or smiling to get things they want. These behaviours are obviously based at least in part on a growing awareness that other people judge your feelings by what they see you expressing. These behaviours wouldn't occur if children were completely incapable of looking at their own behaviour from another person's perspective, as Piaget's assertions about egocentrism would suggest.

APPEARANCE AND REALITY   The young child's movement away from egocentrism seems to be part of a much broader change in her understanding of appearance and reality. Flavell has studied this understanding in a variety of ways (Flavell, Green, & Flavell, 1989; Flavell, Green, Wahl, & Flavell, 1987). In the most famous Flavell procedure, the experimenter shows the child a sponge that has been painted to look like a rock. Three-year-olds will say either that the object looks like a sponge and is a sponge or that it looks like a rock and is a rock. But 4- and 5-year-olds can distinguish between appearance and reality; they realize that the item looks like a rock but is a sponge (Flavell, 1986). Thus, the older children understand that the same object can be represented differently, depending on one's point of view.

Finally, some developmentalists have pointed out that the task of adopting another person's perspective can be challenging even for adults (Kesselring & Müller, 2011). A preschooler's egocentrism may impair his ability to communicate with a person who does not share his physical perspective. Similarly, for instance, the author of a cellphone user's manual may fail to provide users with clear instructions because of her difficulties in adopting the cognitive perspective of those who are unfamiliar with the device. Thus, egocentrism may be best thought of as a lifelong theme of cognitive development that is manifested differently in each of Piaget's stages.

Theories of Mind

Learning Objective 7.7

Describe theory of mind and how it develops.

Evidence like that described in the previous section has led a number of theorists to propose that the 4- or 5-year-old has developed a new and quite sophisticated **theory of mind (ToM)**, or a set of ideas that explains other people's ideas, beliefs, desires, and behaviour (Flavell, 1999).

theory of mind (ToM)

a set of ideas constructed by an individual to explain other people's ideas, beliefs, desires, and behaviour

UNDERSTANDING THOUGHTS, DESIRES, AND BELIEFS   The ToM does not spring forth full-blown at age 4. Infants as young as 10 months have some beginning understanding of the fact that people (but not inanimate objects) operate with goals and intentions (Legerstee & Markova, 2008). By age 3, children understand some aspects of the link between people's thinking or feeling and their behaviour. For example, they know that a person who wants something will try to get it. They also know that a person may still want something even if she can't have it (Lillard & Flavell, 1992). But they do not yet understand the basic principle that each person's actions are based on their own representation of reality, which may differ from what is "really" there. It is this new aspect of the theory of mind that clearly emerges between 3 and 5.

Studies that examine the **false belief principle** illustrate 3-year-olds' shortcomings in this area (Flavell, 1999). In one such study, children were presented with a box on which there were pictures of different kinds of candy. The experimenter shook the box to demonstrate that there was something inside and then asked 3- and 4-year-olds to guess what they would find if they opened it. Regardless of age, the children guessed that the box contained candy. Upon opening the box, though, the children discovered that it actually contained crayons. The experimenter then asked the children to predict what another child who saw the closed box would believe was in it. Three-year-olds thought that the child would believe that the box contained crayons,

false belief principle

the ability to look at a problem or situation from another person's point of view and discern what kind of information would cause that person to believe something that isn't true

but the 4-year-olds realized that the pictures of candy on the box would lead the child to have a false belief that the box contained candy.

Still, there is much that the 4- or 5-year-old doesn't yet grasp about other people's thinking. The child of this age understands that other people think but does not yet understand that other people can think about him. The 4-year-old understands "I know that you know." But he does not yet fully understand that this process is reciprocal—namely, "You know that I know."

Understanding of the reciprocal nature of thought seems to develop between ages 5 and 7 for most children. This understanding is likely particularly important because it is probably necessary for the creation of genuinely reciprocal friendships, which begin to emerge in the elementary school years (Sullivan, Zaitchik, & Tager-Flusberg, 1994). In fact, the rate at which an individual preschooler develops a ToM is a good predictor of her social skills both later in early childhood and during the school years (Moore, Barresi, & Thompson, 1998; Watson, Nixon, Wilson, & Capage, 1999).

Furthermore, it is not until about age 6 that most children realize that knowledge can be derived through inference. For example, researchers in one study showed 4- and 6-year-olds two toys of different colours (Pillow, 1999). Next, they placed the toys in separate opaque containers. They then opened one of the containers and showed the toy to a puppet. When asked whether the puppet now knew which colour toy was in each container, only the 6-year-olds said yes.

INFLUENCES ON THE DEVELOPMENT OF A THEORY OF MIND Developmentalists have found that a child's ToM is correlated with his performance on Piaget's tasks as well as on measures of egocentrism and distinguishing between appearance and reality (Melot & Houde, 1998). Pretend play also seems to contribute to ToM development. Shared pretense with other children, in particular, is strongly related to ToM (Lillard et al., 2013). In addition, researchers have discovered links between working memory development and ToM (Benson & Sabbagh, 2010).

Language skills—such as knowledge of words like *want*, *need*, *think*, or *remember*, which express feelings, desires, and thoughts—are also related to ToM development (Astington & Jenkins, 1995; Tardif, So, & Kaciroti, 2007). Indeed, some level of language facility may be a necessary condition for the development of a ToM. Developmentalists have found that children in the 3-year-old age range must reach a certain threshold of general language skill before they are able to succeed at false belief tasks (Astington & Jenkins, 1999; Watson et al., 1999). Further research found that children with disabilities that affect language development, such as congenital deafness, autism, or a developmental disability, develop a ToM more slowly than others (Martín-García, Gómez-Becerra, & Garro-Espín, 2012; Nilsson & de López, 2016).

Learning Objective 7.8

Describe how information-processing and sociocultural theorists explain changes in young children's thinking.

short-term storage space (STSS)

neo-Piagetian theorist Robbie Case's term for the working memory

operational efficiency

a neo-Piagetian term that refers to the maximum number of schemes that can be processed in working memory at one time

Alternative Theories of Early Childhood Thinking

In recent years, a number of interesting theoretical approaches have attempted to explain both Piaget's original results and the more recent findings that contradict them.

INFORMATION-PROCESSING THEORIES One set of alternative proposals is based on the information-processing model. Robbie Case explained age differences in cognitive development as a function of changes in children's use of their short-term memories (Case, 1985, 1992). Case used the term **short-term storage space (STSS)** to refer to the child's working memory. According to Case, the number of schemes the STSS can attend to is limited. He referred to the maximum number of schemes that may be put into STSS at one time as **operational efficiency**. Improvements in operational efficiency occur through both practice (doing tasks that require memory use, such as learning the alphabet) and brain maturation as the child gets older. Thus, a 7-year-old is better able to handle the processing demands of conservation tasks than is a 4-year-old because of improvements in operational efficiency of the STSS.

Figure 7.5 Neo-Piagetians have used Piaget's matrix classification task in strategy training studies with young children. Before training, most preschoolers say that a blue triangle or red circle belongs in the box with the question mark. After learning a two-step strategy in which they are taught to classify each object first by shape and then by colour, children understand that a red triangle is the figure that is needed to complete the matrix.

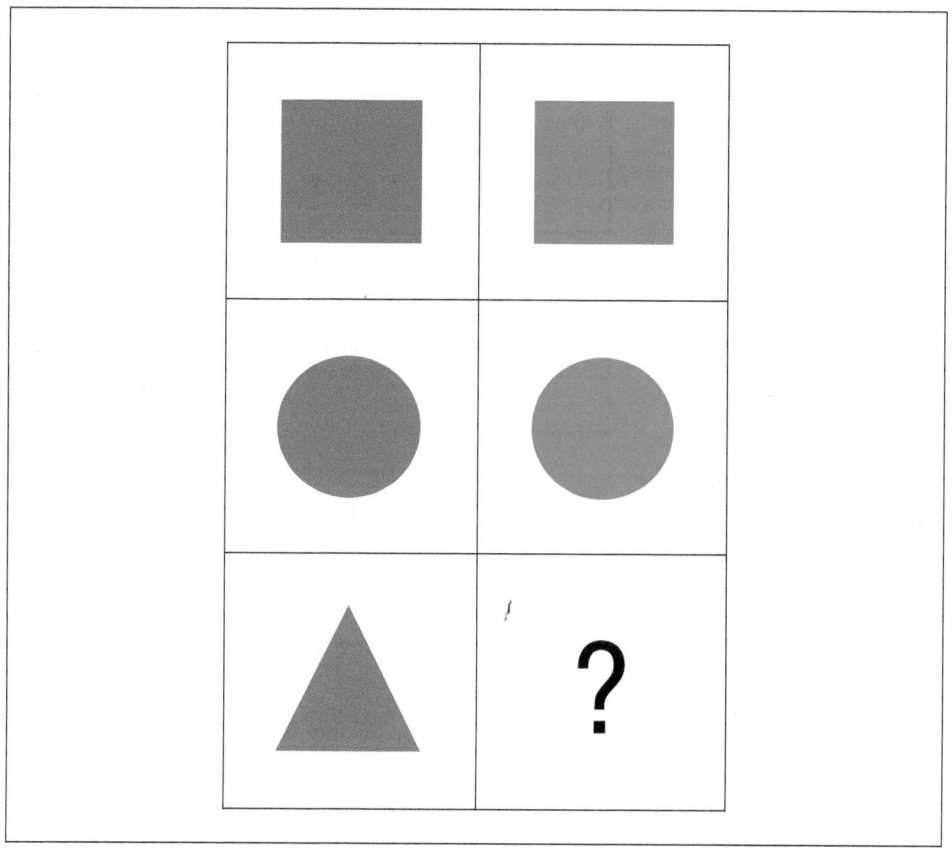

A good example of the function of STSS may be found by examining *matrix classification*, a task Piaget often used with both young and school-aged children (see **Figure 7.5**). Matrix classification requires the child to place a given stimulus in two categories at the same time. Young children fail such tasks because, according to neo-Piagetian theory, they begin by processing the stimulus according to one dimension (either shape or colour) and then either fail to realize that it is necessary to reprocess it along the second dimension or forget to do so.

However, researchers have trained young children to perform correctly on such problems by using a two-step strategy. The children are taught to think of a red triangle, for example, in terms of shape first and colour second. Typically, instruction involves a number of training tasks in which researchers remind children repeatedly to remember to reclassify stimuli with respect to the second variable. According to Case, both children's failure prior to instruction and the type of strategy training to which they respond illustrate the constraints imposed on problem-solving by the limited operational efficiency of the younger child's STSS. There is room for only one scheme at a time in the child's STSS, either shape or colour. The training studies show that younger children *can* learn to perform correctly, but their approach is qualitatively different from that of older children. The older child's more efficient STSS allows her to think about shape and colour at the same time and, therefore, perform successfully without any training.

Young children can solve simple perceptual matching problems like the ones described above but run into difficulty when they are instructed to solve problems

Figure 7.6 On the Flexible Item Selection Task (FIST) children are presented with three cards with pictures of objects that vary on two of four possible dimensions. A child is required to match two cards on one dimension and then to match two cards by using a different dimension. By age 5, children can perform both tasks, which suggests that they are capable of abstraction and cognitive flexibility.

(**SOURCE:** Jacques, S., & Zelazo, P.D. (2001). The Flexible Item Selection Task (FIST): A measure of executive function in preschoolers. *Developmental Neuropsychology*, 20(3), 573–591. Figure 2, p. 578. Reprinted with permission.)

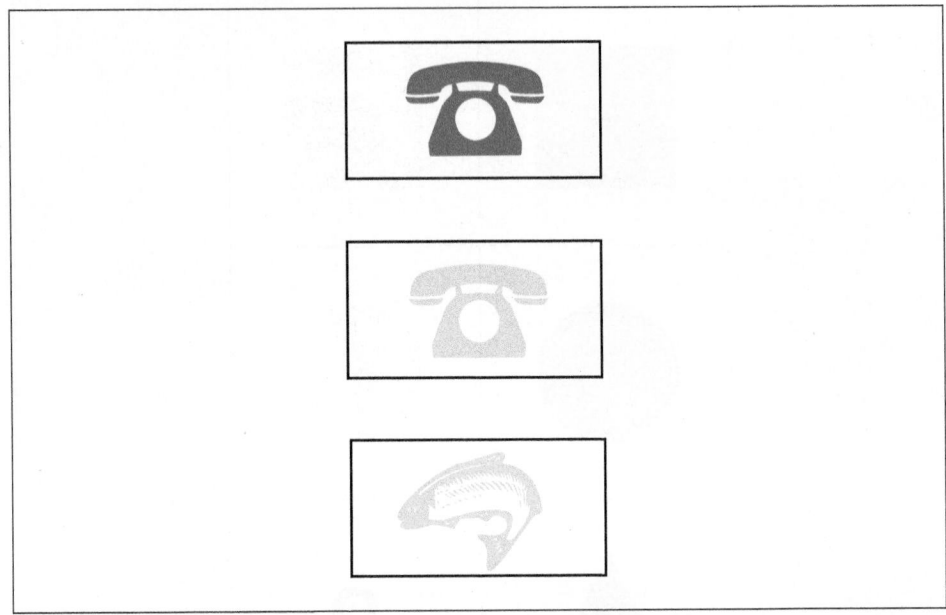

that require higher-level abstract flexible thinking. Sophie Jacques of Dalhousie University and Philip Zelazo of the University of Toronto developed the *Flexible Item Selection Task (FIST)* to measure abstraction and cognitive flexibility (Jacques & Zelazo, 2001). The FIST involves a card-sorting technique to measure if a child can match objects on cards that vary on two of four dimensions (shape, colour, size, and number, as illustrated in **Figure 7.6**). A child is presented with three cards at once and first instructed to pick two cards that match on one of the four dimensions, for example, size (a measure of abstract mental ability), and then to pick two cards that match on a different dimension, for example, shape (a measure of cognitive flexibility—a child has to be able to consider each object on multiple categories). The researchers found that 2-year-olds were unable to grasp the instructions; 3-year-olds could understand the instructions but had difficulty matching cards on even one dimension. The results reflect an underdeveloped abstract reasoning ability in these younger children. By comparison, 4-year-olds could match objects on one dimension but struggled with matching objects on a second dimension, suggesting that although they are capable of abstracting relevant information to solve a problem, they lack the cognitive flexibility to switch between abstract dimensions. However, the 5-year-olds were able to match cards on one or more dimensions. It seems that, even though children as young as 3 years of age can match objects based on concrete perceptual categories, they have a hard time matching objects based on abstract categories required on the FIST. Moreover, it isn't until a child reaches the age of 5 that she demonstrates the ability to show both cognitive abstraction and flexibility.

Jeffrey Bisanz and his colleagues at the University of Alberta have been studying how information-processing capacities affect the development of arithmetic skills in preschoolers. These researchers have been trying to understand what children know about arithmetic prior to formal schooling in terms of the cognitive interplay between arithmetic procedures, concepts, and facts (J. Bisanz, personal communication, July 30,

2001). One problem with testing 4-year-olds' ability to do arithmetic is that they do not have the cognitive ability to use words and symbols to solve number problems. To compensate for their lack of cognitive ability, Klein and Bisanz (2000) developed a novel method of studying arithmetic skills in preschoolers: using poker chips in lieu of numbers for counting. When the researchers studied preschoolers under these new testing procedures, they observed some interesting outcomes. First, in a two-term problem (e.g., a + b or a − b) the "representational set size," the maximum number of units of information that must be held in working memory at the same time during problem solution, is a major constraint on the preschooler's success in solving nonverbal addition and subtraction problems (e.g., 4-year-olds do fairly well on arithmetic problems when the numbers are small [less than 6]). Second, when it comes to solving a three-term problem (e.g., a + b − c), 4-year-olds—although still constrained in their use of larger numbers—can spontaneously invent shortcuts to solve this type of problem (e.g., transforming the problem [a + b] − c to [a − c] + b), thus demonstrating that even at this young age children can apply arithmetic principles to solve nonverbal tasks. Findings such as these may eventually lead to new methods of assessment, early identification, and instruction in the early years.

Information-processing theorists also maintain that children's ability to make efficient use of their memory system influences their performance on problem-solving tasks. For instance, scripts, cognitive structures that underlie behaviours that are often repeated, emerge during early childhood. They are especially useful for managing the memory demands of tasks that involve sequential steps. For example, to brush his teeth, a preschooler must first get his toothbrush. Next, he must apply toothpaste to the brush, and so on. Establishment of a tooth-brushing script frees up the preschooler's information-processing resources so that he can focus on the quality of his brushing rather than the procedure itself.

Information-processing theorists emphasize the importance of metamemory and metacognition. **Metamemory** is knowledge about and control of memory processes. For example, young children know that it takes longer to memorize a list of ten words than a list of five words, but they still aren't very good at coming up with strategies to apply to more difficult memory tasks (Kail, 1990). **Metacognition** is knowledge about and control of thought processes. For example, a child listening to a story may realize he has forgotten the main character's name and ask the reader what it is. Both knowing that the character's name has been forgotten and knowing that the character's name will make the story easier to understand are forms of metacognition.

Children's metamemory and metacognition improve during the early childhood period (Schneider, 2010). Between ages 3 and 5, for example, children figure out that to tell whether a sponge painted like a rock is really a sponge or a rock, a person needs to touch or hold it. Just looking at it doesn't provide enough information (Flavell, 1993; O'Neill, Astington, & Flavell, 1992). Thus, by about age 4 or 5, children seem to have some beginning grasp of these processes, but they still have a long way to go. As a result, their ability to solve complex problems, such as those Piaget used, is limited compared with that of older children.

VYGOTSKY'S SOCIOCULTURAL THEORY Psychologists' interest in Russian psychologist Lev Vygotsky's views on development has grown recently. Vygotsky's theory differs from both Piagetian and information-processing theory in its emphasis on the role of social factors in cognitive development. For example, two preschoolers working on a puzzle together discuss where the pieces belong. After a number of such dialogues, the participants internalize the discussion. It then becomes a model for an internal conversation the child uses to guide himself through the puzzle-solving process. In this way, Vygotsky suggested, solutions to problems are socially generated and learned. Vygotsky did not deny that individual learning takes place. Rather, he suggested that group learning processes are central to cognitive development.

metamemory

knowledge about how memory works and the ability to control and reflect on one's own memory function

metacognition

knowledge about how the mind thinks and the ability to control and reflect on one's own thought processes

Consequently, from Vygotsky's perspective, social interaction is required for cognitive development (Crain, 2011).

The chapter on Theories of Development described two important general principles of Vygotsky's theory: *the zone of proximal development* and *scaffolding*. Vygotsky also proposed specific stages of cognitive development from birth to age 7. Each stage represents a step toward the child's internalization of the ways of thinking used by the adults around him.

In the first period, called the *primitive stage*, the infant possesses mental processes that are similar to those of lower animals. He learns primarily through conditioning, until language begins to develop in the second year. At that point, he enters the *naive psychology stage*, in which he learns to use language to communicate but still does not understand its symbolic character. For example, he doesn't realize that any collection of sounds could stand for the object "chair" as long as everyone agreed—that is, if all English speakers agreed to substitute the word *blek* for *chair*, we could do so because we would all understand what *blek* meant.

Once the child begins to appreciate the symbolic function of language, near the end of the third year of life, he enters the *egocentric speech stage*. In this stage, he uses language as a guide to solving problems. In effect, he tells himself how to do things. For example, a 3-year-old walking down a flight of stairs might say "Be careful" to himself. Such a statement would be the result of his internalization of statements made to him by adults and older children.

Piaget recognized the existence and importance of egocentric speech. However, he believed that such speech disappeared as the child approached the end of the preoperational stage. In contrast, Vygotsky claimed that egocentric speech becomes completely internalized at age 6 or 7, when children enter the final period of cognitive development, the *ingrowth stage*. Thus, he suggested that the logical thinking Piaget ascribed to older children resulted from their internalization of speech routines they had acquired from older children and adults in the social world rather than from schemes children constructed for themselves through interaction with the physical world.

At present, there is insufficient evidence to either support or contradict most of Vygotsky's ideas (Thomas, 2005). However, studies have shown that young children whose parents provide them with more cognitive scaffolding during the preschool years exhibit higher levels of achievement in the early elementary grades than peers whose parents provide less support of this kind (Neitzel & Stright, 2003). In addition, researchers have found that private speech helps children solve problems (Montero & De Dios, 2006; Villegas, Castellanos, & Gutiérrez, 2009). Some intriguing research on children's construction of theory of mind during social interactions lends weight to Vygotsky's major propositions. It seems that children in pairs and groups do produce more sophisticated ideas than individual children who work on problems alone. However, the sophistication of a group's ideas appears to depend on the presence of at least one fairly advanced individual child in the group (Tan-Niam, Wood, & O'Malley, 1998).

By integrating the individualistic "theory of mind" approach (that stemmed from a Piagetian tradition) with Vygotsky's "social interaction" approach, contemporary theorists are attempting to overcome some serious theoretical dilemmas, such as which set of cognitive abilities develops first and which is foremost. The suggestion is that cognitive abilities develop in unison—the child's emerging understanding of the mind helps him interact better with others and, in turn, his social interactions reinforce his understanding of thoughts, desires, and beliefs. In essence, "concepts about the mind are not just passed on from the social group, nor are they completely formed by individual child-theorists" (Carpendale & Lewis, 2004, p. 84). It is only through his regular and routine interactions with others that a child develops a personal understanding of mind that is distinct from his understanding of the minds of others and that is separate from his understanding of objects in the real world.

Test Yourself before going on

1. Match each term with its definition.
  _____ (a) semiotic function
  _____ (b) egocentrism
  _____ (c) centration
  _____ (d) conservation
      (i) thinking that focuses on one variable at a time
      (ii) the belief that matter can change in appearance without changing in quantity
      (iii) the understanding that one thing can stand for another
      (iv) the belief that everyone experiences the world the same way that the self does

2. Some studies show that young children are less _____ than Piaget proposed.

3. The false belief principle is one component of a child's _____ _____ _____.

4. Match each alternative theory or concept of cognitive development with its main emphasis.
  _____ (a) short-term storage space
  _____ (b) awareness and control of memory and thought processes
  _____ (c) Vygotsky's sociocultural theory
      (i) social factors
      (ii) working memory limitations
      (iii) metamemory and metacognition

Critical Thinking

5. Overcoming the egocentrism of early childhood is the foundation of many cognitive tasks later in life. For example, students who are writing research papers have to be able to look at their work from their professor's point of view in order to determine whether what they have written is understandable and in line with the requirements of the assignment. What other situations or tasks can you think of that require taking another person's perspective?

Changes in Language

To his credit, Piaget recognized that the overriding theme of cognitive development in the early childhood years is language acquisition. Of course, the process begins much earlier. Amazingly, though, children enter this period producing only a limited number of words and simple sentences but leave it as accomplished, fluent speakers of at least one language.

Fast-Mapping

The average 2½-year-old's vocabulary of about 600 words is fairly impressive when we compare it with the dozen or so words most 1-year-olds know (Bates et al., 1994). This quantity amounts to the acquisition of one or two new words every day between ages 12 and 24 months. Impressive though this feat is, it pales in comparison to the rate of vocabulary growth among preschoolers. By the time a child goes to school at age 5 or 6, total vocabulary has risen to perhaps 15 000 words—an astonishing increase of 10 words a day (Anglin, 1995; Pinker, 1994). Moreover, word learning appears to be the engine that drives the whole process of language development. That is, the more words a child knows, the more advanced she is with regard to grammar and other aspects of language (McGregor, Sheng, & Smith, 2005). What is the impetus behind this amazing rate of word learning?

Researchers have found that a momentous shift in the way children approach new words happens around age 3. As a result of this shift, children begin to pay attention to words in whole groups, such as words that name objects in a single class (e.g., types of dinosaurs or kinds of fruit) or words with similar meanings. In a sense, understanding of the categorical nature of words helps children develop what we might think of as mental "slots" for new words. Once the slots are in place, they seem to automatically organize the linguistic input children receive from parents, teachers, peers, books, TV programs, advertisements, and every other source of language to extract new words and fill the slots as quickly as possible.

Learning Objective 7.9
Describe how fast-mapping helps children learn new words.

fast-mapping

the ability to categorically link new words to real-world referents

Psychologists use the term **fast-mapping** to refer to this ability to categorically link new words to real-world referents (Carey & Bartlett, 1978). (*Referents* are the real objects and events to which words refer.) At the core of fast-mapping, say researchers, is a rapidly formed hypothesis about a new word's meaning (MacWhinney, 2011). The hypothesis is based on information derived from children's prior knowledge of words and word categories and from the context in which the word is used. Once formed, the hypothesis is tested through use of the word in the child's own speech, often immediately after learning it. The feedback children receive in response to use of the word helps them judge the accuracy of the hypothesis and the appropriateness of the category to which they have assumed that the word belongs. Perhaps this helps explain why preschoolers do so much talking and why they are so persistent at getting their listeners to actively respond to them.

Learning Objective 7.10

Highlight what happens during the grammar explosion.

grammar explosion

period when the grammatical features of children's speech become more similar to those of adult speech

inflections

grammatical markers attached to words to indicate tense, gender, number, and the like, such as the use of the ending *ed* to mark the past tense of a verb in English

overregularization

attachment of regular inflections to irregular words, such as the substitution of *goed* for *went*

The Grammar Explosion

In the chapter on Cognitive Development in Infancy, you learned that the vocabulary explosion of the toddler period begins slowly. Similarly, the **grammar explosion**, the period when the grammatical features of children's speech become more similar to those of adult speech, of the 2- to 6-year-old period starts with several months of simple sentences such "here bottle" or "what that?"

INFLECTIONS   The first spoken sentences typically consist of simple two-word utterances that lack **inflections**. If a child was to say "Mommy sock," for example, the child's sentence is missing the 's that would tell a child's listeners that she is trying to say that the sock belongs to Mommy. Within each language community, children seem to add inflections and more complex word orders in fairly predictable sequences (Legendre, 2006). In a classic early study, Roger Brown found that the earliest inflection used among children learning English is typically -*ing* added to a verb, as in "I playing" or "Doggie running," expressions that are common in the speech of 2½- to 3-year-olds (Brown, 1973). Over the next year or so come (in order) prepositions (such as *on* and *in*), the plural -*s* on nouns, irregular past tenses (such as *broke* or *ran*), possessives, articles (*a* and *the* in English), the -*s* added to third-person verbs (as in "He wants"), regular past tenses (such as *played* and *wanted*), and various forms of auxiliary verbs (as in "I am going").

QUESTIONS AND NEGATIVES   There are also predictable sequences in the child's developing use of questions and negatives. In each case, the child seems to go through periods when he creates types of sentences that he has not heard adults use but that are consistent with the particular set of rules he is using. For example, in the development of questions there is a point at which the child can put a *Wh-* word (*who, what, when, where, why*) at the front end of a sentence, but he doesn't yet put the auxiliary verb in the right place, as in "Where you are going now?" Similarly, in the development of negatives, children go through a stage in which they put in *not* or *no* but omit the auxiliary verb, as in "I not crying."

OVERREGULARIZATION   Another intriguing phenomenon is **overregularization**, or overgeneralization. No language is perfectly regular; every language includes some irregularly conjugated verbs or unusual forms of plurals. What 3- to 4-year-olds do is apply the basic rule to all these irregular instances, thus making the language more regular than it really is (Maratsos, 2000). In English, this is especially clear in children's creation of past tenses, such as "wented," "blowed," and "sitted," or plurals, such as "teeths" and "blockses" (Fenson et al., 1994).

(Photo: Claudia Paulussen/Fotolia)

These 2- to 3-year-olds probably speak to each other in short sentences that include uninflected nouns and verbs.

Such overregularizations illustrate yet again that language development is a rule-governed process that cannot be explained by imitation theories. Children show that they are using rules when they create word forms (such as "wented") that they have not heard. Clearly, children cannot have learned these words by imitation. Instead, their presence in children's speech suggests that children actively infer and use language rules.

COMPLEX SENTENCES   After children have figured out inflections and the basic sentence forms by using negatives and questions, they soon begin to create remarkably complex sentences, using a conjunction such as *and* or *but* to combine two ideas or using embedded clauses. Here are some examples from children aged 30 to 48 months (de Villiers & de Villiers, 1992, p. 379):

- I didn't catch it but Teddy did!
- I'm gonna sit on the one you're sitting on.
- How many more sleeps did you say it is until my birthday?

When you remember that only about 18 months earlier these children were using sentences little more complex than "See doggie," you can appreciate how far they have come in a short time.

Phonological Awareness

Certain aspects of early childhood language development, such as rate of vocabulary growth, predict how easily a child will learn to read and write when she enters school (Wood & Terrell, 1998). However, one specific component, *phonological awareness*, seems to be especially important. **Phonological awareness** is a child's sensitivity to the sound patterns that are specific to the language being acquired. It also includes the child's knowledge of that particular language's system for representing sounds with letters. Researchers measure English-speaking children's phonological awareness with questions such as the following: "What would *bat* be if you took away the *b*? What would *bat* be if you took away the *b* and put *r* there instead?"

A child doesn't have to acquire phonological awareness in early childhood. It can be learned in elementary school through formal instruction (Bus & van IJzendoorn, 1999; Petrill et al., 2010). However, numerous studies have shown that the greater a child's phonological awareness *before* he enters school, the faster he learns to read (Melby-Lervåg, Lyster, & Hulme, 2012; Wood & Terrell, 1998). In addition, phonological awareness in the early childhood years is related to rate of literacy learning in languages as varied as Korean, English, Punjabi, and Chinese (Cheung et al., 2010; Chiappe, Glaeser, & Ferko, 2007; Chiappe & Siegel, 1999; McBride-Chang & Ho, 2000).

Phonological awareness appears to develop primarily through word play. For example, among English-speaking children, learning and reciting nursery rhymes contributes to phonological awareness (Bryant, MacLean, & Bradley, 1990; Layton, Deeny, Tall, & Upton, 1996). For Japanese children, a game called *shiritori*, in which one person says a word and another comes up with a word that begins with its ending sound, helps children develop these skills (Norboru, 1997; Serpell & Hatano, 1997). Educators have also found that using such games to teach phonological awareness skills to preschoolers is just as effective as more formal methods, such as flash cards and worksheets (Brennan & Ireson, 1997). *Shared*, or *dialogic*, *reading* has also been found to contribute to growth in phonological awareness (Burgess, 1997) (see **Development in the Real World**).

Preschoolers with good phonological awareness skills—those who have learned a few basic sound–letter connections informally, from their parents or caregivers—often use a strategy called **invented spelling** when they attempt to write

Learning Objective 7.11

Describe what phonological awareness is, and why it is important.

phonological awareness
children's understanding of the sound patterns of the language they are acquiring

invented spelling
a strategy young children with good phonological awareness skills use when they write

Development in the Real World

Strengthening Language Skills in Preschoolers

Both the quantity and quality of reading experiences that young children have with their parents influence the children's language and reading development (Evans & Shaw, 2008). Researchers at Monique Sénéchal's language lab at Carleton University have been investigating how young children develop language skills, especially in relation to natural experiences such as storybook reading. A study found that parents who change their communication style when reading to infants between 9 and 18 months of age help the infants' language development. Nine-month-old infants vocalized more when parents talked about a picture book they were reading than when parents simply read a story to their infant (Sénéchal, Cornell, & Broda, 1995). Research showed that, although reading a storybook just once to a child improves her **receptive vocabulary** (Sénéchal & Cornell, 1993), children who were read the same book three times did much better in later development of both receptive and **expressive vocabulary** (Sénéchal, 1997). Moreover, when children were asked questions about what was being read, their expressive vocabulary increased even more than their receptive vocabulary. It appears that children who actively participate in story-reading by answering questions comprehend and produce more words than do children who passively listen (Sénéchal, Thomas, & Monker, 1995; Sénéchal & Young, 2008).

During the preschool years, it is important to motivate children to begin preparing for independent reading, and, when children show a delay in vocabulary development, it is especially important to intervene early. A variety of formal reading experiences (e.g., teaching letter names and sounding out words) and informal storybook reading early in a child's life contribute to reading performance later on. Even during the course of routine social interactions, such as dinner table conversation, parents and, to a lesser degree, young children have opportunities to share concepts about language and how it is used (e.g., the concepts of telling stories are reinforced when a mother asks her son, "Did you tell Dad the story about the funny dog you saw today?") (Ely, Gleason, MacGibbon, & Zaretsky, 2001). Research indicates that both formal and informal parental involvement in a child's reading experiences contribute to improved reading skill by the end of Grade 1. Moreover, a child's reading fluency in Grade 1 predicts their vocabulary and listening comprehension in Grade 3 (Sénéchal & LeFevre, 1998, 2002; Sénéchal, LeFevre, Thomas, and Daley, 1998).

As a means of assessing the effects of language skill-development intervention for disadvantaged preschoolers, Hargrave and Sénéchal (2000) studied techniques that could be applied in preschool daycare settings to improve the acquisition of vocabulary for children with poor vocabularies. They studied preschoolers in a standard daycare reading situation where there was a ratio of eight children to every teacher. Children were divided into two groups. One group experienced the standard story-reading situation in which the teacher reads the story and the children listen. The other group was exposed to a *dialogic-reading* intervention.

In the dialogic-reading situation, teachers were trained to actively involve the children. The teacher helped the child become the teller of the story, while the teacher became the audience and listened and questioned the child. Dialogic reading included the following techniques: asking *Wh-* questions (i.e., *what, where, when, why, who, which,* and *how*), asking open-ended questions, and expanding on what the child said (Arnold, Lonigan, Whitehurst, & Epstein, 1994). These techniques were designed to teach vocabulary and encourage children to provide more complete descriptions of what they see.

Another part of the procedure involved the parents. Parents of children in the dialogic-reading group received the same training as the teachers. In addition, the parents were encouraged to read to their children at home.

All the children were assessed before and after the dialogic-reading intervention. A comparison of the children's vocabulary scores showed that the children in the dialogic-reading group demonstrated significantly higher expressive vocabulary scores than children in the regular reading group. The children in the dialogic-reading group were on average 13 months behind in their expressive vocabulary before the intervention but advanced to the point where they were just four months behind after just four weeks of intervention.

Tips for Dialogic Reading

- Repeat what a child says. Let a child know that his answer is correct by restating it: "Yes, that is an elephant."
- Follow answers with questions. When a child names an object, ask a question about it: "What colour is the car?" "Where is the ball hidden?" "Why do we use soap?" "Who works in the hospital?"
- Help a child as needed. If a child is not able to answer your question, then provide a correct answer and ask him to repeat what you have said.
- Expand what a child says. When a child says something about a picture, praise him and add a little to what's been said. For example, if your child says "Doggy bark," then you might say, "Yes, the dog is barking at the kitty." In this

way, you model correct grammar and provide a new piece of information. Later, you might ask a question about this new information: "Who's the dog barking at?"

- Follow a child's interests. If a child shows an interest in a picture either by talking about it or by pointing to it, follow up immediately by asking questions.
- Adapt to a child's growing linguistic abilities. A child who is adept at naming colours should be encouraged to talk about some other aspects of the story.
- Praise and encourage. Tell a child when he is doing well by saying things like "Good answer!" or "That's right. Are you ever brilliant!"
- Have fun. Try to keep reading times fun and like a game. One way to do this is to switch between asking questions and just plain reading. For example, you could read one page and then have a child tell you about the next page.
- Try to read with a child once a day. Pick a time when a child is interested in sharing a book with you. Before bed is a good time for many children and parents. Even 5 to 10 minutes can make a difference.

(**SOURCE:** Adapted from Arnold, Lonigan, Whitehurst, & Epstein, 1994. Copyright © 1994 by the American Psychological Association. Adapted with permission.)

(see **Figure 7.7**). In spite of the many errors they make, researchers have found that invented spelling coupled with corrective feedback from parents and preschool teachers helps children learn their language's system for representing speech sounds with letters (Ouellette & Sénéchal, 2008). Thus, the evidence suggests that one of the best ways parents and preschool teachers can help young children prepare for formal instruction in reading is to engage them in activities that encourage word play and invented spelling.

receptive vocabulary

the words that are understood when heard

expressive vocabulary

the words whose meaning is used correctly when speaking

Figure 7.7 Translation: *A snake came to visit our class.* A 5-year-old used a strategy called "invented spelling" to write this sentence about a snake's visit (accompanied by an animal handler we hope!) to her kindergarten class. Invented spelling requires a high level of phonological awareness. Research suggests that children who have well-developed phonological awareness skills by the time they reach kindergarten learn to read more quickly.

(Courtesy of Jerry and Denise Boyd. Used with permission.)

Language and Numeracy

In a chapter from his book *Outliers*, Canadian author Malcolm Gladwell put forth the idea that language plays a role in our ability to master numbers. To illustrate his point, he compares number words in Chinese with those in English. He contends that they differ in at least two notable ways. For one, Chinese number words are shorter and take less time to pronounce than their English equivalents, and, thus, they use up less short-term memory capacity. "Most of them can be uttered in less than one-quarter of a second (for instance, 4 is 'si' and 7 'qi'). Their English equivalents—'four,' 'seven'—are longer: pronouncing them takes about one-third of a second" (Dehaene, 1997, quoted in Gladwell, 2008, p. 228). Consequently, the ability to remember a larger quantity of numbers in Chinese than in English is entirely due to this difference in length. Add to this the extra challenge of having to learn more English number words for the same numerals in Chinese. For example, in either language counting from 1 to 10 means a child needs to learn 10 numeral words (i.e., 1, 2, 3, 4, 5, 6, 7, 8, 9, and 10), but after that, the Chinese numbering system, unlike the English system, doesn't require a child to learn any new words until he reaches the numeral 100 (e.g., 11 is *eleven*, a new word in English, but simply "ten-one" in Chinese; likewise, 12 is *twelve*, another new word in English, but simply "ten-two" in Chinese). Similarly, counting from 20 to 99 requires learning eight more numeral words in English but none in Chinese (e.g., 30 is *thirty* in English, but simply "three-ten" in Chinese). In sum, to count from 1 to 100 in English, a child must learn 28 words, whereas in Chinese, a child needs only 11—the words for 1 through 10 and for 100 (Cheng, 2009a). This difference gives children who learn numbers in Chinese an early advantage. A 4-year-old Chinese child can usually count to about 40, whereas, their same-age English-speaking peers can count only to 15 (Gladwell, 2008).

Although **numeracy**—the ability to use numbers—is a very different skill set from literacy, there are some parallels. For example, the ability to learn both literacy and numeracy can be enhanced through early parental or caregiver influences. In the case of numeracy, Concordia University developmentalists suggest that young children are capable of and interested in number concepts, and parents can encourage children to think about mathematics in everyday situations (Osana & Rayner, 2010). These researchers emphasize that caregivers can take advantage of preschoolers' eagerness to prepare them for the mathematics they will encounter in school. Moreover, the development of numeracy abilities in preschoolers helps to facilitate the learning of more advanced mathematical concepts in school (Jordan, Kaplan, Locuniak, & Ramineni, 2007; LeFevre et al., 2009). In one Canadian study, researchers found that children who experience more numeracy-related activities at home show greater proficiency at school-based mathematical tasks (LeFevre et al., 2009). Some of these experiences target numeracy skill development directly (e.g., counting objects, sorting objects by category, practising number names, printing numbers). Other experiences involve informal numeracy activities that have quantitative components, such as playing board games with dice, playing card games, measuring quantities while cooking, or setting the table at home. Although both direct and indirect activities in the home are important in promoting numeracy proficiency, these researchers were the first to show a robust relationship between the frequency with which children participate in indirect numeracy activities at home and mathematical proficiency.

numeracy

the knowledge and skills required to effectively manage the mathematical demands of diverse situations (Statistics Canada, 2008b)

Test Yourself before going on

1. _____ _____ is children's ability to rapidly form hypotheses about the meanings of new words.

2. During the grammar explosion, _____ appear in children's speech.

3. Mark "Y" by each example of phonological awareness and "N" by each non-example:
   _____ (a) a child recites the alphabet
   _____ (b) a child says *cat* when asked to suggest a word that rhymes with *hat*

_____ (c) a child recognizes her written name

_____ (d) a child writes *brn* and states that he has written the word *barn*

4. Engaging in activities that possess quantitative elements, such as playing games with dice, playing card games, or measuring quantities while cooking, are indirect ways that parents can encourage the development of _____ skills in their child.

Critical Thinking

5. Suppose you knew a parent who was thrilled that her 5-year-old was beginning to write words but was concerned about the little girl's spelling errors. How would you explain the errors to the mother, and what would you advise her to do about them?

Differences in Intelligence

Thanks to advances in language skills, intelligence testing is far more reliable among preschoolers than among infants. Psychologists have constructed standardized tests of intelligence for preschoolers to measure their vocabulary, reasoning skills, and other cognitive processes that depend on language. However, widespread use of these tests has led to an ongoing debate about the origins of score differences and the degree to which scores can be modified.

Measuring Intelligence

An important assumption in studying differences in intelligence is that these differences can be measured. Thus, it's important to understand something about the tests psychologists use to measure intelligence as well as the meaning and stability of the scores the tests generate.

THE FIRST TESTS   The first modern intelligence test was published in 1905 in France by Alfred Binet and Theodore Simon (Binet & Simon, 1905). From the beginning, the test had a practical purpose—to identify children who might have difficulty in school. For this reason, the tasks Binet and Simon devised for the test were very much like some school tasks, including measures of vocabulary, comprehension of facts and relationships, and mathematical and verbal reasoning. For example, could the child describe the difference between wood and glass? Could the young child identify his nose, his ear, his head? Could he tell which of two weights was heavier?

Lewis Terman and his associates at Stanford University modified and extended many of Binet's original tasks when they translated and revised the test for use in the United States (Terman, 1916; Terman & Merrill, 1937). The Stanford-Binet, the name by which the test is still known, initially described a child's performance in terms of a score called an **intelligence quotient**, later shortened to **IQ**. This score was computed by comparing the child's chronological age (in years and months) with his mental age, defined as the level of questions he could answer correctly. For example, a child who could solve the problems for a 6-year-old but not those for a 7-year-old would have a mental age of 6. The formula used to calculate the IQ was

$$\text{mental age} / \text{chronological age} \times 100 = \text{IQ}$$

This formula results in an IQ above 100 for children whose mental age is higher than their chronological age and an IQ below 100 for children whose mental age is below their chronological age.

This system for calculating IQ is no longer used. Instead, IQ scores for the Stanford-Binet and all other intelligence tests are now based on a direct comparison of a child's performance with the average performance of a large group of other children of the same age. But the scoring is arranged so that an IQ of 100 is still average.

As you can see in **Figure 7.8**, about two-thirds of all children achieve scores between 85 and 115; roughly 96% of scores fall between 70 and 130. Children who score above 130 are often called *gifted*; those who score below 70 may be diagnosed with an *intellectual disability*. A child classified as having an intellectual disability will

Learning Objective 7.13
Describe the strengths and weaknesses of IQ tests.

intelligence quotient (IQ)
the ratio of mental age to chronological age; also, a general term for any kind of score derived from an intelligence test

Figure 7.8 IQ scores form what mathematicians call a normal distribution—the famous "bell curve" you may have heard about. The two sides of a normal distribution curve are mirror images of each other. Thus, 34% of children score between 85 and 100, and another 34% score between 100 and 115. Likewise, 13% score between 70 and 85 and another 13% between 115 and 130. A few other human characteristics, such as height, are normally distributed as well.

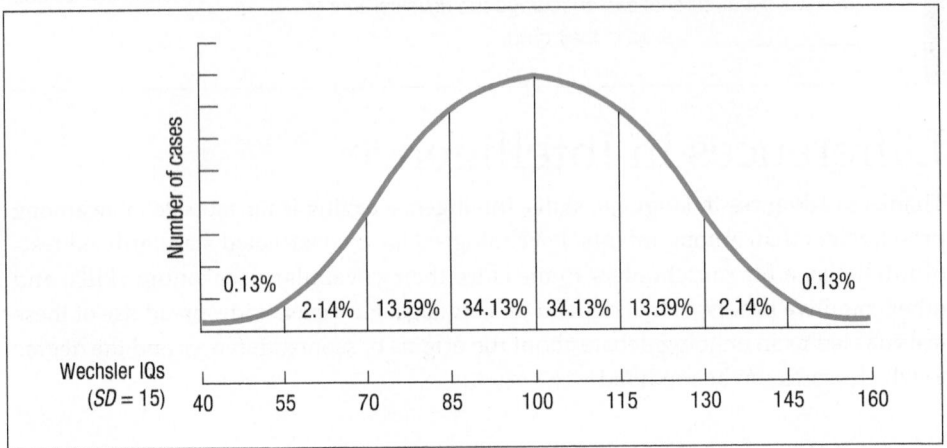

verbal comprehension

the ability to access and apply acquired word knowledge to verbalize meaningful concepts, think about verbal information, and express ideas in words (NCS Pearson, Inc., 2015)

visual spatial

the ability to evaluate visual details and understand visual spatial relationships to construct geometric designs from a model (NCS Pearson, Inc., 2015)

fluid reasoning

the ability to detect the underlying conceptual relationship among visual objects and use reasoning to identify and apply logical rules (NCS Pearson, Inc., 2015)

working memory

the ability to register, maintain, and manipulate visual and auditory information in conscious awareness, which requires attention and concentration, as well as visual and auditory discrimination (NCS Pearson, Inc., 2015)

processing speed

the speed and accuracy of visual identification, decision making, and decision implementation (NCS Pearson, Inc., 2015)

also tend to have a problem with "adaptive behaviour," such as an inability to dress or feed himself, a problem getting along with others, or a significant problem adapting to the demands of a regular school classroom.

MODERN INTELLIGENCE TESTS The tests psychologists use most frequently today were developed by David Wechsler. The Wechsler Intelligence Scales for Children (WISC-V) is the current edition for measuring children's general thinking and reasoning skills (Wechsler, 2014). On the WISC-V, the child is presented different types of problems, each ranging from very easy to very hard on five primary indices: **verbal comprehension, visual spatial, fluid reasoning, working memory,** and **processing speed.** These five indices are derived from recent evidence-based, neurocognitive models of information processing (i.e., the ability to quickly acquire, retain, organize, and apply information) and can be used to indicate intellectual strengths and weaknesses (e.g., learning disabilities and attention disorders) in children (see the chapter on Physical and Cognitive Development in Middle Childhood for details on these conditions). A Full Scale IQ, or measure of overall intellectual ability, is derived from the scores on the subtests of the five indices. The WISC-V[CDN] edition of the test has been standardized to reflect the Canadian norms for children (NCS Pearson, Inc., 2015).

STABILITY AND PREDICTIVE VALUE OF IQ SCORES The correlation between a child's IQ test score and her scores on tests that measure pre-academic skills such as letter knowledge is about 0.70 (Wechsler, 2002). Children with higher IQs are more likely to get good grades, complete high school, and go on to post-secondary education (Konold & Canivez, 2010). On the whole, children with high IQ scores will be among the high achievers in school, and those who score low will be among the low achievers. But success in school also depends on many factors other than IQ, including motivation, interest, and persistence. For this reason, some children with high IQ scores don't excel in school, while some lower-IQ children do.

IQ scores are also quite stable. If two tests are given a few months or a few years apart, the scores are likely to be very similar. The correlations between IQ scores from adjacent years in middle childhood, for example, are typically in the range of 0.80 (Wechsler, 2002). Yet, this high level of predictability masks an interesting fact: Many children show quite wide fluctuations in their scores. In fact, about half of all children show noticeable changes from one testing to another and over time (McCall, 1993). Some show steadily rising scores, and some have declining ones; some show a peak in middle childhood and then a decline in adolescence. In rare cases, the shifts may cover a range as large as 40 points.

Such wide fluctuations are more common in young children. The general rule is that the older the child, the more stable the IQ score—although even in older children, scores may still fluctuate in response to major stresses, such as parental divorce, a change of schools, or the birth of a sibling.

LIMITATIONS OF IQ TESTS   Before moving on to the question of the possible origins of differences in IQ, it is important to emphasize a few key limitations of IQ tests and the scores derived from them. IQ tests do not measure underlying competence. An IQ score cannot tell you (or a teacher, or anyone else) that your child has some specific, fixed, underlying capacity. Traditional IQ tests also do not measure a whole host of skills that are likely to be highly significant for getting along in the world. Originally, IQ tests were designed to measure only the specific range of skills that are needed for success in school. They do this quite well. What they do *not* do is indicate anything about a particular person's creativity, insight, street smarts, ability to read social cues, or understanding of spatial relationships (Baron, 2003; Gardner, 2003).

Origins of Individual Differences in Intelligence

If a couple whom you perceive to be smart conceive a child, what would you predict about their offspring's IQ scores? Most people know that differences in intelligence run in families. But why do related people seem to be alike in this regard? Is nature or nurture responsible?

EVIDENCE FOR HEREDITY   Both twin studies and studies of adopted children show strong hereditary influences on IQ, as you already know from the **Research Report** in the chapter on Prenatal Development and Birth. Identical twins are more like each other in IQ than are fraternal twins, and the IQs of adopted children are better predicted from the IQs of their natural parents than from those of their adoptive parents (Rizzi & Posthuma, 2013). These findings are precisely what researchers would expect if a strong genetic element were at work.

EVIDENCE FOR FAMILY INFLUENCES   Adoption studies also provide some strong support for an environmental influence on IQ scores, because the IQ scores of adopted children are clearly affected by the environment in which they have grown up. The clearest evidence for this comes from a study of 38 French children, all adopted in infancy (Capron & Duyme, 1989). Roughly half the children had been born to better-educated parents from a higher social class, while the other half had been born to working-class or poverty-level parents. Some of the children in each group had then been adopted by parents in a higher social class, while the others grew up in poorer families. The effect of rearing conditions was evident in that the children reared in upper-class homes had IQs 15 to 16 points higher than those reared in lower-class families, regardless of the social class level or education of the birth parents. A genetic effect was evident in that the children born to upper-class parents had higher IQs than those from lower-class families, no matter what kind of environment they were reared in.

When developmentalists observe how individual families interact with their infants or young children and then follow the children over time to see which ones later have high or low IQs, they begin to get some sense of the kinds of specific family interactions that foster higher scores. For one thing, parents of higher-IQ children provide them with an interesting and complex physical environment, including play materials that are appropriate for the child's age and developmental level (Pianta & Egeland, 1994). They also respond warmly and appropriately to the child's behaviour, smiling when the child smiles, answering the child's questions, and in myriad ways reacting to the child's cues (Barnard et al., 1989; Lewis, 1993). These kinds of parental behaviours may even help to limit the effects of poverty and other sources of family

Critical Thinking

In your opinion, how might having a higher IQ make a child more resilient? For example, in what specific ways might the life of a brighter child be different from the life of a less-bright child in the same environment?

Learning Objective 7.14

Identify what kinds of evidence support the nature and nurture explanations for individual differences in IQ.

stress on children's intellectual development (Robinson, Lanzi, Weinberg, Ramey, & Ramey, 2002).

Parents of higher-IQ children also talk to them often, using language that is descriptively rich and accurate (Hart & Risley, 1995; Sigman et al., 1988). And when they play with or interact with their children, they operate in what Vygotsky referred to as the *zone of proximal development*, aiming their conversation, their questions, and their assistance at a level that is just above the level the children could manage on their own, thus helping the children to master new skills (Landry et al., 1996).

On the other hand, one study from the Concordia Longitudinal Risk Project (see the chapter on Basic Concepts and Methods) looked at the intellectual functioning of offspring of mothers who were themselves high-risk children and provides evidence of intergenerational influences on intelligence (Saltaris et al., 2004). Saltaris and her colleagues found that mothers who had a history of aggression in childhood were less likely to provide effective intellectual stimulation for their own preschool-age children. These mothers displayed less constructive feedback during problem-solving activities and less effective teaching strategies. These characteristics, in turn, put the early cognitive development of their offspring at risk.

EVIDENCE FOR PRESCHOOL INFLUENCES Home environments and family interactions are not the only sources of environmental influence. Programs such as Head Start are based squarely on the assumption that it is possible to modify the trajectory of a child's intellectual development, especially if the intervention occurs early enough (Ramey & Ramey, 1998). Children in enriched preschool programs normally show a gain of about 10 IQ points after they are enrolled in them, but this IQ gain typically fades and then disappears within the first few years of school (Zigler & Styfco, 1993).

When the enrichment program is begun in infancy rather than at age 3 or 4, the positive effects persist into adulthood (Campbell et al., 2012; Pungello et al., 2010). One very well-designed and meticulously reported infancy intervention was called the Abecedarian Project (Campbell & Ramey, 1994; Ramey, 1993; Ramey & Campbell, 1987). Infants from poverty-level families whose mothers had low IQs were randomly assigned either to a special daycare program or to a control group that received nutritional supplements and medical care but no special enriched daycare. The special daycare program began when the infants were 6 weeks to 12 weeks old and lasted until they began kindergarten.

Figure 7.9 graphs the average IQ scores of the children in each of these two groups from age 2 to 12. You can see that the IQs of the children who had been enrolled in the special program were higher at every age. Fully 44% of the control group children had IQ scores classified as borderline or developmentally delayed (scores below 85), compared with only 12.8% of the children who had been in the special program. In addition, the enriched daycare group had significantly higher scores on both reading and mathematics tests at age 12 and were only half as likely to have repeated a grade (Ramey, 1992, 1993).

READINESS TO LEARN AT SCHOOL How ready for school is the typical Canadian 3- to 5-year-old? A major Statistics Canada study by Eleanor Thomas (2006) provides an interesting snapshot. Using National Longitudinal Survey of Children and Youth (NLSCY–cycle 5) data, she measured five domains of readiness:

1. Language and communication skill
2. Academic skill

Children who attend enrichment programs typically do not show lasting gains in IQ, but they are more likely to succeed in school.

(Photo: Jonas Unruh/Vetta/Getty Images)

Figure 7.9 In Ramey's study, children from poverty-level families were randomly assigned in infancy to an experimental group that received special daycare or to a control group, with the intervention lasting until age 5. At kindergarten, both groups entered public school. The difference in IQ between the experimental and control groups remained statistically significant even at age 12, seven years after the intervention had ended.

(**SOURCE:** Based on Ramey, C.T., & Campbell, F.A. (1987). The Carolina Abecedarian Project: An educational experiment concerning human malleability. In J.J. Gallagher & C.T. Ramey (Eds.), *The malleability of children* (pp. 127–140). Baltimore, MD: Paul H. Brookes., Figure 3, p. 135, with additional data from Ramey, 1983, Figure 2, p. 29.)

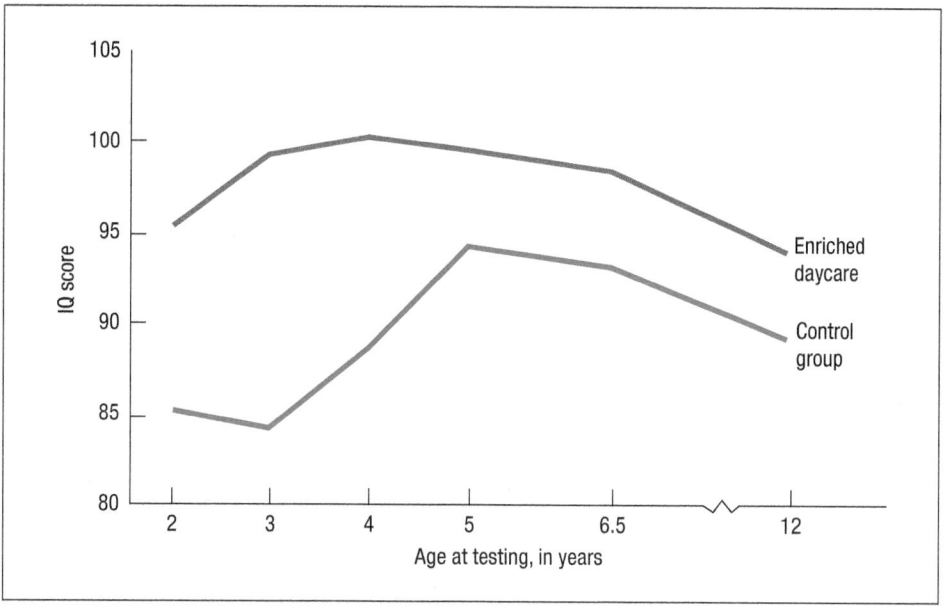

3. Self-regulation of learning

4. Self-control of behaviour

5. Social competence and independence

Girls, she found, enter school with better communication skills, stronger abilities in copying and symbol use, higher scores in attention and in self-control of impulsive behaviour, and higher independence in dressing. Boys were rated above girls on just one measure—curiosity. Although children from lower-income households were generally less ready to learn than children from more affluent households, some aspects of the child's home environment were linked with higher levels of readiness regardless of household income. These activities include daily reading, high positive parent–child interaction, participation in organized sports, lessons in physical activities, and lessons in the arts. But the reality is that children from lower-income households are less likely to have these experiences.

Studies from the Concordia Longitudinal Risk Project indicate that there can also be intergenerational transfer of risk—that is, mothers with a childhood history of social withdrawal can, in turn, put their children's expressive language and language-related academic performance at risk (Campisi, Serbin, Stack, Schwartzman, & Ledingham, 2009; Stack, Serbin, Mantis, & Kingdon, 2015). Two programs in Canada that target high-risk children are Aboriginal Head Start and HighScope. Health Canada (2002b) sponsors several hundred Aboriginal Head Start programs for First Nations, Inuit, Metis, and other Indigenous children. This early intervention program provides young Indigenous children with a half-day preschool experience that prepares them for their school years by focusing on education and school readiness, Indigenous culture and language, parental involvement, health promotion, nutrition, and social support. HighScope, a preschool program that has shown long-term success in high-risk children in the United States, now has three centres across Canada. One HighScope study followed children of poverty into adulthood. The results showed significant differences between those at-risk children who were in the program and those who were not. Children who went through the program had better school readiness skills, spent less time in special education programs, had superior high school graduation rates, had higher employment income, and had lower rates of criminal arrests (Schweinhart, 2003).

COMBINING THE INFORMATION   Virtually all psychologists would agree that heredity is a highly important influence on IQ scores. Studies around the world consistently yield estimates that roughly 40% of the variation in IQ within a given population of children is due to heredity (Rizzi & Posthuma, 2013). The remaining 60% is clearly due to environment or family influences, or interactions between environment and heredity.

reaction range

a range between upper and lower boundaries for traits such as intelligence, which is established by one's genes; one's environment determines where, within those limits, one will fall

One useful way to think about this interaction is to use the concept of **reaction range**, a range between upper and lower boundaries of functioning that is established by one's genetic heritage; exactly where a child will fall within those boundaries is determined by environment. Some developmental psychologists estimate that the reaction range for IQ is about 20 to 25 points (Weinberg, 1989). That is, given a specific genetic heritage, a child's actual IQ test performance may vary as much as 20 or 25 points, depending on the richness or poverty of the environment in which he grows up. When the child's environment is changed for the better, the child moves closer to the upper end of his reaction range. When the environment becomes worse, the child's effective intellectual performance falls toward the lower end of his reaction range. Thus, even though intelligence as measured on an IQ test is highly heritable and falls within the reaction range, the absolute IQ score is determined by environment.

Test Yourself before going on

1. _____ coined the term "IQ."
2. Indicate which of the following factors contribute(s) to IQ scores in early childhood.
    _____ (a) heredity
    _____ (b) family environment
    _____ (c) preschool programs

Critical Thinking

3. What do you think of the notion of providing high IQ infants and preschoolers with publically funded enrichment programming? What would be some benefits and drawbacks of such programs?

Summary

Physical Changes

7.1 Summarize the major milestones of growth and motor development between 2 and 6.

- Physical development is slower from age 2 to 6 than it is in infancy, but it is steady. Large-muscle skills (e.g., running, jumping, galloping) show marked improvement, but small-muscle (fine motor) skills advance more slowly.

7.2 Highlight the important changes that happen in the brain during these years.

- Significant changes in brain lateralization occur in early childhood. Handedness is weakly related to brain lateralization.

7.3 Highlight the nutritional and health care needs of young children.

- Slower rates of growth contribute to declines in appetite. Unintentional injuries are a major cause of harm and death for preschoolers. Parenting, cognitive, and social factors affect injury rates.

7.4 Describe the factors surrounding adverse childhood experiences, and how traumatic events affect children's development.

- Long-term consequences of child maltreatment can include a variety of emotional problems and can result in changes in brain structure and function.

Cognitive Changes

7.5 Summarize the characteristics of children's thought during Piaget's preoperational stage.

- Piaget marked the beginning of the preoperational period as the point when children begin to use mental symbols. In Piaget's view, preschool children are still egocentric, lack understanding of conservation, and are often fooled by appearances.

7.6 Describe how recent research has challenged Piaget's view of this period.

- Research indicates that young children are less egocentric than Piaget thought. By age 4, they can distinguish between appearance and reality in a variety of tasks.

7.7 Describe theory of mind and how it develops.

- By the end of early childhood, children have a well-developed theory of mind. They understand that other people's actions are based on their thoughts and beliefs. The theory of mind includes the false belief principle, an understanding of the factors that cause another person to believe something that isn't true.

7.8 Describe how information-processing and sociocultural theorists explain changes in young children's thinking.

- Information-processing theory explains early childhood cognitive development in terms of limitations on young children's memory systems. Vygotsky's sociocultural theory asserts that children's thinking is shaped by social interaction through the medium of language.

Changes in Language

7.9 Describe how fast-mapping helps children learn new words.

- Fast-mapping, the use of categories to learn new words, enables young children to acquire new words rapidly. It involves the rapid formation of hypotheses about the meanings of new words based on the contexts in which they occur.

7.10 Highlight what happens during the grammar explosion.

- During the grammar explosion (ages 3 to 4), children make large advances in grammatical fluency. Inflections, complex word orders, negatives, and questions appear in their speech.

7.11 Describe what phonological awareness is, and why it is important.

- Development of an awareness of the sound patterns of a particular language during early childhood is important in learning to read during the school years. Children seem to acquire this skill through word play and dialogic reading.

7.12 Describe the similarities and differences in language and numeracy development.

- Although numeracy deals with math skill and literacy with language skill, there are overlaps. Number words impact the short-term memory capacity to learn and manipulate numbers. Both direct and indirect practice activities improve numeracy skills.

Differences in Intelligence

7.13 Describe the strengths and weaknesses of IQ tests.

- Scores on early childhood intelligence tests are predictive of later school performance and are at least moderately consistent over time. However, IQ tests only measure a limited range of skills.

7.14 Identify what kinds of evidence support the nature and nurture explanations for individual differences in IQ.

- Twin and adoption studies indicate that ~40% of the variation in IQ scores is due to genetic differences, the remainder to environment and the interaction of heredity and environment. Family variables and preschool experiences also contribute to variation in IQ scores.

Chapter 8
Social and Personality Development in Early Childhood

EpicStockMedia/Fotolia

 ## Learning Objectives

THEORIES OF SOCIAL AND PERSONALITY DEVELOPMENT

8.1 Summarize the major themes of development proposed by psychoanalytic theorists for the early childhood period.

8.2 Summarize the findings of social-cognitive theorists with respect to young children's understanding of the social world.

FAMILY RELATIONSHIPS AND STRUCTURE

8.3 Describe how attachment changes during the early childhood years.

8.4 Discuss how parenting styles affect children's development.

8.5 Identify how ethnicity and socioeconomic status interact with parenting styles.

8.6 Explain how family structure is related to children's development.

8.7 Describe the impact of divorce on children in early childhood and in later years.

8.8 Identify some possible ways divorce-related changes in family structure affect development.

PEER RELATIONSHIPS

8.9 Trace a child's changing relationship with his or her peers through play.

8.10 Identify the key factors in preschool children's aggressive behaviour.

8.11 Trace the changes in prosocial behaviour and friendship patterns during early childhood.

PERSONALITY AND SELF-CONCEPT

8.12 Describe temperament changes in early childhood.

8.13 Trace the changes in the young child's categorical, emotional, and social selves during the preschool years.

GENDER DEVELOPMENT

8.14 Describe the major theoretical orientations that explain gender development.

8.15 Identify how preschoolers acquire sex-role knowledge.

8.16 Describe the sex-typed behaviour of young children.

If you asked a random sample of adults to tell you the most important characteristics of children between ages 2 and 6, the first thing on the list would probably be their rapidly changing social abilities during these years. Nay-saying, oppositional toddlers who spend most of their playtime alone become skilled, cooperative playmates by age 5 or 6. Thus, the most obvious characteristic of 6-year-olds is how socially "grown up" they seem compared to 2-year-olds. Moreover, their blossoming physical, cognitive, and language skills have led to changes in how preschoolers view themselves and relate to their families. Most have also broadened their social networks to include peers.

In this chapter, we will discuss all of these changes and acquaint you with the major theoretical explanations for them. We begin by reviewing the ideas proposed by psychoanalytic theorists. Next, you will read about the very different explanations of social-cognitive theorists. From there, we turn to the topics of family relationships and structure, young children's relationships with others, and changes in personality and self-concept. Finally, we will address gender role development.

Theories of Social and Personality Development

What is the period of early childhood all about? One way to describe it would be to call it the "stepping out" phase, because that's precisely what 2- to 6-year-olds do. They "step out" from the safety of the strong emotional bonds that they share with their parents into the risky world of relationships with others. How do they do it? The psychoanalysts outlined the broad themes of this foundational time of life, and the work of more recent theorists has provided us with a few details about the skills that children develop in the process of stepping out. Before we get into the details, let's look at the themes.

Learning Objective 8.1

Summarize the major themes of development proposed by psychoanalytic theorists for the early childhood period.

Psychoanalytic Perspectives

Freud's theory of personality development emphasized two *psychosexual* stages of maturation during the preschool years. The developmental task of the *anal stage* (1 to 3 years) is toilet training. The task of the *phallic stage* is to establish a foundation for later gender and moral development by identifying with the same-sex parent. We might sum up Freud's view of the early childhood period as the time in life when young children, first, gain control of their bodily functions and, second, renegotiate their relationships with their parents to prepare for stepping out into the world of peers.

Erikson agreed with Freud's views on bodily control and parental relationships during the preschool years, but he placed the emphasis somewhat differently. Both of the stages he identified in the preschool period (see Erikson's Psychosocial Stages table in the chapter on Theories of Development) are triggered by children's growing physical, cognitive, and social skills. The stage Erikson called *autonomy versus shame and doubt*, for example, centres on the toddler's new mobility and the accompanying desire for autonomy. The stage of *initiative versus guilt* is ushered in by new cognitive skills, particularly the preschooler's ability to plan, which accentuates his wish to take the initiative. However, his developing conscience dictates the boundaries within which this initiative may be exercised (Evans & Erikson, 1967). For example, think about a situation in which one child wants to play with another child's toy. His sense of initiative might motivate him to simply take it, but his conscience will likely prompt him to find a more socially acceptable way to gain the toy. If he fails to achieve the kind of self-control that is required to maintain conformity to his conscience, the child is likely to be hampered by excessive guilt and defensiveness in future psychosocial crises.

For Erikson, the key to healthy development during this period is striking a balance between the child's emerging skills and desire for autonomy and the parents' need to protect the child and control the child's behaviour. Thus, the parents' task changes rather dramatically after infancy. In the early months of life, the parents' primary task is to provide enough warmth, predictability, and responsiveness to foster a secure attachment and to support basic physiological needs. But once the child becomes physically, linguistically, and cognitively more independent, the need to control becomes a central aspect of the parents' task. Too much control and the child will not have sufficient opportunity to explore; too little control and the child will become unmanageable and fail to learn the social skills he will need to get along with peers as well as adults. This is illustrated in Canadian studies in which parents who support autonomy in their children during the early years (e.g., by encouraging independent problem-solving, choice, and engaged decision making), especially in challenging situations (e.g., when a child doesn't get exactly what they want or they are requesting the attention of a busy parent), see improved social and emotional development in their children as they get older (Harvey et al., 2016; Matte-Gagné, Harvey, Stack, & Serbin, 2015).

(Photo: berc/Fotolia)

According to Erikson, young children need opportunities to develop autonomy and show initiative within the bounds of parental guidance and direction.

Social-Cognitive Perspectives

In contrast to the psychoanalytic tradition, **social-cognitive theory** assumes that social and emotional changes in the child are the result of, or at least are facilitated by, the enormous growth in cognitive abilities that happens during the preschool years, especially in the domains of *metacognition* and *theory of mind* (Brosseau-Liard, Penny, & Poulin-Dubois, 2015; Feurer, Sassu, Cimeli, & Roebers, 2015; Poulin-Dubois & Brosseau-Liard, 2016; Salmon, 2016). Over the past few decades, psychologists have devoted a great deal of theoretical and empirical attention to determining just how the social and cognitive domains are connected.

PERSON PERCEPTION   Have you ever heard a child describe a peer as "nice" or "not nice"? Preschoolers' emerging capacity for forming meaningful categories to apply to people is called **person perception**, or the ability to classify others. For example, by age 5 or so, children are capable of using trait labels such as "nice" and "not nice" to describe others (Heyman, 2009), and they describe their peers in terms of traits such as "grumpy" and "mean" (Yuill, 1997). Moreover, children of this age make judgments very similar to those of adults when asked to identify the most intelligent child in their class or play group (Droege & Stipek, 1993). They also make statements about other people's patterns of behaviour—"Grandma always lets me pick the cereal at the grocery store." They use these observations to classify others into groups such as "people I like" and "people I don't like."

However, young children's observations and categorizations of people are far less consistent than those of older children. A playmate they judge to be "nice" one day may be referred to as "mean" the next. Developmentalists have found that young children's judgments about others are inconsistent because they tend to base them on their most recent interactions with those individuals (Ruble & Dweck, 1995). In other words, a 4-year-old girl describes one of her playmates as "nice" on Monday because she shares a cookie but as "mean" on Tuesday because she refuses to share a chocolate bar. Or, the child declares, "I don't like Grandma anymore because she made me go to bed early."

Preschoolers also categorize others on the basis of observable characteristics, such as race, age, and gender (Heyman, 2009). For example, the *cross-race effect*, a phenomenon in which individuals are more likely to remember the faces of people of their own race than those of people of a different race, is established by age 5 (Goodman et al., 2007). Similarly, they talk about "big kids" (school-age children) and "little kids" (their age mates), and seem to know that they fit in best with the latter. Self-segregation by gender—a topic you'll read more about later in the chapter—begins as early as age 2.

UNDERSTANDING RULE CATEGORIES   If you attended a formal dinner at which the forks were on the right side of the plates rather than on the left, would you be upset? Probably not, because social conventions, such as customs that govern where to place flatware, are rules that have nothing to do with our fundamental sense of right and wrong. Consequently, most of us are not troubled when these types of rules are violated and take a dim view of people who are bothered by such trifles. By contrast, we have little tolerance for the breaking of rules that we view as having a basis in morality, such as laws that forbid stealing and unwritten rules such as the one that prohibits you from flirting with your best friend's romantic partner (or with your romantic partner's best friend!). When and how did we learn to make such distinctions?

Researchers have found that children begin to respond differently to violations of social conventions and moral rules between ages 2 and 3 (Smetana, Schlagman, & Adams, 1993). For example, they view taking another child's toy without permission as a more serious violation of rules than forgetting to say "thank you." They also say, just as adults would in response to similar questions, that stealing and physical

Learning Objective 8.2

Summarize the findings of social-cognitive theorists with respect to young children's understanding of the social world.

social-cognitive theory

the theoretical perspective that asserts that social and personality development in early childhood is related to improvements in the cognitive domain

person perception

the ability to classify others according to categories such as age, gender, and race

violence are wrong, even if their particular family or preschool has no explicit rule against them. This kind of understanding seems to develop both as a consequence of preschoolers' increasing capacity for classification and as a result of adults' tendency to emphasize moral transgressions more than social-convention violations when punishing children (Smetana, Jambon, Conry-Murray, & Sturge-Apple, 2012).

UNDERSTANDING OTHERS' INTENTIONS   Would you feel differently about a person who deliberately scratched your car paint with a key than you would about someone who accidentally scratched it while washing your car for you? Chances are you would be far more forgiving of the person who unintentionally scratched your car paint because we tend to base our judgments of others' behaviour and our responses to them on what we perceive to be their intentions. Working from his assumptions about young children's egocentrism, Piaget suggested that young children are incapable of such discriminations.

However, later research has demonstrated that young children do understand intentions to some degree (Zhang & Yu, 2002). For one thing, it's quite common for preschoolers to say "It was an accident . . . I didn't mean to do it" when they are punished. Such protests suggest that children understand that intentional wrongdoing is punished more severely than unintentional transgressions of the rules.

Several studies suggest that children can make judgments about actors' intentions both when faced with abstract problems and when personally motivated by a desire to avoid punishment. For example, in a classic study, 3-year-olds listened to stories about children playing ball (Thompson, 2009). Pictures were used to convey information about intentions (see **Figure 8.1**). The children were more likely to label as "bad" or "naughty" the child who intended to harm a playmate than the child who accidentally hit another child in the head with the ball. However, the children's judgments were also influenced by outcomes. In other words, they were more likely to say a child who wanted to hurt his playmate was "good" if he failed to hit the child with the ball. These results suggest that children know more about intentions than Piaget thought, but, compared to older children, they are still limited in their ability to base judgments entirely on intentions (Jambon & Smetana, 2014).

Figure 8.1 Pictures like these have been used to assess young children's understanding of an actor's intentions.

Test Yourself before going on

1. Classify each developmental milestone as associated with (E) Erikson's theory or (S) social-cognitive theory.
   - _____ (a) resolving the initiative versus guilt crisis
   - _____ (b) distinguishing between social conventions and moral rules
   - _____ (c) understanding others' intentions
   - _____ (d) resolving the autonomy versus shame and doubt crisis
   - _____ (e) categorizing others

Critical Thinking

2. How might the psychoanalytic and social-cognitive perspectives on early childhood development be integrated into a comprehensive explanation of age-related changes during this period?

Family Relationships and Structure

Psychologists agree that family relationships constitute one of the most, if not *the* most, influential factors in early childhood development. These relationships reflect both continuity and change. The preschooler is no less attached to her family than the infant but, at the same time, is struggling to establish independence.

Attachment

By 12 months of age, a baby has normally established a clear attachment to at least one caregiver. By age 2 or 3, the attachment is just as strong, but many attachment behaviours have become less visible. Three-year-olds still want to sit on Mom's or Dad's lap; they are still likely to seek some closeness when Mom returns from an absence. But when she is not afraid or under stress, the 3-year-old is able to wander farther and farther from her safe base without apparent distress. She can also deal with her potential anxiety due to separation by creating shared plans with the parents. For example, a parent might say "I'll be home after your naptime," to which the child may respond "Can we watch a movie then?" (Crittenden, 1992).

Attachment quality also predicts behaviour during the preschool years. Children who are securely attached to parents experience fewer behaviour problems. Specifically, those who are insecurely attached display more anger and aggression toward both peers and adults in social settings such as daycare and preschool (Schmidt, DeMulder, & Denham, 2002). Interestingly, insecurely attached preschoolers are also more likely than their securely attached peers to develop negative, critical attitudes toward themselves (Madigan, Atkinson, Laurin, & Benoit, 2013).

For most children, the attachment relationship, whether secure or not, seems to change at about age 4. Bowlby (1969) described this new stage, or level, as a *goal-corrected partnership.* Just as the first attachment probably requires the baby to understand that his mother will continue to exist when she isn't there, so the preschooler grasps that the *relationship* continues to exist even when the partners are apart. Also at about age 4, the child's internal model of attachment appears to generalize. Bowlby argued that the child's model becomes less a specific property of an individual relationship and more a general property of all the child's social relationships. Thus, it's not surprising that 4- and 5-year-olds who are securely attached to their parents are more likely than their insecurely attached peers to have

Learning Objective 8.3

Describe how attachment changes during the early childhood years.

(Photo: Inu/Shutterstock)

Off he goes, into greater independence. A child this age, especially one with secure attachment, is far more confident about being at a distance from his safe base.

positive relationships with their preschool teachers (DeMulder, Denham, Schmidt, & Mitchell, 2000).

At the same time, advances in the internal working model lead to new conflicts. In contrast to infants, 2-year-olds realize that they are independent contributors to the parent–child relationship. This heightened sense of autonomy brings them into more and more situations in which parents want one thing and children another. However, contrary to popular stereotypes, 2-year-olds actually comply with parents' requests more often than not. They are more likely to comply with safety requests ("Don't touch that; it's hot!") or with prohibitions about care of objects ("Don't tear up the book") than they are with requests to delay ("I can't talk to you now, I'm on the phone") or with instructions about self-care ("Please wash your hands now"). On the whole, however, children of this age comply fairly readily (Gralinski & Kopp, 1993). When they resist, it is most likely to be passive resistance—simply not doing what is asked rather than saying "no."

Parenting Styles

Learning Objective 8.4

Discuss how parenting styles affect children's development.

Families vary in their responses to preschoolers' increasing demands for independence. Psychologists have struggled over the years to identify the best ways of describing the many dimensions along which families may vary. An early conceptualization was offered by developmentalist Diana Baumrind, who focused on four aspects of family functioning: (1) warmth or nurturance; (2) clarity and consistency of rules; (3) level of expectations, which she describes in terms of "maturity demands"; and (4) communication between parent and child (1972).

Children with nurturant and warm parents are more securely attached in the first two years of life than those with more rejecting parents. They also have higher self-esteem and are more empathetic, more altruistic, and more responsive to others' hurts or sufferings. They have higher IQs, are more compliant in preschool and elementary school, do better in school, and are less likely to show criminal behaviour in adolescence or in adulthood (Hoeve et al., 2012; Maccoby, 1980; Rees, 2007; Stormshak, Bierman, McMahon, & Lengua, 2000). Even children from high-risk families (such as low-income, low-parental-education, or dysfunctional families) are less likely to have problems if they are raised in a positive and nurturing environment (Chao & Willms, 1998).

A study of Canadian families by Landy and Tam (1996) found that positive and supportive parenting practices reduced the incidence of problems, especially for children in high-risk family situations (such as low income, family dysfunction, or parental depression). In a later study, Landy and Tam (1998) found that, in children 2 to 3 years of age, the likelihood of problems (such as emotional disorder, aggressive behaviour, and hyperactivity) increased significantly with hostile parenting practices. Positive parenting practices tended to have a buffering effect, showing a reduction in these problems by 25 to 52%.

The degree and clarity of the parents' control over the child are also significant. Parents with clear, consistently applied rules have children who are much less likely to be defiant or noncompliant. Results from the second cycle of the National Longitudinal Survey of Children and Youth (NLSCY) showed that children living in a high-risk family where they are exposed to consistent interactions with parents had fewer behavioural problems (Statistics Canada, 1998). In fact, Landy and Tam (1998) found that the rates of aggressive behaviour and hyperactivity in children of families with consistent parenting styles were less than half the rates found in other families.

Equally important is the form of control the parents use (Barber & Xia, 2013). The most optimal outcomes for the child occur when the parents are not overly restrictive, explain things to the child, and avoid the use of physical punishments. Children whose parents have high expectations—high "maturity demands" in Baumrind's (1971) language—also fare better. Such children have higher self-esteem and show more generosity and altruism toward others.

Finally, open and regular communication between parent and child has been linked to more positive outcomes. Listening to the child is as important as talking to him. Ideally, parents need to convey to the child that what the child has to say is worth listening to, that his ideas are important and should be considered in family decisions. Children of such parents have been found to be more emotionally and socially mature (Baumrind, 1971; Bell & Bell, 1982).

While each of these characteristics of families may be significant individually, they do not occur in isolation but in combinations and patterns. In her early research, Baumrind (1967, 2013) identified three patterns, or styles, of parenting. The **permissive parenting style** is high in nurturance but low in maturity demands, control, and communication. The **authoritarian parenting style** is high in control and maturity demands but low in nurturance and communication. The **authoritative parenting style** is high in all four dimensions: nurturance, communication, clarity and consistency, and maturity demands.

Eleanor Maccoby and John Martin have proposed a variation of Baumrind's category system, shown in **Figure 8.2** (Maccoby & Martin, 1983). They categorize families on two dimensions: the degree of demand or control, and the amount of acceptance versus rejection. The intersection of these two dimensions creates four types, three of which correspond quite closely to Baumrind's authoritarian, authoritative, and permissive types. Maccoby and Martin's conceptualization adds a fourth type, the **uninvolved parenting style**.

THE AUTHORITARIAN TYPE The parent who responds to a child's refusal to go to bed by asserting physical, social, and emotional control over the child is exhibiting the authoritarian style. Children growing up in authoritarian families—with high levels of demand and control but relatively low levels of warmth and communication—do less well in school, have lower self-esteem, and are typically less skilled with peers than are children from other types of families. Some of these children appear subdued; others may show high aggressiveness or other indications of being rebellious or "out of control." These effects are not restricted to preschool-aged children. In a series of large studies of high school students, including longitudinal studies of more than 6000 teens, developmentalists found that teenagers from authoritarian families had poorer grades in school and more negative self-concepts than did teenagers from authoritative families, a finding that has been replicated in more recent cohorts of teens (Steinberg, Blatt-Eisengart, & Cauffman, 2006; Steinberg, Fletcher, & Darling, 1994).

permissive parenting style
a style of parenting that is high in nurturance and low in maturity demands, control, and communication

authoritarian parenting style
a style of parenting that is low in nurturance and communication, but high in control and maturity demands

authoritative parenting style
a style of parenting that is high in nurturance, maturity demands, control, and communication

uninvolved parenting style
a style of parenting that is low in nurturance, maturity demands, control, and communication

Figure 8.2 Maccoby and Martin expanded on Baumrind's categories in this two-dimensional category system.

(**SOURCE:** Based on Maccoby, E.E., & Martin, J.A. (1983). Socialization in the context of the family: Parent-child interaction. In E.M. Hetherington (Ed.), *Handbook of child psychology: Socialization, personality, and social development*, Vol. 4 (pp. 1–102). New York, NY: Wiley.)

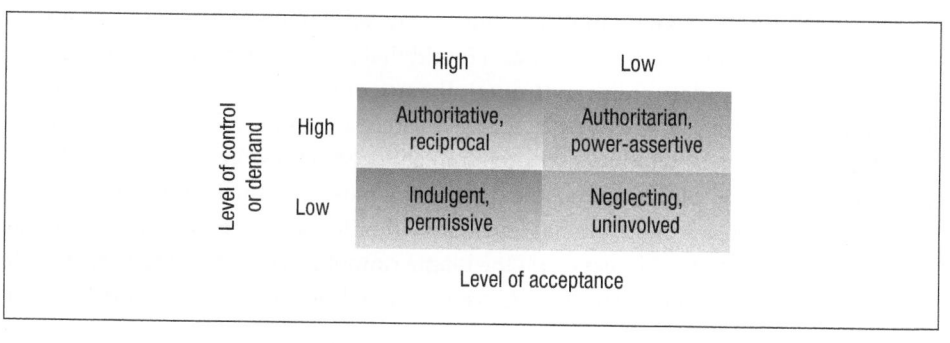

THE PERMISSIVE TYPE The permissive type of parent responds to a child's refusal to go to bed by allowing the child to go to bed whenever she wants to. Children growing up with indulgent or permissive parents also show some negative outcomes. Researchers have found that these children do slightly worse in school during adolescence and are likely to be both more aggressive (particularly if the parents are specifically permissive toward aggressiveness) and somewhat immature in their behaviour with peers and in school. They are less likely to take responsibility and are less independent.

THE AUTHORITATIVE TYPE Authoritative parents respond to undesirable behaviours, such as a child's refusal to go to bed, by firmly sticking to their demands without resorting to asserting their power over the child. The most consistently positive outcomes have been associated with an authoritative pattern in which the parents are high in both control and acceptance—setting clear limits but also responding to the child's individual needs. Children reared in such families typically show higher self-esteem and are more independent, but are also more likely to comply with parental requests and may show more altruistic behaviour as well. They are self-confident and achievement-oriented in school and get better grades than do children whose parents have other parenting styles.

THE UNINVOLVED TYPE Uninvolved parents do not bother to set bedtimes for children or even to tell them to go to bed. They appear to be totally indifferent to children's behaviour and to the responsibilities of parenting. The most consistently negative outcomes are associated with this fourth pattern, the uninvolved or neglecting parenting style. You may remember from the discussion of secure and insecure attachments in the chapter on Social and Personality Development in Infancy that one of the family characteristics often found in infants rated as insecure/avoidant is the "psychological unavailability" of the mother. The mother may be depressed or may be overwhelmed by other problems in her life and may simply have not made any deep emotional connection with the child. Likewise, a parent may be distracted from parenting by more attractive activities. Whatever the reason, such children continue to show disturbances in their social relationships for many years. In adolescence, for example, youngsters from neglecting families are more impulsive and antisocial, less competent with their peers, and much less achievement oriented in school.

CANADIAN PARENTING STYLES Chao and Willms (1998, 2002) analyzed the key dimensions of Canadian parenting practices from the first cycle of the NLSCY and found that the largest portion of parents (about one-third) were authoritative. The *authoritative* parents scored above average on all measures of key parenting practices. About one-quarter of parents were *authoritarian* and another one-quarter were *permissive*. A fourth category, similar to *uninvolved* parenting style, included the remaining 15% of parents who scored low on all key measures of positive parenting. McCain and Mustard (2000) reported that almost half of the children who were raised with this parenting style experienced behavioural problems. In comparison, only one in five children of *authoritative* parents had behavioural problems.

In another study, Canadian researchers analyzed parent–child interactions over the course of two cycles of the NLSCY and found that a *hostile/ineffective* parenting style (e.g., parents manipulate children through the use of sarcasm or put-downs and/or mix anger with punishment) resulted in persistent behavioural problems at a rate nine times higher than what was exhibited in children who were not exposed to this pattern of parenting. Moreover, hostile/ineffective parenting interactions had a stronger negative effect on a child's behaviour than either income level or family structure (Statistics Canada, 1998). However, all the blame cannot be placed on the parents with ineffective discipline styles. Adults who were spanked as children were more likely to use physical punishment of their own children, which points to the intergenerational nature of physical punishment (Gershoff & Grogan-Kaylor, 2016) and marks a good spot for intervention—by breaking the cycle.

Overall, though, it seems Canadian parents are relatively lenient and emotionally warm with their children. In a study lead by Université de Montréal psychologist, Michel Claes, researchers found that, in comparison to European parents, Canadian parents reportedly exerted less behavioural control, were more likely to use permissive disciplinary strategies and were more tolerant of friend-related activities while continuing to have strong emotional bonds (e.g., affection, warmth, closeness, support, and sensitivity) and good communication (e.g., listening ability) with their children (Claes et al., 2011). The challenge for Canadian parents, perhaps, is to maintain respect while still being the ultimate decision makers in the family—easier said than done.

PARENTING AND CHILD DISCIPLINE   The Canadian Paediatric Society (CPS) describes discipline in this way:

> The word discipline means to impart knowledge and skill—to teach. However, it is often equated with punishment and control. There is a great deal of controversy about the appropriate ways to discipline children, and parents are often confused about effective ways to set limits and instill self-control in their child. [The goal of] effective and positive discipline is about teaching and guiding children, not just forcing them to obey. (Nieman, Shea, & CPS, 2016, p. 1)

Through instruction and practice, parents, teachers, and other significant adults help socialize a child in such a way that she has the knowledge, skills, and attitudes required to become a well-functioning person. The purpose of **discipline**, whether physical, mental, or moral, is to develop self-control, moral character, and proper conduct (see how Canadians view discipline in the **Research Report**).

Critical Thinking

Why do you think children of permissive parents are less independent than those from authoritative families?

discipline

training, whether physical, mental, or moral, that develops self-control, moral character, and proper conduct

---

Research Report

Disciplining Children: The Canadian Perspective

Although most Canadian parents would agree that disciplining their offspring is an important yet arduous task, many parents disagree about the best ways to discipline. Parents even interpret the term *discipline* in a variety of ways. It can be a means of assuring conformity, a form of punishment, a corrective tool, or a method of shaping desirable behaviour. Proponents of physical discipline generally argue that it serves a useful purpose and does no lasting harm to children; opponents of physical discipline say it does no good and is associated with negative outcomes.

One retrospective health study by McMaster University researchers looked at a large sample of adults in Ontario (MacMillan et al., 1999). Their analysis revealed a significant relationship between the reported frequency of being slapped and/or spanked during childhood and a prevalence of psychiatric disorders later in life: the higher the reported frequency of being slapped or spanked, the greater the lifetime prevalence of anxiety disorders, alcohol abuse or dependence, drug dependence, antisocial behaviours, and, to a lesser extent, major depression. Similarly, a more recent study by University of Manitoba researchers has found that harsh physical punishment (short of child maltreatment) has been linked to a wide range of mental disorders (Afifi, Mota, Dasiewicz, MacMillan, & Sareen, 2012).

However, based on comprehensive literature reviews, Robert Larzelere found a lack of conclusive evidence that nonabusive spanking causes any more adverse effects in children than do other disciplinary tactics (Larzelere, 2000, 2008; Larzelere, Cox, & Smith, 2010; Larzelere & Kuhn, 2005). Larzelere believed that how and when disciplinary tactics are used may be more important than which tactic is used. On the contrary, other research indicates that the impact of physical punishment cannot be ignored, as evidenced by an extensive study lead by Elizabeth Gershoff that analyzed five decades of research on corporal punishment and behavioural outcomes in children. The conclusion was that both physical abuse and spanking (only to a slightly lessor extent) were linked to the same detrimental outcomes, namely later antisocial behaviour, aggression, and mental health problems (Gershoff & Grogan-Kaylor, 2016).

(Continued)

In January 2004, Canada's highest court ruled that parents, teachers, and caregivers can apply physical force within "reasonable limits" as a form of discipline. The law permits the use of minor corrective force if it "is part of a genuine effort to educate the child, poses no reasonable risk of harm that is more than transitory and trifling, and is reasonable under the circumstances" (Department of Justice Canada, 2004, p. 1). The law disallows hitting a child with objects or delivering blows or slaps to the face or the head. In addition, the use of physical punishment on children under the age of 2 years or over the age of 12 is prohibited. The court has tried to strike a balance between the needs of parents and the rights of children; the judges made it clear that they do not endorse or advocate the use of corporal punishment, such as spanking, but they also don't want to criminalize parents for any and every physical intervention.

University of Manitoba child psychologist Joan Durrant (2004) contends that the Supreme Court's decision affects both parents and child and family professionals alike. She points out that, even though physical discipline is becoming socially unacceptable in Canada, the law still excuses some degree of it, which raises the question: How is a parent to distinguish between physical punishment and physical abuse? How should child welfare professionals advise parents about what is an acceptable degree of and circumstance for physical discipline? For instance, is one spank or two appropriate? Is a tap on the bum or back of the hand permitted? Is it okay to spank with an open hand so long as it leaves no marks or bruising? How calm do parents have to be before they punish? Can you wash a child's mouth out with soap? What about forcing a child to remain motionless in an awkward stance? These are difficult questions to address. In the face of this ambiguity, professionals could give parents the clear message that physical punishment as a form of discipline is not appropriate (Durrant, 2004; Durrant & Ensom, 2012) and that alternate forms of effective discipline are available. This approach has been endorsed in policy statements by the Canadian Psychological Association (2004), the Canadian Paediatric Society (Nieman, Shea, & CPS, 2016), and other child-care organizations. Moreover, nearly 500 Canadian organizations have signed the "Joint Statement on Physical Punishment of Children and Youth," which states "The evidence is clear and compelling—physical punishment of children and youth plays no useful role in their up-bringing and poses only risks to their development. The conclusion is equally compelling—parents should be strongly encouraged to develop alternative and positive approaches to discipline" (Children's Hospital of Eastern Ontario, 2013).

time-out

removing the child from the situation and from attention and rewards for a short period of time, typically one minute for every year of the child's age, in order to stop unwanted behaviour

Two key problems make it hard to establish what constitutes effective discipline. First, it is difficult to establish the harmful or beneficial effects of various forms of discipline. For example, do physical punishments, such as spanking or washing a child's mouth out with soap, work any better than nonphysical corrections, such as giving verbal reprimands, reasoning with an explanation of consequences, or enforcing a **time-out** away from sources of attention or enjoyment? If nonphysical interventions were found to be at least as effective as physical punishment, then it would be hard to justify the continued use of physical intervention because of its potential to cause pain and harm.

Second, research has not concluded how intense and frequent effective discipline needs to be. The differences among mild, moderate, and severe discipline are not clearly delineated. In addition, regardless of the type of discipline, *any* corrective measure that is too extreme or too frequent can become child abuse that contributes to detrimental physical and emotional outcomes (Kazdin & Benjet, 2003; Larzelere, 2003). In fact, punishment is the leading reason given by perpetrators in substantiated cases of child maltreatment in Canada (Trocmé, Durrant, Ensom, & Marwah, 2004). Although research has yet to provide unequivocal answers to address these issues (Baumrind, 2003; Kazdin & Benjet, 2003; Larzelere et al., 2010), Canadian child-care advocates agree that physical interventions are not appropriate. Instead, they advocate the use of minimal nonphysical interventions in the context of a loving family relationship, and they encourage parents to be proactive by improving parenting skills and anticipating and limiting situations that will require intervention (Canadian Psychological Association, 2004; Durrant, 2004; Durrant & Ensom, 2004, 2012; Nieman, Shea, & CPS, 2016).

inductive discipline

a discipline strategy in which parents explain to children why a punished behaviour is wrong

Another area of complexity is evident in the interaction between parenting style and child temperament (Eisenberg, Chang, Ma, & Huang, 2009). For example, authoritative parents often use **inductive discipline**, a discipline strategy in which parents explain to children why a punished behaviour is wrong and typically refrain from physical punishment (Choe, Olson, & Sameroff, 2013; Hoffman, 1970). Inductive discipline helps most preschoolers gain control of their behaviour and learn to look at situations from perspectives other than their own. Likewise, the majority of preschool-aged children whose parents respond to demonstrations of poor self-control, such as temper tantrums, by asserting their social and physical power—as often happens when parents physically punish children—have poorer self-control than preschoolers whose parents use inductive discipline (Houck & Lecuyer-Maus, 2004; Kochanska, 1997b; Kochanska & Kim, 2012).

However, research suggests that inductive discipline is not equally effective for all children. Those who have difficult temperaments or who are physically active and who seem to enjoy risk taking—such as children who like to climb on top of furniture and jump off—seem to have a greater need for firm discipline and to benefit less from inductive discipline than do their peers whose temperamental makeup is different (Kochanska, 1997a). In fact, assumptions about the superiority of inductive discipline, as well as authoritative parenting in general, have been criticized by developmentalists who claim that correlations between discipline strategy and child behaviour may arise simply because parents adapt their techniques to their children's behaviour (Larzelere et al., 2010). Thus, parents of poorly behaved children may be more punitive or author-itarian because they have discovered that this is the kind of parenting their children respond to. In a broader context, corrective intervention for any persistent, severe prob-lem—whether it be for inappropriate behaviour, assistance with homework, a medical condition that requires hospitalization, or a psychological situation, such as suicide risk or delinquency—will demand more intensive intervention, which increases the likeli-hood of detrimental outcomes (Larzelere, Kuhn, & Johnson, 2004).

Ethnicity, Socioeconomic Status, and Parenting Styles

When we consider cultural and social influences in relation to parenting styles, we find that the research reveals some complex patterns. For example, studies in which children provide information about their parents' style as well as those in which researchers conduct direct observation of parents have consistently found that, in general, Asian American parents display an authoritarian style (Chao & Aque, 2009; Wang & Phinney, 1998). The finding that Asian American children score higher than their European American counterparts on almost all measures of cognitive compe-tence argues against the assumption that authoritative parenting is best. In fact, devel-opmentalists have found a link between Asian American children's achievement and authoritarian parenting—that is, parents who have the most authoritarian parenting style have the highest-scoring children (Wang & Phinney, 1998).

However, the key variable in these findings may not be ethnicity. Many stud-ies have shown that parenting styles are grounded in parenting goals (e.g., Cheah & Rubin, 2004). Parenting goals are influenced by cultural values and by the immediate context in which parents are raising children (Choi, Kim, Kim, & Park, 2013; Valentino, Nuttall, Comas, Borkowski, & Akai 2012). Thus, parents may be authoritarian in response to living in an environment that is different from the one in which they grew up, not because they are of a particular ethnic group. Authoritarian parenting may help them achieve two important goals: to help their children succeed economically and to enable them to maintain a sense of ethnic identity. Evidence supporting this interpretation also comes from studies of families who have immigrated to countries such as Canada (Camilleri & Malewska-Peyre, 1997; Chuang & Su, 2009). These stud-ies suggest that parenting style may be dependent on the cultural context in which parents and children live, so that as the cultural context changes, the best correspond-ing type of parenting style changes with it.

Another important aspect to consider is the effect of socioeconomic status (SES) on child development. SES factors such as low family income and low levels of parental education are risk factors that have been associated with an increase in a child's vul-nerability to problems such as aggression or social withdrawal (Landy & Tam, 1998;

Learning Objective 8.5

Identify how ethnicity and socio-economic status interact with parenting styles.

Figure 8.3 Risk factors that are associated with one or more problems for children aged 2 to 3.

(**SOURCE:** Adapted from Landy & Tam, 1998, from Table 1, p. 15, Understanding the contribution of multiple risk factors on child development at various ages (Catalogue No. W098_22E). Human Resources and Social Development Canada. Reproduced with the permission of Her Majesty the Queen in Right of Canada 2013.)

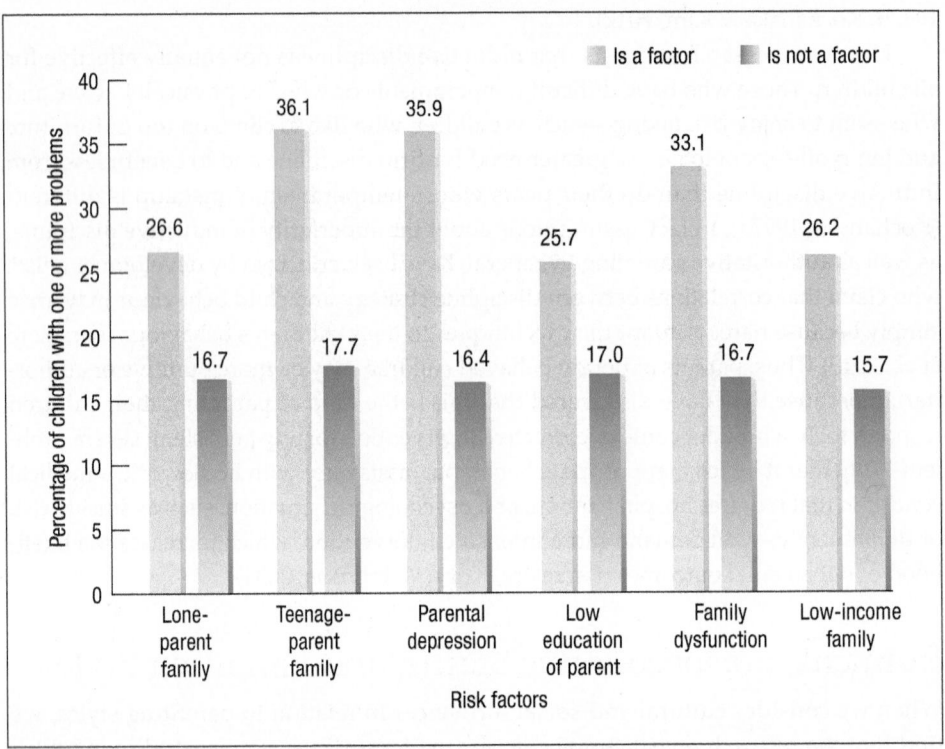

Stack et al., 2015) (see **Figure 8.3**). However, several Canadian studies have shown that parenting style is a better predictor than SES of outcomes in a child. In particular, researchers have found that even when a child was being raised in a high-risk family situation (e.g., low income, parental depression, or family dysfunction), a positive and consistent parenting style acted as a protective factor against these social disadvantages that increase vulnerability for a child (Chao & Willms, 1998, 2002; Landy & Tam, 1998; Miller, Jenkins, & Keating, 2002). Indeed, while good parenting practices are common in all SES levels, hostile/ineffective parenting practices also cross all income levels (Chao & Willms, 1998, 2002). In a study by Brock University psychologist Tanya Martini and others, mothers who held authoritarian beliefs reported that they were less likely to control their hostile emotions in situations where their children were expressing negative emotions. This reaction occurred regardless of whether the mother was from the lower or middle class (Martini, Root, & Jenkins, 2004).

All the same, children raised in families with lower SES are more likely to experience a greater number of risk factors, and this, coupled with hostile or ineffective parenting practices, results in proportionally higher levels of vulnerability in this demographic (see **Figure 8.4**). Therefore, even though effective parenting goes a long way toward compensating for any negative influence associated with the consequences of low SES, the fact remains that increased vulnerability is still associated with low SES. So, the problem remains—without some form of intervention and support, many low SES parents are left in a position where they lack the personal and material resources required to provide effective parenting (refer to the **Policy Question** on poverty in Canada at the end of this chapter). In turn, ineffective parenting contributes to an intergenerational transfer of risk for family poverty and child vulnerability (Serbin & Karp, 2003, 2004; Stack et al., 2015; Véronneau, Serbin, Stack, Ledingham, & Schwartzman, 2015).

Figure 8.4 Lone-parent household income and the degree of vulnerability (lower, moderate, or high) to negative outcomes in children aged 4 to 5.

(**SOURCE:** Adapted from Ross, Roberts, & Scott, 1998, from Table 3.1, p. 20, Mediating factors in child development outcomes: Children in lone-parent families (Catalogue No. W-98-8E). Human Resources and Social Development Canada. Reproduced with the permission of Her Majesty the Queen in Right of Canada 2013.)

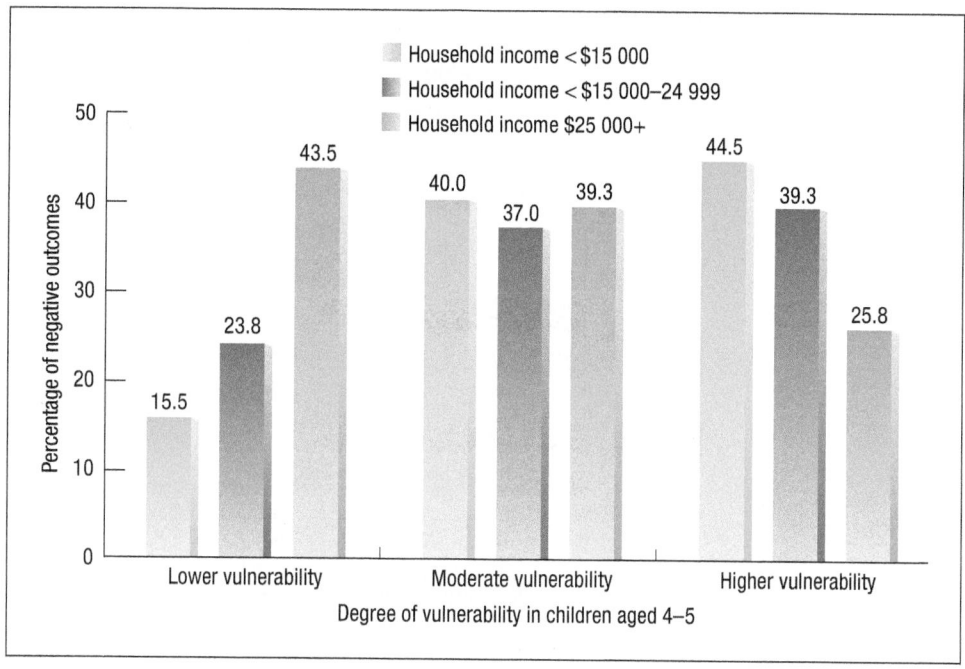

Family Structure

Although in decline, children living with married parents continues to be the dominant structure in Canada. The percentage of children aged 0 to 4 years living in *intact* two-parent homes—a family with biological and/or adopted children of both members of the couple—was ~77%, while 8% lived with stepfamilies and ~16% lived in a lone-parent family (Bohnert, Milan, & Lathe, 2014).

DIVERSITY IN TWO-PARENT AND LONE-PARENT FAMILIES The *blended* two-parent family consists of stepfamilies that were created when a divorced or never-married single biological parent married (or lived common-law with) another single parent or a nonparent. Half of Canadian stepfamilies comprise children living with the biological mother and a stepfather; 10% consist of the biological father and a step-mother; and 40% are blended—a mix of children that both parents brought into the family (8%) or the biological children of one parent and the children born to the new union (32%) (Statistics Canada, 2002a). Roughly half of same-sex couples with children were stepfamilies (Statistics Canada, 2012e).

We find that lone-parent households are no more alike than are two-parent households. The largest proportion of lone-parent households consists of separated or divorced parents (~51%), followed by never-married parents (~32%), and a smaller proportion of widowed parents (~18%). Roughly 80% of lone-parent households were female lone-parent families—a pattern that has remained fairly consistent over the last 50 years (Statistics Canada, 2012f). Additionally, unmarried teenaged parents are likely to live with their own parents (Bowden & Greenberg, 2010).

FAMILY STRUCTURE EFFECTS Most children being raised in lone-parent families do fairly well by all measures, but there is a subset of these families in which children are more vulnerable to a range of problems (Ross, Roberts, & Scott, 1998). Landy and Tam (1998) found that the impact of lone parenthood had different outcomes

Learning Objective 8.6

Explain how family structure is related to children's development.

Figure 8.5 High stress, by household type (age-standardized), age 18+, Canada, 1994–1995.

(**SOURCE:** Adapted from Statistics Canada, *National Population Health Survey*, 1994–1995, special tabulations.)

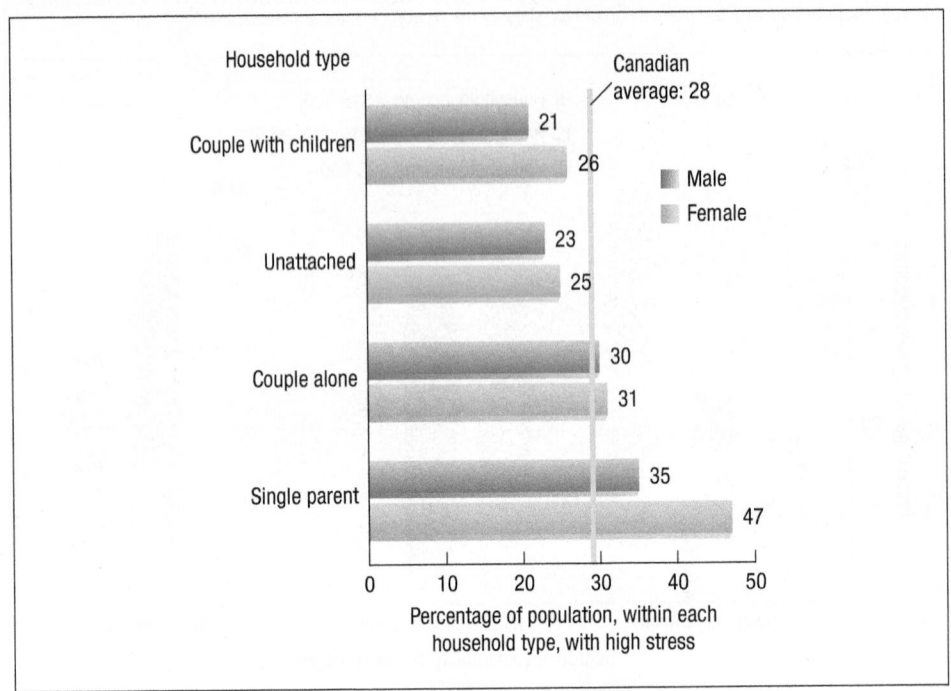

depending on the age of the child. For instance, lone parenthood was not related to any specific problem outcome in children aged 2 or 3. However, for children aged 4 to 11, lone parenthood was associated with double the rates of emotional disorder, conduct disorder, hyperactivity, repeating a grade, relationship problems, and having any one or more of these problems. Not surprisingly, lone parents reported experiencing high levels of chronic stress in comparison with two-parent families (see **Figure 8.5**). Moreover, 80% of lone-parent families are headed by women in Canada, and almost half of the female lone-parent families reported experiencing high levels of chronic stress (Health Canada, 1999b; Statistics Canada, 2012f).

OTHER TYPES OF FAMILY STRUCTURES   To add to the vast quantity of research done on two-parent and lone-parent families, recent research has studied the effects of other family structures on children. For example, through studies on *skip-generation families*—custodial grandparenting— researchers have learned that grandparents' responses to children's problems are quite similar to those of parents (Daly & Glenwick, 2000). Some have suggested that rates of behaviour problems are higher among children who are living in skip-generation families. However, researchers point out that such children are often in the care of their grandparents due to traumatic events that have disrupted their own families (Smith & Palmieri, 2007). These events can include abuse of the children. Thus, developmentalists know very little about how children raised by grandparents fare in the absence of such confounding factors. In Canada, over 12% of grandparents are now raising their grandchildren in skip-generation households, with Indigenous grandparents comprising the highest proportion of skip-generation families (27%) (Milan, Laflamme, & Wong, 2015). Out of necessity, many Indigenous parents move away for work or education. Others may be dealing with health issues or may have died prematurely (Laucius, 2012). The highest numbers of skip-generation families are concentrated in Saskatchewan, Nunavut, and the Northwest Territories, which have a relatively high proportion of Indigenous peoples (CBC News, 2012).

Concerns about children's gender-role identity, personal adjustment, social relationships, and sexual orientation have dominated same-sex parenting research (Patterson,

2009). Parenting by openly same-sex couples is still relatively new in Canada with an estimated 6400 same-sex couples now raising children (Statistics Canada, 2012g). However, more than three decades worth of studies have shown no significant differences in sexual orientation, sexual identity, self-esteem, adjustment, or qualities of social relationships between children raised by gay and lesbian parents and children raised by heterosexual parents (Goldberg & Smith, 2013; Patterson, 2006, 2009).

Furthermore, most studies suggest that children's development depends more on how parental figures interact with them than on any particular family configuration (Goldberg, 2009). A loving, nurturing home environment provided by parents, whether same-sex or other-sex, is an essential ingredient in raising children who grow up to be healthy, competent, and well-adjusted (Goldberg, 2009; Sexualityandu.ca, 2009). A study in the Netherlands has provided some additional insights into the families of lesbian couples (Bos, van Balen, & van den Boom, 2007). Lesbian mothers were found to be more committed and satisfied with their partner as a co-parent than mothers in heterosexual relationships, and satisfaction with the co-parent was positively associated with child adjustment. It seems that lesbian couples have more egalitarian partnerships than heterosexual couples. For example, in terms of division of family tasks, lesbian partners spend roughly equal amounts of time on household work and child care, as compared with heterosexual couples, where one partner (usually the mother) spends a disproportionate amount of time on such tasks. When considering the above research, take note that roughly 80% of same-sex families are headed by lesbian couples in Canada (Statistics Canada, 2012e).

Divorce

The number of divorces in Canada has steadily declined from the all-time peak in 1987; half of all divorces occur within the first 15 years of marriage and one-quarter of all marriages are dissolved by the fourth anniversary (Vanier Institute of the Family, 2011; Statistics Canada, 2012h). For many families, divorce happens during the prime child-rearing period, and there can be little doubt that divorce is traumatic for children. It's important to note, however, that some of the negative effects of divorce are due to factors that were present *before* the divorce, such as difficult temperament in the child or excessive marital conflict between the parents (Bailey & Zvonkovic, 2003). It's also important to keep in mind that divorce is not a single variable; children are probably affected by a multitude of divorce-related factors—parental conflict, poverty, disruptions of daily routine, and so on (Ambert, 2009). For this reason, children whose parents separate or who stay in conflict-ridden marriages may experience many of the same effects as children whose parents actually divorce (Ingoldsby, Shaw, Owens, & Winslow, 1999).

The proportion of children living in post-divorce/separation versus two-parent custody that were found to be experiencing emotional or behavioural problems can

Learning Objective 8.7

Describe the impact of divorce on children in early childhood and in later years.

Many single parents manage to overcome substantial obstacles to give their children the support and supervision they need.

(*Photos:* left, Ilike/Fotolia; right, Silroby/Fotolia)

Figure 8.6 The proportion of children with emotional or behavioural problems, comparing those living with both parents with those in post-divorce/separation custody.

(SOURCE: Human Resources and Social Development Canada, 1998. The proportion of children with emotional or behavioural problems, published in Bulletin — A special Edition on Child Development. www.hrsdc.gc.ca/eng/cs/sp/sdc/pkrf/publications/bulletins/1999-000002/page02.shtml. Reproduced with the permission of the Minister of Public Works and Government Services Canada, 2013.)

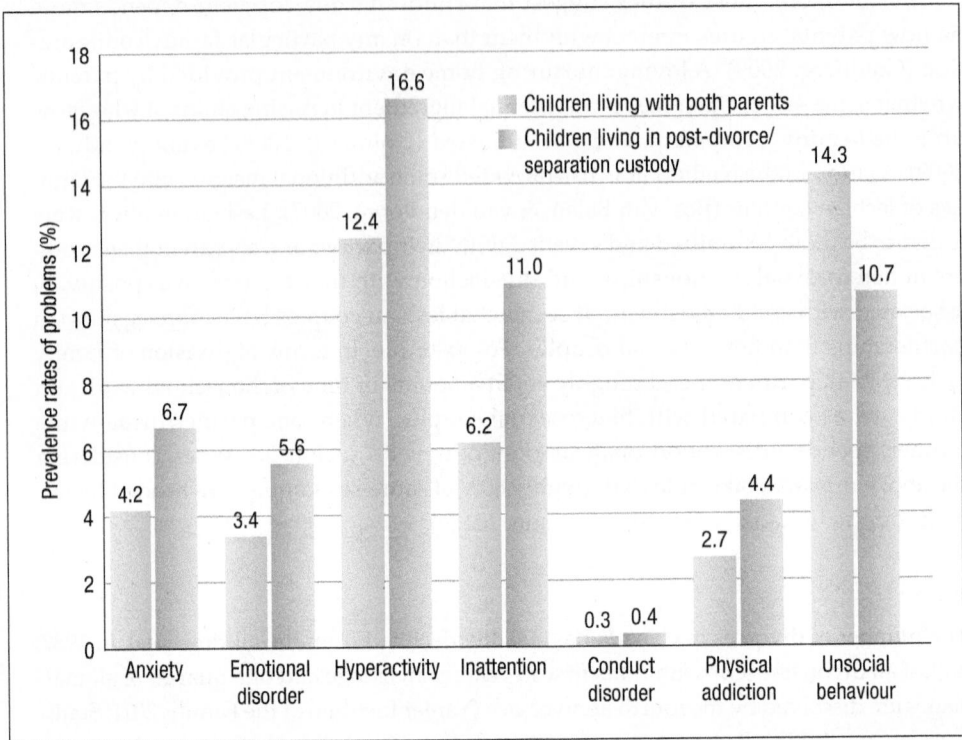

be seen in **Figure 8.6**. Most children in either living arrangement are doing well, although children living in post-divorce/separation situations have a higher prevalence of problems in most areas except unsocial behaviour (low prosocial behaviour) (Human Resources Development Canada, 2001). In the first few years after a divorce, children typically exhibit declines in school performance and show more aggressive, defiant, negative, or depressed behaviour (Greene, Anderson, Doyle, & Ridelbach, 2006). By adolescence, the children of divorced parents are more likely than their peers to engage in criminal behaviour (Price & Kunz, 2003). Children living in step-parent families also have higher rates of delinquency, more behaviour problems in school, and lower grades than do those in intact families (Jeynes, 2006).

The negative effects of divorce seem to persist for many years (Wallerstein, Lewis, & Packer Rosenthal, 2013). For example, about 92% of adult Canadians who had lived in an intact two-parent family from birth to age 15 reported that they had had a very happy childhood. In comparison, only 72% of adult Canadians who had experienced disruption before the age of 15 due to a change in family structure reported that they believe they had been very happy children (Williams, 2001). Moreover, children whose parents divorce have a higher risk of mental health problems in adulthood (Chase-Lansdale, Cherlin, & Kiernan, 1995; Cherlin, Chase-Lansdale, & McRae, 1998; Wallerstein & Lewis, 1998). Many young adults whose parents are divorced lack the financial resources and emotional support necessary to succeed in post-secondary education; a majority report that they struggle with fears of intimacy in relationships; and they are more likely to rely on social assistance income (Ambert, 2009; Cartwright, 2006). Not surprisingly, adults whose parents divorced are themselves more likely to divorce (Ambert, 2009).

As a general rule, these negative effects are more pronounced for boys than for girls. However, some researchers have found that the effects are delayed in girls, making it more difficult to associate the effects with the divorce. Consequently, longitudinal studies often find that girls show equal or even greater negative effects (Amato, 1993; Hetherington, 1991a, 1991b). Age differences in the severity of the reaction have been found in some studies but not others. For example, one longitudinal study found that the effects of divorce were most severe in a group of 12-year-olds who experienced parental divorce in early childhood rather than during their school years (Pagani, Boulerice, Tremblay, & Vitaro, 1997).

Understanding the Effects of Family Structure and Divorce

How are we to understand these various findings? First, lone parenthood or divorce reduces the financial and emotional resources available to support the child (Ambert, 2009). With only one parent, the household typically has only one income and only one adult to respond to the child's emotional needs. Canadian data indicate that a woman's income drops an average of 50% in the first year after a divorce, while a man's drops by 25% (Finnie, 2000). Remarriage does indeed add a second adult to the family system, which alleviates these problems to some degree, but it adds other issues (Ambert, 2009).

Second, any family transition involves upheaval. Both adults and children adapt slowly and with difficulty to the subtraction or addition of new adults to the family system (Ambert, 2009). The period of maximum disruption appears to last several years, during which the parents often find it difficult to monitor their children and maintain control over them.

Perhaps most importantly, lone parenthood, divorce, and step-parenthood all increase the likelihood that the family climate or style will shift away from authoritative parenting (Wallerstein et al., 2013). This shift is not uncommon in the first few years after a divorce, when the custodial parent (usually the mother) is distracted or depressed and less able to set clear limits and continue to be nurturing; it occurs in stepfamilies as well, where rates of authoritative parenting are lower than in intact families.

Many families construct a social network called an **extended family**, a family structure that includes grandparents, aunts, uncles, cousins, and so on. Extended families seem to serve a protective function for children who are growing up in lone-parent homes (Clark & CPS, 2016). Grandmothers, for example, appear to be important sources of emotional warmth for the children of teenaged mothers (Coley & Chase-Lansdale, 1998). Further, extended family members often help single and divorced mothers with financial and emotional support as well as with child care.

Learning Objective 8.8
Identify some possible ways divorce-related changes in family structure affect development.

Critical Thinking
How important was your own extended family to you and your parent(s) during your early childhood years?

extended family
a social network of grandparents, aunts, uncles, cousins, and so on

Test Yourself before going on

1. List the changes in attachment relationships that the text associates with each age in the table below.

Age	Change in Attachment Relationship
2–3	
4	

2. Define each parenting style and summarize its effects on development.

Style	Definition	Effects on Development
Authoritarian		
Permissive		
Authoritative		
Uninvolved		

3. Among what groups is authoritarian parenting associated with positive effects on children's development?
4. Divorce increases the likelihood that the family climate will shift away from _____ parenting.
5. The _____ family serves a protective function for children growing up in single-parent homes.

Critical Thinking

6. In what ways do you think parenting styles and family structure interact to affect development? For instance, might there be differences in how authoritarian parenting influences children in two-parent versus single-parent families?

Peer Relationships

The child's family experience is undeniably a central influence on emerging personality and social relationships, particularly in early childhood when a good portion of the time is still spent with parents and siblings. But over the years from 2 to 6, relationships with non-sibling peers become increasingly important—this is the critical period when brain development and function is most sensitive to social skills development (McCain & Mustard, 2000).

Relating to Peers Through Play

Learning Objective 8.9

Trace a child's changing relationship with his or her peers through play.

In the chapter on Physical and Cognitive Development in Early Childhood, you learned about the cognitive aspects of play. But what about the social features of children's play activities? The social dimensions of play were outlined in a classic observational study conducted by Mildred Parten (1932). If you observe young children who are engaged in free play, you will see that Parten's stages of play continue to be useful today.

At every age, children are likely to spend at least some of their time playing alone—a pattern known as *solitary play*. However, children first begin to show some positive interest in playing with others as early as 6 months of age. If you place two babies that age on the floor facing each other, they will look at each other, touch or pull each other's hair, imitate each other's actions, and smile at each other.

By 14 to 18 months, two or more children play together with toys—sometimes cooperating, but more often simply playing side by side with different toys. Developmentalists refer to this as *parallel play*. Toddlers this age express interest in each other and gaze at or make noises at each other. However, it isn't until around 18 months that children engage in *associative play*. In associative play, toddlers pursue their own activities but also engage in spontaneous, though short-lived, social interactions. For example, one toddler may put down a toy to spend a few minutes chasing another toddler or one may imitate another's action with a toy.

By age 3 or 4, children begin to engage in *cooperative play*, a pattern in which several children work together to accomplish a goal. Cooperative play can be either constructive or symbolic. A group of children may cooperate to build a city out of blocks, or they may assign roles such as "mommy," "daddy," and "baby" to one another to play house.

Play is related to cognitive development. Play is also related to the development of **social skills**, a set of behaviours that usually leads to being accepted as a play partner or friend by others. For example, many researchers have focused on the social skill of *group entry*. Children who are skilled in group entry spend time observing others to find out what they're doing and then try to become a part of it. Children who have poor group-entry skills try to gain acceptance through aggressive behaviour or by interrupting the group. Developmentalists have found that children with poor group-entry skills are often rejected by peers (Fantuzzo, Coolahan, & Mendez, 1998). Peer rejection, in turn, is an important factor in future social development.

social skills

a set of behaviours that usually leads to being accepted as a play partner or friend by peers

Because of the risks associated with poor social skills, developmentalists have turned their attention to social-skills training as a preventive measure. One important finding is that social-skills training improves children's ability to regulate emotions (Calkins & Mackler, 2011). Thus, interventions that help children better manage their feelings and understand those of their peers may improve their social skills. Improving children's communication skills can also help. In one intervention study, socially withdrawn 4- and 5-year-olds were taught specific verbal phrases to use when trying to gain acceptance by a group of peers (Doctoroff, 1997). In addition, their socially accepted peers were taught to remind the trained children to use their new skills. For the most part, social-skills interventions like this one lead to immediate gains in social acceptance. However, the degree to which early childhood social-skills training can prevent later social difficulties is unknown at present.

Aggression

Learning Objective 8.10

Identify the key factors in preschool children's aggressive behaviour.

aggression

behaviour intended to injure another person or damage an object

Just what is aggression and how common is it in children during their early years? The most common definition of **aggression** is behaviour intended to injure another person or damage an object. The emphasis on intentionality helps separate true aggression from rough-and-tumble play in which children sometimes accidentally hurt one another. Almost every young child shows at least some aggressive behaviour toward siblings, peers, and adults, but the form and frequency of aggression changes over the preschool years and beyond (Tremblay, 2000, 2008a; Tremblay et al., 2004).

PATTERNS IN AGGRESSION A number of psychologists at the University of Montreal and their collaborators used Statistics Canada NLSCY data to track patterns in Canadian children's aggressive behaviour over time. Richard Tremblay (2000) found that *physical aggression* (PA) (i.e., direct confrontation such as reacting with anger, fighting, kicking, hitting, or biting) peaks with toddlers at about age two and begins to decline during the preschool years. However, as you can see from **Figure 8.7**, *indirect aggression* (IA) (i.e., indirect harm such as gossiping, saying bad things about another person behind their back, exposing a person's secrets to others, or telling others to exclude someone) begins to increase throughout the preschool years to the age of 11. In one of two later longitudinal studies, Sylvana Côté and her colleagues found that just over half of the children showed occasional PA (52.2%) and about one-third showed infrequent PA (31.1%) in toddlerhood, which declined to an infrequent level of PA and virtually no expression of PA, respectively, by the time they reached pre-adolescence. A small group (~17%), however, frequently displayed PA during toddlerhood and maintained a high level of PA throughout childhood (of this group, two-thirds were boys) (Côté, Vaillancourt, LeBlanc, Nagin, & Tremblay, 2006). In the second of these two studies (the first of its kind to track the joint developmental trajectories of both PA and IA), the researchers made some interesting new observations (Côté, Vaillancourt, Barker, Nagin, & Tremblay, 2007). They found, for example, that between 2 and 8 years

Figure 8.7 Physical and indirect aggression of boys and girls across childhood.

(**SOURCE:** Tremblay, R.E. (2000). The origins of youth violence. *Isuma*, 1 (2), 19–24., Figure 1, p. 20. Reprinted courtesy of Richard E. Tremblay.)

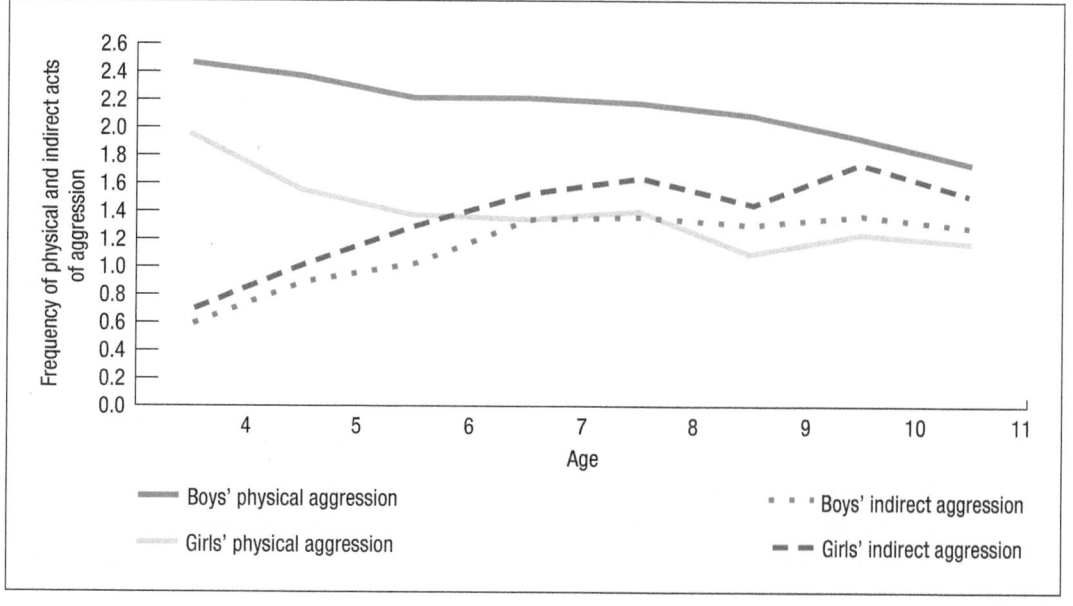

of age, the majority of children (62.1%) followed a trajectory of declining, occasional, or infrequent use of PA (to the point of virtually no PA) coupled with ongoing low levels of IA. They also found that those preschoolers low on PA to begin with demonstrated a low propensity toward using IA as they entered school (~5.0%). In stark contrast, however, both preschool boys and girls with high levels of PA displayed increasingly higher levels of IA during their transition to elementary school (13.5%). Very few boys or girls displayed a pattern in which PA was experienced separately from the use of IA (1.1%).

In the text below, Richard Tremblay from the University of Montreal summarizes the available data on the development of physical aggression:

- the vast majority of preschool children use physical aggression
- the vast majority also learn with age to use other means of solving problems
- some need more time than others to learn
- girls learn more quickly than boys
- by adolescence, not much more than 5% of males can be considered cases of *chronic physical aggression* (CPA), while female cases are exceptional
- most of the CPA cases during adolescence were CPA cases since early childhood

(Tremblay, 2010, p. 346)

AT-RISK FACTORS Canadian researchers interested in the relationship between childhood aggression and the family environment have been making extensive use of NLSCY data. In one study, researchers found that aggressive behaviour tends to run in families (Baillargeon, Tremblay, & Willms, 2002). For example, a second-born child is three to four times more likely to be aggressive if the first-born child is aggressive. The odds are even greater for a third-born child: They are more than 10 times as likely to be aggressive if one or both elder siblings are aggressive. Fortunately, most children become less aggressive during the preschool years. There are a few children, however, whose aggressive behaviour patterns in early childhood become a way of life (Tremblay, 2008a).

Another study found a strong link between harsh, punitive parenting practices and aggressive behaviour in children. Children living in punitive environments at 2 to 3 years of age were rated as significantly more aggressive than children living in nonpunitive families. These children were reassessed when they were 8 to 9 years old and, as was true at the earlier age, a punitive parental environment predicted levels of aggression in children (Thomas, 2004). This finding held true for both genders, all family income levels, and all regions of Canada. Moreover, in cases where the punitive parenting behaviour increased or decreased over time, so did the levels of child aggression. In a follow-up study of the same children, researchers determined that these children also experienced higher levels of anxiety when their parents were more punitive (Statistics Canada, 2005) (see **Figure 8.8**).

Still, it's important to note that the underlying causal relationship between punitive parenting and child aggression is not known. Punitive parenting practices may result in more aggressive children, but it may be that aggressive behaviour in children results in more punitive approaches to parenting, as was found to be the case in a recent Concordia Longitudinal Risk Project study (Serbin, Kingdon, Ruttle, & Stack, 2015). This contention was also supported by an earlier analysis of NLSCY data that showed how parent and child interactions are a two-way street: "Although children presumably respond to their parents' behaviour, it is also true that parents respond to their children's behaviour. That is, more praise may encourage a child to do well, but it is also true that parents may praise more when their children are doing well, censure more severely when the child is misbehaving" (Burton, Phipps, & Curtis, 2005, p. 5).

Figure 8.8 A change in parenting practices over time was associated with changes in children's behaviour rating scores on measures of aggression and anxiety.

(**SOURCE:** Adapted from Statistics Canada, 2005, National Longitudinal Survey of Children and Youth: Home environment, income and child behaviour. *The Daily*, Monday, February 21, 2005, at website www.statcan.ca/Daily/English/050221/d050221b.htm)

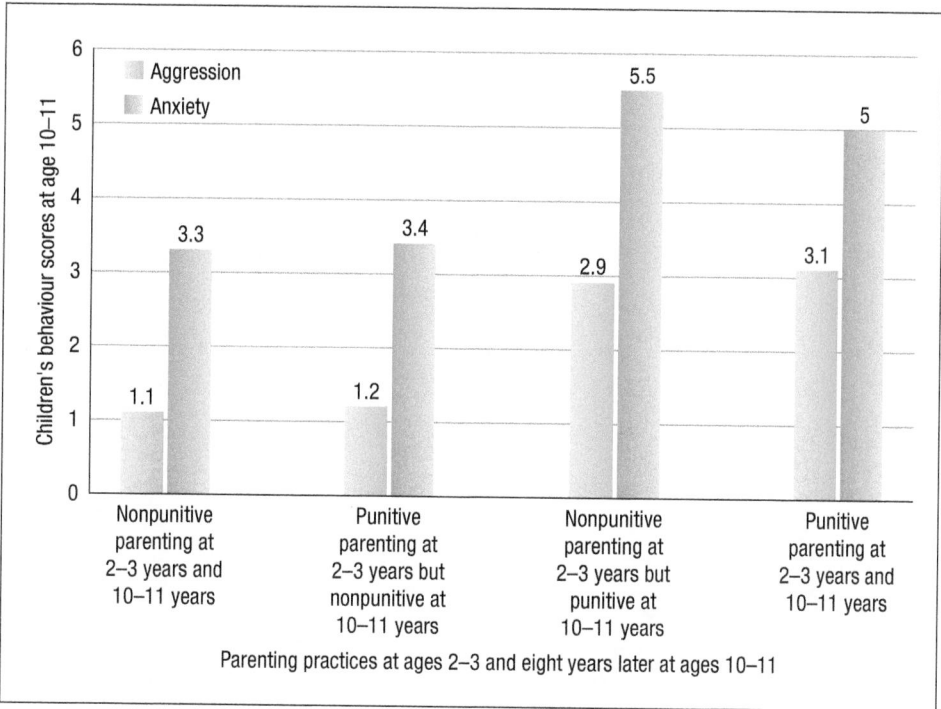

ORIGINS OF AGGRESSION Psychologists have suggested several key factors in aggressive behaviour. On the one hand, they argue that reinforcement is important. For instance, when a child pushes her playmate away and grabs his toy, she is reinforced in her aggression because she gets the toy. In this example, reinforcement clearly plays a vital role in the development of aggressive patterns of behaviour. And when parents give in to their young child's tantrums or aggression, they are reinforcing the very behaviour they deplore, and they thereby unwittingly help to establish a long-lasting pattern of aggression and defiance.

Modelling, too, may play a key role in children's acquisition of aggressive behaviours. In a classic series of studies, psychologist Albert Bandura found that children learn specific forms of aggression, such as hitting, by watching other people perform them (Bandura, Ross, & Ross, 1961, 1963). Although entertainment media offer children many opportunities to observe aggressive behaviour, real-life aggressive models may be more influential. For example, children learn that aggression is a way of solving problems by watching their parents, siblings, and others behave aggressively. A NLSCY analysis revealed that children who are exposed to violence in the home are about twice as likely to be physically and indirectly aggressive, commit delinquent acts, and exhibit higher rates of emotional disorders as children not exposed to such violence (Statistics Canada, 2001a) (see **Figure 8.9**).

Psychologists looking for a heredity basis for trait aggression have produced some supportive data (Hudziak et al., 2003; van Beijsterveldt, Bartels, Hudziak, & Boomsma, 2003; Yaman, Mesman, van IJzendoorn, & Bakermans-Kranenburg, 2010). This alternate view of the development of physical aggression is illustrated in a study which compared gender differences in levels of physical aggression in toddlers in the Québec Longitudinal Study of Child Development (Baillargeon et al., 2007). The

Critical Thinking

Knowing that children's aggressive behaviour or anxiety can change for the better, what does this tell you about the resiliency of children? What does this say about parenting practices over time?

Figure 8.9 Children who witnessed violence in their homes were more likely to exhibit behavioural difficulties.

(**SOURCE:** Statistics Canada. (2001a). The Daily (June 28). Family violence: Focus on child abuse and children at risk. Ottawa, ON: Author. Retrieved from www.statcan.ca/Daily/English/010628/d010628b.htm. Family Violence: Focus on Child Abuse and Children at Risk. Reproduced and distributed on an "as is" basis with the permission of Statistics Canada.)

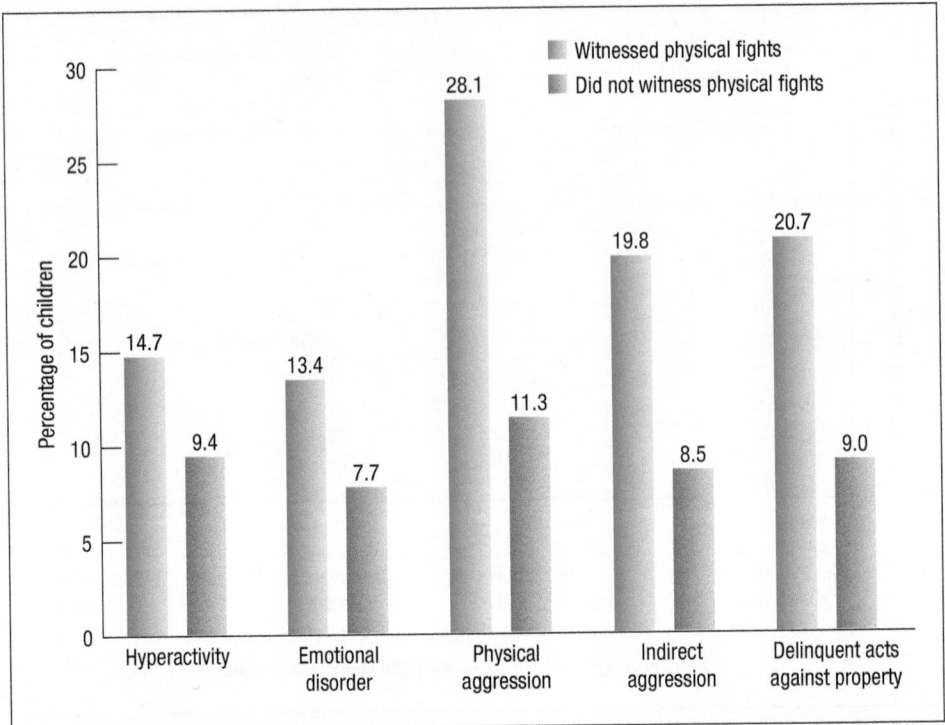

researchers found that the ratio of female to male physical aggression was consistent between 17 and 29 months of age; for every girl, five boys displayed physically aggressive behaviour. The essential point is that aggressiveness was likely established by 17 months of age, before socialization of aggression or gender-stereotypic self-regulatory controls could account for this magnitude and consistency of gender difference in physical aggression. The recent Quebec Newborn Twin Study also found evidence that genetic factors play a pervasive role by setting the stage for both higher levels and growth of physical aggression over the early childhood years (Lacourse, et al., 2014).

A compelling explanation for children's predisposition toward aggression comes from the emerging field of epigenetics (Tremblay, 2008b; Tremblay & Szyf, 2010). As you read above, theories have long focused on how a child develops aggression (i.e., through reinforcement and modelling), but this new model takes a contrary approach by asking how a child fails to gain control over aggression (Tremblay, 2010). This view is based on the premise that children come into the world with aggressive predispositions rather than starting out as "innocents" who acquire aggressiveness. For example, although gene function likely predisposes a child's aggressive tendencies, environmental factors can modify these tendencies from the moment of conception onward (Meaney, 2010; Provençal, Booij, & Tremblay, 2015) (recall from the chapter on Theories of Development that inherited and acquired epigenetic markers can lead to phenotypic changes—such as aggression—without changing the genotype).

Experiments with long-term follow-ups are now needed to determine if early preventive and corrective interventions can lessen aggression during early childhood (Tremblay, 2010). Preventive measures aimed at modifying epigenetic effects that

Social and Personality Development in Early Childhood **223**

predispose children to aggressive behaviour need to take place as close to conception as possible and continue through the prenatal and perinatal periods, especially with mothers who are at risk (i.e., mothers who displayed behaviour problems during adolescence, have a low level of education, had their first pregnancy at a young age, or experienced depression). Interventions beginning after a child is 12 to 17 months of age would need to be more corrective in nature and focus more on the family and preschool environment, especially for high-risk families (i.e., families with low income, family dysfunction, lack of stimulation, or the presence of aggressive siblings). Not only may these early interventions lessen the prevalence of aggression in early childhood, but they may also disrupt the intergenerational transmission of aggression. Already, a recent study has shown that early intervention in the parent–child interactions of high-risk families can prevent physical aggression in early childhood (Brotman et al., 2009). Taking this one step further, future prevention strategies could focus on improving the lifestyle of at-risk pregnant women early in their pregnancy (Tremblay, 2008b, 2010).

Prosocial Behaviour and Friendships

At the other end of the spectrum of peer relationships is a set of behaviours psychologists call *prosocial behaviour*. Like aggression, **prosocial behaviour** is intentional and voluntary, but its purpose is to help another person in some way (Eisenberg, Fabes, & Spinrad, 2006). In everyday language, such behaviour is called *altruism*, and it changes with age, just as other aspects of peer behaviour change.

DEVELOPMENT OF PROSOCIAL BEHAVIOUR Altruistic behaviours first become evident in children of about 2 or 3 years of age—at about the same time as real interest in playing with other children arises. At this age, a child will often share a toy, offer to help another child who is feeling sick, or try to comfort another child who is crying or upset (Baillargeon et al., 2011; Tomasello, 2009). As you read in the chapter on Physical and Cognitive Development in Early Childhood, children this young are only beginning to understand that others feel differently than they do, but they obviously understand enough about the emotions of others to respond in supportive and sympathetic ways when they see other children or adults hurt or sad. In addition, University of British Columbia researchers have found that toddlers, even before the age of 2, experience greater happiness when giving treats to others than when receiving treats themselves, even if it means sacrificing their own treats to give to others (Aknin, Hamlin, & Dunn, 2012).

Beyond these early years, changes in prosocial behaviour show a mixed pattern. Some kinds of prosocial behaviour, such as taking turns, seem to increase with age. If you give children an opportunity to donate some treat to another child who is described as needy, older children donate more than younger children do. Helpfulness, too, seems to increase with age, through adolescence. But not all prosocial behaviours show this pattern. Comforting another child, for example, seems to be more common among preschoolers and children in early elementary grades than among older children (Eisenberg, 2004).

Children vary a lot in the amount of altruistic behaviour they show, and young children who show relatively more empathy and altruism are also those who regulate their own emotions well. They show positive emotions readily and negative emotions less often and are also more popular with peers (Eisenberg et al., 2006). These variations among children's levels of empathy or altruism seem to be related to specific kinds of

Learning Objective 8.11

Trace the changes in prosocial behaviour and friendship patterns during early childhood.

prosocial behaviour

behaviour intended to help another person

(Photo: Tedmiki/Moment/Getty Images)

Prosocial behaviours such as sharing are influenced by cognitive development and the deliberate efforts of parents and teachers to teach children to behave in such ways.

child-rearing. In addition, longitudinal studies indicate that children who display higher levels of prosocial behaviour in the preschool years continue to demonstrate higher levels of such behaviour in adulthood (Eisenberg et al., 1999).

PARENTAL INFLUENCES ON PROSOCIAL BEHAVIOUR   Research suggests that parental behaviour contributes to the development of prosocial behaviour (Eisenberg, 2004). Specifically, parents of altruistic children create a loving and warm family climate. If such warmth is combined with clear explanations and rules about what to do as well as what not to do, then the children are even more likely to behave altruistically. Such parents also often explain the consequences of the child's action in terms of its effects on others—for example, "If you hit Susan, it will hurt her." Stating rules or guidelines positively rather than negatively also appears to be important; for example, "It's always good to be helpful to other people" is more effective guidance than "Don't be so selfish!"

Providing prosocial *attributions*—positive statements about the underlying cause for helpful behaviour—is also useful. For example, a parent might praise a child by saying "You're such a helpful child!" or "You certainly do a lot of nice things for other people." Having heard such statements often during early childhood helps children incorporate them into their self-concepts later in childhood. In this way, parents may help create a generalized, internalized pattern of altruistic behaviour in the child.

Parents of altruistic children also look for opportunities for them to do helpful things. For example, they allow children to help cook, take care of pets, make toys to give away, teach younger siblings, and so forth. Finally, parental modelling of thoughtful and generous behaviour—that is, parents demonstrating consistency between what they say and what they do—is another contributing factor.

FRIENDSHIPS   Beginning at about 18 months, a few toddlers show early hints of playmate preferences or individual friendships (Howes, 1983, 1987); however, by age 3, about 20% of children have a stable playmate. By age 4, more than half spend 30% or more of their time with one other child (Hinde, Titmus, Easton, & Tamplin, 1985). Thus, one important change in social behaviour during early childhood is the formation of stable friendships (Hay, Payne, & Chadwick, 2004).

To be sure, these early peer interactions are still quite primitive. However, it is noteworthy that preschool friend pairs nonetheless show more mutual liking, more reciprocity, more extended interactions, more positive and less negative behaviour, and more supportiveness in a novel situation than do nonfriend pairs at this same age—all signs that these relationships are more than merely passing fancies. Moreover, having had a friend in early childhood is related to social competence (Rubin, Coplan Chen, Bowker, & McDonald, 2011).

Test Yourself before going on

1. Two children are building separate block structures without interacting. They are engaging in _____ play.
2. Which type of aggression is more common between the ages of 2 and 4—indirect or physical—and in what ways do preschoolers display it?
3. Define prosocial behaviour and explain how it changes in early childhood.
4. At what age does each of these milestones in the development of friendship happen?
   _____ (a) More than half of children spend 30% of their time with one peer.
   _____ (b) Most children show hints of playmate preferences.
   _____ (c) About 20% of children have a stable playmate.

Critical Thinking

5. Do you think that peer relationships are necessary to social development in early childhood? That is, do you think that young children who have no exposure to children other than their own siblings are just as likely to emerge from early childhood with adequate social skills as those who have opportunities to interact with peers?

Personality and Self-Concept

As young children gain more understanding of the social environment, their temperaments ripen into true personalities. At the same time, their self-concepts become more complex, allowing them to exercise greater control over their own behaviour.

From Temperament to Personality

Are you familiar with the children's game "Duck, Duck, Goose"? For the benefit of readers who are unfamiliar with the game, here's how it goes. A child who has been assigned the role of "it" walks around the outside of a circle of children who are seated on the floor. As "it" passes by, he touches the head of each child and calls out "duck" until he comes to the child that he chooses to be the "goose." The "goose" then has to jump up and chase "it" around the circle and try to prevent him from taking the goose's seat. If "goose" fails to beat "it," then she becomes "it" for the next round of the game. The difficult part of the game for many young children is waiting to be chosen to be the "goose."

Activities such as "Duck, Duck, Goose" may seem frivolous, but they contribute to the process through which temperament becomes modified into personality during the early childhood years. A child whose temperament includes a low ranking on the dimension of effortful control, for instance, may not be able to tolerate waiting for his turn in a game of "Duck, Duck, Goose" (Li-Grining, 2007). If he obeys his impulse to chase "it" and jumps up from his seat before he is declared the "goose," he will undoubtedly be scolded by his playmates. If his frustration leads him to withdraw from the game with the protest, "I never get to be the goose!", then he will miss out on the fun of participating. Either way, he will learn that controlling his impulses is more beneficial to him than submitting to them. A few such experiences will teach him to moderate the effects of his lack of effortful control on his social behaviour. As a result, his lack of effortful control will become less prominent in the profile of characteristics that constitute his personality and will change how his peers respond to him. Their approval of his modified profile will encourage him to keep his impulses in check.

Likewise, children with difficult temperaments learn that the behaviours associated with difficultness, such as complaining, often result in peer rejection. As a result, many of them change their behaviour to gain social acceptance. Similarly, some shy toddlers are encouraged by their parents to be more sociable, while the timidity of others is amplified by parental overprotectiveness (Kiel & Buss, 2012; Rubin et al., 2011). Thus, personality represents the combination of the temperament with which children are probably born and the knowledge they gain about temperament-related behaviour during childhood (Karreman, de Haas, Van Tuijl, van Aken, & Dekovic, 2010; McCrae, Costa, Ostendord, & Angleitner, 2000). As such, infant temperament doesn't necessarily dictate the kind of personality a child will develop. Instead, it is one factor among many that contribute to an individual child's personality.

Self-Concept

The 18- to 24-month-old is beginning to develop categorical and emotional selves. Between ages 2 and 6, the child continues to develop these two aspects of the self and adds to them a *social self*. Gender differences also begin to appear in self-concept during the preschool years. For instance, Brock University researcher Sandra Bosacki (2001) conducted a longitudinal study of the self-concept–related dimensions of self-knowledge, emotional understanding, and gender-typed play in children aged 3 to 4.

Learning Objective 8.12
Describe temperament changes in early childhood.

(Photo: S.Kobold/Fotolia)

Children with difficult temperaments may show heightened aggressiveness or other behavioural problems in school—but when such behaviour results in peer rejection, they may be motivated to change their behaviour in order to gain social acceptance.

Learning Objective 8.13
Trace the changes in the young child's categorical, emotional, and social selves during the preschool years.

She found that girls scored higher than boys in their cognitive ability to solve false belief tasks, their ability to understand emotions within themselves and in others, and their perceived level of self-control in social situations. Familiarity with the dimensions of preschoolers' self-concepts helps parents, teachers, and others better understand many aspects of their social behaviour.

THE CATEGORICAL SELF   By the end of the preschool period, a child can give you quite a full description of herself on a whole range of dimensions. Still, these early self-concepts remain highly concrete. The self-concept of a preschool child tends to focus on her own visible characteristics—whether she's a boy or girl, what she looks like, what or whom she plays with, where she lives, what she is good at—rather than on more enduring inner qualities.

As you learned earlier in this chapter, categories are also important in young children's perceptions of others—"big kids," "little kids," "boys," "girls," and so on. Preschoolers prefer playmates of their own age and gender. Consequently, the categorical self seems to be as much an internal working model for social relationships as for the self.

THE EMOTIONAL SELF   In a Canadian study of children's emotional knowledge, Bosacki and Moore (2004) found that preschool girls scored higher than boys in the ability to correctly label emotions and understand complex emotions. Both girls and boys were found to be better at understanding their own emotions as opposed to the emotions of others. Preschool children also demonstrated the ability to conceptualize complex emotions, such as pride, before they could understand them (e.g., knowing why a specific situation would lead to a sense of pride). In general, preschool children with better vocabularies were better able to label and explain emotions.

In recent years, research examining development of the emotional self during the early childhood years has focused on the acquisition of **emotional regulation**, or the ability to control emotional states and emotion-related behaviour (Eisenberg & Sulik, 2012). For example, children exhibit emotional regulation when they find a way to cheer themselves up when they are feeling sad, or when they divert their attention to a different activity when they get frustrated with something. Some studies have shown that emotional regulation in early childhood is linked to a variety of social variables. One study showed that level of emotional regulation at age 2 predicted level of aggressive behaviour at age 4 in both boys and girls (Rubin, Burgess, Dwyer, & Hastings, 2003). Predictably, preschoolers who display high levels of emotional regulation are more popular with their peers than those who are less able to regulate their emotional behaviour (Denham et al., 2003; Fantuzzo, Sekino, & Cohen, 2004). Emotional regulation skills appear to be particularly important for children whose temperaments include high levels of anger proneness (Diener & Kim, 2004). Further, longitudinal research has demonstrated that emotional regulation in early childhood is related to children's development of emotional problems and their ability to think about right and wrong during the school years (Kim-Spoon, Cicchetti, & Rogosch, 2013; Kochanska, Murray, & Coy, 1997).

The process of acquiring emotional regulation is one in which control shifts slowly from the parents to the child across the early childhood years (Brophy-Herb, Zajicek-Farber, Bocknek, McKelvey, & Stansbury, 2013; Houck & Lecuyer-Maus, 2004). Here again, the child's temperament is a factor. For example, preschoolers who have consistently exhibited difficult behaviour since infancy are more likely to have self-control problems in early childhood (Schmitz et al., 1999). Similarly, preschoolers who were born prematurely or who were delayed in language development in the second year of life experience more difficulties with self-control during early childhood (Carson, Klee, & Perry, 1998; Schothorst & van Engeland, 1996).

Another aspect of the emotional self involves **empathy**, the ability to identify with another person's emotional state. Empathy has two aspects: apprehending

emotional regulation

the ability to control emotional states and emotion-related behaviour

empathy

the ability to identify with another person's emotional state

another person's emotional state or condition and then matching that emotional state oneself. An empathizing person experiences either the same feeling he imagines the other person to feel or a highly similar feeling. Empathy is negatively associated with aggression in the early childhood years; the more advanced preschoolers' capacity for empathy is, the less aggression they display (Hatakeyama & Hatakeyama, 2012; Strayer & Roberts, 2004). Moreover, the development of empathy in early childhood appears to provide the foundation on which a more sophisticated emotion, *sympathy* (a general feeling of sorrow or concern for another person), is built in later childhood and adolescence (Sallquist, Eisenberg, Spinrad, Eggum, & Gaertner, 2009a).

In addition to empathy, young children's emotional selves include an awareness of emotional states that are linked to their culture's definitions of right and wrong (Thompson & Newton, 2010). These feelings, which are sometimes called the *moral emotions*, include guilt, shame, and pride (Eisenberg, 2000). Guilt is usually thought of as the emotional state that is induced when a child breaks a rule. Consequently, a child who takes a forbidden cookie will experience guilt. Feelings of shame arise when she fails to live up to expectations. For instance, most parents and teachers urge young children to share their toys. Thus, when a child behaves selfishly and is reminded about the sharing rule, he likely feels shame. By contrast, children feel pride when they succeed at meeting such expectations.

Research suggests that the interplay among these three emotions and young children's awareness of them influences the development of behaviour that the children's cultures regard as morally acceptable (Eisenberg, 2000). Thus, they form the foundation of later moral development. Studies suggest that these feelings evolve in the context of parent–child relationships. Young children who do not have warm, trusting relationships with their parents are at risk of failing to develop moral emotions or of developing feelings of guilt, shame, and pride that are too weak to influence their behaviour (Koenig, Cicchetti, & Rogosch, 2004).

THE SOCIAL SELF   Another facet of the child's emerging sense of self is an increasing awareness of herself as a player in the social game. By age 2, the toddler has already learned a variety of social "scripts"—routines of play or interaction with others. The toddler now begins to develop some implicit understanding of her own roles in these scripts (Case, 1991). So she may begin to think of herself as a "helper" in some situations or as "the boss" when she is telling some other child what to do.

You can see this clearly in children's sociodramatic play, as they begin to take explicit roles: "I'll be the daddy and you be the mommy" or "I'm the boss." As part of the same process, the young child also gradually understands her place in the network of family roles. She has sisters, brothers, a father, a mother, and so forth.

Moreover, role scripts help young children become more independent. For example, assuming the "student" role provides a preschooler with a prescription for appropriate behaviour in the school situation. Students listen when the teacher speaks to the class, get out materials and put them away at certain times, help their classmates in various ways, and so on. Once a preschooler is familiar with and adopts the student role, he can follow the role script and is no longer dependent on the teacher to tell him what to do every minute of the day.

While bored toddlers often need to have their attention physically redirected to keep them occupied, by preschool age, most children are able to look for things to do on their own, like looking at a magazine or asking a parent to read to them.

Not all children make the social adjustment to school in the same way. Carlton University psychologists Robert Coplan and Kavita Prakash (2003) looked at three patterns of child–teacher interactions and found that children rated as more aggressive initiated more interactions with teachers; shy and anxious children received, but didn't initiate, interactions with teachers; and a third group of children who were rated as more sociable and less solitary spent the least amount of time interacting with teachers as they spent more time interacting with other students and exploring learning opportunities in the classroom. A closer look at shy students found that their quietness may be due to either social disinterest (a nonfearful preference for solitude) or conflicted shyness (an approach-avoidance conflict—their desire to interact with others is accompanied by fear or anxiety) (Coplan, Prakash, O'Neil, & Armer, 2004; Rubin, Coplan, & Bowker, 2009). Moreover, it seems that children's shyness is related to social anxiety rather than a lack of ability to verbally express themselves (Coplan & Armer, 2005).

Test Yourself before going on

1. Interactions with _____ and _____ can modify children's temperaments.
2. Research on the development of young children's emotional self has focused on _____ _____.
3. The ability to identify with another person's emotional state is _____.
4. Guilt, shame, and pride are _____ emotions that develop during early childhood.

Critical Thinking

5. If parents received a description of their child's temperament at birth (sort of like the owner's manual you get with a new appliance), do you think it would help them to be better parents? Conversely, do you think it would cause them to be overly tolerant of temperamental characteristics that might need to be modified for the child's own benefit, such as irritability?

Gender Development

We noted earlier that preschoolers who are asked to describe themselves are likely to begin by stating whether they are boys or girls. In psychologists' terms, their tendency to do so suggests that "boy-ness" and "girl-ness" are salient, or important, categories for young children. Thus, one of the most fascinating developmental processes of the preschool period is the one that involves children's evolving sense of **gender**—the psychological and social associates and implications of biological sex.

gender
the psychological and social associates and implications of biological sex

Learning Objective 8.14
Describe the major theoretical orientations that explain gender development.

Explaining Gender Concept and Sex-Role Development

Developmentalists have proposed several explanations of gender development.

SOCIAL-COGNITIVE EXPLANATIONS   Social-cognitive theorists have emphasized the role of parents in shaping children's sex-role behaviour and attitudes (Bandura, 1977a; Bandura & Bussey, 2004; Mischel, 1966, 1970). Parents reinforce sex-typed activities in children as young as 18 months, not only by buying different kinds of toys for boys and girls, but also by responding more positively when their sons play with "boy-type" toys, such as tools or trucks, than when their sons play with "girl-type" toys, such as dolls and jewellery, and the opposite is true for daughters (Fagot & Hagan, 1991; Leaper & Friedman, 2007). One study found that an infant's sex affected how mothers interacted with them: The mothers' speech and behaviour varied, even when their infants were as young as 6 months of age. The mothers' speech was more conversational and they engaged in more comforting and hugging with their daughters than with their sons. By comparison, the mothers' speech was more instructional and directive and there was less interaction overall with their sons (Clearfield & Nelson, 2006).

THE COGNITIVE-DEVELOPMENTAL EXPLANATION   A second alternative, Kohlberg's cognitive-developmental theory, suggests that children's understanding of

Figure 8.10 In describing this self-portrait, the 5-year-old artist said, "This is how I will look when I get married to a boy. I am under a rainbow, so beautiful with a bride hat, a belt, and a purse." The girl knows she will always be female and associates gender with externals such as clothing (gender stability). She is also already quite knowledgeable about gender-role expectations.

(Courtesy of Jerry and Denise Boyd. Used with permission.)

gender develops in stages (Kohlberg, 1966; Kohlberg & Ullian, 1974). First comes **gender identity**, which is simply a child's ability to label his or her own sex correctly and to identify other people as men or women, boys or girls. By age 2, most children correctly label themselves as boys or girls, and within six to twelve months, most can correctly label others as well. The second step is **gender stability**, which is the understanding that people stay the same gender throughout life. Researchers have measured this by asking children such questions as "When you were a little baby, were you a little girl or a little boy?" or "When you grow up, will you be a mommy or a daddy?" Most children understand the stability of gender by about age 4 (Slaby & Frey, 1975) (see **Figure 8.10**). The final step is the development of true **gender constancy**, the recognition that someone stays the same gender even though he may appear to change by wearing different clothes or changing his hair length. For example, boys don't change into girls by wearing dresses.

Numerous studies, including studies of children growing up in other cultures such as Kenya, Nepal, Belize, and Samoa, show that children go through this sequence (Martin & Ruble, 2004; Munroe, Shimmin, & Munroe, 1984). Moreover, progression through the sequence is related to general cognitive development (Trautner, Gervai, & Nemeth, 2003). Consequently, Kohlberg asserted that gender constancy is the organizing principle that children use to acquire knowledge of gender and to bring their own behaviour into conformity with cultural standards. However, critics point out that Kohlberg's theory fails to explain why children show clearly different behaviour, such as toy preferences, long before they achieve gender constancy.

gender identity

the ability to correctly label oneself and others as male or female

gender stability

the understanding that gender is a stable, lifelong characteristic

gender constancy

the understanding that gender is a component of the self that is not altered by external appearance

gender schema theory

an information-processing approach to gender concept development that asserts that people use a schema for each gender to process information about themselves and others

THE INFORMATION-PROCESSING APPROACH Information-processing theorists use the term *schema* to refer to mental frameworks, such as categories, that help humans organize processes such as thinking and remembering. **Gender schema theory** assumes that the development of such a framework for gender underlies gender development. According to this perspective, the gender schema begins to develop as soon as the child notices the differences between male and female, knows his own gender, and can label the two groups with some consistency—all of which happens between 18 and 24 months (Zosuls et al, 2009). Perhaps because gender is basically an either/or category, children seem to understand very early that this is a key distinction, so the category serves as a kind of magnet for new information. Once the child has established even a primitive gender schema, a great many experiences can be assimilated to it. Thus, as soon as this schema begins to be formed, children may begin to show preference for same-sex playmates or for gender-stereotyped activities (Martin & Little, 1990; Martin & Ruble, 2004; 2010).

Preschoolers first learn some broad distinctions about what kinds of activities or behaviour "go with" each gender, both by observing other children and through the reinforcements they receive from parents. They also learn a few gender *scripts*—whole sequences of events that are normally associated with a given gender, such as "fixing dinner" or "building with tools"—just as they learn other social scripts at about this age (Levy & Fivush, 1993). Then, between ages 4 and 6, the child learns a more subtle and complex set of associations for his own gender—what children of his own gender like and don't like, how they play, how they talk, what kinds of people they associate with. Only between ages 8 and 10 does the child develop an equivalently complex view of the opposite gender (Martin, Wood, & Little, 1990).

gender constancy theory

Kohlberg's assertion that children must understand that gender is a permanent characteristic before they can adopt appropriate sex roles

The key difference between this theory and Kohlberg's **gender constancy theory** is that gender schema theory asserts that the child need not understand that gender is permanent to form an initial gender schema. When they do begin to understand gender constancy, at about age 5 or 6, children develop a more elaborate rule, or schema, of "what people who are like me do" and treat this rule the same way they treat other rules—as an absolute. Later, the child's application of the gender rule becomes more flexible. She knows, for example, that most boys don't play with dolls, but that they can do so if they like.

BIOLOGICAL APPROACHES For a long time, developmentalists dismissed the idea that biological differences between males and females were responsible for psychological differences between them. Today, though, they are taking a new look at human studies which show that both prenatal and postnatal levels of male hormones, such as testosterone, predict gendered behavioural differences during the preschool years and beyond (Hines, Constantinescu, & Spencer, 2015; Hines et al., 2016). Factors such as children's gender-typical play styles (e.g., rough and tumble play vs. enacting "real life" events like going to school or the doctor's office) and toy interests (e.g., interest in dolls vs. toy vehicles), gender identity and later sexual orientation, show the largest differences.

Hormonal influences have been proposed to explain the outcomes of cases involving boys who carry a genetic defect that causes them to develop deformed genitalia. Decades ago, a few such boys were subjected to plastic surgery to give them female-appearing genitals and were raised as girls. At that time, however, doctors did not realize that the genetic defect in question interferes only with testosterone's effects on the sex organs; the brains of these fetuses were exposed to normal amounts of testosterone throughout prenatal development (Rosenthal & Gitelman, 2002). Follow-up studies found that many of these children, when they learned of their status, sought surgery to masculinize their bodies. Moreover, even those who elected to retain the feminine identities they had been given in infancy possessed many attributes and behaviours that are more typical of males than of females

(Reiner & Gearhart, 2004). Such findings support the view that hormones play some role in gender development.

Sex-Role Knowledge

Learning Objective 8.15

Identify how preschoolers acquire sex-role knowledge.

Figuring out your gender and understanding that it stays constant are only part of the story. Learning what goes with being a boy or a girl in a given culture is also a vital part of the child's task. Researchers have studied this in two ways: by asking children what boys and girls (or men and women) like to do and what they are like (which is an inquiry about gender stereotypes), and by asking children if it is okay for boys to play with dolls or girls to climb trees or do equivalent cross-sex things (an inquiry about roles).

A large study of Canadian children shows that these stereotyped ideas develop early (Serbin, Powlishta, & Gulko, 1993). It would not be uncommon to hear a 3-year-old say "Mommies use the stove, and daddies use the grill." A 4-year-old might define gender roles in terms of competencies: "Daddies are better at fixing things, but mommies are better at tying bows and decorating." Even 2-year-olds already associate certain activities and possessions with men and women, depending on the adult activities they are most often and consistently exposed to in the home. For example, toddlers of both genders can associate feeding a baby, applying makeup, and wearing dresses with women and, to a lesser extent, cars and hammering with men (Serbin, Poulin-Dubois, & Eichstedt, 2002). By age 3 or 4, children can assign stereotypic occupations, toys, and activities to each gender (Blakemore, 2003; Care, Deans, & Brown, 2007). By age 5, children begin to associate certain personality traits, such as assertiveness and nurturance, with males or females (Parmley & Cunningham, 2008).

Studies of children's ideas about how men and women (or boys and girls) ought to behave add an interesting further element. For example, in an early study, a psychologist told a story to children aged 4 to 9 about a little boy named George who liked to play with dolls (Damon, 1977). George's parents told him that only little girls play with dolls; little boys shouldn't. The children were then asked questions about the story, such as "Why do people tell George not to play with dolls?" or "Is there a rule that boys shouldn't play with dolls?"

Four-year-olds in this study thought it was okay for George to play with dolls: There was no rule against it, and he should do it if he wanted to. Six-year-olds, in contrast, thought it was wrong for George to play with dolls. By about age 9, children had differentiated between what boys and girls usually do, and what is "wrong." One boy said, for example, that breaking windows was wrong and bad, but that playing with dolls was not bad in the same way: "Breaking windows you're not supposed to do. And if you play with dolls, well you can, but boys usually don't."

As their gender concept develops, children change their views about whether it is acceptable for boys to play with dolls or for girls to play sports, such as baseball.

(*Photos:* left, MNStudio/Shutterstock; right, Michael Ireland/Fotolia)

Interestingly, more recent studies show that 21st-century children express ideas about gender-typed behaviour that are quite similar to those of their 1970s counterparts (Gee & Heyman, 2007; Gelman, Taylor, Nguyen, Leaper, & Bigler, 2004). These studies suggest that the 5- to 6-year-old has figured out that gender is permanent and is searching for an all-or-none, totally reliable rule about how boys and girls behave (Martin & Ruble, 2004). The child picks up information from watching adults, from watching television, and from listening to the labels that are attached to different activities (e.g., "Boys don't cry" or "Girls act nicely"). Initially, children treat these as absolute, moral rules. Later, they understand that these are social conventions; at this point, sex-role concepts become more flexible and stereotyping declines between ages 5 and 11, although stereotype knowledge and spontaneous stereotyping remain at high levels (Banse, Gawronski, Rebetez, Gutt, & Morton, 2010).

Learning Objective 8.16

Describe the sex-typed behaviour of young children.

sex-typed behaviour

different patterns of behaviour exhibited by boys and girls

Sex-Typed Behaviour

The final element in the development of sex roles is the actual behaviour children show with those of the same and the opposite sex. An unexpected finding is that **sex-typed behaviour**, or different patterns of behaviour among girls and boys, develops earlier than ideas about sex roles (Campbell, Shirley, & Candy, 2004). By 18 to 24 months of age, children begin to show some preference for sex-stereotyped toys, such as dolls for girls or trucks or building blocks for boys, which is some months before they can consistently identify their own gender (O'Toole-Thommessen & Todd, 2010). By age 3, children begin to show a preference for same-sex friends and are much more sociable with playmates of the same sex—at a time when they do not yet have a concept of gender stability (Corsaro, Molinari, Hadley, & Sugioka, 2003) (see **Figure 8.11**).

Figure 8.11 In one study of playmate preferences, researchers counted how often preschool children played with same-sex or opposite-sex playmates. Children as young as 2 years old already showed at least some preference for same-sex playmates.

(**SOURCE:** The Emergence of Same-Sex Affiliative Preferences among Preschool Peers: A Developmental/ Ethological Perspective Child Development Vol. 55, No. 5 (Oct., 1984), pp. 1958–1965. Reproduced by permission of Wiley & Sons, Ltd.)

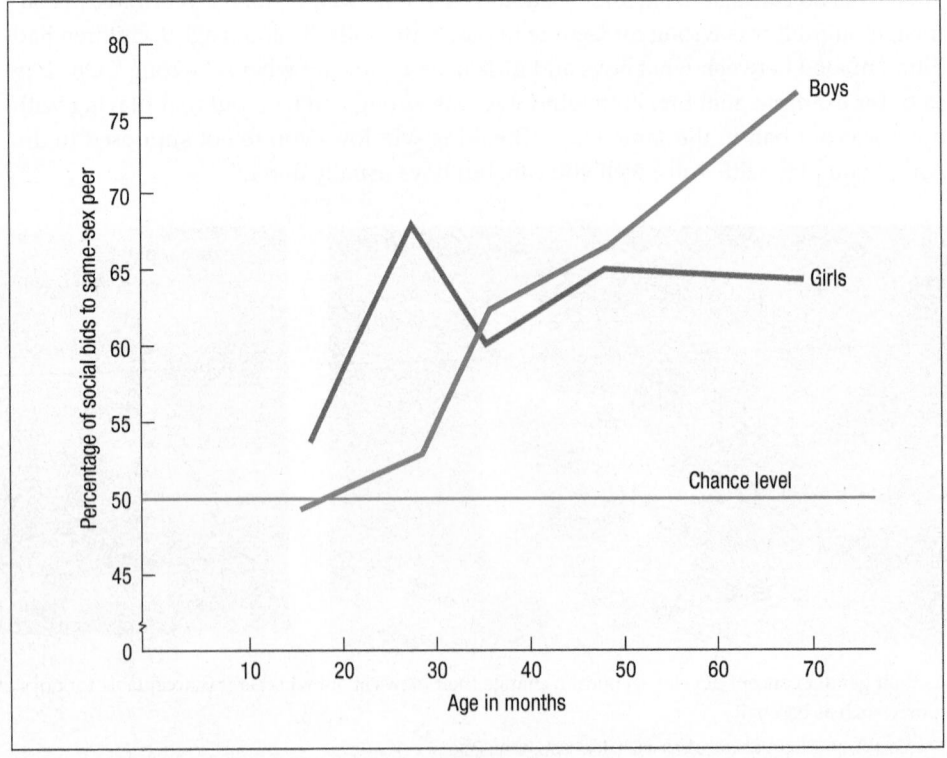

Not only are preschoolers' friendships and peer interactions increasingly sex segregated, but it is also clear that boy–boy interactions and girl–girl interactions differ in quality, even in these early years. One important part of same-sex interactions seems to involve instruction and modelling of sex-appropriate behaviour. In other words, older boys teach younger boys how to be "masculine," and older girls teach younger girls how to be "feminine" (Danby & Baker, 1998).

These "lessons" in sex-typed behaviour are subtle. Eleanor Maccoby, one of the leading theorists in this area, describes the girls' pattern as an *enabling style* (Maccoby, 1990). Enabling includes behaviours such as supporting the friend, expressing agreement, and making suggestions. All these behaviours tend to foster a greater equality and intimacy in the relationship and keep the interaction going. In contrast, boys are more likely to show what Maccoby calls a *constricting, or restrictive, style.* "A restrictive style is one that tends to derail the interaction—to inhibit the partner or cause the partner to withdraw, thus shortening the interaction or bringing it to an end" (1990, p. 517). Contradicting, interrupting, boasting, and other forms of self-display are all aspects of this style.

These two patterns begin to be visible in the preschool years. For example, beginning as early as age 3, boys and girls use quite different strategies in their attempts to influence each other's behaviour (Maccoby, 1990). Girls generally ask questions or make requests; boys are much more likely to make demands or phrase things using imperatives (e.g., "Give me that!"). The really intriguing finding is that even at this early age, boys simply don't respond to the girls' enabling style. Thus, playing with boys yields little positive reinforcement for girls, and they begin to avoid such interactions and band together.

Another kind of learning opportunity happens when children exhibit **cross-gender behaviour**, behaviour that is atypical in their culture for their gender. For example, *tomboyishness*, girls' preference for activities that are more typical for boys, is a kind of cross-gender behaviour. Generally, tomboyishness is tolerated by adults and peers (Sandnabba & Ahlberg, 1999). Not surprisingly, then, cross-gender behaviour is far more common among girls than boys (Etaugh & Liss, 1992). Tomboyishness does not appear to interfere with the development of a "feminine" personality in adulthood, and it may allow girls to acquire positive characteristics such as assertiveness (Hilgenkamp & Livingston, 2002). In contrast, both peers and adults actively discourage boys from engaging in cross-gender behaviour. Specifically, boys who play with dolls or behave in an effeminate manner are likely to elicit expressions of disapproval, or even ridicule, from children, parents, and teachers (Martin & Ruble, 2004, 2010). However, it cannot be assumed that the prevalence of sex-typed

cross-gender behaviour
behaviour that is atypical for one's own sex but typical for the opposite sex

Play may provide children with opportunities to learn about gender-role expectations.

play among boys is strictly the result of adult and peer influence. For one thing, sex-typed play preferences appear earlier and are more consistent in boys, which suggests that these preferences begin to develop before environmental forces have had much chance to influence them (Blakemore, LaRue, & Olejnik, 1979; Fabes, Martin, & Hanish, 2003).

Individual differences in sex-typed behaviour are highly stable across early and middle childhood—that is, among both boys and girls, those who exhibit the greatest amount of sex-typed behaviour at age 2 continue to do so in the middle elementary school years (Golombok et al., 2008). In addition, cross-gender behaviour in early childhood predicts subjective feelings of differentness from peers in adolescence (Golombok, Rust, Zervoulis, Golding, & Hines, 2012). These findings suggest that sex-typed behaviour is part of a complex process of identity development and not just the result of cultural modelling and reinforcement.

Test Yourself before going on

1. Match each theory with its main idea.
   _____ (a) social-cognitive theory
   _____ (b) cognitive-developmental theory
   _____ (c) gender schema theory
   _____ (d) biological approaches
   - (i) gender concept develops in stages
   - (ii) children use a mental framework to organize ideas about gender
   - (iii) gender development is attributable to parental influences
   - (iv) hormones shape gender development

2. Classify each item in the list as (SR) sex-role knowledge, or (ST) sex-typed behaviour.
   _____ (a) enabling style
   _____ (b) belief that boys shouldn't play with dolls
   _____ (c) girls' preference for "feminine" toys
   _____ (d) restrictive style
   _____ (e) associating women with domestic tasks such as cooking and cleaning

Critical Thinking

3. To what degree do you think the enabling and constricting interaction styles are exhibited in adults' social interactions?

Summary

Theories of Social and Personality Development

8.1 Summarize the major themes of development proposed by psychoanalytic theorists for the early childhood period.

- Both Freud's and Erikson's theories of personality development place primary importance on balancing parental control with a child's emerging needs and skills. Erikson described two stages in which autonomy and initiative are developed.

8.2 Summarize the findings of social-cognitive theorists with respect to young children's understanding of the social world.

- Social-cognitive theorists assert that advances in social and personality development are associated with cognitive development. Three topics of interest to social-cognitive theorists are person perception, understanding rule categories, and understanding others' intentions.

Family Relationships and Structure

8.3 Describe how attachment changes during the early childhood years.

- Except in stressful situations, attachment behaviours become less visible as the child gets older. Preschoolers refuse or defy parental influence attempts more than infants do. Outright defiance, however, declines from age 2 to 6. Both these changes are clearly linked to the child's language and cognitive gains.

8.4 Discuss how parenting styles affect children's development.

- Authoritative parenting, which combines warmth, clear rules, and communication with high maturity demands, is associated with the most positive outcomes for children. Authoritarian parenting has some negative effects on development. However, permissive and uninvolved parenting seem to be the least positive styles. Most child development experts recommend minimal nonphysical forms of child discipline.

8.5 Identify how ethnicity and socioeconomic status interact with parenting styles.

- Studies of parenting style and developmental outcomes in ethnic groups suggest that, in some situations, authoritative parenting may not be the best style. Good parenting practices are common in all SES levels, but when children of lower SES are exposed to inadequate parenting practices, they become more vulnerable to a wide range of problems.

8.6 Explain how family structure is related to children's development.

- Canadian studies found that many family structures, other than one that includes two biological parents, experience high levels of stress, yet only a portion of these children have an elevated risk of a range of problems.

8.7 Describe the impact of divorce on children in early childhood and in later years.

- Following a divorce, children typically show disrupted behaviour for several years. Parenting styles also change, becoming less authoritative.

8.8 Identify some possible ways divorce-related changes in family structure affect development.

- To understand the influence of family structure on development, a number of variables, such as poverty, associated with differences in family structure must be taken into account.

Peer Relationships

8.9 Trace a child's changing relationship with his or her peers through play.

- Play with peers is evident before age 2 and becomes increasingly important through the preschool years. At every age, children spend some time in solitary play and may exhibit onlooker play, a pattern in which they watch another child play. By 14–18 months, children engage in parallel play, playing alongside each other but not interacting. At 18 months, associative play—play that includes some interaction—is apparent. By 3 or 4, children begin to engage in cooperative play, in which they work together to accomplish a goal.

8.10 Identify the key factors in preschool children's aggressive behaviour.

- Physical aggression toward peers increases and then declines in most children during these early years, while indirect aggression increases among some children more than others. Some children display chronic physical aggression, a pattern of aggressive behaviour that continues to cause problems for them throughout childhood and adolescence.

8.11 Trace the changes in prosocial behaviour and friendship patterns during early childhood.

- Empathy and prosocial behaviour toward others seems to become more common as the child's ability to take another's perspective increases. Stable friendships develop between children in this age range.

Personality and Self-Concept

8.12 Describe temperament changes in early childhood.

- Young children's temperaments are modified by social experiences both within and outside of the family to form their personalities.

8.13 Trace the changes in the young child's categorical, emotional, and social selves during the preschool years.

- The preschooler continues to define himself along a series of objective dimensions but does not yet have a global sense of self. Children make major strides in self-control and in their understanding of their own social roles in the preschool years, as parents gradually turn over the job of control to the child.

Gender Development

8.14 Describe the major theoretical orientations that explain gender development.

- Social-cognitive explanations suggest a child's sex-role behaviour and attitudes are shaped by the parents. Cognitive-developmental theory claims that gender development depends on children's understanding of the gender concept and that the latter develops in three stages: gender identity, gender stability, and gender constancy. Gender schema theory claims that children organize ideas about gender using a mental framework (schema) that they construct as soon as they can reliably label themselves and others as male and female. Sex hormones also play a role the development of gender development.

8.15 Identify how preschoolers acquire sex-role knowledge.

- Children begin to learn what appropriate behaviour for their gender is at about age 2. By age 5 or 6, most children have developed fairly rigid rules about what boys or girls are supposed to do and be.

8.16 Describe the sex-typed behaviour of young children.

- Children display sex-typed behaviour as early as 18 to 24 months of age. Some theorists think children play in gender-segregated groups because same-sex peers help them learn about sex-appropriate behaviour.

Policy Question

What Are the Effects of Childhood Poverty in Canada?

Almost one in five Canadian children under the age of 18 is living in a low-income family (Statistics Canada, 2015c) and compared to 35 of the wealthiest nations, Canada ranks in the bottom third in overall child inequality—this means we have a large gap between the lowest- and middle-income families as measured by indices such as income, health, education, and life satisfaction (UNICEF Canada, 2016). Plus, poverty in Canada is unequally distributed across various family structures and ethnic groups. Just over half (~52%) of children under the age of 6 in low-income families live in female lone-parent families (Campaign 2000, 2011, 2015). As well, the low-income rates for Indigenous and recent immigrant children in Canada are also persistently much higher than the national rate.

The Effects of Poverty on Families and Children

For Canadian children, low family income is strongly associated with poorer health and social, emotional, and behavioural problems (Huston & Bentley, 2010; Phipps & Lethbridge, 2006). For example, the children of low-income families have higher rates of birth defects and early disabilities; they suffer poorer overall health during the first five months of life and have higher rates of hospital admission; they recover less readily from early problems; they are more often ill and undernourished throughout their childhood years; and they are more likely to experience atypical structural development in several critical areas of the brain that contributes to lower academic achievement (Hair, Hanson, Wolfe, & Pollak, 2015; Qi & Kaiser, 2003; Séguin, Xu, Potvin, Zunzunegui, & Frohlich, 2003).

Children living in low-income families are also more likely to experience hunger. Although children constitute only 22% of the population, 37% of those using food banks are under age 18 (CCSD, 2010). Specifically, children of the working poor, children of lone-parent families, children of Indigenous heritage, and children whose families are on social assistance are two to eight times more likely to go hungry than other Canadian children (McIntyre, Walsh, & Conner, 2001). As a result, these groups of Canadian children are at risk for malnourishment, which is associated with higher rates of both illness and mortality (Health Canada, 1999c).

It's not poverty per se but the negative consequences it creates that put children at greater risk. Among many other things, poverty reduces options for parents. Children of low-income families have less access to health benefits, child care, safe environments, and recreational and physical activities (CCSD, 2001). Low-income families have little access to services not covered by government health plans, for example, dental care, mental health counselling, and prescription drugs (Health Canada, 1999f). When a low-income mother works, she is likely to have fewer choices of affordable child care. Her children spend more time in poor-quality care and shift more frequently from one care arrangement to another. Low-income families also live in smaller and less-than-adequate housing, often in decaying neighbourhoods with high rates of violence. Many such families move frequently, which means their children change schools often. The parents are less likely to feel that they have adequate social support, and the children often lack a stable group of playmates (Dodge, Pettit, & Bates, 1994; Evans, 2004). Parents in these circumstances also tend to be less involved in their children's schools (Griffith, 1998). Overall, the poor live in more chaotic environments, are more highly stressed, and have fewer psychological and social resources than those who are more economically secure (Shonkoff, 2010).

Impetus for Change

There has been continuing interest in the importance of early childhood development and how social policy plays a role (Comley & Mousmanis, 2004; McEwen & Stewart, 2014). For instance, in their seminal report for the Government of Ontario "Early Years Study—Reversing the Real Brain Drain," McCain and Mustard (2000) emphasized the impact of nutrition and stimulation on the rapidly developing neural connections within the brain during the first years of life and how these effects persist throughout life. Further, the pattern for growth and development later in life is mostly set within the first three years of life and thus has an effect on a

(Photo: VictorD/Fotolia)

(Continued)

child's readiness to learn. By age 6, most of the neurological changes that are precursors to lifelong learning, behaviour, and health are complete. Therefore, conditions that contribute to poor neurological development early in life lead to a lifelong disadvantage that is very difficult to reverse and ultimately affects both the individual and Canadian society. The authors of the report called for radical changes in how society supports its young children in all walks of life (McCain & Mustard, 2002). A decade on, the Early Years Study 3 edition began tracking the progress being made toward improving outcomes for children—Quebec, PEI, and Ontario scored highest on the 19-item Early Childhood Education Index 2011 (McCain, Mustard, & McCuaig, 2011).

(Photo: Adrian Wyld/The Canadian Press)

Social Policy Issues

There are many different contentious points of view concerning the issues surrounding poverty (Jackson, 2001; McEwen & Stewart, 2014). One primary issue is how we should define *low income* itself. Some argue that if you give parents more money they will just squander it on nonessentials, and therefore the poverty line should be drawn at the point where the basic necessities are all that can be provided. This idea, however, fails to address just what constitutes a basic necessity. Some argue that physical needs such as food and shelter are the only needs that require attention. Others suggest that those needs beyond the physical (such as recreation, an intellectually stimulating environment, and health care), if ignored, can lead to long-term outcomes that can carry a major economic cost in the future. They question the wisdom of cutting back on social support to save money today only to create even more difficult and expensive problems in the next generation of adults. Still others argue that Canada is a developed nation that values safety, health, civility, and economic and cultural prosperity, and that we who live in such a fair and just society should embrace the ideal that all children should have an equal chance at becoming successful adults.

Generally, as family incomes increase, the children's chances for success increase, but there is no income level below which a child is destined to fail or above which a child is guaranteed to succeed. In addition, it is not just a matter of improving incomes to increase the likelihood of a child's successful transition to adulthood; what is also required is the creation of pathways of opportunity, for example, fair access to public services, education, health care, and recreation. The question of what level of income combined with what level of public support is needed to adequately prepare all Canadian children to meet tomorrow's challenges remains to be answered.

Your Turn

- What are some common perceptions that people have about low-income Canadians and their children?
- In what ways do misconceptions about the poor impede their chances of getting out of poverty?
- Discuss who is responsible for defining the limits of poverty, and justify who should pay for the cost of reducing poverty.
- Explain in what ways it is more than just low family income that creates unfair opportunities for children living in poverty.
- Why should we care about disadvantaged children? Describe how helping all Canadian children to thrive and have the readiness and opportunity to reach their potential can benefit all of society.

Chapter 9
Physical and Cognitive Development in Middle Childhood

Jacek Chabraszewski/Fotolia

 Learning Objectives

PHYSICAL CHANGES

9.1 Identify what kinds of physical changes occur during middle childhood.

9.2 Describe the ways the brain changes during these years.

9.3 Identify what the health risks are for 6- to 12-year-olds.

COGNITIVE CHANGES

9.4 Describe what cognitive advantages children gain as they move through Piaget's concrete operational stage.

9.5 Describe what horizontal decalage is, and how Siegler explains concrete operational thinking.

9.6 Explain how children's information-processing skills improve during middle childhood.

9.7 Explain how vocabulary and other aspects of language change during middle childhood.

SCHOOLING

9.8 Describe what should be included in an effective literacy curriculum.

9.9 Identify the issues related to children who are second-language learners.

9.10 Summarize the benefits of bilingual education.

9.11 Explain the challenges of evaluating students across Canada's educational systems.

9.12 Summarize what kinds of group differences in achievement educational researchers have found.

LEARNERS WITH EXCEPTIONALITIES

9.13 Describe the issues involved with children with learning disabilities.

9.14 Describe how attention-deficit/hyperactivity disorder affects a child's development.

The first day of school is viewed as one of the most important transition points in a child's life. In Canada, parents mark the occasion in a variety of ways—with new clothes, fresh school supplies, and carefully selected backpacks and lunch boxes. Some families take pictures of their children's first ride on the school bus or first classroom. All these ways of recognizing this important milestone say to children that this day is unique, and they begin to think of themselves as "big kids" who are engaged in the serious business of going to school, rather than "little kids" who spend most of their time playing.

Throughout the developed world, as well as in most developing areas, the years between 6 and 12 are devoted to formal education. This universal practice is shaped by the everyday observation that the physical and intellectual skills that formal learning requires begin to blossom around age 6 or 7. Furthermore, formal instruction provides children with learning experiences that both build upon and expand their physical and cognitive abilities.

Physical Changes

Although they are more difficult to observe directly, the physical changes of middle childhood are just as impressive as those of early childhood. Standard growth charts that contain height, weight, and body mass indices-for-age percentiles are commonly used for routine monitoring of ideal or optimal physical development and the detection of growth disorders. A collaboration of Canadian health experts (Dieticians of Canada, Canadian Paediatric Society (CPS), The College of Family Physicians of Canada, and Community Health Nurses Association of Canada) now recommend using the World Health Organization (WHO) growth charts for monitoring the physical development of Canadian infants, children, and adolescents (CPS, 2016).

Growth and Motor Development

Each year between ages 6 and 12, children grow 5 to 8 centimetres and add about 2.75 kilograms. Girls in this age range are ahead of boys in their overall rate of growth—by age 12, girls have attained about 93% of their adult height, while boys have reached only 84% of theirs (WHO, 2010). Girls also have slightly more body fat and slightly less muscle tissue than boys.

Large-muscle coordination continues to improve, and children become increasingly adept at skills such as bike riding; both strength and speed also increase. Hand–eye coordination improves as well (Gabbard, 2012). As a result, school-aged children perform more skilfully in activities requiring coordination of vision with body movements, such as ball-based sports or everyday activities like pouring milk into a glass.

Perhaps even more significant is the school-aged child's improving fine motor coordination. Improvements in fine motor coordination make writing possible, as well as playing most musical instruments, drawing, cutting, and many other tasks and activities. Such accomplished uses of the hands are made possible by maturation of the wrist, which, as you may recall from earlier chapters, occurs more rapidly in girls than in boys (Woolfolk, Winne, & Perry, 2009).

Gender differences in skeletal and muscular maturation cause girls to be better coordinated but slower and somewhat weaker than boys. Thus, girls outperform boys in activities requiring coordinated movement, and boys do better when strength and speed are advantages. Still, the overall gender differences in joint maturation, strength, and speed are small at this age.

(Photo: Ariel Skelley/Getty Images)

When school-aged boys and girls participate in co-ed sports, boys' superior speed and strength is balanced by girls' advantage in coordination.

Learning Objective 9.1

Identify what kinds of physical changes occur during middle childhood.

The Brain and Nervous System

The overall pattern of brain development during middle childhood shows a steady increase in the myelinization of neural axons across the cerebral cortex (Hua et al., 2009). You'll recall from the chapter on Physical and Cognitive Development in Early Childhood that myelinization is linked to the formation of an increasingly complex network of neural connections. At the beginning of middle childhood, myelinization occurs rapidly in the sensory and motor areas of the brain (Lenroot et al., 2007; Shaw et al., 2008) (see the chapter on Physical and Cognitive Development in Adolescence for an illustrated description). Development in these areas may be linked to the striking improvements in fine motor skills and hand–eye coordination that usually occur between 6 and 8 years of age.

Brain growth in the frontal lobes of the cerebral cortex becomes the focus of developmental processes later on in middle childhood (Shaw et al., 2008). Of particular importance is the continued myelinization of the reticular formation and of the nerves that link the reticular formation to the frontal lobes (Sowell et al., 2003). Predictably, the areas of the brain that govern logic and planning, two cognitive functions that improve dramatically during this period, are located primarily in the frontal lobes. These connections are essential if the child is to be able to take full advantage of improvements in frontal lobe functions because, as you may recall, the reticular formation controls attention. It is well documented that the ability to control attention increases significantly during middle childhood (Shaw et al., 2008).

One specific kind of attention, called **selective attention**, is the ability to focus cognitive activity on the important elements of a problem or a situation. As you can probably guess, the development of selective attention is important to children's performance in school (Ma, Le Mare, & Gurd, 2015; Stevens & Bavelier, 2012). For example, suppose your psychology instructor, who usually copies tests on white paper, gives

Learning Objective 9.2

Describe the ways the brain changes during these years.

selective attention

the ability to focus cognitive activity on the important elements of a problem or a situation

you a test printed on blue paper. You won't spend a lot of time thinking about why the test is blue instead of white; this is an irrelevant detail. Instead, your selective attention skills will prompt you to ignore the colour of the paper and focus on the test questions. In contrast, some younger elementary school children might be so distracted by the unusual colour of the test paper that their test performance is affected. As the nerves connecting the reticular formation and the frontal lobes become more fully myelinated between ages 6 and 12, children begin to function more like adults in the presence of such distractions (Aharon-Peretz & Tomer, 2007). To facilitate selective attention, Canadian researchers have found that providing school children with 4-minute high-intensity, classroom-based physical activities is an efficient intervention that not only improves selective attention, but provides children with a much needed extra dose of physical exercise (Ma, Le Mare, & Gurd, 2014, 2015).

Critical Thinking

Think about how you're using selective attention skills as you read this text. What distractions are you screening out?

association areas

parts of the brain where sensory, motor, and intellectual functions are linked

The neurons of the **association areas**—parts of the brain where sensory, motor, and intellectual functions are linked—are myelinized to some degree by the time children enter middle childhood. From 6 to 12, however, the nerve cells in these areas achieve nearly complete myelinization (Shaw et al., 2008). Neuroscientists believe that this advance in the myelinization process contributes to increases in information-processing speed (Chevalier et al., 2015). For example, suppose you were to ask a 6-year-old and a 12-year-old to identify pictures of common items—a bicycle, an apple, a desk, a dog—as rapidly as possible. Both children would know the items' names, but the 12-year-old would be able to produce the names of the items much more rapidly than the 6-year-old. Such increases in processing speed probably contribute to improvements in executive function, working memory, intelligence, and later school performance, which you'll read about later in the chapter (Chevalier et al., 2015; Kail, 1990, 2008).

spatial perception

the ability to identify and act on relationships between objects in space

Another important advance in middle childhood occurs in the right cerebral hemisphere, with the lateralization of **spatial perception**, the ability to identify and act on relationships between objects in space. For example, when you imagine how a room would look with a different arrangement of furniture, you are using spatial perception. Perception of objects such as faces actually lateralizes before age 6; however, complex spatial perception, such as map-reading, isn't strongly lateralized until about age 8.

relative right-left orientation

the ability to identify right and left from multiple perspectives

A behavioural test of the lateralization of spatial perception often involves **relative right-left orientation**, the ability to identify right and left from multiple perspectives. Such a test usually shows that most children younger than 8 years old know the difference between their own right and left. Typically, though, only children older than 8 understand the difference between statements like "It's on *your* right" and "It's on *my* right." Lateralization of spatial perception may also be related to the increased efficiency with which older children learn math concepts and problem-solving strategies.

spatial cognition

the ability to infer rules from and make predictions about the movement of objects in space

Furthermore, some researchers propose that differences in visual experiences explain gender differences in spatial perception and the related function of **spatial cognition**, the ability to infer rules from and make predictions about the movement of objects in space. For example, when you are driving on a two-lane road and you make a judgment about whether you have enough room to pass a car ahead of you, you are using spatial cognition. From an early age, boys score much higher than girls, on average, on such spatial tasks (Casey, 2013). Some researchers suggest that boys' play preferences, such as their greater interest in constructive activities such as building with blocks, help them develop more acute spatial perception and cognition.

One thing that may be becoming apparent as you read about the developing brain is the increasingly organized complexity and interconnectivity of the neurons that is taking place during childhood. Most cognitive functions depend not only on certain regions of the brain, but on various regions working together (Evans et al., 2015; Menon, 2015). This process is similar to the manner in which all instruments in an orchestra work in harmony to produce a symphony concert. The flow of brain activity is like the harmony found in music. And just as the musical score (i.e., the printed notes) represents the sounds heard in a complex piece of music, so too can the patterns of our minds be documented—mathematically and visually (Atasoy, Donnelly, & Pearson, 2016; Smith, 2016). From this point of view, we look for patterns of harmony vs. disharmony in the **human connectome** as we search for clues to differences in brain structure and functioning to tell us about differences in the workings of the mind as reflected in IQ or personality—essentially, our identities (Finn et al, 2015; Seung, 2012). Using neuroimaging research methods to help elucidate this process, researchers have come together in what's known as the Human Connectome Project (HCP) to "construct a map of the complete structural and functional neural connections *in vivo* within and across individuals" (Human Connectome Project, n.d.).

(Photo: Getty Images)

Stunning connectome image(s) illustrating neural networks in the brain

Health Promotion and Wellness

Generally speaking, most school-aged children are very healthy. However, some school-aged children have undiagnosed conditions, such as vision or hearing problems. Another common childhood problem is poor sleep patterns which is associated with many other health concerns. A recent University of Alberta study found that access to and nighttime use of electronic media in the bedroom—TV, computers, smartphones—not only interferes with recommended amounts of sleep for children, but is also related to poorer diets, lower levels of physical activity, and being overweight and obese (Chahal, Fung, Kuhle, & Veugelers, 2013).

Learning Objective 9.3

Identify what the health risks are for 6- to 12-year-olds.

human connectome

the map of the structural and functional neural connections of the human brain and nervous system

IMMUNIZATION Children's immunization history should be reviewed to ensure that optimal vaccination coverage has been achieved. It is also recommended that children age 5 to 13 be vaccinated for Hepatitis B if it was missed during infancy (PHAC, 2015a). Vaccination against Human Papillomavirus (HPV) should also be considered for children between the ages of 9 and 13, before they become sexually active (a topic we'll come back to in the chapter on Physical and Cognitive Development in Adolescence).

UNINTENTIONAL INJURIES Unintentional injury remains the most common cause of death in Canadian children 5 to 9 years old, accounting for ~30% of fatalities (Statistics Canada, 2015d). The injury-related mortality rate increases with age and is higher for males than females in all age categories. More than half (58%) of the fatal injuries in children between ages 5 and 9 are due to motor vehicle crashes, followed by drowning, falls, and fire/flame at 6% each (CPS, 2012b). By far, the majority of nonfatal unintentional injuries are caused by falls, followed by those caused by being struck by or against an object or another person (e.g., being hit by a puck, colliding with a person). In children ages 5 to 9, playground accidents (especially those involving monkey bars, swings, or slides) account for about half of all cases of **traumatic brain injury (TBI)**, an injury to the head that results in diminished brain function such as a loss of consciousness, confusion, or drowsiness (Cheng et al., 2016).

traumatic brain injury (TBI)

an injury to the head that results in diminished brain function such as a loss of consciousness, confusion, or drowsiness

HEALTHY BODIES AND WEIGHTS Although there has been a reduction across Canada in deaths and hospitalizations due to unintentional injuries, it's not because children's environments are necessarily any safer now than in earlier decades. Rather, it's because children are less active: If they don't play outside, walk to school, or ride a bike in their neighbourhood, they are less likely to get injured. Unfortunately, although a convenient and sedentary lifestyle may be safer, it contributes to other health risks (Howard, 2010). Thus, along with unintentional injuries, another significant health risk of the middle childhood period is unhealthy body weights.

An overweight child not only has different kinds of encounters with his peers, but also is more likely to be fat as an adult, with accompanying increased health risks.

underweight

a body weight with a low percentage of body fat, which is associated with an increased risk for health problems (i.e., BMI < 18.5)

overweight

a body weight with a high percentage of body fat, which is associated with an increased risk for health problems (i.e., BMI > 25)

obese

a body weight with a high percentage of body fat, which is associated with an increased risk for serious diseases and health problems (i.e., BMI > 30)

The primary measure of a child's weight category is the *body mass index* (BMI), which is used to estimate the proportion of body fat to lean body mass. Using the BMI allows health care providers to more accurately identify children who are *underweight*, *overweight*, or *obese* (CPS, 2016). A child whose BMI is below the 5th percentile compared to the optimal BMI for his age is considered **underweight**; a BMI above the 85th percentile is generally considered **overweight**; and a child who is above the 95th percentile is classified as **obese**. For optimal growth and health, a child's BMI should fall between the under- and overweight cut-offs.

Over the past few decades, we have witnessed an alarming rise in the proportion of Canadian children who have unhealthy body weights. The rates have nearly tripled during this period, and the rates among First Nations children are 2 to 3 times higher than the Canadian average (PHAC, 2010b). One-quarter of Canadian children between ages 5 and 11 now have unhealthy/suboptimal body weights: 14% of boys and 19% of girls are considered *overweight*, and 8% of boys and 9% of girls are *obese*—the highest levels ever recorded (Statistics Canada, 2015e).

Results from the Quebec Longitudinal Study of Child Development have identified three risk factors for predicting excessive weight gain in childhood—overweight parent(s), large size for gestational age at birth, and early onset of being overweight (age 5 and under) (Pryor et al., 2015). The older a child gets without stopping the pattern of excessive weight gain, the more likely the child is to follow a trajectory of being overweight that will persist into their adolescent and adult years (Roberts, Shields, de Groh, Aziz, & Gilbert, 2012). The concern is that children who are overweight or obese are predisposed to developing a wide range of serious health problems such as type 2 diabetes, sleep apnea, and cardiovascular disease, as well as socio-emotional problems such as low self-esteem, negative body image, depression, and the risk of being teased or bullied (Government of Canada, 2016b; PHAC, 2010b, 2012c; Roberts et al. 2012).

As you might suspect, overeating or eating too much of the wrong foods contributes to obesity in children, just as it does in adults. However, both twin and adoption studies suggest that obesity probably results from a combination of factors: a genetic predisposition, epigenetic modifications set early in life for obesity, and environments that promote overeating and/or low levels of activity (Gluckman & Hanson, 2004a, 2004b; Pryor et al., 2015; PHAC, 2012c). Whatever the genetic contribution might be, research suggests that a cultural pattern of increases in the consumption of high-calorie convenience foods along with decreases in physical activity are connected to the current epidemic of obesity in today's Canadian children (PHAC, 2012c).

It's important to keep in mind, though, that weight-loss diets for children can be risky. Because children are still growing, the nutritional needs of overweight and obese children differ from those of adults with weight problems (Krebs & Primak, 2011). Consequently, these children require special diets developed and supervised by nutritional experts. Furthermore, increasing the amount of exercise children get is just as important as changing their eating habits (CPS, 2012a; PHAC, 2010b).

One serious consequence of low activity levels is found in the results from the first major study in 30 years of Canadian children's fitness levels. It compared several measures of fitness (aerobic, flexibility, muscular endurance, and strength), as well as body composition (BMI, waist size, and skinfold measurements) over time. The researchers found significant deterioration in all measures of fitness, coupled with an unhealthy increase in weight due to body fat in both boys and girls across all ages. In short, children are now not only fatter, but also weaker than in 1981 (see **Figure 9.1**) (Tremblay et al., 2010). This disturbing trend continues—one-quarter of children fail

Figure 9.1 Portrait of Typical 12-year-old Boy and Girl, 1981 and 2007–2009.

(SOURCE: Tremblay, M.S., Shields, M., Laviolette, M., Craig, C.L., Janssen, I., & Connor Gorber, S., 2010. Fitness of Canadian children and youth: Results from the 2007–2009 Canadian Health Measures Survey (Catalogue no. 82-003-X). *Health Reports, 21*(1), 7–20. Figure 3, p. 9.)

Boy

1981	BODY COMPOSITION	2007–2009
150.9 cm	Height	155.8 cm
41.6 kg	Weight	48.0 kg
18.1 kg/m^2	Body mass index	19.2 kg/m^2
64.9 cm	Waist circumference	66.2 cm
78.0 cm	Hip circumference	84.0 cm
0.83	Waist-to-hip ratio	0.82
	FITNESS TEST	
49 kg	Grip strength	44 kg
26.5 cm	Sit and reach	21.4 cm

Girl

1981	BODY COMPOSITION	2007–2009
153.1 cm	Height	155.0 cm
42.7 kg	Weight	47.6 kg
18.4 kg/m^2	Body mass index	19.5 kg/m^2
62.4 cm	Waist circumference	68.0 cm
81.2 cm	Hip circumference	86.0 cm
0.76	Waist-to-hip ratio	0.79
	FITNESS TEST	
43 kg	Grip strength	40 kg
32.0 cm	Sit and reach	28.2 cm

to meet the recommended daily duration of physical activity (i.e., 60 minutes a day or more of moderate to vigorous intensity), while 37% exceed the sedentary behaviour recommendations (i.e., no more than two hours per day of screen time or other passive nonschool related activity) for positive health outcomes as set out in Canadian guidelines (ParticipACTION, 2016; Pujadas Botey, Bayrampour, Carson, Vinturache, & Tough, 2016).

At the other extreme, fear of developing an unattractive body may become a significant problem for some children. Serious eating disorders (which you'll read about in detail in the chapter on Physical and Cognitive Development in Adolescence) don't become common until well into adolescence; however, most 6- to 12-year-olds are quite knowledgeable about weight-loss diets and products. Moreover, research suggests that boys and girls as young as 7 sometimes express dissatisfaction with their weight or physical appearance, and some begin dieting as early as age 9 (Kostanski, Fisher, & Gullone, 2004). This kind of dissatisfaction can lead to *binge eating and purging*, a pattern that increases the risk of obesity (Tanofsky-Kraff et al., 2004).

The challenge for parents is to help children develop good eating habits without overemphasizing physical appearance to the extent that children develop patterns of eating that can threaten their later mental and physical health. One way parents can definitely make a difference for all children, regardless of their weight, is to encourage them to be physically active. Simply limiting the time children may spend on television, on computers, and with video games may lead to increases in physical activity (see the **Research Report**).

Research Report

The Effects of Video Games

Anthropologists propose that video games are one of the many tools developed societies can use to teach children the technological and intellectual skills they need as adults (Greenfield, 1994). But, like any device we invent, they can have beneficial or damaging effects depending on their use.

Several studies suggest that playing video games has a plus side—video gaming can help boys and, more importantly, girls feel more comfortable with technology; promote teamwork and interpersonal skills when played with others; enhance self-esteem and self-confidence through game mastery; foster visual-spatial skills, hand–eye coordination, and fine motor skills; facilitate reading, math, and reasoning and problem-solving skills; and, in the case of educationally based video games, increase knowledge in various subjects, such as health, history, or science (Atwood, 2004; Chaptman, 2004; Kline, 1998; Media Awareness Network, 2004a; Morris, Croker, Zimmerman, Gill, & Romig, 2013). Action video gaming has also been shown to facilitate *neuro network plasticity* marked by increases in grey matter in subcortical areas of the brain, and the pathways that connect them, associated with sensorimotor function, attention, and working memory (Gong et al., 2015; Gong et al., 2016). Despite the positive effects that video gaming can have on learning and development, a strong case has been also made that playing video games has a darker side. For one thing, there is some cause for alarm over the amount of time children spend playing video games at the expense of other activities. Communications psychologist Stephen Kline of Simon Fraser University has been investigating the patterns and risks of video gaming. To begin with, he found that most school-aged children have access to a video game console in the home, and video gaming takes time away from other activities, such as homework, physical activity, and family and peer interactions. Of further concern, most children did not have rules about either the usage time or the content of their video games (Kline, 1998, 2003).

Experts also warn us about the adverse effects that video game content can have on personality development and behaviour—especially games with themes of violence, and gender and racial stereotyping (APA Task Force on Violent Media, 2015; Kline, 2003; Media Awareness Network, 2004b; Mou & Peng, 2009). Violent video games appear to be part of a larger set of influences linking preferences for violent stimuli to aggressive behaviour. The more violent the TV programs children watch and the more violent the video games they prefer, the more aggressively they behave toward peers (Mediascope, Inc., 1999). This finding holds for both boys and girls. However, most girls aren't interested in violent games and respond negatively to the hypersexualized female characters that most such games include (Behm-Morowitz & Mastro, 2009; Ferguson & Olson, 2013). Yet, like boys, the minority of girls who enjoy playing violent video games tend to be more physically aggressive than average. In particular, researchers have demonstrated that playing violent video games leads to increased physiological arousal; increased anger, hostility, aggression, and violent behaviour; decreased prosocial behaviours; and is associated with long-term increases in such behaviours (Anderson, 2004; Anderson et al., 2004; Anderson, Gentile, & Buckley, 2007; Gentile, Lynch, Linder, & Walsh, 2004). The negative outcomes are even more pronounced for those youth who are "addicted" to playing video games (i.e., those who averaged about three hours of video play time a day) (Hauge & Gentile, 2003).

The APA Task Force on Violent Media (2015) has found a clear association between violent video game use and increases in aggressive behaviour, affect, and cognitions; and decreases in prosocial behaviour, empathy, and moral engagement. Consequently, parents who observe that aggressive and violent themes characterize most of their children's leisure-time interests as well as their interactions with peers should worry about their children playing video games with violent content (Gentile, Walsh, Ellison, Fox, & Cameron, 2004). Ironically, in Canada, where television and movie content is highly regulated by the Canadian Radio-television and Telecommunications Commission (CRTC), the video gaming industry remains relatively unchecked (Kline, 2002).

(Photo: Guzimage/Fotolia)

Excessive video gaming cuts into the amount of time that is available for other developmentally important activities, such as homework, physical activity, and family and peer interactions.

Test Yourself before going on

1. List four attention and perceptual skills that are associated with brain maturation during middle childhood.

   (a) _____

   (b) _____

   (c) _____

   (d) _____

2. The two most common causes of injury-related deaths of Canadian children between ages 5 and 9 are _____ and _____.

3. One of the most significant health risks for children is obesity, which is defined as a body mass index (BMI) above the _____ percentile for a child's age and gender.

Cognitive Changes

Along with impressive gains in physical development, children acquire some of the important hallmarks of mature thinking between ages 6 and 12.

Piaget's Concrete Operational Stage

Have you watched a group of children being entertained by a magician? If so, then you may have noticed that younger children, preoperational thinkers in Piaget's terms, don't find magic tricks to be all that interesting. Why? Because preoperational thinkers don't really understand the rules that govern physical reality. In middle childhood, children overcome this limitation and, as a result, they know that rabbits cannot be hidden in hats, and birds don't hide in the sleeves of a magician's jacket and fly out on cue. Knowing that the magician is appearing to do something that is physically impossible is what makes his performance interesting. Like adults, the school-aged child wonders "What's the trick?"

There is no better device for demonstrating the school-aged child's capacity for distinguishing between appearance and reality than Piaget's classic conservation tasks (discussed in the chapter on Physical and Cognitive Development in Early Childhood). By age 6, most children have begun to show some signs of the **concrete operational stage** and can quickly figure out that a lump of clay has the same mass no matter how its appearance is changed. Thus, this stage is devoted to the construction of schemes that enable children to think logically about objects and events in the real world.

The stage takes its name from a set of immensely powerful schemes Piaget called *concrete operations*. These operations include mental processes such as *decentration*. You learned about its opposite, centration (thinking in terms of single variables), in the discussion of preoperational thinking in the chapter on Physical and Cognitive Development in Early Childhood. **Decentration** is thinking that takes multiple variables into account. As a result, the school-aged child can see that a clay ball rolled into a sausage shape is not only wider than it was before, but also shorter. Decentration leads him to conclude that the reduced height of the sausage shape compensates for its increased width and that it still has the same amount of clay.

Preoperational children exhibit *irreversibility*, which is the inability to think of some transformed object as it was prior to the transformation. In contrast, concrete operational thinkers display its opposite, **reversibility**—the ability to mentally undo some kind of physical or mental transformation. Piaget thought that reversibility was the most critical of all the concrete operations. The clay sausage in a conservation experiment can be made back into a ball; the water can be poured back into the shorter, wider glass. Understanding of the basic reversibility of actions lies behind many of the gains made during the middle childhood period. For example, if a child has mastered reversibility, then knowing that A is larger than B also tells him that B is smaller than A. The

Learning Objective 9.4

Describe what cognitive advantages children gain as they move through Piaget's concrete operational stage.

concrete operational stage

Piaget's third stage of cognitive development, during which children construct schemes that enable them to think logically about objects and events in the real world

decentration

thinking that takes multiple variables into account

reversibility

the understanding that both physical actions and mental operations can be reversed

ability to understand hierarchies of classes (such as Fido, spaniel, dog, and animal) also rests on this ability to move both ways in thinking about relationships.

Piaget also proposed that during this stage the child develops the ability to use **inductive logic**. She can go from a specific experience to a general principle. For example, she can make assumptions based on specific facts, such as that her friend's parents live in a mansion and have servants working for them and, therefore, her friend's parents are wealthy.

Elementary school children are fairly good observational scientists, and they enjoy activities such as cataloguing rock samples, counting species of trees or birds, and figuring out the nesting habits of guinea pigs. But they are not yet good at **deductive logic** based on hypothetical premises, which requires starting with a general principle and then predicting some outcome or observation—like going from a theory to a hypothesis. For example, children have a general idea of what a fish is from its shape and habitat; a fish is long and sleek and lives underwater. If you ask a child to determine whether a whale is classified as a fish or a mammal, then he may incorrectly classify a whale as a fish because children at this age struggle with the concept that a whale is not a fish even though it has some outward characteristics of a fish. This kind of task is difficult for 6- to 12-year-olds because they must imagine things they have not experienced. The concrete-operations child is good at dealing with things she can see and manipulate or can imagine seeing or manipulating—that is, she is good with *concrete* things; she does not do well with manipulating ideas, abstract concepts, or possibilities. Thus, as the example above illustrates, children respond to deductive problems by generating ideas that are essentially copies of the things they already know about in the concrete world.

Direct Tests of Piaget's View

Piaget understood that it took children years to apply their new cognitive skills to all kinds of problems, a phenomenon he called *horizontal decalage* (Feldman, 2004). (The French word *décalage* means "a shift.")

HORIZONTAL DECALAGE Researchers have generally found that Piaget was right in his assertion that concrete operational schemes are acquired gradually across the 6- to 12-year-old period. Studies of conservation, for example, consistently show that children grasp conservation of mass or substance by about age 7. That is, they understand that the amount of clay is the same whether it is in a pancake or a ball or some other shape. They generally understand conservation of weight at about age 8, but they don't understand conservation of volume until age 11 (Tomlinson-Keasey, Eisert, Kahle, Hardy-Brown, & Keasey, 1979).

Studies of classification skills show that at about age 7 or 8 the child first grasps the principle of **class inclusion**, the understanding that subordinate classes are included in larger, superordinate classes. Bananas are included in the class of fruit, and fruit is included in the class of food, and so forth. Preschool children understand that bananas are also fruit, but they do not yet fully understand the relationship between the classes.

A good illustration of all these changes comes from an early longitudinal study of concrete operations tasks conducted by Carol Tomlinson-Keasey and her colleagues (Tomlinson-Keasey et al., 1979). They followed a group of 38 children from kindergarten through Grade 3, testing them with five traditional concrete operations tasks each year: conservation of mass, conservation of weight, conservation of volume, class inclusion, and hierarchical classification. (As you recall from the chapter on Physical and Cognitive Development in Early Childhood, *conservation* is the understanding that matter can change in appearance without changing in quantity.) You can see from **Figure 9.2** that the children got better at all five tasks over the three-year period, with a spurt between the end of kindergarten and the beginning of Grade 1 (at about the age Piaget thought that concrete operations really arose) and another spurt during Grade 2.

inductive logic
a type of reasoning in which general principles are inferred from specific experiences

deductive logic
a type of reasoning, based on hypothetical premises, that requires predicting a specific outcome from a general principle

Learning Objective 9.5
Describe what horizontal decalage is, and how Siegler explains concrete operational thinking.

class inclusion
the understanding that subordinate classes are included in larger, superordinate classes

Figure 9.2 In this longitudinal study, children were given the same set of concrete operations tasks five times, beginning in kindergarten and ending in Grade 3.

(**SOURCE:** Data from Tomlinson-Keasey, C., Eisert, D. C., Kahle, L. R., Hardy-Brown, K., & Keasey, B. (1979). The structure of concrete operational thought. Child Development, 50, adapted from Table 2, p. 1158.)

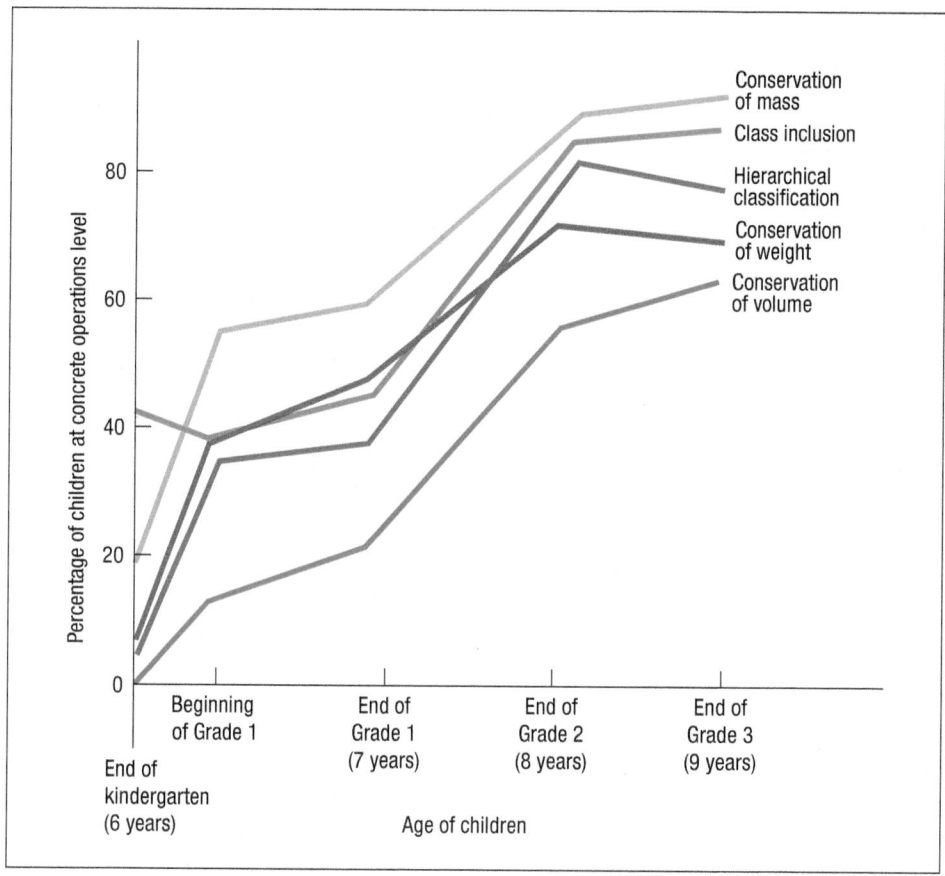

CONCRETE OPERATIONS AS RULES FOR PROBLEM-SOLVING   Other psychologists have conceptualized performance on concrete operational tasks in terms of rules for problem-solving. For example, Robert Siegler's approach is a kind of cross between Piagetian theory and information-processing theory. He argues that cognitive development consists of acquiring a set of basic rules that are then applied to a broader and broader range of problems on the basis of experience (Siegler & Lin, 2010). There are no stages, only sequences. Siegler proposes that problem-solving rules emerge from experience—from repeated trial and error and experimentation (Siegler, 1994).

Some of Siegler's early work on the development of rules illustrates how they may be acquired (Siegler & Chen, 2002). In one test, Siegler used a balance scale with a series of pegs on either side of the centre, like the one in **Figure 9.3**. The child is asked to predict which way the balance will fall, depending on the location and number of disk-shaped weights placed on the pegs. A complete solution requires the child to take into account both the number of disks on each side and the specific location of the disks.

Figure 9.3 This balance scale is similar to what Siegler used in his experiments.

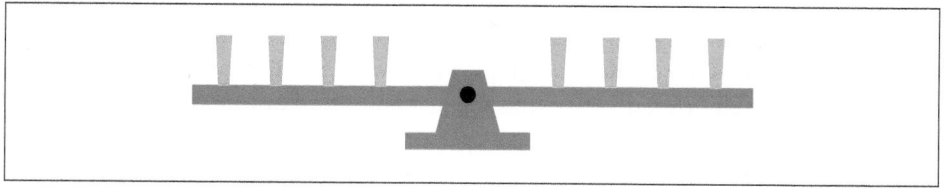

Experience with a teeter-totter, like these children are getting, may be one source of knowledge about how balance scales work.

Children do not develop such a complete solution immediately. Instead, Siegler suggests that they develop four rules, in this order: Rule I is basically a preoperational rule, taking into account only one dimension, the number of weights. Children using this rule will predict that the side with more disks will go down, no matter which peg they are placed on. Rule II is a transitional rule. The child still judges on the basis of number, except when the same number of weights appears on each side; in that case the child takes distance from the fulcrum (point of balance) into account. Rule III is basically a concrete operational rule; the child tries to take both distance and weight into account simultaneously, except that when the information is conflicting (such as when the side with weights closer to the fulcrum has more weights), the child simply guesses. Rule IV involves the understanding of the actual formula for calculating the combined effect of weight and distance for each side of the balance.

Siegler has found that virtually all children perform on this and similar tasks as if they were following one or another of these rules, and that the rules seem to develop in the given order. Very young children behave as if they don't have a rule (they guess or behave randomly); when they do seem to begin using a rule, Rule I always comes first. But progression from one rule to the next depends heavily on experience. If children are given practice with the balance scale so that they can make predictions and then check which way the balance actually falls, many rapidly develop the next rules in the sequence.

Thus, Siegler is attempting to describe a logical sequence children follow, not unlike the basic sequence of stages that Piaget describes—but Siegler's research shows that a particular child's position in the sequence depends not so much on age as on the child's specific experience with a given set of material. In Piaget's terminology, this is rather like saying that when accommodation of some scheme occurs, it always occurs in a particular sequence, but the rate at which the child moves through that sequence depends on experience.

Advances in Information-Processing Skills

Learning Objective 9.6

Explain how children's information-processing skills improve during middle childhood.

As they progress through the middle childhood years, children are able to remember longer and longer lists of numbers, letters, or words, as illustrated in **Figure 9.4**. Moreover, school-aged children's rapidly improving memory skills enable them to acquire new information and skills at a far faster rate, and with greater understanding, than was possible in the early childhood years (Swanson & Alloway, 2012).

processing efficiency

the ability to make efficient use of short-term memory capacity

PROCESSING EFFICIENCY **Processing efficiency**, the ability to make efficient use of short-term memory capacity, increases steadily with age, a change that most developmentalists now see as the basis for cognitive development (Borst, Poirel, Pineau, Cassotti, & Houdé, 2013; Swanson & Kim, 2007). The best evidence that cognitive processing becomes more efficient is that it gets steadily faster with age. Robert Kail has found virtually the same exponential increase in processing speed with age for a wide variety of tasks, including perceptual-motor tasks, such as tapping in response to a stimulus (e.g., pressing a button when you hear a buzzer), and cognitive tasks, such as mental addition (Kail, 1991, 2008; Kail & Hall, 1994). He has found virtually identical patterns of speed increases in cross-cultural studies.

automaticity

the ability to recall information from long-term memory without using short-term memory capacity

AUTOMATICITY One of the most important ways in which processing efficiency grows in middle childhood is through the acquisition of **automaticity**, or the ability to recall information from long-term memory without using short-term memory capacity. For example, when children can respond "49" to the question "How much is

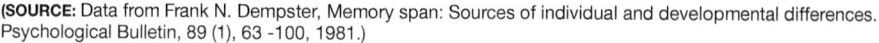

Figure 9.4 Psychologists measure basic memory capacity by asking participants to listen to a list of numbers, letters, or words, and then to repeat back the list in order. This figure shows the number of such items children of various ages are able to remember and report accurately.

(**SOURCE:** Data from Frank N. Dempster, Memory span: Sources of individual and developmental differences. Psychological Bulletin, 89 (1), 63 -100, 1981.)

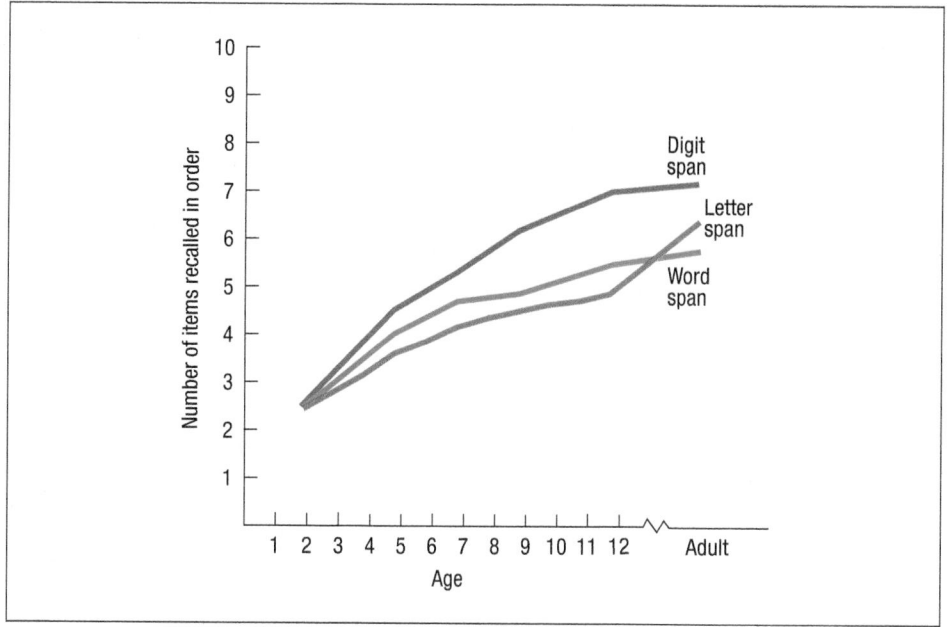

7 times 7?" without thinking about it, they have achieved automaticity with respect to that particular piece of information.

Automaticity is critical to efficient information processing because it frees up short-term memory space for more complex processing. Thus, the child who knows "7 times 7" automatically can use that fact in a complex multiplication or division problem without giving up any of the short-term memory space he is using to solve the problem. As a result, he is better able to concentrate on the "big picture" instead of expending effort trying to recall a simple multiplication fact. Not surprisingly, researchers have found that elementary school children who have *automatized* basic math facts in this way learn complex computational skills more rapidly (Ashkenazi, Rubensten, & Henik, 2009).

Automaticity is achieved primarily through practice. For instance, when children are first learning to read, they have to devote all of their mental effort to linking letters to speech sounds, written words to spoken words, and so on. Once these tasks become automatic, children can devote more attention to the meaning of what they are reading. Likewise, college students who have achieved automaticity with regard to spelling produce higher-quality lecture notes than classmates who are less proficient spellers do (Peverly et al., 2007). Thus, automaticity is important to information processing throughout the lifespan. It is in middle childhood, however, that children seem to begin automatizing large quantities of information and skills at a fairly rapid rate.

EXECUTIVE AND STRATEGIC PROCESSES   If you tried to recall a list of everyday items (e.g., chair, pencil, spaghetti, tree), then you might consciously consider the various alternative strategies for remembering and then select the best one. You could also explain some things about how your mind works, such as which kinds of mental tasks you find most difficult. These are examples of *metacognition*—knowing about knowing or thinking about thinking. Metacognition is part of a large group of skills known as **executive processes**—information-processing skills that allow a person to devise and carry out alternative strategies for remembering and problem-solving. Executive processes are based on a basic understanding of how the mind works. Such skills emerge

executive processes

information-processing skills that involve devising and carrying out strategies for remembering and problem-solving

Table 9.1 Some Common Information-Processing Strategies Used in Remembering

Strategy	Description
Rehearsal	Either mental or vocal repetition; may occur in children as young as 2 years under some conditions, and is common in older children and adults.
Organization	Grouping ideas, objects, or words into clusters to help in remembering them, such as "all animals," or "the ingredients in the lasagna recipe," or "the chess pieces involved in the move called *castling*." This strategy is more easily applied to something a person has experience with or particular knowledge about. Two-year-olds use primitive clustering strategies.
Elaboration	Finding shared meaning or a common referent for two or more things that need to be remembered.
Mnemonic	A device to assist memory; the phrase for the notes of the lines on the musical staff ("Every Good Boy Does Fine") is a mnemonic.
Systematic Searching	"Scanning" one's memory for the whole domain in which a piece of information might be found. Three- and four-year-old children can begin to do this when they search for actual objects in the real world, but they are not good at doing this in memory. So, search strategies may first be learned in the external world and then applied to inner searches.

(**SOURCE:** Flavell, John H. Cognitive Development 2nd Ed., © 1985. Reprinted and Electronically reproduced by permission of Pearson Education, Inc., Upper Saddle River, New Jersey.)

around age 5 and improve a great deal during middle childhood (Blaye & Jacques, 2009). For example, 10-year-olds are more likely than 8-year-olds to understand that attending to a story requires effort (Parault & Schwanenflugel, 2000).

One of the advantages of having good metacognitive and executive processing skills is that they help the individual devise methods for remembering information, or **memory strategies**. Although many people possess their own unique methods for remembering, **Table 9.1** lists a few common memory strategies. For the most part, these memory techniques first appear between ages 6 and 12 (Tam, Jarrold, Baddeley, & Sabatos-DeVito, 2010).

memory strategies

learned methods for remembering information

EXPERTISE A great deal of research shows that the amount of knowledge a person possesses makes a huge difference in how efficiently her information-processing system works. Children and adults who know a lot about a topic (dinosaurs, collectables, mathematics, or whatever it may be) categorize information about that topic in highly complex and hierarchical ways (Posner & Rothbart, 2007; Waters & Waters, 2010).

They are also better at remembering and logically analyzing new information on that topic (Ni, 1998). In addition, children's capacity for creativity appears to greatly depend on how much knowledge they have about a topic (Sak & Maker, 2006).

Even typical age differences in strategy use or memory ability disappear when the younger group has more expertise than the older. For example, psychologist Michelene Chi, in her now-classic early study, showed that expert chess players could remember the placement of chess pieces on a board much more quickly and accurately than novice chess players, even when the expert chess players were children and the novices were adults (Chi, 1978).

Unless they are rank novices, these school-aged chess players will remember a series of chess moves or an arrangement of chess pieces far better than adults who don't play chess.

Many information-processing psychologists now believe that an individual's information-processing skills may depend entirely on the quantity and quality of relevant information stored in long-term memory. Thus, they say, to be able to learn scientific reasoning skills, for example, children must first acquire a body of knowledge about scientific topics (Morris, Croker, Masnick, & Zimmerman, 2012; Zimmerman, 2007). To paraphrase developmental psychologist John Flavell, expertise makes any of us, including children, look very smart; lack of expertise makes us look very stupid (Flavell, 1986).

Language

By age 5 or 6, virtually all children have mastered the basic grammar and pronunciation of their first language, but children of this age still have a fair distance to go before reaching adult levels of fluency. During middle childhood, children become skilled at managing the finer points of grammar (Prat-Sala, Shillcock, & Sorace, 2000). For example, by the end of middle childhood, most children understand various ways of saying something about the past, such as "I went," "I was going," "I have gone," "I had gone," "I had been going," and so on. Moreover, they correctly use such tenses in their own speech. Across the middle childhood years, children also learn how to maintain the topic of conversation, how to create unambiguous sentences, and how to speak politely or persuasively (Anglin, 1993). All these improvements contribute to the school-aged child's emerging mastery of conversation. By age 9, most children are fully capable of engaging in fluent conversation with speakers of any age, and their speech rates approach those of adults (Sturm & Seery, 2007).

Between ages 6 and 12, children also continue to add new vocabulary at a fairly astonishing rate of from 5000 to 10 000 words per year. This estimate comes from several careful studies by developmental psychologist Jeremy Anglin of the University of Waterloo, who estimates children's total vocabularies by testing them on a sample of words drawn at random from a large dictionary (Anglin, 1993, 1995; Skwarchuk & Anglin, 2002). **Figure 9.5** shows Anglin's estimates for Grades 1, 3, and 5. Anglin found that the largest gain between Grades 3 and 5 occurs in knowledge of the type of words he calls *derived words*—words that have a basic root to which some prefix or suffix is added, such as *"unhappy," "happiness," and "happily"*. Once the child grasps these relationships, he can understand and create many new words and his vocabulary thereafter increases rapidly.

Anglin argues that at age 8 or 9 the child shifts to a new level of understanding of the structure of language, figuring out relationships between whole categories of words, such as between adjectives and adverbs (*happy* and *happily*, *sad* and *sadly*), between adjectives and nouns (*happy* and *happiness*), and the like. Once he grasps these relationships, the child can understand and create a whole class of new words, and his vocabulary thereafter increases rapidly.

Learning Objective 9.7

Explain how vocabulary and other aspects of language change during middle childhood.

Figure 9.5 Anglin's estimates of the total vocabulary of children in Grades 1, 3, and 5.

(**SOURCE:** Based on Anglin, Vocabulary Development: A Morphological Analysis (Monographs of the Society for Research in Child Development.)

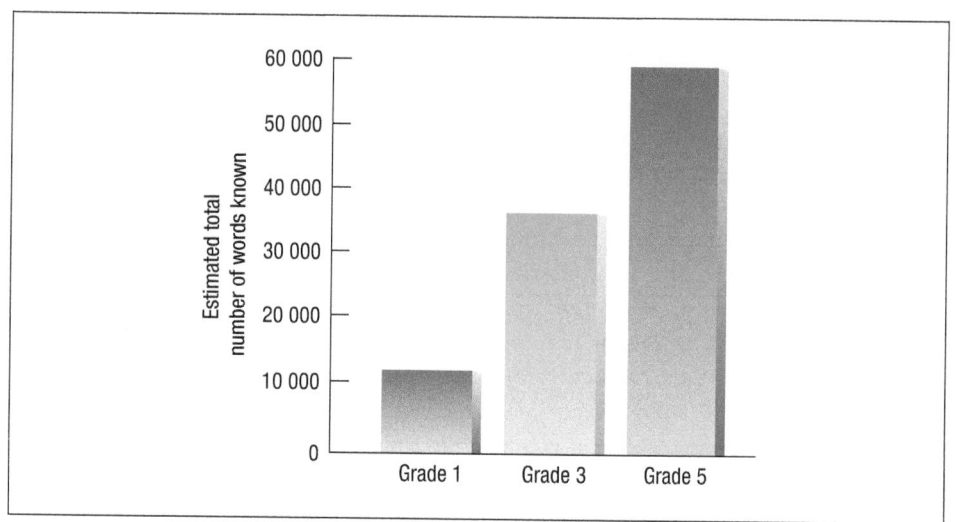

Test Yourself before going on

1. Two distinctive features of concrete operational thinking are _____, thinking that takes multiple variables into account, and _____, the understanding that physical and mental actions can be reversed.

2. In the table below, note the benefits of each advance in information-processing skills.

Advances	Benefits
Greater processing efficiency	
Automaticity	
Executive processes	
Memory strategies	
Expertise	

3. Between 6 and 12, children add _____ to _____ new words to their vocabularies every year.

Critical Thinking

4. In what ways do advances in language, reasoning, and information-processing skills help children succeed in school? How do you think schooling influences these skills?

Schooling

For children all over the world, formal education is well under way by the time they reach the age of 6 or 7. Every society endeavours to find effective ways of teaching children the skills they will need in adulthood. In general, studies show that teachers who display a teaching style similar to the approach that authoritative parents take to raising children—an approach that combines clear goals, good control, good communication, and high nurturance—are the most effective (Kiuru et al., 2012). Still, quality considerations aside, because of its academic focus and the amount of time that children spend in school, formal education is one of the most important influences on the cognitive development of 6- to 12-year-olds.

Literacy

Learning Objective 9.8

Describe what should be included in an effective literacy curriculum.

In the world's developed nations, *literacy*, the ability to read and write, is the focus of education in the 6- to 12-year-old period. As you learned in the chapter on Physical and Cognitive Development in Early Childhood, the skills children bring to school from their early childhood experiences may influence early reading as much as formal instruction does (Crone & Whitehurst, 1999). Especially significant among these skills is the set known as *phonological awareness* (Pearson & Cervetti, 2013). Across the early elementary years, phonological awareness skills continue to increase and serve as the foundation for later-developing skills such as *oral reading fluency*, the ability to read aloud with emotional expressiveness and minimal effort, that strongly predict reading comprehension skills in the later elementary grades (Kim, Petscher, Schatschneider, & Foorman, 2010). Thus, children who lack such expertise at the start of school are likely to fall behind unless some systematic effort is made by teachers to provide them with a base of phonological knowledge (Houston, Al Otaiba, & Torgesen, 2006).

Research indicates that, to be effective, a beginning reading program must include a type of instruction called **systematic and explicit phonics** (Armbruster, Lehr, & Osborn, 2003). *Systematic* means that instruction must follow a plan that begins with simple, one-letter/one-sound correspondences (e.g., the letter *b* for the sound /b/) and moves to those that involve two or more letters. The plan must be carefully developed so that instruction corresponds in meaningful ways to the spelling system of the language being learned. *Explicit* means that letter–sound correspondences are taught intentionally. Effective phonics curricula also provide beginning readers with ample

systematic and explicit phonics

planned, specific instruction in sound–letter correspondences opportunities for daily practice in using their knowledge of sound–symbol correspondences so that they can develop automaticity. Phonics researchers argue that children cannot easily comprehend written language until they can decode it automatically and fluently (Rego, 2006).

Nevertheless, advocates of the **balanced approach** to reading instruction point out that teachers must move beyond basic phonics. In *guided reading* sessions, for instance, teachers work with small groups of children on reading books that are somewhat challenging for them (recall Vygotsky's zone of proximal development) (Phillips, 2013). When a child makes an error, the teacher uses the opportunity to explain a reading strategy or one of the many idiosyncrasies of written English to all the children in the group. Proponents of the balanced approach also point to studies showing that, in the later elementary grades, attainment of reading fluency requires that children learn about meaningful word parts, such as prefixes and suffixes (Berninger, Abbott, Nagy, & Carlisle, 2010). At the same time, instruction in comprehension strategies, such as identifying the purpose of a particular text, also helps (Johnston, Barnes, & Desrochers, 2008). Of course, throughout learning to read, children need to be exposed to good literature, both in their own reading and in what teachers and parents read to them.

Some of the strategies used to teach reading also help children learn writing, the other component of literacy; for example, instruction in sound–letter connections helps children learn to spell as well as to read. Of course, good writing is far more than just spelling; it requires instruction and practice, just as reading does. Specifically, children need explicit instruction in language mechanics, such as how to construct simple, compound, and complex sentences, to become good writers (Saddler, 2007). They also need to learn to organize writing tasks into phases such as planning, drafting, editing, and revising (Graham & Harris, 2007).

Despite educators' best efforts, many children fall behind their classmates in literacy during the early school years. In general, reading researchers have found that poor readers have problems with sound–letter combinations (Gersten et al., 2008). Thus, many children who have reading difficulties benefit from highly specific phonics approaches that provide a great deal of practice in translating letters into sounds and vice versa (Koppenhaver, Hendrix, & Williams, 2007).

Curriculum flexibility is also important in programs for poor readers. Some children do not improve when exposed to phonics approaches. In fact, programs that combine sound–letter and comprehension training have proven to be highly successful in helping poor readers catch up, especially when the programs are implemented in the early elementary years (Gersten et al., 2008). Consequently, teachers need to be able to assess the effectiveness of whatever approach they are using and change it to fit the needs of individual students.

balanced approach
reading instruction that combines explicit phonics instruction with other strategies for helping children acquire literacy

Second-Language Learners

Worldwide patterns of population growth and movement have led to tremendous increases in the number of non-English-speaking children attending school in Canada, the United States, Great Britain, and Australia. Educators in English-speaking countries use the term *Limited English Proficient* (LEP) to refer to non-English-speaking children—either immigrant children or native-born children. There are analogous language challenges for educators in those parts of Canada where French is the dominant language but children are not proficient in French.

Historically, Canada has been host to waves of immigrants from all parts of the world. More recently, immigrant children under age 15 have arrived from Asia and the Pacific region (44%) and Africa and the Middle East (22%). Of these children, 5 in 10 landed in Ontario, 2 in 10 in British Columbia, and slightly more than 1 in 10 in Quebec. More than two-thirds of the children were unable to speak either official language when they arrived (Canadian Council on Social Development [CCSD], 1999; Statistics

Learning Objective 9.9

Identify the issues related to children who are second-language learners.

Canada, 2013b). This immigration resulted in abnormally high levels of official language deficiency in children in our school system, especially in these three provinces. In the lower mainland school districts of British Columbia, for instance, ESL enrolment has more than tripled since 1990, and a large majority of these new students are unfamiliar with both the Roman alphabet and Western cultural practices (British Columbia Ministry of Education, 2001). In the Toronto District School Board (the largest school board in Canada and one of the largest in North America), 41% of the students in elementary schools have a language other than English as their first language. This problem is compounded by the fact that more than 80 languages from all over the world are represented in the Board's schools (Toronto District School Board, n.d.).

Bilingual education is a logistical challenge for most school districts that include LEP children. For one thing, if a school system has only a handful of students who speak a particular language, it is not financially feasible to establish a separate curriculum for them. It may also be impossible to find bilingual teachers for children whose language is spoken by very few people outside their country of origin. For these reasons, most LEP students are enrolled in **English-as-a-second-language (ESL) programs**, or if they intend to learn the French language, they are enrolled in French-as-a-second-language (FSL) programs (Canadian Parents for French [CPF], 2001). In ESL programs, children spend part of the day in classes to learn English and part in academic classes that are conducted entirely in English.

Research has shown that no particular approach to second-language learners is more successful than any other (Mohanty & Perregaux, 1997). There is some indication that programs that include a home-based component, such as those that encourage parents to learn the new language along with their children, may be especially effective (Koskinen et al., 2000). But it seems that any structured program, whether bilingual education or ESL, fosters higher achievement among non-English-speaking children than simply integrating them into English-only classes, an approach called *submersion*. Although most children in submersion programs eventually catch up to their English-speaking peers, many educators believe that instruction that supports children's home language and culture as well as their English-language skills enhances their overall development (Cushner, McClelland, & Safford, 2009).

A cautionary note is necessary, however: An LEP student does not have an increased risk of failure as long as the school provides some kind of transition to English-only instruction and school officials take care to administer all standardized tests in the language with which the child is most familiar (Cushner et al., 2009). Providing a transition to English-only instruction is necessary to optimize the LEP child's potential for achievement. Testing children in their native language ensures that non-English-speaking children will not be misclassified as developmentally delayed or learning disabled because of their limited English skills.

bilingual education

an approach to second-language education in which children receive instruction in two different languages

English-as-a-second-language (ESL) program

an approach to second-language education in which children attend English classes for part of the day and receive most of their academic instruction in English

Learning Objective 9.10

Summarize the benefits of bilingual education.

Bilingual Education

More than 17% of Canadians can now speak both of Canada's official languages—English and French (Statistics Canada, 2012i). Since its experimental roots in St. Lambert, Quebec in 1965, French immersion programs have become a successful fixture of our Canadian education system and a model for teaching a second language throughout the world (Lambert & Tucker, 1972; Safty, 1995). Children enrolled in French immersion programs are taught exclusively in French from kindergarten through to Grade 2. Thereafter, subjects taught in English are incrementally introduced every year until they receive instruction in both languages approximately equally in the senior grades.

Although initially there is some delay in English language development, by the later grades French immersion students' English skills are indistinguishable from those of students taught in English (Holobow, Genesee, & Lambert, 1991). By age 15, French immersion students of both genders have significantly higher reading achievement scores than their nonimmersion counterparts (Allen, 2004). Moreover, Ellen Bialystok (1999, 2011) of York University has found that early immersion education not only facilitates both spoken and written language skills, but also aspects of thinking, such as improved selective attention on nonlanguage tasks.

The process of learning to read, write, and speak a second language instills an appreciation for another culture, provides an alternative way to think about and value the world, and encourages children to become more objective and open-minded (Commissioner of Official Languages, 2009, 2011). There are roughly 200 nonofficial languages spoken in Canada and many heritage language programs are available to help families pass on their language and culture of origin (Settlement.org, 2001; Statistics Canada, 2012i). Inherent in federal, provincial, and territorial legislation and policy is the recognition that heritage languages are fundamental to the preservation of the multicultural nature of our country. There is a particular need to preserve the languages of Canadian Indigenous peoples, since their culture is based on oral tradition and is expressed most fully through their primary heritage language. Historically, more than 60 Indigenous languages were spoken in Canada, but most are either lost or endangered because so few people who can speak these languages are left (Kirkness, 1999). Heritage language education needs to consist of formal, structured programs designed to increase students' knowledge of these languages.

Measuring and Predicting Achievement

Learning Objective 9.11
Explain the challenges of evaluating students across Canada's educational systems.

Canada lacks a single education system, since each province and territory is entitled to establish its own formal curriculum and school organization. Nonetheless, Ministers of Education from across the nation work through the Council of Ministers of Education, Canada (CMEC, 2016), to ensure that all Canadians benefit from the strength and diversity of provincial and territorial education systems. Some of the key projects of the CMEC include pan-Canadian assessments and international comparisons, particularly in the areas of reading, math, and science.

TYPES OF TESTS Standardized **achievement tests** are designed to assess specific information learned in school. Scores are based on the comparison of an individual child's performance with those of other children in the same grade across Canada. Critics of achievement tests point out that, although these tests are intended to measure what children learn in school, they are actually very similar to IQ tests. For example, suppose an achievement test contains the math problem "4 × 4." Bright children who have not yet learned multiplication may reason their way to the correct answer of 16. Others may answer correctly because they have learned it in school. Still others may know the answer because they learned to multiply from their parents. Thus, critics suggest that comprehensive portfolios of children's school work may be better indicators of actual school learning than standardized achievement tests (Neill, 1998). In comparison to achievement measures, educators conducting a student **assessment**

achievement test
a test designed to assess specific information learned in school

assessment
formal and informal methods of gathering information that can be used for programming to improve student learning. No grades or marks are associated with assessment

Children's experiences in school are similar the world over. The similarities help to explain why cognitive-developmental research involving 6- to 12-year-olds yields pretty much the same results in all cultures where children attend school.

(*Photos*, left to right: Digital Vision/Getty Images; paylessimages/Fotolia; Zurijeta/Shutterstock)

will use a variety of formal and informal assessment tools to gather information that can be used to improve student learning at a developmentally appropriate level. Assessment is an ongoing process, and students are encouraged to be involved in the assessment process and in finding ways to improve.

In Canada, the trend is toward evaluating a student in terms of age-appropriate provincial or territorial standards. Accordingly, educators make an **evaluation** by calculating each student's highest, most consistent level of performance for each subject to assign a grade or level at any given point. This approach can offer a student a more valid measure of his achievement in terms of his own performance against the provincial standard rather than comparing his performance with that of his peers in the classroom. In contrast, the old model of evaluation served primarily to differentiate students based solely on their grade averages and to "ultimately determine who [would] be eligible to attend post-secondary education and reap the status and economic rewards that typically result" (Health Canada, 2001b, p. 14).

THEORIES OF INTELLIGENCE   Unlike in previous decades, intellectual assessment in Canadian schools is no longer routinely used to assess students. Intelligence testing (using tools such as the WISC described in the chapter on Physical and Cognitive Development in Early Childhood) is now primarily used to identify a student as exceptional in preparation for special educational programming. In fact, some developmentalists say that the problem with relying on IQ tests to predict achievement is that they fail to provide a complete picture of mental abilities. For example, psychologist Howard Gardner proposed a theory of *multiple intelligences* (Gardner, 1983, 1999). This theory claims there are eight types of intelligence:

- *Linguistic*—the ability to use language effectively. People who are good writers or speakers, who learn languages easily, or who possess a lot of knowledge about language possess greater than average linguistic intelligence.
- *Logical/mathematical*—facility with numbers and logical problem-solving. Logical/mathematical intelligence enables individuals to learn math and to generate logical solutions to various kinds of problems.
- *Musical*—the ability to appreciate and produce music. Musicians, singers, composers, and conductors possess musical intelligence.
- *Spatial*—the ability to appreciate spatial relationships. Spatial intelligence is involved in the production and appreciation of works of art, such as paintings and sculptures.
- *Bodily kinesthetic*—the ability to move in a coordinated way, combined with a sense of one's body in space. Professional athletes and top-notch amateur ones must possess high levels of this kind of intelligence.
- *Naturalist*—the ability to make fine discriminations among the flora and fauna of the natural world or the patterns and designs of human artifacts.
- *Interpersonal*—sensitivity to the behaviour, moods, and needs of others. "Helping" professionals—counsellors, social workers, clergy, and the like—usually need to have relatively high levels of interpersonal intelligence.
- *Intrapersonal*—the ability to understand oneself. People who are good at identifying their own strengths and choosing goals accordingly have high levels of intrapersonal intelligence.

Gardner's theory is based on observations of people with brain damage, an intellectual disability, and other severe mental handicaps. He points out that brain damage usually causes disruption of functioning in very specific mental abilities rather than a general decline in intelligence. He also notes that many individuals with mental deficits have remarkable talents. For example, some are gifted in music, while others can perform complex mathematical computations without using a calculator or pencil and

evaluation

the process of assigning a grade or mark to a student's performance, representing the student's highest, most consistent level of achievement over time

paper. However, critics claim that Gardner's view, although intuitively appealing, has little empirical support (White, 2006).

Robert Sternberg's *triarchic theory of intelligence* proposes three components of human intelligence (Sternberg, 1988). *Contextual intelligence* has to do with knowing the right behaviour for a specific situation. For example, studies of South American street vendors of elementary school age show that they are good at doing practical monetary calculations but perform poorly on more abstract math problems (Schliemann, Carraher, & Ceci, 1997). These children are highly "intelligent" in their daily context, but, in the school context, they appear to lack intellectual ability.

Experiential intelligence, according to Sternberg, involves learning to give specific responses without thinking about them. For example, you can probably respond without thinking to the question "How much is 7 times 7?" Experiential intelligence also enables you to come up with novel solutions to everyday problems that you haven't quite been able to solve and to recognize when a tried-and-true solution is appropriate for a new problem.

Componential intelligence is a person's ability to come up with effective strategies. To Sternberg, this component of intelligence is the most important. He claims that intelligence tests put more emphasis on "correctness" of answers than on the quality of the strategies people use to arrive at them (Sternberg, 2002).

In general, Sternberg says, IQ tests measure how familiar a child is with "school" culture. Thus, children whose cultural background does not include formal schooling perform poorly because they are unfamiliar with the context of the test. Unfortunately, their poor performance is often mistakenly interpreted to mean that they lack intelligence (Sternberg & Grigorenko, 2006).

EMOTIONAL INTELLIGENCE   Both Gardner's and Sternberg's theories have become important in helping educators understand the weaknesses of IQ tests. Moreover, psychologist Daniel Goleman's theory of *emotional intelligence* has also added to scientists' understanding of intelligence and achievement (Goleman, 1995). Emotional intelligence has three components: awareness of one's own emotions, the ability to express one's emotions appropriately, and the capacity to channel emotions into the pursuit of worthwhile goals. Without emotional intelligence, Goleman claims, it is impossible to achieve one's intellectual potential. However, research has yet to provide support for Goleman's hypothesis (Humphrey, Curran, Morris, Farrell, & Woods, 2007). Still, research on the relationship between self-control (the third component of emotional intelligence) in early childhood and achievement in adolescence suggests that Goleman's view is correct. Children's ability to exercise control over their emotions in early childhood is strongly related to measures of academic achievement in high school (Denham, 2006).

Group Differences in Achievement

GENDER DIFFERENCES IN ACHIEVEMENT   Comparisons of overall IQ test scores for boys and girls do not reveal consistent differences. Only when the total scores are broken down into several separate skills do some long-standing and perplexing patterns of gender differences emerge. University of New Brunswick researchers Daniel and Susan Voyer (2014) reviewed a century of international and Canadian data that shows girls have always achieved better school marks than boys for *all* subjects, especially language studies, but also in science and in math courses (although it has been commonly thought that boys were superior in math). The question of where such differences come from remains unanswered. So far, environmental explanations have proven to be more useful than biological theories, particularly in relation to language skills. Some argue that in the early grades boys lack role models with whom they can identify, since most teachers at that level are females. Others suggest that the reading material or learning environment for boys does not match their interests and temperament.

Learning Objective 9.12

Summarize what kinds of group differences in achievement educational researchers have found.

analytical style

a tendency to focus on the details of a task

relational style

a tendency to ignore the details of a task in order to focus on the "big picture"

DIFFERENCES IN LEARNING STYLES Some educators have proposed that group differences in learning styles help to explain variations in achievement (Cushner et al., 2009). Research indicates that children who use an **analytical style** define learning goals and follow a set of orderly steps to reach them. These children are well organized, are good at learning details, and think of information in terms of "right" and "wrong." Other children use a **relational style**. These children focus attention on "the big picture" instead of on individual bits of information. For example, Ayana, who has an analytical style, and Richard, who uses a relational style, both listen carefully as their Grade 4 teacher gives instructions for a complicated project. Ayana lists every detail of the teacher's instructions and how many points each part is worth. In contrast, Richard writes down his general impression of each part of the project. In working on the project, Ayana concentrates her effort on the parts that are worth the most points. Richard pays more attention to the aspects of the project he finds interesting. When it is finished, Ayana's project conforms more exactly to the teacher's instructions than Richard's does, and she receives a higher grade. Ayana's way of approaching school work—her cognitive style—better fits school expectations, giving her an advantage over Richard. In addition, Ayana's way of learning helps her get high scores on achievement tests, which require detailed knowledge of specific information and skills.

Test Yourself before going on

1. Research suggests that an effective literacy program must include _____ _____ _____ _____ instruction.
2. In Canada, children who are not proficient in either English or French can enrol in _____ _____ or _____ classes.
3. Some psychologists claim that conventional achievement and intelligence tests ignore the importance of _____ and _____ intelligences.
4. Children who exhibit a(n) _____ learning style tend to focus on details.

Critical Thinking

5. What is the difference between a bilingual and an ESL/FSL program? Is one approach more effective than the other?

Learners with Exceptionalities

A number of individual and group variables are associated with school performance (see **Table 9.2**). Various disabilities and attention problems are correlated with achievement in some way, as are language proficiency, gender, and culture. Canadian educators are now moving away from the use of labels for learning problems and instead place emphasis on a child's academic strengths and style

exceptional child

a child who has special learning needs; the term refers to students with disabilities as well as gifted students

program accommodation

the adjustment of teaching methods to help a child with special needs achieve the outcomes of the standard curriculum

modified program

changes in the curriculum so that the modified outcomes differ from those of the standard curriculum

Table 9.2 Categories of Exceptionalities in Canadian Schools

Exceptionality Category	Description of Exceptionality
Behaviour Disorders	Conduct disorders, social maladjustment, ADHD, and emotional disorders
Communication Disorders	Language impairment, speech impairment, and learning disability
Sensory Impairments	Deafness and hearing impairment, blindness and low vision
Intellectual Differences	Giftedness, mild intellectual disability, and developmental disability
Pervasive Developmental Disorders	Childhood psychosis, childhood schizophrenia, and infantile autism
Physical Disorders and Impaired Health	Neurological defects, physical disability, and conditions that result from infection and disease
Multiple	Multiple exceptionalities from any of the above categories

(**SOURCES:** Based on Weber, 1993; Winzer, 1993.)

Development in the Real World

Canadian Special Education Practices

Across Canada an **exceptional child** who has special learning needs typically remains integrated in the same class as his same-aged peers. The teacher can introduce a program accommodation or a program modification and adjust her teaching methods to the child's special needs. The exceptional child may also have access to and receive assistance from special education teachers and educational assistants.

In **program accommodations**, an exceptional child is exposed to the same curriculum as his peers and his performance is compared with the same standard outcomes for his grade level, but the classroom teacher makes accommodations for him so that he is allowed to demonstrate his learning in a nonstandard way. Less emphasis is placed on what the student cannot do and more on how he can develop alternative methods of achieving the same outcomes. For example, if a student is required to demonstrate that she understands a specific math concept but she is not good with number functions, then she would be allowed to use a calculator as long as she could explain how she got the answer. In this way, she is measured for her ability to understand math concepts as opposed to being (inadvertently) measured for her ability to use number facts. Other examples include a student who is offered an oral exam because he has difficulty with writing answers down, and a student who is allowed to sit at the front of the classroom because she is easily distracted.

Sometimes a **modified program** is required, whereby the standard curriculum itself is changed so that the modified outcomes are different from the standard outcomes. For example, a student in Grade 5 may be working on a Grade 2 reading program but a Grade 5 program in all other subject areas. Exceptional students are legally designated as such, and require an **individual education plan (IEP)**. The special education teacher, in consultation with the child, the parents, the teacher, and any relevant community partners (e.g., social worker or pediatrician), develops the IEP and reviews it annually.

(Photo: ktmoffitt/E+/Getty Images)

School can be a discouraging and frustrating place for a child with a learning disability.

---

of processing information in order to increase the likelihood of her school success (see **Development in the Real World**).

Learning Disabilities

Some children are born with or develop differences that may significantly interfere with their education unless they receive some kind of special instruction. An estimated 1 in 10 of the Canadian population may experience some kind of learning difficulty that is a continuation of learning disabilities from early childhood (Learning Disabilities Association of Canada [LDAC], n.d.). A **learning disability** is identified when a child has difficulty attaining a specific academic skill, despite possessing average to above-average intelligence, that is not due primarily to physical or sensory disabilities (e.g., uncorrected visual or auditory acuity), mental or neurological disorders, academic instruction in other than the child's first language, a lack of age-appropriate educational instruction, and/or prolonged and intense psychosocial adversity (APA, 2013; LDAC, 2015). It includes a range of conditions that involve perceiving, thinking, remembering, and/or learning that selectively interfere with academic progress, especially in reading (commonly referred to as dyslexia), writing (dysgraphia), and/or math (dyscalculia) (see **Figure 9.6**). It's important to note that a learning disability is distinct from an intellectual disability—a deficit in general or global mental abilities.

Learning Objective 9.13

Describe the issues involved with children with learning disabilities.

learning disability

a disorder in which a child has difficulty mastering a specific academic skill, even though she possesses average to above-average intelligence and has no physical or sensory handicaps

individual education plan (IEP)

a written document containing learning and behavioural objectives for the exceptional student, a description of how the objectives will be achieved, and how the objectives will be evaluated

Figure 9.6 This is a sample of work by a Grade 4 student with a specific learning disorder. On the left are rough research notes for a project on horses. On the right is the intended wording. With support at home and school, this student went on to become an honours student in high school, received entrance scholarships into university, and has successfully completed graduate studies in psychology.

(**SOURCE:** Courtesy of Paul Johnson.)

Where does a horse live?	
Rough work	**Final notes**
bons *stadol* *fidse* *proris* *hlse* *montins* *stobe* *formse*	barn stable fields prairies hills mountains stable farms

What does a horse eat?	
Rough work	**Final notes**
ose *wite* *grone* *vitomis* *bron* *hae* *gasis* *corne* *hoter*	oats wheat grain vitamins bran hay grasses corn water

How do you care for a horse?	
Rough work	**Final notes**
feed Dalle *clin stolle* *prope ncomd* *wascht* *comd and brocte* *Ecesod Dalle*	feed daily clean stall proper nutrition washed combed and brushed exercised daily

What exercise does a horse need?	
Rough work	**Final notes**
A hors nidc I late of Eesel A horse chd es of most of the fome It ndse ronid golpin	A horse needs a lot of exercise. A horse should be out most of the time. It needs to run and gallop.

Learning disabilities are recognized as impairments in one or more processes related to perceiving, thinking, remembering, or learning. Specific learning disorders may include, but are not limited to:

- Inaccurate or slow and effortful word reading
- Difficulty understanding the meaning of what is read
- Difficulties with spelling
- Difficulties with written expression
- Difficulties mastering number sense, number facts, or calculation
- Difficulties in mathematical reasoning (APA, 2013, pp. 66–67)

Moreover, learning disabilities are lifelong, range in severity, and may also involve difficulties with organizational skills, social perception, social interaction, and perspective taking. The way in which they are expressed may vary over an individual's lifetime, depending on the interaction between the demands of the environment and the individual's learning strengths and needs. Learning disabilities are often identified by unexpected academic underachievement or achievement that is maintained only by unusually high levels of effort and support (APA, 2013; LDAC, 2002).

Explanations of the problem are subject to disagreement, which makes for inconsistent special education policies across Canada's provinces and territories (Kozey & Siegel, 2008). Some experts argue that children with learning disabilities (especially reading disabilities) may simply have a more general problem with understanding the sound and structure of language (Torgesen et al., 1999). Others, in particular some Canadian neuropsychologists, contend that a learning disability results from a neurobiological problem (Fiedorowicz et al., 2002). For example, a large number of small abnormalities, such as irregularity of neuron arrangement, clumps of immature brain cells, scars, or congenital tumours, may develop in the brain during prenatal life. The growing brain compensates for these problems by "rewiring" around the problem areas. These rewirings, in turn, may scramble normal information-processing pathways just enough to make reading or calculation or some other specific task very difficult (Farnham-Diggory, 1992). Some evidence also suggests that learning disabilities, especially dyslexia, may have a genetic basis (Bates et al., 2007).

When reading is the problem skill, the term **dyslexia** is often used (even though, technically speaking, *dyslexia* refers to a total absence of reading). Most children with reading disabilities can read but not as well as others their age. Moreover, it appears that their skill deficits are specific to reading, such as an inability to automatize sound–letter correspondences or weak *morphological awareness* (the ability to understand and correctly use small words, letters, and letter combinations, i.e., prefixes, suffixes, and roots, to create new meanings), rather than the result of a general cognitive dysfunction (Siegel, 2008).

For success, individuals with learning disabilities require early identification and timely specialized assessments and interventions involving home, school, community, and workplace settings. The interventions need to be appropriate for each individual's learning disability subtype and, at a minimum, include the provision of:

- Specific skill instruction
- Accommodations
- Compensatory strategies
- Self-advocacy skills (Walcot-Gayda, n.d.)

Attention-Deficit/Hyperactivity Disorder

Some children experience learning difficulties that don't seem to fit the typical special education categories. For example, an estimated 3.7% of Canadian boys and 1.5% of girls aged 6 to 9 have a disorder called **attention-deficit/hyperactivity disorder (ADHD)** (Brault & Lacourse, 2012). Children with ADHD are more physically active, impulsive, and/or less attentive than their peers (APA, 2013). These characteristics often lead to both academic and behavioural problems in school.

CAUSES OF ADHD The cause of ADHD is unknown (Singh, Yeh, Verma, & Das, 2015). However, some developmentalists suggest that children with ADHD are neurologically different from their peers. Twin studies suggesting a genetic basis for the disorder support this hypothesis (Rosenberg, Pennington, Willcutt, & Olson, 2012). Other developmentalists hypothesize that children with ADHD require more sensory stimulation than their peers; thus, they move around more to get the stimulation they need (Antrop, Roeyers, Van Oost, & Buysse, 2000).

Psychologists are fairly sure that diet, environmental toxins, or brain damage are not the causes of ADHD, despite what some promoters of "cures" claim (Barkley, 2005; Singh et al., 2015). At present, most experts believe that each individual case of ADHD is caused by a complex interaction of factors that are unique to the specific child. These factors may include genetics, brain structure, parenting styles, peer relations, interactions with teachers, and stressors in the child's life, such as sleep disturbance, family instability, and parental mental illness (Singh et al., 2015).

dyslexia

problems in reading or the inability to read

Learning Objective 9.14

Describe how attention-deficit/ hyperactivity disorder affects a child's development.

attention-deficit/ hyperactivity disorder (ADHD)

a mental disorder that causes children to have difficulty attending to and completing tasks

Canadian researchers have been investigating the association between ADHD and sleep problems and have determined that one of the challenges of studying this relationship is that both conditions are intertwined with multiple other conditions. Common to anxiety disorders, depressive disorders, and ADHD is a difficulty in falling asleep and/or staying asleep (Corkum, Davidson, & Macpherson, 2011). Despite the difficulties of studying ADHD and sleep problems, there are some consistent findings. For example, children with ADHD display more movements in their sleep than children without the disorder (Corkum, Tannock, & Moldofsky, 1998). Children with ADHD also display instability in sleep onset, sleep duration, and **true sleep** (the number of minutes of sleep time excluding all periods of wakefulness, which can be distinguished by electroencephalograph [EEG] activity), and therefore it may be important to determine the impact that a disturbed sleep has on daytime behaviour (Gruber, Sadeh, & Raviv, 2000). For instance, sleep-deprived children may display hyperactivity, lack of coordination, and learning difficulty, all signs that could be mistaken for ADHD (Divgi, 2000). Low levels of true sleep time have been accurately predicted from teacher-reported behavioural symptoms such as attention and social problems (Aronen, Paavonen, Fjällberg, Soininen, & Törrönen, 2000).

true sleep

the number of minutes of sleep time excluding all periods of wakefulness, which can be distinguished by electroencephalograph (EEG) activity

CHARACTERISTICS OF ADHD On many kinds of attention tasks, children with ADHD do not differ at all from normal children (Lawrence et al., 2004). They seem to vary from their normal peers in activity level, the ability to sustain attention (especially with boring and repetitive tasks), and the ability to control impulses. However, the degree of hyperactivity that children with ADHD exhibit is unrelated to their performance on attention tasks. That is, a child can be very physically active and still be good at controlling his attention. Likewise, a child can be very calm yet have little ability to sustain attention. For this reason, there are now three types of ADHD: (1) the hyperactive-impulsive type, in which a high activity level is the main problem; (2) the inattentive type, in which an inability to sustain attention is the major difficulty; and (3) the combined type which presents symptoms from both (APA, 2013).

Compared to their peers, children with ADHD achieve lower academic grades (Barry, Lyman, & Klinger, 2002; Daley & Birchwood, 2010). Additionally, their hyperactivity and/or inattentiveness often cause other kinds of problems. For one thing, children with both types of ADHD usually produce messy school work that is filled with errors, which further contributes to them getting poorer grades (Barkley, 2005). As well, they may be disruptive in class and are often rejected by other children.

TREATING AND MANAGING ADHD By the time their children are diagnosed with ADHD, usually upon entering school, many parents have lost confidence in their ability to control their children (Barkley, 2005). Some cope with their difficult children by being extremely permissive. Others respond by becoming excessively harsh and, out of frustration, sometimes treat the child abusively. Thus, parent training can be useful in helping parents cope with children who have ADHD.

The goal of such parenting programs is to help parents regain a sense of control (Barkley, 2005). For example, experts recommend that teachers provide parents with daily reports of their children's work in the various school subjects. Parents can then use the information to enforce a standing rule that the child must have completed all school work before watching television or doing other desired activities. Such approaches, when applied consistently, can help parents of children with ADHD manage their children's difficulties, as well as their own emotional reactions, more effectively.

Many children with ADHD take stimulant medications, such as methylphenidate (Ritalin). In fact, an estimated 82 in 1000 Canadian children are using these types of drugs to treat ADHD (Romano et al., 2005). The rate of usage for boys climbs from ~0.6% in 4- to 5-year-olds to a peak of over ~6% in 10- to 11-year-olds. Girls are much less likely to use these drugs—the highest usage is at age 8 to 9 (~1%). Seventy percent of the children who use these drugs are found to be calmer and better able to concentrate. However, some studies show that many children's response to the medication may actually be due to changes in expectations on the part of their teachers and parents—sort of a self-fulfilling prophecy (Spreen, Risser, & Edgell, 1995). In addition, studies suggest that the concentration skills of children with ADHD can be improved with training. For example, one study found that working-memory deficits and the inability to suppress impulses underlie many of the symptoms of ADHD. Moreover, providing children with training and practice in these two domains of cognitive functioning substantially reduces ADHD symptoms (Klingberg et al., 2005).

It's also important to note that medication doesn't always improve the grades of children with ADHD (Currie, Stabile, & Jones, 2013). Rather, for the most part, it seems that stimulant medications reduce such children's activity levels, help them control their impulses, and somewhat improve their social behaviour. These effects usually result in improvements in classroom behaviour and peer acceptance. Medications such as methylphenidate have the greatest effect on school grades among children whose ADHD symptoms are so severe that they interfere with actual learning (Spreen, Risser, & Edgell, 1995). For this reason, the use of stimulant medications for children who have mild or moderate ADHD symptoms is controversial. Furthermore, Canadian pediatricians caution that there is a lack of evidence about the long-term effectiveness of stimulant medications beyond four weeks of treatment (Schachter, Pham, King, Langford, & Moher, 2001).

Test Yourself before going on

1. Most children who receive special education services in Canada have some kind of _____ _____.
2. What are the three types of ADHD?

Critical Thinking

3. Prior to the 1960s, the learning disabilities concept was basically unheard of. How might this have impacted students with unrecognized specific learning disorders?

Summary

Physical Changes

9.1 **Identify what kinds of physical changes occur during middle childhood.**

- Physical development from age 6 to age 12 is steady and slow. Children gain 5 to 8 cm in height and about 2.75 kg of weight each year. Sex differences in skeletal and muscular maturation may lead boys and girls to pursue different activities.

9.2 **Describe the ways the brain changes during these years.**

- Neurological development leads to improvements in selective attention, information-processing speed, and spatial perception. Mapping of the structural and functional neural connections of the human brain and nervous system are now underway.

9.3 **Identify what the health risks are for 6- to 12-year-olds.**

- School-aged children require regular medical checkups. Unintentional injuries and unhealthy weights are the most prevalent health problems of this age group.

Cognitive Changes

9.4 **Describe what cognitive advantages children gain as they move through Piaget's concrete operational stage.**

- Piaget proposed that a major change in the child's thinking occurs at about age 6, when the child begins to understand powerful operations such as reversibility and decentration. The child also learns to use inductive logic, but does not yet use deductive logic.

9.5 Describe what horizontal decalage is, and how Siegler explains concrete operational thinking.

- Children do not master all of Piaget's concrete operational tasks at the same time, a pattern he called horizontal decalage. Moreover, Siegler's research suggests that the "operations" Piaget observed may actually be rules for solving specific types of problems.

9.6 Explain how children's information-processing skills improve during middle childhood.

- Most information-processing theorists conclude that there are no age-related changes in children's information-processing capacity, but there are clearly improvements in speed and efficiency.

9.7 Explain how vocabulary and other aspects of language change during middle childhood.

- Language development continues in middle childhood with vocabulary growth, improvements in grammar, and understanding of the social uses of language.

Schooling

9.8 Describe what should be included in an effective literacy curriculum.

- To become literate, children need specific instruction in sound–symbol correspondences, word parts, and other aspects of written language. They also need to be exposed to good literature and to have lots of opportunities to practice their reading and writing skills.

9.9 Identify the issues related to children who are second-language learners.

- There is an increasing number of children in Canada who are not proficient in either English or French. Where available, these children can learn one of Canada's official languages through bilingual education or English/French-as-a-second-language programs. Transitional

language programming and testing accommodations can help minimize potential academic achievement issues.

9.10 Summarize the benefits of bilingual education.

- Canada's successful model for teaching bilingual education has been adopted throughout the world. Children who participate in bilingual education benefit from improved language skills and thinking skills and a greater appreciation for other cultures.

9.11 Explain the challenges of evaluating students across Canada's educational systems.

- Children's school progress is assessed with both IQ tests and achievement tests. Both types of tests may ignore important aspects of intellectual functioning.

9.12 Summarize what kinds of group differences in achievement educational researchers have found.

- There are no gender differences in overall IQ scores, but girls do consistently better on language, science, and math tasks. There is as yet no clear agreement on how to explain such differences. Differences in achievement may also result from differences in analytic or relational learning styles.

Learners with Exceptionalities

9.13 Describe the issues involved with children with learning disabilities.

- There is considerable dispute about defining and explaining learning disabilities, and some children who are labelled as such have been misclassified. Practically speaking, "learning disability" serves to describe children who do not learn as quickly as their intelligence-test scores suggest they should.

9.14 Describe how attention-deficit/hyperactivity disorder affects a child's development.

- Children with ADHD have problems with both academic learning and social relationships. Medication, parent training, and behaviour modification can be useful in helping children with ADHD overcome these difficulties.

Chapter 10
Social and Personality Development in Middle Childhood

Monkey Business Images/Shutterstock

Learning Objectives

THEORIES OF SOCIAL AND PERSONALITY DEVELOPMENT

10.1 Describe how psychoanalytic theorists characterized the middle childhood years.

10.2 Summarize the main ideas of trait and social-cognitive theorists.

SELF-CONCEPT

10.3 Identify the features of the psychological self.

10.4 Describe the role that self-esteem and meaningfulness have on the valued self.

ADVANCES IN SOCIAL COGNITION

10.5 Describe how children's understanding of others changes in middle childhood.

10.6 Describe how children in Piaget's moral realism and moral relativism stages reason about right and wrong.

SOCIAL RELATIONSHIPS

10.7 Describe how self-regulation affects school-aged children's relationships with their parents.

10.8 Summarize what changes occur in children's understanding of friendships during this period.

10.9 Summarize the ways boys and girls interact during the middle childhood years.

10.10 Identify what types of aggression are most common among school-aged children.

10.11 Describe how popular, rejected, and neglected children differ.

INFLUENCES BEYOND FAMILY AND PEERS

10.12 Describe how self-care affects girls' and boys' development.

10.13 Identify the influences television has on children's development.

Every culture in the world has a *society of childhood*, in which children make up their own social rules that differ from those of adult society. For example, in most Canadian school lunchrooms, food trading is common. A child who refuses to trade may be seen as "stuck-up." But adults who try to talk co-workers into trading lunches are likely to be thought of as pushy or somewhat odd. Such comparisons show that children practise social competence by making up their own social rules rather than simply copying those that exist in the adult world. Creating and enforcing such rules helps children learn to look at things from other people's points of view and to cooperate.

Clearly, cognitive development provides the intellectual foundation required to engage in rule-governed activities. But what makes each child's experiences unique within the context of such universal interactions are the emotional and behavioural responses that their distinctive personalities, self-concepts, and relationship histories contribute to the developmental equation. These are the topics of the present chapter. We begin with a consideration of the major themes of development that uniquely mark social and personality development in the middle childhood years and the different ways in which developmentalists have explained them.

Theories of Social and Personality Development

Development of self-perceived competence is the overarching theme of social and personality development in the middle childhood years. How do children develop this critical attribute? Developmentalists representing different theoretical perspectives emphasize different sets of factors in their explanations.

Learning Objective 10.1

Describe how psychoanalytic theorists characterized the middle childhood years.

Psychoanalytic Perspectives

When you think back to your middle childhood years, what kinds of experiences stand out? Most likely, you remember interacting with your peers and siblings. If Freud were called on to explain how your feelings about your own competence developed, he would appeal to the emotional qualities of these interactions. According to the psychoanalytic perspective, and in line with our everyday experiences with children, children vary greatly in the ways that they respond to social situations. Some become angry and lash out at those who reject them. Others withdraw and develop a general fear of social interactions. For Freud, the challenge of the middle childhood years was to form emotional bonds with peers and to move beyond those that were developed with parents in earlier years. Thus, much of the modern-day research on peer rejection and other emotional features of middle childhood finds its roots in Freud's psychoanalytic approach.

Erikson accepted Freud's view of the central role of peer relationships and the emotions that accompany them in middle childhood. He went beyond Freud's perspective, though, when he further characterized middle childhood as the period during which children experience the crisis of **industry versus inferiority**. During this stage, Erikson said, children develop a sense of their own competence through the achievement of culturally defined learning goals (see the discussion in the chapter on Theories of Development). The psychosocial task of the 6- to 12-year-old is development of industry, or the willingness to work to accomplish goals. To develop industry, the child must be able to achieve the goals her culture sets for all children her age. In most countries, 6- to 12-year-olds must learn to read and write. If they fail to do so, then, Erikson's view claims, they will enter adolescence and adulthood with feelings of inferiority. These feelings of inferiority constitute an emotional mindset that can hamper an individual's ability to achieve for the rest of her life.

Contemporary studies that stress the child's need to feel competent are in tune with Erikson's views. Many of them suggest that he was right about the link between school experiences and an emerging sense of competence. It seems that most 6- to 12-year-olds gradually develop a view of their own competence as they succeed or fail at academic tasks such as reading and arithmetic (Harter, 2012). Thus, their self-assessments and actual achievements are strongly correlated; that is, those who are most successful judge themselves to be competent, while those who have difficulty perceive themselves as less so. However, individual differences in children's responses to success and failure moderate the effects of the experiences themselves. Some of these differences are found in the emotional realm, as suggested earlier.

Erikson also proposed that children who lack success in school can develop it by participating in culturally valued pursuits outside of academic settings. A child who is a mediocre student, for instance, may channel his need to develop self-perceived competence into athletics. Another child who gets poor grades may do so because she spends most of her time reading books that she finds to be more interesting than her school work. Outsiders may worry about her sense of competence, but, internally, she has no doubts about her abilities.

The Trait and Social-Cognitive Perspectives

THE BIG FIVE PERSONALITY TRAITS Psychoanalytic theorists have given us some compelling ideas about how individual differences in emotional responses to childhood experiences shape development and self-perceived competence. However, they tell us little about the origins of those differences. The primary goal of *trait theories*, by contrast, is to do just that. A **trait** is a stable pattern of responding to situations. This definition should remind you of our discussions of temperament in earlier chapters, because the study of infant and early childhood temperament is grounded in trait theory. By middle childhood, trait theorists argue, the various dimensions of temperament have evolved into the five dimensions of personality (**the Big Five** personality traits) shown in **Table 10.1**.

Research suggests that trait theorists are right about the emergence of stable traits in middle childhood. Moreover, these traits are known to contribute to the development of feelings of competence. For instance, a child who is reasonably *extraverted*, or outgoing, responds to peer rejection by becoming more determined to be accepted by the group. One who is *introverted*, or shy, would likely be so emotionally distraught by the taunts of her playmates that she would actively avoid social situations in the future. Still, trait theory leaves us wondering why extraversion doesn't always lead to

industry versus inferiority stage

the fourth of Erikson's psychosocial stages, during which children develop a sense of their own competence through mastery of culturally defined learning tasks

Learning Objective 10.2

Summarize the main ideas of trait and social-cognitive theorists.

trait

a stable pattern of responding to situations

the Big Five

a set of five major dimensions of personality, including extraversion, agreeableness, conscientiousness, neuroticism, and openness/intellect

Table 10.1 The Big Five Personality Traits

Trait	Qualities of Individuals Who Show the Trait	Possible Temperament Components
Extraversion	Active, assertive, enthusiastic, outgoing	High activity level, sociability, positive emotionality, talkativeness
Agreeableness	Affectionate, forgiving, generous, kind, sympathetic, trusting	Perhaps high approach/positive emotionality, effortful control
Conscientiousness	Efficient, organized, prudent, reliable, responsible	Effortful control/task persistence
Neuroticism (also called emotional instability)	Anxious, self-pitying, tense, touchy, unstable, worrying	Negative emotionality, irritability
Openness/Intellect	Artistic, curious, imaginative, insightful, original, having wide interests	Approach new situations and people, low inhibition

(**SOURCES:** Based on Ahadi & Rothbart, 1994; John, Caspi, Robins, Moffitt, & Stouthamer-Loeber, 1994, Table 1, p. 161; McCrae & Costa, 1990.)

social competence, and why some people overcome their tendency toward introversion to become competent in the social arena.

SOCIAL-COGNITIVE PERSPECTIVES From the social-cognitive perspective, both psychoanalytic and trait theorists focus on only one set of factors that shape the development of self-perceived competence in middle childhood. Albert Bandura, for instance, proposed that the emotions described by psychoanalytic theorists and the stable patterns of responding that have been identified by trait theorists, together with cognitive factors, constitute one of three interactive components that influence social and personality development (see the discussion in the chapter on Theories of Development). Recall that Bandura refers to this emotional/cognitive component as the *personal* factor. The other two factors of his model are the person's *behavioural* responses and the *environmental* influences and pressures.

Bandura proposed that the personal, behavioural, and environmental factors interact in a pattern he termed *reciprocal determinism*. Each of the three components influences, and is influenced by, the other two. By organizing the various interactive influences in the way that it does, Bandura's model provides a more comprehensive explanation of how school-aged children develop ideas about the degrees of competence they possess than either psychoanalytic or trait theorists do. Thus, Bandura's social-cognitive approach provides us with a way of taking into account the valuable insights of psychoanalytic theorists relative to children's emotions with those of trait

Test Yourself before going on

1. In the table below, summarize what Erikson believed to be the factors that influence the outcome of the industry versus inferiority stage and the consequences that flow from each outcome.

	Industry	Inferiority
Influences		
Consequences		

2. Classify each behaviour according to the Big Five personality trait that it represents:
   _____ (a) talkativeness
   _____ (b) courteousness
   _____ (c) irritability
   _____ (d) curiosity
   _____ (e) responsibility
      (i) extraversion
      (ii) neuroticism
      (iii) conscientiousness
      (iv) agreeableness
      (v) openness

3. Classify each variable according to the three components of Bandura's reciprocal determinism model of personality development: (P) person, (E) environment, (B) behaviour.
   _____ (a) parents' responses to children's actions
   _____ (b) temperament
   _____ (c) children's actions

theorists. And by integrating both into the three-part model that Bandura proposed, we gain a more comprehensive understanding of the mechanisms that drive the development of self-perceived competence (what Bandura referred to as *self-efficacy*) in the middle childhood years.

Self-Concept

How much insight does a school-aged child really have into her own personality? The answer to this question depends on whether we look at the child at the beginning of this period or near the end of it. Across the years from ages 6 to 12, children's understanding of themselves improves quite a bit and, by the end of the middle childhood period, children's self-concepts include two new components: a *psychological self* and a *valued self*.

The Psychological Self

The **psychological self** is a person's understanding of his or her enduring psychological characteristics. It first appears during the transition from early to middle childhood and becomes increasingly complex as the child approaches adolescence. It includes both basic information about the child's unique characteristics and self-judgments of competency.

PERSONALITY TRAITS   Children don't use the same terminology as the trait theories that you read about earlier in the chapter, but they do describe their own personalities with increasing degrees of precision across the middle childhood years. For example a 6-year-old might use simple psychological self-descriptors, such as "smart" or "dumb." By 10, a child is more likely to use comparisons in self-descriptions: "I'm smarter than most other kids" or "I'm not as talented in art as my friend" (Harter, 2012).

This developmental trend was illustrated in the results of an older study of the self-concepts of 9- to 18-year-olds (Montemayor & Eisen, 1977). Children who participated were asked to give 20 answers to the question "Who am I?" The researchers found that the younger children were still using mostly surface qualities to describe themselves, as in this description by a 9-year-old:

> My name is Bruce C. I have brown eyes. I have brown hair. I have brown eyebrows. I am nine years old. I LOVE! Sports. I have seven people in my family. I have great! eye site. I have lots! of friends. I live on 1923 Pinecrest Dr. I am going on 10 in September. I'm a boy. I have a uncle that is almost 7 feet tall. My school is Pinecrest. My teacher is Mrs. V. I play Hockey! I'm almost the smartest boy in the class. I LOVE! food. I love fresh air. I LOVE school. (Montemayor & Eisen, 1977, p. 317)

In contrast, consider the self-description of this 11-year-old girl in Grade 6:

> My name is A. I'm a human being. I'm a girl. I'm a truthful person. I'm not very pretty. I do so-so in my studies. I'm a very good cellist. I'm a very good pianist. I'm a little bit tall for my age. I like several boys. I like several girls. I'm old-fashioned. I play tennis. I am a very good swimmer. I try to be helpful. I'm always ready to be friends with anybody. Mostly I'm good, but I lose my temper. I'm not well-liked by some girls and boys. I don't know if I'm liked by boys or not. (Montemayor & Eisen, 1977, pp. 317–318)

This girl, like the other 11-year-olds in the study, describes her external qualities, but she also emphasizes psychological factors such as personality traits.

Thus, as a child moves through the concrete operational period, his psychological self becomes more complex, more comparative, less tied to external features, and more centred on feelings and ideas.

Learning Objective 10.3

Identify the features of the psychological self.

psychological self

a person's understanding of his or her enduring psychological characteristics

SELF-EFFICACY   As we noted earlier in the chapter, middle childhood is the time when children develop perceptions about their degree of competence. Bandura has greatly advanced developmentalists' understanding of this crucial aspect of the psychological self. He defines *self-efficacy* as an individual's belief in her capacity to cause an intended event to occur (Bandura, 1997a). How does self-efficacy develop?

Bandura proposed that peer models play a primary role in the development of self-efficacy beliefs (Bandura, 1997a). As an example, consider what it's like for a novice bike rider who is prompted by her friends to try some challenging trail riding. Bandura would predict that, when the girl observes her friends riding up a dirt hill, she probably concludes that she can do likewise. Bandura further argued that, to believe that she could follow her peers' example, the girl had to see herself as similar to them. Thus, *social comparison*, or the process of drawing conclusions about the self based on comparisons to others, plays an integral role in the degree to which children gain insight into their own self-efficacy from observing peers (Thompson, Winer, & Goodvin, 2011). Thus, simply watching other children model success at a task is insufficient for the development of self-efficacy in a child whom outsiders might see as similar to the models. The child herself must perceive that similarity to be influenced by the models.

Encouragement from knowledgeable people that children value and respect also contributes to self-efficacy. For example, the school cycling coach's willingness to let the girl start training for her school's mountain bike club can play a role in her development of self-efficacy. However, nothing influences self-efficacy more than an individual's real life experiences (Britner & Pajares, 2006). In other words, believing that you can do something is less powerful, emotionally and cognitively, than actually doing it. Consequently, the final hurdle in this girl's development of self-efficacy for trail-cycling was surmounted when she successfully competed in her first challenging trail ride.

The Valued Self

Learning Objective 10.4

Describe the role that self-esteem and meaningfulness have on the valued self.

A child can have an accurate view of his personality traits, and even have a solid sense of self-efficacy, but still fail to value himself as an individual. To find out why, developmentalists have studied another aspect of self-concept development in middle childhood: the emergence of the *valued self*.

THE NATURE OF SELF-ESTEEM   A child's ability to evaluate and make judgements has several interesting features. First of all, by the time they reach school age, around age 5, children already possess a *global self-evaluation*. New research using age-appropriate measures (e.g., replacing words related to the "self" with terms like "me" and "not me") has shown that by the time children start school, they already possess an unexpectedly strong sense of *self-esteem* with respect to aspects of their personality, such as gender identity and gender attitude (e.g., boys, and to a greater extent girls, have a strong gender *in-group* preference) (Cvencek, Greenwald, & Meltzoff, 2016). Most children bring a positive sense about themselves to school, a strong foundation on which further self-esteem is nurtured. Later, over the years of elementary school and high school, children's evaluations of their own abilities become increasingly compartmentalized, with quite different judgments made about their academic skills, athletic skills, physical appearance, social acceptance, friendships, romantic appeal, and relationships with parents (Marsh, Craven, & Debus, 1999). By age 7 to 8, children can readily answer questions about how well they like themselves as people, how happy they are, and how well they like the way they are leading their lives. This global evaluation of one's own worth is usually referred to as **self-esteem**.

self-esteem

a global evaluation of one's own worth

HOW SELF-ESTEEM DEVELOPS   Developmental psychologist Susan Harter (1987, 2006, 2012) has studied the development of self-esteem extensively. She has found that self-esteem is strongly influenced by mental comparisons of children's ideal selves and their actual experiences. For example, social self-esteem, the assessment of one's own social skills, is higher in popular children than in those who are rejected by their peers (Jackson & Bracken, 1998). However, each component of self-esteem is valued differently by different children. Thus, a child who perceives herself to have poor social skills because she is unpopular may not necessarily have low self-esteem. The degree to which her social self-assessment affects her self-esteem is influenced by how much she values social skills and popularity. In addition, she may see herself as very competent in another area—such as academic skills—that balances her lack of social skills.

(*Photo*: Michael Ireland/Fotolia)

Hitting a home run will raise this girl's self-esteem only if she places a high value on being good at sports or at baseball specifically.

The key to self-esteem, then, is the amount of discrepancy between what the child desires and what the child thinks he has achieved. Thus, a child who values sports prowess but who isn't big enough or coordinated enough to be good at sports will have lower self-esteem than will an equally small or uncoordinated child who does not value sports skill so highly. Similarly, being good at something, such as singing or playing chess, won't raise a child's self-esteem unless the child values that particular skill.

The second major influence on a child's self-esteem is the overall support the child feels she is receiving from the important people around her, particularly parents, peers, and others in her neighbourhood and school (Hosogi, Okada, Fujii, Noguchi, & Watanabe, 2012). Apparently, to develop high self-esteem, children must first acquire the sense that they are liked and accepted in their families, by both parents and siblings. Next, they need to be able to find friends with whom they can develop stable relationships. Since childhood friendships begin with shared interests and activities, children need to be in an environment in which they can find others who like the same things they do and are similarly skilled. Athletic children need other athletic children to associate with; those who are musically inclined need to meet peers who are also musical, and so on.

The separate influences of the perceived discrepancy between the ideal and actual self and the amount of social support are clear in the results of Harter's research on self-esteem. She asked children in Grades 3, 4, 5, and 6 how important it was to them to do well in each of five domains, and how well they thought they actually did in each. The total discrepancy between these sets of judgments constituted the discrepancy score. A high discrepancy score indicates that children didn't feel they were doing well in areas that mattered to them. The social support score was based on children's replies to a set of questions about whether they thought others (parents and peers) liked them as they were, treated them as people, or felt that they were important. **Figure 10.1** shows the results for children in Grades 3 and 4; the findings for the children in Grades 5 and 6 are virtually identical to these. Both sets of data support Harter's hypothesis. Note that a low discrepancy score alone does not protect children completely from low self-esteem if they lack sufficient social support. Similarly, loving and accepting families and peer groups do not guarantee high self-esteem if youngsters do not feel that they are living up to their own standards.

The criteria by which children learn to evaluate themselves vary considerably from one society to another (Miller, Wang, Sandel, & Cho, 2002; Wang & Ollendick, 2001). In individualistic cultures, like that of Canada, parents focus on helping children develop a sense of self-esteem based on the children's own interests and abilities. In collectivist cultures, such as China's, children are taught to value themselves based on cultural ideals about what a "good" person is.

From all these sources, the child fashions her ideas (her internal model) about what she should be and what she is. Like the internal model of attachment, self-esteem is not fixed in stone. It is responsive to changes in others' judgments as well as to changes in the child's own experience of success or failure. But once created, the

Figure 10.1 For these Grade 3 and 4 children in Harter's studies, self-esteem was about equally influenced by the amount of support the children saw themselves receiving from parents and peers and the degree of discrepancy between the value the children placed on various domains and the skill they thought they had in each of those domains.

(**SOURCE:** Harter, S. (1987). The determinations and mediational role of global self-worth in children. In N. Eisenberg (Ed.), *Contemporary topics in developmental psychology* (pp. 219–242). New York, NY: Wiley-Interscience., Figure 9.2, p. 227. Reproduced with permission of John Wiley & Sons Inc.)

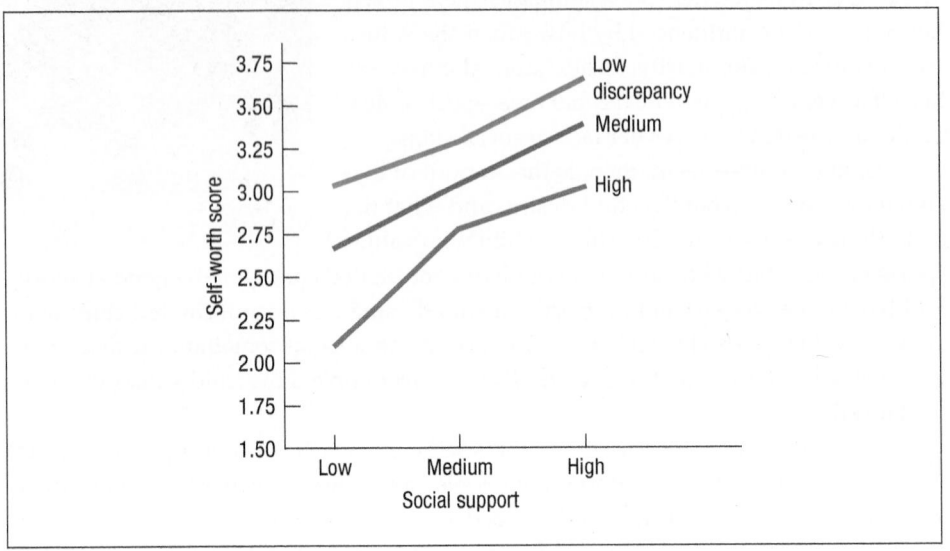

model does tend to persist, both because the child tends to choose experiences that will confirm and support it and because the social environment—including the parents' evaluations of the child—tends to be at least moderately consistent.

MEANINGFULNESS   One challenging and understudied aspect of self-concept in children is the spiritual self (Moore, Talwar, Bosacki, & Park-Saltzman, 2011). Lisa Miller (2015), a Columbia University clinical psychologist, offers that *spirituality*, as distinct from religiosity (i.e., religious activity), is "an inner sense of relationship to a higher power that is loving and guiding" (p. 25). This is not to suggest that religious people aren't spiritual, as for most, the two aspects are intertwined. What's essential to spirituality is that a person's beliefs must be at a "deep personal level for the benefits to be felt" (p. 8), the formation of which is most often traced back to childhood and adolescence, and like any of our other attributes, you either use it or lose it. Further, spirituality is amenable to scientific study and its affects are measurable. As such, spirituality becomes an important aspect of the whole person, potentially benefiting human physical health, mental well-being, and feelings of fulfillment.

Most studies on the topic of spirituality focus on the cognitive and social aspects of spirituality without considering the subjective and experiential elements (Bosacki, 2001a, 2001b; Bosacki, Moore, Talwar, & Park-Saltzman, 2011). The little amount of spiritual education that preadolescents receive commonly focuses more on truisms, facts, and practices than on learning to trust one's intuition and emotions in the quest for a meaningful existence—attributes that are important in the formation of a complete and genuine preadolescent self-concept (Bosacki, 2001b). McGill and Brock University researchers have been looking at Canadian children's perceptions of spirituality and found some interesting common themes (Moore et al., 2011; Moore, Talwar, & Bosacki, 2012). Interviews with children from diverse cultural and religious backgrounds, including those from Baha'i, Christian, Jewish, Hindu, Muslim, and Sikh faiths, as well as no religious faith, found that regardless of their backgrounds, spirituality plays a role in their lives. In particular, it seems children often describe positive feelings when praying to, or thinking about, a divine or higher power as an omnipresent helper, listener, and comforter. Moreover, these feelings seem to play a role in their daily lives: helping them to make decisions, providing guidance or help with coping, especially when facing adversity, and making them grateful for the good things in their lives (e.g., for having a good day or being surrounded by a loving family). Therefore, having a strong sense of spirituality may help shape their perceptions of, and answer questions about, the meaning of life, which can impact their mental health and well-being, as well as set the stage for dealing with the aspirations and challenges they will face in adolescence (issues we'll discuss in the chapters on Physical and Cognitive Development in Adolescence and Social and Personality Development in Adolescence).

Educational strategies that may strengthen the development of the spiritual aspects of preadolescent self-concept, and promote effective coping skills, include the use of experiential exercises, such as meditation and visualization, art and play therapy, psychodrama, and language-based programs such as personal storytelling and journal writing (Bosacki, 2002, 2005; Bosacki et al., 2011). For example, one study found that, for spiritual growth to take place, it was helpful to create an environment in which children were required to be more than just passive learners (Sewell, 2009). In such a setting, teachers and children learned together, shared decisions, and respected and trusted one another. In this environment, the focus was more relational than instructional, which may seem counter to our traditional view of teaching. Still, when children were encouraged to be part of this *community of learning*, the children, and their teachers, developed a stronger sense of who they were as humans in the world—another important aspect in the development of the child's self-concept.

Test Yourself before going on

1. Write "Y" by the statement more likely to have been made by a younger child and "O" by the one likely to have been made by a 6- to 12-year-old.
   _____ (a) I am a boy, and I like to play with trucks.
   _____ (b) I am a nice girl with brown hair, and I like school
2. Match each of the following terms with its definition.
   (a) an individual's belief in her capacity to cause an intended event to occur
   (b) an individual's overall sense of his value
      _____ (i) self-esteem
      _____ (ii) self-efficacy

Critical Thinking

3. If you were a parent who is uncomfortable with religion and/or spirituality, how might you go about providing your child with a sense of personal meaning?

Advances in Social Cognition

Children's ability to understand others is enhanced by the development of a theory of mind in early childhood. But by the end of the middle childhood period, children have developed a much broader understanding of others than they possessed at its beginning. Moreover, they are beginning to understand the moral aspects of social relationships.

The Child as Psychologist

A number of early groundbreaking social-cognitive studies demonstrated that the child of this age looks beyond appearances and searches for deeper consistencies that will help him to interpret both his own and other people's behaviour. Thus, like their understanding of the physical world, 6- to 12-year-olds' descriptions of other people move from the concrete to the abstract. If you ask a 6- or 7-year-old to describe others, then he will focus almost exclusively on external features (e.g., what the person looks

Learning Objective 10.5

Describe how children's understanding of others changes in middle childhood.

like, where he lives, what he does). This description by a 7-year-old boy, taken from a classic study of social-cognitive development, is typical:

> He is very tall. He has dark brown hair, he goes to our school. I don't think he has any brothers or sisters. He is in our class. Today he has a dark orange [sweater] and gray trousers and brown shoes. (Livesley & Bromley, 1973, p. 213)

When young children do use internal or evaluative terms to describe people, they are likely to use quite global ones, such as "nice" or "mean," "good" or "bad." Further, young children do not seem to see these qualities as lasting or general traits of the individual, applicable in all situations or over time (Rholes & Ruble, 1984). In other words, the 6- or 7-year-old has not yet developed a concept that might be called "conservation of personality."

Beginning at about age 7 or 8, a rather dramatic shift occurs in children's descriptions of others. The child begins to focus more on the inner traits or qualities of another person and to assume that those traits will be visible in many situations (Gnepp & Chilamkurti, 1988). Children this age still describe others' physical features, but their descriptions are now used as examples of more general points about internal qualities. You can see the change when you compare the 7-year-old's description given above with this description by a child nearly 10 years old:

> He smells very much and is very nasty. He has no sense of humor and is very dull. He is always fighting and he is cruel. He does silly things and is very stupid. He has brown hair and cruel eyes. He is sulky and 11 years old and has lots of sisters. I think he is the most horrible boy in the class. He has a croaky voice and always chews his pencil and picks his teeth and I think he is disgusting. (Livesley & Bromley, 1973, p. 217)

This description still includes many external physical features but goes beyond such concrete surface qualities to the level of personality traits, such as cruelty and lack of humour.

The movement from externals to internals in descriptions of others is well documented by research. For example, in one important early study, researchers asked 6-, 8-, and 10-year-olds to describe three other children; a year later, they asked them to do the same thing again (Barenboim, 1981). **Figure 10.2** shows the results for two of the

Figure 10.2 These data from Barenboim's study show the change in children's descriptions of their peers during the years of middle childhood. The solid lines represent longitudinal data, the dashed lines cross-sectional comparisons.

(**SOURCE:** Data from Barenboim, C. (1981). The development of person perception in childhood and adolescence: From behavioral comparisons to psychological constructs to psychological comparisons. *Child Development*, 52, 129–144., Figure 1, p. 134.)

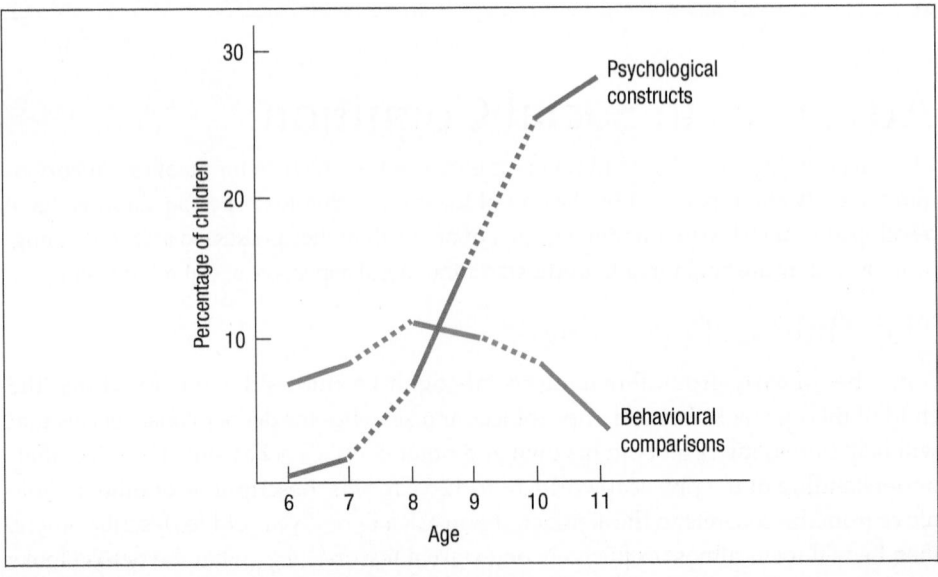

categories used in the study's data analysis. A *behavioural comparison* was any description that involved comparing a child's behaviours or physical features with those of another child or a norm, such as, "Billy runs a lot faster than Jason," or "She draws the best in our whole class." Any statement that involved some internal personality trait was referred to as a *psychological construct*, such as "Sarah is so kind," or "He's a real stubborn idiot!" You can see that behavioural comparisons peaked at around age 8 but psychological constructs increased steadily throughout middle childhood.

Moral Reasoning

Learning Objective 10.6
Describe how children in Piaget's moral realism and moral relativism stages reason about right and wrong.

Children's growing understanding of the internal experiences of other people helps them develop a better understanding of how they and others think about actions that have moral implications. *Moral reasoning* is the process of making judgments about the rightness or wrongness of specific acts. Children learn to discriminate between intentional and unintentional acts between age 2 and 6. However, using this understanding to make moral judgments is another matter. Piaget claimed that the ability to use reasoning about intentions to make judgments about the moral dimensions of behaviour appears to emerge along with concrete operational reasoning.

PIAGET'S MORAL REALISM AND MORAL RELATIVISM   Piaget studied moral development by observing children playing games. He noticed that younger children seemed to have less understanding of the games' rules. Following up on these observations, Piaget questioned children of different ages about rules. Their answers led him to propose a two-stage theory of moral development (Piaget, 1932).

At the beginning of the middle childhood period, children are in what Piaget termed the **moral realism stage**. They believe that the rules of games can't be changed because they come from authorities, such as parents, government officials, or religious figures. For example, one 6-year-old told Piaget that the game of marbles was invented on Noah's ark. He went on to explain that the rules can't be changed because the "big ones," meaning adults and older children, wouldn't like it (Piaget, 1965, p. 60).

moral realism stage
the first of Piaget's stages of moral development, in which children believe rules are inflexible

Moral realists also believe that all rule violations eventually result in punishment. For example, Piaget told children a story about a child who fell into a stream when he tried to use a rotten piece of wood as a bridge. Children younger than 8 years old told him that the child was being punished for something "naughty" he had done in the past.

After age 8, Piaget proposed, children move into the **moral relativism stage**, in which they learn that people can agree to change rules if they want to. They realize that the important thing about a game is that all the players follow the same rules, regardless of what those are. For example, 8- to 12-year-olds know that a group of children playing baseball can decide to give each batter four strikes rather than three. They understand that their agreement doesn't change the game of baseball and that it doesn't apply to other people who play the game. At the same time, children of this age get better at following the rules of games.

moral relativism stage
the second of Piaget's stages of moral development, in which children understand that many rules can be changed through social agreement

Eight- to 12-year-olds also know that you don't get punished for rule violations unless you get caught. As a result, they view events like the one in which the child fell into the stream as accidents. They understand that accidents are not caused by "naughty" behaviour. Children older than 8 also understand the relationship between punishment and intentions. For example, Piaget's research suggests that children over 8 can distinguish between a child who unintentionally left a store without paying for a chocolate bar and another who deliberately took it. Older children are likely to say that both children should return or pay for the candy, but only the one who intentionally stole it should be punished.

Research supports Piaget's claim that school-aged children give more weight to intentions than consequences when making moral judgments (Killen, Mulvey, Richardson, Jampol, & Woodward, 2011). However, although their thinking is more mature than that of preschoolers, 6- to 12-year-olds' moral reasoning is still highly egocentric. For example, every parent has heard the exclamation "It's not fair!" when a child fails to receive the same treat or privilege as a sibling. It is rare, if not completely unknown, for a 6- to 12-year-old to protest the fairness of receiving something that a sibling didn't. Thus, school-aged children still have a long way to go with respect to mature moral reasoning, and we will return to this topic in the chapters on adolescent development (see **Development in the Real World**).

Development in the Real World

Encouraging Moral Reasoning

In his book *Raising Good Children*, developmental psychologist Thomas Lickona reminds readers that the development of mature moral reasoning takes many years (Lickona, 1994). At the same time, he offers parents and teachers several suggestions that will help them assist their 6- to 12-year-olds to prepare for movement to more mature levels. Following are some of his suggestions:

- Require kids to give reasons for what they want.
- Play developmentally appropriate games with them.
- Praise them for observing social conventions, such as saying "please" and "thank you."
- When punishment is necessary, provide them with an explanation, advice on how to avoid punishment in the future, and a way of repairing any damage their misbehaviour has caused.
- Teach them about reciprocity: "We do nice things for you, so you should be willing to help us."
- Give them meaningful chores so that they will think of themselves as important family and community members.
- Help and encourage them to base obedience on love and respect rather than fear.
- Teach them religious and philosophical values, including the idea that some actions are right and others are wrong, regardless of circumstances.
- Challenge their egocentrism by asking questions such as "How would you feel if someone did that to you?" when they violate others' rights.
- Include them in charitable projects, such as food drives, to extend the idea of love and caring beyond their own families.

Test Yourself before going on

1. Circle each characteristic that is not likely to appear in a description of a peer given by a child younger than 6.
   thin   brown hair   smart   happy   mean   tall
2. Piaget claimed that the ability to use reasoning about intentions to make judgments about the moral dimensions of behaviour appears to emerge along with _____ _____.

Critical Thinking

3. Children's understanding of others' traits and behaviours and their understanding of moral dilemmas advances dramatically after age 8. How does each of these important domains of development support the other?

Social Relationships

School-aged children's growing ability to understand others changes their social relationships in important ways. Children continue to be attached to parents, but they are becoming more independent. Relationships with peers become more stable and many ripen into long-term friendships. In fact, the quality of 6- to 12-year-olds' peer relationships shapes their futures in many important ways.

Relationships with Parents

Learning Objective 10.7

Describe how self-regulation affects school-aged children's relationships with their parents.

Middle childhood is a period of increasing independence of child from family. Yet attachments to parents continue to be important (Bokhorst, Sumter, & Westenberg, 2010). Children who have close, warm relationships with their parents tend to be socially competent with peers (Rispoli, McGoey, Koziol, & Schreiber, 2013). Relationships with siblings add another dimension to the social worlds of 6- to 12-year-olds who have them. What does change, though, is the agenda of issues between parent and child. Parents of 6- to 12-year-olds recognize their children's growing capacity for **self-regulation**, the ability to conform to parental standards of behaviour without direct supervision. As a result, as children get older, parents are more likely to allow them to engage in activities such as bicycle riding and skateboarding without supervision (Soori & Bhopal, 2002). Although, cultures vary to some degree in the specific age at which they expect this to occur, most expect 6- to 12-year-olds to be able to supervise their own behaviour at least part of the time.

self-regulation

children's ability to conform to parental standards of behaviour without direct supervision

Some studies suggest that there are sex differences in parents' expectations with respect to self-regulatory behaviour. For example, mothers make different kinds of demands on boys and girls. They appear to provide both with the same types of guidance but are more likely to give boys more autonomy over their own behaviour than girls. Nevertheless, parents are also more likely to hold daughters to a higher standard of accountability for failure than boys (Pomerantz & Ruble, 1998). Developmentalists speculate that this difference may lead to stronger standards of behaviour for girls in later developmental periods.

PARENTING FOR SELF-REGULATION Researchers have learned that several parenting variables contribute to the development of self-regulation (Vazsonyi & Huang, 2010). First, the parents' own ability to self-regulate is important, perhaps because they are providing the child with models of good or poor self-regulation (Sanders & Mazzucchelli, 2013). Also, the degree of self-regulation expected by parents influences the child's self-regulatory behaviour. Higher expectations, together with parental monitoring to make certain the expectations are met, are associated with greater self-regulatory competence (Rodrigo, Janssens, & Ceballos, 1999).

You should recall that such parental behaviours are associated with the authoritative style of parenting. A study of Canadian mothers and their children was conducted by Rosemary Mills of the University of Manitoba and Kenneth Rubin of the University of Maryland to see if maternal methods of control were related to childhood aggression and social withdrawal. They studied children in kindergarten and Grades 2 and 4 and found that mothers who were behaviourally overcontrolling (i.e., gave more compliance commands, punishment, or criticism, or demonstrated greater devaluation of the child than other parents) had children who were socially withdrawn. In comparison, mothers of aggressive children were generally undercontrolling (i.e., were overly permissive and made fewer requests and were less responsive to a child's behaviour) (Mills & Rubin, 1998).

Research suggests that only children are just as well adjusted as those who have siblings.

Friendships

Learning Objective 10.8

Summarize what changes occur in children's understanding of friendships during this period.

The biggest shift in relationships during middle childhood is the increasing importance of peers, particularly close friends. One frequent manifestation of this trend is the appearance of "best-friend" relationships. Cross-cultural studies show that best-friend relationships, and the belief that having a best friend is important, are universal features of school-aged children's social development (Schraf & Hertz-Lazarowitz, 2003). Consequently, it isn't surprising that half to three-quarters of school-aged children tell researchers that they have at least one best friend and that best friendships in this age group persist for months or even years (McChristian, Ray, Tidwell, & LoBello, 2012). Moreover, best friendships are an important indicator of a child's overall social development and competence. That is, children who have a best friend are more likely than those without a best friend to have positive relationships with most of the children they know and to have larger social networks (McChristian et al., 2012). Additional evidence supporting the view that best friendships are developmentally important in middle childhood comes from studies showing that even children who are shy and socially withdrawn report having at least one best friend (Rubin, Wojslawowica, Rose-Krasnor, Booth-LaForce, & Burgess, 2006).

The emphasis on best friendships in middle childhood probably arises from children's increasing understanding of the nature of friendship. Social-cognitive researcher Robert Selman was one of the first to study children's understanding of friendships. He found that if you ask preschoolers and young school-aged children how people make friends, the answer is usually that they "play together" or spend time physically near each other (Damon, 1977, 1983; Selman, 1980).

In the later years of middle childhood, at around age 10, this view of friendship gives way to one in which the key concept seems to be reciprocal trust (Hartup & Abecassis, 2004). Older children see friends as special people who possess desired qualities other than mere proximity, who are generous with each other, who help and trust each other, and so on. **Figure 10.3** is a 10-year-old boy's definition of a friend. His characterization of a friend as someone "you can trust," who "will always be there for you when you are feeling down in the dumps" and "always sits by you at lunch," illustrates the older child's understanding of dimensions of friendships such as trust, emotional support, and loyalty. Thus, as children move through the middle childhood period, they use judgments of peers' trustworthiness to choose their friends (Rotenberg et al., 2004).

Researchers have examined the relationship between children's understanding of friendship and the quantity and quality of their friendships. In one such study, researchers Amanda Rose and Steven Asher (2004) presented Grade 5 students with hypothetical situations in which one friend might have an opportunity to help another. For instance, in one scenario, the researchers described a child who was teased by her

Figure 10.3 This essay on friendship written by a 10-year-old illustrates the way older school-aged children think about friends.

(Courtesy of Denise Boyd. Used with permission.)

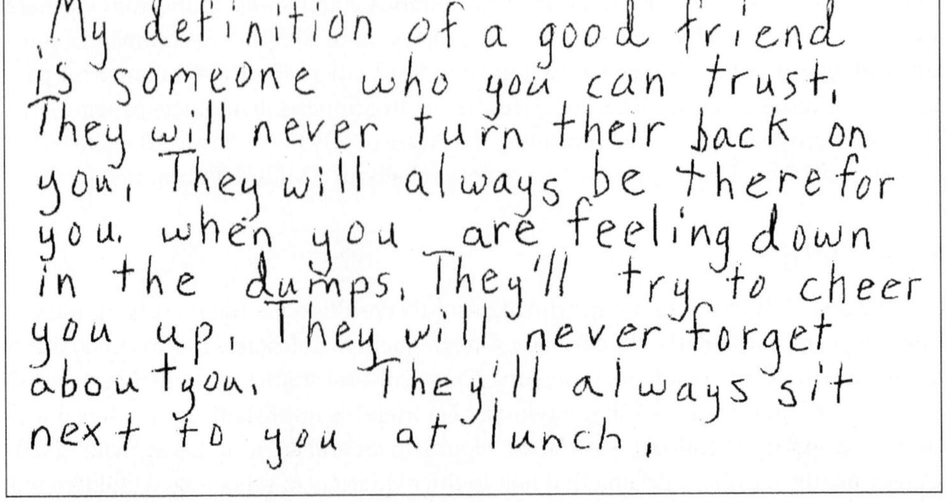
My definition of a good friend is someone who you can trust. They will never turn their back on you. They will always be there for you. when you are feeling down in the dumps. They'll try to cheer you up. They will never forget about you. They'll always sit next to you at lunch.

classmates. Rose and Asher found that children who expressed the view that children should not help others in such situations to avoid putting themselves at risk of being treated similarly by peers had fewer friends than did children who expressed the view that friends should place their relationships above concerns about how their helping behaviour would affect their own social status.

Evidence of the centrality of friends to social development in middle childhood also comes from studies of children's behaviour within friendships. Children are more open and more supportive when with their chums, smiling at, looking at, laughing with, and touching one another more than when they are with nonfriends; they talk more with friends and cooperate and help one another more. Pairs of friends are also more successful than nonfriends are at solving problems or performing some task together. Yet school-aged children are also more critical of friends and have more conflicts with them; they are more polite with strangers (Hartup, 1996). At the same time, when conflicts with friends occur, children are more concerned about resolving them than they are about settling disagreements with nonfriends. Thus, friendship seems to represent an arena in which children can learn how to manage conflicts (Newcomb & Bagwell, 1995).

Critical Thinking

Do you still have any friends from your elementary school years? If not, why do you think those early friendships did not survive? If you do, what do you think differentiates an early friendship that survives from one that does not?

Gender Self-Segregation

Learning Objective 10.9

Summarize the ways boys and girls interact during the middle childhood years.

Possibly the most striking thing about peer group interactions in the elementary school years is how gender-segregated they are. This pattern seems to occur in every culture in the world and is frequently visible in children as young as age 3 or 4. Boys play with boys and girls play with girls, each in their own areas and at their own kinds of games (Cairns & Cairns, 1994). This pattern of preference for same-sex companions appears throughout the lifespan, by the way, although it is far less rigid among adults than among children (Martin & Ruble, 2010; Mehta & Strough, 2009). In fact, gender seems to be more important than age, race, or any other categorical variable in 6- to 12-year-olds' selection of friends; in addition, the strength of children's preference for same-sex associates increases substantially across middle childhood (Graham, Cohen, Zbikowski, & Secrist, 1998). Moreover, gender segregation is unrelated to sex differences in parenting, suggesting that it is a feature of 6- to 12-year-olds' social relationships that they construct for reasons of their own (Martin et al., 2013).

There are some ritualized "boundary violations" between boys' and girls' groups, such as chasing games. For example, in one universal series of interactions, a girl taunts a boy with a statement like "You can't catch me, nyah nyah." Next, a boy chases and catches her, to the delight of both of their fully supportive same-sex peer groups (Thorne, 1986). As soon as the brief cross-gender encounter ends, both girl and boy return to their respective groups. On the whole, however, girls and boys between ages 6 and 12 actively avoid interacting with one another and show strong favouritism toward their own gender and negative stereotyping of the opposite gender (Powlishta, 1995).

Gender segregation patterns are even more pronounced in friendships during middle childhood. For example, when researchers ask children to describe the kind of playmate a fictional child would prefer, school-aged children's predictions are largely gender-based (Halle, 1999). Girls' and boys' friendships also differ in quality in intriguing ways. Boys' friendship groups are larger and more accepting of newcomers than are girls'. Boys play more outdoors and roam over a larger area in their play. Girls are more likely to play in pairs or in small, fairly exclusive groups, and they spend more playtime indoors or near home or school (Benenson, 1994; Gottman, 1986).

Sex differences also characterize the interaction between a pair of friends. Boys' friendships appear to be focused more on competition and dominance than girls' friendships (Ricciardelli & Mellor, 2012). In fact, among school-aged boys, researchers see higher levels of competition between pairs of friends than between strangers—the opposite of what is observed among girls. Friendships between girls include more agreement, more compliance, and more self-disclosure than is true between boys. For

In middle childhood, boys play with boys and girls play with girls. In fact, children's play groups are more sex-segregated at this age than at any other.

(*Photos:* left, Monkey Business Images/Shutterstock; right, Sonya Etchison/Fotolia)

example, "controlling" speech—a category that includes rejecting comments, ordering, manipulating, challenging, defiance, refutation, or resistance of another's attempts to control—is twice as common among pairs of 7- and 8-year-old male friends as among pairs of female friends of that age (Leaper, 1991). Among the 4- and 5-year-olds in Leaper's study, there were no sex differences in controlling speech, suggesting that these differences in interaction patterns arise during middle childhood.

None of this information should obscure the fact that the interactions of male and female friendship pairs have much in common. For example, collaborative and cooperative exchanges are the most common forms of communication in both boys' and girls' friendships in middle childhood. And it is not necessarily the case that boys' friendships are less important to them than girls' are to them. Nevertheless, it seems clear that gender differences, in both form and style, may well have enduring implications for patterns of friendship over the lifespan.

Patterns of Aggression

Learning Objective 10.10

Identify what types of aggression are most common among school-aged children.

Interestingly, results from the Quebec Longitudinal Study of Child Development (QLSCD) found that children whose parents had not used child-care services during their child's preschool years were less physically aggressive upon entry into kindergarten but, within two years, they became as aggressive as their peers. Fortunately, by age 8, levels of physical aggression decline in both groups of children (Pingault et al., 2015).

Although *physical aggression* declines over the elementary school years, *indirect aggression* increases. Research on Canadian children shows that, in middle childhood, physical aggression becomes even less common, as children learn the cultural rules about when displaying anger or aggression is acceptable and how much of a display is acceptable (Brendgen, 2012; Craig, 2004; Pepler et al., 2006; Tremblay, 2000). Boys at every age show more physical aggression and more assertiveness than do girls, both within friendship pairs and in general (Craig, 2004; Tremblay, 2000). Furthermore, school-aged boys often express approval for the aggressive behaviour of peers (Rodkin, Farmer, Pearl, & Van Acker, 2000).

Results like these have been so clear and so consistent that most psychologists have concluded that boys are simply "more aggressive." But that conclusion may turn out to be wrong. Instead, it begins to look as if girls simply express their aggressiveness in a different way, using what has been termed

Why do you think competition is such a strong feature of friendship interactions among boys? Do you think this is true in every culture?

(Photo: Jeanne Provost/Shutterstock)

relational aggression, instead of physical aggression. Physical aggression hurts others physically or poses a threat of such damage; **relational aggression** is aimed at damaging the other person's self-esteem or peer relationships, such as by ostracism or threats of ostracism (e.g., "I won't invite you to my birthday party if you do that."), cruel gossip, or facial expressions of disdain. Children are genuinely hurt by such indirect aggression, and they are likely to shun others who often use this form of aggression (Cillessen & Mayeux, 2004).

relational aggression

aggression aimed at damaging another person's self-esteem or peer relationships, such as by ostracism or threats of ostracism, cruel gossiping, or facial expressions of disdain

Girls are more likely than boys to use relational aggression, especially toward other girls, a difference that begins as early as the preschool years and becomes very marked by fourth or fifth grade (Kawabata, Tseng, Murray-Closse, & Crick, 2013). Some developmentalists suspect that this difference in form of aggression has some hormonal/biological basis (Rhee & Waldman, 2011). Research showing higher rates of physical aggression in males in every human society and in all varieties of primates supports this hypothesis. And scientists know that some link exists between rates of physical aggression and testosterone levels (e.g., Mehta & Beer, 2010). However, cognitive variables contribute to both physical and relational aggression, and the association holds for both boys and girls. Such cognitive variables include the tendency to misjudge others' intentions among children who exhibit more physical and relational aggression than their peers do (Godleski & Ostrov, 2010). Still, gender differences diminish somewhat over time; as boys' cognitive and language skills improve, they rely less on physical aggression and, like girls, resort to using relational aggression (Brendgen, 2012; Card, Stucky, Sawalani, & Little, 2008).

Retaliatory aggression—aggression to get back at someone who has hurt you— increases among both boys and girls during the 6- to 12-year-old period (Astor, 1994). Anger over perceived threats, physical aggression, verbal insults, and the like plays a key role in retaliatory aggression (Hubbard, Romano, McAuliff, & Morrow, 2010). Its development is related to children's growing understanding of the difference between intentional and accidental actions. For example, if a child drops his pencil in the path of another child who is walking by and that child happens to kick the pencil across the floor, most 8-year-olds can identify this action as an accident. Consequently, the child whose pencil was kicked feels no need to get back at the child who did the kicking. However, children over 8 view intentional harm differently. For example, let's say that one child intentionally takes another's pencil off of her desk and throws it across the room. Most children over 8 will try to find a way to get back at a child who does something like this. In fact, children who don't try to retaliate in such situations are also more likely to be seen as socially incompetent and to be bullied by their peers in the future (Astor, 1994), as discussed in the **Research Report**. Quebec Newborn Twin Study (QNTS) data has also shown that when one twin is proactively aggressive, then the other twin is as well, even if the other twin had initially displayed mostly reactive aggression (Dickson et al., 2015).

retaliatory aggression

aggression to get back at someone who has hurt you

Peers may approve of retaliatory aggression, but most parents and teachers strive to teach children that, like other forms of intentional harm, such behaviour is unacceptable. Research suggests that children can learn nonaggressive techniques for managing the kinds of situations that lead to retaliatory aggression. In one international program called PeaceBuilders, early interventions attempt to change individual behaviour by changing a school's overall emotional climate. In the school environment, for example, children, parents, and teachers learn to use positive social and conflict resolution strategies (Flannery et al., 2003)—they are urged to try to praise others more often than they criticize them. Research suggests that when such programs are integrated into students' classes every day for an entire school year or longer, physical and verbal aggression decreases and prosocial behaviour increases. Thus, aggressive interactions between elementary school children may be common, but they do not appear to be an inevitable aspect of development. In Canada's PeaceBuilders (2015) program, interventions also

Research Report

Bullies and Victims

At first glance, aggressive interactions between children might appear to be fairly simple: one child hurts another child. However, Canadian psychologists Wendy Craig of Queen's University (2016 Order of Ontario recipient) and Debra Pepler of York University and their colleagues have found that, in the middle childhood years, aggressive interactions become increasingly complex (Craig, 2004; Pepler et al., 2006). **Bullying** and **victimization** involving physical aggression decline with age in both boys and girls but are replaced with indirect forms of aggression. For example, *sexual harassment*, such as unwanted sexual comments, brushing up against someone in a sexual way, spreading sexual rumours about someone, or calling someone a *faggot* or a *sleaze*, as well as *dating aggression*, such as slapping or kicking a romantic partner, spreading rumours about him, or ignoring or excluding him from the group in anger, emerge in Grades 6 to 8 and peak by Grade 10—in accord with the physical and psychosocial sexual development associated with puberty (Pepler et al., 2006). Nonphysical bullying also becomes more ethnocultural as children age, taking the forms of racial and religious harassment (Craig, 2004).

Electronic media, a primary mode of communication among Canadian youth, has provided a new means of attacking others: *cyberbullying*, which includes such things as sending intentionally abusive text messages and embarrassing photos. The popularity of instant messaging and social network sites such as Facebook have given rise to this new form of aggression (Talwar, Gomez-Garibello, & Shariff, 2014). A Canadian survey of Grade 7 and 8 students found that ~19% of them had been victims of cyberbullying and girls were twice as likely as boys to be victimized (Sampasa-Kanying, Roumeliotis, & Xu, 2014). Canadian researchers found that students pass moral judgement on message content. Situations depicting false stories, an imbalance of power, and an intention to harm were rated as more serious and negative (Talwar et al., 2014). These researchers also found that younger students (i.e., age 12 to 13) were much less able to discriminate between harmless teasing and real online threats. Helping this age cohort distinguish between harmful and harmless *e-posts* is one potential area for intervention.

As children get older, they tend to take on consistent roles across aggressive interactions—perpetrator, victim, assistant to the perpetrator, reinforcing onlooker, nonparticipant onlooker, defender of the victim, and so on (Andreou & Metallidou, 2004). Children's personality traits to some degree determine the roles they assume. For example, shy children usually take the nonparticipant onlooker role, while children who are emotionally unstable are more likely to serve as assistants to the perpetrator or as reinforcing onlookers (Tani, Greenman, Schneider, & Fregoso, 2003). The occupant of each of these roles plays a part in maintaining a particular aggressive incident and in determining whether another aggressive interaction involving the same perpetrator and victim will occur in the future. Sometimes, however, there is an exception to this pattern: in some cases, children who are victimized by others, or who are onlookers, may in turn be drawn into bullying others (Craig, 2004).

Until fairly recently, both research on and interventions aimed at reducing aggression focused on the habitual perpetrators, or "bullies." However, most developmentalists now believe that changing the behaviour of children in the other roles that are a part of aggressive interactions, especially those who are habitual victims, may be just as important as intervening with the aggressive children (Green, 2001). Victims can have certain characteristics in common, including anxiety, passivity, sensitivity, low self-esteem or self-confidence, lack of humour, sadness, and comparative lack of friends (Cuevas, Finkelhor, Clifford, Ormrod, & Turner, 2010; Reijntjes, Kamphuis, Prinzie, & Telch, 2010; Turner, Finkelhor, & Ormrod, 2010).

However, victims also seem to possess characteristics that are less amenable to change and therefore other strategies may be required. In the case of boys, for instance, victims are often physically smaller and/or weaker than their peers (Eslea et al., 2004). As for girls, those with high BMI experience more victimization and those who are victimized risk becoming even more overweight, which invites further victimization (Qualter et al., 2015). Recent results from the QNTS have indicated that certain genetic factors also underlie peer rejection and victimization, for example, hyperactivity, aggression, and impulsiveness. In turn, victimization can foster retaliatory aggression and thereby intensify peer relationship difficulties. Moreover, boys are more likely to be rejected and victimized than girls (Boivin et al., 2013).

Bullying and victimization are complex phenomena that take many forms in boys and girls and at different stages in a child's development. Youths cannot readily solve these behaviours themselves. Teaching victims to be more assertive might seem to be a good way to reduce the prevalence of bullying among school-aged children. However, critics of such programs argue that they send the message that the victim deserves to be bullied. Moreover, by identifying habitual victims and including them in counselling sessions and the like, the adults who are responsible for victim-training programs subject these children to further stigmatization. Thus, critics argue that programs aimed at reducing bullying should focus primarily on the bullies' behaviour and should include the clear message that bullying is wrong, regardless of their victims' behaviour (Temko, 2005). Still, one of the important ways to buffer against continuing victimization is through social support—to have someone to turn to either in person or online. Plus, early intervention and prevention methods involving peers, adults, and schools may be the best first course of action to take (Pepler et al., 2006).

include a community-based *restorative justice approach*. This involves creating a safe and respectful place for having difficult exchanges, taking responsibility, and making amends.

SOCIOECONOMIC STATUS (SES) AND FAMILIAL FACTORS OF AGGRESSION Tremblay et al. (1996) found that there were social class and family differences in rates of aggression in Canadian children. In lower-SES boys, for instance, the incidence of both physical and indirect forms of aggression was higher, appeared at an earlier age (preschool), and persisted throughout childhood. The corresponding rates of aggression were proportionally less in boys who came from families with higher SES. Similarly, it was found that girls in lower-SES families displayed both more physical and indirect aggression than girls from higher-SES families. As well, results from the Concordia Longitudinal Risk Project (CLRP) found that, regardless of SES, childhood aggression is one factor that has been shown to adversely affect upward social mobility in Canada (Véronneau, Serbin, Stack, Ledingham, & Schwartzman, 2015).

In addition to SES, recent results from the CLRP study also found another strong predictor of aggression was negative family influence. Specifically, parents who, when they were young, experienced disadvantaged child-rearing conditions (such as poverty, parental absence, parental mental and physical health problems, aggressive or socially withdrawn mothers, family conflict, and violence) place their offspring at high risk for aggressive behaviour. This pattern of intergenerational transfer of risk for aggression and consequent social disadvantage can be broken through interventions that target and provide economic and social support for high-risk young parents and their children, at home and through child care, school, and community programs (Stack et al., 2015).

Social Status

Developmentalists measure popularity and rejection by asking children to list peers they would not like to play with or by observing which children are sought out or avoided on the playground. These techniques allow researchers to group children according to the degree to which they are accepted by peers—a variable often called **social status**. Typically, researchers find three groups: *popular, rejected,* and *neglected.*

Some of the characteristics that differentiate popular children from those in the other two groups are things outside a child's control. In particular, attractive children and physically larger children are more likely to be popular. Conversely, being very different from her peers may cause a child to be neglected or rejected. For example, shy children usually have few friends (Fordham & Stevenson-Hinde, 1999). Similarly, highly creative children are often rejected, as are those who have difficulty controlling their emotions (Aranha, 1997; Maszk, Eisenberg, & Guthrie, 1999).

However, children's social behaviour seems to be more important than looks or temperament. Most studies show that popular children behave in positive, supporting, nonpunitive, and nonaggressive ways toward most other children. They explain things, take their playmates' wishes into consideration, and take turns in conversation. In addition, popular children are usually good at accurately assessing others' feelings and at regulating their own emotions (Sallquist et al., 2009b). Most are good at looking at situations from others' perspectives as well (Fitzgerald & White, 2003).

There are two types of rejected children. *Withdrawn/rejected* children realize that they are disliked by peers (Harrist, Zaia, Bates, Dodge, & Pettit, 1997). After repeated attempts to gain peer acceptance, these children eventually give up and become socially withdrawn. As a result, they often experience feelings of

Learning Objective 10.11
Describe how popular, rejected, and neglected children differ.

social status
an individual child's classification as popular, rejected, or neglected

bullying
the unjust use of power to wilfully, deliberately, and repeatedly upset or hurt another person, their property, reputation, or social acceptance

victimization
repeated, intentional acts that single someone out for hostile, exploitive, unfair, or vindictive treatment

loneliness. *Aggressive/rejected* children are often disruptive and uncooperative and usually believe that their peers like them (Lansford et al., 2006; Zakriski & Coie, 1996). Many appear to be unable to control the expression of strong feelings (Sallquist et al., 2009b). They interrupt their play partners more often and fail to take turns in a systematic way.

As you learned in the chapter on Social and Personality Development in Early Childhood, aggressive behaviour persists into adulthood in some individuals, and it is most likely to become a stable characteristic among children who are *both* aggressive and rejected by peers. Of course, not all aggressive children are rejected. Among girls, aggression, whether physical or relational, seems to lead to peer rejection consistently. Among boys, however, aggression may result in either popularity or rejection (Rodkin et al., 2000; Xie, Cairns, & Cairns, 1999). For instance, Université Laval psychologists François Poulin and Michel Boivin have studied the role of aggression in the formation and development of boys' friendships in Grades 4 through 6. They found that, irrespective of aggressive boys' general popularity, their close friends tend to be aggressive as well. Furthermore, aggressiveness seems to precede these relationships. In other words, boys who are aggressive seek out boys like themselves as friends, and being friends doesn't seem to make either member of the pair more aggressive (Poulin & Boivin, 2000). Research also suggests that children have more positive attitudes toward aggressive peers whose aggressive acts are seen as mostly retaliatory and toward those who engage in both prosocial and aggressive behaviour (Coie & Cillessen, 1993; Newcomb, Bukowski, & Pattee, 1993; Poulin & Boivin, 1999). Social approval may not increase aggressiveness, but it does seem to help maintain it; interventions to reduce aggressive behaviour typically have little effect on aggressive boys who are popular (Phillips, Schwean, & Saklofske, 1997).

Neglect, when a child is ignored or excluded by his peers, seems to be much less stable over time than rejection; neglected children sometimes move to the popular category when they become part of a new peer group. However, children who experience prolonged neglect are more prone to depression and loneliness than are popular children (Cillessen, van IJzendoorn, van Lieshout, & Hartup, 1992;

Test Yourself before going on

1. Briefly describe how each factor in the table contributes to self-regulation.

Factor	Contribution to self-regulation
Culture	
Gender	
Parenting style	

2. Classify each social behaviour as more typical of (G) girls or (B) boys.
   _____ (a) play more outdoors and roam over a larger area
   _____ (b) play more indoors or near home or school
   _____ (c) interact more in groups rather than in pairs
   _____ (d) more welcoming of newcomers into friendship groups
   _____ (e) interact in pairs or small groups more often than in large groups

3. Which of the following is a boundary violation of children's informal gender-segregation rules?
   (a) A teacher creates mixed-gender groups for a science lesson.
   (b) A boy takes a girl's "Barbie" lunch box, runs away with it to make her chase him, and then gives it back to her.
   (c) Girls play together because they tend to enjoy the same activities.

Critical Thinking

4. If you had to explain an important developmental outcome, such as variations in optimism among adults, as a function of childhood social experiences, what percentage of influence would you assign to each of these factors: relationships with parents, friendships, experiences with gender segregation, experiences with aggression, and social status?

Wentzel & Asher, 1995). The association between peer neglect and depression may be explained by recent brain-imaging studies showing that, among school-aged children, social exclusion stimulates the same area of the brain as physical pain does (Eisenberger, 2003). In addition, this tendency toward depression among neglected children may be fostered by unrealistic expectations about adults' ability to "fix" the social situation—for example, "Why doesn't the teacher make them be my friends?" (Galanaki, 2004).

Influences Beyond Family and Peers

The daily life of the school-aged child is shaped by more than the hours she spends in school. The circumstances in which a child lives also affect her. For example, some parents are at home when children come home from school; others are still at work. A child is also affected by her family's economic circumstances, by the neighbourhood she lives in, and by the media to which she is exposed.

After-School Care

In Canada, many children are at home by themselves after school for an hour or more each weekday. They are often referred to as **self-care children**. Self-care arrangements differ so much from child to child that it is impossible to say whether, as a group, self-care children differ from others. For example, some self-care children are home alone but are closely monitored by neighbours or relatives, while others are completely without supervision of any kind. Developmentalists have learned that the effects of self-care on a child's development depend on behavioural history, maturity, age, gender, the kind of neighbourhood the child lives in, how well parents monitor the child during self-care periods, and the duration and frequency of unsupervised care (Casper & Smith, 2002; Canada Safety Council, 2015; Ruiz-Casares & Radic, 2015).

From a developmental perspective, children younger than age 10 do not have the cognitive abilities necessary to evaluate risks and deal with emergencies. Children who start self-care in the early elementary years are more likely to have adjustment difficulties in school and are vulnerable to older self-care children in their neighbourhoods who may hurt or even sexually abuse them (Pettit, Laird, Bates, & Dodge, 1997). The negative effects of self-care are greatest for children in low-income neighbourhoods with high crime rates (Marshall et al., 1997). Self-care children in such areas may use after-school time to "hang out" with socially deviant peers and older children who are involved in criminal activity or who have negative attitudes about school. Predictably, then, the positive effects of organized, high-quality after-school programs on academic achievement are greater for children in low-income neighbourhoods (Mason & Chuang, 2001).

Children older than age 10 may be cognitively able to manage self-care, but they, too, benefit from participation in well-supervised after-school programs. Even part-time participation in supervised activities after school seems to make a difference in the adjustment of self-care children (Pettit et al., 1997). Good programs provide children with opportunities to play, participate in sports, do

Learning Objective 10.12

Describe how self-care affects girls' and boys' development.

self-care children

children who are at home by themselves after school for an hour or more each day

(*Photo: GeoStock/Photodisc/Getty Images*)

Many Canadian children are at home by themselves after school for an hour or more each weekday.

In North America, children between ages 6 and 12 spend more time watching television than they do playing.

Learning Objective 10.13

Identify the influences television has on children's development.

homework, and get help from adults (Clark, Harris, White-Smith, Allen, & Ray, 2010; Shernoff & Vandell, 2007).

When everything is taken into consideration, the most important factor in self-care seems to be parental monitoring. Many parents, particularly single mothers, enlist the help of neighbours and relatives to keep an eye on their self-care children (Brandon & Hofferth, 2003). Most require children to call them at work when they get home from school to talk about their school day and get instructions about homework and chores. For example, a working mother might tell a fifth-grader, "By the time I get home at 5:00, you should be finished with your math and spelling. Don't work on your history project until I get home and can help you with it. As soon as you finish your math and spelling, start the dishwasher." Research suggests that children whose periods of self-care are monitored in this way are less likely to experience the potential negative effects of self-care (Galambos & Maggs, 1991). Before allowing their child to look after himself or other children, parents can find out what to consider by contacting the Canada Safety Council or St. John Ambulance Home Alone Programs, or the Canadian Red Cross, or other community agencies that offer babysitting training courses for youth.

Media Influences

Another prominent feature of children's environment today is the wide array of informational and entertainment media. Televisions, computers, and video games are found in the majority of homes in the developed world. For Canadian children in Grades 6, 7, and 8, ~62% of boys and ~57% of girls watch an average of two or more hours of television per day. On top of this, more than half of boys and one-quarter of girls spend an average of more than two hours per day playing video games, and by Grade 8, more than half of girls are averaging more than two hours per day on the computer for leisure compared to ~39% of boys (Freeman et al., 2012). For Canadian children, this adds up to an average of more than seven hours per day in front of a screen (ParticipACTION, 2015).

TELEVISION   Nearly every Canadian home has at least one TV set, in addition to internet, smartphones, tablets, and so on. This provides children with access to hundreds of cable, satellite, and internet channels and exposure to a wide variety, and wide quality, of TV programming (Television Bureau of Canada, 2015). Canadian children between ages 2 and 11 spend an average of ~21 hours a week watching television (ThinkTV, 2016). This means television still has a major impact on our children (Mark, Boyce, & Janssen, 2006).

POSITIVE EDUCATIONAL EFFECTS   TV programs specifically designed to be educational and/or to teach children social values do indeed have demonstrable positive effects (Linebarger & Wainwright, 2006). For example, children who regularly watched quality educational programs, such as *Sesame Street*, *Dora the Explorer*, or *Blue's Clues*, developed better early literacy and math skills than did children who did not watch or who watched less often (Ennemoser & Schneider, 2007; Linebarger & Walker, 2005). In fact, one follow-up study, of adolescents whose TV-viewing patterns had been tracked when they were preschoolers, found that those who watched more quality educational programs than entertainment-types of TV programming were less aggressive, had higher grades, read more books, and were more achievement oriented and creative (Anderson, Huston, Schmitt, Linebarger, & Wright, 2001). These studies suggest that the TV content viewed is more important than the raw amount watched.

In addition, children can have learning experiences through TV viewing—such as witnessing the receding Arctic glaciers—that they would not likely have otherwise. As you learned in the chapter on Physical and Cognitive Development in Middle Childhood, the advances in information-processing skills that children undergo between ages 6 and 12 enable them to remember more from such viewing experiences. Moreover, previously acquired knowledge is important to each new learning experience; television can be an important means by which school-aged children acquire experiences that can make them more efficient learners at school. For example, a child who has seen a TV program about retreating glaciers is likely to get more out of a school science lesson about global warming than a student who has no relevant knowledge.

NEGATIVE EFFECTS OF TELEVISION ON COGNITIVE SKILLS   Despite the potential positive effects of watching quality educational television on cognitive development, research has demonstrated that heavy TV viewing is associated with lower scores on achievement tests, including measures of such basic skills as reading, arithmetic, and writing. For example, one study of Grade 3 students found a significant relationship between the type and placement of household media and academic achievement; those students who had no computer in the home but had a television in their bedroom watched more hours of television per week and had the worst test scores on mathematics, reading, and language arts. In contrast, children who had home computer access and use but no bedroom television watched fewer hours of television per week and had the highest achievement test scores (Borzekowski & Robinson, 2005). In a New Zealand longitudinal study, the researchers found that the more hours of television students watched during childhood and adolescence, the lower their academic qualifications achieved by age 26 (Hancox, Milne, & Poulton, 2005). Thus, television can help teach children things they do not already know, but overall, TV-viewing time appears to have a negative effect on school performance, especially television of low educational quality.

TELEVISION AND AGGRESSION   Bandura demonstrated the effects of televised violence on children's behaviour in his classic "Bobo doll" studies (Bandura, Ross, & Ross, 1961, 1963). In these experiments, children were found to imitate adults' violent treatment of an inflatable clown that was depicted on film. Furthermore, it appears that such effects persist into the adult years, whereby individuals who watched the greatest number of violent television programs in childhood were the most likely to engage in actual acts of violence as young adults (Huesmann, Moise-Titus, Podolski, & Eron, 2003). Moreover, results from the QLSCD show that viewing violent television in early childhood was associated with a range of negative socioemotional and academic outcomes by Grade 2, including antisocial behaviour, emotional distress, inattention, and lower academic achievement (Fitzpatrick, Barnett, & Pagani, 2012). Brain-imaging studies suggest that these long-term effects may be the result of patterns of neural activation that underlie emotionally laden behavioural scripts that children learn while watching violent programming (Murray et al., 2006). These patterns of neural activation may also explain the finding that repeated viewing of TV violence leads to a reduction in prosocial behaviour and to long-term aggressive biases, such as emotional desensitization regarding violence, a belief that aggression is a good way to solve problems, and a greater readiness to act aggressively (Bushman, Chandler, & Huesmann, 2010; Ostrov, Gentile, & Crick, 2006).

For parents, the clear message from all the research on television is that television is an "educational" medium: children learn from what they watch—vocabulary words, helpful behaviours, dietary preferences, as well as aggressive behaviours and attitudes. The overall content of television—violence and all—may indeed reflect general cultural values, but parents can pick and choose among the various cultural messages by controlling what their children watch on television and other forms of screen media.

Test Yourself before going on

1. List four factors that influence the effectiveness of after-school self-care:

   (a) _____

   (b) _____

   (c) _____

   (d) _____

2. Which statement below about television viewing is false?

   (a) Heavy TV viewing is linked to lower scores on achievement tests, such as reading, arithmetic, and writing.

   (b) Quality educational TV programs have positive effects on learning.

   (c) The effects of viewing violence have no lasting impact.

   (d) Viewing aggressive behaviour may increase aggressiveness.

Summary

Theories of Social and Personality Development

10.1 Describe how psychoanalytic theorists characterized the middle childhood years.

- Both Freud and Erikson agreed that peer relationships and associated emotions play a key role in middle childhood. Erikson theorized that 6- to 12-year-olds acquire a sense of industry by achieving educational goals determined by their cultures.

10.2 Summarize the main ideas of trait and social-cognitive theorists.

- Trait theories propose that people possess stable characteristics that emerge during middle childhood as experiences modify the dimensions of temperament. Social-cognitive theories, such as Bandura's reciprocal determinism, argue that traits, and the emotional aspects of personality that were emphasized by psychoanalytic theories, represent one of three interaction sets of factors that shape personality: personal factors, environmental factors, and behavioural factors.

Self-Concept

10.3 Identify the features of the psychological self.

- Between ages 6 and 12, children construct a psychological self. As a result, their self-descriptions begin to include personality traits, such as intelligence and friendliness, along with physical characteristics.

10.4 Describe the role that self-esteem and meaningfulness have on the valued self.

- Self-esteem appears to be shaped by two factors: the degree of discrepancy a child experiences between goals and achievements, and the degree of perceived social support from peers and parents. Having a strong sense of meaningfulness helps prepare children for the challenges they will face in adolescence.

Advances in Social Cognition

10.5 Describe how children's understanding of others changes in middle childhood.

- Between ages 6 and 12, children's understanding of others' stable, internal traits improves.

10.6 Describe how children in Piaget's moral realism and moral relativism stages reason about right and wrong.

- Piaget claimed that moral reasoning develops in sequential stages that are correlated with his cognitive-developmental stages. Children in the moral realism stage believe that authority figures establish rules that must be followed, under threat of punishment. Children in the moral relativism stage understand that rules can be changed through social agreement. Their moral judgment is coloured more by intentions than by consequences.

Social Relationships

10.7 Describe how self-regulation affects school-aged children's relationships with their parents.

- Relationships with parents become less overtly affectionate, with fewer attachment behaviours, in middle childhood. The strength of the attachment, however, appears to persist.

10.8 Summarize what changes occur in children's understanding of friendships during this period.

- Friendships become stable in middle childhood. Children's selection of friends depends on variables such as trustworthiness as well as overt characteristics such as play preferences and gender.

10.9 Summarize the ways boys and girls interact during the middle childhood years.

- Gender segregation of peer groups is at its peak in middle childhood and appears in every culture. Individual friendships also become more common and more enduring; boys' and girls' friendships appear to differ in specific ways.

10.10 Identify what types of aggression are most common among school-aged children.

- Physical aggression declines during middle childhood, although verbal aggression increases. Boys show markedly higher levels of physical and direct verbal aggression, and higher rates of conduct disorders, than girls. Girls show higher rates of relational aggression.

10.11 Describe how popular, rejected, and neglected children differ.

- Rejected children are most strongly characterized by high levels of aggression or bullying and low levels of agreeableness and helpfulness, but some aggressive children are very popular.

Influences Beyond Family and Peers

10.12 Describe how self-care affects girls' and boys' development.

- Self-care outcomes are associated with factors such as the child's age, maturity, gender, neighbourhood, and parental monitoring. Children who live in safe neighbourhoods, and children whose parents closely monitor their activities after school are the least likely to be negatively affected by self-care.

10.13 Identify the influences television has on children's development.

- Preschoolers can learn vocabulary, prosocial behaviour, and other social skills from moderated viewing of quality educational television. The more television school-aged children watch, the lower their grades are. Experts agree that watching violence on television increases the level of personal aggression or violence shown by a child.

Chapter 11
Physical and Cognitive Development in Adolescence

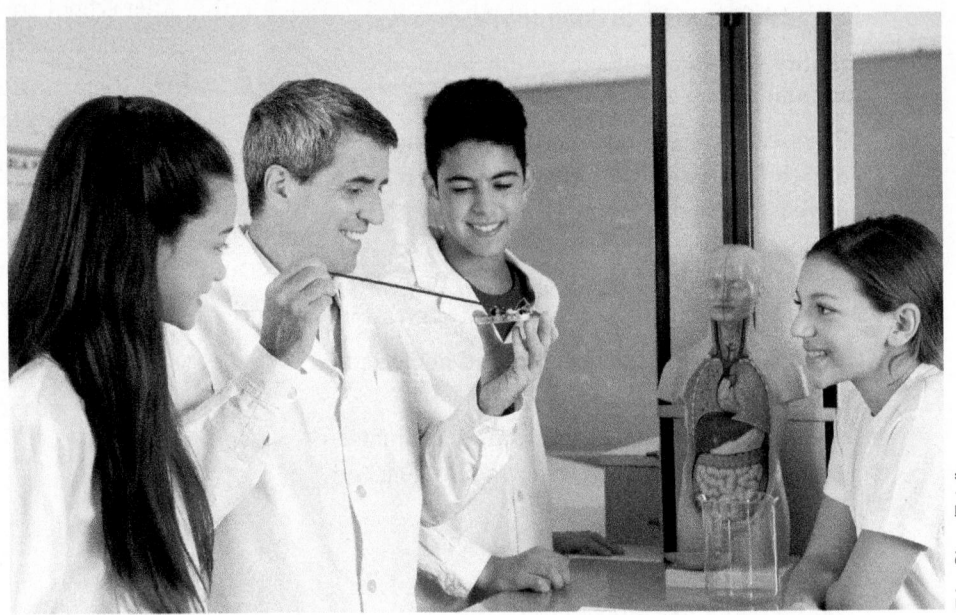

Tyler Olson/Fotolia

 Learning Objectives

PHYSICAL CHANGES

11.1 Identify the major milestones of puberty.

11.2 Discuss how the brains and other body systems of adolescents differ from those of younger children.

ADOLESCENT SEXUALITY

11.3 Identify the issues involved with the sexual behaviour of adolescents.

11.4 Summarize the issues involved in teenaged pregnancy.

11.5 Discuss the emergence of sexual orientation and gender identity in adolescence.

ADOLESCENT HEALTH

11.6   Describe how sensation-seeking affects risky behaviour in adolescents.

11.7   Identify the patterns of drug, alcohol, and tobacco use among adolescents in Canada.

11.8   Describe the characteristics and factors that contribute to eating disorders.

11.9   Identify what factors are involved in adolescent depression and suicide.

CHANGES IN THINKING AND MEMORY

11.10   Describe the characteristics of thought in Piaget's formal operational stage.

11.11   Summarize some major research findings regarding the formal operational stage.

11.12   Describe what kinds of advances in information-processing capabilities occur during adolescence.

SCHOOLING

11.13   Describe how changes in students' goals contribute to the transition to secondary school.

11.14   Identify the gender differences in academic achievement among Canadian adolescents.

11.15   Identify what variables predict the likelihood of dropping out of secondary school.

11.16   Discuss the issues around employed teenagers.

Do you remember making elaborate plans when you were a teenager, plans that usually didn't work out quite the way you thought they would? Perhaps you planned to go to an out-of-town concert with friends, only to find out that the parents of the one licensed driver in your group wouldn't allow her to go. Or you may have mapped out a cross-country motorcycle trip with your best friend, even though neither of you owned nor knew how to operate a motorcycle. Perhaps one of your friends and his romantic partner planned to marry immediately after graduation with little thought about how they would support themselves.

Such actions arise from a new form of thinking that is characteristic of **adolescence**, the transitional period between childhood and adulthood. The powerful intellectual tools that emerge in the early teens allow adolescents to make plans and to mentally project themselves into those plans as a way of testing them. The process is somewhat akin to that of a scientist who formulates a hypothesis and devises an experiment to test it. Armed with this new way of thinking, young adolescents embark upon a period of development characterized by risks and opportunities that compete for their attention. Some of their choices are good ones, but others reflect poor judgment. Most of teenagers' poor choices turn out to have little long-term effect, but others can significantly alter the developmental trajectory of an adolescent's life. How these risks and opportunities are manifested in the physical and cognitive domains is the topic of this chapter.

adolescence

the transitional period between childhood and adulthood

Physical Changes

When we think of the physical changes of adolescence, we usually give the greatest amount of attention to the reproductive system. Reproductive changes are important, as the text will point out. But momentous changes occur in other systems, and we will discuss those as well.

Milestones of Puberty

Learning Objective 11.1

Identify the major milestones of puberty.

puberty

collective term for the physical changes that culminate in sexual maturity

pituitary gland

gland that triggers other glands to release hormones

The growth and development of teenagers' brains and bodies is remarkable. The physical change that most people associate with adolescence is the attainment of sexual maturity. **Puberty** is a collective term that encompasses all the changes, both seen and unseen, that are needed for reproductive maturity. It begins when the **pituitary gland**, the gland that controls all the body's other glands, signals a child's adrenal gland to step up its production of androgen (see **Table 11.1**). This milestone is called *adrenarche* and occurs around age 7 or 8. Next, the pituitary begins secreting hormones that stimulate the growth of the ovaries in girls and the testes in boys. As they grow, these glands secrete hormones that cause the sex organs to develop—testosterone in boys and a form of estrogen called *estradiol* in girls.

The pituitary also secretes two other hormones: *thyroid stimulating hormone* and *general growth hormone*; these, along with adrenal androgen, interact with the specific sex hormones and affect growth. Adrenal androgen, which is chemically very similar to testosterone, plays a particularly important role for girls, triggering the growth spurt and affecting development of pubic hair. For boys, adrenal androgen is less significant, presumably because boys already have so much male hormone in the form of testosterone in their bloodstreams. These hormonal changes trigger two sets of body changes: development of the sex organs and a much broader set of changes in the brain, bones, muscles, and other body organs.

The most obvious changes of puberty are those associated with sexual maturity. Changes in **primary sex characteristics** include growth of the testes and penis in the male and of the ovaries, uterus, and vagina in the female. Changes in **secondary sex characteristics** include breast development in girls, voice pitch changes and beard growth in boys, and body hair growth in both sexes. These physical developments occur in a defined sequence that is customarily divided into five stages, following a system originally suggested by J.M. Tanner (1990), examples from which are shown in **Table 11.2**.

primary sex characteristics

the sex organs: ovaries, uterus, and vagina in the female; testes and penis in the male

secondary sex characteristics

body parts such as breasts in females and pubic hair in both sexes

SEXUAL DEVELOPMENT IN GIRLS Studies of preteens and teens in both Europe and North America show that the various sequential changes are interlocked in a particular pattern in girls. The first steps are the early changes in breasts and pubic hair,

Table 11.1 Major Hormones That Contribute to Physical Growth and Development

Gland	Hormone(s)	Aspects of Growth Influenced
Thyroid gland	Thyroxine	Normal brain development and overall rate of growth
Adrenal gland	Adrenal androgen	Some changes at puberty, particularly the development of secondary sex characteristics in girls
Testes (boys)	Testosterone	Crucial in the formation of male genitals prenatally; also triggers the sequence of changes in primary and secondary sex characteristics in the male
Ovaries (girls)	Estrogen (estradiol)	Development of the menstrual cycle and breasts in girls; has less to do with other secondary sex characteristics than testosterone does for boys
Pituitary gland	General growth hormone, thyroid stimulating hormone, and other activating hormones	Rate of physical maturation; signals other glands to secrete hormones

Table 11.2 Examples of Tanner's Stages of Pubertal Development

Stage	Female Breast Development	Male Genital Development
1	No change except for some elevation of the nipple.	Testes, scrotum, and penis are all about the same size and shape as in early childhood.
2	Breast bud stage: elevation of breast and the nipple as a small mound. Areolar diameter increases compared with stage 1.	Scrotum and testes are slightly enlarged. Skin of the scrotum reddens and changes texture, but little or no enlargement of the penis.
3	Breast and areola both enlarge and elevate more than in stage 2, but no separation of their contours.	Penis slightly enlarged, at first mainly in length. Testes and scrotum are further enlarged. First ejaculation.
4	Areola and nipple form a secondary mound projecting above the contour of the breast.	Penis further enlarged, with growth in breadth and development of glans. Testes and scrotum further enlarged, and scrotum skin still darker.
5	Mature stage. Only the nipple projects, with the areola recessed to the general contour of the breast.	Genitalia achieve adult size and shape.

(**SOURCE:** Based on Handbook of adolescent psychology, Wiley, 1980.)

closely followed by the peak of the growth spurt and by the development of breasts and pubic hair. First menstruation, an event called **menarche** (pronounced men-AR-kee), typically occurs two years after the beginning of other visible changes and is succeeded only by the final stages of breast and pubic hair development (Blake & Davis, 2015). Among girls in Canada today, menarche occurs, on average, at age ~12.7 (Al-Sahab, Ardern, Hamadeh, & Tamim, 2010, 2012).

It is possible to become pregnant shortly after menarche, but irregular menstrual cycles are the norm for some time. In as many as three-quarters of the cycles in the first year and in one-half of the cycles in the second and third years after menarche, the girl's body produces no ovum (Adelman & Ellen, 2002; Blake & Davis, 2015). Full adult fertility thus develops over a period of years. Such irregularity no doubt contributes to the widespread (but false) assumption among younger teenaged girls that they cannot get pregnant.

SECULAR TREND Interestingly, the timing of menarche changed rather dramatically between the mid-19th and the mid-20th centuries. In 1840, the average age of menarche in Western developed countries was roughly 17; the average dropped steadily from that time until the 1950s at a rate of about four months per decade among European populations, an example of what psychologists call a **secular trend** (Bagga & Kulkarni, 2000; Roche, 1979). The change is most likely caused by significant changes in lifestyle and diet, particularly increases in protein and fat intake, along with reductions in physical exercise that resulted in an increase in the proportion of body fat in females.

Data collected over much shorter periods of time in developing countries support the nutritional explanation of the secular trend. In one study, researchers found that the average age of menarche was 16 among North Korean girls who lived in squalid refugee camps (Ku et al., 2006). By contrast, studies involving impoverished groups in which food supplies suddenly increase reveal that the age of menarche can plummet from 16 to 13 within just a few years after improvements in nutrition are experienced (Khanna & Kapoor, 2004). Consequently, any change in eating patterns that affects girls' body fat, which must reach a critical value of 17% before menarche can occur, is likely to lead to a change in the age of menarche (Adelman & Ellen, 2002).

The average ages at which girls show secondary sex characteristics, such as the appearance of breast buds and pubic hair, have also dropped significantly in recent decades (Rosenfield, Lipton, & Drum, 2009). On average, girls now show these signs one to two years earlier than their mothers and grandmothers did, resulting in a lengthening of the average time between the appearance of secondary sex

menarche

the beginning of the menstrual cycle

secular trend

the decline in the average age of menarche, along with changes such as an increase in average height for both children and adults, that happened between the mid-19th and mid-20th centuries in Western countries and occurs in developing nations when nutrition and health improve

characteristics and menarche (Parent et al., 2003). Researchers have found that this trend is attributable to the increased prevalence of overweight children that you read about in the chapter on Physical and Cognitive Development in Middle Childhood (Rosenfield, Lipton, & Drum, 2009). Thus, a girl younger than 7 who exhibits these signs may be diagnosed with *precocious puberty*, a diagnosis that requires follow-up to determine whether a tumour, hormonal disorder, or other condition or disease is responsible (Kaplowitz, 2013).

Being overweight is both a cause and a consequence of early secondary sex characteristic development, because the hormonal changes that trigger the appearance of these characteristics also signal the body's weight regulation mechanisms to increase fat stores (Jasik & Lustig, 2008). Little is known about how these early hormonal shifts affect girls' later health. Several studies are underway to determine whether overweight girls who exhibit early secondary sex characteristic development are at increased risk for breast cancer, adult obesity, and heart disease (National Cancer Institute, 2006). To date these studies have produced mixed results, so researchers are still unsure whether a long-term health risk is entailed (Kaplowitz, 2010).

SEXUAL DEVELOPMENT IN BOYS   In boys, as in girls, the peak of the growth spurt typically comes fairly late in the sequence of physical development. Studies suggest that, on average, a boy completes stages 2, 3, and 4 of genital development and stages 2 and 3 of pubic hair development before reaching the peak of the growth spurt (Blake & Davis, 2011). His first ejaculation, or *spermarche*, occurs between age 13 and 14, but the production of viable sperm does not happen until a few months after the first ejaculation. Most boys do not attain adult levels of sperm production until stage 5 of genital development. The development of a beard and the lowering of the voice occur near the end of the sequence. Precisely when in this sequence the boy begins to produce viable sperm is very difficult to determine, although current evidence places this event some time between ages 12 and 14, usually before the boy has reached the peak of the growth spurt (Adelman & Ellen, 2002).

TIMING OF PUBERTY   Although the order of physical developments in adolescence seems to be highly consistent, there is quite a lot of individual variability. In any random sample of 12- and 13-year-olds, you will find some who are already at stage 5 and others still at stage 1 in the steps of sexual maturation. We have already discussed the contribution of diet, exercise, and body fat to the timing of puberty. Researchers think that hereditary and behavioural factors also contribute to hormonal secretions in the bodies of individual teenagers, thereby controlling the timing of puberty (Dorn, Susman, & Ponirakis, 2003). Discrepancies between an adolescent's expectation and what actually happens determine the psychological effect of puberty. Those whose development occurs outside the desired or expected range are likely to think less well of themselves, to be less happy with their bodies and with the process of puberty. They may also display other signs of psychological distress.

A Canadian study based on NLSCY data determined that girls who are early developers (i.e., experience major body changes before age 10 or

(Photo: racorn /Shutterstock)

Adolescent girls reach adult height sooner than boys because their bones grow and their joints develop more rapidly.

11) showed no problems with self-esteem or academics, and they had fewer behavioural problems than other girls their age (Japal, Tremblay, McDuff, & Willms, 2002). Although early-maturing girls didn't smoke, drink alcohol, or do drugs any

more or less than other girls their age, they did tend to belong to groups of older peers who displayed antisocial behaviours and who smoked, drank alcohol, and did drugs. Associating with older youths who get into trouble may set these early maturing girls up for sexual and school problems later on. Among boys, those who are slightly ahead of their peers in pubertal development exhibit more prosocial behaviour and often occupy leadership roles and are more academically and economically successful in adulthood (Carlo, Crockett, Wolff, & Beal, 2012; Taga, Markey, & Friedman, 2006).

Other Body Systems

For most individuals, adolescence is one of the healthiest periods of life and the changes in other body systems allow adolescents to acquire new cognitive and motor skills (Ernst & Hardin, 2010).

Learning Objective 11.2

Discuss how the brains and other body systems of adolescents differ from those of younger children.

THE BRAIN Although a 6-year-old's brain is approximately 95% of its adult size, many significant anatomical changes continue to unfold in the brain up to adulthood (Lenroot & Giedd, 2006). As you may recall from earlier chapters, postnatal brain development occurs in two basic ways: There are growth spurts that entail *synaptogenesis* (the overproduction of neural branches and connections) followed by synaptic *pruning* (which follows the "use it or lose it" principle whereby neural connections that are not used will wither and die). Evidence to support this comes from brain imaging studies of Mz and Dz twins, which indicate an increasing environmental influence on *grey matter* (GM) volumes in response to *plastic* synapses changing in response to activity (Wallace et al., 2006). The changes in GM are thought to reflect changes in the size and complexity of neurons, not a change in actual number. Accordingly, during adolescence, we observe some dramatic changes in GM volume. The brain's volume of GM follows an inverted U-shaped trajectory from early childhood to early adulthood with peak volumes being reached in different brain regions at different times—and, generally, later in boys than girls (Giedd, 2004; Lenroot & Giedd, 2006; Lenroot et al., 2007). The decreasing amount of GM during early adulthood may reflect the process of pruning. Among the last brain regions to reach adult levels are areas within the frontal cortex that are linked to the control of impulses, judgment, and decision making, which raises concerns about adolescents' degree of responsibility for their actions (Lenroot & Giedd, 2006).

In comparison, the trajectory of volume of *white matter* (WM; myelinated axons that speed up neural processing) steadily increases in the four major lobes of the brain (frontal, temporal, parietal, and occipital)—a developmental pattern that is associated with the cognitive, behavioural, and emotional differences between children and adults (Giedd, 2004; Lenroot & Giedd, 2006). Two other important increases in WM volume take place in areas that are associated with developmental changes during the adolescent years—the corpus callosum (which integrates the activities of the left and right sides of the brain) and the pathways connecting speech reception (Wernicke's area) with speech production (Broca's area). You will find out more about how the brain develops into adulthood in the **Research Report** in the chapter on Physical and Cognitive Development in Early Adulthood.

THE SKELETAL SYSTEM An adolescent may grow 5 to 13 centimetres a year for several years. After the growth spurt, teenagers add height and weight slowly until they reach their adult size. Girls attain most of their height by age 16, while boys continue to grow until they are 18 to 20 years old (Tanner, 1990).

The shape and proportions of the adolescent's body also go through a series of changes. During the growth spurt, the normal *cephalocaudal* and *proximodistal* patterns are reversed. Thus, a teenager's hands and feet are the first body parts to grow to full adult size, followed by the arms and the legs; the trunk is usually the slowest part to grow. In fact, a good signal for a parent that a child is entering puberty is a rapid increase in the child's shoe size. Because of this asymmetry in the body parts, adolescents are often stereotyped as awkward or uncoordinated. Although they may look awkward, they are better coordinated than school-aged children (Gabbard, 2012).

The skeletal system goes through other changes as it increases in size. For example, during the elementary-school years, the size and shape of a child's jaw change when the permanent teeth come in. In adolescence, both jaws grow forward and the forehead becomes more prominent. This set of changes often gives teenagers' faces (especially boys') an angular, bony appearance.

Joint development enables adolescents to achieve levels of coordination that are close to those of adults. As they do at younger ages, boys continue to lag behind girls. You may remember from earlier chapters that boys' fine motor skills are poorer than girls' because their wrists develop more slowly. In early adolescence, this sex difference is very large; girls achieve complete development of the wrist by their mid-teens (Tanner, 1990). A similar pattern of sex differences is evident in other joints as well, enabling early-adolescent girls to outperform boys of the same age on a variety of athletic skills that require coordination, such as pitching a softball. However, by the late teens, at age 17 or 18, boys finally catch up with girls in joint development and, on average, gain superiority over them in coordinated movement.

THE MUSCULAR SYSTEM Muscle fibres also go through a growth spurt at adolescence, becoming thicker and denser, and adolescents become quite a lot stronger in just a few years. Both boys and girls show this increase in strength, but it is much greater in boys (Buchanan & Vardaxis, 2003). For those adolescents of healthy body weight during and after puberty, the proportion of fat rises among girls and declines among boys, while the proportion of weight that is muscle rises in boys and declines in girls as they continue to mature. This sex difference in muscle mass (and accompanying strength) seems to be largely a result of hormone differences. But sex differences in exercise patterns or activities may also be involved.

THE HEART AND LUNGS During the teenaged years, the heart and lungs increase considerably in size, and the heart rate drops. Both of these changes are more marked in boys than in girls—another of the factors that make boys' capacity for sustained physical effort greater than that of girls. Before about age 12, boys and girls have similar endurance limits, although even at these earlier ages, when there is a difference, it is usually boys who have greater endurance because of their lower levels of body fat. After puberty, boys have a clear advantage in endurance, as well as in size, strength, and speed (Klomsten, Skaalvik, & Espnes, 2004).

BODY WEIGHT AND FITNESS Becoming overweight/obese and underfit is an increasing, two-pronged problem in Canadian adolescents (see **Figure 11.1**). Since the early 1980s, the rate of the overweight and obese in 12- to 17-year-olds has risen substantially: the rate of overweight adolescents increased from 12 to ~20%, and the obesity rate tripled, going from 3 to ~10% (Roberts et al., 2012; Shields, 2008). During the same period, fitness levels have declined significantly (i.e., aerobic fitness, flexibility, muscular strength, and endurance) (Tremblay et al., 2010).

It may not be surprising to learn that measures of leisure time and physical activity have shown that obese teens are less active and have a higher screen time (i.e., time spent watching television, playing video games, or using a computer) than non-obese teens. When overweight and obese teens were considered as one group, significant differences were found between those with high and low weekly hours of screen time. Sixty-six percent of youth who clocked more than 20 hours of screen time per week were overweight/obese. In comparison, only 23% of those who logged less than 10 hours per week were overweight/obese (Shields, 2008).

Figure 11.1 Percentage of youth age 15 to 19 years with at-risk levels of body composition and fitness, Canada, 1981 and 2007–2009.

(**SOURCE:** Tremblay, M.S., Shields, M., Laviolette, M., Craig, C.L., Janssen, I., & Connor Gorber, S. (2010). Fitness of Canadian children and youth: Results from the 2007–2009. Canadian Health Measures Survey (Cat. No. 82-003-X). *Health Reports*, 21(1), 7–20.) Reproduced and distributed on an "as is" basis with the permission of Statistics Canada.)

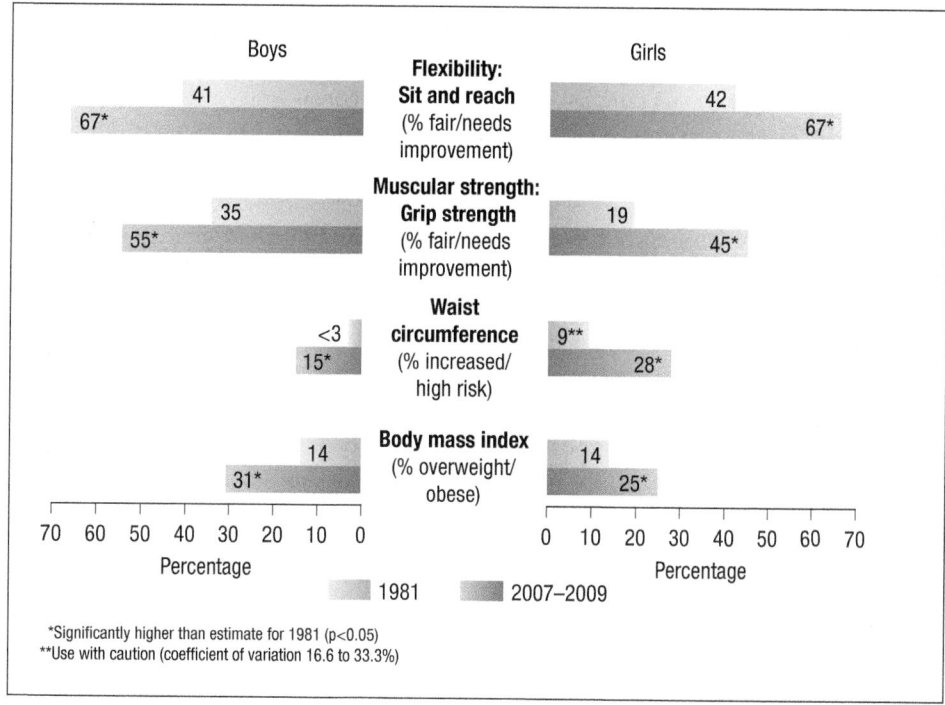

Test Yourself before going on

1. In what order do these milestones of puberty occur in girls?
   _____ (a) menarche
   _____ (b) breast development
   _____ (c) peak of growth spurt
2. In what order do these milestones of puberty occur in boys?
   _____ (a) production of viable sperm
   _____ (b) genitals increase in size
   _____ (c) peak of growth spurt

3. What are some effects of early puberty found in both boys and girls?
4. Changes in the _____ _____ are responsible for improvements in impulse control, judgment, and decision making in late adolescence.
5. The dramatic rise in Canadian adolescents becoming overweight is attributed, in part, to changes _____ in and _____.

Adolescent Sexuality

Puberty brings with it the hormonal changes that underlie both sexual attraction and sexual behaviour. Still, these important domains of experience are not entirely controlled by hormones. Each has psychological and social components, as you will see.

Sexual Behaviour

The proportion of Canadian teen girls and boys who report having had sexual intercourse before age 15 has declined by one-third since the mid-1990s and sits at ~9% (Rotermann, 2008, 2012). The current rate for 15- to 17-year-olds is 30%, and for

Learning Objective 11.3

Identify the issues involved with the sexual behaviour of adolescents.

18- to 19-year-olds, the rate is 68%. Although the rate of 15- to 19-year-old females who reported ever having intercourse has declined, the rate for males at this age has remained constant over the past decade. Females are more likely than males to report having sex without using a condom. For instance, ~37% of females and ~27% of males aged 15 to 24 said they had not used a condom in their recent sexual encounters—a rate of non-use that increases with age for both sexes and puts them at higher risk for unwanted pregnancy and sexually transmitted infections (STIs) (Rotermann, 2008). Three-quarters of Canadian females 15 to 19 years of age who had vaginal intercourse in the six months prior to being asked reported they consistently used some form of birth control: 74% use condoms, 67% use oral contraceptives, and 17% use withdrawal (Black et al., 2009).

Among girls, those who are sexually active are also more likely to have experienced early menarche, to have low interest in school, to have had their first date at a relatively early age, and to have a history of sexual abuse (Buzi, Roberts, Ross, Addy, & Markham, 2003; Ompad et al., 2006). The greater the number of risk factors present in the life of an individual teenager, the greater the likelihood that he or she will be sexually active. There are also common factors that reduce the likelihood of teenagers being sexually active, for example, teenagers who believe that premarital sex is morally wrong and who attend religious services frequently are less likely than their peers to become sexually active before reaching adulthood (Abma, Martinez, & Cohen, 2010). Rates of sexual activity are also lower among teens who are involved in sports or other after-school pursuits than among their peers who do not participate in such activities (Savage & Holcomb, 1999). Moreover, alcohol use is associated with 22% of adolescent sexual encounters; thus, teens who do not use alcohol are less likely to be sexually active than are their peers who drink (Eaton et al., 2010).

pelvic inflammatory disease (PID)

an infection of the female reproductive tract that may result from a sexually transmitted disease and can lead to infertility

SEXUALLY TRANSMITTED INFECTIONS   Even when they are knowledgeable about STIs, many teens may lack the assertiveness necessary to resist sexual pressure from a romantic partner or to discuss condom use—a health risk factor that has become increasingly important for young Canadians. For example, since 2003 in Canada, the rates of new chlamydia, gonorrhea, and syphilis infections have been on the upswing in youth aged 15 to 19 (PHAC, 2015b). Chlamydia, a disease that is preventable through condom use, continues to be the most commonly reported STI in Canada. Infection rates are among the highest in 15- to 19-year-old females, who have an infection rate of ~18 cases per 1000, roughly four times higher than the incidence found in their male peers.

Chlamydia infections are often symptomless (PHAC, 2015b). Thus, routine chlamydia screening of asymptomatic, sexually active teens and young adults is critical to reducing the prevalence of this disease. Left untreated, chlamydia can lead to **pelvic inflammatory disease (PID)**, ectopic pregnancy, and infertility in women and a number of genital and urinary tract disorders in men.

A more serious viral STI is genital warts caused by the human papillomavirus (HPV). The primary symptom of the disease, the presence of growths on the genitals, is not its most serious effect. The virus is strongly associated with cervical cancer, accounting for more than 70% of all cases (Canadian Cancer Society, 2013). Studies indicate that, in Canada, the peak prevalence of HPV of any type tends to occur in adolescent girls and young women (25 years of age or younger) and then decreases with

(Photo: grafikplusfoto/Fotolia)

Teens who date in early adolescence, as these two may be doing, are more likely to become sexually active while still in school than peers who begin dating later.

age (National Advisory Committee on Immunization [NACI], 2007). Canadian public health experts recommend nationwide HPV vaccination of females between ages 9 and 45, as well as continued Pap tests for cervical cancer (Canadian Cancer Society, 2013). HPV vaccination is also recommended for males between ages 9 and 26.

SEX EDUCATION In addition to routine screening, many developmentalists and public health advocates say that more effective sex education programs are needed. Most suggest that programs that include *information* about STIs and pregnancy, *motivation* to use the information (e.g., an awareness of the personal and social consequences of sexual health choices), as well as *behavioural skills* training (e.g., condom acquisition and use and safer-sex negotiation), are more likely than information-only approaches to reduce the prevalence of sexual activity and to increase the number of teens who protect themselves against disease and pregnancy when they do have sex (Johnson, Scott-Sheldon, Huedo-Medina, & Carey, 2011; Sex Information and Education Council of Canada [SIECCAN], 2015).

Some adults object to sex education because they believe it will cause teenagers who are not sexually active to become so. Research suggests that such fears are unfounded (Chin et al., 2012; Johnson et al., 2011). There are also debates over the degree to which sex education programs should emphasize abstaining from sex or using contraceptives. No scientific research has shown that abstinence-only sex-education programs significantly increase the delay of first intercourse or reduce the prevalence of sexual behaviour in teens (Johnson et al., 2011; Kirby, 2000). Moreover, making condoms more readily available to teenagers does not increase their rate of sexual activity but does increase the use of condoms by teenagers who are already sexually active (Schuster, Bell, Berry, & Kanouse, 1998). Despite hot debates about what should and should not be taught in sexual education programs, the large majority of Canadian parents and teens believe that sex education that provides explicit information on topics such as reproduction, birth control, STI/AIDS prevention, relationships, sexual orientation, sexual abuse, and societal beliefs about sexual morals is vitally important and should be provided in our schools (McKay, 2005; SIECCAN, 2015).

Teenaged Pregnancy

Learning Objective 11.4

Summarize the issues involved in teenaged pregnancy.

Among the developed nations of the world, the teenage birth rate is highest in the United States, where it is about three times as high as in Canada, and lowest in Sweden, where it is about seven times lower than in Canada (Luong, 2008). In Canada, the rate of teenage pregnancy for females aged 15 to 19 has declined from ~54 per 1000 in 1974 to ~28 per 1000 in 2010 (McKay, 2012; Statistics Canada, 2000). In comparison, the birth rate for teens aged 15 to 19 is 12 per 1000, which is less than half the pregnancy rate (Statistics Canada, 2016e).

The difference between pregnancy and birth rates is attributed to fetal loss, mostly due to induced abortions. In 1997, the percentage of pregnant teens aged 15 to 19 ending their pregnancy in abortion (50.3%) surpassed the percentage of live births (46.8%) and miscarriages or stillbirths (2.9%) for the first time (see **Figure 11.2**) (Statistics Canada, 2000). This trend has continued for Canadian teens aged 15 to 19, with slightly more than half of all pregnancies being terminated through abortion (McKay, 2012).

Whether a girl becomes pregnant during her teenaged years depends on many of the same factors that predict sexual activity in general. The younger a girl is when she becomes sexually active, the more likely she is to become pregnant. Among teenaged girls who are from poor families, single-parent families, or families with relatively uneducated parents, or whose mothers gave birth to them before age 20, pregnancy rates are higher (Martin et al., 2010). The children of teenaged mothers are more likely to grow up in poverty than children born to older

Figure 11.2 Percentage distribution of outcomes of teenaged pregnancy, women aged 15 to 19, Canada, 1974 to 1997.

(**SOURCE:** Adapted from Statistics Canada, *Health Reports*, Cat. No. 82-003, Vol. 12, No.1, Chart 3, available at www.statcan.ca/english/kits/preg/preg3.htm). This does not constitute an endorsement by Statistics Canada of this product.)

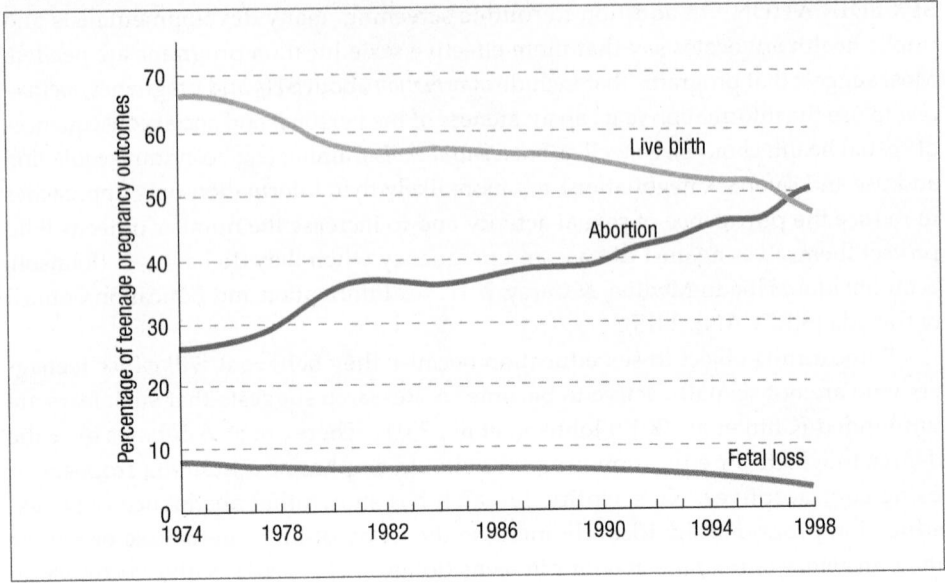

mothers, with all the accompanying negative consequences for the child's optimum development (Burgess, 2005). For instance, they tend to achieve developmental milestones more slowly than infants of older mothers (Pomerleau, Scuccimarri, & Malcuit, 2003).

In contrast, the likelihood of pregnancy is lower among teenaged girls who do well in school and have strong educational aspirations. Such girls are both less likely to be sexually active at an early age and more likely to use contraception if they are sexually active. Girls who have good communication about sex and contraception with their mothers are also less likely to get pregnant.

Learning Objective 11.5

Discuss the emergence of sexual orientation and gender identity in adolescence.

Sexual Minority Youth

The emergence of a physical attraction to members of the opposite sex, or *heterosexuality*, is one of the defining features of adolescence for the great majority of teenagers. For some, though, adolescence is the time when they discover, or confirm a long-standing suspicion, that they are attracted to people of the same sex (*homosexuality*) or to both sexes (*bisexuality*). Still others become increasingly convinced that their psychological gender is inconsistent with their biological sex (*transgenderism*).

GAY, LESBIAN, AND BISEXUAL ADOLESCENTS Surveys involving thousands of teens have found that about 96% identify themselves as exclusively heterosexual in sexual orientation (Kann et al., 2011). About 1.4% of teens report that they are still unsure of their sexual orientation, a status that many researchers call *questioning*. Just under 1% classify themselves as exclusively gay or lesbian, and 3.5% identify as bisexual. By adulthood, 94% of those surveyed report being exclusively heterosexual, and just over 5% describe themselves as gay, lesbian, or bisexual, leaving only a small proportion who are still questioning (Langer, Arnedt, & Sussman, 2004).

Lay people and researchers alike have wondered what causes some people to develop a gay, lesbian, or bisexual orientation. Several twin studies show that when one identical twin is homosexual, the probability that the other twin will also be homosexual is 50 to 60%, whereas the concordance rate is only about 20% for fraternal twins and only about 11% for pairs of biologically unrelated boys adopted into the same family (Dawood, Pillard, Horvath, Revelle, & Bailey, 2000; Kendler, Thornton, Gilman, & Kessler, 2000). Family studies also suggest that male homosexuality runs in families—that is, the families of most gay men have a higher proportion of homosexual males than do the families of heterosexual men (Bailey et al., 1999). Such findings strengthen the hypothesis that homosexuality has a biological basis (Dawood et al., 2000). Such evidence does not mean that environment plays no role in homosexuality. For example, when one of a pair of identical twins is homosexual, the other twin does not share that sexual orientation 40 to 50% of the time. Something beyond biology must be at work, although developmentalists do not yet know what environmental factors may be involved.

Prenatal hormone patterns may be one factor in homosexuality (Rahman & Wilson, 2003). For example, women whose mothers took the drug diethylstilbestrol (DES, a synthetic estrogen) during pregnancy are more likely to be homosexual as adults than are women who were not exposed to DES in the womb (Meyer-Bahlburg et al., 1995). These studies are consistent with the hypothesis that biological factors contribute to sexual orientation.

Whatever the cause of variations in sexual orientation, the process through which an individual comes to realize that he or she is attracted to the same or both sexes appears to be gradual (Hu, Xu, & Tornello, 2016). Some researchers think that the process begins in middle childhood as a feeling of doubt about one's heterosexuality emerges (Wallien & Cohen-Kettenis, 2008). Retrospective studies have found that many gay men and lesbians recall having had homosexual fantasies during their teen years, but few fully accepted their homosexuality while still in adolescence (Wong & Tang, 2004). Instead, the final steps toward full self-awareness and acceptance of one's non-heterosexual orientation appear to take place in early adulthood (Hu, Xu, & Tornello, 2016; Li & Hines, 2016).

TRANSGENDERED TEENS **Transgendered** teens and adults are those whose psychological gender is the opposite of their biological sex. Some studies suggest that transgendered individuals may have been exposed to atypical amounts of androgens in the womb (Lippa, 2005). However, most do not have such histories, so the cause of transgenderism remains a mystery. Transgendered adolescents usually report that, since early childhood, they have been more interested in activities that are associated with the opposite sex than in those that are typical for their own (Lippa, 2005). However, most children who are attracted to cross-gender activities, and even those who express a desire to be the opposite gender, do not exhibit transgenderism after puberty (Wallien & Cohen-Kettenis, 2008). Thus, such behaviours on the part of children are not considered to be predictive of the development of transgenderism in adolescence.

Once individuals accept their transgendered status, some choose to live as the opposite gender on a full-time basis, a pattern called *transsexualism*. Most transsexuals are content with their lives, but others are so anguished by the conflict between their sex and their psychological gender that they seek *sex reassignment*—a process involving hormonal treatment, reconstructive surgery, and psychological counselling—to achieve a match between the two. Typically, sex reassignment is reserved for adults, but some sex reassignment specialists accept teenaged patients (Smith, van Goozen, Kuiper, & Cohen-Kettenis, 2005). Regardless of the age at which sex reassignment is sought, at least half of those who explore this option, with the help of skilled counsellors, ultimately reject it in favour of less drastic ways of coping with their dilemma. Among those who do actually go through the procedure, most are happy with the results and experience relief from their preoperative emotional distress.

transgendered

a person whose psychological gender is the opposite of his or her biological sex

Test Yourself before going on

1. Choose the correct answer in the following sentence:
   In Canada, about (half/two-thirds) of 18- to 19-year-olds
   are sexually experienced.
2. List three factors that increase the risk of adolescent
   pregnancy.
   (a)
   (b)
   (c)
3. When is full acceptance of a homosexual orientation most
   likely to occur?

Critical Thinking

4. Look back at Bronfenbrenner's ecological model of development in the chapter on Theories of Development. Think
   of sexually developing adolescents and explain how their
   families, schools, religious institutions, and neighbourhoods affect sexually active teens, pregnant adolescents,
   and sexual minority youth.

Adolescent Health

Despite the stereotype of adolescence as a period of "storm and stress," most teenagers are well adjusted. However, as adolescents gain independence, they encounter
numerous health risks.

Learning Objective 11.6

Describe how sensation-
seeking affects risky behaviour
in adolescents.

Sensation-Seeking

Teenagers appear to have what many developmentalists describe as a heightened
level of *sensation-seeking*, or a desire to experience increased levels of arousal, such
as those that accompany fast driving or the "highs" that are associated with drugs.
Sensation-seeking leads to recklessness, which, in combination with lifestyle factors and inexperience, leads to increased rates of accidents and injuries in this age
group. For example, adolescents drive faster, follow too closely, switch traffic lanes,
pass other cars more often, and use seat belts less often than adults (Chamberlain &
Solomon, 2006). McGill researchers have found three distinct personality characteristics for repeat risky drivers who are overrepresented in road crashes (Brown et al.,
2016). One group was more stimulation-seeking, another was more fearless, and a
third had poorer behavioural control, and in all groups, risky driving was aggravated
by alcohol misuse.

To reduce the number of accidents among teenaged drivers, provinces have
enacted laws establishing "graduated" driver's licences, and two more have provi-
sional or probationary licence systems (Safety Canada Online, 2000; Traffic Injury
Research Foundation, 2001). Sixteen-year-olds can drive in most provinces (except
Alberta, where 14-year-olds are eligible for a learner's permit), but they must remain
alcohol-, accident-, and ticket-free for a certain period of time before they can have
privileges such as driving at night. Other countermeasures include driver education
programs and advertising campaigns to discourage risk-taking behaviour. Although
car accidents remain the leading cause of death among teens aged 15 to 19, impressive progress has been achieved in reducing road crash death and injury in Canadian
adolescents since 1980. After adjusting for population, the fatality rates have dropped
by 55% and injuries have fallen by 38%. Alcohol-related deaths have also declined. In
1980, nearly 70% of teen drivers killed in motor vehicle accidents had been drinking.
This figure has dropped to around 40% (Chamberlain & Solomon, 2006).

Risky behaviours may be more common in adolescence than other periods
because they help teenagers gain peer acceptance and establish autonomy with respect

to parents and other authority figures (Donenberg, Emerson, Bryant, & King, 2006; Horvath, Lewis, & Watson, 2012). Permissive parenting contributes as well (Tanski, Cin, Stoolmiller, & Sargent, 2010). In addition, adolescents who are not involved in extracurricular activities at school or to whom popularity is important are more likely than their peers who value popularity less to engage in risky behaviour (Latimer & Zur, 2010; Melnick, Miller, Sabo, Barnes, & Farrell, 2010). Lack of maturity in the prefrontal cortex and other brain structures is also viewed by some developmental scientists as the reason that teens exhibit higher levels of sensation-seeking than adults do (Breyer & Winters, 2005; Jensen & Nutt, 2015).

Sensation-seeking and risky behaviours may help teens achieve peer acceptance. Consequently, these behaviours are more likely to happen when adolescents are with peers than when they are alone or with family.

The messages conveyed in the popular media about sex, violence, and drug and alcohol use may influence teens' risky behaviour (Stoolmiller, Gerrard, Sargent, Worth, & Gibbons, 2010). These media messages interact with individual differences in sensation-seeking (Greene, Krcmar, Rubin, Walters, & Hale, 2002). Thus, teens who are highest in sensation-seeking are those who are most strongly influenced by media portrayals of risky behaviour.

Drugs, Alcohol, and Tobacco

What makes a teenager want to use alcohol or drugs? Those who express the most interest in sensation-seeking are most likely to use drugs and consume alcohol (Wu, Liu, & Fan, 2010). Indeed, researchers have found that individual levels of sensation-seeking predict peer associations—that is, teens who are high sensation-seekers choose friends who are similar. Once such groups are formed, sensation-seeking becomes a central feature of their activities. So, for example, if one member tries marijuana or alcohol, others do so as well. However, teens who spend a lot of time alone may also be vulnerable to substance abuse. Researchers have found that shy adolescents, particularly those who are high in neuroticism, are more likely to use alcohol and drugs than are peers who are more outgoing (Kirkcaldy, Siefen, Surall, & Bischoff, 2004).

Sensation-seeking also interacts with parenting style to increase the likelihood of drug use. Authoritative parenting seems to provide high sensation-seeking teenagers with protection against their reckless tendencies (Cablova, Pazderkova, & Miovsky, 2014; Wu, Liu, & Fan, 2010). Parents who have realistic perceptions of the prevalence of teenaged drinking are also less likely to have teenaged children who are drinkers; these parents try to prevent their children from getting into situations, such as unsupervised social events, where drinking is likely to happen (Bogenschneider, Wu, Raffaelli, & Tsay, 1998).

DRUG USE   Drug use among Canadian youth has been steadily declining since the 1970s (Hammond, Ahmed, Yang, Brukhalter, & Leatherdale, 2011). The average age of first-time drug use (including alcohol) is 13 to 14 (Health Canada, 2012a). The use of substances generally increases with age, with alcohol, followed by marijuana and cigarettes, being the top choice of Canadian students who used a substance over a 12-month period. To a lesser degree, students also use prescription drugs (ranging from pain relievers and tranquillizers to stimulants), hallucinogens (ranging from mushrooms [Psilocybin], mescaline, and LSD to newer ones such as *Salvia divinorum* and Jimson weed), inhalants (glue or solvents), and a variety of illicit stimulants (including amphetamines, ecstasy, and cocaine) to "get high" (Health Canada, 2012a;

Learning Objective 11.7

Identify the patterns of drug, alcohol, and tobacco use among adolescents in Canada.

Figure 11.3 The percentage of Canadian students in Grades 7 through 12 who used drugs once or more in the past year.

NOTES: NM = non-medical use, without a doctor's prescription; OTC = over-the-counter drug used for non-medical reasons or to "get high." The use of some drugs has emerged more recently and now is tracked (e.g., non-medical use of prescription opioid pain relievers, *Salvia divinorum*, and others). Over the past decade, there have been noteworthy declines in the use of drugs that have been tracked.

(SOURCE: Data from Paglia-Boak, A., Adlaf, E.M., & Mann, R.E. (2011). Drug use among Ontario Students, 1977-2011: Detailed OSDUHS findings (CAMH Research Document Series No. 32). Toronto, ON: Centre for Addiction and Mental Health.)

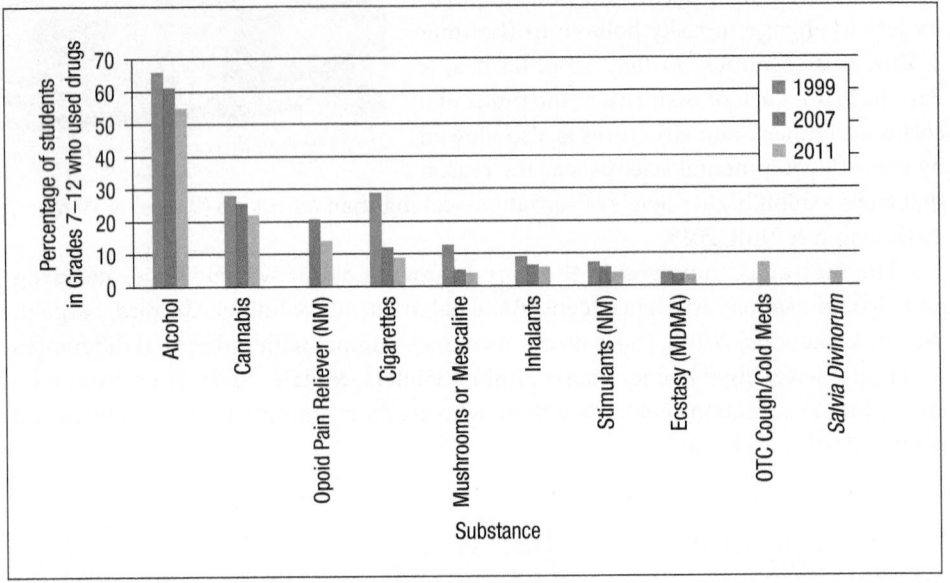

Paglia-Boak, Adlaf, & Mann, 2011). **Figure 11.3** shows the results of the long-running annual survey of Ontario students (average rate of drug use, Grades 7 through 12).

ALCOHOL Alcohol use remains very common among Canadian youth. Slightly more than one in four students in Grades 7 to 9 have used alcohol in the past 12 months, and this figure nearly doubles by the time students reach Grades 10 to 12 (Statistics Canada, 2013). Moreover, ~17% of males and ~11% of females ages 16 to 17 report heavy drinking (defined as consuming five or more drinks on a single occasion at least 12 times in the past year), and these percentages climb to ~39% for males and ~28% for females age 18 to 19 (Statistics Canada, 2013c). One serious consequence of alcohol use is that 16- to 19-year-old youth have the third highest rate of impaired driving charges of any age group in Canada (Perrault, 2013).

Some studies show that there are a few identifiable brain deviations that can predispose teens to initiate alcohol use and later develop problematic alcohol abuse (Wilson, Malone, Thomas, & Iacono, 2015). As well, there are *neurotoxic* effects associated with teen alcohol consumption. Other studies have indicated that early temperament and parenting style jointly affect teen alcohol use. University of Montreal researchers who studied 6-year-olds found that impulsivity combined with a coercive/harsh parenting style predicted higher alcohol use in teens (Rioux et al., 2016). In contrast, though, impulsive children had lower rates of alcohol use as teens compared to low-impulsive children in the absence of coercive parenting. As well, teens with authoritative parents, who have clear rules and monitor their comings and goings, yet allow for independence, have lower frequency of alcohol use.

TOBACCO Cigarette smoking by Canadian youth has declined dramatically since the 1970s and has hit its lowest point in decades. As well, for more than a decade the youth smoking rate has been consistently lower than for the general population (Reid, Hammond, Rynard, & Burkhalter, 2015). The combined daily and occasional smoking rate for teenagers ages 12 to 19 is slightly higher for boys (3.7% daily and 4.6% occasionally) compared to girls (3.8% daily and 3.3% occasionally) (Statistics Canada, 2016f).

In addition to the increased risk for a number of diseases, tobacco use in Canadian youth is correlated with use of a variety of other illicit or harmful substances (Davis, 2006; Health Canada, 2012a). Cigarette smoking has sometimes been referred to as a "gateway" drug to other drugs. Although it's not clear that tobacco use leads to the consumption of other drugs, tobacco is an effective marker of other substance use. For instance, in youth younger than age 20, smokers, in comparison to nonsmokers, are more than 14 times as likely to have used alcohol, 25 times as likely to have used cannabis, and 12.5 times as likely to have used other drugs (e.g., cocaine, heroin, amphetamine, ecstasy, or hallucinogens) in the past year.

Peer influence plays an important role in teen smoking. A nonsmoking teenager who begins associating with a cohesive group of adolescents among whom smoking is a prominent behaviour and a sign of group membership is likely to take up the habit. In fact, some developmentalists advise parents that if their teenaged child's friends smoke, especially close friends with whom the child spends a lot of time, parents should probably assume that their child smokes as well (Holliday, Rothwell, & Moore, 2010). The period between ages 15 and 17 seems to be the time during which a teenager is most susceptible to peer influences with regard to smoking (West, Sweeting, & Ecob, 1999). Clearly, then, monitoring the friends of 15- to 17-year-olds and discouraging these teens from associating with smokers may help parents prevent their teen from smoking (Mott, Crowe, Richardson, & Flay, 1999).

Eating Disorders

Learning Objective 11.8

Describe the characteristics and factors that contribute to eating disorders.

Have you ever tried to lose weight? If so, you have a lot of company. However, dieting is quite different from an *eating disorder*, which is a category of mental disorders in which eating behaviours go far beyond most people's everyday experience with trying to lose weight (American Psychiatric Association, 2013). Eating disorders, once considered rare in Canada, are now among the most significant mental health problems during adolescence. Canadian sources indicate that these disorders, which can be fatal, typically develop during adolescence or early adulthood when the pressures to be thin are the strongest (Jilek, 2001; Government of Canada, 2006). As these social pressures have increased, so too have the rates of eating disorders. About nine out of ten cases occur in women, especially young women (Bitomsky, 2002; HealthyOntario .com, 2003). Although more common among girls than boys, gay and lesbian youth as well as teens who are unsure about their sexual orientation are at higher risk than their heterosexual peers (Austin et al., 2004; Austin et al., 2008).

bulimia

an eating disorder characterized by binge eating and purging

BULIMIA **Bulimia** (sometimes called *bulimia nervosa*) involves an intense concern about weight combined with twice-weekly or more frequent cycles of binge eating followed by purging through self-induced vomiting, excessive use of laxatives, or excessive exercising (Yager, 2013). Bulimics are ordinarily not exceptionally thin, but they are obsessed with their weight, feel intense shame about their abnormal behaviour, and often experience significant depression. The physical consequences of bulimia include marked tooth decay (from repeated vomiting), stomach irritation, lowered body temperature, disturbances of body chemistry, and loss of hair (Yager, 2013).

(*Photo: Gordana Sermek/Shutterstock*)

It is difficult to estimate, but anywhere between 3 and 10% of Canadian adolescent girls and young adult women may experience the full syndrome of bulimia (Canadian Mental Health Association [CMHA], 2003; Polivy & Herman, 2002). One large Ontario study found that as many as one-quarter of girls in high school show at least some bulimic behaviours, such as dieting along with occasional bingeing and purging

When this anorexic 15-year-old looks at herself in the mirror, chances are she sees herself as "too fat," despite being obviously emaciated.

(Jones, Bennett, Olmsted, Lawson, & Rodin, 2001). It's interesting to note that bulimia is essentially unheard of in countries where food is scarce or body thinness is not idealized (Pies, 2003; Mental Health Foundation of New Zealand, 2002).

anorexia nervosa

an eating disorder characterized by self-starvation

ANOREXIA NERVOSA **Anorexia nervosa** is less common but potentially more deadly. Teenagers who suffer from anorexia nervosa usually have a more distorted body image than those who have bulimia. It is characterized by extreme dieting, intense fear of gaining weight, and obsessive exercising. In girls or women, the weight loss eventually produces a variety of physical symptoms associated with starvation: sleep disturbance, cessation of menstruation, insensitivity to pain, loss of hair on the head, low blood pressure, a variety of cardiovascular problems, and reduced body temperature. Estimates are that between 1 and 2% of female adolescents and young adults in Canada develop anorexia (CMHA, 2003). Between 4 and 18% of those with anorexia literally starve themselves to death; others die because of some type of cardiovascular dysfunction (Cushing & Waldrop, 2010).

Although anorexia in women is far more common than in men, an increasing number of young men are suffering from anorexia. Many are involved in sporting activities, such as wrestling and gymnastics, in which they have experienced pressure to maintain a lower weight classification. Similarly, pressure to be thin also comes from the men's fashion industry, where tall, ultra-thin male models have become the norm (Trebay, 2008). In this regard, it seems both young men and women experience similar pressures to achieve weight loss and be lean (Ricciardelli & McCabe, 2004).

RISK FACTORS Some theorists have proposed biological causes for eating disorders, such as some kind of brain dysfunction, and researchers have determined that heredity contributes to the development of eating disorders (Bernstein, 2010; Cushing, 2013; Yager, 2013). Others, however, argue for a psychoanalytic explanation, such as a fear of growing up. But the most promising explanation may lie in the discrepancy between the young person's internal image of a desirable body and her (or his) perception of her (or his) own body.

Some developmentalists suggest that an emphasis on thinness as a characteristic of attractive women, which is common in Western cultures, contributes to the prevalence of eating disorders (Pelletier, Dion, & Levesque, 2004). In one approach to testing this hypothesis, 6- to 12-year-old girls' responses to images of thin, "sexy" women were compared to boys' reactions to images of muscular, hyper-"masculine" men to find out how early children become aware of cultural stereotypes about ideal male and female body types (Murnen, Smolak, Mills, & Good, 2003). Researchers found that even the youngest children in this age group express admiration for the appearance of the models depicted in such images and that children are most interested in idealized images of adults of their own gender. However, girls are more likely than boys to compare their own appearance to that of the models. Moreover, among girls, those who are happiest with their own physical appearance are the least likely to compare their own bodies to media images of "attractive" women (Murnen et al., 2003).

Critical Thinking

If you had the power to change Canadian society to greatly reduce the rates of bulimia and anorexia, what changes would you want to make? Why and how?

These findings support the assertion of many developmentalists that girls internalize images representing what might be called the "thin ideal" during the middle childhood years and use them as standards against which to compare the changes in their bodies that happen during puberty (Hermes & Keel, 2003). In fact, research shows that, by age 11, girls are significantly more dissatisfied with their bodies than boys are with theirs, and the gender gap in body satisfaction increases across the teen years (Sweeting & West, 2002). As you might expect, given these results, researchers have also found that the tendency of girls to compare themselves to the thin ideal increases as they advance through puberty (Hermes & Keel, 2003).

Recent thinking, however, has placed more emphasis on the pre-existing psychological health of people who develop eating disorders than on cultural influences (Cushing, 2013). Some researchers assert that the body images of individuals who suffer from eating disorders are the result of a general tendency toward distorted thinking (Dyl, Kittler, Phillips, & Hunt, 2006). In other words, these researchers say that people who have eating disorders tend to think in distorted ways about many things, not just their bodies. From this perspective, internalized images of the "perfect" body fuel the sales of diet products among psychologically healthy people, but they trigger a far more serious outcome, a true eating disorder, in individuals who have a mentally unhealthy tendency toward thought distortion.

Depression and Suicide

Learning Objective 11.9

Identify what factors are involved in adolescent depression and suicide.

Studies reveal that more women than men experience depression in their late teens, but more male teens commit suicide compared with their female peers. Suicide rates among Canada's Indigenous youth are among the highest in the world.

DEPRESSION   A revealing study by Nancy Galambos and her colleagues at the University of Alberta found that 25% of young women and half as many young men aged 16 to 19 had experienced at least one major depressive episode (MDE) (Galambos, Leadbeater, & Barker, 2004). This sex difference persists throughout adolescence and into adulthood and has been found in a number of developed countries (Pearson, Janz, & Ali, 2013; Petersen et al., 1993).

Neuroimaging studies show that adolescent depression is associated with some kind of dysfunction in the pituitary gland (MacMaster & Kusumakar, 2004). But what causes the pituitary to function inappropriately in the first place? Genetic factors may be involved, as children growing up with depressed parents are much more likely to develop depression than are those growing up with nondepressed parents (Eley et al., 2004; Merikangas & Angst, 1995). The genetic hypothesis has also received support from at least a few studies of twins and adopted children (Petersen et al., 1993). However, the link between parental and child depression may also be explained in terms of the parenting behaviours of depressed parents, which you read about in earlier chapters. Furthermore, the contributions of a variety of family stressors to adolescent depression are just as clear among children whose parents are not depressed. Any combination of stresses—such as the parents' divorce, the death of a parent or another loved person, parental job loss, a move, a change of schools, or lack of sleep—increases the likelihood of depression or other kinds of emotional distress in the adolescent (D'Imperio, Dubow, & Ippolito, 2000; Fredriksen, Rhodes, Reddy, & Way, 2004). Even smoking has been linked to depression—teen smokers were 1.4 times more likely to have an MDE (Galambos et al., 2004).

You'll remember from the chapter on Social and Personality Development in Middle Childhood that low self-esteem is also part of the equation. Harter's studies reveal that a young person who feels she does not measure up to her own standards is much more likely to show symptoms of depression. A great many teenagers are convinced that they do not live up to culturally defined standards of physical appearance and/or achievement. Self-esteem thus drops in early adolescence, and depression rises.

Depression can hinder academic achievement, because it interferes with memory. For example, depressed adolescents are more likely to remember negative information than positive information (Neshat-Doost, Taghavi, Moradi, Yule, & Dalgleish, 1998). If a teacher says to a depressed adolescent, "You're going to fail algebra unless you start handing in your homework on time," the teenager is likely to remember the part about failing algebra and forget that the teacher also provided a remedy: getting homework done on time. Further, depressed adolescents seem to be less able than their nondepressed peers to store and retrieve verbal information (Horan, Pogge, Borgaro, & Stokes, 1997).

SUICIDE   In some teenagers, tragically, the suicidal thoughts that often accompany depression lead to action. Although depression is more common among girls than boys, the likelihood of actually completing a suicide attempt is about three times

Development in the Real World

First Nations Youth Suicide Crisis

The suicide rate for First Nation and Inuit youth in Canada is ~6 and ~11 times higher, respectively, than for non-Indigenous youth (Health Canada, 2013). Moreover, the suicide rate for young Indigenous females is eight times higher than the national rate for same-aged female peers (Health Canada, 2001c, 2003a). Suicide and self-inflicted injury is the leading cause of death (38%) for Indigenous children 10 to 19 years of age (Health Canada, 2003a). In addition, there are some communities in which the incidence of suicide is unmatched in the rest of the world (Lauwers, 2011). For example, the community of Pikangikum in Northwestern Ontario, with a population of about 1700, experienced 12 suicides in the 18 months prior to June 2001 (Kent, 2001). Of these, in the year 2000 alone, eight were young girls and five of them were just 13 years old (Barnsley, 2001; Elliott, 2000). This represents a suicide rate of 470 per 100 000 compared with the Canadian average of 13 per 100 000 (Barnsley, 2001).

Nationwide, comprehensive, community-focused, evidence-based solutions to Indigenous youth suicide are important considerations for dealing with this situation (White, 2015). Crisis support can be supplied in the short term, but a long-term prevention plan that involves significant change is the prime goal. British Columbia psychologists, led by Michael Chandler of University of British Columbia, have shown that factors that promote cultural continuity in Indigenous communities are related to significant suicide reduction in Indigenous youth (Chandler & Lalonde, 1998, 2008; Chandler, Lalonde, Sokol, & Hallet, 2003). The six factors associated with cultural continuity are

- local self-government (the single strongest factor)
- security over traditional lands
- band-controlled school systems
- band-controlled health services
- communal-use cultural facilities
- band-controlled police and fire services

The researchers found that suicide rates varied inversely with the number of indicators of cultural continuity that Indigenous communities embraced to strengthen and preserve their cultural heritage. For example, British Columbia First Nation bands that had established all the factors had no youth suicides. In comparison, bands that had none of the six factors had close to 140 youth suicides per 100 000—a rate about 100 times the provincial average. In the face of nearly two generations of high suicide rates, the challenge of implementing a nationwide strategy to assist Indigenous communities reduce the risk of suicide is daunting.

higher for adolescent boys. Suicide is the second leading cause of death for Canadian young people aged 15 to 19, and the suicide rate is ~6 per 100 000 for females and ~14 per 100 000 for males (Statistics Canada, 2015d). In contrast, suicide attempts are estimated to be three times more common among girls than among boys based on hospital admissions for nonfatal self-inflicted injuries. Girls use methods that are less likely to succeed, such as self-poisoning (Navaneelan, 2015). The major exception to this national trend is the disproportionately high rate of suicide among First Nations youth, girls in particular (Health Canada, 1999c) (see **Development in the Real World**).

Recent results from the QLSCD have found that being victimized by one's peers (i.e., being frequently bullied or excluded) increases the risk for suicidal ideation by ~2.3 times and suicide attempts by ~3 times during mid-adolescence (Geoffroy et al., 2016). Roughly half of suicide attempts are impulsive acts and they are often related to stressful life circumstances, such as the breakup of a relationship or facing a major crisis or dilemma, and are not well planned (Kattimani, Sarkar, Rajkumar, & Menon, 2015). Notably, one key predictor of repeat suicide attempts is the presence of feelings of hopelessness (Menon, Kattimani, Sarkar, & Mathan, 2016).

Although at least three neurobiological systems have been found to be involved in the neurobiology of suicidal behaviour (van Heeringen, 2003), most medical treatment has focused on the treatment of depression associated with suicidal behaviour. The most controversial of these treatments is the use of the newer antidepressant drugs known as *selective serotonin (and noradrenalin) reuptake inhibitors* (SSRIs/SNRIs). Widespread concern about the outcomes of these drugs on children and adolescents have not only cast doubt on their effectiveness for treating depression, but also revealed evidence that SSRIs/SNRIs can contribute to increased suicidal ideation, attempts and risk of suicide, and hostile aggression in these young populations (Garland, 2004; Herxheimer & Mintzes, 2004; Meek, 2004; Sibbald, 2004). In 2003, the United Kingdom banned the use of SSRIs/SNRIs, with the exception of fluoxetine (Prozac), for children and adolescents. In response, Health Canada issued a rare public warning that advised parents to consult with their primary care physician about the risks and benefits of prescribing these drugs for patients under the age of 18 (Health Canada, 2004; Kondro, 2004).

It is obviously very difficult to uncover the contributing factors in completed suicides. Although we know that suicide is related to depression, other factors also play a role. Canadian teens diagnosed with personality disorders, such as antisocial, borderline, and narcissistic personality disorders in particular, have been found to be at increased risk for suicide and suicidal behaviour (Links, Gould, & Ratnayake, 2003). Behaviour problems such as hostility-aggression and impulsivity are also common in the histories of those who complete suicides, as is a family history of psychiatric disorder or suicide or a pattern of drug or alcohol abuse (Korczak & CPS, 2015; Menon, Sarkar, Kattimani, & Mathan, 2015). In addition, experts suggest at least three other contributing factors (Korczak & CPS, 2015; Shaffer, Garland, Gould, Fisher, & Trautman, 1988; Swedo et al., 1991):

- *Some triggering stressful event.* Studies of suicides suggest that this triggering event is often a disciplinary crisis with the parents or some rejection or humiliation, such as breaking up with a girlfriend or boyfriend or failing in a valued activity.

- *An altered mental state.* Such a state might be a sense of hopelessness, reduced inhibitions from alcohol consumption, or rage.

- *An opportunity.* A loaded gun in the house or a bottle of sleeping pills in the parents' medicine cabinet creates an opportunity for a teenager to carry out suicidal plans.

A comprehensive suicide prevention strategy is essential for decreasing suicide and suicide attempts (Canadian Association for Suicide Prevention, 2009). Efforts have focused on education—for example, increasing public awareness and providing training for teachers and teenagers on how to identify students who are at risk for suicide, in the hope that vulnerable individuals might be reached before they attempt suicide. Special training in coping abilities has also been offered to teenaged students so that they might be able to find a nonlethal solution to their problems. Nationwide initiatives, such as community-based suicide prevention, intervention and follow-up care programs, respecting diversity and culture, and reducing the availability and lethality of suicide methods are also required and need to be funded and supported.

Test Yourself before going on

1. List four factors that contribute to adolescent sensation-seeking.
   (a) _____
   (b) _____
   (c) _____
   (d) _____

2. Choose the correct answer in the following sentence: Drug use among teens in Canada has (increased/decreased) since the 1970s.

3. Classify each symptom as characteristic of (A) anorexia nervosa, (B) bulimia nervosa, or (C) both anorexia and bulimia.
   _____ (a) distorted body image
   _____ (b) self-starvation
   _____ (c) bingeing and purging
   _____ (d) increased risk of another psychological disorder

4. Adolescent depression may be associated with dysfunction of the _____ gland.

Changes in Thinking and Memory

At some point in adolescence, most people become capable of several types of thought that appear to be impossible at earlier ages. Piaget was the first psychologist to offer an explanation of this important developmental milestone.

Piaget's Formal Operational Stage

Learning Objective 11.10

Describe the characteristics of thought in Piaget's formal operational stage.

formal operational stage

the fourth of Piaget's stages, during which adolescents learn to reason logically about abstract concepts

systematic problem-solving

the process of finding a solution to a problem by testing single factors

Piaget carried out a number of studies suggesting that an entirely new form of thought emerges between about age 12 and 16. He called the stage associated with this kind of thought the **formal operational stage**. Typically, this stage is defined as the period during which adolescents learn to reason logically about abstract concepts. Formal operational thinking has a number of key elements.

SYSTEMATIC PROBLEM-SOLVING   One important feature of formal operations is **systematic problem-solving**, the ability to search methodically for the answer to a problem. To study this, Piaget and his colleague Barbel Inhelder (Inhelder & Piaget, 1958) presented adolescents with complex tasks, mostly drawn from the physical sciences. In one of these tasks, subjects were given varying lengths of string and a set of objects of various weights that could be tied to the strings to make a swinging pendulum. The teens were shown how to start the pendulum different ways: by pushing the weight with differing amounts of force and by holding the weight at different heights. The subject's task was to figure out which factor or combination of factors—length of string, weight of object, force of push, or height of push—determines the "period" of the pendulum (i.e., the amount of time for one swing). (In case you have forgotten your high school physics, the answer is that only the length of the string affects the period of the pendulum.)

If you give this task to a concrete operational child, then she will usually try out many different combinations of length, weight, force, and height in an inefficient way. She might try a heavy weight on a long string and then a light weight on a short string. Because she has changed both string length and weight in these two trials, there is no way she can draw a clear conclusion about either factor. In contrast, an adolescent using formal operations is likely to be more organized, attempting to vary just one of the four factors at a time. He may try a heavy object with a short string, then with a medium string, and then with a long one. After that, he might try a light object with the three lengths of string. Of course not all adolescents (or all adults, for that matter) are quite this methodical in their approach. Still, there is a very dramatic difference in the overall strategies used by 10-year-olds and 15-year-olds that marks the shift from concrete to formal operations.

hypothetico-deductive reasoning

the ability to derive conclusions from hypothetical premises

personal fable

the belief that the events of one's life are controlled by a mentally constructed autobiography

imaginary audience

an internalized set of behavioural standards usually derived from a teenager's peer group

LOGIC   Another facet of this shift is the appearance in the adolescent's repertoire of skills of what Piaget called **hypothetico-deductive reasoning**, or the ability to derive conclusions from hypothetical premises. You may remember from the chapter on Physical and Cognitive Development in Middle Childhood that Piaget suggested that the concrete operational child can use inductive reasoning, which involves arriving at a conclusion or a rule based on many individual experiences, but performs poorly when asked to reason deductively. Deductive reasoning involves considering hypotheses or hypothetical premises and then deriving logical outcomes. For example, the statement "If all people are equal, then you and I must be equal" involves logic of this type. Although children as young as age 4 or 5 can understand some deductive relationships when the premises given are factually true, both cross-sectional and longitudinal studies support Piaget's assertion that only at adolescence are young people able to understand and use the basic logical relationships (Mueller, Overton, & Reene, 2001; Ward & Overton, 1990).

Piaget suggested that hypothetico-deductive thinking underlies many ideas and behaviours that are common to adolescents (see the **Research Report**). For instance, hypothetico-deductive thinking leads to an outlook he called *naive idealism* in many adolescents (Piaget & Inhelder, 1969). Naive idealism is manifested when adolescents use formal operational thinking to mentally construct an ideal world and then compare the real world with it. Not surprisingly, the real world often falls short. As a result, some teenagers become so dissatisfied with the world that they resolve to change it. For many, the changes they propose are personal. So a teen whose parents have been divorced for years may suddenly decide she wants to live with the noncustodial parent because she expects that her life will be better. Another may express naive idealism by becoming involved in a political or religious organization.

(Photo: Gennadiy Poznyakov/Fotolia)

High school science classes may be one of the first places where adolescents are required to use deductive logic—a skill Piaget did not think was developed until the period of formal operations.

Direct Tests of Piaget's View

In an early cross-sectional study, researchers tested 20 girls in each of four grades (Grades 6, 8, 10, and 12) on 10 different tasks that required one or more of what Piaget called formal operational skills (Martorano, 1977). Indeed, many of the tasks the researchers used were those Piaget himself had devised. Results of performance on two of these tasks are graphed in **Figure 11.4**. The pendulum problem is the one described earlier in this section; the balance problem requires a youngster to predict whether two different weights, hung at varying distances on each side of a scale, will

Learning Objective 11.11

Summarize some major research findings regarding the formal operational stage.

Research Report

Elkind's Adolescent Egocentrism

Psychologist David Elkind hypothesized that another common manifestation of hypothetico-deductive reasoning is a type of thought he called *adolescent egocentrism*, the belief that one's thoughts, beliefs, and feelings are unique. One component of adolescent egocentrism, Elkind said, is the **personal fable**, the belief that the events of one's life are controlled by a mentally constructed autobiography (Elkind, 1967). For example, a sexually active teenage girl might be drawing on such a personal fable when she says "I just don't see myself getting pregnant" in response to suggestions that she use contraception. In contrast to this inappropriately rosy view of the future, a teen who is involved in a violent street gang may say "I'll probably get shot before I make 18" when advised to leave the gang and focus on acquiring the academic skills needed to graduate from high school.

Elkind also proposed that adolescent egocentrism drives teenagers to try out various attitudes, behaviours, and even clothing choices in front of an **imaginary audience**, an internalized set of behavioural standards usually derived from a teenager's peer group. Consider a teenaged girl who is habitually late for school because she changes clothes two or three times every day before leaving home. Each time the girl puts on a different outfit, she imagines how her peers at school will respond to it. If the imaginary audience criticizes the outfit, the girl feels she must change clothes to elicit a more favourable response. Similarly, a boy may spend hours in front of the mirror trimming his facial hair in an effort to achieve a look he thinks his peers will approve of.

Many developmentalists have found Elkind's personal fable and imaginary audience to be helpful in explaining a variety of adolescents' everyday behaviours. However, research examining these constructs has produced mixed results (Bell & Bromnick, 2003; Galanaki, 2012). While it is true that adolescents use idealized mental models to make all kinds of decisions about their own and others' behaviour, researchers have found that school-aged children exhibit similar forms of thought (Vartanian, 2001). Furthermore, studies suggest that older adolescents think in these ways far more often than Elkind originally hypothesized (Schwartz, Maynard, & Uzelac, 2008). Nevertheless, developmentalists agree that the tendency to exaggerate others' reactions to one's own behaviour and to base decisions on unrealistic ideas about the future are two characteristics that distinguish adolescents from younger children (Alberts, Elkind, & Ginsburg, 2007).

Figure 11.4 These are the results from two of the ten different formal operational tasks used in Martorano's cross-sectional study.

(**SOURCE:** Martorano, 1977, p. 670. Copyright by the American Psychological Association.)

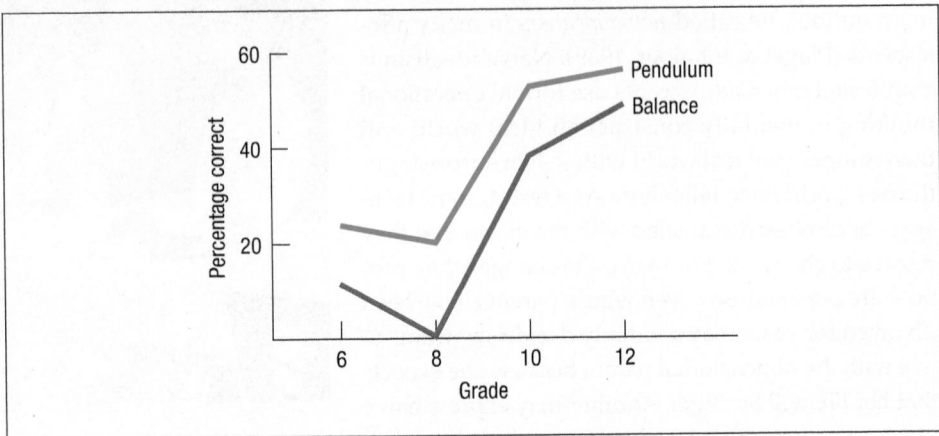

balance. To solve this problem by using formal operations, the teenager must consider both weight and distance simultaneously. You can see from Figure 11.4 that older students generally did better, with the biggest improvement in scores between children in Grades 8 and 10 (i.e., between ages 13 and 15).

Formal operational reasoning also seems to enable adolescents to understand figurative language, such as metaphors, to a greater degree. For example, one early study found that teenagers were much better than younger children at interpreting proverbs (Saltz, 1979). Statements such as "People who live in glass houses shouldn't throw stones" are usually interpreted literally by 6- to 11-year-olds. By age 12 or 13, most adolescents can easily understand them, even though it isn't until much later that teenagers actually use such expressions in their everyday speech (Gibbs & Beitel, 1995).

Take another look at Figure 11.4: Only about 50 to 60% of twelfth-graders solved the two formal operations problems. Furthermore, in this study, only 2 of the 20 Grade 12 participants used formal operational logic on all 10 problems. Recent studies have found rates of formal operational thinking in high school students that are very similar to those found in studies conducted in the 1960s, 1970s, and 1980s (Bradmetz, 1999). The consistency of such findings over several cohorts of adolescents suggests that Piaget's predictions about adolescents' thinking abilities were overly optimistic—in contrast to his overly pessimistic estimates of young children's abilities, which you read about in earlier chapters.

In adulthood, rates of formal operational thinking increase with education. Generally, the better educated the adult participants in a study of formal operational thinking, the greater the percentage who display this kind of reasoning (Mwamwenda, 1999). Piaget's belief in the universality of formal operations may have resulted from his failure to appreciate the role of education in the development of advanced forms of thought. The current consensus among developmentalists is that all teenagers and adults without intellectual disability have the capacity for formal operational thinking, but they actually acquire it in response to specific demands, such as those imposed by higher levels of education. Thus, people whose life situations or cultures do not require formal operational thinking do not develop it.

Critical Thinking

Think of a few real-life examples of tasks that demand systematic problem-solving.

Learning Objective 11.12

Describe what kinds of advances in information-processing capabilities occur during adolescence.

Advances in Information Processing

Adolescents process information faster, use processing resources more efficiently, understand their own memory processes better, and have more knowledge than do elementary school children (Kail, 1990, 1997, 2008). As a result, their working memories function more efficiently and they outperform school-aged children and reach adult-like performance—advances associated with continuing neural development (Chang, Metcalfe, Padmanabhan, Chen, & Menon, 2016; Gathercole, Pickering, Ambridge, & Wearing, 2004). Moreover, they are much better at using strategies to solve problems and help themselves remember things and can more easily understand and remember complex information, such as that presented in a textbook.

METACOGNITION, METAMEMORY, AND STRATEGY USE   By age 13 or 14, the metacognitive and metamemory skills of adolescents far exceed those of younger children, and these skills continue to improve throughout adolescence (and into the adult years, by the way) (Schneider, 2010; van der Stel & Veenman, 2010; Weil et al., 2013). For example, in one classic study, 10- and 14-year-olds were instructed to do a particular activity for exactly 30 minutes (Ceci & Bronfenbrenner, 1985). Experimenters provided them with a clock and instructed them to use it to determine when they should stop. Few of the 10-year-olds periodically checked the time to see if 30 minutes had elapsed, but most of the 14-year-olds did. As a result, less than half of the younger participants succeeded in stopping on time, but more than three-quarters of the teenagers did so.

Training studies, in which children and adolescents are taught to use a particular memory strategy, also suggest that metacognitive abilities enable teenagers to benefit more from training than younger children do. For example, researchers taught elementary school students and secondary school students a strategy for memorizing the manufacturing products associated with different cities (e.g., Detroit—automobiles) (Pressley & Dennis-Rounds, 1980). Once participants had learned the strategy and were convinced of its effectiveness, researchers presented them with a similar task, memorizing Latin words and their English translations. Experimenters found that only the secondary school students made an effort to use the strategy they had just learned to accomplish the new memory task. The elementary school children used the new strategy only when researchers told them to and demonstrated how it could be applied to the new task. Secondary school students' success seemed to be due to their superior ability to recognize the similarity between the two tasks: an aspect of metamemory.

TEXT LEARNING   Differences between younger children's and adolescents' processing of and memory for text are even more dramatic. In a classic study of text processing, experimenters asked 10-, 13-, 15-, and 18-year-olds to read and summarize a 500-word passage. The researchers hypothesized that participants would use four rules in writing summaries (Brown & Day, 1983). First, they would delete trivial information. Second, their summaries would show categorical organization (e.g., they would use terms such as *animals* rather than use the specific names of animals mentioned in the text). Third, the summaries would use topic sentences from the text. Finally, the participants would invent topic sentences for paragraphs that didn't have them.

The results of the study suggested that participants of all ages used the first rule, because all the summaries included more general than detailed or trivial information about the passage. However, the 10-year-olds and 13-year-olds used the other rules far less frequently than did the 15- and 18-year-olds. There were also interesting differences between the two older groups. Fifteen-year-olds used categories about as frequently as 18-year-olds did, but the oldest group used topic sentences far more effectively. This pattern of age differences suggests that the ability to summarize a text improves gradually during the second half of adolescence.

Studies of text outlining reveal a similar pattern (Drum, 1985). Both elementary and secondary school students know that an outline should include the main ideas of a passage along with supporting details. However, research suggests that 17-year-olds generate much more complete outlines than 14-year-olds do. Moreover, 11-year-olds' outlines usually include only a few of the main ideas of a passage and provide little or no supporting details for those main ideas.

Test Yourself before going on

1. The ability to reason from premises that are not necessarily factually true is called _____.

2. Choose the correct answer in the following sentence: Research indicates that formal operational thinking develops (earlier/later) than Piaget hypothesized.

3. List three ways in which teens' information-processing skills differ from those of children.
   (a) _____
   (b) _____
   (c) _____

Schooling

task goals

goals based on a desire for self-improvement

School experiences are clearly formative in middle childhood, but school is no less central a force in the lives of adolescents.

Transition to Secondary School

Learning Objective 11.13

Describe how changes in students' goals contribute to the transition to secondary school.

ability goals

goals based on a desire to be superior to others

In many places in the world, including Canada, children attend elementary school for eight years before moving on to a secondary school for four years. In Canada, the exceptions are British Columbia and Quebec, where students switch from elementary to secondary school after Grade 7 and Grade 6, respectively. Because students typically show achievement declines after entering secondary school, educators have developed a model that includes a transitional school—a junior high school or middle school—between elementary and secondary school. The junior high system typically includes six or seven years of elementary school followed by two or three years of junior high and three or four years of secondary school. As a consequence, the organization and structure of instruction is most likely to vary for Grade 8 across Canada, whereas Grades 6 and 10 are relatively stable.

However, the junior high/middle school approach does not seem to have solved the transition problem. Students show losses in achievement and in self-esteem across both transition points in these systems. Further, students in both of these systems show greater losses during the transition to secondary school than those in standard elementary–secondary track systems (Alspaugh, 1998; Linnenbrink, 2010). Consequently, educators and developmentalists are currently searching for explanations and practical remedies.

(Photo: Phovoir/Shutterstock)

Some developmentalists argue that the transition to middle school or junior high school is difficult for many young adolescents because they are not developmentally ready for the secondary-school model. Children who attend middle and junior high schools where close relationships between teachers and students are encouraged, as they are in elementary school, show smaller declines in achievement and self-esteem.

MIDDLE SCHOOL   One potential explanation for transition-related achievement declines is that students' academic goals change once they enter junior high/middle school. Researchers classify such goals into two very broad categories: *task goals* and *ability goals*. **Task goals** are goals based on personal standards and a desire to become more competent at something. For example, a runner who wants to improve her time in the 100-metre dash has a task goal. An **ability goal** is one that defines success in competitive terms, being better than another person at something. For example, a runner who wants to be the fastest person on her team has an ability goal. Longitudinal research shows that most Grade 5 students have task goals, but by the time they have been in Grade 6 a few months, most children have shifted to ability goals (Anderman & Anderman, 1999; Anderman & Midgley, 1997).

A student's goal influences his behaviour in important ways. Task goals are associated with a greater sense of personal control and more positive attitudes about school (Anderman, 1999; Gutman, 2006). A student who takes a task-goal approach to school work tends to set increasingly higher standards for his performance and attributes success and failure to his own efforts. For example, a task goal-oriented student is likely to say he received an A in a class because he worked hard or because he wanted to improve his performance.

In contrast, students with ability goals adopt relative standards—that is, they view performance on a given academic task as good as long as it is better than someone else's. Consequently, such students are more strongly influenced by the group with which they identify than by internal standards that define good and bad academic performance. Ability goal-oriented students are also more likely than others to attribute success and failure to forces outside themselves. For example, such a student might say he got an A in a class because it was easy or because the teacher liked him. Moreover, such students are likely to have a negative view of school (Anderman, 1999).

Because junior high/middle schools emphasize ability grouping and performance on standardized tests more than elementary schools, it is likely that many middle school students change their beliefs about their own abilities during these years (Anderman & Anderman, 2009). Thus, high-achieving elementary students who maintain their levels of achievement across the Grade 6 transition gain confidence in their abilities (Pajares & Graham, 1999). In contrast, the changes in self-concept experienced by high achievers who fail to meet expectations in middle school as well as average and low-achieving students probably lead to self-esteem losses for many of them. Once an ability goal-oriented student adopts the belief that her academic ability is less than adequate, she is likely to stop putting effort into school work. In addition, such students are likely to use ineffective cognitive strategies when attempting to learn academic material (Young, 1997). Consequently, achievement suffers along with self-esteem. Fortunately, however, educators can increase the chances that middle school students will adopt task goals by making it clear to students that learning is more important than outperforming peers on standardized tests or report card grades (Anderman & Anderman, 2009).

SECONDARY SCHOOL   Regardless of the type of school teenagers attended previously, the early days of secondary school set a general pattern of success or failure for teenagers that continues into their adult years. For example, teenagers who fail one or more courses in the first year of secondary school are far less likely than their peers to graduate (Neild, 2009; Neild & Balfanz, 2006).

However, some psychologists emphasize the positive aspects of transition to secondary school, claiming that participation in activities that are usually offered only in secondary school allows students opportunities to develop psychological attributes that can't be acquired elsewhere. To demonstrate the point, a number of research studies had secondary school students use pagers to signal researchers whenever they were experiencing high levels of intrinsic motivation along with intense mental effort (Larson, 2000). The results showed that students experienced both states in elective classes and during extracurricular activities far more often than in academic classes (Larson & Brown, 2007). In other words, a student engaged in an art project or sports practice is more likely to experience this particular combination of states than one who is in a history class. Consequently, educators may be able to ease the transition to secondary school for many students by offering a wide variety of elective and extracurricular activities and encouraging students to participate. Moreover, academic strategies that promote a prosocial, *self-transcendent* purpose for learning, such as actions that will benefit society and the world, more so than self-oriented motives, such as personal interest or career goals, lead to greater persistence for the more uninteresting and tedious but essential learning tasks (Yeager et al., 2014). Students who developed a self-transcendent purpose for working hard and learning in school had improved grades in science and math courses which later translated into higher levels of enrolment in, and greater persistence at a post-secondary level.

Critical Thinking

What was your first year of high school like? Did your grades and self-esteem decline? What do you think teachers and administrators could do differently to make the transition easier for students?

Learning Objective 11.14

Identify the gender differences in academic achievement among Canadian adolescents.

Programme for International Student Assessment (PISA)

a worldwide assessment of how well 15-year-olds can apply their academic ability to solve real-life problems

Gender and Academic Achievement

Canadian 15-year-olds' academic performance continues to be among the highest of 65 nations on the **Programme for International Student Assessment (PISA)**. The PISA is a measure of the essential knowledge and skills, in subjects such as mathematics, reading, and science, that students will need to successfully compete in a global, knowledge-based economy. Girls perform better than boys in reading skills, while boys outperform girls in math skills and no significant gender differences are seen in science scores (Brochu, Deussing, Houme, & Chuy, 2013).

In addition, consistent relationships have been found between a variety of factors and school achievement. Students who correctly perceived themselves as being higher achievers were more satisfied with school and had better relationships with both schoolmates and parents. In contrast, students who correctly perceived themselves as being lower achievers were moderately associated with high-risk behaviours such as smoking, drinking, and using marijuana. Another factor associated with lower achievement levels was skipping classes. Boys were only slightly more likely to skip classes than girls. In Grade 6 almost one-quarter of students skipped classes, but by Grade 10 over 40% of students were skipping classes. When students skip classes, they are more likely to become involved with high-risk behaviours both during school hours and in the evenings. Consequently, skipping classes is associated with lower levels of academic achievement and strained relationship with parents (Health Canada, 2001b).

(Photo: Ana Abejon/E+/Getty Images)

Family interactive style predicts academic achievement in high school. Adolescents whose parents display authoritative parenting are more likely than those with authoritarian or permissive parents to achieve academic success in high school.

Learning Objective 11.15

Identify what variables predict the likelihood of dropping out of secondary school.

Early School Leavers

The cumulative effect of academic success over many years of schooling fosters a sense of academic confidence in secondary school students. Those who achieve, especially those who achieve despite backgrounds that include poverty and/or other daunting obstacles, are likely to have parents who have high aspirations for them. To be in a position to contribute to today's society and economy, a person without a high school diploma has very limited opportunities (Arriagada, 2015; Heisz & Situ, 2016). For Canadians, "completing high school is now widely considered as a minimal educational requirement for access to the labour market and lifelong learning" (Bushnik, Bar-Telford, & Bussière, 2004, p. 5).

The percentage of Canadian youth who do not have a secondary school diploma has been falling steadily over the last few decades. In 1990, ~17% of Canadian young adults had not completed their secondary school education. In comparison, by 2014, roughly 7% had not completed their secondary school education—about 9% of men and 6% of women 25- to 34-years-old—and these rates were some of the lowest in the world (Statistics Canada, 2012j, 2015f).

Early leavers from secondary school are shaped by a complex interaction of psychosocial variables (Caine, 2013; Camilleri-Cassar, 2014). Children growing up in low-SES families, especially low-income families with a lone parent, are considerably more likely to leave secondary school before graduating than are those from more economically advantaged and/or intact families. Teenagers who are living alone, who come from families that do not provide psychological support for academic achievement, or who have caregivers who have low levels of education or negative attitudes toward education are also more likely to become early school leavers

(HRDC, 2000). Coupled with lack of family or community support, peer influence may also be a factor in early school leaving; when a teenager's peer group puts a low value on achievement, the risk of leaving school early is even higher. Teens who quit school are likely to have friends who have already left school or who are contemplating leaving school early (Bushnik, Bar-Telford, & Bussière, 2004; Statistics Canada, 2008c). Other early school leavers may be those who find it hard to "fit in" with mainstream cultural expectations and feel marginalized, or alternatively, may reject mainstream cultural values (Camilleri-Cassar, 2014). Canadian researchers have also found that secondary school students who are less involved in clubs, sports, and other extracurricular and academic activities are more likely to become early school leavers (Bushnik, Bar-Telford, & Bussière, 2004). These activities are particularly important for Indigenous students, who as a group have among the lowest rates of school completion across Canada (Arriagada, 2015; Caine, 2013).

Whatever its cause, leaving secondary school before graduating is associated with a number of long-term consequences. For instance, unemployment is higher among adults who don't complete high school than among those who graduated, and nongraduates who do manage to find jobs earn lower wages than peers who graduate (Bowlby, 2008; Statistics Canada, 2012k). One successful approach that helps at-risk early school leavers improve their high school graduation rates are *dual credit* programs that help meet the individual student's learning styles and interests. These types of programs help motivate at-risk students by providing them with alternative opportunities to take courses that count toward their high school diploma, such as college or apprenticeship courses. For example, Ontario's Dual Credit School College Work Initiative program has had ~90% rates of retention and course success (School Work College Initiative, 2016).

(Photo: Luna Vandoorne/Fotolia)

Most teenagers with jobs have low-level, low-responsibility, low-paying ones. Some psychologists believe that the negative effects of employment in adolescence may be caused by the type of work teens do.

Working Teens

There is a trend toward staying in the educational system longer because youth employment opportunities are relatively poor and most students are motivated to get a better education to improve their chances of finding a better job. In fact, from age 16, it takes students about eight years to complete the transition from high school to regular employment (Franke, 2003). Another trend among Canadian students is an increase in the hours of employment from ages 15 to 19. These students are employed in mostly "entry-level" minimum wage, part-time and summer jobs. Additionally, almost half of full-time Canadian students are now employed during the school term (Galarneau & Fecteau, 2014; Marshall, 2010).

Research shows that students who have some paid employment have better school performance, but employment beyond 15 to 20 hours per week can be detrimental to academic achievement and contributes to higher levels of personal stress (Jackson & Schetagne, 2001; Marshall, 2007). Those students who seem to benefit from work allocate their time differently than those who experience negative effects. For example, Canadian teens reduce the amount of time they devote to other activities in order to work—male students start to cut back on leisure activities, such as television and video games, whereas female students reduce their time sleeping (Franke, 2003). And, it seems that students who have positive work experiences can develop increased feelings of competence and efficacy (Mortimer, 2010). Overall though, older Canadian teens experience more stress than younger teens and almost half of all women ages 18 to 19 feel constant pressure to accomplish more than they can handle, a rate that is higher than that reported by women, or men, at any other age (Marshall, 2007).

Learning Objective 11.16

Discuss the issues around employed teenagers.

Test Yourself before going on

1. _____ goals are motivated by a desire to outperform others.
2. Canadian girls outperform boys in _____; whereas Canadian boys outperform girls in _____.
3. Poverty, lack of family and peer support for academic achievement, a pattern of aggressive or risky behaviour, and lower involvement with social and extracurricular activities are some the factors associated with _____.
4. Two benefits of having a paid job if you are a secondary school student are _____ and _____, and two drawbacks are _____ and _____.

Summary

Physical Changes

11.1 Identify the major milestones of puberty.

- Puberty is triggered by a complex set of hormonal changes, beginning at about age 7 or 8. Very large increases in gonadotrophic hormones are central to the process. In girls, sexual maturity is achieved as early as age 12 or 13. Sexual maturity is achieved later in boys, with the growth spurt occurring a year or more after the start of genital changes.

11.2 Discuss how the brains and other body systems of adolescents differ from those of younger children.

- Myelination progresses steadily throughout the brain during this period and there is an inverted U-shaped developmental pattern in grey matter volumes from early childhood to adolescence as synaptogenesis is followed by synaptic pruning. Puberty is accompanied by a rapid growth spurt in height and an increase in muscle mass and fat. Boys add more muscle, and girls add more fat. Becoming overweight and less fit is a growing concern for Canadian youth.

Adolescent Sexuality

11.3 Identify the issues involved with the sexual behaviour of adolescents.

- Roughly two-thirds of all Canadian teens have had sexual intercourse by the time they reach 19 years of age.

11.4 Summarize the issues involved in teenaged pregnancy.

- Roughly 3 out of every 100 Canadian teenage girls become pregnant. Less than half of pregnant teenagers give birth. The long-term consequences for the teens that give birth are generally negative, although with support such women may overcome the disadvantages.

11.5 Discuss the emergence of sexual orientation and gender identity in adolescence.

- Hormonal, genetic, and environmental factors have been proposed to explain homosexuality. The process of realizing one's sexual orientation is a gradual one that often isn't completed until early adulthood. Transgendered teens are those whose psychological gender differs from their biological sex.

Adolescent Health

11.6 Describe how sensation-seeking affects risky behaviour in adolescents.

- Teens engage in high rates of various kinds of risky behaviour, including unprotected sex, drug use, and fast driving.

11.7 Identify the patterns of drug, alcohol, and tobacco use among adolescents in Canada.

- The use of alcohol and marijuana remains high among Canadian teenagers, but less so for the use of hard drugs and smoking. Sensation-seeking and neuroticism are associated with alcohol and drug use and abuse.

11.8 Describe the characteristics and factors that contribute to eating disorders.

- Eating disorders, such as bulimia and anorexia, are more common among teenaged girls than teenaged boys. Some theorists have proposed biological and socioeconomic causes. Others hypothesize that media images of thin models and celebrities cause the body-image distortions that underlie eating disorders. Still others emphasize the tendency of individuals with eating disorders to exhibit other kinds of distorted thoughts and be diagnosed with other psychological disorders.

11.9 Identify what factors are involved in adolescent depression and suicide

- Depression and suicide are mental health problems that are common during adolescence. Genetics, social stressors, and low self-esteem are thought to be contributing factors. Although both depression and suicide attempts are more common among girls, boys are more likely to succeed with a suicide attempt.

Changes in Thinking and Memory

11.10 Describe the characteristics of thought in Piaget's formal operational stage.

- For Piaget, the formal operational stage is characterized by the ability to apply basic cognitive operations to ideas and possibilities, in addition to actual objects.

11.11 Summarize some major research findings regarding the formal operational stage.

- Although some adolescents exhibit advanced forms of thinking, formal operational thinking is not universal, nor is it consistently used by those who are able to do it.

11.12 Describe what kinds of advances in information-processing capabilities occur during adolescence.

- Memory function improves in adolescence as teens become more proficient in metacognition, metamemory, and strategy use.

Schooling

11.13 Describe how changes in students' goals contribute to the transition to secondary school.

- The transition to middle school may be accompanied by changes in children's task- and ability-goal orientation. Secondary school offers many teens more opportunities to pursue special interests and extracurricular activities.

11.14 Identify the gender differences in academic achievement among Canadian adolescents.

- When comparing top performing 15-year-old Canadians, females surpass males in literacy, males outperform females in math, and both genders are roughly equivalent in science.

11.15 Identify what variables predict the likelihood of dropping out of secondary school.

- Those who succeed academically in secondary school typically have parents who have high aspirations for them. Those who drop out are less likely to find value in school life.

11.16 Discuss the issues around employed teenagers.

- Teens working more than 15 to 20 hours per week experience more chronic stress and are at risk of getting lower grades or engaging in more risky behaviour than those who work less. Work can be beneficial for students who have positive work experiences.

Chapter 12
Social and Personality Development in Adolescence

Picturenet/Blend Images/Getty Images

 ## Learning Objectives

THEORIES OF SOCIAL AND PERSONALITY DEVELOPMENT

12.1 Describe what happens during Erikson's identity versus role confusion stage.

12.2 Explain Marcia's theory of identity development.

SELF-CONCEPT

12.3 Discuss the ways self-understanding in adolescence differs from that in childhood.

12.4 Describe how self-esteem changes across the teenage years.

12.5 Summarize the gender role concepts of adolescents.

12.6 Describe how ethnic identity develops in Canadian youth.

MORAL DEVELOPMENT

12.7 Describe the features of moral reasoning at each of Kohlberg's stages.

12.8 Identify some important causes and effects in the development of moral reasoning.

12.9 Describe how Kohlberg's theory has been criticized.

12.10 Describe the relationship between moral reasoning abilities and antisocial behaviour.

SOCIAL RELATIONSHIPS

12.11 Describe the changing relationships of adolescents with their parents.

12.12 Discuss the issues involved in adolescents' relationships with peers.

12.13 Describe how interest in romantic relationships emerges among heterosexual and homosexual teens.

Taking their cue from the pioneering work of psychoanalytic theorist Erik Erikson (1968), some developmentalists believe that the absence of formal *rites of passage*—ceremonies that mark the transition from childhood to adulthood—in developed societies makes adolescents more vulnerable to risky behaviours such as alcohol use, unprotected sex, and aggression. Teens who become involved in these activities, say some observers, are attempting to invent their own rites of passage. How adolescents accomplish this goal depends on the peer group with which they identify. For one teenager, the rite may involve preparing college or university applications for admission and scholarships. For another adolescent, it may involve joining a street gang.

Consideration of rites of passage brings to mind Vygotsky's concept of scaffolding. Adolescents are conscious of the need to transition to adulthood, and they take many steps toward this goal on their own. But they need adults to lead the way and to support them when their steps toward maturity turn out to be missteps, whether that support occurs in the context of formal rites of passage or in more informal ways. This chapter begins with an examination of the aspects of the transition to adulthood that occur within adolescents themselves followed by a discussion of how the social world supports them.

Theories of Social and Personality Development

Thirteen-year-old Brendon took a deep breath to steady his nerves and punched in Melissa's cellphone number. He continued to breathe deeply as he waited for her to answer. Over the past few minutes, he had attempted to call her three times. However, the fear of rejection overcame him each time, and he hung up before she could answer. This time he was determined to at least say, "Hi."

Such dramas are played out every day in the world of young adolescents, and there is no denying the fact that the emergence of romantic interests is a prominent feature of this period of development. For Freud, these interests were the central theme of adolescence. Erikson and other theorists proposed models of adolescent development that were much broader in scope.

Learning Objective 12.1

Describe what happens during Erikson's identity versus role confusion stage.

genital stage

in Freud's theory, the period during which people reach psychosexual maturity

identity

an understanding of one's unique characteristics and how they have been, are, and will be manifested across ages, situations, and social roles

identity versus role confusion

in Erikson's theory, the stage during which adolescents attain a sense of who they are

identity crisis

Erikson's term for the psychological state of emotional turmoil that arises when an adolescent's sense of self becomes "unglued" so that a new, more mature sense of self can be achieved

Learning Objective 12.2

Explain Marcia's theory of identity development.

identity achievement

in Marcia's theory, the identity status achieved by a person who has been through a crisis and reached a commitment to ideological or occupational goals

moratorium

in Marcia's theory, the identity status of a person who is in a crisis but who has made no commitment

foreclosure

in Marcia's theory, the identity status of a person who has made a commitment without having gone through a crisis; the person has simply accepted a parentally or culturally defined commitment

Psychoanalytic Perspectives

According to Freud, the postpubertal years constitute the last stage of personality development; both adolescents and adults are in what Freud called the **genital stage**, the period during which psychosexual maturity is reached. Freud believed that puberty awakens the sexual drive that has lain dormant during the latency stage. Thus, for Freud, the primary developmental task of the genital stage is to channel the libido into a healthy sexual relationship.

Erikson, though not denying the importance of achieving sexual maturity, proposed that achievement of a sense of personal *identity* is a far more important developmental task faced by adolescents. He described *identity* as a sense of self-continuity (Erikson, 1968). More recent theorists, elaborating on his idea, define **identity** as an understanding of one's unique characteristics and how they are manifested across ages, situations, and social roles. Thus, in Erikson's model, the central crisis of adolescence is **identity versus role confusion**.

Erikson argued that the child's early sense of identity comes partly "unglued" in early adolescence because of the combination of rapid body growth and the sexual changes of puberty. Erikson claimed that during this period the adolescent's mind is in a kind of moratorium between childhood and adulthood. The old identity will no longer suffice; a new identity must be forged, one that will equip the young person for the myriad roles of adult life—occupational roles, sexual roles, religious roles, and others.

Confusion about all these role choices is inevitable and leads to a pivotal transition Erikson called the *identity crisis*. The **identity crisis** is a period during which an adolescent is troubled by his lack of an identity. Erikson believed that adolescents' tendency to identify with peer groups is a defence against the emotional turmoil engendered by the identity crisis. In a sense, he claimed, teens protect themselves against the unpleasant emotions of the identity crisis by merging their individual identities with that of a group (Erikson, 1980a). The teenaged group thus forms a base of security from which the young person can move toward a unique solution of the identity crisis. Ultimately, however, each teenager must achieve an integrated view of himself, including his own pattern of beliefs, occupational goals, and relationships.

Marcia's Theory of Identity Achievement

Much of the research on the formation of adolescent identity is based on Simon Fraser University professor emeritus James Marcia's descriptions of *identity statuses*. Marcia's early studies confirmed Erikson's general conceptions of the adolescent identity process (Marcia, 1966, 1980, 2001; Schwartz, 2001). Expanding one of Erikson's ideas, Marcia offers that adolescent identity formation has two key parts: a crisis and a commitment. By *crisis*, Marcia means a period of decision making when old values and old choices are re-examined. This may occur as an upheaval—the classic notion of a crisis—or it may occur gradually. The outcome of the re-evaluation is a *commitment* to some specific role, value, goal, or ideology. In sum, the achievement of an "ego identity refers to a sense of who one is, based on who one has been and who one can realistically imagine oneself to be in the future" (Marcia, 2002, p. 202).

If you put these two elements together, as shown in **Figure 12.1**, you can see that four different *identity statuses* are possible:

- **Identity achievement**: The person has been through a crisis and has reached a commitment to ideological, occupational, or other goals.
- **Moratorium**: A crisis is in progress, but no commitment has yet been made.
- **Foreclosure**: The person has made a commitment without having gone through a crisis. No reassessment of old positions has been made. Instead, the young person has simply accepted a parentally or culturally defined commitment.

Figure 12.1 The four identity statuses proposed by Marcia, based on Erikson's theory. For a fully achieved identity, the young person must have both examined her values or goals and reached a firm commitment.

(**SOURCE:** Marcia, J.E. (1980). Identity in adolescence. In J. Adelson (Ed.), *Handbook of adolescent psychology* (pp. 159–187). New York, NY: Wiley. Reproduced with permission of John Wiley & Sons Inc.)

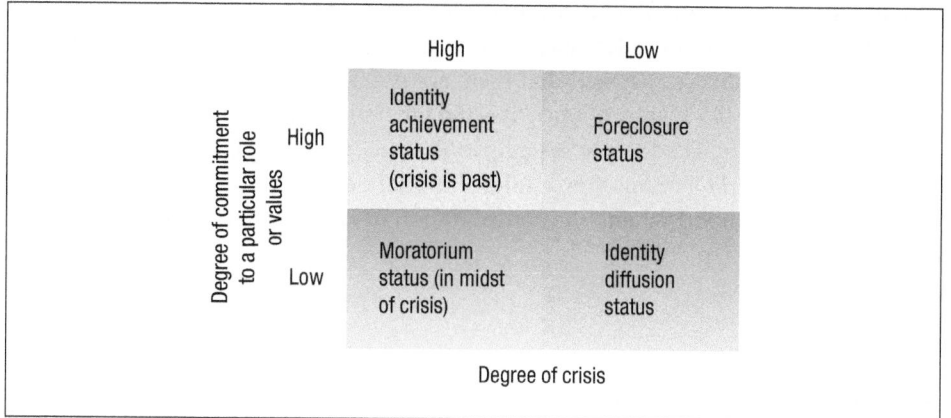

- **Identity diffusion**: The young person is not in the midst of a crisis (although there may have been one in the past) and has not made a commitment. Diffusion may thus represent either an early stage in the process (before a crisis) or a failure to reach a commitment after a crisis.

The whole process of identity formation may occur later than Erikson and Marcia thought, perhaps because cognitive development is more strongly related to identity formation than either believed. Research suggests that teens who are most advanced in the development of logical thinking and other information-processing skills are also the most likely to have attained Marcia's status of identity achievement (Klaczynski, Fauth, & Swanger, 1998). In addition, identity statuses fluctuate during the teen years (Klimstra et al., 2010). That is, a teen who reaches Marcia's identity achievement status doesn't necessarily retain that status over time.

There is also evidence that the quest for personal identity continues throughout the lifespan, with alternating periods of instability and stability (Marcia, 2002, 2010). For example, a person's sense of being "young" or "old" and the integration of that idea into a sense of belonging to a particular generation appears to change several

identity diffusion

in Marcia's theory, the identity status of a person who is not in the midst of a crisis and who has made no commitment

(*Photos:* left, Miriam Reik/Alamy Stock Photo; right, Sabena Jane Blackbird/Alamy Stock Photo)

In the Jewish ceremony called *bar mitzvah* (for boys) or *bat mitzvah* (for girls), 12- or 13-year-olds read from the Torah in Hebrew and are admitted to full adult status in the congregation. This Tanzanian boy has had his face painted with white clay as part of an adolescent rite of passage.

times over the course of the adolescent and adult years (Sato, Shimonska, Nakazato, & Kawaai, 1997). Consequently, adolescence may be only one period of identity formation among several. What makes the formation of an identity during adolescence special is that all the essential elements for the formation of identity are present for the first time in a person's life. The person now possesses a sufficient level of physical, sexual, cognitive, and moral maturity. In conjunction with this, society encourages the individual to take on adult roles, such as worker, parent, and citizen (Marcia, 2002).

Finally, Marcia has suggested that there are two key reasons why adolescence is so important in the life cycle. For one, "it is the time during which a fourth personality structure, an *identity*, is added to the previous structures of ego, self, and superego" (Marcia, 2002, p. 201). For another, adolescence defines the period of transition from childhood to adulthood when "the consolidation of *identity* marks the end of childhood" (Marcia, 1993, p. 3).

Test Yourself before going on

1. According to Erikson, a teen who fails to successfully resolve the identity crisis risks developing a sense of _____ _____.

2. Classify each of these behaviours as indicative of (IA) identity achievement, (M) moratorium, (F) foreclosure, or (ID) identity diffusion.
   _____ (a) Lucy has decided on a pre-med major, because her mother and grandmother are physicians.
   _____ (b) Carl is taking a few college courses in different disciplines to figure out what he wants to major in.
   _____ (c) After considering several different options, Rosa has decided to join the Marines after graduation.
   _____ (d) Sean dropped out of high school at 16 and since then has moved from one minimum-wage job to another. He gives little thought to his future.

Critical Thinking

3. The implication in Marcia's formulation is that foreclosure is a less developmentally mature status—that one must go through a crisis in order to achieve a mature identity. Does this make sense to you? What is your current identity status? Has it changed much over the past few years?

Self-Concept

In the chapter on Physical and Cognitive Development in Adolescence, you read that thinking becomes more abstract in adolescence. Thus, you shouldn't be surprised to find that teenagers' self-concepts are a lot more complex than those of younger children.

Learning Objective 12.3

Discuss the ways self-understanding in adolescence differs from that in childhood.

Self-Understanding

Through the elementary school years, the child's self-concept becomes more focused on enduring internal characteristics: the psychological self. This trend continues in adolescence, with self-definition becoming more abstract. Advances in self-understanding among adolescents are both facilitated by and contribute to the increasing stability of the Big Five personality traits during this period. As a result, enduring traits such as shyness—or *introversion* in Big Five terminology—show up in adolescents' self-descriptions far more often than they do in those of younger children. This change was evident in the replies of a 9-year-old and an 11-year-old to the question "Who am I?" in Montemayor and Eisen's study, cited in the chapter on Social and Personality Development in Middle Childhood. Here's a 17-year-old's answer to the same question:

I am a human being. I am a girl. I am an individual. I don't know who I am. I am a Pisces. I am a moody person. I am an indecisive person. I am an ambitious person. I am a very curious person. I am not an individual. I am a loner.

Figure 12.2 As they get older, children and adolescents define themselves less and less by what they look like and more and more by what they believe or feel.

(**SOURCE:** Based on Montemayor, R., & Eisen, M. (1977). The development of self-conceptions from childhood to adolescence. *Developmental Psychology*, 13, 314–319. Table 1, p. 316.)

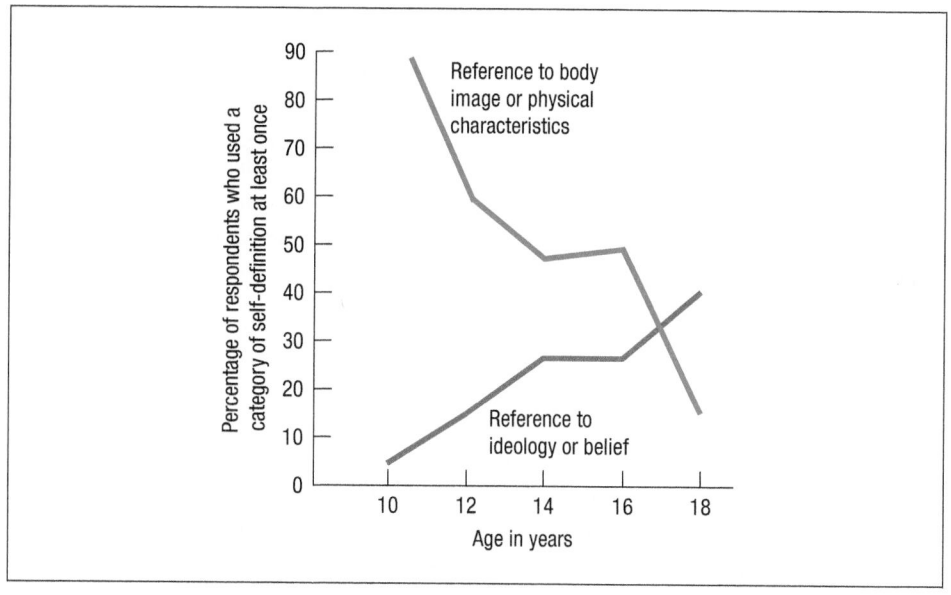

I am an American (God help me). I am a Democrat. I am a liberal person. I am a radical. I am a conservative. I am a pseudoliberal. I am an atheist. I am not a classifiable person (i.e., I don't want to be). (Montemayor & Eisen, 1977, p. 318)

Clearly, this girl's self-concept is even less tied to her physical characteristics or even her abilities than are those of younger children. She is describing abstract traits or ideology.

You can see the change graphically in **Figure 12.2**, which is based on the answers of all 262 participants in Montemayor and Eisen's study. Each of the answers to the "Who am I?" question was categorized as a reference either to physical properties ("I am tall," "I have blue eyes") or to ideology ("I am an environmentalist," "I believe in God"). As you can see, appearance was a highly prominent dimension in the preteen and early teen years but became less dominant in late adolescence, a time when ideology and belief became more important. By late adolescence, most teenagers think of themselves in terms of enduring traits, beliefs, personal philosophy, and moral standards (Damon & Hart, 1988).

At the same time, adolescents' self-concept becomes more differentiated, as they come to see themselves somewhat differently in each of several roles: as a student, with friends, with parents, and in romantic relationships (Harter, 2012). Once these self-concepts are formed, they begin to influence adolescents' behaviour. For example, a longitudinal study of Canadian teens found that a strong self-concept is important to the development of good mental and physical health (Park, 2003). Conversely, a weak self-concept during adolescence puts girls at risk for depression, poor self-perceived health, and obesity, and boys at risk for obesity and inactivity in young adulthood.

Adolescents' academic self-concepts seem to come both from internal comparisons of their performance to a self-generated ideal and from external comparisons to peer performance (Harter, 2012). It also appears that perceived competency in one domain affects how a teenager feels about his ability in other areas. For example, if a high school student fails a math course, it is likely to affect his self-concept in other disciplines as well as in math. This suggests that teens' self-concepts are hierarchical in nature: Perceived competencies in various domains serve as building blocks for creating a global academic self-concept (Cheng, Xiaoyan, Dajun, 2006; Yeung, Chui, & Lau, 1999).

Table 12.1 Influences on Adolescent Self-Esteem

Themes	Sub-themes
Self	Physical appearance, physical state, mental ability, psychological state, personality attributes, aspirations, other
Relationships	Parents, siblings, family, friends, boy-friend/girlfriend/romantic, teachers, other
School	Marks, homework/study, school, post-school plans
Lifestyle	Exercise, relaxing, eating, beer, sex, entertainment, arts, going out, hobbies, shopping, drugs, other
Achievements	Job/work, sports, artistic, housework, financial, other
Experiences and events	Time, events, religion/spirituality, migration, other

(**SOURCE:** Khanlou, 2004, from Table 1, p. 409, Influences on Adolescent Self-Esteem in Multicultural Canadian Secondary Schools. *Public Health Nursing*, Blackwell Publishing, Inc. Reproduced with permission of John Wiley & Sons Inc.)

Self-Esteem

Learning Objective 12.4

Describe how self-esteem changes across the teenage years.

There is an overall rise in self-esteem throughout adolescence which continues to increase, albeit more slowly, throughout early adulthood (Erol & Orth, 2011). A study of students in multicultural Canadian secondary schools found that many factors act variously upon a teen's self-esteem, especially personal characteristics, relationships with significant others, lifestyle factors, and achievements (Khanlou, 2004) (see **Table 12.1**). As well, several studies have found that high self-esteem is correlated with positive developmental outcomes. For example, teens with high self-esteem are better able to resist peer pressure and achieve higher grades in school (Moksnes, Moljord, Espnes, & Byrne, 2010). Conversely, low self-esteem is associated with poorer mental and physical health, including antisocial behaviour, eating disorders, anxiety, depression, and suicidal thinking (Erol & Orth, 2011; Obeid, Buchholz, Boerner, Henderson, & Norris, 2013; Sowislo & Orth, 2013; Trzesniewski et al., 2006).

Gender Roles

Learning Objective 12.5

Summarize the gender role concepts of adolescents.

gender role identity

gender-related aspects of the psychological self

Developmentalists use the term **gender role identity** to refer to gender-related aspects of the psychological self. In contrast to younger children, adolescents understand that gender roles are social conventions, so their attitudes toward them are more flexible (Katz & Ksansnak, 1994). Parental attitudes and parental behaviour become increasingly important in shaping teens' ideas about gender and sex roles (Cox, Mezulis, & Hyde, 2010; Ridolfo, Chepp, & Milkie, 2013). In addition, concepts that were largely separate earlier in development, such as beliefs about gender roles and sexuality, seem to become integrated into a conceptual framework that teens use to formulate ideas about the significance of gender in personal identity and social relationships (Mallet, Apostolidis, & Paty, 1997).

In the early days of research on gender role identity, psychologists conceived of masculinity and femininity as polar opposites. A person could be masculine or feminine, but couldn't be both. However, theories first advanced in the 1970s by Sandra Bem and others have resulted in a large body of research in support of the notion that masculinity and femininity are dimensions along a continuum and each may be found in varying quantities in the personalities of both men and women (Bem, 1974; Spence & Helmreich, 1978). A male or a female can be high or low on masculinity or femininity, or both. Indeed, if people are categorized as high or low on each of these two dimensions, based on their self-descriptions, four basic gender role types emerge: *masculine, feminine, androgynous,* and *undifferentiated* (see **Figure 12.3**).

Figure 12.3 This diagram illustrates how the dimensions of masculinity and femininity interact to produce four types of gender role orientation.

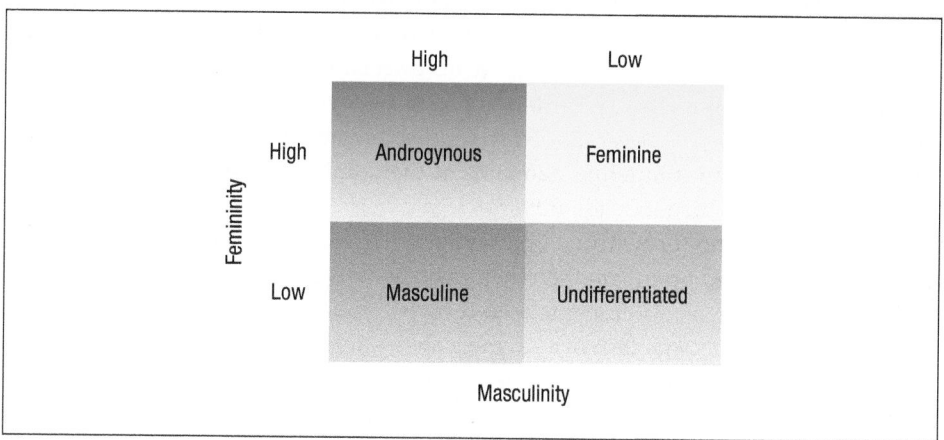

The masculine and feminine types are the traditional categories; a person in either of these categories sees himself or herself as high in one and low in the other. A "masculine" teenager or adult, according to this view, is thus one who perceives himself (or herself) as having many traditional masculine qualities and few traditional feminine qualities. A feminine teenager or adult shows the reverse pattern. In contrast, androgynous individuals see themselves as having both masculine and feminine traits; undifferentiated individuals describe themselves as lacking both.

Interestingly, research suggests that either an androgynous or a masculine gender role identity is associated with higher self-esteem among both boys and girls (Huang, Zhu, Zheng, Zhang, & Shiomi, 2012; Woo & Oei, 2006). Similarly, girls with a feminine gender identity are more prone to rumination, a thought process that focuses on anxiety-inducing stimuli (e.g., peer judgments of physical attractiveness) and can lead to depression (Cox et al., 2010). These findings make sense in light of the existence of a "masculine bias" in North American and other Western societies, which causes both men and women to value traditionally masculine qualities, such as independence and competitiveness, more than many traditionally feminine qualities, such as nurturance and gracefulness.

Ethnic Identity

There are more than 200 distinct ethnic identities in Canada, and Canadian identities vary along linguistic, national, regional, racial, and religious groupings (Statistics Canada, 2013b). Minority teenagers, especially recent immigrant youth, face the task of creating two identities in adolescence. Like other teens, they must develop a sense of individual identity that they believe sets them apart from others. In addition, they must develop an **ethnic identity** that includes self-identification as a member of their specific group, commitment to that group and its values and attitudes, and some attitudes (positive or negative) about the group to which they belong (Phinney, Ferguson, & Tate, 1997). Moreover, the process of developing an ethnic identity can be at variance with a social environment that is dominated by the concerns of the majority (Phinney, Ong, & Madden, 2000). For example, immigrant parents' expectations about helping out with family obligations, obeying parents, and dating or socializing can differ from the views of the adolescents who have been exposed to majority cultural values (Sodhi Kalsi, 2003). Furthermore, intergenerational differences tend to become more pronounced the longer the term of residency.

Psychologist Jean Phinney has proposed that, in adolescence, the development of a complete ethnic identity moves through three stages (Phinney, 1990; Phinney & Rosenthal, 1992). The first stage is an *unexamined ethnic identity* and is typical of

Learning Objective 12.6

Describe how ethnic identity develops in Canadian youth.

ethnic identity

a sense of belonging to an ethnic group

younger children who haven't paid attention to or haven't shown much interest in their ethnic identity. Phinney's second stage is the *ethnic identity search*. This search is typically triggered by some experience that makes ethnicity relevant—perhaps an example of blatant prejudice or merely the widening experience of high school. At this point, the young person begins to compare his own ethnic group with others, to try to arrive at his own judgments. This exploration stage is eventually followed by the third stage, *ethnic identity achievement*, in which adolescents develop strategies for solving conflicts between the competing demands of the dominant culture and those of the ethnic group with which they identify.

Adolescents who form strong and favourable ethnic identities have higher levels of self-esteem and optimism than their peers with weak ethnic identities (Phinney et al., 1997). Moreover, adolescents who form a combined identity based on strong identification and participation in both their own ethnic culture and the larger culture have the highest self-esteem and the best outcomes. Teens who possess a **bicultural identity** not only feel more positive about their own ethnic group, but they have more favourable relationships with people from other ethnic groups as well (Phinney et al., 1997; Phinney & Kohatsu, 1997).

Recent-immigrant youth experience mixed feelings toward Canadian society. Although they enjoy the freedom associated with Canadian youth culture, they feel "somewhat overwhelmed and alienated by what they perceive to be its rampant consumerism and superficiality" (CCSD, 2000a). Those who speak neither English nor French face the extra challenge of learning a new language as well as overcoming social isolation when they arrive in Canada. A Canadian Council on Social Development report on cultural diversity (CCSD, 2000b) found that new arrivals have to contend with developing new relationships with friends in whom they can confide. More than one-quarter of immigrant youth aged 12 to 14 who have been in Canada less than 10 years reported that they do not have someone on whom they can rely during a crisis or when making important decisions. Consequently, immigrant youth often seek social support through formal social groups such as volunteer and religious organizations, and actively participate in religious organizations in part as a way to establish a social network (see **Development in the Real World**). Once they have lived in Canada for at least a decade, immigrant youth adopt patterns of lifestyle behaviours similar to those of Canadian-born youth (CCSD, 2000b). Specifically, immigrant youth who have lived in Canada for more than 10 years have about as many friends in whom they can confide as Canadian-born youth.

bicultural identity
personal identification and satisfaction with more than one culture

Young recent immigrants often develop two identities: a psychological sense of self and an ethnic identity. Those who succeed at both tasks often think of themselves as "bicultural" and have an easier time relating to peers of the same and other ethnicities.

(*Photos:* left, DragonImages/Fotolia; right, William Perugini/Shutterstock)

Development in the Real World

The Students Commission

The Students Commission, a diverse, global-minded organization that is run by youth for youth across Canada, was established in 1991 to bring students together to discuss issues and direct public policy both nationally and internationally. Delegates of The Students Commission have had a voice at the tables of the Prime Minister, the Governor General, cabinet ministers, provincial premiers, and business, education, community, and labour leaders across Canada, as well as at many prominent international organizations, such as the United Nations, APEC, and UNESCO (Students Commission, 1995, 2004).

The Students Commission:

- holds conferences for youth, and for adults who work with youth, to learn skills, share information, and address barriers.
- supports young people to develop projects to assist people in their communities.
- delivers workshops in schools, community organizations, and at our offices.
- trains young people in office skills, research and evaluation, facilitation, desk-top publishing, web design, and video production.
- develops programs with youth in the areas of substance abuse, violence prevention, mental health, stress management, and tobacco prevention.
- engages youth in discussion groups, consultations, and youth advisories to amplify the ideas of young people.
- conducts research and evaluation on meaningful youth engagement, communicates results, and develops policies and guidelines.
- develops and distributes tools and resources for youth and adults who work with youth.

(**SOURCE:** http://www.studentscommission.ca/aorg/aboutusref_e.php The Students Commission, 2016.)

Test Yourself before going on

1. Which of the following characteristics are likely to be included in a teenager's self-description but not in a school-aged child's self-description (T), and which might be included in both (B)?
   _____ (a) happy
   _____ (b) honest
   _____ (c) tall
   _____ (d) friendly
   _____ (e) environmentalist
2. Choose the correct answer in the following sentence: Self-esteem is (higher/lower) in early adolescence than in the later teen years.
3. Classify each description as indicative of one of the following gender role identities: (A) androgynous, (M) masculine, (F) feminine, or (U) undifferentiated sex role.
   _____ (a) Luis views self-reliance as the defining characteristic of his personality.
   _____ (b) Sandra's ability to offer compassionate and caring responses to her friends' problems is the trait she feels best defines her personality.
   _____ (c) Montel prides himself on responding according to the demands of different situations. If a problem calls for assertiveness, he can tackle it head

on. If a problem calls for empathy or patience, he feels that he can handle that as well.
   _____ (d) Keisha has a poorly developed sense of self and has trouble describing her identity in terms of personality traits.

4. In the table below, briefly summarize Phinney's stages of ethnic identity development.

Stage	Summary
Unexamined	
Search	
Achievement	

Critical Thinking

5. Which of Bem's gender role identity categories best describes you? (Look back at Figure 12.3.) Do you think your gender role identity has changed since you were a teenager?

Moral Development

As you learned in the chapter on Social and Personality Development in Middle Childhood, theorists representing various orientations think differently about moral development. The theorist whose work has had the most powerful impact has been psychologist Lawrence Kohlberg (Bergman, 2002; Colby, Kohlberg, Gibbs, & Lieberman, 1983; Kohlberg, 1976, 1981). Theories of moral reasoning have also been important in explanations of adolescent antisocial behaviour.

Kohlberg's Theory of Moral Reasoning

Learning Objective 12.7

Describe the features of moral reasoning at each of Kohlberg's stages.

Piaget proposed two stages in the development of moral reasoning. Working from Piaget's basic assumptions, Kohlberg devised a way of measuring moral reasoning based on research participants' responses to moral dilemmas such as the following:

> In Europe, a woman was near death from a special kind of cancer. There was one drug that the doctors thought might save her. It was a form of radium that a druggist in the same town had recently discovered. The drug was expensive to make, but the druggist was charging ten times what the drug cost him to make. He paid $200 for the radium and charged $2000 for a small dose of the drug. The sick woman's husband, Heinz, went to everyone he knew to borrow the money, but he could only get together about $1000.... He told the druggist that his wife was dying, and asked him to sell it cheaper or let him pay later. But the druggist said, "No, I discovered the drug and I'm going to make money from it." So Heinz got desperate and broke into the man's store to steal the drug for his wife. (Kohlberg & Elfenbein, 1975, p. 621)

Kohlberg analyzed participants' answers to questions about such dilemmas (e.g., "Should Heinz have stolen the drug? Why?") and concluded that there were three levels of moral development, each made up of two substages, as summarized in **Table 12.2**. It is important to understand that what determines the stage or level of a person's moral judgment is not any specific moral choice but the form of reasoning used to justify that choice. For example, either response to Kohlberg's dilemma—that Heinz should steal the drug or that he should not—could be justified with logic at any given stage.

Table 12.2 Kohlberg's Stages of Moral Development

Level	Stages	Description
Level I: Preconventional	Stage 1: Punishment and Obedience Orientation	The child or teenager decides what is wrong on the basis of what is punished. Obedience is valued for its own sake, but the child obeys because the adults have superior power.
	Stage 2: Individualism, Instrumental Purpose, and Exchange	Children and teens follow rules when it is in their immediate interest. What is good is what brings pleasant results.
Level II: Conventional	Stage 3: Mutual Interpersonal Expectations, Relationships, and Interpersonal Conformity	Moral actions are those that live up to the expectations of the family or other significant group. "Being good" becomes important for its own sake.
	Stage 4: Social System and Conscience (Law and Order)	Moral actions are those so defined by larger social groups or the society as a whole. One should fulfill duties one has agreed to and uphold laws, except in extreme cases.
Level III: Postconventional	Stage 5: Social Contract or Utility and Individual Rights	This stage involves acting so as to achieve the "greatest good for the greatest number." The teenager or adult is aware that most values are relative and laws are changeable, although rules should be upheld to preserve the social order. Still, there are some basic absolute values, such as the importance of each person's life and liberty.
	Stage 6: Universal Ethical Principles	The small number of adults who reason at stage 6 develop and follow self-chosen ethical principles in determining what is right. These ethical principles are part of an articulated, integrated, carefully thought-out, and consistently followed system of values and principles.

(SOURCES: Based on Kohlberg, 1976; Lickona, 1978.)

Figure 12.4 These findings are from Colby and Kohlberg's long-term longitudinal study of a group of boys who were asked about Kohlberg's moral dilemmas every few years from age 10 through early adulthood. As they got older, the stage or level of their answers changed, with conventional reasoning appearing fairly widely at high school age. Postconventional, or principled, reasoning was not very common at any age.

(**SOURCE**: Colby et al., 1983, Figure 1, p. 46. © The Society for Research in Child Development. Reproduced by permission of Wiley & Sons, Ltd.)

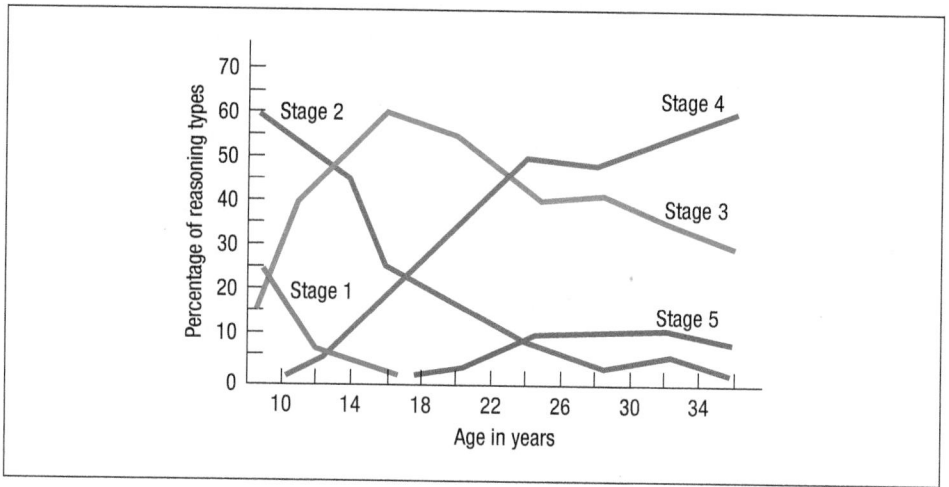

AGE AND MORAL REASONING   The stages are correlated somewhat loosely with age. Very few children reason beyond stage 1 or 2, and stage 2 and stage 3 reasoning are the types most commonly found among adolescents (Walker, de Vries, & Trevethan, 1987). Among adults, stages 3 and 4 are the most common (Gibson, 1990). Two research examples illustrate these overall age trends. The first, shown in **Figure 12.4**, comes from Kohlberg's own longitudinal study of 58 boys, first interviewed when they were age 10 and then followed for more than 20 years (Colby et al., 1983). **Table 12.3** shows cross-sectional data from a study by Lawrence Walker and his colleagues (1987). They studied 10 boys and 10 girls at each of four ages, interviewing the parents of each child as well. The results of these two studies, although not identical, point to remarkably similar conclusions about the order of emergence of the various stages and about the approximate ages at which they predominate. In both studies, stage 2 reasoning dominates at around age 10, and stage 3 reasoning is most common at about age 16.

PRECONVENTIONAL REASONING   At level I, **preconventional morality**, the child's judgments are based on sources of authority who are close by and physically superior—usually the parents. Just as descriptions of others are largely external at this level, so the standards the child uses to judge rightness or wrongness are external

Critical Thinking

How would you respond to the Heinz dilemma? What does your response suggest about your level of moral reasoning?

preconventional morality

in Kohlberg's theory, the level of moral reasoning in which judgments are based on authorities outside the self

Table 12.3 Percentages of Children and Parents Who Show Moral Reasoning at Each of Kohlberg's Stages

Age	Stage								
	1	1–2	2	2–3	3	3–4	4	4–5	5
6 (Grade 1)	10%	70%	15%	5%	—	—	—	—	—
9 (Grade 4)	—	25%	40%	35%	—	—	—	—	—
12 (Grade 7)	—	—	15%	60%	25%	—	—	—	—
15 (Grade 10)	—	—	—	40%	55%	5%	—	—	—
Parents	—	—	—	1%	15%	70%	11%	3%	—

(**SOURCE**: Walker et al., 1987, from Table 1, p. 849, "Moral stages and moral orientations in real-life and hypothetical dilemmas," *Child Development*, 60, 842–858. Reproduced with permission of Wiley & Sons, Ltd.)

rather than internal. In particular, the outcome or consequence of an action determines the rightness or wrongness of the action.

In stage 1 of this level—the *punishment and obedience orientation*—the child relies on the physical consequences of some action to decide whether it is right or wrong. If he is punished, then the behaviour was wrong; if he is not punished, then it was right. He is obedient to adults because they are bigger and stronger.

In stage 2—*individualism, instrumental purpose, and exchange*—the child or adolescent operates on the principle that you should do things that are rewarded and avoid things that are punished. For this reason, the stage is sometimes called *naive hedonism*. If it feels good, or brings pleasant results, then it is good. Some beginning of concern for other people is apparent during this stage, but only if that concern can be expressed as something that benefits the child or teenager himself as well. So he can enter into agreements such as "If you help me, I'll help you."

To illustrate, here are some responses to variations of the Heinz dilemma, drawn from studies of children and teenagers in a number of different cultures, all of whom were at stage 2:

> He should steal the drug for his wife because if she dies he'll have to pay for the funeral, and that costs a lot. [Taiwan]

> [He should steal the drug because] he should protect the life of his wife so he doesn't have to stay alone in life. [Puerto Rico] (Snarey, 1985, p. 221)

conventional morality

in Kohlberg's theory, the level of moral reasoning in which judgments are based on rules or norms of a group to which the person belongs

CONVENTIONAL REASONING   At the next major level, the level of **conventional morality**, rules or norms of a group to which the individual belongs become the basis of moral judgments, whether that group is the family, the peer group, a church, or the nation. What the chosen reference group defines as right or good is right or good in the individual's view. Again, very few children exhibit conventional thinking, but many adolescents are capable of this kind of moral reasoning.

Stage 3 (the first stage of level II) is the stage of *mutual interpersonal expectations, relationships, and interpersonal conformity* (sometimes also called the *good boy/nice girl stage*). Regardless of age, individuals who reason at this stage believe that good behaviour is what pleases other people. They value trust, loyalty, respect, gratitude, and maintenance of mutual relationships. Andy, a boy Kohlberg interviewed who was at stage 3, said:

> I try to do things for my parents, they've always done things for you. I try to do everything my mother says, I try to please her. Like she wants me to be a doctor and I want to, too, and she's helping me get up there. (Kohlberg, 1964, p. 401)

Another mark of this third stage is that the individual makes judgments based on intentions as well as on outward behaviour. If someone "didn't mean to do it," then the wrongdoing is seen as less serious than if the person did it "on purpose."

Stage 4, the second stage of the conventional morality level, incorporates the norms of a larger reference group into moral judgments. Kohlberg labelled this the stage of *social system and conscience*. It is also sometimes called the *law-and-order orientation*. People reasoning at this stage focus on doing their duty, respecting authority, and following rules and laws. The emphasis is less on what is pleasing to particular people (as in stage 3) and more on adhering to a complex set of regulations. However, the regulations themselves are not questioned, and morality and legality are assumed to be equivalent. Therefore, for a person at stage 4, something that is legal is right, whereas something that is illegal is wrong. Consequently, changes in law can effect changes in the moral views of individuals who reason at stage 4.

postconventional morality

in Kohlberg's theory, the level of moral reasoning in which judgments are based on an integration of individual rights and the needs of society

POSTCONVENTIONAL REASONING   The transition to level III, **postconventional morality**, is marked by several changes, the most important of which is a shift in the source of authority. Individuals who reason at level I see authority as totally outside of themselves; at level II, the judgments or rules of external authorities are internalized, but they are not questioned or analyzed; at level III, a new kind of personal authority emerges, in which an individual makes choices and judgments based on self-chosen principles or on principles that are assumed to transcend the needs and concerns of any individual or group. Postconventional thinkers represent only a minority of adults and an even smaller minority of adolescents.

In stage 5 at this level, which Kohlberg called the *social contract orientation*, such self-chosen principles begin to be evident. Rules, laws, and regulations are not seen as irrelevant; they are important ways of ensuring fairness. But people operating at this level also acknowledge that there are times when the rules, laws, and regulations need to be ignored or changed.

The American civil rights movement of the 1950s and 1960s is a good example of stage 5 reasoning in action. *Civil disobedience*—deliberately breaking laws that were believed to be immoral—arose as a way of protesting racial segregation. For example, in restaurants, African Americans intentionally took seats that were reserved for whites. It is important to note that the practice of civil disobedience does not usually involve avoiding the penalties that accompany criminal behaviour. Indeed, some of the most effective and poignant images from that period of U.S. history are photographs of individuals who surrendered and were jailed for breaking segregation laws. This behaviour illustrates the stage 5 view that, as a general principle, upholding the law is important, even though a specific law that is deemed to be immoral can, or even should, be broken when breaking it will serve to promote the common good.

(Photo: The Herald/AP Images)

Civil disobedience involves intentionally breaking laws one believes to be immoral. For example, in the early years of the U.S. civil rights movement, African Americans broke laws that excluded them from certain sections of restaurants by "sitting in" at whites-only lunch counters. Practitioners of civil disobedience do not try to evade the consequences of their actions, because they believe in upholding the law as a general principle even though they may view some specific laws as immoral. Thus, the thinking that underlies acts of civil disobedience represents Kohlberg's postconventional level of moral reasoning.

In his original writing about moral development, Kohlberg also included a sixth stage, the *universal ethical principles orientation*. Stage 6 reasoning involves balancing equally valid, but conflicting, moral principles against one another in order to determine which should be given precedence with respect to a specific moral issue. For example, in arguing against capital punishment, some people say that an individual's right to life is more important than society's right to exact justice from those who are convicted of heinous crimes. Such a claim might or might not be an example of stage 6 reasoning. Remember, the key to assessing an individual's stage of moral development is to fully probe the reasoning behind her answer to a question about a moral dilemma. Sometimes this kind of probing reveals that arguments that, on first glance, appear to represent stage 6 thinking are actually based on the authority of a religious tradition or a highly respected individual, in which case the reasoning is conventional rather than postconventional. Occasionally, though, the individual making such an argument is able to explain it in terms of a universal ethical principle that must always be adhered to regardless of any other considerations. In the case of opposition to the death penalty, the universal ethical principle would be the idea that the maintenance of human life is the highest of all moral principles. Note, however, that a person reasoning at stage 6 would not argue that society has no right to punish criminals. Instead, she would say that, in situations where upholding such rights involves termination of a human life, that person's right to life takes precedence.

Kohlberg argued that this sequence of reasoning is both universal and hierarchically organized. That is, each stage grows out of the preceding one. Kohlberg did not suggest that all individuals eventually progress through all six stages, or even that each stage is tied to specific ages. But he insisted that the order is invariant and universal. He also believed that the social environment determines how slowly or rapidly individuals move through the stages.

The evidence seems fairly strong that the stages follow one another in the sequence Kohlberg proposed. Long-term longitudinal studies of teenagers and young adults in the United States, Israel, and Turkey show that changes in participants' reasoning nearly always occur in the hypothesized order (Colby et al., 1983; Nisan & Kohlberg, 1982; Snarey, Reimer, & Kohlberg, 1985; Walker, 1989). People do not skip stages, and movement down the sequence rather than up occurs only about 5 to 7% of the time.

Variations of Kohlberg's dilemmas have been used with children in a wide range of countries, including both Western and non-Western, developed and developing (Snarey, 1985). In every culture, researchers find higher stages of reasoning among older children, but cultures differ in the highest level of reasoning observed. In urban cultures (both Western and non-Western), stage 5 is typically the highest stage observed; in agricultural societies and those in which there is little opportunity for formal education, stage 4 is typically the highest. Collectively, this evidence seems to provide quite strong support for the universality of Kohlberg's stage sequence.

Learning Objective 12.8

Identify some important causes and effects in the development of moral reasoning.

Causes and Consequences of Moral Development

The most obvious reason for the general correlations between Kohlberg's stages and chronological age is cognitive development. Specifically, it appears that children must have a firm grasp of concrete operational thinking before they can develop or use conventional moral reasoning. Likewise, formal operations appears to be necessary for advancement to the postconventional level.

To be more specific, Kohlberg and many other theorists suggest that the decline of egocentrism that occurs as an individual moves through Piaget's concrete and formal operational stages is the cognitive-developmental variable that matters most in moral reasoning. The idea is that the greater a child's or adolescent's ability to look at a situation from another person's perspective, the more advanced he is likely to be in moral reasoning. Psychologists use the term **role-taking** to refer to this ability (Selman, 1980). Research has provided strong support for the hypothesized link between role-taking and moral development (Kuhn, Kohlberg, Languer, & Haan, 1977; Walker, 1980).

role-taking

the ability to look at a situation from another person's perspective

Nevertheless, cognitive development isn't enough. Kohlberg thought that the development of moral reasoning also required support from the social environment. Specifically, he claimed that to foster mature moral reasoning, a child's or teenager's social environment must provide him with opportunities for meaningful, reciprocal dialogue about moral issues.

Longitudinal research relating parenting styles and family climate to levels of moral reasoning suggest that Kohlberg was right (Pratt, Arnold, & Pratt, 1999). Parents' ability to identify, understand, and respond to children's and adolescents' less mature forms of moral reasoning seems to be particularly important to the development of moral reasoning. This ability on the part of parents is important because people of all ages have difficulty understanding and remembering moral arguments that are more advanced than their own level (Pratt, Norris, Hebblethwaite, & Arnold, 2008). Thus, a parent who can express her own moral views in words that reflect her child's level of understanding is more likely to be able to influence the child's moral development.

Perhaps most importantly, teenagers' level of moral reasoning appears to be positively correlated with prosocial behaviour and negatively related to antisocial behaviour (Ma, 2012; Schonert-Reichl, 1999). In other words, the highest levels of prosocial behaviour are found among teens at the highest levels of moral reasoning (compared with their peers). Alternatively, the highest levels of antisocial behaviour are found among adolescents at the lowest levels of moral reasoning.

Criticisms of Kohlberg's Theory

Criticisms of Kohlberg's theory have come from theorists representing different perspectives.

Learning Objective 12.9

Describe how Kohlberg's theory has been criticized.

CULTURE AND MORAL REASONING   Cross-cultural research provides strong support for the universality of Kohlberg's stage sequence (Snarey, 1985, 1995). Nevertheless, some cross-cultural researchers have argued that his approach is too narrow to be considered truly universal. These critics point out that many aspects of moral reasoning found in non-Western cultures do not fit in well with Kohlberg's approach (Branco, 2012; Eckensberger & Zimba, 1997). The root of the problem, they say, is that Kohlberg's theory is strongly tied to the idea that justice is an overriding moral principle. To be sure, say critics, justice is an important moral concept throughout the world, and thus it isn't surprising that Kohlberg's stage sequence has been so strongly supported in cross-cultural research. These critics argue, however, that the notion that justice supersedes all other moral considerations is what distinguishes Western from non-Western cultures. These criticisms would predict, and research has shown, that the responses of individuals in non-Western cultures to Kohlberg's classic dilemmas often include ideas that are not found in his scoring system (Baek, 2002).

For example, in many cultures, respect for one's elders is an important moral principle that often overrides other concerns (Eckensberger & Zimba, 1997). Thus, if researchers alter the Heinz dilemma such that the sick woman is Heinz's mother rather than his wife, Western and non-Western research participants are likely to respond quite differently. Such differences are difficult to explain from the justice-based, stage-oriented perspective of Kohlberg's theory. Advocates for the theory have argued that respect for elders as the basis of moral reasoning represents Kohlberg's conventional level. Critics, by contrast, say that this classification underestimates the true moral reasoning level of individuals from non-Western cultures.

MORAL REASONING AND EMOTIONS   Researchers studying the link between moral emotions and moral reasoning have also criticized the narrowness of Kohlberg's justice-based approach (Keller, 2012). Psychologist Nancy Eisenberg, for example, suggests that empathy, the ability to identify with others' emotions, is both a cause and a consequence of moral development (Eisenberg, 2000; Eisenberg, Eggum, & Edwards, 2010). Similarly, Eisenberg suggests that a complete explanation of moral development should include age-related and individual variations in the ability to regulate emotions (such as anger) that can motivate antisocial behaviour.

Likewise, Carol Gilligan claims that an ethic based on caring for others and maintaining social relationships may be as important to moral reasoning as ideas about justice. Gilligan's theory argues that there are at least two distinct "moral orientations": justice and care (Gilligan, 1982; Gilligan & Wiggins, 1987). Each has its own central injunction—not to treat others unfairly (justice) and not to turn away from someone in need (caring). Research suggests that adolescents do exhibit a moral orientation based on care and that care-based reasoning about hypothetical moral dilemmas is related to reasoning about real-life dilemmas (Skoe et al., 1999). In response, Kohlberg acknowledged in his later writings that his theory deals specifically with development of reasoning about justice and does not claim to be a comprehensive account of moral development (Kohlberg, Levine, & Hewer, 1983). Thus, some developmentalists view Gilligan's ideas about moral development as an expansion of Kohlberg's theory rather than a rejection of it (Jorgensen, 2006).

Possible sex differences in moral reasoning are another focus of Gilligan's theory. According to Gilligan, boys and girls learn both the justice and care orientations, but girls are more likely to operate from the care orientation, whereas boys are more likely to operate from a justice orientation. Because of these differences, girls and boys tend to perceive moral dilemmas quite differently.

Given the emerging evidence on sex differences in styles of interaction and in friendship patterns, Gilligan's hypothesis makes some sense; perhaps girls, focused more on intimacy in their relationships, judge moral dilemmas by different criteria. But, in fact, research on moral dilemmas has not consistently shown that boys are more likely to use justice reasoning or that girls more often use care reasoning. Several studies of adults do show such a pattern (e.g., Wark & Krebs, 1996); however, studies of children and teenagers generally have not (e.g., Jadack, Hyde, Moore, & Keller, 1995).

MORAL REASONING AND BEHAVIOUR   Finally, critics have questioned the degree to which moral reasoning predicts moral behaviour (Krebs & Denton, 2006). Researchers have found that moral reasoning and moral behaviour are correlated, but the relationship is far from perfect. To explain inconsistencies between reasoning and behaviour, learning theorists suggest that moral reasoning is situational rather than developmental (van IJzendoorn, Bakermans-Kranenburg, Pannebakker, & Out, 2010). They point to a variety of studies to support this assertion.

First, neither adolescents nor adults reason at the same level in response to every hypothetical dilemma (Rique & Camino, 1997). An individual research participant might reason at the conventional level in response to one dilemma and at the postconventional level with respect to another. Second, the types of characters in moral dilemmas strongly influence research participants' responses to them, especially when the participants are adolescents. For example, hypothetical dilemmas involving celebrities as characters elicit much lower levels of moral reasoning from teenagers than those involving fictional characters (Einerson, 1998).

In addition, research participants show disparities in levels of moral reasoning in response to hypothetical dilemmas compared with real-life moral issues. For example, Israeli Jewish, Israeli Bedouin, and Palestinian youths living in Israel demonstrate different levels of moral reasoning when responding to hypothetical stories, such as the Heinz dilemma, than they exhibit in discussing the moral dimensions of the long-standing conflicts among their ethnic groups (Elbedour, Baker, & Charlesworth, 1997). In addition, situational variables such as perceived anonymity strongly influence decisions about moral behaviour (Zhong, Bohns, & Gino, 2010). Thus, as learning theorists predict, it appears that situational factors may be more important variables for decisions about actual moral behaviour than the level of moral reasoning exhibited in response to hypothetical dilemmas.

Moral Development and Antisocial Behaviour

Learning Objective 12.10

Describe the relationship between moral reasoning abilities and antisocial behaviour.

cyberbullying

a form of aggression in which information and communication technology (ICT) messages are used to intentionally inflict harm on others

The consistent finding of low levels of moral reasoning among adolescents who engage in serious forms of antisocial behaviour has been of particular interest to developmentalists (e.g., Ashkar & Kenny, 2007; Brugman, 2010; Ma, 2003, 2012). As well, teens who are aggressive typically lack empathy and are especially vulnerable to situational factors that contribute to poor moral decision making. These factors are prominent in research that has examined why some adolescents engage in **cyberbullying**, a form of aggression in which *information and communication technology* (ICT) messages are used to intentionally inflict harm on others (Ang & Goh, 2010; Mishna et al., 2016; Talwar et al., 2014). In fact, two-thirds of cyberbullies exhibit aggressive behaviour in other contexts as well (Twyman, Saylor, Taylor, & Comeaux, 2010). Because they lack empathy, cyberbullies typically have little sensitivity to the speed with which ICT messages of an aggressive nature, such as digitally altered or embarrassing photos, can spread throughout a peer context such as a school or neighbourhood (Renati, Berrone, & Zanetti, 2012; Smith & Slonje, 2010). They may even regard the spreading of such information as a measure of cyberbullying success and display little concern about how such experiences affect their victims. Being able to act aggressively with relative degrees of anonymity and in a way that distances the perpetrator from a victim's immediate responses may also contribute to cyberbullying.

A young person who commits a crime is distinguished from other youth who engage in other forms of antisocial behaviour, such as cyberbullying, on the basis of actual lawbreaking (**criminality**). Canada's new *Youth Criminal Justice Act* (YCJA), which addresses youth criminality, focuses in part on rehabilitation and reintegration of a young person into society. Thus, the YCJA avoids the previous practice of labelling a youth as a criminal, delinquent, or a young offender and instead focuses on the young person's offensive actions, which are malleable to change (see **Development in the Real World**). Additionally, there is a distinction between teens whose criminal acts are isolated incidents and those for whom criminality is only one feature of a pattern that includes other antisocial behaviours such as cyberbullying.

School-aged children and youth who display a consistent pattern of antisocial behaviour may be diagnosed with **conduct disorder** (American Psychiatric Association [APA], 2013). Youth with conduct disorder appear to be behind their peers in moral reasoning because of deficits in role-taking skills (Barnett & Mann, 2013). For example, researchers have found that teenagers who can look at actions they are contemplating from their parents' perspective are less likely to engage in antisocial behaviour than adolescents who cannot do so (Wyatt & Carlo, 2002). Most youths with conduct disorder also seem to be unable to look at their crimes from their victims'

criminality

antisocial behaviour that includes lawbreaking

conduct disorder

a psychological disorder in which the social and/or academic functioning of children and youth is impaired by patterns of antisocial behaviour that include bullying, destruction of property, theft, deceitfulness, and/or violations of social rules

Development in the Real World

Youth Criminal Justice

Since the *Youth Criminal Justice Act* (YCJA) was enacted in 2003, there has been a downward trend in the number of court cases involving youth across most jurisdictions in Canada—in part because the YCJA allows for a wider range of *extrajudicial measures and sanctions*, such as warnings or referrals to agencies and community programs (Allen & Superle, 2016). Most cases that do make it to court involve nonviolent offences (71%), such as break and enter, theft, and mischief. The remaining cases (29%) consist of violent crimes or offences such as robbery, sexual assault, and homicide (Alam, 2015).

Rates for crimes committed by youth vary with location, age, and sex. Demographic data shows that the three territories and Saskatchewan experience the highest rates of youth crime, while British Columbia, Prince Edward Island, and Ontario experience the lowest rates. Canadian youth crime rates increase with age and peak at age 17 (Allen & Superle, 2016). Further, males have higher crime rates at every age and account for nearly four out of five youth court cases; males 16 and 17 years of age account for almost half of all youth court cases (Alam, 2015).

Rates for crimes committed against youth also reveal some interesting findings. A disproportionately high number of youth are crime victims compared to adults. Youth are more likely to be victims of crimes committed by other youth than by adults. Boys are more likely to be victims of physical assault and other violent offences, whereas girls are more likely to be victims of sexual assault (Hotton Mahony, 2011; Ogrodnik, 2010).

As with conduct disorder, two key socializing factors that predict youth crime rates are peer influences and parenting style. The percentage of children engaging in high-risk behaviours such as smoking, fighting, and stealing was four to nine times higher when children were part of a peer group "doing bad things" than when children were not. Children who witnessed violence at home or who were raised by a parent who had either an ineffective or aversive parenting style were very often likely to exhibit conduct disorder behaviours (Statistics Canada, 2001b). Moreover, the rate of violent offences by youth was almost five times higher in families where parents failed to consistently monitor where their children were and whom they were with (Fitzgerald, 2010).

It is difficult to understand the motivations that underlie criminal activity, especially violent offences, but Canada's new approach to youth crime has resulted in a major restructuring of our youth justice system that appears to be a step in the right direction. Canada's YCJA is based on "the values, rights and responsibilities of both society and young people in relation to crime [and has three main objectives:] to prevent crime, rehabilitate and reintegrate offenders into society, and ensure meaningful consequences for offences committed by young people" (Department of Justice Canada, 2001b, p. 1). All the same, it is not easy to balance what should be done to satisfy our need for justice for the suffering of victims of violence against the personal consequences of violent behaviour for the young perpetrators of these crimes, while at the same time reducing future violent offences. Interventions require a considerable commitment of time and resources. Developmentalists play an important role by providing research-based guidance regarding the mental development factors of individuals, as well as the social factors, associated with criminality.

perspectives or to assess hypothetical crimes from a victim's perspective. Thus, programs aimed at helping youths with conduct disorder develop more mature levels of moral reasoning usually focus on heightening their awareness of a victim's point of view. However, few such programs have been successful (Armstrong, 2003; Barnett & Mann, 2013). Consequently, psychologists believe that there is far more to youth criminality than just a lack of role-taking and moral reasoning skills.

One important factor in conduct disorder is the age at which a child or teenager's antisocial behaviour begins (APA, 2013). The symptoms of individuals with *childhood-onset conduct disorder*, those whose pattern of antisocial behaviour appears before puberty, are more serious and are more likely to persist into adulthood than those of individuals whose problems began after puberty. The antisocial behaviours of teens with *adolescent-onset conduct disorder* are typically milder and more transitory, apparently more a reflection of peer-group processes or a testing of the limits of authority than a deeply ingrained behaviour problem.

The developmental pathway for childhood-onset conduct disorder seems to be directed by factors inside the child, such as temperament and personality. In early life, these children throw tantrums and defy parents; they may also develop insecure attachments (Klein et al., 2012). Once the defiance appears, if the parents are not up to the task of controlling the child, the child's behaviour worsens. He may begin to display overt aggression toward others, who then reject him, which aggravates the problem. A Canadian study found a genetic vulnerability associated with a substantial number of kindergarteners who display disruptive behaviours, such as aggression and hyperactivity, that contribute to peer rejection and victimization and, in turn, foster further peer relation difficulties. It is important to identify these at-risk youngsters and intervene before the disruptive behaviours and peer difficulties become entrenched (Boivin et al., 2012; Boivin et al., 2013). Otherwise, the seriously aggressive child begins to associate with other children with similar problems, who soon become the child's only supportive peer group (Powers & Bierman, 2013).

By adolescence, youngsters with childhood-onset conduct disorder often exhibit serious behavioural problems. Most have friends drawn almost exclusively from the ranks of other antisocial teens (Lansford et al., 2009). Of course, this situation is reinforced by frequent rejection by non-antisocial peers (Brendgen, Vitaro, & Bukowski, 1998; Véronneau, Vitaro, Brendgen, Dishion, & Tremblay, 2010). Teens with childhood-onset conduct disorder are also highly likely to display a large cluster of other problem behaviours, including drug and alcohol use, truancy or dropping out of school, and early and risky sexual behaviour, including having multiple sexual partners (Mason & Spoth, 2012).

For young people whose pattern of antisocial behaviour appears first in adolescence, the pathway is different. They, too, have friends who frequently exhibit antisocial behaviour. However, associating with such peers worsens the behaviour of teens whose antisocial behaviour did not appear until after puberty, while the behaviour of those with childhood-onset conduct disorder remains essentially the same whether they have antisocial friends or are "loners" (Vitaro, Tremblay, Kerr, Pagani, & Bukowski, 1997). Moreover, the antisocial behaviour patterns of teens with adolescent-onset conduct disorder often change as their relationships change (Laird, Pettit, Dodge, & Bates, 1999). In light of this, peer influence seems to be the most important factor in the development of adolescent-onset youth conduct disorder.

Apart from peer influence, several personal factors contribute to the development of adolescent-onset conduct disorder. Personality is one important factor. Teens who are low in agreeableness, low in self-efficacy for emotional regulation, and high in neuroticism are more likely to exhibit antisocial behaviour than peers with different trait profiles (Caprara, Alessandri, Di Giunta, Panerai, & Eisenberg, 2010; Savina, 2009). *Narcissism*, the tendency to exaggerate one's importance, is also associated with conduct disorder (Fossati, Borroni, Eisenberg, & Maffei, 2010; Muris, Meesters, & Timmermans, 2013).

Social variables also contribute to conduct disorder. Most teens with the disorder have parents who do not monitor them sufficiently and many of these adolescents have parents with histories of antisocial behaviour (Wachlarowicz, Snyder, Low, Forgatch, & Degarmo, 2012). As well, their individual friendships are not very supportive or intimate, and they are drawn to peer groups that include some teens who are experimenting with drugs or mild lawbreaking (Lansford et al., 2009). However, when parents do provide good monitoring and emotional support, their adolescent child is unlikely to get involved in criminal acts or drug use, even if she hangs around with a tougher crowd or has a close friend who engages in such behaviour (Brown & Huang, 1995; Mounts & Steinberg, 1995).

Test Yourself before going on

1. List the factors that influence progression through Kohlberg's stages.
   (a) _____
   (b) _____
   (c) _____
   (d) _____
2. A person's ability to look at a situation from another's perspective is called _____.
3. Learning theorists argue that moral decision making is more influenced by _____ factors than by stages of moral reasoning.

4. Choose the correct answers in the following sentence: Criminal behaviours that emerge during (childhood/adolescence) are generally more serious than those that develop during (childhood/adolescence).

Critical Thinking

5. How might Kohlberg's views and those of his critics be integrated to explain variations in moral behaviour among adolescents?

Social Relationships

As you can see from the solutions for peer conflicts listed in **Table 12.4**, adolescents' ideas about other people and their understanding of social situations are more complex than those of children. These advances in interpersonal understanding lead to changes in family and peer relationships.

Relationships with Parents

Teenagers have two apparently contradictory tasks in their relationships with their parents: to establish autonomy from them and to maintain a sense of relatedness with them.

Learning Objective 12.11

Describe the changing relationships of adolescents with their parents.

Table 12.4 Children's and Adolescents' Comments About How to Solve Disagreements Between Friends

Age	Comments
5-year-olds	Go away from her and come back later when you're not fighting.
8-year-olds	Well, if you say something and don't really mean it, then you have to mean it when you take it back.
14-year-olds	Sometimes you got to get away for a while. Calm down a bit so you won't be so angry. Then get back and try to talk it out.
16-year-olds	Well, you could talk it out, but it usually fades itself out. It usually takes care of itself. You don't have to explain everything. You do certain things and each of you knows what it means. But if not, then talk it out.

(**SOURCE:** Based on Selman, 1980, pp. 107–113. *The growth of interpersonal understanding.* New York: Academic Press.)

While it is true that the physical changes of puberty are often followed by an increase in the number of conflicts, it is a myth that conflict is the main feature of the parent–adolescent relationship.

CONFLICTS WITH PARENTS The rise in conflict between parents and teenagers has been documented by a number of researchers (e.g., Flannery, Montemayor, & Eberly, 1994; Laursen, 1995). University of Lethbridge sociologist Reginald Bibby found that Canadian teens disagree with their parents most when it comes to everyday issues such as chores around the house, school, their parents' reaction to the way they talk to them, and their parents' concern about their safety. These issues account for roughly half of the conflicts. It's interesting that there was less parent–teen conflict over issues such as who they are dating, drugs, their appearance (clothing and hairstyle), and sex (about one-fifth of the conflicts) (Bibby, 2001).

Although this increase in discord is widely observed, you should not assume that it signifies a major disruption of the quality of the parent–child relationships. For most Canadian teens, their families are still important to them, especially as a source of enjoyment and support (Bibby, 2001). Furthermore, parent–teen conflicts appear to cause more distress for parents than for adolescents (Dekovic, 1999).

ATTACHMENT Teenagers' underlying emotional attachment to their parents remains strong on average. Virtually all the researchers who have explored this question find that a teenager's sense of well-being or happiness is more strongly correlated with the quality of her attachment to her parents than with the quality of her relationships with peers (e.g., Nichikawa, Hägglöf, & Sundbom, 2010; Raja, McGee, & Stanton, 1992). Moreover, research findings regarding the centrality of parent–teen relationships have been consistent across a variety of cultures (Okamoto & Uechi, 1999).

Research in several countries has also found that teens who remain closely attached to their parents have less difficulty resolving conflicts with them (García-Ruiz, Rodrigo, Hernández-Cabrera, Máiquez, Deković, 2013). They are also more likely to be academically successful and to enjoy good peer relations (e.g., Mayseless & Scharf, 2007; Zimmermann, 2004). They are less likely than less securely attached teens to engage in antisocial behaviour (Ma, Shek, Cheung, & Oi Bun Lam, 2000). Further, the quality of attachment in early adolescence predicts drug use in later adolescence and early adulthood (Brook, Whiteman, Finch, & Cohen, 2000). Teens who are close to their parents are less likely to use drugs than peers whose bonds with their parents are weaker. Thus, even while teenagers are becoming more autonomous, they need their parents to provide a psychological safe base.

Learning Objective 12.12

Discuss the issues involved in adolescents' relationships with peers.

Relationships with Peers

Despite the importance of family relationships to adolescents, it is evident that peer relationships become far more significant in adolescence than they have been at any earlier period, and perhaps than they will be at any time later in life.

FRIENDSHIPS For many adolescents, ICT platforms of various types serve as hubs around which their social networks revolve. Surveys indicate that 69% of 11- to 14-year-olds and 85% of 15- to 18-year-olds have their own cellphones (Rideout, Foehr, & Roberts, 2010). Teens in both age groups spend an average of about two hours a day talking with and texting peers on their cellphones. They devote an additional 45 minutes or so each day to communicating with friends via instant messaging and social networking websites. Moreover, many teenagers have one group of friends with whom they communicate by phone, another with whom they exchange online instant messages and email, and yet another with whom they associate through social networking (Foehr, 2006). As a result, teenagers have a wider range of acquaintances than their parents did in adolescence. However, they do not necessarily have more close friends.

Cross-sectional studies suggest children's belief in the importance of popularity and peer acceptance strengthens slowly over the elementary school years and peaks during early adolescence (LaFontana & Cillessen, 2010). During these years—age 12 to 15 or so—teens place more emphasis on popularity and peer acceptance than on any other dimension of peer relations. As adolescents get older, the quality of peer relationships becomes more important to them than popularity. Consequently, as they approach adulthood, their friendships become increasingly intimate, in the sense that adolescent friends share more and more of their inner feelings and secrets and are more knowledgeable about each other's feelings. Loyalty and faithfulness become more valued characteristics of friendship. However, the ability to display intimacy, loyalty, and faithfulness in the context of a friendship doesn't come automatically with age. In fact, teens vary considerably in these interpersonal skills. The variation may be the result of individual differences in temperament and personality or of teens' experiences with family relationships (Updegraff & Obeidallah, 1999).

Adolescent friendships are also more stable than those of younger children (Bowker, 2004). In one longitudinal study, researchers found that only about 20% of friendships among children in Grade 4 lasted as long as a year, whereas about 40% of friendships formed by these same youngsters when they were in Grade 10 were long-lasting (Cairns & Cairns, 1994). Friendship stability probably increases in adolescence because older teens work harder than younger teens and elementary school children at maintaining positive relationships with friends through negotiation of conflicts (Nagamine, 1999).

Adolescents tend to choose friends who share their social status (Dijkstra, Cillessen, & Borch, 2013). That is, popular teens are most likely to be friends with others who are popular, and rejected teens are likely to associate with others who have been rejected. In addition, teens often choose friends who are committed to the same activities they are. For example, many teens, especially boys, report that peer companionship is their primary motive for playing computer and video games (Chou & Tsai, 2007; Colwell & Kato, 2005). Some studies suggest that shared video game-playing experiences promote the development of a masculine gender role among male teens (Sanford & Madill, 2006). Some developmentalists also argue that playing these games in group settings helps male adolescents learn to channel aggressive and competitive impulses into socially acceptable ways of expressing them (Jansz & Martens, 2005).

Finally, adolescents' reasons for ending friendships reflect the influence of individual differences in rate of development of social skills. For example, a change in identity status from a less mature to a more mature level often leads to acquisition of new friends (Akers, Jones, & Coyl, 1998). Likewise, girls seem to prefer friendships with other girls whose romantic status is the same as their own—that is, girls who have boyfriends prefer female friends who also have boyfriends. In fact, a girl who gets a boyfriend is likely to spend less time with female peers and to end long-standing friendships with girls who haven't yet acquired a romantic partner (Benenson & Benarroch, 1998; Zimmer-Gembeck, 1999). For boys, differences in athletic achievements can lead to the end of previously important friendships. Both boys and girls tend to end relationships with peers who show a propensity for socially victimizing others by means such as spreading rumours (Sijtsema, Rambaran, & Ojanen, 2013).

PEER GROUPS Like friendships, peer groups become relatively stable in adolescence. Although peer influences are often thought of as primarily negative in nature, social networks have both positive and negative influences on teenagers' development (Eccles & Roeser, 2011; Ulmer, Desmond, Jang, & Johnson, 2012). For

As adolescents age, the structures of their peer groups change.

(Photo: Monkey Business Images/Shutterstock.com)

one thing, adolescents typically choose to associate with a group that shares their values, attitudes, behaviours, and identity status (Mackey & La Greca, 2007). When the values that drive peer associations are those that lead to adaptive developmental outcomes, such as graduating from high school, peers become an important source of reinforcement that keeps teens on developmentally positive pathways. Moreover, researchers have found that if the discrepancy between their own ideas and those of their friends becomes too great, teens are more likely to switch to a more compatible group of friends than to be persuaded to adopt the first group's values or behaviours (Verkooijen, de Vries, & Nielsen, 2007).

CHANGES IN PEER-GROUP STRUCTURE   Peer-group structures change over the years of adolescence. The classic, widely quoted early study is that of Dunphy (1963) on the formation, dissolution, and interaction of teenaged groups in a high school in Sydney, Australia, between 1958 and 1960. Dunphy identified two important subvarieties of groups. The first type, which he called a **clique**, is made up of four to six young people who appear to be strongly attached to one another. Cliques have strong cohesiveness and high levels of intimate sharing. However, most cliques also feature a considerable amount of within-group aggression aimed at maintaining the group's status hierarchies (Closson, 2010). Typically, aggressive acts within cliques are perpetrated by dominant members against lower-status members (Closson, 2010). Furthermore, research suggests that cliques that are perceived as highly popular by nonmembers tolerate higher levels of within-group aggression than less popular cliques do. Thus, even though teens may enhance their popularity by associating with popular cliques, being accepted by these groups may require adolescents to endure being targeted by the groups' high-status members.

In the early years of adolescence, cliques are almost entirely same-sex groups— a holdover from the preadolescent pattern. Gradually, however, the cliques combine into larger sets that Dunphy called **crowds**, which include both males and females. Finally, the crowd breaks down again into heterosexual cliques and then into loose associations of couples. In Dunphy's study, the period during which adolescents socialized in crowds was roughly between ages 13 and 15—the very years when they display the greatest conformity to peer pressure.

Later researchers on adolescence changed Dunphy's labels somewhat (Brown, 1990; Brown, Mory, & Kinney, 1994). They use the word *crowd* to refer to the *reputation-based group* with which a young person is identified, either by choice or by peer designation. In Canadian schools, these groups have labels such as "populars," "jocks," "emos," "geeks," "nerds," "skaters," "gamers," "gangsters," "stoners," "preps," "hipsters," and "loners," just to name a few. Studies in junior high and high schools make it clear that teenagers can readily identify each of the major crowds in their school and have quite stereotypical descriptions of them (e.g., "The partiers goof off a lot more than the jocks do, but they don't come to school stoned like the burnouts do") (Brown et al., 1994, p. 133). Each of these descriptions serves as what Brown calls an *identity prototype*: Labelling others and oneself as belonging to one or more of these groups helps to create or reinforce the adolescent's own identity (Brown et al., 1994). Such labelling also helps the adolescent identify potential friends or foes.

Within any given school, the various crowds are organized into a fairly clear, widely understood pecking order. In North American schools, the groups labelled as some variant of "populars" or "jocks" are typically at the top of the heap, with "brains" somewhere in the middle, and "druggies," "loners," and "nerds" at the bottom (Brown et al., 1994).

Throughout the years of junior high and high school, the social system of crowds becomes increasingly differentiated, with more and more distinct groups (Kinney, 1993). Within (and sometimes between) these crowds, Kinney found, adolescents created smaller cliques. As Dunphy observed, social groups were almost entirely

clique

four to six young people who appear to be strongly attached to one another

crowd

a combination of cliques, which includes both males and females

Critical Thinking

Think back to your own high school years and draw a diagram or map to describe the organization of crowds and cliques. Were those crowds or cliques more or less important in the last few years of high school than they had been earlier?

same-sex in early adolescence but, by late adolescence, they had become mixed in gender, often composed of groups of dating couples. Mutual friendships and dating pairs become more central to social interactions in later adolescence than are cliques or crowds (Urberg, Degirmencioglu, Tolson, & Halliday-Scher, 1995).

Romantic Relationships

Learning Objective 12.13

Describe how interest in romantic relationships emerges among heterosexual and homosexual teens.

Heterosexual and homosexual teens follow somewhat different pathways. For both, though, the ups and downs that are associated with early romances are an important theme of development during adolescence.

HETEROSEXUAL TEENS Most teens display a gradual progression from same-sex friendships to heterosexual relationships. The change happens gradually, but it seems to proceed at a somewhat more rapid pace in girls than in boys. At the beginning of adolescence, teens are still fairly rigid about their preferences for same-sex friends (Bukowski, Sippola, & Hoza, 1999). Over the next year or two, they become more open to opposite-sex friendships (Kuttler, LaGreca, & Prinstein, 1999). The skills they gain in relating to opposite-sex peers in such friendships and in mixed-gender groups, as well as interactions with opposite-sex parents, prepare them for romantic relationships, which begin to become common among teens at around age 15 or so (Bucx, & Seiffge-Krenke, 2010; Seiffge-Krenke & Connolly, 2010). Thus, although adults often assume that sexual desires are the basis of emergent romantic relationships, it appears that social factors are just as important (Rauer, Pettit, Lansford, Bates, & Dodge, 2013).

Interpretations of research on couple formation must take into account the general finding that the development of romantic relationships in adolescence varies across cultures (Seiffge-Krenke & Connolly, 2010). In one study that compared Chinese and Canadian 16- and 17-year-olds, researchers found that far fewer Chinese than Canadian teens were involved in or desired to be involved in romantic relationships (Li, Connolly, Jiang, Pepler, & Craig, 2010). Analyses of these findings suggested that the underlying variable was cross-cultural variation in the centrality of peer and parental relationships. Chinese teens, on average, felt emotionally closest to their parents, while their Canadian counterparts reported greater emotional closeness to friends. However, among Chinese teens who reported being emotionally closer to friends than to parents, romantic relationships were more frequent than among peers who felt closer to their parents. Thus, these findings suggest that, across cultures, peer associations in early adolescence are foundational to the development of romantic relationships later in the teen years.

By age 12 or 13, most adolescents have a basic conception of what it means to be "in love," and the sense of being in love is an important factor in adolescent dating patterns (Montgomery & Sorel, 1998). Thus, many teenagers prefer to date those with whom they believe they are in love, and they view falling out of love as a reason for ending a dating relationship. However, other teens form romantic attachments that are based on a desire for companionship rather than romantic love (Bucx & Seiffge-Krenke, 2010). In addition, for girls (but not for boys), romantic relationships are seen as a context for self-disclosure. Put another way, girls seem to want more psychological intimacy from these early relationships than their partners do (Feiring, 1999).

Early dating and early sexual activity are more common among the poor of every ethnic group and among those who experience relatively early puberty. Religious teachings and individual attitudes about the appropriate age for dating and sexual behaviour also make a difference, as does family structure. Girls with parents who are divorced or remarried, for example, report earlier dating and higher levels of sexual experience than do girls from intact families, and those with a strong religious identity report later dating and lower levels of sexuality (Bingham, Miller, & Adams, 1990; Ivanova, Mills, & Veenstra, 2011). But for every group, these are years of experimentation with romantic relationships.

HOMOSEXUAL TEENS Romantic relationships emerge somewhat differently in the lives of homosexual teens. Researchers have found that homosexual teenagers are more comfortable about revealing their sexual orientation to their parents and to their peers than was true in past cohorts (Riley, 2010). Like their heterosexual peers, homosexual teenagers become aware of same-sex attraction at around age 11 or 12 (Rosario, Scrimshaw, & Hunter, 2004). In contrast to heterosexual teens, boys notice and act on same-sex attraction at somewhat earlier ages than girls do (Grov, Bimbi, Nanin, & Parsons, 2006). However, girls who ultimately commit to a homosexual orientation express more certainty about their sexual identity than boys do (Rosario, Scrimshaw, Hunter, & Braun, 2006).

Many boys and girls, however, experience some degree of attraction to both sexes prior to self-identifying as gay or lesbian. Thus, many homosexual teens go through a period of sexual discovery that begins with experimentation with heterosexual relationships. Shortly thereafter, these teenagers begin to experiment with same-sex relationships. By age 15 or so, most have classified themselves as primarily heterosexual or committed to a gay, lesbian, or bisexual orientation (Rosario et al., 2004). Many of those who are gay, lesbian, or bisexual participate in clubs and extracurricular activities that are designed to help sexual minority youth form social connections. In the company of these like-minded peers, gay, lesbian, and bisexual teens meet potential romantic partners and find important sources of social support (Rosario et al., 2004).

Test Yourself before going on

1. Most parent–teen conflicts involve _____ issues.
2. Today's teens have more _____ than their parents did but not necessarily more close friends.
3. Status hierarchies within cliques are maintained through within-group _____.

4. Both heterosexual and homosexual adolescents become aware of sexual attraction at around the age of _____.

Summary

Theories of Social and Personality Development

12.1 Describe what happens during Erikson's identity versus role confusion stage.

- For Erikson, adolescence is a period when a person faces a crisis of identity versus role confusion, out of which the teenager must develop a sense of who he is and where he belongs in his culture.

12.2 Explain Marcia's theory of identity development.

- Building on Erikson's notion of an adolescent identity crisis, Marcia identified four identity statuses: identity achievement, moratorium, foreclosure, and identity diffusion. Research suggests that the process of identity formation may take place somewhat later than either Erikson or Marcia believed. Moreover, it continues throughout the lifespan.

Self-Concept

12.3 Discuss the ways self-understanding in adolescence differs from that in childhood.

- Self-definitions become increasingly abstract at adolescence, with more emphasis on enduring, internal qualities and ideology.

12.4 Describe how self-esteem changes across the teenage years.

- Self-esteem drops somewhat at the beginning of adolescence and then rises steadily throughout the teenaged years.

12.5 Summarize the gender role concepts of adolescents.

- Teenagers increasingly define themselves in terms that include both masculine and feminine traits. When high levels of both masculinity and femininity are present, the individual is described as androgynous. Androgyny is associated with higher self-esteem in both male and female adolescents.

12.6 Describe how ethnic identity develops in Canadian youth.

- Young people in clearly identifiable minority groups, bicultural teens, and teens in immigrant families have the additional task in adolescence of forming an ethnic identity. Phinney proposed a series of ethnic identity stages that are similar to those in Marcia's model of general identity development. Phinney's stages are unexamined ethnic identity, ethnic identity search, and ethnic identity achievement. For immigrant teens, the process of identity development includes reconciling differences in their own and their parents' views of the cultural values of their new and former homes.

Moral Development

12.7 Describe the features of moral reasoning at each of Kohlberg's stages.

- Kohlberg proposed six stages of moral reasoning, organized into three levels. Preconventional moral reasoning includes reliance on external authority: What is punished is bad, and what feels good is good. Conventional morality is based on rules and norms provided by outside groups, such as the family, church, or society. Postconventional morality is based on self-chosen principles. Research evidence suggests that these levels and stages are loosely correlated with age, develop in a specified order, and appear in this same sequence in all cultures studied so far.

12.8 Identify some important causes and effects in the development of moral reasoning.

- The acquisition of cognitive role-taking skills is important to moral development, but the social environment is important as well. Specifically, to foster moral reasoning, adults must provide children with opportunities for discussion of moral issues. Moral reasoning and moral behaviour are correlated, though the relationship is far from perfect.

12.9 Describe how Kohlberg's theory has been criticized.

- Kohlberg's theory has been criticized by theorists who place more emphasis on learning moral behaviour and others who believe that moral reasoning may be based more on emotional factors than on ideas about justice and fairness.

12.10 Describe the relationship between moral reasoning abilities and antisocial behaviour.

- Youth who commit antisocial acts are usually found to be far behind their peers in both role-taking and moral reasoning. Factors linked to the development of conduct disorders include age, temperament, personality, parenting style, and having antisocial peers.

Social Relationships

12.11 Describe the changing relationships of adolescents with their parents.

- Adolescent–parent interactions typically become somewhat more conflicted in early adolescence. Strong attachments to parents remain so and are predictive of good peer relations.

12.12 Discuss the issues involved in adolescents' relationships with peers.

- Thanks to ICT, teens today have more acquaintances than their parents did. Over the teen years, friendships become increasingly intimate and stable. Adolescents value loyalty, intimacy, and faithfulness in their friends and typically form friendships with peers who share their interests and are their equals with regard to social skill development. In the early years of adolescence, *cliques* are almost entirely same-sex groups. Between 13 and 15, cliques combine into *crowds* that include both males and females. This is the time when teens are most susceptible to peer influences. Crowds break down into mixed-gender cliques and then into small groups of couples.

12.13 Describe how interest in romantic relationships emerges among heterosexual and homosexual teens.

- Heterosexual teens gradually move from same-sex peer groups to heterosexual couples. The feeling of being "in love" is important to the formation of couple relationships. Many homosexual teens experiment with heterosexual and homosexual relationships before committing to a gay, lesbian, or bisexual orientation in mid-adolescence.

Policy Question

What Can Be Done About Gambling Among Canadian Youth?

Today's youth are the first generation of Canadians to live within a culture that views gambling as an everyday and acceptable form of entertainment. Not surprisingly, gambling and wagering are popular and on the rise among children and adolescents alike (Derevensky, 2012; Shaffer & Hall, 2001). Canadian researchers have discovered some startling facts about gambling among Canadian youth and why it is a concern. One factor is that gambling often begins at an earlier age than other high-risk behaviours such as alcohol or drug use—McGill University researchers found that "pathological gamblers" started serious gambling by age 10 to 11 (Derevensky & Gilbeau, 2015; Gupta and Derevensky, 1998a, 2000). Adolescents also have a higher incidence of gambling problems than adults, and youth are two to four times more likely than adults to have a *serious* gambling problem (Derevensky, Gupta, & Winters, 2003; Gupta & Derevensky, 2000; Gupta, Pinzon, & CPS, 2016). Gambling, like many high-risk behaviours, is consistently more prevalent in males than females, and boys are two to four times as likely as girls to have a serious gambling problem (Carbonneau, Vitaro, Brendgen, & Tremblay, 2015a, 2015b; Derevensky, 2015).

Older adolescents and adults prefer to wager money, and a significant number of underage youth illegally engage in age-restricted gambling activities such as lotteries, instant-win tickets, pull-tabs, and online sports betting in addition to informal and unregulated gambling (e.g., making wagers among peers [cards, games of skill, etc.] and on international online gaming sites) (Carbonneau et al., 2015b; Derevensky & Gilbeau, 2015). A vast majority of adolescents surveyed by researchers acknowledged that they have participated in gaming activities—roughly three-quarters or more of teenagers report that they have wagered money in the previous year and anywhere between 9 and 35% did so at least once a week (Derevensky & Gupta, 1998; Gupta & Derevensky, 1998b; Lawrence, Yardley, Root, Canham, & McPhee, 2002). Of these youths, 55% are considered casual gamblers, 13% have some gambling problems, and 4 to 6% have serious problems with gambling.

Problem gambling is now classified as a *substance-related and addictive disorder* (namely, *gambling disorder*) in the DSM-V, similar to other high-risk behaviours such as alcohol or drug use (APA, 2013). Like other addictive behaviours, gambling offers a way to temporarily escape problems, boredom, and stress. At the same time, these benefits are mixed with the excitement of winning. In fact, most adolescents do not gamble primarily for money but for the excitement and sensations of dissociation and escape (Derevensky & Gupta, 1998; Gupta & Derevensky, 1998b). Young problem gamblers have been found to dissociate more frequently when gambling compared with peers who do not have a gambling problem (Gupta & Derevensky, 2000). It has also been shown that when young problem gamblers are away from the gambling situation (a video lottery terminal, for instance), they can experience withdrawal-like symptoms that make them more likely to want to play again in order to escape these undesirable sensations (Noonan, Turner, & Macdonald, 1999). Not surprisingly, adolescents with serious gambling problems have an increased risk for the development of multiple addictions. They also have higher rates of depression, which puts them at a heightened risk for suicidal thoughts and suicide attempts (Derevensky & Gilbeau, 2015; Dussault et al., 2015). Furthermore, within a social context, adolescents with gambling problems report having a support group, but old friends are often replaced by gambling associates (Gupta & Derevensky, 2000).

Cognitively, children and young adolescents are at a disadvantage because they lack an understanding of what the odds of winning are and they have an overly optimistic view of the probability of winning (St-Pierre & Derevensky, 2016). Moreover, for most teens and adults (including parents and community leaders) gambling is perceived as a relatively benign activity. Well-intentioned social groups such as schools and religious groups may inadvertently endorse gambling by sponsoring fundraising events such as bingo or casino nights that are supported by parents and the community (Derevensky & Gupta, 2004). Consequently, children are not as informed about the inherent dangers of gambling as they are about the dangers of smoking, drugs, and alcohol use (Derevensky & Gupta, 1998). Moreover, children and adolescents often gamble with their parents or other family members. For example, they go together to buy and play lottery tickets, play cards, or play bingo (Gupta & Derevensky, 1997). When children are exposed to family members, peers, neighbours, or celebrities who relish gambling, youth may acquire favourable expectations about gambling (Gupta & Derevensky, 1997).

Although most adult problem gamblers reported that their problem with gambling began in their youth, it hasn't been clear how gambling problems develop. Recent models, however, suggest there are three main pathways that lead to a gambling disorder (Allami & Vitaro, 2015; Milosevic & Ledgerwood, 2010; Nower & Blaszczynski, 2005). The lower-risk "*behaviourally conditioned*" route encompasses teens who are attracted by the excitement and socialization of gaming and they are the most responsive to interventions. The "*emotionally vulnerable*" route is characterized by teens who gamble (akin to using drugs and alcohol) as a way to cope, albeit not so effectively, with pre-existing affective disorders (e.g., anxiety and depression). These teens require a somewhat more complex treatment plan that addresses their emotional difficulties before dealing with their gambling problems. The highest-risk "*biologically vulnerable*" route involves teens with a biological, and possibly genetic, susceptibility associated with neurologically-based impulsivity (e.g., inattentiveness, distractibility, hyperactivity, and an underlying propensity for thrill-seeking and risk-taking behaviour). Teens with ADHD or antisocial behaviour fall within in this category (Fatseas et al., 2016). Moreover, biologically vulnerable teens are least likely to recognize they have a gambling problem, and thus, least likely to seek help; additionally, they are more resistant to treatment (Allami & Vitaro, 2015).

Reportedly, youth gambling treatment program research remains wanting (Derevensky & Gupta, 1998, 2004; St-Pierre & Derevensky, 2016). Although research into gambling prevention programs is in the formative stages of development, some practical measures can help to inoculate children against the risk of developing a gambling dependence—especially youth who are on the behaviourally conditioned or emotionally vulnerable pathways noted above (Allami & Vitaro, 2015). Parents and caregivers need to first become aware of the seriousness of the problem and then advise and instruct their children accordingly, just as they would with the dangers of other risk-taking behaviours such as smoking and alcohol use or unsafe sexual activity. In terms of social learning theory, "actions speak louder than words." Therefore, if parents believe that they are important role models against gambling, they need to act in ways that are consistent with what they say. Another preventive measure is teaching children about the nature of random events and statistical probability at a level that they can understand. Other cognitive preventive measures include giving a child facts that counter unrealistic expectations and changing inappropriate ideas a child may have concerning the roles of skill, luck, and the illusion of control in gambling activities. It should also be emphasized that gambling is not a method of making money; rather it is another way of spending money. The aim of discussion should be to help modify and change the attitude that gambling is a harmless behaviour.

The school system can provide another important venue for implementing prevention activities that increase knowledge about youth gambling problems (St-Pierre & Derevensky, 2016). Indeed, recent studies show that instructional videos can increase the level of accurate knowledge and reduce misconceived attitudes about gambling in students from Grades 6 to 8 (Ferland, Ladouceur, & Vitaro, 2002; Lavoie & Ladouceur, 2004). There is also a need to develop a protocol for the identification, assessment, and referral of students who are at risk of developing a serious gambling problem, especially those with the highest risk, such as those who are biologically vulnerable (Allami & Vitaro, 2015). Students need to be introduced to both alternative and effective ways of coping with problems and need to improve the skills that would prevent the development of problematic gambling. It would be appropriate for these school-based programs to be integrated into both the elementary and secondary school levels.

(Photo: Lucky Business/Shutterstock)

Your Turn

- Explain whether there is a relationship between the proliferation of gambling opportunities for adults, such as casinos and lottery ticket sales, and adolescent gambling.
- Describe the ways that problem gambling can be harmful to more than just the gambler.
- Explain why youth are more vulnerable to problem gambling than adults.
- Explain how gambling on a computer (no stakes) could help inoculate children against false beliefs they may have about the odds of winning.
- Some young problem gamblers are driven by the excitement and sensations of dissociation they experience when they gamble. What kinds of intervention would help them overcome their dependence on gambling?
- Where do youth get the money to gamble?

Chapter 13
Physical and Cognitive Development in Early Adulthood

Technotr/E+/Getty Images

Learning Objectives

PHYSICAL FUNCTIONING

13.1 Explain the difference between primary and secondary aging.

13.2 Identify what changes take place in the brain in early adulthood.

13.3 Identify the ways other body systems change during early adulthood.

HEALTH PROMOTION AND WELLNESS

13.4 Identify what habits and personal factors are associated with good health.

13.5 Describe the risks associated with sexually transmitted infections during early adulthood.

13.6 Discuss the risk factors for intimate partner violence.

13.7 Discuss the issues involved in sexual assault.

13.8 Identify which mental disorders occur most frequently in early adulthood.

COGNITIVE CHANGES

13.9 Describe what types of postformal thought developmentalists have proposed.

13.10 Describe how the concepts of crystallized and fluid intelligence help to explain age-related changes in IQ scores.

POST-SECONDARY EDUCATION

13.11 Describe the developmental impact of post-secondary education.

Have you kept up with your high school friends via Facebook or some other social networking platform? If you have, then you are very aware of how divergent developmental pathways become in early adulthood. When you were 10 years old, everyone you knew was in school, and the schools they attended were very similar to one another. The same was true when you were 14. Now, however, you're studying at the post-secondary level, but some of your high school friends have taken their lives in other directions. Some may be parents already, while others may be joining the workforce or taking a gap year to travel or earn extra money. Don't be surprised if your friends' lives become even more diverse over the next few years.

Despite the variations in adult developmental pathways, most developmental scientists agree that it is still useful to divide the adult years into three roughly equal parts: early adulthood, from 20 to 40; middle adulthood, from 40 to about 65; and late adulthood, from 65 until death. This way of dividing adulthood reflects the fact that optimum physical and cognitive functioning, achieved in the 20s and 30s, begins to wane in some noticeable and measurable ways in the 40s and 50s. We will follow this way of dividing the adult years and define early adulthood as the period from age 20 to 40. In this chapter, you will read about the changes that occur during these years, along with a number of variables that are associated with variation from the "typical" pathway.

Physical Functioning

When developmentalists study children's development, they look at increases or improvements. When developmentalists study adults, especially adults' physical functioning, they ask questions about loss of function, or decline. Of course, factors such as diet and exercise slow down these declines, but many of them are inevitable.

Primary and Secondary Aging

"Some Canadians live their lives in excellent health with one of the highest life expectancies in the world; paradoxically others spend their life in poor health, with a life expectancy similar to some third world countries" (Keon & Pépin, 2009, p. 1).

SOCIAL DETERMINANTS OF HEALTH   Researchers distinguish between two types of aging. The basic, underlying, inevitable aging process is called **primary aging**, sometimes called **senescence**, by most developmentalists. Gray hair, wrinkles, and changes in visual acuity, for example, are attributable to primary aging.

Critical Thinking

Before you read the rest of the chapter, think about how you might answer the following question for yourself: In what ways have your body and mind changed since you were younger? How do you expect them to change as you get older? How has attending post-secondary school affected your life, and what difference will it make in your future?

Learning Objective 13.1

Explain the difference between primary and secondary aging.

primary aging (senescence) age-related physical changes that have a biological basis and are universally shared and inevitable

secondary aging

age-related changes that are due to social and environmental influences, poor health habits, or disease

Secondary aging, in contrast, is the product of socioeconomic and environmental influences, health habits, or disease and is neither inevitable nor experienced by all adults. Statistics on age differences in health and death rates reveals the expected pattern. For example, 20- to 34-year-olds rarely die from disease (Statistics Canada, 2015d). However, researchers have found that age interacts with other variables to influence health, a pattern suggesting the influence of secondary aging.

Most developmentalists believe that the income-status differences in health, where the rich are generally healthier and live longer than the poor, are caused by secondary aging (Hertzman & Frank, 2006; Raphael, 2016). A closer look at the differences in levels of health among developed nations reveals that it is not just a simple case that the wealthy members of a population are healthier than those who are less well off. Rather, the degree of *socioeconomic inequality* (i.e., the distribution of income and wealth—the spread between the rich and poor) of a country is related to the overall health of its citizens (Keon & Pépin, 2009; United Nations Development Programme [UNDP], 2009). Prosperous nations with high levels of socioeconomic inequality, most notably the United States and the United Kingdom, experience poorer overall health than less wealthy but more egalitarian societies, such as Japan and Sweden (Pickett & Wilkinson, 2010). By comparison, in the past, Canada distributed its social and economic resources fairly equitably among its citizens (through public funding of and relatively universal access to health care, housing, and education) and as a consequence, Canadians enjoyed relatively good health (Ross et al., 2000; Siddiqi, Kawachi, Keating, & Hertzman, 2013; UNDP, 2009). Unfortunately, income inequality in Canada has been increasing since the 1980s—the percentages of Canadian families who are either very rich or very poor have been increasing which, in turn, is adversely impacting our collective health. Indeed, it's the living conditions that Canadians experience, more so than medical treatments or lifestyle choices, that are shaping our health outcomes (Kondro, 2012; Mikkonen & Raphael, 2010; Siddiqi et al., 2013).

For example, 2010 CIHR "Health Researcher of the Year" Clyde Hertzman (1953–2013), coined the term *biological embedding* to describe how social circumstances in the first few years of a child's life can cause epigenetic modifications in the brain and body systems that determine the trajectory—for better or worse—of a person's health through adulthood (Essex et al., 2013; Hertzman, 2013; Hertzman & Boyce, 2010; Suderman et al., 2013). This notion is underscored by a Canadian Senate Committee report that determined that our health care system only accounts for an estimated 25% of health outcomes (Keon & Pépin, 2009). The other 75% of health is shaped by a variety of socioeconomic and environmental factors and influences (see **Table 13.1**). These

Table 13.1 Determinants of Health

Factors and Influences	Percent Contribution	Examples
Socioeconomic	50%	Early childhood development, education, socioeconomic status, personal health behaviours, culture, gender, employment, and social support
Health care system	25%	Medical services, hospitals and medical clinics, community and home-based health care services, as well as medical and health care professionals (e.g., physicians, nurses, dentists, optometrists, laboratory and medical technicians, therapists, psychologists, pharmacists, public health inspectors, speech language pathologists, audiologists, and so on)
Biology and genetics	15%	Organs and body systems, DNA
Physical environment	10%	Adequate housing, safe workplaces and communities, and clean air, water, and soil

(**SOURCE:** Data from Keon, W.J., & Pépin, L. (2009). *A Healthy, Productive Canada: A Determinant of Health Approach. The Standing Senate Committee on Social Affairs, Science and Technology Final Report of Senate Subcommittee on Population Health*. Ottawa, ON: Senate Subcommittee on Population Health.)

social determinants of health include factors such as early childhood experiences, education, socioeconomic status, culture, gender, quality of housing, employment, and safe workplaces and communities.

The study of the factors associated with secondary aging can be viewed in relation to an individual, which we look at later in this chapter, and with respect to a population, an approach that looks at the health indicators that influence populations as a whole. Common indicators of the *population health approach* include mortality statistics and rates of hospitalization, although measures of morbidity are also important because morbidity measures tap into "a key health policy challenge facing Western developed nations: that some health interventions may be adding years of sickness to life, rather than years of health" (Chomik, 2001, p. 9). From this perspective it becomes important to measure the health status of populations by looking at *aggregate health indicators* that measure quality of life, such as **disability-adjusted life years (DALY)**, **health-adjusted life expectancy (HALE)**, and **quality-adjusted life years (QALY)**. For example, a Canadian study has shown that there are considerable HALE disparities among socioeconomic groups (McIntosh, Finès, Wilkins, & Wolfson, 2009; PHAC, 2012d). At age 25, the average difference in HALE between the highest and lowest income group was 14.1 years for men and 9.5 years for women and, for both sexes, life expectancy tended to rise in step with income (see **Figure 13.1**).

disability-adjusted life years (DALY)

a measure of the gap between a population's ideal and actual levels of health. It is derived from the number of life-years lost to premature death, illness, or injury and the number of years living with a disability. It assumes a potential life limit of 82½ years for women and 80 for men

health-adjusted life expectancy (HALE)

an estimate of life expectancy at birth. It is the number of years that a newborn can expect to live in full health given current rates of morbidity and mortality

quality-adjusted life years (QALY)

a measure of how much benefit is gained, and at what cost, for any particular physical or mental intervention. It provides an estimate of the time a person will live at different levels of health over his remaining years of life

Figure 13.1 Remaining health-adjusted life expectancy (years) at age 25, by income decile and sex, Canada, 1991–2001.

(**SOURCE:** Adapted from Table 4 in "Income disparities in health-adjusted life expectancy for Canadian adults, 1991 to 2001" by McIntosh, Finès, Wilkins, & Wolfson, 2009.)

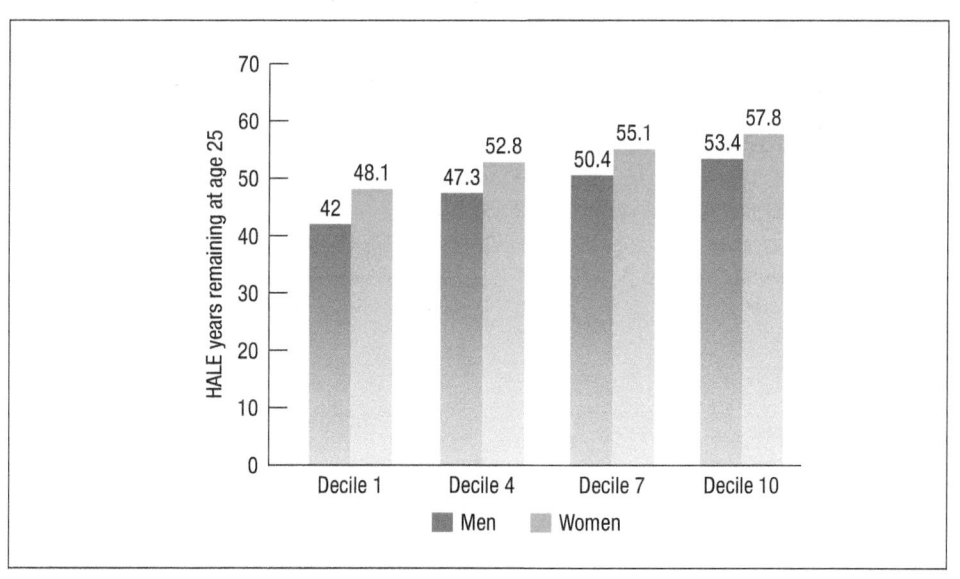

The Brain and Nervous System

No matter what age an individual is, new synapses are forming, myelinization is occurring, and old connections are dying off. Further, there is now evidence that, contrary to what neurologists have believed for a long time, some parts of the brain produce new neurons to replace those that die, even in the brains of older adults (Gould, Reeves, Graziano, & Gross, 1999; Leuner & Gould, 2010). Interestingly, too, animal research suggests that production of these new neurons is stimulated by an enriched environment, as well as by physical exercise (Cao et al., 2004; Rhodes et al., 2003). Thus, just as is true in childhood and adolescence, a challenging environment probably supports brain development. At some point in development, though, usually in the late teens, developmental processes reach a balance and the brain attains a stable

Learning Objective 13.2

Identify what changes take place in the brain in early adulthood.

size and weight. Similarly, by early adulthood, most functions have become localized in specific areas of the brain (Gaillard et al., 2000).

Neurologists have found that the pattern of peaks and valleys in the development of brain functions that begins during the fetal period continues into adulthood (see the **Research Report**). In fact, neuroscientists have now found evidence, based on MRI studies, that the human brain continues to mature throughout early adulthood (Giedd et al., 1999; Gogtay et al., 2004; Lebel & Beaulieu, 2011; Sowell, Thompson, Tessner, & Toga, 2001). As you may remember from the chapter on Physical and Cognitive Development in Adolescence, a second major growth spurt of the grey matter of frontal lobes—the area of the brain devoted to logic, planning, and emotional control—begins during preadolescence. The overproduction of neural tissue is followed by a maturing of the frontal lobes that is characterized by the synaptic pruning and myelination that continues through to young adulthood. Many neuropsychologists believe that this pattern of neural development is strongly connected to the increases in the capacity for formal operational thinking and other kinds of abstract reasoning that occur in late adolescence.

Response inhibition is another cognitive skill that emerges in early adulthood that seems to be linked to changes in the brain. For example, when you take a multiple-choice test, you need to be able to keep yourself from responding too quickly to the options in order to carefully weigh all of them. Response inhibition also helps you "bite your tongue" to keep from putting your "foot in your mouth" as often as you did at a younger age. Neuropsychologists suggest that response inhibition may

Research Report

The Brain Matures into Adulthood

The brain contains two types of tissue: grey matter and white matter. Grey matter is made up of neuron cell bodies and axon and dendrite terminals that "connect" neurons to one another (refer back to the discussion in the chapter on Prenatal Development and Birth); white matter is the myelinated axons. Normal brain development seems to follow a cyclical pattern of development. It starts with the rapid proliferation of grey matter and is followed by the simultaneous processes of synaptic pruning and myelination. Synaptic pruning is a process that results in a decline in grey matter density as unused synapses—neural circuits—are discarded. Any unused neural cells and synaptic connections wither away while those that are used become stronger and more efficient with the help of myelination. During myelination, white matter density increases as a cholesterol-rich fatty substance coats the axons to improve neural transmission. A period of relative stability follows once this stage of brain maturation is reached, usually around age 30 (Sowell et al., 2003).

Maturation of the brain does not happen all at once—the human brain matures in uneven patterns whereby specific regions of the brain develop at different times and rates than others (Gogtay et al., 2004). For example, the first stage of grey matter proliferation occurs during the first 18 months of life in the parts of the brain that control basic somatosensory functions. The next major cycle of brain development begins just prior to puberty, when there is a surge in grey matter production in areas of the brain associated with higher mental processes, namely the frontal lobes (Giedd et al., 1999; Gogtay et al., 2004). In both instances, the surge in grey matter production is followed by synaptic pruning and myelination. The time-lapse MRI scans in **Figure 13.2** illustrate a part of this process—you can see that over time, grey matter recedes at the same time that white matter advances across the surface of the brain (Sowell et al., 2001).

The human brain seems to mature in the primitive areas first and in the newer parts of the brain last (Gogtay et al., 2004). One exception to this pattern is the development of the areas of the brain that are associated with language and vocabulary. Although grey matter formation develops early in life in these brain regions, growth continues until a person reaches middle adulthood. This fits the research that shows that language skills improve continuously through to middle age (Sowell et al., 2003).

A final cycle of brain development is associated with the overall natural degenerative process that occurs in later adulthood (Sowell et al., 2003). This phase is characterized by a decline in grey matter density coupled with an end to white matter growth, resulting in an overall decline in brain volume. In this last stage of development, brain function begins to slow and becomes gradually less efficient, as you'll read later in the chapters on Physical and Cognitive Development in Middle and Late Adulthood.

Figure 13.2 Selected slides from MRI scans that tracked brain maturation from ages 5 to 20 (a time-lapse movie can be viewed at http://www.pnas.org/content/suppl/2004/05/13/0402680101.DC1#F1). Grey matter (red) diminishes as the brain matures because of synaptic pruning and myelination (blue). Notice that the region at the front of the brain (the prefrontal cortex that is associated with higher mental functioning) matures last.

(**SOURCE:** Gogtay, N., Giedd, J.N., Lusk, L., Hayashi, K.M., Greenstein, D., Vaituzis, A.C., . . . Thompson, P.M. (2004). Dynamic mapping of human cortical development during childhood through early adulthood. *Proceedings of the National Academy of Sciences of the United States of America*, 101, 8174–8179., Figure 3, p. 8178. Copyright 2004 National Academy of Sciences, U.S.A.)

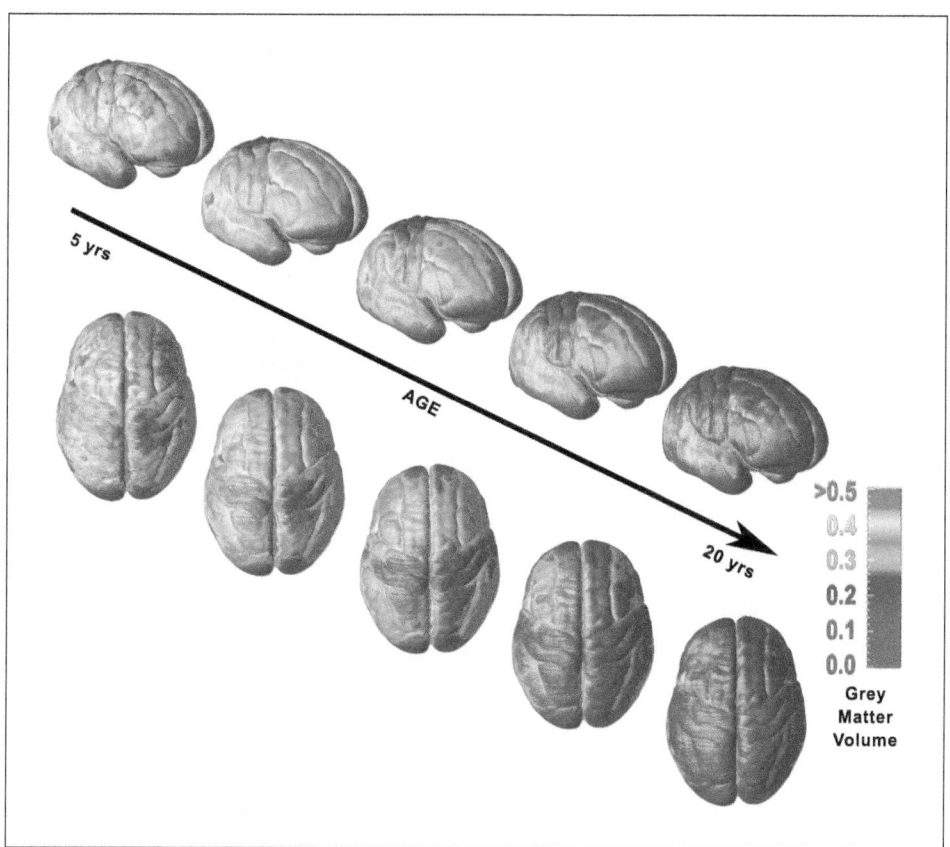

depend on the ability of the frontal lobes of the brain to regulate the **limbic system**, or the emotional part of the brain. Many scientists believe that the capacity to integrate various brain functions in this way does not become fully developed until early adulthood (Lebel & Beaulieu, 2011).

limbic system

the part of the brain that regulates emotional responses

Other Body Systems

Young adults perform better than do the middle-aged or old on virtually every physical measure. Compared with older adults, adults in their 20s and 30s have more muscle tissue; maximum bone calcium; more brain mass; better eyesight, hearing, and sense of smell; greater oxygen capacity; and a more efficient immune system. The young adult is stronger, faster, and better able to recover from exercise or to adapt to changing conditions, such as alterations in temperature or light levels.

DECLINES IN PHYSICAL FUNCTIONING After this early peak, there is a gradual decline in almost every measure of physical functioning through the years of adulthood. **Table 13.2** summarizes these changes. Most of the summary statements in the table are based on both longitudinal and cross-sectional data; many are based on studies in which both experimental and control groups consisted of participants in good health. So developmentalists can be reasonably confident that most of the age changes

Learning Objective 13.3

Identify the ways other body systems change during early adulthood.

Critical Thinking

If teenagers lack the neurological capacity to fully control their emotions, then should they be held to the same level of culpability as adults for committing impulsive criminal acts, such as knifing someone during a brawl?

Table 13.2 A Summary of Age Changes in Physical Functioning

Body Function	Age at Which Change Begins to Be Clear or Measurable	Nature of Change
Vision	Mid-40s	Lens of eye thickens and loses accommodative power, resulting in poorer near vision and more sensitivity to glare
Hearing	50 or 60	Loss of ability to hear very high and very low tones
Smell	About 40	Decline in ability to detect and discriminate among different smells
Taste	None	No apparent loss in taste discrimination ability
Muscles	About 50	Loss of muscle tissue, particularly in "fast twitch" fibres used for bursts of strength or speed
Bones	Mid-30s (women)	Loss of calcium in the bones, called *osteoporosis*; also wear and tear on bone in joints, called *osteoarthritis*; more marked after about 60
Heart and lungs	35 or 40	Most functions (such as aerobic capacity or cardiac output) do not show age changes at rest but do show age changes during work or exercise
Nervous system	Probably gradual throughout adulthood	Some loss (but not clear how much) of neurons in the brain; gradual reduction in density of dendrites; gradual decline in total brain volume and weight
Immune system	Adolescence	Loss in size of thymus; reduction in number and maturity of T cells; not clear how much of this change is due to stress and how much is primary aging
Reproductive system	Mid-30s (women)	Increased reproductive risk and lowered fertility
	Early 40s (men)	Gradual decline in viable sperm beginning at about age 40; very gradual decline in testosterone from early adulthood
Cellular elasticity	Gradual	Gradual loss of elasticity in most cells, including skin, muscle, tendon, and blood vessel cells; faster deterioration in cells exposed to sunlight
Height	40	Compression of disks in the spine, with resulting loss of height of 2.5 to 5.0 cm by age 80
Weight	Nonlinear	In American studies, weight reaches a maximum in middle adulthood and then gradually declines in old age
Skin	40	Increase in wrinkles, as a result of loss of elasticity; oil-secreting glands become less efficient
Hair	About 50	Becomes thinner and may grey

(**SOURCES:** Based on Bartoshuk & Weiffenbach, 1990; Blatter et al., 1995; Braveman, 1987; Briggs, 1990; Brock, Guralnik, & Brody, 1990; Doty et al., 1984; Fiatarone & Evans, 1993; Fozard, 1990; Fozard, Metter, & Brant, 1990; Gray, Berlin, McKinlay, & Longcope, 1991; Hallfrisch, Muller, Drinkwater, Tobin, & Adres, 1990; Hayflick, 1994; Ivy, MacLeod, Petit, & Marcus, 1992; Kallman, Plato, & Tobin, 1990; Kline & Scialfa, 1996; Kozma, Stones, & Hannah, 1991; Lakatta, 1990; Lim, Zipursky, Watts, & Pfefferbaum, 1992; McFalls, 1990; Miller, 1996; Mundy, 1994; Scheibel, 1992, 1996; Shock et al., 1984; Weisse, 1992.)

It's hard to draw a clear line between "early adulthood" and "middle adulthood" because the physical and mental changes are so gradual; even at age 30, adults may find that it takes a bit more work to get into or stay in shape than it did at age 20.

(Photo: WavebreakmediaMicro/Fotolia)

listed reflect primary aging and not secondary aging. The centre column of the table lists the approximate age at which the loss or decline reaches the point where it becomes fairly readily apparent. Virtually all these changes begin in early adulthood. But the early losses or declines are not typically noticeable in everyday physical functioning during these years.

Another way to think of this change is in terms of a balance between physical demand and physical capacity (Welford, 1993). In early adulthood, almost all of us have ample physical capacity to meet the physical demands we encounter in everyday life. We can read the fine print without bifocals, we can carry heavy boxes or furniture when we move, our immune systems are strong enough to fight off most illnesses, and we recover quickly from sickness. As we move into middle adulthood, the balance sheet changes. We find more and more areas in which our physical capacities no longer quite meet the demands.

HEART AND LUNGS   The most common measure of overall aerobic fitness is **maximum oxygen uptake (VO₂ max)**, which reflects the ability of the body to take in and transport oxygen to various body organs. When VO_2 max is measured in a person at rest, scientists find only minimal decrements associated with age. But when they measure VO_2 max during exercise (such as during a treadmill test), it shows a systematic decline with age of about 1% per year, beginning between ages 35 and 40 (Goldberg, Dengel, & Hagberg, 1996).

    VO_2 max during exercise declines more with age than does VO_2 max at rest for a variety of reasons. Primary aging effects have been demonstrated in studies showing that, even in healthy individuals who exercise regularly, age is associated with a loss of arterial elasticity and with calcification of the valves that regulate the flow of blood to and from the heart (Cheitlin, 2003). As a result, the older adult's heart responds less efficiently to the demands of exercise than the younger adult's. In addition, the ability of muscle tissue to utilize oxygen declines with age (Betik & Hepple, 2008). Research has also revealed, however, that aerobic exercise can improve VO_2 max in both younger and older adults (Wilmore et al., 2001). Thus, age-related declines in this variable may reflect the cumulative effects of a sedentary lifestyle.

maximum oxygen uptake (VO₂ max)

a measure of the body's ability to take in and transport oxygen to various body organs

Research on peak performance in various sports suggests that elite athletes reach peak performance levels in their early 20s.

STRENGTH AND SPEED   The collective effect of changes in muscles and cardiovascular fitness is a general loss of strength and speed with age—not just in top athletes, but in all of us. **Figure 13.3** shows both cross-sectional and nine-year longitudinal changes in grip strength in a group of men who participated in the Baltimore Longitudinal Studies of Aging (Kallman et al., 1990). Clearly, strength was at its peak in the men's 20s and early 30s and then declined steadily. Once again, though, such

Figure 13.3 These data, from the Baltimore Longitudinal Study of Aging, show both cross-sectional data (the dots) and longitudinal data (the lines) for grip strength among men.

(**SOURCE:** Kallman, D.A., Plato, C.C., & Tobin, J.D. (1990). The role of muscle loss in the age-related decline of grip strength: Cross-sectional and longitudinal perspectives. *Journals of Gerontology: Medical Sciences*, 45, M82–88., Figure 2, p. M84. Reproduced by permission of Oxford University Press.)

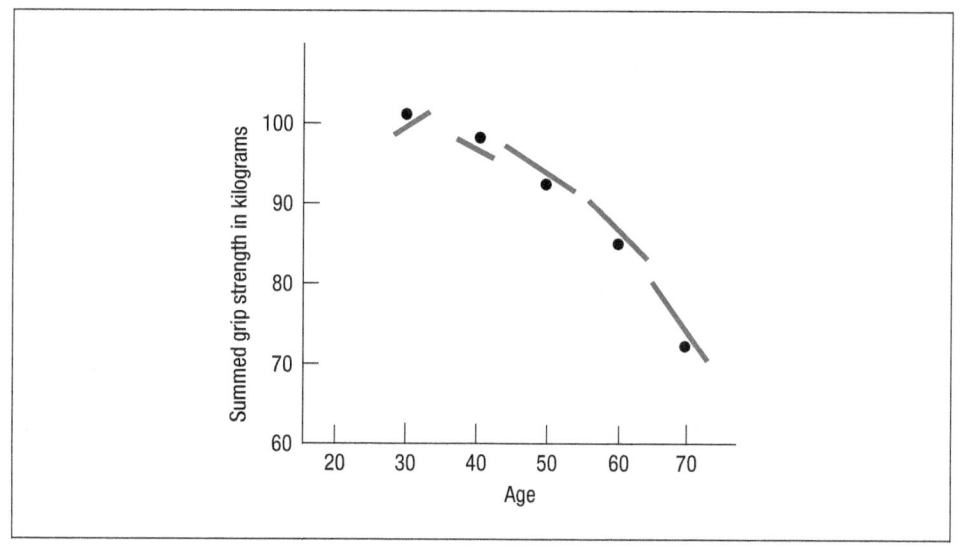

a difference might be the result of the fact that younger adults are more physically active or more likely to be engaged in activities or jobs that demand strength. Arguing against this conclusion, however, are studies of physically active older adults, who also show loss of muscle strength (e.g., Phillips, Bruce, Newton, & Woledge, 1992).

REPRODUCTIVE CAPACITY The risk of miscarriage and other complications of pregnancy is higher in a woman's 30s than in her 20s. An equivalent change occurs in fertility—the ability to conceive—which is at its highest in the late teens and early 20s and drops steadily thereafter (Johnson & Tough, 2012). Men's reproductive capacity declines as well, but far more slowly than is common for women. Even though older men have a diminished sperm count, as long as their reproductive organs remain disease free, they retain the ability to father children throughout their lives. However, with increasing paternal age, the risk of passing on genetic mutations associated with congenital disorders and maladies, ranging from cancers to schizophrenia and autism, to offspring increases exponentially (Goriely & Wilkie, 2012; Kong et al., 2012).

As you will learn in the chapter on Physical and Cognitive Development in Middle Adulthood, in preparation for menopause, ovulation becomes sporadic and unpredictable in many women, sometimes as soon as the early 30s. Consequently, the natural process of reproductive aging leads many women to experience periods of time during which conception is impossible. However, because menstrual cycles continue to occur, many women who are ovulating intermittently are unaware of this. Thus, to achieve conception, many women in their 30s turn to specialists in reproductive medicine who can help them identify the times when they are fertile or can prescribe drugs that stimulate the ovaries to produce more eggs.

IMMUNE SYSTEM FUNCTIONING The two key organs in the immune system are the thymus gland and the bone marrow. Between them, they create two types of cells, B cells and T cells, each of which plays a distinct role. B cells fight against external threats by producing antibodies against such disease organisms as viruses or bacteria; T cells defend against essentially internal threats, such as transplanted tissue, cancer cells, and viruses that live within the body's cells (Kiecolt-Glaser & Glaser, 1995). It is T cells that decline most in number and efficiency with age (Nikolich-Žugich, 2005).

Changes in the thymus gland appear to be central to the aging process (Cohen, 2006). This gland is largest in adolescence and declines dramatically thereafter in both size and mass. By age 45 or 50, the thymus has only about 5 to 10% of the cellular mass it had at puberty (Braveman, 1987). This smaller, less functional thymus is less able to turn the immature T cells produced by the bone marrow into fully "adult" cells. Additionally, the hormone-producing cells of the thymus in many adults are no longer capable of maintaining optimum immune-system functioning (Yang et al., 2009). As a result, both of the basic protective mechanisms work less efficiently. Adults produce fewer antibodies than do children or teenagers. And T cells partially lose the ability to "recognize" a foreign cell, so that the body may fail to fight off some disease cells (cancer cells, for example). Thus, one of the key physical changes over the years of adulthood is an increasing susceptibility to disease.

It is not entirely clear whether this susceptibility is due to primary or secondary aging. These changes in the immune system are found in healthy adults, which makes them look like part of primary aging. But there is also growing evidence that the functioning of the immune system is impaired by chronic conditions to which lifestyle factors contribute, such as diabetes (Nikolich-Žugich, 2005). The system is also highly responsive to psychological stress and depression (Hawkley & Cacioppo, 2004). College and university students, for example, show lower levels of one variety of T cells ("natural killer" T cells) during exam periods than at other times (Glaser et al., 1992). And adults who have recently been widowed show a sharp drop in immune system functioning (Irwin & Pike, 1993). Chronic stress, too, has an effect on the immune system, initially stimulating an increase in immune efficiency, followed by a drop (Hawkley & Cacioppo, 2004).

Collectively, this research points to the possibility that life experiences that demand high levels of change or adaptation will affect immune system functioning. Over a period of years and many stresses, the immune system may become less and less efficient. It may well be that the immune system changes with age in basic ways regardless of the level of stress. But it is also possible that what is thought of as normal aging of the immune system is a response to cumulative stress.

Test Yourself before going on

1. Label each age-related change as (P) primary aging, (S) secondary aging, or (B) influenced by both.
   _____ (a) decline in ability to detect and discriminate among various smells
   _____ (b) reduction in the density of dendrites
   _____ (c) lowered fertility of women
   _____ (d) obesity
   _____ (e) thinning of hair

2. Response inhibition is linked to maturation of the _____ _____, the emotional part of the brain.

3. Measured in a person at rest, VO$_2$ max begins to decline between the ages of _____ and _____.

Critical Thinking

4. How do social class differences and income disparity influence secondary aging?

Health Promotion and Wellness

Early adulthood is a relatively healthy period of life, but risky behaviours—having multiple sex partners or engaging in substance use, for example—along with generally poor health habits can be problematic.

Health Habits and Personal Factors

As you might expect, individual health habits, such as exercise, influence health in the early adult years and beyond. Social support networks and attitudes also affect health.

HEALTH HABITS   The best evidence for the long-term effects of various health habits comes from the Alameda County Study, a major longitudinal epidemiological study conducted in a county in California (Housman & Dorman, 2005). The study began in 1965, when a random sample of all residents of the county, a total of 6928 people, completed an extensive questionnaire about many aspects of their lives, including their health habits and their health and disability. These participants were contacted again in 1974 and in 1983, when they again described their health and disability. The researchers also monitored death records and were able to specify the date of death of each of the participants who died between 1965 and 1983. They could then link health practices reported in 1965 to later death, disease, or disability. The researchers initially identified seven good health habits that they thought might be critical: getting physical exercise; not smoking, drinking, over- or undereating, or snacking; eating breakfast; and getting regular sleep.

Data from the first nine years of the Alameda study show that five of these seven practices were independently related to the risk of death. Only snacking and eating breakfast were unrelated to mortality. When the five strong predictors were combined in the 1974 data, researchers found that, in every age group, those with poorer health habits had a higher risk of mortality. Not surprisingly, poor health habits were also related to disease and disability rates over the 18 years of the study. Those who described poorer health habits in 1965 were more likely to report disability or disease

Learning Objective 13.4

Identify what habits and personal factors are associated with good health.

symptoms in 1974 and in 1983 (Breslow & Breslow, 1993; Guralnik & Kaplan, 1989; Strawbridge, Camacho, Cohen, & Kaplan, 1993). Moreover, the study showed that a sedentary lifestyle in early adulthood predisposes people to develop life-threatening illnesses such as diabetes in later years (Hu, Li, Colditz, Willet, & Manson, 2003).

The Alameda study is not the only one to show these connections between health habits and mortality. For example, a 20-year longitudinal study in Sweden confirms the link between physical exercise and lower risk of death (Lissner, Bengtsson, Bjorkelund, & Wedel, 1996). In addition, the Nurses' Health Study, a longitudinal investigation that examined the health behaviours of more than 115 000 nurses in the United States for almost two decades, found that the lower a woman's initial body mass index (BMI—the ratio of weight to height), the lower her likelihood of death (Manson et al., 1995).

These longitudinal studies suggest that the lifestyle choices of early adulthood have cumulative effects. For example, the effect of a high-fat diet coupled with a sedentary lifestyle appears to add up over time. However, reducing levels of saturated fats in the diet may reverse the process of cholesterol buildup in the blood vessels (Citkowitz, 2012). Similarly, the effects of smoking begin to reverse themselves shortly after a person quits. Thus, the long-term effects of lifestyle choices made in early adulthood may be either negative or positive. So there is likely to be a payoff for changing your health habits.

SOCIAL SUPPORT   Abundant research shows that adults with adequate *social support* have lower risk of disease, death, and depression than do adults with weaker social networks or less supportive relationships (Baker, 2005). The link between social support and health was revealed in some of the findings from the Alameda study. In this study, the *social network index* reflected an objective measurement—number of contacts with friends and relatives, marital status, and church and group membership. Even using this less-than-perfect measure of support, the relationship was vividly clear: Among both men and women in three different age groups (30 to 49, 50 to 59, and 60 to 69), those with the fewest social connections had higher death rates than those with more social connections. Since similar patterns have been found in other countries, including Sweden and Japan, this link between social contact and physical hardiness is not restricted to Western cultures (Orth-Gomér, Rosengren, & Wilhelmsen, 1993; Sugisawa, Liang, & Liu, 1994).

How does social support contribute to health? One reason may be that the size and perceived adequacy of a person's social network is correlated with the functioning of her immune system (Bouhuys, Flentge, Oldehinkel, & van den Berg, 2004). Likewise, adults who have adequate social support are less likely than their peers to be depressed, a factor that indirectly affects the immune system (Symister & Friend, 2003).

A SENSE OF CONTROL   Another personal characteristic that affects health is an individual's level of *self-efficacy*, the belief in one's ability to perform some action or to control one's behaviour or environment, to reach some goal or to make something happen (Bandura, 1977b, 1986, 1997a, 1997b). As you learned in the chapter on Social and Personality Development in Middle Childhood, this aspect of the psychological self first appears in middle childhood. In adulthood, it is linked to many health outcomes. For instance, individuals who are high in self-efficacy are more likely than those who are low in self-efficacy to follow medical advice with regard to health problems such as cardiac rehabilitation following a heart attack (Rodgers, Murray, Selzler, & Norman, 2013).

locus of control

a set of beliefs about the causes of events

A similar variable, **locus of control**, which is an individual's set of beliefs about the causes of events, also contributes to health. A person who has an *internal* locus of control sees herself as capable of exerting some control over what happens to her (Rotter, 1990). One who has an *external* locus of control believes that other people or uncontrollable forces, such as luck, determine the future.

To understand how locus of control influences health, think about what would happen if you had an ear infection for which a doctor prescribed an antibiotic that you took for only half as long as directed. How would you explain your ear infection if it failed to go away? If you have an internal locus of control, then you would have no difficulty acknowledging the fact that your failure to take the medicine as directed was responsible for your still-aching ear. However, if you have an external locus of control, then you might respond to the pain in your ear with a remark such as "Just my luck! Nothing ever goes my way."

Research suggests that the tendency to make realistic attributions is what counts when it comes to health (Frick, Fegg, Tyroller, Fischer, & Bumeder, 2007). The best outcomes for patients happen when they are able to accurately determine which aspects of their conditions are controllable and which are not. For instance, with regard to our ear infection example, a person who is able to balance attributions in this way would realize that taking medicine is under his control and would take responsibility for that aspect of his treatment. However, he would understand that the physician is responsible for determining which antibiotic to prescribe. Balancing his thinking about the reasons for his recovery or his failure to recover helps him cope with the stress of being ill.

Both self-efficacy and locus of control are related to yet another control-related psychological characteristic, the continuum that ranges from *optimism* to *pessimism* (Seligman, 2006). The pessimist, who feels helpless, believes that misfortune will last a long time, will undermine everything, and is her own fault. The optimist believes that setbacks are temporary and usually caused by circumstances; he is convinced that there is always some solution and that he will be able to work things out. Confronted by defeat, the optimist sees it as a challenge and tries harder, whereas the pessimist gives up. Not surprisingly, optimism affects health in many ways, including enhancing the effects of medication (Geers, Kosbab, Helfer, Weiland, & Wellman, 2007). That is, optimists show larger benefits from medication than pessimists do. These results are in line with other studies showing that optimism has positive effects on the immune system (Low, Bower, Moskowitz, & Epel, 2011). In addition, it fits with the results of a classic longitudinal study that found that pessimism at age 25 was correlated with poor health in middle and late adulthood (Peterson, Seligman, & Vaillant, 1988).

Sexually Transmitted Infections

In contrast to other types of disease, most sexually transmitted infections (STIs), including chlamydia (by far the most widespread) and gonorrhea, are more common among young adults than in any other age group (PHAC, 2011a). Rates of syphilis are relatively low throughout adolescence but climb steadily beginning in early adulthood until about age 60. After declining for two decades, the number of reported new cases of these infections has been increasing, especially for chlamydia. The other disease that is more common in young adults than in other age groups is HIV/AIDS.

The precise measurement of HIV infection in the Canadian population is difficult because it relies on individuals to come forward and be tested. This means that HIV infection may be present but remain undiagnosed. Another challenge in determining the levels of current and new HIV infections is that estimates are based on data from major Canadian cities and therefore do not reflect local trends. Even so, we see some disturbing trends appearing from the data that is available.

Early in the Canadian HIV epidemic, those most affected were men who had sex with men (MSM) and, to a lesser extent, unsuspecting victims who received HIV-contaminated blood products in the 1980s. The rate of new infections for the MSM population has levelled off after steady increases in the 2000s. The rate of new HIV infection for another high-risk group, injection drug users (IDU), has declined after peaking in the early 2000s (PHAC, 2012e) (see **Figure 13.4**). The HIV epidemic has recently invaded other segments of the population, with new infections on the rise in heterosexuals, women, and, to a disproportionately high level, Indigenous people (~12.2%), a rate that is almost four times higher than among non-Indigenous people (PHAC, 2010c, 2012e).

Learning Objective 13.5

Describe the risks associated with sexually transmitted infections during early adulthood.

Critical Thinking

After waning for two decades, what factors do you think have been contributing to the resurgence of STIs in Canada?

Figure 13.4 Estimated number of new HIV infections per year over time period in Canada by exposure category (range of uncertainty omitted). Estimates were subclassified according to the following exposure categories: men who have had sex with men (MSM), injection drug users (IDU), heterosexual/endemic (non-IDU heterosexual with origin in a country where heterosexual sex is the predominant mode of HIV transmission and HIV prevlence is high, primarily countries in sub-Saharan Africa and the Caribbean), heterosexual/non-endemic (heterosexual contact with a person who is either HIV infected or at risk of HIV, or heterosexual as the only identified risk).

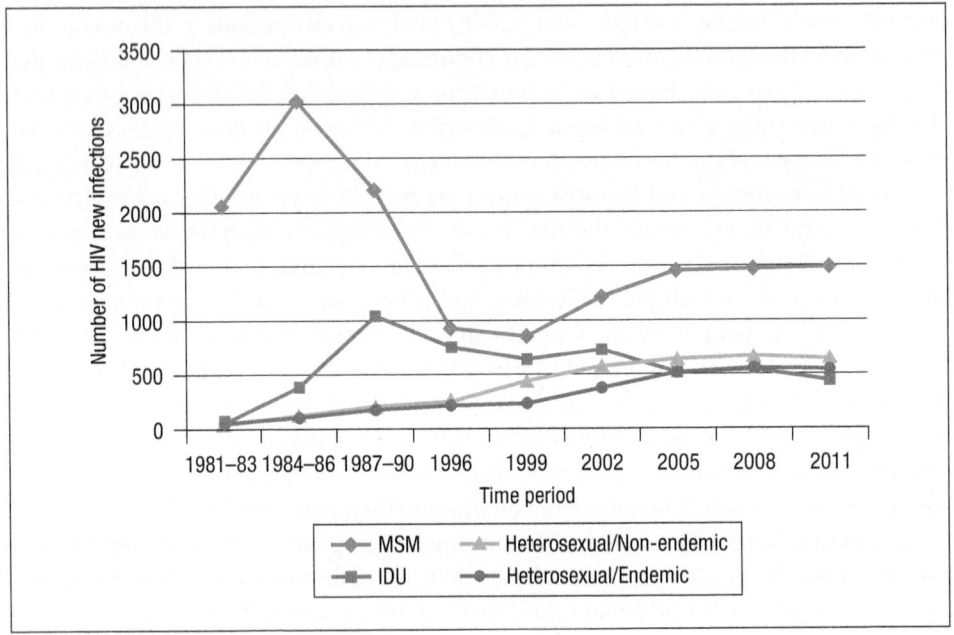

It is estimated that more than 71 300 Canadians now live with HIV and/or AIDS, of which almost 17 000 are women. Three-quarters of the new HIV infections in women are due to heterosexual contact (~76%), while the remainder is attributable to IDU (PHAC, 2012e). Women are most likely to test positive for HIV between ages 20 and 49, peaking in their 30s. In comparison, men are more likely to be diagnosed at relatively steady rates beginning in their 20s and continuing beyond their 50s. The highest percentage of newly diagnosed AIDS cases occurs in women in their 30s and in men in their 40s. Age determinants are difficult to measure because of the lengthy delay between exposure and diagnosis. In many cases, the onset of AIDS occurs in individuals who were exposed to HIV infection in their early 20s.

PREVENTION Like adolescents, many young adults engage in high-risk behaviours that are specifically linked to STIs: having multiple sexual partners, having sex without adequate protection, and frequently using drugs or alcohol. However, for most young adults, STIs remain one of the taboo topics. Many young adults are unwilling to insist on the use of condoms; many do not seek medical attention when they develop symptoms and do not inform their partners of potential problems (CDC, 2011; PHAC 2013b). The risks of these behaviours are considerable, especially with the increase in drug-resistant strains of gonorrhea and syphilis. So take note: Safe sex practices—including knowledge of your partner's sexual history—are worth the effort.

Sexually transmitted diseases are one of the most significant health risks of young adulthood. Casual sexual encounters with multiple partners carry with them a higher risk of contracting such diseases than do more careful relationship choices.

Intimate Partner Violence

Researchers define **intimate partner violence** as physical acts or other behaviour intended to cause physical, psychological, or sexual harm to an intimate partner. Intimate partners are couples who are dating, cohabiting, engaged, or married, or who were formerly partners. The more common term, *domestic violence*, refers only to incidents involving individuals who live in the same household.

PREVALENCE When intimate partners get into a physical altercation, men and women are about equally likely to push, slap, or kick their partners. However, analyses of medical records show that, throughout the world, women are more likely than men to be injured during physical confrontations between intimate partners (McHugh, 2005). Intimate partner violence is one of the most common forms of violence against women both in Canada and globally (Sinha, 2012). And as **Figure 13.5** reveals, the rates of violence against women vary significantly across Canada, but overall, roughly 8 in 10 victims of police-reported intimate partner violence are women (~6 per 1000 women) (Sinha, 2013). Both men and women are at higher risk of violence from dating partners than spouses, but in comparison to heterosexual spouses, gay, lesbian, or bisexual Canadians are roughly three times as likely to be victims of spousal violence (Sinha, 2013). Spousal violence within the Indigenous population is also higher than average, with 25% of Indigenous women and 13% of Indigenous men being assaulted by their spouse (Statistics Canada, 2001b). In both Indigenous and non-Indigenous populations, people living in common-law relationships are more likely to be victims of lethal and nonlethal spousal violence than those who are legally married (Hotton, 2001). Both women (28%) and men (22%) who had contact with an ex-marital or ex-common-law partner reported violence committed by the ex-partner (Statistics Canada, 2001d). Moreover, violence by former partners is reportedly more severe and lethal than assault by a current partner (Sinha, 2013).

Learning Objective 13.6

Discuss the risk factors for intimate partner violence.

intimate partner violence

physical acts or other behaviour intended to intimidate or harm an intimate partner

Figure 13.5 Victims of police-reported intimate partner violence, by sex of victim and province.

NOTE: Intimate partner violence refers to violence committed by legally married, separated, divorced, opposite- and same-sex common-law, dating partners (current and previous), and other intimate partners. Intimate partner category includes victims aged 15 to 89. Excludes incidents where the sex and/or age of the victim was unknown. Rates are calculated on the basis of 100 000 population.

(SOURCE: Statistics Canada, Canadian Centre for Justice Statistics, Incident-based Uniform Crime Reporting Survey. In: Sinha, M. (2013). Measuring violence against women: Statistical trends (Statistics Canada Cat. No. 85-002-XWE). Juristat, (Feb 25). Ottawa, ON: Minister of Industry. Chart 1.5 Victims of police-reported intimate partner violence, by sex of victim and province, 2011. Reproduced and distributed on an "as is" basis with the permission of Statistics Canada.)

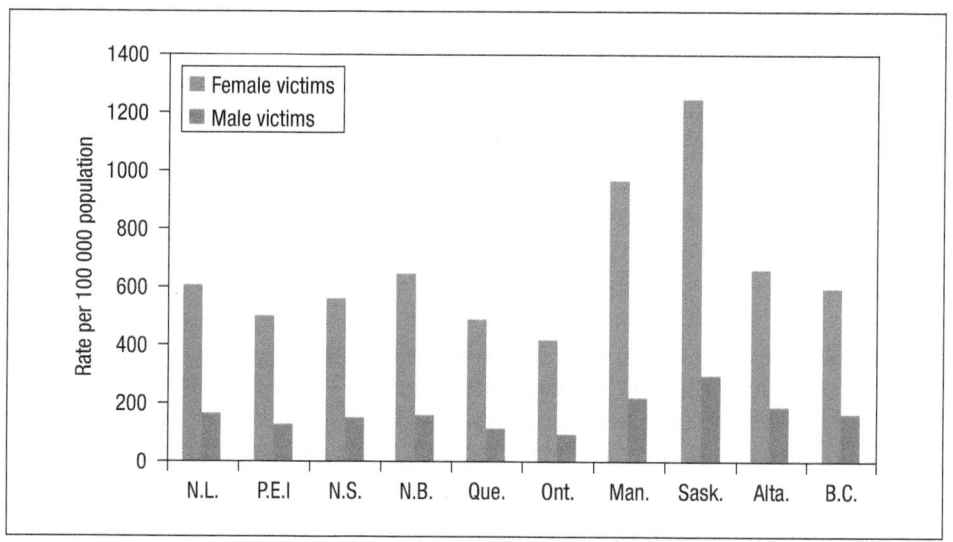

CAUSES OF PARTNER VIOLENCE Cultural attitudes contribute to rates of partner violence (McHugh, 2005). Specifically, in many societies, women were regarded as property, and a man's "right" to beat his partner was at times protected by law (Dabby, 2007). In fact, there was a time when, based on English common-law traditions, this was true in British-governed parts of North America. This factor may help explain why nearly three-quarters of male victims report the incident to police, compared to only half of female victims (Catalano, Smith, Snyder, & Rand, 2009).

In addition to cultural beliefs, a number of characteristics of perpetrators of violence and their victims are associated with intimate partner violence. For example, the same cluster of personality traits contributes to violence in both heterosexual and homosexual couples (Burke & Follingstad, 1999). The cluster includes a tendency toward irrational jealousy, a need for dependency in the partner and control in a relationship, sudden mood swings, and a quick temper (Landolt & Dutton, 1997). Men who are generally more aggressive than others are also more likely than less aggressive men to use violence against their partners (Kane, Staiger, & Ricciardelli, 2000). In addition, men who are high school dropouts or who are frequently unemployed are violent toward their partners more often than other men (Kyriacou et al., 1999).

(Photo: Ana Blazic Pavlovic/Fotolia)

Criminologists point out that intimate partner abuse happens most often in the context of arguments over long-standing disagreements that take place when partners are home from work in the evening, on holidays, or on weekends, and/or when partners have been drinking or using drugs.

Victims of violence are more likely to have been the target of violent acts as children than are their peers who are not involved in violent relationships (Catalano, 2012; Smith, White, & Holland, 2003). Age is also a factor. Young women between ages 16 and 24 are more likely to be victims of violence than those who are older (Catalano, 2012). This pattern of age differences may result from younger women's lesser ability to function independently from violent partners. They may lack the education or work experience necessary to gain employment. Finally, younger women are more likely to be caring for infants and young children for whom they cannot obtain daycare. As a result, many such women remain in violent relationships, believing they have no other choice (Kaplan & Sadock, 1991).

Alcohol and drug problems are more common amongst both perpetrators of violence and victims than among nonviolent partners (Iverson et al., 2013). One extensive study of more than 8000 intrafamily killings found that, in about half of spousal homicides, the perpetrator had been drinking alcohol or using drugs (Dawson & Langan, 1994). Similarly, in 50% of cases, the victim had been using alcohol or drugs.

EFFECTS OF PARTNER VIOLENCE ON INDIVIDUALS Women who are victims of violence are at risk for physical injury, sexual and reproductive disorders, and homicide (Heise & Garcia-Moreno, 2002). They often react by being upset, confused, frustrated, and angry and may develop feelings of fear, anxiety, depression, and low self-esteem (Sinha, 2013). Such feelings are intensified when victims believe they cannot escape from the violent relationship. Some become so despondent that they consider or attempt suicide as an escape (Iverson et al., 2013). Employment and productivity on the job may also suffer. As well, there is a social cost to family, friends, and community support networks that provide assistance to victims (Sinha, 2013).

Witnessing violence also influences children's development. One study involving 420 adults who had witnessed physical violence between their parents as children suggested that there are strong relationships between parental violence and a variety of negative developmental outcomes (McNeal & Amato, 1998). For one thing, many of these adults were found to have poor relationships with their own partners and children. Moreover, many had become perpetrators or victims of partner violence themselves.

PREVENTION Vigorous law enforcement is one approach to prevention (Dugan, Nagin, & Rosenfeld, 2003). Advocates of this approach suggest that the stigma of arrest may force perpetrators of violence to face the reality that they have a serious problem. Training programs for law enforcement officials and hospital emergency room personnel that teach them to recognize signs of violence are also essential (Hamberger & Minsky, 2000). Many experts also recommend training physicians and nurses to recognize and question patients about signs of violence during routine medical exams (Scholle et al., 2003). As a result of such training, advocates claim, perpetrators may be identified and prosecuted even when victims do not voluntarily report violent incidents.

A different approach is to provide victims with problem-solving skills and temporary shelters that may prevent their revictimization (Dutton, 2012). Further, community-wide and school-based approaches to prevention seek to educate the public about intimate partner violence and to change attitudes about the acceptability of violence in intimate relationships, so that violence will not happen in the first place.

Sexual Assault

Sexual assault is any form of sexual activity with another person without his or her consent. Engaging in sex with a person who is incapable of consenting or of understanding what is happening to him or her because of a mental disability or a temporary altered state of consciousness is also defined as sexual assault.

Canadian law prescribes three levels of sexual assault: level 1—sexual assault (i.e., kissing, touching, oral or anal sex, intercourse, or other forms of penetration); level 2—sexual assault with a weapon or resulting in bodily harm; and level 3—aggravated sexual assault (i.e., wounding, maiming, disfiguring, or endangering the life of the victim).

PREVALENCE The rate of reported sexual assault incidents was 86 per 100 000 in 2002 (Kong, Johnson, Beattie, & Cardillo, 2003). Of these, 91% are level 1 sexual assaults, whereas level 2 sexual assaults account for 2%, and there are fewer than 1% level 3 sexual assaults (see **Figure 13.6**) (Sinha, 2013). Of those aged 15 and older, women are far more likely than men to be sexually assaulted, accounting for ~92% of reported sexual offence cases in Canada.

Learning Objective 13.7

Discuss the issues involved in sexual assault.

sexual assault

any form of sexual activity with another person without his or her consent

---

Figure 13.6 The rates of police-reported sexual offences peaked during the 1990s and then declined in Canada.

(**SOURCE:** Adapted from Statistics Canada, 2003, available at: http://www.statcan.ca/Daily/English/030725/d030725.pdf. This does not constitute an endorsement by Statistics Canada of this product.)

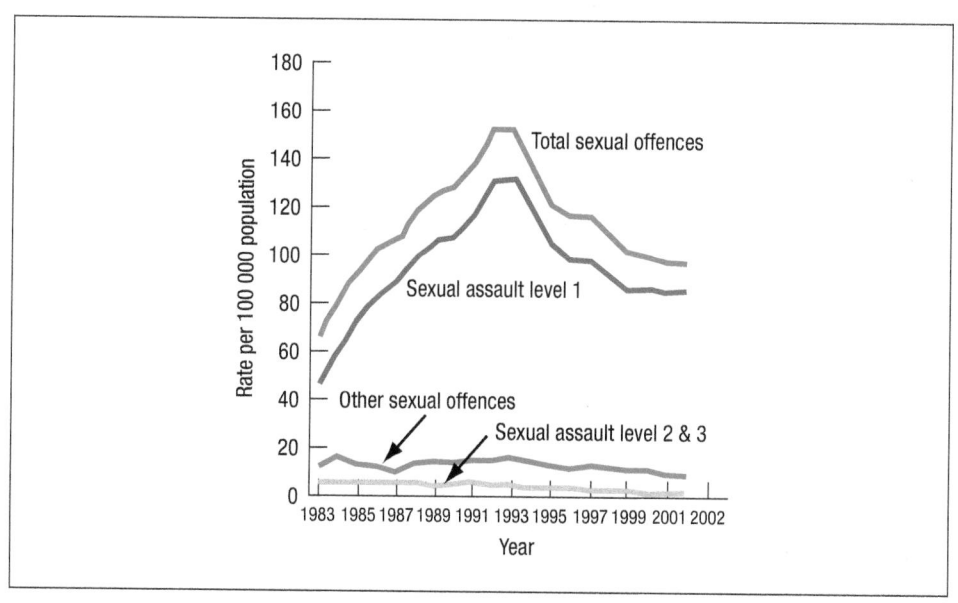

Most sexual violence occurs within the context of established social or romantic relationships; one-quarter of all sexual assaults are committed by strangers. For the female victims of reported cases who knew their assailants, 45% of the sexual assaults were committed by an acquaintance or friend, 17% by an intimate partner, and 13% by a nonspousal family member (Sinha, 2013). Like sexual assault by men against women, male rape against males usually involves men who are acquaintances or who are intimate partners (Hodge & Canter, 1998).

EFFECTS The psychological effects of being a victim of sexual violence include the development of sexual dysfunctions and post-traumatic stress disorder, as well as the possibility of physical trauma and pregnancy (Elliott, Mok, & Briere, 2004). Men who are raped by other men also sometimes experience doubts about their sexual orientation (Kaplan & Sadock, 1991). Moreover, the psychological effects of sexual violence have been found to persist for more than a decade in many victims (Elliott et al., 2004). Thus, being victimized by sexual violence can, overall, be one of the most traumatic episodes in a young adult's life.

One particularly troubling type of sexual violence among young adults is *date rape*, or rape that occurs in the context of a date. Many cases of date rape are premeditated and involve the use of alcohol and drugs to loosen the inhibitions of the victim. Research indicates that such episodes may be more traumatic than rapes perpetrated by strangers because victims of date rape believe they should have been able to prevent the assault. Victims who were coerced with drugs and/or alcohol also frequently have incomplete memories of the event, a factor that increases their vulnerability to long-term negative emotional consequences (Gauntlett-Gilbert, Keegan, & Petrak, 2004).

Prevention of sexual violence often involves training potential victims to avoid situations in which such episodes are likely to occur (Kalmuss, 2004). Training in self-defence techniques, both verbal and physical, can also help women learn how to deal effectively with the initial phases of a threatened sexual assault (Hollander, 2004).

Learning Objective 13.8

Identify which mental disorders occur most frequently in early adulthood.

Mental Health Problems

Studies in a number of developed countries show that the risk of virtually every kind of emotional disturbance is higher in early adulthood than in middle age (Kessler et al., 2005).

CAUSES OF MENTAL DISORDERS The most plausible explanation for the differing rates of mental disorder between young adults and middle-aged adults is that early adulthood is the period in which adults have both the highest expectations and the highest levels of role conflict and role strain. These are the years when each of us must learn a series of major new roles (e.g., spouse, parent, worker). If we fall short of our expectations, then emotional difficulties such as anxiety and depression become more likely.

Some people respond very effectively to the challenges of young adulthood, while others do not. For example, the personal factors you read about in an earlier section are important to mental health as well as physical health. However, with respect to mental disorder, researchers' attention is becoming more focused on biological causes.

First, mental disorders tend to run in families, suggesting a hereditary factor. In fact, the number of close relatives a person has who suffer from depression or other mood disorders is the best predictor of the likelihood that the individual will develop a mood disorder (Kendler et al., 1995). In addition, an increasing number of studies demonstrate links between mental disorders and disturbances in specific brain functions (Drevets et al., 1997; Monarch, Saykin, & Flashman, 2004). Consequently, the current view of most psychologists is that mental disorders result from an interaction of biological, psychological, and sociocultural factors.

When a young adult develops a mental health problem, the long-term impact of the problem depends on the degree to which it diverts her from an adaptive developmental pathway. For instance, if a college student develops one of these problems, then she may have to leave school. Thus, many mental health professionals believe that once an effective treatment has been identified, educational and vocational rehabilitation services are critical to the young adult's full recovery. Longitudinal studies involving young adults with mental illnesses who have participated in educational/vocational rehabilitation programs support this view (Ellison, Danley, Bromberg, & Palmer-Erbs, 1999; Gralinski-Bakker et al., 2005).

ANXIETY AND MOOD DISORDERS   The most common mental disorders that affect Canadians are those that are associated with intense or prolonged fear and anxiety (Government of Canada, 2006). For example, anxiety disorders, such as *phobias*, *generalized anxiety disorder*, *obsessive-compulsive disorder*, and *panic disorder*, affect a reported 12% of the Canadian adult population in any given year. Anxiety disorders are of such severity as to interfere with normal daily functioning, and because they are so common they also contribute to lost productivity from both absenteeism and unemployment.

After anxiety disorders, problems associated with moods are the most common type of mental difficulty. Depression is the most frequent of these disorders, with the most debilitating type, called *major depression*, affecting between 4 and 5% of Canadians annually (Government of Canada, 2006). Rates of depression are higher in early adulthood than in either adolescence or middle age. Thus, paradoxically, the time of life in which people experience their peak of physical and intellectual functioning is also the time when they may be most prone to feelings of sadness. Depression rates may be higher in early adulthood because these are the years when people must create new attachment relationships while at the same time separating from parents (Erikson's task of *intimacy*). Consequently, brief periods during which a person is alone may result in feelings of loneliness and social failure that may lead to depression (Jaremka et al., 2013).

PERSONALITY DISORDERS   In a few cases, the stresses of young adulthood, presumably in combination with some type of biological factor, lead to serious disturbances in cognitive, emotional, and social functioning that are not easily treated. For example, a **personality disorder** is an inflexible pattern of behaviour that leads to difficulties in social, educational, and occupational functioning. In many cases, the problems that are associated with these disorders appear early in life. However, the behaviour pattern is usually not diagnosed as a mental disorder until late adolescence or early adulthood (APA, 2013). The five most common types of personality disorders are listed in **Table 13.3**.

personality disorder
an inflexible pattern of behaviour that leads to difficulty in educational, occupational, and social functioning

Some young adults may exhibit behaviour that suggests a personality disorder because of stressors such as the breakup of a long-term relationship. For this reason, mental health professionals have to assess an individual's long-term and current levels of functioning in order to diagnose personality disorders. Ethnic and cultural standards of behaviour also have to be taken into account, and physical illnesses that can cause

Table 13.3 Personality Disorders

Type	Characteristics
Antisocial	Difficulty forming emotional attachments; lack of empathy; little regard for the rights of others; self-centred; willingness to violate the law or social rules to achieve a desired objective
Paranoid	Suspicious of others' behaviour and motives; emotionally guarded and highly sensitive to minor violations of personal space or perceived rights
Histrionic	Irrational, attention-seeking behaviour; inappropriate emotional responses; sexually seductive behaviour and clothing
Narcissistic	Exaggerated sense of self-importance; craves attention and approval; exploits others; lack of empathy
Borderline	Unstable moods and relationships; fear of abandonment; tendency to self-injury; highly dependent on others; impulsive and reckless behaviour

(**SOURCE:** Based on APA, 2013.)

abnormal behaviour, such as disturbances in the endocrine system, have to be ruled out. Clinicians also have to keep in mind that some of these disorders are closely related, such as the narcissistic and histrionic disorders, and that some individuals have more than one.

Generally, to be diagnosed with any of the disorders in Table 13.3, a young adult has to have been exhibiting the associated behaviour since mid- or late adolescence. In addition, the person should demonstrate the behaviour consistently, across all kinds of situations. For example, a person who steals from an employer but generally respects the property rights of others outside the work environment would probably not be diagnosed with antisocial personality disorder. The individual's functioning at work, at school, or in social relationships also must be impaired to some degree. Psychological tests can be helpful in distinguishing whether an individual simply has a troublesome personality trait, such as suspiciousness, or a genuine mental disorder, such as paranoid personality disorder.

Some personality disorders, such as antisocial and borderline disorders, become less severe in their manifestations with age (APA, 2013). However, most of these disorders remain problematic throughout adult life. In addition, they are not easily treated. They often do not respond to psychotherapy, because those who suffer from them seem to believe their problems result from others' behaviour rather than their own.

schizophrenia

a serious mental disorder characterized by disturbances of thought such as delusions and hallucinations

SCHIZOPHRENIA   One of the most serious mental disorders that is often first diagnosed in early adulthood is **schizophrenia**. This mental disorder affects an estimated 1% of Canadians and is characterized by confused thinking, false beliefs known as *delusions*, and false sensory experiences called *hallucinations* (Government of Canada, 2006). For example, a first-year biology student who breaks into a laboratory on his university campus to work on a cure for cancer he has just thought of may suffer from a *delusion of grandeur*. Likewise, a young woman who hears voices that guide her behaviour is likely to be experiencing hallucinations.

For most people with schizophrenia, these disturbances of thought become so severe that they can no longer function at work, at school, or in social relationships. In fact, many engage in behaviour that endangers themselves or others. For example, a person with schizophrenia may believe that he can fly and jump out of an upper-storey window. Consequently, people with schizophrenia are frequently hospitalized and powerful antipsychotic medications are used to help them regain some degree of normal functioning (Lauriello, McEvoy, Rodriguez, Bossie, & Lasser, 2005). Yet many continue to experience recurring episodes of disturbed thinking, even when medication helps them gain control over their behaviour.

Scientists have recently made an important discovery of a critical, underlying biological mechanism that may be involved in the development of schizophrenia. It appears genes related to *synaptic pruning* play a role in schizophrenia (National Institute of Mental Health [NIMH], 2016; Sekar, et al., 2016). In particular, the gene *complement component 4* (C4) found on chromosome 6 is overactive, causing excessive and inappropriate synaptic pruning and results in reduced numbers of synapse connections in the brains of those with schizophrenia. As discussed earlier in the chapter, synaptic pruning is normally prevalent in late adolescence and early adulthood in the association areas of the cerebral cortex, such as the pre-frontal cortex. The result is the loss of grey matter and abnormal amounts of cortical thinning that are evident in schizophrenia. Thus, too much pruning is the problem and this may also be implicated in other neurodegenerative disorders, such as *dementias* that will be discussed in the chapter on Physical and Cognitive Development in Late Adulthood. Stopping the runaway pruning may prove to be pivotal in the long-sought-after turning point in the prevention, detection, and treatment of such disorders (NIMH, 2016).

ALCOHOL AND SUBSTANCE USE DISORDERS   Rates of alcoholism and significant drug addiction also peak between ages 18 and 40, after which they decline gradually. The rates of addiction are higher for men than for women, but the age pattern is very similar in both genders (Thompson & Lande, 2007). Canadian data show the rate of **binge drinking** to be ~31% for young adults aged 20 to 34, compared with ~24% among 35- to 44-year-olds, and ~6% for those over age 65. The greatest disparity between gender drinking rates was found for the age group 20 to 34, with ~38% of male drinkers and ~24% of female drinkers considered to be binge drinkers (Statistics Canada, 2016f). For most, binge drinking peaks in the late teens and early 20s, which corresponds with the age at which drinking becomes legal and when youth are becoming more independent. Rates then taper off gradually as young adults take on new roles and responsibilities (e.g., career, marriage, parenthood) (Wellman, Contreras, Dugas, O'Loughlin, & O'Loughlin, 2014). For some though, heavy drinking continues, especially for those who score high on sensation-seeking traits (those who desire exciting, novel, and varied experiences) (Ashenhurst, Harden, Corbin, & Fromme, 2015).

binge drinking

a pattern of behaviour in which a man consumes five or more drinks, or a woman consumes four or more drinks, on one occasion, at least once a month over the past year

Binge drinking is particularly common among college and university students in Canada (Hunter & Francescutti, 2013). Notably, students typically overestimate the alcohol consumption norms (quantity and frequency) on their campus. This, in turn, predicts their personal rates of alcohol consumption (Perkins, 2007). Although most binge drinkers do not think of themselves as having a problem with alcohol, they clearly display a variety of problem behaviours, including substantially higher rates of unprotected sex, physical injury, driving while intoxicated, and trouble with the police (Hunter & Francescutti, 2013; Perkins, 2002). As well, the brain is still developing and alcohol consumption interferes with brain development and can worsen emerging psychiatric conditions (Silveri, 2012).

Binge drinking is one of several substance use behaviours that can lead to **substance abuse**, a pattern of behaviour in which a person continues to use a substance even though doing so interferes with psychological, occupational, educational, and social functioning. Substances of abuse interact with risk factors and environmental cues to produce life-long alterations to the epigenetic state of the brain's reward circuitry that, in turn, further alters the behavioural response to substances of abuse (Walker, Cates, Heller, & Nestler, 2015). The journey from first use of a drug to abuse may be long or short. Four factors influence the addictive potential of a drug:

substance abuse

a pattern of behaviour in which a person continues to use a substance even though it interferes with psychological, occupational, educational, and social functioning

- How fast the effects of the drug are felt
- How pleasurable the drug's effects are in producing euphoria or in extinguishing pain
- How long the pleasurable effects last
- How much discomfort is experienced when the drug is discontinued

Test Yourself before going on

1. The _____ _____ _____ was a longitudinal study that discovered the association between health habits and aging.
2. List high-risk behaviours linked to STIs that young adults engage in.
   (a) _____
   (b) _____
   (c) _____
3. List four factors that contribute to intimate partner abuse.
   (a) _____
   (b) _____
   (c) _____
   (d) _____

4. _____ is a serious mental disorder that is characterized by confused thinking, false beliefs, and false sensory experiences.
5. Women consuming four, or men consuming five, or more drinks on one occasion, at least once a month over the past year is _____ _____.

Critical Thinking

6. How would you rate your own health habits and personal factors, and how vulnerable do you think you are to sexually transmitted diseases, intimate partner abuse, mental health problems, and substance abuse? What behavioural changes might you make to reduce your risk?

Cognitive Changes

Like most aspects of physical functioning, intellectual processes are at their peak in early adulthood. Indeed, it now seems clear that the intellectual peak lasts longer than many early researchers had thought and that the rate of decline is quite slow. Current research also makes it clear that the rate and pattern of cognitive decline varies widely—differences that appear to be caused by a variety of environmental and lifestyle factors, as well as by heredity.

Learning Objective 13.9

Describe what types of postformal thought developmentalists have proposed.

postformal thought

types of thinking that are associated with a hypothesized fifth stage of cognitive development

relativism

the idea that some propositions cannot be adequately described as either true or false

dialectical thought

a form of thought involving recognition and acceptance of paradox and uncertainty

reflective judgement

the ability to identify the underlying assumptions of differing perspectives on controversial issues

Formal Operations and Beyond

Piaget's formal operational stage emerges in mid- to late adolescence, but some theorists dispute Piaget's hypothesis that the formal operations stage is the last stage of cognitive development (Labouvie-Vief, 2006). These theorists hypothesize that a fifth stage emerges in early adulthood, typically in the early 20s, in response to the kinds of problems that are unique to adult life. The term **postformal thought** is collectively applied to the types of thinking that these theorists propose to be characteristic of the fifth stage of cognitive development.

The work of postformal theorists owes its origins to the ideas of Lawrence Kohlberg, whose theory of moral development you read about in the chapter on Social and Personality Development in Adolescence, and William Perry (Labouvie-Vief, 2006). Kohlberg and Perry emphasized the shift toward **relativism**, the idea that some propositions cannot be adequately described as either true or false, that occurs in early adulthood (Kohlberg, 1969; Perry, 1968). Perry studied undergraduates at Harvard University in the 1960s and concluded that they began their studies with the view that knowledge comprises truthful statements and that the purpose of education is to accumulate an increasing number of such propositions. As young adults progress through higher education, Perry's work suggested, conflicts among the many ideas to which they are exposed push them toward a relativistic approach that enables them to evaluate propositions in terms of their underlying assumptions and the contexts in which they occur. For example, in the United States, most high school history students learn that slavery was the main cause of the Civil War (1861–1865). According to Perry's view, a student who is presented with a different idea about the main cause of the war is likely to dismiss it as "false" rather than to analyze it with regard to the supporting evidence that is cited by the person who advocates it. Perry argued that higher education classes reframe the "facts" that students acquired in earlier years in just this way and, in the process, help students develop a postformal approach to such complex issues.

Another theorist, Michael Basseches, points out that many young adults turn away from a purely logical, analytic approach toward a more open, perhaps deeper, mode of understanding that accepts paradox and uncertainty. He calls this new adult type of thinking **dialectical thought** (Basseches, 1984, 1989). According to this view, adults do not give up their ability to use formal reasoning. Instead, they acquire a new ability to deal with the fuzzier problems that make up the majority of the problems of adulthood—problems that do not have a single solution or in which some critical pieces of information may be missing. Choosing what type of refrigerator to buy might be a decision aided by formal operational thought. But such forms of logical thought may not be helpful in making a decision about whether to adopt a child or whether to place an aging parent in a nursing home. Basseches argues that such problems demand a different kind of thinking—not a "higher" kind of thinking, but a different one.

Psychologists Patricia King and Karen Kitchener (2004) have proposed that **reflective judgment**, the capacity to identify the underlying assumptions of differing perspectives on controversial issues, is an important feature of postformal thought.

For example, reflective thinkers are capable of ascertaining that a person who argues that the key to reducing drug use is to educate people about the adverse effects of drugs is assuming that those who use drugs do so because they lack such knowledge. According to the studies that King and Kitchener have carried out, the capacity to analyze arguments in this way develops in a series of seven stages across childhood, adolescence, and adulthood (King & Kitchener, 2004). Like Kohlberg's stages of moral judgment, these stages are loosely tied to age and are influenced by an individual's level of education.

Many of these theories of adult cognition are intriguing, but they remain highly speculative, with little empirical evidence to back them up. More generally, psychologists do not yet agree on whether these new types of thinking represent "higher" forms of thought, built on the stages Piaget described, or whether it is more appropriate simply to describe them as different forms of thinking that may or may not emerge in adulthood. What may be most important about such theories is the emphasis on the fact that the normal problems of adult life, with their inconsistencies and complexities, cannot always be addressed fruitfully by using formal operational logic. It seems entirely plausible that adults are pushed toward more pragmatic, relativistic forms of thinking and use formal operational thinking only occasionally, if at all. Postformal theorists agree that this change should not be thought of as a loss or a deterioration, but rather as a reasonable adaptation to a different set of cognitive tasks.

Critical Thinking

List two personal problems you have had to solve in the past six months. What kind of logic or thought process did you use to solve each one? Did your mode of thinking change in response to the nature of the problem?

Intelligence

Learning Objective 13.10

Describe how the concepts of crystallized and fluid intelligence help to explain age-related changes in IQ scores.

Examination of intelligence and memory in early adulthood suggests that both continuity and change characterize these components of cognitive functioning (Schroeder & Salthouse, 2004). Verbal abilities, such as the number of words in one's vocabulary, grow during early adulthood. By contrast, spatial skills decline a bit. Thus, you may be wondering—does an individual become more intelligent or less so over the years from 20 to 40? The answer to this question depends on how intellectual functioning is measured.

IQ SCORES   IQ scores remain quite stable across middle childhood, adolescence, and early adulthood. For example, a classic study of Canadian army veterans, first tested when they were in their early 20s and then again in their early 60s, yielded similar results; there was a correlation of 0.78 between verbal IQ scores achieved at the two ages (Gold et al., 1995). Over shorter intervals, the correlations were even higher.

The best single source of evidence on the stability of IQ in adulthood is a remarkable 50-year study by Warner Schaie, referred to as the Seattle Longitudinal Study (Schaie, 2013). Schaie's study has provided developmentalists with a number of important insights into how intellectual functioning changes across adulthood. One is the finding that longitudinal and cross-sectional data yield somewhat different pictures of these changes, a phenomenon first reported by Schaie in 1983 (Schaie, 2009; Schaie & Hertzog, 1983). He began in 1956 with a set of cross-sectional samples; the participants in different samples were seven years apart in age and ranged in age from 25 to 67. All participants took an IQ test at the outset of the study; a subset of the participants in each age group was then followed over 35 years and retested every seven years. In 1963, another set of cross-sectional samples, covering the same age ranges, was tested, and a subset of these was retested 7, 14, 21, and 28 years later. Further samples were added in 1970, 1977, 1984, and 1991. This remarkable data-collection process enabled Schaie to look at IQ changes over 7-, 14-, 21-, and 28-year intervals for several sets of participants, each from a slightly different cohort. **Figure 13.7** graphs one set of cross-sectional comparisons made in 1977 as well as 14-year longitudinal

Figure 13.7 These results from the Seattle Longitudinal Study show both cross-sectional and longitudinal data for a measure of overall intellectual skill (average score = 50).

(**SOURCE:** Schaie, 1983, Tables 4.5 and 4.9, pp. 89 and 100.)

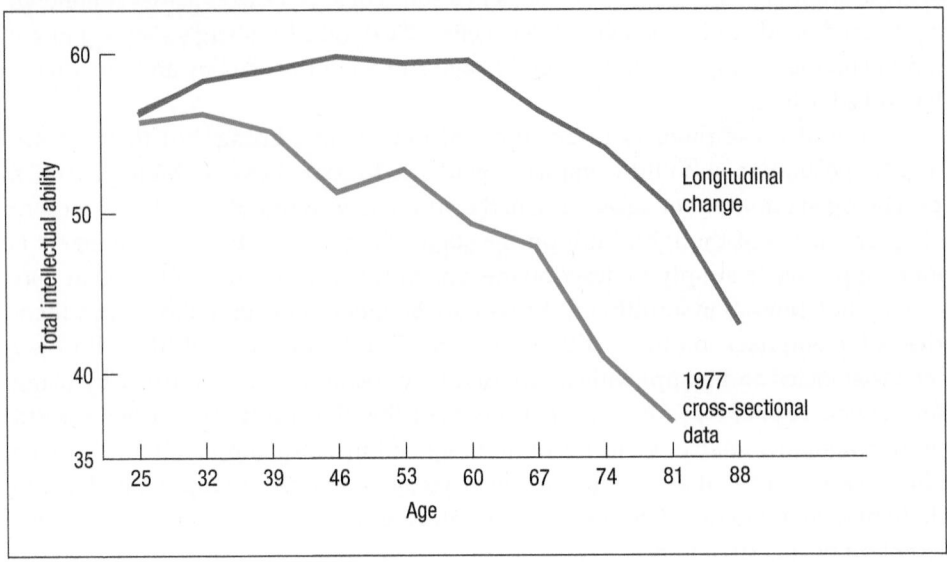

results smoothed over the whole age range. The test involved in this case is a measure of global intelligence on which the average score is set at 50 points (equivalent to an IQ of 100 on most other tests).

You can see that the cross-sectional comparisons show a steady drop in IQ. But the longitudinal evidence suggests that overall intelligence test scores actually rise in early adulthood and then remain quite constant until perhaps age 60, when they begin to decline. Since this pattern has also been found by other researchers (e.g., Sands, Terry, & Meredith, 1989; Siegler, 1983), there is good support for the temptingly optimistic view that intellectual ability remains essentially stable through most of adulthood.

CRYSTALLIZED AND FLUID INTELLIGENCE   Looking at different components of intellectual ability gives a clearer picture of change and stability across the adult years.

Crystallized intelligence depends heavily on education and experiences (Horn, 1982). It consists of the set of skills and bits of knowledge that every adult learns as part of growing up in any given culture, such as vocabulary, the ability to read and understand the newspaper, and the ability to evaluate experience. Technical skills you may learn for your job or your life—balancing a chequebook, using a computer, making change, finding the mayonnaise in the grocery store—also represent crystallized intelligence.

Fluid intelligence, in contrast, involves more "basic" abilities—it is the aspect of intelligence that depends more on the efficient functioning of the central nervous system and less on specific experience (Horn, 1982). A common measure of fluid intelligence is a "letter series test," in which a participant is given a series of letters (e.g., A C F J O) and must figure out what letter should go next. This problem demands abstract reasoning rather than reasoning about known or everyday events. Most tests of memory also measure fluid intelligence, as do many tests measuring response speed and those measuring higher-level or abstract mathematical skills. Schaie's results, and the results of many other investigators, suggest that adults maintain crystallized intelligence throughout early and middle adulthood, but that fluid intelligence declines fairly steadily over adulthood, beginning at perhaps age 35 or 40 (Schaie, 2013).

So where does this leave us in answering the question about intellectual maintenance or decline over adulthood? It seems safe to conclude, at least tentatively, that

crystallized intelligence

knowledge and judgment acquired through education and experience

fluid intelligence

the aspect of intelligence that reflects fundamental biological processes and does not depend on specific experiences

intellectual abilities show essentially no decline in early adulthood except at the very top levels of intellectual demand. In middle adulthood, though, declines on fluid intelligence abilities—those tasks that are thought to represent the efficiency of the basic physiological process—become evident (Salthouse, 2010, 2012a).

Test Yourself before going on

1. Some researchers have proposed that a new stage of cognitive development called _____ _____ emerges in early adulthood.
2. Choose the correct answers in the following sentence: Research indicates that (crystallized/fluid) intelligence increases in adulthood, but (crystallized/fluid) intelligence declines.

Critical Thinking

3. Earlier in the chapter you learned that most people reach their physical peak during early adulthood. What would you conclude about the development of a cognitive peak? When is it likely to occur and in what ways is the process similar to and different from the development of one's physical peak?

Post-Secondary Education

In today's knowledge- technology- and innovation-intensive global economy, **post-secondary education**—any formal educational experience that follows high school—is an important consideration for virtually everyone. This need for more education helps to explain why the number of students enrolled in post-secondary education in Canada continues to rise. Not only do almost two-thirds of all Canadian adults aged 25 to 64 now possess a post-secondary credential, but Canada remains top-ranked in the world when it comes to post-secondary completion rates (OECD, 2015; Statistics Canada, 2016g). This is not necessarily all good in that there is a relatively fixed demand for high-knowledge jobs and young Canadians run the risk of becoming *overqualified* and *underemployed*, working in jobs requiring less education than they've attained (Gillis & Sorenson, 2013; Morissette, Garnett, & Lu, 2013). Canada's Parliamentary Budget Officer [PBO] (2015) warns that roughly 40% of recent university graduates ages 25 to 34 are overqualified for their job, a mismatch that has been trending upward since the 1990s. Those who did not go beyond a bachelor's degree and university-educated immigrants who graduated from a university outside of Canada or the USA are especially affected. Being a graduate in certain fields also mattered—those who graduated in education, health-related, and architectural- and engineering-related fields were the least likely to be overqualified or inappropriately educated (Uppal & LaRochelle-Côté, 2014a). Somewhat ironically, there is a shortage of youth who possess the higher-level skills needed in sectors where there is high job demand, such as in the skilled trades. Plus, it seems that in addition to specific vocational knowledge, skills, and techniques, employers favour employees with so-called *"soft skills"* which include having a positive attitude and people and relationship skills, as well as numeracy, analytical, and problem-solving skills (Grant, 2016). Reflecting on this, two Canadian educators offer a poignant insight:

post-secondary education
any formal educational experience that follows high school

Critical Thinking

What reasons can you think of to explain why so many new graduates are overqualified and underemployed?

> The top performing students, particularly those in high-demand technical and professional fields, have very good employment prospects and will likely make impressive incomes. Students in more general areas of study and, particularly, those who fall short in skill level, motivation and work ethic, will likely struggle after graduation. Many students will, if academically capable, have to continue to an advanced degree; a growing number will have to continue their studies at a community college in order to prepare for the workforce. Plan accordingly. (Coates & Morrison, 2013, p. 45)

Learning Objective 13.11

Describe the developmental impact of post-secondary education.

Developmental Impact

Canada's adult population has the world's highest proportion of college (25%) and university (28%) graduates combined (53%) (OECD, 2015; Statistics Canada, 2016g). Notably, more Canadian women than men 25 to 34 years of age now possess a college diploma (~56%), a bachelor's degree (~59%), a medical degree (~62%), or a master's degree (~58%), although slightly fewer women than men have doctoral degrees (~47%) (Statistics Canada, 2013e). On the flip side, fewer than one in ten students has left high school before graduating (Statistics Canada, 2016g).

Although the wage gap between higher educated and high school–only educated Canadians has been declining since 2000 (mostly due to the rapidly rising wages of the less educated), the economic value of post-secondary education remains solid. To be sure, those who possess a post-secondary education earn much more than those who don't (Morissette, Garnett, & Lu, 2013; Statistics Canada, 2016g) as **Figure 13.8** suggests. Further, although some post-secondary education is better than none, people who succeed in completing a post-secondary credential have a clear employment advantage—this is especially true for women. Of those Canadians aged 25 to 34 who have not completed high school, roughly 57% are employed compared with an employment rate of 85% for college and university graduates (Statistics Canada, 2016g). Interestingly, although there are sex differences in the earnings of men and women at all educational levels, the advantage of a post-secondary education is now greater for women than it is for men, especially for younger women (Uppal & LaRochelle-Côté, 2014b). (We will return to the issue of sex differences in earnings in the chapter on Social and Personality Development in Early Adulthood.)

College and university graduates earn more than nongraduates for a variety of reasons (Statistics Canada, 2012k). First, graduates get more promotions and are far less likely than nongraduates to be unemployed for prolonged periods of time. In addition, college and university graduates have higher status. This means that they are more likely than nongraduates to get high-status managerial, technical, and professional positions, and they are viewed by those who make hiring decisions as more desirable employees than are nongraduates. This finding raises the question of whether graduates of post-secondary schools are really different from nongraduates or are simply perceived to be. One uncomfortable reality is that family background is major predictor of future earnings and career success: "…a substantial portion of the income boost connected to a university degree is due in fact to a combination of

Figure 13.8 Average real hourly wages (2010 dollars) by education level, full-time workers aged 17 to 34 in 2011.

(**SOURCE:** Data from Morissette, R., Garnett, P., & Lu, Y. (2013). The Evolution of Canadian Wages over the Last Three Decades (Cat. no. 11F0019MWE - Issue 349). Ottawa, ON: Minister of Industry. Reproduced and distributed on an "as is" basis with the permission of Statistics Canada.)

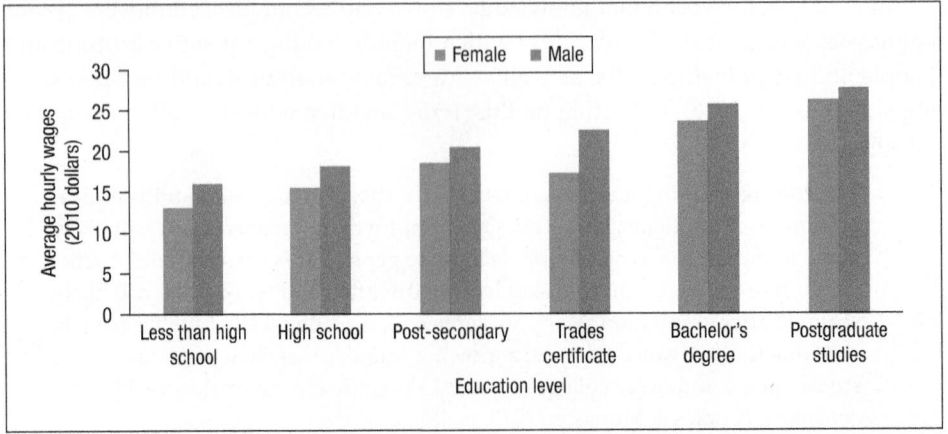

personal qualities and family background, assisted by the university education" (Coates & Morrison, 2013).

During their years of post-secondary school enrolment, students' academic and vocational aspirations change (Sax & Bryant, 2006). For example, a woman may enter university with the goal of becoming a biology teacher but graduate with the intention of going on to medical school. What seems critical about post-secondary education for making such decisions is that college- and university-level classes enable students to make realistic assessments of their academic abilities. Thus, another student who may have intended to be a doctor when he began his first year may soon conclude that becoming a biology teacher is a more realistic, attainable goal, given his performance in university-level classes. This is reflected in data that found only about one-third of Canadian students at age 25 still had the same career goal that they made at age 21. By age 25, slightly more than half of students were either still undecided (~13%) or had chosen another career (~38%) from what they had previously decided on pursuing (Statistics Canada, 2015g).

(Photo: Robert Kneschke/Shutterstock)

College and university attendance is associated with developmental advances in both the cognitive and social domains.

Test Yourself before going on

1. Identify which trends in post-secondary education are either (T) true or (F) false.
   _____ (a) Canada has among the highest proportion of post-secondary educated adults in the world.
   _____ (b) Overall, for those ages 25–34, Canadian men with university degrees outnumber women.
   _____ (c) In addition to cognitive and career benefits, post-secondary education provides new socialization opportunities.
   _____ (d) By the end of high school, most young adults have predictable and consistent career paths.

Critical Thinking

2. Review Erikson's and Marcia's research on identity processes, discussed in the chapter on Social and Personality Development in Adolescence. What would you predict about the link between identity formation and academic and vocational aspirations?

Summary

Physical Functioning

13.1 Explain the difference between primary and secondary aging.

- It is important to distinguish between the unavoidable effects of primary aging and the preventable consequences of secondary aging. Primary aging is a consequence of biological factors that are largely uncontrollable. Secondary aging can be influenced by lifestyle changes.

13.2 Identify what changes take place in the brain in early adulthood.

- The brain reaches a stable size and weight in early adulthood. There is strong evidence that the frontal lobes of the brain do not fully mature until young adulthood. This mirrors the development of cognitive abilities, such as abstract reasoning, logic, planning, and emotional control.

13.3 Identify the ways other body systems change during early adulthood.

- Adults are at their peak physically between ages 20 and 40—that is, a person has more muscle tissue, more calcium in the bones, better sensory acuity, greater aerobic capacity, and a more efficient immune system.

Health Promotion and Wellness

13.4 Identify what habits and personal factors are associated with good health.

- Several longitudinal studies have shown that habits and personal factors influence good health. Lifestyle factors include avoiding smoking, drinking, overeating, undereating, and a sedentary lifestyle; exercising; getting regular sleep; and having a low BMI. Personal factors include social support, self-efficacy, an internal locus of control, and optimism.

13.5 Describe the risks associated with sexually transmitted infections during early adulthood.

- Sexually transmitted infections are more common among young adults than among older adults. High-risk behaviours linked to STIs include multiple sex partners, unsafe sex practices, and frequent substance use.

13.6 Discuss the risk factors for intimate partner violence.

- Intimate partner abuse is a significant global health problem. Causal factors include cultural beliefs about gender roles, as well as personal variables such as alcohol and drug use. Women who are abused develop feelings of anxiety, shame, and low self-esteem. Witnessing abuse negatively affects children's development.

13.7 Discuss the issues involved in sexual assault.

- Sexual assault usually involves individuals who are acquaintances or intimate partners.

13.8 Identify which mental disorders occur most frequently in early adulthood.

- Rates of mental disorder are higher in early adulthood than in middle adulthood; young adults are more likely to be depressed, anxious, or lonely than are the middle-aged. Early adulthood is the period during which personality disorders and schizophrenia are usually diagnosed. Addiction to alcohol and drugs peaks between ages 18 and 40. Binge drinking is a common problem in young adulthood.

Cognitive Changes

13.9 Describe what types of postformal thought developmentalists have proposed.

- There may be a change in cognitive structure in adult life, and theorists have suggested that cognitive development goes beyond Piaget's formal operational stage. Postformal thought, a proposed fifth stage of cognitive development, includes various types of thinking. These types of thinking are relativism, dialectical thought, and reflective judgment.

13.10 Describe how the concepts of crystallized and fluid intelligence help to explain age-related changes in IQ scores.

- Intellectual decline occurs quite late for well-exercised abilities (crystallized abilities), such as recall of vocabulary, everyday memory use, and normal problem-solving. A measurable decline occurs earlier for so-called fluid abilities.

Post-Secondary Education

13.11 Describe the developmental impact of post-secondary education.

- Post-secondary education has beneficial effects on socioeconomic and career opportunities.

Chapter 14
Social and Personality Development in Early Adulthood

goodluz/Shutterstock

Learning Objectives

THEORIES OF SOCIAL AND PERSONALITY DEVELOPMENT

14.1 Explain what Erikson meant when he described early adulthood as a crisis of intimacy versus isolation.

14.2 Describe what a life structure is, and how it changes.

14.3 Describe the characteristics of emerging adulthood.

INTIMATE RELATIONSHIPS

14.4 Identify what factors evolutionary and social role theorists emphasize in their theories of mate selection.

14.5 Identify what factors are involved in predicting marriage quality.

14.6 Discuss how divorce affects the lives of Canadian adults.

14.7 Describe the relationship between cohabitation and subsequent success in marriage.

14.8 Describe the ways in which gay and lesbian couples are similar to and different from heterosexual couples.

14.9 Describe how singles accomplish Erikson's psychosocial developmental task of intimacy.

PARENTHOOD AND OTHER RELATIONSHIPS

14.10 Summarize what happens during the transition to parenthood.

14.11 Discuss the ways in which family and friends are important to young adults.

THE ROLE OF WORKER

14.12 Identify what factors influence an individual's occupational choices.

14.13 Describe how career goals and job satisfaction change over time.

14.14 Describe in what ways women's work patterns differ from those of men.

How many family roles do you occupy? At the very least, you're a son or daughter. Perhaps you're also a boyfriend, girlfriend, fiancé(e), or even a spouse or a parent. And what about your nonfamily roles? You're a student, but you may also be a roommate, an employee, or a volunteer. What's clear about early adulthood is that it is the time in people's lives when the number of roles in which they must function effectively grows by leaps and bounds. As you will learn in this chapter, even under the best of circumstances, the role transitions of early adulthood can be stressful. Part of the stress comes from the fact that so many transitions occur in such a relatively short time. Still, each transition brings with it new opportunities for personal growth.

Theories of Social and Personality Development

Psychoanalytic theories view adult development, like development at younger ages, as a result of a struggle between a person's inner thoughts, feelings, and motives and society's demands. Other perspectives provide different views of this period. Integrating ideas from all of them allows us to better understand early adult development.

Erikson's Stage of Intimacy Versus Isolation

Learning Objective 14.1

Explain what Erikson meant when he described early adulthood as a crisis of intimacy versus isolation.

intimacy versus isolation
Erikson's early adulthood stage, in which an individual must find a life partner or supportive friends to avoid social isolation

intimacy
the capacity to engage in a supportive, affectionate relationship without losing one's own sense of self

For Erikson, the central crisis of early adulthood is **intimacy versus isolation**. The young adult must find a life partner or supportive friends from outside her own family with whom she can share her life, or face the prospect of being isolated from society. More specifically, **intimacy** is the capacity to engage in a supportive, affectionate relationship without losing one's own sense of self. Intimate partners can share their views and feelings with each other without fearing that the relationship will end. They can also allow each other some degree of independence without feeling threatened.

As you might suspect, successful resolution of the intimacy versus isolation stage depends on a good resolution of the identity versus role confusion crisis you read about in the chapter on Social and Personality Development in Adolescence (Beyers & Seiffge-Krenke, 2010). Erikson predicted that individuals who reached early

Social scientists have not done very well at devising theories to explain lovely romantic moments like these.
(*Photos:* left, Jenner/Fotolia; right, tracyhornbrook/Fotolia)

adulthood without having established a sense of identity would be incapable of intimacy—that is, such young adults would be, in a sense, predestined to social isolation.

Still, a poor sense of identity is only one barrier to intimacy. Misunderstandings stemming from sex differences in styles of interaction can also get in the way. To women, intimacy is bound up with self-disclosure. Thus, a woman who is involved with a partner who does not reveal much that is personal perceives the relationship as lacking in intimacy. However, most men don't see self-disclosure as essential to intimacy. Consequently, many men are satisfied with relationships that their female partners see as inadequate.

Though many people involved in intimate relationships wish their relationships were better, most adults succeed in establishing some kind of close relationship. Not everyone marries, of course, but many adults develop affectionate, long-lasting friendships that are significant sources of support for them and may, in some cases, serve the same functions as an intimate life partner.

Levinson's Life Structures

Daniel Levinson's concept of *life structure* represents a different approach to adult development (Levinson, 1978, 1990). A **life structure** includes all the roles an individual occupies, all his relationships, and the conflicts and balance that exist among them.

Like Erikson, Levinson theorized that each of these periods presents adults with new developmental tasks and conflicts. He believed that individuals respond psychologically to these tasks and conflicts by creating new life structures. Consequently, adults cycle through periods of stability and instability.

As adults enter a period in which a new life structure is required, there is a period of adjustment, which Levinson called the *novice* phase. In the *mid-era* phase, adults become more competent at meeting the new challenges through reassessment and reorganization of the life structure they created during the novice phase. Stability returns in the *culmination* phase, when adults have succeeded in creating a life structure that allows them to manage the demands of the new developmental challenges with more confidence and less distress.

For example, marriage requires a new life structure. Even if the newlyweds have known each other for a very long time or have been living together, they have not known each other in the roles of husband and wife. Moreover, they have never had in-laws. So, young adults who marry acquire a whole new set of relationships. At the same time, they face many new day-to-day, practical issues, such as how finances will be managed, how housekeeping chores will be done, and whose family they will visit on which holidays.

Critical Thinking

Have you experienced periods of loneliness? If so, how do you think the state of your love life at the time contributed to your feelings?

Learning Objective 14.2

Describe what a life structure is, and how it changes.

life structure
a key concept in Levinson's theory: the underlying pattern or design of a person's life at a given time, which includes roles, relationships, and behaviour patterns

As Levinson's theory predicts, newlyweds usually go through a period of adjustment, during which they experience more conflict than before the wedding and after which things are much calmer. The calm comes, as Levinson would put it, when each spouse has achieved a new life structure that is adapted to the demands of marriage.

Emerging Adulthood

Learning Objective 14.3

Describe the characteristics of emerging adulthood.

emerging adulthood

the period from the late teens to early 20s when individuals explore options prior to committing to adult roles

Like Levinson, a growing number of developmentalists view the period between ages 17 and 22 as a transitional one. Psychologist Jeffrey Arnett has proposed that the educational, social, and economic demands that modern cultures make on individuals in this age range have given rise to a new developmental period he calls **emerging adulthood**. Arnett defines this phase as the period from the late teens to the early twenties when individuals experiment with options prior to taking on adult roles (Arnett, 2000, 2004). He argues that emerging adulthood is not necessarily a universal phase of development. Instead, it arises in cultures where individuals in their late teens face a wide array of choices about the occupational and social roles they will occupy in adulthood (Jensen & Arnett, 2012). Research examining the self-concepts of men and women in this age group support Arnett's view. His studies and those of other researchers indicate that, at least in Canada and the United States, young people do not tend to think of themselves as having fully attained adulthood until age 25 or so (Galambos, Turner, & Tilton-Weaver, 2005; Kins & Beyers, 2010).

Neuroimaging studies have provided some support for the notion that emerging adulthood is a unique period of life. These studies suggest that the parts of the brain that underlie rational decision making, impulse control, and self-regulation mature during these years (Crone, Wendelken, Donohue, van Leijenhorst, & Bunge, 2006; Gotay et al., 2004). As a result, early on in this phase of life, individuals make poorer decisions about matters such as risky behaviours (e.g., unprotected sex) than they do when these brain areas reach full maturity in the early to mid-20s.

The neurological changes of the emerging adult period combine with cultural demands to shape the psychosocial features of this period of development. Researcher Glenn Roisman and his colleagues have hypothesized that emerging adults must address developmental tasks in five domains: academic, friendship, conduct, work, and romantic (Roisman, Masten, Coatsworth, & Tellegen, 2004). Roisman's research suggests that skills within the first three of these domains transfer easily from adolescence to adulthood. Useful study skills (academic) acquired in high school, for instance, are just as helpful in college. Likewise, the skills needed to make and keep friends (friendship) are the same in both periods, and the process of adapting to rules (conduct) is highly similar as well.

By contrast, emerging adults must approach the work and romantic domains differently than they did as adolescents, according to Roisman. Certainly, many teenagers have jobs and are involved in romances. However, the cultural expectations associated with emerging adulthood require them to commit to a career path that will enable them to achieve full economic independence from their families. Likewise, emerging adults must make decisions about the place of long-term romantic relationships in their present and future lives, as well as participate in such relationships. As predicted by his hypothesis, Roisman's findings and those of other researchers suggest that emerging adults experience more adjustment difficulties related to these two domains than they do in the academic, friendship, and conduct domains (Korobov & Thorne, 2006).

Finally, psychologists speculate that the tendency of emerging adults to push the limits of the independence from their families that most acquire in the late teens contributes to the remarkable neurological changes that occur during this phase. Thus, the road that leads to fulfillment of the developmental tasks outlined by Roisman is often a bumpy one. The hope of most parents and teachers of emerging adults is that each of these bumps further opens, rather than closes, the doors of opportunity to emerging adults.

Test Yourself before going on

1. According to Erikson, an adult who fails to establish an intimate relationship risks _____ from society.
2. In what order do these periods of adjustment occur in Levinson's theory of life structures?
   _____ (a) culmination phase
   _____ (b) mid-era phase
   _____ (c) novice phase

3. Emerging adults face developmental tasks in the domains of _____, _____, _____, _____, and _____.

Critical Thinking

4. What is a life structure and how does it change? What are the characteristics of emerging adulthood?

Intimate Relationships

Theories help to explain what everyday observations of adults reveal: an intimate relationship forms the secure base from which most young adults move out into the adult world. In many cases, marriage is the context in which such a relationship is established. Marriages in Canada are quickly starting to mirror our sociodemographic diversity. In addition to the legalization of same-sex marriages, we've seen a dramatic increase in mixed unions among those with differing sociodemographic and cultural characteristics, such as age, education, religion, or ethnic origin (Maheux, 2014; Milan, Maheux & Chui, 2010). The largest shift is in the number of intermarriages of visible minorities, which has increased more than threefold over the past 25 years (see **Figure 14.1**). Also, as society has become more accepting of nonmarital relationships—gay and lesbian partners and cohabiting heterosexual couples—behavioural scientists

Figure 14.1 This figure shows the proportion of all the married or partnered couples within a visible minority group who are in mixed unions.* Overall, men and women who belong to visible minority groups and are in couples are equally likely to be in mixed-union relationships, although there are some differences within specific minority groups.

*Common-law or marital relationships made up of one spouse or partner who is a member of a visible minority group and the other who is not, as well as couples composed of two different visible minority group members.

(**SOURCE:** Milan, Maheux, & Chui, 2010. *A portrait of couples in mixed unions* (Statistics Canada—11-008-X, "Canadian Social Trends"). Reproduced and distributed on an "as is" basis with the permission of Statistics Canada.)

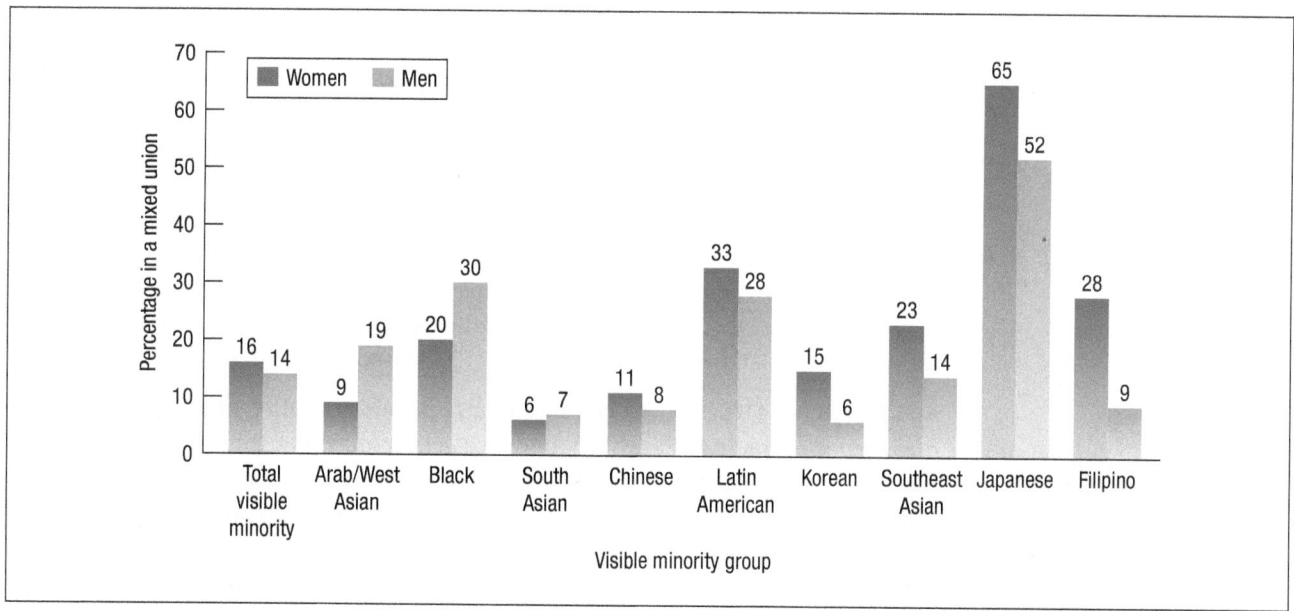

have had to expand research on intimacy to include these relationships as well. Further, internet relationships have added a new dimension to courtship and dating.

Theories of Mate Selection

Learning Objective 14.4

Identify what factors evolutionary and social role theorists emphasize in their theories of mate selection.

What are the characteristics that men and women look for in an intimate partner? Some theorists claim that males and females answer this question differently because of evolutionary pressures. Others argue that the roles that men and women occupy in the cultures in which they live shape their ideas about what kind of person would be an ideal mate.

EVOLUTIONARY THEORIES   As you should remember from the chapter on Theories of Development, evolutionary explanations of behaviour focus on survival value. Heterosexual relationships ensure the survival of the species, of course, because they are the context in which conception takes place. However, when choosing a mate, heterosexuals don't simply look for someone of the opposite sex. Instead, mating is a selective process, and evolutionary theorists often cite research on sex differences in mate preferences and mating behaviour in support of their views. Cross-cultural studies conducted over a period of several decades suggest that men prefer physically attractive, younger women, while women look for men whose socioeconomic status is higher than their own, who offer earning potential and stability (Crompton, 2005; Schmitt, Shackelford, & Buss, 2001).

parental investment theory

the theory that sex differences in mate preferences and mating behaviour are based on the different amounts of time and effort men and women must invest in child-rearing

The reasons behind men's and women's divergent mating goals are explained by **parental investment theory** (Trivers, 1972). This theory proposes that men value health and availability in their mates and are less selective because their minimum investment in parenting offspring—a single act of sexual intercourse—requires only a few minutes. In contrast, women's minimum investment in child-bearing involves nurturing an unborn child in their own bodies for nine months, as well as enduring the potentially physically traumatic experience of giving birth. Given their minimum investments, men seek to maximize the likelihood of survival of the species by maximizing the number of their offspring; whereas, women seek to minimize the number of offspring because their investment is so much greater.

Further, evolutionary theorists argue that both men and women realize that a truly adaptive approach to child-rearing requires much more than a minimum investment (Buss, 1999). Human offspring cannot raise themselves. Therefore, men value health and youth in their mates not only because these traits suggest fertility, but also because a young, healthy woman is likely to live long enough to raise the children. Similarly, women realize that to be able to nurture children to adulthood, they must have an economic provider so that they will be able to invest the time needed to raise offspring. Consequently, they look for men who seem to be capable of fulfilling these requirements.

As mentioned above, consistent sex differences in mate preferences and mating behaviour have been found across many cultures, and evolutionary theorists suggest that this cross-cultural consistency is strong evidence for a genetic basis for the behaviour (Frederick, Reynolds, & Fisher, 2013). However, these claims take us back to the basic nature-versus-nurture arguments we have examined so many times before (Eagly & Wood, 2013). Certainly, these sex differences are consistent, but they could be the result of variations in gender roles that are passed on within cultures.

social role theory

the idea that sex differences in mate preferences and mating behaviour are adaptations to gender roles

SOCIAL ROLE THEORY   Social role theory provides a different perspective on sex differences in mating (Eagly & Wood, 2012). According to this view, such sex differences are adaptations to gender roles that result from present-day social realities rather than from natural selection pressures that arose in a bygone evolutionary era. To test this hypothesis, social role theorists reanalyzed a very large set of cross-cultural data, a data set produced and interpreted by evolutionary psychologist David Buss in support of parental investment theory (Buss et al., 1990). In their re-analysis, advocates of social role theory found that both men's and women's mate preferences changed as women gained economic power (Wood & Eagly, 2007). Women's emphasis on potential mates' earning power declined, and men's focus on potential mates' domestic skills decreased.

Researchers have also found that higher-educated women with high earning potential prefer to date and marry men whose income potential is higher than their own (Wiederman & Allgeier, 1992). In fact, the more a woman expects to earn herself, the higher are her income requirements in a prospective mate. This study was widely cited by evolutionary theorists as supporting their view that such preferences are genetic and are not influenced by cultural conditions. However, a different perspective on the same study, proposed by social role theorists, led to a different conclusion (Wood & Eagly, 2007). These theorists suggest that many of today's high-income women desire to take time off to have and raise children. To be able to do so without lowering their standard of living substantially, these women require a mate who can earn a lot of money. Thus, social role theorists say, such research findings can be explained by social role theory just as well as by evolutionary theory.

In addition, social role theorists point out that high-income women desire high-income husbands because members of both sexes prefer mates who are like themselves. People are drawn to those who are similar in age, education, social class, ethnic group membership, religion, attitudes, interests, and temperament. Sociologists refer to this tendency as **assortative mating, or homogamy**. Further, partnerships based on homogamy are much more likely to endure than are those in which the partners differ markedly (Smith, Maas, & van Tubergen, 2012).

assortative mating (homogamy)

a sociologist's term for the tendency to mate with someone who has traits similar to one's own

Psychological Aspects of Marriage

The average age for first marriage among women in Canada rose from about 22.6 in the 1960s and 1970s to 29.1 by 2008. The average age of first marriage for men similarly rose from about 25 to 31.1 during the same time period (HRSDC, 2011a). Marriage remains an important milestone of the young adult years, as evidenced by the fact that only 12% of Canadians aged 25 to 29 do not expect to marry and, in fact, nine in ten do get legally married by age 50 (Crompton, 2005). In predicting who will mate with whom as well as the quality of these relationships, several psychological factors seem to be of importance—attachment, love, and conflict management.

Learning Objective 14.5

Identify what factors are involved in predicting marriage quality.

RELATIONSHIP QUALITY While we often discuss differences across sociocultural groups, there is a remarkable amount of agreement across groups about what makes a marriage work (Taylor, Funk, & Clark, 2007). Importantly, a large majority of adults in all groups believe that intimacy issues, that is, faithfulness and a satisfactory sexual relationship, are more important than the material aspects of marriage, such as dividing labour and having an adequate income. Thus, relationship quality appears to be what most people look for to judge whether their marriages are satisfactory.

Many powerful influences on marital success are in place long before a marriage even begins. Each partner brings to the relationship certain skills, resources, and traits that affect the emerging partnership system. The personality characteristics of the partners seem especially important. For example, shyness in one or both spouses is associated with low levels of marital satisfaction, presumably because of the link between shyness and unassertive communication skills (Baker & McNulty, 2010). In addition, Canadian researchers have found some interesting long-term patterns among couples who have been married for an average of 34 years (O'Rourke, Claxton, Chou, Smith, & Hadjistavropoulos, 2011):

- higher levels of extraversion predict mutual marital satisfaction in both partners
- higher levels of conscientiousness predict higher levels of satisfaction in husbands

- similar levels of openness to experience predict higher levels of satisfaction in husbands
- similar levels of agreeableness predict higher levels of satisfaction in wives

As well, Canadian studies show that attitudes toward marriage affect marital stability (Clark & Crompton, 2006). Couples who do not believe that marriage is important for them to be happy are at greater risk of marital breakdown (170% higher risk) than those who believe it is very important.

THE ROLE OF ATTACHMENT   Another important factor appears to be the security of each partner's attachment to his or her family of origin. Theorists speculate that the parental attachment relationship contributes to the construction of an internal model of intimate relationships that children bring with them into adulthood and into their marriages (Fraley, Roisman, Booth-LaForce, Owen, & Holland, 2013). Research supports this hypothesis to some degree (Simpson, Collins, Tran, & Haydon, 2008). However, the relationship between attachment security early in life and intimate relationships in adulthood is not a simple, direct one (Dinera, Conger, Shaver, Widaman, & Larsen-Rife, 2008). Research suggests that attachment security is one of several variables that work together to influence relationship satisfaction later in life. These variables include the quality of partners' peer relationships, life stresses such as unemployment, and patterns of interaction between partners that develop over the duration of the relationship (Dinera et al., 2008; Neff & Karney, 2009).

THE ROLE OF LOVE   Emotional affection contributes to relationship quality as well. The most compelling theory of romantic love comes from Robert Sternberg, who argues that love has three key components: (1) *intimacy*, which includes feelings that promote closeness and connectedness; (2) *passion*, which includes a feeling of intense longing for union with the other person, including sexual union; and (3) *commitment to a particular other*, often over a long period of time (Sternberg, 1987). When these three components are combined in all possible ways, you end up with the seven subvarieties of love listed in **Figure 14.2**. Sternberg's theory suggests that the characteristics of the emotional bond that holds a couple together influence the unique pattern of interaction that develops in each intimate relationship.

CONFLICT MANAGEMENT   How a couple manages conflict is also an important predictor of relationship quality. Drawing on a large body of research, psychologists have identified three quite different types of stable, or enduring, marriages (Gottman, 1994). **Validating couples** have disagreements, but the disagreements rarely escalate. Partners express mutual respect, even when they disagree, and listen well to each other. **Volatile couples** squabble a lot, disagree, and don't listen to each other very well when they argue, but they still have more positive than negative encounters, showing high levels of laughter and affection. **Avoidant couples**, called *conflict minimizers*, don't try to persuade each other; they simply agree to disagree, without apparent rancour, a pattern sometimes described as "devitalized."

Similarly, psychologists find two types of unsuccessful marriages. Like volatile couples, **hostile/engaged couples** have frequent hot arguments, but they lack the balancing effect of humour and affection. **Hostile/detached couples** fight regularly (although the arguments tend to be brief), rarely look at each other, and lack affection and support. In both unsuccessful types, the ratio of negative to positive encounters gets out of balance, and the marriage spirals downward toward dissolution.

Finally, there appears to be a parallel between the qualities of a successful marriage and the qualities of a secure attachment. Adults in good marriages have a high level of the same kind of responsiveness to the other's signals that developmentalists see between securely attached infants and their parents. Satisfied partners take turns, read each other's cues, and respond positively. Whatever internal model of

validating couples

partners who express mutual respect, even in disagreements, and are good listeners

volatile couples

partners who argue a lot and don't listen well, but still have more positive than negative interactions

avoidant couples

partners who agree to disagree and who minimize conflict by avoiding each other

hostile/engaged couples

partners who have frequent arguments and lack the balancing effect of humour and affection

hostile/detached couples

partners who fight regularly, rarely look at each other, and lack affection and support

Figure 14.2 Sternberg's theory postulates three components of love: passion, intimacy, and commitment. Relationships can be classified according to which of the three components is present.

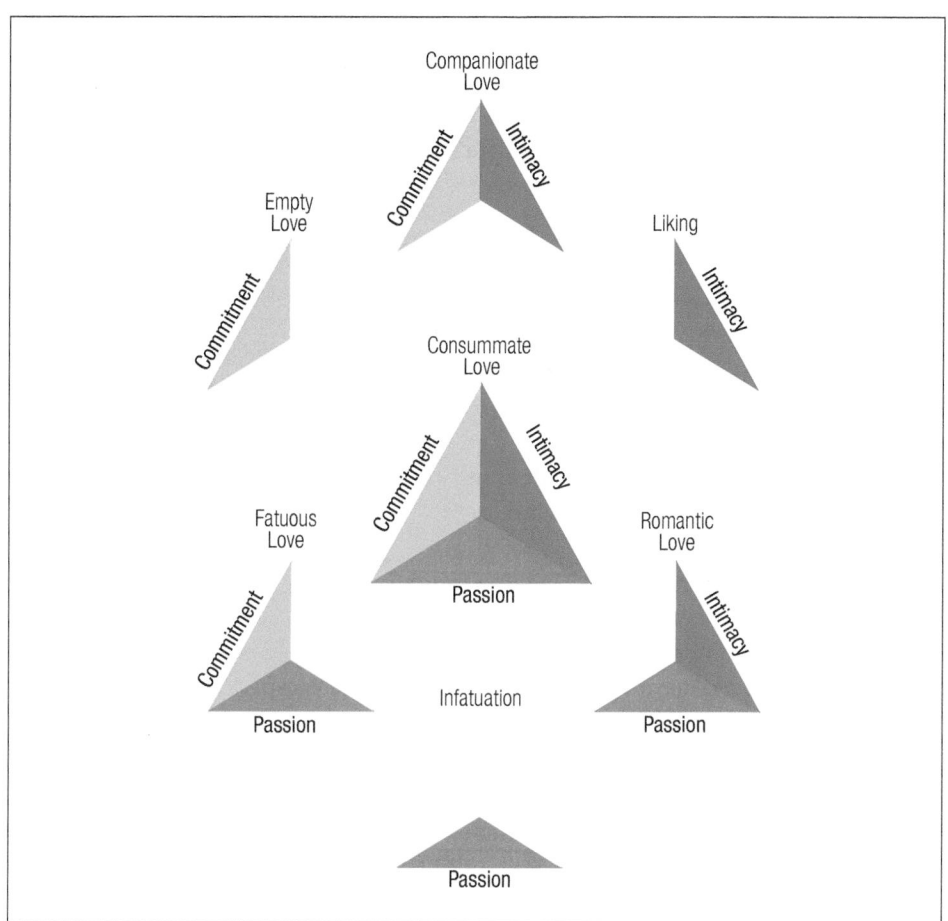

attachment each individual may bring to a marriage, the ability of the partners to create such a mutually interlocking and supportive interactive system seems to be critical to the survival of the marriage. Many of the same qualities characterize both heterosexual and homosexual couples in long-term relationships.

Divorce

York University sociologist emeritus Anne-Marie Ambert (2009) describes how different ways of computing the divorce rate can distort our ideas about how frequently divorce happens. The figure usually cited, 50%, is the ratio of divorces to marriages in a given year. In other words, a divorce rate of 50% means that there is one divorce for every two marriages. However, when married couples are followed longitudinally, the actual likelihood is that roughly 38% of marriages in Canada will end in divorce within 30 years of marriage. And, the divorce rate only increases by about 3% by the time the 50th wedding anniversary is reached (41%) (Statistics Canada, 2008d). Still, the rate of divorce peaks before the fifth wedding anniversary and the average marriage lasts almost 15 years. The average age when men divorce is 44 years and the average age for women is 41 years. These average ages may seem high, but they include both single and multiple divorces and it's important to note that the likelihood of divorcing is lower for a first marriage than it is for a remarriage (Ambert, 2009).

PSYCHOLOGICAL EFFECTS At a psychological level, divorce is clearly a major stressor. It is associated with increases in mental health problems, especially

Learning Objective 14.6

Discuss how divorce affects the lives of Canadian adults.

depression. For example, results from a National Population Health Survey of Canadian couples between ages 20 and 64 found that men who experienced marital breakup were six times more likely to exhibit symptoms of depression within two years of a breakup than men who remained married (Rotermann, 2007). Women who divorced were three-and-a-half times more likely to experience depression in this time period than those who remained married. Even after controlling for other factors that are associated with depression, such as the effects of changes in income and employment status, social support, presence of children, as well as education, age, and a history of depression, the rates of depression remained significant for both sexes—men were still three times more likely to become depressed following marital breakdown and women were two and a half times more likely.

ECONOMIC EFFECTS   The psychological effects of divorce are often significantly worsened by serious economic effects, particularly for women. Because most men have had continuous work histories, they commonly leave a marriage with far greater earning power than do women. Women not only typically lack high earning capacity, but also usually retain custody of any children, with attendant costs. Several longitudinal studies in Canada, the United States, and European countries show that divorced men slightly improve in their economic position, while divorced women are strongly adversely affected (Ambert, 2009). For example, men's incomes were above the average Canadian household income following a breakup, whereas women's incomes declined to below average (Rotermann, 2007). Furthermore, this negative economic effect does not disappear quickly—and for some women, it doesn't disappear at all. Such a long-term economic loss from divorce is especially likely for working-class women or those with relatively low levels of education, especially if they do not remarry. Women who were earning above-average incomes before their divorce are more likely to recover financially, even if they do not remarry (Ambert, 2009).

Cohabiting Heterosexual Couples

Learning Objective 14.7

Describe the relationship between cohabitation and subsequent success in marriage.

With today's high divorce rate, many young people want to be sure the person they marry is someone they want to be with for the rest of their lives. Thus, although the numbers are declining, it is still relatively common for couples to live in common-law unions. The latest Canadian census shows that roughly 12% of adults in their early 20s lived in common-law relationships and the rates were higher for those in their late twenties, ~23%—about the same percentage as those who were married (Statistics Canada, 2012l).

Given the opportunity, a majority of young adults would live common-law (Milan, 2003). Many such couples conceive of cohabitation as a final "filter," a sort of "test" before marriage: Can we really get along together? Are we sexually compatible? In Levinson's terms, they believe that cohabitation will lessen the likelihood of divorce because it will provide them with an opportunity to build a life structure they can use in adapting to marriage. Interestingly, the great bulk of the evidence shows exactly the opposite.

Studies in Canada, the United States, and several European countries show that those who cohabit before marriage are less satisfied with their subsequent marriages. Research has also shown that this relationship exists across historical cohorts. That is, couples who cohabited prior to marriage during the 1980s and 1990s display the same rates of marital dissatisfaction and divorce as those who cohabited in the 1960s and 1970s (Dush, Cohan, & Amato, 2003; Goodwin, Mosher, & Chandra, 2010). In Canada, the divorce rate for those who lived together before marriage is double that of those who did not cohabitate prior to marriage (Ambert, 2005; Clark & Crompton, 2006). The most likely explanation of this surprising set of findings is twofold.

First, cohabiting leads to development of a life structure for cohabiting, not for marriage, because the two relationships are fundamentally different (Ambert, 2003,

2005, 2009). For example, moving in together is seldom accompanied by the public announcements and celebratory fanfare that are associated with marriage (Lindsay, 2000). Further, cohabiting couples regard their relationships as ambiguous in nature—it may or may not be permanent. In contrast, marriage involves a public declaration of lifelong commitment to another person. Thus, when a cohabiting couple marries, the social and psychological aspects of the relationship change because of the deepened sense of commitment and the expectation that the relationship is permanent.

Second, adults who choose to live together before marriage are different, in key ways, from those who marry without cohabiting (Ambert, 2003, 2005). For example, couples who cohabit are less *homogamous* (similar) than those who do not. That is, cohabitating couples are more dissimilar in ethnicity, religious beliefs, educational attainment, and socioeconomic status than married couples are (Blackwell & Lichter, 2000; Mäenpää & Jalovaara, 2013; Morgan, 2012). Homogamy contributes to relationship stability. Thus, the difference in marital stability between premarital cohabitants and noncohabitants may be a matter of self-selection, not a result of some causal process attributable to cohabitation itself.

Other developmentalists believe that these findings result from the tendency of researchers to lump all kinds of cohabiting couples into a single category. This kind of aggregation, they say, may distort a study's findings because it ignores that there are two rather distinct types of heterosexual cohabitation (Kline, Stanley, Markman, & Olmos-Gallo, 2004). One type involves couples who are fully committed to a future marriage. In most cases, these couples have firm wedding plans and choose to live together for convenience or for economic reasons. In the second type of cohabitation, the relationship between the two partners is more ambiguous. Many such couples regard future marriage as a possibility but also believe that the relationship may be temporary.

Sociologist Jay Teachman points out that one important difference between these two types of couples is previous cohabitation and premarital sexual experience (Teachman, 2003). His findings are derived from the National Survey of Family Growth, a longitudinal study that focuses on women's family transitions. Teachman's analyses of these data show that married women whose premarital cohabitation and sexual experience was limited to their future husband are no more likely to divorce than women who did not cohabit prior to marriage. Thus, says Teachman, the critical variable at work in the cohabitation–divorce relationship is the fact that a large proportion of cohabitants have been in prior cohabiting or sexual relationships.

Researchers have also identified interaction differences between cohabitants with firm intentions to marry and those whose future plans are less clear. For instance, cohabiting men who intend to marry their partners do more housework than men who are not so committed (Ciabattari, 2004). This difference may be the result of communication patterns that distinguish cohabiting women of the two types. In other words, cohabiting women who intend to marry their partners may do a better job of communicating their expectations about a fair division of labour. Another important finding is that cohabiting couples who are clear about their intentions to marry are happier during the period of cohabitation than couples whose future plans are more ambiguous (Brown, 2003; Goodwin, Mosher, & Chandra, 2010). Thus, looking at the kinds of interaction patterns that exist among cohabitants who intend to marry helps us understand why, after marriage, they differ little in satisfaction and stability from those who do not cohabit until after marriage.

Gay and Lesbian Couples

Canadian census data indicated that about one in three same-sex couples are married (~21 000), while the majority are in common-law relationships (~43 600) (Statistics Canada, 2015h). One factor that appears to be just as important in same-sex unions

Learning Objective 14.8

Describe the ways in which gay and lesbian couples are similar to and different from heterosexual couples.

as it is in opposite-sex relationships is attachment security—higher levels of insecurity within same-sex partners is linked with lower satisfaction, commitment, trust, and communication, and higher problem intensity (Mohr, Selterman, & Fassinger, 2013). Homosexual couples argue about the same things as heterosexual couples, and, like heterosexual marriages, gay and lesbian relationships are of higher quality if the two partners share similar backgrounds and are equally committed to the relationship (Mackey, Diemer, & O'Brien, 2004; Quam, Whitford, Dziengel, & Knochel, 2010; Solomon, Rothblum, & Balsam, 2004).

Despite these similarities, there are important differences between the two kinds of relationships. Homosexual couples seem to be more egalitarian than heterosexual couples, with less-specific role prescriptions. For example, one study of gay, lesbian, and heterosexual couples who had recently adopted a child found that the homosexual couples were more likely to share parental responsibilities equally (Goldberg, Smith, & Perry-Jenkins, 2012). Homosexual and heterosexual partners appear to differ with regard to expectations for monogamy. Both men and women in heterosexual relationships overwhelmingly state that they expect their partners to be sexually faithful to them. Similarly, lesbian partners often insist on sexual exclusivity. However, gay men, even those who are married or in long-term partnerships, do not necessarily regard sexual fidelity as essential to their relationships (Parsons, Starks, Garnarel, & Grov, 2012). Couples therapists report that monogamy is important to gay men, but it is an issue that is considered to be negotiable by most (Bonello & Cross, 2010; Garza-Mercer, Christenson, & Doss, 2006). What is the cause of this difference?

Some evolutionary psychologists suggest that the openness of gay relationships is an adaptation to the finding that males, both heterosexual and homosexual, desire sex more frequently than females do (Buss, 2011). Thus, sexual contact with individuals outside the partnership is less likely to lead to termination of relationships among gay couples than among heterosexuals or lesbians (Bonello & Cross, 2010).

Learning Objective 14.9

Describe how singles accomplish Erikson's psychosocial developmental task of intimacy.

Singlehood

Many adults are single by preference. The impact of singlehood on an adult's life often depends on the reason for her relationship status. For example, *continuous singlehood* is associated with greater individual autonomy and capacity for personal growth than is a life path that has included divorce or loss of a spouse (Marks & Lamberg, 1998). As well, one Canadian study found that mature singles who do not intend to marry have less conventional views about the importance of love, marriage, and family: They don't value being part of a couple or a family as highly as singles who do expect to marry (Crompton, 2005).

Although close relationships with their families of origin are an important source of psychological and emotional intimacy, close friends are likely to play a more prominent role in the personal relationship networks of Canadian singles than either family or acquaintances (Vézina, 2011). Another important point to keep in mind is that many single adults participate in intimate relationships that do not involve either cohabitation or marriage—these **living apart together** couples make up roughly 1 in 13 adult Canadians (Turcotte, 2013b). Overall though, Canadians living alone experience more social loneliness and have poorer quality social networks compared to those living in a couple (Vézina, 2011). As well, large-scale surveys suggest that single adults are less healthy and satisfied with their lives than their peers who are married (Robards, Evandrou, Falkingham, & Vlachantoni, 2013).

The number of years an individual has been single appears to be an important factor in the influence of singlehood on his development. Developmentalists have found that there is a transition time during which long-term singles move from thinking of themselves as people who will be married or partnered in the future to viewing themselves as single by choice (Davies, 2003). Afterwards, singlehood becomes an

living apart together

intimate partners who do not cohabitate

important, positive component of the individual's identity. This kind of self-affirmation may protect singles from some of the negative health consequences associated with singlehood that you read about earlier.

Test Yourself before going on

1. Write "E" beside each factor in mate selection that evolutionary theory emphasizes and "S" beside those factors that social role theory emphasizes.
   _____ (a) women's physical attractiveness
   _____ (b) homogamy
   _____ (c) economic opportunities for women
   _____ (d) men's financial resources
   _____ (e) parental investment
2. List three factors that contribute to marital success and satisfaction.
   (a)
   (b)
   (c)
3. What are the two types of cohabiting couples?
   (a)
   (b)

4. What two factors predict higher quality gay/lesbian relationships?
   (a)
   (b)
5. Which group of singles experiences the most positive adult life path, on average—continuous singles, divorced singles, or widowed singles?

Critical Thinking

6. A statement widely attributed to anthropologist Margaret Mead is, "One of the oldest human needs is having someone to wonder where you are when you don't come home at night." In what way does the research in this section suggest that Mead made a profoundly accurate statement about human nature?

Parenthood and Other Relationships

Referring to couples who do not have children, comedian Bill Cosby once said, "Why shouldn't you be miserable like the rest of us?" Yet, despite all the trials and tribulations of parenting, 85% of parents cite relationships with their children as the most fulfilling aspect of their lives (Taylor, Funk, & Clark, 2007). Even so, the transition to parenthood is not easy, and to make matters more complicated, it usually happens at a time when most other social relationships are in transition as well.

Parenthood

Most parents would agree that parenthood is a remarkably mixed emotional experience. On one hand, the desire to become a parent is, for many adults, extremely strong; thus, fulfilling that desire is an emotional high point for most. On the other hand, parenthood results in a number of stressful changes.

Learning Objective 14.10
Summarize what happens during the transition to parenthood.

THE DESIRE TO BECOME A PARENT   In Canada, the vast majority of both young men and young women expect to have at least one child; only about 6 to 9% of 20- to 34-year-olds report that they do not expect to have children (Ravanera & Roderic, 2009; Stobert & Kemeny, 2003). Not surprisingly, a major Canadian survey found that most parents (92%) believe that parenting is the most important thing they could do and most individuals enjoyed the role of being a parent (94%) (Oldershaw, 2002). The percentage of men who strongly feel they want to become parents and view parenting as a life-enriching experience is actually greater than the percentage of women who feel this way (Horowitz, McLaughlin, & White, 1998; Muzi, 2000). Furthermore, Canadian fathers are increasingly stay-home parents (~12%) and/or take paternity leave (~76% in Quebec and ~26% in the rest of Canada), and three-quarters claim to be more involved in parenting their children than their father was (Hoffman, 2010; Findlay & Kohen, 2012; Statistics Canada, 2012m).

For most couples in long-term relationships, especially those who are married, having a child is an important goal.

THE TRANSITION EXPERIENCE   The transition to parenthood can be very stressful (Doss, Rhoades, Stanley, & Markman, 2009; Umberson, Pudrovska, & Reczek, 2010). New parents may argue about child-rearing philosophy as well as how, when, where, and by whom child-care tasks should be done. Both parents are usually physically exhausted, perhaps even seriously sleep-deprived, because their newborn keeps them up for much of the night. Predictably, new parents report that they have much less time for each other—less time for conversation, sex, simple affection, or even doing routine chores together (Belsky, Lang, & Rovine, 1985). Couples without children who reported conflict management and communication problems saw these problems intensify after birth, which contributed to further relationship difficulties (Doss et al., 2009). However, the quality of the new parents' relationship can help moderate the stresses associated with caring for a newborn—the more secure and committed the relationship is, the more resilient the parents (Bouchard, 2014).

POSTPARTUM DEPRESSION   After delivery, upwards of 85% of new mothers may experience fluctuating mood, tearfulness, irritability, and anxiety—symptoms that usually dissipate within several days. Between 10 and 15% of new mothers experience a more persistent and severe mood disturbance called *postpartum depression (PPD)*. Women who develop PPD suffer from feelings of sadness for several weeks after the baby's birth and some women suffer for a year or more. Moreover, women who have PPD after their first pregnancy are at risk for experiencing the disorder again following subsequent deliveries (Joy, Templeton, & Mattingly, 2016).

The presence of major life stressors during pregnancy or immediately after the baby's birth—such as a move to a new home, the death of someone close, or job loss—also increases the risk of PPD (Swendsen & Mazure, 2000). Fatigue and difficult temperament in the infant can also contribute to PPD (Fisher, Feekery, & Rowe-Murray, 2002). However, the best predictor of PPD is depression during pregnancy (Martinez-Schallmoser, Telleen, & MacMullen, 2003). Thus, many cases of PPD can probably be prevented by training health professionals to recognize depression in pregnant women. Similarly, family members of women with absent or unsupportive partners can help them locate agencies that provide material and social support.

DEVELOPMENTAL IMPACT OF PARENTHOOD   Despite its inherent stressfulness, the transition to parenthood is associated with positive behavioural changes. Sensation-seeking and risky behaviour decline considerably when young adults become parents (Arnett, 1998). However, marital satisfaction tends to decline after the birth of a child. The general pattern is that such satisfaction is at its peak before the birth of the first child, after which it can drop quite suddenly (Doss et al., 2009) and remain at a lower level until the last child leaves home (Rollins & Feldman, 1970). Nevertheless, recent studies that examine the relationship between marital satisfaction and parenthood in a more complex fashion suggest that it is neither universal nor inevitable (Lachman, Teshale, & Agrigoroaei, 2015). Longitudinal studies show that the length of time that a couple has been together before having their first child, the amount of education they have, and the number of children they have are all positively related to marital satisfaction (Jose & Alfons, 2007). It's important to keep in mind, though, that new parents who are married or cohabiting experience a much smaller decline in overall life satisfaction than new single parents, whose lives are far more complicated and stressful (Copeland & Harbaugh, 2010). Instead of focusing on declines in relationship satisfaction, some developmentalists suggest that more attention should be paid to the consistent finding that having a parenting partner—especially one to whom one is married—is a significant protective factor in managing the stressful transition to parenthood.

LIFE WITHOUT CHILDREN   Like parenthood, having no children affects the shape of an adult's life, both within marriage and in employment patterns. To begin with, those Canadians who place less value on the importance of marriage or being part of a couple are more likely to expect to remain without children than those who do value committed relationships (Stobert & Kemeny, 2003). For couples who marry and remain without children, marital satisfaction fluctuates little over time. However, as is true of all couples, those without children are also likely to experience some drop in satisfaction in the first months and years of marriage. But over the range of adult life, the curve of marital satisfaction for couples without children is much flatter than it is for those with children (Doss et al., 2009; Keizer & Schenk, 2012). Couples in their 20s and 30s without children consistently report higher cohesion in their marriages than do couples with children.

For Canadian women from ages 30 to 39, the most common reasons given for not having children are that children don't fit in with their lifestyle (~20 to 31%), they are too old (~14%), and infertility (~13%) (Ravanera & Roderic, 2009). For example, not having children affects employment patterns, especially for women. Women without children are much more likely to have full-time, continuous careers (Abma & Martinez, 2006; Zhang, 2009). Moreover, a study comparing Canadian women with and without children found some sizable earnings differences (Zhang, 2009). This so-called **motherhood earnings gap** shows how much the earnings of women with children fall below those of women without children. For example, at any given age, women with children averaged roughly 12% lower hourly earnings than their counterparts without children and this gap increases with the number of children. As well, the earnings gap was larger yet for mothers with higher education than those with no more than a high school education. Thus, raising children affects not only marital satisfaction, but also income.

motherhood earnings gap
a measure showing how much the earnings of women with children are below those of women without children

Social Networks

Learning Objective 14.11
Discuss the ways in which family and friends are important to young adults.

Creating a partnership may be the most central task of the process of achieving intimacy, but it is certainly not the only reflection of that basic process. In early adult life, each of us creates a social network made up of family and friends as well as our life partner.

FAMILY   If you ask "Who is the person you don't like to be away from?" or "Who is the person you know will always be there for you?" children and teenagers most often list their parents, while adults most often name their spouses or partners and almost never mention their parents (Hazan, Hutt, Sturgeon, & Bricker, 1991). However, most adults feel emotionally close to their parents and see or talk to them regularly (Belsky, Jaffee, Caspi, Moffitt, & Silva, 2003).

Not surprisingly, the amount and kind of contact an adult has with kin is strongly influenced by proximity. Adults who live within two hours of their parents and siblings see them far more often than those who live farther away. But distance does not prevent a parent or sibling from being part of an individual adult's social network. These relationships can provide support in times of need, even if physical contact is infrequent.

FRIENDS   Friends, too, are important members of a social network, even those with whom young adults interact exclusively online (Sherman, Lansford, & Volling, 2006). We choose our friends as we choose our partners, from among those who are similar to us in education, social class, interests, family background, or family life-cycle stage. Cross-sex friendships are more common among adults than they are among 10-year-olds, but they are still outnumbered by same-sex friendships. Young adults' friends are also overwhelmingly drawn from their own age group. Beyond this basic requirement of similarity, close friendship seems to rest on mutual openness and personal disclosure.

Critical Thinking

List all the people in your current social network. What is the relative importance of family and friends for you?

Because of the centrality of the task of intimacy in early adulthood, most researchers and theorists assume that young adults have more friends than do middle-aged or older adults. Research has offered some hints of support for this idea, but it has been a difficult assumption to test properly. Developmentalists lack longitudinal data and do not agree on definitions of friendship, which makes combining data across studies very difficult.

SEX DIFFERENCES IN RELATIONSHIP STYLES As in childhood, there are very striking sex differences in both the number and quality of friendships in the social network of young adults (Radmacher & Azmitia, 2006). Women have more close friends, and their friendships are more intimate, with more self-disclosure and more exchange of emotional support. Young men's friendships, like those of boys and older men, are more competitive. Male friends are less likely to agree with each other or to ask for or provide emotional support to each other (Dindia & Allen, 1992; Maccoby, 1990). Adult women friends talk to each other; adult men friends do things together.

Another facet of this difference is that women most often fill the role of **kin-keeper** (Moen, 1996; Salari & Zhang, 2006). They write the letters, make the phone calls, and arrange the gatherings of family and friends. (In later stages of adult life, it is also the women who are likely to take on the role of caring for aging parents—a pattern you'll learn more about in the chapter on Social and Personality Development in Middle Adulthood.)

Taken together, all this means that women have a much larger "relationship role" than men do. In virtually all cultures, it is part of the female role to be responsible for maintaining the emotional aspects of relationships—with a spouse, with friends, with family, and, of course, with children.

kin-keeper

a family role, usually occupied by a woman, which includes responsibility for maintaining family and friendship relationships

Test Yourself before going on

1. List three factors that influence the impact of having a child on a couple's levels of relationship satisfaction/dissatisfaction.
   (a)
   (b)
   (c)
2. In addition to a romantic partner, the social networks of most young adults include _____ and _____.

Critical Thinking

3. Having children often means that a couple's social networks change such that the parents of their children's playmates take the place of other adults with whom they have associated in the past. What are the long-term advantages and disadvantages of this trend for parents' future post-child-rearing lives?

The Role of Worker

In addition to the roles of "spouse" or "partner" and of "parent," a large percentage of young adults are simultaneously filling yet another major and relatively new role, that of "worker." Most young people need to take on this role to support themselves economically, but that is not the only reason for the centrality of this role. Satisfying work also seems to be an important ingredient in mental health and life satisfaction for both men and women (Galambos, Fang, Krahn, Johnson, & Lachman, 2015; Howard, Galambos, & Krahn, 2014). Before looking at what developmentalists know about career steps and sequences in early adulthood, let's examine how young people choose an occupation.

Learning Objective 14.12

Identify what factors influence an individual's occupational choices.

Choosing an Occupation

As you might imagine, a multitude of factors influence a young person's choice of job or career. For instance, some young adults base their choices on the financial rewards associated with various careers, while others are more concerned about factors such as community service (Schlosser, Safran, & Sbaratta, 2010). Other contributing variables include family background and values, intelligence, education, gender, personality, ethnicity, self-concept, and school performance.

FAMILY INFLUENCES Typically, young people tend to choose occupations at the same general social class level as their parents, although this is less true today than it was in decades past (Leemann, 2002). In part, this effect is perpetuated through the medium of education. Canadian parents who have higher-than-average levels of education typically influence the aspirations and preparedness of their children for post-secondary education over the course of their children's lives (Finnie, Mueller, Sweetman, & Usher, 2010). This ongoing influence engenders motivation, engagement with school, good study habits, and academic success in high school that increases a student's preparedness for, and decision to attend, post-secondary education.

Families also influence job choices through their value systems (Jacobs, Chin, & Bleeker, 2006). In particular, parents who value academic and professional achievement are far more likely to have children who attend a post-secondary school and choose professional-level jobs (Flouri & Hawkes, 2008). This effect is not just social-class difference in disguise. Among working-class families, the children of those who place the strongest emphasis on achievement are most likely to move up into middle-class jobs (Finnie et al., 2010). Further, families whose career aspirations for their children are high tend to produce young adults who are more intrinsically motivated as employees (Cotton, Bynum, & Madhere, 1997).

GENDER Canadian researchers Thiessen and Nickerson (2001) contend that "the nature and extent of women's and men's educational and labour market activities evolves continuously" (p. 10). Academically, for instance, more women than men are now enrolled in all the major fields of study except for architecture and engineering; mathematics and computer sciences; and personal, protective, and transportation services (Parsons & McMullen, 2009). Nonetheless, specific job selection remains strongly affected by gender. Despite the women's movement and despite the vast increase in the proportion of women working, about 70% of women occupy traditionally female occupations, such as nursing, teaching, and clerical (Cooke-Reynolds & Zukewich, 2004; McMullen, Gilmore, & Le Petit, 2010; Statistics Canada, 2004). However, the trend is shifting—Canadian women are increasing their presence in traditionally male-dominated jobs, such as medicine, dentistry, and senior management, as well as doubling their ranks in agriculture and manufacturing (see **Figure 14.3**) (Cooke-Reynolds & Zukewich, 2004; McMullen et al., 2010). It is not surprising that, in Canada, the gap between women's income and that of their male counterparts has been decreasing steadily—the average weekly earnings of women working full-time is roughly ~82% of men's wages (Statistics Canada, 2016h).

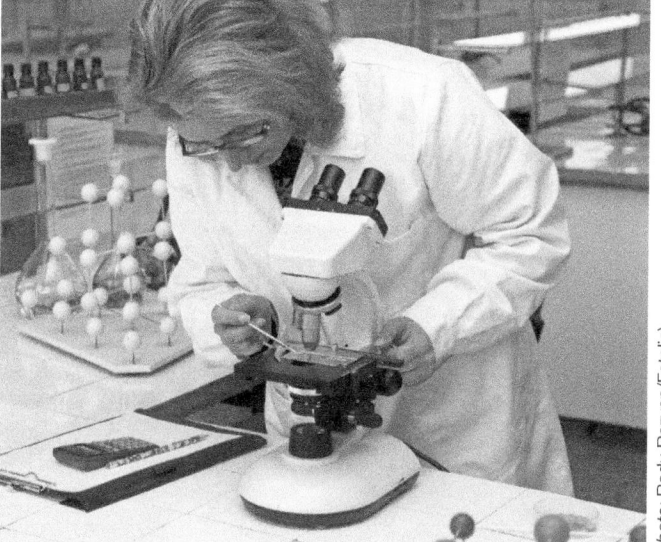

(Photo: Radu Razvan/Fotolia)

Parents who have higher-than-average levels of education themselves are more likely to encourage their children to pursue post-secondary studies.

PERSONALITY Another important influence on job choice is the young adult's personality. John Holland, whose work has been the most influential in this area, proposes six basic personality types, summarized in **Table 14.1** (Holland, 1973, 1992). Holland's basic hypothesis is that each of us tends to choose and be most successful at an occupation that matches our personality.

Research in non-Western as well as Western cultures has generally supported Holland's proposal (Joeng, Turner, & Lee, 2013; Spokane & Cruza-Guet, 2005). Ministers,

Figure 14.3 In Canada, the proportion of women in most occupational fields has been steadily increasing, although many occupations still reflect historical gender roles.

(**SOURCE:** McMullen, K., Gilmore, J., & Le Petit, C., 2010. Occupations and Fields of Study. (Statistics Canada—81-004-X). Chart 3. *Education Matters: Insights on Education, Learning and Training in Canada* April 29, 7(1). Retrieved from http://www.statcan.gc.ca/pub/81-004-x/2010001/article/11151-eng.htm. Reproduced and distributed on an "as is" basis with the permission of Statistics Canada.)

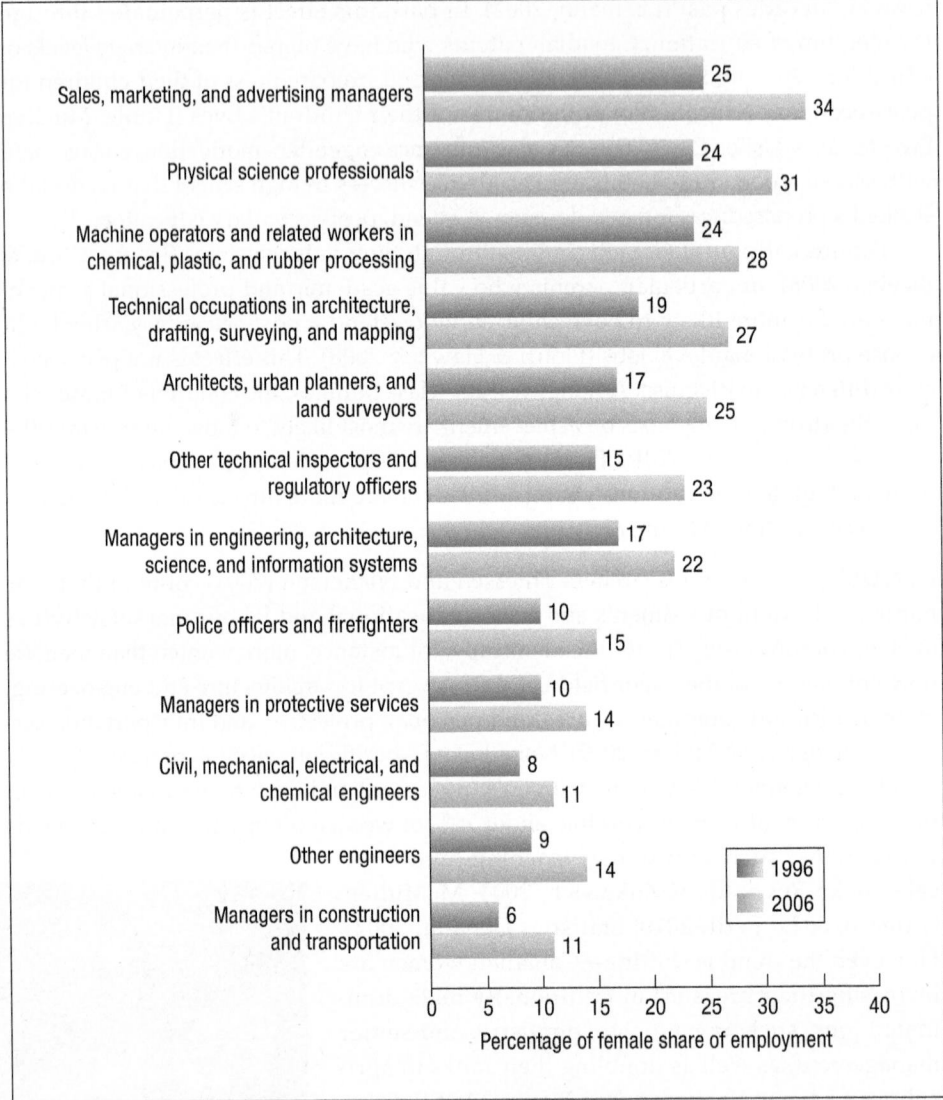

Table 14.1 Holland's Personality Types and Work Preferences

Type	Personality and Work Preferences
Realistic	Aggressive, masculine, physically strong, often with low verbal or interpersonal skills; prefer mechanical activities and tool use, choosing jobs such as mechanic, electrician, or surveyor
Investigative	Oriented toward thinking (particularly abstract thinking), organizing, and planning; prefer ambiguous, challenging tasks but are low in social skills; are often scientists or engineers
Artistic	Social; prefer unstructured, highly individual activity; are often artists
Social	Extraverts; people-oriented, sociable, and attention-seeking; avoid intellectual activity and dislike highly ordered activity; prefer to work with people, choosing service jobs such as nursing and education
Enterprising	Highly verbal and dominating; enjoy organizing and directing others; are persuasive and strong leaders, often choosing careers in sales
Conventional	Prefer structured activities and subordinate roles; like clear guidelines and see themselves as accurate and precise; may choose occupations such as bookkeeping or filing

(**SOURCES:** Data from Holland, 1973, 1992.)

for example, generally score highest on Holland's social scale, engineers highest on the investigative scale, car salespeople on the enterprising scale, and career army officers on the realistic scale. Moreover, people whose personalities match their jobs are more likely to be satisfied with their work.

Career Development

Once the job or career has been chosen, what kinds of experiences do young adults have in their work life? **Career development** is the process of adapting to the workplace, managing career transitions, and pursuing personal goals through employment. Psychologists who study career development focus on issues such as the phases of workplace adaptation and job satisfaction, and the ways in which individuals integrate work with other aspects of their lives.

SUPER'S STAGES OF CAREER DEVELOPMENT Psychologist Donald Super claims that the roots of the career development process are found in infancy. Between birth and age 14, Super says, we are in the *growth stage*, a period during which we learn about our abilities and interests. Next comes the *exploratory stage*, roughly from age 15 to 24. In this stage, the young person must decide on a job or a career; he searches for a fit between his interests and personality and the jobs available. The whole process involves a good deal of trial and error as well as luck or chance. Perhaps because many of the jobs available to those in this age range are not terribly challenging and because many young adults have not yet found the right fit, job changes are at their peak during this period.

Next comes the *establishment stage* (also called the *stabilization stage*), roughly from age 25 to 45. Having chosen an occupation, the young person must learn the ropes and begin to move up the early steps on the career ladder as he masters the needed skills, perhaps with a mentor's help. In this period, the worker also focuses on fulfilling whatever aspirations or goals he may have set for himself. The young scientist pushes himself to make an important discovery; the young attorney strives to become a partner; the young business executive tries to move as far up the ladder as he can; the young blue-collar worker may aim for job stability or promotion to foreman. It is in these years that most promotions occur.

The final phase of career development in Super's model is the *maintenance stage*. It begins around age 45 and ends at retirement. The primary goals of the maintenance stage are to protect and maintain the gains that were made during the establishment stage. To accomplish these goals, older workers must keep up with new developments in their fields. They must also acquire new skills to avoid becoming obsolete. Moreover, individuals in the maintenance phase must make preparations for retirement.

Super's model is useful for describing the challenges that individuals face in the various phases of their careers. However, to be validly applied in today's rapidly changing economy, Super's stages must be thought of independently from the ages to which he originally linked them (Super, 1990). This is necessary because of the frequency with which adults now change careers or move from one workplace to another. Thus, regardless of age, a person who makes a major career change probably exhibits the characteristics of Super's exploratory stage prior to doing so and experiences some of the features of his establishment and maintenance phases in the years following the change.

JOB SATISFACTION Some researchers have found that job satisfaction is lowest at mid-career, usually toward the end of the early adulthood period (Fullerton & Wallace, 2007; Larson, 2012). This trend is attributable, in part, to changes in workers' perceptions of job security. In the past, security increased with time on the job. But, nowadays, job security is more elusive because of the speed with which job requirements and employers' priorities shift. Thus, workers who have been on the job for some time are no longer assured of having greater security, higher incomes, or higher

Learning Objective 14.13

Describe how career goals and job satisfaction change over time.

career development

the process of adapting to the workplace, managing career transitions, and pursuing goals through employment

status positions than beginning workers. The impact of job insecurity is illustrated in a joint University of Ottawa and University of Alberta longitudinal study which found that having periods of unemployment is associated with lower job satisfaction, and depression, for in those in their 20s and 30s (Howard et al., 2014). Interestingly, those with a university education, in comparison to high school–educated young adults, were more adversely affected by periods of unemployment—perhaps because of the higher expectations they've attributed to having higher education (Galambos et al., 2015). On the plus side, though, a recent Canadian longitudinal study has found that overall happiness was at its lowest level in early adulthood and then rose steadily toward midlife (Galambos et al., 2015). And, as you might expect, those with higher occupational status and income had a higher sense of life and career satisfaction by midlife (Howard et al., 2014).

The degree to which a worker perceives his career as consistent with his personality also predicts his level of job satisfaction (Harzer & Ruch, 2013). Plus, workers who are satisfied have lower turnover rates, meaning that companies are spared the expense of searching for and training replacements (Castle, Engberg, & Anderson, 2007; Wright & Bonett, 2007). This factor influences an organization's efficiency and profitability. Therefore, job satisfaction can be just as important to employers as it is to their employees.

Another important factor that contributes to job satisfaction is achieving a balance between work and family (Marshall, 2006). Canadian workers value this balance even more than a range of other factors, such as job challenges, levels of responsibility, and salary (Ipsos-Reid/Globe and Mail, 2003). However, achieving balance seems to be an ever-elusive goal. General Social Survey (GSS) data show that Canadians have less time to spend with their families as their number of hours of paid work increases (Turcotte, 2007). Today, roughly seven of ten Canadian families with at least one child have two employed parents, the majority of whom are both working full-time (~75%) (Statistics Canada, 2016i). Despite this new reality, the majority of Canadian parents report that they are satisfied with their *work–life balance* (Statistics Canada, 2016j).

work–life balance

the balance between an employee's work and nonwork roles

quality of work–life (QWL) movement

an approach to enhancing job satisfaction by basing job and workplace design on analyses of the quality of employee experiences in an organization

In an effort to enhance job satisfaction among some employees, employers have developed new policies that consider a variable called **work–life balance**, that is, the balance between an employee's work and nonwork roles. Research has shown that work–life balance issues affect not only workers' mental and physical health, but also their job performance (Thompson, Brough, & Schmidt, 2006). Moreover, workers are more satisfied with their jobs when they believe that their supervisors share their views on work–life balance. To address the work–life needs of today's employees, psychologists have developed the **quality of work–life (QWL) movement**. Advocates of the QWL movement promote the development of job practices and workplace designs based on analyses of the quality of employees' experiences in an organization. The idea is that when people are happier at work, they will be more productive. For example, the on-site child-care centre is an innovation that has come about because of concern for the quality of work–life balance. Even though providing it can be expensive, QWL advocates argue that on-site child care will pay for itself in terms of reduced absences and lower stress levels among employees who are parents.

Other QWL innovations include *telecommuting* and *flextime*. Telecommuters work in their homes part- or full-time and are connected to their workplaces by *information and communication technology* (ICT). Employees of organizations that offer flextime benefits are allowed to create their own work schedules. Most organizations that use flextime have certain times (usually called "core hours") when all employees must be present. At other times, though, employees are free to come and go, as long as their work is done and they put in the required number of hours. Many employees take advantage of the flextime option to reduce work–family conflicts (Shockley & Allen, 2012) and Canadian data has found that parents who have flexible work schedules express slightly more work–life balance satisfaction than those parents who don't have it (Statistics Canada, 2016j).

Gender Differences in Work Patterns

Learning Objective 14.14

Describe in what ways women's work patterns differ from those of men.

It is estimated that it now takes the average Canadian youth about seven years to make the transition from school to full-time work. The transition begins at the point at which most young people are attending only school, continues through a period of schooling mixed with part-time work, and reaches the point at which more than half are working full-time (Beaujot, 2004). This transitional delay has meant that young men today are economically worse off than young men of previous generations (Drolet, 2011). Young women, however, especially if they have continued to advance their education, are better off than young women of earlier generations. From a heterosexual couple's standpoint, the woman's greater financial contribution compensates for the man's lower contribution, as most couples form a two-worker family.

Women's work experience in early adulthood differs from men's in one strikingly important respect: The great majority of women move in and out of the workforce at least once, usually to have and raise children (Moen, 2005; Yerkes, 2010). This pattern has numerous repercussions for working women. For example, Canadian women who work continuously or delay motherhood to keep working have higher salaries and achieve higher levels in their jobs than do those who have moved in and out of employment (Drolet, 2003). Of women who have not worked continuously, those who worked for several short bursts during their in-and-out stage do better economically than those who were unemployed for a single long stretch, even when the total months or years of employment are the same in the two groups (Gwartney-Gibbs, 1988). Very likely these short bursts of work allow the woman to keep up her work skills, especially if she works at the same type of job each time she re-enters the workforce. Continuous part-time work also seems to serve the same function. It seems that some strategies can help a woman maximize her work success while still allowing her to spend time with her family, but accomplishing both takes a good deal of thought and planning.

The evidence on women's patterns of discontinuous employment raises the more general question of how individuals and couples balance the roles of worker, parent, and spouse. In Canada, at least, the division of labour in the home is steadily diminishing (Marshall, 2006, 2011). **Figure 14.4** shows that women between ages 25 and 54 now spend more time in paid work than their coequals in 1986. In comparison, men in the same age category, whether single or married with or without children, have increased their time spent on housework. To be sure, married women, especially those

Canadian women have one of the highest labour force participation rates in the world.
(*Photos:* left, Phovoir/Shutterstock; right, spwidoff/Fotolia)

Figure 14.4 Daily participation in, and time spent on, paid work and housework, by living arrangements of Canadian men and women ages 25 to 54. (Note: Except paid work for those living alone, all other differences between men and women are statistically significant.)

(**SOURCE:** Marshall, 2006. Converging gender roles. *Perspectives on Labour and Income*, 18[2], p. 10. Cat. No. 75-001-XPE. Reproduced and distributed on an "as is" basis with the permission of Statistics Canada.)

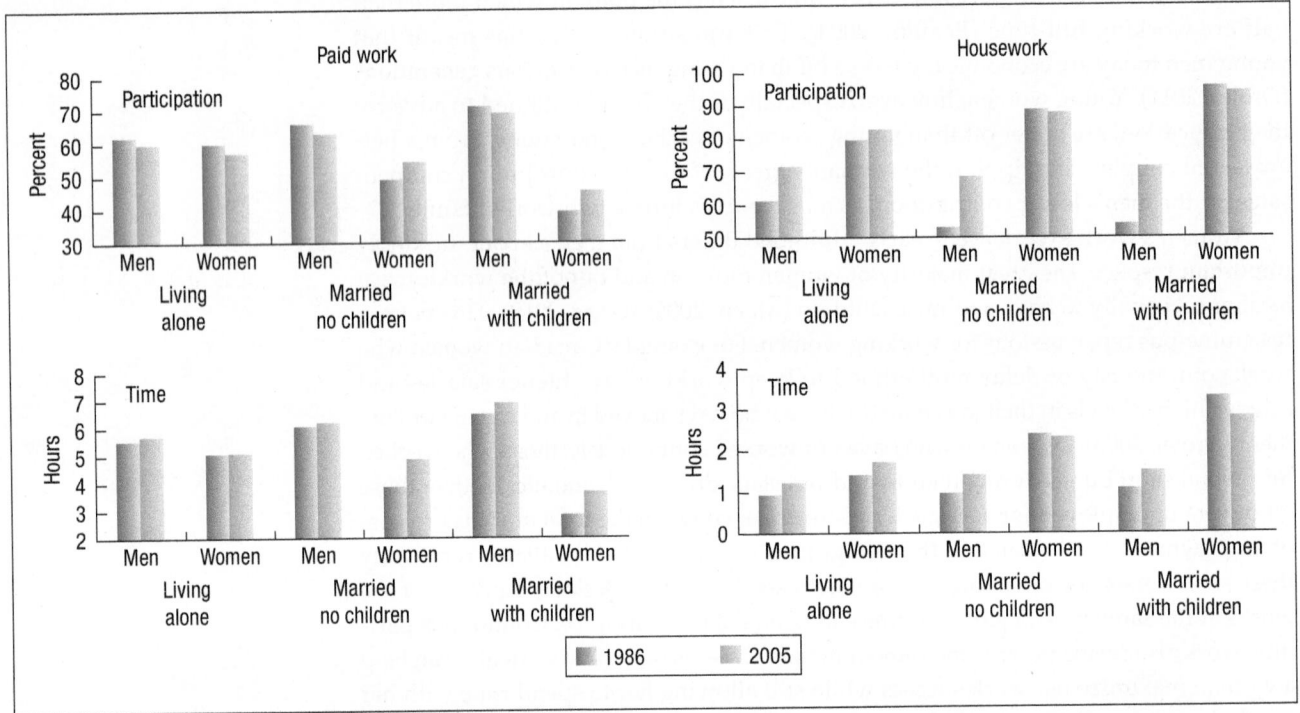

with children, still continue to do more of the housework than married men, but the overall difference is narrowing.

Kerry Daly (2000) of the University of Guelph found that Canadian adults aged 25 to 44 experience the most time pressure of all age groups. Both single mothers and married parents who were employed full time reported the highest levels of time-related stress. In addition, Daly determined that there was a curvilinear relationship between age and leisure time, whereby youth and late middle-aged adults had the highest proportion of leisure time per day and 35- to 44-year-olds reported the least amount. Men in this latter age bracket averaged 4.8 hours and women averaged 4.5 hours of leisure per day over a week. Of course, parents with children had even less leisure time than average. In many respects, this complex intersection of spousal, parental, and work roles is the defining feature of early adult life in developed societies (Crompton, 2011) (see **Development in the Real World**).

Development in the Real World

Strategies for Coping with Conflict Between Work and Family Life

If you are like many of today's college or university students, then you view your future as including marriage, parenthood, and a successful career (Hoffnung, 2004; Turcotte, 2007), much like the ~69% of dual-, full-time-earner Canadian families that have at least one child (Statistics Canada, 2016j). Fortunately, three-quarters of parents are satisfied with their work–life balance, although men with a partner (~78%) and women with a partner (~73%) still have slightly higher satisfaction rates than single parent fathers (~73%) and single parent mothers (~66%). While there is no magic formula for creating such a balance and eliminating conflict and distress, some strategies can help. These suggestions are phrased as advice to women, because it is women who experience the greatest role conflict. But men can certainly profit from the same information.

The most helpful strategy overall is something psychologists call *cognitive restructuring*—recasting or reframing the situation for yourself in a way that identifies the positive elements. Cognitive restructuring might include reminding yourself that you had good reasons for choosing to have both a job and a family and recalling other times when you have coped successfully with similar problems (Liossis, Shochet, Millear, & Biggs, 2009).

Another related restructuring involves redefining family roles. A working couple could begin the process by making a list of household chores, child-care responsibilities, and other tasks, noting which person does each chore. If the couple agree that responsibilities are unbalanced, then the couple can work toward finding a more equitable distribution of labour. As a side note of some merit, a recent study found that when the male partner's share of housework is *perceived* as being fair, the couple reported more frequent and more satisfying sexual relations (Johnson, Galambos, & Anderson, 2016). If economic resources are sufficient, reassure yourself that it is all right to hire others to help with housework. In fact, as Canadians work longer hours, they see their household incomes rise, which provides the means to get some relief from housework by hiring someone to do it, as you can see in **Figure 14.5**.

Figure 14.5 A greater percentage of higher-income Canadian households are more likely to hire and spend more money annually on domestic help than lower-income households.

(**SOURCE:** Marshall, 2006. Converging gender roles. *Perspectives on Labour and Income*, 18[2], p. 10. Cat. No. 75-001-XPE. Reproduced and distributed on an "as is" basis with the permission of Statistics Canada.)

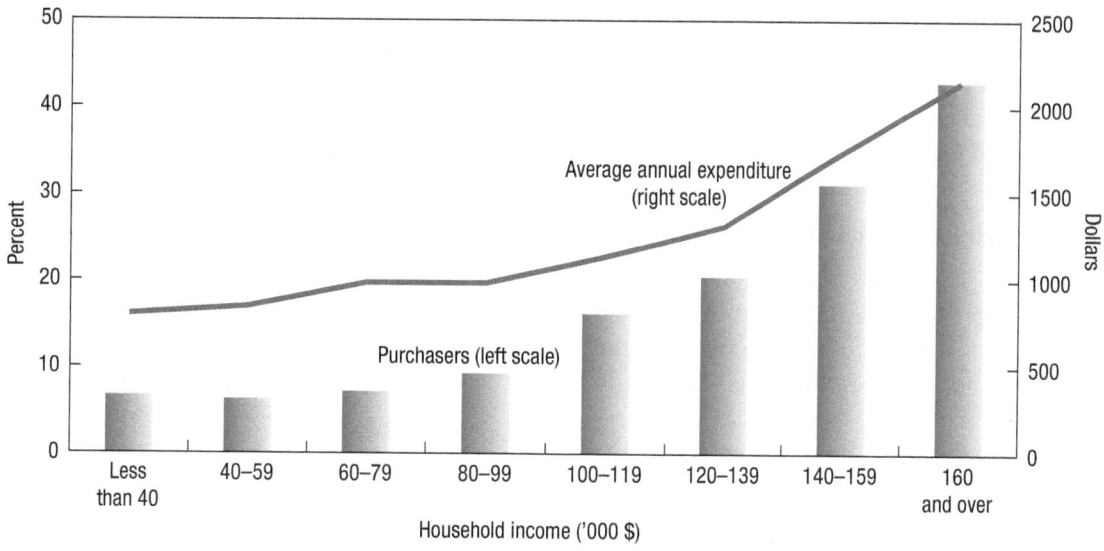

Finally, you have probably already heard lots of advice about how to organize things better. Easier said than done! But there are techniques that can help (APA, 2016), and many of these are available online and in self-help books and are taught in workshops and classes in most cities. What does not help is simply trying harder to do it all yourself. At best, you may manage a delicate balance. At worst, you will find yourself overwhelmed.

Test Yourself before going on

1. List three influences on career choice.
   (a)
   (b)
   (c)
2. According to Super, the career-development process begins between the ages of _____ and _____.
3. What is the goal of the quality of work–life movement?
4. Conflict between _____ and _____ goals strongly influences Canadian women's pattern of employment.

Critical Thinking

5. What are your own plans for achieving a satisfactory work–life balance after completing your post-secondary education? Based on the research in this section, how realistic do you think your goals are?

Summary

Theories of Social and Personality Development

14.1 Explain what Erikson meant when he described early adulthood as a crisis of intimacy versus isolation.

- Erikson proposed that young adults who fail to establish a stable relationship with an intimate partner or a network of friends become socially isolated.

14.2 Describe what a life structure is, and how it changes.

- Levinson's concept of the life structure includes all of the roles that a person occupies, all of her relationships, and the conflicts and balance that exist among them. He hypothesized that adult development involves alternating periods of stability and instability, through which adults construct and refine life structures.

14.3 Describe the characteristics of emerging adulthood.

- The parts of the brain involved in decision making and self-control mature between the late teens and early 20s. Emerging adults use skills they acquired earlier in life to accomplish developmental tasks in the academic, conduct, and friendship domains. New skills are required for tasks in the work and romantic domains.

Intimate Relationships

14.4 Identify what factors evolutionary and social role theorists emphasize in their theories of mate selection.

- Evolutionary theories of mate selection suggest that sex differences in mate preferences and mating behaviour are the result of natural selection. Social role theory emphasizes gender roles, similarity, and economic exchange in explaining sex differences in mating.

14.5 Identify what factors are involved in predicting marriage quality.

- Personality characteristics, as well as attachment and love, contribute to marital success. In general, married adults are happier, healthier, live longer, and have lower rates of psychological disorders than singles do.

14.6 Discuss how divorce affects the lives of Canadian adults.

- Divorce tends to increase young adults' risk of depression, suicide, and adverse outcomes such as accidents, absenteeism from work, illness, loss of self-esteem, feelings of failure, and loneliness.

14.7 Describe the relationship between cohabitation and subsequent success in marriage.

- People who cohabit prior to marriage are more likely to divorce. However, research has shown that among cohabiting couples in which the intention to marry is firm and the woman has had no prior cohabitation experience, divorce or dissatisfaction with the relationship is no more likely than among couples who do not live together before marriage.

14.8 Describe the ways in which gay and lesbian couples are similar to and different from heterosexual couples.

- The factors that contribute to relationship satisfaction are similar across homosexual and heterosexual couples. However, the two types of couples often differ in the power relation within the partnership. Further, monogamy is not as important to gay male couples as it is to lesbian or heterosexual partners.

14.9 Describe how singles accomplish Erikson's psychosocial developmental task of intimacy.

- People who do not have intimate partners rely on family and friends for intimacy. After many years of singlehood, unpartnered adults tend to incorporate "singleness" into their sense of personal identity. Continuous singles are more likely to experience a positive adult developmental path than divorced or widowed singles.

Parenthood and Other Relationships

14.10 Summarize what happens during the transition to parenthood.

- Most men and women want to become parents because they view raising children as a life-enriching experience. The transition to parenthood is stressful and can lead to a decline in relationship satisfaction. Factors such as the division of labour between mother and father, individual personality traits, and the availability of help from extended family members contribute to relationship satisfaction.

14.11 Discuss the ways in which family and friends are important to young adults.

- Young adults' relationships with their parents tend to be steady and supportive, even if they are less central to the young adults' lives than they were at earlier ages. The quality of attachment to parents continues to predict a number of important variables in early adulthood. Each young adult creates a network of relationships with friends as well as with a partner and family members.

The Role of Worker

14.12 Identify what factors influence an individual's occupational choices.

- The specific job or career a young adult chooses is affected by family background and values, personality, and gender. The majority of adults choose jobs that fit the cultural norms for their social class and gender. Young people with more education are more upwardly mobile.

14.13 Describe how career goals and job satisfaction change over time.

- Super's stage theory proposes that career development involves the growth, exploratory, establishment, and maintenance stages. Many factors influence job satisfaction including job security, personality, job status, and work–life balance. The QWL movement includes innovations that help employees achieve a balance between work and nonwork roles.

14.14 Describe in what ways women's work patterns differ from those of men.

- For many women, the work role also includes an "in-and-out" stage in which periods of focusing on family responsibilities alternate with periods of employment. The more continuous a woman's work history, the more successful she is likely to be at her job. When both partners work, the family responsibilities are not always divided fairly, although in Canada, each partner's share of household tasks is steadily equalizing.

Chapter 15
Physical and Cognitive Development in Middle Adulthood

alvarez /E+/Getty Images

 ## Learning Objectives

PHYSICAL CHANGES

15.1 Summarize what researchers know about brain function in middle age.

15.2 Describe how reproductive function changes in men and women in middle age.

15.3 Describe what osteoporosis is, and what factors are associated with it.

15.4 Describe how vision and hearing change in middle age.

HEALTH PROMOTION AND WELLNESS

15.5 Describe mid-life health trends.

15.6 Identify what factors contribute to cancer.

15.7   Summarize the risks of cardiovascular disease in middle age.

15.8   Identify some important differences in the health of middle-aged men and women.

15.9   Discuss mental health trends and alcohol consumption in middle age.

COGNITIVE FUNCTIONING

15.10   Discuss how Denney's and the Balteses' models explain the relationship between health and cognitive functioning in middle age.

15.11   Describe the relationship between health and cognitive functioning.

15.12   Describe how young and middle-aged adults differ in performance on memory tests.

15.13   Discuss what the research suggests about age-related changes in creativity.

The great baseball player Satchel Paige, who was still pitching in the major leagues at age 62, once said, "Age is mind over matter. If you don't mind, it doesn't matter."

It's a nice summary of the physical changes of the middle years. Yes, there are changes. Memory does get less efficient in some situations in mid-life; vision and hearing get worse; people slow down slightly and become somewhat weaker. But among adults who are otherwise healthy, the amount of loss is far less than folklore would have us believe. Further, along with obvious losses come important gains. Indeed, although early adulthood may be the physical high point of adulthood, there is a great deal of evidence that middle adulthood is the intellectual and creative peak.

In this chapter you will learn that, with advancing age, the story of human development seems to become more an account of differences than a description of universals. This happens because so many factors—behavioural choices, poor health, and so on—determine the specific developmental pathway an adult follows. Most middle-aged adults are healthy, energetic, and intellectually productive, but others are in decline. Moreover, because developmental psychology has focused more on younger individuals, there simply isn't as much knowledge about universal changes in adulthood.

Physical Changes

For a quick overview of the common physical changes of middle age, take another look at the table in the chapter on Physical and Cognitive Development in Early Adulthood, which summarizes most of the evidence. Changes or declines in many physical functions occur very gradually through the 40s and 50s. For a few physical functions, however, change or decline is already substantial in the middle adult years.

The Brain and Nervous System

Learning Objective 15.1

Summarize what researchers know about brain function in middle age.

Our knowledge of what happens to the normal, undamaged brain during middle adulthood has increased dramatically over the past few years because of the findings of recent MRI studies. One of the first studies of its kind, based at the UCLA Department of Neurology, compared brain development in a cross-sectional study of people

Figure 15.1 These graphs illustrate the changes that take place in the brain across the lifespan. White matter volume increases until middle adulthood and then declines. Grey matter volume declines from childhood and then levels off at the end of middle adulthood. Cerebrospinal fluid (CSF) increases at a regular rate across the lifespan.

(**SOURCE:** Image courtesy of Elizabeth R. Sowell, Ph.D., UCLA Laboratory of Neuro Imaging. From Sowell et al, 2003, Figure 6, p. 314.)

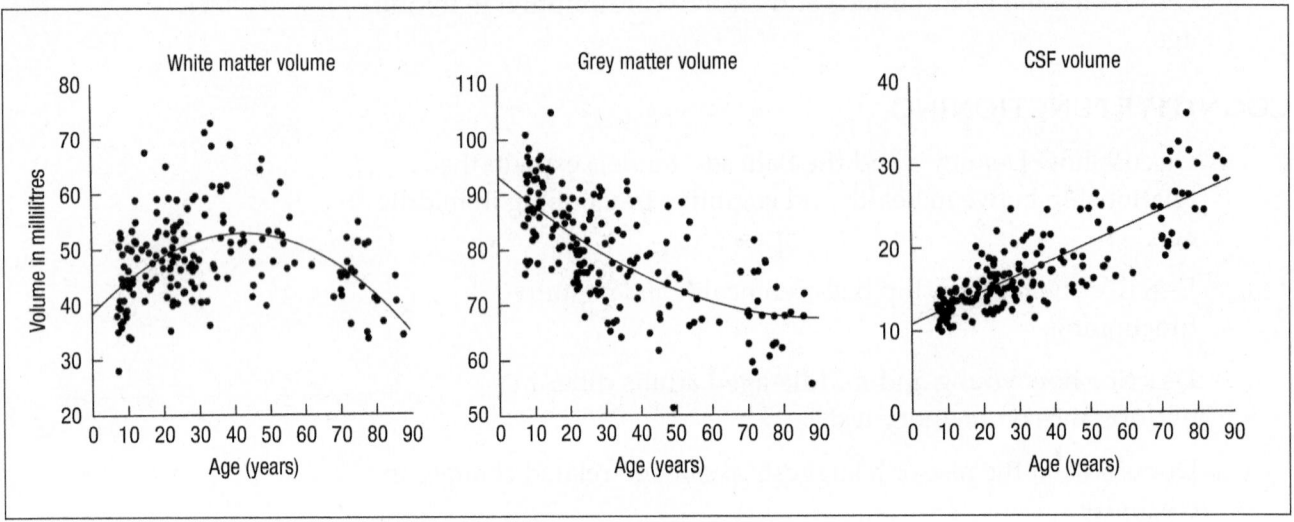

ranging from their first to their ninth decade of life (Sowell et al., 2003). For example, **Figure 15.1** shows significant changes in two main components of the brain. Broadly speaking, it shows that white matter volume crests during middle adulthood and that grey matter volume continues the decline that it began in childhood and does not level off until about age 60. The volume of *cerebrospinal fluid* (CSF) also increases steadily across the lifespan (CFS primarily serves to add buoyancy to protect the brain and spinal cord, and to transport nutrients and hormones and remove waste products across the nervous system). It is important to note that new synapses are continuing to form in middle age. Earlier in life, though, new synapses form more rapidly or at the same rate as old connections are lost. In middle age, it appears, more synapses are lost than are formed; this net loss is associated with the cognitive declines seen in older adults.

As noted in the chapter on Physical and Cognitive Development in Early Adulthood, hidden within the global changes depicted in Figure 15.1 are localized changes that occur in various parts of the brain at different times and rates. It is suspected that the decline in grey matter density that occurs after age 40 is associated with subtle degenerative processes—this is the time when white matter growth peaks and total brain weight begins to decline (Sowell et al., 2003; Sowell, Thompson, & Toga, 2004). With the exception of specific regions in the left temporal lobe that are associated with language comprehension skills, the general rule of brain maturation is that the areas of the brain that develop last are the ones that begin to decline first, namely areas located within the frontal and parietal lobes. You will read more about the associated changes in cognitive function later in the chapter.

In addition, developmentalists know that mental health affects the adult brain. For example, alcoholics and nonalcoholics differ in both grey matter volume and in the distribution of electrical activity in the brain (Courtney & Polich, 2010; Ide et al., 2014; Porjesz & Begleiter, 2003). The brains of adults who experience long-term negative stress differ as well (Zannas et al., 2013). Further, a number of serious mental illnesses, such as depression and schizophrenia, are associated with structural variations in the brain (Andreasen, Liu, Ziebell, Vora, & Ho, 2013; Zannas et al., 2013). What researchers don't know yet is whether the brains of those with alcoholism, stress, depression, or schizophrenia were different from others before the onset of these difficulties. The longitudinal research necessary to answer such questions has yet to be done.

Besides studying the effects of trauma and disease, neuropsychologists are also involved in investigating a very important issue in the study of aging—whether declines in cognitive functions are caused by a loss of neurological processing resources. To find out, researchers examine how the brains of young and middle-aged people respond to cognitive tasks. Such studies have produced a rather complex set of findings.

One fairly consistent finding is that middle-aged adults' brains respond more slowly to cognitive tasks than those of younger adults (Zysset, Schroeter, Neumann, & von Cramon, 2007). By using neuroimaging techniques, researchers have found that such tasks activate a larger area of brain tissue in middle-aged adults than they do in younger adults (Marques et al., 2016; Marques, Soares, Magalhães, Santos, & Sousa, 2015; Reuter-Lorenz & Park, 2014). At this time, neuropsychologists don't know why this happens, but they speculate that cognitive processing in middle-aged adults is less selective than it is in younger adults. It's as if the middle-aged brain has a more difficult time finding just the right neurological tool to carry out a particular function, and so it *compensates* by activating more tools than are necessary. This lack of selectivity could account for differences between age groups in the speed at which cognitive tasks are carried out.

The brains of middle-aged and younger adults also respond differently to sensory stimuli (Cheng & Lin, 2012). For example, when participants are presented with a simple auditory stimulus such as a musical tone, patterns of brain waves in different areas vary across age groups (Yordanova, Kolev, & Basar, 1998). Research along this line has suggested that middle-aged adults may have less ability to control attention processes by inhibiting brain responses to irrelevant stimuli (Amenedo & Diaz, 1998, 1999; Lorenzo-López et al., 2016). Their difficulty with attentional control could be another reason for the average difference in processing speed between young and middle-aged adults.

Such findings might lead you to conclude that, in everyday situations requiring intense concentration and rapid judgments, middle-aged adults would perform more poorly than their younger counterparts. Interestingly, though, researchers seldom find differences in everyday memory function that distinguish young from middle-aged adults (Salthouse, 2012b). In fact, some studies show that middle-aged adults outperform those who are younger. For example, researchers have found that younger drivers exhibit more lapses in attention and make more driving errors than middle-aged drivers (Dobson, Brown, Ball, Powers, & McFadden, 1999). These lapses and errors, combined with younger drivers' greater likelihood of driving after drinking alcohol, help account for the different accident rates of young and middle-aged adults. Such findings, when considered with those on age differences in brain function, illustrate the difficulty researchers face in finding direct relationships between age-related brain differences and cross-age variations in behaviour.

Another point to keep in mind about studies of the middle-aged brain is that the results of these studies are likely due to both primary and secondary aging. That is, part of the difference in brain function between young and middle-aged adults is due to natural aging processes. The remainder is attributable to the effects of health. Studies show, for example, that health-related changes in the circulatory system cause damage in the parts of the brain that are critical to processing speed, planning, and memory in middle age (Raz & Rodrigue, 2006; Raz, Rodrigue, Kennedy, & Acker, 2007). Consequently, healthy middle-aged adults exhibit both neurological and cognitive functioning that is more similar to that of young adults than their peers who suffer from health conditions that affect the circulatory system.

The Reproductive System

If you were asked to name a single significant physical change occurring in the years of middle adulthood, chances are you'd say *menopause*—especially if you're a woman.

Learning Objective 15.2
Describe how reproductive function changes in men and women in middle age.

climacteric

the years of middle or late adulthood in both men and women during which reproductive capacity declines or is lost

The term **climacteric** refers to the years of middle or late adulthood in both men and women during which reproductive capacity declines or is lost.

MALE CLIMACTERIC   In men, the climacteric is extremely gradual, with a slow loss of reproductive capacity, although the rate of change varies widely from one man to the next, and there are documented cases of men in their 90s fathering children. On average, the quantity of viable sperm produced declines slightly, beginning perhaps at about age 40. The testes also shrink very gradually, and the volume of seminal fluid declines after about age 60.

The causal factor is most likely a very slow drop in testosterone levels, beginning in early adulthood and continuing well into old age. This decline in testosterone is implicated in the gradual loss of muscle tissue (and hence strength) that becomes evident in the middle and later years, as well as in the increased risk of heart disease in middle and old age. It also appears to affect sexual function. In particular, in the middle years, the incidence of *erectile dysfunction* (the inability to achieve or maintain an erection) begins to increase—although many things other than the slight decline in testosterone contribute to this change, including an increase in poor health (especially heart disease), obesity, use of blood-pressure medication (and other medications), alcohol abuse, and smoking.

Lifestyle changes can sometimes restore sexual function. In one study, researchers enrolled 35- to 55-year-old obese men with erectile dysfunction in a two-year weight-loss program that required participants to make changes in their diets and exercise habits (Esposito et al., 2004). About one-third of the men experienced improvements in erectile dysfunction along with reductions in body fat.

Among healthy middle-aged men, performance anxiety is a frequent cause of erectile dysfunction. The drugs sildenafil (Viagra), tadalafil (Cialis), and vardenafil (Levitra) have been found to be effective in treating this condition (Kim, 2013). However, physicians warn that men with erectile dysfunction should avoid so-called natural treatments such as food supplements because most of them have not been studied in placebo-controlled experiments (Rowland & Tai, 2003). Moreover, men who turn to supplements for symptom relief may delay seeking medical attention and, as a result, may continue to suffer from a serious underlying condition without realizing it.

During middle age, supportive partners help each other cope with the changes in sexual function that are brought about by the natural aging of the reproductive system.

menopause

the cessation of monthly menstrual cycles in middle-aged women

MENOPAUSE   Declines in key sex hormones are also clearly implicated in the set of changes in women called **menopause**, which means literally the cessation of the menses. Secretion of several forms of *estrogen* by the ovaries increases rapidly during puberty, triggering the onset of menstruation as well as stimulating the development of breasts and secondary sex characteristics. In the adult woman, estrogen levels are high during the first 14 days of the menstrual cycle, stimulating the release of an ovum and the preparation of the uterus for possible implantation. *Progesterone*, which is secreted by the ruptured ovarian follicle from which the ovum emerges, rises during the second half of the menstrual cycle and stimulates the sloughing off of accumulated material in the uterus each month if conception has not occurred (see the **Research Report**).

The transition phase of menopause, called *perimenopause*, can be expected to begin after age 40 and may last five to eight years (sometimes symptoms may appear earlier than age 40 or extend beyond age 55). Menopause usually occurs when a woman is between her late 40s and early 50s (Society of Obstetricians and Gynaecologists of Canada [SOGC], n.d.). This suggests that about one in five, or more than 2.6 million, Canadian women are experiencing a menopausal phase (Statistics Canada, 2015i).

Research Report

The Pros and Cons of Menopausal Hormone Therapy

Most of the physical symptoms and effects of menopause—including hot flashes, thinning of the vaginal wall, and loss of vaginal lubrication—can be dramatically reduced by taking estrogen and progesterone.

However, *menopausal hormone therapy* (MHT) has had a somewhat checkered history. In the 1950s and 1960s, estrogen therapy became extremely common. In some surveys, as many as half of all postmenopausal women in the United States reported using replacement estrogen, many of them over periods of 10 years or more (Stadel & Weiss, 1975). In the 1970s, however, new evidence showed that the risk of endometrial cancer (cancer of the lining of the uterus) increased threefold to tenfold in women taking replacement estrogen (Nathanson & Lorenz, 1982). Not surprisingly, when this information became public, the use of estrogen therapy dropped dramatically.

The third act in this drama was the discovery that a combination of estrogen and progesterone, at quite low dosages, had the same benefits as estrogen alone and eliminated the increased risk of endometrial cancer. Furthermore, studies also made clear that the use of replacement estrogen significantly retards the bone loss of osteoporosis (Barrett-Connor & Bush, 1991; Ross, Paganini-Hill, Mack, & Henderson, 1987). Research reveals that this benefit occurs with the newer estrogen–progesterone combinations as well as with estrogen alone (e.g., Cauley et al., 1995; Stampfer et al., 1991; Working Group for the PEPI Trial, 1995).

This sounds almost too good to be true, doesn't it? Why shouldn't every postmenopausal woman be on a program of MHT? There are serious counter-arguments: First, many women consider the process of aging, including the changes of menopause, to be natural physical processes with which they do not want to tinker. Second, although scientists have evidence that MHT is linked to slightly lower overall cancer risks, some studies have found that it is associated with somewhat higher rates of breast cancer and very slightly higher rates of ovarian cancer (Posthuma, Westendorp, & Vandenbroucke, 1994). In the Nurses' Health Study (which you read about in the chapter on Physical and Cognitive Development in Early Adulthood), researchers found that for every woman diagnosed with breast cancer who did not take replacement hormones, there were roughly 1.4 cases of

breast cancer diagnosed among women who did use MHT (Colditz et al., 1995). The equivalent comparison for ovarian cancers, drawn from another study (Rodriguez et al., 1995), was 1.0 case of ovarian cancer in women who did not take hormones and 1.15 cases in women who did. Third, the next milestone in this story is the NIH's Women's Health Initiative (WHI) study of MHT. Findings included increased risk of heart attack, stroke, blood clots, dementia, and breast cancer. There was so much concern that certain parts of the study were stopped. With the release and wide media coverage of these findings, prescriptions of estrogen–progesterone for MHT dropped off the charts (Heiss et al., 2008; National Institute of Health [NIH], 2005; Toh et al., 2010; WHI Steering Committee, 2004).

However, after a decade of concern about the risks associated with MHT, a closer look at the earlier WHI research found it was misleading. Further analysis revealed that the original research sample included a large number of women who were postmenopausal (two-thirds of the women were over the age of 60) and therefore well beyond the age when MHT is needed. When compared to the target group of newly menopausal women, it became apparent that for women in their 50s who have moderate to severe menopausal symptoms, MHT is a safe and effective option for use up to five years. The caveat is that with longer-term use in older women, the risk of adverse effects starts to rise (Reid et al., 2014; SOGC, n.d.).

How can an individual woman add up these various benefits and risks? Among other things, a woman should consider not only her present discomfort, but also her overall risk of heart disease and cancer (heart disease is actually the larger overall risk in the years of middle and late adulthood), which includes her family history of these diseases. Above all, a woman entering menopause should commit herself to seeking information beyond what can be learned from television and women's magazines. For example, Canadian experts advise that women should discuss their concerns with health care professionals in order to make an informed choice based on their unique medical history. Moreover, it is recommended that MHT should be used primarily for the treatment of menopausal symptoms rather than solely for the prevention of disease, especially among postmenopausal women in whom healthy lifestyle changes should be encouraged, including exercising, eating a healthy diet, smoking cessation, and the like (Reid et al., 2014).

MENOPAUSAL PHASES   Menopause, like puberty, is often thought of as a single event. However, it actually occurs over several years, and researchers generally agree that it consists of three phases. First, during the **premenopausal phase**, estrogen levels begin to fluctuate and decline, typically in the late 30s or early 40s, producing irregular menstrual periods in many women. The ovaries are less sensitive to cyclical hormonal signals, and many women experience *anovulatory cycles*, or cycles in which no

premenopausal phase

the stage of menopause during which estrogen levels fall somewhat, menstrual periods are less regular, and anovulatory cycles begin to occur

ovum is released. Even though no ovum is produced, estrogen levels are high enough in premenopausal women to produce periodic bleeding. However, the lack of ovulation results in a dramatic drop in progesterone. As a result, women are exposed to high levels of estrogen for prolonged periods of time during and after menopause. This is significant because estrogen exposure increases cancer risk (Coney, 2013).

perimenopausal phase

the stage of menopause during which estrogen and progesterone levels are erratic, menstrual cycles may be very irregular, and women begin to experience symptoms such as hot flashes

During the **perimenopausal phase**, a period that can last up to six years before complete cessation of menstruation, estrogen levels decrease and women experience more extreme variations in the timing of their menstrual cycles (Coney, 2013). In addition, about 75% of perimenopausal women experience *hot flashes*, sudden sensations of feeling hot. It is hypothesized that fluctuating levels of estrogen and other hormones cause a woman's blood vessels to expand and contract erratically, thus producing hot flashes.

During a hot flash, the temperature of the skin can rise as much as 4°C in some parts of the body, although the core body temperature actually drops (Kronenberg, 1994). Hot flashes last, on average, a few minutes and may recur as seldom as daily or as often as three times per hour (Coney, 2013). Most women learn to manage these brief periods of discomfort if they occur during the day. However, hot flashes frequently disrupt women's sleep. When this happens, it sets in motion a series of changes that are actually due to sleep deprivation rather than menopause. For example, lack of sleep can lead to mental confusion, difficulty with everyday memory tasks, and emotional instability (Philip et al., 2012). Thus, perimenopausal women may have the subjective feeling that they are "going crazy" when the real problem is that hot flashes are preventing them from getting enough sleep. The general light-headedness and shakiness that accompany some women's hot flashes can add to this sensation.

postmenopausal phase

the last stage of menopause; a woman is postmenopausal when she has had no menstrual periods for at least a year

Eventually, estrogen and progesterone drop to consistently low levels and menstruation ceases altogether. Once a woman has ceased to menstruate for a year, she is in the **postmenopausal phase**. In postmenopausal women, estradiol and estrone, both types of estrogen, drop to about one-quarter or less of their premenopausal levels. Progesterone decreases even more, as a result of the cessation of ovulation, although the adrenal glands continue to provide postmenopausal women with some progesterone.

The reduction in estrogen during the perimenopausal and postmenopausal phases also has effects on genital and other tissue. The breasts become less firm, the genitals and the uterus shrink somewhat, and the vagina becomes both shorter and smaller in diameter. The walls of the vagina also become somewhat thinner and less elastic and produce less lubrication during intercourse (Coney, 2013).

PSYCHOLOGICAL EFFECTS OF MENOPAUSE   One other aspect of the climacteric in women deserves some mention. It has been part of folklore for a very long time that menopause involves major emotional upheaval, as well as clear physical changes. However, research findings are mixed. Longitudinal studies show that depressive symptoms increase during menopause (Bromberger et al., 2010). Nevertheless, experts note that depression is no more frequent among menopausal women than among those who are nonmenopausal (Judd, Hickey, & Bryant, 2012).

A woman's overall negativity and number of life stressors before entering menopause contribute to her emotional state (Dennerstein, Lehert, & Guthrie, 2002). In other words, a woman's negativity may be attributed to menopause when, in reality, it may be a longstanding component of her personality. Alternatively, she may have a particularly stressful life, and menopausal symptoms are just one more source of difficulty.

In addition, the actual level of symptoms women experience makes a difference (Bromberger et al., 2010). It isn't surprising that women who are most uncomfortable because of hot flashes and other physical changes, and whose symptoms last the longest, experience the most depression and negative mood. Researchers have also found that menopausal women who suffer from sleep deprivation because of hot flashes at night, or *night sweats*, may be misdiagnosed with generalized anxiety disorder. Not only are the symptoms of the two conditions similar, but electroencephalographic studies reveal that the patterns of brain activity across the two conditions are quite similar too (Terashima et al., 2004).

SEXUAL ACTIVITY   Despite changes in the reproductive system, the great majority of middle-aged adults remain sexually active, although the frequency of sex declines somewhat during these years. It is unlikely that this decline during mid-life is due wholly or even largely to drops in sex hormone levels. To be sure, researchers are now taking a more holistic, *biopsychosocial* view of sexuality and aging whereby biological (e.g., chronic conditions and overall poorer health), psychological (e.g., sexual expectations and mental disorders), and social (e.g., differing partner expectations about sexual activity) factors interact to predispose us to problems with sexual functioning as we age (Brotto et al., 2016; Lee, Nazroo, O'Connor, Blake, & Pendleton, 2016).

Chronic conditions that develop toward the latter part of middle age account for much of the decline in the frequency of sexual activity among people in their 50s. In particular, biological factors related to chronic medical conditions, such as diabetes, obesity, arthritis, cardiovascular disease, and neurological diseases (e.g., Parkinson's disease and multiple sclerosis), have an impact (Basson & Bronner, 2015; Basson, Rees, Wang, Montejo, & Incrocci, 2010; Corona et al., 2010; Hackett et al., 2016; Lee et al., 2016; Steptoe, Jackson, & Wardle, 2016; Wylie & Kenny, 2010). Psychosocial factors, such as mental disorders (e.g., depression, anxiety, and substance use disorders), concerns over one's sexual performance or activity, and relationship concerns (e.g., a lack of emotional intimacy during sex) are also implicated (Brotto et al., 2016; Holloway & Wylie, 2015; Lee et al., 2016). Of note, regardless of frequency of sex, there is a steady decline in sexual satisfaction with relationship duration in heterosexual couples, although relationship satisfaction and intimacy have a mediating effect on sexual satisfaction (McNulty, Wenner, & Fisher, 2016; Schmiedeberg & Schröder, 2016).

In many instances, it's difficult to separate cause from effect—depression may both contribute to and be a consequence of sexual dysfunction (Brotto et al., 2016; Lee et al., 2016; Wylie & Kenny, 2010). Even some of the drugs used to treat diseases and disorders (e.g., antidepressant, heart disease, and painkiller medication) can contribute to sexual dysfunction (Basson, 2005; Basson et al., 2010; Lee et al., 2016). On top of all this, the daily stresses and demands of other roles can be simply so pressing or distracting that middle-aged adults find it hard to find time, and the proper ambiance, for sex (Basson, 2005; Brotto et al., 2016). Sometimes, given the choice, the promise of a good night's sleep wins out over sex. Couples may also take some solace in knowing that even though problems with sexual functioning may increase in mid-life, overall concerns about sex diminish over time—it becomes less of an issue.

The Skeletal System

Another change that begins to be quite significant in middle adulthood is a loss of calcium from the bones, resulting in reduced bone mass and more brittle and porous bones. This process is called **osteoporosis**. Bone loss begins at about age 30 for both men and women, but in women the process is accelerated by menopause. The major consequence of this loss of bone density is a significantly increased risk of fractures, beginning as early as age 50 for women, and much later for men. Among older women (and men), such fractures can be a major cause of disability and reduced activity, so osteoporosis is not a trivial change.

In women, it is clear that bone loss is linked quite directly to estrogen and progesterone levels. Researchers know that these hormones fall dramatically after menopause, and it is the timing of menopause, rather than age, that signals the increase in rate of bone loss (Jacobs-Kosmin, 2013). Researchers also know that the rate of bone loss drops to premenopausal levels among women who take replacement hormones, all of which makes the link quite clear (Rossouw et al., 2002). While the overall pattern

Learning Objective 15.3

Describe what osteoporosis is, and what factors are associated with it.

osteoporosis

loss of bone mass with age, resulting in more brittle and porous bones

Table 15.1 Risk Factors for Osteoporosis

Risk Factor	Explanation
Race	Whites are at higher risk than other races.
Gender	Women have considerably higher risk than men.
Weight	Those who are underweight are at higher risk.
Timing of climacteric	Women who experience early menopause and those who have had their ovaries removed are at higher risk, presumably because their estrogen levels decline at earlier ages.
Family history	Those with a family history of osteoporosis are at higher risk.
Diet	A diet low in calcium during adolescence and early adulthood results in lower peak levels of bone mass, and hence greater risk of falling below critical levels later. Whether there is any benefit in increasing intake of calcium postmenopausally remains in debate. Diets high in either caffeine (especially black coffee) or alcohol are also linked to higher risk.
Exercise	Those with a sedentary lifestyle are at higher risk. Prolonged immobility, such as bedrest, also increases the rate of bone loss. Exercise reduces the rate of bone loss.

(**SOURCE:** Based on Duursma, Raymakers, Boereboom, & Scheven, 1991; Gambert, Schultz, & Hamdy, 1995; Goldberg & Hagberg, 1990; Gordon & Vaughan, 1986; Lindsay, 1985; Morrison et al., 1994; Smith, 1982.)

of bone loss seems to be a part of primary aging, the amount of such loss nonetheless varies quite a lot from one individual to another. **Table 15.1** lists the known risk factors for osteoporosis.

Aside from taking replacement hormones, women can help prevent osteoporosis by using one or all of the following strategies. First, they can get enough calcium during early adulthood, so that peak levels of bone mass are as robust as possible. Second, throughout adult life women can get regular exercise, particularly weight-bearing exercise such as walking or strength training (Tolomio, Ermolao, Lalli, & Zaccaria, 2010). In one study, a group of middle-aged or older women were randomly assigned to a strength-training program consisting of twice-weekly sessions for a year. They showed a gain in bone density over the year, whereas women in a control group without such weight training showed a loss (Nelson et al., 1994). Third, *bone mineral density* (BMD) tests can identify osteoporosis long before it causes serious damage to bones. Once it is diagnosed, women can take bone-building medications such as *alendronate sodium* (Fosamax). Studies show that the combination of BMD testing and medication dramatically reduces the risk of fractures among women over the age of 50 (Jaglal et al., 2005).

Learning Objective 15.4

Describe how vision and hearing change in middle age.

presbyopia

normal loss of visual acuity with aging, especially the ability to focus the eyes on near objects

Vision and Hearing

One of the most noticeable physical changes occurring in the middle years is a loss of visual acuity. Two changes in the eyes, collectively called **presbyopia**, are involved. First, the lens of the eye thickens. In a process that begins in childhood but produces noticeable effects only in middle adulthood, layer after layer of slightly pigmented material accumulates on the lens. Because light coming into the eye must pass through this thickened, slightly yellowed material, the total light reaching the retina decreases, which reduces a person's overall sensitivity to light waves, particularly to short wavelengths that are perceived as blue, blue-green, and violet (Schachar, 2010).

Because of this thickening of the lens, it is also harder and harder for the muscles surrounding the eye to change the shape of the lens to adjust the focus. In a young eye, the shape of the lens readily adjusts for distance, so no matter how near or far away some object may be, the light rays passing through the eye converge where they should, on the retina in the back of the eye,

(Photo: Robert Kneschke/Shutterstock)

Any weight-bearing exercise— including walking—will help prevent osteoporosis.

giving a sharp image. But as the thickening increases, the elasticity of the lens declines and it can no longer make these fine adjustments. Many images become blurry. In particular, the ability to focus clearly on near objects deteriorates rapidly in the 40s and early 50s. As a result, middle-aged adults often hold books and other items farther and farther away, because only in that way can they get a clear image. Finally, of course, they cannot read print at the distance at which they can focus, and they are forced to wear reading glasses or bifocals. These same changes also affect the ability to adapt quickly to variations in levels of light or glare, such as from passing headlights when driving at night or in the rain, so driving may become more stressful. All in all, these changes in the eyes, which appear to be a genuine part of primary aging, require both physical and psychological adjustment.

The equivalent process in hearing is called **presbycusis**. The auditory nerves and the structures of the inner ear gradually degenerate as a result of basic wear and tear, resulting primarily in losses in the ability to hear sounds of high and very low frequencies. But these changes do not accumulate to the level of significant hearing loss until somewhat later in life than is typical for presbyopia. Hearing loss is quite slow until about age 50. After age 50 or 55, however, the rate of hearing loss accelerates. Some of this loss is due to conditions that are more common among older adults than among younger individuals, such as excessive earwax, chronic fluid in the ear, or abnormal growth of the bones of the inner ear (National Institute on Aging, 2010). Most commonly, however, hearing loss in adulthood appears to be the result of lifelong exposure to excessive noise (Rabinowitz, 2000).

By age 45 or 50, nearly everyone needs glasses, especially for reading.

Test Yourself before going on

1. Middle-aged adults are most likely to perform more poorly than young adults on tasks involving _____.
2. The _____ is the time in middle or late adulthood when the reproductive capacity declines or is lost.
3. _____ _____ _____ tests identify osteoporosis before it seriously damages the bones.
4. Match each term with its definition.
   _____ (a) presbycusis
   _____ (b) presbyopia
   (i) age-related vision decline of near vision
   (ii) age-related hearing loss

Critical Thinking

5. Given the changes in the brain, reproductive system, bones, and sensory abilities that you have learned about in this section, how would you evaluate a statement such as "age is just a state of mind"?

Health Promotion and Wellness

No single variable affects the quality of life in middle and late adulthood as much as health. A middle-aged person in good health often functions as well and has as much energy as much younger adults. However, mid-life is the era during which the poor health habits and risky behaviours of earlier years begin to catch up with us.

Health Trends at Mid-Life

In general, most 40-year-old Canadians' *health-related quality of life* (HRQL)—a measure of physical, mental, and social health—remains relatively high and stable through to

presbycusis

normal loss of hearing with aging, especially of high-frequency tones

Learning Objective 15.5

Describe mid-life health trends.

Figure 15.2 In Canada, disease-related deaths become increasingly common during middle adulthood.

(**SOURCE:** Adapted from Health Canada, 2000a, Table—Leading Causes of Death and Hospitalization in Canada, p. 1.)

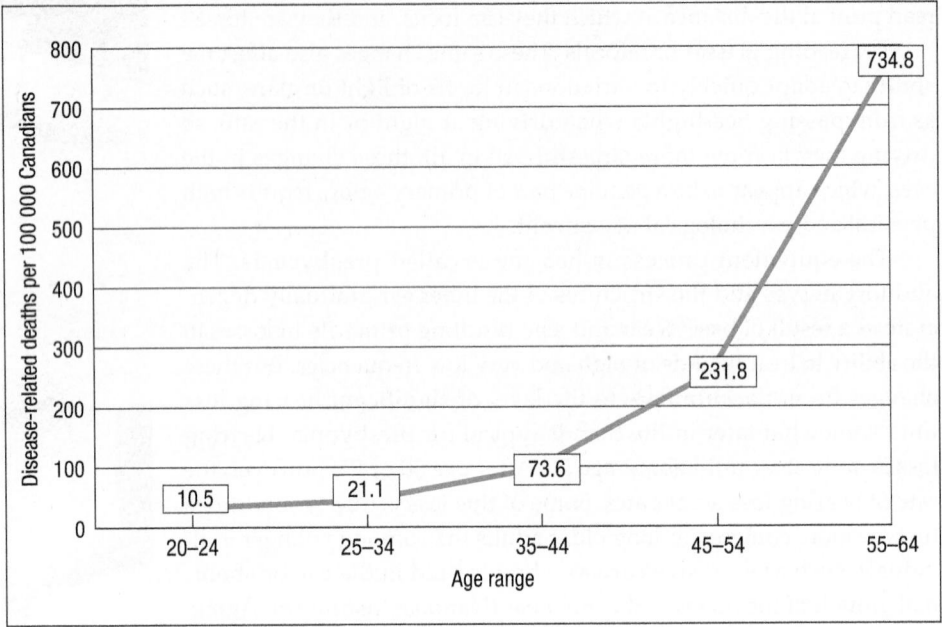

roughly age 70, when it begins to decline (Orpana et al., 2009). Still, across the mid-life years, adults report that they experience annoying aches and pains with greater frequency than when they were younger (Helme & Gibson, 2001), and many middle-aged adults, especially women, are unhappy with their bodies (i.e., most would prefer to be thinner) (Zerbe & Domnitei, 2004). In addition, the number of truly healthy adults declines in mid-life—middle-aged adults have more chronic diseases and disabilities, such as diabetes and arthritis, than those who are younger (Crompton, 2000). As well, disease-related death rates increase significantly later in middle adulthood, as you can see in **Figure 15.2**—with the two leading causes of death in middle age being cancer and heart disease (Statistics Canada, 2015d).

However, middle-agers can choose to stack the odds of longevity in their favour—there is a link between longevity and level of physical activity. One particularly large and well-designed study of the effects of exercise on physical health involved 17 321 Harvard alumni who had been students between 1916 and 1950. In 1962 or 1966, when the men were in their 30s, 40s, or 50s, each man provided information about his daily levels of physical activity (Lee, Hsieh, & Paffenbarger, 1995). (The measures of physical activity were quite detailed. Each man reported how many blocks he normally walked each day, how often he climbed stairs, the amount of time per week he normally engaged in various sports, and so on. All the answers were then converted into estimates of calories expended per week. For example, walking 1 mile [1.6 kilometres] on level ground uses roughly 100 calories; climbing one flight of stairs uses about 17.) The researchers tracked all these men until 1988 to identify who had died and of what cause. The link between the level of physical activity and death rates over the succeeding 25 years is shown clearly in **Figure 15.3**: The more exercise a man reported, the lower his mortality risk.

Researchers were careful to exclude from the study any man who was known to suffer from heart disease or other disease at the outset of the study, in the 1960s. Furthermore, the groups differed *only* in level of energy expenditure; they did not differ in age, or whether they smoked, had high blood pressure, were overweight, or had a family history of early death—which makes the effect of exercise even clearer. To be sure, because the level of exercise was each man's own choice, there may have been

Figure 15.3 Results from the Harvard Alumni Study show clearly that those who are more physically active in middle adulthood have lower risk of mortality over the next decades.

(**SOURCE:** Lee, I.-M., Hsieh, C., & Paffenbarger, R.S. (1995). Exercise intensity and longevity in men. *Journal of the American Medical Association*, 273, 1179–1184. Adapted from data from Table 2, p. 1181.)

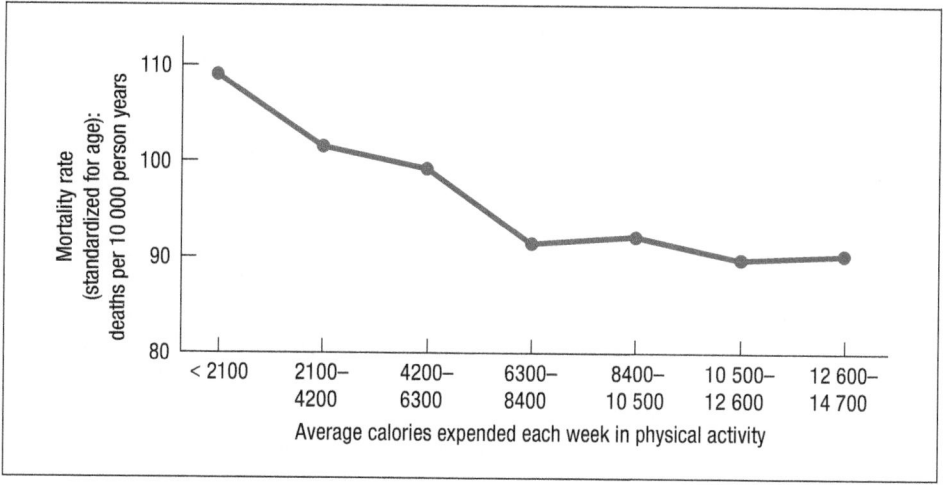

other differences that separated the various exercise groups that could account for the different death rates. But the pattern, which has been replicated in other groups of both men and women, is so substantial and striking that alternative explanations are hard to come by (e.g., Byberg et al., 2009; Lissner et al, 1996). By far, the most likely explanation is that there is a causal connection between longevity and level of physical activity.

Cancer

The leading cause of death of Canadians in middle and old age is cancer (Statistics Canada, 2015d). The lifetime probability of developing cancer is 45% for men and 42% for women. In addition, men have a 29% and women have a 24% lifetime probability of dying from cancer (Canadian Cancer Society's Advisory Committee on Cancer Statistics [CCSACCS], 2015).

Lung cancer remains the number one type of cancer death in Canada and accounts for ~27% of cancer deaths in both men and women (CCSACCS, 2015). For men, the incidence of new cases of lung cancer peaked in the 1980s and has been dropping steadily; for women, the bad news is that the number of new cases of lung cancer has jumped ~50% since the 1980s, although the good news is that the incidence rate has recently begun to level off. After lung cancer, the next leading type of cancer deaths for Canadians is colorectal cancer in men (12.4%) and breast cancer in women (13.6%). The third major type of cancer death in Canadian men is prostate cancer (10.1%) and colorectal cancer in women (11.5%).

Like heart disease, which you'll read about next, cancer does not strike in a totally random fashion. Indeed, as you can see in **Table 15.2**, some of the same risk factors are implicated in both diseases. Most of these risk factors are at least partially under the individual's control. It helps to have established good health habits in early adulthood, but it is also clear from the research that improving health habits in middle age can reduce the risks of both cancer and heart disease.

The most controversial item listed in Table 15.2 is diet; in particular, scientists debate the role of dietary fat as a potential risk factor. Some evidence suggests that reducing consumption of red meat may decrease the risk of colorectal cancer (Kushi & Giovannucci, 2002).

Learning Objective 15.6

Identify what factors contribute to cancer.

Table 15.2 Risk Factors for Cancer and Heart Disease

Risk	Cancer	Heart Disease
Smoking	Substantially increases the risk of lung cancer; also implicated in other cancers.	Major risk; the more you smoke, the greater the risk. Quitting smoking reduces risk.
Blood pressure	No known risk.	Systolic pressure above 140 or diastolic pressure above 90 linked to higher risk.
Weight	Being overweight is linked to increased risk of several cancers, including breast cancer, but the risk is smaller than for heart disease.	Some increased risk with any weight above the normal range; risk is greater for those with weight 20% or more above recommended weight.
Cholesterol	No known risk.	Clear risk with elevated levels of low-density lipoproteins.
Inactivity	Inactivity is associated in some studies with higher rates of colon cancer.	Inactive adults have about twice the risk as those who exercise.
Diet	Results are still unclear; a high-fat diet is linked to risks of some cancers; high-fibre diets appear to be protective for some cancers.	High-fat, low-fibre diet increases risk; antioxidants, such as vitamin E, vitamin C, or beta-carotene, may decrease risk.
Alcohol	Heavy drinking is associated with cancers of the digestive system.	Moderate intake of alcohol, especially wine, is linked to decreased cardiovascular disease (CVD) risk; heavy drinking can weaken the heart muscle.
Heredity	Some genetic component with nearly every cancer.	Those with first-degree relatives with CVD have seven to ten times the risk; those who inherit a gene for a particular protein are up to twice as likely to have CVD.

(**SOURCE:** Based on Centers for Disease Control, 1994; Dwyer et al., 2004; Gaziano & Hennekens, 1995; Hunter et al., 1996; Lee, Manson, Hennekens, & Paffenbarger, 1993; Manson et al., 1995; Morris, Kritchevsky, & Davis, 1994; Rich-Edwards, Manson, Hennekens, & Buring, 1995; Risch, Jain, Marrett, & Howe, 1994; Rose, 1993; Stampfer et al., 1993; Woodward & Tunstall-Pedoe, 1995.)

While the debate over the role of diet continues, there is now little doubt that several types of cancers are caused by infectious agents (Ewald, 2000). For example, in the chapter on Physical and Cognitive Development in Adolescence you learned about the link between the human papillomavirus (HPV) and cervical cancer (Canadian Cancer Society, 2007; Castellsagué et al., 2002). This sexually transmitted disease is apparently also responsible for many cancers of the mouth, nose, and throat, presumably because of oral sex, and for some cases of anal cancer in gay men (Frisch et al., 1997; Mork et al., 2001).

Studies have shown that Epstein-Barr virus is also associated with cancers of the nose and throat, as well as one type of non-Hodgkin's lymphoma (Antonsson et al., 2015). Other viruses, hepatitis B and C, are linked to liver cancer. Thus, screening people who do not yet have symptoms of these viral infections may help to identify cancers at very early stages of development, when they are most curable.

Correlations between bacterial infections and cancer have also been identified. For example, *Helicobacter pylori* has been implicated in many studies of stomach cancer and one type of non-Hodgkin's lymphoma (Antonsson et al., 2015; Uemura et al., 2001). This micro-organism also causes stomach ulcers. Typically, antibiotic treatment clears up both the infection and the ulcers and, coincidentally, reduces the risk of stomach cancer. However, most people who carry *H. pylori* do not have ulcers or any other symptoms. Moreover, a fairly high proportion of people, especially those in developing nations with poor water purification systems, carry the infection (Brown, 2000). Research indicates that antibiotic treatment of people with *H. pylori* infections who do not have symptoms may reduce rates of stomach cancer in these areas; however, more research is needed before investigators can be certain about the effectiveness of such treatments (Wong et al., 2004).

Studies of the role of infection in the development of cancer provide yet another example of the importance of health-related choices. Specifically, safe sex practices can

(Photo: LifesizeImages/E+/Getty Images)

The Japanese, whose diet is very low in fat, have lower rates of some kinds of cancer than North Americans and Europeans.

limit an individual's risk of contracting sexually transmitted diseases and the cancers in which they have been implicated. Moreover, vaccines against many viruses, including HPV and hepatitis B and C, are widely available.

Cardiovascular Disease

The term **cardiovascular disease (CVD)** covers a group of disease processes in the heart and circulatory system, but the key problem is in the arteries. In individuals suffering from CVD, *plaque* (a waxy combination of fats, cholesterol, calcium, fibrin, and other substances) forms in the inner lining of the arteries, in a process called **athero-sclerosis**. Eventually, vital arteries may become completely blocked, producing what laypeople call a *heart attack* (if the blockage is in the coronary arteries) or a *stroke* (if the blockage is in the brain). Although the risk of atherosclerosis increases with age, it is important to keep in mind that it is a disease that is strongly associated with lifestyle factors such as smoking, diet, and exercise rather than a natural consequence of aging. Therefore, it is preventable.

The rate of CVD has been dropping steadily in Canada over the past half century. Between 1956 and 2002, for example, it decreased by 70%, a fairly startling decline that has contributed greatly to the increased life expectancy among today's adults (Health Canada, 2002c; Heart & Stroke Foundation, 2010). Although the CVD mortality rate has been declining at roughly 3% annually since the mid-1990s (Tu et al., 2009), CVD remains a leading cause of death among middle-aged adults in Canada, accounting for 20% of deaths among those ages 45 to 54 and 24% among those ages 55 to 64 (PHAC, 2009b).

GENERAL RISK FACTORS The best information about who is at risk for CVD comes from a number of long-term epidemiological studies, such as the Framingham Heart Study and the Nurses' Health Study, in which the health and habits of large numbers of individuals have been tracked over time. In the Framingham study, 5209 adults were first studied in 1948, when they were 30 to 59 years old. Their health (and mortality) has since been assessed repeatedly, which makes it possible to identify characteristics that predict CVD (Anderson, Castelli, & Levy, 1987; Dawber, Kannel, & Lyell, 1963; Garrison, Gold, Wilson, & Kannel, 1993; Kannel & Gordon, 1980). Table 15.2 lists the well-established risk factors that emerged from the Framingham study and similar studies, along with a few other risk factors that are more speculative. More recent studies continue to suggest the same risk factors (Heart and Stroke Foundation of Canada, 2010; PHAC, 2009c).

Because lists like the one in Table 15.2 have appeared in numerous popular magazines and newspapers, the list does not likely contain information that will be new to you, but a couple of critical points must still be made. First, many Canadians have the risk factors listed in Table 15.2. In fact, one-third of Canadians older than age 20 have three or more risk factors for CVD, and the risks increase as we age (Canadian Heart Health Strategy and Action Plan, 2009). Canadian researchers have found that the prevalence of most of the major CVD risk factors (including high blood pressure, diabetes mellitus, and obesity) have increased dramatically over the last decade (Lee et al., 2009). So, although mortality rates have declined, national trends indicate a rise in the risk factors, particularly among younger Canadians. Such trends have significant implications: The presence of the risk factors in young and middle-aged adults predisposes them to earlier onset of CVD and increases the potential that they will lose quality life-years. This trend has the potential of reducing life expectancy in the 21st century, something that has not occurred in two centuries (Bibbins-Domingo, Coxson, Pletcher, Lightwood, & Goldman, 2007; Lee et al., 2009; Olshansky et al., 2005). Thus, it is important to do a much better job of reducing heart disease risks in younger age groups (Heart and Stroke Foundation of Canada, 2010).

Learning Objective 15.7

Summarize the risks of cardio-vascular disease in middle age.

cardiovascular disease (CVD)

a set of disease processes in the heart and circulatory system

atherosclerosis

narrowing of the arteries caused by deposits of plaque, a fatty substance

Second, it is important to understand that these risks are cumulative in the same way that the health habits investigated in the Alameda County Study (which you learned about in the chapter on Physical and Cognitive Development in Early Adulthood) seem to be cumulative: The more high-risk behaviours or characteristics you have, the higher your risk of heart disease; the effect is not just additive. For example, high cholesterol is more serious for a person who has diabetes and high blood pressure than it is for adults who do not suffer from these conditions (Cohen, Hailpern, & Alderman, 2004).

PERSONALITY AND HEALTH   Personality may also contribute to heart disease. The **type A personality pattern** was first described by two cardiologists, Meyer Friedman and Ray Rosenman (1974; Rosenman & Friedman, 1983). They were struck by the apparently consistent presence among patients who suffered from heart disease of several other characteristics, including competitive striving for achievement, a sense of time urgency, and hostility or aggressiveness. These people, whom Friedman and Rosenman named *type A personalities*, were perpetually comparing themselves with others, always wanting to win. They scheduled their lives tightly, timed themselves in routine activities, and often tried to do such tasks faster each time. They had frequent conflicts with their co-workers and family. *Type B personality* people, in contrast, were thought to be less hurried, more laid back, less competitive, and less hostile.

Early research by Friedman and Rosenman suggested that type A behaviour was linked to higher levels of cholesterol, and hence to increased risk of CVD, even among people who did not suffer from observable heart disease. Contradictory results from more extensive studies since then, however, have forced some modifications in the original hypothesis (e.g., Miller, Turner, Tindale, Posavac, & Dugoni, 1991; O'Connor, Manson, O'Connor, & Buring, 1995). However, not all facets of the type A personality, as originally described, seem to be equally significant for CVD. The most consistent link has been found between CVD and hostility (Mohan, 2006; Olson et al., 2005). Moreover, careful studies have shown that hostility may be part of a larger complex of variables that includes anger, anxiety, cynicism, and other negative emotions (Kubzansky, Cole, Kawachi, Vokonas, & Sparrow, 2006; Olson et al., 2005). The finding that negative emotions are correlated with CVD has led some researchers to propose a new classification, *type D personality* (D for distress) (Denollet, 1997). People with this profile exhibit a chronic pattern of emotional distress combined with a tendency to suppress negative emotions. In one study of men who were enrolled in a rehabilitative therapy program after having had a heart attack, those with the type D profile were found to have four times the risk of death as other patients in the program (Sher, 2004).

Most people who have analyzed this research would now agree that there is some kind of connection between personality and CVD. What is less clear is just which aspect(s) of personality are most strongly predictive. Some research suggests that measures of neuroticism or depression may be even better risk predictors than hostility (e.g., Cramer, 1991).

type A personality pattern

a personality type associated with greater risk of coronary heart disease. It includes competitive achievement striving, a sense of time urgency, and, sometimes, hostility or aggressiveness

Learning Objective 15.8

Identify some important differences in the health of middle-aged men and women.

Gender and Health

It's clear that women's life expectancy is greater than men's. But what is not evident is an interesting paradox: Women live longer, but they have more diseases and disabilities (Orpana et al., 2009). Women are more likely to describe their health as poor, to have more chronic conditions such as arthritis, and to be more limited in their daily activities. Such differences have been found in every country in which the pattern has been studied, including developing countries.

This difference is already present in early adulthood and grows larger with age. By old age, women are substantially more likely than men to be chronically ill (Guralnik, Land, Blazer, Fillenbaum, & Branch, 1993; Kunkel & Applebaum, 1992). In early adulthood, this gender difference in disease rate can be largely attributed to health problems associated with child-bearing. At later ages, the difference cannot be explained in this same way.

How is it possible that men die younger but are healthier while they are alive? Researchers suggest that the apparent paradox can be resolved by considering sex differences in potentially fatal conditions such as CVD (Verbrugge, 1989). In Canada, 101 of every 100 000 men between ages 45 and 54 die of heart disease annually, compared with only 35 of every 100 000 women (Health Canada, 2002c). This difference in rates of heart disease diminishes once women are past menopause, although it does not disappear totally, even in late old age.

It isn't just that men have higher rates of CVD; they are also more likely to die from the disease once they have it. One reason for this may be that the heart muscles of women who have CVD seem to be better able to adapt to stresses such as physical exertion (van Doornen, Snieder, & Boomsma, 1998). In addition, once they suffer a heart attack, women recover to a higher level of physical functioning than men do (Bosworth et al., 2000). Sex differences in health habits also seem to contribute to women's greater ability to recover from CVD. For example, women are more likely to get regular checkups and seek help earlier in an illness than men are (Addis & Mahalik, 2003).

By contrast, women are more likely than men to suffer from nonfatal chronic ailments, such as arthritis. Because chronic pain is characteristic of arthritis, the activities of women who suffer from it are often limited. Understandably, too, living with chronic pain affects their general sense of well-being.

(Photo: Goodluz/Fotolia)

Chances are this man will die before his wife does, but she will be more troubled by chronic illnesses in her middle and later years.

Mental Health

Most types of mental health problems are considerably more common in early adulthood than in the middle years of adult life. In fact, both Canadian men and women report improved mental health with increasing age. One measure of mental health in particular, self-esteem, reportedly peaks around age 60 (Orth, Trzesniewski, & Robins, 2010). However, about two-thirds of adults diagnosed with serious mental disorders in early adulthood continue to have difficulties in middle age (Meeks, 1997). Further, though most addictive disorders begin in adolescence or early adulthood, they frequently go undiagnosed until the middle adulthood years, when they begin to have dramatic effects on health and other areas of functioning that sufferers or their families can no longer deny.

ALCOHOL USE DISORDERS As is true throughout adulthood (Statistics Canada, 2015j), Canadian men are more likely than women to engage in *binge drinking*. For instance, between ages 35 to 54, ~24% of men versus ~14% of women reported binge drinking in the previous year. Notably, after peaking in early adulthood, the rates begin to steadily decline thereafter in both men and women.

Alcoholism, defined as physical and psychological dependence on alcohol, can develop at any age. However, during the middle adulthood years, as the toxic effects of heavy drinking combine with the physical and psychological changes resulting from primary and secondary aging, alcoholism begins to take a heavy toll on the body (Thompson, 2013).

Long-term heavy drinking damages every organ in the body. It is especially harmful to the liver, and it weakens the heart muscle and the valves and walls of the blood vessels. Individuals with alcoholism are also more likely to smoke than those without the disorder (Thompson, 2013). Thus, rates of liver disease, cardiovascular disease, and cancers of the digestive and urinary systems are higher among alcoholics than they are among nonalcoholics (Thompson, 2013). Heavy alcohol use

Learning Objective 15.9

Discuss mental health trends and alcohol consumption in middle age.

alcoholism

physical and psychological dependence on alcohol

also damages the brain, causing impairments in memory and language functions (Daurignac et al., 2005).

The result of this interaction between aging and alcohol abuse is that alcoholics face an increased risk of health problems and death (Thompson, Lande, & Kalapatapu, 2010). A longitudinal study involving more than 40 000 males in Norway found that the rate of death prior to age 60 was significantly higher among alcoholics than among nonalcoholics (Rossow & Amundsen, 1997). Studies further indicate that the death rates of men with alcoholism who are in their 50s and early 60s are five to six times higher than those of nonalcoholics in the same age group (Kristenson, Österling, Nilsson, & Lindgärde, 2002). Thankfully, the effects of alcohol on the brain may be reversible if an alcoholic quits drinking (Kensinger, Clarke, & Corkin, 2003). Likewise, giving up alcohol is essential to stopping the progression of alcohol-induced liver damage. A drug called acamprosate can be prescribed to help recovering alcoholics deal with withdrawal symptoms and maintain abstinence from alcohol (Mason, Goodman, Chabac, & Lehert, 2006).

Test Yourself before going on

1. In Canada, the lifetime probability of developing cancer is between _____ and the probability of dying from cancer lies between _____.
   (a) 15–25%; 5–15%
   (b) 30–40%; 10–20%
   (c) 40–50%; 20–30%

2. Write "CVD" beside each risk factor for cardiovascular disease, "C" beside each risk factor for cancer, and "Both" beside each risk factor that applies to both.
   _____ (a) high-fat diet
   _____ (b) smoking
   _____ (c) high blood pressure
   _____ (d) heavy drinking
   _____ (e) heredity

3. Women are more likely than men to have _____ _____ ailments.

4. Which diseases and disorders are more common among alcoholics than nonalcoholics?

Cognitive Functioning

In the middle adult years, some cognitive abilities improve, while others slow down a bit. Still, many adults have acquired large bodies of knowledge and skill that help them compensate for losses and solve problems within their areas of expertise more efficiently than younger adults do.

A Model of Physical and Cognitive Aging

Learning Objective 15.10

Discuss how Denney's and the Balteses' models explain the relationship between health and cognitive functioning in middle age.

Many of the various bits and pieces of information you've encountered so far about physical and cognitive changes in adulthood can be combined in a single model, suggested by Nancy Denney and illustrated in **Figure 15.4** (Denney, 1982, 1984). Denney proposed that, on nearly any measure of physical or cognitive functioning, age-related changes follow a typical curve, like those shown in the figure. But she also argued that the height of this curve varies depending on the amount an individual exercises some ability or skill. Denney used the word *exercise* very broadly, to refer not only to physical exercise, but also to mental exercise and behavioural tasks and skills. Unexercised abilities generally have a lower peak level of performance; exercised abilities generally have a higher peak. Recent studies seem to support this. For example when adults persist with challenging and engaging cognitive training, such as taking up

Figure 15.4 Denney's model suggests both a basic decay curve and a fairly large gap between actual level of performance on exercised and unexercised abilities.

(**SOURCE:** Based on Denney, N.W. (1982). Aging and cognitive changes. In B.B. Wolman (Ed.), *Handbook of developmental psychology* (pp. 807–827). Englewood Cliffs, NJ: Prentice-Hall; Denney, N.W. (1984). Model of cognitive development across the life span. *Developmental Review*, 4, 171–191.)

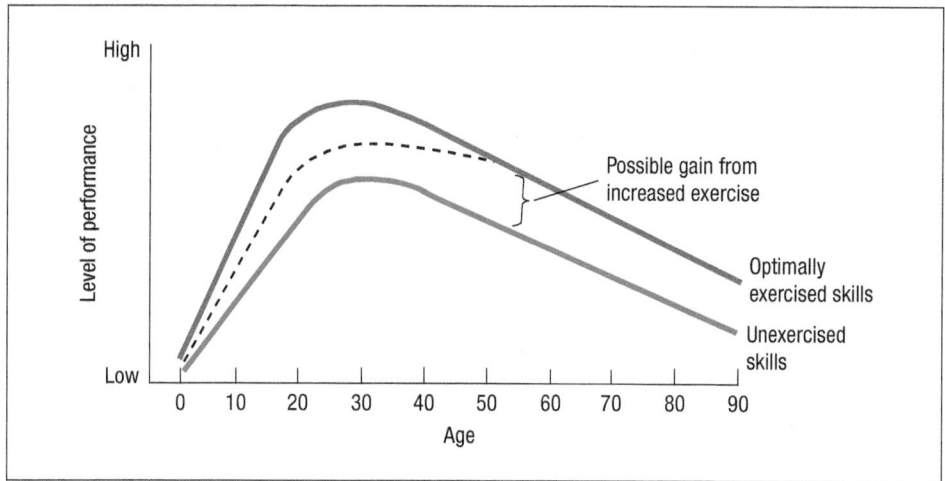

new hobbies and crafts or acquiring and using new strategies to solve problems, they maintain or improve cognition (Reuter-Lorenz & Park, 2014).

Many laboratory tests of memory, for example, memorizing lists of names, tap unexercised abilities. Everyday memory tasks, such as recalling details from a newspaper column, tap much more exercised abilities. The distinction is somewhat similar to the distinction between crystallized and fluid intelligence (see the chapter on Physical and Cognitive Development in Early Adulthood). Most crystallized abilities are at least moderately exercised, whereas many fluid abilities are relatively unexercised. But Denney was making a more general point: Whether abilities are crystallized or fluid, those that are more fully exercised will have a higher peak.

The gap between the curve for unexercised abilities and the curve for maximally exercised abilities represents the degree of improvement that would be possible for any given skill. Any skill that is not fully exercised can be improved if the individual begins to exercise that ability. There is clear evidence, for example, that aerobic capacity (VO$_2$ max) can be increased at any age if a person begins a program of physical exercise (Cheitlin, 2003). Nonetheless, in Denney's model, the maximum level an adult will be able to achieve, even with optimum exercise, will decline with age, just as performance of top athletes declines, even with optimum training regimens. One implication of this is that young adults are more likely to be able to get away with laziness or poor study habits and still perform well; as adults age, this becomes less and less true, because they are fighting against the basic decay curve of aging.

A somewhat different approach was taken by researchers Paul Baltes (1939–2006) and Margaret Baltes (1939–1999). In their view, the physical declines of middle age give rise to a strategy they call **selective optimization with compensation**, the process of balancing the gains and losses associated with aging (Baltes & Baltes, 1990). The idea is that since a body's resources, such as physical agility and working memory capacity, decrease as the body ages, aging adults, to manage the demands of competing tasks, select one task to which they devote most or all of their resources. Moreover, adults optimize the skills that they believe can be improved by exercising them as much as possible. At the same time, they use compensatory strategies to offset the effects of aging.

Selection occurs when a middle-aged adult reduces distractions to more efficiently carry out a cognitive task. For example, a middle-aged post-secondary student

selective optimization with compensation

the process of balancing the gains and losses associated with aging

might be more likely than a younger student to turn off the television when she studies. Optimization is involved when middle-aged adults work to improve their physical fitness or expand their knowledge. Compensation takes many forms, including the use of reading glasses to correct for presbyopia and the development of organizational strategies, such as being diligent about recording important events on a calendar, to offset declines in memory.

Learning Objective 15.11

Describe the relationship between health and cognitive functioning.

Health and Cognitive Functioning

It is often difficult to separate the effects of primary and secondary aging because they happen at the same time. Research examining correlations between health and cognition helps developmentalists understand the effects of secondary aging. Specifically, many of the same characteristics that are linked to increased or decreased risk of heart disease and cancer are also linked to the rate of change or the maintenance of intellectual skill in the middle years.

One illustration of this relationship comes from Walter Schaie's analysis of data from the Seattle Longitudinal Study (which has now passed the 60-year mark) (Schaie, 2013). He found that those research participants who had some kind of CVD (either coronary heart disease or high blood pressure) showed earlier and larger declines on intellectual tests than did those who were disease-free. Canadian researchers have found similar linkages between hypertension in mid-life and the risk of cognitive decline in aging (Desjardins-Crépeau & Bherer, 2016).

As well, physical exercise is another factor that seems to be related to cognitive abilities in the middle adult years. A detailed analysis of four longitudinal studies, including Schaie's, that are investigating the association between physical activity and cognitive function has provided us with a clearer picture of possible connections (Lindwall et al., 2012). In all four studies researchers found that changes in physical activity corresponded to changes in cognition, especially reasoning ability. Two of three studies that measured fluency also found a connection. These longitudinal studies suggest that increased physical activity leads to improved cognition and that physical activity may be instrumental in moderating some functions associated with age-related cognitive decline, such as executive control processes and working memory. Moreover, specific physical exercise interventions (e.g., cardiovascular, resistance, and coordination exercises) may actually improve various cognitive processes and may be critical to an individual's overall cognitive performance during middle adulthood (Erickson & Liu-Ambrose, 2016; Voelcker-Rehage & Niemann, 2013). It remains a matter of developing and testing the best interventions.

Learning Objective 15.12

Describe how young and middle-aged adults differ in performance on memory tests.

Changes in Memory and Cognition

When developmentalists study changes in cognitive functioning in middle age, they find almost precisely what Denney's model and Schaie's longitudinal study suggest. That is, lack of mental exercise tends to be correlated with declines in memory and cognitive skills, but these declines can be reversed and then sustained for many of those who undergo cognitive training and exercises (Mitchell et al., 2012; Schaie & Willis, 2010).

MEMORY FUNCTION Drawing conclusions about memory function in middle age is difficult because studies of age differences in adult memory rarely include middle-aged people. Typically, researchers compare very young adults, such as college students, to adults in their 60s and 70s. When the two groups are found to differ, psychologists often infer that middle-aged adults' performance falls somewhere between the two. In other words, they assume that memory function declines steadily, in linear fashion, across the adult years—an assumption that may not be true.

One thing developmentalists do know about memory is that the subjective experience of forgetfulness clearly increases with age. The older we get, the more forgetful we think we are (Scheibner & Leathem, 2012). However, it may be that the memory demands of middle-aged adults' everyday lives are greater than those of young adults. Remember, working memory is limited, and the more you try to remember at one time, the more you will forget.

Nevertheless, there seem to be some real differences in the memory performance of young and middle-aged adults. For example, performance on memory tasks such as remembering lists of words and passages of text declines with age, but usually not until after about age 55. In contrast, recognition of words and texts appears to remain stable throughout adulthood (Zelinski & Burnight, 1997). Such findings suggest that there are age differences in working memory. Research examining short-term memory capacity at various ages shows that it remains very stable throughout early, middle, and late adulthood. What changes, apparently, is the ability to make efficient use of available capacity (Lincourt, Rybash, & Hoyer, 1998).

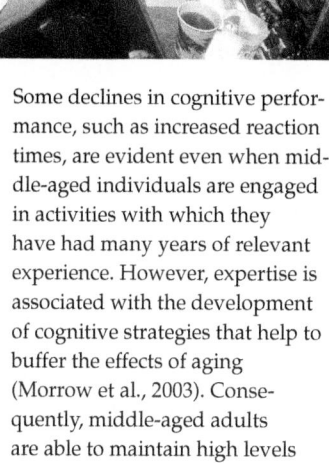

(Photo: Jeff Greenberg/The Image Works)

Some declines in cognitive performance, such as increased reaction times, are evident even when middle-aged individuals are engaged in activities with which they have had many years of relevant experience. However, expertise is associated with the development of cognitive strategies that help to buffer the effects of aging (Morrow et al., 2003). Consequently, middle-aged adults are able to maintain high levels of performance on cognitively demanding tasks, such as flying a commercial airliner.

SEMANTIC AND EPISODIC MEMORIES   Researchers can gain additional insight into age-related memory changes by studying how well young and middle-aged adults encode different kinds of memories. In the 1960s at the University of Toronto, Endel Tulving (1972, 2004) was the first to distinguish between two important types of memory. **Episodic memories** have to do with the ability to re-experience personal events or episodes (Tulving, 1999); **semantic memories** represent our general knowledge of the world, facts, and the meaning of words. For example, a person's memories of a vacation in Newfoundland and Labrador are episodic, and her knowledge that Newfoundland became the last Canadian province in 1949 is semantic.

Researchers find that young and middle-aged adults differ more with respect to new episodic memories than they do with respect to semantic memories (Gallo & Wheeler, 2013). For example, a middle-aged person attending a hockey game may forget where he parked his car (episodic memory). However, he is unlikely to forget the basic rules of the game (semantic memory).

Middle-aged adults are very proficient at overcoming episodic memory limitations by using reminders, or cues, to help themselves remember information. Thus, the middle-aged person who knows that he may forget where his car is parked makes a point of noting nearby landmarks that will help him remember its location. The tendency to use cues may exist because middle-aged adults, in contrast to those who are older, continue to have a high sense of self-efficacy with respect to memory (Lineweaver & Hertzog, 1998). In other words, they believe their efforts will make a difference, so they actively work to improve their memories. This effect is strengthened when the person perceives himself as belonging to a positive aging stereotype category, such as those who are self-accepting, fun-loving, sociable, and independent (Lineweaver, Berger, & Hertzog, 2009).

episodic memories

recollections of personal events

semantic memories

recollections of general knowledge, facts, and word meanings

USE IT OR LOSE IT?   In general, most adults maintain or even gain in skill on any task that they practise often or that is based on specific learning. For example, verbal abilities increase in middle age (Howieson, 2015; Salthouse, 2004). It appears that vocabulary—or, more precisely, performance on vocabulary tests—doesn't begin to decline until about age 65. And the "use it or lose it" dictum seems to hold true for cognitive abilities. That is, adults who engage in intellectually challenging activities show fewer losses in cognitive skills than those who do not (Howieson, 2015; Salthouse, 2004).

Similarly, expertise in a particular field helps to compensate for age-related deficits in cognitive functioning (Howieson, 2015; Morrow et al., 2003; Tsang, 1998). For example, in one study, researchers examined 17- to 79-year-old participants' ability to recognize melodies performed at varying tempos (Andrews, Dowling, Bartlett,

& Halpern, 1998). Some tunes were played very rapidly and then slowed until participants could recognize them. Both age and years of musical training predicted participants' ability to recognize melodies presented in this way, but the relationship between age and recognition was much weaker than the relationship between recognition and musical training. Other melodies were played too slowly to be recognized at the beginning and then sped up. Interestingly, only musical training correlated with recognition of tunes played this way; there was no association with age whatsoever.

NEW LEARNING Owing to the accumulated effects of many years of using some cognitive skills and the development of a large body of relevant information in long-term memory, middle-aged adults outperform those who are younger on tasks that involve comprehending and remembering reading material. For instance, researchers have found that middle-aged and younger adults take different approaches to learning from expository text (the kind of text you're reading right now!) (Matzen & Benjamin, 2013). Younger adults focus on creating a word-for-word representation of the text in their memories. By contrast, middle-aged adults pay more attention to overarching themes than to details. In memory, this difference might be reflected in a decline in memory for surface detail, accompanied by an increase in memory for themes and meanings.

Creativity

Learning Objective 15.13

Discuss what the research suggests about age-related changes in creativity.

creativity

the ability to produce original, appropriate, and valuable ideas and/or solutions to problems

A somewhat different question about cognitive functioning in the middle years of adulthood has to do with **creativity**, the ability to produce original, appropriate, and valuable ideas and/or solutions to problems. One psychologist, Dean Simonton, looked at the lifetime creativity and productivity of thousands of notable scientists from the 19th century and earlier (Simonton, 1991, 2000). Simonton identified the age at which these individuals (nearly all men) published their first significant work, their best work, and their last work. In every scientific discipline represented, the thinkers produced their best work at about age 40, on average. But most of them were publishing significant, even outstanding, research through their 40s and into their 50s.

Lifetime creative output of modern-day scientists follows a similar pattern. Mathematicians, psychologists, physicists, and other scientists born in the 20th century have consistently shown their maximum productivity (usually measured by the number of papers published in a single year) when they were about 40 years old. But research quality (as measured by the number of times each research paper is cited by peers) remains high through age 50 or even age 60 (Gingras, 2015; Simonton, 1988, 2013, in press; Rietzschel, Zacher, & Stroebe, 2016). Among musicians or other artists, peak creativity may occur later or be maintained far longer. For example, in one study, researchers asked judges to rate the aesthetic qualities of musical compositions by the 172 composers whose works are most often performed (Simonton, 1988). Works created late in life ("swan songs") were most likely to be evaluated as masterpieces by the judges.

Critical Thinking

Why do you think that some people associate creativity with youth, when there are so many highly creative middle-aged and older adults?

You might be wondering how the creative process actually works (see **Development in the Real World**). Psychologists have been studying it for some time and still have much to learn. However, one useful approach describes creativity as a type of thought process called *divergent thinking* (Guilford, 1967). A person who uses divergent thinking can provide multiple solutions to problems that have no clear answer. Thus, divergent thinking is as vital to science as it is to art. For instance, when scientists were faced with the problem of identifying the cause of AIDS, they proposed and tested many hypotheses before it became clear that the disease was caused by a virus (HIV). Likewise, a novelist who wants to provide readers with insight into

Development in the Real World

Maintaining the Creative "Edge" in Mid-Life and Beyond

The songwriting career of music legend Willie Nelson began when he started writing poetry at age 5. When his grandparents gave him a guitar, he figured out how to set his poems to music. Nearly 3000 songs later, Nelson continues to be inspired more by lyrics than he is by melodies. And even though Nelson is in his late 70s, he doesn't seem to have lost his creative edge. What is the secret to maintaining one's creativity and productivity through middle age and into the later years?

In a fascinating set of interviews, a number of highly successful and creative people described how they viewed creativity (Bassior et al., 2000). Interestingly, all reported that they viewed themselves as more creative than they had been when they were younger. Their comments suggested that the creative process is a highly individualized intellectual activity. However, what was remarkable was that, by middle age, all had arrived at firm conclusions about what did and did not work for them. So, some part of the maintenance of creativity included acceptance of their own creative idiosyncrasies. Some, for example, expressed the need for external motivation, such as a deadline. Guitarist B.B. King, who was 74 at the time of the interview and is still performing in his late 80s, emphasized his need for a deadline. Others were more motivated by self-imposed standards than by external influences. For example, writer Isabel Allende, age 57, reported that she always begins a new work on January 8, because the date is a personally meaningful anniversary for her. Advertising writer Stan Freberg, age 73, claimed that when he needs an idea, he takes a shower, because he often gets inspiration while in the shower.

A second theme pervaded these reports. Each creative person, in one way or another, recognized the value of accumulated knowledge and experience. They also tended to acknowledge important sources of this knowledge, such as parents, spouses, and friends. Consequently, these people saw their creative work not only as the product of their own abilities, but also as the result of a complex network of influential individuals, life experiences, and their own capacity to reflect on their lives. This is a principle that is supported by research that suggests creativity doesn't just happen in a vacuum—contextual factors, such as an environment that encourages and supports creativity and innovation, are beneficial as well (Rietzschel et al., 2016).

From these extraordinary individuals, we can learn two important things about maintaining creativity and productivity in the middle and late adult years: First, being consciously aware of one's own creative process—and accepting its boundaries—seems to be critical. Second, some degree of humility, a sense of indebtedness to those who have contributed to and supported one's creative development, appears to be associated with continuing productivity in the middle and late adult years.

a character's motivations tries out several ways of communicating the information before she settles on the one that works best.

Creative solutions sometimes pop into the mind of a creative person fully formed, but most of the time they arise from bits and pieces of several solutions that he has been mulling over for a while. Psychologist Daniel Goleman describes this mulling over process as involving four stages when it is used to solve problems (Goleman, Kaufman, & Ray, 1992). During *preparation*, relevant information is gathered. The next phase, *incubation*, involves digesting the information without actually trying to work on the problem. *Illumination* occurs when this digestive process produces an "aha!" moment in which the solution to the problem becomes clear. Finally, during *translation*, the solution is applied to the problem and adjustments are made as needed. As you probably know from experience, the last step is the most difficult and time-consuming because, in the real world, things don't often go as we imagine they will. As Thomas Edison put it, "Genius is 1% inspiration and 99% perspiration." Edison should know; after working out how to design a commercially viable electric light bulb theoretically, he spent over a year making prototypes before he finally found the design that worked. Thus, Edison believed that failure was essential to the creative process.

Test Yourself before going on

1. Would Denney agree or disagree with the following statement? "Through lifestyle changes, a middle-aged adult can regain the peak levels of fitness he or she enjoyed in early adulthood."

2. What was the main finding of studies that looked at the relationship between physical activity and cognitive function?

3. Write "Y" by memory functions that decline with age and "N" by those which do not.
   _____ (a) episodic memory
   _____ (b) semantic memory
   _____ (c) performance on memory tasks, e.g., remembering lists of words
   _____ (d) recognition of words and texts

   _____ (e) comprehending and remembering reading material
   _____ (f) efficient use of working memory capacity

4. Creativity often involves _____ thinking.

Critical Thinking

5. Given what you have learned in this section, where would you place cognitive functioning in middle age on a 10-point scale ranging from "age and health have no effect on cognitive functioning" at the low end to "age and health cause inevitable declines in cognitive functioning" at the high end? What reasons would you give if you were asked to explain your assessment?

Summary

Physical Changes

15.1 Summarize what researchers know about brain function in middle age.

- Brain volume peaks during the middle adult years and grey matter density starts to decline. The speed at which cognitive tasks are carried out begins to slow. Middle-aged adults often outperform younger adults on everyday tasks that require concentration and rapid judgments, such as driving.

15.2 Describe how reproductive function changes in men and women in middle age.

- The loss of reproductive capacity, *climacteric*, occurs very gradually in men, but more rapidly in women. Menopause is a three-phase process that results from a series of hormonal changes. Biopsychosocial conditions begin to adversely affect sexual activity.

15.3 Describe what osteoporosis is, and what factors are associated with it.

- Bone mass declines significantly after age 30; accelerated declines in women at menopause are linked to decreased levels of estrogen and progesterone. Faster bone loss occurs in women who experience early menopause, who are underweight, who exercise little, or who have low-calcium diets.

15.4 Describe how vision and hearing change in middle age.

- Thickening of the lens of the eye, with accompanying loss of elasticity, reduces visual acuity noticeably in the 40s or 50s. Hearing loss is more gradual.

Health Promotion and Wellness

15.5 Describe mid-life health trends.

- Chronic illness and death rates rise noticeably toward the end of middle adulthood. The two major causes of death in middle adulthood are cancer and heart disease.

15.6 Identify what factors contribute to cancer.

- Risk factors for cancer include smoking, obesity, and an inactive lifestyle. The role of a high-fat diet has been debated, but most evidence supports the hypothesis that such a diet contributes to the risk. Recent research shows that several cancers are caused by infectious agents (viral and bacterial).

15.7 Summarize the risks of cardiovascular disease in middle age.

- Cardiovascular disease is not a normal part of aging; it is a disease for which there are known risk factors, include smoking, high blood pressure, high blood cholesterol, obesity, and a high-fat diet.

15.8 Identify some important differences in the health of middle-aged men and women.

- Women tend to live longer than men but are more likely to suffer from chronic illnesses. Women recover more readily from heart attacks because of gender differences in the heart itself and women's greater tendency to get follow-up care.

15.9 Discuss mental health trends and alcohol consumption in middle age.

- Middle-aged adults have lower rates of mental health problems of virtually every kind than young adults. Alcoholism usually starts at younger ages but often remains undiagnosed until middle age.

Cognitive Functioning

15.10 Discuss how Denney's and the Balteses' models explain the relationship between health and cognitive functioning in middle age.

- Denney's model of aging suggests that exercising either physical or cognitive abilities can improve performance at any age, but the upper limit on improvement declines with increasing age. Paul and Margaret Baltes assert that

middle-aged adults balance the gains and losses associated with aging by selecting tasks on which to focus limited resources, optimizing some skills through practice, and compensating for declines.

15.11 Describe the relationship between health and cognitive functioning.

- Some studies suggest that differences in health contribute to variations in cognitive functioning among middle-aged adults. Exercise clearly affects the physical health of middle-aged adults and has been shown to help maintain and improve cognitive functioning.

15.12 Describe how young and middle-aged adults differ in performance on memory tests.

- Verbal abilities continue to grow in middle age. Some loss of memory speed and skill occurs, but by most measures the loss is quite small until fairly late in the middle adult years. Expertise helps middle-aged adults compensate for losses in processing speed.

15.13 Discuss what the research suggests about age-related changes in creativity.

- Creative productivity also appears to remain high during middle adulthood, at least for adults in challenging jobs (the category of adults on whom most of this research has focused).

Chapter 16
Social and Personality Development in Middle Adulthood

Monkey Business Images/Shutterstock

 ## Learning Objectives

THEORIES OF SOCIAL AND PERSONALITY DEVELOPMENT

16.1 Explain how the views of Erikson and Vaillant differ with regard to generativity.

16.2 Explain how the concept of the mid-life crisis evolved into the life events perspective of middle age.

CHANGES IN RELATIONSHIPS AND PERSONALITY

16.3 Identify what factors contribute to the "mellowing" of partnerships in middle adulthood.

16.4 Describe how multigenerational caregiving and caregiver burden affect middle-aged adults' lives.

16.5 Describe how the grandparent role affects middle-aged adults.

16.6 Describe important qualities of social networks during middle adulthood.

16.7 Summarize the research on personality continuity and change in mid-life.

MID-LIFE CAREER ISSUES

16.8 Describe how work satisfaction and job performance change in middle adulthood.

16.9 Identify what factors contribute to career transitions in mid-life.

16.10 Describe how Baby Boomers are preparing for retirement.

Think about the social roles that are prominent in each phase of life. Peer and family relationships are of primary importance to the social lives of adolescents and young adults. Peers and families matter to middle-aged adults, too. However, the role of worker is typically the centre of a middle-aged adult's social network. Despite the centrality of work in mid-life, in order to understand the changes that happen during this phase of life, it's important to keep in mind that most middle-aged adults occupy several social roles throughout this period, and middle-aged adults must often deal with conflicts among these roles. By the end of middle age, however, these roles have begun to shift dramatically. Children leave home, job promotions have usually reached their limit, and aging parents often make new demands on middle-aged adults' financial, psychological, and social resources. The prospect of preparing for the next phase of life also looms large as the middle adult years draw to a close. In this chapter, you will read about how adults between ages 40 and 65 progress through and adapt to all these changes.

Theories of Social and Personality Development

You should remember from the chapter on Theories of Development that Erik Erikson viewed middle age as a period when attention turns to creation of a legacy that nurtures and guides the next generation. Adults do this by influencing the lives of those in younger generations. Yet many have characterized middle age less positively, suggesting that it is a period of intense crisis.

Erikson's Generativity Versus Stagnation Stage

Middle-aged adults are in Erikson's **generativity versus stagnation stage**. Their developmental task is to acquire a sense of **generativity**, which involves an interest in establishing and guiding the next generation. Generativity is expressed not only in bearing or rearing one's own children, but also through teaching, serving as mentor, or taking on leadership roles in various civic, religious, or charitable organizations. Merely having children is not enough for developing generativity in Erikson's terms. The optimum expression of generativity requires turning outward from a preoccupation with self, a kind of psychological expansion toward caring for others. Those who fail to develop generativity often suffer from a "pervading sense of stagnation and personal impoverishment [and indulge themselves] as if they were their own one and only child" (Erikson, 1963, p. 267).

RESEARCH ON GENERATIVITY Research has produced hints of such a developmental stage, but the findings are much less clear than data on changes in earlier

Learning Objective 16.1

Explain how the views of Erikson and Vaillant differ with regard to generativity.

generativity versus stagnation stage
the seventh of Erikson's stages, in which middle-aged adults find meaning in contributing to the development of younger individuals

generativity
a sense that one is making a valuable contribution to society by bringing up children or mentoring younger people in some way

years. One cross-sectional study of young, mid-life, and older women found that generativity increased in middle age, as Erikson's theory suggests (Zucker, Ostrove, & Stewart, 2002). Contrary to what his theory would predict, however, the oldest group of participants, whose average age was 66, cited generative concerns as being important to them just as frequently as the middle-aged group did. These findings support Erikson's claim that generativity is more common in middle age than in early adulthood, but they also indicate that generativity continues to be important in old age. Other research suggests that generativity is a more prominent theme in the lives of middle-aged women than in the lives of middle-aged men (Jones & McAdams, 2013).

Despite these inconsistencies, several studies support Erikson's belief that generativity is related to mental health in middle-aged adults. Researchers have found that generativity is positively linked to satisfaction in life and work, altruistic behaviour, successful marriage, close friendships, and to emotional well-being (Ackerman, Zuroff, & Moskowitz, 2000; Westermeyer, 2004, 2013). Further, it seems that generativity is something of a two-way street in that cultures that support generativity foster individuals who internalize the value of generativity and who, in turn, show more generativity, and life satisfaction, in middle age (Hofer et al., 2016). As well, cultures that encourage respect for elders by its younger citizens have higher levels of generative acts and well-being in older citizens. Thus, the perceived appreciation and respect from younger generations supports the development of generativity in its older adults (Tabuchi, Nakagawa, Miura, & Gondo, 2015).

VAILLANT'S REVISION OF ERIKSON'S THEORY Psychiatrist George Vaillant has spent the past three decades chronicling the development of several hundred adults through early, middle, and late adulthood. His research emphasizes resilience and has included measures of change in the physical, cognitive, personality, and social domains (Vaillant, 2012). His findings for the middle adulthood period prompted him to propose a modification of Erikson's theory of lifespan development (Vaillant, 2002).

Vaillant offered that there is a stage between intimacy and generativity called *career consolidation*. Like Erikson, Vaillant tended to define the domains of life fairly broadly, so *career* may mean a paid vocation or it could involve a decision to be a stay-at-home mother or father. The outcome of this phase is the creation of a new social network for which the middle-aged adult's primary work serves as a hub. Involvement with this social network helps the individual meet the psychosocial needs of this substage. Such needs include contentment, compensation, competence, and commitment (Vaillant, 2002). Individuals need to be happy with the work-related choices they have made, to feel that they are adequately compensated, to view themselves as competent in their chosen field, and to be able to maintain a sense of commitment to their work.

Following generativity versus stagnation, Vaillant offered, is another stage called *keeper of the meaning*. In this phase, middle-aged adults focus on preserving the institutions and values of their culture that they believe will benefit future generations. For some, religious organizations become paramount. Others focus on the arts, educational institutions, historical preservation societies, or political organizations. The key is that participation in these institutions is motivated by the desire to ensure their survival rather than by a concern for how the institution can benefit the individual middle-aged adult. In other words, the well-adjusted adult in the keeper-of-the-meaning stage wants to give something to the institution rather than to get something from it. Moreover, the social networks that are created through middle-aged adults' associations with institutions support their need to feel that the work they are doing will make a difference for future generations.

Learning Objective 16.2

Explain how the concept of the mid-life crisis evolved into the life events perspective of middle age.

Mid-Life Crisis: Fact or Fiction?

Canadian psychoanalyst Elliot Jacques (1965) popularized the term *mid-life crisis* in the 1960s, an era when the occurrence of major events along the timeline of life was relatively lockstep and predictable, especially for men. The landmarks of life (particularly in developed countries such as Canada) included finishing school, going to work, retiring, and, ultimately, dying. Midway between completing school and death there was a change in a person's time perspective that shifted from "time since birth" to "time left till death." At this point, any perceived gap between what one had accomplished thus far in life and where one had expected to be, coupled with the realization that only so much time was left to close the gap, was therefore thought to be responsible for creating a sense of urgency, a sense of having just one last chance at a fulfilled life. The realization of the inevitability of death, along with other tangible indicators of time passing, such as noticeable body aging, children leaving home, or elderly or deceased parents, seemed to be a universal phenomenon that hit people during their 40s.

Decades later, of course, the timing and nature of major life events have changed dramatically. The progression from formal secondary schooling to late adulthood is far less predictable than it was in the 1960s, and it is certainly not a universal, worldwide experience as thought previously. In Canada, for instance, both women and men engage in lifelong learning, have different family living arrangements at various times in their lives, and generally hit the major milestones later in life—if at all. By the 1980s, the concept of a mid-life crisis was being challenged. For example, by using a mid-life crisis scale, including items about inner turmoil, marital or job dissatisfaction, and a sense of declining power, researchers compared the responses of over 500 participants in a cross-sectional study of men ranging in age from 35 to 70 (Costa & McCrae, 1980; McCrae & Costa, 1984). The researchers could find no distinct ages at which measures of "mid-life crisis" occurred.

Researcher Susan Krauss Whitbourne would agree—she traced the developmental pathways of 182 people longitudinally over 40 years and concluded that resolution of crises evolves continuously and cumulatively at least through to our mid-50s (Whitbourne, 2009; Whitbourne, Sneed, & Sayer, 2009). For example, in terms of Erikson's theory, psychosocial crises usually associated with childhood (i.e., trust, autonomy, and initiative) can show gradual growth throughout adulthood. Those who experience late resolution of industry, identity, intimacy, and generativity can overcome their earlier psychosocial deficits to catch up and sometimes exceed their initially advantaged peers. Conversely, ego integrity, which is usually considered a late life crisis, may become important at earlier ages in a person's life. Thus, it seems that in many cases, psychosocial issues must be continually revisited and reworked as a person's circumstances change. Based on the evidence, it seems that we all go through Erickson's psychosocial crises, although not necessarily in the same sequence or at the same times in our lives. Moreover, by engaging in ongoing evaluation of our identity, in particular, we can maximize our potential for well-being (Sneed, Whitbourne, Schwartz, & Huang, 2012; Whitbourne, 2009).

In Whitbourne's (2009) longitudinal study, she found that, at least through to their 50s, adults generally followed one of five *life pathways*:

- The Meandering Way: A life based on a low sense of identity—this type of person felt lost and thus was unable to commit to a clear set of goals.

- The Straight and Narrow Path: Predictability and routine were paramount, risk was avoided.

- The Downward Slope: Life started out great, but after making some regrettable decisions, it took a turn for the worse.

- The Triumphant Trail: Early life was a challenge, but through inner resilience those challenges were overcome.

- The Authentic Road: A life characterized by self-examination and redirection to get back on a track toward a strong sense of purpose and satisfaction.

life events approach

a theoretical perspective on middle adulthood that focuses on normative and non-normative events and how adults in this age group respond to them

A LIFE EVENTS APPROACH For many middle-aged and older adults crises seem to have been triggered by specific events, such as the loss of a job or the death of a close friend or relative (Lachman, 2004). Thus, some developmentalists offer that a **life events approach** to explaining the unique stresses of the middle adulthood period is preferable to a theoretical perspective that proposes a universal crisis. The life events approach focuses on normative and non-normative events and middle-aged adults' responses to them.

The physical changes of middle age are the backdrop against which the major life events of this period are played out. Consequently, all middle-aged adults are dealing with new stressors for which they must develop new ways of coping, and research shows that concerns about the limitations imposed by these physical changes increase across the middle adulthood years (Cate & John, 2007). In addition, most middle-aged adults experience the loss of a parent or must cope with major declines in their parents' ability to care for themselves. Most are also dealing with work-related issues. At the same time, for those who have children, major shifts are occurring in the nature of parent–child relationships. Another important factor, one that adds another layer of complexity, is that many of these stressors last for some time. A middle-aged person can spend years, for example, caring for an incapacitated parent. With all these changes going on at the same time, it isn't surprising that middle-aged adults often feel stressed. Thus, some developmentalists contend that the best way to understand middle adulthood is to study how people in this age group manage to integrate all of these changes and their interpretations of them into the coherent stories of their own middle adulthood experiences (Farrow, 2012).

role conflict

any situation in which two or more roles are at least partially incompatible, either because they call for different behaviours or because their separate demands add up to more hours than there are in the day

Finally, the stresses associated with the events of middle age are often complicated by **role conflict**—any situation in which two or more roles are at least partially incompatible, either because they call for different behaviours or because their separate demands add up to more hours than there are in the day. Role conflict happens, for example, when a middle-aged father must choose between helping his aging parents with financial or health problems and attending his teenaged son's football games. A person experiences *role strain* when her own qualities or skills do not measure up to the demands of some role. For example, a 40-year-old worker who is forced to return to college to acquire new skills after a job layoff and who feels anxious about her ability to succeed is experiencing role strain.

Test Yourself before going on

1. Match each term with its major emphasis.
   _____ (a) normative and non-normative events and adults' responses to them
   _____ (b) the need to make a valuable contribution to society
   _____ (c) social networks for which an individual's work serves as the hub
   _____ (d) preserving institutions and values for future generations
   _____ (e) a life characterized by self-examination and redirection to keep moving toward a strong sense of purpose and satisfaction

   (i) generativity
   (ii) life events approach
   (iii) authentic road life pathway
   (iv) keeper of the meaning
   (v) career consolidation

Critical Thinking

2. How could the stage models of Erikson and Vaillant be integrated with the life events approach to provide a more comprehensive description of middle adulthood than any of them could alone?

Changes in Relationships and Personality

As suggested previously, family roles are still an important part of Canadian life in middle age (Beaujot & Ravanera, 2008). However, these roles change significantly during this period of life.

Partnerships

Several lines of evidence suggest that, on average, marital stability and satisfaction increase in mid-life as conflicts over child-rearing and other matters decline (Huber, Navarro, Wombie, & Mumme, 2010). In addition, as couples get older, the number of shared friends they have increases and the number of nonshared friends decreases (Kalmijn, 2003). As a result, the social network tends to get a bit tighter—and probably more supportive—in middle age, which may be one reason for age-related improvements in relationship satisfaction. So, despite considerable diversity among mid-life marriages or partnerships, overall, they are less conflicted than those of young adults.

Improvements in marital satisfaction may derive from middle-aged adults' increased sense of control—a kind of marital self-efficacy (Lachman & Weaver, 1998). It is likely that middle-aged partners' identification of successful problem-solving strategies contributes to the sense that they have control over their relationship. Research has provided useful illustrations of this point. For example, researchers typically find that marital problem themes among middle-aged couples are remarkably similar to those of younger adults. Wives complain of an unjust division of labour; husbands express dissatisfaction with limits on their freedom. Yet, relationship stability among middle-aged couples is maintained through the practice of what one researcher called *skilled diplomacy*, an approach to solving problems that involves confrontation of the spouse about an issue, followed by a period during which the confronting spouse works to restore harmony (Perho & Korhonen, 1999). Skilled diplomacy is practised more often by wives than by husbands, but it appears to be an effective technique for marital problem solving no matter which spouse uses it.

As age-related increases in marital satisfaction would predict, middle-aged Canadian couples are far less likely to divorce than those who are younger (Kelly, 2012). Even so, compared to previous generations, there is a larger proportion of Canadians aged 50 and over who have divorced or separated and have had multiple unions (Milan, Wong, & Vézina, 2014). For women who do divorce, research suggests that middle-aged women are better able to cope with divorce than younger women (Marks & Lamberg, 1998). Perhaps a "mellowing" of personality (which you will read about later in this chapter) renders the middle-aged woman more resilient in the face of such traumatic events. Moreover, some women remain in unsatisfactory marriages through their 20s and 30s because they think that divorce will be harmful to their children. Once the children are grown, such women feel free to move out of these relationships and report that the stress associated with divorce was less problematic than the emotional turmoil they experienced in the years prior to splitting from their husbands (Enright, 2004).

Learning Objective 16.3

Identify what factors contribute to the "mellowing" of partnerships in middle adulthood.

(Photo: Monkey Business Images/Shutterstock)

Once the children are grown and gone, many couples find it easier to spend time together—perhaps one of the reasons that marital satisfaction generally rises in middle age.

The Role of the Caregiver

The discussion of the relationship between young adults and their families in the chapter on Social and Personality Development in Early Adulthood focused almost

Learning Objective 16.4

Describe how multigenerational caregiving and caregiver burden affect middle-aged adults' lives.

entirely on connections *up* the chain of family generations—that is, relationships between the young adults and their own middle-aged parents. When looking at family relationships from the perspective of middle age, we have to look in both directions: down the generational chain to relationships with grown children (see **Development in the Real World** below) and up the chain to relationships with aging parents (see **Development in the Real World** on caring for aging parents). On average, it is clear that middle adulthood is likely to be a time when more help is given than is received.

SANDWICH GENERATION   Each of the positions in a family's generational chain has certain role prescriptions (Lachman, 2015; Lachman et al., 2015). In middle adulthood, for current age cohorts at least, the role requires giving assistance in both directions in the generational chain. These responsibilities produce what is sometimes called the mid-life *squeeze*, and those being squeezed are called **multigenerational caregivers**, often referred to as the *sandwich generation*. Nearly 30% of Canadian caregivers are in this position (Sinha, 2013).

More than one in three middle-aged Canadians are now caring for a senior—most likely an aging parent or parent-in-law. This trend is likely to continue with the rise in life expectancy (Sinha, 2013; Turcotte, 2013a; Turner & Findlay, 2012). Slightly more than half of these caregivers reported experiencing a variety of difficulties and challenges. For example, many found caregiving to be emotionally demanding and time consuming, leaving them with little time for self and/or family, thereby producing stress and fatigue. For some, caregiving caused or worsened a health condition and added to financial hardship. Collectively, these effects are often termed **caregiver burden**. On the flip side, however, the vast majority of caregivers reported that they derived personal satisfaction or enjoyment from providing assistance to a care recipient.

multigenerational caregivers

middle-aged adults who are caring both for elderly parents and young adult children at the same time; also called the *sandwich generation*

caregiver burden

the cumulative negative effects of caring for an elderly or disabled person

Development in the Real World

Emptying the Nest, Failure-to-Launch, and the Revolving Door

EMPTYING THE NEST Folklore in Western cultures postulates that many women become anxious or depressed once the "nest" is empty because they are losing their central role of "mother." Of course, it is possible that such a pattern exists in some cultures, but it seems not to be true for Canadian society, at least not for the great majority of middle-aged parents (Mitchell & Lovegreen, 2009). Still, Simon Fraser University researchers have found that parents' feelings about their children leaving home are shaped by ethnocultural values, relationship quality, living arrangements, and financial circumstances when their grown children reach this milestone (Mitchell & Wister, 2015).

The timing of the "empty nest" stage in the family life cycle obviously depends on a person's (or couple's) age when the last child is born. In conjunction with women delaying child-bearing, men are delaying parenting, which pushes the empty-nest stage to a later age in a pattern typical of today's Canadian adults. This pattern is quite different from the historical parenting trends in Canada. For example, McMaster University researchers Carolyn Rosenthal and James Gladstone have been studying trends in contemporary families. They reported that women born in the mid-1800s had their last child, on average, when they were about 40 (Rosenthal & Gladstone, 2000). If we assume that this last child left home when he was between 20 and 25, then women in this cohort were roughly 60 years old when their last child left. Since the life expectancy for women during the first decades of the 1900s was less than 60 years (Health Reports, 2001), there was little possibility for women to experience what we now call the empty-nest stage. By comparison, women born during the 1930s and later were only about 30 when they bore their last child and were in their 50s when the last child left home (Beaujot & Ravanera, 2001). Their life expectancy was somewhat beyond 60 years. Thus, there was greater likelihood that they would experience the empty-nest stage. This stage will likely be prolonged even more in the near future because of a number of other factors associated with women born in the late 1940s and 1950s: These women started having fewer, more closely spaced babies at an earlier age (Rosenthal & Gladstone, 2000). This cohort also enjoys a much longer projected lifespan, which increases the likelihood of living well beyond the time when the youngest child leaves home.

A study by University of Western Ontario researchers Ravanera and Rajulton (1998) found that male parenting in Canada parallels the female pattern, whereby male parenting patterns in the latter half of the 20th century have been more variable than prior to that time. Both men and women experience nontraditional family patterns, including sole-parenting and step-parenting. Moreover, since Canadian men are living longer, they too experience the empty nest. Interestingly, men of lower status start parenting younger but end parenting at an older age.

The role of parent does not cease when the child leaves home. Support and advice continue to be expected and offered. But the content of the parental role in this "postparental" phase is clearly quite different from what it was when the children were still living at home. The child does not need daily care or supervision. As a result, adults have much more time for their spousal roles, a change that undoubtedly contributes to the higher reported marital satisfaction in this stage of family life.

FAILURE-TO-LAUNCH AND THE REVOLVING DOOR What happens when adult children either don't leave or later return home? Researchers have recently turned their attention to adult children who remain at home longer (often termed "failure-to-launch"), as well as those who return to their parents' home after living elsewhere independently (the "revolving door"). Studies show that conflicts between parents and resident adult children are common (Burn & Szoeke, 2016; Dennerstein, Dudley, & Guthrie, 2002; Dykstra et al., 2014; Muzi, 2000). Adult children may put extra pressure on their parents if they take on a childlike stance (e.g., expecting their parents to cater to their needs and not doing their fair share of household chores). Further, both parents and adult children feel that they have inadequate privacy. Middle-aged parents' sense of obligation to their adult children may cause them to feel that they can't pursue their own goals until they have helped their late-blooming children become self-sufficient. As a child's departure is further and further delayed, frustrations can accumulate.

The percentage of adult children living with their middle-aged parents is increasing (Milan, 2016). Gerontologist Barbara Mitchell (2000, 2006) of Simon Fraser University reported that 20- to 34-year-olds are staying at home longer. In fact, about half of this age group are still living with their parents. Further, about 24% of Canadian parents have an adult child living with them who is part of this so-called *boomerang generation* (i.e., an adult child who has left home and later returned) (Turcotte, 2006). Financial difficulties associated with unemployment, extended postsecondary schooling, delayed marriage, and a rise in the divorce rate probably explain this increase (Milan, 2016; Mitchell, 2006; Turcotte, 2006).

Contrary to popular belief, when this woman's daughter leaves the nest in a few years, it will be a joyful experience.

The degree of infirmity of the aging parents, the nature of the relationship the middle-aged adult has with those aging parents, and the degree of help required by the young adult children make a difference in the level of intensity of care. A 50-year-old whose divorced daughter has returned with her children to live at home or a 50-year-old who has a parent with dementia living nearby is far more likely to experience major caregiver burden than someone of the same age who sometimes babysits her grandchildren or helps her aging parents by doing occasional shopping, snow shovelling, or housecleaning. In addition to the strain, Canadian high-intensity sandwich generation caregivers who spend more time on elder care than low-intensity caregivers also incur extra expenses, are absent from work more often, and have a reduced quality of life in terms of cancelled holiday plans, reduced social activities, and less time for their own families (Vézina & Turcotte, 2010).

Grandparenting

Middle-aged adults typically move into several new roles, such as becoming in-laws and grandparents as their children get married and have children. Almost 6 in 10 Canadian adults become grandparents by the end of middle adulthood (Milan,

Learning Objective 16.5

Describe how the grandparent role affects middle-aged adults.

Development in the Real World

Who Provides Care for Aging Parents in Canada?

One of the most difficult dilemmas of mid-life arises when elderly parents become incapable of caring for themselves. Inevitably, the issue of who will care for them creates conflict. Following some form of needs assessment, the caregiver must choose between several care options, each of which carries its own unique blend of quality, convenience, and cost. Options in Canada include in-home care (private and publicly funded); independent-supportive living, for example, full-service residences or apartments and retirement homes; nursing homes and homes for the aged; and palliative care and hospice care facilities. Ultimately, even if elders move to long-term care facilities, someone has to take primary responsibility for overseeing their care (Turcotte & Sawaya, 2015).

Families typically negotiate the caregiving task along a number of dimensions, including each family member's competing demands and availability of resources. Among siblings, making decisions about how the tasks of caregiving should be shared can become contentious and evoke old sibling rivalries. Sometimes a sibling may come to resent doing most of the work; in other cases a sibling may feel left out (Russo, 2010).

Anne Martin-Matthews (2001), a University of British Columbia gerontologist, points out that Canadian women are the ones most likely to be actively involved in the caregiving of their elderly parents and, in their later years, an elderly spouse. Moreover, women have traditionally married older men, and since men have a shorter life expectancy, proportionally more women than men will outlive their spouse. This means that, if they require care, these women will be dependent on alternative (rather than spousal) sources of care in their senior years (Turcotte & Sawaya, 2015).

Some studies have found that as many as 90% of the primary caregivers for elders with Alzheimer's disease are either daughters or daughters-in-law (Daire, 2004). One factor that increases daughters' involvement in parental care is simple proximity. Perhaps because of greater emotional closeness to their parents or their socialization for the role of kin-keeping, daughters are more likely to live near their parents. And parents, when they approach their later years, are more likely to move to be close to a daughter than to a son.

Even when sons are involved in the care of an elder, research indicates that they experience far less caregiver burden than daughters do (Pinquart & Sorensen, 2006a). This difference results from the tendency of daughters to provide more hours of care and more personal types of care, such as bathing; daughters are also more likely to view the recipient of care as more difficult to deal with than sons do. The psychological and physical aspects of the types of care that daughters give and their attitudes toward their role of caregiver result in increases in depressive symptoms and decreases in health.

Researchers have found that multi-dimensional interventions can ease the strain of the caregiver burden (Pinquart & Sorensen, 2006b). These interventions should include information for the caregiver about the care recipient's condition or illness. The educational component should include information on the availability of resources such as daycare and home health aides, both of which can provide the caregiver with a much needed respite from the physical aspects of caring for an elderly parent. Similarly, counselling sessions and support groups can help with the emotional aspects of caregiving.

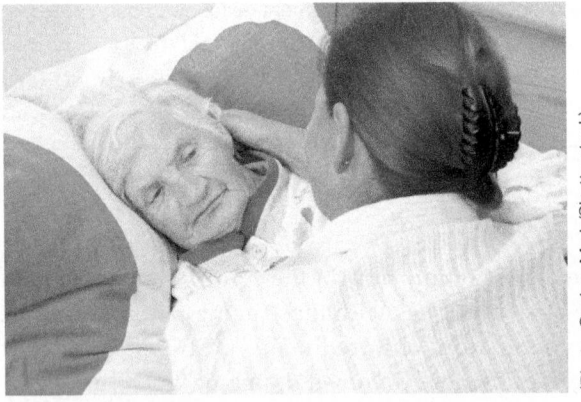

(Photo: Ocskay Mark/Shutterstock)

Daughters, far more than sons, are likely to take on the role of significant caregiver for a disabled or demented parent as this daughter has done, now that her mother is suffering from Alzheimer's disease.

Laflamme, & Wong, 2015) (see **Figure 16.1**). In Canada, there are about 7 million grandparents, each having ~4.2 grandchildren. Nearly 600 000 grandparents live in the same household as their grandchildren. As well, a fair number of these children (72 700) live with only their grandparent(s) in *skip-generation families*.

Most grandparents express high levels of satisfaction with this role (Goyer, 2012; Thiele & Whelan, 2008). A majority see or talk to their grandchildren regularly. They may write, call, or visit as often as every couple of weeks, and most describe their relationships as warm and loving. Likewise, many studies have demonstrated the

Figure 16.1 The likelihood of being a grandparent increases with age. In Canada, two-thirds of women and over one-half of men 55 to 64 years of age are grandparents.

(**SOURCE:** Adapted from Statistics Canada, 2003, *Canadian Social Trends Winter [71]*, 2–7, Cat. No. 11-008 [Milan & Hamm, 2003].)

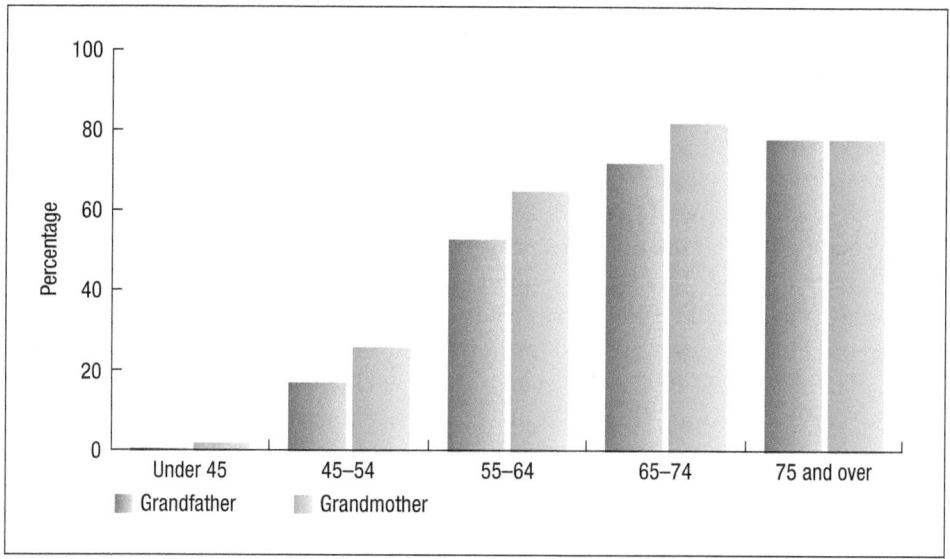

positive impact of warm relationships with grandparents on children's development (Attar-Schwartz, Tan, & Buchanan, 2009; Buchanan, 2014; Dunifon & Bajracharya, 2012).

Grandparents seem to be an especially important source of stability in the lives of children of divorced parents (Attar-Schwartz, Tan, Buchanan, Flouri, & Griggs, 2009). In most provinces and Yukon, there are statutes that provide grandparents, and other individuals, with a legal basis for matters such as visitation or access to their grandchildren if it is in the *best interests of the child* (Adcox, 2016; Spencer, 2008).

Fortunately, most parents welcome the involvement of their own parents in their children's lives, and surveys suggest that grandparents and grandchildren engage in many of the same activities—watching television, shopping, attending religious services—that parents and children share (Goyer, 2012). However, while parenthood clearly involves full-time responsibility, there are many degrees of being a grandparent.

Most behavioural scientists place grandparents in one of several categories derived from a classic study in which researchers interviewed a nationally representative sample of over 500 grandparents (Cherlin & Furstenberg, 1986).

- *Companionate relationship.* The most common pattern is when grandparents have frequent contact and warm interactions with grandchildren.

- *Remote relationship.* The next most common pattern is when grandparents do not see their grandchildren, often due to remoteness caused by physical distance.

- *Involved relationship.* The least common pattern is when grandparents are directly involved in the everyday care of grandchildren or have close emotional ties with them.

(Photo: bst2012/Fotolia)

This girl seems delighted with her grandmother, with whom she seems to have what Cherlin and Furstenberg would call a companionate relationship.

Friends

The scant research on friendships in middle adulthood suggests that the total number of friendships is lower in these years than in young adulthood (Kalmijn, 2003). At the same time, other bits of research suggest that mid-life friendships are as intimate and close as those at earlier ages. For example, researchers have analyzed information from the files of 50 participants in the now-familiar Berkeley/Oakland Longitudinal Study, who had been interviewed or tested repeatedly from adolescence through age 50 (Carstensen, 1992). These analyses revealed that the frequency of interaction with best friends dropped between ages 17 and 50, but that the best-friend relationships remained very close.

Such studies suggest that the social network of middle-aged adults is relatively small, although relationships are just as intimate as they were at earlier ages (Due, Holstein, Lund, Modvig, & Avlund, 1999). More importantly, however, a longitudinal study of 6500 British people born in the late 1950s determined there is a strong correlation between friendships in mid-life and mental health (Cable, Bartley, Chandola, & Sacker, 2013). For both men and women in their 50s, having larger friendship networks and seeing friends regularly—once a month or more frequently—was associated with better psychological health and well-being. Conversely, mental health was found to be especially poor among those who had no friends or relatives.

Continuity and Change in Personality

Learning Objective 16.7

Summarize the research on personality continuity and change in mid-life.

Can developmentalists tell what kind of person someone will be in middle adulthood, based on what is known about his childhood, adolescence, or early adult life? A stable set of personality traits that psychologists call the *Big Five* emerge during middle childhood. Notice in this brief review of the traits that they can be easily remembered by using the acronym *CANOE*:

- **C**onscientiousness: need for order in the environment
- **A**greeableness: ease with which a person gets along with others
- **N**euroticism: emotional negativity, pessimism, and irritability
- **O**penness: willingness to try new things
- **E**xtraversion: sociability

Many studies show that the Big Five are relatively stable from childhood to old age (Hampson & Goldberg, 2006; Kandler et al., 2010). Such findings are consistent with the proposition that the five factors are determined very early in life and are stable throughout the lifespan (Shiner & Caspi, 2012). However, there are subtle age-related changes in the five factors across the years of adulthood (Lucas & Donnellan, 2011; Wortman, Lucas, & Donnellan, 2012). Longitudinal research indicates that openness, extraversion, and neuroticism decline as adults age. Agreeableness increases, as does conscientiousness, up until around age 70 when it begins to show declines. Thus, the best statement that we can make about the stability of the Big Five is that these traits follow a general pattern of stability in most people but that they are also subject to some degree of modification.

Studies of negative and positive emotionality suggest a similar pattern. Even though negative emotionality in early adulthood is moderately to strongly correlated with negative emotionality in middle adulthood, longitudinal studies show that many individuals, particularly women, become *less* negative over time (Kopala-Sibley, Mongrain, & Zuroff, 2013; Srivastava, John, Gosling, & Potter, 2003). Similarly, agreeableness appears to increase with age (Srivastava et al., 2003), whereas tolerance for risk-taking and impulsivity decline with age (Deakin, Aitken, Robbins, & Sahakian, 2004).

However, when researchers consider large groups, which they must do to correlate variables such as personality factors, they find that these large group correlations can mask a number of individual cases in which there is a great deal of change. Consequently, the best conclusion to draw is that stability is the general pattern, but individual variability in personality typically found among middle-aged adults is clearly possible. Notably, a dramatic change is not necessarily desirable; for example, it's becoming evident that personality stability is associated with better cognitive performance as well as psychological and physical health in mid-life. But, a shift toward higher neuroticism and lower conscientiousness signals poorer health and well-being outcomes (Graham & Lachman, 2012; Human et al., 2013). In particular, personality is an important contributor to middle-aged adults' capacity for managing stress. For example, in one study, researchers found that adults who were higher in extraversion and conscientiousness were less likely to feel strained by work-related stressors (Grant & Langan-Fox, 2007). By contrast, those who were high in neuroticism were less able to cope with on-the-job problems. Other researchers have found that individuals who are high in neuroticism are more likely than peers to have stress-related conditions such as chronic fatigue syndrome (Poeschla, Strachan, Dansie, Buchwald, & Afari, 2013).

Critical Thinking

Has your personality changed since you were younger? In what ways? How do you expect it to change as you get older?

Test Yourself before going on

1. Many middle-aged adults occupy four family roles. What are they?

   (a) _____
   (b) _____
   (c) _____
   (d) _____

2. Choose the correct answer to complete the following sentence:
   Studies of negative and positive emotionality show that adults become (more/less) negative as they move through the middle adult years.

Critical Thinking

3. In your view, how do the changes in social relationships that are described in this section contribute to maintaining some personality traits while modifying others in middle age?

Mid-Life Career Issues

Work in mid-life is characterized by two paradoxes: First, work satisfaction is at its peak in these years, despite the fact that most adults receive few work promotions in middle age. Second, the quality of work performance remains high, despite declines in some cognitive or physical skills.

Quality of Work Life

As we have noted before, many aspects of life improve with age. Interestingly, middle-aged workers are less likely than younger workers to experience work-related **burnout**, especially those who are *engaged* in their work in a meaningful way (Freudenberger & Richelson, 1980; James, McKechnie, & Swanberg, 2011). People with burnout lack energy, feel emotionally drained, and are pessimistic about the possibility of changing their situations. People who feel that their work is unappreciated are more subject to burnout than others. For example, one survey suggested that nearly half of the social workers in the United Kingdom suffer from burnout, and the sense of being unappreciated was the best predictor of the condition (Evans et al., 2006). Developmentalists suggest that middle-aged workers who have avoided burnout in high-stress professions are those who have learned to pace themselves and to rely less on external sources of job satisfaction (Randall, 2007).

Learning Objective 16.8

Describe how work satisfaction and job performance change in middle adulthood.

burnout

lack of energy, exhaustion, and pessimism that results from chronic stress

WORK SATISFACTION   In addition, despite the plateau in promotions that occurs for most adults in the middle years, job satisfaction is typically at its peak, as is a sense of power, or job clout. One reason for these increases may be that careers become more stable in middle age, with fewer interruptions caused by either voluntary or involuntary job changes (Bonikowska & Schellenberg, 2013; Saad, 2008). As well, both men and women in mid-life have a greater sense of control over their work lives than younger adults do (Lachman & Weaver, 1998). One reason for the increased feeling of control may be that social-cognitive skills improve from early to middle adulthood (Blanchard-Fields, Chen, Schocke, & Hertzog, 1998; Hess, Bolstad, Woodburn, & Auman, 1999). Middle-aged adults are better than they were when younger at "sizing up" people, relationships, and situations. At the same time, by middle age, they have become proficient at directing their own behaviour in ways that allow them to maintain levels of personal satisfaction even in unpleasant circumstances.

Job performance researchers Paul and Margaret Baltes have offered that maintaining high job productivity or performance is possible because adults, faced with small but noticeable erosions of cognitive or physical skill, engage in a process the Balteses call *selective optimization with compensation* (Baltes & Baltes, 1990). Three subprocesses are involved:

- *Selection.*   Workers narrow their range of activities—for example, by focusing on only the most central tasks, delegating more responsibilities to others, or giving up or reducing peripheral job activities.
- *Optimization.*   Workers deliberately "exercise" crucial abilities—such as by taking added training or polishing rusty skills—so as to remain as close to maximum skill levels as possible.
- *Compensation.*   Workers adopt pragmatic strategies for overcoming specific obstacles—for example, getting stronger glasses or hearing aids, making lists to reduce memory loads, or even carefully emphasizing strengths and minimizing weaknesses when talking to co-workers or bosses.

A growing body of evidence supports the Balteses' view of the importance of prioritizing goals (selection) in order to maximize gains (optimization) and minimize losses (compensation) (SOC) in order to achieve successful aging (Baltes & Heydens-Gahir, 2003; Young, Baltes, & Pratt, 2007; Freund, 2008). Across adulthood, though, there is shift in goal orientation—younger adults have more growth oriented goals whereas older workers focus more on maintenance and loss prevention (Ebner, Freund, & Baltes, 2006). Adopting SOC strategies seems to be especially important for older employees who have worked at less complex jobs throughout their working careers (e.g., those jobs that are less mentally demanding such as semiskilled and unskilled work) as it affords them more work-related opportunities in light of their declining abilities and work-related constraints (Zacher & Frese, 2011).

Researchers also look at other factors to explain changes in older workers' approach to job performance. For example, it is apparent that people's motivations change as they age (Kooij, De Lange, Jansen, Kanfer, & Dikkers, 2011). With increasing age, people become more motivated by *intrinsic* job characteristics such as accomplishment or achievement, use of skills, doing interesting work, autonomy, helping others or contributing to society, and job security. Compared to their younger peers, older workers are less motivated by development or challenge, advancement or promotion, working with people, recognition and prestige, and compensation and benefits. More to the point, one Canadian study found that having "insider status" that fosters a true sense of belonging resulted in higher retention of older workers (Armstrong-Stassen & Schlosser, 2011). In particular, when older workers have a sense that they are making a meaningful contribution it benefits both the individual and the organization.

Interestingly, older employees who hold negative stereotypes toward aging perform worse on a range of memory, psychomotor, physiological, and social measures (Levy, 2003; Levy & Leifheit-Limson, 2009; Levy, Zonderman, Slade, & Ferrucci, 2010, 2012; Meisner, 2012). In fact, negative age stereotyping impacts performance and perception more strongly than positive age stereotypes by a magnitude of three to one (Meisner, 2012). Unfortunately, in developed countries like Canada, negative age stereotypes are pervasive, persistent, and rigid, and outnumber positive age stereotypes. Keep in mind that negative stereotypes may be perpetuated by a self-fulfilling prophecy, in that, even though older workers are quite capable of learning and developing new skills, they fall victim to the stereotype by internalizing it and then conforming to it, thus helping to perpetuate it (Buyens, Hans, Dewilde, & De Vos, 2009; Maurer, Barbeite, Weiss, & Lippstreu, 2008). Common negative age stereotypes imply that older workers are less motivated, reluctant to change, less trusting, less healthy, and more vulnerable to family–work conflict—none of which is supported by research evidence (Ng & Feldman, 2012). The only age-related stereotype studied that received some support was that older workers are less keen on participating in training and career development activities.

Unemployment and Career Transitions

Learning Objective 16.9

Identify what factors contribute to career transitions in mid-life.

In today's competitive job market, it is not unusual for men and women to change occupations. However, career transitions can be more difficult in middle age than earlier in adulthood. For one thing, potential employers tend to believe that young adults are more capable of learning a new job than middle-aged applicants, even though research suggests that this generalization is untrue (Maurer et al., 2008; Wrenn & Maurer, 2004). Employers give middle-aged applicants higher ratings on variables such as dependability, but they tend to think that younger applicants will be able to acquire new skills (especially computer skills) more rapidly. Thus, mid-life career changers must often overcome ageism in obtaining new employment.

Career counsellors also point out that to understand mid-life career changes, it is useful to categorize workers on the basis of their reasons for changing occupations (Hom, Mitchell, Lee, & Griffeth, 2012; Zunker, 2016). They suggest that people change careers for either external or internal reasons and can thus be classified as either *involuntary* or *voluntary* career changers.

INVOLUNTARY CAREER CHANGERS Involuntary career changers are people who are in transition because of external reasons: Their skills have become obsolete, their jobs have been eliminated through organizational restructuring, or they have been laid off because of shifting economic conditions. They experience heightened levels of anxiety, depression, and substance abuse, and are at higher risk of physical illness in the months after the job loss (He, Colantonio, & Marshall, 2003; Mandal, Ayyagari, & Gallo, 2011; Mandal & Roe, 2008).

The effects of job loss include changes in family relationships and loss of self-esteem. Most strikingly, marital relationships deteriorate rapidly after one or the other spouse has been laid off. The number of hostile or negative interactions increases, and the number of warm and supportive interactions declines—which means that the crucial ratio of positive to negative interactions spirals downward. Separation and divorce become much more common as a result (Ahituv & Lehman, 2004). Interestingly, just as remarriage alleviates many of the stresses associated with divorce, re-employment seems to restore health, emotional stability, and a sense of well-being quite rapidly.

Involuntary career changers must confront a series of stressful situations, such as retraining and relocating to find work.

(Photo: Jim West/Alamy Stock Photo)

Predictably, the Big Five personality dimensions, especially neuroticism and openness to experience, contribute to mental health during involuntary career transitions across all racial and ethnic groups (Heppner, Fuller, & Multon, 1998). Nevertheless, mental health professionals suggest that the impact of an involuntary career change on an individual's life may be more directly affected by his coping skills (Zunker, 2016). For example, the person must be able to assess the situation realistically. If new work skills are needed, then the person must be able to formulate and carry out a plan for obtaining such skills. Researchers have found that mid-life career changers who have good coping skills and use them to manage involuntary transitions are less likely to become depressed (Cook & Heppner, 1997).

As with all types of stress, the effects of unemployment can be partially buffered by having adequate social support (Vinokur & van Ryn, 1993). Further, involuntary career changers benefit from career counselling that addresses both their occupational needs and their psychosocial development. Counsellors can help people who are forced to change jobs learn to think of the transition as an opportunity to re-examine goals and priorities—to treat the crisis as an opportunity (Zunker, 2016).

VOLUNTARY CAREER CHANGERS   Voluntary career changers leave one career to pursue another for a variety of personal reasons (Zunker, 2016). For example, they may believe that the new job will be more meaningful, fulfilling, and *self-actualizing* (Phanse & Kaur, 2015). Others believe the career change will enable them to do something new and creative as a way of expressing aspects of their personalities that they believe aren't utilized in their present jobs.

Twin studies and gene–environment studies suggest that the tendency to change careers voluntarily in adulthood may have a genetic basis (Chi, Li, Wang, & Song, 2016; Li, Zhang, Song, & Arvey, 2016). These findings further suggest that such transitions are a by-product of personality. Specifically, voluntary job changers appear to have a higher tolerance for risk-taking than do people who generally do not actively seek to change jobs (Roth, 2003). Most also appear to be people who do not regard either working or job-seeking as particularly stressful (Mao, 2003). However, voluntary job changers who exhibit the *honeymoon-hangover effect* seem to be chronically dissatisfied with their jobs. They experience high levels of satisfaction immediately after changing jobs (the "honeymoon"), closely followed by feelings of regret over having left behind the parts of their former jobs that they enjoyed (the "hangover"). This pattern increases the likelihood of frequent voluntary job changes (Boswell, Shipp, Payne, & Culbertson, 2009).

Although voluntary career changers have a better sense of control over their situation than do people whose job changes are forced on them, the transition may still be stressful. Spouses and family members may not understand why the person wants to change careers. Moreover, changing careers can involve periods of unemployment and, often, a reduction in income. Thus, voluntary career changers manifest many of the same symptoms of anxiety and depression seen in involuntary career changers (Ahituv & Lehman, 2004). Consequently, they, too, benefit from social support and career counselling.

In comparison to those who change careers, some workers remain locked into their current job, especially in times of high unemployment. This *involuntary non-mobility*—particularly when a worker remains in a non-preferred work situation, coupled with the perception of low employability, negatively impacts well-being. The associated depressive symptoms and lower self-ratings of their general state of health, could adversely affect both the individual and the employer (Stengård, Bernhard-Oettel, Berntson, Leineweber, & Aronsson, 2016).

Preparing for Retirement

Learning Objective 16.10

Describe how Baby Boomers are preparing for retirement.

Many middle-aged Canadians begin to prepare for retirement over a span of years before their anticipated retirement date (Bonikowska & Schellenberg, 2014). This notion of retirement is relatively new and tends to be exclusive to developed nations.

As well, the retirement preparations of the Baby Boom cohort—the large cohort of individuals who were born between 1946 and 1964—are quite different from those of their parents (Monroy, 2000; Phillipson, 2013). For their parents, retirement planning was primarily a male responsibility. In contrast, Baby Boom wives are also doing retirement planning, sometimes with their husbands and sometimes independently (Dietz, Carrozza, & Ritchey, 2003). Further, instead of transitioning directly from a full-time career to full-time retirement, most Baby Boomers seek *bridge employment*, typically a job that is related to the retiree's career but is less demanding than the job from which she is retiring (Bonikowska & Schellenberg, 2014; Gobeski & Beehr, 2009). Also, many Boomers have changed their retirement plans somewhat and plan to continue working longer than they thought they would (Anrig & Parekh, 2010). Nevertheless, the typical Boomer expects to be retired for 20 years or more, far longer than earlier generations. What do Boomers plan to do with all that time?

In a survey involving more than 3000 Baby Boomers, gerontologist Ken Dychtwald found that virtually all the respondents intended to continue working into retirement, but most intended to combine paid work with other pursuits (Mauldin, 2005). Dychtwald identified five distinct approaches to what those nonwork pursuits would be (Mauldin, 2005). *Wealth Builders* (31%) intend to spend their spare time finding new ways to make money and building on the wealth that they have already accumulated. Predictably, this group plans to devote more hours to paid work than their peers in other groups do. *Anxious Idealists* (20%) would like to do volunteer work and give money to charity after they retire, but they recognize that their tendency toward impracticality has left them with insufficient economic resources to do either. *Empowered Trailblazers* (18%) expect to spend time travelling, taking classes, and doing volunteer work, and they believe that they are financially secure enough to meet these goals. *Stretched and Stressed Boomers* (18%) are in deep trouble financially, and they are well aware of it. Most are worried about how they will be able to pay for basic necessities such as food and health care. *Leisure Lifers* (13%) intend to spend most of their time engaging in recreational pursuits and are geared toward very early retirement in their early to mid-50s.

(Photo: michaeljung/Fotolia)

One difference between Baby Boomers and earlier cohorts is that more women are involved in retirement planning.

Clearly, Baby Boomers have devoted a great deal of thought to what they would like to do during their retirement years. And, data shows retirement preparation and *financial literacy* (e.g., knowing how much to save for retirement) increase with age. Even so, of the majority of Canadians aged 55 to 64 who said they are preparing for retirement (~80%), fewer than half have indicated they know how much to save for their retirement (Uppal, 2016). Not surprisingly, fewer than half of all Boomers have actually saved enough money to be able to do what they say they wanted to do in retirement (Insured Retirement Institute, 2013; Mauldin, 2005). Further, Old Age Security and Canada Pension Plan benefits will likely be inadequate to meet their desired lifestyle needs. As well, there are declining numbers of men working at jobs that have workplace *registered pension plans*. Women, however, work predominantly in public sector jobs that offer pension plans and are still holding their own (Drolet & Morissette, 2014). Overall though, many Baby Boomers appear to be headed on a path toward disappointment when financial realities set in just a few years from now.

Nevertheless, economic analysts predict that as a group Baby Boomers are likely to enjoy levels of affluence in retirement that far exceed those of their parents

(Brucker & Leppel, 2013). Further, they are projected to be the healthiest, best-educated, and longest-living retirees in history. Thus, they are likely to substantially change their ideas about both preparing for retirement and retirement itself.

Test Yourself before going on

1. Identify which of the following statements about middle adulthood are true (T) or false (F).

   _____ (a) Adults who find their work meaningful are less likely to experience burnout.

   _____ (b) Increased feelings of control may be due to improved social-cognitive skills from early to middle adulthood.

   _____ (c) Maintaining high job productivity or performance is difficult because middle-aged adults experience noticeable erosions of cognitive and physical skills.

   _____ (d) Compared to their younger peers, older workers are highly motivated by development or challenge, advancement or promotion, working with people, recognition and prestige, and compensation and benefits.

   _____ (e) In developed countries, negative age stereotypes are pervasive, persistent, and rigid, and outnumber positive age stereotypes.

2. Both voluntary and involuntary career changers experience symptoms of _____ and _____.

3. List two ways in which Baby Boomers differ from their parents' generation with regard to preparing for retirement.

   (a)

   (b)

Critical Thinking

4. How do the retirement plans of Baby Boomers fit in with the stage and life events approaches to middle age that you learned about at the beginning of the chapter?

Summary

Theories of Social and Personality Development

16.1 Explain how the views of Erikson and Vaillant differ with regard to generativity.

- Erikson proposed that the primary developmental task of middle adulthood is to acquire a sense of generativity through mentoring younger individuals. Vaillant proposed that the stage of career consolidation precedes Erikson's generativity stage, and that the stage of keeper of the meaning follows it.

16.2 Explain how the concept of the mid-life crisis evolved into the life events perspective of middle age.

- Earlier models of the "mid-life crisis" don't seem to fit the more variable life courses we see today. A life events approach to understanding the unique stresses of middle age is more useful.

Changes in Relationships and Personality

16.3 Identify what factors contribute to the "mellowing" of partnerships in middle adulthood.

- Marital satisfaction is typically higher at mid-life than it is earlier. This higher level of satisfaction appears to be due primarily to a decline in problems and conflicts.

16.4 Describe how multigenerational caregiving and caregiver burden affect middle-aged adults' lives.

- Middle-aged adults have significant family interactions both up and down the generational chain. The two-way responsibilities of multigenerational caregiving can create a mid-life "squeeze," or a "sandwich generation." It is common for middle-aged Canadians to take on the caregiver role for an aging parent. Those who do report feeling a considerable burden and increased stress, particularly if the parent being cared for suffers from some form of dementia. Still, most caregivers report they were coping very well.

16.5 Describe how the grandparent role affects middle-aged adults.

- Most adults become grandparents in middle age. The majority have warm, affectionate relationships with their grandchildren, although there are also many remote relationships. A minority of grandparents are involved in day-to-day care of grandchildren.

16.6 Describe important qualities of social networks during middle adulthood.

- Friendships at this age continue to be intimate and central to the individual. Friendships appear to be somewhat less numerous in middle adulthood, although having many friends and visiting with them on a regular basis is linked with better mental health outcomes.

16.7 Summarize the research on personality continuity and change in mid-life.

- The Big Five personality traits and other aspects of personality are correlated across early and middle adulthood. There is evidence that a change toward higher neuroticism and lower conscientiousness in middle age is linked to poorer health and well-being.

Mid-Life Career Issues

16.8 Describe how work satisfaction and job performance change in middle adulthood.

- Middle-aged workers who are engaged in their work are less likely to experience work-related burnout. Job satisfaction is at its peak in middle adulthood, and productivity remains high. There is a shift toward being more internally motivated in mid-life. Ageism stereotypes are mostly unfounded, but can adversely influence the performance expectations and actions of self and others.

16.9 Identify what factors contribute to career transitions in mid-life.

- Involuntary career changes result from job skill obsolescence, organizational restructuring, or economic downturns. Middle-aged adults who make voluntary career transitions do so to pursue personal fulfillment or career advancement or because they are prone to risk taking.

16.10 Describe how Baby Boomers are preparing for retirement.

- Middle-aged adults prepare for retirement in several ways, such as considering retirement finances, employment options, and recreational and volunteer activities.

Policy Question

What Is Canada's Position on Stem Cell Research?

Stem cells are partially developed, unspecialized cells. In response to biochemical signals that scientists don't yet fully understand, they develop into mature, specialized cells (Campbell, Perez-Iratxeta, Andrade-Navarro, & Rudnicki, 2007). The potential of stem cells for curing neurodegenerative disorders associated with disease and disability, such as Alzheimer's, Parkinson's, or stroke, has received a great deal of attention in recent years (e.g., Luarte, Bátiz, Wyneken, & Lafourcade, 2016). For instance, a remarkable decade-long study led by Canadian researchers has shown that the stem cell treatment they developed has led to a dramatic improvement in the treatment of, and recovery from, an aggressive form of multiple sclerosis in many patients (Atkins et al., 2016). Such clinical advances have resulted in widespread public interest in stem cell research. Policy-makers are especially interested in age-related applications of stem cell research because of the anticipated health care costs associated with the demographic crisis you will read about in the chapter on Physical and Cognitive Development in Late Adulthood.

Canadian Stem Cell Research Regulations

The Canadian Institutes of Health Research (CIHR) have led the development and implementation of the policy and guidelines that govern human stem cell research. Accordingly, the Stem Cell Oversight Committee (SCOC) ensures that no research with human stem cells is funded without prior approval. Research undertaken must have

- potential health benefits for Canadians;
- free and informed consent;
- respect for privacy and confidentiality;
- no direct or indirect payment for tissues collected and no financial incentives;
- no creation of embryos for research purposes;
- respect for individual and community notions of human dignity and physical, spiritual, and cultural integrity.
  (CIHR, 2007)

Relatedly, new international stem cell research guidelines have been developed by scientists and ethicists from across the globe, including Canada (Kimmelman et al., 2016). The International Society for Stem Cell Research's *Guidelines for Stem Cell Research and Clinical Translation* is available at http://www.isscr.org/docs/default-source/guidelines/isscr-guidelines-for-stem-cell-research-and-clinical-translation.pdf?sfvrsn=2.

Types of Stem Cells

The zygote, which results from the union of a sperm and an egg, is a kind of stem cell scientists refer to as *totipotent* because it is capable of developing into an entire human being. As the zygote divides, each resulting cell retains the characteristic of totipotentiality until the eight-cell stage is reached. In other words, each of the cells in an eight-cell embryo can develop into an entire human body (see **Figure 16.2** for an illustration of the kinds of stem cells).

Once the number of cells exceeds eight, each cell can develop into one of the body's 216 different cell types, but none can become an entire human body. Stem cells of this kind are *pluripotent*. Both totipotent and pluripotent cells are known as **embryonic stem cells**. As the embryo develops, cells become committed to specific tissues and lose their pluripotent characteristics. Applying this knowledge to the treatment of disease and injury is the goal of embryonic stem cell research. Such research involves extracting undifferentiated stem cells from embryos and experimenting with them.

Some cells that are committed to a particular kind of tissue retain a degree of plasticity, even though they are not pluripotent. Such cells represent a second kind of stem cell called **somatic or adult stem cells**. One subtype of somatic cells, *multipotent*, are present in the body at all stages of development, including adulthood. For example, multipotent stem cells in bone marrow can become any kind of blood cell the body needs. The least plastic somatic stem cells, *unipotent*, normally produce only one type of mature cell, for example, liver stem cells can give rise to only liver cells. When tissues are damaged by injury, disease, or the natural aging process, the body initiates a developmental process through which these somatic stem cells mature into precisely the kind of tissue the body needs to repair itself. In the stem cell research debate, when people talk about "adult" stem cells, they are referring to these multipotent or unipotent cells.

embryonic stem cells
undifferentiated cells found in the zygote and blastocyst that are capable of indefinite self-replication and differentiation into specialized cells

somatic or adult stem cells
non-embryonic stem cells found in differentiated tissue that are capable of self-replicating and differentiating into the kind of tissue from which they originated

Figure 16.2 *Totipotent* stem cells will develop into any human cell. *Pluripotent* stem cells will grow into three very broad categories of cells: endoderm (e.g., gastrointestinal and respiratory); ectoderm (e.g., nerves and skin); and mesoderm (e.g., bones, muscle, and blood). *Multipotent* stem cells descend from pluripotent stem cells but have a more limited range of development. For example, multipotent nerve stem cells can form into only neural and glial cells. *Unipotent* stem cells can produce only one type of cell. Embryonic stem cells are of particular interest to researchers because of their potential to treat a wide range of human diseases and disorders. Scientists have also found that it is possible to manipulate somatic stem cells into forming other cell types.

(**SOURCE:** Artwork copyright © Alexandra Johnson. Printed with permission.)

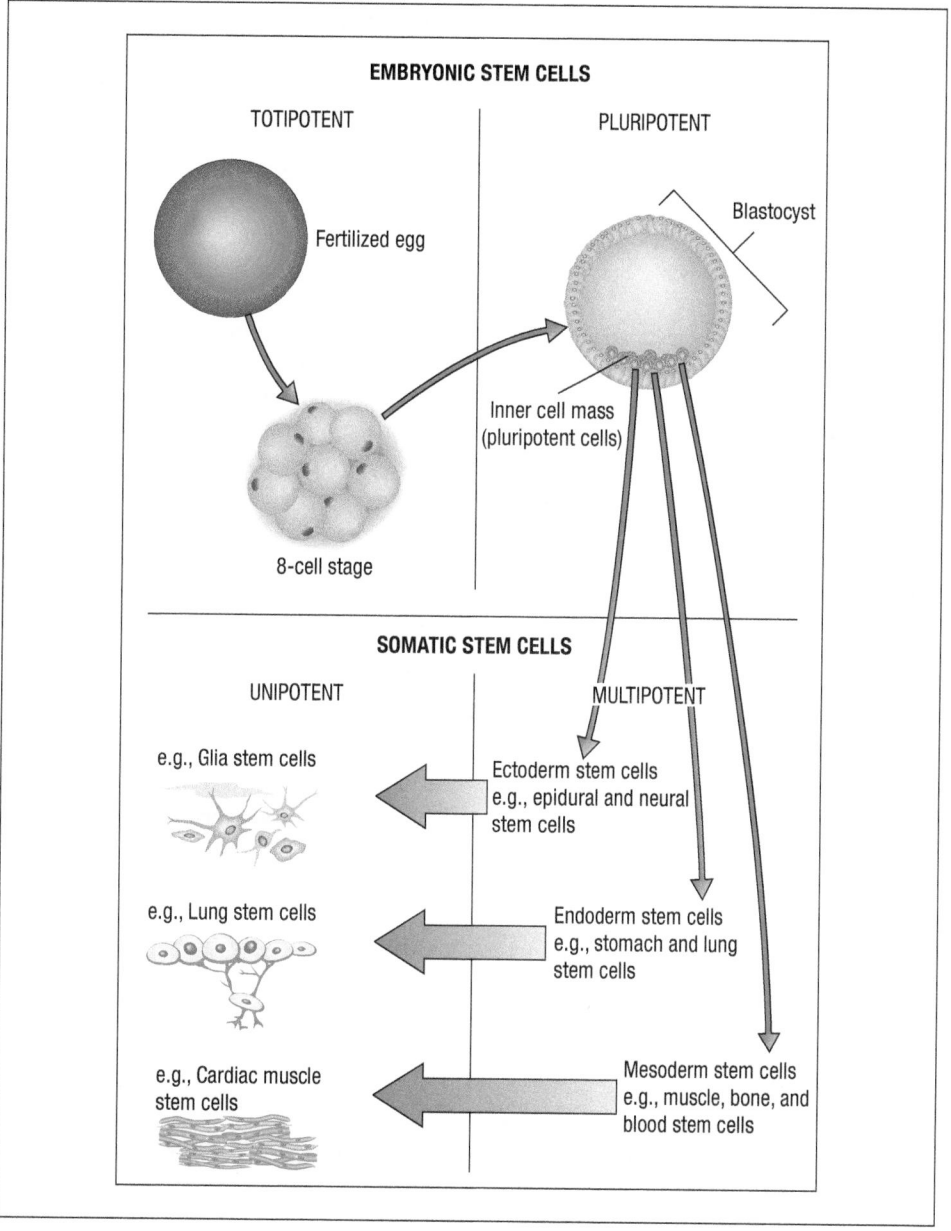

Why Is Stem Cell Research Controversial?

Many people object to embryonic stem cell research because it requires the destruction of a human embryo, which they equate with killing a human being (Santos & Ventura-Juncá, 2012; Shannon, 2004). They argue that destruction of human life is always wrong, regardless of its stage of development.

In response, advocates of embryonic stem cell research argue that the human embryo is not yet a person (Santos & Ventura-Juncá, 2012; Shannon, 2004). Furthermore, because embryonic stem cell research involves excess embryos that

(Continued)

are created for in vitro fertilization (IVF), many argue that they would be destroyed whether they were used for research or not. Thus, advocates ask, why not use them to benefit others?

The debate takes a turn when the issue of creating embryos strictly for research is raised. Many who would endorse using excess IVF embryos for research balk at the idea that sperm and ova might be joined in a test tube for the sole purpose of experimentation. They argue that leftover embryos from IVF were conceived with the intention of allowing them to develop into human beings. For this reason, they say, using leftover tissue to help others is morally acceptable, much like organ donation and transplant.

By contrast, research involving somatic stem cells extracted from the tissues of children and/or adults is unhampered by such ethical dilemmas (Stewart, 2004). The procedure for developing such cells, known as *induced pluripotent stem* (iPS) cells, was pioneered by Shinya Yamanaka (Takahashi & Yamanaka, 2006). It means that somatic cells can be reprogrammed to be like embryonic stem cells, although, epigenetic markings can remain and subtly alter the genetic structure (Scudellari, 2016). Caution in proceeding with clinical trials using iPS cells is advised until the effects of these variations can be controlled.

Can Stem Cells Cure Diseases?

Experiments have shown that it is possible to extract pluripotent cells from developing embryos and grow them in the laboratory. In fact, a few such cells can turn into millions in a matter of weeks (National Institute of Health, 2009). Moreover, scientists have learned how to keep them from differentiating into specialized cells. In other words, they know how to maintain the cells' pluripotent characteristics indefinitely. What isn't known, though, is exactly how to initiate and control specialization.

Still, there is no doubt that stem cells can be used to treat diseases. In fact, bone marrow stem cells have been used in the treatment of blood diseases for decades (Stewart, 2004). And in recent years, scientists have identified many new somatic stem cell "populations"—in muscle tissue, the liver, the brain, skin, hair follicles, and many other tissues, including menstrual blood, which contains 30 times more stem cells than bone marrow (Kerr, 2006; National Institute of Health, 2009). Thus, most experts agree that the potential for using stem cells to treat disease—or even to moderate the effects of aging—is tremendous.

Even so, the most ardent advocates of stem cell research warn that much remains to be learned before similar clinical experiments can be carried out with human beings. For one thing, they caution that stem cell transplants, like organ transplants, can be rejected by the body that receives them. Moreover, studies suggest that laboratory-grown cells can develop into malignant tumours (e.g., Laird, 2005; Tai et al., 2005). Consequently, stem cells must be used with caution to treat diseases in humans until more is known about controlling the tissue rejection and tumour development.

Moreover, Canadian scientists affiliated with the Ottawa Health Research Institute have identified a single gene, *Oct4*, that regulates the formation, self-renewal, and differentiation of embryonic stem cells (Campbell et al., 2007; Campbell & Rudnicki, 2013). The *Oct4* gene is not normally active in mature stem cells but has been found to be active in cancerous cells. In many ways this supports the theory that cancer is a disease related to stem cell division—that is, the greater the number of organ tissue cell divisions, the greater the cancer risk (Tomasetti & Vogelstein, 2015). Thus, the discovery that *Oct4* is a master regulator has implications for finding new approaches to fighting cancer.

Stem Cell Research Policies

Stem cell research policy in Canada can be summarized as follows: (1) emphasis on public rather than private funding for stem cell research, (2) strict regulation of stem cell research, and (3) prioritization of embryonic over somatic stem cell research.

Your Turn

- Think about some of the risks associated with stem cell therapy, such as immune rejection and tumour formation. If you had a debilitating medical condition, such as a spinal cord injury, liver disease, multiple sclerosis, or Parkinson's disease, explain why you would or wouldn't be willing to participate in clinical trials.
- Of what benefit is it to society to develop and implement stem cell cures?
- As a Canadian taxpayer, you help fund stem cell research. (1) What benefits, assurances, and protection would you expect to receive from any treatment or cures that result from publicly funded research? (2) What would be a fair price to pay for any needed stem cell therapy? (3) Should stem cell therapy be available to all Canadians regardless of their ability to pay? (4) What impact would making stem cell therapy available to non-Canadians (so-called "medical tourists") have on the universality of our Canadian health care system?
- Other than the treatment of diseases, what applications might there be for stem cell research?

Chapter 17

Physical and Cognitive Development in Late Adulthood

Gina Sanders/Fotolia

 ## Learning Objectives

VARIABILITY IN LATE ADULTHOOD

17.1 Identify the life expectancy and longevity trends in Canadian seniors.

17.2 Describe contemporary theories of biological aging.

17.3 Describe the health of older adults in Canada.

PHYSICAL CHANGES

17.4 Describe how the brain changes in late adulthood.

17.5 Describe the common types of sensory changes that occur in late adulthood.

17.6 Summarize the behavioural effects of changes in the body systems of older adults.

MENTAL HEALTH

17.7   Differentiate Alzheimer's disease from other dementias.

17.8   Describe what the research suggests about depression among older adults.

COGNITIVE CHANGES

17.9   Identify how older and younger adults differ in memory function.

17.10   Describe what wisdom and creativity theory and research reveals about cognitive functioning in late adulthood.

How long do you expect to live? You may be one of the increasing number of people who live to be 100 years of age or more. Centenarians (people who live to the age of 100) are one of the fastest-growing segments of the population in developed countries. In 2011, there were 5825 centenarians living in Canada, and if current trends continue, there will be close to 80 000 by the year 2061 (Statistics Canada, 2012n). An online quiz can help you determine your chances of living to 100 (https://www.livingto100.com/calculator).

Most people, when they think about the prospect of living 80, 90, or 100 years, worry about age-related declines in health, mobility, and cognitive functioning. Certainly, there are some very real physical declines as we age. But for many people, as you will learn in this chapter, even very old age is a time of continuing health and enthusiasm for life.

Variability in Late Adulthood

gerontology

the scientific study of aging

The scientific study of aging is known as **gerontology**. For many years, gerontologists thought about old age almost exclusively in terms of decline and loss. However, perspectives on seniors are rapidly changing, and late adulthood is now thought of as a period of tremendous individual variability rather than one of universal decline. To study the changes that occur in people's lives over time, Canadian researchers have embarked on a project called the Canadian Longitudinal Study on Aging (CLSA). Data is being collected about changes that occur in the key areas of people's lives, including physical and psychological health as well as social and economic factors (CLSA, 2016; Kirkland et al., 2015). They plan to track 50 000 Canadians aged 45 to 85 for at least 20 years. The researchers will be looking at factors that affect how adults age, why some people stay healthy as they get older and others develop health problems, and the life-changing events people face as they get older and how they cope. The CLSA website is www.clsa-elcv.ca.

Learning Objective 17.1

Identify the life expectancy and longevity trends in Canadian seniors.

Life Expectancy and Longevity

Animal species vary widely in their expected lifespans. Fruit flies, for instance, live for only a few weeks, while giant Galapagos turtles often live to be more than 100 years old. Among humans, cases such as that of Jeanne Calmet, a French woman who lived to be 122 years old, suggest that the maximum lifespan is about 120 years, but this estimate may change as more individuals pass the centenarian mark. Still, there is no denying that death rates increase dramatically when humans reach their 60s, and scientists are learning more about the variables that distinguish individuals who die in their 60s from those who live for 100 years or more. These differences in life length have persuaded some biologists that there may be a universal genetic process that triggers age-related declines and limits the lifespan (e.g., Hayflick, 1977, 1987).

SUBGROUPS   The 65 and older age group is the fastest growing segment of the Canadian population and, as of 2015, it surpassed the 14 and younger segment—a trend that is predicted to continue (Statistics Canada, 2015k). Gerontologists divide older adults into subgroups of the *young old* (aged 60 to 75), the *old old* (aged 75 to 85), and the *oldest old* (aged 85 and over). And, it's the oldest old who are the fastest-growing subgroup of the senior population in Canada. This means that terms such as *octogenarian* (a person in his 80s) and *centenarian* (a person over 100 years of age) will be used far more often than in the past. As mentioned above, throughout the developed world, including Canada, the subgroup of seniors who are 100 years old or older is growing at a more rapid rate than any other segment of the population. Demographers project that within fifty years the centenarian population in Canada will approach 80 000—more than a 13-fold increase (Statistics Canada, 2012o). As in all periods of older adulthood, the overwhelming majority of these 100-year-olds will be women.

LIFE EXPECTANCY   There are more elderly women than men because of a sex difference in life expectancy from birth. Of note, the gender gap has been narrowing in Canada since 1981, at which time women outlived men by 7.1 years (Statistics Canada, 2001c). The latest estimates indicate that a male baby born in 2012 can expect to live to be 79.4 years old and a female baby can expect to live to be 83.6 years old, a difference of only 4.2 years (Statistics Canada, 2016k).

You may be surprised to learn that once you reach young adulthood your odds of dying during a given year remain quite constant—doubling every eight years—at least to the age of roughly 107 (Gavrilov & Gavrilova, 2011). On average, a 65-year-old Canadian man lives close to age 84, and once a man reaches his mid-80s, he is likely to live to be around 91 (Statistics Canada, 2016k). Life expectancy among Canadian women is somewhat longer. The average 65-year-old woman is likely to live to almost age 87, and the women who make it to this age can expect to live close to age 94.

LONGEVITY   The general tendency to live a long life is partly inherited (Govindaraju, 2015; Xiao et al., 2015). Identical twins are more similar in length of life than are fraternal twins, and adults whose parents and grandparents were long-lived are also likely to live longer (Plomin & McClearn, 1990). Overall though, genetic influences on longevity found in twin and family studies have shown that only a modest 20–30% of the overall variation in lifespan is accounted for by genetic factors (Gavrilova & Gavrilov, 2009; Fraga, 2009; Kahn & Fraga, 2009; Xiao et al., 2015). Furthermore, it now appears that genetic influences on longevity are minimal before the age of 60, but increase thereafter (Hjelmborg et al., 2006). This means that factors other than genetics play a large role in us making it to late adulthood.

Theories of Biological Aging

Current explanations of **senescence**—the gradual deterioration of body systems that happens as an organism ages after reaching maturity—look to changes on multiple levels, including cellular and molecular. Although we are still in search of a universally accepted explanation of biological aging, most researchers agree it is caused by changes in genetic and epigenetic mechanisms that are shaped by environmental and *stochastic* (random or unpredictable) variables (Berdasco & Esteller, 2012; Govindaraju, 2015; Kahn & Fraga, 2009; Rodriguez-Rodero et al., 2011; Xiao et al., 2015). Although the aging process itself is not a disease, it increases vulnerability to disease (Hayflick, 2007). Therefore, there is now hope that through a better understanding of basic aging mechanisms, it may become possible to postpone the degenerative diseases associated with aging, and thus increase human longevity (Li, Daniel, & Tollefsbol, 2012).

THE HAYFLICK LIMIT   Until half a century ago, it was believed that human body cells were immortal—they could continue to divide indefinitely. From this perspective,

Learning Objective 17.2

Describe contemporary theories of biological aging.

senescence

physical changes and declines associated with aging

age-related degeneration was thought to be due to wear and tear (Goldsmith, 2011). This belief changed when Hayflick and Moorhead (1961) demonstrated that human body cells have a limited lifespan—they divide a specific number of times and then stop. Their findings were reinforced by research demonstrating that cells taken from the embryos of different species and placed in a nutrient solution divide only a fixed number of times, after which the cell colony degenerates. Human embryo cells divide about 50 times; those from the Galapagos tortoise divide roughly 100 times; chicken cells divide only about 25 times. Furthermore, cells taken from human adults divide only about 20 times, as if they have already "used up" some of their genetic capacity (Norwood, Smith, & Stein, 1990). The theoretical proposal that emerged from such observations is that each species is subject to a time limit, beyond which cells simply lose their capacity to replicate themselves (Hayflick, 2000, 2007). This phenomenon, known as the **Hayflick limit** after its discoverer, transformed our understanding of the biological aging process.

TELOMERES   The Hayflick limit theory was further strengthened by the discovery that each chromosome in the human body (and in other species, too) has, at its tip, a string of repetitive DNA called a **telomere** (Blackburn, 2012; Blackburn & Gall, 1978; Olovnikov, 1971, 1996). Among other functions, telomeres serve as a kind of timekeeping mechanism for the organism. Researchers have found that the length of telomeres is reduced slightly each time a cell divides, so that the remaining length in a 70-year-old is much shorter than what is found in a child. Thus, it seems that there is a crucial minimum telomere length; when the telomere length falls below a certain threshold, disease or death comes fairly quickly.

TELOMERASE   Within a decade after the discovery of the role of telomeres in aging, another breakthrough in our understanding of cellar aging was made. Certain cells, such as stem cells and germ line cells (gametes), make use of an enzyme, *telomerase*, to restore telomeres to the ends of their chromosomes, ensuring that these cells can continue to replicate themselves (Greider & Blackburn, 1985). However, most *adult cells* (somatic cells) in the body lack the capacity to produce high levels of telomerase, and so the telomeres of these cells inevitably shorten until they reach a critical length, stop replicating, and eventually die. This eventually leads to the death of the entire organism (Jin, 2010). Thus, telomerase, or the lack of it, helps to explain why most adult cells have a finite capacity to replicate.

CELLULAR DAMAGE   Another variable of aging focuses on the cells' ability to repair breaks in DNA. Breaks in DNA strands are common events, resulting from unknown metabolic processes. Because the organism is apparently unable to repair all the damage, the theory proposes, the accumulation of unrepaired breaks results over time in a loss of cellular function, and the organism ages (Tice & Setlow, 1985). A related theory focuses on another cellular process called **cross-linking**, which occurs more often in cell proteins of older adults than in those of younger adults. Cross-linking occurs when undesirable chemical bonds form between proteins or fats. In skin and connective tissue, for example, two proteins called collagen and elastin form cross-linkages, either between their molecules or within a given molecule. The resulting molecules cannot assume the correct shape for proper function, leading to effects such as wrinkling of the skin and arterial rigidity.

Yet another type of cellular process that may contribute to aging relates to the body's ability to deal with **free radicals** (Kenyon, 2010; Liu, Cao, & Finkel, 2011; Rattan, 2006). Free radicals, which are molecules or atoms that possess an unpaired electron, are a normal by-product of body metabolism and can arise, for example, as a result of exposure to certain substances in foods, sunlight, X-rays, and air pollution. Free radicals also occur more frequently in older than in younger people's bodies because of age-related deterioration of the mitochondria, the cell structures that convert food into

Hayflick limit
the theoretical proposal that each species is subject to a genetically programmed time limit after which cells no longer have any capacity to replicate themselves accurately

telomere
string of repetitive DNA at the tip of each chromosome in the body that appears to serve as a kind of timekeeping mechanism

cross-linking
the formation of undesirable bonds between proteins or fats

free radicals
molecules or atoms that possess an unpaired electron

energy (Nichols & Melov, 2004). These radicals, especially the subgroup called *oxygen free radicals*, enter into many potentially harmful chemical reactions, resulting in irreparable cellular damage that accumulates with age. For example, oxidation reactions caused by free radicals can damage cell membranes, thereby reducing the cell's protection against toxins and carcinogens.

STEM CELLS As you will recall from the Policy Question in the chapter on Social and Personality Development in Middle Adulthood, *stem cells* are undifferentiated cells that are capable of self-renewal and differentiation into specialized adult cells. Unlike adult cells, stem cells will divide an unlimited number of times and for this reason are referred to as immortal. In the absence of stem cells, an organism would waste away once the existing adult cells had reached the Hayflick limit.

For the most part, human tissues are composed of adult cells that have a finite lifespan (Hayflick limit). These cells will die and the tissue will shrink, unless replenished by a fresh supply of cells. The only source of these new cells is stem cells, which make up only a very small portion of our tissue's cells. Stem cells help keep human tissue healthy by replacing adult cells that have become senescent or damaged. Stem cells are present in tissue in an undifferentiated state, but can be triggered to divide indefinitely as needed. For instance, after a tissue injury that results in cell loss (a torn muscle, for example), a stem cell can divide asymmetrically by generating a copy of itself (stem cell self-renewal) and an adult cell at the same time. The newly created cells replace the lost cells and after regeneration is complete, the stem cell returns to a dormant state. Since there is only a small pool of stem cells, they ensure survivability by producing high levels of telomerase, which maintains telomere length which, in turn, inhibits stem cell death (Smith & Daniel, 2012).

Throughout life, stem cells are subject to the same environmental stresses and intracellular damages that impact all cells over time (Childs, Durik, Baker, & van Deursen, 2015; Jung & Brack, 2014; Koliada, Krasnenkov, & Vaiserman, 2015; Oh, Lee, & Wagers, 2014; Pollina & Brunet, 2011; Schultz & Sinclair, 2016; Wong, Solis, Chen, & Huang, 2015). Some stem cells may display an age-dependent decrease in number. But more importantly, just as the adult cells in any part of the body can become damaged over time, so too can stem cells. For example, damage to aged stem cells may result from the accumulation of irreversible modifications, including genetic alterations, mitochondrial DNA damage, and telomere shortening. These modifications contribute to a decline in stem cell functioning, wherein damaged adult cells are not repaired or replaced quickly enough, which leaves the body more vulnerable to disease processes and breakdown. Thus, over time, it seems stem cells gradually lose their ability to effectively sustain the body's cells.

THE ROLE OF EPIGENETICS IN STEM CELL AGING The genotype determines the maximum lifespan of different species, whereas the variation in longevity of individuals within a species seems to be affected by the accumulation over time of epigenetic errors that compromise adult stem cell function (Fraga, 2009). Epigenetic changes do not affect the actual makeup of a cell's DNA, but rather, how that DNA functions or expresses itself. In other words, epigenetics can be thought of as changes in gene expression caused by factors that do not change the actual DNA makeup. The evidence is mounting that suggests epigenetic mechanisms regulate nearly every aspect of cell biology, including stem cell senescence. It has been shown, for example, that epigenetic changes, in response to environmental cues and stochastic stresses, can degrade the capacity of stem cells to regenerate new cells to replace or repair old or damaged adult cells which, in turn, contributes to disease vulnerability and foreshortened longevity (Berdasco & Esteller, 2012; Pollina & Brunet, 2011; Fraga, 2009; Rodriguez-Rodero et al., 2011; Smith & Daniel, 2012). In fact, it is now possible to predict a person's age based on their epigenetic status (Bocklandt et al., 2011).

Critical Thinking

Like stem cells, cancer cells also contain high levels of telomerase. What challenges does this pose for developing treatments for cellular aging?

Figure 17.1 Most Canadian seniors rated their health as good to excellent.

(**SOURCE:** Adapted from Statistics Canada, July 2012, Health Facts Sheets, 2012, Chart 2— Percentage reporting very good or excellent health, by age group and sex, household population aged 12 or older, Canada, 2011 – description, Cat. No. 82-625-XWE [Statistics Canada, 2012q.)

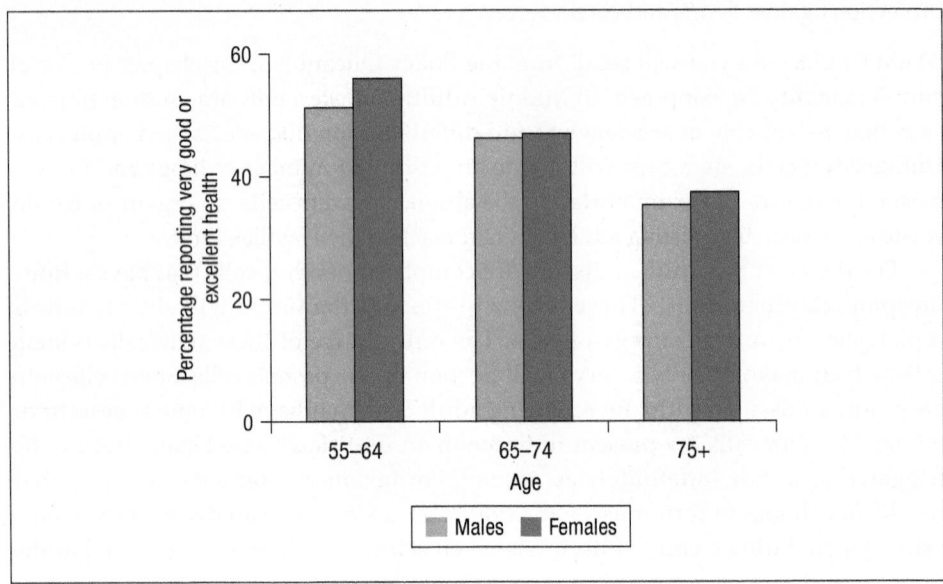

Learning Objective 17.3

Describe the health of older adults in Canada.

Health

Stereotypes may lead you to think that most seniors are in poor health. However, the majority of older adults do not suffer from ailments that seriously impair their day-to-day functioning (FIFARS, 2012). Moreover, the inevitable physical declines that are associated with aging do not seem to decrease older adults' satisfaction with their lives.

SELF-RATED HEALTH As **Figure 17.1** indicates, a substantial number of older adults across all three age subgroups regard their health as very good to excellent (Statistics Canada, 2016l). These data contradict stereotypes of old age as a period of illness. Still, the proportion of seniors with fair or poor health is a great deal higher than the equivalent proportions for young and middle-aged adults. For instance, the proportion of fair or poor self-rated health scores jumped from ~6% in Canadians aged 20 to 34 up to ~22% in seniors aged 65 and older (Statistics Canada, 2016l). Thus, as you might suspect, health is the single largest factor determining the trajectory of an adult's physical and mental status over the years beyond age 65. As you read more about the prevalence of disability and disease among older adults, keep Figure 17.1 in mind. You will see that these data are a testimony to the emotional resilience of older adults, a majority of whom are able to maintain an optimistic view of themselves and their lives in the face of growing physical challenges.

Further, their optimistic view seems to help protect older adults against the long-term effects of serious health threats, such as strokes. Researchers have found that seniors who rate their health as good, regardless of how an objective observer might rate it, recover more physical and cognitive functions after a stroke than their peers who rate their health more poorly (Hillen, Davies, Rudd, Kieselbach, & Wolfe, 2003). Older adults who are already suffering from one or more chronic diseases at 65 show far more rapid declines than do those who begin late adulthood with no disease symptoms. In part, of course, this is an effect of the disease processes themselves. Cardiovascular disease results, among other things, in restricted blood flow to many organs, including the brain, with predictable effects on an adult's ability to learn or remember. Longitudinal studies show that adults with this disease show earlier declines in all mental abilities (Schaie & Willis, 2005). And, of course, those suffering from the early stages of Alzheimer's disease or another disease that causes dementia will experience far more rapid declines in mental abilities than will those who do not have such diseases.

LIMITATIONS ON ACTIVITIES   University of Manitoba health care researchers Betty Havens and Marcia Finlayson (1999) define **functional status** as a measure of an individual's ability to perform certain roles and tasks, particularly self-help tasks and other chores of daily living. Daily living tasks are grouped into two categories: **activities of daily living (ADLs)** include bathing, dressing, using the toilet, and so forth; **instrumental activities of daily living (IADLs)** include doing housework, cooking, and managing money.

As you can see from **Figure 17.2**, more than half of older Canadians reported being overweight or obese—a factor that is implicated in an increased risk for other health conditions including diabetes, hypertension, and arthritis (Health Canada, 2012b; Statistics Canada, 2016l). Of these, the physical diseases and conditions that are most likely to contribute to some functional disability in late adulthood and lower health-adjusted life expectancy (HALE) are arthritis and hypertension (Turcotte & Schellenberg, 2007; PHAC, 2012d). Although arthritis is very common in both genders, women aged 65 or higher are considerably more likely than men to suffer from arthritis, so they are also more often limited in their ability to carry out the various movements and tasks necessary for independent life (Gilmour & Park, 2006; Statistics Canada, 2016l). Since women are more likely to be widowed and thus to lack a partner who can assist with these daily living tasks, it is not surprising that more women than men live with their children or in nursing homes.

functional status

a measure of an individual's ability to perform certain roles and tasks, particularly self-help tasks and other chores of daily living (Havens & Finlayson, 1999)

activities of daily living (ADLs)

self-help tasks such as bathing, dressing, and using the toilet

instrumental activities of daily living (IADLs)

more complex daily living tasks such as doing housework, cooking, and managing money

Figure 17.2   This graph shows the proportions of Canadian seniors who suffer from select chronic conditions that limit their activity and may necessitate help for activities of daily living.

(**SOURCE:** Adapted from Statistics Canada, March 13, 1996, Health Reports 8(3), pp. 7–15, Table 5, Cat. No. 82-003 [Wilkins & Park, 1996].)

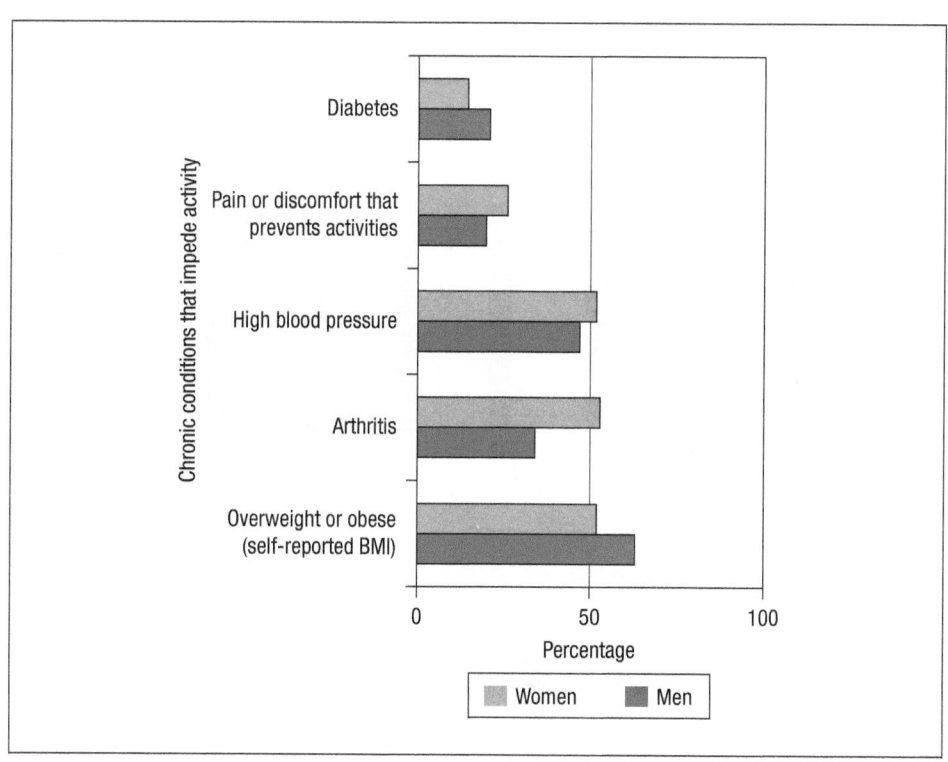

As you would probably predict, disability rates increase dramatically as seniors get older—71% of Canadians aged 60 to 79 and 82% of those over age 80 experienced at least one chronic health condition, and more than half reported having two or more (Broemeling, Watson, & Prebtani, 2008). As well, seniors with chronic health conditions, especially when accompanied by chronic pain, are significantly more likely to experience difficulty performing basic daily life activities (Gilmour & Park, 2006; Statistics Canada, 2016l). Consequently, the increase in the number of the oldest old means that the population of **frail elderly**, older adults who cannot care for themselves, is also likely to grow significantly. As a result, demographers and economists have become concerned about the ability of young and middle-aged adults to support the growing number of seniors.

frail elderly

seniors whose physical and/or mental impairments are so extensive that they cannot care for themselves

HEALTH HABITS   The same health habits that are important predictors of health and longevity in early adulthood continue to be significant predictors in late adulthood (Turcotte & Schellenberg, 2007). Those health habits that are within one's control can prevent the development of chronic conditions or limit their severity (Ramage-Morin, Shields, & Martel, 2010) (see **Figure 17.3**). Of these, perhaps high levels of physical activity, not smoking, and maintaining a healthy weight are the most effective ways to extend life expectancy (Nusselder, Franco, Peeters, & Mackenbach, 2009). In fact, a recent study found that modifiable lifestyle factors were responsible for dramatically shortened life expectancy. The study began by comparing health risk factors between Ontarians and British Columbians (Canada's healthiest population) to determine what factors might account for the difference in life expectancy. Next the researchers analyzed the top risk factors among Ontarians and found that five factors (smoking, physical activity, diet, alcohol, and stress) accounted for an estimated 60% of all deaths and shaved 7.5 years off Ontarians' life expectancy and almost 10 years off their health-adjusted life expectancy (i.e., quality of life years). Even more pronounced, there was a remarkable 20-year life

Figure 17.3   Prevalence of good health that is positively associated with eight potentially modifiable factors in Canadians aged 65 years and older.

(**SOURCE:** Adapted from Statistics Canada, 2010, 2009 Canadian Community Heath Survey—Healthy Aging. In Ramage-Morin, M. & Martel, L. (2010). Health-promoting factors and good health among Canadians in mid- to late life. *Health Reports, 21* (3), 1–9. Table 2, Cat. No. 82-003-X,)

1. Never smoked daily/Quit for 15 or more years
2. Not obese
3. Five or more times per day

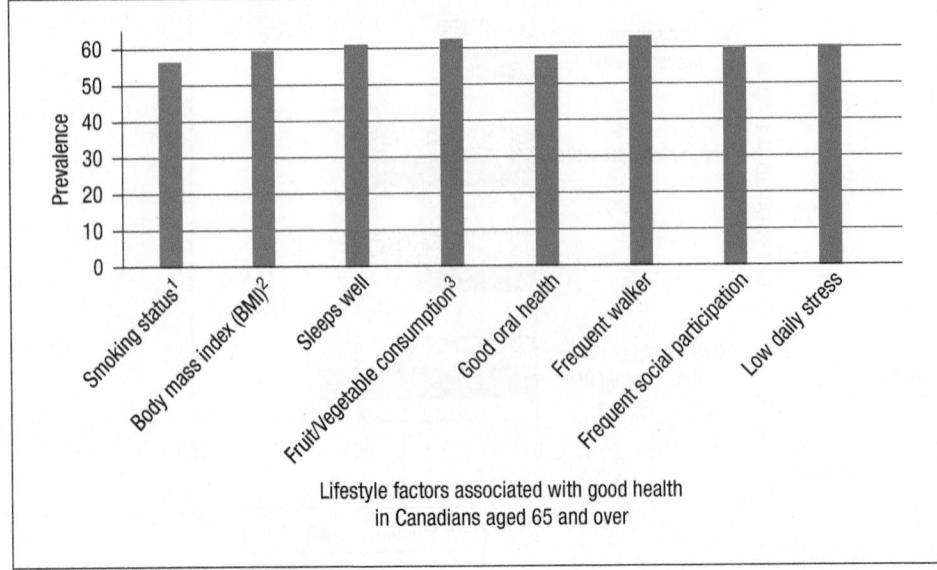

Lifestyle factors associated with good health
in Canadians aged 65 and over

expectancy difference between those individuals who had all five behavioural risks and those with none. Of the five risk factors, physical activity, proper diet, and not smoking contribute the most to increasing life expectancy and health-adjusted life expectancy in Ontarians—a finding that may also apply across Canada. (Calculate your own life expectancy at http://www.projectbiglife.ca/life/.)

The notion that physical exercise is a key contributor to good health in people over 65 is familiar enough. Not only has it been clearly linked to greater longevity (Manini et al., 2006), but also to lower rates of diseases such as heart disease, stroke, some cancers, osteoporosis, type 2 diabetes, gastrointestinal problems, and arthritis (PHAC, 2012f; Reimers, Knapp, & Reimers, 2012). If anything, physical exercise seems to be even more important in the later years than at earlier ages.

In addition to the many benefits for the aging body, physical activity also appears to be one of the more promising preventive strategies for cognitive impairment and decline in seniors. A review of the research has shown that people who are more physically active in later life have a reduced incidence of dementia and cognitive impairment (Erickson & Liu-Ambrose, 2016; Jedrziewski, Ewbank, Wang, & Trojanowski, 2010, 2014; Kirk-Sanchez & McGough, 2014). Plus, people who participate in higher levels of physical activity have slower rates of cognitive decline compared to those who are less active. Some studies have even provided evidence that regular exercise of moderate intensity, including aerobic, resistance, and multicomponent exercises (e.g., Tai Chi that involves balance, coordination, and movement) improve performance across a broad range of cognitive areas, such as attention, information processing speed, executive function (e.g., decision making), working memory, and motor control and coordination (Bauman et al., 2016; Bherer, 2015; Hagovská, Takáč, & Dzvoník, 2016; Kirk-Sanchez & McGough, 2014; Voelcker-Rehage & Niemann, 2013).

Healthy exercise strategies for older adults, including those in the overweight and obese categories, should focus on improving physical fitness and function more so than on weight loss. Although a combination of aerobic and resistance exercise appears to be the most effective strategy for achieving physical fitness (Decaria, Sharp, & Petrella, 2012), older adults can still achieve a significant reduction in mortality risk and lower rates of functional decline by regularly performing less vigorous physical activities, such as walking, gardening, and household chores (Hirsch et al., 2010). Helpful guidelines for increasing the fitness levels of inactive seniors include the *Canadian Physical Activity Guidelines for Older Adults* (Canadian Society for Exercise Physiology, 2012) and *Physical Activity Tips for Older Adults (65 Years and Older)* (PHAC, 2012f). These guides are readily available to provide practical information about getting active. They promote the attitude that physical activity for health can easily be built into a person's daily routine, regardless of current level of activity.

There are many ways to maintain physical fitness in old age. In China, seniors can often be found practicing Tai Chi in the early morning.

A complement to these guides is *Eating Well with Canada's Food Guide*, which provides advice about eating healthy portions based on the four basic food groups (Health Canada, 2011). Eating well and being physically active are important factors in controlling the rising levels of obesity in Canadian seniors (Turcotte & Schellenberg, 2007). In addition to having higher levels of daily caloric energy expenditure and healthier diets, researchers have also found that having a good appetite seems to put seniors at a lower mortality risk (Shahar et al., 2009).

Critical Thinking

How would you characterize your own chances for a long life based on the genes you have inherited and on your health habits?

Physical Changes

Despite variability in health and functioning among seniors, several changes in physical functioning characterize the late adult years for almost everyone.

The Brain and Nervous System

Learning Objective 17.4
Describe how the brain changes in late adulthood.

Four main changes occur in the brain during the adult years: a reduction of brain weight, a loss of grey matter, a decline in the density of dendrites, and slower synaptic transmission speed (i.e., the rate at which information flows among neurons). The most central of these changes is the loss of dendritic density. Dendrites are "pruned" during the first few years after birth, so that redundant or unused pathways are eliminated. The loss of dendrites in middle and late adulthood does not seem to be the same type of pruning. Rather, it appears to be a decrease in useful dendritic connections (Sowell et al., 2003).

Research suggests that experience as well as aging is involved in the loss of dendritic density. Neurologists have found that seniors with higher levels of education show significantly less atrophy of the cerebral cortex, as well as more efficient processing of information, than those who have fewer years of schooling (Farfel et al., 2013; Marques et al., 2016; Marques et al., 2015). Moreover, the brains of well- and poorly educated seniors do not differ in areas that are less involved in academic learning than the cerebral cortex is. This finding suggests that education itself is the cause of the reduced atrophying of the cerebral cortex rather than some general factor, such as socioeconomic status, which is coincidentally related to education.

Dendritic loss also results in a gradual slowing of synaptic speed, with a consequent increase in reaction time for many everyday tasks. Neural pathways are redundant enough that it is nearly always possible for a nerve impulse to move from neuron A to neuron B, or from neuron A to some muscle cell. Neurologists usually refer to this redundancy as **synaptic plasticity**. But with the increasing loss of dendrites, the shortest route may be lost, so plasticity decreases and reaction time increases.

synaptic plasticity
the redundancy in the nervous system that ensures that it is nearly always possible for a nerve impulse to move from one neuron to another or from a neuron to another type of cell (e.g., a muscle cell)

The Senses

Learning Objective 17.5
Describe the common types of sensory changes that occur in late adulthood.

In the chapter on Physical and Cognitive Development in Middle Adulthood, you read about declines in sensory and other physical functions that occur in middle age. Such deficits become larger in late adulthood, and several more serious threats to the health of these systems arise.

VISION   In addition to presbyopia (farsightedness), late adulthood can bring other vision defects due to body changes. For example, blood flow to the eye decreases (perhaps as a side effect of atherosclerosis), which results in an enlarged "blind spot" on the retina and thus a reduced field of vision. The pupil does not widen or narrow as much or as quickly as it previously did, which means that the older adult has more difficulty seeing at night and responding to rapid changes in brightness (Kline & Scialfa, 1996).

In addition, a significant minority of older adults suffer from diseases of the eye that further diminish visual acuity and adaptability. For example, among Canadians aged 65 and over, roughly one in five have *cataracts* (a condition in which the lens inside the eye becomes clouded and obscures vision) and 6% have *glaucoma* (a progressive loss of vision caused by optic nerve damage that is often associated with increased fluid pressure buildup in the eye) (Millar, 2004). The leading cause of field restriction for older Canadians is *macular degeneration*, a type of age-related deterioration of the retina that results in loss of central vision. An estimated 20% of those aged 65 to 75, and 37% of those over age 75, have the condition (Somani et al., 2009). Thus, many older adults must adapt to significant impairments of vision, and the process of adaptation doesn't always go smoothly. Researchers have found that middle-aged adults adjust more easily than older adults to the difficulties associated with living with a serious vision impairment (Lindo & Nordholm, 1999). Moreover, vision loss has a greater negative effect on a senior's sense of well-being. Fortunately, many age-related diseases of the eye can be effectively treated with medications and/or surgery.

HEARING   Wear and tear on the auditory system results in some hearing loss (*presbycusis*) beginning in middle adulthood, but these gradual losses don't typically add up to functionally significant loss until late adulthood. Auditory problems, unlike many other disabilities of old age, are more likely to be experienced by men than by women. This sex difference is normally attributed to differential exposure to noise: More men have worked in environments with high levels of noise (at least in current cohorts of older adults in developed countries).

Hearing difficulties in late adulthood have several components: First, there is the loss of ability to hear high-frequency sounds (Roland & Kutz, 2015). Both cross-sectional and longitudinal studies suggest that, for the range of sounds used in normal human speech, the loss after age 60 is such that a given sound has to be about 1 to 2 decibels louder each year for the individual to report that he hears it (Fozard, 1990; Kline & Scialfa, 1996).

Second, most older adults develop difficulties with word discrimination sounds (Roland & Kutz, 2015). Even when the sound is loud enough, older adults have more difficulty identifying individual words they have just heard (Schieber, 1992). In addition, many adults over age 60 have problems hearing under noisy conditions. The loss of ability to discriminate individual words is even greater in such situations, so large gatherings become increasingly difficult for older adults.

tinnitus

a persistent ringing in the ears

Tinnitus is a persistent ringing in the ears that, among seniors, peaks in early old age and decreases somewhat thereafter (McCormack, Edmondson-Jones, Somerset, & Hall, 2016; Negrila-Mezei, Enache, & Sarafoleanu, 2011). It is believed that tinnitus is a symptom associated with many conditions, including those pertaining to the ear, nose and nasal sinuses, hypertension, and arteriosclerosis (Canadian Hearing Society, 2013; Negrila-Mezei et al., 2011). An estimated 14 to 42% of seniors worldwide experience tinnitus (McCormack et al., 2016) and many patients with annoying tinnitus report a strongly diminished *quality of life* because of it (Carlsson et al, 2015). Furthermore, it seems that the higher the age of tinnitus onset, the greater the tinnitus-related distress (Schlee et al., 2011).

Hearing aids improve many adults' quality of life.

(Photo: Lisa F. Young/Shutterstock)

Even mild hearing loss can pose communication problems in some situations. Those with such problems may also be perceived by others as disoriented or suffering from poor memory, especially if the person with the hearing loss is unwilling to admit the problem and ask for a comment or an instruction to be repeated. Nonetheless, the older adult with a hearing impairment is *not* necessarily socially isolated or unhappy. Mild and moderate hearing losses, even if uncorrected with a hearing aid, are simply not correlated with measures of general social, emotional, or psychological health among seniors. Only severe hearing loss is associated with an increase in social or psychological problems, including heightened rates of anxiety and depression (Carlsson et al., 2015).

Presbycusis and the other changes in hearing seem to result from gradual degeneration of virtually every part of the auditory system. Older adults secrete more ear wax, which may block the ear canal; the bones of the middle ear become calcified and less elastic; the cochlear membranes of the inner ear become less flexible and less responsive; and the nerve pathways to the brain show some degeneration (Roland & Kutz, 2015). Notably, many studies are now discovering that hearing loss in seniors is associated with structural and functional changes in the brain that seem to accelerate cognitive decline and increase the risk of developing dementia (e.g., Cardin, 2016; Deal et al., 2016; Mudar & Husain, 2016).

Critical Thinking

How do you think a hearing impairment is likely to affect the life of an older adult? Aside from wearing a hearing aid, how could a person with a moderate hearing impairment adapt her life so as to reduce the impact of the disability?

TASTE, SMELL, AND TOUCH   The ability to taste the five basic flavours (sweet, sour, bitter, salty, and umami) does not seem to decline over the years of adulthood. Taste receptor cells (taste buds) have short lives and are constantly replaced (Bornstein, 1992). But other changes in the taste system affect older adults, such as the secretion of somewhat less saliva, producing a sensation of "woolly mouth" for some. Many seniors also report that flavours seem blander than in earlier years, leading them to prefer more intense concentrations of flavours, particularly sweetness (de Graaf, Polet, & van Staveren, 1994). But it may well be that this perception of flavour blandness is largely due to a loss of the sense of smell.

The sense of smell clearly deteriorates in old age. The best information comes from a cross-sectional study in which researchers tested nearly 2000 children and adults on their ability to identify 40 different smells—everything from pizza to gasoline (Doty et al., 1984). As **Figure 17.4** reveals, young and middle-aged adults had equally good scores on this smell identification test, but scores declined rapidly after

Figure 17.4   Doty's data show a very rapid drop in late adulthood in the ability to identify smells.

(**SOURCE:** Based on Doty, R.L., Shaman, P., Appelbaum, S.L., Bigerson, R., Sikorski, L., & Rosenberg, L. (1984). Smell identification ability: Changes with age. *Science, 226,* 1441–1443.)

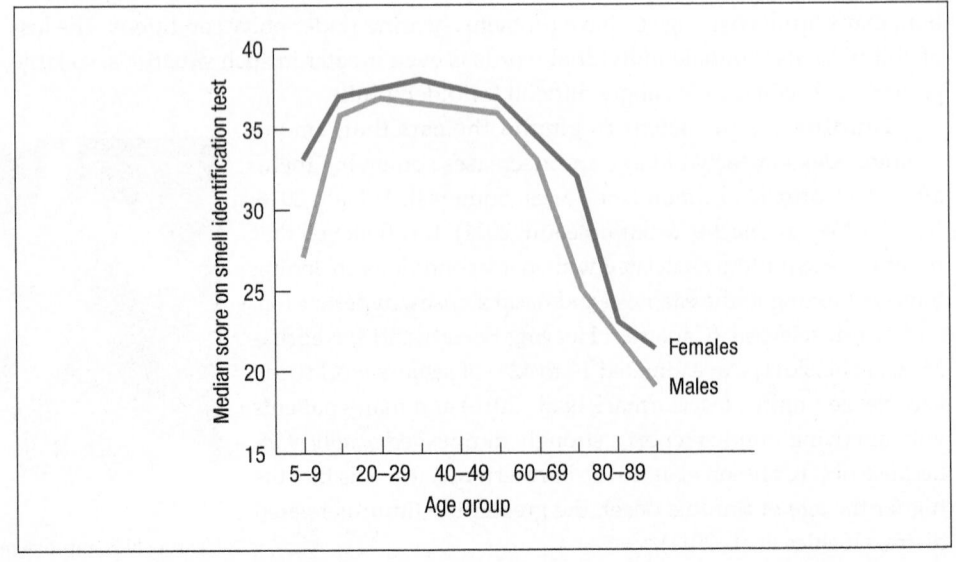

age 60. However, the loss of sensitivity to odours is far greater among elderly men than women (Morgan, Covington, Geisler, Polich, & Murphy, 1997).

These changes in taste and smell can reduce many pleasures in life. But they can also have practical health consequences. Smells enhance the pleasure of food, so as the sense of smell becomes less acute, seniors are less motivated to prepare tasty food. In some cases, this can result in inadequate nutrition or significant dietary imbalances.

The skin of elderly adults is less responsive to cold and heat (Johnson, Minson, & Kellogg, 2014). Research suggests that the loss of sensitivity occurs in a pattern that is a reversal of the proximodistal principle of growth. In other words, the extremities, usually the feet, are the first body parts that decline in sensitivity. Consequently, seniors are less able to benefit from the potential comforts associated with physical stimuli. For example, for an elderly person to be able to feel a warm bath, the water temperature may have to be so high that it will burn the skin. Similarly, older adults have an increased risk of hypothermia because their skin doesn't signal the brain efficiently when it is exposed to low temperatures that would make younger people quickly pull on a jacket or cover up with a blanket (Kingma, Frijns, Saris, van Steenhoven, & van Marken Lichtenbelt, 2010).

Behavioural Effects of Physical Changes

Learning Objective 17.6

Summarize the behavioural effects of changes in the body systems of older adults.

The great majority of older adults cope effectively with most everyday tasks—buying groceries, managing their finances, reading bus schedules, planning their lives, and so on—despite changes in vision, hearing, and other physical functions. Thus, in addition to knowing what these changes are and how they might be explained, it's important to know just how they affect older adults' daily lives.

GENERAL SLOWING The biggest single behavioural effect of age-related physical changes is a general slowing down. Dendritic loss at the neuronal level clearly contributes substantially to this general slowing, but other factors are also involved, including arthritic changes in the joints and loss of elasticity in the muscles. Everything takes longer—writing things down, tying one's shoes, and adapting to changes in temperature or changes in light conditions (Schaie & Willis, 2005). Even tasks that involve executive functions (e.g., using working memory and planning tasks), which tend to decline very little at earlier ages, nonetheless are done more slowly (Turner & Spreng, 2012, 2015).

Further, many developmentalists believe that the decline in the speed of nerve impulses is responsible for age-related difficulties in translating thoughts into action. For example, neurologists sometimes assess nervous system functioning by having patients demonstrate a physical action involving a tool, such as hammering. Demonstrating an appropriate hand posture and moving the arm in an appropriate way are taken as indicators of neurological health. Developmentalists have found that healthy individuals in late adulthood make more initial errors than younger adults in trying to carry out such activities (Peigneux & van der Linden, 1999). However, they correct their errors just as quickly as those who are younger. Consequently, neuropsychologists think that general slowing of brain activity interferes with older adults' retrieval of the knowledge they need to accomplish the task and that they use behavioural feedback to compensate for mistakes.

This older man has bought himself a very sporty car and doubtless thinks of himself as still a skilful driver. But it is nonetheless true that many of the physical changes associated with aging will make it harder for him to respond quickly, to see clearly in glare, and to adapt rapidly to changing driving conditions.

(Photo: ysbrandcosijn/Fotolia)

Age-related physical changes add up to really significant differences in functioning in a complex motor activity, such as driving. Young adults have more auto accidents than any other age group, primarily because they drive too fast. But older adults have more accidents per kilometres driven (Market Wire, 2003). Of course, other physical changes beyond general slowing contribute to driving problems in old age. Changes in the eyes mean that older adults have more trouble reading signs at night and adjusting to the glare of oncoming headlights. In addition, reduced range of motion in the neck, which often accompanies arthritis, may contribute to automobile accidents involving elderly drivers. The general increase in reaction time affects a senior's ability to switch attention from one thing to the next and, therefore, react quickly and appropriately when a vehicle or obstacle appears unexpectedly. Unfortunately, researchers have found that older adults are typically unaware of the ways in which their driving skills have diminished since they were younger (Horswill, Sullivan, Lurie-Beck, & Smith, 2013). For many, the first indication that their driving skills are impaired is a serious accident.

Changes in temperature sensitivity, together with general slowing, lead to increases in accidental burns. For example, seniors are more likely to burn themselves when they mistakenly pick up a hot pan while cooking. The neurological message "Put down this pan because it's going to burn your skin" moves from the hand to the brain almost instantaneously in a young or middle-aged adult. Among older adults, however, a greater amount of heat is required to initiate the message, the message itself travels to the brain more slowly, and the response from the brain that signals the hand to let go of the pan travels more slowly as well. Consequently, burns are far more common in late adulthood than earlier.

SLEEPING AND EATING PATTERNS Another common effect of physical change is a shift in sleep patterns in old age, which occurs among both healthy and less healthy seniors (Maglione & Ancoli-Israel, 2012). Adults older than age 65 typically wake up more frequently in the night and show decreases in rapid eye movement (REM) sleep, the lighter sleep state in which dreaming occurs. Older adults are also more likely to wake early in the morning and go to bed early at night. They become "morning people" instead of "night people." And because their night sleep is more often interrupted, older adults also nap more during the day to accumulate the needed amount of sleep. These changes in sleep and activity patterns are presumed to be related to changes in nervous system functioning.

The ability of the brain to regulate appetite also changes with advancing age (Cheah et al., 2014). When you eat, your blood sugar rises, resulting in a chemical message to the brain that creates a sensation called **satiety**, the sense of being full. The feeling of satiety continues until your blood sugar drops, at which time another chemical message is sent to the brain that causes you to feel hunger. In older adults, the satiety part of the pattern seems to be impaired (De Vadder & Mithieux, 2015). As a result, older adults may feel hungry all the time and may overeat. Or, conversely, they may often feel satiated which can contribute to the so called *anorexia of aging* and malnutrition (Atalayer & Astbury, 2013; Benelam, 2009; Kmieć, Pétervári, Balaskó, & Székely, 2013; Volkert, 2013). In addition to changes in the physiological regulation of satiation, the risks of obesity, being underweight, and malnutrition are higher in seniors who live and/or eat alone for whom loneliness and/or depression may play a role (Arganini & Sinesio, 2015; Tani et al., 2015; Tani, Sasaki, Haseda, Kondo, & Kondo, 2015). Still, whether they live in the community or in long-term care, seniors, especially those with dementia and/or low physical self-feeding capability, are at risk for unhealthy eating behaviours and would benefit from interventions provided by trained caregivers (Liu et al., 2016; Liu, Galik, Boltz, Nahm, & Resnick, 2015).

MOTOR FUNCTIONS The various physical changes associated with aging also combine to produce a reduction in stamina, dexterity, and balance. The loss of stamina clearly arises in large part from the changes in the cardiovascular system, as well as from changes in muscles. Dexterity is lost primarily as a result of arthritic changes in the joints.

Another significant change, one with particularly clear practical ramifications, is a gradual loss of the sense of balance (Flores, 2012; Speechley, 2011). Older adults, who may be quite mobile in their home environments, are likely to have greater difficulty

satiety

the feeling of fullness that follows a meal

Critical Thinking

How might age-related changes in facial muscles contribute to stereotypes about "grumpiness" in seniors?

Research Report

Falls in Seniors: A Major Public Health Concern

Falls are a leading cause of injury, disability, and injury-related deaths in seniors, making falls and the associated complications among the most serious problems that face older adults (Billette & Janz, 2011). Across Canada, it is estimated that 20 to 30% of seniors are likely to fall at least once each year, and half of those who fall will fall more than once in a year. This makes falls the leading cause of hospitalization due to injury (85%) for seniors (PHAC, 2014a, 2016b; Scott, Wagar, & Elliott, 2010).

Falls can be lethal in themselves or lead to conditions that increase the likelihood of death; for example, 20% of seniors with hip injuries die within a year of the fracture (Billette & Janz, 2011). Although most seniors who suffer falls eventually heal from their injuries, many never fully recover. Non-fatal fall injuries can contribute to a loss of independence, confusion, immobilization, fear of falling, depression, chronic pain, and functional decline (i.e., the ability to perform ADLs such as meal preparation, housework, and personal care). As well, there is often a greater reliance on family members and other caregivers for support and a significant use of a range of health care and social services, including both short-term and long-term care placement (Do, Chang, Kuran, & Thompson, 2015; Finlayson & Peterson, 2010; Flores, 2012).

A large proportion of falls and fall-related injuries in older people results from multiple risk factors acting either singularly or in complex interactions. Biological risk factors include those due to natural age-related decline, as well as the effects of acute and chronic health conditions. Aspects of physical health that increase the risk of falling include muscle weakness or impairment, joint pain, reduced physical fitness (particularly in the lower body), difficulty with gait and balance, visual or hearing impairment, breathing difficulties,

hypotension, dizziness, and vertigo (Do et al., 2015; Flores, 2012; Speechley, 2011). Chronic illnesses and conditions, such as arthritis, stroke, cardiovascular disease, osteoporosis, and physical disabilities, are seen as underlying factors for many of these physical risk factors. As well, seniors suffering from cognitive impairment due to, for example, depression, anxiety, dementia, or delirium, also have a higher falling risk.

Many illnesses and conditions are treated with medications that can result in adverse reactions, either on their own or in combination with other medications, that increase the risk of falls. For example, the psychotropics—sedative, anti-anxiety, and antipsychotic drugs that reduce mental alertness or impair perception and coordination—are often implicated. As well, many cardiac drugs can cause a drop in blood pressure when standing or leaning over leading to dizziness and/or loss of consciousness. So too, alcohol consumption, regardless of quantity and particularly in connection with other medical conditions, raises the risk of falls (Finlayson & Peterson, 2010; Flores, 2012; Tremblay & Barber, 2013).

The presence of environmental hazards increases susceptibility to falls in older people. Common tripping and stumbling hazards include clutter and obstacles on the floor, including loose rugs and pets; slippery floors and stairs; poor lighting, especially on stairs; a lack of or poorly positioned grab bars, especially in the bathroom; and cracked, uneven, or ice- and snow-covered walkways. As well, certain situations or risky behaviours can increase the likelihood of falling for those who are prone to mobility or balance difficulties. These may involve climbing, reaching, bending, standing on unsteady chairs, non-use of prescribed assistive devices such as canes and walkers, wearing loose-fitting clothing or shoes, carrying heavy or awkward objects, or even engaging in vigorous activities such as skiing or tennis (Billette & Janz, 2011; Do et al., 2015; Tremblay & Barber, 2013).

---

handling an uneven sidewalk or adapting their bodies to a swaying bus. Such situations require the ability to adjust rapidly to changing body cues and the muscular strength to maintain body position, both of which decline in old age. As a result, older adults fall more often (see **Research Report**).

Older adults also have increasing difficulty with fine motor movements (Voelcker-Rehage, 2008). Such losses are small and gradual with respect to well-practised skills, such as handwriting. Moreover, fine motor skills with older adults' areas of expertise, such as playing a musical instrument, decline little and actually can continue to improve in old age with additional practice (Krampe, 2002). However, research suggests that some fine motor activities, especially those that require learning a new pattern of movement, may be extremely difficult for seniors—even with practice (Voelcker-Rehage, 2008). For example, an older adult may take far longer than a young or middle-aged adult to learn complex computer mouse skills, such as clicking and dragging objects across the screen. Even with much practice, older adults would likely perform with less accuracy and speed than when they were younger.

Chapter 17

SEXUAL ACTIVITY   Another behaviour that is affected by the cumulative physical changes of aging is sexual behaviour. You read in the chapter on Physical and Cognitive Development in Middle Adulthood that the frequency of sexual activity declines gradually in middle adulthood. Both cross-sectional and longitudinal data suggest that this trend continues in late adulthood (Lindau et al., 2007).

The decline in the frequency of sexual activity in late adulthood doubtless has many causes (Basson, 2010; Lee et al., 2016; Steptoe et al., 2016). The continuing decline in testosterone levels among men clearly plays some role. The state of one's overall health plays an increasingly larger role with advancing age. For example, antidepressants and blood pressure medication sometimes produce impotence as a side effect; chronic pain and illnesses (e.g., arthritis, CVD, and diabetes) may also affect sexual desire. Stereotypes that portray old age as an essentially asexual period of life may also have some effect.

Despite declining frequency, though, the majority of adults continue to be sexually active in old age (Lee et al., 2016; Lindau et al., 2007; Thomas, Hess, & Thurston, 2015). Moreover, the physiological capacity to respond to sexual stimulation, unlike other aspects of functioning, appears not to diminish with age. As you may imagine, this creates some complications for long-term care residents, especially those with dementia and/or those who are still married to another person (Simpson, Horne, Brown, Dickinson, & Wilson, 2016; Wiskerke & Manthorpe, 2016). Greater acknowledgement of, and ways of addressing, sexuality and intimacy needs in care homes is much overdue.

Test Yourself before going on

1. The brain loses interconnectivity as a result of the decreases in _____.
2. An older adult is most likely to perform at the same levels as she did in earlier adulthood on tasks involving the sense of _____.
3. Match each term with its definition.
   _____ (a) macular degeneration
   _____ (b) tennitus
   _____ (c) satiety
   _____ (d) psychotropics
      (i) feeling of fullness after eating
      (ii) loss of central vision caused by retinal deterioration
      (iii) drugs that reduce mental alertness or impair perception and coordination
      (iv) continuous ringing in the ears

Mental Health

dementia

a neurological disorder involving problems with memory and thinking that affect an individual's emotional, social, and physical functioning

Learning Objective 17.7

Differentiate Alzheimer's disease from other dementias.

Alzheimer's disease

a very severe form of dementia, the cause of which is unknown

The best-known mental health problems of old age are the **dementias**, a group of *major neurocognitive disorders* (APA, 2013) involving problems with memory and thinking that affect an individual's emotional, social, and physical functioning. Dementia is the leading cause of institutionalization of seniors in Canada, especially women (Alzheimer Society of Canada, 2010) (see **Development in the Real World**). However, depression is also a concern in the late adult years.

Alzheimer's Disease and Other Dementias

Alzheimer's disease is a severe form of dementia. The early stages of Alzheimer's disease usually become evident very slowly, beginning with subtle memory difficulties, repetitive conversation, and disorientation in unfamiliar settings. Then memory for recent events begins to go. Memory for long-ago events or for well-rehearsed cognitive procedures, such as simple calculations, is often retained until late in the illness,

Development in the Real World

Institutionalization Among Canadian Seniors

Research results, such as those graphed in Figure 17.2, suggest that the average older adult will spend at least a few years with some kind of disability or chronic disease. How often do such problems require nursing-home care? There are several answers to that question, depending on what statistics you look at.

In Canada, roughly the same number of women and men aged 65 to 74 are in long-term care—less than 3% of seniors in this age group (McGregor & Ronald, 2011). However, when we look at the oldest old, the number rises to about 20%, and of these, there are 50% more women than men living in institutions. Still, these numbers may be lower than you would have guessed.

There are many factors that predict whether a senior in Canada will need institutional care (Statistics Canada, 2012r; Ramage-Morin, 2006; Tanuseputro et al., 2015). First off, two health conditions have been found to be predictive. Those seniors with a serious cognitive impairment and those with uncorrected visual impairment were, respectively, 3.2 and 3.0 times more likely to be institutionalized. Second, seniors with low or lower-middle household income had more than a twofold chance of being institutionalized compared to the higher income groups. And third, the odds of being institutionalized for those seniors who perceived themselves as having only fair or poor health were 2.6 times higher than for seniors who had good to excellent self-perceived health status.

It is true that placement in a nursing home is often followed by death within a relatively short time. One Canadian study found that nearly 12% of seniors died within a year of admission (Tanuseputro et al., 2015). However, it is not true that nursing-home care shortens a person's life. There is evidence that the move to a care facility itself is a contributing factor in rapid decline and death as it can be extremely challenging to adapt to a new environment, especially when it is beyond one's ability to understand why one is moving, and/or residents can have difficulties communicating their needs, level of distress, or ill health (Aneshensel, Pearlin, Levy-Storms, & Schuler, 2000). Still, significant differences are found between the two main types of long-term care facilities in Canada. Residents living in for-profit homes had a 10% higher risk of mortality and an ~25% higher risk of hospitalization compared to those in not-for-profit facilities (Tanuseputro et al., 2015). These are important considerations for Canadian policy makers to consider when contemplating the development and construction of new nursing home beds (Ronald, McGregor, Harrington, Pollock, & Lexchin, 2016).

In Canada, there is a growing need to create alternatives to institutionalization as the number of seniors increases over the next several decades, many of whom will have some form of dementia in their later years (Alzheimer Society of Canada, 2010). Two suggested preventative measures include increasing the physical activity levels for all Canadians over age 65 and delaying the onset of dementia through healthy diet and lifestyle programs that target dementia-free Canadian adults. Two supportive measures include the development of informal caregiver skill-building and support programs, as well as linking newly diagnosed dementia patients and their informal caregivers with case managers to coordinate care.

presumably because these memories can be accessed through many alternative neural pathways (Anderson, 2013).

Eventually, however, an individual with Alzheimer's disease may fail to recognize family members and may be unable to remember the names of common objects or how to perform routine activities such as brushing her teeth or dressing. Those afflicted with Alzheimer's suffer declines in the ability to communicate, as well as the ability to carry out daily self-care routines. The changes in appetite regulation you read about earlier in this chapter are particularly problematic for those with Alzheimer's, because they can't rely on habit to regulate their eating behaviour, as healthy older people do. Left to their own devices, Alzheimer's victims may consume as many as three or four complete meals at one sitting without realizing how much they have eaten. Consequently, their eating behaviour must be closely supervised.

People with Alzheimer's also have difficulty processing information about others' emotions, such as facial expressions (Burnham & Hogervorst, 2004). Some have problems controlling their own emotions and display sudden bursts of anger or even rage. Others exhibit an increased level of dependency and clinginess toward family or friends (McLaughlin et al., 2010). In addition, research suggests that the incidence of depression among seniors with Alzheimer's disease may be as high as 40% (Guo et al., 2016).

DIAGNOSING AND TREATING ALZHEIMER'S DISEASE Alzheimer's disease can be definitively diagnosed only after a person has died. At autopsy, the brains of Alzheimer's victims are far more likely to contain extensive *neurofibrillary tangles* than are the brains of individuals with other kinds of dementia (Anderson, 2013). Neurofibrillary tangles are stringy masses of tissue that appear to "clog" connections between neurons. They are typically surrounded by deposits of proteins and other substances called *plaques.*

The difficulty involved in diagnosing Alzheimer's disease is magnified by the fact that nearly 80% of seniors complain of memory problems (Anderson, 2013). As a result, researchers are currently looking for a set of predictors that may distinguish individuals who are in the process of developing Alzheimer's from those who are suffering from the effects of normal aging. A few indicators, such as the syndrome known as *mild cognitive impairment*, show promise. At present, though, a diagnosis of Alzheimer's disease represents a health professional's best educated guess about the source of an individual's cognitive difficulties.

A few drugs appear to slow down the progress of Alzheimer's disease. Cholinesterase inhibitor drugs such as *donepezil*, *rivastigmine*, and *galantamine*, although not a cure, benefit some Alzheimer's patients by helping to preserve the ability of damaged neural endings to transmit neural impulses from one neuron to the next (Anderson, 2013; Bannon, Boswell, & Schneider, 2010; Diamond, 2011).

Experimental studies have shown that training Alzheimer's sufferers to use specific strategies (e.g., making notes in a journal, having a readily accessible daily planner, making lists, etc.) can to some degree improve their performance of everyday memory-related tasks, such as being ready for appointments and remembering to take medication (Lowenstein, Acevedo, Czaja, & Duara, 2004). As mentioned earlier in the Health Habits section, there is much emerging evidence that daily physical activity and physical exercise (aerobic in particular) are by far the best natural way to keep the brain healthy. In particular, regular physical activity is associated with reducing the risk of, and delaying or slowing the development of cognitive impairment and dementia including Alzheimer's disease (Beeri & Middleton, 2012; Buchman et al., 2012; Voss et al., 2013). Unfortunately, a major challenge is getting sedentary seniors engaged in safe, enjoyable, regular exercise and physical activity—caregiver support is often required to initiate and maintain activity routines (McCurry et al., 2010).

HEREDITY AND ALZHEIMER'S DISEASE Genetic factors seem to be important in some, but not all, cases of Alzheimer's (Anderson, 2013; Bannon et al., 2010). Researchers have found a gene variant on chromosome 19 (*apoliprotein E4* or *ApoE4*) that controls production of a protein that is linked to Alzheimer's disease (Diamond, 2011). When errors in the production of this protein occur, the dendrites and axons of neurons in the brain become tangled and, as a result, do not function as efficiently. However, this gene does not act alone. Many other genes combine with *ApoE4* in ways that researchers don't yet fully understand to trigger the onset of the disease (Elias-Sonnenschein, Bertram, & Visser, 2012; Reiman et al., 2007).

Even in families with very high prevalences of Alzheimer's disease, ages of onset are highly variable. In one family study, age of onset ranged from age 44 to age 67, and in another, onset ranged from the early 60s to the mid-80s (Silverman, Ciresi, Smith, Marin, & Schnaider-Beeri, 2005). Moreover, there were wide variations in the severity of the disease's behavioural effects and in the length of time the victims lived once they developed Alzheimer's.

OTHER TYPES OF DEMENTIA Strictly speaking, dementia is a symptom and not a disease, and neurological research indicates that Alzheimer's and non-Alzheimer's dementias involve very different disease processes. For example, signs of dementia frequently appear after a person suffers multiple small strokes; in this case, the condition is called **vascular dementia** (Kannayiram, 2012). The brain damage caused by such strokes is irreversible. However, in contrast to most cases of Alzheimer's disease, various forms of therapy—occupational, recreational, and physical—can improve victims' functioning.

vascular dementia

a form of dementia caused by one or more strokes

In addition, dementia can be caused by depression, metabolic disturbances, drug intoxication, Parkinson's disease, hypothyroidism, multiple blows to the head (frequent among boxers), a single head trauma, some kinds of tumours, vitamin B_{12} deficiency, anemia, or alcohol abuse (Anthony & Aboraya, 1992; Butters et al., 2004; Suryadevara, Storey, Aronow, & Ahn, 2003). Clearly, many of these causes are treatable; indeed, roughly 10% of all patients who are evaluated for dementia turn out to have some reversible problem. So, when an older person shows signs of dementia, it is critical to arrange for a careful diagnosis.

INCIDENCE OF ALZHEIMER'S AND OTHER DEMENTIAS Experts also agree that the rates of all kinds of dementias, including Alzheimer's disease, rise rapidly among people after age 85 (Tom et al., 2015). Evidence from research indicates that roughly 1 in 11 Canadian adults over age 65 show significant symptoms of some kind of dementia, and by the time they reach age 85, about 1 in 3 suffered from moderate to severe symptoms of dementia. Of those with dementia, almost two-thirds (64%) have Alzheimer's disease (Alzheimer Society of Canada, 2010; Lindsay, Sykes, McDowell, Verreault, & Laurin, 2004).

Depression

The earliest studies of age differences in depression suggested that older adults were at higher risk for this disorder than any other age group, which contributed to a widespread cultural stereotype of the inevitably depressed senior. However, several Canadian studies have shown the rate of depression declines with age (e.g., CIHI, 2010; Statistics Canada, 2002b; Streiner, Cairney, & Velhuizen, 2006). **Figure 17.5** shows the declining prevalence rates for depressive and anxiety disorders in older Canadians.

Learning Objective 17.8

Describe what the research suggests about depression among older adults.

Figure 17.5 Prevalence of lifetime mood disorders for Canadian men and women age 55 years and over.

(SOURCE: Streiner, D.L., Cairney, J., & Veldhuizen, S. (2006). The epidemiology of psychological problems in seniors. *Canadian Journal of Psychiatry*, 51(3), 185–191. Printed with permission of Canadian Psychiatric Association.)

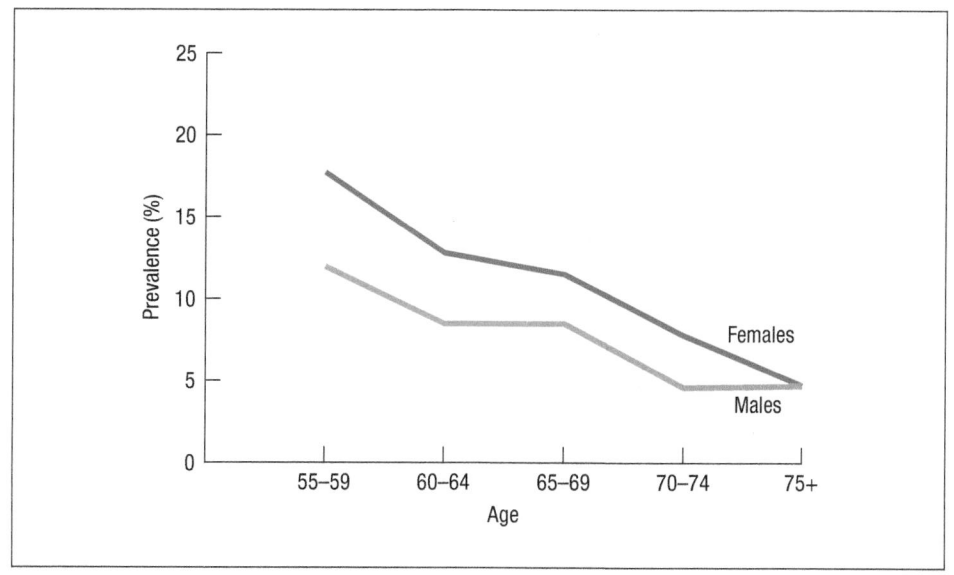

Still, the full story on depression in late adulthood is complex—although seniors living independently in the community have the lowest levels (~6%) (Østbye et al., 2005), roughly one in four older Canadians with serious medical conditions or those in the early stages of Alzheimer's disease experience depression (Cappeliez, 2009). Further, the rates of depression (diagnosed and/or symptoms of) are almost double that (45%) for those seniors living in residential care settings such as long-term care or nursing homes (CIHI, 2010).

DIAGNOSIS Ageism can influence the diagnosis of depression in seniors. Signs of depression in older adults may be dismissed as old-age "grumpiness" by family members. It can also be difficult for health care providers to recognize the signs of depression in seniors; when seniors seek help for their depression, they are most likely to access medical services (hospitals and family doctor) rather than mental health services, and to focus more on their physical symptoms than emotional concerns (Canadian Coalition for Seniors' Mental Health (CCSMH) (2009). As well, as noted earlier, depression may be mistaken for dementia because it can cause confusion and memory loss. It is also important to distinguish between depressed mood and full-fledged clinical depression. The latter involves problems (e.g., feelings of hopelessness, insomnia, lack of appetite, loss of interest in social activities) that are of long duration and are severe enough to interfere with a person's ability to carry out normal activities (APA, 2013; CCSMH, 2009). By contrast, chronic depressed mood among seniors, known as **geriatric dysthymia**, typically does not progress to clinical depression and has been found to be related to life stresses (Kocsis, 1998).

geriatric dysthymia

chronic depressed mood in older adults

RISK FACTORS The risk factors for depression and dysthymia among seniors are not difficult to identify: inadequate social support, inadequate income, emotional loss (such as following the deaths of a spouse, family, or friends), and nagging health problems. However, the strongest predictor appears to be health status. Across all ethnic and socioeconomic groups, the more disabling conditions older adults have, the more depressive symptoms they have (Patten et al., 2006, 2010; PHAC, 2010d). Determining the direction of causation in the association between health status and depression is difficult because depression impairs an older adult's ability to respond to therapeutic interventions that might be helpful (Mast, Azar, MacNeil, & Lichtenberg, 2004). To put it differently, seniors who have chronic health conditions, such as arthritis, are more likely to be depressed than their peers who do not, but depression is a risk factor for a poor response to therapy. Thus, for many seniors, the link between health and depression becomes circular.

Gender is also a risk factor; in Canada, depressed women outnumber men two to one among seniors, just as they do at younger ages (Patten et al., 2006, 2010). However, sorting out the causes of this difference is difficult. For one thing, women appear to be more resilient in response to many life stressors. The death of a spouse, for example, is more likely to lead to depression in a man than in a woman (Byrne & Raphael, 1999; Chen et al., 1999). Such findings suggest that depression in women may more often be the result of an accumulation of everyday stresses, while traumatic events are more likely to bring on feelings of depression in men. Another possible explanation is that women are more willing to seek help for depression and, as a result, are more often diagnosed.

There is a fair amount of consistency in findings that seniors living in poverty are at higher risk for depression than others (Areán et al., 2010). Education is also independently related to depression; that is, poorly educated older adults are more likely to be depressed (Gallagher-Thompson, Tazeau, & Basilio, 1997; Miech & Shanahan, 2000). The association between education and depression exists among seniors at all levels of income and in all racial and ethnic groups.

Figure 17.6 Suicide rates in Canada are more than three times higher for males than for females, but the difference for those aged 65-plus increases to more than six times higher for males than for females.

(SOURCE: Adapted from Statistics Canada, 2001, Health Reports 13(2), Table 2, p. 15, Cat. No. 82-003 [Langlois & Morrison, 2002].)

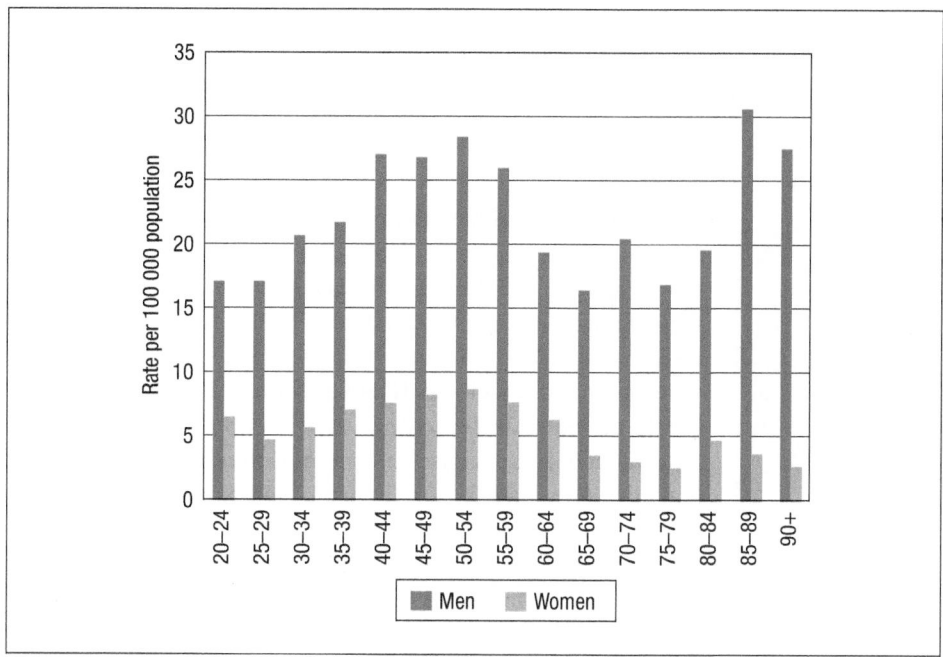

SUICIDE Suicide rates per 100 000 for all age groups of Canadians have increased almost 75% since the 1950s (Navaneelan, 2012; Statistics Canada, 2012s; WHO, 2011). Historically, Canadian seniors had higher than average rates of suicide until the late 1980s. Since that time, the suicide rate for seniors has declined to a level slightly below the national average, except for those 85 and older. Despite higher rates of depression among women in Canada, elderly men are more than six times as likely to commit suicide, as illustrated in **Figure 17.6**.

The reasons for this dramatic gender difference are not entirely clear. The loss of economic status through retirement may be more troubling for men than for women in present cohorts of seniors, because traditional socialization patterns may have led men to equate earnings with self-worth (Mooney, Knox, & Schacht, 2013). Similarly, declining health may cause an elderly man to view himself as a burden on others. The death of a spouse may also be a factor in many male suicides, because, as you will learn in the chapter on Death, Dying, and Bereavement, men do not adjust as well as women do to the death of a spouse (Stroebe & Stroebe, 1993). Finally, as is true of younger people, older women attempt suicide more often than older men do, but the men complete the act more often, mostly because they are more likely than women to choose more violent methods such as firearms.

PREVENTION AND INTERVENTIONS Therapies for depression are the same for older adults as for those who are younger. Treatment can include the enhancement of lifestyle and social supports, counselling and psychotherapy, and antidepressant medication (CCSMH, 2009). A combination of these treatments is often recommended.

Exercise has proven effective in reducing major depressive symptoms in as little as 16 weeks, even among older patients with chronic illnesses (Blumenthal et al., 1999; Blumenthal et al., 2012; Herring, Puetz, O'Conner, & Dishman, 2012). Given that poor overall health status predicts depression in seniors, one important aspect of preventing and reducing depression is to help older adults improve their overall health. A program of regular exercise is a relatively cost-effective strategy for both preventing and alleviating symptoms of depression, as well as improving overall health (e.g., as outlined in *Canadian Physical Activity Guidelines for Older Adults* [CSEP, 2012]).

Social involvement is also important in preventing depression and loneliness in seniors (National Seniors Council, 2014; Pitkala, 2016). For example, studies have found that nursing home residents' participation in planned, supervised intergenerational programs, such as playing games, singing, or reading with children, improved participants' emotional and general well-being (Heerema, 2016; Morita & Kobayashi, 2013; Sakurai et al., 2016; Yasunaga et al., 2016). So, periodic involvement with children might be an effective way to treat depression in institutionalized seniors. Likewise, *pet therapy* or *animal-assisted therapy* has been shown to be effective at improving quality of life for institutionalized seniors (Menna et al., 2012). Unfortunately, some research has shown that these efforts may not suit some seniors who experience loneliness (Pitkala, 2016).

In addition, research has consistently shown that religious beliefs and practices play a protective role in preventing and alleviating depression (Bonelli, Dew, Koenig, Rosmarin, & Vasegh, 2012; Kasen, Wickramaratne, Gameroff, & Weissman, 2012; Miller et al., 2012). This suggests an opportunity for caregivers to help seniors avoid or reduce depression by supporting their spiritual needs. Many older adults need help getting to religious services; those who live in institutions may need to have services brought to them. Declines in vision may mean that an elderly person can no longer read religious books and may deeply appreciate having someone read to him or provide him with recordings. Helping seniors maintain religious faith and practices may be an important key to reducing depression rates.

Of course, a wide range of psychological therapies are available—some focus on changing the interactions of negative thoughts, feelings, and behaviours. Others focus on improving interpersonal relationships and/or developing and putting into practice problem-solving strategies for improving ADLs, for example (Hunsley, Elliot, & Therrien, 2013). Psychological treatments are safe and effective for mild to moderate depression, whereas a combination of antidepressant drugs and psychotherapy is usually recommended for severe depression. Experts point out that appropriate use of antidepressant medications among seniors is critical. For one thing, antidepressants may reduce the effectiveness of the life-sustaining drugs some older adults take (NIA, 2000).

(Photo: Courtesy of Richard Robert Burrowes and Michael and Alexandra Enns)

Interacting with children may help prevent depression in late adulthood.

Test Yourself before going on

1. Declines in cognitive functioning that appear after a person has several small strokes are called _____ _____.

2. Among seniors, inadequate social support, inadequate income, emotional loss, and disabling health conditions are risk factors for _____ _____.

Critical Thinking

3. Many of the techniques that mental health professionals use require them to empathize with and develop trusting relationships with the people whom they are trying to help. In what ways do the characteristics of Alzheimer's disease and depression interfere with mental health professionals' efforts to do so with those who have them?

Cognitive Changes

Although there is an increased likelihood of cognitive and intellectual disorders as we age, cognitive decline is not inevitable for all (Cohen, 2012). Among the young old (aged 60 to 75) cognitive changes are still fairly small, and these older adults show little or no decline on some measures, e.g., numeric ability. But the old old and the oldest old show average declines on virtually all measures of intellectual skill, with the largest declines evident on any measures that involve speed or unexercised abilities (Schaie & Willis, 2005). Still, poorer performance on standardized tests of cognition and intelligence does not necessarily equate to poorer performance on everyday skills—there is more to living life than what we can measure on a test (Stuart-Hamilton, 2012).

Memory

Learning Objective 17.9

Identify how older and younger adults differ in memory function.

Forgetfulness becomes more frequent with age (Ballard, 2010). However, it's important to remember that the same basic rules seem to apply to memory processes among both older and younger adults. For both groups, for example, recognition is easier than recall, and tasks that require speed are more difficult. Further, metamemory and metacognition skills are just as important to memory function in old age as they are earlier in life (Olin & Zelinski, 1997). In many studies, older adults achieve scores very similar to those of younger adults on tests of memory accuracy, although they typically take longer to complete memory tasks and make more errors (Babiloni et al., 2004). Nevertheless, training programs designed to increase seniors' information-processing speed have demonstrated the role that experience plays in the speed with which individuals perform memory tasks (Edwards, Ruva, O'Brien, Haley, & Lister, 2013). Consequently, we should not assume that losses in speed of processing are entirely due to biological aging, nor are they necessarily inevitable or permanent.

SHORT-TERM MEMORY FUNCTION   One area in which researchers see significant late adulthood changes is in short-term, or working, memory capacity (Artuso, Cavallini, Bottiroli, Palladino, 2016; Hester, Kinsella, & Ong, 2004). You should remember from earlier chapters that there is a limitation on the number of items a person can retain in her memory at once. The more pieces of information she has to handle, the more she forgets, and the poorer her performance on memory and other kinds of cognitive tasks. Thus, the more any given cognitive task makes demands on working memory, the larger the decline with age.

A good illustration comes from a study involving a familiar, everyday task—remembering telephone numbers (West & Crook, 1990). Participants were shown a series of seven-digit or ten-digit telephone numbers on a computer screen, one at a time. The participant said each number as it appeared; then the number disappeared from the screen and the participant had to dial the number he had just seen on a push-button phone attached to the computer. On some trials, the participants got a busy signal when they first dialled and then had to dial the number over again. **Figure 17.7** shows the relationship between age and the correct recall of the phone numbers under these four conditions.

Notice that there is essentially no decline with age in immediate recall of a normal seven-digit telephone number (the equivalent of what you do when you look a number up in the phone book, say it to yourself as you read it, and then dial it immediately). When the length of the number increases to the 10 digits used for long-distance numbers, however, a decline with age becomes evident, beginning at about age 60. And with even a brief delay between saying the number and dialling it, the decline occurs earlier.

Patterns of age differences are not identical for all memory tasks. For example, older adults typically perform more poorly than younger adults on tasks involving *retrospective memory*, or recalling something that has happened recently (Henry, MacLeod, Phillips, & Crawford, 2004). By contrast, older adults outperform younger adults on *prospective memory* tasks in a natural setting, such as their home (Henry et al., 2004;

Figure 17.7   The graph shows the results from West and Crook's study of memory for telephone numbers. Notice that there is no loss of memory in middle adulthood for the most common condition: a seven-digit number dialled immediately. But if the number of digits increases, or if you have to remember the number a bit longer, some decline in memory begins around age 50 or 60.

(**SOURCE:** Data from West, R.L., & Crook, T.H. (1990). Age differences in everyday memory: Laboratory analogues of telephone number recall. *Psychology and Aging*, 5, 520–529. Data from Table 3, p. 524.)

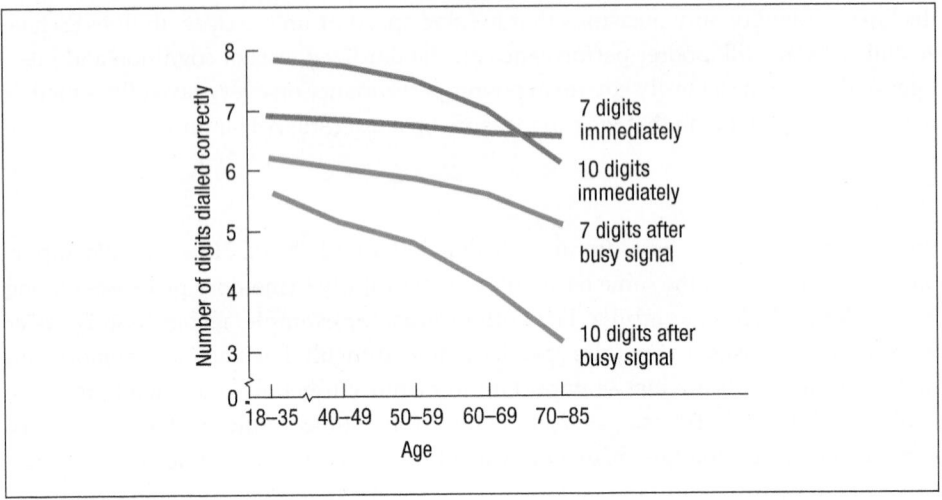

Rendell & Thomson, 1999). Prospective tasks require a person to remember an event into the future—for example, remembering to take their medication, show up for a doctor's appointment, or pay a bill. However, University of Victoria memory researchers have found that seniors generally underperform young and middle-aged adults on such tasks when in a controlled laboratory setting where there are no external memory cues, such as a calendar or reminder note (Cohen, Dixon, Lindsay, & Masson, 2003).

STRATEGY LEARNING   A study of older adults in Germany provides a good example of research findings on strategy learning and memory in older adults (Baltes & Kliegl, 1992; Kliegl, Smith, & Baltes, 1990). Researchers tested 18 college students and 19 old, but physically healthy, adults between ages 65 and 80, with an average age of 71.7 years. Participants were shown sets of pictures of 30 familiar buildings in Berlin and were asked to use the pictures to create associations that would help them remember a list of 30 words. For example, a castle might be paired with the word "bicycle." A typical association would be to imagine someone riding a bicycle in front of a castle. The pictures in each set were displayed for different amounts of time, ranging from 20 seconds each to 1 second each. After participants attempted to learn each list of words, the experimenters asked what images they had used and suggested possible improvements. Training sessions were interspersed with test sessions to check on the participants' progress.

Figure 17.8 shows the results for pictures and words presented at five-second intervals. You can see that the older adults showed improvement after training, but their performance was poorer than that of younger adults. These findings suggest that the learning process simply takes longer for older adults—longer to create the mental image and longer to link that image up with the word in the list. However, when allowed more time to associate each picture and word, older adults' performance was more similar to that of younger participants.

EVERYDAY MEMORY   One common argument from those who take an optimistic view of the effects of aging on cognitive functioning is that older adults may be able to remember just as well as younger adults but may simply be less motivated to memorize lists of unrelated words given to them by researchers in a laboratory. However, on virtually all everyday tasks—remembering the main points of a story or

Figure 17.8 These results from Kliegl's study show that older adults can learn complex information-processing skills and improve their performance after training but that they don't gain as much as younger adults do. However, this study also suggested that, given enough time, older adults can learn new strategies.

(**SOURCE:** Kliegl, R., Smith, J., & Baltes, P.B. (1990). On the locus and process of magnification of age differences during mnemonic training. *Developmental Psychology*, 26, 894–904. Adapted from figure on p. 899.)

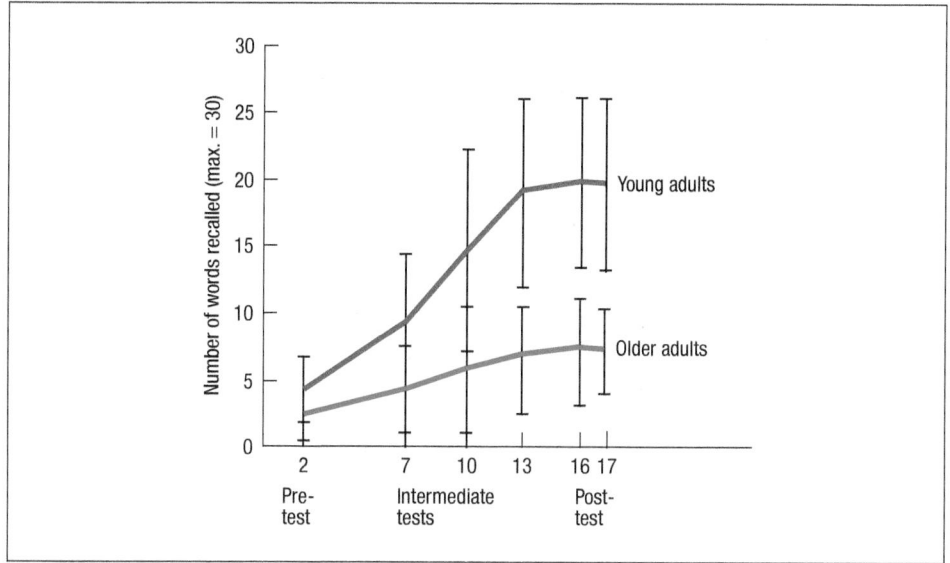

a newspaper article; recalling movies, conversations, grocery lists, or recipes; recalling the information from a medicine label; remembering whether they did something ("Did I turn off the stove before I left the house?"); or remembering where they heard something (called *source memory*)—older adults perform less well than younger adults (Dixon, Rust, Feltmate, & See, 2007). These results have been found in longitudinal as well as cross-sectional studies (Craik, 2002). However, researchers have found that many older adults are quite skilled at using strategies such as written reminders that help them compensate for some of these losses (Delprado, Kinsella, Ong, & Pike, 2013).

PRELIMINARY EXPLANATIONS How do researchers account for these changes in memory? Neuroimaging studies show that age-related memory decline is associated with changes in the ratio of grey to white matter in the brain (Kramer et al., 2007). In addition, a reduction in the volume of the hippocampus is associated with memory deficits among seniors.

Functionally speaking, forgetfulness among seniors may result from the kind of general slowing that you read about earlier in the chapter. Older adults take longer to register some new piece of information, encode it, and retrieve it. Some of the clearest evidence of the important role of speed in memory decline in old age comes from an extensive series of studies by Timothy Salthouse (e.g., Salthouse, 2004, 2011).

Salthouse has tested both basic reaction speed and memory or other cognitive skills in adults of various ages. According to him, a very large portion of the age decline in memory can be accounted for simply by slower reaction times in older adults. He is convinced that the loss of speed occurs at the level of the central nervous system and not in the peripheral nerves. So physiological changes in neurons and the accompanying loss of nerve conductance speed may be the root causes of these changes in memory.

Use it or lose it? These men keep their minds sharp by playing games that require complex memory and strategy skills.

(Photo: Budimir Jevtic/Shutterstock)

Virtually all experts now agree with Salthouse that loss of speed is a key aspect of the process of memory decline, and studies have shown that quantitative losses in speed of information-processing very strongly predict qualitative changes in memory function (Verhaegen, 2013). But most also believe that speed is not the entire explanation. There appear to be other factors as well, such as changes in attention strategies that lead to less effective processing of information.

Wisdom and Creativity

Theorists who study cognition in older adults have also begun to ask whether seniors might have some advantages over the young because of their accumulation of knowledge, skills, and life experiences. In other words, older adults might be wiser. Researchers have not yet agreed on a common definition of wisdom, but most authors emphasize that it goes beyond mere accumulations of facts. **Wisdom** reflects understanding of "universal truths" or basic laws or patterns. It is knowledge that is blended with values and meaning systems; it is knowledge based on the understanding that clarity is not always possible, that unpredictability and uncertainty are part of life (Baltes & Kunzmann, 2004).

You may be wondering how researchers measure wisdom. The pioneering researcher in this field, the late Paul Baltes, devised one useful technique (Baltes & Staudinger, 2000). Baltes presented research participants with stories about fictional characters who were trying to make a major life decision. For example, one dilemma Baltes used involved a 15-year-old girl who wants to get married. Participants' responses to the stories are judged according to five criteria Baltes hypothesized to be central to wisdom as it relates to solving practical life problems:

- factual knowledge
- procedural knowledge
- understanding of relevance of context
- understanding of relevance of values
- recognition that it is impossible to know in advance how any decision will ultimately affect one's life

A person would be judged to be low in wisdom if her response to the 15-year-old's desire to marry were something like "A 15-year-old getting married? That's stupid. I would tell the girl to forget about it until she's older." The answer of a person judged to be high in wisdom would be more complex. A wise person might point out, "There are circumstances when marriage at such a young age might be a good decision. Is she motivated by a desire to make a home for a child she is expecting? Also, the girl might come from a culture where marriage at 15 is quite common. You have to consider people's motivations and their backgrounds to understand their decisions. You also have to know how the person involved views the situation to be able to give advice."

Virtually all theorists who have written about wisdom assume that it is more likely to be found in the middle-aged and the elderly. However, Baltes has found that younger adults perform as well as older adults in response to the fictional dilemma task. In fact, Baltes has found that, rather than age, intelligence and professional experience are correlated with responses to the dilemma task. So, Baltes's research seems to suggest that the popular idea that age and wisdom are associated is probably not true. Wisdom does not appear to be a characteristic of the elderly that distinguishes them from other subgroups of adults.

Critics have suggested that Baltes is simply measuring general cognitive ability rather than what is usually thought of as wisdom. Nevertheless, Baltes's research has produced an important finding about wisdom and old age: In contrast to performance

Learning Objective 17.10
Describe what wisdom and creativity theory and research reveals about cognitive functioning in late adulthood.

wisdom
a hypothesized cognitive characteristic of older adults that includes accumulated knowledge and the ability to apply that knowledge to practical problems of living

on information-processing tasks, such as memorizing nonsense words, performance on wisdom tasks does not decline with age (Baltes & Staudinger, 2000). Moreover, the speed of accessing wisdom-related knowledge remains constant across adulthood, unlike speed of information-processing in other domains. In addition, other researchers have found that older adults who ranked high in wisdom and retained a sense of mastery and purpose in life were more likely to rank high in *subjective well-being* (Ardelt & Edwards, 2015), which might be considered what Erikson called *ego integrity*, a concept we'll revisit in the chapter on Social and Personality Development in Late Adulthood.

Enhanced creativity may also be an element of cognition in older adults. As you learned in the chapter on Physical and Cognitive Development in Middle Adulthood, some highly creative individuals, especially composers and artists, reach their peak in late adulthood. To describe the potential for creative work in the later years, a leading gerontologist, Gene Cohen, has developed a four-stage theory of mid- to late-life creativity (Cohen, 2000). Cohen's theory has been the basis of successful art therapy programs for seniors with a variety of psychological problems (Malchiodi, 2012).

Cohen proposes that at around age 50, creative individuals enter a *re-evaluation phase*, during which they reflect on past accomplishments and formulate new goals. The re-evaluation process, along with an increasing sense of time limitations, leads to an intensification of the desire to create and produce. During the next stage, the *liberation phase*, individuals in their 60s become freer to create, because most have retired from everyday work. Most are also more tolerant of their own failures, and thus are willing to take risks that they would not have taken at earlier ages. In the *summing-up phase*, creative people in their 70s have a desire to knit their accomplishments together into a cohesive, meaningful story. They begin to view their early accomplishments in terms of how those accomplishments prefigured later achievements. Finally, in the *encore phase*, during the 80s and beyond, there is a desire to complete unfinished works or to fulfill desires that have been put aside in the past.

(Photo: KidStock/Blend Images/Getty Images)

Seeking advice from a senior who is presumed to be wise is one way young adults act on the belief that those who are older have accumulated knowledge and information that can benefit them.

Test Yourself before going on

1. What two factors were found to influence older adults' ability to recall digits in West and Crook's study?
2. According to Baltes, what are the five elements of wisdom?

Critical Thinking

3. Make a list of the people you think of as wise. How old are they? Is old age necessary for wisdom? If not, how do you think wisdom is acquired?

Summary

Variability in Late Adulthood

17.1 Identify the life expectancy and longevity trends in Canadian seniors.

- Developmentalists group seniors into three subgroups: the young old (60–75), the old old (75–85), and the oldest old (85 and older).

The oldest old are the fastest-growing group of seniors in the Canada.

17.2 Describe contemporary theories of biological aging.

- Theories of biological aging focus on the decline in stem cell functioning that involves genetic and epigenetic processes shaped by environmental and random variables over time. One such mechanism involves the Hayflick limit—a shortening of telomeres that imposes time limits on the capacity of the body's cells to reproduce. Other contributing factors include molecular damage caused by DNA breakage, cross-linking, and free radicals.

17.3 Describe the health of older adults in Canada.

- Most seniors view their health status positively. With increasing age, the proportion of seniors whose health interferes with activities of daily living rises. Chronic diseases such as arthritis and hypertension afflict many older adults. Heredity, overall health, current and prior health habits (particularly exercise), and availability of adequate social support influence longevity.

Physical Changes

17.4 Describe how the brain changes in late adulthood.

- Changes in the brain associated with aging include, most centrally, a loss of dendritic density of neurons, which has the effect of slowing reaction time for almost all tasks.

17.5 Describe the common types of sensory changes that occur in late adulthood.

- Older adults have more difficulty adapting to darkness and light. Loss of hearing is more common and more noticeable after 65 than at earlier ages. Taste discrimination remains largely unchanged with age, but ability to discriminate smells declines substantially in late adulthood.

17.6 Summarize the behavioural effects of changes in the body systems of older adults.

- General slowing alters behaviour in old age and makes tasks such as driving more dangerous. Older adults also change their sleeping and eating patterns. Motor abilities decline, causing more accidents due to falls. Sexual activity also decreases in frequency, although most older adults continue to be sexually active.

Mental Health

17.7 Differentiate Alzheimer's disease from other dementias.

- Dementia is rare before late adulthood, becoming steadily more common with advancing age. The most common cause of dementia is Alzheimer's disease. It is difficult to diagnose definitively, and its causes are not fully understood. Neurofibrillary tangles are far more likely to be present in the brains of individuals with Alzheimer's disease than in those of people with other types of dementia.

17.8 Describe what the research suggests about depression among older adults.

- The prevalence of depression appears to decline in Canadians over age 65. However, rates increase for seniors living in an institutional setting or who also suffer from serious medical conditions and/or dementia. Enhancement of lifestyle and social supports, counselling and psychotherapy, and antidepressant medication are recommended treatments.

Cognitive Changes

17.9 Identify how older and younger adults differ in memory function.

- Although not inevitable, seniors experience difficulties in a variety of mental processes, which appear to reflect a general slowing of the nervous system and perhaps a loss of working-memory capacity.

17.10 Describe what wisdom and creativity theory and research reveals about cognitive functioning in late adulthood.

- Wisdom and creativity may be important aspects of cognitive functioning in old age. According to Baltes, decision making that is characterized by wisdom includes factual knowledge, procedural knowledge, an understanding of the relevance of context, an understanding of the relevance of values, and recognition that it is impossible to know in advance how a decision will affect one's life. Cohen proposed that creative individuals over the age of 50 pass through a series of stages in which they evaluate and reshape their lives.

Chapter 18
Social and Personality Development in Late Adulthood

Alexander Nicholson/Digital Vision/Getty Images

 ## Learning Objectives

THEORIES OF SOCIAL AND PERSONALITY DEVELOPMENT

18.1 Describe what the research says about Erikson's stage of ego integrity versus despair.

18.2 Characterize the main ideas of activity theory, disengagement theory, and continuity theory.

INDIVIDUAL DIFFERENCES

18.3 Describe how successful aging is manifested in the lives of older adults.

18.4 Describe how religious coping influences physical and mental health in late adulthood.

SOCIAL RELATIONSHIPS

18.5 Identify the living arrangements of elderly people in Canada.

18.6 Describe how intimate partnerships contribute to development in late adulthood.

18.7 Identify the significance of family relationships and friendships for older adults.

18.8 Identify gender differences in older adults' social networks.

CAREER ISSUES IN LATE LIFE

18.9 Identify what factors contribute to the decision to retire.

18.10 Describe how retirement affects the lives of older adults.

18.11 Describe what the research says about the decision not to retire.

Can you imagine being married for 80 years? Thanks to increases in longevity and the relatively young ages at which couples married in times past, an increasing number of elderly couples are celebrating their 60th, 70th, and even 80th anniversaries. Among the list of people with the longest marriages are several Canadians. An up-to-date listing can be found online (http://en.wikipedia.org/wiki/List_of_people_with_the_longest_marriages).

No matter how long an older couple has been together, the emotional support that most elders derive from an intimate partnership helps them cope with the loudly ticking biological clock that reminds them every day that they aren't as young as they used to be. As you will learn in this chapter, changes in roles and relationships are perhaps just as significant as physical ones. And for many older adults, these changes are perceived not as losses but as opportunities to create new roles and to make old age a time of personal and social gains.

Theories of Social and Personality Development

If the social and personality changes of young adulthood can be described as "individuation" and those of middle adulthood can be described (more tentatively) as "mellowing," how might the changes of late adulthood be described? Several theorists have hypothesized specific forms of change, but there is little agreement among them and very little information supporting any of their theories.

Erikson's Stage of Ego Integrity Versus Despair

Learning Objective 18.1

Describe what the research says about Erikson's stage of ego integrity versus despair.

ego integrity versus despair stage

the last of Erikson's psychosocial stages, in which older adults must achieve a sense of satisfaction with their lives

ego integrity

the feeling that one's life has been worthwhile

reminiscence

reflecting on past experience

Erikson termed the last of his eight life crises the **ego integrity versus despair stage**. He thought that the task of achieving **ego integrity**, the sense that one has lived a useful life, began in middle adulthood but was most central in late adulthood. To achieve ego integrity, the older adult must come to terms with who she is and has been, how her life has been lived, the choices that she made, the opportunities gained and lost. The process also involves coming to terms with death and accepting its imminence. Erikson hypothesized that failure to achieve ego integrity in late adulthood would result in feelings of hopelessness and despair because there would be too little time to make changes before death.

One aspect of Erikson's theory that has received a great deal of attention from researchers is the notion that the process of **reminiscence**, thinking about the past, is a necessary and healthy part of achieving ego integrity, and thus important during old age and in preparing for death. However, few developmentalists today would say that the only, or even the most important, purpose of this process is to help an individual prepare for death. Instead, recent research has examined the link between reminiscence and well-being. For example, developmentalists at Simon Fraser University have been conducting longitudinal research on reminiscence in the elderly and the results, so far, suggest autobiographical memories impact psychological well-being (O'Rourke, Bachner, Cappeliez, Chaudhury, & Carmel, 2015; O'Rourke, Cappeliez, & Claxton, 2011). In particular, experiencing *self-positive reminiscences* in later life are associated with better mental health—perhaps by restoring, maintaining, or enhancing a sense of meaning and purpose in life (Reker, Birren, & Svensson, 2012). Conversely, having *self-negative reminiscences*, such as apathy, absence of purpose, and dwelling on unresolved conflicts and losses seems to undermine well-being (O'Rourke et al., 2011).

It's important to note that adults of all ages engage in reminiscence. For older adults, though, reminiscence can be a way of communicating their experiences to younger individuals. Interestingly, studies from across cultures have found what's called a *reminiscence bump*: a higher frequency of memories derived from young adulthood (ages 15–30) than from other stages in life (Bohn & Bertsen, 2011; Dickson, Pillemer, & Bruehl, 2011). The reasons for a reminiscence bump—which tends to favour positive memories—seem to be related not only to memory encoding processes, but also to the influence of cultural life scripts, i.e., memories that fit one's internalized cultural expectations and are largely drawn from events that are concentrated in this period of life, such as dating, leaving home, getting a job, marriage, etc. (Dickson et al., 2011).

Among older adults, reminiscence is also the foundation for the process of **life review**, an evaluative process in which seniors make judgments about their past behaviour (Butler, 1963, 2002). Consistent with Erikson's view of the ego integrity/ despair crisis, life review results in both positive and negative emotional outcomes, and the overall balance of positive and negative emotions that results from the life review process is correlated with seniors' mental health. Researchers have found that seniors whose life reviews produce more regrets over past mistakes and missed opportunities than satisfaction with how they handled problems earlier in life are more prone to depression than those who have generally positive feelings about their lives. Fortunately, both reminiscence-based and life-review interventions that help seniors re-evaluate past life events have been shown to have preventative and therapeutic effects on mental health—especially depression and anxiety (Gaggioli et al., 2014a; Korte, Westerhof, & Bohlmeijer, 2012; Pinquart & Forstmeier, 2012).

Some intriguing interventions that involve primary school students interacting with seniors over the course of several reminiscence sessions have resulted in positive outcomes for both groups. In particular, students develop a more positive attitude toward seniors and seniors report an improved sense of well-being and decreased feelings of loneliness (Gaggioli et al., 2014b). Relatedly, teaching and encouraging seniors, both on their own and jointly with young students, to use e-technologies to digitally capture and archive personal histories and memorabilia (e.g., newspaper clippings, postcards, photos, and videos) has proven to be a novel and effective way of enhancing the quality of life for seniors (Morganti et al., 2016; Riva et al., 2016). One such international program that promotes the use of information and communication technology for active healthy aging is the Active and Assisted Living Programme (http:// www.aal-europe.eu/).

The success of these reminiscence sessions supports what Erikson wrote about later in his life: the quest for *generativity* that was prominent in middle age likely continues in importance well into old age (Tabuchi et al., 2015; Wink & Staudinger, 2014). Even those living in long-term care settings and those who are living with dementia seem to benefit from generative opportunities (Doyle, Rubinstein, & de Medeiros, 2015). One caveat seems to be that the social and cultural context matters (Cheng, 2009b; Tabuchi et al., 2015). Seniors retain the desire to be generative and nurturing

life review

an evaluative process in which elders make judgments about past behaviour toward others, often in personally unique ways, but there needs to be someone on the receiving end or it's no more meaningful than "unrequited love." Whether or not a person has come to terms with the life they've lived, the point is, they are still alive, and if alive, they are still driven to be of value—to continue to share with and contribute to others. Alas, if no one really cares, then what's the use of going on? It's somewhat akin to the child who makes a craft for their parent and proudly presents it as a gift; the parent's response to the child's effort is critical to the child's sense of worth. So too, seniors have a need to feel that their efforts are valued and respected by others, not only past efforts, but also, and perhaps just as importantly, those of the present. Maybe this is why many seniors baulk at transitioning to long-term care; it may symbolize being "put on a shelf" and no longer serving any useful purpose.

Two cautionary notes: "empty" efforts to express respect toward the generativity of seniors can be interpreted as patronizing and insincere, and thus diminish their sense of worth. Secondly, the generativity of seniors can also make them vulnerable to being taken advantage of, or worse, leave them open to abuse. The struggle for generativity in old age underscores many concepts that we'll explore throughout the chapter.

Other Theories of Late-Life Psychosocial Functioning

Learning Objective 18.2

Characterize the main ideas of activity theory, disengagement theory, and continuity theory.

As you learned in the chapter on Social and Personality Development in Middle Adulthood, the ideas of Paul and Margaret Baltes about selection, optimization, and compensation have been important in the study of middle-aged adults' psychosocial functioning. They are often applied to the study of older adults as well. Recall that the Balteses proposed that, as adults get older, they maintain high levels of performance by focusing on their strengths. In this way, they compensate for weaknesses.

Another theoretical perspective on old age focuses on the question of whether it is normal, necessary, or healthy for older adults to remain active as long as possible, or whether the more typical and healthy pattern is some kind of gradual turning inward. The perspective typically referred to as **activity theory** argues that the psychologically and physically healthiest response to old age is to maintain the greatest possible level of activity and involvement in the greatest possible number of roles.

activity theory

the idea that it is normal and healthy for older adults to try to remain as active as possible for as long as possible

Activity theorists often cite research demonstrating that the most active older adults report slightly greater satisfaction with themselves or their lives, are healthiest, and have the highest morale (McIntosh & Danigelis, 1995; Park, 2009; Winstead, Yost, Cotten, Berkowsky, & Anderson, 2015). The effect is not large, but its direction is consistently positive: More social involvement is linked to better outcomes, even among seniors who suffer from disabilities, such as arthritis, for whom active social participation may be physically painful (e.g., Maniecka-Bryla, Gajewska, Burzynska, & Bryla, 2013). Yet, it is also true that every in-depth study of lifestyles of older adults identifies at least a few who lead socially isolated lives but remain contented, sometimes because they are engaged in an all-consuming hobby (e.g., Maas & Kuypers, 1974; Rubinstein, 1986).

An alternative theory of social and personality development in old age is disengagement theory, first proposed as a formulation of the central psychological process for older adults (Cumming, 1975; Cumming & Henry, 1961). In its current form, **disengagement theory** proposes that aging has three aspects:

disengagement theory

the theory that it is normal and healthy for older adults to scale down their social lives and to separate themselves from others to a certain degree

- *Shrinkage of life space:* As people age, they interact with fewer and fewer people and fill fewer and fewer roles.

- *Increased individuality:* In the roles and relationships that remain, the older individual is much less governed by strict rules or expectations.

- *Acceptance of these changes:* The healthy older adult actively disengages from roles and relationships, turning increasingly inward and away from interactions with others.

The first two of these aspects seem largely beyond dispute. What has been controversial about disengagement theory is the third aspect. Advocates argue that the normal and healthy response to the shrinkage of roles and relationships is for the older adult to step back still further, to stop seeking new roles, spend more time alone, and turn inward. In essence, they propose a kind of personality change, not just a decline in involvement.

Although it is possible to choose a highly disengaged lifestyle in late adulthood and to find satisfaction in it, such disengagement is neither normal for the majority of older adults nor necessary for overall mental health in the later years. For most seniors, some level of social involvement is a sign—and probably a cause—of higher morale and lower levels of depression and other psychiatric symptoms (Zunzunegui, Alvarado, Del Ser, & Otero, 2003).

Finally, **continuity theory** argues that the primary means by which seniors adjust to aging is by engaging in the same kinds of activities that interested and challenged them in their earlier years (Atchley, 1989). For instance, an older woman who was an avid gardener during early and middle adulthood, but whose physical condition renders continuation of this hobby impossible, may adjust to her body's decline by limiting her passion for gardening to a small selection of potted plants. Research supports continuity theorists' assertions that aging adults work to maintain consistency of this kind and that achieving such consistency is essential to older adults' maintenance of a positive outlook on the aging process (Greenfield & Marks, 2007; Palmore, 2016; Winstead et al., 2015). Therefore, they argue, providing ways in which seniors can meet these continuity goals should be integral to their care.

(Photo: Anna Lurye/Fotolia)

Some older adults are quite content with solitary lives, but disengagement from social contacts is neither a typical nor optimal choice for most elders.

continuity theory

the idea that older adults adapt lifelong interests and activities to the limitations imposed on them by physical aging

Critical Thinking

Think about the oldest person you know. How are the themes of ego integrity, reminiscence, life review, activity, disengagement, and continuity manifested in their life?

Test Yourself before going on

1. Match each term with its definition.
   _____ (a) ego integrity
   _____ (b) reminiscence
   _____ (c) life review
   (i) reflecting on past experience
   (ii) the feeling that one's life has been worthwhile
   (iii) judgments about past behaviour

2. The main idea of _____ theory is that seniors adjust to aging by engaging in the same kinds of activities that interested them in their earlier years.

Individual Differences

Individual differences continue to make substantial contributions to the experiences of older men and women. In fact, research suggests that differences in a variety of behaviours are related to overall quality of life as well as to longevity. Similarly, individual differences in reliance on religious beliefs and institutions as sources of support are also correlated with well-being in late adulthood.

The Successful Aging Paradigm

In recent years, one of the dominant themes in gerontology literature has been the concept of **successful aging**. As defined by authors John Rowe and Robert Kahn, successful aging has three components: good physical health, retention of cognitive abilities, and continuing engagement in social and productive activities (Rowe &

Learning Objective 18.3

Describe how successful aging is manifested in the lives of older adults.

successful aging

the term gerontologists use to describe maintaining one's physical health, mental abilities, social competence, and overall satisfaction with one's life as one ages

Table 18.1 The Components of Successful Aging

Health	Good health must be maintained through middle and late adulthood.
Mental activity	Engaging in cognitively stimulating activities and hobbies helps older adults retain mental abilities.
Social engagement	Remaining socially active is critical; social contacts that involve helping others are especially important.
Productivity	Volunteer activities can help by engaging retired adults in productive pursuits.
Life satisfaction	Older adults must learn how to adjust expectations such that life satisfaction remains high.

Kahn, 1987, 1998). An additional aspect of successful aging is an individual's subjective sense of life satisfaction (**Table 18.1** describes these components). The concept of successful aging is referred to as a *paradigm* because it presents patterns for or examples of such aging. Rather than stating a theory of development, the paradigm of successful aging offers a way of thinking about late adulthood and about how earlier decisions and patterns of behaviour contribute to quality of life at later ages.

STAYING HEALTHY AND ABLE By now, you should be familiar with the factors that predict health and physical functioning across the lifespan: diet, exercise, avoidance of tobacco, and so on. Even getting a good night sleep is considered a priority by seniors for successful aging (Crawford-Achour et al., 2012). In a sense, older people reap the consequences of the behavioural choices they made when they were younger. Thus, it isn't surprising that making wise choices in this domain during early and middle adulthood, especially with regard to the factors that influence cardiovascular health, is essential to successful aging later in life (Hughes & Hayman, 2007).

However, there are other aspects to staying healthy and able that most of us never face until old age. For example, when an older adult suffers an event such as a stroke or fractured bone, his willingness to engage in the sometimes painful process of rehabilitation significantly affects his degree of recovery. Researchers have found that older adults, more so than those who are younger, vary considerably in their willingness to comply with physicians and therapists who supervise their rehabilitations after such events. Predictably, patients who participate in all recommended rehabilitation activities are healthier at follow-up than those who do not participate (Leung et al., 2011). Thus, lifelong health habits contribute to successful aging, but individuals' responses to the health crises of old age also matter. According to Dalhousie University researchers, for example, successful agers tend to develop new, meaningful leisure-based activities to replace activities they abandoned because of negative changes in their health (Hutchinson & Nimrod, 2012).

Still, physical activity, in addition to leisure activity, is positively associated with successful aging in later life. Canadian researchers have found that physical inactivity was a stronger predictor of functional limitations in performing daily tasks (IADLs or ADLs) than was either chronic disease or being socially unengaged with life (Baker, Meisner, Logan, Kungl, & Weir, 2009; Meisner, Dogra, Logan, Baker, & Weir, 2010; Weir, Meisner, & Baker, 2010). These studies suggest that even moderate levels of physical activity benefit seniors.

RETAINING COGNITIVE ABILITIES The degree to which seniors maintain cognitive functioning is a crucial component of successful aging (Fiocco & Yaffe, 2010). Those seniors who are the best educated show the least cognitive decline (Marques et al., 2016; Marques et al., 2015).

In addition to education, the complexity of the cognitive challenges older adults are willing to take on also influences their cognitive functioning. Psychologists suggest that self-stereotyping contributes to this reluctance; older people may believe that they can't learn as well as younger people can, and so they stick to established routines and disengage from new challenges (Ennis, Hess, & Smith, 2013). However, neuropsychologists suggest that such avoidance of learning may actually contribute to cognitive decline (Volz, 2000). New learning, these scientists hypothesize, helps to establish new connections between neurons, connections that may protect the aging brain against deterioration (Calero & Navarro, 2007). Thus, what might be called *cognitive adventurousness*, a willingness to learn new things, appears to be a key component of successful aging.

SOCIAL ENGAGEMENT Social connectedness and participation in activities that involve interactions with others are clearly important to successful aging (Huxhold, Fiori, & Windsor, 2013). With regard to maintaining a social life, for example, nursing home residents report greater satisfaction with their lives when they have frequent contact with family and friends (Guse & Masesar, 1999). Similarly, seniors with disabilities who have frequent contact with family and friends have reduced feelings of loneliness (Liu & Richardson, 2012).

Social engagement contributes to successful aging because it provides opportunities for older adults to give support as well as to receive it. Researchers studying Japanese elders, for example, found that a majority of them say that helping others contributes to their own health and personal sense of well-being (Krause, Ingersoll-Dayton, Liang, & Sugisawa, 1999). In addition, researchers who have asked U.S. nursing home residents to rate various quality-of-life factors have found that they often give high ratings to "opportunities to help others" (Guse & Masesar, 1999). Thus, even when elderly adults have significant disabilities, many are still oriented toward helping others and feel more satisfied with their lives when they can do so.

Findings such as these helped set the stage for the launch of the WHO *Global Network of Age-friendly Cities and Communities* (PHAC, 2016c; WHO, 2014). This active aging initiative emphasizes eight overlapping domains that cities and communities can focus on in order to develop environments that enhance quality of life as people age. Three of the domains, in particular, focus on social engagement: social participation, respect and social inclusion, and civic participation and employment. University of Manitoba researchers have also found age-friendly community initiatives work well in rural contexts and are associated with better life satisfaction and perceived health in seniors (Menec, Newall, & Nowicki, 2016; Menec & Nowicki, 2014). Unfortunately, extending such programs to remote communities has some logistical challenges, such as limited community resources and geographic distance (Menec et al., 2015; Spina & Menec, 2015). Of note, Canada hosts two age-friendly world programs: Municipalité Amie des Aînés (MADA) and the Pan-Canadian Age-Friendly Communities Initiative.

PRODUCTIVITY Contributing to a social network may be one important way of remaining productive, especially for older adults who are retired. **Volunteerism**, performing unpaid work for altruistic reasons, has been linked to successful aging as it provides seniors with opportunities to socialize, be physically active, and engage in personally meaningful activity that provides psychological health benefits (Godbout, Filiatrault, & Plante, 2012). Neena Chappell, past director of the University of Victoria Centre on Aging, conducted an extensive review of the literature on volunteerism in North America and concluded that people who volunteer, especially with helping others, are happier and healthier in their elder years. The social interaction aspect in particular has a beneficial impact on both quality of life and mortality. This finding may not be surprising, since seniors indicate that their relationships with others are what they value the most in life (Chappell, 1999).

Although the percentage of Canadians volunteering has declined in all age groups over the past decade, those aged 65 to 74 consistently clocked the highest number of annual volunteer hours of any age group (234 hours), and those 75 and older came in a close second (218 hours) (Statistics Canada, 2012t). So it seems the volunteer activities

volunteerism

performance of unpaid work for altruistic motives

Figure 18.1 This graph shows the participation in social and leisure organizations and activities by Canadians age 65 and older.

* age 65 to 74

(**SOURCE:** Adapted from Turcotte & Schellenberg, 2007, Table 4.3.2, Table 4.4.1 and Table 4.4.2; Veenhof & Timusk, 2009, Chart 1.)

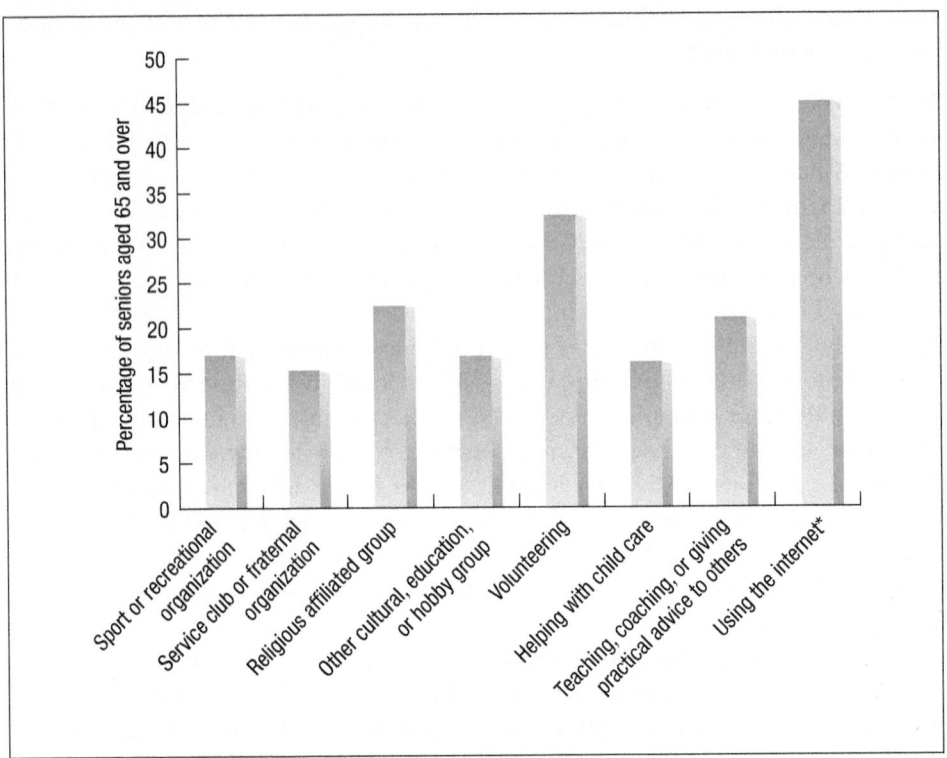

of older adults have the potential to benefit society as well as enhance the volunteers' own physical and mental health (National Seniors Council, 2010). As you can see from **Figure 18.1**, older adults in Canada are involved in their communities through a wide range of activities.

Some older adults remain productive by venturing into new pursuits, such as taking music lessons, attending college classes, or learning to paint or sculpt (Malchiodi, 2012; Sherrod, 2012). Researchers conducting a study of 36 artists over age 60 asked them to explain how artistic productivity contributed to their successful aging (Fisher & Specht, 1999). Their responses contained several themes: Producing art gave them a purpose in life, opportunities to interact with like-minded peers, and a sense of competence. The older artists also claimed that creating art helped them stay healthy. Thus, creative productivity may help older adults maintain an optimistic outlook, which, as you have learned, contributes to physical and mental health (Flood, 2007).

LIFE SATISFACTION *Life satisfaction*, or a sense of personal well-being, is also an important component of successful aging. What is critical to life satisfaction in almost all cases is an individual's perception of her own situation, which seems to be more important than objective measures (Gana, Alphilippe, & Bailly, 2004). Perceived adequacy of social support and perceived adequacy of income are critical. Moreover, self-ratings of health, rather than objective measures of health, may be the most significant predictors of life satisfaction and morale (Abu-Bader, Rogers, & Barusch, 2002; Draper, Gething, Fethney, & Winfield, 1999).

For some elders, remaining productive means venturing into new hobbies, such as painting, sculpting, or other artistic pursuits.

Research also suggests that social comparisons—how well an older adult thinks he is doing compared with others his age—are just as important to these perceptions as the older adult's awareness of the changes he has undergone since his younger years (Robinson-Whelen & Kiecolt-Glaser, 1997). A majority of older adults, no matter what their personal circumstances, believe that most others their age are worse off than they are (Heckhausen & Brim, 1997). Developmentalists speculate that the tendency to see others as having more problems is an important self-protective psychological device employed by those who are aging successfully (Frieswijk, Buunk, Steverink, & Slaets, 2004).

CRITICISMS OF THE SUCCESSFUL AGING PARADIGM Critics of the successful aging paradigm suggest that the concept can be misleading. For one thing, they say, the paradigm has the potential to become a new kind of ageist stereotype, one that portrays older adults who suffer from disabilities as incompetent (Dillaway & Byrnes, 2009; Minkler & Fadem, 2012; van Dyk, 2014). Such critics point out that, for many elderly adults, no amount of optimism, willingness to rehabilitate, social support, or involvement in intellectually demanding activities can moderate their physical limitations. For example, studies of performance on reading comprehension tests that compared university professors over age 70 and graduate students show that some degree of age-based cognitive decline can be expected, even among very bright, highly experienced, and productive adults (Christensen, Henderson, Griffiths, & Levings, 1997). Thus, these critics claim, the danger of the successful aging paradigm is that it can give the erroneous impression that all the effects of aging are under one's control (Holstein & Minkler, 2003).

Canadian gerontologists point out that it's not easy to determine which comes first—do good physical health, retention of cognitive abilities, and continuing engagement in social and productive activities lead to successful aging or are there predispositions, such as personality characteristics, that drive some seniors to be more engaged in successful aging activities, which in turn contributes to a greater sense of *subjective well-being* (a blend of happiness and life satisfaction) (Stones, Kozma, McNeil, & Worobetz, 2011)? Longitudinal evidence is leaning toward the latter: That is, stable personality characteristics (such as higher extraversion and agreeableness and lower neuroticism) contribute to a lifelong approach to living characterized by a propensity to be active and socially engaged. A good part of this predisposition is hereditary in nature—genetics contributes to roughly half of the variability in the personality traits that influence subjective well-being. Thus, it seems that some people have an advantage from an early age—they come into the world more prepared to both shape and react to their environment in ways that will contribute to successful aging and subjective well-being later in life. This may account for the finding that, despite declines in physical and cognitive functioning and shrinking social networks, healthy seniors can maintain high levels of well-being (Suri & Gross, 2012).

Nevertheless, critics concede that the successful aging paradigm has broadened gerontologists' approaches to studying old age. Thus, they agree that its influence has been largely positive. Still, keeping their criticisms in mind can help balance the optimism of the successful aging paradigm against the realities of life in late adulthood and the need to continue to encourage researchers to search for treatments for age-related diseases, such as Alzheimer's.

Religious Coping

Religion appears to be one factor contributing to individual differences in life satisfaction among seniors (Sørensen, Lien, Holmen, & Danbolt, 2012). Psychologists use the term **religious coping** to refer to the tendency to turn to religious beliefs and institutions in times of stress or trouble. People of all ages use religious coping. However, many developmentalists suggest that religious coping may be particularly important

Learning Objective 18.4

Describe how religious coping influences physical and mental health in late adulthood.

religious coping

the tendency to turn to religious beliefs and institutions for support in times of difficulty

in the later years because of the high number of life stressors, including deaths of loved ones, chronic illnesses, and declining sensory abilities. And seniors themselves often cite religious coping as their primary and preferred means of managing anxiety and depression (Huang, Hsu, & Chen, 2012).

SEX DIFFERENCES Canadian data suggest that women make more use of religious coping than men do (Bibby, 2001; Lindsay, 2008). Most developmentalists attribute this finding to sex differences in social behaviour that are observed across the lifespan. However, it's important to keep in mind that, even though the frequency with which religious coping is used may differ according to ethnicity and gender, its effects seem to be similar in all racial and ethnic groups and for both women and men. These effects are best examined by separating the psychological and social components of religious coping.

Strong religious beliefs appear to be positively associated with elders' health and well-being.

(Photo: Stacy Barnett/Shutterstock)

RELIGIOUS BELIEFS The psychological component of religious coping involves people's beliefs and attitudes. A number of investigators have examined links between religious beliefs and various measures of well-being among the elderly. For example, seniors who place a great deal of emphasis on religious faith worry much less than those who do not (Tapanya, Nicki, & Jarusawad, 1997). Moreover, associations between religious faith and physical and mental health have been found among older adults of diverse faiths—Christians, Buddhists, Muslims, Hindus, Taoists, and Sikhs—and from a variety of cultures and ethnic groups (Krause et al., 1999; Meisenhelder & Chandler, 2000; Tapanya et al., 1997; Zhou, Yao, & Xu, 2002). Thus, the positive effects of religious faith may have more to do with a general attitude of *spirituality*, a tendency to focus on the aspects of life that transcend one's physical existence, than on any particular set of doctrines or teachings.

The positive effects of religious coping seem to arise from its influence on how seniors think about their lives (Park, Edmondson, & Mills, 2010). For example, older adults who rate their religious beliefs as highly important to them are more likely than others to think that their lives serve an important purpose (Gerwood, LeBlanc, & Piazza, 1998). In addition, religious faith seems to provide older adults with a theme that integrates the various periods of their lives (Ko, Mehta, & Meng, 2006; Mehta, 1997). As a result, religious seniors are more likely than their nonreligious peers to view old age as a chapter in an ongoing story rather than as primarily a period of loss of capacities.

ATTENDANCE AT RELIGIOUS SERVICES The social aspect of religious coping most often examined by researchers is attendance at religious services. Across all ages, adult women attend religious services more regularly than men (Clark & Schellenberg, 2006; Statistics Canada, 2010b). Regular religious service attendance dips during early adulthood but rises steadily once Canadians reach their mid-adult years. It is highest for seniors, with roughly four in ten attending at least once a week (Lindsay, 2008). Research has shown that Canadian adults who regularly attend such services are more optimistic, are physically healthier, are longer living, are very satisfied with their lives, and have less stressful lives than their nonattending peers (Clark, 1998; Koenig, 2009, 2012). These findings correspond with research on religious people that emphasizes the positive connection between a sense of belonging and a sense of well-being (Idler, McLaughlin, & Kasl, 2009). As well, there appears to be a causal connection wherein feelings of belonging improve a person's level of health. Religious seniors who regularly attend religious services live healthier lives, and this is associated with a strong sense of connectedness to their community and a better personal support network (Clark, 2000; Idler et al., 2009). Interestingly, longitudinal studies suggest that patterns of attendance change little even if seniors become ill or disabled (Idler & Kasl, 1997; Idler, McLaughlin, & Kasl, 2009).

Longitudinal studies also suggest that the mortality rate is lower among religious participants (Gillum, King, Obisesan, & Koenig, 2008; Li, Stampfer, Williams, & VanderWeele, 2016). In one study, researchers examined the association between religious attendance and mortality in nearly 75 000 older adult women over a 20-year period (Li et al., 2016). Researchers found that the mortality rate of death from all causes, including cardiovascular and cancer disease, during the 20-year period was significantly lower among the older adult women who frequently (weekly or more often) attended religious services.

Seniors themselves cite a number of reasons for the benefits of religious involvement. For example, many say that religious institutions provide them with opportunities to help others (la Cour, Avlund, & Schultz-Larsen, 2006; Krause et al., 1999). Intergenerational involvement is another aspect of religious participation often mentioned by older adults. For many, religious institutions provide a structure within which they can pass on their knowledge and beliefs to younger individuals. Whatever the reasons, the research evidence suggests that supporting the spiritual needs of the elderly may be just as important to maintaining their health and functioning as meeting their physical and material needs.

Critical Thinking

How might you explain the associations between religious faith and physical and mental health?

Test Yourself before going on

1. According to critics, the successful aging paradigm is a new kind of _____ _____ that portrays elders with disabilities as incompetent.
2. The psychological component of religious coping is _____, and the social aspect is _____.

Critical Thinking

3. How do the concepts of successful aging and religious coping apply to people who have not yet reached late adulthood?

Social Relationships

The social roles older adults occupy are usually different from those they held at younger ages. The greatest proportion of seniors' social activities involve contacts with family and friends (Turcotte & Schellenberg, 2007). For widowed or unmarried seniors, relationships with adult children and other family members may become more central than they were in earlier years. However, an older adult who is no longer able to live alone may be reluctant to live with an adult child with whom she has long-standing disagreements or does not trust. Canadian statistics give credence to this wariness as adult children are identified as the perpetrators in most cases of family violence against seniors (Sinha, 2012) (see the **Research Report**). Nevertheless, most elderly adults cite meaningful social roles as essential to life satisfaction (Bowling et al., 2003). Moreover, there is no doubt that social relationships contribute to older adults' sense of well-being. Both consistency and change characterize social relationships during this period.

Living Arrangements

Only a small percentage of women (5.6%) and men (3%) over age 65 reside in long-term care institutions, although the percentage increases substantially in seniors who are aged 85 and older (Statistics Canada, 2012u, 2013c). Most older adults prefer to live independently in private households. However, the physical changes associated

Learning Objective 18.5

Identify the living arrangements of elderly people in Canada.

Research Report

Elder Abuse in Canada

Abuse and/or neglect of seniors is an extreme manifestation of conflict and strain between older adults and someone in a relationship of trust, such as a family member, a friend, a service provider, or health care providers in institutional settings. This abuse/neglect can be psychological, emotional, verbal, physical, sexual, financial, or any combination thereof (Government of Canada, 2015a; Yon, Wister, Mitchell, & Gutman, 2014). Although most Canadians (93%) (EKOS, 2011) are aware of the term *elder abuse*, and the maltreatment of seniors has occasionally received a great deal of media coverage, it is largely a hidden and challenging problem in Canada and worldwide (Podnieks, Rietschlin, & Walsh, 2012; Walsh & Yon, 2012; Yon et al., 2014). Canadian surveys have indicated that 7% of seniors reported emotional abuse (such as yelling, insulting, threatening, or ignoring) and/or financial exploitation (Yon et al., 2014). Additionally, roughly 10% of Canadian seniors are victims of crime each year. Of these, ~9% are victims of property crime and ~1% are victims of physical abuse or violent crime (Government of Canada, 2015b). Of the ~4000 seniors who were victims of violent crime, ~34% were victimized by a family member (i.e., a grown child, spouse, or extended family member), ~40% by casual acquaintances or neighbours, and ~25% by strangers (Ibrahim, 2016a). Notably, data indicates police-reported violence, ranging from uttering threats to homicide, committed by a current spouse increases with age and is highest among Canadians 65 years and older (Ibrahim, 2016b). Collectively, the impact of any form of abuse involves a range of emotional reactions that affect seniors more intensely than adults at other ages (Brennon, 2012; Hayman, 2011).

Researchers have identified several risk factors for elder abuse, including mental illness or alcoholism in the abuser, financial dependency of the abuser on the victim, social isolation, and external stresses (Pillemer & Suitor, 1990, 1992; Swanson, 1999). There are gender differences as well—male abusers are more likely to commit physical abuse, whereas female abusers are more likely to fail to provide needed aid (neglect) (Swanson, 1999). A likely victim of abuse is an elderly widow sharing her household with a dependent son who has a mental disorder or a drug or alcohol problem; the mother is typically too dependent on her son to kick him out and too ashamed of the abuse to tell others about it (Bengtson, Rosenthal, & Burton, 1996). Abuse is also more likely when a senior with dementia is physically violent and when a husband has physically abused his wife throughout their adult lives and simply continues to do so in old age.

The existence of such destructive forms of interaction is a clear reminder that older adults' relationships with their kin are not all sweetness and light. But it is also important to remember that these highly negative patterns are the exception rather than the rule. For most seniors, relationships with children and other family may be a mixture of positive and negative, but the scale most often tips toward the positive.

More recently, the risk of mass marketing fraud and internet victimization has been increasing (Brennon, 2012). Those Canadians between the ages of 60 and 69 are now the largest target of mass marketing fraud—most often by means of telephone/facsimile, followed by email, internet, and text messaging, and also by mail (Canadian Anti-Fraud Centre, 2015). In addition to financial losses, seniors are also at risk for identity fraud.

with aging mean that some kind of change in living arrangements generally must be made at some point in an individual's later years. Many housing options are available to seniors depending upon their level and type of care needs, living preferences, and financial resources. A guide to seniors housing in Canada can be found online (http://www.aplaceformom.com/canada/canada-seniors-housing-guide).

Figure 18.2 shows the marital status of the old and oldest old in Canada. Because men, at least in the past, typically married younger women and because women live longer than men, a man can normally expect to have a spouse or intimate partner until he dies. The normal expectation for an elderly woman is that she will eventually be without such a partner, often for many years. Clearly, the percentages in Figure 18.2 support these expectations.

The difference is also clearly reflected in **Figure 18.3**, which shows the living arrangements of seniors in Canada. As you can see, older women are more likely to live alone than older men. Although this pattern is typical in other developed countries as well, it is changing in Canada. Increasingly, couples are closer in age to each other than they were just a generation ago and men are living proportionally longer. This means that one partner (usually the woman) is less likely to outlive the other partner (usually the man) for as long a period of time as in the past (Milan, Wong, & Vézina, 2014).

Figure 18.2   As seniors age, women are more likely to become widowed and can expect to spend their final years without their spouse.

(**SOURCE:** Adapted from Statistics Canada, *2006 Census of Population*, Statistics Canada catalogue no. 97-552-XCB2006007. Retrieved from http://www12.statcan.gc.ca/census-recensement/2006/dp-pd/index-eng.cfm)

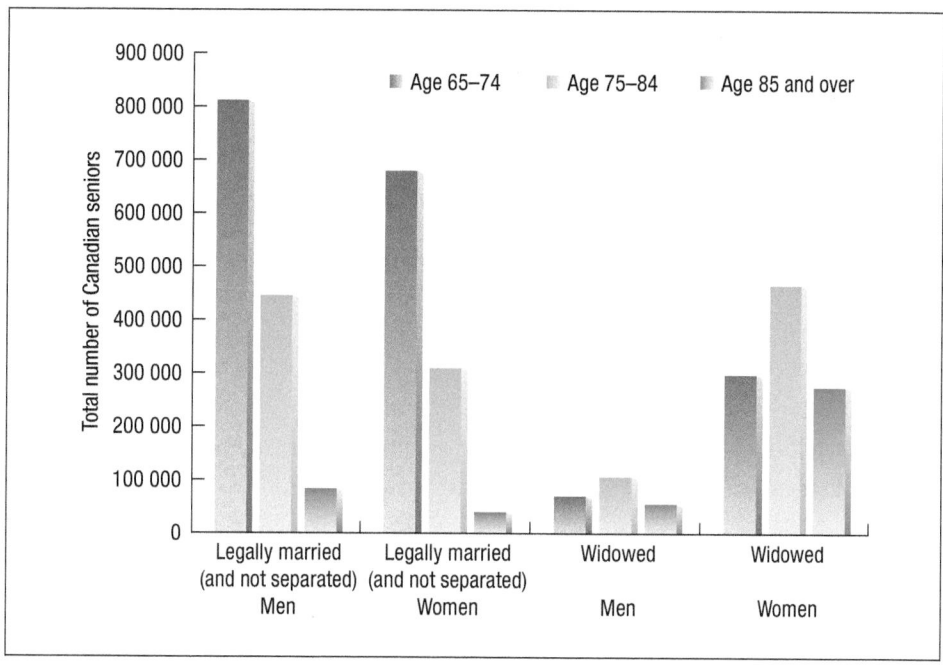

Figure 18.3   This graph shows the living arrangements of Canadian seniors. You can see that for those seniors who were not living with a spouse, living alone was the most common alternative, followed by living with extended families.

(**SOURCES:** http://statcan.gc.ca/tables-tableaux/sum-som/l01/cst01/famil52a-eng.htm)

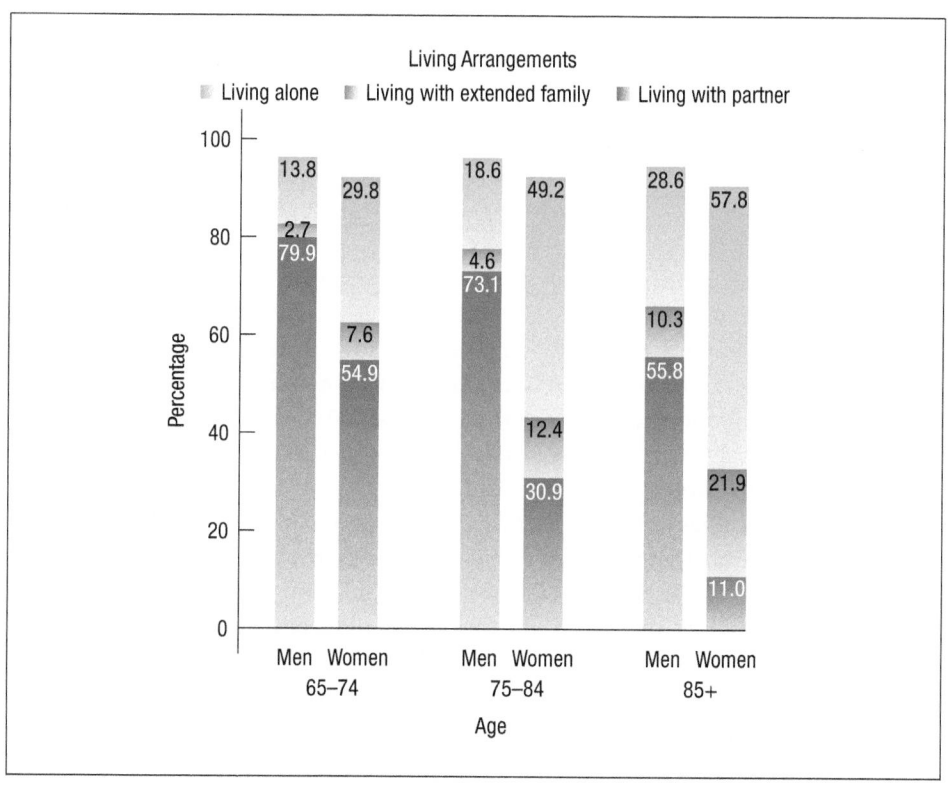

This is partially reflected in the corresponding increase in seniors who are now living in private households, in part because both partners can provide support for each other. It is expected that living arrangements will become increasingly more diverse as the number of same-sex couples, individuals who have remarried and also may now have an extended family, and those who live in common-law relationships increases. How this will impact the living arrangements of the next generation of seniors is not yet clear.

Several factors affect the probability that an unattached older adult will live with a child, with other relatives, or in a long-term care setting:

- *Health.* Older adults with higher levels of functional health are less likely to move in with family or into institutional living arrangements (Sarma, Hawley, & Basu, 2009). Seniors who need help with activities of daily living (ADLs) are more likely to live in the homes of family members than are those who can manage the physical demands of living independently (Choi, 2003). However, as self-reported health status declines, the probability of institutionalization increases (Sarma et al., 2009).
- *Income.* Older adults with higher household incomes are more likely to live independently or with family members (Sarma et al., 2009).
- *Adult children's characteristics.* Older adults with several daughters are more likely than those with few daughters to live with grown children (Soldo, Wolf, & Agree, 1990). Married adults are more likely than those who are single to take in their aging parents (Choi, 2003).
- *Public home care and social support services.* Older adults who receive home care services are less likely to become institutionalized, and older adults with social support services are less likely to have either family or institutional living arrangements (Sarma et al., 2009).

What do these factors suggest about the roles and relationships of older adults? First and foremost, of course, they point to a sharp divergence of experience for men and women in the later years. They also indicate that developmentalists need to look beyond the spousal or partnership relationship if they are to understand the patterns of social interactions that are central to the aging individual.

Partnerships

Learning Objective 18.6

Describe how intimate partnerships contribute to development in late adulthood.

Cross-sectional comparisons show that marital satisfaction is higher in the late adult years than when children are still at home (Ito & Sagara, 2012). But this high marital satisfaction may have a somewhat different basis than that of the early years of marriage. In late adulthood, marriages tend to be based less on passion and mutual disclosure and more on loyalty, familiarity, and mutual investment in the relationship (Fouquereau & Baudoin, 2002). In Sternberg's terms (refer to the discussion in the chapter on Social and Personality Development in Early Adulthood), late adult marriages are more likely to reflect companionate love than romantic or even consummate love. In addition to the intimacy portion of companionate love, a deep level of commitment—characterized by determination, some degree of sacrifice, and taking the effort to resolve conflicts—was found to be associated with lasting and happy marriages (Schoebi, Karney, & Bradbury, 2012).

Of course, this does not mean that the marriages of older adults are necessarily devitalized or neutral. That may well be true of some marriages, but there is evidence to the contrary for many. You'll recall from the chapter on Physical and Cognitive Development in Late Adulthood that the majority of older adult couples are still sexually active and may be somewhat more sexually adventurous than younger adults. Collectively, older couples also report higher levels of pleasure and lower levels of conflict in their relationships than do middle-aged couples. A recent longitudinal study found that couples who believe marriage should be forever and had a more egalitarian relationship—e.g., shared decision making and husbands who shared in the housework—had an increased likelihood of being happy in the relationship and had a low level of conflict (Kamp Dush & Taylor, 2012). When older couples do have conflicts, they resolve them in more affectionate and less negative ways. Older couples also spend more time with each other than with family or friends, and although much of this time is spent in passive or basic maintenance activities—watching TV, doing housework, running errands—it is also true that those married seniors who spend more time with their spouses report high levels of happiness (Anderson, Van Ryzin, & Doherty, 2010).

Affection between married partners and pleasure in each other's company clearly do not disappear in old age.

Further evidence of the deep bond that continues to exist in late-life marriages is the remarkable degree of care and assistance older spouses give each other when one or the other is disabled. For married seniors with some kind of disability, by far the largest source of assistance is the spouse, not children or friends. Many husbands and wives continue to care for spouses who are ill or who suffer from dementia for very long periods of time. And even when both spouses suffer from significant disabilities, they nonetheless continue to care for each other "until death do us part." Marriages may thus be less romantic or less emotionally intense in late adulthood than they were in earlier years, but they are typically satisfying and highly committed.

Researchers have found similar characteristics and effects in long-term gay and lesbian relationships (Grossman, Daugelli, & Hershberger, 2000). Like heterosexuals, an elderly homosexual who has a long-term partner typically identifies the partner as his most important source of emotional support. In addition, those who live with a partner report less loneliness and better physical and mental health.

The loss of the marriage or partnership relationship through the death of a spouse or partner alters this pattern for many older adults. The gender difference in marital status among seniors illustrated in Figure 18.2 is further increased by a higher rate of remarriage for men than for women, a pattern found among both the widowed and the divorced at every age. In Canada, 76% of divorced or separated men over 65 engage in another union, compared to only 55% of women in this age group. Likewise, a larger portion of older men (31%) remarry or enter a second union following the death of their spouse than do women (13%) (Milan et al., 2014). This difference is due, in large part, to the lack of available partners for women as they outlive men. This is especially the case in the latter parts of old age (Hudon & Milan, 2016).

Married older adults, like married adults of any age, have certain distinct advantages: They have higher life satisfaction, better health, and lower rates of institutionalization (Iwashyna & Christakis, 2003; Waldinger & Schulz, 2010). Such differential advantages are generally greater for married older men than for married older women (again, this is also true among younger adults). This difference might be interpreted as indicating that marriage affords more benefits to men than to women or that men rely more on their marriage relationship for social support and are thus more affected by its loss. Whatever the explanation, it seems clear that, for older women, marital status is less strongly connected to health or life satisfaction, but still strongly connected to financial security.

Elderly newlyweds report higher levels of personal happiness than either long-married or single peers.

The protective nature of marriage for older adults is supported by research showing that single adults over age 65 have higher mortality rates, even when factors such as poverty are controlled (Manzoli, Villari, Pironec, & Boccia, 2007). Moreover, these rates are consistent across gender and culture. Interestingly, though, seniors whose single status is the result of divorce have higher mortality rates than either those who have been widowed or peers who have never married. In addition, divorced older adults have higher rates of alcohol abuse, depression, and suicide (Hahn, Yong, Shih, & Lo, 2004; Lorant, Kunst, Huisman, Bopp, & Mackenbach, 2005; Onen et al., 2005). These rates may be higher because divorced seniors, especially men, are more likely to be disconnected from their families than their never-married or widowed peers are (Tomassini et al., 2004). However, participation in religious activities and other forms of social engagement appear to moderate the associations among single status, substance abuse, depression, poor health, and mortality risk (Hahn et al., 2004). Thus, the key advantage of intimate partnerships for older adults is that they provide them with readily available sources of support (Landis, Peter-Wight, Martin, & Bodenmann, 2013). For single seniors, more effort is required to identify and connect with sources of support, and physical disabilities are more likely to interfere with maintaining them than is the case for partnered seniors who share the same household.

Family Relationships and Friendships

Learning Objective 18.7

Identify the significance of family relationships and friendships for older adults.

Folklore and descriptions of late adulthood in the popular press suggest that family, particularly children and grandchildren, form the core of the social life of older adults, perhaps especially those who are widowed. Older adults do describe intergenerational bonds as strong and important; most report a renewed sense of purpose and enjoyment from their grandchildren, and a sense of family solidarity and support (Milan & Hamm, 2003). These bonds are reflected, among other things, in regular contact between seniors and family members. Moreover, researchers have found that family relationships become more harmonious as adults get older (Akiyama, Antonucci, Takahashi, & Langfahl, 2003). Thus, they represent an important component of most seniors' overall life satisfaction.

CONTACTS WITH ADULT CHILDREN Canadian studies show that at least half of older parents said their children see them at least once a week (Connidis, 1989; Turcotte & Schellenberg, 2007). The distance between where a senior parent and adult child live has an effect on the frequency of visitation. University of Alberta sociologist Susan McDaniel (1994) reported that, of those Canadians who lived within 10 kilometres of one of their parents, 80% visited daily or at least once a week. Of those who lived between 11 and 50 kilometres away, 52% visited daily or weekly, but the rate of regular visitations dropped to 23% when the parent and child lived 51 to 100 kilometres apart.

For those children who do not visit frequently, close family ties are maintained with telephone calls, letters, and email. In addition, it is important to emphasize that the frequency of contact is not the only measure of the closeness of family relationships.

Perhaps more important than the frequency of visitation is the satisfaction seniors experience with family contacts. Havens and Finlayson (1999) reported that seniors do not need to have frequent contact with family members to feel close to them. Regardless of frequency of visitation, 88% of seniors report that they feel close to family members. Moreover, about three-quarters of seniors aged 65 and above are very satisfied with the level of family contact, while fewer than 4% are less than satisfied with the level of contact with family members.

(Photo: bst2012/Fotolia)

Most elders enjoy maintaining relationships with younger family members. However, research suggests that such connections are not essential to life satisfaction in old age.

Part of the regular contact between the elderly and their adult children, of course, involves giving aid to or receiving it from the elder person. Most of the time, when older adults need help that cannot be provided by a spouse, it is provided by other family members, principally children. However, relationships between older parents and their adult children cannot be reduced simply to the exchange of aid. A great deal of the interaction is social as well as functional, and the great majority of older adults describe their relationships with their adult children in positive terms. Most see their children not only out of a sense of obligation or duty but because they take pleasure in such contact, and a very large percentage describe at least one child as a confidant (Taylor, Funk, Craighill, & Kennedy, 2006).

EFFECTS OF RELATIONSHIPS WITH ADULT CHILDREN   Some studies indicate that when relationships between elders and adult children are warm and close, they are more important to elders' sense of well-being than any other kind of social relationship (Pinquart & Soerensen, 2000). By contrast, other researchers have found that seniors who see their children more often or report more positive interactions with their children do not describe themselves as happier or healthier overall than do those who have less frequent or less positive relationships with their children (e.g., Mullins & Mushel, 1992). Moreover, such results have been obtained in very different cultural settings, for example, in India and among Mexican Americans (Lawrence, Bennett, & Markides, 1992; Venkatraman, 1995). In all these studies, the older adults reported regular contact with their children and said that they enjoyed it, but these relationships did not seem to enhance happiness or health. Moreover, research has shown that childless seniors are just as happy and well-adjusted as those who have children (Taylor et al., 2006). Many developmentalists have concluded that good relationships and regular contact with adult children can add to an elderly adult's quality of life but are not necessary for it.

One possible explanation for this inconsistency in findings is that the relationship with one's children is still governed by role prescriptions, even in old age. It may be friendly, but it is not chosen in the same way that a relationship with a friend is. With your friend, you feel free to be yourself and feel accepted as who you are. With your children, you may feel the need to live up to their demands and expectations. This hypothesis may explain why elders' levels of distress increase whenever their adult children experience problems with their careers or intimate relationships (Milkie, Bierman, & Scheiman, 2008). That is, threats to adult children's independence such as job loss and divorce may cause elders to become anxious about being thrust back into an active parenting role.

GRANDCHILDREN AND SIBLINGS   As you learned in the chapter on Social and Personality Development in Middle Adulthood, interactions between grandchildren and middle-aged grandparents are beneficial to both. However, in late adulthood, contact between grandchildren and grandparents declines as the grandchildren become adults themselves (Barer, 2001; Silverstein & Long, 1998). Thus, grandchildren are rarely part of an elderly adult's close family network.

Interestingly, though, it appears that relationships with siblings may become more important in late adulthood, especially after both parents have died (Taylor et al., 2006). Siblings seldom provide much practical assistance to each other in old age, but they can and often do serve two other important functions. First, siblings can provide a unique kind of emotional support for each other, based on shared reminiscences and companionship. Once parents are gone, no one else knows all the old stories, all the family jokes, the names and history of former friends and neighbours. Second, many seniors see their siblings as a kind of "insurance policy" in old age, a source of support of last resort (Connidis, 1994).

FRIENDSHIPS   Mounting evidence suggests that contact with friends has a significant impact on overall life satisfaction, self-esteem, health, and the amount of loneliness reported by older adults (Antonucci, Lansford, & Akiyama, 2001; Turcotte &

Friends seem to play an important role in late adulthood, perhaps because they share the same background and memories—like favourite old tunes and dances.

Schellenberg, 2007). Moreover, for those seniors whose families are unavailable, friendships seem to provide an equally effective support network (Takahashi, Tamura, & Tokoro, 1997). The importance of friendships is particularly true for unmarried seniors but is at least somewhat true for married ones as well.

Friends meet different kinds of needs for older adults than do family members. For one thing, relationships with friends are likely to be more reciprocal or equitable, and developmentalists know that equitable relationships are more valued and less stressful. Friends provide companionship, opportunities for laughter, and shared activities. Canadian studies have found, for example, friends were second only to spouses as sources of companionship and emotional support among those over age 65 (Turcotte & Schellenberg, 2007). Friends may also provide assistance with daily tasks, such as shopping or housework, although they typically provide less help of this kind than do family members.

Learning Objective 18.8

Identify gender differences in older adults' social networks.

Gender Differences in Social Networks

As at earlier ages, women and men in late adulthood appear to form different kinds of social networks, with men's friendships involving less disclosure and less intimacy than women's. In addition, older women's networks tend to be larger and closer than those of older men. Developmentalists attribute these findings to a continuation of a pattern evident across most of the lifespan (Taylor et al., 2006). Thus, if you think back on what you learned about sex differences in the chapters on childhood, adolescence, early adulthood, and middle adulthood, sex differences in late adulthood social networks should not be surprising.

It would be a mistake to assume, however, that because men have smaller social networks, their relationships are unimportant to them. Some developmentalists suggest that research on social networks may be biased in such a way that women will always be found to have stronger networks. This bias, critics say, originates from the fact that research emphasizes shared activities and frequency of contact more than the quality of the relationships. Indeed, when quality of relationships is considered, research shows that men's social networks are just as important to them and provide them with the same kinds of emotional support as women's networks do, even though men's networks tend to be smaller (Hall, Havens, & Sylvestre, 2003; Riggs, 1997).

Test Yourself before going on

1. What two living arrangements are most common among older adults living in Canada?
2. A married older adult with a disability or dementia is most likely to be cared for by a(n) _____.
3. For most seniors, friends provide (more/less) help than family members.
4. Older men have (larger/smaller) social networks than older women do.

Critical Thinking

5. What kinds of physical and social barriers are there to creating new social relationships in late adulthood?

Career Issues in Late Life

A remarkable capacity for adaptation marks the transition from work to retirement. Although this transition certainly brings the loss of a major role, the research points to a collection of "pushes" and "pulls" that combine to influence each person's decision to retire.

Timing of and Reasons for Retirement

Until a few years ago the normal retirement age was 65 in Canada. With few exceptions (e.g., those in physically demanding jobs, such as firefighting and police work), mandatory retirement has been eliminated across the country (*CBC News*, 2009). Ironically, survey results of employed Canadians under age 40 found that only 18% were willing to postpone their retirement (Langlois, 2004); this trend was contradicted by those nearing retirement age (aged 50 to 59), of whom 57% indicated they would rather work longer rather than forego their current lifestyle (CIBC, 2012a). Furthermore, until recently, the average age of retirement had been dropping in most developed countries; in Canada, the average age of retirement went from age 64.9 in 1982 to a low of 61.0 in 2000 (Statistics Canada, 2001d). Now, however, it seems the trend is reversing and the age of retirement is creeping back up. It rose to above 63 years of age by 2015 and continues edging upwards (Statistics Canada, 2016m). And, at least half of workers in their 50s say they'll continue working at least part-time in retirement (CIBC, 2012b).

AGE   Age itself is obviously an important ingredient in the retirement equation. Internal models play an important role here. If a person's "expected life history" includes retirement at age 55 or 65, he will be strongly inclined to retire at that age, regardless of other factors.

HEALTH   Poor health provides a particularly strong push toward early retirement (Carrière & Galaneau, 2011). Poor health lowers the average age of retirement by one to three years; this trend is commonly found in developed countries (Hayward, Friedman, & Chen, 1996; McDonald & Wanner, 1990; Stanford, Happersett, Morton, Molgaard, & Peddecord, 1991). However, among those who retire at age 65 or later, health is a less powerful factor, presumably because most of these later retirees are in good health.

FAMILY CONSIDERATIONS   Family composition is important in the decision to retire (McDonald & Donahue, 2011). Those who are still supporting minor children retire later than do those in the postparental stage. Thus, men and women who bear their children very late, those who acquire a second and younger family in a second marriage, and those rearing grandchildren are likely to continue to work until these children have left home.

FINANCIAL SUPPORT   Equally important in the timing of retirement is the availability of adequate financial support for retirement (McDonald & Donahue, 2011; Schellenberg & Ostrovsky, 2008). Those who anticipate receiving pension support in addition to Canada Pension Plan (CPP) or Québec Pension Plan (QPP) benefits, or who have personal savings to draw on, retire earlier than do those who have no such financial backup.

Anticipated pension and health frequently work in opposite directions, because many working-class men and women who have worked in unskilled jobs can expect little supplementary retirement income and are in poor health. In general, working-class adults retire earlier than do middle-class and upper-class adults, often as a result of ill health and social norms, but many poor and working-class adults continue to work well past the normal retirement age to supplement their incomes.

On the other end of the social class scale, health and the adequacy of pensions work against each other in the opposite way. Adults in higher socioeconomic groups generally have both better health and better pensions; they also tend to have more interesting jobs. The three factors combine to produce somewhat later retirement for this group.

WORK CHARACTERISTICS   The ranks of Canadian seniors who are employed has been trending upward since 1996 and is hovering around 12% with twice as many senior

Learning Objective 18.9

Identify what factors contribute to the decision to retire.

men as women in the workforce (Statistics Canada, 2012v). Median retirement ages across industry categories are different. For example, more non-unionized or self-employed people expect to work beyond age 65 than those who aren't (Schellenberg & Ostrovsky, 2008). People who are highly committed to work they enjoy, including many self-employed adults, retire later—often quite a lot later—than do those who are less gratified by their work. As well, self-employed seniors tend to be better educated and work in jobs that are more intellectually challenging and less physically demanding (Duchesne, 2004; Park, 2011; Uppal, 2011). People in challenging and interesting jobs are likely to postpone retirement until they are pushed by ill health or attracted by some extra financial inducement. For them, availability of a pension is less of an influence (Hayward & Hardy, 1985).

SEX DIFFERENCES On average, women in Canada retire about one-and-a-half years before men retire (Statistics Canada, 2016m). Just when women will retire cannot be predicted by retirement benefits, health, or job characteristics. One factor that tends to keep women in the labour force is the lure of higher earnings that will augment future CPP/QPP benefits—a factor that may be especially important for women who took several years off from full-time work to raise children. However, financial experts point out that even if retirement-aged women have as many years of full-time employment as men do, they are still likely to receive less money from pensions because, on average, their earnings are lower (Powell, 2006).

Effects of Retirement

Learning Objective 18.10

Describe how retirement affects the lives of older adults.

A number of shifts, both positive and negative, take place at retirement. But, overall, retirement seems to have positive effects on the lives of older adults.

INCOME One potentially significant change that occurs at retirement is related to the availability of alternative sources of income. Canadian seniors have several potential sources of income: government pensions, such as Old Age Security (OAS) and CPP/QPP; other pensions, such as those offered through an employer; income from savings, such as registered retirement savings plans (RRSPs), or other assets; and earnings from continued work. For most seniors in Canada, nongovernment sources now provide the largest portion of retirement income (Brown, 2011), which means that young workers need to plan well ahead to ensure that they will have enough retirement income to meet their retirement lifestyle expectations. A common estimation is that you will need between 60% and 80% of your preretirement earnings to maintain your standard of living in retirement; for example, if you are earning $100,000 before you retire, you can expect to require roughly $70,000 in annual income once you retire (*Globe and Mail*, n.d.). To assist in planning for one's future financial security, Service Canada (2016) has created an interactive website to help Canadians estimate their retirement income needs with the aid of the Canadian Retirement Income Calculator (http://www.esdc.gc.ca/en/cpp/cric.page).

POVERTY It used to be that postretirement income losses resulted in high poverty rates among the elderly. However, over the past several decades, poverty rates among the elderly have declined substantially (Brown, 2011). Health Canada (2003b) reported that, after adjusting for inflation, senior men's income rose 21% and senior women's by 22% between 1981 and 1998. In line with this, the incidence of seniors who were living below Statistics Canada's low income cut-offs (LICOs), a measure of poverty, fell sharply from 34% in the early 1980s, to 20% by the late 1990s where it has remained relatively constant (Murphy, Zhang & Dionne, 2015).

A variety of factors were responsible for the declining poverty rates among the elderly. For one thing, there were significant improvements in work-related pensions. As well, there were moderate improvements in CPP/QPP and regular cost-of-living increases for pension incomes (Health Canada, 2003c). Equivalent progress was made in reducing the rates of poverty among the elderly in many other countries.

Figure 18.4 This graph illustrates how unattached older adults, in particular, continue to be poorer than their peers who live in families. Among unattached seniors, women are more likely to be poor than men. Poverty among seniors has been rising after dropping to historic lows in the 1990s.

(**SOURCE:** Adapted from Statistics Canada. (2012w). Persons in low income families-annual (CANSIM Table 202-0802). Ottawa, ON: Author. Retrieved from http://www5.statcan.gc.ca/cansim/a01?lang=eng. Reproduced with permission of Minister for Statistics Canada, 2012)

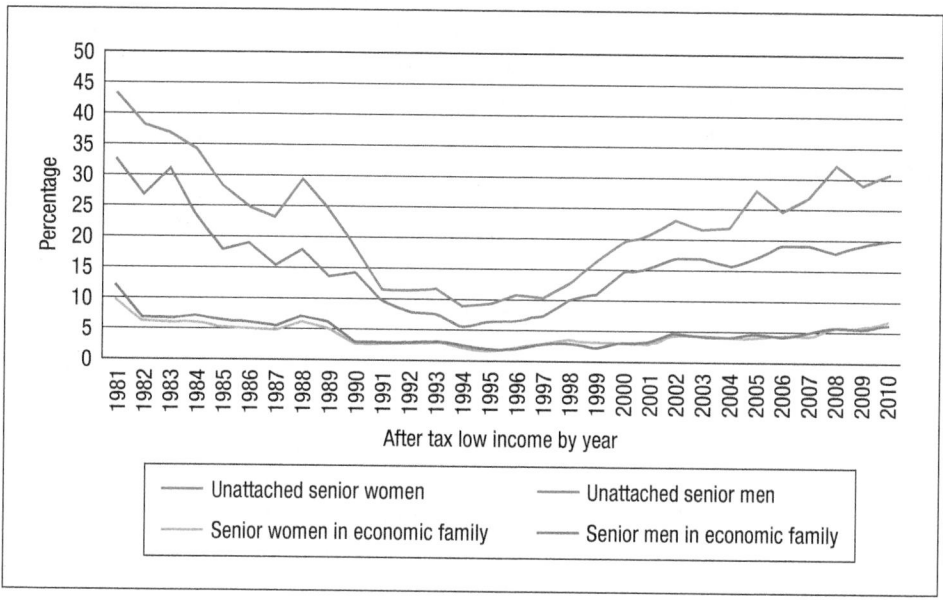

Unfortunately, the rates of poverty in the elderly have recently been moving upward (Conference Board of Canada (CBoC), 2012; Statistics Canada, 2012w). As well, the rising numbers of seniors living below the LICOs obscures much higher rates of poverty in two subgroups—unattached and female seniors (CBoC, 2012). **Figure 18.4** shows persistent disparities in the poverty rates for senior men and women who are unattached. Unattached older adults are more likely to be poor than their peers who live in families, and among unattached seniors, women are more likely to be poor than men (~31% versus 20%, respectively) (Statistics Canada, 2012w). Varying poverty rates for elderly unattached men and women arise from a number of differences in adult life experiences. Current cohorts of older women are much less likely than their male peers to have had paid employment, are less likely to have earned retirement benefits even if they did work, and generally worked for lower wages (Powell, 2006). As a result, many older widows rely entirely on CPP/QPP and OAS income. Younger women are more likely to have been employed and to have participated in a retirement plan, but, as you learned in earlier chapters, gender differences in work patterns still exist. Moreover, many more retirement-age women today are divorced than in past cohorts. The combination of income inequality and the increased prevalence of divorce are likely to lead to a dramatic rise in the number of women who live in poverty after retirement (Powell, 2006).

HEALTH, ATTITUDES, AND EMOTIONS Longitudinal studies indicate quite clearly that health simply does not change, for better or worse, because of retirement (van Solinge, 2007). When ill health accompanies retirement, the causal sequence is nearly always that the individual retired because of poor health. Among those in good health at retirement age, retirement itself has little or no effect on health status over the succeeding years.

In fact, Canadian research suggests that retirement can have a positive impact on overall life satisfaction, especially in situations where dissatisfaction stems from a work–life imbalance (Uriarte-Landa & Hébert, 2009). The most common causes of work–life conflict are caregiving, (e.g., for elderly parents, elderly relatives, and/or grandchildren); disability onset; coping with emotional demands, such as a change in marital status or loss of a spouse or a parent; and changing priorities, where spending time with family or on recreational pursuits or volunteering becomes more valuable than pursuing a career. Unfortunately, given a choice, dissatisfied older workers elect to continue working the same number of hours rather than sacrifice pay.

Other evidence suggests that those who respond least well to retirement are those who had the least control over the decision (Smith & Moen, 2004). For example, those who go into retirement because of a late-career job loss show declines in physical and mental health (Halleröd, Örestig, & Stattin, 2013). Similarly, those who are forced to retire because of poor health typically adjust more poorly to retirement (Hardy & Quadagno, 1995). Even workers who accept special early retirement offers from their employers are likely to report lower satisfaction and higher levels of stress than do those who feel they had more control over the retirement decision (Herzog, House, & Morgan, 1991). But for those for whom retirement is anticipated and on time, this role loss is not stressful.

It appears that what predicts life satisfaction in late adulthood is not whether a person has retired, but whether she was satisfied with life in earlier adulthood. We take ourselves with us through the years: Grumpy, negative young people tend to be grumpy, negative old people, and satisfied young adults find satisfaction in retirement as well. The consistency of this finding is quite striking and provides very good support for continuity theories of adulthood. Work does shape daily life for 40 years or more of adulthood, but a person's happiness or unhappiness with life, her growth or stagnation, seems less a function of the specifics of the work experience than a function of the attitudes and qualities she brings to the process.

(Photo: Susan Chiang/E+/Getty Images)

Elders who have moved to resort communities specifically designed for retired people have made what social scientists call an *amenity move*.

amenity move

postretirement move away from kin to a location that has some desirable feature, such as year-round warm weather

GEOGRAPHIC MOBILITY   For many adults, retirement brings an increase in choices about where to live. When your job or your spouse's job no longer ties you to a specific place, you can choose to move to sunnier climes or to live nearer to one of your children. Surprisingly, however, most retirees stay fairly close to the place they have called home for many years (Northcott & Petruik, 2011). In fact, Northcott and Petruik (2011) reported that only about 30% of Canadian seniors moved within a five-year period. When seniors aged 65 and over did move, most did so because their house was too big or too small; they or a spouse retired; they wanted to be near to their adult children and grandchildren; there was a decline in their health or the health of a spouse; and/or they wanted access to recreation or leisure. Regardless of whether they moved or remained where they lived before retirement, about seven of every ten seniors lived in Canadian urban centres with a population of 50 000 or more (Turcotte & Schellenberg, 2007).

Charles Longino (1938–2008), who was one of the most diligent investigators of residential moves among the elderly, suggests that elderly adults make three types of moves (Longino, 2003). The first type, which he calls an *amenity move*, is the one most of us probably think of when we think of older adults changing residences. If an older adult makes such a move, it is almost always right around the time of retirement. Most typically, an **amenity move** is in a direction away from the older person's children, frequently to a warmer climate. The department of Foreign Affairs and International Trade (FAIT) (2008) suggests that Florida and Arizona are popular destinations for amenity moves to the United States. Other popular international destinations include Mexico, Latin American countries, and islands in the Caribbean, especially where there is a Canadian expatriate community.

Seniors who make amenity moves are likely to be still married and relatively healthy and to have adequate or good retirement income (Cress, 2007). Often the relocating couple has vacationed in the new location; many have planned the move carefully over a number of years (Longino, Bradley, Stoller, & Haas, 2008). Most report higher levels of life satisfaction or morale after such a move, although some move back to where they came from because they find themselves too isolated from family and friends.

Another kind of amenity move is to move seasonally rather than making a permanent move to a new location. Some seniors, often called *snowbirds*, spend the winter months in sunnier areas and the summer months at home, nearer their families. Permanent movers away from Canada and seasonal retirees both have to contend with many essential issues when they leave the country, namely immigration and citizenship, taxation, health care, and real estate matters (FAIT, 2008).

The second type of move, which Longino calls **compensatory (kinship) migration**, occurs when the older adult—most often, a widow living alone—develops such a level of chronic disability that she has serious difficulty managing an independent household. When a move of this type occurs, it is nearly always a shift to be closer to a daughter, son, or some other relative who can provide regular assistance. In some cases, this means moving in with that daughter or son, but often the move is to an apartment or house nearby or into a retirement community in which the individual can live independently but has supportive services available. The final type of move in late adulthood is what Longino calls **institutional migration** to nursing-home care (see **Development in the Real World**).

Of course, very few older adults actually move three times. Longino's point is that these are three very different kinds of moves, made by quite different subsets of the population of elderly, and at different times in the late adult years. Amenity moves usually occur early, kinship or compensatory migration is likely to occur in middle to late old age, and institutional migration clearly occurs late in life. Only the first of these types of moves reflects the increase in options that may result from retirement.

compensatory (kinship) migration

a move to a location near family or friends that happens when an elder requires frequent help because of a disability or a disease

institutional migration

a move to an institution, such as a nursing home, that is necessitated by a disability

Development in the Real World

Deciding on Long-Term Care in Canada

In the chapter on Physical and Cognitive Development in Late Adulthood you read about the numbers of older adults living in long-term care institutions. A long-term care home in Canada usually denotes either not-for-profit homes for the aged or not-for-profit and for-profit nursing homes. The economics of long-term institutional care can make it unattractive for many older adults, especially seniors in low-income households (Sarma et al., 2009). Such care in Canada now starts at a minimum cost of about $2000 per month and goes up from there—these costs are only partially covered by government or most health insurance plans. A stay of as long as a year is likely to exhaust the disposable assets of the majority of older adults. To be eligible for government subsidization for such care, a person must first use all his own disposable assets, which may leave a surviving spouse in very difficult financial straits. Most Canadian jurisdictions permit ownership of certain assets, such as a home, to be transferred to a surviving spouse, so that this asset need not be disposed of before the partner in the long-term care institution is eligible for government subsidy—an alternative that leaves the surviving spouse in somewhat better financial condition. But the spouse may still suffer significant impoverishment.

The problem for individual families is balancing the older adult's need for independence and control against the needs of younger family members who have lives of their own to lead. What often tips the balance, one way or the other, is whether any family member is able or willing to provide assistance, and whether other community services are available. For some families, Meals on Wheels, visiting nurses, adult day programs, and other help may make it possible to continue to care for a frail or demented senior at home. An intermediate alternative, which is becoming more available, is some kind of "supportive housing," where the older person can have an individual apartment, and thus live independently, but has nursing and meal services available in the building or complex (Social Data Research/Pollara, 2005).

(Continued)

Beyond cost considerations, provincial and territorial agencies that serve older adults have suggested several criteria for evaluating a long-term care facility (Government of Canada, 2008). Here are a few:

- Be certain that the facility has the staff and equipment required to meet your elder's physical needs.
- Check with authorities to see whether any complaints have been filed and how they were resolved; avoid facilities with many outstanding complaints.
- Research the results of provincial/territorial inspections and the extent to which any deficiencies were corrected; do not admit your elder to a facility that has any current deficiencies.
- Visit at different times, such as during meals, recreation periods, early morning, and late evening, to note how residents are cared for in different situations.
- Talk to family members of other residents if possible.
- Ask about the facility's policies regarding medical emergencies.

Of course, a facility can receive high marks on these criteria and still not be the best one for an older adult. Thus, once a facility has satisfied these basic criteria, families must determine whether it can meet their older loved one's cognitive, social, and spiritual needs. Moreover, once an elder has been admitted, family members should closely monitor their care and be prepared to make a change if needed.

Learning Objective 18.11

Describe what the research says about the decision not to retire.

Choosing Not to Retire

A small number of adults continue working past the typical retirement age. In 2011, 16.5% of men and 8.1% of women over age 65 were employed in Canada (Statistics Canada, 2012v). This subgroup actually includes two types of people: those who have never retired from their long-time occupations and those who retired from their regular occupations and ventured into new lines of work, often part-time.

CONTINUING IN A LIFELONG OCCUPATION Recent research has focused on those over age 65 who are still employed. Some are seniors with very limited education and poor retirement benefits who would therefore have very low retirement incomes. Consequently, many of these seniors continue working out of economic necessity (McDonald & Donahue, 2011; Park, 2011). Yet, there's a large fraction of those who shun retirement who are highly educated, healthy, work-committed professionals. Many of them have been greatly invested in their careers their entire adult lives. For these seniors, work continues to provide more satisfaction than they expect retirement to offer.

Only 16.5% of men and 8.1% of women over age 65 are employed in Canada. However, a fairly high proportion of middle-aged people say they plan to work at least part-time after retirement. Consequently, employers are eager to learn how best to train older workers.

(*Photos:* left, Minerva Studio/Shutterstock; right, © StockLite/Shutterstock.com)

LEARNING NEW JOB SKILLS AND WORKPLACE FUNCTIONING Perhaps the greatest obstacle to employment for older adults is that many potential employers express concerns about older adults' ability to learn new job skills (Government of Alberta, 2010; HRSDC, 2011b). However, research shows that, with appropriately designed training, older adults can acquire new work-related skills. Pacing is an important element of instructional design, because older adults learn more efficiently when smaller chunks of information are presented than is typical in many job-training programs (Foos & Goolkasian, 2010). In addition, designers of computer-based training must take into account the increased prevalence of visual difficulties among older trainees by creating visual interfaces that include high contrast and larger text than is typically used with younger workers (Rivera-Nivar & Pomales-García, 2010).

With respect to aspects of job functioning other than learning of new skills, supervisors typically give older adults higher ratings than younger adults (Government of Alberta, 2010). For example, they view older employees as more loyal, reliable, safety conscious, literate, and flexible. In addition, managers typically report that, although younger workers produce a greater quantity of work, the quality of older employees' work is better, especially in various white-collar positions. Consequently, many employers view older adults as desirable employees.

Research suggests that older adults respond to computer training very much the way younger adults do. Most get over any anxieties they have about using computers after receiving training. In addition, they can become as proficient as younger adults, although they may require slower-paced training.

Test Yourself before going on

1. Those who were satisfied with their lives when they were working are (more/less) likely to be satisfied with their lives during their retirement years.
2. An older adult who moves in order to be closer to an adult child who can provide supportive care has made a type of move that Longino calls a(n) _____ _____.
3. Why is pacing important in job-training programs for older adults?

Critical Thinking

4. In what ways do the educational and career decisions that people make in their 20s and 30s shape the decisions they make about retirement in late adulthood?

Summary

Theories of Social and Personality Development

18.1 Describe what the research says about Erikson's stage of ego integrity versus despair.

- Erikson's concept of ego integrity has been influential, but research does not indicate that the development of ego integrity is necessary to adjustment in old age. The notions of reminiscence, life review, and continuing generativity have been helpful in researchers' attempts to understand development in late adulthood.

18.2 Characterize the main ideas of activity theory, disengagement theory, and continuity theory.

- Activity theory proposes that it is both normal and healthy for older adults to try to stay as active as possible. Disengagement theory asserts that it is normal for older adults to separate themselves from others. In addition, the theory argues that aging has three components: shrinkage of life space, increased individuality, and acceptance of age-related changes. Continuity theory views later adulthood as a time when elders cope with age-related changes by continuing to engage in activities that interested and challenged them earlier in life.

Individual Differences

18.3 Describe how successful aging is manifested in the lives of older adults.

- Successful aging encompasses maintenance of health, cognitive and social functioning, productivity, and life satisfaction.

18.4 Describe how religious coping influences physical and mental health in late adulthood.

- Religious coping has psychological and social components. It is associated with a lower mortality rate as well as with better physical and mental health.

Social Relationships

18.5 Identify the living arrangements of elderly people in Canada.

- Among Canadian seniors who were not living with a spouse, living alone was the most common alternative, followed by living with extended families.

18.6 Describe how intimate partnerships contribute to development in late adulthood.

- Marriages in late adulthood are, on average, highly satisfying for both spouses, who exhibit strong loyalty, mutual affection, and an egalitarian attitude. Married seniors, as a group, are somewhat healthier and more satisfied with their lives than are single seniors.

18.7 Identify the significance of family relationships and friendships for older adults.

- The majority of seniors see their adult children regularly. Relationships with siblings may become more significant in late adulthood than at earlier ages. Degree of contact with friends is correlated with overall life satisfaction among older adults.

18.8 Identify gender differences in older adults' social networks.

- Women in this age group continue to have larger social networks than men do.

Career Issues in Late Life

18.9 Identify what factors contribute to the decision to retire.

- The typical retirement age in Canada is roughly age 63 and rising. Time of retirement is affected by health, family responsibilities, adequacy of anticipated pension income, and satisfaction with one's job.

18.10 Describe how retirement affects the lives of older adults.

- Income typically decreases with retirement. Unattached seniors, especially women, are more likely to live with lower income than married couples. Retirement appears not to be a stressful life change for most people. The minority of older adults who find retirement stressful are likely to be those who feel they had little control over the decision to retire. Many older adults move at some time during retirement. Types of moves include amenity moves, compensatory migrations, and institutional migrations.

18.11 Describe what the research says about the decision not to retire.

- Those who choose not to retire do so for economic reasons or because of particularly strong commitments to work. Research indicates that older adults can learn new job skills. Supervisors rate older workers as desirable because they are reliable and they produce high-quality output.

Chapter 19
Death, Dying, and Bereavement

RubberBall Productions/Brand X Pictures/Getty Images

 Learning Objectives

THE EXPERIENCE OF DEATH

19.1 Differentiate among the processes of clinical death, brain death, and social death.

19.2 Compare how hospital and hospice palliative care differ with respect to their effects on terminally ill patients.

THE MEANING OF DEATH ACROSS THE LIFESPAN

19.3 Describe the characteristics of children's and adolescents' ideas about death.

19.4 Describe how young, middle-aged, and older adults think about death.

19.5 Identify what factors are related to fear of death in adults.

19.6 Describe how adults prepare for death.

THE PROCESS OF DYING

19.7 Summarize how Kübler-Ross explained the process of dying.

19.8 Identify some other views of the process of dying.

19.9 Describe how people vary in the ways they adapt to impending death.

THE EXPERIENCE OF GRIEVING

19.10 Describe how funerals and ceremonies help survivors cope with grief.

19.11 Identify what factors influence the grieving process.

19.12 Describe how grief affects the physical and mental health of widows and widowers.

We began our study of the human lifespan with an examination of birth and went on to consider the multitude of changes in the physical, cognitive, and social domains from infancy to late adulthood. Now we turn to the end of life. A particularly eloquent expression of the inevitability of death came from Stewart Alsop, a writer who kept a diary of the last years of his life as he was dying of leukemia. In one of the very late entries in this journal, he said, "A dying man needs to die as a sleepy man needs to sleep, and there comes a time when it is wrong, as well as useless, to resist" (1973, p. 299). Alsop's statement calls to mind one of the important individual variables you have read about often in earlier chapters: the timing of a universal developmental event in a particular individual's life.

Like Alsop, many people contract fatal diseases and consciously face the inevitability of impending death for a period of months or years. Sometimes an unexpected event—perhaps an accident or a crime—ends a child's or young adult's life prematurely. For most of us, though, death comes in late adulthood and results from the subtle interplay between primary and secondary aging. Consequently, a good deal of what you will learn about dying and death will concern older adults. But the story must begin earlier, with an examination of people's understanding of and attitudes toward dying and death.

The Experience of Death

Most of us use the word *death* as if it described a simple phenomenon: You are either alive or dead. In fact, death is a process as well as a state, and physicians have different labels for different aspects of this process. Moreover, for both the deceased and the bereaved, the experience of death is shaped by the circumstances surrounding the end of life.

Death Itself

Learning Objective 19.1

Differentiate among the processes of clinical death, brain death, and social death.

clinical death

a period during which vital signs are absent but resuscitation is still possible

brain death

irreversible absence of brain function

The term **clinical death** refers to the few minutes after the heart has stopped pumping, when breathing has stopped and there is no evident brain function, but during which resuscitation is still possible. Heart attack patients are sometimes brought back from clinical death; presumably, those who report near-death experiences were in a state of clinical death.

Brain death (referred to as *whole-brain death* in some jurisdictions) describes a state in which a person no longer has reflexes or any response to vigorous external stimuli and shows no electrical activity in the brain—essentially, irreversible failure of the cerebrum, cerebellum, limbic system, and brain stem. When the cerebral cortex, but not the brain stem, is affected, the person may still be able to breathe without assistance and may survive for long periods in a vegetative state or on life-support systems. However, when the brain stem irreversibly ceases to function, no body functioning can occur independently, and, in Canada, the individual is said to be *legally dead* (Daniels, 2014; Shaw 2014). Brain death most often occurs after a period of eight to ten minutes of clinical death, but there are cases in which brain death has occurred because of brain injury, as in an auto accident or a stroke, and other body functions can still be maintained artificially. In such cases, other body organs, such as the heart and kidneys, can be used for organ donation, as long as they are removed without delay.

Social death occurs at the point when the deceased person is treated like a corpse by others; for instance, someone may close the eyes or sign a death certificate. Once social death has been acknowledged, family and friends must begin to deal with the loss.

social death

the point at which family members and medical personnel treat the deceased person as a corpse

End-of-Life Care

Although the majority of Canadians die in hospitals, changing views about the process of dying means more families are turning toward an alternate form of end-of-life care for their terminally ill loved ones: hospice palliative care.

HOSPITAL CARE Almost two-thirds of Canadians die in hospitals rather than at home or in long-term care facilities (Statistics Canada, 2015l). Where people die depends on such factors as age, gender, and type of disease or injury (CIHI, 2007a, 2007b). For example, hospital death is more prevalent for older adults, and somewhat more so for women than men, than it is for their younger counterparts. People with a terminal illness, such as cancer, are more likely to die in a hospital than those with organ failure or frailty, or those who die suddenly because of, for example, accidents or trauma. As well, adults with terminal illness or chronic conditions, such as heart disease or organ failure, typically spend more time in the hospital in the year before death than those dying of other causes, such as those who are hospitalized with an acute problem such as a heart attack or an injury and who die soon thereafter, having had no prior hospitalization.

HOSPICE PALLIATIVE CARE In recent years, an alternative form of end-of-life care that has become common is **hospice care**, a holistic approach to caring for the dying that embraces individual and family control of the process. The modern-day hospice care movement emerged in England in the late 1960s and in Canada in the mid-1970s (van Bommel, 2002). The hospice care movement was given a boost by the writings of Elisabeth Kübler-Ross, who emphasized the importance of a "good death," or a "death with dignity," in which the patient and the patient's family have an active role in the process (1974). Many health care professionals, particularly in England, Canada, and the United States, believe that death with dignity is more likely if the dying person remains at home, or in a home-like setting, in which contact with family and friends is part of the daily experience. The philosophy that underlies this alternative approach to the dying patient has several aspects (van Bommel, 2002):

- Death should be viewed as normal, as something not to be avoided but to be faced and accepted.

- The patient and family should be encouraged to prepare for the death by examining their feelings, planning for after the death, and talking openly about the death.

- The family should be involved in the patient's care as much as is physically possible, not only because this participation gives the patient the emotional support of loved ones, but also because it allows family members to resolve their relationships with the dying person.

Learning Objective 19.2

Compare how hospital and hospice palliative care differ with respect to their effects on terminally ill patients.

hospice care

a holistic approach to care for the terminally ill that emphasizes individual and family control of the process of dying

- Control over the patient's care should be in the hands of the patient and the family. They decide what types of medical treatment they will ask for or accept; they decide whether the patient will remain at home or be hospitalized.
- Care should be aimed at satisfying the physical, emotional, spiritual, and psychosocial needs of a person with a life-threatening or terminal condition and his family.
- Medical care should be primarily *palliative care* rather than curative. The emphasis is on controlling pain and maximizing comfort, not on invasive or life-prolonging measures.

palliative care

a form of care that seeks to prevent, relieve, or soothe the patients' symptoms rather than cure their diseases or disorders

A related and more bilingual term, **palliative care**, was first coined in 1975 by Canadian oncology specialist Balfour Mount, following his inspiring 1974 visit to Dame Cicely Saunders's St. Christopher's Hospice in England. Founded in 1967, this establishment was the first modern-day hospice. Shortly after his return to Canada, two Canadian palliative care units were opened late in 1974, the first at St. Boniface General Hospital in Winnipeg and weeks later, under the direction of Balfour Mount, the second at the Royal Victoria Hospital in Montreal (McBurney, 2008; *Ottawa Citizen*, 2005). Although the terms *hospice care* and *palliative care* are still used independently by some organizations in Canada, we have seen the terms converge, and *hospice palliative care* is now widely used across the country (Canadian Hospice Palliative Care Association [CHPCA], 2016a). The philosophy that underlies hospice palliative care focuses on both the relief of suffering and the improvement of the quality of living and dying. Hospice palliative care helps dying patients and their families to

- address physical, psychological, social, spiritual, and practical issues and their associated expectations, needs, hopes, and fears;
- prepare for and manage self-determined life closure and the dying process; and
- cope with loss and grief during illness and bereavement (BC Ministry of Health, 2006).

End-of-life care for terminally ill patients in Canada has shifted away from the purely curative to include hospice palliative care, as illustrated in **Figure 19.1**. While hospice palliative care complements traditional curative biomedical care, it has more of a wellness, whole-person orientation—that is, it encompasses a person's existential/spiritual needs in addition to their physical and psychosocial ones—and is intended to optimize the quality of life for individuals and their families who are living with life-threatening progressive illnesses or are bereaved. This shift has spawned a new field of research to determine how to best alleviate distress and optimize end-of-life well-being (Chochinov, 2007; Chochinov et al., 2005; Chochinov et al., 2006; Chochinov et al., 2009).

Indeed, research studies are now beginning to demonstrate the tangible value of whole-person end-of-life care (Chochinov, 2006). For example, University of Manitoba research psychiatrist Harvey Chochinov has developed a Model of Dignity that shows that a loss of dignity is associated with increased levels of distress in the terminally ill (Chochinov et al., 2008; Chochinov et al., 2009; Chochinov et al., 2016). In this Model of Dignity, a person's perception of dignity is intertwined with physical, psychological, existential, and spiritual challenges. Subsequently, Chochinov developed the Patient Dignity Inventory (PDI) to objectively measure dignity-related distress in palliative care for the purpose of fostering psychotherapeutic interventions to help patients die with greater dignity (Chochinov et al., 2008; Chochinov et al., 2016). So far, evidence suggests that patients who participate in *dignity-based care* report a heightened sense of dignity, an increased sense of purpose, a heightened sense of meaning, better pain endurance, and an increased will to

Balfour Mount is considered the founder of the palliative care movement in North America that focuses on improving the quality of life for people with terminal illnesses and their families.

(Photo: Courtesy of McGill University/Dr. Balfour M. Mount)

Figure 19.1 This model represents the relative proportions of concurrent therapies at different phases of the dying process. The dashed line distinguishes therapies intended to modify disease (curative care) from therapies intended to relieve suffering and/or improve quality of life (labelled *Hospice palliative care*). The lines are straight for simplicity. In reality, the total quantity of therapy and the mix of concurrent therapies would fluctuate based on the patient's and family's issues, and their goals for care and treatment priorities. At times, there may not be any therapy in use at all.

(**SOURCE:** Ferris, F.D., Balfour, H.M., Bowen, K., Farley, J., Hardwick, M., Lamontagne, C. ... West, P. (2005). A Model to Guide Hospice Palliative Care: Based on National Principles and Norms of Practice. Ottawa, ON: Canadian Hospice Palliative Care Association. Retrieved from www.chpca.net/resource_doc_ library/model_to_guide_hpc/A+Model+to+Guide+Hospice+Palliative+Care+2002-URLUpdate-August2005.pdf page 18. Printed with permission.)

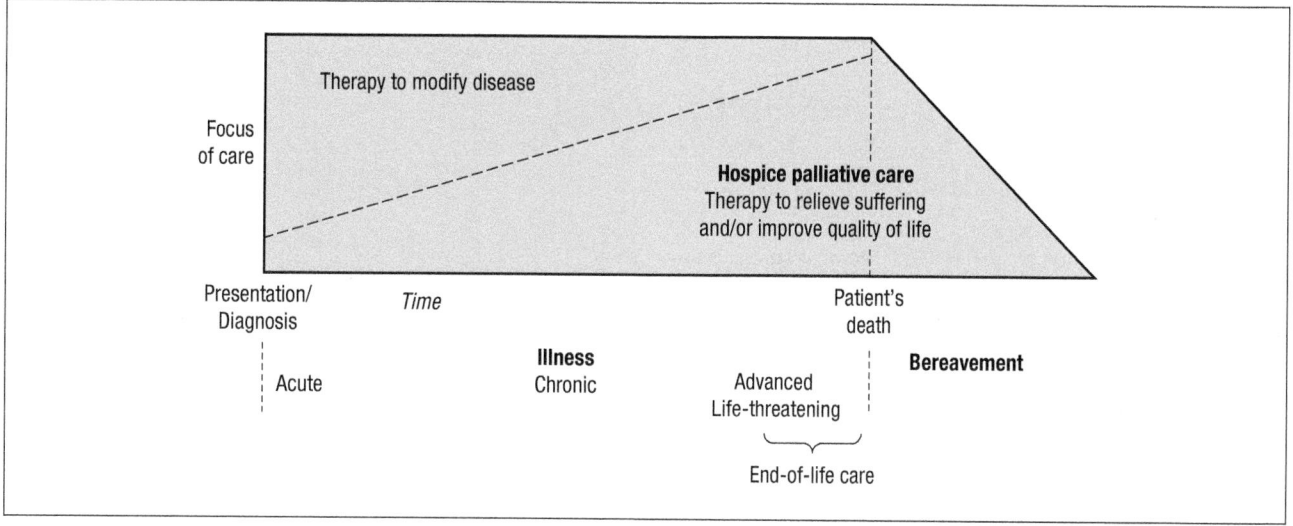

live (Chochinov et al., 2012, 2013; Ho et al., 2013; Thompson et al., 2009). In addition, the families of terminally ill patients were better prepared for the future.

Today, most communities in Canada provide some form of hospice palliative care, serving thousands of terminally ill patients and their families (CHPCA, 2016b). And yet, no more than four out of ten Canadians who are dying have access to quality hospice palliative care (Bacon, 2008).

CAREGIVER SUPPORT Hospice palliative care providers now recognize that caregivers have needs as well (CHPCA, 2013; Kristjanson & Aoun, 2004). This is particularly important for the roughly one in five Canadians in their 50s and 60s who provide end-of life care for a parent, spouse, grandparent, or other family member or friend (Statistics Canada, 2014). For example, the majority of those caring for a dying loved one, particularly someone with cancer or dementia, induces a *grief response* both in anticipation of and following the death of their loved one (Coelho & Barbosa, 2016; Dionne-Odom et al., 2016). For some caregivers, the grief response can be persistent and involve serious psychological disorders, such as depression, anxiety, PTSD, and/or substance abuse (Rumpold et al., 2016a, 2016b; Schulz, Hebert, & Boerner, 2008; Zisook et al., 2014). Consequently, an important element of palliative hospice care is grief support for caregivers, support that includes both psychosocial and educational components. Similarly, palliative hospice care providers also often require support services because of the emotional strain involved in caring for patients who are terminally ill. For many, though, caring for those who are dying is seen as an opportunity to address questions about the meaning and purpose of life which benefits them personally as well as their patients (Hospice Friendly Hospitals Programme, 2013; Karlsson, Kasén, & Wärnå-Furu, 2016; Sinclair, 2011).

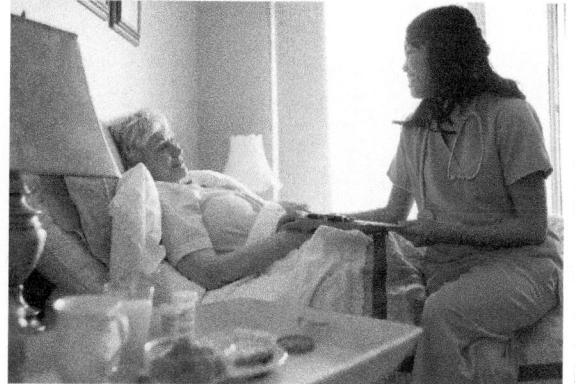

(Photo: Hero Images/Getty Images)

This woman, who is dying of cancer, has chosen to stay at home during her last months, supported by regular visits from hospice nurses.

In 2004, the Winnipeg Regional Health Authority was instrumental in launching the Canadian Virtual Hospice (CVH) website (2015a) to help support palliative hospice care providers, their patients, the patients' families, and researchers across Canada. The Canadian Virtual Hospice enables palliative hospice care experts to interact directly with informal caregivers and palliative hospice care providers, provide access to a wide range of palliative hospice care services, and bring medical expertise to the home, and to rural and remote areas of Canada. There is also help available for Canadians considering palliative care at home (Stenekes & Streeter, 2015).

Test Yourself before going on

1. A person who has survived on a life-support system for several years has probably experienced _____ death.
2. A growing number of families are turning to hospice _____ care for their dying loved ones, a form of care that focuses on both the relief of suffering and the improvement of the quality of living and dying.

Critical Thinking

3. What is the value of emphasizing care that seeks to prevent, reduce, or soothe the patients' symptoms rather than care that uses life-prolonging treatments at the end of life?

The Meaning of Death Across the Lifespan

Life teaches us how to survive, while death teaches us how to live. Life is a taskmaster, while death is a master teacher. We cannot learn how to appreciate the preciousness of life without coming to grips with the reality of death. (Wong, 2000, p. 27)

As an adult, you understand that death is irreversible, that it comes to everyone, and that it means a cessation of all function. But do children and teenagers understand these aspects of death? And what does death mean to adults of different ages?

Learning Objective 19.3

Describe the characteristics of children's and adolescents' ideas about death.

Children's and Adolescents' Understanding of Death

Results from a variety of studies suggest that preschool-aged children typically understand none of these aspects of death. They believe that death can be reversed, for instance, through prayer, magic, or wishful thinking; they believe that dead persons can still feel or breathe. Research shows that young children's ideas about death are rooted in their lack of understanding of life (Slaughter & Lyons, 2003). This link between understanding life and understanding death has been illustrated in a series of studies showing that teaching young children about the nature of biological life helps them understand what causes death and why it is irreversible.

By the time they start school, just about the time Piaget described as the beginning of concrete operations, most children seem to understand both the permanence and the universality of death. Children 6 to 7 years of age comprehend death as a biological event in which the heart ceases to beat, the lungs no longer take in air, and brain activity stops (Barrett & Behne, 2005; Slaughter, 2005).

As is true of so many other milestones of this age range, the child's specific experience seems to make a good deal of difference. Young children who have had direct experience with the death of a family member are more likely to understand the permanence of death than are those who have had no such personal experience (Bonoti,

(Photo: Design Pics Inc/Alamy Stock Photo)

This child being comforted by an adult at a loved one's grave is likely to have far more mature concepts of death than others her age who have not encountered death first-hand.

Leondari, & Mastora, 2013). Experiences in which children discover a dead animal, lose a pet, or are exposed to a story in which a character dies (e.g., *Bambi*, *The Lion King*) can also speed up their understanding of death (Cox, Garrett, & Graham, 2004–2005). Such experiences influence children's understanding of death because they serve as the catalyst for discussions of death with children's parents. Such discussions, when they focus on the concrete, biological aspects of death, provide children with the scaffolding they need to achieve a cognitive understanding of death (Moore & Moore, 2010). Linking death to broader values with which children are familiar helps them grasp the social aspects of death.

Adolescents understand the finality of death better than children do. Moreover, in an abstract sense, they understand that death is inevitable. Nevertheless, adolescents tend to overestimate their own chances of death (Fischoff, de Bruin, Parker, Millstein, & Halpern-Felsher, 2010). This phenomenon is most pronounced among teens who have personal experience with death, particularly those who live in high-crime neighbourhoods.

Unrealistic beliefs about personal death also appear to contribute to adolescent suicide. Typically, teens who attempt suicide claim to understand that death is final, but many tell researchers and counsellors that the purpose of their suicidal behaviour was to achieve a temporary escape from a stressful personal problem (Blau, 1996). Further, researchers have found that some teenagers who attempt suicide believe that death is a pleasurable experience for most people who die (Gothelf et al., 1998). Certainly, such distorted beliefs may be the result of the powerful emotions that lead teens to attempt suicide rather than the product of adolescent thinking. However, suicidal adults typically think of death, even when it is desired, as painful and unpleasant. So there may be a developmental difference between suicidal adolescents' and suicidal adults' understanding of death.

Like those of children, adolescents' ideas about death are affected by their personal experiences. Experiencing the death of a family member or a friend, especially someone who is near the teenager's own age, tends to shake an adolescent's confidence in her own immortality. In fact, research suggests that the loss of someone close, such as a sibling, may lead an adolescent to re-examine critically her ideas about death—both as a general concept and as something that is inevitable for herself (Batten & Oltjenbruns, 1999).

The Meaning of Death for Adults

Adults' ideas about death vary with age. Death seems remote to most young adults. The notion of personal mortality is a more common focus of thought in middle age, and by the later years, the idea of death becomes very personally relevant for most adults.

EARLY ADULTHOOD   In recent years, research examining young adults' views on death has been guided by a theoretical concept similar to the personal fable. Psychologists point out that young adults have a sense of **unique invulnerability**—a belief that bad things, including death, happen to others but not to themselves. Although young adults are more realistic about personal mortality than adolescents are, researchers find that many believe that they possess unique personal characteristics that somehow protect them against death. Some studies suggest that many young adults engage in high-risk activities such as rock-climbing because succeeding at them reinforces invulnerability beliefs (Popham, Kennison, & Bradley, 2011).

However, the loss of a loved one appears to shake a young adult's belief in unique invulnerability and, as a result, is often more traumatic for younger than for older adults (Liu & Aaker, 2007). In fact, such losses frequently lead to suicidal thoughts in young adults. Young adults who have recently lost a loved one in an accident or because of a homicide or a suicide are about five times as likely to formulate a suicide

Learning Objective 19.4

Describe how young, middle-aged, and older adults think about death.

unique invulnerability

the belief that bad things, including death, happen only to others

plan as young adults who have not had such a loss, although most never follow through with their plans (Prigerson et al., 1999).

Analyses of public reactions to the deaths of relatively young "celebrities," such as *Marathon of Hope* legend Terry Fox, former Toronto mayor Rob Ford, and pop music stars Amy Winehouse and Prince, provide additional insight into young adults' ideas about death. As you may notice, public interest in the events surrounding celebrities' deaths, as evidenced by the frequency of tabloid headline stories devoted to them, continues for many years afterward (Gibson, 2007a, 2007b, 2011a). Likewise, purchases of products that are associated with a celebrity who dies in early adulthood typically increase dramatically immediately after his or her death (Radford & Bloch, 2013). Psychologists hypothesize that such early deaths challenge young people's beliefs in unique invulnerability and, therefore, provoke defensive reactions that cause them to place those who die young in a special category. In other words, to maintain belief in their own unique invulnerability, young adults must come up with reasons why death came early to others but will not happen to them. As a result, they elevate such figures to near-sainthood.

(Photo: Frank Gunn/The Canadian Press)

Images of flag-draped caskets holding the remains of Canadian soldiers killed in the line of duty promote intense feelings of pride. Here, people line Highway 401 to honour Canada's fallen soldiers as they are repatriated.

MIDDLE AND LATE ADULTHOOD In middle and late adulthood, an understanding of death goes well beyond the simple acceptance of finality, inevitability, and universality. A death changes the roles and relationships of everyone else in a family. For example, when an elder dies, everyone else in that particular lineage "moves up" in the generational system. The death of a parent can be particularly unsettling for a middle-aged adult if the adult does not yet consider himself ready to assume the elder role.

An individual's death also affects the roles of people beyond the family, such as younger adults in a business organization, who then can take on new and perhaps more significant roles. Retirement serves some of the same function, as an older adult steps aside for a younger one. But death brings many permanent changes in families and social systems. At an individual level, the prospect of death may shape one's view of time (Kalish, 1985). In middle age, most people exhibit a shift in their thinking about time, thinking less about "time since birth" and being more aware of "time until death."

Such an "awareness of finitude" is not a part of every middle-aged or older adult's view of death (Marshall, 1975). One study of a group of adults aged 72 and older found that only about half thought in terms of "time remaining" (Keith, 1981/1982). Interestingly, those who did think of death in these terms had less fear of death than did those who thought of their lives as "time lived." Other research confirms this: Middle-aged and older adults who continue to be preoccupied with the past are more likely to be fearful and anxious about death (Pollack, 1979/1980).

Critical Thinking

When you think of your own age, do you think of time since birth, or time until death, or both? If you think in terms of time until death, can you remember when you switched to this view?

DEATH AS LOSS The most pervasive meaning of death for adults of all ages is loss (Dysvik & Furnes, 2010). Which of the many potential losses is feared or dreaded the most seems to change with age. Young adults are more concerned about loss of opportunity to experience things and about the loss of family relationships; older adults worry more about the loss of time to complete inner work. Such differences are evident in the results of a classic study in which researchers interviewed roughly 400 adults (Kalish & Reynolds, 1976). Among many other questions, researchers asked, "If you were told that you had a terminal disease and six months to live, how would you want to spend your time until you died?" (Think about this question for a moment yourself before reading on.) Age differences were substantial: Younger adults were more likely to say that they would seek out new experiences; older adults were considerably more likely to say that they would turn inward—an interesting piece of support for disengagement theory.

Fear of Death

Learning Objective 19.5

Identify what factors are related to fear of death in adults.

The Canadian existentialist researcher, Paul T.P. Wong, discusses the nature of death anxiety in the following way:

> Death is the only certainty in life. All living organisms die; there is no exception. However, human beings alone are burdened with the cognitive capacity to be aware of their own inevitable mortality and to fear what may come afterwards. Furthermore, their capacity to reflect on the meaning of life and death creates additional existential anxiety. (Wong, 2003, para. 16)

Wong goes on to suggest that our fear of death stems from six existential uncertainties, as described in **Table 19.1**.

Researchers have typically tried to measure fear of death with questionnaires. For example, one strategy is to ask participants to indicate, on a five-point scale, how disturbed or anxious they feel when thinking about various aspects of death or dying, such as "the shortness of life" or "never thinking or experiencing anything again" or "your lack of control over the process of dying" (Lester, 1990). Another approach asks participants to respond to statements such as "I fear dying a painful death" or "Coffins make me anxious" or "I am worried about what happens to us after we die" (Thorson & Powell, 1992).

FEAR OF DEATH ACROSS ADULTHOOD Although you might think that the oldest old, those closest to death, would fear it the most, research suggests that middle-aged adults are most fearful of death (Kumabe, 2006). For young adults, the sense of unique invulnerability probably prevents intense fears of death. In middle age, though, belief in one's own immortality begins to break down, resulting in increasing anxiety about the end of life. However, by late life, the inevitability of death has been accepted, and anxieties are focused on how death will actually come about.

Still, older adults do not become less preoccupied with death, and most would prefer to extend their lives as long as possible (Cicirelli, 2011). To an older person, particularly one who has a strong sense of having lived for some higher purpose, death is highly important, but it is apparently not as frightening as it was at mid-life (Cicirelli, 2006). Older adults are more likely to fear the period of uncertainty before death than they are to fear death itself (Sullivan, Ormel, Kempen, & Tymstra, 1998). They are anxious about where they may die, who will care for them until they do, and whether

Table 19.1 Sources of Fear of Death

Aspects of Death	Implications
The finality of death	There is no reversal, no remedy, no more tomorrow. Therefore, death signifies the cessation of all hope with respect to this world.
The uncertainty of what follows	Socrates has made the case that, since we really don't know what will happen, we should not fear. But uncertainty coupled with finality can create a potential for terror.
Annihilation anxiety or fear of nonexistence	The concept of nonbeing can be very threatening, because it seems to go against a strong and innate conviction that life should not be reduced to nonbeing.
The ultimate loss	When death occurs, we are forced to lose everything we have ever valued. Those with the strongest attachments toward things of this world are likely to fear death most. Loss of control over affairs in the world and loss of the ability to care for dependents also contribute to death anxiety.
Fear of the pain and loneliness in dying	Many are afraid that they will die alone or die in pain, without any family or friends around them.
Fear of failing to complete life work	According to Goodman's (1981) interviews with eminent artists and scientists, many people are more afraid of a meaningless existence than death itself; their fear of death stems from fear of not being able to complete their mission or calling in life.

(**SOURCE:** Wong, P.T.P. [2003]. From death anxiety to death acceptance: A meaning management model. Langley, BC: International Network on Personal Meaning. Retrieved September 9, 2004, from http://www.meaning.ca/articles/death_acceptance.htm. Courtesy of Paul T.P. Wong, Graduate Program in Counselling Psychology, Trinity Western University.)

they will be able to cope with the pain and loss of control and independence that may be part of the last months or years of life (Marshall & Levy, 1990).

RELIGIOUS BELIEFS Researchers typically find that adults who are deeply religious or who regularly go to their place of worship for spiritual reasons are less afraid of death than those who describe themselves as less religious or who participate less regularly in religious activities (Ardelt & Koenig, 2006; Landes & Ardelt, 2011; Pyne, 2008). In some instances, however, researchers have found that both those who are deeply religious and those who are totally irreligious report less fear of death. Thus, the most fearful may be those who are uncertain about or uncommitted to any religious or philosophical tradition.

Religious beliefs may moderate fears of death because religious people tend to view death as a transition from one form of life to another, from physical life to a spiritual one. Sociologist Reginald Bibby of the University of Lethbridge has been tracking the attitudes of thousands of Canadians of all ages since 1975. His survey in 2000 revealed some curious intergenerational differences in conventional and less-conventional religious beliefs (see **Figure 19.2**). For one, the belief that God exists increases with each age group, from 73% of teens to 85% of grandparents. Yet, at the same time, belief in life after death decreases with age, from a high of 78% in teens to a low of 64% in grandparents (Bibby, 2001). This suggests that although youth may be somewhat less eager to participate in an organized set of religious practices, they do have a strong sense of spirituality. Two pioneers of hospice palliative care in Canada, Dorothy Ley and Harry van Bommel, remind us that the spiritual search for meaning in our lives is often intensified by the reality of death. This spiritual struggle is arguably an important philosophical cornerstone of the dying process and thus an important factor behind providing palliative care (Ley & van Bommel, 1994).

In addition to framing death as a transition rather than an end, religious beliefs provide adults with death stories that help them cope with both their own deaths and

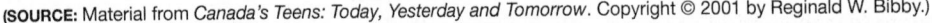

Figure 19.2 This graph shows the prevalence of some conventional beliefs (belief in God and life after death), unconventional beliefs (belief in astrology), religious participation (weekly attendance), and spirituality (very important) of four generations of Canadians in 2000. Involvement in and traditional expression of spirituality tend to be somewhat higher among older adults than others.

(**SOURCE:** Material from *Canada's Teens: Today, Yesterday and Tomorrow*. Copyright © 2001 by Reginald W. Bibby.)

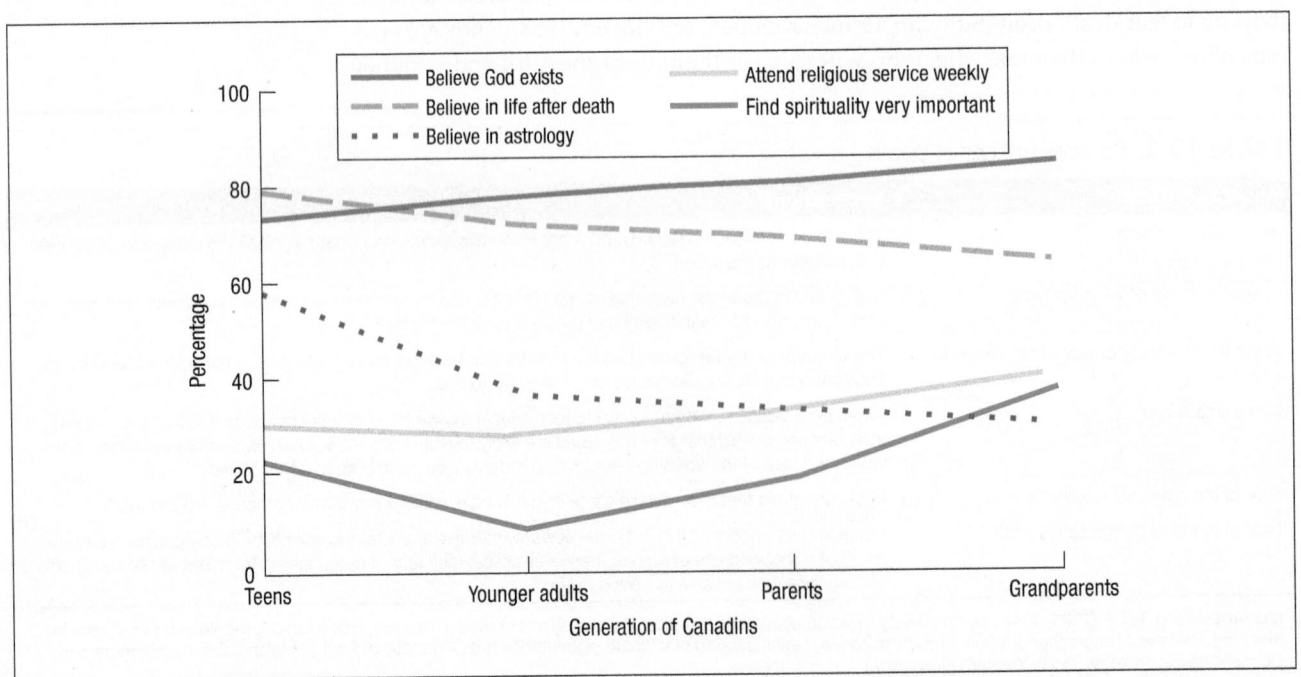

those of loved ones (Winter, 1999). For example, Jewish scriptures, the Christian Bible, and the Muslim Quran all contain many stories that convey the idea that death comes when one's purpose in life has been fulfilled. Many such stories also teach that each individual life is part of a larger, multigenerational story. In this larger context, death is portrayed as a necessary part of the transfer of responsibility from one generation to another. This kind of philosophical approach to death leads believers to focus on the contributions to family and community that they have made during their lives rather than on the losses they will experience at their deaths.

PERSONAL WORTH   Feelings about death are also linked to one's sense of personal worth or competence (Tam, 2013). Adults who feel that they have achieved the goals they set out to achieve, or who believe that they have become the persons they wanted to be, are less anxious about death than are those who are disappointed in themselves (Ardelt & Koenig, 2006). Adults who believe that their lives have had some purpose or meaning also appear to be less fearful of death, as do those who have some sense of personal competence (Neimeyer, Wittkowski, & Moser, 2004).

Such findings suggest that adults who have successfully completed the major tasks of adult life, who have adequately fulfilled the demands of the roles they occupied, and who have developed inwardly are able to face death with greater equanimity. Adults who have not been able to resolve the various tasks and dilemmas of adulthood face their late adult years more anxiously, even with what Erikson described as despair. Fear of death may be merely one facet of such despair.

Preparation for Death

Preparation for death occurs on a number of levels. At a practical level, regardless of age, most adults agree that it is important to make preparations for death (Fowler & Hammer, 2013; CVH, 2015b). Such preparations typically include purchasing life insurance, making a will, and issuing advanced care directives regarding end-of-life care, often called a *living will*. Individuals can use living wills to make clear to health care professionals and to their families that they either do or do not wish to have their lives prolonged with feeding tubes and other devices. Similarly, a *health-care power of attorney* specifies who can make decisions for an individual in the event that he or she becomes unable to do so. Moreover, most people agree that advance funeral planning can help bereaved family members deal with the many decisions they must make in the hours and days following the death of a loved one. However, researchers have found that older adults are far more likely than younger adults to have actually made such preparations (Moorman & Inoue, 2013).

Learning Objective 19.6

Describe how adults prepare for death.

TERMINAL DECLINE   At a somewhat deeper level, older adults may prepare for death through some process of reminiscence. Deeper still, there may be unconscious changes that occur in the years just before death, which might be thought of as a type of preparation. Research has pointed to the possibility that terminal psychological changes may occur. For example, in a still-influential study, researchers studied older adults longitudinally, interviewing and testing each participant regularly over a period of three years (Lieberman, 1965; Lieberman & Coplan, 1970). By comparing the psychological test scores obtained by each participant over the three-year period, researchers could detect differences—those nearer to death became increasingly more conventional, docile, dependent, and non-introspective, a pattern that did not occur among those of the same age who were further from death.

More recently, in a German longitudinal study spanning 22 years, researchers examined another psychological attribute, life satisfaction, in a representative population sample of 70- to 100-year-olds (Gerstorf et al., 2008). The researchers set out to identify and describe well-being at the end of life. They found sharp declines in life satisfaction, commencing in the four years prior to death. They also found that individuals dying at older ages spend more time in the terminal period of life satisfaction decline than individuals dying at younger ages.

A Canadian research team has observed a pattern of change in mental functioning that is characteristic of a **terminal decline**—there tends to be a gradual, but accelerating, decline in overall cognitive functioning over the course of roughly six years (MacDonald, Hultsch, & Dixon, 2011). However, it is important to note that other longitudinal research has shown that not all cognitive abilities decline at the same rate (Muniz-Terrera, van den Hout, Piccinin, Matthews, & Hofer, 2013; Wilson et al., 2012). For instance, a sudden, steep drop in crystalized intellectual ability, in particular, seems to signal that death is imminent (Johansson et al., 2004; Thorvaldsson et al., 2011).

terminal decline

an individual's decline in mental functioning accelerates a few years immediately preceding death

---

Test Yourself before going on

1. Children begin to understand that death is a biological event at about age _____.
2. Young adults' thinking about death is often influenced by a set of beliefs called _____ _____.
3. Which age group, middle-aged or elderly, fears death the most?
4. As a result of the terminal psychological changes that occur in the three years prior to death, individuals become more _____, _____, _____, and _____.

Critical Thinking

5. What role do age and fear of death play in people's decisions about death preparations such as living wills and prepaid funeral arrangements?

The Process of Dying

Elisabeth Kübler-Ross (1926–2004) was a Swiss-American psychiatrist who studied the experiences of the dying and their loved ones. In the 1960s, she formulated a model that asserted that those who are dying go through a series of psychological stages. These stages of dying, which were formulated on the basis of interviews with approximately 200 adults who were dying of cancer, continue to be highly influential, although Kübler-Ross's model has its critics. For example, research suggests that individual differences affect the process of dying in important ways.

Kübler-Ross's Stages of Dying

Learning Objective 19.7

Summarize how Kübler-Ross explained the process of dying.

In Kübler-Ross's early writings, she proposed that those who know they are dying move through a series of steps, or stages, arriving finally at the stage she called *acceptance*. Kübler-Ross's ideas and her terminology are still widely used (Roos, 2013). In fact, surveys of death education programs suggest that Kübler-Ross's model is the only systematic approach to the dying process to which health professionals-in-training are exposed (Downe-Wamboldt & Tamlyn, 1997). Thus, you should at least be familiar with the stages she proposed.

Kübler-Ross's model predicts that most people who are confronted with a terminal diagnosis react with some variant of "Not me!" "It must be a mistake," "I'll get another opinion," or "I don't feel sick." All these reactions are forms of *denial*, a psychological defence that may be highly useful in the early hours and days after such a diagnosis. Denial of this kind may be helpful in insulating a person's emotions from the trauma of hearing such news. Keeping emotions in check in this way may help an individual formulate a rational plan of action based on "What if it's true?" Having a plan of action may help moderate the effects of acknowledging the reality of the diagnosis. Kübler-Ross thought that these extreme forms of denial would fade within a few days, to be replaced by *anger.*

The model suggests that anger among the dying expresses itself in thoughts such as "It's not fair!" but a dying person may also express anger toward God, the doctor who made the diagnosis, nurses, or family members. The anger seems to be a response not only to the diagnosis itself, but also to the sense of loss of control and helplessness that many patients feel in impersonal medical settings.

Bargaining follows anger in the Kübler-Ross model. In this form of defence, the patient tries to make "deals" with doctors, nurses, family, or God: "If I do everything you tell me, then I'll live till spring." Kübler-Ross gave a particularly compelling example of this defence reaction: A patient with terminal cancer wanted to live long enough to attend the wedding of her eldest son. The hospital staff, to help her try to reach this goal, taught her self-hypnosis to deal with her pain and she was able to attend the wedding. Kübler-Ross reported, "I will never forget the moment when she returned to the hospital. She looked tired and somewhat exhausted and—before I could say hello—said, 'Now don't forget; I have another son!'" (1969, p. 83).

Bargaining may be successful as a defence for a while, but the model predicts that, eventually, bargaining breaks down in the face of signs of declining health. At this point, Kübler-Ross's theory predicts, the patient enters the stage of *depression.* According to Kübler-Ross, depression, or despair, is a necessary preparation for the final stage of *acceptance.* To reach acceptance, the dying person must grieve for all that will be lost with death.

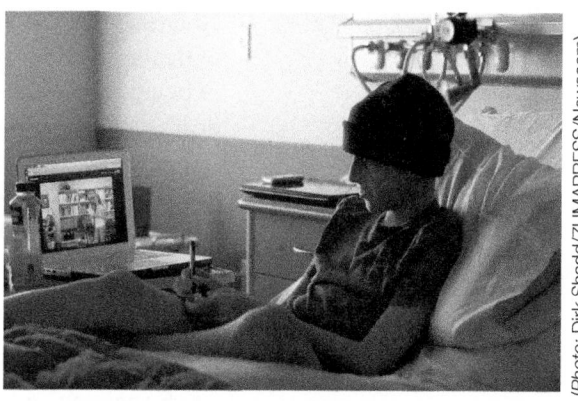

Children use some of the same defences to deal with impending death as adults. Young cancer patients may deny or bargain—for instance, "If I take my medicine, then I'll be able to go back to school in the fall."

Criticisms and Alternative Views

Kübler-Ross's model has provided a common language for those who work with dying patients, and her highly compassionate descriptions have, without doubt, sensitized health care workers and families to the complexities of the process of dying. At some moments, what the patient needs is cheering up; at other moments, he simply needs someone to listen to him. There are times to hold his hand quietly and times to provide encouragement or hope. Many new programs for terminally ill patients are clearly outgrowths of this greater sensitivity to the dying process.

These are all worthwhile changes. But Kübler-Ross's basic thesis—that the dying process necessarily involves these specific five stages in this specific order—has been widely criticized (Roos, 2013). Kübler-Ross responded to critics by pointing out that she had not meant the stages she proposed to be interpreted as rigidly as some researchers and practitioners suggested they should be. Nevertheless, criticisms of her model go beyond concerns about its stages, in part because Kübler-Ross bases her hypothesized sequence on a somewhat narrow sample (i.e., 200 individuals who were mostly adult cancer patients with Westernized, individualistic cultural values). This small sample raises questions about the generalizability and cross-cultural relevance of her findings.

The most potent criticism of Kübler-Ross's model, however, centres on the issue of stages. Many clinicians and researchers who have attempted to study the process systematically have found that not all dying patients exhibit these five emotions, let alone in a specific order. Of the five, only depression seems to be common among Western patients. Edwin Shneidman (1980, 1983), a major theorist and clinician in the field of **thanatology** (the scientific study of death and dying), argues that people who are dying display a wide range of emotional responses and do not all have the same needs. Instead of stages, Shneidman suggests that the dying process has many

Learning Objective 19.8

Identify some other views of the process of dying.

thanatology

the scientific study of death and dying

"themes" that can appear, disappear, and reappear in any one patient in the process of dealing with death. These themes include terror, pervasive uncertainty, fantasies of being rescued, incredulity, feelings of unfairness, a concern with reputation after death, and fear of pain.

Another alternative to Kübler-Ross's model is the "task-based" approach suggested by Charles Corr (1991/1992). In his view, coping with dying is like coping with any other problem or dilemma: You need to take care of certain specific tasks. Corr suggests four such tasks for the dying person:

- Satisfying bodily needs and minimizing physical stress
- Maximizing psychological security, autonomy, and richness of life
- Sustaining and enhancing significant interpersonal attachments
- Identifying, developing, or reaffirming sources of spiritual energy, and thereby fostering hope

Corr does not deny the importance of the various emotional themes described by Shneidman. Rather, he argues that for health professionals who deal with dying individuals, it is more helpful to think in terms of the patient's tasks, because the dying person may need help in performing some or all of them.

Whichever model one uses, what is clear is that no common patterns typify most or all reactions to impending death. Common themes exist, but they are blended together in quite different patterns by each person who faces this last task. Still, when it comes to end-of-life care, Canadians are saying they prefer to focus on comfort more so than aggressive technologically-based interventions (Fowler & Hammer, 2013). As a starting point for dealing with this desire, Canadian researchers have begun to study compassionate care from the dying person's perspective (Sinclair et al., 2016a, 2016b). The hope is that this will inform the training of health care providers and guide clinical practice that is compatible with the perceptions of the patient's and their family's concept of, and desire for, compassion to ameliorate suffering. Secondly, such research could provide data to objectively and consistently measure quality of care and support a more empathetic care culture.

Responses to Impending Death

Learning Objective 19.9

Describe how people vary in the ways they adapt to impending death.

Individual variations in responding to imminent death have themselves been the subject of a good deal of research interest in the past few decades. In one study involving 26 terminally ill men, researchers found that many of the men believed that they could avoid entering into the process of actively dying by continuing to engage in their favourite hobbies (Vig & Pearlman, 2003). Such findings raise questions about whether attitudes and behavioural choices can influence the course of a terminal disease.

Some of the early influential research on responses to impending death has been the work of British psychiatrist Steven Greer and his colleagues (Greer, 1991; Greer, Morris, & Pettingale, 1979; Pettingale, Morris, Greer, & Haybittle, 1985). They followed 62 women diagnosed with early stages of breast cancer in the 1970s. Three months after her original diagnosis, each woman was interviewed at some length and her reaction to the diagnosis and her treatment was classed in one of five groups:

- *Denial (positive avoidance)*. The person rejects evidence about diagnosis; she insists that surgery was just precautionary.
- *Fighting spirit*. The person maintains an optimistic attitude and searches for more information about the disease. These patients often see their disease as a challenge and plan to fight it with every method available.

- *Stoic acceptance (fatalism).* The person acknowledges the diagnosis but makes no effort to seek any further information; or, the person ignores the diagnosis and carries on normal life as much as possible.

- *Helplessness/hopelessness.* The person acts overwhelmed by diagnosis; she sees herself as dying or gravely ill and as devoid of hope.

- *Anxious preoccupation.* Women in this category had originally been included in the helplessness group, but they were separated out later. The category includes those whose response to the diagnosis is strong and persistent anxiety. If they seek information, they interpret it pessimistically. They monitor their body sensations carefully, interpreting each ache or pain as a possible recurrence.

Greer then checked on the survival rates of these five groups after 5, 10, and 15 years. Only 33% of the women whose initial reaction had been a fighting spirit had died of cancer 15 years later, compared with 76% of the women whose initial reaction had been denial, stoic acceptance, anxious preoccupation, or helplessness/hopelessness. Because those in the five groups did not differ initially in the stage of their disease or in their treatment, these results support the hypothesis that psychological responses contribute to disease progress—just as coping strategies more generally affect the likelihood of disease in the first place. However, in a subsequent study in the 1990s, Greer reported that the link between the fighting spirit and cancer survival was likely to have been due to an absence of an anxious or hopeless approach to the disease (Greer, 1999). That is, having a fighting spirit does not necessarily increase a cancer patient's chances of survival, but an anxious or hopeless attitude reduces it. As a result, Greer has been a strong advocate for psychotherapeutic interventions that help patients with anxiety or hopelessness develop a more positive outlook (Greer, 2002, 2008).

More recently, Canadian cancer psychologist Alistair Cunningham and his colleagues have been involved in longitudinal studies that have provided a very clear indication of how a patient's involvement in psychological self-help can prolong life (Cunningham, 2008; Cunningham, Phillips, Stephen, & Edmonds, 2002; Cunningham & Watson, 2004). In a longitudinal analysis, 22 patients with medically incurable metastatic cancers were tracked as they went through group therapy (Cunningham & Watson, 2004). At the start of the study, expert oncologists examined data on patients' medical charts and predicted each patient's probability of length of survival. The patients' attitudes and behaviours were tracked by using their written homework and therapists' notes. From this, the researchers developed a measure of how engaged the patients became in their self-help work (e.g., their levels of motivation, confidence, and openness to change). In essence, the researchers wanted to look at how much better each person did than expected, and how this correlated with their engagement in the self-help work.

What they found was that the one-third of patients who became most engaged in self-help lived much longer (about three times on average) than the one-third who were least engaged, despite the expectation of similar survival length (see **Figure 19.3**). Ten of the patients with medically incurable cancers outlived their prognosis from 2.2 to 12.5 years and two of the patients had complete remission of their disease—the difference being that those with the higher survival rates displayed a much higher degree of early involvement in their psychological self-help than did most of their nonsurviving peers. The survivors' mental state following the self-help routine was characterized by "equanimity and social harmony" and increased "meaning and spiritual connection." Long-term survivors also saw their lives as having changed profoundly: They came to understand what was important and meaningful to them (authenticity); to exercise freedom of choice in determining how to live their lives (autonomy); and they exhibited greater "acceptance,"

Figure 19.3 Predicted and observed survival for subgroups rated low, medium, and high for level of involvement in self-help.

(**SOURCE:** Cunningham, A.J., Phillips, C., Lockwood, G.A., Hedley, D.W., & Edmonds, C.V. [2000]. Association of involvement in psychological self-regulation with longer survival in patients with metastatic cancer: an exploratory study. *Advances in Mind-Body Medicine*. Fall; 16(4):276–87. (Table 1 Relationship of subjects' characteristics to survival). Used with the permission of InnoVision Health Media.)

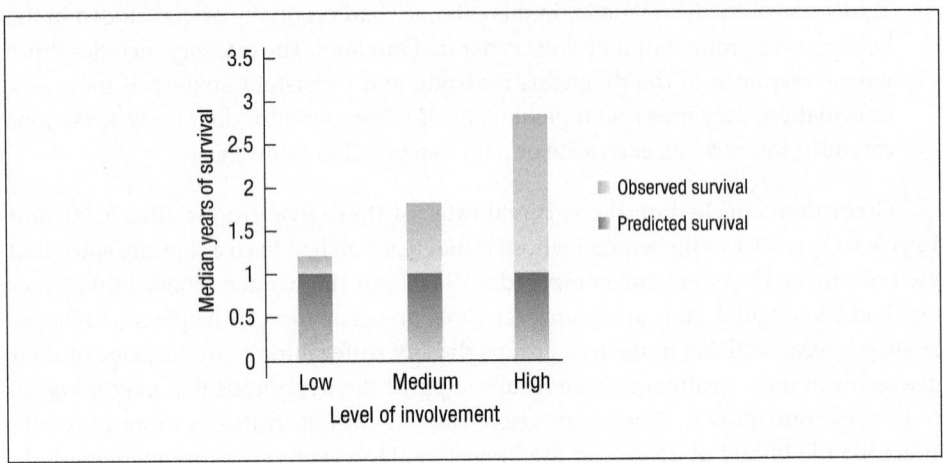

evidenced by enhanced self-esteem, greater tolerance for and emotional closeness to others, and an affective experience described as more peaceful and joyous. These were common themes among long survivors but were largely absent from the interviews with the comparison groups, who seemed preoccupied with their disease to the relative exclusion of other aspects of their lives.

Studies such as these highlight the growing body of evidence suggesting that suffering can be lessened while survival can be prolonged by psychological interventions. A word of caution: There is no conclusive evidence that the mind can cure cancer or other diseases. All the same, research shows that, along with the body's own healing mechanisms and medical treatment, mental state and attitude are associated with healing and can cause people to live longer in some cases (Cunningham, 2004, 2005; Greer, 2000, 2002). When Canadian researchers recently reviewed the last 30 years of research on mind–body connections in cancer outcomes, they concluded that the mind–cancer survival question must be seen as a legitimate and important area worthy of further exploration (Stephen, Rahn, Verhoef, & Leis, 2007).

Test Yourself before going on

1. Number Kübler-Ross's stages of dying in the order in which they occur.
    _____ (a) acceptance
    _____ (b) denial
    _____ (c) bargaining
    _____ (d) anger
    _____ (e) depression
2. The scientific study of death is called _____.
3. Canadian researchers have indicated that a cancer patient's involvement in _____ _____ can prolong life.

Critical Thinking

4. In what ways is Kübler-Ross's model helpful to health care professionals who work with terminal patients, and in what ways might the model interfere with their responses to the needs of patients?

The Experience of Grieving

In virtually every culture, the immediate response to a death is some kind of funeral ritual. However, a death ritual is only the first step in the process of **grieving**—the emotional response to a death—which may take months or years to complete.

Psychosocial Functions of Death Rituals

Funerals, wakes, and other death rituals help family members and friends manage their grief by giving them a specific set of roles to play. Like all roles, these include both expected behaviours and prohibited or discouraged behaviours. The content of these roles differs markedly from one culture to the next, but their clarity in most cases provides a shape to the days or weeks immediately following the death of a loved person. In Canadian society, depending on one's ethnic or religious background, the rituals prescribe what one should wear, who should be called, who should be fed, what demeanour one should show, and far more.

Death rituals also bring family members together as no other occasion does (with the possible exception of weddings). Frequently, cousins and other distant relatives see one another for the first time in many years at funerals. Such occasions typically inspire shared reminiscences and renew family relationships that have been inactive for a long time. In this way, death rituals can strengthen family ties, clarify the new lines of influence or authority within a family, and "pass the torch" in some way to the next generation. Likewise, funerals help to establish deaths as shared milestones for family members—"that was before Grandpa died" or "the last time I saw her was at Grandma's funeral." A death can become an important organizer of experience that separates the past from the present. Dividing time in this way seems to help survivors cope with grief (Katz & Bartone, 1998).

Death rituals are also designed to help the survivors understand the meaning of death itself, in part by emphasizing the meaning of the life of the person who has died. It is not accidental that most death rituals include testimonials, biographies, and witnessing. By telling the story of a person's life and describing that life's value and meaning, others can more readily accept the person's death.

Finally, death rituals may give some transcendent meaning to death itself by placing it in a philosophical or religious context (Pang & Lam, 2002). In this way, they provide comfort to the bereaved by offering answers to that inevitable question "Why?"

The Process of Grieving

The ritual of a funeral, in whatever form it occurs, can provide structure and comfort in the days immediately following a death. But what happens when that structure is gone? How do people handle the sense of loss? Answering that question requires a look at a number of factors associated with grief.

Each culture has its own death rituals. The customarily quiet graveside service in Canada would seem strange to people in many other societies.

grieving

the emotional response to a death

Learning Objective 19.10

Describe how funerals and ceremonies help survivors cope with grief.

Critical Thinking

Do the various funerals or death rituals you have participated in seem to have served the purposes described in the text?

Learning Objective 19.11

Identify what factors influence the grieving process.

AGE OF THE BEREAVED   Children express feelings of grief very much the way teens and adults do (Auman, 2007). Like adults, children demonstrate grief through sad facial expressions, crying, loss of appetite, and age-appropriate displays of anger, such as temper tantrums (Oatley & Jenkins, 1996). Funerals seem to serve the same adaptive function for children as for adults, and most children resolve their feelings of grief within the first year after the loss. In addition, knowing that a loved one or even a pet is ill and in danger of death helps children cope with the loss in advance, just as it does for those who are older (Jarolmen, 1998).

Although the behavioural aspects of adolescents' grief responses vary little from those of adults, teens may be more likely to experience prolonged grief than children or adults. One study found that more than 20% of a group of high school students who had a friend killed in an accident continued to experience intense feelings of grief nine months after the death (Dyregrov, Gjestad, Bie Wikander, & Vigerust, 1999). Adolescents may also grieve longer than children or adults for lost siblings; in some cases, teens continue to have problems with grief-related behaviours, such as intrusive thoughts about the deceased, for as long as two years after the death of a sibling (Lohan & Murphy, 2001/2002). Other research suggests that adolescent girls whose mothers have died run a particularly high risk of developing long-term, grief-related problems (Lenhardt & McCourt, 2000). Teenagers may also be more likely than adults to experience grief responses to the deaths of celebrities or to idealize peers' suicides.

Adolescents' grief responses are probably related to their general cognitive characteristics. You should remember from the chapters on development in adolescence that adolescents often judge the real world by idealized images. Consequently, a teenager may become caught up in fantasizing about how the world would be different if a friend or loved one had not died. Prolonged grieving among adolescents may be rooted in their tendency to engage in this kind of "what if" thinking. This may lead teens to believe that they could have prevented the death and, thus, cause them to develop irrational guilt feelings (Cunningham, 1996).

MODE OF DEATH   How an individual dies also contributes to the grief process of those who are in mourning. For example, widows who have cared for spouses during a period of illness prior to death are less likely to become depressed after the death than those whose spouses die suddenly (Carnelley, Wortman, & Kessler, 1999; Schaan, 2013). Grief-related depression seems to emerge during the spouse's illness rather than after the death. The spouse's death is thought of as an escape from suffering for the one who dies and a release from grieving for the caregiver. Similarly, a death that has intrinsic meaning, such as that of a young soldier who dies defending his country, is not necessarily easier to cope with but does provide the bereaved with a sense that the death has not been without purpose (Malkinson & Bar-Tur, 1999). Consequently, mourners have a built-in cognitive coping device—a rational explanation for the death—that allows them to grieve but also protects them from long-term depression.

Sudden and violent deaths evoke more intense grief responses (Brent, Melhelm, Donohoe, & Walker, 2009; Lichtenthal, Neimeyer, Currier, Roberts, & Jordan, 2013). For some, private memorials in public spaces (e.g., mementos placed at a roadside death site) can act as a meaningful commemoration to survivors whose loved ones have died unexpectedly and tragically (Gibson, 2011b). Still, one study found that 36% of widows and widowers whose spouses had died in accidents or by suicide were suffering from post-traumatic stress disorder (PTSD) symptoms (e.g., nightmares) two months after the death, compared with only 10% of widows and widowers whose spouses had died of natural causes (Zisook, Chentsova-Dutton, & Shuchter, 1998). Moreover, almost all those whose spouses had died unnaturally and who had PTSD symptoms were also depressed.

Death in the context of a natural disaster is also associated with prolonged grieving and development of symptoms of PTSD (Rajkumar, Mohan, & Tharyan, 2013). Such events bring to mind the inescapable reality of the fragility of human life. Public memorial services in which the common experiences of survivors are recognized and the differences between controllable and noncontrollable aspects of life are emphasized can help survivors cope with this kind of grief.

By contrast, the most frustrating aspect of the grieving process for people who have lost a loved one through a violent crime is the inability to find meaning in the event (Currier, Holland, & Neimeyer, 2006; Lichtenthal et al., 2013). In the initial phases of the grief process, survivors protect themselves against such frustration through cognitive defences, such as denial, and by focusing on tasks that are immediately necessary (Goodrum, 2005). Next, survivors often channel their grief and anger into the criminal justice process through which they hope that the perpetrator of the crime will be justly punished. Oftentimes, survivors eventually become involved in organizations that support crime victims and survivors of murdered loved ones or those that seek to prevent violence (Stetson, 2002).

Finally, suicide is associated with a unique pattern of responses among survivors (Bailley, Kral, & Dunham, 1999). In general, family and close friends of someone who commits suicide experience feelings of rejection and anger. Moreover, their grief over the loss of the loved one is complicated by the feeling that they could or should have done something to prevent the suicide. They are also less likely to discuss the loss with other family members or with friends because of their sense that a suicide in the family is a source of shame. For these reasons, suicide survivors may be more likely than others who have lost loved ones to experience long-term negative effects.

Widowhood

The relationship between the deceased and those who are in mourning affects the grieving process. For example, bereaved parents often report that their health is poorer after a child's death than it was before the death, and many parents continue to experience intense feelings of sadness for several years (Song, Floyd, Seltzer, Greenberg, & Hong, 2010). Similarly, children who lose a sibling sometimes worry that thoughts produced by sibling rivalry, such as wishing a brother or sister would die, caused the death (Crehan, 2004). As a general rule, though, the most difficult death to recover from is that of a spouse (Kaslow, 2004).

WIDOWHOOD AND PHYSICAL HEALTH   The experience of widowhood appears to have both immediate and longer-term effects on the immune system (Callaway, 2010; Utz, Caserta, & Lund, 2012). (The term *widowhood* applies to both men and women; *widow* refers to women and *widower* to men.) In one Norwegian study, researchers measured immune functioning in widows twice, shortly after their husbands' deaths and a year later (Lindstrom, 1997). Investigators found that the widows' immune systems were suppressed somewhat immediately after the death but in most cases had returned to normal a year later.

Similarly, a study comparing widows with married women in the Netherlands found that widows' immune responses continued to differ from those of married participants seven months after the spouses' deaths, even though psychological differences (such as feelings of sadness) between the two groups had disappeared (Beem et al., 1999). Thus, the bereaved may continue to suffer at a biochemical level even after obvious signs of grieving have subsided (O'Connor et al., 2013). Moreover, the association between death of a spouse and ensuing illness in the surviving partner may be the result of the effects of grief on the body's defences against disease agents such as viruses and bacteria (see the **Research Report**).

WIDOWHOOD AND MENTAL HEALTH   Researchers have found that the mental health of older adults whose spouses have died may differ for several years following the death from the mental health of peers whose spouses are still alive. Changes in mental health are most pronounced in the year following bereavement, when the incidence of depression among widows and widowers rises substantially (Onrust & Cuijpers, 2006; Schaan, 2013). It appears that declines in mental health follow

Learning Objective 19.12

Describe how grief affects the physical and mental health of widows and widowers.

Research Report

The Widowhood Effect

In celebration of their 50th wedding anniversary, British couple Brian and Betty Eckersley took their children and grandchildren on a vacation to Spain. The day before the family was scheduled to return home, Betty suffered a brain hemorrhage which doctors said was fatal. Her family faced the agonizing decision to discontinue artificial means of maintaining her life. Shortly thereafter, Brian suffered a heart attack. Within hours, both of the Eckersleys had passed away.

Brian Eckersley's heart attack is an extreme example of the widowhood effect, a phenomenon in which the death of one spouse is soon followed by the other. This effect was first reported by Ciocco (1940), who discovered a high correlation between the lifespans of married couples. Since that time, researchers have confirmed there is a substantial rise in mortality for both men and women following the death of their spouse. This relationship appears worldwide and is not influenced by the cause of death of the spouse (Boyle, Feng, & Raab, 2011; Moon, Kondo, Glymour, & Subramanian, 2011).

For example, researchers were astonished by the results of a study of the widowhood effect in which the medical records of nearly half a million widows and widowers were examined (Elwert & Christakis, 2006, 2008a). Consistent with earlier research, the risk of death from any cause increased by 30 to 90% among widows and widowers during the first three months of bereavement. Based on further analysis, researchers were able to account for possible biases in the increased mortality rates by examining the impact of death of both wives and ex-wives on husbands. They found a significant effect between a man's mortality and his current wife's death, but no such significant evidence was seen between a man's mortality and his ex-wife's death. This helped to rule out bias due to spousal similarity and lifestyle habits, such as diet and smoking, or bias from sharing a common environment for many years with the ex-wife (Elwert & Christakis, 2008b).

A more recent study of some 120 000 Scottish couples adds further evidence to support the causal nature of the widowhood effect. In this case, researchers found a 40% higher risk of death following widowhood for a six-month period along with a lower, but elevated, mortality risk for the surviving spouse for at least 10 years after the death of the partner (Boyle, Feng, & Raab, 2011). Finally, a meta-analysis of almost 2.3 million partners verified that people experiencing bereavement have an increased risk for premature mortality, especially within six months after spousal loss, after which, the risk declines (Moon et al., 2011).

What accounts for the widowhood effect remains unknown, but the sudden loss of whatever social and emotional buffering effects that marriage provides may play a role, ranging from economic advantages to encouraging mutual healthy lifestyles (FIFARS, 2012). And, possibly, the effect may result from the immune system's response to emotional trauma (Callaway, 2010).

---

bereavement fairly consistently, but how long such effects last may be highly variable. Several factors contribute to this variability.

One such factor is mental health history. Older adults who enter widowhood with a history of depression or poor health are more likely to experience depression after the death of their spouse (Utz et al., 2012; Zisook, Paulus, Shuchter, & Judd 1997). However, regardless of prior mental health, several variables have been associated with mental health problems following widowhood (Onrust, Cuijpers, Smit, & Bohlmeijer, 2007). In particular, depressive symptomology, anxiety, and somatic complaints were predicted by a combination of risk factors, including lower age, shorter duration of widowhood, lack of social support (both actual and perceived), more physical illness/disabilities, and a lower sense of mastery (i.e., their perceived sense of influence over outcomes). Moreover, the quality of the relationship of the widow or widower with the deceased spouse is related to depressive symptoms. Widows who report high levels of marital satisfaction are more likely than less satisfied widows to experience depression (Schaan, 2013). Economic changes accompany the loss of a spouse and add to the overall stress involved in the transition to widowhood. Generally, women suffer greater economic losses after the death of a spouse than men do, usually because they lose their husbands' income or pension (Zick & Holden, 2000). Thus, the degree to which an individual's economic status changes as a result of a spouse's death is probably another factor that contributes to individual differences in the long-term effects of bereavement.

pathological grief

persistent symptoms of depression brought on by the death of a loved one

PATHOLOGICAL GRIEF Some psychologists argue that **pathological grief**, depression-like symptoms following the death of a loved one, should be thought of as a separate disorder from depression (Doka, 2013). They suggest that adults who continue to experience grief symptoms, such as intense sorrow and a persistent yearning or preoccupation with the deceased, for more than twelve months following the loss of a loved one may be developing pathological grief (a condition under consideration for further study in the DSM-5 as *Persistent Complex Bereavement Disorder* [APA, 2013]).

Identifying and treating pathological grief may be important for preventing problems in both mental and physical health among widows and widowers. Researchers have found that widows and widowers whose grief symptoms continue for six months or longer are more likely to suffer long-term depression as well as physical ailments, such as cancer and heart disease (Prigerson et al., 1997). Moreover, they continue to show important differences in physical and mental functioning for up to two years after their spouse's death.

It's important to keep in mind, however, that many aspects of grief are culturally determined. Beliefs about how long mourning should last and how the bereaved should behave vary widely from one culture to another (Braun & Nichols, 1997; Rubin & Schechter, 1997). Thus, mental health professionals are advised to learn about an individual's cultural beliefs before forming conclusions about grief-related behaviour. Likewise, friends, neighbours, and co-workers of someone who is mourning the death of a spouse or other close family member should also be careful to interpret any grief-related behaviours within the context of the person's cultural background. Moreover, it is not unusual for nondepressed widows and widowers to express feelings of grief even decades after their spouses have died (Carnelley, Wortman, Bolger, & Burke, 2006).

PREVENTING LONG-TERM PROBLEMS Some research suggests that the "talk-it-out" approach to managing grief can be helpful in preventing grief-related depression, especially when feelings are shared with others who have had similar experiences in the context of a support group (Francis, 1997; Schneider, 2006). Research also indicates that developing a coherent personal narrative of the events surrounding the spouse's death helps widows and widowers manage grief (Haase & Johnston, 2012; Neimeyer, Prigerson, & Davies, 2002). Participating in support groups, or even jointly recalling relevant events with close family members, can facilitate the formation of such stories. These interventions suggest the most important preventions of depression are those actions that promote a sense of mastery, or an internal locus-of-control, as well as actual and perceived social support (Onrust et al., 2007).

Clearly, this kind of psychosocial management of grief requires time. Mental health professionals advise employers that providing bereaved employees (especially those whose spouses have died) with sufficient time off to grieve may be critical to their physical and mental health. In the long run, illness and depression among bereaved workers who return to their jobs too soon may be more costly to employers than providing additional time off (Eyetsemitan, 1998).

Test Yourself before going on

1. How do funerals help grieving individuals manage grief?
2. Write "Y" beside each factor that increases a bereaved person's risk of prolonged grief and "N" by each factor that does not increase it.
   _____ (a) the bereaved is a middle-aged adult
   _____ (b) the deceased died after a long illness
   _____ (c) the bereaved is a teenager
   _____ (d) the deceased committed suicide
   _____ (e) the deceased died in a natural disaster

3. Persistent depression-like symptoms that follow the death of a loved one are called _____ _____.

Critical Thinking

4. Given what you have learned in this section, what kinds of factors would lead you to make different predictions about how long a person who has lost a loved one will grieve?

Summary

The Experience of Death

19.1 Differentiate among the processes of clinical death, brain death, and social death.

- *Death* is a somewhat nonspecific term. Medical personnel refer to *clinical death* and *brain death*; *social death* occurs when the deceased person is treated like a corpse by those around him.

19.2 Compare how hospital and hospice palliative care differ with respect to their effects on terminally ill patients.

- Two-thirds of adults in Canada die in hospitals. Rather than providing curative treatment, hospice palliative care emphasizes patient and family control of the dying process. It is a holistic approach that focuses on the relief of suffering and improvement of the quality of living and dying.

The Meaning of Death Across the Lifespan

19.3 Describe the characteristics of children's and adolescents' ideas about death.

- Until about age 6 or 7, children do not understand that death is permanent and inevitable and involves loss of function. Teens understand the physical aspects of death much better than children do, but they sometimes have distorted ideas about it, especially in regard to their own mortality.

19.4 Describe how young, middle-aged, and older adults think about death.

- Many young adults believe they possess unique characteristics that protect them from death. For middle-aged and older adults, death has many possible meanings: a signal of changes in family roles, a transition to another state (such as a life after death), and a loss of opportunity and relationships. Awareness of death may help a person organize her remaining time.

19.5 Identify what factors are related to fear of death in adults.

- Fear of death appears to peak in mid-life, after which it drops rather sharply. Older adults talk more about death but are less afraid of it. Deeply religious adults are typically less afraid of death.

19.6 Describe how adults prepare for death.

- Many adults prepare for death in practical ways, such as by buying life insurance, writing wills, and making living wills. Reminiscence may also serve as mental preparation. Within a few years

prior to death, a person can seem less physically active and more psychologically disengaged.

The Process of Dying

19.7 Summarize how Kübler-Ross explained the process of dying.

- Kübler-Ross suggested five stages of dying: denial, anger, bargaining, depression, and acceptance. Research fails to support the hypothesis that all dying adults go through all five stages or that the stages necessarily occur in this order.

19.8 Identify some other views of the process of dying.

- Critics of Kübler-Ross suggest that her findings may be culture specific and the process of dying is less stagelike than her theory claims. Alternate views focus on the importance of taking care of tasks and end-of-life care.

19.9 Describe how people vary in the ways they adapt to impending death.

- Research with terminally ill patients suggests that those who are most pessimistic and docile in response to diagnosis and treatment have shorter life expectancies. Those who are less anxious or depressed, engage in self-help efforts, and live more authentically live longer.

The Experience of Grieving

19.10 Describe how funerals and ceremonies help survivors cope with grief.

- Funerals and other rituals after death serve important functions, including defining roles for the bereaved, bringing family together, and giving meaning to the deceased's life and death.

19.11 Identify what factors influence the grieving process.

- Grief responses depend on a number of variables. The age of the bereaved and the mode of death shape the grief process.

19.12 Describe how grief affects the physical and mental health of widows and widowers.

- In general, the death of a spouse evokes the most intense and long-lasting grief. Widows and widowers show high levels of illness and death in the months immediately after the death of a spouse, perhaps as a result of the effects of grief on the immune system.

Policy Question

Exercising One's Right to Die

One element of having greater control over the process of dying is having the legal right to choose the timing of death—a deeply personal topic. Today, most medical ethicists distinguish between two forms of assisted dying. *Passive assisted dying* occurs when a person (typically, a physician) hastens a death by not using life support systems or medication that would prolong life or by withdrawing life support or other treatment that may be keeping a terminally ill patient alive. *Active assisted dying* (medical assistance in dying) occurs when a physician or nurse practitioner hastens an eligible patient's death by active means, such as by administering a fatal dose of a drug (voluntary euthanasia) or giving or prescribing a drug that is self-administered to an eligible patient to cause death (medically assisted suicide). As of June 2016, these active forms of assisted dying are legal in Canada using procedural guidelines for eligible adults, i.e., those who are 18 years and older, mentally competent, and have a "grievous and irremediable" medical condition for whom death is "reasonably foreseeable" (Government of Canada, 2016c).

Living Will Directives

There is little controversy about passive euthanasia. Most people agree that individuals should be able to determine the degree to which life-support technology will be used to delay their own deaths. Thus, an increasing number of adults have made *living wills*, specifying that life-support systems or resuscitation should not be used in the case of their clinical death or near death. Such living wills essentially ask physicians to participate in passive euthanasia.

All Canadian jurisdictions have legislation that recognizes the directives expressed in living wills, which are known variously as an *advanced directive*, a *health care directive*, or *powers of attorney for personal care*. A living will generally contains two essential elements: a proxy directive, which specifies who you deem to be responsible to make health care decisions on your behalf if you are no longer able to make your wishes known to others; and an instruction directive, which specifies the health care or other personal care choices that can be fulfilled by you, or your designated proxy, on your behalf. The living will can include any combination of consent or refusal to consent to a diagnostic, therapeutic, preventative, or palliative treatment (CVH, 2015b).

Medical Assistance in Dying Considerations

The debate over physician-assisted suicide/dying was brought to public attention in North America by the actions of Dr. Jack Kevorkian (1928–2011), a physician who helped several terminally ill or severely handicapped individuals end their own lives. Those who favour medical assistance in dying note that modern medical technology has increasingly made it possible to prolong life well past the point at which death, in earlier decades, would naturally have occurred. Further, proponents of assisted suicide argue that many terminal patients are unable to carry out their own suicides, and therefore require the help of a physician. However, opponents counter that asking another person to help with a suicide is a far cry from giving a person "death with dignity."

Many of those who oppose medical assistance in dying believe that each individual life is sacred. They believe that decisions about when to end life should be subject only to divine authority. These critics also view assisted suicide/dying as just another form of suicide—a practice they consider immoral.

Other opponents argue against medical assistance in dying on the grounds that it might be extremely difficult to set limits on the practice even with strict guidelines. Advocates for people with disabilities have been particularly vocal in putting forward this point of view. They claim that once assisted suicide becomes widely viewed as not just legally, but morally acceptable, society may come to the point where those who are infirm or have severe disabilities will be subtly (or not so subtly) encouraged to end their own lives in order to relieve others of the burden of their care (Gallagher, 2015; Watt, 2009). Others, such as Justice Minister Jody Wilson-Raybould, caution that expanding the eligibility of medically assisted dying can send the wrong message—that it's appropriate to choose death to address suffering in life, which may encourage those who are in an emotional crisis and already considering taking their life to act on these suicidal thoughts (Bryden, 2016).

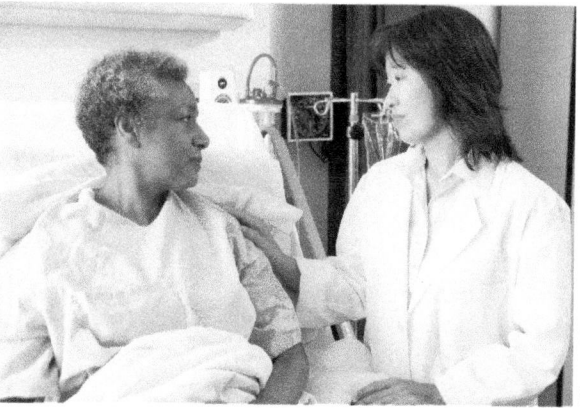

Many hospitals now specifically ask terminal patients during the admission process how they want to be treated in the event that they become mentally incapacitated.

(Continued)

Another argument against medical assistance in dying is that modern pain management techniques allow even those with extremely painful terminal illnesses to be comfortable in the last days or weeks of their lives (Fowler & Hammer, 2013; Gallagher, 2015). Thus, it is not necessary to hasten death to prevent pain. For example, long-time Canadian hospice care advocate Harry van Bommel (1992, 2002) reasoned that it's not only the fear of death, but also the fear of dying alone or in pain or of creating hardship for others that helped to feed the pro-euthanasia movement. He suggested that the real fears about the quality of life that a dying person holds could be assuaged with an alternate form of care—namely, a Canadian style of hospice palliative care that meets the full range of human needs, in which the patient and family are the primary decision makers.

Therefore, those who oppose medically assisted dying advocate palliative-care education for Canadians to make them aware of the benefits of palliative care, as well as the most effective ways of relieving patients' pain. They also suggest that physicians treating terminal patients engage their patients in frank discussions about pain relief as early in the course of their illness as possible. Through such discussions, doctors and patients can decide together what pain relief measures will be taken.

Opponents also question terminally ill patients' psychological fitness for making the decision to end their lives (Gallagher, 2015). Some fear that such patients may be depressed and that a request to hasten death is really no different from any other kind of suicide attempt. In other words, it is an act born of emotional despair, not rationality. The distinction is important, they say, because the philosophical rationale inherent in the medical assistance in dying law is that choosing to die involves a rational decision-making process. To help address this concern, assisted suicide legislation includes a mandatory waiting period between a request for death and the fulfilment of the request.

Now that medical assistance in dying is available as a legal option for those who are eligible, the decision to proceed, or not, lies with the individual. After careful and informed consultation and deliberation, which may include health care, legal and spiritual professionals, loved ones, and others, it is ultimately a decision that is made alone.

Your Turn

- Find out from a local medical association or health unit whether hospitals and physicians in your area generally honour living wills. Does your province or territory require medical personnel to ask all hospitalized people whether they have a living will?
- The medical association or health unit should also be able to tell you whether your province or territory allows family members to authorize health professionals to terminate aspects of care, such as tube feeding, in cases where a terminally ill or seriously injured individual can't speak for himself.
- Do you think the Canadian medical assistance in dying legislation has gone too far/not far enough? What are your reasons?
- Under what circumstances, if any, would you consider medical assistance in dying? What would be the deciding factors?

Glossary

ability goals goals based on a desire to be superior to others

accommodation changing a scheme as a result of some new information

achievement test a test designed to assess specific information learned in school

activities of daily living (ADLs) self-help tasks such as bathing, dressing, and using the toilet

activity theory the idea that it is normal and healthy for older adults to try to remain as active as possible for as long as possible

adaptive reflexes reflexes, such as sucking, that help newborns survive; some adaptive reflexes persist throughout life

adolescence the transitional period between childhood and adulthood

adverse childhood experiences (ACEs) childhood stressors, ranging from day-to-day maltreatment to traumatic events, that increase the risk of wide-ranging, negative health and social consequences over the life course

ageism a prejudicial view of older adults that characterizes them in negative ways

aggression behaviour intended to injure another person or damage an object

alcoholism physical and psychological dependence on alcohol

Alzheimer's disease a very severe form of dementia, the cause of which is unknown

ambivalent attachment a pattern of attachment in which the infant shows little exploratory behaviour, is greatly upset when separated from the parent, and is not reassured by the parent's return or efforts to comfort him

amenity move postretirement move away from kin to a location that has some desirable feature, such as year-round warm weather

amnion fluid-filled sac in which the fetus floats until just before it is born

amygdala an almond-shaped brain structure that plays a key role in the regulation of defensive emotions like fear and anger

analytical style a tendency to focus on the details of a task

anorexia nervosa an eating disorder characterized by self-starvation

anoxia oxygen deprivation experienced by a fetus during labour and/or delivery

assessment formal and informal methods of gathering information that can be used for programming to improve student learning. No grades or marks are associated with assessment

assimilation the process of using schemes to make sense of events or experiences

assisted human reproduction (AHR) "any activity undertaken for the purpose of facilitating human reproduction" (Health Canada, 2001a)

association areas parts of the brain where sensory, motor, and intellectual functions are linked

assortative mating (homogamy) a sociologist's term for the tendency to mate with someone who has traits similar to one's own

atherosclerosis narrowing of the arteries caused by deposits of plaque, a fatty substance

attachment the emotional tie to a parent experienced by an infant, from which the child derives security

attachment theory the view that the ability and need to form an attachment relationship early in life are genetic characteristics of all human beings

attention-deficit/hyperactivity disorder (ADHD) a mental disorder that causes children to have difficulty attending to and completing tasks

atypical development development that deviates from the typical developmental pathway

auditory acuity how well one can hear

authoritarian parenting style a style of parenting that is low in nurturance and communication, but high in control and maturity demands

authoritative parenting style a style of parenting that is high in nurturance, maturity demands, control, and communication

autism spectrum disorders (ASDs) a group of disorders that impair an individual's ability to understand and engage in the give-and-take of social relationships

automaticity the ability to recall information from long-term memory without using short-term memory capacity

avoidant attachment a pattern of attachment in which an infant avoids contact with the parent and shows no preference for the parent over other people

avoidant couples partners who agree to disagree and who minimize conflict by avoiding each other

axons tail-like extensions of neurons

babbling the repetitive vocalizing of consonant-vowel combinations by an infant

balanced approach reading instruction that combines explicit phonics instruction with other strategies for helping children acquire literacy

behaviour genetics the study of the role of heredity in individual differences

behavioural epigenetics the study of how the environment and personal behaviour can cause epigenetic changes that affect gene expression resulting in changes to behaviour and psychological processes over the course of a life and across generations

behaviourism the view that defines development in terms of behaviour changes caused by environmental influences

bicultural identity personal identification and satisfaction with more than one culture

bilingual education an approach to second-language education in which children receive instruction in two different languages

binge drinking a pattern of behaviour in which a man consumes five or more drinks, or a woman consumes four or more drinks, on one occasion, at least once a month over the past year

bioecological systems theory Bronfenbrenner's theory that explains development in terms of the relationships among individuals and their environments, or interconnected contexts

body mass index (BMI) a ratio of weight to height that estimates healthy and unhealthy body composition

brain death irreversible absence of brain function

bulimia an eating disorder characterized by binge eating and purging

bullying the unjust use of power to wilfully, deliberately, and repeatedly upset or hurt another person, their property, reputation, or social acceptance

burnout lack of energy, exhaustion, and pessimism that results from chronic stress

Caesarean section (C-section) delivery of an infant through incisions in the abdominal and uterine walls

cardiovascular disease (CVD) a set of disease processes in the heart and circulatory system

career development the process of adapting to the workplace, managing career transitions, and pursuing goals through employment

caregiver burden the cumulative negative effects of caring for an elderly or disabled person

case study an in-depth examination of a single individual

cell bodies the part of a neuron that contains the nucleus and is the site of vital cell functions

cell migration the movement of cells to their genetically predetermined destinations in the body

cell proliferation the increase in cell numbers by means of cell growth and cell division

centration the young child's tendency to think of the world in terms of one variable at a time

cephalocaudal pattern growth that proceeds from the head downward

chromosomes strings of genetic material in the nuclei of cells

class inclusion the understanding that subordinate classes are included in larger, superordinate classes

classical conditioning learning that results from the association of stimuli

climacteric the years of middle or late adulthood in both men and women during which reproductive capacity declines or is lost

clinical death a period during which vital signs are absent but resuscitation is still possible

clique four to six young people who appear to be strongly attached to one another

cognitive domain changes in thinking, memory, problem-solving, and other intellectual skills

cognitive theories theories that emphasize mental processes in development, such as logic and memory

cohort a group of individuals who share the same historical experiences at the same times in their lives

colic an infant behaviour pattern involving intense, inconsolable bouts of crying, totalling three or more hours a day

compensatory (kinship) migration a move to a location near family or friends that happens when an elder requires frequent help because of a disability or a disease

concrete operational stage Piaget's third stage of cognitive development, during which children construct schemes that enable them to think logically about objects and events in the real world

conduct disorder a psychological disorder in which the social and/or academic functioning of children and youth is impaired by patterns of antisocial behaviour that include bullying, destruction of property, theft, deceitfulness, and/or violations of social rules

congenital anomaly an abnormality present at birth

conservation the understanding that matter can change in appearance without changing in quantity

contingent responsiveness being sensitive to the child's verbal and nonverbal cues and responding appropriately

continuity theory the idea that older adults adapt lifelong interests and activities to the limitations imposed on them by physical aging

control group the group in an experiment that receives either no special treatment or a neutral treatment

conventional morality in Kohlberg's theory, the level of moral reasoning in which judgments are based on rules or norms of a group to which the person belongs

cooing making repetitive vowel sounds, particularly the *uuu* sound

corpus callosum the structure that connects the right and left hemispheres of the cerebral cortex

correlation a relationship between two variables that can be expressed as a number ranging from −1.00 to +1.00

creativity the ability to produce original, appropriate, and valuable ideas and/or solutions to problems

criminality antisocial behaviour that includes lawbreaking

critical period a specific period in development when an organism is especially sensitive to the presence (or absence) of some particular kind of experience

cross-gender behaviour behaviour that is atypical for one's own sex but typical for the opposite sex

cross-linking the formation of undesirable bonds between proteins or fats

cross-sectional design a research design in which groups of different ages are compared

crowd a combination of cliques, which includes both males and females

cryopreservation preserving cells or tissues through a freezing process that stops all biological activity

crystallized intelligence knowledge and judgment acquired through education and experience

cyberbullying a form of aggression in which information and communication technology (ICT) messages are used to intentionally inflict harm on others

decentration thinking that takes multiple variables into account

deductive logic a type of reasoning, based on hypothetical premises, that requires predicting a specific outcome from a general principle

defence mechanisms strategies for reducing anxiety, such as repression, denial, or projection, proposed by Freud

deferred imitation imitation that occurs in the absence of the model who first demonstrated it

dementia a neurological disorder involving problems with memory and thinking that affect an individual's emotional, social, and physical functioning

dendrites branch-like protrusions from the cell bodies of neurons

deoxyribonucleic acid (DNA) a chemical material that makes up chromosomes and genes

dependent variable the characteristic or behaviour that is expected to be affected by the independent variable

depth perception ability to judge the relative distances of objects

developmental milestones near-universal, age-related events whose first appearance signals noteworthy change or growth (Eaton, 2015)

dialectical thought a form of thought involving recognition and acceptance of paradox and uncertainty

disability-adjusted life years (DALY)   a measure of the gap between a population's ideal and actual levels of health. It is derived from the number of life-years lost to premature death, illness, or injury and the number of years living with a disability. It assumes a potential life limit of 82½ years for women and 80 for men

discipline   training, whether physical, mental, or moral, that develops self-control, moral character, and proper conduct

disengagement theory   the theory that it is normal and healthy for older adults to scale down their social lives and to separate themselves from others to a certain degree

dishabituation   recurrence of a response to a stimulus that has undergone habituation

disorganized/disoriented attachment   a pattern of attachment in which an infant seems confused or apprehensive and shows contradictory behaviour, such as moving toward the parent while looking away from him or her

dominant-recessive pattern   a pattern of inheritance in which a single dominant gene influences a person's phenotype but two recessive genes are necessary to produce an associated trait

dyslexia   problems in reading or the inability to read

Eating Well with Canada's Food Guide   guidelines for a balanced and healthy diet based on the four major food groups: vegetables and fruits, grain products, milk and alternatives, and meat and alternatives

ego   according to Freud, the thinking element of personality

ego integrity   the feeling that one's life has been worthwhile

ego integrity versus despair stage   the last of Erikson's psychosocial stages, in which older adults must achieve a sense of satisfaction with their lives

egocentrism   the young child's belief that everyone sees and experiences the world the way she does

embryonic stage   the second stage of prenatal development, from week 2 through week 8, during which the embryo's organ systems form

embryonic stem cells   undifferentiated cells found in the zygote and blastocyst that are capable of indefinite self-replication and differentiation into specialized cells

emerging adulthood   the period from the late teens to early 20s when individuals explore options prior to committing to adult roles

emotional regulation   the ability to control emotional states and emotion-related behaviour

empathy   the ability to identify with another person's emotional state

empiricists   theorists who argued that perceptual abilities are learned

English-as-a-second-language (ESL) program   an approach to second-language education in which children attend English classes for part of the day and receive most of their academic instruction in English

enriched daycare   daycare that provides structured programming to build skills, such as literacy, numeracy, social, art, and physical skills

epigenetic factors   inheritable and acquired gene regulation patterns that alter gene function (phenotype) without changing gene structure (genotype)

epigenetics   the study of the gene regulation patterns that alter gene function (phenotype) without changing gene structure (genotype)

epigenome   the sum total of inherited and acquired molecular modifications to the genome that leads to changes in gene regulation without changing the DNA sequence of the genome

epimutagens   agents that cause abnormal gene silencing or expression without changing the genomic DNA

episodic memories   recollections of personal events

equilibration   the process of balancing assimilation and accommodation to create schemes that fit the environment

esteem needs   the need for a person to have a sense of value and acceptance based, in part, on their experience of respect and admiration from others and on their perceived self-confidence and self-worth

ethnic identity   a sense of belonging to an ethnic group

ethnography   a detailed description of a single culture or context

ethology   a perspective on development that emphasizes genetically determined survival behaviours presumed to have evolved through natural selection

evaluation   the process of assigning a grade or mark to a student's performance, representing the student's highest, most consistent level of achievement over time

evolutionary developmental psychology   the view that genetically inherited cognitive and social characteristics that promote survival and adaptation appear at different times across the lifespan

evolutionary psychology   the view that genetically inherited cognitive and social traits have evolved through natural selection

exceptional child   a child who has special learning needs; the term refers to students with disabilities as well as gifted students

executive processes   information-processing skills that involve devising and carrying out strategies for remembering and problem-solving

experiment   a study that tests a causal hypothesis

experimental group   the group in an experiment that receives the treatment the experimenter thinks will produce a particular effect

expressive language   the ability to use sounds, signs, or symbols to communicate meaning

expressive vocabulary   the words whose meaning is used correctly when speaking

extended family   a social network of grandparents, aunts, uncles, cousins, and so on

extinction   the gradual elimination of a behaviour through repeated nonreinforcement

false belief principle   the ability to look at a problem or situation from another person's point of view and discern what kind of information would cause that person to believe something that isn't true

fast-mapping   the ability to categorically link new words to real-world referents

fetal stage   the third stage of prenatal development, from week 9 to birth, during which growth and organ refinement take place

fluid intelligence   the aspect of intelligence that reflects fundamental biological processes and does not depend on specific experiences

fluid reasoning   the ability to detect the underlying conceptual relationship among visual objects and use reasoning to identify and apply logical rules (NCS Pearson, Inc., 2015)

foreclosure   in Marcia's theory, the identity status of a person who has made a commitment without having gone through a crisis; the person has simply accepted a parentally or culturally defined commitment

formal operational stage   the fourth of Piaget's stages, during which adolescents learn to reason logically about abstract concepts

frail elderly   seniors whose physical and/or mental impairments are so extensive that they cannot care for themselves

free radicals molecules or atoms that possess an unpaired electron

functional magnetic resonance imaging (fMRI) a form of magnetic resonance imaging (MRI) that records what regions of the brain are active during specific mental activities

functional status a measure of an individual's ability to perform certain roles and tasks, particularly self-help tasks and other chores of daily living (Havens & Finlayson, 1999)

gametes cells that unite at conception (ova in females; sperm in males)

gender constancy the understanding that gender is a component of the self that is not altered by external appearance

gender constancy theory Kohlberg's assertion that children must understand that gender is a permanent characteristic before they can adopt appropriate sex roles

gender identity the ability to correctly label oneself and others as male or female

gender role identity gender-related aspects of the psychological self

gender schema theory an information-processing approach to gender concept development that asserts that people use a schema for each gender to process information about themselves and others

gender stability the understanding that gender is a stable, lifelong characteristic

gender the psychological and social associates and implications of biological sex

gene expression when a gene sequence is activated ("turned on") and ready to be translated into gene products—proteins, for the most part

gene silencing when a gene sequence is made inactive ("turned off") and is prevented from being translated into gene products—proteins, for the most part

generativity a sense that one is making a valuable contribution to society by bringing up children or mentoring younger people in some way

generativity versus stagnation stage the seventh of Erikson's stages, in which middle-aged adults find meaning in contributing to the development of younger individuals

genes complex chemical units of a chromosome that control or influence inherited traits

genital stage in Freud's theory, the period during which people reach psychosexual maturity

genome all the DNA that an organism possesses

genotype an individual's unique genetic blueprint

geriatric dysthymia chronic depressed mood in older adults

germinal stage the first stage of prenatal development, beginning at conception and ending at implantation (approximately two weeks)

gerontology the scientific study of aging

glial cells specialized cells in the brain that support neurons

gonads sex glands (ovaries in females; testes in males)

goodness of fit the degree to which an infant's temperament is adaptable to his environment, and vice versa

grammar explosion period when the grammatical features of children's speech become more similar to those of adult speech

grammatical words words that pertain to the rules of language and proper sentence construction, such as articles, prepositions, and auxiliaries

grieving the emotional response to a death

gut microbiota the population of microbes that colonizes the gastrointestinal tract

habituation the decline in responding that occurs as a stimulus becomes familiar

handedness a strong preference for using one hand or the other that develops between 3 and 5 years of age

Hayflick limit the theoretical proposal that each species is subject to a genetically programmed time limit after which cells no longer have any capacity to replicate themselves accurately

health-adjusted life expectancy (HALE) an estimate of life expectancy at birth. It is the number of years that a newborn can expect to live in full health given current rates of morbidity and mortality

hippocampus a brain structure that is essential for the formation of memories

holism the view that the whole is greater than the sum of its parts

holophrases combinations of gestures and single words that convey more meaning than just the word alone

hospice care a holistic approach to care for the terminally ill that emphasizes individual and family control of the process of dying

hostile/detached couples partners who fight regularly, rarely look at each other, and lack affection and support

hostile/engaged couples partners who have frequent arguments and lack the balancing effect of humour and affection

human connectome the map of the structural and functional neural connections of the human brain and nervous system

human development the scientific study of age-related changes in our bodies, behaviour, thinking, emotions, social relationships, and personalities

human epigenomics the study of the human epigenome including the location of all acquired and inherited epigenetic markers, their function, and their role in human physical and mental health

human genomics the study of the human genome including the location of genes, their function, and their role in human physical and mental health

hypothetico-deductive reasoning the ability to derive conclusions from hypothetical premises

id in Freud's theory, the part of the personality that comprises a person's basic sexual and aggressive impulses; it contains the libido and motivates a person to seek pleasure and avoid pain

identity an understanding of one's unique characteristics and how they have been, are, and will be manifested across ages, situations, and social roles

identity achievement in Marcia's theory, the identity status achieved by a person who has been through a crisis and reached a commitment to ideological or occupational goals

identity crisis Erikson's term for the psychological state of emotional turmoil that arises when an adolescent's sense of self becomes "unglued" so that a new, more mature sense of self can be achieved

identity diffusion in Marcia's theory, the identity status of a person who is not in the midst of a crisis and who has made no commitment

identity versus role confusion in Erikson's theory, the stage during which adolescents attain a sense of who they are

imaginary audience an internalized set of behavioural standards usually derived from a teenager's peer group

implantation attachment of the blastocyst to the uterine wall

independent variable the presumed causal element in an experiment

individual education plan (IEP) a written document containing learning and behavioural objectives for the exceptional student, a description of how the objectives will be achieved, and how the objectives will be evaluated

inductive discipline   a discipline strategy in which parents explain to children why a punished behaviour is wrong

inductive logic   a type of reasoning in which general principles are inferred from specific experiences

industry versus inferiority stage   the fourth of Erikson's psychosocial stages, during which children develop a sense of their own competence through mastery of culturally defined learning tasks

infant-directed speech (IDS)   the simplified, higher-pitched speech that adults use with infants and young children

infant mortality   death within the first year of life

infantile amnesia   the inability of adults and older children to remember more than a few events that took place before they were 3 years of age

inflections   grammatical markers attached to words to indicate tense, gender, number, and the like, such as the use of the ending *ed* to mark the past tense of a verb in English

information-processing theory   theoretical perspectives that use the computer as a model to explain how the mind manages information

institutional migration   a move to an institution, such as a nursing home, that is necessitated by a disability

instrumental activities of daily living (IADLs)   more complex daily living tasks such as doing housework, cooking, and managing money

intelligence   the ability to take in information and use it to adapt to the environment

intelligence quotient (IQ)   the ratio of mental age to chronological age; also, a general term for any kind of score derived from an intelligence test

interactionist model   the theory that development results from complex reciprocal interactions between multiple personal and environmental factors

interactionists   theorists who argue that language development is a subprocess of general cognitive development and is influenced by both internal and external factors

intermodal perception   formation of a single perception of a stimulus that is based on information from two or more senses

intimacy   the capacity to engage in a supportive, affectionate relationship without losing one's own sense of self

intimacy versus isolation   Erikson's early adulthood stage, in which an individual must find a life partner or supportive friends to avoid social isolation

intimate partner violence   physical acts or other behaviour intended to intimidate or harm an intimate partner

invented spelling   a strategy young children with good phonological awareness skills use when they write

joint attention   when two people are focusing their attention on an object and each is aware that the other is attending to that same object

kin-keeper   a family role, usually occupied by a woman, which includes responsibility for maintaining family and friendship relationships

language acquisition device (LAD)   an innate language processor, theorized by Chomsky, that contains the basic grammatical structure of all human language

lateralization   the process through which brain functions are divided between the two hemispheres of the cerebral cortex

learning disability   a disorder in which a child has difficulty mastering a specific academic skill, even though she possesses average to above-average intelligence and has no physical or sensory handicaps

learning theories   theories that assert that development results from an accumulation of experiences

lexical words   words with a high level of meaning, such as nouns, verbs, adjectives, and adverbs

libido   in Freud's theory, an instinctual drive for physical pleasure present at birth that forms the motivating force behind virtually all human behaviour

life events approach   a theoretical perspective on middle adulthood that focuses on normative and non-normative events and how adults in this age group respond to them

life review   an evaluative process in which elders make judgments about past behaviour

life structure   a key concept in Levinson's theory: the underlying pattern or design of a person's life at a given time, which includes roles, relationships, and behaviour patterns

lifespan perspective   the current view of developmentalists that changes happen throughout the entire human lifespan and that changes must be interpreted in light of the culture and context in which they occur; thus, interdisciplinary research is critical to understanding human development

limbic system   the part of the brain that regulates emotional responses

living apart together   intimate partners who do not cohabitate

locus of control   a set of beliefs about the causes of events

longitudinal design   a research design in which people in a single group are studied at different times in their lives

low birth weight (LBW)   newborn weight below 2500 grams

macronutrients   large amounts of carbohydrates, fats, and proteins that are needed for energy and for body- and brain-building elements

maturation   the gradual unfolding of a genetically programmed sequential pattern of change

maximum oxygen uptake (VO$_2$ max)   a measure of the body's ability to take in and transport oxygen to various body organs

means–end behaviour   purposeful behaviour carried out in pursuit of a specific goal

memory strategies   learned methods for remembering information

menarche   the beginning of the menstrual cycle

menopause   the cessation of monthly menstrual cycles in middle-aged women

metacognition   knowledge about how the mind thinks and the ability to control and reflect on one's own thought processes

metamemory   knowledge about how memory works and the ability to control and reflect on one's own memory function

micronutrients   essential vitamins and minerals that are needed in small amounts to regulate physical and mental processes

mitochondrial inheritance   a pattern of inheritance in which a cell's mitochondrial DNA (mtDNA) is inherited from the mother's egg and not the father's sperm

modified program   changes in the curriculum so that the modified outcomes differ from those of the standard curriculum

moral realism stage   the first of Piaget's stages of moral development, in which children believe rules are inflexible

moral relativism stage   the second of Piaget's stages of moral development, in which children understand that many rules can be changed through social agreement

moratorium in Marcia's theory, the identity status of a person who is in a crisis but who has made no commitment

motherhood earnings gap a measure showing how much the earnings of women with children are below those of women without children

motives internal factors or conditions that tend to initiate, direct, or sustain behaviour

multifactorial inheritance a pattern of inheritance affected by both genes and the environment

multigenerational caregivers middle-aged adults who are caring both for elderly parents and young adult children at the same time; also called the *sandwich generation*

mutagens agents that cause changes (mutations) in genomic DNA

myelinization a process in neuronal development in which sheaths made of a substance called myelin gradually cover individual axons and electrically insulate them from one another to improve the conductivity of the nerve

naming explosion the period when toddlers experience rapid vocabulary growth, typically beginning between 16 and 24 months

nativists theorists who claimed that perceptual abilities are inborn

naturalistic observation the process of studying people in their normal environments

neonate baby between birth and 1 month of age

neo-Piagetian theory an approach that uses information-processing principles to explain the developmental stages identified by Piaget

neurobehavioural disorders cognitive and behavioural disorders that are associated with brain dysfunction, such as autism spectrum disorder, ADHD, and dyslexia

neurons specialized cells of the nervous system

neuroplasticity the ability of the brain to reorganize its neural structures and functioning in response to experiences

niche-picking the process of selecting experiences on the basis of temperament

norm-referenced tests standardized tests that compare an individual's score to the average score of same-aged peers

norms average ages at which developmental milestones are reached

numeracy the knowledge and skills required to effectively manage the mathematical demands of diverse situations (Statistics Canada, 2008b)

obese a body weight with a high percentage of body fat, which is associated with an increased risk for serious diseases and health problems (i.e., BMI > 30)

obesogenic environments environments in which social influences and context contribute to obesity in individuals or populations

object concept an infant's understanding of the nature of objects and how they behave

object individuation the process by which an infant differentiates and recognizes distinct objects based on their mental images of objects in the environment

object permanence the understanding that objects continue to exist when they can't be seen

objective (categorical) self the toddler's understanding that she is defined by various categories, such as gender, or qualities, such as shyness

observational learning, or modelling learning that results from seeing a model reinforced or punished for a behaviour

operant conditioning learning to repeat or stop behaviours because of their consequences

operational efficiency a neo-Piagetian term that refers to the maximum number of schemes that can be processed in working memory at one time

organogenesis process of organ development

osteoporosis loss of bone mass with age, resulting in more brittle and porous bones

overregularization attachment of regular inflections to irregular words, such as the substitution of *goed* for *went*

overweight a body weight with a high percentage of body fat, which is associated with an increased risk for health problems (i.e., BMI > 25)

palliative care a form of care that seeks to prevent, relieve, or soothe the patients' symptoms rather than cure their diseases or disorders

parental investment theory the theory that sex differences in mate preferences and mating behaviour are based on the different amounts of time and effort men and women must invest in child-rearing

pathological grief persistent symptoms of depression brought on by the death of a loved one

pelvic inflammatory disease (PID) an infection of the female reproductive tract that may result from a sexually transmitted disease and can lead to infertility

perimenopausal phase the stage of menopause during which estrogen and progesterone levels are erratic, menstrual cycles may be very irregular, and women begin to experience symptoms such as hot flashes

permissive parenting style a style of parenting that is high in nurturance and low in maturity demands, control, and communication

person perception the ability to classify others according to categories such as age, gender, and race

personal fable the belief that the events of one's life are controlled by a mentally constructed autobiography

personality a pattern of responding to people and objects in the environment

personality disorder an inflexible pattern of behaviour that leads to difficulty in educational, occupational, and social functioning

phenotype an individual's whole set of observable characteristics

phonological awareness children's understanding of the sound patterns of the language they are acquiring

physical domain changes in the size, shape, and characteristics of the body

pituitary gland gland that triggers other glands to release hormones

placenta specialized organ that allows substances to be transferred from mother to embryo and from embryo to mother without their blood mixing

polygenic inheritance a pattern of inheritance in which many genes influence a trait

postconventional morality in Kohlberg's theory, the level of moral reasoning in which judgments are based on an integration of individual rights and the needs of society

postformal thought types of thinking that are associated with a hypothesized fifth stage of cognitive development

postmenopausal phase the last stage of menopause; a woman is postmenopausal when she has had no menstrual periods for at least a year

post-secondary education any formal educational experience that follows high school

post-traumatic stress disorder (PTSD) a disorder that involves extreme levels of anxiety, emotional discomfort and/or numbness, flashback memories of episodes of abuse, nightmares, and other sleep disturbances in response to traumatic life events

preconventional morality in Kohlberg's theory, the level of moral reasoning in which judgments are based on authorities outside the self

predictive-adaptive responses the prenate's ability to use information about the current environment to adjust its physiology in anticipation that it will match future environmental conditions and optimize the chances to survive and reproduce in adulthood

preference technique a research method in which a researcher keeps track of how long a baby looks at each of two objects shown

premenopausal phase the stage of menopause during which estrogen levels fall somewhat, menstrual periods are less regular, and anovulatory cycles begin to occur

preoperational stage Piaget's second stage of cognitive development, during which children become proficient in the use of symbols in thinking and communicating but still have difficulty thinking logically

presbycusis normal loss of hearing with aging, especially of high-frequency tones

presbyopia normal loss of visual acuity with aging, especially the ability to focus the eyes on near objects

primary aging (senescence) age-related physical changes that have a biological basis and are universally shared and inevitable

primary circular reactions Piaget's phrase to describe a baby's simple repetitive actions in substage 2 of the sensorimotor stage; the actions are organized around the baby's own body

primary sex characteristics the sex organs: ovaries, uterus, and vagina in the female; testes and penis in the male

primitive reflexes reflexes, controlled by "primitive" parts of the brain, that disappear during the first year of life

processing efficiency the ability to make efficient use of short-term memory capacity

processing speed the speed and accuracy of visual identification, decision making, and decision implementation (NCS Pearson, Inc., 2015)

program accommodation the adjustment of teaching methods to help a child with special needs achieve the outcomes of the standard curriculum

Programme for International Student Assessment (PISA) a worldwide assessment of how well 15-year-olds can apply their academic ability to solve real-life problems

prosocial behaviour behaviour intended to help another person

protein-coding genes genes that direct the production of proteins

proteins organic compounds, consisting of amino acids, that perform most life functions and make up the majority of cellular structures

proximodistal pattern growth that proceeds from the middle of the body outward

psychoanalytic theories theories proposing that developmental change happens because of the influence of internal drives and emotions on behaviour

psychological self a person's understanding of his or her enduring psychological characteristics

psychosexual stages Freud's five stages of personality development through which children move in a fixed sequence determined by maturation; the libido is centred on a different body part in each stage

psychosocial stages Erikson's eight stages, or crises, of personality development in which inner instincts interact with outer cultural and social demands to shape personality

puberty collective term for the physical changes that culminate in sexual maturity

punishment any immediate consequence that follows a behaviour and decreases the likelihood that the behaviour will be repeated

qualitative change a change in kind or type

quality of work–life (QWL) movement an approach to enhancing job satisfaction by basing job and workplace design on analyses of the quality of employee experiences in an organization

quality-adjusted life years (QALY) a measure of how much benefit is gained, and at what cost, for any particular physical or mental intervention. It provides an estimate of the time a person will live at different levels of health over his or remaining years of life

quantitative change a change in amount

reaction range a range between upper and lower boundaries for traits such as intelligence, which is established by one's genes; one's environment determines where, within those limits, one will fall

receptive language comprehension of spoken language

receptive vocabulary the words that are understood when heard

reciprocal determinism a process of human development based on the interaction of personal, behavioural, and environmental factors

reflective judgement the ability to identify the underlying assumptions of differing perspectives on controversial issues

reinforcement any immediate consequence that follows a behaviour and increases the likelihood that the behaviour will be repeated

relational aggression aggression aimed at damaging another person's self-esteem or peer relationships, such as by ostracism or threats of ostracism, cruel gossiping, or facial expressions of disdain

relational style a tendency to ignore the details of a task in order to focus on the "big picture"

relative right-left orientation the ability to identify right and left from multiple perspectives

relativism the idea that some propositions cannot be adequately described as either true or false

religious coping the tendency to turn to religious beliefs and institutions for support in times of difficulty

reminiscence reflecting on past experience

research ethics the guidelines researchers follow to protect the rights of animals used in research and humans who participate in studies

retaliatory aggression aggression to get back at someone who has hurt you

reticular formation the part of the brain that regulates attention

reversibility the understanding that both physical actions and mental operations can be reversed

role conflict any situation in which two or more roles are at least partially incompatible, either because they call for different behaviours or because their separate demands add up to more hours than there are in the day

role-taking the ability to look at a situation from another person's perspective

satiety the feeling of fullness that follows a meal

scaffolding a process in which the learning of new cognitive skills is guided by someone who is more skilled

schematic learning   organization of experiences into expectancies, called *schemas*, which enable infants to distinguish between familiar and unfamiliar stimuli

scheme   in Piaget's theory, an internal cognitive structure that provides an individual with a procedure to follow in a specific circumstance

schizophrenia   a serious mental disorder characterized by disturbances of thought such as delusions and hallucinations

secondary aging   age-related changes that are due to social and environmental influences, poor health habits, or disease

secondary circular reactions   Piaget's phrase to describe the repetitive actions in substage 3 of the sensorimotor period; the actions are oriented around external objects

secondary sex characteristics   body parts such as breasts in females and pubic hair in both sexes

secular trend   the decline in the average age of menarche, along with changes such as an increase in average height for both children and adults, that happened between the mid-19th and mid-20th centuries in Western countries and occurs in developing nations when nutrition and health improve

secure attachment   a pattern of attachment in which an infant readily separates from the parent, seeks proximity when stressed, and uses the parent as a safe base for exploration

selective attention   the ability to focus cognitive activity on the important elements of a problem or a situation

selective optimization with compensation   the process of balancing the gains and losses associated with aging

self-actualization   the process of fulfilling one's unique personal potential

self-care children   children who are at home by themselves after school for an hour or more each day

self-efficacy   the belief in one's own capacity to cause an intended event to occur or to perform a task

self-esteem   a global evaluation of one's own worth

self-regulation   children's ability to conform to parental standards of behaviour without direct supervision

semantic memories   recollections of general knowledge, facts, and word meanings

semiotic (symbolic) function   the understanding that one object or behaviour can represent another

senescence   physical changes and declines associated with aging

sensitive period   a span of months or years during which a child may be particularly responsive to specific forms of experience or particularly influenced by their absence

sensorimotor stage   Piaget's first stage of development, in which infants use information from their senses and motor actions to learn about the world

separation anxiety   expressions of discomfort, such as crying, when separated from an attachment figure

sequential design   a research design that combines cross-sectional and longitudinal examinations of development

sex-typed behaviour   different patterns of behaviour exhibited by boys and girls

sexual assault   any form of sexual activity with another person without his or her consent

shaping   the reinforcement of intermediate steps until an individual learns a complex behaviour

short-term storage space (STSS)   neo-Piagetian theorist Robbie Case's term for the working memory

social clock   a set of age norms that defines a sequence of life experiences that is considered normal in a given culture and that all individuals in that culture are expected to follow

social death   the point at which family members and medical personnel treat the deceased person as a corpse

social domain   changes in variables that are associated with the relationship of an individual to others

social referencing   infants' use of others' facial expressions as a guide to their own emotions

social role theory   the idea that sex differences in mate preferences and mating behaviour are adaptations to gender roles

social skills   a set of behaviours that usually leads to being accepted as a play partner or friend by peers

social status   an individual child's classification as popular, rejected, or neglected

social-cognitive theory   the theoretical perspective that asserts that social and personality development in early childhood is related to improvements in the cognitive domain

sociocultural theory   Vygotsky's view that complex forms of thinking have their origins in social interactions rather than in an individual's private explorations

somatic or adult stem cells   non-embryonic stem cells found in differentiated tissue that are capable of self-replicating and differentiating into the kind of tissue from which they originated

spatial cognition   the ability to infer rules from and make predictions about the movement of objects in space

spatial perception   the ability to identify and act on relationships between objects in space

stages   qualitatively distinct periods of development

states of consciousness   different states of sleep and wakefulness in infants

stranger anxiety   expressions of discomfort, such as clinging to the mother, in the presence of strangers

subjective self   an infant's awareness that he is a separate person who endures through time and space and can act on the environment

substance abuse   a pattern of behaviour in which a person continues to use a substance even though it interferes with psychological, occupational, educational, and social functioning

successful aging   the term gerontologists use to describe maintaining one's physical health, mental abilities, social competence, and overall satisfaction with one's life as one ages

sudden infant death syndrome (SIDS)   the term used to describe the sudden and unexpected death of an apparently healthy infant

superego   Freud's term for the part of personality that is the moral judge

survey   a data collection method in which participants respond to questions

synapses   tiny spaces across which neural impulses flow from one neuron to the next

synaptic plasticity   the redundancy in the nervous system that ensures that it is nearly always possible for a nerve impulse to move from one neuron to another or from a neuron to another type of cell (e.g., a muscle cell)

synaptic pruning   process by which unused or unnecessary neural pathways and connections are eliminated

synaptogenesis   the process of synapse development

synchrony   a mutual, interlocking pattern of attachment behaviours shared by a parent and a child

systematic and explicit phonics planned, specific instruction in sound–letter correspondences

systematic problem-solving the process of finding a solution to a problem by testing single factors

systems approach the view that personal factors together with external factors form a dynamic integrated system

task goals goals based on a desire for self-improvement

telegraphic speech simple two- or three-word sentences that usually include a noun and a verb

telomere string of repetitive DNA at the tip of each chromosome in the body that appears to serve as a kind of timekeeping mechanism

temperament inborn predispositions, such as activity level, that form the foundations of personality

teratogens substances such as viruses and drugs that can cause congenital anomalies

terminal decline an individual's decline in mental functioning accelerates a few years immediately preceding death

tertiary circular reactions deliberate experimentation with variations of previous actions that occurs in substage 5 of the sensorimotor period

thanatology the scientific study of death and dying

the Big Five a set of five major dimensions of personality, including extraversion, agreeableness, conscientiousness, neuroticism, and openness/intellect

theory of mind (ToM) a set of ideas constructed by an individual to explain other people's ideas, beliefs, desires, and behaviour

time-out removing the child from the situation and from attention and rewards for a short period of time, typically one minute for every year of the child's age, in order to stop unwanted behaviour

tinnitus a persistent ringing in the ears

toxic stress response persistently elevated physiological arousal caused by recurring and/or unabated adversity that threatens healthy development

tracking the smooth movements of the eye used to follow the track of a moving object

trait a stable pattern of responding to situations

transgendered a person whose psychological gender is the opposite of his or her biological sex

traumatic brain injury (TBI) an injury to the head that results in diminished brain function such as a loss of consciousness, confusion, or drowsiness

true sleep the number of minutes of sleep time excluding all periods of wakefulness, which can be distinguished by electroencephalograph (EEG) activity

type A personality pattern a personality type associated with greater risk of coronary heart disease. It includes competitive achievement striving, a sense of time urgency, and, sometimes, hostility or aggressiveness

umbilical cord organ that connects the embryo to the placenta

underweight a body weight with a low percentage of body fat, which is associated with an increased risk for health problems (i.e., BMI < 18.5)

uninvolved parenting style a style of parenting that is low in nurturance, maturity demands, control, and communication

unique invulnerability the belief that bad things, including death, happen only to others

validating couples partners who express mutual respect, even in disagreements, and are good listeners

vascular dementia a form of dementia caused by one or more strokes

verbal comprehension the ability to access and apply acquired word knowledge to verbalize meaningful concepts, think about verbal information, and express ideas in words (NCS Pearson, Inc., 2015)

viability ability of the fetus to survive outside the womb

victimization repeated, intentional acts that single someone out for hostile, exploitive, unfair, or vindictive treatment

violation-of-expectancy a research strategy in which researchers move an object in one way after having taught an infant to expect it to move in another

visual acuity how well one can see details at a distance

visual spatial the ability to evaluate visual details and understand visual spatial relationships to construct geometric designs from a model (NCS Pearson, Inc., 2015)

vitrification the use of cryoprotectants along with rapid cooling to prevent the fluid in biological tissues (e.g., eggs, semen, embryos) from forming ice crystals (that act like glass shards on cell structures) and from dehydrating; the tissue becomes an intact, noncrystalline, glass-like solid that can be preserved for years

volatile couples partners who argue a lot and don't listen well, but still have more positive than negative interactions

volunteerism performance of unpaid work for altruistic motives

wellness a measure of optimal holistic health

wisdom a hypothesized cognitive characteristic of older adults that includes accumulated knowledge and the ability to apply that knowledge to practical problems of living

working memory the ability to register, maintain, and manipulate visual and auditory information in conscious awareness, which requires attention and concentration, as well as visual and auditory discrimination (NCS Pearson, Inc., 2015)

work–life balance the balance between an employee's work and nonwork roles

zone of proximal development signifies tasks that are too hard for a child to do alone but that can be managed with guidance

zygote a single cell created when sperm and ovum unite

References

Chapter 1

Auerback, S. (2014). *Dr. Toy's smart play smart toys: How to select and use the best toys and games* (4th ed.). Berkeley, CA: Regent Press.

Baltes, P.B., Lindenberger, U., & Staudinger, U. (2006). Lifespan theory in developmental psychology. In W. Damon & R.M. Lerner (Eds.), *Handbook of child psychology: Vol. 1. Theoretical models of human development* (6th ed., pp. 569–664). New York, NY: Wiley.

Baltes, P.B., Reese, H.W., & Lipsitt, L.P. (1980). Life-span developmental psychology. *Annual Review of Psychology, 31,* 65–70.

Canadian Child Care Federation. (2009). *Toy safety.* Retrieved from www.cccf-fcsge.ca/docs/cccf/RS_26-e.pdf

Canadian Heritage. (2001). *Multiculturalism: Strength through diversity.* Ottawa, ON: Author. Retrieved from www.pch.gc.ca/multi/reports/ann98-99/multic_e.shtml

Canadian Psychological Association. (2000). *Canadian Code of Ethics for Psychologists.* (3rd ed.). Ottawa, ON: Author.

Canadian Psychological Association. (2015). *Canadian Code of Ethics for Psychologists* (4th ed.) (Draft – February 2015). Retrieved from http://www.cpa.ca/docs/File/Ethics/CPA_Code_Feb2015Draft-DIST.pdf

Canadian Toy Testing Council. (2016). *Canadian toy testing council: About the CTTC.* Retrieved from www.toy-testing.org/aboutus.html

Canadian Toy Testing Council. (n.d.). *Learn to play, play to learn.* Retrieved from: http://www.cfc-efc.ca/docs/toytc/00001_en.htm

Cavanaugh, J., & Whitbourne, S. (1999). *Gerontology: An interdisciplinary perspective.* New York, NY: Oxford University Press.

Charlesworth, W.R. (1992). Darwin and developmental psychology: Past and present. *Developmental Psychology, 28,* 5–16.

Crain, W. (2011). *Theories of development* (6th ed.). Upper Saddle River, NJ: Pearson Prentice-Hall.

Cuffaro, D.F., Paige, D., Blackman, C.J., Laituri, D., Covert, D.E., Sears, L.M., Nehez-Cuffaro, A. & Zaksenberg, I. (2013). *The industrial design reference & specification book.* Beverly, MA: Rockport Publishers.

Dewsbury, D. (2009). Charles Darwin and psychology at the bicentennial and sesquicentennial: An introduction. *American Psychologist, 64*(2), 67–74. doi:10.1037/a0013205

Ferguson, G.A. (1993). Psychology in Canada 1939–1945. *Canadian Psychology, 33*(2), Abstract.

Froberg Mortensen, T. (2012). *LEGO history timeline.* Retrieved from http://aboutus.lego.com/en-us/lego-group/the_lego_history/

Gesell, A. (1925). *The mental growth of the preschool child.* New York, NY: Macmillan.

Helson, R., Mitchell, V., & Moane, G. (1984). Personality and patterns of adherence and nonadherence to the social clock. *Journal of Personality and Social Psychology, 46,* 1079–1096.

Hess, E.H. (1972). "Imprinting" in a natural laboratory. *Scientific American, 227,* 24–31.

Hoff, T.L. (1992). Psychology in Canada one hundred years ago: James Mark Baldwin at the University of Toronto. *Canadian Psychology, 33*(2), Abstract.

Human Resources Development Canada. (1996). *National Longitudinal Survey of Children and Youth (NLSCY).* (Cat. No. SPAH036E-10-96). Ottawa, ON: Author. Retrieved from www11.hrdc-drhc.gc.ca/edd/NLSCY_172000.htm

Isaacowitz, D., Löckenhoff, C., Lane, R., Wright, R., Sechrest, L., Riedel, R., & Costa, P. (2007). Age differences in recognition of emotion in lexical stimuli and facial expressions. *Psychology and Aging, 22*(1), 147–159. doi:10.1037/0882-7974.22.1.147

Iverson, T., Larsen, L., & Solem, P. (2009). A conceptual analysis of ageism. *Nordic Psychology, 61*(3), 4–22. doi:10.1027/1901-2276.61.3.4

Lerner, R.M. (2008). The contributions of Paul B. Baltes to the transformation of the field of child development: From developmental psychology to developmental science. *Research in Human Development, 5*(2), 69–70. doi:10.1080/15427600802034744

Neugarten, B.L. (1979). Time, age, and the life cycle. *American Journal of Psychiatry, 136,* 887–894.

Ozmon, H.A. (2012). *Philosophical foundations of education* (9th ed.). Upper Saddle River, NJ: Pearson.

Pisani, J. (2006, November 29). The making of . . . a LEGO. *Bloomberg Business Week.* Retrieved from www.businessweek.com/bwdaily/dnflash/content/nov2006/db20061127_153826.htm

Riediger, M., Freund, A.M., & Baltes, P.B. (2005). Managing life through personal goals: Intergoal facilitation and intensity of goal pursuit in younger and older adulthood. *The Journals of Gerontology. Series B, Psychological sciences and social sciences, 60*(2), 84–91.

Schonert-Reichl, K. (1999). Relations of peer acceptance, friendship adjustment, and social behavior to moral reasoning during early adolescence. *Journal of Early Adolescence, 19,* 249–279.

Serbin, L.A., Cooperman, J.M., Peters, P.L., Lehoux, P.M., Stack, D.M. & Schwartzman A.E. (1998). Intergenerational transfer of psychosocial risk in women with childhood histories of aggression, withdrawal. *Developmental Psychology, 34,* 1246–1262.

Statistics Canada. (2008a). *Window on the National Longitudinal Survey of Children and Youth.* Ottawa, ON: Author. Retrieved from www.statcan.gc.ca/imdb-bmdi/document/4450_D3_T9_V2-eng.pdf

Statistics Canada. (2010a). *National longitudinal survey of children and youth (NLSCY).* Retrieved from http://www23.statcan.gc.ca/imdb/p2SV.pl?Function=getSurvey&SDDS=4450&lang=en&db=imdb&adm=8&dis=2

Statistics Canada. (2012a). *Life expectancy at birth, by sex, by province* [CANSIM data]. Retrieved from http://www.statcan.gc.ca/tables-tableaux/sum-som/l01/cst01/health26-eng.htm

Statistics Canada. (2015a). *Centenarians in Canada.* Retrieved from http://www12.statcan.gc.ca/census-recensement/2011/as-sa/98-311-x/98-311-x2011003_1-eng.cfm

Statistics Canada. (2016a). *Canada at a glance 2016* (Catalogue No. 12-581-XIE). Retrieved from http://www.statcan.gc.ca/pub/12-581-x/12-581-x2016000-eng.pdf

Thelen, E., & Adolph, K.E. (1992). Arnold L. Gesell: The paradox of nature and nurture. *Developmental Psychology, 28,* 368–380.

Thomas, M. (2005). *Comparing theories of child development* (6th ed.). Pacific Grove, CA: Wadsworth/Cengage.

Toy Retailers Association (n.d.) *Toy of the Century.* Retrieved from www.toyretailersassociation.co.uk/toty/totc20.htm

Tzschentke, B., & Plagemann, A. (2006). Imprinting and critical periods in early development. *World's Poultry Science Journal, 62*(4), 626–637.

White, W.H. (1992). G. Stanley Hall: From philosophy to developmental psychology. *Developmental Psychology, 28,* 25–34.

Willms, J.D. (2002a). Research findings bearing on Canadian social policy. In J.D. Willms (Ed.), *Vulnerable children* (pp. 331–358). Edmonton, AB: The University of Alberta Press.

Willms, J.D. (2002b). Socioeconomic gradients for childhood vulnerability. In J.D. Willms (Ed.), *Vulnerable children* (pp. 71–102). Edmonton, AB: The University of Alberta Press.

World Health Organization. (2015a). *Life expectancy data by country.* Retrieved from http://apps.who.int/gho/data/node.main.688

Wright, M.J, & Myers, C. (1982). *History of academic psychology in Canada.* Toronto, ON: C.J. Hogrefe, Inc.

Wright, M.J. (1993). Women groundbreakers in Canadian psychology: World War II and its aftermath. *Canadian Psychology, 33*(2), Abstract.

Chapter 2

American Psychiatric Association, (2013). *Diagnostic and Statistical Manual of Mental Disorder: DSM-5* (5th ed.). Washington, DC: American Psychiatric Publishing.

Anway, M.D., Cupp, A.S., Uzumcu, M., & Skinner, M.K. (2005). Epigenetic transgenerational actions of endocrine disruptors and male fertility. *Science, 308* (5727), 1466–1469.

Bandura, A. (1977a). *Social learning theory*. Englewood Cliffs, NJ: Prentice-Hall.

Bandura, A. (1977b). Self-efficacy: Toward a unifying theory of behavioral change. *Psychological Review, 84,* 91–125.

Bandura, A. (1982). The psychology of chance encounters and life paths. *American Psychologist, 37,* 747–755.

Bandura, A. (1986). *Social foundations of thought and action: A social cognitive theory*. Englewood Cliffs, NJ: Prentice-Hall.

Bandura, A. (1989). Social cognitive theory. *Annals of Child Development, 6,* 1–60.

Bandura, A. (2001). Social cognitive theory: An agentic perspective. *Annual Review of Psychology, 52*(2), 1–26.

Bandura, A. (2006). Toward a Psychology of Human Agency. *Perspectives on Psychological Science, 1*(2), 164–180. Retrieved from http://www.jstor.org/stable/4021216

Barsh, G.S. (2003). What controls variation in human skin color? *PLOS: Biology, 1*(1), e27. doi:10.1371/journal.pbio.0000027

Bjorklund, D.F., & Ellis, B.J. (2014). Children, childhood, and development in evolutionary perspective. *Developmental Review, 34*(3), 225–264. doi:10.1016/j.dr.2014.05.005

Bjorklund, D.F., & Pellegrini, A.D. (2002). *The origins of human nature: Evolutionary developmental psychology*. Washington, DC: American Psychological Association.

Bjorklund, D.F., Hernández Blasi, C., & Ellis, B.J. (2016). Evolutionary developmental psychology. In D.M. Buss (Ed.), *The Evolutionary Psychology handbook* (2nd Ed.). New York, NY: John Wiley & Sons.

Bowlby, J. (1969). *Attachment and loss: Vol. 1. Attachment*. New York, NY: Basic Books.

Bowlby, J. (1980). *Attachment and loss: Vol. 3. Loss, sadness, and depression*. New York, NY: Basic Books.

Bronfenbrenner, U. (1979). *The ecology of human development*. Cambridge, MA: Harvard University Press.

Bronfenbrenner, U. (2005). The bioecological theory of human development (2001). In U. Bronfenbrenner (Ed.), *Making human beings human: Bioecological perspectives on human development* (pp. 3–15). Thousand Oaks, CA: Sage Publications, Inc.

Buss, D.M. (1999). *Evolutionary psychology: The new science of the mind*. Boston, MA: Allyn & Bacon.

Buss, D.M. (2016). Introduction: The Emergence and Maturation of Evolutionary Psychology. In D. M. Buss (Ed.), *The Handbook of Evolutionary Psychology, Volume 1: Foundation* (2nd ed.) (pp. xxiii–xxvi). Hoboken, NJ: Wiley. doi:10.1002/9781119125563.evpsych101

Case, R. (1985). *Intellectual development: Birth to adulthood*. New York, NY: Academic Press.

Case, R. (1997). The development of conceptual structures. In B. Damon (General Ed.) and D. Kuhn & R. S. Siegler (Series Eds.), *Handbook of child psychology, Vol. 2: Cognitive, language, and perceptual development*. New York, NY: Wiley.

Champagne, F.A., & Rissman, E.F. (2011). Behavioral epigenetics: A new frontier in the study of hormones and behavior. *Hormones and Behavior, 59*(3), 277–278. doi:10.1016/j.yhbeh.2011.02.011

Chen, B.S., & Li, C.W. (2016). Constructing an integrated genetic and epigenetic cellular network for whole cellular mechanism using high-throughput next-generation sequencing data. *BMC Systems Biology, 10*(Feb), 18. doi:10.1186/s12918-016-0256-5

Cosmides, L. & Tooby, J. (2013). Evolutionary psychology: New perspectives on cognition and motivation. *Annual Review of Psychology, 64*(Jan), 201–229. doi:10.1146/annurev.psych.121208.131628

Cropley, J.E., Suter, C.M., Beckman, K.B., & Martin, D.I. (2006). Germ-line epigenetic modification of the murine A vy allele by nutritional supplementation. *Proceedings of the National Academy of Sciences of the United States of America, 103*(46), 17308–17312.

Erikson, E.H. (1950). *Childhood and society*. New York, NY: Norton.

Erikson, E.H. (1959). *Identity and the life cycle*. New York, NY: Norton. (Reissued, 1980.)

Erikson, E.H. (1963). *Childhood and society* (2nd ed.). New York, NY: Norton.

Erikson, E.H. (1980b). Themes of adulthood in the Freud-Jung correspondence. In N.J. Smelser & E. Erikson (Eds.), *Themes of work and love in adulthood* (pp. 43–76). Cambridge, MA: Harvard University Press.

Erikson, E.H. (1982). *The life cycle completed*. New York, NY: Norton.

Erikson, E.H., Erikson, J.M., & Kivnick, H.Q. (1986). *Vital involvement in old age*. New York, NY: Norton.

Garner, A.S., & Shonkoff, J.P. (2012). Early childhood adversity, toxic stress, and the role of the pediatrician: Translating developmental science into lifelong health. *Pediatrics, 129*(1), e224–231. doi:10.1542/peds.2011-2662

Garner, A.S., Forkey, H, & Szilagyi, M. (2015). Translating developmental science to address childhood adversity. *Academic Pediatrics, 15*(5), 493–502. doi:10.1016/j.acap.2015.05.010

Gluckman, P., & Hanson, M. (2006a). *Mismatch: Why our world no longer fits our bodies*. New York, NY: Oxford University Press.

Gluckman, P.D., & Hanson, M.A. (2004a). Living with the past: Evolution, development, and patterns of disease. *Science, 305,* 1733–1736.

Gluckman, P.D., & Hanson, M.A. (2004b). *The fetal matrix: evolution, development and disease*. New York, NY: Cambridge University Press.

Gluckman, P.D., & Hanson, M.A. (2006b). Adult disease: echoes of the past. *European Journal of Endocrinology, 155*(S1), S47–S50. doi:10.1530/eje.1.02233

Gluckman, P.D., & Hanson, M.A. (2007). Developmental plasticity and human disease: Research directions. *Journal of Internal Medicine, 261*(5), 461–471.

Gluckman, P.D., Hanson, M.A., & Beedle, A.S. (2007). Early life events and their consequences for later disease: A life history and evolutionary perspective. *American Journal of Human Biology, 19*(1), 1–19.

Gluckman, P.D., Hanson, M.A., & Spencer, H.G. (2005). Predictive adaptive responses and human evolution. *Trends in Ecology and Evolution, 20*(10), 527–33. doi:10.1016/j.tree.2005.08.001

Gluckman, P.D., Hanson, M.A., Bateson, P., Beedle, A.S., Law, C.M., Bhutta, Z.A., . . . West-Eberhard, M.J. (2009). Towards a new developmental synthesis: adaptive developmental plasticity and human disease. *Lancet, 373*(9675), 1654–1657.

Godfrey, K.M., Costello, P.M. & Lillycrop, K.A. (2015). The developmental environment, epigenetic biomarkers and long-term health. *Journal of Developmental Origins of Health and Disease, 6*(May), 399–406. doi:10.1017/S204017441500121X

Hackett, F., Abonyi, S., & Dyck, R. (2016). Anthropometric indices of First Nations children and youth on first entry to Manitoba/Saskatchewan residential schools -1919 to 1953. *International Journal of Circumpolar Health, 75*(June 27). doi:10.3402/ijch.v75.30734

Hall, W.D., Morley, K.I., & Lucke, J.C. (2004). The prediction of disease risk in genomic medicine. *EMBO reports, 5*(S1), S22–S26.

Hanson, M.A., & Gluckman, P.D. (2014). Early Developmental Conditioning of Later Health and Disease: Physiology or Pathophysiology? *Physiological Reviews, 94*(4), 1027–1076. doi:10.1152/physrev.00029.2013

Hanson, M.A., & Gluckman, P.D. (2015). Developmental origins of health and disease–global public health implications. *Best Practice & Research Clinical Obstetrics & Gynaecology, 29*(1), 24–31. doi:10.1016/j.bpobgyn.2014.06.007

Health Canada. (2010). First Nations, Inuit and Aboriginal health—diabetes. Ottawa, ON: Author. Retrieved from www.hc-sc.gc.ca/fniah-spnia/diseases-maladies/diabete/index-eng.php#a71

Hegele, R.A., Cao, H., Harris, S.B., Hanley, A.J.G., & Zinman, B. (1999). The hepatic nuclear factor—1% G319S variant is associated with early-onset type 2 diabetes in Canadian Oji-Cree. *The Journal of Clinical Endocrinology and Metabolism, 84*(3), 1007–1082.

Heindel, J.J., & Lawler, C. (2006). Role of exposure to environmental chemicals in developmental origins of health and disease.

In P. Gluckman, Hanson, M (Eds.), *Developmental origins of health and disease* (pp. 82–97). New York, NY: Cambridge University Press.

Heller, E.A., Cates, H.M., Peña, C.J., Sun, H., Shao, N., Feng, J., . . . Nestler, E.J. (2014). Locus-Specific Epigenetic Remodeling Controls Addiction- and Depression-Related Behaviors (NN-A50213-T). *Nature Neuroscience, 17*(12), 1720–1727. doi.org/10.1038/nn.3871

Hertzman, C. (2013). Commentary on the symposium: Biological embedding, life course development, and the emergence of a new science. *Annual Review of Public Health, 34*, 1–5. doi:10.1146/annurev-publhealth-031912-114500

Hertzman, C. (2013). The significance of early childhood adversity. *Paediatrics & Child Health, 18*(3), 127–128.

Heyn, H., Li, N., Ferreira, H.J., Moran, S., Pisano, D.G., Gomez, A., . . . Esteller, M. (2012). Distinct DNA methylomes of newborns and centenarians. *Proceedings of the National Academy of Sciences of the United States of America, 109*(26), 10522–10527. doi:10.1073/pnas.1120658109

Holtzman, N.A., & Marteau, T.M. (2000). Will genetics revolutionize medicine? *The New England Journal of Medicine, 343*(2), 141–144.

International Cancer Genome Consortium (2010). International network of cancer genome projects. *Nature, 464*, 993–998.

International Human Epigenome Consortium (n.d.). *About IHEC Objectives*. Retrieved from http://ihec-epigenomes.org/

Isles, A.R. (2015), Neural and behavioral epigenetics; what it is, and what is hype. *Genes, Brain and Behavior, 14*(1), 64–72. doi:10.1111/gbb.12184

Jablonka, E., & Lamb, M.J. (2005). *Evolution in Four Dimensions.* Cambridge, MA: MIT Press.

Jablonka, E., & Lamb, M.J. (2015). The inheritance of acquired epigenetic variations. *International Journal of Epidemiology, 44*(4), 1094–1103. doi:10.1093/ije/dyv020

Jensen, P. (2015). Adding 'epi-' to behaviour genetics: Implications for animal domestication. *The Journal of Experimental Biology, 218*(Pt 1), 32–40. doi:10.1242/jeb.106799

John P. Robarts Research Institute. (2000). *New gene helps fight diabetes in Canada's Aboriginal population*. London, ON: Diabetes Research Centre.

Jospe, N. (2015). Endocrinology. In Marcdante, K., Kliegman, R., Jenson, H., & Behrman, R. (Eds), *Nelson essentials of pediatrics* (7th ed., pp. 625–670). Philadelphia, PA: Saunders Elsevier.

Kaminsky, Z., Wilcox, H.C., Eaton, W.W., Van Eck, K., Kilaru, V., Jovanovic, T., . . . Smith, A.K. (2015). Epigenetic and genetic variation at *SKA2* predict suicidal behavior and post-traumatic stress disorder. *Translational Psychiatry, 5*(8), e627. doi:10.1038/tp.2015.105

Keshavan, M.S., Nasrallah, H.A., & Tandon, R. (2011). Schizophrenia, "Just the Facts" 6. Moving ahead with the schizophrenia concept: From the elephant to the mouse. *Schizophrenia Research, 127*(1–3), 3–13. doi:10.1016/j.schres.2011.01.011

Keverne, E.B., Pfaff, D.W., & Tabansky, I. (2015). Epigenetic changes in the developing brain: Effects on behavior. *PNAS USA, 112*(22), 6789–6795. doi:10.1073/pnas

Khoury, M.J. (2003). Genetics and genomics in practice: The continuum from genetic disease to genetic information in health and disease. *Genetics in Medicine, 5*(4), 261–268.

Kimmins, S., & Sassone-Corsi, P. (2005). Chromatin remodeling and epigenetic features of germ cells. *Nature, 434* (7033), 583–589.

Lahiri, D.K., Maloney, B., Bayon, B.L., Chopra, N., White, F.A., Greig, N.H., & Nurnberger, J.I. (2016). Transgenerational latent early-life associated regulation unites environment and genetics across generations. *Epigenomics, 8*(3), 373–387. doi:10.2217/epi.15.117

Landry, S.H., Garner, P.W., Swank, P.R., & Baldwin, C.D. (1996). Effects of maternal scaffolding during joint toy play with preterm and full-term infants. *Merrill-Palmer Quarterly, 42*, 177–199.

Lester, B.M., Conradt, E., & Marsit, C. (2016), Introduction to the special section on epigenetics. *Child Development, 87*(1), 29–37. doi:10.1111/cdev.12489

Levy, P., & Marion, R. (2015). Human genetics and dysmorphology. In Marcdante, K., Kliegman, R., Jenson, H., & Behrman, R. (Eds),

Nelson essentials of pediatrics (7th ed., pp. 167–186). Philadelphia, PA: Saunders Elsevier.

Liu, A., Wollstein, A., Hysi, P., Ankra-Badu, G., Spector, T., Park, D., . . . Kayser, M. (2010). Digital quantification of human eye color highlights: Genetic association of three new loci. *PLOS: Genetics, 6*(5): e1000934. doi:10.1371/journal.pgen.1000934

Lomanowska, A.M., Boivin, M., Hertzman, C., & Fleming, A.S. (2015). Parenting begets parenting: A neurobiological perspective on early adversity and the transmission of parenting styles across generations. *Neuroscience,* (Sep 16). pii: S0306-4522(15)00848-9. doi:10.1016/j.neuroscience.2015.09.029

Martin, G.M. (2005). Epigenetic drift in aging identical twins. *Proceedings of the National Academy of Sciences of the United States of America, 102*(30), 10413–10414.

Maslow, A.H. (1968). *Toward a psychology of being* (2nd ed.). New York, NY: Van Nostrand Reinhold.

Maslow, A.H. (1970). *Motivation and personality* (2nd ed.). New York, NY: Harper & Row.

McGowan, P.O., & Roth, T.L. (2015). Epigenetic pathways through which experiences become linked with biology. *Development and Psychopathology, 27*(2), 637–648. doi:10.1017/S0954579415000206

Meaney, M.J., & Szyf, M. (2005). Maternal care as a model for experience-dependent chromatin plasticity? *Trends in Neuroscience, 28*(9), 456–463.

Moore, D.S. (2013). Behavioral genetics, genetics, & epigenetics. In P.D. Zelazo (Ed.), *Oxford handbook of developmental psychology* (pp. 91–128). New York, NY: Oxford University Press.

Moore, D.S. (2015). *The developing genome: An introduction to behavioral epigenetics.* New York, NY: Oxford University Press.

Munakata, Y. (2006). Information processing approaches to cognitive development. In W. Damon, R. Lerner, D. Kuhn, & R. Sieglers (Eds.), *Handbook of child psychology: Vol 2: Cognition, perception, and language* (6th ed., pp. 426–463). New York, NY: John Wiley & Sons.

Nagle, G.A., & Usry, L.R. (2016). Using public health strategies to shape early childhood policy. *American Journal of Orthopsychiatry, 86*(2), 171–178. doi:10.1037/ort0000088

Pajares, F. (2004). *Albert Bandura: Biographical sketch*. Retrieved from Dision of Educational Studies website: www.des.emory.edu/mfp/banconversion.html

Pal, M., Ebrahimi, S., Oh, G., Khare, T., Zhang, A., Kaminsky, Z.A., . . . Petronis, A. (2016). High precision DNA modification analysis of *HCG9* in major psychosis. *Schizophrenia Bulletin, 42*(1), 170–177. doi:10.1093/schbul/sbv079

Park, J., & Peters, P.A. (2014). Mortality from diabetes mellitus, 2004 to 2008: A multiple-cause-of-death analysis. *Health Reports, 25*(3), 12–16.

Park, J., Tjepkema, M., Goedhuis, N., & Pennock, J. (2015). Avoidable mortality among First Nations adults in Canada: A cohort analysis. *Health Reports, 26*(8), 10–16.

Pascual-Leone, J. (1987). Organismic processes for Neo-Piagetian theories: A dialectical causal account of cognitive development. *International Journal of Psychology, 22*, 531–570.

Pembrey, M., Saffery, R., & Bygren, L.O. (2014). Human transgenerational responses to early-life experience: Potential impact on development, health and biomedical research. *Journal of Medical Genetics, 51*(9), 563–572. doi:10.1136/jmedgenet-2014-102577

Petronis, A. (2003). Epigenetics and bipolar disorder: New opportunities and challenges. *American Journal of Medical Genetics, 123*(1), 65–75.

Petronis, A. (2004). The origin of schizophrenia: Genetic thesis, epigenetic antithesis, and resolving synthesis. *Biological Psychiatry, 55*(10), 965–970.

Petronis, A. (2006). Epigenetics and twins: Three variations on the theme. *Trends in Genetics, 22*(7), 347–350.

Piaget, J. (1952). *The origins of intelligence in children*. New York, NY: International Universities Press.

Piaget, J. (1970). Piaget's theory. In P.H. Mussen (Ed.), *Carmichael's manual of child psychology: Vol. 1* (3rd ed., pp. 703–732). New York, NY: Wiley.

Piaget, J. (1977). *The development of thought: Equilibration of cognitive structures.* New York, NY: Viking.

Piaget, J., & Inhelder, B. (1969). *The psychology of the child*. New York, NY: Basic Books.

Picard, A. (2010, March 4). The budget's fine print matters to health. *The Globe and Mail*. Retrieved from www.theglobeand-mail.com/life/health/the-budgets-fine-print-matters-to-health/article1489327/

Pinker, S. (1997). *How the mind works*. New York, NY: Norton.

Pinker, S. (2002). *The blank slate: The modern denial of human nature*. New York, NY: Viking.

Pinker, S. (2013). Deep commonalities between life and mind. In S. Pinker (Ed.), *Language, Cognition, and Human Nature: Selected Articles* (pp. 293-301). New York, NY: Oxford University Press.

Plomin, R., DeFries, J.C., Knopik, V.S., & Neiderhiser, J.M. (2016). Top 10 replicated findings from behavioral genetics. *Perspectives on Psychological Science, 11*(1), 3-23. doi:10.1177/1745691615617439

Ramsay, M. (2015). Epigenetic epidemiology: Is there cause for optimism? *Epigenomics, 7*(5), 683–685. doi:10.2217/epi.15.48

Roemer, I., Reik, W., Dean, W., & Klose, J. (1997). Epigenetic inheritance in the mouse. *Current Biology, 7*(4), 277–280.

Rogers, C.R. (1961). *On becoming a person*. Boston, MA: Houghton Mifflin.

Rogoff, B. (1990). *Apprenticeship in thinking: Cognitive development in social contexts*. New York, NY: Oxford University Press.

Shah, S.P., Morin, R.D., Khattra, J., Prentice, L., Pugh, T., Burleigh, A., ... Aparicio, S. (2009). Mutational evolution in a lobular breast tumour profiled at single nucleotide resolution. *Nature, 461*, 809–813.

Shonkoff, J.P. (2010). Building a new biodevelopmental framework to guide the future of early childhood policy. *Child Development, 81*(1), 357–367. doi:10.1111/j.1467-8624.2009.01399.x

Skinner, B.F. (1953). *Science and human behavior*. New York, NY: Macmillan.

Skinner, B.F. (1980). The experimental analysis of operant behavior: A history. In R.W. Riebes & K. Salzinger (Eds.), *Psychology: Theoretical-historical perspectives*. New York, NY: Academic Press.

Szyf, M. (2006). Letter from the editor. *Epigenetics, 1*(1), i–i.

Tanner, J.M. (1990). *Foetus into man: Physical growth from conception to maturity* (2nd ed.). Cambridge, MA: Harvard University Press.

Tharp, R.G., & Gallimore, R. (1988). *Rousing minds to life*. New York, NY: Cambridge University Press.

Thiele, D.K., & Anderson, C.M. (2016). Developmental origins of health and disease: A challenge for nurses. *Journal of Pediatric Nursing, 31*(1), 42–46. doi:10.1016/j.pedn.2015.10.020

Thomas, M. (2005). *Comparing theories of child development* (6th ed.). Pacific Grove, CA: Wadsworth/Cengage.

Tooby, J. & Cosmides, L. (2016). The theoretical foundations of evolutionary psychology. In D.M. Buss (Ed.), *The handbook of evolutionary psychology* (2nd ed.) (pp. 3–87). Hoboken, NJ: Wiley. doi:10.1002/9781119125563.evpsych101

Tooby, J., Cosmides, L. & Barrett, H. C. (2005). Resolving the debate on innate ideas: Learnability constraints and the evolved interpenetration of motivational and conceptual functions. In Carruthers, P., Laurence, S. & Stich, S. (Eds.), *The Innate Mind: Structure and Content*. New York, NY: Oxford University Press.

Uhlén, M., Fagerberg, L., Hallstrom, B.M., Lindskog, C., Oksvold, P., Mardinoglu, A., ... Pontén, F. (2015). Tissue-based map of the human proteome. *Science, 347*(6220), 394–403. doi:10.1126/science.1260419

Vaiserman, A. (2015a). Epidemiologic evidence for association between adverse environmental exposures in early life and epigenetic variation: A potential link to disease susceptibility? *Clinical Epigenetics, 7*(1), 96. doi:10.1186/s13148-015-0130-0 eCollection 2015

Vaiserman, A.M. (2015b), Epigenetic programming by early-life stress: Evidence from human populations. *Developmental Dynamics, 244*(3), 254–265. doi:10.1002/dvdy.24211

Vygotsky, L.S. (1978). *Mind and society: The development of higher mental processes*. Cambridge, MA: Harvard University Press. (Original works published 1930, 1933, and 1935.)

Waterman, R.A. (2006). Critical experiments to determine if early nutritional influences on epigenetics mechanisms cause metabolic imprinting in humans. In M.E. Wintour & J.A. Owens (Eds.), *Early life origins of health and disease. Advances in Experimental medicine and biology: Vol. 573* (pp. 79–86). New York, NY: Springer Science & Business Media.

Weaver, I.C., Meaney, M.J., & Szyf, M. (2006). Maternal care effects on the hippocampal transcriptome and anxiety-mediated behaviors in the offspring that are reversible in adulthood. *Proceedings of the National Academy of Sciences of the United States of America, 103*(9), 3480–3485.

Weaver, I.C.G., Cervoni, N., Champagne, F.A., D'Alessio, A.C., Sharma, S., Seck, J.R., ... Meaney, M.J. (2004). Epigenetic programming by maternal behavior. *Nature Neuroscience, 7*(8), 847–854.

Weaver, I.C.G., Champagne, F.A., Brown, S.E., Dymov, S., Sharma, S., Meaney, M.J., & Szyf, M. (2005). Reversal of maternal programming of stress responses in adult offspring through methyl supplementation: Altering epigenetic marking later in life. *The Journal of Neuroscience, 25*(47), 11045–11054.

Weaver, I.C.G., D'Alessio, A.C., Brown, S.E., Hellstrom, I.C., Dymov, S., Sharma, S., ... Meaney, M.J. (2007). The transcription factor nerve growth factor-inducible protein a mediates epigenetic programming: Altering epigenetic marks by immediate–early genes. *The Journal of Neuroscience, 27*(7), 1756–1768.

Wei, Y., Schatten, H., & Sun, Q.Y. (2015). Environmental epigenetic inheritance through gametes and implications for human reproduction. *Human Reproduction Update, 21*(2), 194–208. doi:10.1093/humupd/dmu061

Whitelaw, N.C., & Whitelaw, E. (2006). How lifetimes shape epigenotype within and across generations. *Human Molecular Genetics, 15* (Review Issue No. 2), 131–137.

Wong, A.H.C., Gottesman, I.I., & Petronis, A. (2005). Phenotypic differences in genetically identical organisms: The epigenetic perspective. *Human Molecular Genetics, 14* (Review Issue 1), R11–R18.

World Health Organization. (2012). *Developmental difficulties in early childhood: Prevention, early identification, assessment and intervention in low- and middle-income countries: A review*. Retrieved from http://whqlibdoc.who.int/publications/2012/9789241503549_eng.pdf

Wu, L., Lu, Y., Jiao, Y., Liu, B., Li, S., Li, Y., ... Li, X. (2016). Paternal psychological stress reprograms hepatic gluconeogenesis in offspring. *Cell Metabolism, 23*(4), 735–743. doi:10.1016/j.cmet.2016.01.014

Young, T.K, Reading, J., Elias, B. & O'Neil, J.D. (2000). Type 2 diabetes mellitus in Canada's First Nations: Status of an epidemic in progress. *Canadian Medical Association Journal, 163*(5), 561–566.

Zeidán-Chuliá, F., Rybarczyk-Filho, J., Slmina, A., Neves de Oliveira, B., Noda, M., & Moreira, J. (2013). Exploring the multifactorial nature of autism through computational systems biology: Calcium and the Rho GTPase RAC1 under the spotlight. *Journal of Molecular Neuroscience, 15*(2), 364–383. doi:10.1007/s12017-013-8224-3

Zimmerman, B.J., & Schunk, D.H. (2002). Albert Bandura: The man and his contributions to educational psychology. In B.J. Zimmerman, & H. Schunk (Eds.), *Educational psychology: A century of contributions* (pp. 431–459). Mahwah, NJ: L. Erlbaum Associates.

Chapter 3

Accardo, P., Tomazic, T., Fete, T., Heaney, M., Lindsay, R., & Whitman, B. (1997). Maternally reported fetal activity levels and developmental diagnoses. *Clinical Pediatrics, 36*, 279–283.

Amato, S. (1998). Human genetics and dysmorphy. In R. Behrman & R. Kliegman (Eds.), *Nelson essentials of pediatrics* (3rd ed., pp. 129–146). Philadelphia, PA: W.B. Saunders.

American Psychiatric Association, (2013). *Diagnostic and Statistical Manual of Mental Disorder: DSM-5* (5th ed.). Washington, DC: American Psychiatric Publishing.

Apgar, V.A. (1953). A proposal for a new method of evaluation of the newborn infant. *Current Research in Anesthesia and Analgesia, 32*, 260–267.

Arabin, B. (2009). Development of the senses. In Levene, M., & Chervenak, F. (Eds), *Fetal and neonatal neurology and neurosurgery*,

(4th ed., pp. 111–127). Philadelphia, PA: Churchill Livingstone Elsevier.

Auyeung, B., Lombardo, M.V., & Baron-Cohen, S. (2013). Prenatal and postnatal hormone effects on the human brain and cognition. *Pflugers Archives, 465*(5), 557–571. doi:10.1007/s00424-013-1268-2

Behrman, R.E., & Butler, A.S. (Eds.). (2007b). *Preterm birth: causes, consequences, and prevention.* Retrieved from http://www.nap.edu/catalog.php?record_id=11622

Benn, P.A., & Egan, J.F.X. (2000). Letters to the Editor: Survival of Down syndrome in utero. *Prenatal Diagnosis, 20*(5), 432–433.

Bertrand, J., Floyd, R.L., Weber, M.K., O'Connor, M., Riley, E.P., Johnson, K.A., et al.; National Task Force on FAS/FAE. (2004). *Fetal Alcohol Syndrome: Guidelines for Referral and Diagnosis.* Atlanta, GA: Centers for Disease Control and Prevention.

Best Start: Ontario's Maternal, Newborn and Early Child Development Resource Centre (n.d.). *Reducing the impact-working with pregnant women who live in difficult situations.* Retrieved from http://www.beststart.org/resources/anti_poverty/pdf/REDUCE.pdf

Best, R., & Gregg, A. (2009). *Patau syndrome.* Retrieved from http://emedicine.medscape.com/article/947706-overview

Biswas, M.K., & Craigo, S.D. (1994). The course and conduct of normal labor and delivery. In A.H. DeCherney & M.L. Pernoll (Eds.), *Current obstetric and gynecologic diagnosis & treatment* (pp. 202–227). Norwalk, CT: Appleton & Lange.

Braun, K., & Champagne, F.A. (2014). Paternal influences on offspring development: Behavioural and epigenetic pathways. *Journal of Neuroendocrinology, 26*(10), 697–706. doi:10.1111/jne.12174

Brazelton, T.B., & Nugent, J.K. (1995). *Neonatal Behavioral Assessment Scale.* London, England: MacKeith Press.

Brent, R.L. (2004a). Environmental causes of human congenital malformations: The pediatrician's role in dealing with these complex clinical problems caused by a multiplicity of environmental and genetic factors. *Pediatrics, 113*(4 S), 957–968.

Brent, R.L. (2004b). Teratology in the 20th century environmental causes of congenital malformations in humans and how they were established by Harold Kalter. *Neurotoxicology and Teratology, 26*(1), 1–12.

Breslau, N., Johnson, E., & Lucia, V. (2001). Academic achievement of low birthweight children at age 11: The role of cognitive abilities at school entry. *Journal of Abnormal Child Psychology, 29*(4), 273–279.

Brockington, I. (1996). *Motherhood and mental health.* Oxford, England: Oxford University Press.

Brown, L., Karrison, T., & Cibils, L. (1994). Mode of delivery and perinatal results in breech presentation. *American Journal of Obstetrics & Gynecology, 171*(1), 28–34.

Buckett, W., & Tan, S.L. (2004). What is the most relevant standard of success in assisted reproduction? The importance of informed choice. *Human Reproduction, 19*(5), 1043–1045.

Bushnik. T., & Garner, R. (2008). The children of older first-time mothers in Canada: Their health and development. (89-599-M). Ottawa, ON: Statistics Canada. Retrieved from Women's Health Resources website: http://thesurvey.womenshealthdata.ca/pdf_files/89-599-MIE2008005.pdf

Calderon-Margalit, R., Qiu, C., Ornoy, A., Siscovick, D.S., & Williams, M.A. (2009). Risk of preterm delivery and other adverse perinatal outcomes in relation to maternal use of psychotropic medications during pregnancy. *American Journal of Obstetrics & Gynecology, 201*(6), 579.

Canadian Association of Genetic Counsellors. (n.d.). *Genetic Counselling: A brochure for Canadians seeking Assisted Human Reproduction.* Retrieved from http://cagc.mindzplay.ws/cagc/index.php?page=185

Canadian Fertility and Andrology Society, The. (2015). *2015 AHR live birth rates for Canada News Release - Canadian IVF Clinics achieve their objective of reducing multiple pregnancy rate less than 15% even earlier than projected.* [Media Release]. Retrieved from https://cfas.ca/public-affairs/canadian-art-register/

Canadian Institute of Child Health. (n.d.). *The health of Canada's children: A CICH profile* (3rd ed.). Ottawa, ON: Author.

Centre for Addiction and Mental Health. (2010). *Cannabis.* Retrieved from http://knowledgex.camh.net/primary_care/guidelines_materials/Pregnancy_Lactation/Pages/per_cannabis.aspx

Chen, H. (2009). *Trisomy 18.* Retrieved from http://emedicine.medscape.com/article/943463-overview

Chen, H. (2010). *Down syndrome.* Retrieved from http://emedicine.medscape.com/article/943216-overview

Chen, X., Wen, S.W., Fleming, N., Yang, Q., & Walker, M.C. (2007). Teenage pregnancy and congential anomalies: Which system is vulnerable? *Human Reproduction, 22*(6), 1730–1735.

Chen, X., Wen, S.W., Krewski, D., Fleming, N., Yang, Q., & Walker, M.C. (2008). Paternal age and adverse birth outcomes: teenager or 40+, who is at risk? *Human Reproduction, 23*(6), 1290–1296.

Chia, S.E., & Shi L.M. (2002). Review of recent epidemiological studies on paternal occupations and birth defects. *Occupational and Environmental Medicine, 59,* 149–155.

Christian, P., & Stewart, C.P. (2010). Maternal micronutrient deficiency, fetal development, and risk of chronic disease. *The Journal of Nutrition, 140*(3), 437–445. doi:10.3945/?jn.109.116327

Chudley, A.E. (2006). *Birth defects and fetal alcohol spectrum disorder.* Winnipeg, MB: Public Health Agency of Canada.

Clement, T. (2006). *Assisted Human Reproduction Agency of Canada 2006–2007 Report on Plans and Priorities.* Ottawa, ON: Health Canada. Retrieved from Treasury Board of Canada Secretariat website: www.tbs-sct.gc.ca/rpp/0607/ahrac-accpa/ahrac-accpa_e.pdf

Communication Canada (2004). *Statutes of Canada 2004 Chapter 2: An Act respecting assisted human reproduction and related research Bill C-6.* Retrieved from Health Canada website: www.hc-sc.gc.ca/english/pdf/protection/ahr/C-6_4_RA.pdf

Corbet, A., Long, W., Schumacher, R., Gerdes, J., & Cotton, R. (1995). Double-blind developmental evaluation at 1-year corrected age of 597 premature infants with birth weights from 500 to 1350 grams enrolled in three placebo-controlled trials of prophylactic synthetic surfactant. *Journal of Pediatrics, 126,* S5–12.

Cox, J., Bota, G.W., Carter, M., Bretzlaff-Michaud, J.A., Sahai, V., & Rowe, B.H. (2004). Domestic violence. Incidence and prevalence in a northern emergency department. *Canadian Family Physician, 50*(1), 90–97.

Cropley, J.E., Suter, C.M., Beckman, K.B., & Martin, D.I. (2006). Germ-line epigenetic modification of the murine A vy allele by nutritional supplementation. *Proceedings of the National Academy of Sciences of the United States of America, 103*(46), 17308–17312.

Davies, M.J., Moore, V.M., Willson, K.J., Van Essen, P., Priest, K., Scott, H., . . . Chan, A. (2012). Reproductive technologies and the risk of birth defects. *The New England Journal of Medicine, 366*(19), 1803–1813. doi:10.1056/NEJMoa1008095

Day, P.E., Ntani, G., Crozier, S.R., Mahon, P.A., Inskip, H.M., Cooper, C., . . . Cleal, J.K. (2015). Maternal factors are associated with the expression of placental genes involved in amino acid metabolism and transport. *PLoS ONE, 10*(12), e0143653. doi:10.1371/journal.pone.0143653

De Vries, G.J., & Forger, N.G. (2015). Sex differences in the brain: A whole body perspective. *Biology of Sex Differences, 6*(Aug), 15. http://doi.org/10.1186/s13293-015-0032-z

DeCasper, A.J., & Spence, M.J. (1986). Prenatal maternal speech influences newborns' perception of speech sounds. *Infant Behavior and Development, 9,* 133–150.

Dell, C.A., & Roberts, G. (2006). *Research update: Alcohol use and pregnancy: An important Canadian public health and social issue.* Ottawa, ON: Public Health Agency of Canada.

Department of Justice Canada. (2001a). *Criminal Code. R.S., c. C-34, s. 1.* Ottawa, ON: Author. Retrieved from http://lois.justice.gc.ca/en/C-46/text.html

Dharan, V., & Parviainen, E. (2009). *Psychosocial and environmental pregnancy risks.* Retrieved from http://emedicine.medscape.com/article/259346-overview

Dieni, S., & Rees, S. (2003). Dendritic morphology is altered in hippocampal neurons following prenatal compromise. *Journal of Neurobiology, 55,* 41–52.

DiPietro, J.A. (2010). Psychological and psychophysiological considerations regarding the maternal-fetal relationship. *Infant and Child Development, 19*(1), 27–38. doi:10.1002/icd.651

DiPietro, J.A., Ghera, M.M., & Costigan, K.A. (2008). Prenatal origins of temperamental reactivity in early infancy. *Early Human Development, 84*(9), 569–575. doi:10.1016/j.earlhumdev.2008.01.004

DiPietro, J.A., Kivlighan, K.T., Costigan, K.A., Rubin, S.E., Shiffler, D.E., Henderson, J.L., & Pillion, J.P. (2010). Prenatal antecedents of newborn neurological maturation. *Child Development, 81*(1), 115–130. doi:10.1111/j.1467-8624.2009.01384.x

Dyack, S. (2004). Expanding newborn screening: Lessons learned from MCAD deficiency. *Paediatrics & Child Health, 9*(4), 241–243.

Eaton, S.A., Jayasooriah, N., Buckland, M.E., Martin, D.I., Cropley, J.E. & Suter, C.M. (2015). Roll over Weismann: Extracellular vesicles in the transgenerational transmission of environmental effects. *Epigenomics, 7*(7), 1165–1171. doi:10.2217/epi.15.58

Edwards, G. (n.d.). *Health and environmental issues linked to the nuclear fuel chain: Health effects* (Section B). Montreal: Canadian Coalition for Nuclear Responsibility. Retrieved from www.ccnr.org/ceac_B.html#b.14

Eliot, L. (1999). *What's going on in there?: How the brain and mind develop in the first five years of life.* New York, NY: Bantom Books.

Evans, J.A., & Fortier, A. (2006). *Congenital malformations in infants born to young mothers.* Winnipeg, MB: Public Health Agency of Canada.

Fear, N.T., Hey, K., Vincent, T., & Murphy, M. (2007). Paternal occupation and neural tube defects: A case-control study based on the Oxford Record Linkage Study register. *Paediatric and Perinatal Epidemiology, 21*(2), 163–168.

Feil, R. (2006). Environmental and nutritional effects on the epigenetic regulation of genes. *Mutation Research/Fundamental and Molecular Mechanisms of Mutagenesis, 600*(1–2), 46–57.

Feil, R. (2008). Epigenetics, an emerging discipline with broad implications. *Molecular Biology and Genetics, 331*(11), 837–843.

Finnell, R.H., Waes, J.G., Eudy, J.D., & Rosenquist, T.H. (2002). Molecular basis of environmentally induced birth defects. *Annual review of Pharmacology and Toxicology, 42*, 181–208.

Fleming, N., O'Driscoll, T., Becker, G., Spitzer, R.F., CANPAGO Committee, Allen, L., . . . Society of Obstetricians and Gynaecologists of Canada. (2015). Adolescent pregnancy guidelines. *Journal of Obstetrics and Gynaecology Canada, 37*(8), 740–759. doi:10.1016/S1701-2163(15)30180-8

Forster, P., Hohoff, C., Dunkelmann, B., Schürenkamp, M., Pfeiffer, H., Neuhuber, F., & Brinkmann, B. (2015). Elevated germline mutation rate in teenage fathers. *Proceedings of the Royal Society B: Biological Sciences, 282*(1803), 20142898. doi:10.1098/rspb.2014.2898

Fraga, M.F. (2009). Genetic and epigenetic regulation of aging. *Current Opinion in Immunology, 21*(4), 446–453.

Fraga, M.F., Ballestar, E., Paz, M.F., Ropero, S., Setien, F., Ballestar, M.L., . . . Esteller, M. (2005). Epigenetic differences arise during the lifetime of the monozygotic twins. *Proceedings of the National Academy of Sciences of the United States of America, 102*(30), 10604–10609.

Francis, P.L., Self, P.A., & Horowitz, F.D. (1987). The behavioral assessment of the neonate: An overview. In J.D. Osofsky (Ed.), *Handbook of infant development* (2nd ed., pp. 723–779). New York, NY: Wiley-Interscience.

Frans, E., MacCabe, J.H., & Reichenberg, A. (2015). Advancing paternal age and psychiatric disorders. *World Psychiatry, 14*(1), 91–93. doi:10.1002/wps.20190

Georgieff, M. K. (1994). Nutritional deficiencies as developmental risk factors: Commentary on Pollitt and Gorman. In C. A. Nelson (Ed.). *The Minnesota Symposia on Child Development,* (Vol. 27, pp. 145–159). Hillsdale, NJ: Erlbaum.

Gordon, L., Joo, J.E., Powell, J.E., Ollikainen, M., Novakovic, B., Li, X., . . . Saffery, R. (2012). Neonatal DNA methylation profile in human twins is specified by a complex interplay between intrauterine environmental and genetic factors, subject to tissue-specific influence. *Genome Research, 22*(8), 1395–1406. doi:10.1101/gr.136598.111

Gowen, C. (2011). Fetal and neonatal medicine. In Marcdante, K., Kliegman, R., Jenson, H., & Behrman, R. (Eds). *Nelson essentials of pediatrics* (6th ed., pp. 213–264). Philadelphia, PA: Saunders Elsevier.

Grandjean, P., & Landrigan, P.J. (2014). Neurobehavioural effects of developmental toxicity. *The Lancet. Neurology, 13*(3), 330–338. doi:10.1016/S1474-4422(13)70278-3

Grandjean, P., Barouki, R., Bellinger, D.C., Casteleyn, L., Chadwick, L.H., Cordier, S., . . . Heindel, J.J. (2015). Life-long implications of developmental exposure to environmental stressors: New perspectives. *Endocrinology, 156*(10), 3408–3415. doi:10.1210/EN.2015-1350

Green, R.F., Devine, O., Crider, K.S., Olney, R.S., Archer, N., Olshan, A.F., & Shapira, S.K. (2010). Association of paternal age and risk for major congenital anomalies from the nation birth defects prevention study, 1997 to 2004. *Annals of Epidemiology, 20*(3), 241–249.

Groome, L., Mooney, D., Holland, S., Smith, L., Atterbury, J., & Dykman, R. (1999). Behavioral state affects heart rate response to low-intensity sound in human fetuses. *Early Human Development, 54*, 39–54.

Groome, L., Mooney, D., Holland, S., Smith, L., Atterbury, J., & Dykman, R. (1999). Behavioral state affects heart rate response to low-intensity sound in human fetuses. *Early Human Development, 54*(1), 39–54. doi:10.1016/S0378-3782(98)00083-8

Guintivano, J., & Kaminsky, Z.A. (2016). Role of epigenetic factors in the development of mental illness throughout life. *Neuroscience Research, 102*(Jan), 56–66. doi:10.1016/j.neures.2014.08.003

Haque, F.N., Gottesman, I.I., & Wong, A.H.C. (2009). Not really identical: Epigenetic differences in monozygotic twins and implications for twin studies in psychiatry. *American Journal of Medical Genetics Part C: Seminars in Medical Genetics, 151C*(2), 136–141.

Health Canada. (2001a). *Proposal for legislation governing assisted human reproduction: An overview.* Ottawa, ON: Author. Retrieved from www.hc-sc.gc.ca/english/archives/releases/2001/2001_44ebk1.htm

Health Canada. (2002a). *Congenital anomalies in Canada—A perinatal health report, 2002* (H39-641/2002E). Ottawa, ON: Minister of Public Works and Government Services Canada.

Health Canada. (2003a). *Canadian perinatal health report* (H49-142/2003E). Ottawa, ON: Minister of Public Works and Government Services Canada.

Health Canada. (2009). *Canadian gestational weight gain recommendations.* Ottawa, ON: Author. Retrieved from www.hc-sc.gc.ca/fn-an/nutrition/prenatal/qa-gest-gros-qr-eng.php

Health Canada. (2011). *Eating well with Canada's food guide.* Retrieved from http://www.hc-sc.gc.ca/fn-an/food-guide-aliment/order-commander/index-eng.php

Health Canada. (2011a). *Canada's food guide: Pregnancy and breastfeeding.* Retrieved from http://www.hc-sc.gc.ca/fn-an/food-guide-aliment/choose-choix/advice-conseil/women-femmes-eng.php

Heaman, M.I., & Chalmers, K. (2005). Prevalence and correlates of smoking during pregnancy: A comparison of Aboriginal and non–Aboriginal women in Manitoba. *Birth, 32*(4), 299–305.

Hill, J., Brooks–Gunn, J., & Waldfogel, J. (2003). Sustained effects of high participation in an early intervention for low-birth-weight premature infants. *Developmental Psychology, 39*(4), 730–744. doi:10.1037/0012-1649.39.4.730

Hines, M., Constantinescu, M., & Spencer, D. (2015). Early androgen exposure and human gender development. *Biology of Sex Differences, 6*(Feb), 3. doi:10.1186/s13293-015-0022-1

Hochberg, Z., Feil, R., Constancia, M., Fraga, M., Junien, C., Carel, J.C., . . . Albertsson-Wikland K. (2011). Child health, developmental plasticity, and epigenetic programming. *Endocrine Reviews, 32*(2), 159–224. doi:10.1210/er.2009-0039

Horsthemke, B. (2006). Epimutations in human disease. *Current Topics in Microbiology and Immunology, 310*, 45–59.

Huang, C., Lee, T., Chen, S., Chen, H., Cheng, T., Liu, C., . . . Lee, M. (2005). Successful pregnancy following blastocyst cryopreservation using super-cooling ultra-rapid vitrification. *Human Reproduction, 20*(1), 122–128.

Huntington Society of Canada. (2013). *Learn about HD*. Retrieved from http://www.huntingtonsociety.ca/learn-about-hd/what-is-huntingtons/

Ierardi-Curto, L. (2013). *Lipid storage disorders*. Retrieved from http://emedicine.medscape.com/article/945966-overview#a0199

Ivorra, C., Fraga, M. F., Bayón, G. F., Fernández, A. F., Garcia-Vicent, C., Chaves, F. J., . . . Lurbe, E. (2015). DNA methylation patterns in newborns exposed to tobacco in utero. *Journal of Translational Medicine, 13*(Jan), 25. doi:10.1186/s12967-015-0384-5

Janssen, P.A., Saxell, L., Page, L.A., Llien, M.C., Liston, R.M., & Lee, S.K. (2009). Outcomes of planned home birth with registered midwife versus planned hospital birth with midwife of physician. *Canadian Medical Association Journal, 181*(6–7), 377–383.

Jewell, J. (2009). *Fragile X syndrome*. Retrieved from http://emedicine.medscape.com/article/943776-overview

Johnson, E., & Breslau, N. (2000). Increased risk of learning disabilities in low birth weight boys at age 11 years. *Biological Psychiatry, 47*, 490–500.

Johnson, J.A., & Tough, S. (2012). Delayed child-bearing. *Journal of Obstetrics and Gynaecology Canada, 34*(1), 80–93. Retrieved from http://www.jogc.com/abstracts/full/201201_SOGCClinical-PracticeGuidelines_1.pdf

Johnson, J.A., & Tough, S. (2012). Delayed child-bearing. *Journal of Obstetrics and Gynaecology Canada, 34*(1), 80–93. Retrieved from http://www.jogc.com/abstracts/full/201201_SOGCClinical-PracticeGuidelines_1.pdf

Johnson, M. (2011). Developmental neuroscience, psychophysiology, and genetics. In M. Bornstein & M. Lamb (Eds.), *Developmental science: An advanced textbook* (6th ed., pp. 201–240). New York, NY: Psychology Press.

Joseph, R. (2000). Fetal brain behavior and cognitive development. *Developmental Review, 20*, 81–98.

Kalter, H. (2003). Teratology in the 20th century: Environmental causes of congenital malformations in humans and how they were established. *Neurotoxicology and Teratology, 25*(2), 131–282.

Kaminsky, Z.A., Tang, T., Wang, S., Ptak, C., Oh, G.H.T., Wong, A. H.C., . . . Petronis, A. (2009). DNA methylation profiles in monozygotic and dizygotic twins. *Nature Genetics, 41*, 240–245.

Kilpatrick, S.J., & Laros, R.K. (1989). Characteristics of normal labor. *Obstetrics and Gynecology, 74*, 85–87.

Kim, T.J., Laufer, L.R., & Wook Hong, S. (2010). Vitrification of oocytes produces high pregnancy rates when carried out in fertile women. *Fertility and Sterility, 93*(2), 467–474.

Kisilevsky, B.S., Hains, S.M.J., Lee, K., Xie, X., Huang, H., Ye, H.-H., . . . Wang, Z. (2003). Effects of experience on fetal voice recognition. *Psychological Science, 14*(3), 220–224.

Kivlighan, K., DiPietro, J., Costigan, K., & Laudenslager, M. (2008). Diurnal rhythm of cortisol during late pregnancy: Associations with maternal psychological well-being and fetal growth. *Psychoneuroendocrinology, 33*(9), 1225–1235. doi:10.1016/j.psyneuen.2008.06.008

Kliegman, R. (1998). Fetal and neonatal medicine. In R. Behrman & R. Kliegman (Eds.), *Nelson essentials of pediatrics* (3rd ed., pp. 167–225). Philadelphia, PA: W.B. Saunders.

Kong, A., Frigge, M.L., Masson, G., Besenbacher, S., Sulem, P., Magnusson, G., . . . Stefansson, K. (2012). Rate of de novo mutations and the importance of father's age to disease risk. *Nature, 488*(7412), 471–475. doi:10.1038/nature11396

Kong, A., Frigge, M.L., Masson, G., Besenbacher, S., Sulem, P., Magnusson, G., . . . Stefansson, K. (2012). Rate of *de novo* mutations, father's age, and disease risk. *Nature, 488*(7412), 471–475. doi:10.1038/nature11396

Kovac, J.R., Addai, J., Smith, R.P., Coward, R.M., Lamb, D.J., & Lipshultz, L.I. (2013). The effects of advanced paternal age on fertility. *Asian Journal of Andrology, 15*(6), 723–728. doi:10.1038/aja.2013.92

Kyser, K.L., Morriss, F.H., Bell, E.F., Klein, J.M., & Dagle, J.M. (2012). Improving survival of extremely preterm infants born between 22 and 25 weeks of gestation. *Obstetrics & Gynecology, 119*(4), 795–800. doi:10.1097/AOG.0b013e31824b1a03

Lahiri, D.K., Maloney. B., Bayon, B.L., Chopra, N., White, F.A., Greig, N.H., & Nurnberger, J.I. (2016). Transgenerational latent early-life associated regulation unites environment and genetics across generations. *Epigenomics, 8*(3), 373–387. doi:10.2217/epi.15.117

Lange, S., Probst, C., Quere, M., Rehm, J., & Popova, S. (2015). Alcohol use, smoking and their co-occurrence during pregnancy among Canadian women, 2003 to 2011/12. *Addictive Behaviors, 50*(Nov), 102–109. doi:10.1016/j.addbeh.2015.06.018

Langille, D.B. (2007). Teenage pregnancy: Trends, contributing factors and the physician's role. *Canadian Medical Association Journal, 176*(11), 1601–1602.

Levy, P., & Marion, R. (2015). Human genetics and dysmorphology. In Marcdante, K., Kliegman, R., Jenson, H., & Behrman, R. (Eds), *Nelson essentials of pediatrics* (7th ed., pp. 167–186). Philadelphia, PA: Saunders Elsevier.

Lewis, D. (2011). Neurology. In Marcdante, K., Kliegman, R., Jenson, H., & Behrman, R. (Eds),. *Nelson essentials of pediatrics* (6th ed., pp. 671–712). Philadelphia, PA: Saunders Elsevier.

Liebermann, J. (2009). Vitrification of human blastocysts: An update. *Reproductive Biomedicine Online, 19*(Suppl 4), 4328.

Liebermann, J. (2015). Vitrification: A simple and successful method for cryostorage of human blastocysts. *Methods in Molecular Biology, 1257*, 305–319. doi:10.1007/978-1-4939-2193-5_12

Lippa, R. (2005). *Gender, nature, and nurture*. Hillsdale, NJ: Lawrence Erlbaum Associates.

Loutfy, M.R., Hart, T.A., Mohammed, S.S., Su, D., Ralph, E.D., Walmsley, S.L., . . . Yudin, M.H. (2009). Fertility desires and intentions of HIV-positive women of reproductive age in Ontario, Canada: A cross-sectional study. *PLoS One, 4*(12), 1–7.

Loutfy, M.R., Margolese, S., Money, D.M., Gysler, M., Hamilton, S., & Yudin, M.H. (2012). Canadian HIV pregnancy planning guidelines. *Journal of Obstetrics and Gynaecology Canada, 34*(6), 575–590. Retrieved from http://www.sogc.org/guidelines/documents/gui278CPG1206E.pdf

Maakaron, J. (2013). *Sickle cell anemia*. Retrieved from http://emedicine.medscape.com/article/205926-overview#a0156

Mamayson, S. (2009). *What is down syndrome?* Retrieved from Canadian Down Syndrome Society website: www.cdss.ca/information/general-information/what-is-down-syndrome.html

Martin, D.I., Ward, R., & Suter, C.M. (2005). Germline epimutation: A basis for epigenetic disease in humans. *Annals of the New York Academy of Sciences, 1054*(1), 68–77.

McCarthy, M.M. (2015). Sex differences in the brain. *The Scientist, 29*(10).

McCarthy, M.M. (2016). Multifaceted origins of sex differences in the brain. *Philosophical Transactions of the Royal Society. Biological Sciences, 371*(1688), pii: 20150106. doi:10.1098/rstb.2015.0106

Melamed, N., Meizner, I., Mashiach, R., Wiznitzer, A., Glezerman, M., & Yogev, Y. (2013). Fetal sex and intrauterine growth patterns. *Journal of Ultrasound in Medicine, 32*(1), 35–43.

Millar, W.J., & Hill, G. (2004). Pregnancy and smoking (Cat. No. 82–003). *Health Reports, 15*(4), 53–56.

Min, J., Breheny, S., MacLachlan, V., & Healy, D. (2004). What is the most relevant standard of success in assisted reproduction? The singleton, term gestation, live birth rate per cycle initiated: the BESST endpoint for assisted reproduction. *Human reproduction, 19*(1), 3–7.

Min, J., Claman, P., & Hughes, E. (2006). Guidelines for the number of embryos to transfer following in vitro fertilization. *Journal of Obstetrics Gynaecology Canada, 28*(9), 799–813.

Moore, K.L., Persaud, T.V.N., & Torchia, M.G. (2011). *The developing human: Clinically oriented embryology* (9th ed.). Philadelphia, PA: Saunders.

Muhajarine, N., & D'Arcy, C. (1999). Physical abuse during pregnancy: prevalence and risk factors. *Canadian Medical Association Journal, 160*(4), 1007–1011.

Murphy, C.C., Schei, B., Myhr, T.L., & Du Mont, J. (2001). Abuse: a risk factor for low birth weight? A systematic review and meta-analysis. *Canadian Medical Association Journal, 164*(11), 1567–1572.

Mutch, L., Leyland, A., & McGee, A. (1993). Patterns of neuropsychological function in a low-birth-weight population. *Developmental Medicine & Child Neurology, 35*, 943–956.

Myerowitz, R., & Hogikyan, N.D. (1987). A deletion involving Alu sequences in the beta-hexosaminidase alpha-chain gene of French Canadians with Tay-Sachs disease. *Journal of Biological Chemistry, 15* :262(32), 15396–15399.

Nijhuis, J.G. (2003). Fetal behavior. *Neurobiology of Aging, 24*, S41–S46. doi:10.1016/S0197-4580(03)00054-X

Nygren, K.G. (2007). Single embryo transfer: The role of natural cycle/minimal stimulation IVF in the future. *Reproductive Biomedicine Online, 14*(5), 626–627.

Olds, D.L., Sadler, L., & Kitzman, H. (2007). Programs for parents of infants and toddlers: Recent evidence from randomized trials. *Journal of Child Psychology and Psychiatry, 48*(3–4), 355–391.

Olson, J.M., Vernon, P.A., Aitken Harris, J., & Jang, K.L. (2001). The heritability of attitudes: A study of twins. *Journal of Personality and Social Psychology, 80*(6), 845–860.

Ontario Hospital Association. (2009). *Cytomegalovirus surveillance protocol for Ontario hospitals* (#295). Toronto, ON: Author.

Organization of Teratology Information Specialists. (2005). *Acetaminophen and pregnancy*. Retrieved from www.otispregnancy.org/pdf/acetaminophen.pdf

Organization of Teratology Information Specialists. (2010). *Parental exposures and pregnancy*. Retrieved from www.otispregnancy.org/files/paternal.pdf

Paul, C., & Robaire, B. (2015). Ageing of the male germ line. *Nature Reviews. Urology, 10*(4), 227–234. doi:10.1038/nrurol.2013.18

Pembrey, M., Saffery, R., Bygren, L. O., & Network in Epigenetic Epidemiology. (2014). Human transgenerational responses to early-life experience: Potential impact on development, health and biomedical research. *Journal of Medical Genetics, 51*(9), 563–572. doi:10.1136/jmedgenet-2014-102577

Pembrey, M., Saffery, R., Bygren, L.O., & Network in Epigenetic Epidemiology. (2014). Human transgenerational responses to early-life experience: Potential impact on development, health and biomedical research. *Journal of Medical Genetics, 51*(9), 563–572. doi:10.1136/jmedgenet-2014-102577

Petronis, A. (2006). Epigenetics and twins: Three variations on the theme. *Trends in Genetics, 22*(7), 347–350.

Prasad, K.N., Cole, W.C., & Hasse, G.M. (2004). Health risks of low dose ionizing radiation in humans: A review. *Experimental Biology and Medicine, 229*(5), 378–382.

Public Health Agency of Canada. (2008). *Canadian perinatal health report* (2008 ed.) (HP10-12/2008E-PDF). Ottawa, ON: Ministry of Health. Retrieved from www.phac-aspc.gc.ca/publicat/2008/cphr-rspc/pdf/cphr-rspc08-eng.pdf

Public Health Agency of Canada. (2012a). *Perinatal health indicators for Canada 2011* (Catalogue No. HP7-1/2011). Retrieved from http://publications.gc.ca/collections/collection_2012/aspc-phac/HP7-1-2011-eng.pdf

Public Health Agency of Canada. (2012b). *Population-Specific HIV/AIDS Status Report: Women* (Catalogue No. HP40-43/2-2012E-PDF). Retrieved from http://library.catie.ca/pdf/ATI-20000s/26407.pdf

Raj, A., & Bertolone, S. (2010). *Sickle cell anemia*. Retrieved from http://emedicine.medscape.com/article/958614-overview

Ray, J.G., Vermeulen, M.J., Schull, M.J., Singh, G., Shah, R., & Redelmeier, D.A. (2007). Results of the recent immigrant pregnancy and perinatal long-term evaluation study (RIPPLES). *Canadian Medical Association Journal, 176*(10), 1419–1426.

Regidor, E., Ronda, E., Garcia, A.M., & Dominguez, V. (2004). Paternal exposure to agricultural pesticides and cause specific fetal death. *Occupational and Environmental Medicine, 61*, 334–339.

Righetti, P. (1996). The emotional experience of the fetus: A preliminary report. *Pre- & Peri-Natal Psychology Journal, 11*, 55–65.

Rivera, D., & Frye, R. (2010). *HIV infection*. Retrieved from http://emedicine.medscape.com/article/965086-overview

Roberts, M. (May 22, 2007). Canadian women offered chance to delay motherhood. *BioNews*. Retrieved from www.bionews.org.uk/new.lasso?storyid=3447

Rosenblith, J.F. (1992). *In the beginning* (2nd ed.). Thousand Oaks, CA: Sage.

Ross, M., & Mansano, R. (2010). *Fetal growth restriction*. Retrieved from http://emedicine.medscape.com/article/261226-overview

Rutter, M. (2007). Gene-environment interdependence. *Developmental Science, 10*(1), 12–18.

Sandman, C., Wadhwa, P., Hetrick, W., Porto, M., & Peeke, H. (1997). Human fetal heart rate dishabituation between thirty and thirty-two weeks. *Child Development, 68*, 1031–1040.

Sarkar, N.N. (2008). The impact of intimate partner violence on women's reproductive health and pregnancy outcome. *Journal of Obstetricians and Gynaecology, 28*(3), 266–271.

Sartorius, G.A., & Nieschlag, E. (2010). Paternal age and reproduction. *Human Reproduction Update, 16*(1), 65–79.

Schaal, B., Marlier, L., & Soussignan, R. (1998). Olfactory function in the human fetus: Evidence from selective neonatal responsiveness to the odor of amniotic fluid. *Behavioral Neuroscience, 112*, 1438–1449.

Schwartz, R.M., Anastasia, M.L., Scanlon, J.W., & Kellogg, R.J. (1994). Effect of surfactant on morbidity, mortality, and resource use in newborn infants weighing 500 to 1500 g. *New England Journal of Medicine, 330*, 1476–1480.

Sharma, R., Agarwal, A., Rohra, V.K., Assidi, M., Abu-Elmagd, M., & Turki, R.F. (2015). Effects of increased paternal age on sperm quality, reproductive outcome and associated epigenetic risks to offspring. *Reproductive Biology and Endocrinology, 13*(Apr), 35. doi:10.1186/s12958-015-0028-x

Society of Obstetricians and Gynaecologists of Canada. (2004). C-sections on demand—SOGC's position. *SOGC Advisory* (March 10, 2004). Retrieved from www.sogc/org/sogcnet/sogc%5Fdocs/press/releases2004/pdfs/electivecaesareanspart%20ii.pdf

Society of Obstetricians and Gynaecologists of Canada. (2011). *HIV testing in pregnancy*. Retrieved from http://www.sogc.org/health/pregnancy-hiv_e.asp

Springer, S. (2010). *The fetus as a patient, prenatal diagnosis and fetal therapy*. Retrieved from http://emedicine.medscape.com/article/947706-overview

Statistics Canada. (2012b). *Live births and fetal deaths (stillbirths), by place of birth (hospital and non-hospital), Canada, provinces and territories* (CANSIM Table 102-4516). Retrieved from http://www5.statcan.gc.ca/cansim/a05?lang=eng&id=1024516

Statistics Canada. (2012c). *Low birth weight (less than 2,500 grams) and borderline viable birth weight-adjusted low birth weight (500 to less than 2,500 grams), by sex, Canada, provinces and territories* (CANSIM Table 102-4005). Retrieved from http://www5.statcan.gc.ca/cansim/a05?lang=eng&id=1024005

Statistics Canada. (2015b). *Father's Day... by the numbers*. Retrieved from http://www.statcan.gc.ca/eng/dai/smr08/2015/smr08_201_2015

Statistics Canada. (2016a). *Canada at a glance 2016* (Catalogue No. 12-581-XIE). Retrieved from http://www.statcan.gc.ca/pub/12-581-x/12-581-x2016000-eng.pdf

Statistics Canada. (2016b). *Live births, weeks of gestation indicators, by characteristics of the mother and child, Canada* [Table 102-4513]. Retrieved from http://www5.statcan.gc.ca/cansim/pick-choisir?lang=eng&p2=33&id=1024513

Statistics Canada. (2016c). *Health Fact Sheets: Trends in Canadian births, 1992 to 2012*. Retrieved from http://www.statcan.gc.ca/pub/82-625-x/2016001/article/14314-eng.htm

Sultana, R., Chen, X.K., Lee, C., & Hader, J. (2011). Outcomes in multiple gestation pregnancies among Canadian women age 35 years and older. *Healthcare Quarterly, 14*(4), 22–24.

Susser, E., St. Clair, D., & He, L. (2008). Latent effects of prenatal malnutrition on adult health. *Annals of the New York Academy of Sciences, 1136*, 185–192. doi:10.1196/annals.1425.024

Szyf, M. (2009). The early life environment and the epigenome. *Biochimica et Biophysica Acta (BBA)—General Subjects, 1790*(9), 878–885.

Talge, N.M., Neal, C., & Glover, V. (2007). Antenatal maternal stress and long-term effects on child neurodevelopment: How and why? *Journal of Child Psychology and Psychiatry and Allied Disciplines*, 48(3–4), 245–261.

Tanner, J.M. (1990). *Foetus into man: Physical growth from conception to maturity* (2nd ed.). Cambridge, MA: Harvard University Press.

Tortora, G., & Grabowski, S. (1993). *Principles of anatomy and physiology*. New York, NY: HarperCollins.

Trasler, J.M., & Doerksen, T. (1999). Teratogen update: Paternal exposures-reproductive risks. *Teratology*, 60(3), 161–172.

Triggs-Raine, B., Richard, M., Wasel, N., Prence, E.M., & Natowicz, M.R. (1995). Mutational analyses of Tay-Sachs disease: Studies on Tay-Sachs carriers of French Canadian background living in New England. *American Journal of Human Genetics*, 56(4), 870–879.

Vaudry, W., Lee. B., Rosychuk, R., & Pelletier, L. (2009). Congenital cytomegalovirus infection. *Canadian Paediatric Surveillance Program (CPSP) 2008 Results*, 17–20.

Vézina, M., & Turcotte, M. (2009). *Forty-year-old mothers of pre-school children: A profile*. (11-008-XWE). Ottawa, ON: Statistics Canada. Retrieved from www.statcan.gc.ca/pub/11-008-x/2009002/article/10918-eng.htm

Vogin, J. (2005). Taking medication while pregnant. Retrieved from www.medicinenet.com/script/main/art.asp?articlekey=51639

Walmsley, S. (2003). Opt in or opt out: What is optimal for prenatal screening for HIV infection? *Canadian Medical Association Journal*, 168(6), 707–708.

Walusinski, O., Kurjak, A., Andonotopo, W., & Azumendi, G. (2005). Fetal yawning: A behavior's birth with 4D US revealed. *The Ultrasound Review of Obstetrics & Gynecology*, 5, 210–217.

Wang, L., & Xu, R. (2007). The effects of perinatal protein malnutrition on spatial learning and memory behaviour and brain-derived neurotrophic factor concentration in the brain tissue in young rats. *Asia Pacific Journal of Clinical Nutrition*, 16(S1), 467–472. Retrieved from http://apjcn.nhri.org.tw/server/APJCN/Volume16/vol-16suppl.1/LingWang%28467-472%29.pdf

Wedding, D., Kohout, J., Mengel, M.B., Ohlemiller, M., Ulione, M., Cook, K., . . . Braddock, S. (2007). Psychologists' knowledge and attitudes about fetal alcohol syndrome, fetal alcohol spectrum disorder, and alcohol use during pregnancy. *Professional Psychology: Research and Practice*, 38(2), 208–213.

Weindrich, D., Jennen-Steinmetz, C., Laucht, M., & Schmidt, M.H. (2003). Late sequelae of low birthweight: mediators of poor school performance at 11 years. *Developmental Medicine and Child Neurology*, 45(7), 463–469.

Xu, M., Sun, W., Liu, B., Feng, G., Yu, L., Yang, L., . . . He, L. (2009). Prenatal malnutrition and adult schizophrenia: Further evidence from the 1959–1961 Chinese famine. *Schizophrenia Bulletin*, 35(3), 568–576. doi:10.1093/schbul/sbn168

Yang, Q., Wen, S.W., Leader, A., Chen, X.K., Lipson, J., & Walker, M. (2007). Paternal age and birth defects: how strong is the association? *Human Reproduction*, 22(3), 696–701.

Yonkers, K., Wisner, K., Steart, D., Oberlander, T., Dell, D., Stotland, N.,... Lockwood, C. (2009). The management of depression during pregnancy: A report from the American psychiatric association and the American college of obstetricians and gynecologists. *Obstetrics & Gynecology*, 114(3), 703–713. doi:10.1097/AOG.0b013e3181ba0632

Zaiden, R.A. (2016). *Hemophilia A-Epidemiology*. Retrieved from http://emedicine.medscape.com/article/779322-overview#a5

Chapter 4

Adolph, E., & Berger, S. (2011). Physical and motor development. In M. Bornstein & M. Lamb (Eds.), *Developmental science: An advanced textbook* (6th ed., pp. 241–302). New York, NY: Psychology Press.

Adolph, K.E., & Tamis-LeMonda, C.S. (2014). The costs and benefits of development: The transition from crawling to walking. *Child Development Perspectives*, 8(4), 187–192. doi.org/10.1111/cdep.12085

Amit, M., & Canadian Paediatric Society (2009). Position statement: Vision screening in infants, children and youth. *Paediatrics & Child Health*, 14(4), 246–248.

Archer, J. (2004). Sex differences in aggression in real-world settings: A meta-analytic review. *Review of General Psychology*, 8(4), 291–322. doi:10.1037/1089-2680.8.4.291

Asbjornsen, A., Obrzut, J., Boliek, C., Myking, E., Holmefjord, A., Reisaeter, S., . . . & Moller, P. (2005). Impaired auditory attention skills following middle-ear infections. *Child Neuropsychology*, 11, 121–133.

Aslin, R. (1987). Motor aspects of visual development in infancy. In N. P. Salapatek & L. Cohen (Eds.), *Handbook of infant perception: Vol. 1. From sensation to perception* (pp. 43–113). Orlando, FL: Academic Press.

Azad, M.B., Konya, T., Maughan, H., Guttman, D.S., Field, C.J., Chari, R.S., . . . Kozyrskyj, A.L. (2013). Gut microbiota of healthy Canadian infants: Profiles by mode of delivery and infant diet at 4 months. *Canadian Medical Association Journal*, 185(5), 385–394. doi.org/10.1503/cmaj.121189

Bahrick, L., & Lickliter, R. (2000). Intersensory redundancy guides attentional selectivity and perceptual learning in infancy. *Developmental Psychology*, 36, 190–201.

Beaton, G.H., Martorell, R., L'Abbe, K.A., Edmonston, B., McCabe, G., . . . Harvey, B. (1993). Effectiveness of Vitamin A supplementation in the control of young child morbidity and mortality in developing countries. *Final report to the Canadian International Development Agency (CIDA)*. Toronto, ON: University of Toronto.

Behrman, R.E., & Butler, A.S. (Eds.). (2007a). *Mortality and acute complications in preterm infants*. Institute of Medicine (US) Committee on Understanding Premature Birth and Assuring Healthy Outcomes; Preterm Birth: Causes, Consequences, and Prevention. Washington (DC): National Academies Press (US). Retrieved from http://www.ncbi.nlm.nih.gov/books/NBK11385/

Bhimji, A. (2000). Infant male circumcision: A violation of the Canadian Charter of Rights and Freedoms. *Health Care Law (Toronto)*, (January 1), 1–33. Retrieved from http://www.cirp.org/library/legal/Canada/court1/

Bodnarchuk, J.L., Eaton, W.O., & Martens, P.J. (2006). Transitions in breastfeeding: Daily parent diaries provide evidence of behavior over time. *Journal of Human Lactation*, 22(2), 166–74. doi:10.1177/0890334406286992

Bornstein, M., Arterberry, M., & Mash, C. (2011). Perceptual development. In M. Bornstein & M. Lamb (Eds.), *Developmental science: An advanced textbook* (6th ed., 303–352). New York, NY: Psychology Press.

Bornstein, M.H. (1992). Perception across the life span. In M.H. Bornstein & M.E. Lamb (Eds.), *Developmental psychology: An advanced textbook* (3rd ed., pp. 155–210). Hillsdale, NJ: Erlbaum.

Brown, G., & Dixson, A. (2000). The development of behavioral sex differences in infant rhesus macaques. *Primates*, 41, 63–77.

Bruderer, A.G., Danielson, D K., Kandhadai, P., & Werker, J.F. (2015). Sensorimotor influences on speech perception in infancy. *Proceedings of the National Academy of Sciences of the United States of America*, 112(44), 13531–13536. doi.org/10.1073/pnas.1508631112

Cabrera-Rubio, R. Mira-Pascual, L. Mira A. & Collado M.C. (2016). Impact of mode of delivery on the milk microbiota composition of healthy women. *Journal of Developmental Origins of Health and Disease*, 7(1), 54–60. doi:10.1017/S2040174415001397

Campbell, D.W., & Eaton, W.O. (1999). Sex differences in the activity levels of infants. *Infant and Child Development*, 8(1), 1–17.

Canadian Children's Rights Council. (n.d.). *Circumcision of males/females*. Retrieved from http://canadiancrc.com/Circumcision_Genital_Mutilation_Male-Female_Children.aspx

Canadian International Development Agency. (2000). *Micronutrient malnutrition*. Author. Retrieved from www.acdi-cida.gc.ca/cida_ind.nsf/vLUallDocByIDEn/D1509FA7EF751EDF8525686C006D06B8?OpenDocument

Canadian Ophthalmological Society (n.d.). *When should you see an ophthalmologist?* Retrieved from http://www.cos-sco.ca/visionhealth-information/when-should-you-see-an-ophthalmologist/

Canadian Paediatric Society. (2009). *Recommendation for safe sleeping environments for infants and children*. Retrieved from www.cps.ca/english/statements/cp/cp04-02.htm

Canadian Paediatric Society. (2015). *Newborn male circumcision* [Position Statement]. Retrieved from http://www.cps.ca/documents/position/circumcision

Caron, A.J., & Caron, R.F. (1981). Processing of relational information as an index of infant risk. In S. Friedman & M. Sigman (Eds.), *Preterm birth and psychological development* (pp. 219–240). New York, NY: Academic Press.

Carpenter, R.G., Irgens, L.M., Blair, P.S., England, P.D., Fleming, P., Huber, J., . . . Schreuder, P. (2004). Sudden unexplained infant death in 20 regions in Europe: Case control study. *Lancet, 363*, 185–191.

Castanes, M.S. (2003). Major review: The underutilization of vision screening (for amblyopia, optical anomalies and strabismus) among preschool age children. *Binocular Vision & Strabismus Quarterly, 18*(4), 217–32.

Ceponiene, R., Kuchnerenko, E., Fellman, V., Renlund, M., Suominen, K., & Naeaetaenen, R. (2002). Event-related potential features indexing central auditory discrimination by newborns. *Cognitive Brain Research, 13*, 101–113.

Cole, M., & Packer, M. (2011). Culture and development. In M. Bornstein & M. Lamb (Eds.), *Developmental science: An advanced textbook* (6th ed., pp. 51–108). New York, NY: Psychology Press.

Cole, W.G., Robinson, S.R., & Adolph, K.E. (2016). Bouts of steps: The organization of infant exploration. *Developmental Psychobiology, 58*(3), 341–354. doi:10.1002/dev.21374

Collet, J.P., Burtin, P., Gillet, J., Bossard, N., Ducruet, T., & Durr, F. (1994). Risk of infectious diseases in children attending different types of day-care setting. Epicreche Research Group. *Respiration, 61*, 16–19.

Conference Board of Canada. (2016a). *Infant mortality*. Retrieved from http://www.conferenceboard.ca/hcp/details/health/infant-mortality-rate.aspx

Cooper, L.G., Gooding, J.S., Gallagher, J., Sternesky, L., Ledsky, R., & Berns, S.D. (2007). Impact of a family-centered care initiative on NICU care, staff and families. *Journal of Perinatology, 27*, s32–s37.

Cooper, P.A., Geldart, S.S., Mondloch, C.J., & Maurer, D. (2006). Developmental changes in perceptions of attractiveness: A role of experience? *Developmental Sciences, 9*(5), 530–543.

Dammeijer, P., Schlundt, B., Chenault, M., Manni, J., & Anteunis, L. (2002). Effects of early auditory deprivation and stimulation on auditory brainstem responses in the rat. *Acta Oto-Laryngologica, 122*, 703–708.

DeCasper, A., & Fifer, W. (1980). Of human bonding: Newborns prefer their mothers' voices. *Science, 208*, 1174–1176.

DeRegnier, R., Wewerka, S., Georgieff, M., Mattia, F., & Nelson, C. (2002). Influences of postconceptional age and postnatal experience on the development of auditory recognition memory in the newborn infant. *Developmental Psychobiology, 41*, 215–225.

Domínguez, P.R. (2011). The study of postnatal and later development of the taste and olfactory systems using the human brain mapping approach: An update. *Brain Research Bulletin, 84*(2), 118–124. doi:10.1016/j.brainresbull.2010.12.010

Ganchrow, J.R., Steiner, J.E., & Daher, M. (1983). Neonatal facial expressions in response to different qualities and intensities of gustatory stimuli. *Infant Behavior & Development, 6*(2–3), 189–200.

Eaton, W. (2003, Fall). *Infant milestones newsletter*. Winnipeg, MB: University of Manitoba Milestone Study. Retrieved from www.umanitoba.ca/outreach/milestones/fallnewsletter2003.shtml

Eaton, W. (2013). *Early words and milestones study*. Retrieved from http://www.milestoneshome.org/

Eaton, W. (2015). *Developmental milestones defined*. Retrieved from http://milestoneshome.org/whats-a-milestone/

Espy, K., Stalets, M., McDiarmid, M., Senn, T., Cwik, M., & Hamby, A. (2002). Executive functions in preschool children born preterm: Application of cognitive neuroscience paradigms. *Child Neuropsychology, 8*, 83–92.

Fantz, R.L. (1956). A method for studying early visual development. *Perceptual & Motor Skills, 6*, 13–15.

Gahagan, S. (2011). Behavioral disorders. In K. Marcdante, R. Kliegman, H. Jensen, & R. Behrman (Eds.), *Nelson's essentials of pediatrics* (6th ed., pp. 45–62). New York, NY: Elsevier Health Publishers.

Galland, B.C., Taylor, B.J., Elder, D.E., & Herbison, P. (2012). Normal sleep patterns in infants and children: A systematic review of observational studies. *Sleep Medicine Reviews, 16*(3), 213–222. doi:10.1016/j.smrv.2011.06.001

Geldart, S., Mondloch, C.J., Maurer, D., de Schonen, S., & Brent, H.P. (2002). The effect of early visual deprivation on the development of face processing. *Developmental Science, 5*(4), 490–501.

Gelfand, A.A. (2015). Infant colic. *Seminars in Pediatric Neurology, 23*(1), 79–82. doi:10.1016/j.spen.2015.08.003

Gelfand, A.A. (2016). Infant colic—a baby's migraine? *Cephalalgia, 35*(14), 1243–1245. doi:10.1177/0333102415576224

Gelfand, A.A., Goadsby, P.J., & Allen, I.E. (2015). The relationship between migraine and infant colic: A systematic review and meta-analysis. *Cephalalgia, 35*(1), 63–72. doi:10.1177/0333102414534326

Gerken, L., & Aslin, R. (2005) Thirty years of research on infant speech perception: The legacy of Peter W. Jusczyk. *Language Learning and Development, 1*(1), 5–21.

Gervain, J., Werker, J.F, Black, A., & Geffen, M.N. (2016). The neural correlates of processing scale-invariant environmental sounds at birth. *NeuroImage, 133*(June), 144–150. doi:10.1016/j.neuroimage.2016.03.001

Gionet, L. (2013). Breastfeeding trends in Canada (Cat. no. 82-624-X). *Health at a Glance*. Ottawa, ON: Statistics Canada.

Gouvernement du Québec. (2012). *Final report on the provincial outbreak of measles in 2011*. Retrieved from http://www.msss.gouv.qc.ca/en/sujets/prob_sante/measles/portrait2011.php

Government of Canada. (2016a). *Canada's provincial and territorial routine (and catch-up) vaccination programs for infants and children*. Retrieved from http://healthycanadians.gc.ca/healthy-living-vie-saine/immunization-immunisation/schedule-calendrier/infants-children-vaccination-enfants-nourrissons-eng.php

Harkness, S. (1998). Time for families. *Anthropology Newsletter, 39*, 1, 4.

Health Canada. (1999a). Positive mental health. In *Statistical report on the health of Canadians* (Cat. No. H39-467/1999E) (pp. 220–222). Ottawa, ON: Author. Retrieved from www.hc-sc.ca/hppb/phdd/report/stat/pdf/english/all_english/pdf

Health Canada. (2015b). *Nutrition for healthy term infants: recommendations from birth to six months—A joint statement of Health Canada, Canadian Paediatric Society, Dietitians of Canada, and Breastfeeding Committee for Canada*. Ottawa, ON: Minister of Public Works and Government Services. Retrieved from http://www.hc-sc.gc.ca/fn-an/nutrition/infant-nourisson/recom/index-eng.php

Henderson, J.M., France, K.G., & Blampied, N.M. (2011). The consolidation of infants' nocturnal sleep across the first year of life. *Sleep Medicine Reviews, 15*(4), 211–220. doi:10.1016/j.smrv.2010.08.003

Hubel, D.H., & Weisel, T.N. (1963). Receptive fields of cells in striate cortex of very young, visually inexperienced kittens. *Journal of Neurophysiology, 26*, 994–1002.

Humphreys, A., & Smith, P. (1987). Rough and tumble, friendship, and dominance in school children: Evidence for continuity and change with age. *Child Development, 58*, 201–212.

Hyde, J.S. (2005). The gender similarities hypothesis. *American Psychologist, 60*(6), 581–592. doi:10.1037/0003-066X.60.6.581

James, A. (2010). *Respiratory infections in infants: RSV*. Retrieved from http://www.aboutkidshealth.ca/En/News/NewsAndFeatures/Pages/Respiratory-infections-in-infants-RSV.aspx

Johnson, M. (2011). Developmental neuroscience, psychophysiology, and genetics. In M. Bornstein & M. Lamb (Eds.), *Developmental science: An advanced textbook* (6th ed., pp. 201–240). New York, NY: Psychology Press.

Johnson, M.H., & de Haan, M. (2015). *Developmental cognitive neuroscience: An introduction* (4th ed.). New York, NY: John Wiley & Sons.

Johnston, C., Campbell-Yeo, M., Fernandes, A., Inglis, D., Streiner, D., & Zee, R. (2014). Skin-to-skin care for procedural pain in neonates. *Cochrane Database of Systematic Reviews, 23*(1), CD008435. doi:10.1002/14651858.CD008435.pub2

Johnston, C.C., Filion, F., Campbell-Yeo, M., Goulet, C., Bell, L., McNaughton, K., . . .Walker, C.D. (2008). Kangaroo mother care diminishes pain from heel lance in very preterm neonates: A cross-over trial. *BMC Pediatrics, 8*(13), 1–9.

Karasik, L.B., Tamis-LeMonda, C.S., Adolph, K.E., & Bornstein, M.H. (2015). Places and postures: A cross-cultural comparison of sitting in 5-month-olds. *Journal of Cross-Cultural Psychology, 46*(8), 1023–1038. doi.org/10.1177/0022022115593803

Kercsmar, C. (1998). The respiratory system. In R. Behrman & R. Kliegman (Eds.), *Nelson essentials of pediatrics* (3rd ed.). Philadelphia, PA: W.B. Saunders.

Kliegman, R. (1998). Fetal and neonatal medicine. In R. Behrman & R. Kliegman (Eds.), *Nelson essentials of pediatrics* (3rd ed., pp. 167–225). Philadelphia, PA: W.B. Saunders.

Koleva, P.T., Bridgman, S.L., & Kozyrskyj, A.L. (2015). The infant gut microbiome: Evidence for obesity risk and dietary intervention. *Nutrients, 7*(4), 2237–2260. doi.org/10.3390/nu7042237

Koleva, P.T., Kim, J.S., Scott, J.A., & Kozyrskyj, A.L. (2015). Microbial programming of health and disease starts during fetal life. *Birth defects research. Part C, Embryo today 105*(4), 265–277. doi:10.1002/bdrc.21117

Kozyrskyj A.L. & Sloboda D.M. (2016). Perinatal programming of gut microbiota and immunity. *Journal of Developmental Origins of Health and Disease, 7*(Feb), 2–4. doi:10.1017/S2040174415007916

Kozyrskyj, A.L. (2015). Can we predict future allergies from our infant gut microbiota? *Expert Review of Respiratory Medicine, 9*(6), 667–670. doi:10.1586/17476348.2015.1098538

Krebs, N., & Primak, L. (2011). Pediatric nutrition and nutritional disorders. In K. Marcdante, R. Kliegman, H. Jensen, & R. Behrman (Eds.), *Nelson's essentials of pediatrics* (pp. 103–122). New York, NY: Elsevier Health Publishers.

Langlois, J.H., Kalakanis, L.E., Rubenstein, A.J., Larson, A.D., Hallam, M.J., & Smoot, M.T. (2000). Maxims and myths of beauty: A meta-analytic and theoretical review. *Psychological Bulletin, 126*, 390–423.

Langlois, J.H., Ritter, J.M., Roggman, L.A., & Vaughn, L.S. (1991). Facial diversity and infant preferences for attractive faces. *Developmental Psychology, 27*, 79–84.

Langlois, J.H., Roggman, L.A., & Rieser-Danner, L.A. (1990). Infants' differential social responses to attractive and unattractive faces. *Developmental Psychology, 26*, 153–159.

Langlois, J.H., Roggman, L.A., Casey, R.J., Ritter, J.M., Rieser-Danner, L.A., & Jenkins, V.Y. (1987). Infant preferences for attractive faces: Rudiments of a stereotype? *Developmental Psychology, 23*, 363–369.

Lau, A., Uba, A., & Lehman, D. (2002). Infectious diseases. In A. Rudolph, R. Kamei, & K. Overby (Eds.), *Rudolph's fundamental of pediatrics* (3rd ed., pp. 289–399. New York, NY: McGraw-Hill.

Le Grand, R., Mondloch, C.J., Maurer, D., & Brent, H.P. (2001). Early visual experiences and face processing. *Nature, 410*, 890.

Le Grand, R., Mondloch, C.J., Maurer, D., & Brent, H.P. (2004). Impairment in holistic face processing following early visual deprivation. *Psychological Science, 15*(11), 762–768.

Le Grand, R., Mondloch, C.J., Maurer, D., & Brent, H.P. (2003). Expert face processing requires visual input to the right hemisphere during infancy. *Nature Neuroscience, 6*(10), 1108–1112.

Levine, D. (2011). Growth and development. In K. Marcdante, R. Kliegman, H. Jensen, & R. Behrman (Eds.), *Nelson's essentials of pediatrics* (6th ed., pp. 13–44). New York, NY: Elsevier Health Publishers.

Lewis, T.L., & Maurer, D. (2005). Multiple sensitive periods in human visual development: Evidence from visually deprived children. *Developmental Psychobiology, 46*(3), 163–183.

Lippé, R., Perchet, C., & Lassonde, M. (2007). Electrophysical markers of visocortical development. *Cerebral Cortex, 17*(1), 100–107. doi:10.1093/cercor/bhj130

Lofti, M. (2001). *Experiences and issues in controlling micronutrient malnutrition.* Ottawa, ON: International Development Research Centre.

Luo, Z.C., Wilkins, R., Heaman, M., Martens, P., Smylie, J., Hart, L., . . . Fraser, W.D. (2010). Birth outcomes and infant mortality by the degree of rural isolation among First Nations and non-First Nations in Manitoba, Canada. *The Journal of Rural Health, 26*(2), 175–181. doi:10.1111/j.1748-0361.2010.00279.x

Maurer, D., Ellemberg, D., & Lewis, T.L. (2006). Repeated measurements of contrast sensitivity reveal limits to visual plasticity after early binocular deprivation in humans. *Neuropsychologia, 44*, 2104–2112.

Maurer, D., Mondloch, C.J., & Lewis, T.L. (2007). Sleeper effects. *Developmental Science, 10*(1), 40–47.

McIntosh, C.G., Tonkin, S.L., & Gunn, A.J. (2009). What is the mechanism of sudden infant deaths associated with co-sleeping? *New Zealand Medical Journal, 122*, 69–75.

McNally, E., Hendricks, S., & Horowitz, I. (1985). A look at breast-feeding trends in Canada (1963–1982). *Canadian Journal of Public Health, 76*, 101–107.

McShane, K., Smylie, J., & Adomako, P. (2009). Health of First Nations, Inuit, and Métis children in Canada. In J. Smylie & P. Adomako (Eds.), *Indigenous Children's Health Report: Health Assessment in Action.* Ottawa, ON: Health Canada.

Mondloch, C.J., Dobson, K.S., Parsons, J., & Maurer, D. (2004). Why 8-year-olds cannot tell the difference between Steve Martin and Paul Newman: Factors contributing to the slow development of sensitivity to the spacing of facial features. *Journal of Experimental Child Psychology, 89*, 159–181.

Mondloch, C.J., Geldart, S., Maurer, D., & Le Grand, R. (2003). Developmental changes in face processing skills. *Journal of Experimental Child Psychology, 86*, 67–84.

Mondloch, C.J., Le Grand, R., & Maurer, D. (2002). Configural face processing develops more slowly than featural face processing. *Perception, 31*, 553–566.

Mondloch, C.J., Leis, A., & Maurer, D. (2006). Recognizing the face of Johnny, Suzy, and me: Insensitivity to the spacing among features at 4 years of age. *Child Development, 77*(1), 234–243.

Mondloch, C.J., Maurer, D., & Ahola, S. (2006). Becoming a face expert. *Psychological Science, 17*(11), 930–934.

Mondloch, C.J., Segalowitz, S.J., Lewis, T.L., Dywan, J., Le Grand, R., & Maurer, D. (2013). The effect of early visual deprivation on the development of face detection. *Developmental Science, 16*(5), 728–742. doi:10.1111/desc.12065

Moore, E.R., Anderson G.C., Bergman, N., Dowswell, T. (2012). Early skin-to-skin contact for mother and their healthy newborn infants. *Cochrane Database of Systematic Reviews, 16*(5), CD003519. doi:10.1002/14651858.CD003519.pub3

Morrongiello, B.A., Fenwick, K.D., & Chance, G. (1990). Sound localization acuity in very young infants: An observer-based testing procedure. *Developmental Psychology, 24*, 75–84.

Nicklaus, S., Boggio, V., & Issanchou, S. (2005). Gustatory perceptions in children. *Archives of Pediatrics, 12*(5), 579–584.

O'Connor, D., Khan, S., Vaughan, J., Jefferies, A., Asztalos, E., Rovet, J., & Whyte, H. (2008). Growth and nutrient intakes of human milk-fed preterm infants provided with extra energy and nutrients after hospital discharge. *Pediatrics, 121*(4), 766–776. doi:10.1542/peds.2007-0054

Pascalis, O., de Schonen, S., Morton, J., Derulle, C., & Fabre-Grenet, M. (1995). Mother's face recognition by neonates: A replication and extension. *Infant Behavior and Development, 18*, 79–85.

Pereverzeva, M., Hui-Lin Chien, S., Palmer, J., & Teller, D. (2002). Infant photometry: Are mean adult isoluminance values a sufficient approximation to individual infant values? *Vision Research, 42*, 1639–1649.

Persaud, R.R., Azad, M.B., Chari, R.S., Sears, M.R., Becker, A.B., & Kozyrskyj, A.L. (2015). Perinatal antibiotic exposure of neonates in Canada and associated risk factors: A population-based study. *Journal of Maternal–Fetal & Neonatal Medicine, 28*(10), 1190–1195. doi:10.3109/14767058.2014.947578

Polka, L., & Werker, J.F. (1994). Developmental changes in perception of nonnative vowel contrasts. *Journal of Experimental Psychology: Human Perception and Performance, 20*, 421–435.

Public Health Agency of Canada (2009a). *Breastfeeding and infant nutrition.* Ottawa, ON: Ministry of Health. Retrieved from www.phac-aspc.gc.ca/dca-dea/prenatal/nutrition-eng.php

Public Health Agency of Canada. (2008). *Canadian perinatal health report* (2008 ed.) (HP10-12/2008E-PDF). Ottawa, ON: Ministry of Health. Retrieved from www.phac-aspc.gc.ca/publicat/2008/cphr-rspc/pdf/cphr-rspc08-eng.pdf

Public Health Agency of Canada. (2013a). *Highlights of 2011–2012 selected indicators describing the birthing process in Canada*. Retrieved from https://secure.cihi.ca/free_products/Childbirth_Highlights_2010-11_EN.pdf

Public Health Agency of Canada. (2015a). *Canadian immunization guide*. Retrieved from http://www.phac-aspc.gc.ca/publicat/cig-gci/index-eng.php

Qubty, W., & Gelfand, A.A. (2016). The link between infantile colic and migraine. *Current Pain and Headache Reports, 20*(5), 31. doi:10.1007/s11916-016-0558-8

Quinn, P., Kelly, D., Lee, K., Pascalis, O., & Slater, A. (2009). Preference for attractive faces in human infants extends beyond conspecifics. *Developmental Science, 11*(1), 76–83. doi:10.1111/j.1467-7687.2007.00647.x

Reisman, J.E. (1987). Touch, motion, and proprioception. In P. Salapatek & L. Cohen (Eds.), *Handbook of infant perception: Vol. 1. From sensation to perception* (pp. 265–304). Orlando, FL: Academic Press.

Rhodes, G. (2006). The evolutionary psychology of facial beauty. *Annual Review of Psychology, 57*, 199–226.

Rhodes, G., Lee, K., Palermo, R., Weiss, M., Yoshikawa, S., Clissa, P., ... Jeffery, L. (2005). Attractiveness of own-race, other-race and mixed-race faces. *Perception, 34*, 319–340.

Rhodes, G., Nishimura, M., de Heering, A., Jeffery, L., & Maurer, D. (2016). Reduced adaptability, but no fundamental disruption, of norm-based face coding following early visual deprivation from congenital cataracts. *Developmental Science, 29*(Jan). doi:10.1111/desc.12384 [Epub ahead of print]

Rhodes, G., Yoshikawa, S., Palermo, R., Simmons, L.W., Peters, M., Les, K., ... Crawford, J.R. (2007). Perceived health contributions to the attractiveness of facial symmetry, averageness and sexual dimorphism. *Perception, 36*, 1244–1252.

Romanello, S., Spiri, D., Marcuzzi, E., Zanin, A., Boizeau, P., Riviere, S., ... Titomanlio, L. (2013). Association between childhood migraine and history of infantile colic. *Journal of the American Medical Association, 309*(15), 1607–1612. doi:10.1001/jama.2013.747

Rose, S.A., & Ruff, H.A. (1987). Cross-modal abilities in human infants. In J.D. Osofsky (Ed.), *Handbook of infant development* (2nd ed., pp. 318–362). New York, NY: Wiley-Interscience.

Schwartz, C., Chabanet, C., Laval, C., Issanchou, S., & Nicklaus, S. (2012). Breast-feeding duration: Influence on taste acceptance over the first year of life. *The British Journal of Nutrition, 4*, 1–8. Advanced online publication. doi: http://dx.doi.org/10.1017/S0007114512002668

Sillanpää, M., & Saarinen, M. (2015). Infantile colic associated with childhood migraine: A prospective cohort study. *Cephalalgia: An International Journal of Headache, 35*(14), 1246–1251. doi:10.1177/0333102415576225

Sola, A., Rogido, M., & Partridge, J. (2002). The perinatal period. In A. Rudolph, R. Kamei, & K. Overby (Eds.), *Rudolph's fundamental of pediatrics* (3rd ed., pp. 125–183). New York, NY: McGraw-Hill.

Sorokan, S.T., Finlay, J.C., Jefferies, A.L., & Canadian Paediatric Society, Fetus and Newborn Committee, Infectious Diseases and Immunization Committee. (2015). Newborn male circumcision. *Paediatrics & Child Health, 20*(6), 311–315.

Steiner, J.E. (1979). Human facial expressions in response to taste and smell stimulation. In H. W. Reese & L. P. Lipsitt (Eds.), *Advances in child development and behavior: Vol. 13* (pp. 257–296). New York, NY: Academic Press.

Sulkes, S. (1998). Developmental and behavioral pediatrics. In R. Behrman & R. Kliegman (Eds.), *Nelson essentials of pediatrics* (3rd ed., pp. 1–55). Philadelphia, PA: W.B. Saunders.

Suman, R. P.N., Udani, R., & Nanavati, R. (2008). Kangaroo mother care for low birth weight infants: A randomized controlled trial. *Indian Pediatrics, 45*, 17–23.

Tanner, J.M. (1990). *Foetus into man: Physical growth from conception to maturity* (2nd ed.). Cambridge, MA: Harvard University Press.

Tau, G.Z., & Peterson, B.S. (2010). Normal development of brain circuits. *Neuropsychopharmacology, 35*(1), 147–168. doi.org/10.1038/npp.2009.115

Tessier, R., Charpak, N., Giron, M., Cristo, M., de Calume, Z.F., & Ruiz-Palaez, J.G. (2009). Kangaroo mother care, home environment and father involvement in the first year of life: a randomized controlled study. *Acta Paediatrica, 98*, 1444–1450.

Thelen, E. (1995). Motor development: A new synthesis. *American Psychologist, 50*, 79–95.

Trehub, S.E., & Rabinovitch, M.S. (1972). Auditory-linguistic sensitivity in early infancy. *Developmental Psychology, 6*, 74–77.

Trehub, S.E., Bull, D., & Thorpe, L.A. (1984). Infants' perception of melodies: The role of melodic contour. *Child Development, 55*, 821–830.

Trehub, S.E., Plantinga, J., & Brcic, J. (2009). Infants detect cross-modal cues to identity in speech and singing. *Annals of the New York Academy of Sciences, 1169*, 508–511.

Trehub, S.E., Thorpe, L.A., & Morrongiello, B.A. (1985). Infants' perception of melodies: Changes in a single tone. *Infant Behavior & Development, 8*, 213–223.

Trifunov, W. (2009). *The practice of bed sharing: A systematic literature and policy review*. Ottawa, ON: Public Health Agency of Canada. Retrieved from www.phac-aspc.gc.ca/dca-dea/prenatal/pbs-ppl-eng.php

Trovato, F. (1991). Early childhood mortality 1926–1986. *Canadian Social Trends (Summer)*, 6–10. Ottawa, ON: Statistics Canada.

Uylings, H. (2006). Development of the human cortex and the concept of "critical" or "sensitive" periods. *Language Learning, 56*, 59–90.

Wagner, C. (2009). *Counseling the breastfeeding mother*. Retrieved from http://emedicine.medscape.com/article/979458-overview

Walker, S., & Harris, Z. (2012). Detecting the serious visual disorders of childhood. *Paediatrics and Child Health, 22*(1), 25–30. doi:10.1016/j.paed.2011.04.009

Wallace, J.G., Gohir, W., & Sloboda, D.M. (2016). The impact of early life gut colonization on metabolic and obesogenic outcomes: What have animal models shown us? *Journal of Developmental Origins of Health and Disease, 7*(1), 15–24. doi:10.1017/S2040174415001518

Waseem, M., & Aslam, M. (2010). *Otitis media*. Retrieved from http://emedicine.medscape.com/article/994656-overview

Weissbluth, M., & Weissbluth, L. (1992a). Colic, sleep inertia, melatonin and circannual rhythms. *Medical Hypotheses, 38*(3), 224–228.

Weissbluth, M., & Weissbluth, L. (1992b). Infant colic: The effect of serotonin and melatonin circadian rhythms on the intestinal smooth muscle. *Medical Hypotheses, 39*(2), 164–167.

Werner, L.A., & Gillenwater, J.M. (1990). Pure-tone sensitivity of 2- to 5-week-old infants. *Infant Behavior & Development, 13*, 355–375.

White-Traut, R., Nelson, M., Silvestri, J., Vasan, U., Littau, S., Meleedy-Rey, P., ... Patel, M. (2002). Effect of auditory, tactile, visual, and vestibular intervention on length of stay, alertness, and feeding progression in preterm infants. *Developmental Medicine & Child Neurology, 44*, 91–97.

White-Traut, R., Norr, K.F., Fabiyi, C., Rankin, K.M., Li, Z., & Liu, L. (2013). Mother–infant interaction improves with a developmental intervention for mother–preterm infant dyads. *Infant Behavior & Development, 36*(4), 1–15. doi:10.1016/j.infbeh.2013.07.004

Wilkins, R., Houle, C., Berthelot, J., & Ross, N. (2000). The changing health status of Canada's children. *Isuma, 1*(2), 57–63.

Woldemicael, G. (2009, October). *Breastfeeding practices of immigrant mothers in Canada: The role of immigration status, length of residence, and ethnic minority*. Presented at the Health over the Life Course Conference, London, ON.

Wright, C., & Birks, E. (2000). Risk factors for failure to thrive: A population-based survey. *Child: Care, Health & Development, 26*, 5–16.

Yonas, A., & Owsley, C. (1987). Development of visual space perception. In P. Salpatek & L. Cohen (Eds.), *Handbook of infant perception: Vol. 2. From perception to cognition* (pp. 80–122). Orlando, FL: Academic Press.

Yonas, A., Elieff, C., & Atterberry, M. (2002). Emergence of sensitivity to pictorial depth cues: Charting development in individual infants. *Infant Behavior & Development, 25*, 495–514.

Zelazo, N.A., Zelazo, P.R., Cohen, K.M., & Zelazo, P.D. (1993). Specificity of practice effects on elementary neuromotor patterns. *Developmental Psychology, 29*, 686–691.

Zelazo, P.R., Zelazo, N.A., & Kolb, S. (1972). "Walking" in the newborn. *Science, 176*, 314–315.

Chapter 5

Aksu-Koc, A.A., & Slobin, D.I. (1985). The acquisition of Turkish. In D.I. Slobin (Ed.), *The crosslinguistic study of language acquisition: Vol. 1: The data* (pp. 839–878). Hillsdale, NJ: Erlbaum.

Anderson, R.T. (1997). Examining language loss in bilingual children. *Perspectives on Communication Disorders and Sciences in Culturally and Linguistically Diverse Populations, 3*(1), 2–5. doi:10.1044/cds3.1.2

Anisfeld, M. (2005). No compelling evidence to dispute Piaget's timetable of the development of representational imitation in infancy. In S. Hurley & N. Chater (Eds.), *Perspectives on imitation: From neuroscience to social science: Volume 2: Imitation, human development, and culture* (pp. 107–131). Cambridge, MA: MIT Press.

Archibald, L., & Joanisse, M. (2013). Domain-specific and domain-general constraints on word and sequence learning. *Memory & Cognition, 41*(2), 268–280. doi:10.3758/s13421-012-0259-4

Baillargeon, R. (2004). Infants' reasoning about hidden objects: Evidence for event-general and event-specific expectations. *Developmental Science, 7*, 391–424.

Barr, R., Marrott, H., & Rovee-Collier, C. (2003). The role of sensory preconditioning in memory retrieval by preverbal infants. *Learning & Behavior, 31*, 111–123.

Bates, E., O'Connell, B., & Shore, C. (1987). Language and communication in infancy. In J.D. Osofsky (Ed.), *Handbook of infant development* (2nd ed., pp. 149– 03). New York, NY: Wiley.

Bauer, P., Schwade, J., Wewerka, S., & Delaney, K. (1999). Planning ahead: Goal-directed problem solving by 2-year-olds. *Developmental Psychology, 35*, 1321–1337.

Bayley, N. (1969). *Bayley scales of infant development*. New York, NY: Psychological Corporation.

Bayley, N. (1993). *Bayley scales of infant development: Birth to two years*. New York, NY: Psychological Corporation.

Bayley, N. (2006). *Bayley scales of infant and toddler development* (3rd ed). San Antonio, TX: Harcourt Assessment, Inc.

Bearce, K., & Rovee-Collier, C. (2006). Repeated priming increases memory accessibility in infants. *Journal of Experimental Child Psychology, 93*(4), 357–376.

Bialystok, E. (1997). Effects of bilingualism and biliteracy on children's emerging concepts of print. *Developmental Psychology, 33*(3), 429–440.

Bialystok, E. (2007). Acquisition of literacy in bilingual children: A framework for research. *Language Learning, 57*, 45–77. doi:10.1111/j.1467-9922.2007.00412.x

Bialystok, E., & Majumder, S. (1998). The relationship between bilingualism and the development of cognitive processes in problem solving. *Applied Psycholinguistics, 19*, 69–85.

Bialystok, E., Craik, F.I., & Luk, G. (2012). Bilingualism: Consequences for mind and brain. *Trends in Cognitive Sciences, 16*(4), 240–250. doi:10.1016/j.tics.2012.03.001

Bialystok, E., Shenfield, T., & Codd, J. (2000). Languages, scripts, and the environment: Factors in developing concepts of print. *Developmental Psychology, 36*, 66–76.

Birney, D., & Sternberg, R. (2011). The development of cognitive abilities. In M. Bornstein & M. Lamb (Eds.), *Developmental science: An advanced textbook* (6th ed., pp. 353–388). New York, NY: Psychology Press.

Bloom, L. (1973). *One word at a time*. The Hague: Mouton.

Bode, M.M., D'Eugenio, D.B., Mettelman, B.B., & Gross, S.J. (2014). Predictive validity of the Bayley, Third Edition at 2 years for intelligence quotient at 4 years in preterm infants. *Journal of Developmental and Behavioral Pediatrics, 35*(9), 570–575. doi:10.1097/DBP.0000000000000110

Bremner, J. (2002). The nature of imitation by infants. *Infant Behavior & Development, 25*, 65–67.

Brown, R., & Bellugi, U. (1964). Three processes in the acquisition of syntax. *Harvard Educational Review, 334*, 133–151.

Burns, T.C., Yoshida, K.A., Hill, K., & Werker, J.F. (2007). The development of phonetic representation in bilingual and monolingual infants. *Applied Psycholinguistics, 28*(3), 455–474.

Campanella, J.L., & Rovee-Collier, C. (2005). Latent learning and deferred imitation at 3 months. *Infancy, 7*, 243–262.

Canadian Paediatric Society. (2012a). Healthy active living: Physical activity guidelines for children and adolescents. Retrieved from http://www.cps.ca/documents/position/physical-activity-guidelines

Carey, S., & Xu, F. (2001). Infants' knowledge of objects: Beyond object files and object tracking. *Cognition, 80*(1–2), 179–213.

Casasola, M., & Cohen, L. (2000). Infants' association of linguistic labels with causal actions. *Developmental Psychology, 36*, 155–168.

Certain, L.K., & Kahn, R.S. (2002). Prevalence, correlates and trajectory of television viewing among infants and toddlers. *Pediatrics, 109*(4), 634–642.

Cevasco, A., & Grant, R. (2005). Effects of the Pacifier Activity Lullaby (PAL) on weight gain in premature infants. *Journal of Music Therapy, 42*, 123–139.

Cheour, M., Martynova, O., Naeaetaenen, R., Erkkola, R., Sillanpaeae, M., Kero, P., . . . Haemaelaeinen, H. (2002). Speech sounds learned by sleeping newborns. *Nature, 415*, 599–600.

Chincotta, D., & Underwood, G. (1997). Estimates, language of schooling and bilingual digit span. *European Journal of Cognitive Psychology, 9*, 325–348.

Choi, A.L., Sun, G., Zhang, Y., & Grandjean, P. (2012). Developmental fluoride neurotoxicity: A systematic review and meta-analysis. *Environmental Health Perspectives, 120*(10), 1362–1368. doi:10.1289/ehp.1104912

Christakis, D.A. (2009). The effects of infant media usage: What do we know and what should we learn? *Acta Paediatrica, 98*, 8–16.

Collisson, B.A., Graham, S.A., Preston, J.L., Rose, M.S., McDonald, S., & Tough, S. (2016). Risk and protective factors for late talking: An epidemiologic investigation. *Journal of Pediatrics, 172*(May), 168–174. e1. doi:10.1016/j.jpeds.2016.02.020

Cooper, R.P., & Aslin, R.N. (1994). Developmental differences in infant attention to the spectral properties of infant-directed speech. *Child Development, 65*, 1663–1677.

Courage, M., & Howe, M. (2002). From infant to child: The dynamics of cognitive change in the second year of life. *Psychological Bulletin, 128*, 250–277.

Craik, F.I., Bialystok, E., & Freedman, M. (2010). Delaying the onset of Alzheimer disease: Bilingualism as a form of cognitive reserve. *Neurology, 75*(19), 1726–1729. doi:10.1212/WNL.0b013e3181fc2a1c

Cristia, A. (2013). Input to language: The phonetics and perception of infant-directed speech. *Language and Linguistics Compass, 7*(3), 157–170. doi:10.1111/lnc3.12015

Cuevas, K., Rovee-Collier, C., & Learmonth, A. E. (2006). Infants form associations between memory representations of stimuli that are absent. *Psychological Science, 17*, 543–549.

Dezoete, J., MacArthur, B., & Tuck, B. (2003). Prediction of Bayley and Stanford-Binet scores with a group of very low birthweight children. *Child: Care, Health, & Development, 29*, 367–372.

Diesendruck, G., & Shatz, M. (2001). Two-year-olds' recognition of hierarchies: Evidence from their interpretation of the semantic relation between object labels. *Cognitive Development, 16*, 577–594.

Ellis, E., & Thal, D. (2008). Early language delay and risk for language impairment. *Perspectives on Language Learning and Education, 15*, 93–100.

Elsner, B., Jeschonek, S., & Pauen, S. (2013). Event-related potentials for 7-month-olds' processing of animals and furniture items. *Developmental Cognitive Neuroscience, 3*(Jan), 53–60. doi:10.1016/j.dcn.2012.09.002

Fagan, J. (2000). A theory of intelligence as processing: Implications for society. *Psychology, Public Policy, & Law, 6*, 168–179.

Fagan, J.F., & Detterman, D.K. (1992). The Fagan Test of Infant Intelligence: A technical summary. *Journal of Applied Developmental Psychology, 13*, 173–193.

Farrar, M.J. (1992). Negative evidence and grammatical morpheme acquisition. *Developmental Psychology, 28*, 90–98.

Fenson, L., Dale, P.S., Reznick, J.S., Bates, E., Thal, D.J., & Pethick, S.J. (1994). Variability in early communicative development. *Monographs of the Society for Research in Child Development, 59*(5, Serial No. 242).

Fluoride Action Network. (2016). *Fluoride & IQ: The 49 studies.* Retrieved from http://fluoridealert.org/studies/brain01/

Gardner, J., Karmel, B., Freedland, R., Lennon, E., Flory, M., Miroschnichenko, I., . . . Harm, A. (2006). Arousal, attention, and neurobehavioral assessment in the neonatal period: Implications for intervention and policy. *Journal of Policy and Practice in Intellectual Disabilities, 3*, 22–32.

Gaultney, J., & Gingras, J. (2005). Fetal rate of behavioral inhibition and preference for novelty during infancy. *Early Human Development, 81*, 379–386.

Gervain J. (2015). Plasticity in early language acquisition: The effects of prenatal and early childhood experience. *Current Opinion in Neurobiology, 35*(Dec), 13–20. doi:10.1016/j.conb.2015.05.004

Gleitman, L.R., & Gleitman, H. (1992). A picture is worth a thousand words, but that's the problem: The role of syntax in vocabulary acquisition. *Current Directions in Psychological Science, 1*, 31–35.

Goertz, C., Lamm, B., Graf, F., Kolling, T., Knopf, M., & Keller, H. (2011). Deferred imitation in 6-month-old German and Cameroonian Nso infants. *Journal of Cognitive Education and Psychology, 10*(1), 44–55. doi.org/10.1891/1945-8959.10.1.44

Grandjean, P., Barouki, R., Bellinger, D.C., Casteleyn, L., Chadwick, L.H., Cordier, S., . . . Heindel, J.J. (2015). Life-long implications of developmental exposure to environmental stressors: New perspectives. *Endocrinology, 156*(10), 3408–3415. doi:10.1210/EN.2015-1350

Gunther, M. (1955). Instinct and the nursing couple. *Lancet, 265*(6864), 575–578.

Gunther, M. (1961). Infant behavior at the breast. In B. Foss (Ed.), *Determinants of infant behavior* (pp. 37–44). London: Methuen.

Gupta, N., Gupta, N., & Chhabra, P. (2016). Image diagnosis: Dental and skeletal fluorosis. *The Permanente Journal, 20*(1), e105–e106. doi:10.7812/TPP/15-048

Hakansson, G., Salameh, E., & Nettelbladt, U. (2003). Measuring language development in bilingual children: Swedish-Arabic children with and without language impairment. *Linguistics, 41*, 255–288.

Hanna, E., & Meltzoff, A.N. (1993). Peer imitation by toddlers in laboratory, home, and day-care contexts: Implications for social learning and memory. *Developmental Psychology, 29*, 701–710.

Hauf, P., Aschersleben, G. & Prinz, W. (2007). Baby do—baby see! How action production influences action perception in infants. *Cognitive Development, 22*, 16–32.

Health Canada. (2015c). *Fluoride and human health.* Retrieved from http://www.hc-sc.gc.ca/hl-vs/iyh-vsv/environ/fluor-eng.php

Herbert, J., Gross, J., & Hayne, H. (2006). Age-related changes in deferred imitation between 6 and 9 months of age. *Infant Behavior & Development, 29*, 136–139.

Hespos, S., & Baillargeon, R. (2008). Young infants' actions reveal their developing knowledge of support variables: Converging evidence for violation-of-expectation findings. *Cognition, 107*, 304–316.

Holowka, S., & Petitto, L.A. (2002). Left hemisphere cerebral specialization for babies while babbling. *Science, 297*(5586), 1515.

Johnson, S., Moore, T., & Marlow, N. (2014). Using the Bayley-III to assess neurodevelopmental delay: Which cut-off should be used? *Pediatric Research, 75*(5), 670–674. doi:10.1038/pr.2014.10

Josephson, W.L. (1995). *Television violence: A review of the effects on children of different ages.* (CH4-1/8-1995E). Retrieved from The Department of Canadian Heritage website: http://dsp-psd.communication.gc.ca/Collection/CH4-1-8-1995E.pdf

Júlvez, J, & Grandjean, P. (2009). Neurodevelopmental toxicity risks due to occupational exposure to industrial chemicals during pregnancy. *Industrial Health, 47*(5), 459–468. doi:10.2486/indhealth.47.459

Júlvez, J., Paus, T., Bellinger, D., Eskenazi, B., Tiemeier, H., Pearce, N., . . . Sunyer, J. (2016). Environment and brain development: Challenges in the global context. *Neuroepidemiology, 46*(2), 79–82. doi:10.1159/000442256

Kavšek, M., & Bornstein, M.H. (2010). Visual habituation and dishabituation in preterm infants: A review and meta-analysis. *Research in Developmental Disabilities, 31*(5), 951–975. doi:10.1016/j.ridd.2010.04.016

Kavšek, M., (2004). Predicting later IQ from infant visual habituation and dishabituation: A meta-analysis. *Journal of Applied Developmental Psychology, 25*, 369–393.

Lapierre, M., Piotrowski, J., & Linebarger, D. (2012). Background television in the homes of U. S. children. *Pediatrics, 130*(5), 2011–2581. doi:10.1542/peds.2011-2581

Lefebvre, F., Gagnon, M.M., Luu, T.M., Lupien, G., & Dorval, V. (2016). In extremely preterm infants, do the Movement Assessment of Infants and the Alberta Infant Motor Scale predict 18-month outcomes using the Bayley-III? Early *Human Development, 94*(Mar), 13–17. doi:10.1016/j.earlhumdev.2016.01.012

Levine, D. (2011). Growth and development. In K. Marcdante, R. Kliegman, H. Jensen, & R. Behrman (Eds.), *Nelson's essentials of pediatrics* (6th ed., pp. 13–44). New York, NY: Elsevier Health Publishers.

MacWhinney, B. (2011). Language development. In M. Bornstein & M. Lamb (Eds.), *Developmental science: An advanced textbook* (6th ed., pp. 389–424). New York, NY: Psychology Press.

Maitel, S., Dromi, E., Sagi, A., & Bornstein, M. (2000). The Hebrew Communicative Development Inventory: Language-specific properties and cross-linguistic generalizations. *Journal of Child Language, 27*, 43–67.

Malabonga, V., & Pasnak, R. (2002). Hierarchical categorization by bilingual Latino children: Does a basic-level bias exist? *Genetic, Social, & General Psychology Monographs, 128*, 409–441.

Maratsos, M. (1998). The acquisition of grammar. In W. Damon (Ed.), *Handbook of child psychology: Vol. 2, Cognition, perception, and language* (5th ed., pp. 421–466). New York, NY: Wiley.

Mares, M.L., & Woodard, E. (2005). Positive effects of television on children's social interactions: A meta-analysis. *Media Psychology, 7*(3), 301–322.

Mares, M.L., & Woodard, E.H. (2001). Prosocial effects on children's social interactions. In: D.G. Singer & J.D. Singer (Eds.), *Handbook of Children and the Media* (pp. 183–205). Thousand Oaks, CA: Sage Publications.

Meltzoff, A.N., & Moore, M.K. (1977). Imitation of facial and manual gestures by human neonates. *Science, 198*, 75–78.

Mitchell, P.R., & Kent, R.D. (1990). Phonetic variation in multisyllable babbling. *Journal of Child Language, 17*, 247–265.

Morales, J., Calvo, A., & Bialystok, E. (2013). Working memory development in monolingual and bilingual children. *Journal of Experimental Child Psychology, 114*(2), 187–202. doi:10.1016/j.jecp.2012.09.002

Morales, J., Calvo, A., & Bialystok, E. (2013). Working memory development in monolingual and bilingual children. *Journal of Experimental Child Psychology, 114*(2), 187–202. doi:10.1016/j.jecp.2012.09.002

Nelson, K. (1977). Facilitating children's syntax acquisition. *Developmental Psychology, 13*, 101–107.

Nicoladis, E., & Genesee, F. (1996). A longitudinal study of pragmatic differentiation in young bilingual children. *Language Learning, 46*, 439–464.

Nicoladis, E., & Genesee, F. (1997). Language development in preschool bilingual children. *Journal of Speech-Language Pathology and Audiology, 21*(4), 258–270.

Oller, D.K. (1981). Infant vocalizations: Exploration and reflectivity. In R.E. Stark (Ed.), *Language behavior in infancy and early childhood* (pp. 85–104). New York, NY: Elsevier North-Holland.

Omiya, A., & Uchida, N. (2002). The development of children's thinking strategies: The retrieval of alternatives based on the categorization with conditional reasoning tasks. *Japanese Journal of Psychology*, 73, 10–17.

Oulhote, Y., & Grandjean, P. (2016). Association between child poverty and academic achievement. *JAMA Pediatrics*, 170(2), 179–180. doi:10.1001/jamapediatrics.2015.3856

Parekh, S.A., Boyle, E.M., Guy, A., Blaggan, S., Manktelow, B.N., Wolke, D., & Johnson, S. (2016). Correcting for prematurity affects developmental test scores in infants born late and moderately preterm. *Early Human Development*, 94(Mar), 1–6. doi:10.1016/j.earlhumdev.2016.01.002

Patel, S., Gaylord, S., & Fagen, J. (2013). Generalization of deferred imitation in 6-, 9-, and 12-month-old infants using visual and auditory contexts. *Infant Behavior & Development*, 36(1), 25–31. doi:10.1016/j.infbeh.2012.09.006

Pauen, S. (2002). The global-to-basic level shift in infants' categorical thinking: First evidence from a longitudinal study. *International Journal of Behavioral Development*, 26(6), 492–499.

Pegg, J.E., Werker, J.F., & McLeod, P.J. (1992). Preference for infant-directed over adult-directed speech: Evidence from 7-week-old infants. *Infant Behavior & Development*, 15, 325–345.

Petitto, L.A., & Holowka, S. (2002). Evaluating attributions of delay and confusion in young bilinguals: Special insights from infants acquiring a signed and spoken language. *Sign Language Studies*, 3(1), 4–34.

Picciolini, O., Squarza, C., Fontana, C., Giannì, M. L., Cortinovis, I., Gangi, S., . . . Mosca, F. (2015). Neurodevelopmental outcome of extremely low birth weight infants at 24 months corrected age: A comparison between Griffiths and Bayley Scales. *BMC Pediatrics*, 15(Sep), 139. doi:10.1186/s12887-015-0457-x

Poulson, C.L., Nunes, L.R.D., & Warren, S.F. (1989). Imitation in infancy: A critical review. In H.W. Reese (Ed.), *Advances in child development and behavior: Vol. 22* (pp. 272–298). San Diego, CA: Academic Press.

Protzko, J. (2015). The environment in raising early intelligence: A meta-analysis of the fadeout effect. *Intelligence*, 53(Dec), 202–210. doi:10.1016/j.intell.2015.10.006

Protzko, J. (2016). Does the raising IQ/raising g distinction explain the fadeout effect? *Intelligence*, 56(May–June), 65–71. doi:10.1016/j.intell.2016.02.008

Protzko, J., Aronson, J., & Blair, C. (2013). How to make a young child smarter: Evidence from the database of raising intelligence. *Perspectives on Psychological Science*, 8(1), 25–40. doi:10.1177/1745691612462585

Provasi, J., Dubon, C., & Bloch, H. (2001). Do 9- and 12-month-olds learn means–ends relation by observing? *Infant Behavior & Development*, 24, 195–213.

Räsänen, O. (2012). Computational modeling of phonetic and lexical learning in early language acquisition: Existing models and future directions. *Speech Communication*, 54(9), 975–997. doi:10.1016/j.specom.2012.05.001

Rose, S., Feldman, J., & Jankowski, J. (2004). Infant visual recognition memory. *Developmental Review*, 24(1), 74–100.

Rovee-Collier, C. (1993). The capacity for long-term memory in infancy. *Current Directions in Psychological Science*, 2, 130–135.

Rovee-Collier, C., & Cuevas, K. (2009). The development of infant memory. In M. Courage & N. Cowan. (Eds.), *The development of memory in infancy and childhood* (2nd ed.). New York, NY: Psychology Press.

Schweizer, T.A., Craik, F.I., & Bialystok, E. (2012). Bilingualism, not immigration status, is associated with maintained cognitive level in Alzheimer's disease. *Cortex*, 48(8), 991–996. doi:10.1016/j.cortex.2011.04.009

Sebastián-Gallés, N., Albareda-Castellot, B., Weikum, W.M., & Werker, J.F. (2012). A bilingual advantage in visual language discrimination in infancy. *Psychological Science*, 23(9), 994–999. doi:10.1177/0956797612436817

Shi, R., & Werker, J.F. (2001). Six-month-old infants' preference for lexical over grammatical words. *Psychological Science*, 12(1), 70–75.

Shi, R., Werker, J.F., & Morgan, J.L. (1999). Newborn infants' sensitivity to perceptual cues to lexical and grammatical words. *Cognition*, 72, B11–B12.

Singh, L., Nestor, S., Parikh, C., & Yull, A. (2009). Influences of infant-directed speech on early word recognition. *Infancy*, 14(6), 654–666.

Smith, L., Fagan, J., & Ulvund, S. (2002). The relation of recognition memory in infancy and parental socioeconomic status to later intellectual competence. *Intelligence*, 30, 247–259.

Spelke, E., & Hespos, S. (2001). Continuity, competence, and the object concept. In E. Dupoux (Ed.), *Language, brain, and cognitive development: Essays in honor of Jacques Mehler* (pp. 325–340). Cambridge, MA: MIT Press.

Spelke, E.S. (1982). Perceptual knowledge of objects in infancy. In J. Mehler, E.C.T. Walker, & M. Garrett (Eds.), *Perspectives on mental representation* (pp. 409–430). Hillsdale, NJ: Erlbaum.

Spelke, E.S. (1991). Physical knowledge in infancy: Reflections on Piaget's theory. In S. Carey & R. Gelman (Eds.), *The epigenesis of mind. Essays on biology and cognition* (pp. 133–169). Hillsdale, NJ: Erlbaum.

Stager, C.L., & Werker, J.F. (1997). Infants listen for more phonetic detail in speech perception than in word learning tasks. *Nature*, 388, 381–382.

Statistics Canada. (2012d). *Linguistics characteristics of Canadians*. Retrieved from http://www12.statcan.gc.ca/census-recensement/2011/as-sa/98-314-x/98-314-x2011001-eng.pdf

Statistics Canada. (2016d). *The evolution of English–French bilingualism in Canada from 1901 to 2011*. Retrieved from http://www.statcan.gc.ca/pub/11-630-x/11-630-x2016001-eng.htm

Suk, W.A., Ahanchian, H., Asante, K.A., Carpenter, D.O., Diaz-Barriga, F., Ha, E.H., . . . Landrigan, P.J. (2016). Environmental pollution: An under-recognized threat to children's health, especially in low- and middle-income countries. *Environmental Health Perspectives*, 124(3), A41–A45. doi:10.1289/ehp.1510517

Tanimura, M., Okuma, K., & Kyoshima, K. (2007). Television viewing, reduced parental utterance, and delayed speech development in infants and young children. *Archives of Pediatric & Adolescent Medicine*, 161(6), 618–619.

Thomas, M. (2005). *Comparing theories of child development* (6th ed.). Pacific Grove, CA: Wadsworth/Cengage.

Thorn, A., & Gathercole, S. (1999). Language-specific knowledge and short-term memory in bilingual and non-bilingual children. *Quarterly Journal of Experimental Psychology: Human Experimental Psychology*, 52A, 303–324.

Tincoff, R., & Jusczyk, P. (2012). Six-month-olds comprehend words that refer to parts of the body. *Infancy*, 17(4), 432–444. doi:10.1111/j.1532-7078.2011.00084.x

Valenza, E., Leo, I., Gava, L., & Simion, F. (2006). Perceptual completion in newborn human infants. *Child Development*, 8, 1–12.

Vouloumanos, A., & Werker, J.F. (2004). Tuned to the signal: The privileged status of speech for young infants. *Developmental Science*, 7(3), 270–276.

Vouloumanos, A., & Werker, J.F. (2007a). Listening to language at birth: Evidence for a bias for speech in neonates. *Developmental Science*, 10(2), 159–164.

Vouloumanos, A., & Werker, J.F. (2007b). Why voice melody alone cannot explain neonates' preference for speech. *Developmental Science* 10(2), 170–172.

Vuorenkoski, L., Kuure, O., Moilanen, I., & Peninkilampi, V. (2000). Bilingualism, school achievement, and mental wellbeing: A follow-up study of return migrant children. *Journal of Child Psychology & Psychiatry & Allied Disciplines*, 41, 261–266.

Werker, J., Pons, F., Dietrich, C., Kajikawa, S., Fais, L., & Amano, S. (2007). Infant directed speech supports phonetic category learning in English and Japanese. *Cognition*, 103, 147–162.

Werker, J.F. (1989). Becoming a native listener: A developmental perspective on human speech perception. *American Scientist*, 77(1), 54–59.

Werker, J.F. (1995). Exploring developmental changes in cross-language speech perception. In D.N. Osherson (Ed.), *An invitation to cognitive science: Language: Vol. 1*. Cambridge, MA: MIT Press.

Werker, J.F., & Hensch, T.K. (2015). Critical periods in speech perception: New directions. *Annual Review of Psychology*, 3(66), 173–196. doi:10.1146/annurev-psych-010814-015104

Werker, J.F., & Tees, R.C. (1984). Phonemic and phonetic factors in adult cross-language speech perception. *Journal of the Acoustical Society of America*, 75(6), 1866–1878.

Werker, J.F., Byers-Heinlein, K., & Fennell. C.T. (2009). Bilingual beginnings to learning words. *Philosophical Transactions of the Royal Society of London. Series B, Biological sciences, 364*(1536), 3649–3663.

Werker, J.F., Cohen, L.B., Lloyd, V., Casosola, M., & Stager, C. (1998). Acquisition of word-object associations by 14-month-old infants. *Developmental Psychology, 34*(6), 1289–1309.

Werker, J.F., Pegg, J.E., & McLeod, P.J. (1994). A cross-language investigation of infant preference for infant-directed communication. *Infant Behavior & Development, 17*, 323–333.

Xu, F. (2003). The development of object individuation in infancy. In H. Hayne & J. Fagen (Eds.), *Progress in Infancy Research: Vol. 3* (pp. 159–192). Mahwah, NJ: Lawrence Erlbaum.

Xu, F. (2005). Categories, kinds, and object individuation in infancy. In L. Gershkoff-Stowe and D. Rakison (Eds.), *Building object categories in developmental time* (pp. 63–89). Papers from the 32nd Carnegie Symposium on Cognition. New Jersey: Lawrence Erlbaum.

Xu, F., & Baker, A. (2005). Object individuation in 10-month-old infants using a simplified manual search method. *Journal of Cognition and Development, 6*(3), 307–323.

Xu, F., & Carey, S. (1996). Infants' metaphysics: the case of numerical identity. *Cognitive Psychology, 30*(2), 111–153.

Yildiz, A., & Arikan, D. (2012). The effects of giving pacifiers to premature infants and making them listen to lullabies on their transition period for total oral feeding and sucking success. *Journal of Clinical Nursing, 21*(5–6), 644–656. doi: 10.1111/j.1365-2702.2010.03634.x

Yu, C., & Ballard, D. (2007). A unified model of early word learning: Integrating statistical and social cues. *Neurocomputing: An International Journal, 70*, 2149–2165.

Zimmerman, F.J., & Christakis, D.A. (2005). Children's television viewing and cognitive outcomes: A longitudinal analysis of national data. *Archives of Pediatric & Adolescent Medicine, 159*(7), 619–625.

Zimmerman, F.J., Christakis, D.A., & Meltzoff, A.N. (2007). Television and DVD/video viewing in children younger than 2 years. *Archives of Pediatrics and Adolescent Medicine, 161*(5), 473–479.

Zmyj, N., Buttelmann, D., Carpenter, M., & Daum, M. (2010). The reliability of a model influences 14-month-olds' imitation. *Journal of Experimental Child Psychology, 106*, 208–220.

Chapter 6

Abraham, E., Hendler, T., Shapira-Lichter, I., Kanat-Maymon, Y., Zagoory-Sharon, O., & Feldman, R. (2014). Father's brain is sensitive to childcare experiences. *Proceedings of the National Academy of Sciences of the United States of America, 111*(27), 9792–9797. doi:10.1073/pnas.1402569111

Adamson, K. (2016). *Commonalities and diversities of fathering. Overall commentary on fathering. encyclopedia on early childhood development.* Retrieved from http://www.child-encyclopedia.com/father-paternity/according-experts/commonalities-and-diversities-fathering-overall-commentary

Adi-Japha, E., & Klein, P.S. (2009). Relations between parenting quality and cognitive performance of children experiencing varying amounts of childcare. *Child Development, 80*(3), 893–906.

Ahnert, L. & Lamb, M.E. (2011). Child care and its impact on young children (2–5). In R.E. Tremblay, M. Boivin, & R. Peters (Eds). *Encyclopedia on early childhood development.* Montreal, Quebec: Centre of Excellence for Early Childhood Development. Retrieved from http://www.child-encyclopedia.com/documents/Ahnert-LambANGxp2.pdf

Ainsworth, M.D.S. (1989). Attachments beyond infancy. *American Psychologist, 44*, 709–716.

Ainsworth, M.D.S., & Marvin, R.S. (1995). On the shaping of attachment theory and research: An interview with Mary D.S. Ainsworth (Fall 1994). *Monographs of the Society for Research in Child Development, 60*(244, Nos. 2–3), 3–21.

Ainsworth, M.D.S., Blehar, M., Waters, E., & Wall, S. (1978). *Patterns of attachment.* Hillsdale, NJ: Erlbaum.

American Psychiatric Association, (2013). *Diagnostic and Statistical Manual of Mental Disorder: DSM-5* (5th ed.). Washington, DC: American Psychiatric Publishing.

Ames, E.W. (1997). *The development of Romanian orphanage children adopted to Canada: Final report.* Ottawa, ON: National Welfare Grants Program, Human Resources Development Canada.

Apter-Levi, Y., Zagoory-Sharon, O., & Feldman, R. (2014). Oxytocin and vasopressin support distinct configurations of social synchrony. *Brain Research, 1580*(Sep), 124–132. doi:10.1016/j.brainres.2013.10.052

Asendorpf, J.B., Warkentin, V., & Baudonnière, P. (1996). Self-awareness and other-awareness. II: Mirror self-recognition, social contingency awareness, and synchronic imitation. *Developmental Psychology, 32*, 313–321.

Atzil, S., Hendler, T., & Feldman, R. (2014). The brain basis of social synchrony. *Social Cognitive and Affective Neuroscience, 9*(8), 1193–1202. doi:10.1093/scan/nst105

Audet, K., & Le Mare, L. (2011). Mitigating effects of the adoptive caregiving environment on inattention/overactivity in children adopted from Romanian orphanages. *International Journal of Behavioral Development, March, 35*(2), 107–115. doi:10.1177/0165025410373313

Bagner, D.M., Sheinkopf, S.J., Vohr, B.R., & Lester, B.M. (2010). A preliminary study of cortisol reactivity and behavior problems in young children born premature. *Developmental Psychobiology, 52*(6), 574–582. doi.org/10.1002/dev.20464

Baker, M., & Milligan, K. (2007, April). *Maternal employment, breastfeeding and health: Evidence from maternity leave mandates* (Working Paper). Toronto, ON: National Bureau of Economic Research. Retrieved from ww.chass.utoronto.ca/cepa/breastfeeding2.9.pdf

Baker, M., Gruber, J., & Milligan, K. (2008). Universal child care, maternal labor supply and family well-being. *Journal of Political Economy, 116*(4), 709–745.

Balaban, M.T. (1995). Affective influences on startle in five-month-old infants: Reactions to facial expressions of emotion. *Child Development, 66*, 28–36.

Ball, J., & Moselle, S. (2016). Aboriginal fathers in Canada. *Encyclopedia on early childhood development.* Retrieved from http://www.child-encyclopedia.com/father-paternity/according-experts/aboriginal-fathers-canada

Bearss, K., Johnson, C., Handen, B., Smith, T., & Scahill, L. (2013). A pilot study of parent training in young children with autism spectrum disorders and disruptive behavior. *Journal of Autism and Developmental Disorders, 43*(4), 829–840. doi:10.1007/s10803-012-1624-7

Beaujot, R., & Ravanera, Z.R. (2009). Family models for earning and caring: Implications for child care and for family policy. *Canadian Studies in Population, 36*(1–2), 145–166.

Beaupré, P., & Cloutier, E. (2007). Navigating family transitions: Evidence from the General Social Survey, *Cycle 20: Family Transitions Survey* (89–625–XIE, no. 2). Ottawa, ON: Statistics Canada. Retrieved from www.statcan.ca/english/research/89-625-XIE/89-625-XIE2007002.pdf

Belsky, J. (1985). Prepared statement on the effects of day care. In Select Committee on Children, Youth, and Families, House of Representatives, 98th Congress, Second Session, *Improving child care services: What can be done?* Washington, DC: U.S. Government Printing Office.

Belsky, J. (2009). Early day care and infant-mother attachment security. In R.E. Tremblay, R.G. Barr, R.D. Peters, & M. Boivin (Eds.), *Encyclopedia on early childhood development.* Montreal, QC: Centre of Excellence for Early Childhood Development. Retrieved from www.child-encyclopedia.com/documents/BelskyANGxp-Child_care2.pdf

Belsky, J. (2011). Child care and its impact on young children. (2nd rev ed.). In R.E. Tremblay, M. Boivin, & R. Peters (Eds) *Encyclopedia on Early Childhood Development [online].* Montreal, Quebec: Centre of Excellence for Early Childhood Development and Strategic Knowledge Cluster on Early Child Development. Retrieved from: http://www.child-encyclopedia.com/documents/Belsky-ANGxp3-Child_care.pdf

Belsky, J., Vandell, D.L., Burchinal, M., Clarke-Stewart, K.A., McCartney, K., & Owen, M.T. (2007). Are there long-term effects of early child care? *Child Development, 78*(2), 681–701.

Benoit, D., & Parker, K.C.H. (1994). Stability and transmission of attachment across three generations. *Child Development, 65,* 1444–1456.

Berry, D., Blair, C., Ursache, A., Willoughby, M., Garrett-Peters, P., Vernon-Feagans, L., . . . Granger, D.A. (2014). Child care and cortisol across early childhood: Context matters. *Developmental Psychology, 50*(2), 514–525. doi:10.1037/a0033379

Biringen, Z. (2000). Emotional availability: Conceptualization and research findings. *American Journal of Orthopsychiatry, 70,* 104–114.

Blatný, M., Millová, K., Jelínek, M., & Osecká, T. (2015). Personality predictors of successful development: Toddler temperament and adolescent personality traits predict well-being and career stability in middle adulthood. *PLoS ONE, 10*(4), e0126032. doi:10.1371/journal.pone.0126032

Blehar, M.C., Lieberman, A.F., & Ainsworth, M.D. (1977). Early face-to-face interaction and its relation to later infant–mother attachment. *Child Development, 48*(1), 182–194. doi:10.2307/1128897

Bohlin, G., & Hagekull, B. (2009). Socio-emotional development: From infancy to young adulthood. *Scandinavian Journal of Psychology, 50,* 592–601. doi:10.1111/j.1467-9450.2009.00787.x

Bos, K., Zeanah, C.H., Fox, N.A., Drury, S.S., McLaughlin, K.A., & Nelson, C.A. (2011). Psychiatric outcomes in young children with a history of institutionalization. *Harvard Review of Psychiatry, 19*(1), 15–24. doi:10.3109/10673229.2011.549773

Bowlby, J. (1969). *Attachment and loss: Vol. 1. Attachment.* New York, NY: Basic Books.

Brisch, K.H. (2015). Attachment and adoption: Diagnostics, psychopathology, and therapy [Article in German]. *Praxis der Kinderpsychologie und Kinderpsychiatrie, 64*(10), 793–815. doi:10.13109/prkk.2015.64.10.793

Brumariu, L., & Kerns, K. (2010). Parent–child attachment and internalizing symptoms in childhood and adolescence: A review of empirical findings and future directions. *Development and Psychopathology, 22,* 177–203. doi: http://dx.doi.org/10.1017/S0954579409990344

Burger, K. (2010). How does early childhood care and education affect cognitive development? An international review of the effects of early interventions for children from different social backgrounds. *Early Childhood Research Quarterly 25*(2), 140–165.

Bushnik, T. (2006). *Child Care in Canada* (89–599–MIE2006003). Ottawa, ON: Minister of Industry. Retrieved from Statistics Canada website: www.statcan.ca/english/research/89-599-MIE/89-599-MIE2006003.pdf

Buss, A.H., & Plomin, R. (1984). *Temperament: Early developing personality traits.* Hillsdale, NJ: Erlbaum.

Carlson, E., Sroufe, A., & Egeland, B. (2004). The construction of experience: A longitudinal study of representation and behavior. *Child Development, 75,* 66–83.

Carpendale, J.I.M., & Lewis, C. (2004). Constructing an understanding of mind: The development of children's understanding of mind within social interaction. *Behavioral and Brain Sciences, 27*(1), 79–96.

Carver, L.J., & Cornew, L. (2009). The development of social information gathering in infancy: A model of neural substrates and developmental mechanisms. In M. de Haan, M., & M.R. Gunnar, M. (Eds.), *Handbook of developmental social neuroscience* (pp. 122–141). New York, NY: Guilford Press.

Caspi, A., & Shiner, R. (2006). Personality development. In W. Damon & R. Lerner (Eds.), *Handbook of child psychology, Volume 3: Social, emotional, and personality development* (6th ed., pp. 300–365). New York, NY: John Wiley Publishers.

Cassibba, R., van IJzendoorn, M.H., & Coppola, G. (2012). Emotional availability and attachment across generations: Variations in patterns associated with infant health risk status. *Child: Care, Health and Development, 38*(4), 538–544. doi:10.1111/j.1365-2214.2011.01274

Cassidy, J., & Berlin, L.J. (1994). The insecure/ambivalent pattern of attachment: Theory and research. *Child Development, 65,* 971–991.

Centre of Excellence for Early Childhood Development (CEECD) (2009a). High quality child care services: A stimulating and caring environment for children. In R.E. Tremblay, R.G. Barr, R.D. Peters, & M. Boivin (Eds.), *Encyclopedia on Early Childhood Development.* Montreal, QC: Centre of Excellence for Early Childhood Development. Retrieved from www.child-encyclopedia.com/pages/PDF/Child_careANGmcP.pdf

Centre of Excellence for Early Childhood Development (CEECD) (2009b). Synthesis on child care (0–5 years). In R.E. Tremblay, R.G. Barr, R.D. Peters, & M. Boivin (Eds.), *Encyclopedia on Early Childhood Development.* Montreal, QC: Centre of Excellence for Early Childhood Development. Retrieved from www.child-encyclopedia.com/pages/PDF/child_care.pdf

Cernoch, J.M., & Porter, R.H. (1985). Recognition of maternal axillary odors by infants. *Child Development, 56,* 1593–1598.

Chaudhary, N., Tuli, M., & Sharda, S. (2015). Fathers. *Encyclopedia on Early Childhood Development.* Retrieved from http://www.child-encyclopedia.com/father-paternity/according-experts/fathers

Cleveland, G., Forer, B., Hyatt, D., Japel, C., & Krashinsky, M. (2008). New evidence about child care in Canada: Use patterns, affordability and quality. *IRPP Choices, 14*(12), 1–42.

Cole, P., Martin, S., & Dennis, T. (2004). Emotion regulation as a scientific construct: Methodological challenges and directions for child development research. *Child Development, 75,* 317–333.

Co-ordinated Access for Child Care (2009). *Choosing quality child care. The Regional Municipality of Hamilton-Wentworth, ON: Arthur.* Retrieved from www.cafcc.on.ca/quality.php?subs=/choose.php

Corapci, F. (2010). Child-care chaos and child development. In G. Evens & T. Wachs (Eds.), *Chaos and its influence on children's development: An ecological perspective* (pp. 67–82). Washington, DC: American Psychological Association.

Crockenberg, S. (2003). Rescuing the baby from the bathwater: How gender and temperament (may) influence how child care affects child development. *Child Development, 74,* 1034–1038.

Crockenberg, S., Leerkes, E., & Lekka, S. (2007). Pathways from marital aggression to infant emotion regulation: The development of withdrawal in infancy. *Infant Behavior & Development, 30,* 97–113.

D'Entremont, B. (2000). A perceptual-attentional explanation of gaze following in 3- and 6-month-olds. *Developmental Science, 3,* 302–311.

D'Entremont, B., & Hartung, C. (2003). *A longitudinal investigation of joint attention, emotion regulation and attachment.* Poster presented at the Society for Research in Child Development, Tampa, FL.

D'Entremont, B., Hains, S.M.J., & Muir, D.W. (1997). A demonstration of gaze following in 3- to 6-month-olds. *Infant Behavior and Development, 20,* 560–572.

Davies, P.T., Cicchetti, D., Hentges, R.F., & Sturge-Apple, M.L. (2013). The genetic precursors and the advantageous and disadvantageous sequelae of inhibited temperament: An evolutionary perspective. *Developmental Psychology, 49*(12), 2285–2300. doi:10.1037/a0032312

Ellsworth, C.P., Muir, D.W., & Hains, S.M.J. (1993). Social competence and person-object differentiation: An analysis of the still-face effect. *Developmental Psychology, 29,* 63–73.

Emde, R.N., Plomin, R., Robinson, J., Corley, R., DeFries, J., Fulker, D.W., . . . Zahn-Waxler, C. (1992). Temperament, emotion, and cognition at fourteen months: The MacArthur longitudinal twin study. *Child Development, 63,* 1437–1455.

Fagan, J., & Palm, G. (2016). Interventions with fathers. *Encyclopedia on Early Childhood Development.* Retrieved from http://www.child-encyclopedia.com/father-paternity/according-experts/interventions-fathers

Feldman, R. (2003). Paternal socio-psychological factors and infant attachment: The mediating role of synchrony in father-infant interactions. *Infant Behavior & Development, 25,* 221–236.

Feldman, R. (2016). The neurobiology of mammalian parenting and the biosocial context of human caregiving. *Hormones and Behavior, 77*(Jan), 3–17. doi:10.1016/j.yhbeh.2015.10.001

Flom, R., & Bahrick, L. (2007). The development of infant discrimination of affect in multimodal and unimodal stimulation: The role of intersensory redundancy. *Developmental Psychology, 43*(1), 238–252. doi:10.1037/0012-1649.43.1.238

Fox, N., Henderson, H., Rubin, K., Calkins, S., & Schmidt, L. (2001). Continuity and discontinuity of behavioral inhibition and exuberance: Psychophysiological and behavioral influences across the first four years of life. *Child Development, 72*, 1–21.

Fraley, R.C., Roisman, G.I., Booth-LaForce, C., Owen, M.T., & Holland, A.S. (2013). Interpersonal and genetic origins of adult attachment styles: A longitudinal study from infancy to early adulthood. *Journal of Personality and Social Psychology, 104*(5), 817–838. doi:10.1037/a0031435

George, M., Cummings, E., & Davies, P. (2010). Positive aspects of fathering and mothering, and children's attachment in kindergarten. *Early Child Development and Care, 180*, 107–119. doi:10.1080/03004430903414752

Goodman, S., & Brand, S. (2009). Infants of depressed mothers: Vulnerabilities, risk factors, and protective factors for the later development of psychopathology. In C. Zeanah (Ed.), *Handbook of infant mental health* (3rd ed., pp. 153–170). New York, NY: Guilford Press.

Government of Ontario (2010). *Full-day learning for 4- and 5-year-olds: Time to learn, grow and play.* Toronto, ON: Ministry of Education, Government of Ontario. Retrieved from www.edu.gov.on.ca/earlylearning/EL_FactSheet_Jan2010.pdf

Gray, P.B., & Anderson, K.G. (2016). The impact of fathers on children. *Encyclopedia on Early Childhood Development.* Retrieved from http://www.child-encyclopedia.com/father-paternity/according-experts/impact-fathers-children

Gunnar, M., Kryzer, E., Van Ryzin, M., & Phillips, D. (2010). The rise in cortisol in family day care: Association with aspects of care quality, child behavior, and child sex. *Child Development, 81*(3), 851–869. doi:10.1111/j.1467-8624.2010.01438.x

Hamilton, C.E. (1995, March). *Continuity and discontinuity of attachment from infancy through adolescence.* Paper presented at the biennial meetings of the Society for Research in Child Development, Indianapolis, IN.

Hammond, M., Landry, S., Swank, P., & Smith, K. (2000). Relation of mothers' affective development history and parenting behavior: Effects on infant medical risk. *American Journal of Orthopsychiatry, 70*, 95–103.

Harlow, H., & Zimmerman, R. (1959). Affectional responses in the infant monkey. *Science, 130*, 421–432.

Harrison, L.J., & Ungerer, J.A. (2002). Maternal employment and infant-mother attachment security at 12 months postpartum. *Developmental Psychology 38*(5), 758–773.

Hasenfratz, L., Benish-Weisman, M., Steinberg T., & Knafo-Noam, A. (2015). Temperament and peer problems from early to middle childhood: Gene–environment correlations with negative emotionality and sociability. *Development and Psychopathology, 27*(4 Pt 1), 1089–1109. doi:10.1017/S095457941500070X

Henderson, H., Marshall, P., Fox, N., & Rubin, K. (2004). Psychophysiological and behavioral evidence for varying forms and functions of nonsocial behavior in preschoolers. *Child Development, 75*, 236–250.

Hou, J., Chen, H., & Chen, X. (2005). The relationship of parent–children interaction in the free play session and copy-modeling session with the development of children's behavioral inhibition in Chinese families. *Psychological Science (China), 28*, 820–825.

Human Resources Development Canada. (2003). *A new generation of Canadian families raising young children* (Cat. No. SP-579-09-03E). Retrieved from www11.sdc.gc.ca/en/cs/sp/arb/publications/research/2003-001330/2003-001330.pdf

Huth-Bocks, A., Levendosky, A., Bogat, G., & von Eye, A. (2004). The impact of maternal characteristics and contextual variables on infant-mother attachment. *Child Development, 75*, 480–496.

Isabella, R.A. (1995). The origins of infant–mother attachment: Maternal behavior and infant development. *Annals of Child Development, 10*, 57–81.

Izard, C.E., & Harris, P. (1995). Emotional development and developmental psychopathology. In D. Cicchetti & D.J. Cohen (Eds.), *Developmental psychopathology: Vol. 1. Theory and methods* (pp. 467–503). New York, NY: Wiley.

Izard, C.E., Fantauzzo, C.A., Castle, J.M., Haynes, O.M., Rayias, M.F., & Putnam, P.H. (1995). The ontogeny and significance of infants' facial expressions in the first 9 months of life. *Developmental Psychology, 31*, 997–1013.

Johnson, M. (2003). Development of human brain functions. *Biological Psychiatry, 54*, 1312–1316.

Juffer, F., Finet, C., Vermeer, H., & van den Dries, L. (2015). Attachment and cognitive and motor development in the first years after adoption: A review of studies on internationally adopted children from China [Article in German]. *Praxis der Kinderpsychologie und Kinderpsychiatrie, 64*(10), 774–792. doi:10.13109/prkk.2015.64.10.774

Juffer, F., Van IJzendoorn, M.H., & Palacios, J. (2011). Children's recovery after adoption. *Journal for the Study of Education and Development, 34*(1), 3–18. doi:10.1174/021037011794390102

Kagan, J., & Herschkowitz, N. (2005). *A young mind in a growing brain.* Hillsdale, NJ: Lawrence Erlbaum.

Kagan, J., Snidman, N., & Arcus, D. (1993). On the temperamental categories of inhibited and uninhibited children. In K.H. Rubin & J.B. Asendorpf (Eds.), *Social withdrawal, inhibition, and shyness in childhood* (pp. 19–28). Hillsdale, NJ: Erlbaum.

Kahana-Kalman, R., & Walker-Andrews, A. (2001). The role of person familiarity in young infants' perception of emotional expressions. *Child Development, 72*, 352–369.

Kim, G., Walden, T., & Knieps, L. (2010). Impact and characteristics of positive and fearful emotional messages during infant social referencing. *Infant Behavior & Development, 33*(2), 189–195. doi: http://dx.doi.org/10.1016/j.infbeh.2009.12.009

Kobak, R., Zajac, K., & Smith, C. (2009). Adolescent attachment and trajectories of hostile/impulsive behavior: Implications for the development of personality disorders. *Development and Psychopathology, 21*, 839–851. doi:10.1017/S0954579409000455

Lamb, M., & Lewis, C. (2011). The role of parent-child relationships in child development. In M. Bornstein & M. Lamb (Eds.), *Developmental science: An advanced textbook* (6th ed., pp. 469–518). New York, NY: Psychology Press.

Lamb, M.E. (1981). The development of father-infant relationships. In M.E. Lamb (Ed.), *The role of the father in child development* (2nd ed., pp. 459–488). New York, NY: Wiley.

Laurin, J.C., Geoffroy, M.C., Boivin, M., Japel, C., Raynault, M.F., Tremblay, R.E., & Côté, S.M. (2015). Child care services, socioeconomic inequalities, and academic performance. *Pediatrics, 136*(6), 1112–1124. doi:10.1542/peds.2015-0419

Le Mare, L., & Audet, K.N. (2014). Behaviour problems in post-institutionalized Romanian adoptees: Explanatory parameters in the adoptive home. *Merrill-Palmer Quarterly: Journal of Developmental Psychology, 60*(3), 245–273. doi:10.1353/mpq.2014.0017

Le Mare, L., Fernyhough, L., & Warford, L. (2001, April 19–22). *Intellectual and academic performance of Romanian orphans 10 years after being adopted to Canada.* Poster presented at the Biennial Meeting of the Society for Research in Child Development, Minneapolis, MN.

Legerstee, M., Anderson, D., & Schaffer, A. (1998). Five- and eight-month-old infants recognize their faces and voices as familiar and social stimuli. *Child Development, 69*, 37–50.

Legerstee, M., Pomerleau, A., Malcuit, G., & Feider, H. (1987). The development of infants' response to people and a doll: Implications for research communication. *Infant Behavior and Development, 10*, 82–95.

Lemery-Chalfant, K., Kao, K., Swann, G., & Goldsmith, H.H. (2013). Childhood temperament: Passive gene-environment correlation, gene-environment interaction, and the hidden importance of the family environment. *Development and Psychopathology, 25*(1), 51–63. doi:10.1017/S0954579412000892

Levendosky, A.A., Bogat, G.A., Huth-Bocks, A.C., Rosenblum, K., & von Eye, A. (2011). The effects of domestic violence on the stability of attachment from infancy to preschool. *Journal of Clinical Child and Adolescent Psychology, 40*(3), 398–410. doi:10.1080/15374416.2011.563460

Levine, D. (2011). Growth and development. In K. Marcdante, R. Kliegman, H. Jensen, & R. Behrman (Eds.), *Nelson's essentials of pediatrics* (6th ed., pp. 13–44). New York, NY: Elsevier Health Publishers.

Levtov, R., van der Gaag, N., Greene, M., Kaufman, M., & Barker, G. (2015). State of the world's fathers: Summary and recommendations. *A MenCare Advocacy Publication.* Washington, DC: Promundo, Rutgers, Save the Children, Sonke Gender Justice, and the MenEngage Alliance. Retrieved from http://sowf.men-care.org/download/

Lewis, C., & Lamb, M.E. (2003). Fathers' influences on children's development: The evidence from two-parent families. *European Journal of Psychology of Education, 18,* 211–228.

Lewis, M. (1990). Social knowledge and social development. *Merrill-Palmer Quarterly, 36,* 93–116.

Lewis, M. (1991). Ways of knowing: Objective self-awareness of consciousness. *Developmental Review, 11,* 231–243.

Lewis, M., & Brooks, J. (1978). Self-knowledge and emotional development. In M. Lewis & L.A. Rosenblum (Eds.), *The development of affect* (pp. 205–226). New York, NY: Plenum.

Lewis, M., Allesandri, S.M., & Sullivan, M.W. (1992). Differences in shame and pride as a function of children's gender and task difficulty. *Child Development, 63,* 630–638.

LoBue, V., Coan, J.A., Thrasher, C., & DeLoache, J.S. (2011). Prefrontal asymmetry and parent-rated temperament in infants. *Public Library of Science ONE, 6*(7), e22694. doi:10.1371/journal.pone.0022694

Love, J., Harrison, L., Sagi-Schwartz, A., van IJzendoorn, M., Ross, C., Ungerer, J., . . . Chazan-Cohen, R. (2003). Child care quality matters: How conclusions may vary with context. *Child Development, 74,* 1021–1033.

Lugo-Gil, J., & Tamis-LeMonda, C.S. (2008). Family resources and parenting quality: Links to children's cognitive development across the first three years. *Child Development, 79*(4), 1065–1085.

Lyons, D., Parker, K., & Schatzberg, A. (2010). Animal models of early life stress: Implications for understanding resilience. *Developmental Psychobiology, 52*(5), 402–410. doi:10.1002/dev.20429

Maccoby, E., & Lewis, C. (2003). Less day care or different day care? *Child Development, 74,* 1069–1075.

Main, M., & Hesse, E. (1990). Parents' unresolved traumatic experiences are related to infant disorganized attachment status: Is frightened and/or frightening parental behavior the linking mechanism? In M.T. Greenberg, D. Cicchetti, & E.M. Cummings (Eds.), *Attachment in the preschool years: Theory, research, and intervention* (pp. 161–182). Chicago, IL: University of Chicago Press.

Main, M., & Solomon, J. (1990). Procedures for identifying infants as disorganized/disoriented during the Ainsworth Strange Situation. In M.T. Greenberg, D. Cicchetti, & E.M. Cummings (Eds.), *Attachment in the preschool years: Theory, research, and intervention* (pp. 121–160). Chicago, IL: University of Chicago Press.

Maki, P., Veijola, J., Rantakallio, P., Jokelainen, J., Jones, P., & Isohanni, M. (2004). Schizophrenia in the offspring of antenatally depressed mothers: A 31-year follow-up of the Northern Finland 1966 Birth Cohort. *Schizophrenia Research, 66,* 79–81.

Markova, M., & Legerstee, M. (2008). How infants come to learn about the minds of others. *Zero to Three Journal, 28*(3), 26–31.

Marshall, K. (2003). Parental leave: More time off for baby. (11–008–XPE) in *Canadian Social Trends, Winter* (71), 13–18.

Marshall, K. (2008). Fathers' use of paid parental leave. In *Perspectives* (75-001-X). Ottawa, ON: Statistics Canada. Retrieved from www.statcan.gc.ca/pub/75-001-x/2008106/pdf/10639-eng.pdf

Marwick, H., Doolin, O., Allely, C.S., McConnachie, A., Johnson, P., Puckering, C., Golding, J., . . . Wilson, P. (2013). Predictors of diagnosis of child psychiatric disorder in adult–infant social-communicative interaction at 12 months. *Research in Developmental Disabilities, 34*(1), 562–572. doi:10.1016/j.ridd.2012.09.007

McCartney, K., Burchinal, M., Clarke-Stewart, A., Bub, K.L., Owen, M.T., & Belsky, J. (2010). Testing a series of causal propositions relating time in child care to children's externalizing behavior. *Developmental Psychology, 46*(1), 1–17a.

McCrae, R., & Costa, P. (2013). Introduction to the empirical and theoretical status of the five-factor model of personality traits. In T. Widiger, T., & P. Costa, P. (Eds.), *Personality disorders and the five-factor model of personality* (3rd ed., pp. 15–27). Washington, DC: American Psychological Association.

McKim, M.K., Cramer, K.M., Stuart, B., & O'Connor, D.L. (1999). Infant care decisions and attachment security: The Canadian transition to child care study. *Canadian Journal of Behavioural Science, 31*(2), 92–106.

McMillan, R. (2010). Voices from the field—Early learning care and education: Applying an integrated approach. In R.E. Tremblay, R.G. Barr, R.D. Peters, & M. Boivin (Eds.), *Encyclopedia on Early Childhood Development.* Montreal, QC: Centre of Excellence for Early Childhood Development. Retrieved from www.childencyclopedia.com/documents/McMillanANGps.pdf

Minzi, M. (2010). Gender and cultural patterns of mothers' and fathers' attachment and links with children's self-competence, depression and loneliness in middle and late childhood. *Early Child Development and Care, 180,* 193–209. doi:10.1080/03004430903415056

Moore, C. & D'Entremont, B. (2001). Developmental changes in pointing as a function of attentional focus. *Journal of Cognition and Development, 2,* 109–129.

Moore, C. (2007). Maternal behavior, infant development, and the question of developmental resources. *Developmental Psychobiology, 49,* 45–53.

Müller, U., Carpendale, J.I.M., Bibok, M., & Racine, T.P. (2006). Subjectivity, identification and differentiation: Key issues in early social development. *Monographs of the Society for Research in Child Development, 71*(2), 167–179.

Murray, L., Sinclair, D., Cooper, P., Ducournau, P., Turner, P. & Stein, A. (1999). The socioemotional development of 5-year-old children of postnatally depressed mothers. *Journal of Child Psychology & Psychiatry & Allied Disciplines, 40,* 1259–1271.

National Institute of Child Health and Human Development Early Child Care Research Network. (Eds.). (2005). *Child care and child development: Results of the NICHD Study of early child care and youth development.* New York, NY: Guilford Press.

National Institute of Child Health and Human Development Early Child Care Research Network. (2006). Child-care effect sizes for the NICHD study of early child care and youth development. *American Psychologist, 61*(2), 99–116.

Neppl, T.K., Donnellan, M.B., Scaramella, L.V., Widaman, K.F., Spilman, S.K., Ontai, L.L., & Conger, R.D. (2010). Differential stability of temperament and personality from toddlerhood to middle childhood. *Journal of Research in Personality, 44*(3), 386–396. doi:10.1016/j.jrp.2010.04.004

Nuttall, A.K., Valentino, K., Borkowski, J.G. (2012). Maternal history of parentification, maternal warm responsiveness, and children's externalizing behavior. *Journal of Family Psychology, 26*(5), 767–775. doi:10.1037/a0029470

Orenstein, W.A., Paulson, J.A., Brady, M.T., Cooper, L.Z., & Seib, K. (2012). Global vaccination recommendations and thimerosal. *Pediatrics, 131*(1), 149–151. doi:10.1542/peds.2012-1760

Owen, M.T. (2011). Child care and the development of young children (0–2). (2nd rev ed.). In R.E. Tremblay, M. Boivin, & R. Peters, (Eds). *Encyclopedia on Early Childhood Development [online].* Montreal, Quebec: Centre of Excellence for Early Childhood Development and Strategic Knowledge Cluster on Early Child Development. Retrieved from: http://www.child-encyclopedia.com/documents/OwenANGxp2.pdf

Palacios, J., Román, M., Moreno, C., León, E., & Peñarrubia, M.G. (2014). Differential plasticity in the recovery of adopted children after early adversity. *Child Development Perspectives, 8*(3), 169–174. doi:10.1111/cdep.12083

Pederson, D., & Moran, G. (1996). Expressions of the attachment relationship outside of the Strange Situation. *Child Development, 67,* 915–927.

Pederson, D.R., & Moran, G. (1995). A categorical description of infant–mother relationships in the home and its relation to Q-sort measures of infant-mother interaction. *Monographs of the Society for Research in Child Development, 60*(244, Nos. 2–3), 111–132.

Pederson, D.R., Gleason, K.E., Moran, G., & Bento, S. (1998). Maternal attachment representations, maternal sensitivity, and the infant-mother attachment relationship. *Developmental Psychology, 34*, 925–933.

Pederson, D.R., Moran, G., Sitko, C., Campbell, K., Ghesquire, K., & Acton, H. (1990). Maternal sensitivity and the security of infant–mother attachment: A Q-sort study. *Child Development, 61*, 1974–1983.

Pesonen, A., Raikkonen, K., Strandberg, T., Kelitikangas-Jarvinen, & L., Jarvenpaa, A. (2004). Insecure adult attachment style and depressive symptoms: Implications for parental perceptions of infant temperament. *Infant Mental Health Journal, 25*, 99–116.

Phillips, A., Wellman, H., & Spelke, E. (2002). Infants' ability to connect gaze and emotional expression to intentional action. *Cognition, 85*, 53–78.

Plomin, R., Emde, R.N., Braungart, J.M., Campos, J., Corley, R., Fulker, D.W., . . . DeFries, J.C. (1993). Genetic change and continuity from fourteen to twenty months: The MacArthur longitudinal twin study. *Child Development, 64*, 1354–1376.

Pluess, M., & Belsky J. (2009). Differential susceptibility to rearing experience: The case of childcare. *Journal of Child Psychology and Psychiatry, 50*(4), 396–404. doi:10.1111/j.1469-7610.2008.01992.x

Pluess, M., & Belsky, J. (2010). Differential susceptibility to parenting and quality child care. *Developmental Psychology, 46*(2), 379–90.

Pluess, M., & Belsky, J. (2010). Differential susceptibility to parenting and quality child care. *Developmental Psychology, 46*(2), 379–90.

Pungello, E., Kainz, K., Burchinal, M., Wasik, B., Sparling, J., Ramey, C., & Campbell, F. (2010). Early educational intervention, early cumulative risk, and the early home environment as predictors of young adult outcomes within a high-risk sample. *Child Development, 81*(1), 410–426. doi: 10.1111/j.1467-8624.2009.01403.x

Quitmann, J.H., Krison, L., Romer, G., & Ramsauer, B. (2012). The capacity to see things from the child's point of view—assessing insightfulness in mothers with and without a diagnosis of depression. *Clinical Psychology & Psychotherapy, 19*(6), 508–517. doi:10.1002/cpp.759

Racine, T.P., & Carpendale, J.I.M. (2007). The role of shared practice in joint attention. *British Journal of Developmental Psychology, 25*(1), 3–25.

Ramchandani, P.G., Domoney, J., Sethna, V., Psychogiou, L., Vlachos, H., & Murray, L. (2013). Do early father—infant interactions predict the onset of externalizing behaviours in young children? Findings from a longitudinal cohort study. *Journal of Child Psychology and Psychiatry, 54*(1), 56–64. doi:10.1111/j.1469-7610.2012.02583

Rose, K., & Elickere, J. (2010). Maternal child care preferences for infants, toddlers, and preschoolers: The disconnect between policy and preference in the USA. *Community, Work, & Family, 13*(2), 205–229. doi:10.1080/13668800903314366

Rosenkrantz, S., Aronson, S., & Huston, A. (2004). Mother–infant relationship in single, cohabiting, and married families: A case for marriage? *Journal of Family Psychology, 18*, 5–18.

Rothbart, M.K., (2012). Advances in temperament: History, concepts, and measures. In M. Zentner, M., & R. Shiner, R.L. (Eds.), *Handbook of temperament.* (pp. 3–20). New York, NY: Guilford Press.

Roy, F. (2006). From she to she: Changing patterns of women in the Canadian labour force. (11-010-XPB) in *Canadian Economic Observer, 19*(6), 1–10. Ottawa, ON: Statistics Canada.

Rutgers, A.H, Bakermans-Kranenburg, M.J., Van IJzendoorn, M.H., & Van Bercklelaer-Onnes, I.A. (2004). Autism and attachment: A meta-analytic review. *Journal of Child Psychology and Psychiatry, 45*(6), 1123–1134. doi:10.1111/j.1469-7610.2004.t01-1-00305.x

Rutter, M., Sonuga-Barke, E., Beckett, C., Castle, J., Kreppner, J., Kumsta, R., Schlotz, W., Stevens, S., & Bell, C. (2010). Deprivation-specific psychological patterns: Effects of institutional deprivation. *Monographs of the Society for Research in Child Development, 75*, 1–231.

Sagi, A., Koren-Karie, N., Gini, M., Ziv, Y., & Joels, T. (2002). Shedding further light on the effects of various types and quality of early child care on infant-mother attachment relationship: The Haifa Study of early child care. *Child Development, 73*(4), 1166.

Scarr, S., & McCartney, K. (1983). How people make their own environments: A theory of genotype/environment effects. *Child Development, 54*, 424–435.

Schaffer, H., & Emerson, P. (1964). The development of social attachments in infancy. *Monographs of the Society for Research in Child Development, 29*(3, Serial No. 94).

Shaver, P.R., & Mikulincer, M. (2012). An attachment perspective on morality: Strengthening authentic forms of moral decision making. In M. Mikulincer, M., & P. Shaver, P.R. (Eds.), *The social psychology of morality: Exploring the causes of good and evil.* (pp. 257–274). Washington, DC: American Psychological Association.

Smyke, A.T. (2015). Adoptive parents can be unprepared for the challenges in caring for children with reactive attachment disorder. *Evidence-based Nursing, 18*(2), 53. doi:10.1136/eb-2014-101907

Soken, N., & Pick, A. (1999). Infants' perception of dynamic affective expressions: Do infants distinguish specific expressions? *Child Development, 70*, 1275–1282.

Statistics Canada. (2009). *The Canadian labour market at a glance 2007* (71-222-X). Ottawa, ON: Minister of Industry. Retrieved from www.statcan.gc.ca/pub/71-222-x/71-222-x2008001-eng.pdf

Steele, M., Hodges, J., Kaniuk, J., Hillman, S., & Henderson, K. (2003). Attachment representations and adoption: Associations between maternal states of mind and emotion narratives in previously maltreated children. *Journal of Child Psychotherapy, 29*, 187–205.

Stilberg, J., San Miguel, V., Murelle, E., Prom, E., Bates, J., Canino, G., Egger, H., & Eaves, L. (2005). Genetic environmental influences on temperament in the first year of life: The Puerto Rico Infant Twin Study (PRINTS). *Twin Research and Human Genetics, 8*, 328–336.

Stipek, D., Gralinski, J., & Kopp, C. (1990). Self-concept development in the toddler years. *Developmental Psychology, 26*, 972–977.

Striano, T., & Rochat, P. (1999). Developmental link between dyadic and triadic social competence in infancy. *British Journal of Developmental Psychology, 17*, 551–562.

Sumner, M., Bernard, K., & Dozier, M. (2010). Young children's full-day patterns of cortisol production on child care days. *Archives of Pediatrics & Adolescent Medicine, 164*(6), 567–571. doi:10.1001/archpediatrics.2010.85

Teti, D.M., Gelfand, D.M., Messinger, D.S., & Isabella, R. (1995). Maternal depression and the quality of early attachment: An examination of infants, preschoolers, and their mothers. *Developmental Psychology, 31*, 364–376.

Thomas, A., & Chess, S. (1977). *Temperament and development.* New York, NY: Brunner/Mazel.

Thompson, R. (2008). Early attachment and later development: Familiar questions, new answers. In J. Cassidy & P. Shaver (Eds.), *Handbook of attachment: Theory, research, and clinical applications* (2nd ed., pp. 317–332). New York, NY: Guilford Press.

Thompson, R., Winer, A., & Goodvin, R. (2011). The individual child. In M. Bornstein & M. Lamb (Eds.), *Developmental science: An advanced textbook* (6th ed., pp. 427–468). New York, NY: Psychology Press.

Tremblay, D.G. (2010). Paid parental leave: An employee right or still an ideal? An analysis of the situation in Quebec in comparison with North America. *Employee Responsibilities and Rights Journal, 22*(2), 83–100.

Uppal, S. (2015). Employment patterns of families with children. *Insights on Canadian Society* (Cat. no. 75-006-X). Ottawa, ON: Statistics Canada.

van IJzendoorn, M. (2005). Attachment at an early age (0–5) and its impact on children's development. In Centres of Excellence for Children's Well-Being (Ed.), *Encyclopedia on Early Childhood Development*. Retrieved from www.excellence-earlychildhood.ca/documents/van_I JzendoornANGxp.pdf

Vandell, D., Belsky, J., Burchinal, M., Steinberg, L., & Vandergrift, N. (2010). Do the effects of early child care extend to age 15 years? Results from the NICHD study of early child care and youth development. *Child Development, 81*(3), 737–756. doi:10.1111/j.1467-8624.2010.01431.x

Walker-Andrews, A.S. (1997). Infants' perception of expressive behaviors: Differentiation of multimodal information. *Psychological Bulletin, 121*(3), 437–456.

Walker-Andrews, A.S., & Lennon, E. (1991). Infants' discrimination of vocal expressions: Contributions of auditory and visual information. *Infant Behavior and Development, 14,* 131–142.

Walton, G.E., Bower, N.J.A., & Bower, T.G.R. (1992). Recognition of familiar faces by newborns. *Infant Behavior and Development, 15,* 265–269.

Warren, S., Gunnar, M., Kagan, J., Anders, T., Simmens, S., Rones, M., . . . Sroufe, A. (2003). Maternal panic disorder: Infant temperament, neurophysiology, and parenting behaviors. *Journal of the American Academy of Child & Adolescent Psychiatry, 42,* 814–825.

Washburn, R. (1929). A study of the smiling and laughing of infants in the first year of life. *Genetic Psychology Monographs, 6,* 397–535.

Waters, E., Treboux, D., Crowell, J., Merrick, S., & Albersheim, L. (1995, March). *From the Strange Situation to the Adult Attachment Interview: A 20-year longitudinal study of attachment security in infancy and early adulthood.* Paper presented at the biennial meetings of the Society for Research in Child Development, Indianapolis, IN.

Weinfield, N., & Egeland, B. (2004). Continuity, discontinuity, and coherence in attachment from infancy to late adolescence: Sequelae of organization and disorganization. *Attachment & Human Development, 6,* 73–97.

Weitlauf, A.S., McPheeters, M.L., Peters, B., Sathe, N., Travis, R., Aiello, R., . . . Warren, Z. (2014). *Therapies for children with autism spectrum disorder: Behavioral interventions update. Comparative effectiveness review no. 137.* (Prepared by the Vanderbilt Evidence-based Practice Center under Contract No. 290-2012-00009-I.) AHRQ Publication No. 14-EHC036-EF. Rockville, MD: Agency for Healthcare Research and Quality. Retrieved from www.effectivehealthcare.ahrq.gov/reports/final.cfm

Wong, D. (1993). *Whaley & Wong's essentials of pediatric nursing.* St. Louis, MO: Mosby-Yearbook, Inc.

Woodhouse, S., Ramos-Marcuse, F., Ehrlich, K., Warner, S., & Cassidy, J. (2010). The role of adolescent attachment in moderating and mediating the links between parent and adolescent psychological symptoms. *Journal of Clinical Child & Adolescent Psychology, 39*(1), 51–63. doi:10.1080/15374410903401096

Chapter 7

Anderson, L.M., & Anderson, J. (2010). Barney and breakfast: Messages about food and eating in preschool television shows and how they may impact the development of eating behaviours in children. *Early Child Development and Care, 180*(10), 1323–1336. doi:10.1080/03004430903040516

Anglin, J.M. (1995, March). *Word learning and the growth of potentially knowable vocabulary.* Paper presented at the biennial meetings of the Society for Research in Child Development, Indianapolis, IN.

Arning, L., Ocklenburg, S., Schulz, S., Ness, V., Gerding, W.M., Hengstler, J.G., . . . Beste, C. (2013). PCSK6 VNTR polymorphism is associated with degree of handedness but not direction of handedness. *Public Library of Science One, 8,* e67251. doi:10.1371/journal.pone.0067251

Arnold, D.H., Lonigan, C.J., Whitehurst, G.J., & Epstein, J.N. (1994). Accelerating language development through picture book reading: Replication and extension to a videotape training format. *Journal of Educational Psychology, 86* (2), 235–243.

Astington, J., & Jenkins, J. (1999). A longitudinal study of the relation between language and theory-of-mind development. *Developmental Psychology, 35,* 1311–1320.

Astington, J.W., & Jenkins, J.M. (1995, March). *Language and theory of mind: A theoretical review and a longitudinal study.* Paper presented at the biennial meetings of the Society for Research in Child Development, Indianapolis, IN.

Barnard, K.E., Hammond, M.A., Booth, C.L., Bee, H.L., Mitchell, S.K., & Spieker, S.J. (1989). Measurement and meaning of parent-child interaction. In J.J. Morrison, C. Lord, & D.P. Keating (Eds.), *Applied developmental psychology: Vol. 3* (pp. 40–81). San Diego, CA: Academic Press.

Baron, I. (2003). *Neuropsychological evaluation of the child.* New York, NY: Oxford University Press.

Barthélémy-Musso, A., Tartas, V., & Guidetti, M. (2013). Taking objects' uses seriously: Developmental approach of children's co-construction of semiotic convention. *Psychologie Française, 58*(1), 67–88. doi:10.1016/j.psfr.2012.10.001

Bates, E., Marchman, V., Thal, D., Fenson, L., Dale, P., Reznick, J.S., . . . Hartung, J. (1994). Developmental and stylistic variation in the composition of early vocabulary. *Journal of Child Language, 21,* 85–123.

Baucal, A., Arcidiacono, F., & Budjevac, N. (2013). "Is there an equal amount of juice?" Exploring the repeated question effect in conservation through conversation. *European Journal of Psychology of Education, 28*(2), 475–495. doi:10.1007/s10212-012-0124-7

Bellis, M.A., Hughes, K., Leckenby, N., Hardcastle, K.A., Perkins, C., & Lowey, H. (2015). Measuring mortality and the burden of adult disease associated with adverse childhood experiences in England: A national survey. *Journal of Public Health (Oxford, England), 37*(3), 445–454. doi:10.1093/pubmed/fdu065

Benson, J., & Sabbagh, M. (2010). Theory of mind and executive functioning: A developmental neuropsychological approach. In P. Zelazo, M. Chandler, & E. Crone (Eds.), *Developmental social cognitive neuroscience.* New York, NY: Psychology Press.

Binet, A., & Simon, T. (1905). Méthodes nouvelles pour le diagnostic du niveau intellectuel des anormaux [New methods for diagnosing the intellectual level of the abnormal]. *L'Année Psychologique, 11,* 191–244.

Bittner, S., & Newberger, E. (1981). Pediatric understanding of child abuse and neglect. *Pediatric Review, 2,* 198.

Boivin, M., & Hertzman, C. (Eds.). (2012). *Early childhood development: Adverse experiences and developmental health.* Royal Society of Canada - Canadian Academy of Health Sciences Expert Panel (with Ronald Barr, Thomas Boyce, Alison Fleming, Harriet MacMillan, Candice Odgers, Marla Sokolowski, & Nico Trocmé). Ottawa, ON: Royal Society of Canada. Retrieved from: https://rsc-src.ca/sites/default/files/pdf/ECD%20Report_0.pdf

Brennan, F., & Ireson, J. (1997). Training phonological awareness: A study to evaluate the effects of a program of metalinguistic games in kindergarten. *Reading & Writing, 9,* 241–263.

Brown, R. (1973). *A first language: The early stages.* Cambridge, MA: Harvard University Press.

Brownell, C.A. (1990). Peer social skills in toddlers: Competencies and constraints illustrated by same-age and mixed-age interaction. *Child Development, 61,* 836–848.

Bryant, P., MacLean, M., & Bradley, L. (1990). Rhyme, language, and children's reading. *Applied Psycholinguistics, 11,* 237–252.

Burgess, S. (1997). The role of shared reading in the development of phonological awareness: A longitudinal study of middle to upper class children. *Early Child Development & Care, 127/128,* 191–199.

Bus, A., & van IJzendoorn, M. (1999). Phonological awareness and early reading: A meta-analysis of experimental training studies. *Journal of Educational Psychology, 91,* 403–414.

Callaghan, T., & Corbit, J. (2015). The development of symbolic representation. In R.M. Lerner (Ed.). *Handbook of child psychology and developmental science* (7th ed., Vol. 2 Cognitive Processes, pp. 1–46). New York, NY: Wiley.

Callaghan, T., & Rankin, M. (2002). Emergence of graphic symbol functioning and the question of domain specificity: A longitudinal training study. *Child Development, 73,* 359–376.

Callaghan, T.C., Rochat, P., & Corbit, J. (2012). Young children's knowledge of the representational function of pictorial symbols: Development across the preschool years in three cultures. *Journal of Cognition and Development, 13*(3), 320–353. doi:10.1080/15248372.2011.587853

Campbell, D.W., Eaton, W.O., & McKeen, N.A. (2002). Motor activity level and behavioural control in young children. *International Journal of Behavioral Development, 26*(4), 289–296.

Campbell, F.A., & Ramey, C.T. (1994). Effects of early intervention on intellectual and academic achievement: A follow-up study of children from low-income families. *Child Development, 65*, 684–698.

Campbell, F.A., Pungello, E.P., Burchinal, M. Kainz, K., Pan, Y., Wasik, B.H., . . . Ramey, C.T. (2012). Adult outcomes as a function of an early childhood educational program: An Abcedarian Project follow-up. *Developmental Psychology, 48*(4), 1033–1043. doi:10.1037/a0026644

Campbell, J.A., Walker, R.J., & Egede, L.E. (2016). Associations between adverse childhood experiences, high-risk behaviors, and morbidity in adulthood. *American Journal of Preventive Medicine, 50*(3), 344–352. doi.org/10.1016/j.amepre.2015.07.022

Campisi, L., Serbin, L.A., Stack, D.M., Schwartzman, A.E., & Ledingham, J.E. (2009). Precursors of language ability and academic performance: An intergenerational, longitudinal study of at-risk children. *Infant and Child Development, 18*(5), 377–403.

Capron, C., & Duyme, M. (1989). Assessment of effects of socioeconomic status on IQ in a full cross-fostering study. *Nature, 340*, 552–554.

Carey, S., & Bartlett, E. (1978). Acquiring a single new word. *Papers & Reports on Child Language Development, 15*, 17–29.

Carpendale, J.I.M., & Lewis, C. (2004). Constructing an understanding of mind: The development of children's understanding of mind within social interaction. *Behavioral and Brain Sciences, 27*(1), 79–96.

Carroll, M.D., Navaneelan, T., Bryan, S., & Ogden, C.L. (2015). *Prevalence of obesity among children and adolescents in Canada and the United States. NCHS data brief, no 211*. Hyattsville, MD: National Center for Health Statistics.

Case, R. (1985). *Intellectual development: Birth to adulthood*. New York, NY: Academic Press.

Case, R. (1992). *The mind's staircase: Exploring thought and knowledge*. Hillsdale, NJ: Erlbaum.

Centre of Excellence for Early Childhood Development. (2011). *Physical Activity in Early Childhood: Setting the stage for lifelong healthy habits* (Parenting Series April 2011). Retrieved from: http://www.excellence-arlychildhood.ca/documents/Parenting_2011-04.pdf

Cheng, L. (2009a). Thinking about thinking, how language and math intersect: Chinese v. English. Philosophy, Pop Culture Blog. Retrieved from http://larrycheng.com/2009/10/07/how-languageand-math-intersect-chinese-v-english/

Cheung, H., Chung, K., Wong, S., McBride-Chang, C., Penney, T., & Ho, C. (2010). Speech perception, metalinguistic awareness, reading, and vocabulary in Chinese-English bilingual children. *Journal of Educational Psychology, 102*(2), 367–380. doi:10.1037/a0017850

Chiappe, P., & Siegel, L. (1999). Phonological awareness and reading acquisition in English- and Punjabi-speaking Canadian children. *Journal of Educational Psychology, 91*, 20–28.

Chiappe, P., Glaeser, B., & Ferko, D. (2007). Speech perception, vocabulary, and the development of reading skills in English among Korean- and English-speaking children. *Journal of Educational Psychology, 99*, 154–166.

Christian, C., & Bloom, N. (2011). In K. Marcdante, R. Kliegman, H. Jensen, & R. Behrman (Eds.), *Nelson's essentials of pediatrics* (pp. 81–103). New York, NY: Elsevier Health Publishers.

Ciancio, D., Sadovsky, A., Malabonga, V., Trueblood, L., & Pasnak, R. (1999). Teaching classification and seriation to preschoolers. *Child Study Journal, 29*, 193–205.

Coley, R.L., Lynch, A.D., & Kull, M. (2015). Early exposure to environmental chaos and children's physical and mental health. *Early Childhood Research Quarterly, 32*(3rd quarter), 94–104. doi:10.1016/j.ecresq.2015.03.001

Connolly, K., & Dalgleish, M. (1989). The emergence of a tool-using skill in infancy. *Developmental Psychology, 25*, 894–912.

Crain, W. (2011). *Theories of development* (6th ed.). Upper Saddle River, NJ: Pearson Prentice-Hall.

Cronholm, P.F., Forke, C.M., Wade, R., Bair-Merritt, M.H., Davis, M., Harkins-Schwarz, M., . . . Fein, J.A. (2015). Adverse childhood experiences: Expanding the concept of adversity. *American Journal of Preventive Medicine, 49*(3), 354–361. doi:10.1016/j.amepre.2015.02.001

Daniels, J.K., Coupland, N.J., Hegadoren, K.M., Rowe, B.H., Densmore, M., Neufeld, R.W., & Lanius, R.A. (2012). Neural and behavioral correlates of peritraumatic dissociation in an acutely traumatized sample. *The Journal of Clinical Psychiatry, 73*(4), 420–426. doi:10.4088/JCP.10m06642

de Lacoste, M., Horvath, D., & Woodward, J. (1991). Possible sex differences in the developing human fetal brain. *Journal of Clinical and Experimental Neuropsychology, 13*, 831.

de Villiers, P.A., & de Villiers, J.G. (1992). Language development. In M.H. Bornstein & M.E. Lamb (Eds.), *Developmental psychology: An advanced textbook* (3rd ed., pp. 337–418). Hillsdale, NJ: Erlbaum.

DeLoache, J.S. (1995). Early understanding and use of symbols: The model model. *Current Directions in Psychological Science, 4*, 109–113.

Desrochers, S. (2008). From Piaget to specific Genevan developmental models. *Child Development Perspectives, 2*(1), 7–12. doi:10.1111/j.1750-8606.2008.00034.x

Diagram Group, The (1977). *Child's body*. New York, NY: Paddington.

Dubois, L., Farmer, A., Girard, M., & Peterson, K. (2008). Social factors and television use during meals and snacks is associated with higher BMI among preschool children. *Public Health Nutrition, 11*(12), 1–13. doi:10.1017/S1368980008002887

Dunn, J. (1994). Experience and understanding of emotions, relationships, and membership in a particular culture. In P. Ekman & R.J. Davidson (Eds.), *The nature of emotion: Fundamental questions* (pp. 352–355). New York, NY: Oxford University Press.

Eaton, W.O. (1994). Temperament, development, and the five factor model: Lessons from activity level. In C.F. Halverson, G.A. Kohnstamm, & R.P. Martin (Eds.), *The developing structure of temperament and personality from infancy to adulthood* (pp. 173–187). Hillsdale, NJ: Erlbaum.

Eaton, W.O., McKeen, N.A., & Campbell, D.W. (2001). The waxing and waning of movement: Implications for psychological development. *Developmental Review, 21*(2), 205–223.

Ely, R., Gleason, J.B., MacGibbon, A., & Zaretsky, E. (2001). Attention to language: Lessons learned at the dinner table. *Social Development, 10*(3), 355–373.

Evans, M.A., & Shaw, D. (2008). Home grown for reading: Parental contributions to young children's emergent literacy and word recognition. *Canadian Psychology, 49*(2), 89–95. doi:10.1037/0708-5591.49.2.89

Fagard, J., & Jacquet, A. (1989). Onset of bimanual coordination and symmetry versus asymmetry of movement. *Infant Behavior and Development, 12*, 229–235.

Fenson, L., Dale, P.S., Reznick, J.S., Bates, E., Thal, D.J., & Pethick, S.J. (1994). Variability in early communicative development. *Monographs of the Society for Research in Child Development, 59*(5, Serial No. 242).

Fitzpatrick, C., Pagani, L.S., & Barnett, T.A. (2012). Early childhood television viewing predicts explosive leg strength and waist circumference by middle childhood. *The International Journal of Behavioral Nutrition and Physical Activity, 9*(1), 87. doi:10.1186/1479-5868-9-87

Flavell, J. (1999). Cognitive development: Children's knowledge about the mind. *Annual Review of Psychology, 50*, 21–45.

Flavell, J.H. (1986). The development of children's knowledge about the appearance–reality distinction. *American Psychologist, 41*, 418–425.

Flavell, J.H. (1993). Young children's understanding of thinking and consciousness. *Current Directions in Psychological Science, 2*, 40–43.

Flavell, J.H., Everett, B.A., Croft, K., & Flavell, E.R. (1981). Young children's knowledge about visual perception: Further evidence for the Level 1–Level 2 distinction. *Developmental Psychology, 17*, 99–103.

Flavell, J.H., Green, F.L., & Flavell, E.R. (1989). Young children's ability to differentiate appearance-reality and level 2 perspectives in the tactile modality. *Child Development, 60*, 201–213.

Flavell, J.H., Green, F.L., & Flavell, E.R. (1990). Developmental changes in young children's knowledge about the mind. *Cognitive Development, 5*(1), 1–27.

Flavell, J.H., Green, F.L., Wahl, K.E., & Flavell, E.R. (1987). The effects of question clarification and memory aids on young children's performance on appearance-reality tasks. *Cognitive Development, 2*, 127–144.

Forrester, G.S., Quaresmini, C., Leavens, D.A., Mareschal, D., & Thomas, M.S. (2013). Human handedness: An inherited evolutionary trait. *Behavioural Brain Research, 237*(Jan), 200–206. doi:10.1016/j.bbr.2012.09.037

Francks, C., Maegawa, S., Lauren, J., Abrahams, B., Velayos-Baeza, A., Medland, S., . . . Monaco, A. (2007). LRRTM1 on chromosome 2p12 is a maternally suppressed gene that is associated paternally with handedness and schizophrenia. *Molecular Psychiatry, 12*, 1129–1139.

Gardner, H. (2003). Three distinct meanings of intelligence. In Sternberg, R., Lautrey, J., & Lubart, T. (Eds.), *Models of intelligence: International perspectives.* (pp. 43–54). Washington, DC: American Psychological Association.

Garner, A.S., & Shonkoff, J.P. (2012). Early childhood adversity, toxic stress, and the role of the pediatrician: Translating developmental science into lifelong health. *Pediatrics, 129*(1), e224–231. doi:10.1542/peds.2011-2662

Garner, A.S., Forkey, H., & Szilagyi, M. (2015). Translating developmental science to address childhood adversity. *Academic pediatrics, 15*(5), 493–502. doi:10.1016/j.acap.2015.05.010

Gladwell, M. (2008). *Outliers: The story of success.* New York, NY: Little, Brown and Company.

Guralnik, J.M., & Paul-Brown, D. (1984). Communicative adjustments during behavior-request episodes among children at different developmental levels. *Child Development, 55*, 911–919.

Gzesh, S.M., & Surber, C.F. (1985). Visual perspective-taking skills in children. *Child Development, 56*, 1204–1213.

Hargrave, A.C. & Sénéchal, M. (2000). Book reading interventions with language-delayed preschool children: The benefits of regular reading and dialogic reading. *Early Childhood Research Quarterly, 15*(1), 75–90.

Harris, P.L. (1989). *Children and emotion: The development of psychological understanding.* Oxford, England: Blackwell.

Hart, B., & Risley, T.R. (1995). *Meaningful differences in the everyday experience of young American children.* Baltimore, MD: Paul H. Brookes.

Harvey, A., Towner, E., Peden, M., Soori, H., & Bartolomeos, K. (2009). Injury prevention and the attainment of child and adolescent health. *Bulletin of the World Health Organization, 87*(5), 390–394. doi:10.2471/BLT.08.059808

Health Canada. (2002b). *A Report on Mental Illnesses in Canada* (Cat. No. 0-662-32817-5). Ottawa, ON: Health Canada Editorial Board Mental Illnesses in Canada. Retrieved from www.hc-sc.gc.ca/pphb-dgspsp/publicat/miic-mmac/pdf/men_ill_e.pdf

Howard, A.W. (2006). Injury in childhood: A vexingly simple problem. *Canadian Medical Association Journal, 175*(8), 899–900.

Howard, A.W. (2010). Keeping children safe: Rethinking how we design our surroundings. *Canadian Medical Association Journal, 182*(6), 573.

Hughes, K., Lowey, H., Quigg, Z., & Bellis, M.A. (2016). Relationships between adverse childhood experiences and adult mental well-being: Results from an English national household survey. *BMC Public Health, 16*(1), 222–233. doi:10.1186/s12889-016-2906-3

Jacques, S., & Zelazo, P.D. (2001). The Flexible Item Selection Task (FIST): A measure of executive function in preschoolers. *Developmental Neuropsychology, 20*(3), 573–591.

Jawahar, M.C., Murgatroyd, C., Harrison, E.L., & Baune, B.T. (2015). Epigenetic alterations following early postnatal stress: A review on novel aetiological mechanisms of common psychiatric disorders. *Clinical Epigenetics, 7*(1), 122. doi:10.1186/s13148-015-0156-3

Jimenez, M.E., Wade, R, Lin, Y., Morrow, L.M., & Reichman, N.E. (2016). Adverse experiences in early childhood and kindergarten outcomes. *Pediatrics, 137*(2), 1–9. doi:10.1542/peds.2015-1839

Jordan, N.C., Kaplan, D., Locuniak, M.N., & Ramineni, C. (2007). Predicting first-grade math achievement from developmental number sense trajectories. *Disabilities Research and Practice, 22*, 36–46.

Kail, R. (1990). *The development of memory in children* (3rd ed.). New York, NY: Freeman.

Kesselring, T., & Müller, U. (2011). The concept of egocentrism in the context of Piaget's theory. *New Ideas in Psychology, 29*(3), 327–345.

Klar, A. (2003). Human handedness and scalp hair-whorl direction develop from a common genetic mechanism. *Genetics, 165*, 269–276.

Klein, J.S., & Bisanz, J. (2000). Preschoolers doing arithmetic: The concepts are willing but the working memory is weak. *Canadian Journal of Experimental Psychology, 54*(2), 105–115.

Konold, T.R., & Canivez, G.L. (2010). Differential relationships between WISC-IV and WIAT-II scales: An evaluation of potentially moderating child demographics. *Educational and Psychological Measurement, 70*(4), 613–627. doi:10.1177/0013164409355686

Landry, S.H., Garner, P.W., Swank, P.R., & Baldwin, C.D. (1996). Effects of maternal scaffolding during joint toy play with preterm and full-term infants. *Merrill-Palmer Quarterly, 42*, 177–199.

Lanius, R.A., Williamson, P.C., Densmore, M., Boksman, K., Neufeld, R.W., Gati, J.S., & Menon, R.S. (2004). The nature of traumatic memories: A 4-T fMRI functional connectivity analysis. *American Journal of Psychiatry, 16* (1), 36–44.

Lanius, R.A., Williamson, P.C., Hopper, J., Densmore, M., Boksman, K., Gupta, M.A., . . . Menon, R.S. (2003). Recall of emotional states in posttraumatic stress disorder: An fMRI investigation. *Biological Psychiatry, 53*(3), 204–210.

Layton, L., Deeny, K., Tall, G., & Upton, G. (1996). Researching and promoting phonological awareness in the nursery class. *Journal of Research in Reading, 19*, 1–13.

LeBlanc, J.C., Pless, I.B., King, W.J., Bawden, H., Bernard-Bonnin, A., Klassen, T., . . . Tenenbein, M. (2006). Home safety measure and the risk of unintentional injury among young children: a multicenter case-control study. *Canadian Medical Association Journal, 175*(8), 883–887.

LeFevre, J., Skwarchuk, S., Smith-Chant, B. L., Fast, L., Kamawar, D., & Bisanz, J. (2009). Home numeracy experiences and children's math performance in the early school years. *Canadian Journal of Behavioural Science, 41*(2), 55–66.

Legendre, G. (2006). Early child grammars: Qualitative and quantitative analysis of morphosyntactic production. *Cognitive Science, 30*, 803–835.

Legerstee, M., & Markova, G. (2008). Variations in 10-month-old infant imitation of people and things. *Infant Behavior and Development, 31*(1), 81–91.

Levine, D. (2011). Growth and development. In K. Marcdante, R. Kliegman, H. Jensen, & R. Behrman (Eds.), *Nelson's essentials of pediatrics* (6th ed., pp. 13–44). New York, NY: Elsevier Health Publishers.

Lewis, M.D. (1993). Early socioemotional predictors of cognitive competence at 4 years. *Developmental Psychology, 29*, 1036–1045.

Lillard, A. S., & Flavell, J. H. (1992). Young children's understanding of different mental states. *Developmental Psychology, 28*, 626–634.

Lillard, A.S., Lerner, M.D., Hopkins, E.J., Dore, R.A., Smith, E.D., & Palmquist, C.M. (2013). The impact of pretend play on children's development: A review of the evidence. *Psychological Bulletin, 139*(1), 1–34. doi:10.1037/a0029321

MacWhinney, B. (2011). Language development. In M. Bornstein & M. Lamb (Eds.), *Developmental science: An advanced textbook* (6th ed., pp. 389–424). New York, NY: Psychology Press.

Maratsos, M. (2000). More overregularizations after all: New data and discussion on Marcus, Pinker, Ullman, Hollander, Rosen & Xu. *Journal of Child Language, 27*, 183–212.

Martín-García, M.J., Gómez-Becerra, I., & Garro-Espín, M.J. (2012). Teoría de la mente en un caso de autismo: ¿cómo entrenarla? [Theory of Mind in a child with autism: How to train her?] *Psicothema, 24*(4), 542–547.

Mathew, A., & Cook, M. (1990). The control of reaching movements by young infants. *Child Development, 61*, 1238–1257.

McBride-Chang, C., & Ho, C. (2000). Developmental issues in Chinese children's character acquisition. *Journal of Educational Psychology, 92*, 50–55.

McCall, R.B. (1993). Developmental functions for general mental performance. In D.K. Detterman (Ed.), *Current topics in human intelligence: Vol. 3. Individual differences and cognition* (pp. 3–30). Norwood, NJ: Ablex.

McGregor, K., Sheng, L., & Smith, B. (2005). The precocious two-year-old: Status of the lexicon and links to the grammar. *Journal of Child Language, 32*, 563–585.

Melby-Lervåg, M., Lyster, S.A., & Hulme, C. (2012). Phonological skills and their role in learning to read: A meta-analytic review. *Psychological Bulletin, 138*(2), 322–352. doi:10.1037/a0026744

Melot, A., & Houde, O. (1998). Categorization and theories of mind: The case of the appearance/reality distinction. *Cahiers de Psychologie Cognitive/Current Psychology of Cognition, 17*, 71–93.

Mills, D.L., Coffey-Corina, S.A., & Neville, H. (1994). Variability in cerebral organization during primary language acquisition. In G. Dawson & K. Fischer (Eds.), *Human behavior and the developing brain.* New York, NY: Guilford Press.

Montero, I., & De Dios, M. (2006). Vygotsky was right: An experimental approach to the relationship between private speech and task performance. *Estudios de Psicologíia, 27*, 175–189.

Mooney, L., Knox, D., & Schacht, C. (2010). *Understanding social problems* (7th ed.). Thousand Oaks, CA: Wadsworth.

Moore, C., Barresi, J., & Thompson, C. (1998). The cognitive basis of future-oriented prosocial behavior. *Social Development, 7*, 198–218.

Morrongiello, B., Corbett, M., & Bellissimo, A. (2008). "Do as I say, not as I do': Family influences on children's safety and risk behaviors. *Health Psychology, 27*(4), 498–503.

Morrongiello, B.A., & Dawber, T. (1999). Parental influences on toddlers' injury-risk behaviors: Are sons and daughters socialized differently? *Journal of Applied Developmental Psychology, 20*, 227–251.

Morrongiello, B.A., & House, K. (2004). Measuring parent attributes and supervision behaviors relevant to child injury risk: Examining the usefulness of questionnaire measures. *Injury Prevention, 10*(2), 114–119.

Morrongiello, B.A., & Kiriakou, S. (2004). Mothers' home-safety practices for preventing six types of childhood injuries: What do they do, and why? *Journal of Pediatric Psychology, 29*(4), 285–297.

Morrongiello, B.A., & Rennie, H. (1998). Why do boys engage in more risk taking than girls? The role of attributions, beliefs, and risk appraisal. *Journal of Pediatric Psychology, 23*, 33–44.

Morrongiello, B.A., Fenwick, K.D., & Chance, G. (1990). Sound localization acuity in very young infants: An observer-based testing procedure. *Developmental Psychology, 24*, 75–84.

Morrongiello, B.A., Kane, A., & Bell, M. (2011). Advancing our understanding of mothers' safety rules for school-age children. *Canadian Journal of Public Health, 102*(6), 455–458.

Morrongiello, B.A., Kane, A., & Zdzieborski, D. (2011). "I think he is in his room playing a video game": Parental supervision of young elementary-school children at home. *Journal of Pediatric psychology, 36*(6), 708–717. doi:10.1093/jpepsy/jsq065

Morrongiello, B.A., Midgett, C., & Shields, R. (2001). Don't run with scissors: Young children's knowledge of home safety rules. *Journal of Pediatric Psychology, 26*, 105–115.

Morrongiello, B.A., Sandomierski, M., Zdzieborski, D., & McCollam, H. (2012). A randomized controlled trial evaluating the impact of the supervising for home safety program on parent appraisals of injury risk and need to actively supervise. *Health Psychology, 31*(5), 601–611. doi:10.1037/a0028214

Morrongiello, B.A., Schwebel, D.C., Bell, M., Stewart, J., & Davis, A.L. (2012). An evaluation of the great escape: Can an interactive computer game improve young children's fire safety knowledge and behaviors? *Health Psychology, 31*(4), 496–502. doi: org/10.1037/a0027779

Morrongiello, B.A., Walpole, B., & McArthur, B.A. (2009). Young children's risk of unintentional injury: A comparison of mothers' and fathers' supervision beliefs and reported practices. *Journal of Pediatric Psychology, 34*(10), 1063–1068. doi:10.1093/jpepsy/jsp011

Morrongiello, B.A., Zdzieborski, D., Sandomierski, M., & Munroe, K. (2013). Results of a randomized controlled trial assessing the efficacy of the supervising for home safety program: Impact on mothers' supervision practices. *Accident Analysis and Prevention, 50*, 587–595. doi:10.1016/j.aap.2012.06.007

NCS Pearson, Inc. (2015). *WISC-V CDN interpretive considerations for sample child #2 (08/27/2015).* Retrieved from http://www.pearsonassess.ca/content/dam/ani/clinicalassessments/ca/programs/pdfs/WISC-V-CDN-QG-Interpretive-Report-Gifted.pdf

Neitzel, C., & Stright, A. (2003). Mothers' scaffolding of children's problem solving: Establishing a foundation of academic self-regulatory competence. *Journal of Family Psychology, 17*, 147–159.

Nilsson, K.K., & de López, K.J. (2016). Theory of mind in children with specific language impairment: A systematic review and meta-analysis. *Child Development, 87*(1), 143–53. doi:10.1111/cdev.12462

Norboru, T. (1997). A developmental study of wordplay in pre-school children: The Japanese game of "Shiritori." *Japanese Journal of Developmental Psychology, 8*, 42–52.

O'Neill, D.K., Astington, J.W., & Flavell, J.H. (1992). Young children's understanding of the role that sensory experiences play in knowledge acquisition. *Child Development, 63*, 474–490.

Osana, H. P., & Rayner, V. (2010). Developing numeracy: Promoting a rich learning environment for young children. In *Encyclopedia of Language and Literacy Development* (pp. 1–12). London, ON: Canadian Language and Literacy Research Network. Retrieved from www.literacyencyclopedia.ca/pdfs/topic.php?topId=286

Ouellette, G., & Sénéchal, M. (2008). Pathways to literacy: A study of invented spelling and its role in learning to read. *Child Development, 79*, 899–913.

Perry, B.D. (2002). *Stress, trauma and post-traumatic stress disorders in children: An introduction.* Houston, TX: ChildTrauma Academy. Retrieved from Child Trauma Academy website: www.childtrauma.org/CTAMATERIALS/PTSDfn_03_v2.pdf

Perry, B.D. (2009). Examining child maltreatment through a neurodevelopmental lens: Clinical application of the neurosequential model of therapeutics. *Journal of Loss and Trauma, 14*(4), 240–255. doi:10.1080/15325020903004350

Perry, B.D., & Pollard, R. (1998). Homeostasis, stress, trauma, and adaptation. A neurodevelopmental view of childhood trauma. *Child and Adolescent Psychiatric Clinics of North America, 7*(1), 33–51.

Petrill, S., Hart, S., Harlaar, N., Logan, J., Justice, L., Schatschneider, C., . . . Cutting, L. (2010). Genetic and environmental influences on the growth of early reading skills. *Journal of Child Psychology and Psychiatry, 51*, 660–667.

Piaget, J. (1954). *The construction of reality in the child.* New York, NY: Basic Books. (Originally published 1937.)

Pianta, R.C., & Egeland, B. (1994). Predictors of instability in children's mental test performance at 24, 48, and 96 months. *Intelligence, 18*, 145–163.

Pillow, B. (1999). Children's understanding of inferential knowledge. *Journal of Genetic Psychology, 160*, 419–428.

Pinker, S. (1994). *The language instinct: How the mind creates language.* New York, NY: Morrow.

Prichard, E., Propper, R.E., & Christman, S.D. (2013). Degree of handedness, but not direction, is a systematic predictor of cognitive performance. *Frontiers in Psychology, 4*(Jan), 9. doi:10.3389/fpsyg.2013.00009

Public Health Agency of Canada. (2010a). *Canadian incidence study of reported child abuse and neglect – 2008: Major findings.* Retrieved from: http://www.phac-aspc.gc.ca/ncfv-cnivf/pdfs/nfntscis-2008-rprt-eng.pdf

Public Health Agency of Canada. (2016a). *Leading causes of death and hospitalization in Canada.* Ottawa, ON: Author. Retrieved from http://www.phac-aspc.gc.ca/publicat/lcd-pcd97/table1-eng.php#tbl1fn2

Pujadas Botey, A., Bayrampour, H., Carson, V., Vinturache, A., & Tough, S. (2016). Adherence to Canadian physical activity and sedentary behaviour guidelines among children 2 to 13 years of age. *Preventive Medicine Reports, 3*(June), 14–20. doi:10.1016/j.pmedr.2015.11.012

Pungello, E., Kainz, K., Burchinal, M., Wasik, B., Sparling, J., Ramey, C., & Campbell, F. (2010). Early educational intervention, early cumulative risk, and the early home environment as predictors of young adult outcomes within a high-risk sample. *Child Development, 81*(1), 410–426. doi:10.1111/j.1467-8624.2009.01403.x

Ramey, C., & Ramey, S. (1998). Early intervention and early experience. *American Psychologist, 53*, 109–120.

Ramey, C.T. (1992). High-risk children and IQ: Altering intergenerational patterns. *Intelligence, 16*, 239–256.

Ramey, C.T. (1993). A rejoinder to Spitz's critique of the Abecedarian experiment. *Intelligence, 17*, 25–30.

Ramey, C.T. (1993). A rejoinder to Spitz's critique of the Abecedarian experiment. *Intelligence, 17*, 25–30.

Ramey, C.T., & Campbell, F.A. (1987). The Carolina Abecedarian Project: An educational experiment concerning human malleability. In J.J. Gallagher & C.T. Ramey (Eds.), *The malleability of children* (pp. 127–140). Baltimore, MD: Paul H. Brookes.

Ramsay, M. (2013). Feeding skill, appetite and feeding behaviours of infants and young children and their impact on growth and psychosocial development. *Encyclopedia on Early Childhood Development.* Montreal, QC: Centre of Excellence for Early Childhood Development. Retrieved from http://www.child-encyclopedia.com/child-nutrition/according-experts/feeding-skill-appetite-and-feeding-behaviours-infants-and-young

Rizzi, T.S., & Posthuma, D. (2013). Genes and intelligence. In D. Reisberg (Ed.), *The Oxford handbook of cognitive psychology* (pp. 823–841). New York, NY: Oxford University Press.

Robinson, N., Lanzi, R., Weinberg, R., Ramey, S., & Ramey, C. (2002). Family factors associated with high academic competence in former Head Start children at third grade. *Gifted Child Quarterly, 46*, 278–290.

Rolls, E. (2000). Memory systems in the brain. *Annual Review of Psychology, 51*, 599–630.

Saltaris, C., Serbin, L.A., Stack, D.M., Karp, J.A., Schwartzman, A.E., & Ledingham, J.E. (2004). Nurturing cognitive competence in preschoolers: A longitudinal study of intergenerational continuity and risk. *International Journal of Behavioral Development, 28*(20), 105–115.

Saluja, G., Brenner, R., Morrongiello, B.A., Haynie, D., Rivera, M., Cheng, T.L. (2004). The role of supervision in child injury risk: Definition, conceptual and measurement issues. *Injury Control & Safety Promotion, 11*(1), 17–23.

Schneider, W. (2010). Metacognition and memory development in childhood and adolescence. In H. Waters & W. Schneider (Eds.), *Metacognition, strategy use, and instruction* (pp. 54–81). New York, NY: Guilford Press.

Schweinhart, L.J. (2003, April). *Benefits, costs, and explanation of the High/Scope Perry Preschool Program.* Paper presented at the Meeting of the Society for Research in Child Development, Tampa, FL. Retrieved from www.highscope.org/Research/Perry-Project/Perry-SRCD-2003.pdf

Sénéchal, M. (1997). The differential effect of storybook reading on preschooler's expressive and receptive vocabulary acquisition. *Journal of Child Language, 24*, 123–138.

Sénéchal, M., & Cornell, E.H. (1993). Vocabulary acquisition through shared reading experiences. *Reading Research Quarterly, 28*, 360–374.

Sénéchal, M., & LeFevre, J. (1998). *Long-term consequences of early home literacy experiences.* Paper presented at the annual meeting of the Canadian Psychological Conference, Edmonton, AB.

Sénéchal, M., & LeFevre, J. (2002). Parental involvement in the development of children's reading skill: A 5-year longitudinal study. *Child Development, 73*(2), 445–460.

Sénéchal, M., & Young, L. (2008). The effect of family literacy interventions on children's acquisition of reading from kindergarten to grade 3: A meta-analytic review. *Review of Educational Research, 78*, 880–890.

Sénéchal, M., Cornell, E.H., & Broda, L.S. (1995). Age-related differences in the organization of parent–infant interactions during picture-book reading. *Early Childhood Research Quarterly, 10*, 317–337.

Sénéchal, M., LeFevre, J., Thomas, E., & Daley, K. (1998). Differential effects of home literacy experiences on the development of oral and written language. *Reading Research Quarterly, 32*, 96–116.

Sénéchal, M., Thomas, E., & Monker, J. (1995). Individual differences in 4-year-old children's acquisition of vocabulary during storybook reading. *Journal of Educational Psychology, 87*, 218–229.

Serpell, R., & Hatano, G. (1997). Education, schooling, and literacy. In J. Berry, P. Dasen, & T. Saraswathi (Eds.), *Handbook of cross-cultural psychology: Vol. 2. Basic processes and human development.* Needham Heights, MA: Allyn & Bacon.

Shonkoff, J.P., & Garner, A.S. (2012). The lifelong effects of early childhood adversity and toxic stress. *Pediatrics, 129*(1), e23–246. doi:10.1542/peds.2011-2663

Sigman, M., Neumann, C., Carter, E., Cattle, D.J., D'Souza, S., & Bwibo, N. (1988). Home interactions and the development of Embu toddlers in Kenya. *Child Development, 59*, 1251–1261.

Song, H.J., & Baillargeon, R. (2008). Infants' reasoning about others' false perceptions. *Developmental Psychology, 44*(6), 1789–1795.

Stack, D.M., Serbin, L.A, Mantis, I., & Kingdon, D. (2015). Breaking the cycle of adversity in vulnerable children and families: A thirty-five year study of at-risk lower income families. *International Journal for Family Research and Policy, 1*(1), 31–56. doi:10.1177/0165025416631836

Statistics Canada. (1994). *1993 General Social Survey-Cycle 8 Personal Risk* (Public Microdata File Documentation and User's Guide). Ottawa: Statistics Canada.

Statistics Canada. (1995). *National Population Health Survey Overview 1994-95* (Catalogue no. 82-567). Ottawa, ON: Minister of Industry.

Statistics Canada. (2008b). *Numeracy.* Ottawa, ON: Minister of Industry. Retrieved from www.statcan.gc.ca/pub/81-004-x/def/4068737-eng.htm

Steele, J., & Mayes, S. (1995). Handedness and directional asymmetry in the long bones of the human upper limb. *International Journal of Osteoarchaeology, 5*, 39–49.

Stiles, J., & Jernigan, T.L. (2010). The basics of brain development. *Neuropsychology Review, 20*(4), 327–348. doi:10.1007/s11065-010-9148-4

Stroganova, T., Posikera, I., Pushina, N., & Orekhova, E. (2003). Lateralization of motor functions in early human ontogeny. *Human Physiology, 29*, 48–58.

Suderman, M., Borghol, N., Pappas, J.J., Pinto Pereira, S.M., Pembrey, M., Hertzman, C., . . . Szyf, M. (2014). Childhood abuse is associated with methylation of multiple loci in adult DNA. *BMC Medical Genomics, 7*(Mar), 13. doi:10.1186/1755-8794-7-13

Sullivan, K., Zaitchik, D., & Tager-Flusberg, H. (1994). Preschoolers can attribute second-order beliefs. *Developmental Psychology, 30*, 395–402.

Tanner, J.M. (1990). *Foetus into man: Physical growth from conception to maturity* (2nd ed.). Cambridge, MA: Harvard University Press.

Tan-Niam, C., Wood, D., & O'Malley, C. (1998). A cross-cultural perspective on children's theories of mind and social interaction. *Early Child Development & Care, 144*, 55–67.

Tardif, T., So, C., & Kaciroti, N. (2007). Language and false belief: Evidence for general, not specific, effects in Cantonese-speaking preschoolers. *Developmental Psychology, 43*, 318–340.

Taylor, M., Cartwright, B.S., & Carlson, S.M. (1993). A developmental investigation of children's imaginary companions. *Developmental Psychology, 29*, 276–285.

Teicher, M.H. (2002). Scars that won't heal: The neurobiology of child abuse. *Scientific American, 286*(3), 68–75.

Teicher, M.H. (2010). Commentary: Childhood abuse: new insights into its association with posttraumatic stress, suicidal ideation, and aggression. *Journal of Pediatric Psychology, 35*(5), 578–580. doi:10.1093/jpepsy/jsq018

Teicher, M.H., & Samson, J.A. (2016). Annual research review: Enduring neurobiological effects of childhood abuse and neglect. *Journal of Child Psychology and Psychiatry, 57*(3), 241–266. doi:10.1111/jcpp.12507

Terman, L. (1916). *The measurement of intelligence.* Boston, MA: Houghton Mifflin.

Terman, L., & Merrill, M.A. (1937). *Measuring intelligence: A guide to the administration of the new revised Stanford-Binet tests*. Boston, MA: Houghton Mifflin.

Thomas, E.M. (2006). *Readiness to learn at school among five-year-old children in Canada*. (89-599-MIE-no. 004). Ottawa, ON: Special Surveys Division, Statistics Canada.

Thomas, M. (2005). *Comparing theories of child development* (6th ed.). Pacific Grove, CA: Wadsworth/Cengage.

Thomas, R.M. (Ed.). (1990). *The encyclopedia of human development and education: Theory, research, and studies*. Oxford, England: Pergamon Press.

Toomela, A. (1999). Drawing development: Stages in the representation of a cube and a cylinder. *Child Development, 70*, 1141–1150.

Vaiserman, A. (2015a). Epidemiologic evidence for association between adverse environmental exposures in early life and epigenetic variation: A potential link to disease susceptibility? *Clinical Epigenetics, 7*(1), 96. doi:10.1186/s13148-015-0130-0

Vaiserman, A.M. (2015b), Epigenetic programming by early-life stress: Evidence from human populations. *Developmental Dynamics, 244*(3), 254–265. doi:10.1002/dvdy.24211

Villegas, J., Castellanos, E., & Gutiérrez, J. (2009). Representations in problem solving: A case study with optimization problems. *Electronic Journal of Research in Educational Psychology, 17*, 279–308.

Wade, R., Cronholm, P.F., Fein, J.A., Forke, C.M., Davis, M.B., Harkins-Schwarz, M., . . . Bair-Merritt, M.H. (2016). Household and community-level adverse childhood experiences and adult health outcomes in a diverse urban population. *Child Abuse & Neglect, 52*(Feb), 135–145. doi:10.1016/j.chiabu.2015.11.021

Walker-Andrews, A., & Kahana-Kalman, R. (1999). The understanding of pretence across the second year of life. *British Journal of Developmental Psychology, 17*, 523–536.

Watson, A., Nixon, C., Wilson, A., & Capage, L. (1999). Social interaction skills and theory of mind in young children. *Developmental Psychology, 35*, 386–391.

Wechsler, D. (2002). *The Wechsler preschool and primary scale of intelligence* (3rd ed.). San Antonio, TX: The Psychological Corporation.

Wechsler, D. (2014). *Wechsler Intelligence Scale for Children-Fifth Edition: Canadian* (WISC-V CDN). Toronto, ON: NCS Pearson, Inc.

Weinberg, R.A. (1989). Intelligence and IQ: Landmark issues and great debates. *American Psychologist, 44*, 98–104.

Wong, D. (1993). *Whaley & Wong's essentials of pediatric nursing*. St. Louis, MO: Mosby-Yearbook, Inc.

Wood, C., & Terrell, C. (1998). Pre-school phonological awareness and subsequent literacy development. *Educational Psychology, 18*, 253–274.

Yanchar, N.L., Warda, L.J., & Fuselli, P. (2012). Child and youth injury prevention: A public health approach. *Paediatrics & Child Health, 17*(9), 511–512.

Zigler, E., & Styfco, S.J. (1993). Using research and theory to justify and inform Head Start expansion. *Social Policy Report, Society for Research in Child Development, VII*(2), 1–21.

Zola, S., & Squire, L. (2003). Genetics of childhood disorders: Learning and memory: Multiple memory systems. *Journal of the American Academy of Child and Adolescent Psychiatry, 42*, 504–506.

Chapter 8

Afifi, T.O., Mota, N.P., Dasiewicz, P., MacMillan, H.L., & Sareen, J. (2012). Physical punishment and mental disorders: Results from a nationally representative US sample. *Pediatrics, 130*(2), 184–192. doi:10.1542/peds.2011-2947

Aknin, L.B., Hamlin, J.K., & Dunn, E.W. (2012). Giving leads to happiness in young children. *PLoS One, 7*(6), e39211. doi:10.1371/journal.pone.0039211

Amato, P.R. (1993). Children's adjustment to divorce: Theories, hypotheses, and empirical support. *Journal of Marriage and the Family, 55*, 23–38.

Ambert, A. (2009). *Divorce: Facts, causes & consequences*. Retrieved from www.vanierinstitute.ca/include/get.php?nodeid=190

Bailey, S., & Zvonkovic, A. (2003). Parenting after divorce: Nonresidential parents' perceptions of social and institutional support. *Journal of Divorce & Remarriage, 39*, 59–80.

Baillargeon, R., Tremblay, R., & Willms, J.D. (2002). Physical aggression among toddlers: Does it run in families? In J. D. Willms (Ed.), *Vulnerable Children: Findings from Canada's National Longitudinal Survey of Children and Youth* (pp. 71–102). Edmonton, AB: The University of Alberta Press.

Baillargeon, R.H., Morisset, A., Keenan, K., Normand, C.L., Jeyaganth, S., Boivin, M., & Tremblay, R.E. (2011). The development of prosocial behaviors in young children: A prospective population-based cohort study. *The Journal of Genetic Psychology, 172*(3), 221–251. doi:10.1080/00221325.2010.533719

Baillargeon, R.H., Zoccolillo, M., Keenan, K., Côté, S., Pérusse, D., Wu, H.X., . . . Tremblay, R.E. (2007). Gender differences in the prevalence of physical aggression: A prospective population-based survey of children before and after two years of age. *Developmental Psychology, 43*, 13–26.

Bandura, A. & Bussey, K. (2004). On broadening the cognitive, motivational, and sociocultural scope of theorizing about gender development and functioning: Comment on Martin, Ruble, and Szkrybalo (2002). *Psychological Bulletin, 130*, 691–701.

Bandura, A. (1977a). *Social learning theory*. Englewood Cliffs, NJ: Prentice-Hall.

Bandura, A., Ross, D., & Ross, S.A. (1961). Transmission of aggression through imitation of aggressive models. *Journal of Abnormal and Social Psychology, 63*, 575–582.

Bandura, A., Ross, D., & Ross, S.A. (1963). Imitation of film-mediated aggressive models. *Journal of Abnormal and Social Psychology, 66*, 3–11.

Banse, R., Gawronski, B., Rebetez, C., Gutt, H., & Morton, J.B. (2010). The development of spontaneous gender stereotyping in childhood: Relations to stereotype knowledge and stereotype flexibility. *Developmental Science, 13*(2), 298–306.

Barber, B.K., & Xia, M. (2013). The centrality of control to parenting and its effects. In R.E. Larzelere, A.S. Morris, & A.W. Harrist (Eds.), *Authoritative parenting: Synthesizing nurturance and discipline for optimal child development* (pp. 61–87). Washington, DC: American Psychological Association.

Baumrind, D. (1967). Child care practices anteceding three patterns of preschool behavior. *Genetic Psychology Monographs, 75*, 43–88.

Baumrind, D. (1971). Current patterns of parental authority. *Developmental Psychology Monograph, 4*(1, Part 2).

Baumrind, D. (1972). Socialization and instrumental competence in young children. In W.W. Hartup (Ed.), *The young child: Reviews of research* (Vol. 2, pp. 202–224). Washington, DC: National Association for the Education of Young Children.

Baumrind, D. (2003, March). *When are causal inferences justified in the debate about physical discipline "effects"?* Paper presented at the Institute of Human Development University of California, Berkeley, CA.

Baumrind, D. (2013). Authoritative parenting revisited: History and current status. In R.E. Larzelere, A.S. Morris, & A.W. Harrist (Eds.), *Authoritative parenting: Synthesizing nurturance and discipline for optimal child development* (pp. 11–34). Washington, DC: American Psychological Association.

Bell, L.G., & Bell, D.C. (1982). Family climate and the role of the female adolescent: Determinants of adolescent functioning. *Family Relations, 31*, 519–527.

Blakemore, J., LaRue, A., & Olejnik, A. (1979). Sex-appropriate toy preference and the ability to conceptualize toys as sex-role related. *Developmental Psychology, 15*, 339–340.

Blakemore, J.E.O. (2003). Children's beliefs about violating gender norms: Boys shouldn't look like girls and girls shouldn't act like boys. *Sex Roles, 48*(9/10), 411–415.

Bohnert, N., Milan, A., & Lathe, H. (2014). Enduring diversity: Living arrangements of children in Canada over 100 years of the census. *Insights on Canadian Society* (Catalogue no. 91F0015M—No. 11). Ottawa, ON: Statistics Canada. Retrieved from http://www.statcan.gc.ca/pub/75-006-x/2014001/article/11919-eng.pdf

Bos, H.M.W, van Balen, F., & van den Boom, D.C. (2007). Child adjustment and parenting in planned lesbian-parent families. *American Journal of Orthopsychiatry, 7*(1), 38–48. doi:10.1037/0002-9432.77.1.38

Bosacki, S. (2001a). "Theory of Mind" or "Theory of the Soul"? The role of spirituality in children's understanding of minds and emotions. In J. Erricker, C. Ota, & C. Erricker (Eds.), *Spiritual Education: Cultural, Religious and Social Differences* (pp. 156–169). Portland, OR: Sussex Academic Press.

Bosacki, S., & Moore, C. (2004). Preschoolers' understanding of simple and complex emotions: Links with gender and language. *Sex Roles, 50*(9–10), 659–675.

Bowden, V., & Greenberg, C. (2010). *Children and their families: The continuum of care* (2nd ed.). New York, NY: Lippincott, Williams, & Wilkins.

Bowlby, J. (1969). *Attachment and loss: Vol. 1. Attachment.* New York, NY: Basic Books.

Brophy-Herb, H.E., Zajicek-Farber, M.L., Bocknek, E.L., McKelvey, L.M., & Stansbury, K. (2013). Longitudinal connections of maternal supportiveness and early emotion regulation to children's school readiness in low-income families. *Journal of the Society for Social Work and Research, 4*(1), 2–19. doi:10.5243/jsswr.2013.1

Brosseau-Liard, P., Penney, D., & Poulin-Dubois, D. (2015). Theory of mind selectively predicts preschoolers' knowledge-based selective word learning. *British Journal of Developmental Psychology, 33*(4), 464–75. doi:10.1111/bjdp.12107

Brotman, L.M., O'Neal, C.R., Huang, K-Y., Gouley, K.K., Rosenfelt, A., & Shrout, P.E. (2009). An experimental test of parenting practices as mediator of early childhood physical aggression. *Journal of Child Psychology and Psychiatry, 50* (3), 235–245.

Burton, P., Phipps, S., & Curtis, L. (2005). All in the family: A simultaneous model of parenting style and child conduct (11F0019MIE). Ottawa, ON: Statistics Canada. Retrieved from www.statcan.gc.ca/pub/11f0019m/11f0019m2005261-eng.pdf

Calkins, S.D., & Mackler, J.S. (2011). Temperament, emotion regulation, and social development. In M. Underwood, & L. Rosen (Eds.), *Social development: Relationships in infancy, childhood, and adolescence* (pp. 44–70). New York, NY: Guilford Press.

Camilleri, C., & Malewska-Peyre, H. (1997). Socialization and identity strategies. In J. Berry, P. Dasen, & T. Saraswathi (Eds.), *Handbook of cross-cultural psychology, Vol. 2: Basic processes and human development.* Boston, MA: Allyn & Bacon.

Campaign 2000 (2011). *2011 report card on child and family poverty in Canada.* Retrieved from http://www.campaign2000.ca/report-Cards/national/2011EnglishRreportCard.pdf

Campaign 2000. (2015). *2015 report card on child and family poverty in Canada.* Retrieved from http://www.campaign2000.ca/reportCards/2015RepCards/NationalReportCardEn2015.pdf

Campbell, A., Shirley, L., & Candy, J. (2004). A longitudinal study of gender-related cognition and behaviour. *Developmental Science, 7,* 1–9.

Canadian Council on Social Development. (2001). *Highlights: The progress of Canada's children 2001.* Ottawa, ON: Author. Retrieved from www.ccsd.ca/pubs/2001/pcc2001/hl.htm

Canadian Council on Social Development. (2010). *Hard truths: Canada's social deficit.* Retrieved from http://www.ccsd.ca/Hard_Truths_ENG.pdf

Canadian Psychological Association. (2004). Policy statement on *physical punishment of children and youth.* Ottawa, ON: Author. Retrieved from www.cpa.ca/documents/policy.html

Care, E., Deans, J., & Brown, R. (2007). The realism and sex type of four to five-year-old children's occupational aspirations. *Early Childhood Research, 5*(2), 155–68.

Carson, D., Klee, T. & Perry, C. (1998). Comparisons of children with delayed and normal language at 24 months of age on measures of behavioral difficulties, social and cognitive development. *Infant Mental Health Journal, 19,* 59–75.

Cartwright, C. (2006). You want to know how it affected me? Young adults' perceptions of the impact of parental divorce. *Journal of Divorce & Remarriage, 44,* 125–143.

Case, R. (1991). Stages in the development of the young child's first sense of self. *Developmental Review, 11,* 210–230.

CBC News. (2012, Sept 19). *More Sask. grandparents taking care of kids: Census.* Retrieved from http://www.cbc.ca/news/canada/saskatchewan/story/2012/09/19/sk-grandparents-1209.html

Chao, R.K., & Aque, C. (2009). Interpretations of parental control by Asian immigrant and European American youth. *Journal of Family Psychology, 23*(3), 342–354. doi:10.1037/a0015828

Chao, R.K., & Willms, J.D. (1998). *Do parenting practices make a difference?* (Cat. No. W-98-32Es). Retrieved from Human Resources Development Canada website: www.hrdc-drhc.gc.ca/stratpol/arb/conferences/nlscyconf/chao-e.shtml

Chao, R.K., & Willms, J.D. (2002). The effects of parenting practices on children's outcomes. In J.D. Willms (Ed.), *Vulnerable children* (pp. 71–102). Edmonton, AB: The University of Alberta Press.

Chase-Lansdale, P.L., Cherlin, A.J., & Kiernan, K.E. (1995). The long-term effects of parental divorce on the mental health of young adults: A developmental perspective. *Child Development, 66,* 1614–1634.

Cheah, C.S.L., & Rubin, K.H. (2004). European American and mainland Chinese mothers' responses to aggression and social withdrawal in preschoolers. *International Journal of Behavioral Development, 28*(1), 83–94. doi:10.1080/01650250344000299

Cherlin, A., Chase-Lansdale, P., & McRae, C. (1998). Effects of parental divorce on mental health throughout the life course. *American Sociological Review, 63,* 239–249.

Children's Hospital of Eastern Ontario. (2013). *Joint Statement on Physical Punishment of Children and Youth.* Ottawa, ON: Author. Retrieved from www.cheo.on.ca/en/physicalpunishment

Choe, D.E., Olson, S.L., & Sameroff, A.J. (2013). The interplay of externalizing problems and physical and inductive discipline during childhood. *Developmental Psychology, 49*(11), 2029–2039. doi:10.1037/a0032054

Choi, Y., Kim, Y.S., Kim, S.Y., & Park, I.K. (2013). Is Asian American parenting controlling and harsh? Empirical testing of relationships between Korean American and Western parenting measures. *Asian American Journal of Psychology, 4*(1), 19–29. doi.org/10.1037/a0031220

Chuang, S.S., & Su, Y. (2009). Do we see eye to eye? Chinese mothers' and fathers' parenting beliefs and values for toddlers in Canada and China. *Journal of Family Psychology, 23*(3), 331–341. doi:10.1037/a0016015

Claes, M., Perchec, C., Miranda, D., Benoit, A., Bariaud, F., Lanz, M., Marta, E., & Lacourse, E. (2011). Adolescents' perceptions of parental practices: A cross-national comparison of Canada, France, and Italy. *Journal of Adolescence, 34*(2), 225–38. doi:10.1016/j.adolescence.2010.05.009

Clark, B., & Canadian Paediatric Society. (2016). *Supporting the mental health of children and youth of separating parents.* Retrieved from http://www.cps.ca/documents/position/mental-health-children-and-youth-of-separating-parents

Clearfield, M.W., & Nelson, N.M. (2006). Sex differences in mothers' speech and play behavior with 6-, 9-, and 14-month-old infants. *Sex Roles, 54,*(1/2) doi:10.1007/s11199-005-8874-1

Coley, R., & Chase-Lansdale, L. (1998). Adolescent pregnancy and parenthood: Recent evidence and future directions. *American Psychologist, 53,* 152–166.

Comley, L., & Mousmanis, P. (2004). *Improving the odds: Healthy child development.* Toronto, ON: Ontario College of Physicians. Retrieved from Best Start website: www.beststart.org/resources/hlthy_chld_dev/pdf/HCD_complete.pdf

Coplan, R.J., & Armer, M. (2005). 'Talking yourself out of being shy': Shyness, expressive vocabulary, and adjustment in preschool. *Merrill-Palmer Quarterly. 51*(1), 20–41.

Coplan, R.J., & Prakash, K. (2003). Spending time with teacher: Characteristics of preschoolers who frequently elicit versus initiate interactions with teachers. *Early Childhood Research Quarterly, 18* (1), 143–158.

Coplan, R.J., Prakash, K., O'Neil, K., & Armer, M. (2004). Do you 'want' to play? Distinguishing between conflicted-shyness and social disinterest in early childhood. *Developmental Psychology, 40*(2), 244–258.

Corsaro, W., Molinari, L., Hadley, K., & Sugioka, H. (2003). Keeping and making friends: Italian children's transition from preschool to elementary school. *Social Psychology Quarterly, 66,* 272–292.

Côté, S.M., Vaillancourt, T., Barker, E.D., Nagin, D., & Tremblay, R.E. (2007). The joint development of physical and indirect aggression: Predictors of continuity and change during childhood. *Development and Psychopathology, 19*(1), 37–55.

Côté, S.M., Vaillancourt, T., LeBlanc, J.C., Nagin, D.S., & Tremblay, R.E. (2006). The development of physical aggression from toddlerhood to pre-adolescence: A nationwide longitudinal study of Canadian children. *Journal of Abnormal Child Psychology, 34*(1), 71–85.

Crittenden, P.M. (1992). Quality of attachment in the preschool years. *Development and Psychopathology, 4,* 209–241.

Daly, S., & Glenwick, D. (2000). Personal adjustment and perceptions of grandchild behavior in custodial grandmothers. *Journal of Clinical Child Psychology, 29,* 108–118.

Damon, W. (1977). *The social world of the child.* San Francisco, CA: Jossey-Bass.

Danby, S., & Baker, C. (1998). How to be masculine in the block area. *Childhood: A Global Journal of Child Research, 5,* 151–175.

DeMulder, E., Denham, S., Schmidt, M., & Mitchell, J. (2000). Q-sort assessment of attachment security during the preschool years: Links from home to school. *Developmental Psycholgy, 36,* 274–282.

Denham, S., Blair, K., DeMulder, E., Levitas, J., Sawyer, K., & Queenan, P. (2003). Preschool emotional competence: Pathway to social competence. *Child Development, 74,* 238–256.

Department of Justice Canada. (2004). *Fact sheet—Section 43 of the Criminal Code (Corporal Punishment): The Canadian Foundation for Children, Youth and the Law v. The Attorney General of Canada.* Ottawa, ON: Author. Retrieved from http://canada.justice.gc.ca/en/news/fs/2004/doc_31114.html

Diener, M., & Kim, D. (2004). Maternal and child predictors of preschool children's social competence. *Journal of Applied Developmental Psychology, 25,* 3–24.

Doctoroff, S. (1997). Sociodramatic script training and peer role prompting: Two tactics to promote sociodramatic play and peer interaction. *Early Child Development & Care, 136,* 27–43.

Dodge, K.A., Pettit, G.S., & Bates, J.E. (1994). Socialization mediators of the relation between socioeconomic status and child conduct problems. *Child Development, 65,* 649–665.

Droege, K., & Stipek, D. (1993). Children's use of dispositions to predict classmates' behavior. *Developmental Psychology, 29,* 646–654.

Durrant, J. (2004). Distinguishing physical punishment from physical abuse: Implications for professionals. *Ontario Association of Children's Aid Societies Journal, 48*(2), 15–20.

Durrant, J., & Ensom, R. (2004). *Physical punishment of children* (CECW Information Sheet #7E). Ottawa, ON: Child Welfare League of Canada. Retrieved from www.cecw-cepb.ca/DocsEng/PhysPun7E.pdf

Durrant, J., & Ensom, R. (2012). Physical punishment of children: lessons from 20 years of research. *Canadian Medical Association Journal, 184*(12), 1373–1377. doi:10.1503/cmaj.101314

Eisenberg, N. (2000). Emotion, regulation, and moral development. *Annual Review of Psychology, 51,* 665–697.

Eisenberg, N. (2004). Prosocial and moral development in the family. In T. Thorkildsen & H. Walberg (Eds.), *Nurturing morality: Issues in children's and families' lives* (pp. 119–135). New York, NY: Kluwer Academic/Plenum Publishers.

Eisenberg, N., & Sulik, M.J. (2012). Emotion-related self-regulation in children. *Teaching of Psychology, 39*(1), 77–83. doi:10.1177/0098628311430172

Eisenberg, N., Chang, L., Ma, Y., & Huang, X. (2009). Relations of parenting style to Chinese children's effortful control, ego resilience, and maladjustment. *Development and Psychopathology, 21,* 455–477.

Eisenberg, N., Fabes, R., & Spinrad, T. (2006). Prosocial development. In N. Eisenberg (Ed.), *Handbook of Child Psychology, Volume 3: Social, Emotional, and Personality Development* (6th ed., pp. 646–718). Hoboken, NJ: John Wiley & Sons.

Eisenberg, N., Guthrie, I., Murphy, B., Shepard, S., Cumberland, A., & Carlo. G. (1999). Consistency and development of prosocial dispositions: A longitudinal study. *Child Development, 70,* 1360–1372.

Etaugh, C., & Liss, M. (1992). Home, school, and playroom: Training grounds for adult gender roles. *Sex Roles, 26,* 129–147.

Evans, G. (2004). The environment of childhood poverty. *American Psychologist, 59,* 77–92.

Evans, R., & Erikson, E. (1967). *Dialogue with Erik Erikson.* New York, NY: Harper & Row.

Fabes, R., Martin, C., & Hanish, L. (2003). Young children's play qualities in same-, other-, and mixed-sex peer groups. *Child Development, 74,* 921–932.

Fagot, B.I., & Hagan, R. (1991). Observations of parent reactions to sex-stereotyped behaviors: Age and sex effects. *Child Development, 62,* 617–628.

Fantuzzo, J., Coolahan, K., & Mendez, J. (1998). Contextually relevant validation of peer play constructs with African American Head Start children: Penn Interactive Peer Play Scale. *Early Childhood Research Quarterly, 13,* 411–431.

Fantuzzo, J., Sekino, Y., & Cohen, H. (2004). An examination of the contributions of interactive peer play to salient classroom competencies for urban Head Start children. *Psychology in the Schools, 41,* 323–336.

Feurer, E., Sassu, R., Cimeli, P., & Roebers, C.M. (2015). Development of meta-representations: Procedural metacognition and the relationship to Theory of Mind. *Journal of Educational and Developmental Psychology, 5*(1), 6–18. doi:10.5539/jedp.v5n1p6

Finnie, R. (2000). *Earnings of post-secondary graduates in Canada: Holding their own* (Cat. No. MP 32-29/99-12-1E). Retrieved from Human Resources Development Canada website: www.hrdc-drhc.gc.ca/arb/publications/research/1999docs/r-99-12ea.pdf

Gee, C., & Heyman, G. (2007). Children's evaluation of other people's self- descriptions. *Social Development, 16,* 800–818.

Gelman, S., Taylor, M., Nguyen, S., Leaper, C., & Bigler, R. (2004). Mother-child conversations about gender: Understanding the acquisition of essentialist beliefs. *Monographs of the Society for Research in Child Development, 69,* 1–127.

Gershoff, E.T., & Grogan-Kaylor, A. (2016). Spanking and child outcomes: Old controversies and new meta-analyses. *Journal of Family Psychology, 30*(4), 453–469. doi:10.1037/fam0000191

Goldberg, A.E. (2009). Claiming a place at the family table: Gay and lesbian families in the 21st century. *PsycCritiques, 55*(7), 233–235.

Goldberg, A.E., & Smith, J.Z. (2013). Predictors of psychological adjustment in early placed adopted children with lesbian, gay, and heterosexual parents. *Journal of Family Psychology, 27*(3), 431–442. doi:10.1037/a0032911

Golombok, S., Rust, J., Zervoulis, K., Croudace, T., Golding, J., & Hines, M. (2008). Developmental trajectories of sex-typed behavior in boys and girls: A longitudinal general population study of children aged 2.5–8 years. *Child Development, 79,* 1583–1593.

Golombok, S., Rust, J., Zervoulis, K., Golding, J., & Hines, M. (2012). Continuity in sex-typed behavior from preschool to adolescence: A longitudinal population study of boys and girls aged 3–13 years. *Archives of Sexual Behavior, 41*(3), 591–597. doi:10.1007/s10508-011-9784-7

Goodman, G.S., Sayfan, J.S., Lee, M., Sandhai, A., Walle-Olsen, S., Magnussen, K., & Pezdek, P.A. (2007). The development of memory for own and other-race faces. *The Journal of Experimental Child Psychology, 98*(4), 233–242.

Gralinski, J.H., & Kopp, C.B. (1993). Everyday rules for behavior: Mothers' requests to young children. *Developmental Psychology, 29,* 573–584.

Greene, S., Anderson, E., Doyle, E., & Ridelbach, H. (2006). Divorce. In Bear, G., & Minke, K. (Eds.), *Children's needs III: Development, prevention, and intervention.* Washington, DC: National Association of School Psychologists.

Griffith, J. (1998). The relation of school structure and social environment to parent involvement in elementary schools. *Elementary School Journal, 99,* 53–80.

Hair, N.L., Hanson, J.L., Wolfe, B.L., & Pollak, S.D. (2015). Association of child poverty, brain development, and academic achievement. *JAMA Pediatrics, 169*(9), 822–829. doi:10.1001/jamapediatrics.2015.1475

Harvey, B., Matte-Gagné, C., Stack, D.M., Serbin, L.A., Ledingham, J.E., & Schwartzman, A.E. (2016). Risk and protective factors for autonomy-supportive and controlling parenting in high-risk families. *Journal of Applied Developmental Psychology, 43*(Mar–Apr), 18–28. doi:10.1016/j.appdev.2015.12.004

Hatakeyama, M., & Hatakeyama, H. (2012). Developmental study of empathy, moral judgment, and social information processing in preschoolers with relational aggression. *Japanese Journal of Developmental Psychology, 23*(1), 1–11.

Hay, D., Payne, A., & Chadwick, A. (2004). Peer relations in childhood. *Journal of Child Psychology & Psychiatry & Allied Disciplines, 45*, 84–108.

Health Canada. (1999b). *Toward a healthy future: Second report on the health of Canadians* (Cat. No. H39-468/1999E). Ottawa, ON: Minister of Public Works and Government Services Canada. Retrieved from www.hc-sc.gc.ca/hppb/phdd/report/toward/pdf/english/toward_a_healthy_english.PDF

Health Canada. (1999c). *Suicide.* Ottawa, ON: Author. Retrieved from www.hc-sc.gc.ca/hpb/lcdc/brch/measuring/mu_y_e.html

Hetherington, E.M. (1991a). Presidential address: Families, lies, and videotapes. *Journal of Research on Adolescence, 1*, 323–348.

Hetherington, E.M. (1991b). The role of individual differences and family relationships in children's coping with divorce and remarriage. In P.A. Cowen & M. Hetherington (Eds.), *Family transitions* (pp. 165–194). Hillsdale, NJ: Erlbaum.

Heyman, G. (2009). Children's reasoning about traits. In P. Bauer (Ed.). *Advances in child development, Volume 37* (pp. 105–144). San Diego, CA: Academic Press.

Hilgenkamp, K., & Livingston, M. (2002). Tomboys, masculine characteristics, and self-ratings of confidence in career success. *Psychological Reports, 90*(3 Pt 1), 743–749.

Hinde, R.A., Titmus, G., Easton, D., & Tamplin, A. (1985). Incidence of "friendship" and behavior toward strong associates versus non-associates in preschoolers. *Child Development, 56*, 234–245.

Hines, M., Constantinescu, M., & Spencer, D. (2015). Early androgen exposure and human gender development. *Biology of Sex Differences, 6*(Feb), 3. doi:10.1186/s13293-015-0022-1

Hines, M., Spencer, D., Kung, K.T., Browne, W.V., Constantinescu, M., & Noorderhaven, R.M. (2016). The early postnatal period, mini-puberty, provides a window on the role of testosterone in human neurobehavioural development. *Current Opinion in Neurobiology, 38*(June), 69–73. doi:10.1016/j.conb.2016.02.008

Hoeve, M., Stams, G.J.J.M., van der Put, C.E., Dubas, J.S., van der Laan, P.H., & Gerris, J.R.M. (2012). A meta-analysis of attachment to parents and delinquency. *Journal of Abnormal Child Psychology, 40*(5), 771–785. doi:10.1007/s10802-011-9608-1

Hoffman, M. (1970). Moral Development. In P. Mussen (Ed.), *Carmichael's manual of child psychology: Vol. 2.* New York, NY: Wiley.

Houck, G., & Lecuyer-Maus, E. (2004). Maternal limit setting during toddlerhood, delay of gratification and behavior problems at age five. *Infant Mental Health Journal, 25*, 28–46. doi:10.1002/imhj.10083

Howes, C. (1983). Patterns of friendship. *Child Development, 54*, 1041–1053.

Howes, C. (1987). Social competence with peers in young children: Developmental sequences. *Developmental Review, 7*, 252–272.

Hudziak, J.J., van Beijsterveldt, C.E.M., Bartels, M., Rietveld, M.J.V., Rettew, D.C., Derks, E.M., & Boomsma, D.I. (2003). Individual differences in aggression: Genetic analyses by age, gender, and informant in 3-, 7-, and 10-year-old Dutch twins. *Behavior Genetics, 33*(5), 575–589. doi:10.1023/A:1025782918793

Human Resources Development Canada. (2001). *Does parental separation affect children's behaviour?* Ottawa, ON: Author. Retrieved from www.hrdc-drhc.gc.ca/stratpol/arb/publications/bulletin/child_dev/chi_dev2.shtml

Huston, A.C., & Bentley, A.C. (2010). Development in societal context. *Annual Review of Psychology, 61*(Jan), 411–438. doi:10.1146/annurev.psych.093008.100442

Ingoldsby, E., Shaw, D., Owens, E., & Winslow, E. (1999). A longitudinal study of interparental conflict, emotional and behavioral reactivity, and preschoolers' adjustment problems among low-income families. *Journal of Abnormal Child Psychology, 27*, 343–356.

Jackson, A. (2001). *The incidence and depth of child poverty in recession and recovery: Some preliminary lessons on child benefits.* Ottawa, ON: Canadian Council on Social Development. Retrieved from www.ccsd.ca/pubs/2001/ajncb.htm

Jambon, M., & Smetana, J.G. (2014). Moral complexity in middle childhood: Children's evaluations of necessary harm. *Developmental Psychology 50*(1), 22–33. doi:10.1037/a0032992

Jeynes, W. (2006). The impact of parental remarriage on children: A meta-analysis. *Marriage & Family Review, 40*(4), 75–102.

Karreman, A., de Haas, S., Van Tuijl, C., van Aken, M., & Dekovic, M. (2010). Relations among temperament, parenting, and problem behavior in young children. *Infant Behavior & Development, 33*, 39–49.

Kazdin, A.E., & Benjet, C. (2003). Spanking children: Evidence and issues. *Current Directions in Psychological Science, 12*(3), 99–103.

Kiel, E.J., & Buss, K.A. (2012). Associations among context-specific maternal protective behavior, toddler fearful temperament, and maternal accuracy and goals. *Social Development (Oxford, England), 21*(4), 742–760. doi:10.1111/j.1467-9507.2011.00645.x

Kim-Spoon, J., Cicchetti, D., & Rogosch, F.A. (2013). A longitudinal study of emotion regulation, emotion lability-negativity, and internalizing symptomatology in maltreated and nonmaltreated children. *Child Development, 84*(2), 512–527. doi:10.1111/j.1467-8624.2012.01857.x

Kochanska, G. (1997a). Multiple pathways to conscience for children with different temperaments: From toddlerhood to age 5. *Developmental Psychology, 33*, 228–240.

Kochanska, G. (1997b). Mutually responsive orientation between mothers and their young: Implications for early socialization. *Child Development, 68*, 94–112.

Kochanska, G., & Kim, S. (2012). Toward a new understanding of legacy of early attachments for future antisocial trajectories: Evidence from two longitudinal studies. *Development and Psychopathology, 24*(3), 783–806. doi: http://dx.doi.org/10.1017/S0954579412000375

Kochanska, G., Murray, K., & Coy, K. (1997). Inhibitory control as a contributor to conscience in childhood: From toddler to early school age. *Child Development, 68*, 263–277.

Koenig, A.L., Cicchetti, D., & Rogosch, F.A. (2004). Moral development: The association between maltreatment and young children's prosocial behaviors and moral transgressions. *Social Development, 13*(1), 87–106.

Kohlberg, L. (1966). A cognitive-developmental analysis of children's sex-role concepts and attitudes. In E.E. Maccoby (Ed.), *The development of sex differences* (pp. 82–172). Stanford, CA: Stanford University Press.

Kohlberg, L., & Ullian, D.Z. (1974). Stages in the development of psychosexual concepts and attitudes. In R.C. Friedman, R.M. Richart, & R.L. Vande Wiele (Eds.), *Sex differences in behavior* (pp. 209–222). New York, NY: Wiley.

Lacourse, E., Boivin, M., Brendgen, M., Petitclerc, A., Girard, A., Vitaro, F., . . . Tremblay, R.E. (2014). A longitudinal twin study of physical aggression during early childhood: Evidence for a developmentally dynamic genome. *Psychological Medicine, 44*(12), 2617–2627. doi:10.1017/S0033291713003218

Landy, S., & Tam, K.K. (1996). "Yes, parenting does make a difference to the development of children in Canada." In *Growing up in Canada: National longitudinal survey of children and youth.* Ottawa, ON: Human Resources Development Canada and Statistics Canada.

Landy, S., & Tam, K.K. (1998). *Understanding the contribution of multiple risk factors on child development at various ages* (Cat. No. W-98-22E). Ottawa, ON: Human Resources Development Canada.

Larzelere, R.E. (2000). Child outcomes of non-abusive and customary physical punishment by parents: An updated literature review. *Clinical Child and Family Psychology Review, 3*(4), 199–221.

Larzelere, R.E. (2003, April). *A meta-analysis comparing the effect sizes and correlates of corporal punishment with alternative disciplinary tactics.* Paper presented at the Society for Research in Child Development, Tampa, FL.

Larzelere, R.E. (2008). Disciplinary spanking: The scientific evidence. *Journal of Developmental and Behavioral Pediatrics, 29*(4), 334–335. doi:10.1097/DBP.0b013e3181829f30

Larzelere, R.E., & Kuhn, B.R. (2005). Comparing child outcomes of physical punishment and alternative disciplinary tactics: A meta-analysis. *Clinical Child and Family Psychology Review, 8*(1), 1–37. doi:10.1007/s10567-005-2340-z

Larzelere, R.E., Cox, R.B., & Smith, G.L. (2010). Do nonphysical punishments reduce antisocial behavior more than spanking? A comparison using the strongest previous causal evidence against spanking. *BMC Pediatrics, 10*(Feb), 10. doi:10.1186/1471-2431-10-10

Larzelere, R.E., Kuhn, B.R., & Johnson, B. (2004). The intervention selection bias: An underrecognized confound in intervention research. *Psychological Bulletin, 130*(2), 289–303.

Laucius, J. (2012, Sept 19). The 'skip-generation' family. *Ottawa Citizen.* Retrieved from http://www.ottawacitizen.com/life/skip+generation+family/7268651/story.html

Leaper, C., & Friedman, C.K. (2007) The socialization of gender. In J.E. Grusec & P.D. Hastings (Eds.), *Handbook of socialization: Theory and research* (pp. 561–587). New York, NY: Guilford.

Levy, G.D., & Fivush, R. (1993). Scripts and gender: A new approach for examining gender-role development. *Developmental Review, 13,* 126–146.

Li-Grining, C. (2007). Effortful control among low-income preschoolers in three cities: Stability, change, and individual differences. *Developmental Psychology, 43,* 208–221.

Maccoby, E.E. (1990). Gender and relationships: A developmental account. *American Psychologist, 45,* 513–520.

Maccoby, E.E., & Martin, J.A. (1983). Socialization in the context of the family: Parent–child interaction. In E.M. Hetherington (Ed.), *Handbook of child psychology: Socialization, personality, and social development: Vol. 4* (pp. 1– 102). New York, NY: Wiley.

MacMillan, H.L., Boyle, M.H., Wong, M.Y.Y., Duku, E.K., Fleming, J.E., & Walsh, C.A. (1999). Slapping and spanking in childhood and its association with lifetime prevalence of psychiatric disorders in a general population sample. *Canadian Medical Association Journal, 161*(7), 805–809.

Madigan, S., Atkinson, L., Laurin, K., & Benoit, D. (2013). Attachment and internalizing behavior in early childhood: A meta-analysis. *Developmental Psychology, 49*(4), 672–689. doi:10.1037/a0028793

Martin, C.L., & Little, J.K. (1990). The relation of gender understanding to children's sex-typed preferences and gender stereotypes. *Child Development, 61,* 1427–1439.

Martin, C.L., & Ruble, D.N. (2004). Children's search for gender cues: Cognitive perspectives on gender development. *Current Directions in Psychological Science, 13,* 67–70.

Martin, C.L., & Ruble, D.N. (2010). Patterns of Gender Development. *Annual Review of Psychology, 61,* 353–381. doi:10.1146/annurev.psych.093008.100511

Martin, C.L., Wood, C.H., & Little, J.K. (1990). The development of gender stereotype components. *Child Development, 61,* 1891–1904.

Martini, T.S., Root, C.A., & Jenkins, J.M. (2004). Low and middle income mothers' regulation of negative emotion: Effects of children's temperament and situational emotional responses. *Social Development, 13*(4), 515–530.

Matte-Gagné, C., Harvey, B., Stack, D.M., & Serbin, L.A. (2015). Contextual specificity in the relationship between maternal autonomy support and children's socio-emotional development: A longitudinal study from preschool to preadolescence. *Journal of Youth and Adolescence, 44*(8), 1528–1541. doi:10.1007/s10964-014-0247-z

McCain, M., & Mustard, F. (2000). *Early years study: Reversing the real brain drain: Final report.* Toronto, ON: Government of Ontario.

McCain, M.N., & Mustard, J.F. (2002). *The early years study three years later.* Toronto, ON: The Founders' Network.

McCain, M.N., Mustard, J.F., & McCuaig, K. (2011). *Early years study 3: Making decisions, taking action.* Toronto, ON: Margaret & Wallace McCain Family Foundation.

McCrae, R., Costa, P., Ostendord, F., & Angleitner, A. (2000). Nature over nurture: Temperament, personality, and life span development. *Journal of Personality & Social Psychology, 78,* 173–186.

McEwen, M., & Stewart, J. (2014). The relationship between income and children's outcomes: A synthesis of Canadian evidence (CRDCN Synthesis Series). *Canadian Public Policy, 40*(1), 99–109.

McIntyre, L., Walsh, G., & Conner, S.K. (2001). *A follow-up study on child hunger in Canada* (Cat. No. W-01-1-2E). Ottawa, ON: Human Resources Development Canada. Retrieved from www.hrdc-drhc.gc.ca/stratpol/arb/publications/research/2001docs/abw-01-1-2e.shtml

Meaney, M. (2010). Epigenetics and the biological definition of Gene x Environment interactions. *Child Development, 81,* 41–79.

Milan, A., Laflamme, N., & Wong, I. (2015). Diversity of grandparents living with their grandchildren. *Insights on Canadian Society* (Catalogue no. 75-006-X). Ottawa, ON: Statistics Canada. Retrieved from http://www.statcan.gc.ca/pub/75-006-x/2015001/article/14154-eng.pdf

Miller, F., Jenkins, J., & Keating, D. (2002). Parenting and children's behaviour problems. In J.D. Willms (Ed.), *Vulnerable children* (pp. 71–102). Edmonton, AB: The University of Alberta Press.

Mischel, W. (1966). A social learning view of sex differences in behavior. In E.E. Maccoby (Ed.), *The development of sex differences* (pp. 56–81). Stanford, CA: Stanford University Press.

Mischel, W. (1970). Sex typing and socialization. In P.H. Mussen (Ed.), *Carmichael's manual of child psychology: Vol. 2* (pp. 3–72). New York, NY: Wiley.

Munroe, R.H., Shimmin, H.S., & Munroe, R.L. (1984). Gender understanding and sex role preference in four cultures. *Developmental Psychology, 20,* 673–682.

Nieman, P., Shea, S., & Canadian Paediatric Society. (2016). *Effective discipline for children.* Retrieved from http://www.cps.ca/documents/position/discipline-for-children

Nieman, P., Shea, S., & Canadian Paediatric Society. (2016). *Effective discipline for children.* Retrieved from http://www.cps.ca/documents/position/discipline-for-children

O'Toole-Thommessen. S., & Todd B. (2010). *Revisiting sex differences in play: Very early evidence of stereotypical preferences in infancy.* Paper presented at the annual meeting of the British Psychological Society. Stratford-upon-Avon, UK, April, 2010.

Pagani, L., Boulerice, B., Tremblay, R., & Vitaro, F. (1997). Behavioural development in children of divorce and remarriage. *Journal of Child Psychology & Psychiatry & Allied Disciplines, 38,* 769–781.

Parmley, M., & Cunningham, J.G. (2008). Children's gender-emotion stereotypes in the relationship of anger to sadness and fear. *Sex Roles, 58*(5), 358–370. doi:10.1199-007-9335-9

Parten, M. (1932). Social participation among preschool children. *Journal of Abnormal and Social Psychology, 27*(3), 243–269.

Patterson, C.J. (2006). Children of lesbian and gay parents. *Current Directions in Psychological Science, 15*(5), 241–243.

Patterson, C.J. (2009). Children of lesbian and gay parents: Psychology, law and policy. *American Psychologist, 64*(8), 727–36.

Phipps, S., & Lethbridge, L. (2006). *Incomes and the outcomes of children* (11F0019MIE—No. 281). Ottawa, ON: Ministry of Industry.

Poulin-Dubois, D., & Brosseau-Liard, P. (2016). The developmental origins of selective social learning. *Current Directions in Psychological Science, 25*(1), 60–64. doi:10.1177/0963721415561396

Price, C., & Kunz, J. (2003). Rethinking the paradigm of juvenile delinquency as related to divorce. *Journal of Divorce & Remarriage, 39,* 109–133.

Provençal, N., Booij, L., & Tremblay, R.E. (2015). The developmental origins of chronic physical aggression: Biological pathways triggered by early life adversity. *Journal of Experimental Biology, 218*(Pt 1), 123–33. doi:10.1242/jeb.111401

Qi, C.H., & Kaiser, A.P. (2003). Behavior problems of preschool children from low-income families: Review of the literature. *Early*

Childhood Special Education, 23(4), 188–216. doi:10.1177/02711214030230040201

Rees, C. (2007). Childhood attachment. *The British Journal of General Practice, 57*(544), 920–922. doi:10.3399/096016407782317955

Reiner, W., & Gearhart, J. (2004). Discordant sexual identity in some genetic males with cloacal extrophy assigned to female sex at birth. *The New England Journal of Medicine, 350,* 333–341.

Rosenthal, S., & Gitelman, S. (2002). Endocrinology. In A. Rudolph, R. Kamei, & K. Overby (Eds.), *Rudolph's fundamentals of pediatrics* (3rd ed.) (pp. 747–795). New York, NY: McGraw-Hill.

Ross, D.P., Roberts, P.A., & Scott, K. (1998). *Mediating factors in child development outcomes: Children in lone-parent families* (Cat. No. W-98-8E). Ottawa, ON: Human Resources Development Canada.

Rubin, K., Burgess, K., Dwyer, K., & Hastings, P. (2003). Predicting preschoolers' externalizing behaviors from toddler temperament, conflict, and maternal negativity. *Developmental Psychology, 39,* 164–176.

Rubin, K., Coplan, R., Chen, X, Bowker, J., & McDonald, K. (2011). Peer relationships in childhood. In M. Bornstein & M. Lamb (Eds.), *Developmental science: An advanced textbook* (6th ed., pp. 519–570). New York, NY: Psychology Press.

Rubin, K.H., Coplan, R.J., & Bowker, J.C. (2009). Social withdrawal in childhood. *Annual Review of Psychology, 60,* 141–171. doi:10.1146/annurev.psych.60.110707.163642

Ruble, D., & Dweck, C. (1995). Self-conceptions, person conceptions, and their development. In N. Eisenberg (Ed.), *Social development, Volume 15* (pp. 109–135). Thousand Oaks, CA: Sage.

Sallquist, J., Eisenberg, N., Spinrad, T., Eggum, N., & Gaertner, B. (2009a). Assessment of preschoolers' positive empathy: Concurrent and longitudinal relations with positive emotion, social competence, and sympathy. *The Journal of Positive Psychology, 4,* 223–233.

Salmon, A.K. (2016). Learning by thinking during play: The power of reflection to aid performance. *Early Child Development and Care, 186*(3), 480–496. doi:10.1080/03004430.2015.1032956

Sandnabba, N., & Ahlberg, C. (1999). Parents' attitudes and expectations about children's cross-gender behavior. *Sex Roles, 40,* 249–263.

Schmidt, M., DeMulder, E., & Denham, S. (2002). Kindergarten social-emotional competence: Developmental predictors and psychosocial implications. *Early Child Development & Care, 172,* 451–461.

Schmitz, S., Fulker, D., Plomin, R., Zahn-Waxler, C., Emde, R., & DeFries, J. (1999). Temperament and problem behavior during early childhood. *International Journal of Behavioral Development, 23,* 333–355.

Schothorst, P., & van Engeland, H. (1996). Long-term behavioral sequelae of prematurity. *Journal of the American Academy of Child & Adolescent Psychiatry, 35,* 175–183.

Séguin, L., Xu, Q., Potvin, L., Zunzunegui, M.V., & Frohlich, K.L. (2003). Effects of low income on infant health. *Canadian Medical Association Journal, 168*(12), 1533–1538.

Serbin, L.A., & Karp, J. (2003). Intergenerational studies of parenting and the transfer of risk from parent to child. *Current Directions in Psychological Science. 12*(4), 138–142. doi:10.1111/1467-8721.01249

Serbin, L.A., & Karp, J. (2004). The intergenerational transfer of psychosocial risk: Mediators of vulnerability and resilience. *Annual Review of Psychology, 55*(Feb), 333–363. doi:10.1146/annurev.psych.54.101601.145228

Serbin, L.A., Kingdon, D., Ruttle, P.L., & Stack, D.M. (2015). The impact of children's internalizing and externalizing problems on parenting: Transactional processes and reciprocal change over time. *Development and psychopathology, 27*(4 Pt 1), 969-986. doi:10.1017/S0954579415000632

Serbin, L.A., Poulin-Dubois, D., & Eichstedt, J.A. (2002). Infants' responses to gender-inconsistent events. *Infancy, 3*(4), 531–542.

Serbin, L.A., Powlishta, K.K., & Gulko, J. (1993). The development of sex typing in middle childhood. *Monographs of the Society for Research in Child Development, 58*(2, Serial No. 232).

Sexualityandu.ca (2009). *Talking contraception and sexuality with your child same-sex parenting: Creating a strong family life as a gay couple.* Ottawa, ON: Society of Obstetricians and Gynaecologists of Canada. Retrieved from www.sexualityandu.ca/parents/talk-7.aspx

Shonkoff, J.P. (2010). Building a new biodevelopmental framework to guide the future of early childhood policy. *Child Development, 81*(1), 357–367. doi:10.1111/j.1467-8624.2009.01399.x

Slaby, R.G., & Frey, K.S. (1975). Development of gender constancy and selective attention to same-sex models. *Child Development, 46,* 849–856.

Smetana, J., Schlagman, N., & Adams, P. (1993). Preschool children's judgments about hypothetical and actual transgressions. *Child Development, 64,* 202–214.

Smetana, J.G., Jambon, M., Conry-Murray, C., & Sturge-Apple, M.L. (2012). Reciprocal associations between young children's developing moral judgments and theory of mind. *Developmental Psychology, 48*(4), 1144–1155. doi:10.1037/a0025891

Smith, G., & Palmieri, P. (2007). Risk of psychological difficulties among children raised by custodial grandparents. *Psychiatric Services, 58,* 1303–1310.

Stack, D.M., Serbin, L.A, Mantis, I., & Kingdon, D. (2015). Breaking the cycle of adversity in vulnerable children and families: A thirty-five year study of at-risk lower income families. *International Journal for Family Research and Policy, 1*(1), 31–56. doi:10.1177/0165025416631836

Statistics Canada (2012h). *Data table for chart 1 number of marriages and divorces, Canada, 1926 to 2008.* Retrieved from http://www.statcan.gc.ca/pub/85-002-x/2012001/article/11634/c-g/desc/desc01-eng.htm

Statistics Canada. (1998). *National Longitudinal Survey of Children and Youth, Cycle 2, 1996* (The Daily, October 28). Ottawa, ON: Author. Retrieved from www.statcan.ca:80/Daily/English/981028/d981028.htm

Statistics Canada. (2001a). *The Daily* (June 28). Family violence: Focus on child abuse and children at risk. Ottawa, ON: Author. Retrieved from www.statcan.ca/Daily/English/010628/d010628b.htm

Statistics Canada. (2002a). *General Social Survey—Cycle 15: Changing conjugal life in Canada* (Cat. No. 89-576-XIE). Ottawa, ON: Author. Retrieved from www.statcan.ca/english/freepub/89-576-XIE/89-576-XIE2001001.pdf

Statistics Canada. (2005). *National Longitudinal Survey of Children and Youth: Home environment, income and child behaviour.* Ottawa, ON: The Daily (February 21). Retrieved from www.statcan.ca/Daily/English/050221/d050221b.htm

Statistics Canada. (2012e). *2011 census of population: Families, households, marital status, structural type of dwelling, collectives* (Catalogue No. 98-312-XWE2011001). Retrieved from http://www.statcan.gc.ca/daily-quotidien/120919/dq120919a-eng.pdf

Statistics Canada. (2012f). *Fifty years of families in Canada: 1961 to 2011* (Catalogue No. 98-312-X2011003). Retrieved from http://www12.statcan.gc.ca/census-recensement/2011/as-sa/98-312-x/98-312-x2011003_1-eng.pdf

Statistics Canada. (2012g). *Conjugal status (3), opposite/same-sex status (5) and presence of children (5) for the couple census families in private households of Canada, provinces, territories and census metropolitan areas, 2011 census* (Catalogue No. 98-312-XWE2011046). Retrieved from http://www5.statcan.gc.ca/bsolc/olc-cel/olc-cel?catno=98-312-X2011046&lang=eng

Statistics Canada. (2015c). *Family characteristics, Low Income Measures (LIM), by family type and family type composition* (Table 111-0015). Retrieved from http://www.statcan.gc.ca/daily-quotidien/150626/dq150626c-cansim-eng.htm

Steinberg, L., Blatt-Eisengart, I., & Cauffman, E. (2006). Patterns of competence and adjustment among adolescents from authoritative, authoritarian, indulgent, and neglectful homes: A replication in a sample of serious juvenile offenders. *Journal of Research on Adolescence, 16,* 47–58.

Steinberg, L., Fletcher, A., & Darling, N. (1994). Parental monitoring and peer influences on adolescent substance use. *Pediatrics, 93,* 1060–1064.

Stormshak, E., Bierman, K., McMahon, R., & Lengua, L. (2000). Parenting practices and child disruptive behavior problems in early elementary school. *Journal of Clinical Child Psychology, 29*, 17–29.

Strayer, J., & Roberts, W. (2004). Empathy and observed anger and aggression in five-year-olds. *Social Development, 13*, 1–13.

Thomas, E.M. (2004). *Aggressive behaviour outcomes for young children: Change in parenting environment predicts change in behaviour* (Cat. No. 89-599-MIE2004001). Ottawa, ON: Statistics Canada.

Thompson, R. (2009). Early foundations: Conscience and the development of moral character. In D. Narvaez & D. Lapsley (Eds.), *Personality, identity, and character: Explorations in moral psychology* (pp. 159–184). New York, NY: Cambridge University Press.

Thompson, R., & Newton, E. (2010). Emotion in early conscience. In W. Arsenio & E. Lemerise (Eds.), *Emotions, aggression, and morality in children: Bridging development and psychopathology* (pp. 13–31). Washington, DC: American Psychological Association.

Tomasello, M. (2009). *Why we cooperate.* Cambridge, MA: MIT Press.

Trautner, H., Gervai, J., & Nemeth, R. (2003). Appearance-reality distinction and development of gender constancy understanding in children. *International Journal of Behavioral Development, 27*, 275–283.

Tremblay, D.G. (2010). Paid parental leave: An employee right or still an ideal? An analysis of the situation in Quebec in comparison with North America. *Employee Responsibilities and Rights Journal, 22*(2), 83–100.

Tremblay, R.E. (2000). The origins of youth violence. *Isuma, 1*(2), 19–24.

Tremblay, R.E. (2008a). Development of physical aggression from early childhood to adulthood. In Centres of Excellence for Children's Well-Being (Eds.), *Encyclopedia on Early Childhood Development.* Retrieved from www.enfant-encyclopedie.com/pages/PDF/TremblayANGxp_rev.pdf

Tremblay, R.E. (2008b). Understanding development and prevention of chronic physical aggression: Towards experimental epigenetic studies. *Philosophical Transaction of the Royal Society B, 363*, 2613–2622.

Tremblay, R.E. (2010). Developmental origins of disruptive behaviour problems: The "original sin" hypothesis, epigenetics and their consequences for prevention. *Journal of Child Psychology and Psychiatry, 51*(4), 341–367.

Tremblay, R.E., & Szyf, M. (2010). Developmental origins of chronic physical aggression and epigenetics. *Epigenomics, 2*(4), 495–499. doi:10.2217/epi.10.40

Tremblay, R.E., Nagin, D.S., Séguin, J.R., Zoccolillo, M., Zelazo, P.D., Boivin, M., . . . Japel, C. (2004). Physical aggression during early childhood: trajectories and predictors. *Canadian Child and Adolescent Psychiatry Review, 14*(1), 3–9.

Trocmé, N., Durrant, J., Ensom, R., & Marwah, I. (2004). *Physical abuse of children in the context of punishment* (CECW Information Sheet #8E). Toronto, ON: Faculty of Social Work, University of Toronto.

UNICEF Canada. (2016). *Report Card 13: Fairness for children-Canada's challenge. Comparing inequality across rich countries.* Retrieved from http://www.unicef.ca/sites/default/files/imce_uploads/images/advocacy/rc/rc13_infographen_media.pdf

Valentino, K., Nuttall, A.K., Comas, M., Borkowski, J.G., & Akai, C.E. (2012). Intergenerational continuity of child abuse among adolescent mothers: Authoritarian parenting, community violence, and race. *Child Maltreatment, 17*(2), 172–181. doi:10.1177/1077559511434945

van Beijsterveldt, C.E.M., Bartels, M., Hudziak, J.J., & Boomsma, D.I. (2003). Causes of stability of aggression from early childhood to adolescence: A longitudinal genetic analysis in Dutch twins. *Behavior Genetics, 33*(5), 591–605. doi:10.1023/A:1025735002864

Vanier Institute of the Family (2011). *Four in ten marriages end in divorce.* Ottawa, ON: Author. Retrieved from http://www.vanierinstitute.ca/modules/news/newsitem.php?ItemId=74#.UnbPCl-EhxI

Véronneau, M.H., Serbin, L.A., Stack, D.M., Ledingham, J., & Schwartzman, A.E. (2015). Emerging psychopathology moderates upward social mobility: The intergenerational (dis)continuity of

socioeconomic status. *Development and psychopathology, 27*(4 Pt 1), 1217–1236. doi:10.1017/S0954579415000784

Wallerstein, J., & Lewis, J. (1998). The long-term impact of divorce on children: A first report from a 25-year study. *Family & Conciliation Courts Review, 36*, 368–383.

Wallerstein, J., Lewis, J., & Packer Rosenthal, S. (2013). Mothers and their children after divorce: Report from a 25-year longitudinal study. *Psychoanalytic Psychology, 30*(2), 167–184. doi:10.1037/a0032511

Wang, C., & Phinney, J. (1998). Differences in child rearing attitudes between immigrant Chinese mothers and Anglo-American mothers. *Early Development & Parenting, 7*, 181–189.

Williams, C. (2001). Family disruptions and childhood happiness (Cat. No. 11-008-XPE). *Canadian Social Trends, Autumn*, 2–4.

Yaman, A., Mesman, J., van IJzendoorn, M.H., & Bakermans-Kranenburg, M.J. (2010). Parenting and toddler aggression in second-generation immigrant families: The moderating role of child temperament. *Journal of Family Psychology, 24*(2), 208–211. doi:10.1037/a0019100

Yuill, N. (1997). English children as personality theorists: Accounts of the modifiability, development, and origin of traits. *Genetic, Social & General Psychology Monographs, 123*, 5–26.

Zhang, R., & Yu, Y. (2002). A study of children's coordinational ability for outcome and intention information. *Psychological Science* (China), *25*, 527–530.

Zosuls, K.M., Ruble, D.N., Tamis-LeMonda, C.S., Shrout, P.E., Bornstein, M.H., & Greulich, F.K. (2009). The acquisition of gender labels in infancy: Implications for sex-typed play. *Developmental Psychology, 45*, 688–701.

Chapter 9

Aharon-Peretz, J., & Tomer, R. (2007). Traumatic brain injury. In B. Miller & J. Cummings (Eds.), *The human frontal lobes: Functions and disorders* (2nd ed., pp. 540–551). New York, NY: Guilford Press.

Allen, M. (2004). Minority language school systems: A profile of students, schools and communities. *Education Quarterly Review, 9*(4), 9–29.

American Psychiatric Association. (2013). *Diagnostic and Statistical Manual of Mental Disorder: DSM-5* (5th ed.). Washington, DC: American Psychiatric Publishing.

Anderson, C.A. (2004). An update on the effects of violent video games. *Journal of Adolescence, 27*(1), 113–122.

Anderson, C.A., Carnagey, N.L., Flanagan, M., Benjamin, A.J., Eubanks, J., & Valentine, J.C. (2004). Violent video games: Specific effects of violent content on aggressive thoughts and behavior. In M. Zane (Ed.), *Advances in experimental social psychology, Vol. 36.* New York, NY: Elsevier.

Anderson, C.A., Gentile, D.A., & Buckley, K.E. (2007). *Violent video game effects on children and adolescents: Theory, research, and public policy.* New York, NY: Oxford University Press.

Anglin, J.M. (1993). Vocabulary development: A morphological analysis. *Monographs of the Society for Research in Child Development, 58* (Serial No. 238).

Anglin, J.M. (1995, March). *Word learning and the growth of potentially knowable vocabulary.* Paper presented at the biennial meetings of the Society for Research in Child Development, Indianapolis, IN.

Antrop, I., Roeyers, H., Van Oost, P., & Buysse, A. (2000). Stimulation seeking and hyperactivity in children with ADHD. *Journal of Child Psychology, Psychiatry & Allied Disciplines, 41*, 225–231.

APA Task Force on Violent Media. (2015). *Technical report on the review of the violent video game literature.* Retrieved from http://www.apa.org/pi/families/violent-media.aspx

Armbruster, B., Lehr, F., & Osborn, J. (2003). *A child becomes a reader: Kindergarten through grade 3.* Washington, DC: National Institute for Literacy.

Aronen, E.T., Paavonen, E., Fjällberg, J., Soininen, M., & Törrönen, J. (2000). Sleep and psychiatric symptoms in school-age children. *Journal of the American Academy of Child & Adolescent Psychiatry, 39*(4), 502–508.

Ashkenazi, S., Rubinsten, O., & Henik, A. (2009). Attention, automaticity, and developmental dyscalculia. *Neuropsychology, 23*(4), 535–540. doi:10.1037/a0015347

Atasoy, S., Donnelly, I., & Pearson, J. (2016). Human brain networks function in connectome-specific harmonic waves. *Nature Communications, 7*(Jan), 10340. doi:10.1038/ncomms10340

Atwood, S. (2004, June). Education Arcade: MIT researchers are creating academically driven computer games that rival commercial products and make learning fun. *Technology Review.* Cambridge, MA. Retrieved from Technology Review website: http://www.technologyreview.com/news/402780/education-arcade

Barkley, R. (2005). *Attention-deficit hyperactivity disorder: A handbook for diagnosis and treatment* (3rd ed.). New York, NY: Guilford Press.

Barry, T.D., Lyman, R.D., & Klinger, L.G. (2002). Academic underachievement and attention-deficit/hyperactivity disorder: The negative impact of symptom severity on school performance. *Journal of School Psychology, 40*(3), 259–283. doi:10.1016/S0022-4405(02)00100-0

Bates, T.C., Lucian, M., Castles, A., Coltheart, M., Wright, M.J., & Martin, NAG. (2007). Replication of reported linkages for dyslexia and spelling and suggestive evidence for novel regions on chromosomes 4 and 17. *European Journal of Human Genetics, 15*(2), 194–203.

Behm-Morawitz, E., & Mastro, D. (2009). The effects of the sexualization of female video game characters on gender stereotyping and female self-concept. *Sex Roles, 61*(11), 808–823. doi:10.1007/s11199-009-9683-8

Berninger, V., Abbott, R., Nagy, W., & Carlisle, J. (2010). Growth in phonological, orthographic, and morphological awareness in grades 1 to 6. *Journal of Psycholinguistic Research, 39*(2), 141–163. doi:10.1007/s10936-009-9130-6

Bialystok, E. (1999). Cognitive complexity and attentional control in the bilingual mind. *Child Development, 70*, 636–644.

Bialystok, E. (2011). Reshaping the mind: The benefits of bilingualism. *Canadian Journal of Experimental Psychology, 65*(4), 229–35. doi:10.1037/a0025406

Blaye, A., & Jacques, S. (2009). Categorical flexibility in preschoolers: Contributions of conceptual knowledge and executive control. *Developmental Science, 12*(6), 863–873. doi:10.1111/j.1467-7687.2009.00832.x

Borst, G., Poirel, N., Pineau, A., Cassotti, M., & Houdé, O. (2013). Inhibitory control efficiency in a Piaget-like class inclusion task in school-age children and adults: A developmental negative priming study. *Developmental Psychology, 49*(7), 1366–1374. doi:org/10.1037/a0029622

Brault, M.C., & Lacourse, É. (2012). Prevalence of prescribed attention-deficit hyperactivity disorder medications and diagnosis among Canadian preschoolers and school-age children: 1994–2007. *Canadian Journal of Psychiatry, 57*(2), 93–101.

British Columbia Ministry of Education. (2001). English as a second language. Victoria, BC: Author. Retrieved from www.bced.gov.bc.ca/esl/policy/introduction.htm

Canadian Council on Social Development. (1999). *Immigrant youth in Canada: Arriving in Canada.* Ottawa, ON: Author. Retrieved from www.ccsd.ca/subsites/cd/docs/iy/arriving.htm

Canadian Paediatric Society. (2012a). *Healthy active living: Physical activity guidelines for children and adolescents.* Retrieved from http://www.cps.ca/documents/position/physical-activity-guidelines

Canadian Paediatric Society. (2012b). *Child and youth injury prevention: A public health approach.* Retrieved from http://www.cps.ca/documents/position/child-and-youth-injury-prevention

Canadian Paediatric Society. (2016). *Promoting optimal monitoring of child growth in Canada: Using the new World Health Organization growth charts - executive summary.* Retrieved from http://www.cps.ca/en/documents/position/child-growth-charts

Canadian Parents for French. (2001). *The state of French second language in Canada 2001.* Ottawa, ON: Author. Retrieved from www.cpf.ca/English/resources/FSL%202001%20Report/stateoffsl2001.htm

Casey, B.M. (2013). Individual and group differences in spatial ability. In D. Waller, & L. Hadel (Eds.), *Handbook of spatial cognition* (pp. 117–134). Washington, DC: American Psychological Association.

Chahal, H., Fung, C., Kuhle, S., & Veugelers, P.J. (2013). Availability and night-time use of electronic entertainment and communication devices are associated with short sleep duration and obesity among Canadian children. *Pediatric Obesity, 8*(1), 42–51. doi:10.1111/j.2047-6310.2012.00085.x

Chaptman, D. (2004, January 24). Education Arcade aims for videogame literacy, markets. *Wisconsin Week.* Madison, WI: University of Wisconsin. Retrieved from www.news.wisc.edu/9333.html

Cheng, T.A., Bell, J.M., Haileyesus, T., Gilchrist, J., Sugerman, D.E., & Coronado, V.G. (2016). Nonfatal playground-related traumatic brain injuries among children, 2001–2013. *Pediatrics, 137*(6). doi:10.1542/peds.2015-2721.R3

Chevalier, N., Kurth, S., Doucette, M.R., Wiseheart, M., Deoni, S.C.L., Dean, D.C., . . . LeBourgeois, M.K. (2015). Myelination is associated with processing speed in early childhood: Preliminary insights. *PLoS ONE, 10*(10), e0139897. doi:10.1371/journal.pone.0139897

Chi, M.T. (1978). Knowledge structure and memory development. In R.S. Siegler (Ed.), *Children's thinking: What develops?* (pp. 73–96). Hillsdale, NJ: Erlbaum.

Commissioner of Official Languages. (2009). *Two languages, a World of Opportunities: Second-language learning in Canada's universities.* Retrieved from http://www.ocol-clo.gc.ca/docs/e/uni_e.pdf

Commissioner of Official Languages. (2011). *Discussion forum on the perspectives of Canadians of diverse backgrounds on linguistic duality.* Retrieved from http://www.ocol-clo.gc.ca/docs/e/discussion_forum_halifax_e.pdf

Corkum, P., Davidson, F., & Macpherson, M. (2011). A framework for the assessment and treatment of sleep problems in children with attention-deficit/hyperactivity disorder. *Pediatric Clinics of North America. 58*(3), 66–683. doi:10.1016/j.pcl.2011.03.004

Corkum, P., Tannock, R. & Moldofsky, H. (1998). Sleep disturbances in children with attention-deficit/hyperactivity disorder. *Journal of the American Academy of Child and Adolescent Psychiatry, 37*(6), 637–646.

Council of Ministers of Education, Canada. (2016). *Council of Ministers of Education, Canada (CMEC).* Retrieved from http://www.cmec.ca/en/

Crone, D., & Whitehurst, G. (1999). Age and schooling effects on emergent literacy and early reading skills. *Journal of Educational Psychology, 91*, 594–603.

Currie, J., Stabile, M., & Jones, L.E. (2013). *Do stimulant medications improve educational and behavioral outcomes for children with ADHD?* National Bureau of Economic Research Working Paper No. 19105. Retrieved from http://www.nber.org/papers/w19105.pdf

Cushner, K., McClelland, A., & Safford, P. (2009). *Human diversity in education: An integrative approach.* Boston, MA: McGraw-Hill.

Cushner, K., McClelland, A., & Safford, P. (2009). *Human diversity in education: An integrative approach.* Boston, MA: McGraw-Hill.

Daley, D., & Birchwood, J. (2010). ADHD and academic performance: Why does ADHD impact on academic performance, and what can be done to support ADHD children in the classroom? *Child: Care, Health and Development, 36*(4), 455–464. doi:10.1111/j.1365-2214.2009.01046.x

Dempster, F.N. (1981). Memory span: Sources of individual and developmental differences. *Psychological Bulletin, 89*(1), 63–100.

Denham, S. (2006). Social-emotional competence as support for school readiness: What is it and how do we assess it? *Early Education and Development, 17*, 57–89.

Divgi, V. (2000). What about sleep? *Archives of Pediatrics & Adolescent Medicine, 154*(6), 636.

Evans, T.M., Kochalka, J., Ngoon, T.J., Wu, S.S., Qin, S., Battista, C., & Menon, V. (2015). Brain structural integrity and intrinsic functional connectivity forecast 6 year longitudinal growth in children's numerical abilities. *The Journal of Neuroscience, 35*(33), 11743–11750. doi.org/10.1523/JNEUROSCI.0216-15.2015

Farnham-Diggory, S. (1992). *The learning-disabled child.* Cambridge, MA: Harvard University Press.

Feldman, D. (2004). Piaget's stages: The unfinished symphony of cognitive development. *New Ideas in Psychology, 22,* 175–231.

Ferguson, C.J., & Olson, C.K. (2013). Friends, fun, frustration and fantasy: Child motivations for video game play. *Motivation and Emotion, 37*(1), 154–164. doi:10.1007/s10964-013-9986-5

Fiedorowicz, C., Benezra, E., MacDonald, W., McElgunn, B., Wilson, A., & Kaplan, B. (2002). The neurobiological basis of learning disabilities: An update. *Learning Disabilities: A Multidisciplinary Focus, 11*(2), 61–73.

Flavell, J.H. (1985). *Cognitive development* (2nd ed.). Englewood Cliffs, NJ: Prentice-Hall.

Flavell, J.H. (1986). The development of children's knowledge about the appearance-reality distinction. *American Psychologist, 41,* 418–425.

Gabbard, C.P. (2012). *Lifelong motor development* (6th ed.). San Francisco, CA: Pearson Benjamin Cummings.

Gardner, H. (1983). *Frames of mind: The theory of multiple intelligence.* New York, NY: Basic Books.

Gardner, H. (1999). *Intelligence reframed.* New York, NY: Basic Books.

Gentile, D.A., Lynch, P.J., Linder, J.R., & Walsh, D.A. (2004). The effects of violent video game habits on adolescent aggressive attitudes and behaviors. *Journal of Adolescence, 27*(1), 5–22.

Gentile, D.A., Walsh, D.A., Ellison, P.R., Fox, M., & Cameron, J. (2004, May). *Media violence as a risk factor for children: A longitudinal study.* Paper presented at the American Psychological Society 16th Annual Convention, Chicago, IL.

Gersten, R., Compton, D., Connor, C., Dimino, J., Santoro, L., Linan-Thompson, S., & Tilly, W. (2008). *Assisting students struggling with reading: Response to intervention and multi-tier intervention for reading in the primary grades. A practice guide.* Retrieved from http://ies.ed.gov/ncee/wwc/pdf/practiceguides/rti_reading_pg_021809.pdf

Gluckman, P.D., & Hanson, M.A. (2004a). Living with the past: Evolution, development, and patterns of disease. *Science, 305,* 1733–1736.

Gluckman, P.D., & Hanson, M.A. (2004b). *The fetal matrix: Evolution, development and disease.* New York, NY: Cambridge University Press.

Goleman, D. (1995). *Emotional intelligence.* New York, NY: Bantam.

Gong, D., He, H., Liu, D., Ma, W., Dong, L., Luo, C., & Yao, D. (2015). Enhanced functional connectivity and increased gray matter volume of insula related to action video game playing. *Scientific reports, 5*(Apr), 9763. doi:10.1038/srep09763

Gong, D., He, H., Ma, W., Liu, D., Huang, M., Dong, L., . . . Yao, D. (2016). Functional integration between salience and central executive networks: A role for action video game experience. *Neural Plasticity, 2016*(Sep), 9803165. doi:10.1155/2016/9803165

Government of Canada. (2016b). *Childhood obesity.* Retrieved from http://healthycanadians.gc.ca/healthy-living-vie-saine/obesity-obesite/risks-risques-eng.php

Graham, S., & Harris, K. (2007). Best practices in teaching planning. In S. Graham, C. MacArthur, & J. Fitzgerald (Eds.), *Best practices in writing instruction* (pp. 119–140). New York, NY: Guilford Press.

Greenfield, P. (1994). Video games as cultural artifacts. *Journal of Applied Developmental Psychology, 15,* 3–12.

Gruber, R., Sadeh, A., & Raviv, A. (2000). Instability of sleep patterns in children with attention-deficit/hyperactivity disorder. *Journal of the American Academy of Child and Adolescent Psychiatry, 379*(4), 495–501.

Hauge, M.R., & Gentile, D.A. (2003, April). *Video game addiction among adolescents: Associations with academic performance and aggression.* Paper presented at the Society for Research in Child Development Conference, Tampa, FL.

Health Canada. (2001b). *Coping with life. Trends in the health of Canadian youth.* Ottawa, ON: Author. Retrieved from www.hc-sc.gc.ca/hppb/childhood-youth/spsc/e_trends.html

Holobow, N., Genesee, F., & Lambert, W. (1991). The effectiveness of a foreign language immersion program for children from different ethnic and social class backgrounds: Report 2. *Applied Psycholinguistics, 12,* 179–198.

Houston, D., Al Otaiba, S., & Torgesen, J. (2006). Learning to read: Phonics and fluency. In D. Browder, & F. Spooner (Eds.), *Teaching language arts, math & science to students with significant cognitive disabilities* (pp. 93–123). Baltimore, MD: Paul H. Brookes Publishing.

Howard, A.W. (2010). Keeping children safe: Rethinking how we design our surroundings. *Canadian Medical Association Journal, 182*(6), 573.

Hua, X., Leow, A.D., Levitt, J.G., Caplan, R., Thompson, P.M., & Toga, W.A. (2009). Detecting brain growth patterns in normal children using tensor-based morphometry. *Human Brain Mapping, 30,* 209–219.

Human Connectome Project. (n.d.). *About the Human Connectome Project.* Retrieved from http://www.humanconnectomeproject.org/about/

Humphrey, N., Curran, A., Morris, E., Farrell, P., & Woods, K. (2007). Emotional intelligence and education: A critical review. *Educational Psychology, 27,* 235–254.

Johnston, A.M., Barnes, M.A., & Desrochers, A. (2008). Reading comprehension: Developmental processes, individual differences, and interventions. *Canadian Psychology, 49*(2), 125–133.

Kail, R. (1990). *The development of memory in children* (3rd ed.). New York, NY: Freeman.

Kail, R. (2008). Speed of processing in childhood and adolescence: Nature, consequences, and implications for understanding atypical development. In J. DeLuca & J. Kalmar (Eds.), *Studies on neuropsychology, neurology, and cognition* (pp. 101–123). Philadelphia, PA: Taylor & Francis.

Kail, R., & Hall, L.K. (1994). Processing speed, naming speed, and reading. *Developmental Psychology, 30,* 949–954.

Kim, Y., Petscher, Y., Schatschneider, C., & Foorman, B. (2010). Does growth rate in oral reading fluency matter in predicting reading comprehension achievement? *Journal of Educational Psychology, 102*(3), 652–667. doi:10.1037/a0019643

Kirkness, V.J. (1999). The critical state of aboriginal languages in Canada. *Canadian Journal of Native Education, 22,* 1–15.

Kiuru, N., Aunola, K., Torppa, M., Lerkkanen, M.K., Poikkeus, A.M., Niemi, P., . . . Nurmi, J.E. (2012). The role of parenting styles and teacher interactional styles in children's reading and spelling development. *Journal of School Psychology, 50*(6), 799–823. doi:10.1016/j.jsp.2012.07.001

Kline, S. (1998). *Video game culture: Leisure and play preferences of BC teens.* Vancouver, BC: Simon Fraser University Media Analysis Laboratory.

Kline, S. (2002). *Moral panics and video games.* Vancouver, BC: Simon Fraser University Media Analysis Laboratory. Retrieved from www2.sfu.ca/media-lab/

Kline, S. (2003). *Media consumption as a health and safety risk factor.* Vancouver, BC: Simon Fraser University Media Analysis Laboratory. Retrieved from www2.sfu.ca/media-lab/risk/docs/kline_media_risk_reduction5.doc

Klingberg, T., Fernell, E., Olesen, P., Johnson, M., Gustafsson, P., Dahlstrom, K., . . . Westerberg, H. (2005). Computerized training of working memory in children with ADHD: A randomized, controlled trial. *Journal of the American Academy of Child and Adolescent Psychiatry, 44*(2), 177–186.

Koppenhaver, D., Hendrix, M., & Williams, A. (2007). Toward evidence-based literacy interventions for children with severe and multiple disabilities. *Seminars in Speech & Language, 28,* 79–90.

Koskinen, P., Blum, I., Bisson, S., Phillips, S., Creamer, T., & Baker, T.K. (2000). Book access, shared reading, and audio models: The effects of supporting the literacy learning of linguistically diverse students in school and at home. *Journal of Educational Psychology, 92,* 23–36.

Kostanski, M., Fisher, A., & Gullone, E. (2004). Current conceptualization of body image dissatisfaction: Have we got it wrong? *Journal of Child Psychology and Psychiatry, 45*(7), 1317–1325. doi:10.1111/j.1469-7610.2004.00315.x

Kozey, M., & Siegel, L.S. (2008). Definitions of learning disabilities in Canadian provinces and territories. *Canadian Psychology, 49*(2), 162–172.

Krebs, N., & Primak, L. (2011). Pediatric nutrition and nutritional disorders. In K. Marcdante, R. Kliegman, H. Jensen, & R. Behrman (Eds.), *Nelson's essentials of pediatrics* (pp. 103–122). New York, NY: Elsevier Health Publishers.

Lambert, W., & Tucker, G.R. (1972). *Bilingual education of children: The St. Lambert experiment*. Rowley, MA: Newbury House.

Lawrence, V., Houghton, S., Douglas, G., Durkin, K., Whiting, K., & Tannock, R. (2004). Executive function and ADHD: A comparison of children's performance during neuropsychological testing and real-world activities. *Journal of Attention Disorders, 7*(3), 137–149. doi:10.1177/108705470400700302

Learning Disabilities Association of Canada (2002). *Official definition of learning disabilities*. Ottawa, ON: Author. Retrieved from www.ldac-taac.ca/english/defined/jan02eng.pdf

Learning Disabilities Association of Canada (2015). *Official definition of learning disabilities*. Retrieved from http://www.ldac-acta.ca/learn-more/ld-defined/official-definition-of-learning-disabilities

Learning Disabilities Association of Canada (n.d.). *Prevalence of learning disabilities*. Retrieved http://www.ldac-acta.ca/learn-more/ld-basics/prevalence-of-lds

Lenroot, R.K., Gogtay, N., Greenstein, D.K., Wells, E.M., Wallace, G.L., Clasen, L.S., . . . Giedd, J. (2007). Sexual dimorphism of brain developmental trajectories during childhood and adolescence. *Neuroimage, 36*(4), 1065–1073.

Ma, J.K., Le Mare, L., & Gurd, B.J. (2014). Classroom-based high-intensity interval activity improves off-task behaviour in primary school students. *Canadian Journal of Applied Physiology, 39*(12), 1332–1337, doi:10.1139/apnm-2014-0125

Ma, J.K., Le Mare, L., & Gurd, B.J. (2015). Four minutes of in-class high-intensity interval activity improves selective attention in 9- to 11-year olds. *Canadian Journal of Applied Physiology, 40*(3), 238–244. doi:10.1139/apnm-2014-0309

Media Awareness Network. (2004a). *Video games*. Retrieved from www.media-awareness.ca/english/parents/video_games/index.cfm

Media Awareness Network. (2004b). *Young Canadians in a wired world—Phase II: A qualitative research report*. Ottawa, ON: Author. Retrieved from www.media-awareness.ca/english/special_initiatives/surveys/phase_two/index.cfm

Mediascope, Inc. (1999). *The social effects of electronic interactive games: An annotated bibliography*. Studio City, CA: Mediascope Press.

Menon, V. (2015). Large-scale functional brain organization. In A.W. Toga (Ed.), *Brain mapping: An encyclopedic reference* (Vol 2, pp. 449–459). San Diego, CA: Academic Press-Elsevier B.V.

Mohanty, A. & Perregaux, C. (1997). Language acquisition and bilingualism. In J. Berry, P. Dasen, & T. Saraswath (Eds.), *Handbook of cross-cultural psychology: Vol. 2*. Boston, MA: Allyn & Bacon.

Morris, B.J., Croker, S., Masnick, A., & Zimmerman, C. (2012). The emergence of scientific reasoning. In H. Kloos, B.J. Morris, & J. Amaral (Eds.), *Trends in cognitive development* (pp. 61–82). Rijeka, Croatia: InTech Pub. doi:10.5772/53885

Morris, B.J., Croker, S., Zimmerman, C., Gill, D., & Romig, C. (2013). Gaming science: The "Gamification" of scientific thinking. *Frontiers in Psychology, 4*(Sep), 607. doi:10.3389/fpsyg.2013.00607

Mou, Y., & Peng, W. (2009). Gender and racial stereotypes in popular video games. In R. Ferdig (Ed.), *Handbook of research on effective electronic gaming in education* (pp. 922–937). Hershey, PA: IGI Global.

Neill, M. (1998). *High stakes tests do not improve student learning*. Retrieved from National Center for Fair & Open Testing website: www.fairtest.org

Ni, Y. (1998). Cognitive structure, content knowledge, and classificatory reasoning. *Journal of Genetic Psychology, 159*, 280–296.

Parault, S., & Schwanenflugel, P. (2000). The development of conceptual categories of attention during the elementary school years. *Journal of Experimental Child Psychology, 75*, 245–262.

ParticipACTION. (2016). *Physical activity guidelines*. Retrieved from https://www.participaction.com/en-ca/thought-leadership/benefits-and-guidelines/5-11

Pearson, P.D., & Cervetti, G.N. (2013). The psychology and pedagogy of reading processes. In W. Reynolds, G. Miller, & I. Weiner (Eds). *Handbook of psychology, Vol. 7: Educational psychology (2nd ed.)*. (pp. 257–281). Hoboken, NJ: John Wiley & Sons Inc.

Peverly, S., Ramaswamy, V., Brown, C., Sumowski, J., Alidoost, M., & Garner, J. (2007). What predicts skill in lecture note taking? *Journal of Educational Psychology, 99*(1), 167–180. doi:10.1037/0022-0663.99.1.167

Phillips, E. (2013). A case study of questioning for reading comprehension during guided reading. *Education 3–13, 41*(1), 110–120. doi:10.1080/03004279.2012.710106

Posner, M., & Rothbart, M. (2007). Expertise. In M. Posner & M. Rothbart (Eds.), *Educating the human brain* (pp. 189–208). Washington, DC: American Psychological Association.

Prat-Sala, M., Shillcock, R., & Sorace, A. (2000). Animacy effects on the production of object-dislocated descriptions by Catalan-speaking children. *Journal of Child Language, 27*, 97–117.

Pryor, L.E., Brendgen, M., Tremblay, R.E., Pingault, J.B., Liu, X., Dubois, L., . . . Côté, S.M. (2015). Early risk factors of overweight developmental trajectories during middle childhood. *PLoS ONE, 10*(6), e0131231. doi:10.1371/journal.pone.0131231

Public Health Agency of Canada. (2010b). *Childhood obesity and the role of the Government of Canada*. Ottawa, ON: Author. Retrieved from www.phac-aspc.gc.ca/ch-se/obesity/obesityeng.php

Public Health Agency of Canada. (2012c). *Curbing childhood obesity*. Retrieved from http://www.phac-aspc.gc.ca/hp-ps/hl-mvs/framework-cadre/pdf/ccofw-eng.pdf

Public Health Agency of Canada. (2015a). *Canadian immunization guide*. Retrieved from http://www.phac-aspc.gc.ca/publicat/cig-gci/index-eng.php

Pujadas Botey, A., Bayrampour, H., Carson, V., Vinturache, A., & Tough, S. (2016). Adherence to Canadian physical activity and sedentary behaviour guidelines among children 2 to 13 years of age. *Preventive Medicine Reports, 3*(3), 14–20. doi:10.1016/j.pmedr.2015.11.012

Rego, A. (2006). The alphabetic principle, phonics, and spelling: Teaching students the code. In J. Schumm (Ed.), *Reading assessment and instruction for all learners* (pp. 118–162). New York, NY: Guilford Press.

Roberts, K.C., Shields, M., de Groh, M., Aziz, A., & Gilbert, J.A. (2012). Overweight and obesity in children and adolescents: results from the 2009 to 2011 Canadian Health Measures Survey. *Health Reports, 23*(3), 37–41.

Romano, E., Baillargeon, R.H., Fortier, I., Wu, H.X., Robaey, P., Zoccolillo, M., Tremblay, R.E. (2005). Individual change in methylphenidate use in a national sample of children aged 2 to 11 years. *Canadian Journal of Psychiatry, 50* (3), 144–152.

Rosenberg, J., Pennington, B.F., Willcutt, E.G., & Olson, R.K. (2012). Gene by environment interactions influencing reading disability and the inattentive symptom dimension of attention deficit/hyperactivity disorder. *Journal of Child Psychology and Psychiatry, 53*(3), 243–251. doi:10.1111/j.1469-7610.2011.02452.x

Saddler, B. (2007). Improving sentence construction skills. In S. Graham, C. MacArthur, & J. Fitzgerald (Eds.), *Best practices in writing instruction* (pp. 163–178). New York, NY: Guilford Press.

Safty, A. (1995). French immersion and the making of a bilingual society: A critical review and discussion. In L.W. Roberts & R.A. Clifton (Eds.), *Contemporary Canadian educational issues*. Toronto, ON: Nelson.

Sak, U., & Maker, C. (2006). Developmental variation in children's creative mathematical thinking as a function of schooling, age, and knowledge. *Creativity Research, 18*, 279–291.

Schachter, H.M., Pham, B., King, J., Langford, S., & Moher, D. (2001). How efficacious and safe is short-acting methylphenidate for the treatment of attention-deficit disorder in children and adolescents? A meta-analysis. *Canadian Medical Association Journal, 165*(11), 1475–1488.

Schliemann, A., Carraher, D., & Ceci, S. (1997). Everyday cognition. In J. Berry, P. Dasen, & T. Saraswathi (Eds.), *Handbook of cross-cultural psychology: Vol. 2. Basic processes and human development*. Needham Heights, MA: Allyn & Bacon.

Settlement.org (2001). *First-language literacy and heritage: Heritage language programs.* Retrieved from www.settlement.org/site/LL/firstlanguage_heritage.asp

Seung, S. (2012). *Connectome – how the brain's wiring makes us who we are.* New York, NY: Houghton Mifflin Harcourt.

Shaw, P., Kabani, N.J., Lerch, J.P., Eckstrand, K., Lenroot, R., Gogtay, N., . . . Wise, S.P. (2008). Neurodevelopmental trajectories of the human cerebral cortex. *Journal of Neuroscience, 28*(14), 3586–3594.

Siegel, L.S. (2008). Morphological awareness skills of English language learners and children with dyslexia. *Topics in Language Disorders, 28*(1), 15–27. doi:10.1097/01.adt.0000311413.75804.60

Siegler, R., & Chen, Z. (2002). Development of rules and strategies: Balancing the old and the new. *Journal of Experimental Child Psychology, 81,* 446–457.

Siegler, R., & Lin, X. (2010). Self-explanations promote children's learning. In H. Waters & W. Schneider (Eds.), *Metacognition, strategy use, and instruction* (pp. 85–112). New York, NY: Guilford Press.

Siegler, R.S. (1994). Cognitive variability: A key to understanding cognitive development. *Current Directions in Psychological Science, 3,* 1–5.

Singh, A., Yeh, C.J., Verma, N., & Das, A.K. (2015). Overview of attention deficit hyperactivity disorder in young children. *Health Psychology Research, 3*(2), 2115. doi:10.4081/hpr.2015.2115

Skwarchuk, S., & Anglin, J. (2002). Children's acquisition of the English cardinal number words: A special case of vocabulary development. *Journal of Educational Psychology, 94*(1), 107–125. doi:10.1037/0022-0663.94.1.107

Smith, D. (2016). Theory linking brain activity to brain shape could throw light on human consciousness. *UNSW Australia Newsroom.* Retrieved from http://newsroom.unsw.edu.au/news/science-tech/theory-linking-brain-activity-brain-shape-could-throw-light-human-consciousness

Sowell, E.R., Peterson, B.S., Thompson, P.M., Welcome, S.E., Henkenius, A.L., & Toga, A.W. (2003). Mapping cortical change across the human life span. *Nature Neuroscience, 6*(3), 309–315.

Spreen, O., Risser, A., & Edgell, D. (1995). *Developmental neuropsychology.* New York, NY: Oxford University Press.

Statistics Canada. (2012i). *Linguistic characteristics of Canadians* (Cat. no. 98-314-X2011001). Ottawa, ON: Ministry of Industry. Retrieved from http://www12.statcan.gc.ca/census-recensement/2011/as-sa/98-314-x/98-314-x2011001-eng.pdf

Statistics Canada. (2013b). *Immigration and ethnocultural diversity in Canada* (Catalogue no. 99-010-X2011001). Retrieved from http://www12.statcan.gc.ca/nhs-enm/2011/as-sa/99-010-x/99-010-x2011001-eng.pdf

Statistics Canada. (2015d). *Leading causes of death, total population, by age group and sex, Canada, annual* (CANSIM Table 102-0561). Retrieved from http://www5.statcan.gc.ca/cansim/a26?lang=eng&id=1020561

Statistics Canada. (2015e). *Body mass index of children and youth, 2012 to 2013.* Retrieved from http://www.statcan.gc.ca/pub/82-625-x/2014001/article/14105-eng.htm

Sternberg, R. (1988). *The triarchic mind: A new theory of intelligence.* New York, NY: Viking Press.

Sternberg, R. (2002). A broad view of intelligence: The theory of successful intelligence. *Consulting Psychology Journal: Practice and Research, 55*(3), 139–154. doi:10.1037/1061-4087.55.3.139

Sternberg, R., & Grigorenko, E. (2006). Cultural intelligence and successful intelligence. *Group & Organization Management, 31,* 37–39.

Stevens, C., & Bavelier, D. (2012). The role of selective attention on academic foundations: A cognitive neuroscience perspective. *Developmental Cognitive Neuroscience, 2*(Suppl 1), S30–S48. doi:10.1016/j.dcn.2011.11.001

Sturm, J., & Seery, C. (2007). Speech and articulatory rate of school-aged children in conversation and narrative contexts. *Language, Speech, and Hearing Services in Schools, 38,* 47–59.

Swanson, H.L., & Alloway, T.P. (2012). Working memory, learning and academic achievement. In K.R. Harris, S. Graham, T. Urdan, C.B. McCormick, G.M. Sinatra, & J. Sweller (2012). *APA educational psychology handbook, Volume 1: Theories, constructs, and critical issues* (pp. 327–366). Washington, DC: American Psychological Association.

Swanson, L., & Kim, K. (2007). Working memory, short-term memory, and naming speed as predictors of children's mathematical performance. *Intelligence, 35,* 151–168.

Tam, H., Jarrold, C., Baddeley, A., & Sabatos-De Vito, M. (2010). The development of memory maintenance: Children's use of phonological rehearsal and attentional refreshment in working memory tasks. *Journal of Experimental Child Psychology, 107*(3), 306–324. doi:http://dx.doi.org/10.1016/j.jecp.2010.05.006

Tanofsky-Kraff, M., Yanovski, S., Wilfley, D., Marmarosh, C., Morgan, C., & Yanovski, J. (2004). Eating-disordered behaviors, body fat, and psychopathology in overweight and normal-weight children. *Journal of Consulting and Clinical Psychology, 72,* 53–61.

Tomlinson-Keasey, C., Eisert, D.C., Kahle, L.R., Hardy-Brown, K., & Keasey, B. (1979). The structure of concrete operational thought. *Child Development, 50,* 1153–1163.

Torgesen, J., Wagner, R., Rashotte, C., Rose, E., Lindamood, P., Conway, T. & Garvan, C. (1999). Preventing reading failure in young children with phonological processing disabilities: Group and individual responses to instruction. *Journal of Educational Psychology, 91,* 594–603.

Toronto District School Board (n.d.). *Facts and figures about the TDSB.* Retrieved from http://www.tdsb.on.ca/communications/tdsb-facts.html

Tremblay, M.S., Shields, M., Laviolette, M., Craig, C.L., Janssen, I., & Connor Gorber, S. (2010). Fitness of Canadian children and youth: Results from the 2007–2009 Canadian Health Measures Survey. *Health Reports, 21*(1), 7–20.

Voyer, D., & Voyer, S.D. (2014). Gender differences in scholastic achievement: A meta-analysis. *Psychological Bulletin, 140*(4), 1174–1204. doi:10.1037/a0036620

Walcot-Gayda, E. (n.d.). *Understanding learning disabilities.* Retrieved from http://www.ldac-acta.ca/learn-more/ld-basics/understanding-learning-disabilities

Waters, H., & Waters, T. (2010). Bird experts: A study of child and adult knowledge utilization. In H. Waters & W. Schneider (Eds.), *Metacognition, strategy use, and instruction* (pp. 113–134). New York, NY: Guilford Press.

Weber, K. (1993). *Special Education in Ontario Schools.* Thornhill, ON: Highland Press.

White, J. (2006). Multiple invalidities. In J. Schaler (Ed.), *Howard Gardner under fire: The rebel psychologist faces his critics* (pp. 45–72). Chicago, IL: Open Court.

Winzer, M. (1993). *Children with exceptionalities* (3rd ed.). Scarborough, ON: Prentice-Hall Canada.

Woolfolk, A. E., Winne, P. H., & Perry, N. E. (2009). *Educational Psychology* (3rd CDN ed.). Toronto, ON: Pearson Education Canada.

World Health Organization. (2010). *The WHO child growth standards.* Retrieved from www.who.int/childgrowth/en/

Zimmerman, C. (2007). The development of scientific thinking skills in elementary and middle school. *Developmental Review, 27*(2), 172–223. doi:10.1016/j.dr.2006.12.001

Chapter 10

Ahadi, S.A., & Rothbart, M.K. (1994). Temperament, development, and the Big Five. In C.F. Halverson, Jr., G.A. Kohnstamm, & R.P. Martin (Eds.), *The developing structure of temperament and personality from infancy to adulthood* (pp. 189–207). Hillsdale, NJ: Erlbaum.

Anderson, D.R., Huston, A.C., Schmitt, K.L., Linebarger, D.L., & Wright, J.C. (2001). Early childhood television viewing and adolescent behavior: The recontact study. *Monographs of the Society for Research in Child Development, 66*(1):I–VIII, 1–147.

Andreou, E., & Metallidou, P. (2004). The relationship of academic and social cognition to behaviour in bullying situations among Greek primary school children. *Educational Psychology, 24*(1), 27–41.

Aranha, M. (1997). Creativity in students and its relation to intelligence and peer perception. *Revista Interamericana de Psicologia, 31,* 309–313.

Astor, R. (1994). Children's moral reasoning about family and peer violence: The role of provocation and retribution. *Child Development, 65*, 1054–1067.

Bandura, A. (1997a). *Self-efficacy: The exercise of control.* New York, NY: W.H. Freeman.

Bandura, A., Ross, D., & Ross, S.A. (1961). Transmission of aggression through imitation of aggressive models. *Journal of Abnormal and Social Psychology, 63*, 575–582.

Bandura, A., Ross, D., & Ross, S.A. (1963). Imitation of film-mediated aggressive models. *Journal of Abnormal and Social Psychology, 66*, 3–11.

Barenboim, C. (1981). The development of person perception in childhood and adolescence: From behavioral comparisons to psychological constructs to psychological comparisons. *Child Development, 52*, 129–144.

Benenson, J.F. (1994). Ages four to six years: Changes in the structures of play networks of girls and boys. *Merrill-Palmer Quarterly, 40*, 478–487.

Boivin, M., Brendgen, M., Vitaro, F., Forget-Dubois, N., Feng, B., Tremblay, R.E., & Dionne, G. (2013). Evidence of gene-environment correlation for peer difficulties: Disruptive behaviors predict early peer relation difficulties in school through genetic effects. *Development and Psychopathology, 25*(1), 79–92. doi:10.1017/S0954579412000910

Bokhorst, C., Sumter, S., & Westenberg, P. (2010). Social support from parents, friends, classmates, and teachers in children and adolescents aged 9 to 18 years: Who is perceived as most supportive? *Social Development, 19*(2), 417–426. doi:10.1111/j.1467-9507.2009.00540.x

Borzekowski, D.G.L., & Robinson, T.N. (2005). The remote, the mouse and the No. 2 pencil: The household media environment and academic achievement among third grade students. *Archives of Pediatrics and Adolescent Medicine, 159*(7), 607–613.

Bosacki, S. (2001a). "Theory of Mind" or "Theory of the Soul"? The role of spirituality in children's understanding of minds and emotions. In J. Erricker, C. Ota, & C. Erricker (Eds.), *Spiritual Education: Cultural, Religious and Social Differences* (pp. 156–169). Portland, OR: Sussex Academic Press.

Bosacki, S. (2005). Religiosity in children and youth: Psychoeducational approaches. In C. Frisby & C.R. Reynolds (Eds.), *Comprehensive handbook of multicultural school psychology* (pp. 611–650). New York, NY: Wiley & Sons.

Bosacki, S.L. (2001b). Spirituality, gendered subjectivities, and education in preadolescents: Canadian preadolescents' reflections on gender-roles and their sense of self. *International Journal of Children's Spirituality, 6*(20), 207–221.

Bosacki, S.L. (2002). Spirituality and self in preadolescents: Implications for a connected curriculum. *Journal of Beliefs & Values, 23*(1), 55–67.

Bosacki, S.L., Moore, K., Talwar, V., & Park-Saltzman, J. (2011). Preadolescents' gendered spiritual identities and self-regulation. *Journal of Beliefs & Values, 32*(3), 303–316. doi:10.1080/13617672.2011.627679

Brandon, P., & Hofferth, S. (2003). Determinants of out-of-school childcare arrangements among children in single-mother and two-parent families. *Social Science Research, 32*, 129–147.

Brendgen, B. (2012). Development of indirect aggression before school entry. In R.E Tremblay, M. Boivin, & R. Peters (Eds.), *Encyclopedia on early childhood development [online].* Montreal, Quebec: Centre of Excellence for Early Childhood Development. Retrieved from www.child-encyclopedia.com/documents/BrendgenANGxp1.pdf

Britner, S., & Pajares, F. (2006). Sources of science self-efficacy beliefs in middle school students. *Journal of Research in Science Teaching, 43*(5), 485–499.

Bushman, B.J., Chandler, J., & Huesmann, L.R. (2010). Do violent media numb our consciences? In W. Koops, D. Brugman, T.J. Ferguson, & A.F. Sanders, (Eds.), *The development and structure of conscience* (pp. 237–251). New York, NY: Psychology Press.

Cairns, R.B., & Cairns, B.D. (1994). *Lifelines and risks: Pathways of youth in our time.* Cambridge, England: Cambridge University Press.

Canada Safety Council. (2015). *Preparation and communication the key for children home alone.* Ottawa, ON: Author. Retrieved from https://canadasafetycouncil.org/child-safety/preparation-and-communication-key-children-home-alone

Card, N.A., Stucky, B.D., Sawalani, G.M., & Little, T.D. (2008). Direct and indirect aggression during childhood and adolescence: A meta-analytic review of gender differences, intercorrelations, and relations to maladjustment. *Child Development, 79*(5), 1185–229. doi:10.1111/j.1467-8624.2008.01184.x

Casper, L., & Smith, K. (2002). Dispelling the myths: Self-care, class, and race. *Journal of Family Issues, 23*(6), 716–727.

Cillessen, A., & Mayeux, L. (2004). From censure to reinforcement: Developmental changes in the association between aggression and social status. *Child Development, 75*(1), 147–163.

Cillessen, A.H.N., van IJzendoorn, H.W., van Lieshout, C.F.M., & Hartup, W.W. (1992). Heterogeneity among peer-rejected boys: Subtypes and stabilities. *Child Development, 63*, 893–905.

Clark, R., Harris, A., White-Smith, K., Allen, W., & Ray, B. (2010). Promising practices: The positive effects of after-school programs for African American male development and educational progress. In W. Johnson (Ed.), *Social work with African American males: Health, mental health, and social policy* (pp. 117–146). New York, NY: Oxford University Press.

Coie, J.D., & Cillessen, A.H.N. (1993). Peer rejection: Origins and effects on children's development. *Current Directions in Psychological Science, 2*, 89–92.

Craig, W.M. (2004). Bullying in Canada. In *The Canadian World Health Organization report on young people in Canada and their health and well being* (pp. 87–96). Ottawa, ON: Health Canada.

Cuevas, C.A., Finkelhor, D., Clifford, C., Ormrod, R.K., & Turner, H.A. (2010). Psychological distress as a risk factor for re-victimization in children. *Child Abuse and Neglect, 34*(4), 235–243. doi:10.1016/j.chiabu.2009.07.004

Cvencek, D., Greenwald, A.G., & Meltzoff, A.N. (2016). Implicit measures for preschool children confirm self-esteem's role in maintaining a balanced identity. *Journal of Experimental Social Psychology, 62*(1), 50–57. doi:10.1016/j.jesp.2015.09.015

Damon, W. (1977). *The social world of the child.* San Francisco, CA: Jossey-Bass.

Damon, W. (1983). The nature of social-cognitive change in the developing child. In W.F. Overton (Ed.), *The relationship between social and cognitive development* (pp. 103–142). Hillsdale, NJ: Erlbaum.

Dickson, D.J., Richmond, A.D., Brendgen, M., Vitaro, F., Laursen, B., Dionne, G. & Boivin, M. (2015). Aggression can be contagious: Longitudinal associations between proactive aggression and reactive aggression among young twins. *Aggressive Behavior, 41*(5), 455–466. doi:10.1002/ab.21582

Eisenberger, N. (2003). Does rejection hurt? An fMRI study of social exclusion. *Science, 302*(5643), 290–292.

Ennemoser, M., & Schneider, W. (2007). Relations of television viewing and reading: Findings from a 4-year longitudinal study. *Journal of Educational Psychology, 99*(2), 349–368.

Eslea, M., Menesini, E., Morita, Y., O'Moore, M., Mora-Merchan, J., Pereira, B., & Smith, P. (2004). Friendship and loneliness among bullies and victims: Data from seven countries. *Aggressive Behavior, 30*(1), 71–83. doi:10.1002/ab.20006

Fitzgerald, D., & White, K. (2003). Linking children's social worlds: Perspective taking in parent–child and peer contexts. *Social Behavior and Personality: An International Journal, 31*(5), 509–522.

Fitzpatrick, C., Barnett, T., & Pagani, L.S. (2012). Early exposure to media violence and later child adjustment. *Journal of Developmental and Behavioral Pediatrics, 33*(4), 291–7. doi:10.1097/DBP.0b013e31824eaab3

Flannery, D.J., Vazsonyi, A.T., Liau, A.K., Guo, S., Powell, K.E., Atha, H., . . . Embry, D. (2003). Initial behavior outcomes for the PeaceBuilders universal school-based prevention program. *Developmental Psychology*, 39(2), 292–308. doi:10.1037/0012-1649.39.2.292

Fordham, K., & Stevenson-Hinde, J. (1999). Shyness, friendship quality, and adjustment during middle childhood. *Journal of Child Psychology & Psychiatry & Allied Disciplines*, 40, 757–768.

Freeman, J.G., King, M., Pickett, W., Craig, W., Elgar, F., Janssen, I., & Klinger, D. (2012). *The health of Canada's young people: A mental health focus*. Retrieved from: http://www.phac-aspc.gc.ca/hp-ps/dca-dea/publications/hbsc-mental-mentale/index-eng.php

Galambos, N., & Maggs, J. (1991). Out-of-school care of young adolescents and self-reported behavior. *Developmental Psychology*, 27, 644–655.

Galanaki, E. (2004). Teachers and loneliness: The children's perspective. *School Psychology International*, 25(1), 92–105.

Gnepp, J., & Chilamkurti, C. (1988). Children's use of personality attributions to predict other people's emotional and behavioral reactions. *Child Development*, 50, 743–754.

Godleski, S., & Ostrov, J. (2010). Relational aggression and hostile attribution biases: Testing multiple statistics methods and models. *Journal of Abnormal Child Psychology*, 38(4), 447–458. doi:10.1007/s10802-010-9391-4

Gottman, J.M. (1986). The world of coordinated play: Same- and cross-sex friendship in young children. In J.M. Gottman & J.G. Parker (Eds.), *Conversations of friends: Speculations on affective development* (pp. 139–191). Cambridge, England: Cambridge University Press.

Graham, J., Cohen, R., Zbikowski, S., & Secrist, M. (1998). A longitudinal investigation of race and sex as factors in children's classroom friendship choices. *Child Study Journal*, 28, 245–266.

Green, S. (2001). Systemic vs. individualistic approaches to bullying. *Journal of the American Medical Association*, 286(7), 787.

Halle, T. (1999). Implicit theories of social interactions: Children's reasoning about the relative importance of gender and friendship in social partner choices. *Merrill-Palmer Quarterly*, 45, 445–467.

Hancox, R.J., Milne, B.J., & Poulton, R. (2005). Association of television viewing during childhood with poor educational achievement. *Archives of Pediatrics & Adolescent Medicine*, 159(7), 614–618.

Harrist, A., Zaia, A., Bates, J., Dodge, K., & Pettit, G. (1997). Subtypes of social withdrawal in early childhood: Sociometric status and social-cognitive differences across four years. *Child Development*, 68, 278–294.

Harter, S. (1987). The determinations and mediational role of global self-worth in children. In N. Eisenberg (Ed.), *Contemporary topics in developmental psychology* (pp. 219–242). New York, NY: Wiley-Interscience.

Harter, S. (2006). Developmental and individual difference perspectives on self-esteem. In D. Mroczek & T. Little (Eds.), *Handbook of personality development* (pp. 311–334). Mahwah, NJ: Lawrence Erlbaum Associates Publishers.

Harter, S. (2012). *The construction of the self: Developmental and sociocultural foundations* (2nd ed.). New York, NY: Guilford Press.

Hartup, W.W. (1996). The company they keep: Friendships and their developmental significance. *Child Development*, 67, 1–13.

Hartup, W.W., & Abecassis, M. (2004). Friends and enemies. In P.K. Smith & C.H. Hart (Eds.), *Blackwell handbook of childhood social development* (pp. 285–306). Maiden, MA: Blackwell.

Hosogi, M., Okada, A., Fujii, C., Noguchi, K., & Watanabe, K. (2012). Importance and usefulness of evaluating self-esteem in children. *Biopsychosocial Medicine*, 6(Mar), 9. doi:10.1186/1751-0759-6-9

Hubbard, J.A., Romano, L.J., McAuliffe, M.D., & Morrow, M.T. (2010). Anger and the reactive–proactive aggression distinction in childhood and adolescence. In M. Potegal, G. Stemmler, & C. Spielberger (Eds.), *International handbook of anger: Constituent and concomitant biological, psychological, and social processes* (pp. 231–239). New York, NY: Springer Science & Business Media.

Huesmann, L.R., Moise-Titus, J., Podolski, C.L., & Eron, L.D. (2003). Longitudinal relations between children's exposure to TV violence and their aggressive and violent behaviour in young adulthood: 1977–1992. *Developmental Psychology*, 39(2), 201–221.

Jackson, L., & Bracken, B. (1998). Relationship between students' social status and global and domain-specific self-concepts. *Journal of School Psychology*, 36, 233–246.

John, O.P., Caspi, A., Robins, R.W., Moffitt, T.E., & Stouthamer-Loeber, M. (1994). The "little five": Exploring the nomological network of the five-factor model of personality in adolescent boys. *Child Development*, 65, 160–178.

Kawabata, Y., Tseng, W.L., Murray-Close, D., & Crick, N.R. (2012). Developmental trajectories of Chinese children's relational and physical aggression: Associations with social-psychological adjustment problems. *Journal of Abnormal Child Psychology*, 40(7), 1087–1097. doi:10.1007/s10802-012-9633-8

Killen, M., Mulvey, K., Richardson, C., Jampol, N., & Woodward, A. (2011). The accidental transgressor: Morally-relevant theory of mind. *Cognition*, 119(2), 197–215. doi:10.1016/j.cognition.2011.01.006

Lansford, J., Putallaz, M., Grimes, C., Schiro-Osman, K., Upersmidt, J., & Coie, J. (2006). Perceptions of friendship quality and observed behaviors with friends: How do sociometrically rejected, average, and popular girls differ? *Merrill-Palmer Quarterly: Journal of Developmental Psychology*, 52(4), 694–720. doi:10.1353/mpq.2006.0036

Leaper, C. (1991). Influence and involvement in children's discourse: Age, gender, and partner effects. *Child Development*, 62, 797–811.

Lickona, T. (1994). *Raising good children*. New York, NY: Bantam Books.

Linebarger, D.L. & Walker, D. (2005). Infants' and toddlers' television viewing and language outcomes. *American Behavioral Scientist*, 48(5), 624–645.

Linebarger, D.L., & Wainwright, D.K. (2006). *Television can teach: Elements of effective educational television*. Philadelphia, PA: Annenberg School for Communication, University of Pennsylvania.

Livesley, W.J., & Bromley, D.B. (1973). *Person perception in childhood and adolescence*. London, England: Wiley.

Mark, A.E., Boyce, W.F., & Janssen, I. (2006). Television viewing, computer use, and total screen time in Canadian youth. *Paediatrics & Child Health*, 11(9), 595–599.

Marsh, H., Craven, R., & Debus, R. (1999). Separation of competency and affect components of multiple dimensions of academic self-concept: A developmental perspective. *Merrill-Palmer Quarterly*, 45, 567–601.

Marshall, N., Coll, C., Marx, F., McCartney, K., Keefe, N., & Ruh, J. (1997). After-school time and children's behavioral adjustment. *Merrill-Palmer Quarterly*, 43, 497–514.

Martin, C.L., & Ruble, D.N. (2010). Patterns of gender development. *Annual Review of Psychology*, 61, 353–381. doi:10.1146/annurev.psych.093008.100511

Martin, C.L., Kornienko, O., Schaefer, D.R., Hanish, L.D., Fabes, R.A., & Goble, P. (2013). The role of sex of peers and gender-typed activities in young children's peer affiliative networks: A longitudinal analysis of selection and influence. *Child Development*, 84(3), 921–937. doi:10.1111/cdev.12032

Mason, J., & Chuang, S. (2001). Culturally-based after-school arts programming for low-income urban children: Adaptive and preventive effects. *Journal of Primary Prevention*, 22(1), 45–54.

Maszk, P., Eisenberg, N., & Guthrie, I. (1999). Relations of children's social status to their emotionality and regulation: A short-term longitudinal study. *Merrill-Palmer Quarterly*, 454, 468–492.

McChristian, C.L., Ray, G.E., Tidwell, P.S., & LoBello, S.G. (2012). Classroom friends and very best friends: A short-term longitudinal analysis of relationship quality. *The Journal of Genetic Psychology*, 173(4), 463–469. doi:10.1080/00221325.2011.626000

McCrae, R., & Costa, P. (1990). *Personality in adulthood*. New York, NY: Guilford.

Mehta, P., & Beer, J. (2010). Neural mechanisms of the testosterone-aggression relation: The role of orbitofrontal cortex. *Journal of Cognitive Neuroscience*, 22(10), 2357–2368. doi:10.1162/jocn.2009.21389

Mehta, P., & Strough, J. (2009). Sex segregation in friendships and normative contexts across the life span. *Developmental Review*, 29 (3), 201–220. doi: http://dx.doi.org/10.1016/j.dr.2009.06.001

Miller, L. (2015). *The spiritual child. The new science on parenting for health and lifelong thriving.* New York, NY: St. Martin's Press.

Miller, P., Wang, S., Sandel, T., & Cho, G. (2002). Self-esteem as folk theory: A comparison of European American and Taiwanese mothers' beliefs. *Science & Practice, 2*(3), 209–239.

Mills, R.S.L., & Rubin, K.H. (1998). Are behavioural and psychological control both differentially associated with childhood aggression and social withdrawal? *Canadian Journal of Behavioural Science, 30*(2), 132–136.

Montemayor, R., & Eisen, M. (1977). The development of self-conceptions from childhood to adolescence. *Developmental Psychology, 13*, 314–319.

Moore, K., Talwar, V., & Bosacki, S. (2012). Canadian children's perceptions of spirituality: Diverse voices. *International Journal of Children's Spirituality, 17*(3), 217–234. doi:10.1080/1364436X.2012.742040

Moore, K., Talwar, V., Bosacki, S., & Park-Saltzman, J. (2011). Diverse voices: Children's perceptions of spirituality. *Alberta Journal of Educational Research, 57*(1), 107–110. doi:10.1080/1364436X.2012.742040

Murray, J., Liotti, M., Ingmundson, P., Mayberg, H., Pu, U., Zamarripa, F., . . . Fox, T. (2006). Children's brain activations while viewing televised violence revealed by MRO. *Media Psychology, 8*(1), 25–37.

Newcomb, A.F., & Bagwell, C.L. (1995). Children's friendship relations: A meta-analytic review. *Psychological Bulletin, 117*, 306–347.

Newcomb, A.F., Bukowski, W.M., & Pattee, L. (1993). Children's peer relations: A meta-analytic review of popular, rejected, neglected, controversial, and average sociometric status. *Psychological Bulletin, 113*, 99–128.

Ostrov, J.M., Gentile, D.A., & Crick, N.R. (2006). Media exposure, aggression and prosocial behavior during early childhood: A longitudinal study. *Social Development, 15*(4), 612–627.

ParticipACTION. (2015). *The biggest risk is keeping kids indoors. The 2015 ParticipACTION report card on physical activity for children and youth.* Toronto, ON: ParticipACTION.

Peacebuilders. (2015). *About Peacebuilders.* Retrieved from http://peacebuilders.ca/peacebuilders/

Pepler, D.J., Craig, W.M., Connolly, J.A., Yuill, A., McMaster, L., & Jiang, D. (2006). A developmental perspective on bullying. *Aggressive Behavior, 32*(4), 376–384.

Pettit, G., Laird, R., Bates, J., & Dodge, K. (1997). Patterns of after-school care in middle childhood: Risk factors and developmental outcomes. *Merrill-Palmer Quarterly, 43*, 515–538.

Phillips, D., Schwean, V., & Saklofske, D. (1997). Treatment effect of a school-based cognitive-behavioral program for aggressive children. *Canadian Journal of School Psychology, 13*, 60–67.

Piaget, J. (1932). *The moral judgment of the child.* New York, NY: Macmillan.

Piaget, J. (1965). *The moral judgment of the child.* New York, NY: Free Press.

Pingault, J.B., Tremblay, R.E., Vitaro, F., Japel, C., Boivin, M., & Côté, S.M. (2015). Early nonparental care and social behavior in elementary school: Support for a social group adaptation hypothesis. *Child Development, 86*(5), 1469–1488. doi:10.1111/cdev.12399

Pomerantz, E., & Ruble, D. (1998). The role of maternal control in the development of sex differences in child self-evaluative factors. *Child Development, 69*, 458–478.

Poulin, F., & Boivin, M. (1999). Proactive and reactive aggression and boys' friendship quality in mainstream classrooms. *Journal of Emotional & Behavioral Disorders, 7*, 168–177.

Poulin, F., & Boivin, M. (2000). The role of proactive and reactive aggression in the formation and development of boys' friendships. *Developmental Psychology, 36*(2), 233–240.

Powlishta, K.K. (1995). Intergroup processes in childhood: Social categorization and sex role development. *Developmental Psychology, 31*, 781–788.

Qualter, P., Murphy, S.M., Abbott, J., Gardner, K.J., Japel, C., Vitaro, F., . . . Tremblay, R.E. (2015). Developmental associations between victimization and body mass index from 3 to 10 years in a population sample. *Aggressive Behavior, 41*(2), 109–122. doi:10.1002/AB.21580

Reijntjes, A., Kamphuis, J.H., Prinzie, P., & Telch, M.J. (April 2010). "Peer victimization and internalizing problems in children: A meta-analysis of longitudinal studies". *Child Abuse & Neglect, 34*(4): 244–252. doi:10.1016/j.chiabu.2009.07.009

Rhee, S., & Waldman, I. (2011). Genetic and environmental influences on aggression. In P. Shaver & M. Mikulincer (Eds.), *Human aggression and violence: Causes, manifestations, and consequences.* Washington, DC: American Psychological Association.

Rholes, W.S., & Ruble, D.N. (1984). Children's understanding of dispositional characteristics of others. *Child Development, 55*, 550–560.

Ricciardelli, L.A., & Mellor, D. (2012). Influence of peers. In N. Rumsey, & D. Harcourt (Eds.). *The Oxford handbook of the psychology of appearance* (pp. 253–272). New York, NY: Oxford University Press.

Rispoli, K.M., McGoey, K.E., Koziol, N.A., & Schreiber, J.B. (2013). The relation of parenting, child temperament, and attachment security in early childhood to social competence at school entry. *Journal of School Psychology, 51*(5), 643–658. doi:10.1016/j.jsp.2013.05.007

Rodkin, P., Farmer, T., Pearl, R., & Van Acker, R. (2000). Heterogeneity of popular boys: Antisocial and prosocial configurations. *Developmental Psychology, 36*, 14–24.

Rodkin, P., Farmer, T., Pearl, R., & Van Acker, R. (2000). Heterogeneity of popular boys: Antisocial and prosocial configurations. *Developmental Psychology, 36*, 14–24.

Rodrigo, M., Janssens, J., & Ceballos, E. (1999). Do children's perceptions and attributions mediate the effects of mothers' child rearing actions? *Journal of Family Psychology, 13*, 508–522.

Rose, A.J., & Asher, S.R. (2004). Children's strategies and goals in response to help-giving and help-seeking tasks within a friendship. *Child Development, 75*(3), 749–763.

Rotenberg, K., McDougall, P., Boulton, M., Vaillancourt, T., Fox, C., & Hymel, S. (2004). Cross-sectional and longitudinal relations among peer-reported trustworthiness, social relationships, and psychological adjustment in children and early adolescents from the United Kingdom and Canada. *Journal of Experimental Child Psychology, 88*(1), 46–67. doi: http://dx.doi.org/10.1016/j.jecp.2004.01.005

Rubin, K.H., Wojslawowica, J.C., Rose-Krasnor, L., Booth-LaForce, C., & Burgess, K.B. (2006). The best friendships of shy/withdrawn children: Prevalence, stability, and relationship quality. *Journal of Abnormal Child Psychology, 34*(2), 143–157. doi:10.1007/s10802-005-9017-4

Ruiz-Casares, M., & Radic, I. (2015). *Legal age for leaving children unsupervised across Canada* (CWRP information sheet #144E). Montreal, QC: McGill University, Centre for Research on Children and Families.

Sallquist, J., Eisenberg, N., Spinrad, T., Reiser, M. Hofer, C., Zhou, Q., Liew, J., & Eggum, N. (2009b). Positive and negative emotionality: Trajectories across six years and relations with social competence. *Emotion, 9*, 15–28. doi:10.1037/a0013970

Sampasa-Kanyinga, H., Roumeliotis, P., & Xu, H. (2014). Associations between cyberbullying and school bullying victimization and suicidal ideation, plans and attempts among Canadian schoolchildren. *PLoS ONE, 9*(7), e102145. doi:10.1371/journal.pone.0102145

Sanders, M.B., & Mazzucchelli, T.G. (2013). The promotion of self-regulation through parenting interventions. *Clinical Child and Family Psychology Review, 16*(1), 1–17. doi:10.1007/s10567-013-0129-z

Schraf, M., & Hertz-Lazarowitz, R. (2003). Social networks in the school context: Effects of culture and gender. *Journal of Social & Personal Relationships, 20*, 843–858.

Selman, R.L. (1980). *The growth of interpersonal understanding.* New York, NY: Academic Press.

Sewell, A. (2009). Evoking children's spirituality in the reciprocal relationships of a learning community. *International Journal of Children's Spirituality, 14*(1), 5–16.

Shernoff, D., & Vandell, D. (2007). Engagement in after-school program activities: Quality of experience from the perspective of participants. *Journal of Youth and Adolescence, 36*(7), 891–903. doi:10.1007/s10964-007-9183-5

Soori, H., & Bhopal, R. (2002). Parental permission for children's independent outdoor activities: Implications for injury prevention. *European Journal of Public Health, 12*, 104–109.

Stack, D.M., Serbin, L.A, Mantis, I., & Kingdon, D. (2015). Breaking the cycle of adversity in vulnerable children and families: A thirty-five year study of at-risk lower income families. *International Journal for Family Research and Policy, 1*(1), 31–56. doi:10.1177/0165025416631836

Talwar, V., Gomez-Garibello, C., & Shariff, S. (2014). Adolescents' moral evaluations and ratings of cyberbullying: The effect of veracity and intentionality behind the event. *Computers in Human Behavior, 36*(July), 122–128. doi:10.1016/j.chb.2014.03.046

Tani, F., Greenman, P.S., Schneider, B.H., & Fregoso, M. (2003). Bullying and the Big Five: A study of childhood personality and participant roles in bullying incidents. *School Psychology International, 24*(2), 131–146.

Television Bureau of Canada. (2015). *The Canadian TV industry.* Retrieved from http://www.tvb.ca/page_files/pdf/infocentre/tvbasics.pdf

Temko, N. (2005). *Anti-bullying protests force policy u-turn.* Retrieved from www.guardian.co.uk/child/story/0,7369,1557999,00.html

ThinkTV. (2016). *Reach & time spent by media.* Retrieved from http://thinktv.ca/wp-content/uploads/2015/10/Reach-Time-Spent-by-Media_2015-Broadcast-Year.pdf

Thompson, R., Winer, A., & Goodvin, R. (2011). The individual child. In M. Bornstein & M. Lamb (Eds.), *Developmental science: An advanced textbook* (6th ed., pp. 427–468). New York, NY: Psychology Press.

Thorne, B. (1986). Girls and boys together . . . but mostly apart: Gender arrangements in elementary schools. In W.W. Hartup & Z. Rubin (Eds.), *Relationships and development* (pp. 167–184). Hillsdale, NJ: Erlbaum.

Tremblay, R.E. (2000). The origins of youth violence. *Isuma, 1*(2), 19–24.

Tremblay, R.E., Boulerice, B., Harden, P.W., McDuff, P., Perusse, D., Pihl, R.O., & Zoccolillo, M. (1996). Do children in Canada become more aggressive as they approach adolescence? In Human Resources Development Canada & Statistics Canada, *Growing up in Canada: National longitudinal survey of children and youth.* Ottawa, ON: Author.

Turner, H.A., Finkelhor, D., & Ormrod, R. (2010). Child mental health problems as risk factors for victimization. *Child Maltreatment, 15*(2), 132–143. doi:10.1177/1077559509349450

Vazsonyi, A., & Huang, L. (2010). Where self-control comes from: On the development of self-control and its relationship to deviance over time. *Developmental Psychology, 46*(1), 245–257. doi:10.1037/a0016538

Véronneau, M.H., Serbin, L.A., Stack, D.M., Ledingham, J., & Schwartzman, A.E. (2015). Emerging psychopathology moderates upward social mobility: The intergenerational (dis)continuity of socioeconomic status. *Development and Psychopathology, 27*(4 Pt 1), 1217–1236. doi:10.1017/S0954579415000784

Wang, Y., & Ollendick, T. (2001). A cross-cultural and developmental analysis of self-esteem in Chinese and Western children. *Clinical Child and Family Psychology Review, 4*(3), 253–271.

Wentzel, K.R., & Asher, S.R. (1995). The academic lives of neglected, rejected, popular, and controversial children. *Child Development, 66*, 754–763.

Xie, H., Cairns, R., & Cairns, B. (1999). Social networks and configurations in inner-city schools: Aggression, popularity, and implications for students with EBD. *Journal of Emotional & Behavioral Disorders, 7*, 147–155.

Zakriski, A., & Coie, J. (1996). A comparison of aggressive-rejected and nonaggressive-rejected children's interpretation of self-directed and other-directed rejection. *Child Development, 67*, 1048–1070.

Chapter 11

Abma, J., Martinez, G., & Copen, C. (2010). Teenagers in the United States: Sexual activity, contraceptive use, and childbearing. *Vital Health Statistics, 23*, 1–86.

Adelman, W., & Ellen, J. (2002). Adolescence. In A. Rudolph, R. Kamei, & K. Overby (Eds.), *Rudolph's fundamentals of pediatrics* (3rd ed., pp. 70–109). New York, NY: McGraw-Hill.

Alberts, A., Elkind, D., & Ginsberg, S. (2007). The personal fable and risk-taking in early adolescence. *Journal of Youth and Adolescence, 36*, 71–76.

Al-Sahab, B., Ardern, C.I., Hamadeh, M.J., & Tamim, H. (2010). Age at menarche in Canada: Results from the National Longitudinal Survey of Children & Youth. *BMC Public Health, 12*(11), 736. doi:10.1186/1471-2458-10-736

Al-Sahab, B., Ardern, C.I., Hamadeh, M.J., & Tamim, H. (2012). Age at menarche and current substance use among Canadian adolescent girls: Results of a cross-sectional study. *BMC Public Health, 12*(3), 195. doi:10.1186/1471-2458-12-195

Alspaugh, J. (1998). Achievement loss associated with the transition to middle school and high school. *Journal of Educational Research, 92*, 20–25.

American Psychiatric Association. (2013). *Diagnostic and Statistical Manual of Mental Disorder: DSM-5* (5th ed.). Washington, DC: American Psychiatric Publishing.

Anderman, E., & Midgley, C. (1997). Changes in achievement goal orientations, perceived academic competence, and grades across the transition to middle-level schools. *Contemporary Educational Psychology, 22*, 269–298.

Anderman, L. (1999). Classroom goal orientation, school belonging and social goals as predictors of students' positive and negative affect following the transition to middle school. *Journal of Research & Development in Education, 32*, 89–103.

Anderman, L., & Anderman, E. (1999). Social predictors of changes in students' achievement goal orientations. *Contemporary Educational Psychology, 24*, 21–37.

Anderman, L., & Anderman, E. (2009). Oriented towards mastery: Promoting positive motivational goals for students. In R. Gilman, E. Huebner, & M. Furlong (Eds.), *Handbook of positive psychology in schools.* (pp. 161–173). New York, NY: Routledge/Taylor & Francis Group.

Arriagada, P. (2015). Participation in extracurricular activities and high school completion among off-reserve First Nations people. *Insights on Canadian Society* (Cat. no. 75-006-X). Ottawa, ON: Statistics Canada.

Austin, S., Ziyadeh, N., Farman, S., Prokop, L., Keliher, A., & Jacobs, D. (2008). Screening high school students for eating disorders: Results of a national initiative. *Prevention of Chronic Disease, 5*, 1–10.

Austin, S., Ziyadeh, N., Kahn, J., Camargo, C., Colditz, G., & Field, A. (2004). Sexual orientation, weight concerns, and eating-disordered behaviors in adolescent girls and boys. *Journal of the American Academy of Child & Adolescent Psychiatry, 43*, 1115–1123.

Bagga, A., & Kulkarni, S. (2000). Age at menarche and secular trend in Maharashtrian (Indian) girls. *Acta Biologica Szegediensis, 44*(1–4), 53–57.

Bailey, J., Pillard, R., Dawood, K., Miller, M., Farrer, L., Trivedi, S., & Murphy, R. (1999). A family history study of male sexual orientation using three independent samples. *Behavior Genetics, 29*, 7986.

Barnsley, P. (2001). Native youth remain in distress. *Windspeaker News.* Retrieved from The Aboriginal Multi-Media Society website: www.ammsa.com/windspeaker/children/JAN2001-youthindistress.html

Bell, J., & Bromnick, R. (2003). The social reality of the imaginary audience: A ground theory approach. *Adolescence, 38*, 205–219.

Bernstein, B. (2010). *Eating disorder, anorexia.* Retrieved from http://emedicine.medscape.com/article/805152-overview

Bitomsky, M. (2002). Men often untreated for eating disorders. *The Medical Post, 38*(37), 53.

Black, A., Yang, Q., Wen, S.W., Lalonde, A.B., Guilbert, E., & Fisher, W. (2009). Contraceptive use among Canadian women of reproductive age: Results of a national survey. *Journal of Obstetrics and Gynaecology Canada, 31*(7), 627–640.

Blake, K., & Davis, V. (2011). Adolescent medicine. In K. Marcdante, R. Kliegman, H. Jensen, & R. Behrman (Eds.), *Nelson's essential of pediatrics* (6th ed., pp. 265–284). New York, NY: Elsevier Health Publishers.

Blake, K., & Davis, V. (2015). Adolescent medicine. In K. Marcdante, R. Kliegman, H. Jenson, & R. Behrman (Eds.) *Nelson essentials of pediatrics* (7th ed., Section XII). Philadelphia, PA: Saunders Elsevier.

Bogenschneider, K., Wu, M., Raffaelli, M., & Tsay, J. (1998). "Other teens drink, but not my kid": Does parental awareness of adolescent alcohol use protect adolescents from risky consequences? *Journal of Marriage & the Family, 60*, 356–373.

Bowlby, G. (2008). Provincial drop-out rates—trends and consequences (81-004-XIE). In *Education Matters*, Ottawa, ON: Statistics Canada. Retrieved from www.statcan.gc.ca/pub/81-004-x/2005004/8984-eng.htm

Bradmetz, J. (1999). Precursors of formal thought: A longitudinal study. *British Journal of Developmental Psychology, 17*, 61–81.

Breyer, J., & Winters, K. (2005). *Adolescent brain development: Implications for drug use prevention*. Retrieved from http://www.mentorfoundation.org/pdfs/prevention_perspectives/19.pdf

Brochu, P., Deussing, M.A., Houme, K., & Chuy, M. (2013). *Measuring up: Canadian results of the OECD PISA Study; no. 3* (CS81-590-XPE). Ottawa, ON: Minister of Industry.

Brown, A., & Day, J. (1983). Macrorules for summarizing text: The development of expertise. *Journal of Verbal Learning and Verbal Behavior, 22*, 1–14.

Brown, T.G., Ouimet, M.C., Eldeb, M., Tremblay, J., Vingilis, E., Nadeau, L., . . . Bechara, A. (2016). Personality, executive control, and neurobiological characteristics associated with different forms of risky driving. *PLoS ONE, 11*(2), e0150227. doi:10.1371/journal.pone.0150227

Buchanan, P., & Vardaxis, V. (2003). Sex-related and age-related differences in knee strength of basketball players ages 11–17 years. *Journal of Athletic Training, 38*, 231–237.

Burgess, S. (2005). The preschool home literacy environment provided by teenage mothers. *Early Child Development & Care, 175*, 249–258.

Bushnik, T., Bar-Telford, L., & Bussière, P. (2004). *In and out of school: First results from the second cycle of Youth in Transition Survey, 2002* (Cat. No. 81-595). Ottawa, ON: Statistics Canada.

Buzi, R., Roberts, R., Ross, M., Addy, R., & Markham, C. (2003). The impact of a history of sexual abuse on high-risk sexual behaviors among females attending alternative schools. *Adolescence, 38*, 595–605.

Cablova, L., Pazderkova, K., & Miovsky, M. (2014). Parenting styles and alcohol use among children and adolescents: A systematic review. *Drugs—Education Prevention and Policy, 21*(1), 1–13. doi:10.3109/09687637.2013.817536

Caine, V. (2013). Literature Review. In D.J. Clandinin, P. Steeves, & V. Caine (Eds.). *Composing lives in transition: A narrative inquiry into the experiences of early school leavers* (pp. 15–42). Bingley, UK: Emerald Group Publishing.

Camilleri-Cassar, F. (2014). Education strategies for social inclusion or marginalising the marginalised? *Journal of Youth Studies, 17*(2), 252–268. doi:org/10.1080/13676261.2013.834312

Canadian Association for Suicide Prevention. (2009). *The CASP Blueprint for a Canadian National Suicide Prevention Strategy* (2nd ed.). Retrieved from http://suicideprevention.ca/wp-content/uploads/2014/05/SuicidePreventionBlueprint0909.pdf

Canadian Cancer Society. (2013). *HPV vaccines*. Retrieved from http://www.cancer.ca/en/cancer-information/cancer-101/what-isa-risk-factor/viruses-bacteria-and-other-infectious-agents/hpvvaccines/?region=on

Carlo, G., Crockett, L.J., Wolff, J.M., & Beal, S.J. (2012). The role of emotional reactivity, self-regulation, and puberty in adolescents' prosocial behaviors. *Social Development, 21*(4), 667–685. doi:10.1111/ j.1467–9507.2012.00660.x

Ceci, S., & Bronfenbrenner, U. (1985). "Don't forget to take the cupcakes out of the oven": Prospective memory, strategic time- monitoring, and context. *Child Development, 56*, 152–164.

Chamberlain, E., & Solomon, R. (2006). *Youth and impaired driving in Canada: Opportunities for progress*. Oakville, ON: MADD Canada.

Retrieved from www.madd.ca/english/research/youth_and_impaired_driving_may_2006.pdf

Chandler, M. and Lalonde, C. (2008). Cultural Continuity as a protective factor against suicide in First Nations youth. *Horizons. 10*(1), 68–72.

Chandler, M.J., & Lalonde, C. (1998). Cultural continuity as a hedge against suicide in Canada's First Nations. *Transcultural Psychiatry, 35*(2), 193–211.

Chandler, M.J., Lalonde, C.E., Sokol, B., & Hallett, D. (2003). Personal persistence, identity development, and suicide: A study of native and non-native North American adolescents. *Monographs of the Society for Research in Child Development, 68*(2), 1–130.

Chang, T., Metcalfe, A., Padmanabhan, A., Chen, T., & Menon, V. (2016). Heterogenous and nonlinear development of human posterior parietal cortex function. *NeuroImage, 126*(1 Feb), 184–195. doi:10.1016/j.neuroimage.2015.11.053

Chin, H.B., Sipe, T.A., Elder, R., Mercer, S.L., Chattopadhyay, S.K., Jacob, V. . . .Community Preventive Services Task Force. (2012). The effectiveness of group-based comprehensive risk reduction and abstinence education interventions to prevent or reduce the risk of adolescent pregnancy, human immunodeficiency virus, and sexually transmitted infections. *American Journal of Preventive Medicine, 42*(3), 272–294. doi:10.1016/j.amepre.2011.11.006

Cushing, T. (2013). *Emergent management of anorexia nervosa*. Retrieved from http://emedicine.medscape.com/article/805152-overview#aw2aab6b2b5

Cushing, T., & Waldrop, R. (2010). *Anorexia nervosa*. Retrieved from http://emedicine.medscape.com/article/912187-overview

D'Imperio, R., Dubow, E., & Ippolito, M. (2000). Resilient and stress-affected adolescents in an urban setting. *Journal of Clinical Child Psychology, 29*, 129–142.

Davis, C.G. (2006). *Risks associated with tobacco use in youth aged 15–19*. Ottawa, ON: Canadian Centre on Substance Abuse. Retrieved from www.ccsa.ca/2006%20CCSA%20Documents/ccsa-011346-2006.pdf

Donenberg, G., Emerson, E., Bryant, F., & King, S. (2006). Does substance use moderate the effects of parents and peers on risky sexual behavior? *AIDS Care, 18*, 194–200.

Dorn, L.D., Susman, E.J., & Ponirakis, A. (2003). Pubertal timing and adolescent adjustment and behavior: Conclusions vary by rater. *Journal of Youth and Adolescence, 32*(3), 157–167. doi:10.1023/A:1022590818839

Drum, P. (1985). Retention of text information by grade, ability and study. *Discourse Processes, 8*, 21–52.

Dyl, J., Kittler, J., Phillips, K., & Hunt, J. (2006). Body dysmorphic disorder and other clinically significant body image concerns in adolescent psychiatric inpatients: Prevalence and clinical characteristics. *Child Psychiatry and Human Development, 36*, 369–382.

Eaton, D., Kann, L., Kinchen, S., Shanklin, S., Ross, J., Hawkins, J., . . . Wechsler, H. (2010). Youth risk behavior surveillance—United States, 2009. *Morbidity and Mortality Weekly Report, 59*, 1–148.

Eley, T., Liang, H., Plomin, R., Sham, P., Sterne, A., Williamson, R., & Purcell, S. (2004). Parental familial vulnerability, family environment, and their interactions as predictors of depressive symptoms in adolescents. *Journal of the American Academy of Child Psychiatry, 43*, 298–306.

Elkind, D. (1967). Egocentrism in adolescence. *Child Development, 38*, 1025–1033.

Elliott, L. (2000). Aboriginal girls taking their lives in record numbers across Ontario's north. *Canadian Aboriginal News*. Retrieved from www.canadianaboriginal.com/health/health15b.htm

Ernst, M., & Hardin, M. (2010). Neurodevelopment underlying adolescent behavior: A neurobiological model. In P. Zelazo, M. Chandler, & E. Crone (Eds.), *Developmental social cognitive neuroscience. The Jean Piaget symposium series* (pp. 165–189). New York, NY: Psychology Press.

Franke, S. (2003). Studying and working: The busy lives of students with paid employment (Cat. No. 11-008). *Canadian Social Trends, Spring*(68), 22–25.

Fredriksen, K., Rhodes, J., Reddy, R., & Way, N. (2004). Sleepless in Chicago: Tracking the effects of adolescent sleep loss during the middle school years. *Child Development, 75*(1), 84–95. doi:10.1111/j.1467-8624.2004.00655.x

Gabbard, C.P. (2012). *Lifelong motor development* (6th ed.). San Francisco, CA: Pearson Benjamin Cummings.

Galambos, N.L., Leadbeater, B.J., & Barker, E.T. (2004). Gender differences in and risk factors for depression in adolescence: A 4-year longitudinal study. *International Journal of Behavioral Development, 28*(1), 16–25.

Galanaki, E.P. (2012). The imaginary audience and the personal fable: A test of Elkind's theory of adolescent egocentrism. *Psychology, 3*(6), 457–466. doi:10.4236/psych.2012.36065

Galarneau, D. & Fecteau, E. (2014). The ups and downs of minimum wage. *Insights on Canadian Society* (Cat. no. 75-006-X). Ottawa, ON: Statistics Canada. Retrieved from http://www.statcan.gc.ca/pub/75-006-x/2014001/article/14035-eng.pdf

Garland, E.J. (2004). Facing the evidence: Antidepressant treatment in children and adolescents. *Canadian Medical Association Journal, 170*(4), 489–491.

Gathercole, S., Pickering, S., Ambridge, B., & Wearing, H. (2004). The structure of working memory from 4 to 15 years of age. *Developmental Psychology, 40*, 177–190.

Geoffroy, M.C., Boivin, M., Arseneault, L., Turecki, G., Vitaro, F., Brendgen, M., . . . Côté, S.M. (2016). Associations between peer victimization and suicidal ideation and suicide attempt during adolescence: Results from a prospective population-based birth cohort. *Journal of the American Academy of Child and Adolescent Psychiatry, 55*(2), 99–105. doi:10.1016/j.jaac.2015.11.010

Gibbs, R., & Beitel, D. (1995). What proverb understanding reveals about how people think. *Psychological Bulletin, 118*, 133–154.

Giedd, J.N. (2004). Structural magnetic resonance imaging of the adolescent brain. *Annals of the New York Academy of Sciences, 1021*, 77–85.

Government of Canada. (2006). *The human face of mental health and mental illness in Canada* (HP5-19/2006E). Ottawa, ON: Minister of Public Works and Government Services Canada. Retrieved from www.phac-aspc.gc.ca/publicat/human-humain06/pdf/human_face_e.pdf

Greene, K., Krcmar, M., Rubin, D., Walters, L., & Hale, J. (2002). Elaboration in processing adolescent health messages: The impact of egocentrism and sensation seeking on message processing. *Journal of Communication, 52*, 812–831.

Gutman, L. (2006). How student and parent goal orientations and classroom goal structures influence the math achievement of African Americans during the high school transition. *Contemporary Educational Psychology, 31*, 44–63.

Hammond, D., Ahmed, R., Yang, W.S., Brukhalter, R., & Leatherdale, S. (2011). Illicit substance use among Canadian youth: Trends between 2002 and 2008. *Canadian Journal of Public Health, 102*(1), 7–12.

Health Canada. (1999c). *Suicide*. Ottawa, ON: Author. Retrieved from www.hc-sc.gc.ca/hpb/lcdc/brch/measuring/mu_y_e.html

Health Canada. (2001b). Coping with life. *Trends in the health of Canadian youth*. Ottawa, ON: Author. Retrieved from www.hc-sc.gc.ca/hppb/childhood-youth/spsc/e_trends.html

Health Canada. (2001c). *National Report—Canada: Ten-year review of the world summit for children*. Ottawa, ON: Author. Retrieved from www.hc-sc.gc.ca/hppb/childhood-youth/spsc/pdf/WSC10FinalEnglish.pdf

Health Canada. (2003a). *Canadian perinatal health report* (H49-142/2003E). Ottawa, ON: Minister of Public Works and Government Services Canada.

Health Canada. (2004). *Health Canada advises Canadians under the age of 18 to consult physicians if they are being treated with newer anti-depressants*. Ottawa, ON: Author. Retrieved from www.hc-sc.gc.ca/english/protection/warnings/2004/2004_02.htm

Health Canada. (2012a). *Canadian tobacco use monitoring survey (CTUMS): Supplementary tables, youth smoking survey 2010-11*. Retrieved from http://www.hc-sc.gc.ca/hc-ps/tobac/tabac/research-recherche/stat/_survey-sondage_2010-2011/table-eng.php

Health Canada. (2013). *First Nations & Inuit health: Suicide prevention*. Retrieved from http://www.hc-sc.gc.ca/fniah-spnia/promotion/suicide/index-eng.php

HealthyOntario.com. (2003). *Eating disorders: The facts*. Toronto, ON: Ministry of Health and Long-Term Care. Retrieved from www.healthyontario.com/english/printVersion.asp?which=features&text_id=91&channel_id=0

Heisz, A., & Situ, J. (2016). The association between skills and low income. *Insights on Canadian Society* (Cat. no. 75-006-X). Ottawa, ON: Statistics Canada. Retrieved from http://www5.statcan.gc.ca/cansim/a26?lang=eng&id=1024505&p2=17

Hermes, S., & Keel, P. (2003). The influence of puberty and ethnicity on awareness and internalization of the thin ideal. *International Journal of Eating Disorders, 33*, 465–467.

Herxheimer, A., & Mintzes, B. (2004). Antidepressants and adverse effects in young patients: Uncovering the evidence. *Canadian Medical Association Journal, 170*(4), 487–488.

Holliday, J., Rothwell, H., & Moore, L. (2010). The relative importance of different measures of peer smoking on adolescent smoking behavior: Cross-sectional and longitudinal analyses of a large British cohort. *Journal of Adolescent Health, 47*, 58–66.

Horan, W., Pogge, D., Borgaro, S., & Stokes, J. (1997). Learning and memory in adolescent psychiatric inpatients with major depression: A normative study of the California Verbal Learning Test. *Archives of Clinical Neuropsychology, 12*, 575–584.

Horvath, C., Lewis, I., & Watson, B. (2012). The beliefs which motivate young male and female drivers to speed: A comparison of low and high intenders. *Accident Analysis and Prevention, 45*(Mar), 334–341. doi:10.1016/j.aap.2011.07.023

Hu, Y., Xu, Y., & Tornello, S.M. (2016). Stability of self-reported same-sex and both-sex attraction from adolescence to young adulthood. *Archives of Sexual Behavior, 45*(3), 651–659. doi:10.1007/s10508-015-0541-1

Human Resources Development Canada. (2000). *Dropping out of high school: Definitions and costs* (Cat. No. R-01-1E). Ottawa, ON: Author.

Inhelder, B., & Piaget, J. (1958). *The growth of logical thinking from childhood to adolescence*. New York, NY: Basic Books.

Jackson, A., & Schetagne, S. (2001). *Still struggling: An update on teenagers at work*. Ottawa, ON: Canadian Council on Social Development. Retrieved from www.ccsd.ca/pubs/2001/pcc2001/employ.htm

Japal, C., Tremblay, R., McDuff, P., & Willms, J.D. (2002). Preadolescent girls and the onset of puberty. In J.D. Willms (Ed.), *Vulnerable children* (pp. 305–316). Edmonton, AB: The University of Alberta Press.

Jasik, C., & Lustig, R. (2008). Adolescent obesity and puberty: The "perfect storm." *Annals of the New York Academy of Sciences, 1135*, 265–279.

Jensen, F.E., & Nutt, A.E. (2015). *The teenage brain: A neuroscientist's survival guide to raising adolescents and young adults*. New York, NY: HarperCollins.

Jilek, W.G. (2001). *Anorexia nervosa: Cultural factors in psychiatric disorders*. Paper presented at the 26th Congress of the World Federation for Mental Health, July, 2001. Retrieved from Internet Mental Health website: www.mentalhealth.com/mag1/wolfgangex.html

Johnson, B.T., Scott-Sheldon, L.A., Huedo-Medina, T.B., & Carey, M.P. (2011). Interventions to reduce sexual risk for HIV in adolescents: A meta-analysis of trials, 1985–2008. *Archives of Pediatrics & Adolescent Medicine, 165*(1), 77–84. doi:10.1001/archpediatrics.2010.251

Jones, J.M., Bennett, S., Olmsted, M.P., Lawson, M.L., & Rodin, G. (2001). Disordered eating attitudes and behaviours in teenaged girls: A school-based study. *Canadian Medical Association Journal, 165*(5), 547–552.

Kail, R. (1990). *The development of memory in children* (3rd ed.). New York, NY: Freeman.

Kail, R. (1997). Processing time, imagery, and spatial memory. *Journal of Experimental Child Psychology, 64*, 67–78.

Kail, R. (2008). Speed of processing in childhood and adolescence: Nature, consequences, and implications for understanding atypical development. In J. DeLuca & J. Kalmar (Eds.), *Studies on neuropsychology, neurology, and cognition* (pp. 101–123). Philadelphia, PA: Taylor & Francis.

Kann, L., Olsen, E.O., McManus, T., Kinchen, S., Chyen, D., Harris, W.A., & Wechsler, H. (2011). Sexual identity, sex of sexual contacts, and health-risk behaviors among students in grades 9-12: Youth risk behavior surveillance, selected sites, United States, 2001–2009. *Surveillance Summaries, 60*(7), 1–133.

Kaplowitz, P. (2010). *Precocious puberty.* Retrieved from http:// emedicine.medscape.com/article/924002-overview

Kaplowitz, P. (2013). *Precocious puberty.* Retrieved from http:// emedicine.medscape.com/article/924002-overview#a0199

Kattimani, S., Sarkar, S., Rajkumar, R.P., & Menon, V. (2015). Stressful life events, hopelessness, and coping strategies among impulsive suicide attempters. *Journal of Neurosciences in Rural Practice, 6*(2), 171–176. doi:org/10.4103/0976-3147.153222

Kendler, K., Thornton, L., Gilman, S., & Kessler, R. (2000). Sexual orientation in a U.S. national sample of twin and nontwin sibling pairs. *American Journal of Psychiatry, 157*, 1843–1846.

Kent, H. (2001). Eighteen months, 12 suicides. *Canadian Medical Association Journal, 164*(13), 1940.

Khanna, G., & Kapoor, S. (2004). Secular trend in stature and age at menarche among Punjabi Aroras residing in New Delhi, India. *Collegium Antropologicum, 28*, 571–575.

Kirby, D. (2000). School-based interventions to prevent unprotected sex and HIV among adolescents. In J. Peterson & D. Diclemente (Eds.), *Handbook of HIV prevention* (pp. 83–97). New York, NY: Plenum Publishers.

Kirkcaldy, B.D., Siefen, G., Surall, D., & Bischoff, R.J. (2004) Predictors of drug and alcohol abuse among children and adolescents. *Personality and Individual Differences, 36*, 247–265.

Klomsten, A., Skaalvik, E., & Espnes, G. (2004). Physical self-concept and sports: Do gender differences still exist? *Sex Roles: A Journal of Research, 50*, 119–127.

Kondro, W. (2004). UK bans, Health Canada warns about antidepressants. *Canadian Medical Association Journal, 170*(4), 23.

Korczak, D.J., & Canadian Paediatric Society, Mental Health and Developmental Disabilities Committee. (2015). Suicidal ideation and behaviour. *Paediatrics & Child Health, 20*(5), 257–260.

Ku, S., Kang, J., Kim, H., Kim, Y., Jee, B., Suh, C., . . . Kim, S. (2006). Age at menarche and its influencing factors in North Korean female refugees. *Human Reproduction, 21*, 833–836.

Langer, G., Arnedt, C., & Sussman, D. (2004). Primetime Live poll: American sex survey analysis. Retrieved from http://abcnews. go.com/Primetime/PollVault/story?id=156921&page=1 Dawood, K., Pillard, R., Horvath, C., Revelle, W., & Bailey, J. (2000). Familial aspects of male homosexuality. *Archives of Sexual Behavior, 29*, 155–163.

Larson, R. (2000). Toward a psychology of positive youth development. *American Psychologist, 55*, 170–183.

Larson, R., & Brown, J. (2007). Emotional development in adolescence: What can be learned from a high school theater program? *Child Development, 78*, 1083–1099.

Latimer, W. & Zur, J. (2010). Epidemiologic trends of adolescent use of alcohol, tobacco, and other drugs. *Child and Adolescent Psychiatric Clinics of North America, 19*, 451–464.

Lauwers, B. (2011). *The office of the chief coroner's death review of the youth suicides at the Pikangikum First Nation 2006–2008.* Retrieved from the Ministry of Community Safety & Correctional Services Website at http://www.mcscs.jus.gov.on.ca/stellent/groups/public/ @mcscs/@www/@com/documents/webasset/ec093490.pdf

Lenroot, R.K., & Giedd, J.N. (2006). Brain development in children and adolescents: Insights from anatomical magnetic resonance imaging. *Neuroscience and Biobehavioral Reviews, 30*(6), 718–729.

Lenroot, R.K., Gogtay, N., Greenstein, D.K., Wells, E.M., Wallace, G.L., Clasen, L.S., . . . Giedd, J. (2007). Sexual dimorphism of brain developmental trajectories during childhood and adolescence. *Neuroimage, 36*(4), 1065–1073.

Li, G., & Hines, M. (2016). In search of emerging same-sex sexuality: Romantic attractions at age 13 years. *Archives of Sexual Behavior,* Apr 18. doi:10.1007/s10508-016-0726-2 [Epub ahead of print.]

Links, P.S., Gould, B., & Ratnayake, R. (2003). Assessing suicidal youth with antisocial, borderline, or narcissistic personality disorder. *Canadian Journal of Psychiatry, 48*(5), 301–310.

Linnenbrink, M. (2010). *Transition to the middle school building and academic achievement in Iowa.* Retrieved from http://intersect.iowa. gov/admin/ckfinder/userfiles/files/Intersect%20Middle%20Sch. pdf

Lippa, R. (2005). *Gender, nature, and nurture.* Hillsdale, NJ: Lawrence Erlbaum Associates.

Luong, M. (2008). Life after teenage motherhood (75-001-X). *Perspectives on Labour and Income, 9*(5), 5–13. Retrieved from Statistics Canada website: www.statcan.gc.ca/pub/75-001-x/2008105/ pdf/10577-eng.pdf

MacMaster, F.P., & Kusumakar, V. (2004). Hippocampal volume in early onset depression. *BMC Medicine, 2*, 2. http://doi. org/10.1186/1741-7015-2-2

Marshall, K. (2007). The busy lives of teens. *Perspectives on Labour and Income, 8*(5), 5–25.

Marshall, K. (2010). Employment patterns of postsecondary students. *Perspectives* (75-001-X). Ottawa, ON: Statistics Canada. Retrieved from http://www.statcan.gc.ca/pub/75-001-x/ 2010109/pdf/11341-eng.pdf

Martin, J., Hamilton, B., Sutton, P., Ventura, S., Mathews, T., Kirmeyer, S., & Osterman, M. (2010). Births: Final data for 2007. *National Vital Statistics Report, 58*, 1–125.

Martorano, S.C. (1977). A developmental analysis of performance on Piaget's formal operations tasks. *Developmental Psychology, 13*, 666–672.

McKay, A. (2005). *Sexual health education in the schools: Questions & answers.* Toronto, ON: Sex Information and Education Council of Canada (SIECCAN). Retrieved from www.sieccan.org/pdf/ SHES_QA.pdf

McKay, A. (2012). Trends in Canadian national and provincial/ territorial teen pregnancy rates: 2001–2010. *Canadian Journal of Human Sexuality, 21*(3/4), 161–175.

Meek, C. (2004). UK psychiatrists question SSRI warnings for under-18s. *Canadian Medical Association Journal, 170* (4), 455.

Melnick, M., Miller, K., Sabo, D., Barnes, G., & Farrell, M. (2010). Athletic participation and seatbelt omission among U.S. high school students. *Health Education & Behavior, 37*, 23–36.

Menon, V., Kattimani, S., Sarkar, S., & Mathan, K. (2016). How do repeat suicide attempters differ from first timers? An exploratory record based analysis. *Journal of Neurosciences in Rural Practice, 7*(1), 91–96. doi:10.4103/0976-3147.168435

Menon, V., Sarkar, S., Kattimani, S., & Mathan, K. (2015). Do personality traits such as impulsivity and hostility-aggressiveness predict severity of intent in attempted suicide? Findings from a record based study in South India. *Indian Journal of Psychological Medicine, 37*(4), 393–398. doi:10.4103/0253-7176.168563

Mental Health Foundation of New Zealand. (2002). *Bulimia Nervosa.* Auckland, NZ: Author. Retrieved from www.mentalhealth.org. nz/conditions/docs/pdf8.pdf

Merikangas, K.R., & Angst, J. (1995). The challenge of depressive disorders in adolescence. In M. Rutter (Ed.), *Psychosocial disturbances in young people: Challenges for prevention* (pp. 131–165). Cambridge, England: Cambridge University Press.

Meyer-Bahlburg, H.F.L., Ehrhardt, A.A., Rosen, L.R., Gruen, R.S., Veridiano, N.P., Vann, F.H., & Neuwalder, H.F. (1995). Prenatal estrogens and the development of homosexual orientation. *Developmental Psychology, 31*, 12–21.

Mortimer, J.T. (2010). The benefits and risks of adolescent employment. *The Prevention Researcher, 17*(2), 8–11.

Mott, J., Crowe, P., Richardson, J., & Flay, B. (1999). After-school supervision and adolescent cigarette smoking: Contributions of the setting and intensity of after-school self-care. *Journal of Behavioral Medicine, 22,* 35–58.

Mueller, U., Overton, W., & Reene, K. (2001). Development of conditional reasoning: A longitudinal study. *Journal of Cognition & Development, 2,* 27–49.

Murnen, S., Smolak, L., Mills, J., & Good, L. (2003). Thin, sexy women and strong, muscular men: Grade-school children's responses to objectified images of women and men. *Sex Roles, 49,* 427–437.

Mwamwenda, T. (1999). Undergraduate and graduate students' combinatorial reasoning and formal operations. *Journal of Genetic Psychology, 160,* 503–506.

National Advisory Committee on Immunization. (2007). *Statement on human papillomavirus vaccine. Canadian Communicable Disease Report 2007, 33(ACS–2),* 1–32. Ottawa, ON: Author. Retrieved from Public Health Agency of Canada website: www.phac-aspc.gc.ca/publicat/ccdr-rmtc/07pdf/acs33-02.pdf

National Cancer Institute. (2006). *Breast cancer and the environment research centers chart new territory.* Retrieved from www.nci.nih.gov/ncicancerbulletin/NCI_Cancer_Bulletin_081506/page9

Navaneelan, T. (2015). Suicide rates: An overview (Cat. no. 82-624-X). Retrieved from http://www.statcan.gc.ca/pub/82-624-x/2012001/article/11696-eng.htm

Neild, R. (2009). Falling off track during the transition to high school: What we know and what can be done. *The Future of Children, 19,* 53–76.

Neild, R., & Balfanz, R. (2006). An extreme degree of difficulty: The educational demographics of urban neighborhood high schools. *Journal of Education for Students Placed at Risk, 11,* 123–141.

Neshat-Doost, H., Taghavi, M., Moradi, A., Yule, W., & Dalgleish, T. (1998). Memory for emotional trait adjectives in clinically depressed youth. *Journal of Abnormal Psychology, 107,* 642–650.

Ompad, D., Strathdee, S., Celentano, D., Latkin, C., Poduska, J., Kellam, S., & Ialongo, N. (2006). Predictors of early initiation of vaginal and oral sex among urban young adults in Baltimore, Maryland. *Archives of Sexual Behavior, 35,* 53–65.

Paglia-Boak, A., Adlaf, E.M., & Mann, R.E. (2011). *Drug use among Ontario students, 1977–2011: Detailed OSDUHS findings (CMHA Research Document Series No. 32).* Toronto, ON: Centre for Addiction and Mental Health.

Pajares, F., & Graham, L. (1999). Self-efficacy, motivation constructs, and mathematics performance of entering middle school students. *Contemporary Educational Psychology, 24,* 124–139.

Parent, S., Tillman, G., Jule, A., Skakkebaek, N., Toppari, J., & Bourguignon, J. (2003). The timing of normal puberty and the age limits of sexual precocity: Variations around the world, secular trends, and changes after migration. *Endocrine Review, 24,* 668–693.

Pearson, C., Janz, T., & Ali, J. (2013). Mental and substance use disorders in Canada (Cat. no. 82-624-X). *Health at a Glance.* Ottawa, ON: Statistics Canada.

Pelletier, L., Dion, S., & Levesque, C. (2004). Can self-determination help protect women against sociocultural influences about body image and reduce their risk of experiencing bulimic symptoms? *Journal of Social & Clinical Psychology, 23,* 61–88.

Perrault, S. (2013). *Impaired driving in Canada, 2011* (Catalogue No. 85-002-X). Retrieved from Statistics Canada Website http://www.statcan.gc.ca/pub/85-002-x/2013001/article/11739-eng.pdf

Petersen, A.C., Compas, B.E., Brooks-Gunn, J., Stemmler, M., Ey, S., & Grant, K.E. (1993). Depression in adolescence. *American Psychologist, 48,* 155–168.

Peterson, A.C., & Taylor, B. (1980). The biological approach to adolescence. In J. Adelson (Ed.), *Handbook of adolescent psychology* (pp. 117–158). New York, NY: Wiley.

Piaget, J., & Inhelder, B. (1969). *The psychology of the child.* New York, NY: Basic Books.

Pies, R. (2003). *Body image.* Irvine, CA: Continuing Medical Education. Inc. Retrieved from www.mhsource.com/expert/exp1090803c.html

Polivy, J., & Herman, P. (2002). Causes of eating disorders. *Annual Review of Psychology, 53,* 187–213.

Pomerleau, A., Scuccimarri, C., & Malcuit, G. (2003). Mother–infant behavioral interactions in teenage and adult mothers during the first six months postpartum: Relations with infant development. *Infant Mental Health Journal, 24*(5). 495–509.

Pressley, M., & Dennis-Rounds, J. (1980). Transfer of a mnemonic keyword strategy at two age levels. *Journal of Educational Psychology, 72,* 575–582.

Public Health Agency of Canada. (2015b). *Report on Sexually Transmitted Infections in Canada: 2012.* Retrieved from http://www.phac-aspc.gc.ca/sti-its-surv-epi/rep-rap-2012/index-eng.php

Rahman, Q., & Wilson, G. (2003). Born gay? The psychobiology of human sexual orientation. *Personality and Individual Differences, 34,* 1337–1382.

Reid, J.L., Hammond, D., Rynard, V.L., & Burkhalter, R. (2015). *Tobacco Use in Canada: Patterns and Trends, 2015 Edition.* Waterloo, ON: Propel Centre for Population Health Impact, University of Waterloo.

Ricciardelli, L.A., & McCabe, M.P. (2004). A biopsychosocial model of disordered eating and the pursuit of muscularity in adolescent boys. *Psychological Bulletin, 130*(2), 179–205.

Rioux, C., Castellanos-Ryan, N., Parent, S., Vitaro, F., Tremblay, R.E., & Séguin, J.R. (2016). Differential susceptibility to environmental influences: Interactions between child temperament and parenting in adolescent alcohol use. *Development and Psychopathology, 28*(1), 265–275. doi:10.1017/S0954579415000437

Roberts, K.C., Shields, M., de Groh, M., Aziz, A., & Gilbert, J.A. (2012). Overweight and obesity in children and adolescents: Results from the 2009 to 2011 Canadian Health Measures Survey. *Health Reports, 23*(3), 37–41.

Roche, A.F. (1979). Secular trends in human growth, maturation, and development. *Monographs of the Society for Research in Child Development, 44* (3–4, Serial No. 179).

Rosenfield, R., Lipton, R., & Drum, M. (2009). Thelarche, pubarche, and menarche attainment in children with normal and elevated body mass index. *Pediatrics, 123,* 84–88.

Rotermann, M. (2008). Trends in teen sexual behaviour and condom use. *Health Reports, 19*(3), 1–5.

Rotermann, M. (2012). Sexual behaviour and condom use of 15- to 24-year-olds in 2003 and 2009/2010. *Health Reports, 23*(1), 41–45.

Safety Canada Online. (2000). *Youth and road crashes.* Ottawa, ON: Canada Safety Council, (Vol. XLIV, No. 2). Retrieved from: www.safety-council.org/index.html

Saltz, R. (1979). Children's interpretation of proverbs. *Language Arts, 56,* 508–514.

Savage, M., & Holcomb, D. (1999). Adolescent female athletes' sexual risk-taking behaviors. *Journal of Youth and Adolescence, 28,* 583–594.

Schneider, W. (2010). Metacognition and memory development in childhood and adolescence. In H. Waters & W. Schneider (Eds.), *Metacognition, strategy use, and instruction* (pp. 54–81). New York, NY: Guilford Press.

School Work College Initiative. (2016). *Dual Credit: School Work College Initiative.* Retrieved from http://www.scwi.ca/

Schuster, M., Bell, R., Berry, S., & Kanouse, D. (1998). Impact of a high school condom availability program on sexual attitudes and behaviors. *Family Planning Perspectives, 30,* 67–72.

Schwartz, P., Maynard, A., & Uzelac, S. (2008). Adolescent egocentrism: A contemporary view. *Adolescence, 43,* 441–448.

Sex Information and Education Council of Canada. (2015). *Sexual health education in the schools: Questions and answers. Updated 2015 Ontario edition.* Toronto, ON: Sex Information and Education Council of Canada (SIECCAN).

Shaffer, D., Garland, A., Gould, M., Fisher, P., & Trautman, P. (1988). Preventing teenage suicide: A critical review. *Journal of the American Academy of Child and Adolescent Psychiatry, 27,* 675–687.

Shields, M. (2008). *Measured obesity: Overweight Canadian children and adolescents.* (Cat. No. 82-620-MWE2005001). Ottawa, ON: Statistics

Canada. Retrieved from www.statcan.ca/english/research/82-620-MIE/2005001/pdf/cobesity.pdf

Sibbald, B. (2004). Legal action against GSK over SSRI data. *Canadian Medical Association Journal, 170*(4), 23.

Smith, Y., van Goozen, S., Kuiper, A., & Cohen-Kettenis, P. (2005). Sex reassignment: Outcomes and predictors of treatment for adolescent and adult transsexuals. *Psychological Medicine, 35*, 89–99.

Statistics Canada. (2000). *The Daily* (October 20). Teenage pregnancy. Ottawa, ON: Author. Retrieved from www.statcan.ca/Daily/English/001020/d001020b.htm

Statistics Canada. (2008c). Early indicators of students at risk of dropping out of high school (81-004-XIE). In *Education Matters*, Ottawa, ON: Author. Retrieved from www.statcan.gc.ca/pub/81-004-x/2004006/7781-eng.htm

Statistics Canada. (2012j). *Learning – school drop-outs. Labour Force Survey 2012*. Retrieved from: http://well-being.esdc.gc.ca/misme-iowb/.3ndic.1t.4r@-eng.jsp?iid=32

Statistics Canada. (2012k). *Economic downturn and educational attainment. Education Indicators in Canada: Fact Sheets* (Cat. no. 81-599-X). Retrieved from http://www.statcan.gc.ca/pub/81-599-x/81-599-x2012009-eng.htm

Statistics Canada. (2013). *Crude birth rate, age-specific and total fertility rates (live births), Canada, provinces and territories. Table 102-4505.* Retrieved from http://www5.statcan.gc.ca/cansim/pickchoisir?lang=eng&p2=33&id=1024505

Statistics Canada. (2015d). *Leading causes of death, total population, by age group and sex, Canada, annual* (CANSIM Table 102-0561). Retrieved from http://www5.statcan.gc.ca/cansim/a26?lang=eng&id=1020561

Statistics Canada. (2015f). *Education indicators in Canada: An international perspective*. Retrieved from http://www.statcan.gc.ca/pub/81-604-x/81-604-x2015001-eng.pdf

Statistics Canada. (2016e). *Crude birth rate, age-specific and total fertility rates (live births), Canada, provinces and territories* (Table 102-4505). Retrieved from http://www5.statcan.gc.ca/cansim/a26?lang=eng&id=1024505

Statistics Canada. (2016f). *Health indicator profile, annual estimates, by age group and sex, Canada, provinces, territories, health regions (2013 boundaries) and peer groups* (CANSIM Table 105-0501). Retrieved from http://www5.statcan.gc.ca/cansim/a26?lang=eng&id=1050501

Stoolmiller, M., Gerrard, M., Sargent, J., Worth, K., & Gibbons, F. (2010). R-rated movie viewing, growth in sensation seeking and alcohol initiation: Reciprocal and moderation effects. *Prevention Science, 11*, 1–13.

Swedo, S.E., Rettew, D.C., Kuppenheimer, M., Lum, D., Dolan, S., & Goldberger, E. (1991). Can adolescent suicide attempters be distinguished from at-risk adolescents? *Pediatrics, 88*, 620–629.

Sweeting, H., & West, P. (2002). Gender differences in weight related concerns in early to late adolescence. *Journal of Family Issues, 23*, 728–747.

Taga, K., Markey, C., & Friedman, H. (2006). A longitudinal investigation of associations between boys' pubertal timing and adult behavioral health and well-being. *Journal of Youth and Adolescence, 35*, 401–411.

Tanner, J.M. (1990). *Foetus into man: Physical growth from conception to maturity* (2nd ed.). Cambridge, MA: Harvard University Press.

Tanski, S., Cin, S., Stoolmiller, M., & Sargent, J. (2010). Parental R-rated movie restriction and early-onset alcohol use. *Journal for the Study of Alcohol and Drugs, 71*, 452–459.

Traffic Injury Research Foundation. (2001). *Graduated licensing: A blueprint for North America*. Ottawa, ON: Author.

Trebay, G. (2008, February 7). The Vanishing Point. *The New York Times*. Retrieved from www.nytimes.com/2008/02/07/fashion/shows/07DIARY.html?pagewanted=1

Tremblay, M.S., Shields, M., Laviolette, M., Craig, C.L., Janssen, I., & Connor Gorber, S. (2010). Fitness of Canadian children and youth: Results from the 2007–2009 Canadian Health Measures Survey. *Health Reports, 21*(1), 7–20.

van der Stel, M., & Veenman, M. (2010). Development of metacognitive skillfulness: A longitudinal study. *Learning and Individual Differences, 20*, 220–224.

van Heeringen, K. (2003). The neurobiology of suicide and suicidality. *Canadian Journal of Psychiatry, 48*(5), 292–300.

Vartanian, L. (2001). Adolescents' reactions to hypothetical peer group conversations: Evidence for an imaginary audience? *Adolescence, 36*, 347–380.

Wallace, G.L., Schmitt, E.J., Lenroot, R., Viding, E., Ordaz, S., Rosenthal, M.A., et al. (2006). A pediatric twin study of brain morphometry. *Journal of child psychology and psychiatry, and allied disciplines, 47*(10), 987–993.

Wallien, M., & Cohen-Kettenis, P. (2008). Psychosexual outcome of gender-dysphoric children. *Journal of the American Academy of Child & Adolescent Psychiatry, 47*, 1413–1423.

Ward, S.L., & Overton, W.F. (1990). Semantic familiarity, relevance, and the development of deductive reasoning. *Developmental Psychology, 26*, 488–493.

Weil, L.G., Fleming, S.M., Dumontheil, I., Kilford, E.J., Weil, R.S., Rees, G., . . . Blakemore, S.J. (2013). The development of metacognitive ability in adolescence. *Consciousness and Cognition: An International Journal, 22*(1), 264–271. doi:10.1016/j.concog.2013.01.004

West, P., Sweeting, H., & Ecob, R. (1999). Family and friends' influences on the uptake of regular smoking from mid-adolescence to early adulthood. *Addiction, 97*, 1397–1411.

White, J. (2015). *Preventing youth suicide: A guide for practitioner*. Victoria, BC: Ministry of Children and Family Development.

Wilson, S., Malone, S.M., Thomas, K.M., & Iacono, W.G. (2015). Adolescent drinking and brain morphometry: A co-twin control analysis. *Developmental Cognitive Neuroscience, 16*(Dec), 130–138. doi:10.1016/j.dcn.2015.07.005

Wong, C., & Tang, C. (2004). Coming out experiences and psychological distress of Chinese homosexual men in Hong Kong. *Archives of Sexual Behavior, 33*, 149–157.

Wu, P., Liu, X., & Fan, B. (2010). Factors associated with initiation of ecstasy use among US adolescents: Findings from a national survey. *Drug and Alcohol Dependence, 106*, 193–198.

Yager, J., (2013). *Bulimia nervosa*. Retrieved from http://emedicine.medscape.com/article/286485-overview

Yeager, D.S., Henderson, M.D., D'Mello, S., Paunesku, D., Walton, G.M., Spitzer, B.J., & Duckworth, A.L. (2014). Boring but important: A self-transcendent purpose for learning fosters academic self-regulation. *Journal of Personality and Social Psychology, 107*(4), 559–580. http://doi.org/10.1037/a0037637

Young, A. (1997). I think, therefore I'm motivated: The relations among cognitive strategy use, motivational orientation and classroom perceptions over time. *Learning & Individual Differences, 9*, 249–283.

Chapter 12

Akers, J., Jones, R., & Coyl, D. (1998). Adolescent friendship pairs: Similarities in identity status development, behaviors, attitudes, and interests. *Journal of Adolescent Research, 13*, 178–201.

Alam, S. (2015). *Youth court statistics in Canada, 2013/2014* (Cat. no. 85-002-X). Retrieved from http://www.statcan.gc.ca/pub/85-002-x/2015001/article/14224-eng.pdf

Allami, Y., & Vitaro, F. (2015). Pathways model to problem gambling: Clinical implications for treatment and prevention among adolescents. *Canadian Journal on Addictions, 6*(2), 13–19.

Allen, M.K., & Superle, T. (2016). *Youth crime in Canada, 2014* (Cat. no. 85-002-X). Retrieved from http://www.statcan.gc.ca/pub/85-002-x/2016001/article/14309-eng.pdf

American Psychiatric Association. (2013). *Diagnostic and Statistical Manual of Mental Disorder: DSM-5* (5th ed.). Washington, DC: American Psychiatric Publishing.

Ang, R., & Goh, D. (2010). Cyberbullying among adolescents: The role of affective and cognitive empathy, and gender. *Child*

Psychiatry and Human Development, 41(4), 387–397. doi:10.1007/s10578-010-0176-3

Armstrong, T.A. (2003). Effect of moral reconation therapy on the recidivism of youthful offenders: A randomized experiment. *Criminal Justice & Behavior, 30*(6), 668–687. doi:10.1177/0093854803256452

Ashkar, P., & Kenny, D. (2007). Moral reasoning of adolescent male offender: Comparison of sexual and nonsexual offenders. *Criminal Justice and Behavior, 34*, 108–118.

Baek, H. (2002). A comparative study of moral development of Korean and British children. *Journal of Moral Education, 31*, 373–391.

Barnett, G., & Mann, R.E. (2013). Empathy deficits and sexual offending: A model of obstacles to empathy. *Aggression and Violent Behavior, 18*(2), 228–239. doi:10.1016/j.avb.2012.11.010

Bem, S.L. (1974). The measurement of psychological androgyny. *Journal of Consulting and Clinical Psychology, 42*, 155–162.

Benenson, J., & Benarroch, D. (1998). Gender differences in responses to friends' hypothetical greater success. *Journal of Early Adolescence, 18*, 192–208.

Bergman, R. (2002). Why be moral? A conceptual model from developmental psychology. *Human Development, 45*, 104–124.

Bibby, R.W. (2001). *Canada's teens: Today, yesterday and tomorrow.* Toronto, ON: Stoddart Publishing Co. Limited.

Bingham, C.R., Miller, B.C., & Adams, G.R. (1990). Correlates of age at first sexual intercourse in a national sample of young women. *Journal of Adolescent Research, 5*, 18–33.

Boivin, M., Brendgen, M., Vitaro, F., Dionne, G., Girard, A., Pérusse, D., & Tremblay, R.E. (2012). Strong genetic contribution to peer relationship difficulties at school entry: Findings from a longitudinal twin study. *Child Development*, Dec 4. doi:10.1111/cdev.12019. [Epub ahead of print]

Boivin, M., Brendgen, M., Vitaro, F., Forget-Dubois, N., Feng, B., Tremblay, R.E., & Dionne, G. (2013). Evidence of gene-environment correlation for peer difficulties: Disruptive behaviors predict early peer relation difficulties in school through genetic effects. *Development and Psychopathology, 25*(1), 79–92. doi:10.1017/S0954579412000910

Bowker, A. (2004). Predicting friendship stability during early adolescence. *Journal of Early Adolescence, 24*, 85–112.

Branco, A.U. (2012). Values and socio-cultural practices: Pathways to moral development. In J. Valsiner, (Ed.). *The Oxford handbook of culture and psychology* (pp. 749–766). New York, NY: Oxford University Press.

Brendgen, M., Vitaro, F., & Bukowski, W. (1998). Affiliation with delinquent friends: Contributions of parents, self-esteem, delinquent behavior, and rejection by peers. *Journal of Early Adolescence, 18*, 244–265.

Brook, J., Whiteman, M., Finch, S., & Cohen, P. (2000). Longitudinally foretelling drug use in the late twenties: Adolescent personality and social-environmental antecedents. *Journal of Genetic Psychology, 161*, 37–51.

Brown, B.B. (1990). Peer groups and peer cultures. In S.S. Feldman & G.R. Elliott (Eds.), *At the threshold: The developing adolescent* (pp. 171–196). Cambridge, MA: Harvard University Press.

Brown, B.B., & Huang, B. (1995). Examining parenting practices in different peer contexts: Implications for adolescent trajectories. In L.J. Crockett & A.C. Crouter (Eds.), *Pathways through adolescence* (pp. 151–174). Mahwah, NJ: Erlbaum.

Brown, B.B., Mory, M.S., & Kinney, D. (1994). Casting adolescent crowds in a relational perspective: Caricature, channel, and context. In R. Montemayor, G.R. Adams, & T.P. Gullotta (Eds.), *Personal relationships during adolescence* (pp. 123–167). Thousand Oaks, CA: Sage.

Brugman, D. (2010). Moral reasoning competence and the moral judgment-action discrepancy in young adolescents. In W. Koops, D. Brugman, T. Ferguson, & A. Sanders (Eds.), *The development and structure of conscience* (pp. 119–133). New York, NY: Psychology Press.

Bucx, F., & Seiffge-Krenke, I. (2010). Romantic relationships in intra-ethnic and inter-ethnic adolescent couples in Germany: The role of attachment to parents, self-esteem, and conflict resolution skills. *International Journal of Behavioral Development, 34*, 128–135.

Bukowski, W., Sippola, L., & Hoza, B. (1999). Same and other: Interdependency between participation in same- and other-sex friendships. *Journal of Youth & Adolescence, 28*, 439–459.

Cairns, R.B., & Cairns, B.D. (1994). *Lifelines and risks: Pathways of youth in our time.* Cambridge, England: Cambridge University Press.

Canadian Council on Social Development. (2000a). Immigrant youth in Canada: Highlights. In *Cultural diversity: A CCSD research program.* Ottawa, ON: Author. Retrieved from www.ccsd.ca/subsites/cd/docs/iy/hl.htm

Canadian Council on Social Development. (2000b). Immigrant youth in Canada: Lifestyle patterns of immigrant youth. In *Cultural diversity: A CCSD research program.* Ottawa, ON: Author. Retrieved from www.ccsd.ca/subsites/cd/docs/iy/lifestyl.htm

Caprara, G.V., Alessandri, G., Di Giunta, L., Panerai, L., & Eisenberg, N. (2010). The contribution of agreeableness and self-efficacy beliefs to prosociality. *European Journal of Personality, 24*(1), 36–55. doi:10.1002/per.739

Carbonneau, R., Vitaro, F., Brendgen, M., & Tremblay, R.E. (2015a). Trajectories of gambling problems from mid-adolescence to age 30 in a general population cohort. *Psychology of Addictive Behaviors, 29*(4), 1012–1021. doi:10.1037/adb0000102

Carbonneau, R., Vitaro, F., Brendgen, M., & Tremblay, R.E. (2015b). Variety of gambling activities from adolescence to age 30 and association with gambling problems: A 15-year longitudinal study of a general population sample. *Addiction, 110*(12), 1985–1993. doi:10.1111/add.13083

Cheng, G., Xiaoyan, H., & Dajun, Z. (2006). A review of academic self-concept and its relationship with academic achievement. *Psychological Science (China), 29*, 133–136.

Chou, C., & Tsai, M. (2007). Gender differences in Taiwan high school students' computer game playing. *Computers in Human Behavior, 23*, 812–824.

Closson, R.B. (2010). Critical race theory and adult education. *Adult Education Quarterly, 60*(3), 261–283. doi:10.1177/0741713609358445

Colby, A., Kohlberg, L., Gibbs, J., & Lieberman, M. (1983). A longitudinal study of moral judgment. *Monographs of the Society for Research in Child Development, 48*(1–2, Serial No. 200).

Colwell, J., & Kato, M. (2005). Video game play in British and Japanese adolescents. *Simulation & Gaming, 36*, 518–530.

Cox, S., Mezulis, A., & Hyde, J. (2010). The influence of child gender role and maternal feedback to child stress on the emergence of the gender difference in depressive rumination in adolescence. *Developmental Psychology, 46*, 842–852.

Damon, W., & Hart, D. (1988). *Self understanding in childhood and adolescence.* New York, NY: Cambridge University Press.

Dekovic, M. (1999). Parent-adolescent conflict: Possible determinants and consequences. *International Journal of Behavioral Development, 23*, 977–1000.

Department of Justice Canada. (2001b). *Backgrounder: Youth Criminal Justice Act.* Ottawa, ON: Author. Retrieved from http://canada.justice.gc.ca/en/news/nr/2001/doc_25948.html

Derevensky, J. (2012). *Teen gambling: Understanding a growing epidemic.* New York, NY: Rowman & Littlefield Publishing.

Derevensky, J. (2015). Youth gambling: Some current misconceptions. *Austin Journal of Psychiatry and Behavioral Sciences, 2*(2), 1039.

Derevensky, J., & Gilbeau, L. (2015). Adolescent gambling: Twenty-five years of research. *Canadian Journal of Addiction, 6*(2), 4–12.

Derevensky, J.L. & Gupta, R. (1998). Youth gambling: Lack of public awareness is contributing to the increasing number. *Psynopsis*, Fall. Retrieved from Canadian Psychological Association website: www.cpa.ca/Psynopsis/Gambling.html

Derevensky, J.L., & Gupta, R. (2004, February). Adolescents with gambling problems: A synopsis of our current knowledge. *eGambling: The Electronic Journal of Gambling Issues, 10*, 1–22. Retrieved from Centre for Addiction and Mental Health website: www.camh.net/egambling/issue10/ejgi_10_derevensky_gupta.html

Derevensky, J.L., Gupta, R., & Winters, K. (2003). Prevalence rates of youth gambling problems: Are the current rates inflated? *Journal of Gambling Studies, 19*(4), 405–425.

Dijkstra, J.K., Cillessen, A.H., & Borch, C. (2013). Popularity and adolescent friendship networks: Selection and influence dynamics. *Developmental Psychology, 49*(7), 1242–1252. doi:10.1037/a0030098

Dunphy, D.C. (1963). The social structure of urban adolescent peer groups. *Sociometry, 26*, 230–246.

Dussault, F., Brendgen, M., Vitaro, F., Carbonneau, R., Boivin, M., & Tremblay, R.E. (2015). Co-morbidity between gambling problems and depressive symptoms: A longitudinal perspective of risk and protective factors. *Journal of Gambling Studies, 32*(2), 547–565. doi:10.1007/s10899-015-9546-x

Eccles, J., & Roeser, R. (2011). School and community influences on human development. In M. Bornstein & M. Lamb (Eds.), *Developmental science: An advanced textbook* (6th ed., pp. 571–644). New York, NY: Psychology Press.

Eckensberger, E., & Zimba, R. (1997). The development of moral judgment. In J. Berry, P. Dasen, & T. Saraswathi (Eds.), *Handbook of cross-cultural psychology: Vol. 2* (pp. 299–328). Boston, MA: Allyn & Bacon.

Einerson, M. (1998). Fame, fortune, and failure: Young girls' moral language surrounding popular culture. *Youth & Society, 30*, 241–257.

Eisenberg, N. (2000). Emotion, regulation, and moral development. *Annual Review of Psychology, 51*, 665–697.

Eisenberg, N., Eggum, N., & Edwards, A. (2010). Empathy-related responding and moral development. In W. Arsenio & E. Lemerise (Eds.), *Emotions, aggression, and morality in children: Bridging development and psychopathology* (pp. 115–135). Washington, DC: American Psychological Association.

Elbedour, S., Baker, A., & Charlesworth, W. (1997). The impact of political violence on moral reasoning in children. *Child Abuse & Neglect, 21*, 1053–1066.

Erikson, E.H. (1968). *Identity: youth and crisis.* New York, NY: W.W. Norton.

Erikson, E.H. (1980a). *Identity and the life cycle.* New York, NY: Norton. (Originally published 1959.)

Erol, R.Y., & Orth, U. (2011). Self-esteem development from age 14 to 30 years: A longitudinal study. *Journal of Personality and Social Psychology, 101*(3), 607–19. doi:10.1037/a0024299

Fatseas, M., Alexandre, J.M., Vénisse, J.L., Romo, L., Valleur, M., Magalon, D., . . . Bronnec, M. (2016). Gambling behaviors and psychopathology related to Attention-Deficit/Hyperactivity Disorder (ADHD) in problem and non-problem adult gamblers. *Psychiatry Research, 239*(May 30), 232–238. doi:10.1016/j.psychres.2016.03.028

Feiring, C. (1999). Other-sex friendship networks and the development of romantic relationships in adolescence. *Journal of Youth & Adolescence, 28*, 495–512.

Ferland, F., Ladouceur, R., & Vitaro, F. (2002). Prevention of problem gambling: Modifying misconception and increasing knowledge. *Journal of Gambling Studies, 18*(10), 19–29.

Fitzgerald, R. (2010). *Parenting, school contexts and violent delinquency* (85-561-M, no. 19). Ottawa, ON: Ministry of Industry. Retrieved from www.statcan.gc.ca/pub/85-561-m/85-561-m2010019-eng.pdf

Flannery, D.J., Montemayor, R., & Eberly, M.B. (1994). The influence of parent negative emotional expression on adolescents' perceptions of their relationships with their parents. *Personal Relationships, 1*, 259–274.

Foehr, U. (2006). *Media multitasking among American youth: Prevalence, predictors and pairings.* Menlo Park, CA: Henry J. Kaiser Foundation. Retrieved from http://kff.org/entmedia/upload/7592.pdf

Fossati, A., Borroni, S., Eisenberg, N., & Maffei, C. (2010). Relations of proactive and reactive dimensions of aggression to overt and covert narcissism in nonclinical adolescents. *Aggressive Behavior, 36*(1), 21–27. doi:10.1002/ab.20332

Garcáa-Ruiz, M., Rodrigo, M.J., Hernández-Cabrera, J.A., Máiquez, M.L., & Dekoviæ, M. (2013). Resolution of parent-child conflicts in the adolescence. *European Journal of Psychology of Education, 28*(2), 173–188. doi:10.1007/s10212-012-0108-7

Gibson, D.R. (1990). Relation of socioeconomic status to logical and sociomoral judgment of middle-aged men. *Psychology and Aging, 5*, 510–513.

Gilligan, C. (1982). *In a different voice: Psychological theory and women's development.* Cambridge, MA: Harvard University Press.

Gilligan, C., & Wiggins, G. (1987). The origins of morality in early childhood relationships. In J. Kagan & S. Lamb (Eds.), *The emergence of morality in young children* (pp. 277–307). Chicago, IL: University of Chicago Press.

Grov, C., Bimbi, D., Nanin, J., & Parsons, J. (2006). Race, ethnicity, gender, and generational factors associated with the coming-out process among gay, lesbian, and bisexual individuals. *Journal of Sex Research, 43*, 115–121.

Gupta, R., & Derevensky, J.L. (1997). Familial and social influences on juvenile gambling. *Journal of Gambling Studies, 13*, 179–192.

Gupta, R., & Derevensky, J.L. (1998a). Adolescent gambling behaviour: A prevalence study and examination of the correlates associated with excessive gambling. *Journal of Gambling Studies, 14*, 227–244.

Gupta, R., & Derevensky, J.L. (1998b). An empirical examination of Jacob's General Theory of Addictions: Do adolescent gamblers fit the theory? *Journal of Gambling Studies, 14*, 17–49.

Gupta, R., & Derevensky, J.L. (2000). Adolescents with gambling problems: From research to treatment. *Journal of Gambling Studies, 16*(2–3), 315–342.

Gupta, R., Pinzon, J.L., & CPS. (2016). *Gambling in children and adolescents: Canadian Paediatric Society position statement.* Retrieved from http://www.cps.ca/documents/position/gambling-children-adolescents

Harter, S. (2012). *The construction of the self: Developmental and sociocultural foundations* (2nd ed.). New York, NY: Guilford Press.

Hotton Mahony, T. (2011). *Women and the criminal justice system* (Cat no. 89-503-X). Retrieved from http://www.statcan.gc.ca/pub/89-503-x/2010001/article/11416-eng.pdf

Huang, X., Zhu, X., Zheng, J., Zhang, L., & Shiomi, K. (2012). Relationships among androgyny, self-esteem, and trait coping style of Chinese university students. *Social Behavior and Personality, 40*(6), 1005–1014. doi:10.2224/sbp.2012.40.6.1005

Ivanova, K., Mills, M., & Veenstra, R. (2011). The initiation of dating in adolescence: The effect of parental divorce. The TRAILS study. *Journal of Research on Adolescence, 21*(4), 769–775. doi:10.1111/j.1532-7795.2010.00734.x

Jadack, R.A., Hyde, J.S., Moore, C.F., & Keller, M.L. (1995). Moral reasoning about sexually transmitted diseases. *Child Development, 66*, 167–177.

Jansz, J., & Martens, L. (2005). Gaming at a LAN event: The social context of playing video games. *New Media & Society, 7*, 333–355.

Jorgensen, G. (2006). Kohlberg and Gilligan: Duet or duel? *Journal of Moral Education, 35*, 179–196.

Katz, P.A., & Ksansnak, K.R. (1994). Developmental aspects of gender role flexibility and traditionality in middle childhood and adolescence. *Developmental Psychology, 30*, 272–282.

Keller, M. (2012). Moral developmental science between changing paradigms. *International Journal of Developmental Science, 6*(12), 65–69. doi:10.3233/DEV-2012-11090

Khanlou, N. (2004). Influences on adolescent self-esteem in multicultural Canadian secondary schools. *Public Health Nursing, 21*(5), 404–411.

Kinney, D.A. (1993). From "nerds" to "normals": Adolescent identity recovery within a changing social system. *Sociology of Education, 66*, 21–40.

Klaczynski, P.A., Fauth, J.M., & Swanger, A. (1998). Adolescent identity: Rational vs. experiential processing, formal operations and critical thinking beliefs. *Journal of Youth and Adolescence, 27*(2), 185–207.

Klein, R.G., Mannuzza, S., Olazagasti, M.A., Roizen, E., Hutchison, J.A., Lashua, E.C., & Castellanos, F.X. (2012). Clinical and functional outcome of childhood attention-deficit/hyperactivity disorder 33 years later. *JAMA Psychiatry, 69*(12), 1295–1303. doi:10.1001/archgenpsychiatry.2012.271

Klimstra, T., Luyckx, K., Hale, W., Frijns, T., van Lier, P., & Meeus, W. (2010). Short-term fluctuations in identity: Introducing a microlevel approach to identity formation. *Journal of Personality and Social Psychology, 99*, 191–202.

Kohlberg, L. (1964). Development of moral character and moral ideology. In M.L. Hoffman & L.W. Hoffman (Eds.), *Review of child development research: Vol. 1* (pp. 283–332). New York, NY: Russell Sage Foundation.

Kohlberg, L. (1976). Moral stages and moralization: The cognitive developmental approach. In T. Lickona (Ed.), *Moral development and behavior: Theory, research, and social issues* (pp. 31–53). New York, NY: Holt.

Kohlberg, L. (1981). *Essays on moral development: Vol. 1. The philosophy of moral development.* New York, NY: Harper & Row.

Kohlberg, L., & Elfenbein, D. (1975). The development of moral judgments concerning capital punishment. *American Journal of Orthopsychiatry, 54*, 614–640.

Kohlberg, L., Levine, C., & Hewer, A. (1983). *Moral stages: A current formulation and a response to critics.* Basel, Switzerland: S. Karger.

Krebs, D., & Denton, K. (2006). Explanatory limitations of cognitive-developmental approaches to morality. *Psychological Review, 113*, 672–675.

Kuhn, D., Kohlberg, L., Languer, J., & Haan, N. (1977). The development of formal operations in logical and moral judgment. *Genetic Psychology Monographs, 95*, 97–188.

Kuttler, A., LaGreca, A., & Prinstein, M. (1999). Friendship qualities and social-emotional functioning of adolescents with close, cross-sex friendships. *Journal of Research on Adolescence, 9*, 339–366.

LaFontana, K., & Cillessen, A. (2010). Developmental changes in the priority of perceived status in childhood and adolescence. *Social Development, 19*, 130–147.

Laird, R., Pettit, G., Dodge, K., & Bates, J. (1999). Best friendships, group relationships, and antisocial behavior in early adolescence. *Journal of Early Adolescence, 19*, 413–437.

Lansford, J., Costanzo, P., Grimes, C., Putallaz, M., Miller, S,. & Malone, P. (2009). Social network centrality and leadership status: Links with problem behaviors and tests of gender differences. *Merrill-Palmer Quarterly: Journal of Developmental Psychology, 55*, 1–25.

Laursen, B. (1995). Conflict and social interaction in adolescent relationships. *Journal of Research on Adolescence, 5*, 55–70.

Lavoie, M., & Ladouceur, R. (2004, February). Prevention of gambling among youth: Increasing knowledge and modifying attitudes towards gambling. *eGambling: The Electronic Journal of Gambling Issues, 10*, 1–10. Retrieved from www.camh.net/egambling/issue10/ejgi_10_lavoie_ladouceur.html

Lawrence, K., Yardley, J., Root, L., Canham, B., & McPhee, J. (2002). *Report on adolescent gambling: Attitudes and behaviours of Niagara Region youth.* St. Catharines, ON: Brock University. Retrieved from Ontario Problem Gambling website: www.gamblingresearch.org/download.sz/037%20Report%20web%20version.pdf?docid=5372

Li, Z., Connolly, J., Jiang, D., Pepler, D., & Craig, W. (2010). Adolescent romantic relationships in China and Canada: A cross-national comparison. *International Journal of Behavioral Development, 34*, 113–120.

Lickona, T. (1978). Moral development and moral education. In J.M. Gallagher & J.J.A. Easley (Eds.), *Knowledge and development: Vol. 2* (pp. 21–74). New York, NY: Plenum.

Ma, H. (2003). The relation of moral orientation and moral judgement to prosocial and antisocial behaviour of Chinese adolescents. *International Journal of Psychology, 38*(2), 101–111.

Ma, H., Shek, D., Cheung, P., & Oi Bun Lam, C. (2000). Parental, peer and teacher influences on the social behavior of Hong Kong Chinese adolescents. *Journal of Genetic Psychology, 161*, 65–78.

Ma, H.K. (2012). Internet addiction and antisocial internet behavior of adolescents. *International Journal of Child Health and Human Development, 5*, 123–130.

Mackey, E., & La Greca, A. (2007). Adolescents' eating, exercise, and weight control behaviors: Does peer crowd affiliation play a role? *Journal of Pediatric Psychology, 32*, 13–23.

Mallet, P., Apostolidis, T., & Paty, B. (1997). The development of gender schemata about heterosexual and homosexual others during adolescence. *Journal of General Psychology, 124*, 91–104.

Marcia, J. (2010). Life transitions and stress in the context of psychosocial development. In T. Miller (Ed.)., *Handbook of stressful transitions across the lifespan* (pp. 19–34). New York, NY: Springer Science & Business Media.

Marcia, J.E. (1966). Development and validation of ego identity status. *Journal of Personality and Social Psychology, 3*, 551–558.

Marcia, J.E. (1980). Identity in adolescence. In J. Adelson (Ed.), *Handbook of adolescent psychology* (pp. 159–187). New York, NY: Wiley.

Marcia, J.E. (2001). A commentary on Seth Schwartz's review of identity theory and research. *Identity: An International Journal of Theory and Research, 1*(1), 59–65.

Marcia, J.E. (2002). Adolescence, identity, and the Bernardone family. *Identity: An International Journal of Theory and Research, 2*(3), 199–209.

Mason, W.A., & Spoth, R.L. (2012). Sequence of alcohol involvement from early onset to young adult alcohol abuse: Differential predictors and moderation by family-focused preventive intervention. *Addiction, 107*(12), 2137–2148. doi:10.1111/j.1360-0443.2012.03987.x

Mayseless, O., & Scharf, M. (2007). Adolescents' attachment representations and their capacity for intimacy in close relationships. *Journal of Research on Adolescence, 17*, 23–50.

Milosevic, A., & Ledgerwood, D.M. (2010). The subtyping of pathological gambling: A comprehensive review. *Clinical Psychology Review, 30*(8), 988–998. doi:10.1016/j.cpr.2010.06.013

Mishna, F., McInroy, L.B., Lacombe-Duncan, A., Bhole, P., Van Wert, M., Schwan, K., . . . Johnston, D. (2016). Prevalence, motivations, and social, mental health and health consequences of cyberbullying among school-aged children and youth: Protocol of a longitudinal and multi-perspective mixed method study. *JMIR Research Protocols, 5*(2), e83 doi:10.2196/resprot.5292

Moksnes, U., Moljord, I., Espnes, G., & Byrne, D. (2010). The association between stress and emotional states in adolescents: The role of gender and self-esteem. *Personality and Individual Differences, 49*, 430–435.

Montemayor, R., & Eisen, M. (1977). The development of self-conceptions from childhood to adolescence. *Developmental Psychology, 13*, 314–319.

Montgomery, M., & Sorel, G. (1998). Love and dating experience in early and middle adolescence: Grade and gender comparisons. *Journal of Adolescence, 21*, 677–689.

Mounts, N.S., & Steinberg, L. (1995). An ecological analysis of peer influence on adolescent grade point average and drug use. *Developmental Psychology, 31*, 915–922.

Muris, P., Meesters, C., & Timmermans, A. (2013). Some youths have a gloomy side: Correlates of the dark triad personality traits in non-clinical adolescents. *Child Psychiatry and Human Development, 44*(5), 658–665. doi:10.1007/s10578-013-0359-9

Nagamine, S. (1999). Interpersonal conflict situations: Adolescents' negotiation processes using an interpersonal negotiation strategy model: Adolescents' relations with their parents and friends. *Japanese Journal of Educational Psychology, 47*, 218–228.

Nichikawa, S., Hägglöf, B., & Sundbom, E. (2010). Contributions of attachment and self-concept on internalizing and externalizing problems among Japanese adolescents. *Journal of Child and Family Studies, 19*, 334–342.

Nisan, M., & Kohlberg, L. (1982). Universality and variation in moral judgment: A longitudinal and cross-sectional study in Turkey. *Child Development, 53*, 865–876.

Noonan, G., Turner, N.E., & Macdonald, J. (1999). *Gambling and problem gambling amongst students in grades 5 to 11.* Centre for Addiction and Mental Health, May, 1–22. Retrieved from www.cfcg.org/search/documents/Gambling_and_problem_gambling_amongst_students_in_grades_5_to_11-14_02_2000-15_11_09.pdf

Nower, L., & Blaszczynski, A.A. (2005). Pathways Approach to Treating Youth Gamblers. In J. Derevensky, & R. Gupta (Eds.). *Gambling problems in youth: Theoretical and applied perspectives* (pp. 189–209). New York, NY: Springer.

Obeid, N., Buchholz, A., Boerner, K.E., Henderson, K.A., & Norris, M. (2013). Self-esteem and social anxiety in an adolescent female eating disorder population: Age and diagnostic effects. *Eating Disorders, 21*(2), 140–153. doi:10.1080/10640266.2013.761088

Ogrodnik, L. (2010). *Child and youth victims of police-reported violent crime, 2008* (Cat. no. 85F0033M, no. 2). Retrieved from http://www.statcan.gc.ca/pub/85f0033m/85f0033m2010023-eng.pdf

Okamoto, K., & Uechi, Y. (1999). Adolescents' relations with parents and friends in the second individuation process. *Japanese Journal of Educational Psychology, 47*, 248–258.

Park, J. (2003). Adolescent self-concept and health into adulthood (Cat. No. 82-003). *Health Reports, 14*(Supplement), 41–52.

Phinney, J.S. (1990). Ethnic identity in adolescents and adults: Review of research. *Psychological Bulletin, 108*, 499–514.

Phinney, J.S., & Kohatsu, E.L. (1997). Ethnic and racial identity development and mental health. In J. Schulenberg, J.L. Maggs, & K. Hurrelmann (Eds.), *Health risks and developmental transitions during adolescence* (pp. 420–443). Cambridge, England: Cambridge University Press.

Phinney, J.S., & Rosenthal, D.A. (1992). Ethnic identity in adolescence: Process, context, and outcome. In G. R. Adams, T. P. Gullotta, & R. Montemayor (Eds.), *Adolescent identity formation* (pp. 145–172). Newbury Park, CA: Sage.

Phinney, J.S., Ferguson, D.L., & Tate, J.D. (1997). Intergroup attitudes among ethnic minority adolescents: A causal model. *Child Development, 68*(5), 955–969.

Phinney, J.S., Ong, A., & Madden, T. (2000). Cultural values and intergenerational value discrepancies in immigrant and nonimmigrant families. *Child Development, 71*(2), 528–539.

Powers, C.J., & Bierman, K.L. (2013). The multifaceted impact of peer relations on aggressive-disruptive behavior in early elementary school. *Developmental Psychology, 49*(6), 1174–1186. doi:10.1037/a0028400

Pratt, M., Arnold, M., & Pratt, A. (1999). Predicting adolescent moral reasoning from family climate: A longitudinal study. *Journal of Early Adolescence, 19*, 148–175.

Pratt, M.W., Norris, J.E., Hebblethwaite, S., & Arnold, M.L. (2008). Intergenerational transmission of values: Family generativity and adolescents' narratives of parent and grandparent value teaching. *Journal of Personality, 76*(2), 171–198. doi:10.1111/j.1467-6494.2007.00483.x

Raja, S.N., McGee, R., & Stanton, W.R. (1992). Perceived attachments to parents and peers and psychological well-being in adolescence. *Journal of Youth and Adolescence, 21*, 471–485.

Rauer, A.J., Pettit, G.S., Lansford, J.E., Bates, J.E., & Dodge, K.E. (2013). Romantic relationship patterns in young adulthood and their developmental antecedents. *Developmental Psychology 49*(11), 2159–2171. doi:10.1037/a0031845

Renati, R., Berrone, C., & Zanetti, M.A. (2012). Morally disengaged and unempathic: Do cyberbullies fit these definitions? An exploratory study. *Cyberpsychology, Behavior, and Social Networking, 15*(8), 391–398. doi:10.1089/cyber.2012.0046

Rideout, V., Foehr, U., & Roberts, D. (2010). *Generation M2: Medial in the lives of 8- to 18-year-olds*. Retrieved from http://www.kff.org/entmedia/upload/8010.pdf

Ridolfo, H., Chepp, V., & Milkie, M.A. (2013). Race and girls' self-evaluations: How mothering matters. *Sex Roles, 68*(7–8), 496–509. doi:10.1007/s11199-013-0259-2

Riley, B. (2010). GLB adolescent's "coming out." *Journal of Child and Adolescent Psychiatric Nursing, 23*(1), 3–10. doi:10.1111/j.1744-6171.2009.00210.x

Rique, J., & Camino, C. (1997). Consistency and inconsistency in adolescents' moral reasoning. *International Journal of Behavioral Development, 21*, 813–836.

Rosario, M., Schrimshaw, E., & Hunter, J. (2004). Ethnic/racial differences in the coming-out process of lesbian, gay, and bisexual youths: A comparison of sexual identity development over time. *Cultural Diversity and Ethnic Minority Psychology, 10*, 215–228.

Rosario, M., Schrimshaw, E., Hunter, J., & Braun, L. (2006). Sexual identity development among lesbian, gay, and bisexual youths: Consistency and change over time. *Journal of Sex Research, 43*, 46–58.

Sanford, K., & Madill, L. (2006). Resistance through video game play: It's a boy thing. *Canadian Journal of Education, 29*, 287–306.

Sato, S., Shimonaka, Y., Nakazato, K., & Kawaai, C. (1997). A life-span developmental study of age identity: Cohort and gender differences. *Japanese Journal of Developmental Psychology, 8*, 88–97.

Savina, N.N. (2009). Endogenous factors of juvenile delinquency and the perspectives of its prognosing. *International Journal of Academic Research, 1*(2), 195–198.

Schonert-Reichl, K. (1999). Relations of peer acceptance, friendship adjustment, and social behavior to moral reasoning during early adolescence. *Journal of Early Adolescence, 19*, 249–279.

Schwartz, S.J. (2001). The evolution of Eriksonian and Neo-Eriksonian identity theory and research: A review and integration. *Identity: An International Journal of Theory and Research, 1*(1), 7–58.

Seiffge-Krenke, I., & Connolly, J. (2010). Adolescent romantic relationships across the globe: Involvement, conflict management, and linkages to parents and peer relationships. *International Journal of Behavioral Development, 34*, 97.

Selman, R.L. (1980). *The growth of interpersonal understanding.* New York, NY: Academic Press.

Shaffer, H.J., & Hall, M.N. (2001). Updating and refining prevalence estimates of disordered gambling behaviour in the United States and Canada. *Canadian Journal of Public Health, 92*(3), 168–172.

Sijtsema, J.J., Rambaran, A.J., & Ojanen, T.J. (2013). Overt and relational victimization and adolescent friendships: Selection, de-selection, and social influence. *Social Influence, 8*(2–3), 177–195. doi:10.1080/15534510.2012.739097

Skoe, E., Hansen, K., Morch, W., Bakke, I., Hoffman, T., Larsen, B., & Aasheim, M. (1999). Care-based moral reasoning in Norwegian and Canadian early adolescents: A cross-national comparison. *Journal of Early Adolescence, 19*, 280–291.

Smith, P., & Slonje, R. (2010). Cyberbullying: The nature and extent of a new kind of bullying, in and out of school. In S. Jimerson, S. Swearer, & D. Espelage (Eds.), *Handbook of bullying in schools: An international perspective* (pp. 249–262). New York, NY: Routledge/Taylor & Francis Group.

Snarey, J. (1995). In communitarian voice: The sociological expansion of Kohlbergian theory, research, and practice. In W.M. Kurtines & J.L. Gerwitz (Eds.), *Moral development: An introduction* (pp. 109–134). Boston, MA: Allyn & Bacon.

Snarey, J.R. (1985). Cross-cultural universality of social-moral development: A critical review of Kohlbergian research. *Psychological Bulletin, 97*, 202–232.

Snarey, J.R., Reimer, J., & Kohlberg, L. (1985). Development of social-moral reasoning among kibbutz adolescents: A longitudinal cross-sectional study. *Developmental Psychology, 21*, 3–17.

Sodhi Kalsi, P. (2003). *"The best of both worlds": Bicultural identity formation of Punjabi women living in Canada.* Canadian Association for the Study of Adult Education—Online Proceedings 2003. University of Toronto. Retrieved from www.oise.utoronto.ca/CASAE/cnf2003/2003_papers/psodhiCAS03.pdf

Sowislo, J.F, & Orth, U. (2013). Does low self-esteem predict depression and anxiety? A meta-analysis of longitudinal studies. *Psychological Bulletin, 139*(1), 213–240. doi:10.1037/a0028931

Spence, J.T., & Helmreich, R.L. (1978). *Masculinity and femininity.* Austin, TX: University of Texas Press.

Statistics Canada (2013b). *Immigration and ethnocultural diversity in Canada* (Cat. no. 99-010-X2011001). Retrieved from http://www12.

statcan.gc.ca/nhs-enm/2011/as-sa/99-010-x/99-010-x2011001-eng.pdf

Statistics Canada. (2001b). *Family violence in Canada: A statistical profile* (Cat. No. 85-224-XIE). Ottawa, ON: Author. Retrieved from www.statcan.ca/english/freepub/85-224-XIE/0100085-224-XIE.pdf

St-Pierre, R., & Derevensky, J.L. (2016). Youth gambling behavior: Novel approaches to prevention and intervention. *Adolescent Substance Abuse, 3*(2), 157–165. doi:10.1007/s40429-016-0104-0

Students Commission. (1995). History. Students commission. Retrieved from http://collections.ic.gc.ca/sharing/history_e.html

Students Commission. (2004). *The Students Commission.* Toronto, ON: Author. Retrieved from Tiny Giant Magazine website: www.tgmag.ca/index_e.htm

Students Commission. (2016). *The students commission: Who we are.* Retrieved from http://www.tgmag.ca/aorg/aboutusref_e.php

Talwar, V., Gomez-Garibello, C., & Shariff, S. (2014). Adolescents' Moral Evaluations and Ratings of Cyberbullying: The effect of veracity and intentionality behind the event. *Computers in Human Behavior, 36*(July), 122–128. doi:10.1016/j.chb.2014.03.046

Trzesniewski, K.H., Donnellan, M.B., Moffitt, T.E., Robins, R.W., Poulton, R., & Caspi, A. (2006). Low self-esteem during adolescence predicts poor health, criminal behavior, and limited economic prospects during adulthood. *Developmental Psychology, 42*(2), 381–390.

Twyman, K., Saylor, C., Taylor, L., & Comeaux, C. (2010). Comparing children and adolescents engaged in cyberbullying to matched peers. *Cyberpsychology, Behavior, and Social Networking, 13,* 195–199.

Ulmer, J.T., Desmond, S.A., Jang, S.J., & Johnson, B.R. (2012). Religious involvement and dynamics of marijuana use: Initiation, persistence, and desistence. *Deviant Behavior, 33*(6), 448–468. doi:10.1080/01639625.2011.636653

Updegraff, K., & Obeidallah, D. (1999). Young adolescents' patterns of involvement with siblings and friends. *Social Development, 8,* 52–69.

Urberg, K.A., Degirmencioglu, S.M., Tolson, J.M., & Halliday-Scher, K. (1995). The structure of adolescent peer networks. *Developmental Psychology, 31,* 540–547.

van IJzendoorn, M., Bakermans-Kranenburg, M., Pannebaker, F., & Out, D. (2010). In defence of situational morality: Genetic, dispositional and situational determinants of children's donating to charity. *Journal of Moral Education, 39,* 1–20.

Verkooijen, K., de Vries, N., & Nielsen, G. (2007). Youth crowds and substance use: The impact of perceived group norm and multiple group identification. *Psychology of Addictive Behaviors, 21,* 55–61.

Véronneau, M.H., Vitaro, F., Brendgen, M., Dishion, T.J, & Tremblay, R.E. (2010). Transactional analysis of the reciprocal links between peer experiences and academic achievement from middle childhood to early adolescence. *Developmental Psychology, 46*(4), 773–790. doi:10.1037/a0019816

Vitaro, F., Tremblay, R., Kerr, M., Pagani, L., & Bukowski, W. (1997). Disruptiveness, friends' characteristics, and delinquency in early adolescence: A test of two competing models of development. *Child Development, 68,* 676–689.

Wachlarowicz, M., Snyder, J., Low, S., Forgatch, M., & Degarmo, D. (2012). The moderating effects of parent antisocial characteristics on the effects of Parent Management Training-Oregon (PMTOTM). *Prevention Science, 13*(3), 229–240. doi:10.1007/s11121-011-0262-1

Walker, L. (1980). Cognitive and perspective-taking prerequisites for moral development. *Child Development, 51,* 131–139.

Walker, L.J. (1989). A longitudinal study of moral reasoning. *Child Development, 60,* 157–160.

Walker, L.J., de Vries, B., & Trevethan, S.D. (1987). Moral stages and moral orientations in real-life and hypothetical dilemmas. *Child Development, 58,* 842–858.

Wark, G.R., & Krebs, D.L. (1996). Gender and dilemma differences in real-life moral judgment. *Developmental Psychology, 32,* 220–230.

Woo, M., & Oei, T. (2006). The *MMPI-2* gender-masculine and gender-feminine scales: Gender roles as predictors of psychological

health in clinical patients. *International Journal of Psychology, 41,* 413–422.

Wyatt, J.M., & Carlo, G. (2002). What will my parents think? Relations among adolescents' expected parental reactions, prosocial moral reasoning, and prosocial and antisocial behaviours. *Journal of Adolescent Research, 17*(6), 646–66.

Yeung, A., Chui, H., & Lau, I. (1999). Hierarchical and multidimensional academic self-concept of commercial students. *Contemporary Educational Psychology, 24,* 376–389.

Zhong, C.B., Bohns, V.K., & Gino, F. (2010). Good lamps are the best police: Darkness increases dishonesty and self-interested behavior. *Psychological Science, 21*(3), 311–314. doi:10.1177/0956797609360754

Zimmer-Gembeck, M. (1999). Stability, change and individual differences in involvement with friends and romantic partners among adolescent females. *Journal of Youth & Adolescence, 28,* 419–438.

Zimmermann, P. (2004). Attachment representations and characteristics of friendship relations during adolescence. *Journal of Experimental Child Psychology, 88*(1), 83–101.

Chapter 13

American Psychiatric Association. (2013). *Diagnostic and Statistical Manual of Mental Disorder: DSM-5* (5th ed.). Washington, DC: American Psychiatric Publishing.

Ashenhurst, J.R., Harden, K.P., Corbin, W.R., & Fromme, K. (2015). Trajectories of binge drinking and personality change across emerging adulthood. *Psychology of Addictive Behaviors: Journal of the Society of Psychologists in Addictive Behaviors, 29*(4), 978–991. doi:10.1037/adb0000116

Baker, E.D. (2005). Social support and physical health: Understanding the health consequences of relationships. *American Journal of Epidemiology, 161*(3), 297–298. doi:10.1093/aje/kwi036

Bandura, A. (1977b). Self-efficacy: Toward a unifying theory of behavioral change. *Psychological Review, 84,* 91–125.

Bandura, A. (1986). *Social foundations of thought and action: A social cognitive theory.* Englewood Cliffs, NJ: Prentice-Hall.

Bandura, A. (1997a). *Self-efficacy: The exercise of control.* New York, NY: W.H. Freeman.

Bandura, A. (1997b). Self-efficacy. *Harvard Mental Health Letter, 13*(9), 4–6.

Bartoshuk, L.M., & Weiffenbach, J.M. (1990). Chemical senses and aging. In E.L. Schneider & J.W. Rowe (Eds.), *Handbook of the biology of aging* (3rd ed., pp. 429–444). San Diego, CA: Academic Press.

Basseches, M. (1984). *Dialectical thinking and adult development.* Norwood, NJ: Ablex.

Basseches, M. (1989). Dialectical thinking as an organized whole: Comments on Irwin and Kramer. In M.L. Commons, J.D. Sinnott, F.A. Richards, & C. Armon (Eds.), *Adult development: Vol. 1. Comparisons and applications of developmental models* (pp. 161–178). New York, NY: Praeger.

Betik, A., & Hepple, R. (2008). Determinants of VO 2 max decline with aging: An integrated perspective. *Applied Physiology, Nutrition, and Metabolism, 33*(1), 130–140. doi: 10.1139/H07-174

Blatter, D.D., Bigler, E.D., Gale, S.D., Johnson, S.C., Anderson, C.V., Burnett, B.M., . . . & Horn, S.D. (1995). Quantitative volumetric analysis of brain MR: Normative database spanning 5 decades of life. *American Journal of Neuroradiology, 16*(2), 241–251.

Bouhuys, A., Flentge, F., Oldehinkel, A., & van den Berg, M. (2004). Potential psychosocial mechanisms linking depression to immune function in elderly subjects. *Psychiatry Research, 127,* 237–245.

Braveman, N.S. (1987). Immunity and aging immunologic and behavioral perspectives. In M.W. Riley, J.D. Matarazzo, & A. Baum (Eds.), *Perspectives in behavioral medicine: The aging dimension* (pp. 94–124). Hillsdale, NJ: Erlbaum.

Breslow, L., & Breslow, N. (1993). Health practices and disability: Some evidence from Alameda County. *Preventive Medicine, 22,* 86–95.

Briggs, R. (1990). Biological aging. In J. Bond & P. Coleman (Eds.), *Aging in society* (pp. 48–61). London, England: Sage.

Brock, D.B., Guralnik, J.M., & Brody, J.A. (1990). Demography and the epidemiology of aging in the United States. In E.L. Schneider & J.W. Rowe (Eds.), *Handbook of the biology of aging* (3rd ed., pp. 3–23). San Diego, CA: Academic Press.

Burke, L., & Follingstad, D. (1999). Violence in lesbian and gay relationships: Theory, prevalence, and correlational factors. *Clinical Psychology Review, 19*, 487–512.

Canada's Parliamentary Budget Officer [PBO] (2015). *Labour market assessment 2015*. Ottawa, ON: Office of the Parliamentary Budget Officer. Retrieved from http://www.pbo-dpb.gc.ca/en/blog/news/Labour_Market_Assessment_2015

Cao, L., Jiao, X., Zuzga, D., Liu, Y., Fong, D., Young, D., & During, M. (2004). VEGF links hippocampal activity with neurogenesis, learning and memory. *Nature Genetics, 36*(8), 827–835. doi:10.1038/ng1395

Catalano, S. (2012). *Intimate partner violence, 1993—2010*. Retrieved from http://www.bjs.gov/content/pub/pdf/ipv9310.pdf

Catalano, S., Smith, E., Snyder, H., & Rand, M. (2009). *Female victims of violence*. Retrieved from http://bjs.ojp.usdoj.gov/content/pub/pdf/fvv.pdf

Centers for Disease Control. (2011). *2010 STD Treatment Guidelines: Clinical prevention guidance*. Retrieved from http://www.cdc.gov/std/treatment/2010/clinical.htm

Cheitlin, M. (2003). Cardiovascular physiology: Changes with aging. *American Journal of Geriatric Cardiology, 12*, 9–13.

Chomik, T.A. (2001). *The population health template*. Ottawa, ON. Retrieved from Health Canada website: www.hc-sc.gc.ca/hppb/phdd/pdf/discussion_paper.pdf

Citkowitz, E. (2012). *Polygenic hypercholesterolemia*. Retrieved from http://emedicine.medscape.com/article/121424-overview

Coates, K., & Morrison, B. (2013, January 21). The graduate's million-dollar promise. *Maclean's*, 42–45.

Cohen, S. (2006). *Aging changes in immunity. Medline: Medical encyclopedia*. Retrieved www.nlm.nih.gov/medlineplus/ency/article/004008.htm

Dabby, F. (2007). *Domestic violence against Asian and Pacific Islander women*. Retrieved from http://www.vaw.umn.edu/documents/dvagainstapi/dvagainstapi.pdf

Dawson, J., & Langan, P. (1994). *Murder in families*. Washington, DC: U.S. Department of Justice.

Doty, R.L., Shaman, P., Appelbaum, S.L., Bigerson, R., Sikorski, L., & Rosenberg, L. (1984). Smell identification ability: Changes with age. *Science, 226*, 1441–1443.

Drevets, W., Price, J., Simpson, J., Todd, R., Reich, T., Vannier, M., & Raichle, M. (1997). Subgenual prefrontal cortex abnormalities in mood disorders. *Nature, 386*, 824–827.

Dugan, L., Nagin, D., & Rosenfeld, R. (2003). Do domestic violence services save lives? *National Institute of Justice Journal, 250*, 1–6.

Dutton, D.G. (2012). The prevention of intimate partner violence. *Prevention Science, 13*(4), 395–397. doi:10.1007/s11121-012-0306-1

Elliott, D., Mok, D., & Briere, J. (2004). Adult sexual assault: Prevalence, symptomatology, and sex differences in the general population. *Journal of Traumatic Stress, 17*, 203–211.

Ellison, M., Danley, K., Bromberg, C., & Palmer-Erbs, V. (1999). Longitudinal outcome of young adults who participated in a psychiatric vocational rehabilitation program. *Psychiatric Rehabilitation Journal, 22*, 337–341.

Essex, M.J., Boyce, T., Hertzman, C., Lam, L.L., Armstrong, J.M., Neumann, S.M., & Kobor, M.S. (2013). Epigenetic vestiges of early developmental adversity: Childhood stress exposure and DNA methylation in adolescence. *Child Development, 84*(1), 58–75. doi:10.1111/j.1467-8624.2011.01641.x

Fiatarone, M.A., & Evans, W.J. (1993). The etiology and reversibility of muscle dysfunction in the aged. *The Journals of Gerontology, 48*(Special Issue), 77–83.

Fozard, J.L. (1990). Vision and hearing in aging. In J.E. Birren & K.W. Schaie (Eds.), *Handbook of the psychology of aging* (3rd ed., pp. 150–171). San Diego, CA: Academic Press.

Fozard, J.L., Metter, E.J., & Brant, L.J. (1990). Next steps in describing aging and disease in longitudinal studies. *Journals of Gerontology: Psychological Sciences, 45*, P116–127.

Frick, E., Fegg, M., Tyroller, M., Fischer, N., & Bumeder, I. (2007). Patients' health beliefs and coping prior to autologous peripheral stem cell transplantation. *European Journal of Cancer Care, 16*, 156–163.

Gaillard, W., Hertz-Pannier, L., Mott, S., Barnett, A., LeBihan, D., & Theodore, W. (2000). Functional anatomy of cognitive development: fMRI of verbal fluency in children and adults. *Neurology, 54*, 180–185.

Gauntlett-Gilbert, J., Keegan, A., & Petrak, J. (2004). Drug-facilitated sexual assault: Cognitive approaches to treating the trauma. *Behavioral & Cognitive Psychotherapy, 32*, 211.

Geers, A., Kosbab, K., Helfer, S., Weiland, P., & Wellman, J. (2007). Further evidence for individual differences in placebo responding: An interactionist perspective. *Journal of Psychosomatic Research, 62*, 563–570.

Giedd, J.N., Blumenthal, J., Jeffries, N.O., Castellanos, F.X., Liu, H., Zijdenbos, A., . . . Rapoport, J.L. (1999). Brain development during childhood and adolescence: A longitudinal MRI study. *Nature Neuroscience, 2*(10), 861–863.

Gillis, C., & Sorensen, C. (2013, January 21). The new underclass. *Maclean's*, 38–42.

Glaser, R., Kiecolt-Glaser, J.K., Bonneau, R.H., Malarkey, W., Kennedy, S., & Hughes, J. (1992). Stress-induced modulation of the immune response to recombinant hepatitis B vaccine. *Psychosomatic Medicine, 54*, 22–29.

Gogtay, N., Giedd, J.N., Lusk, L., Hayashi, K.M., Greenstein, D., Vaituzis, A.C., . . . Thompson, P.M. (2004). Dynamic mapping of human cortical development during childhood through early adulthood. *Proceedings of the National Academy of Sciences of the United States of America, 101*, 8174–8179.

Gold, D.P., Andres, D., Etezadi, J., Arbuckle, T., Schwartzman, A., & Chaikelson, J. (1995). Structural equation model of intellectual change and continuity and predictors of intelligence in older men. *Psychology and Aging, 10*, 294–303.

Goldberg, A.P., Dengel, D.R., & Hagberg, J.M. (1996). Exercise physiology and aging. In E.L. Schneider & J.W. Rowe (Eds.), *Handbook of the biology of aging* (4th ed., pp. 331–354). San Diego, CA: Academic Press.

Goriely, A., & Wilkie, A.O. (2012). Paternal age effect mutations and selfish spermatogonial selection: Causes and consequences for human disease. *American Journal of Human Genetics, 90*(2), 175–200. doi:10.1016/j.ajhg.2011.12.017

Gould, E., Reeves, A., Graziano, M., & Gross, C. (1999). Neurogenesis in the neocortex of adult primates. *Science, 286*, 548–552.

Government of Canada (2006). *The human face of mental health and mental illness in Canada* (HP5-19/2006E). Ottawa, ON: Minister of Public Works and Government Services Canada. Retrieved from www.phac-aspc.gc.ca/publicat/human-humain06/pdf/human_face_e.pdf

Gralinski-Bakker, J., Hauser, S., Billings, R., Allen, J., Lyons, P., & Melton, G. (2005). Transitioning to adulthood for young adults with mental health issues. *Network on Transitions to Adulthood Policy Brief, 21*, 1–3.

Grant, M. (2016). *Aligning skills development with labour market need*. Ottawa, ON: The Conference Board of Canada.

Gray, A., Berlin, J.A., McKinlay, J.B., Longcope, C. (1991). An examination of research design effects on the association of testosterone and male aging: Results of a meta-analysis. *Journal of Clinical Epidemiology, 44*(7), 671–684.

Guralnik, J.M., & Kaplan, G.A. (1989). Predictors of healthy aging: Prospective evidence from the Alameda County Study. *American Journal of Public Health, 79*, 703–708.

Hallfrisch, J., Muller, D., Drinkwater, D., Tobin, J., & Adres, R. (1990). Continuing diet trends in men: The Baltimore Longitudinal Study of Aging. *Journals of Gerontology: Medical Sciences, 45*(6), M186–191.

Hamberger, K., & Minsky, D. (2000, August). *Evaluation of domestic violence training programs for health care professionals.* Paper presented at the annual meeting of the American Psychological Association, Washington, DC.

Hawkley, L., & Cacioppo, J. (2004). Stress and the aging immune system. *Brain, Behavior, and Immunity, 18*, 114–119.

Hayflick, L. (1994). *How and why we age.* New York, NY: Ballantine Books. Ivy, G.O., MacLeod, C.M., Petit, T.L., & Marcus, E.J. (1992). A physiological framework for perceptual and cognitive changes in aging. In F.I.M. Craik & T.A. Salthouse (Eds.), *The handbook of aging and cognition* (pp. 273–314). Hillsdale, NJ: Erlbaum.

Heise, L. & Garcia-Moreno, C. (2002). Violence by intimate partners. In E.G. Krug, L.L. Dahlberg, J.A. Mercy, A.B. Zwi, & R. Lozano (Eds.), *World report on violence and health* (pp. 87–121). Geneva: World Health Organization. Retrieved from www.who.int/violence_injury_prevention/violence/world_report/en/full_en.pdf

Hertzman, C. & Frank, J. (2006). Biological pathways linking the social environment, development, and health. In J. Heymann, C. Hertzman, M.L. Barer, & R.G. Evans (Eds.), *Healthier societies: From analysis to action* (pp. 35–57). New York, NY: Oxford University Press.

Hertzman, C. (2013). Commentary on the symposium: Biological embedding, life course development, and the emergence of a new science. *Annual Review of Public Health, 34*, 1–5. doi:10.1146/annurev-publhealth-031912-114500

Hertzman, C., & Boyce, T. (2010). How experience gets under the skin to create gradients in developmental health. *Annual Review of Public Health, 31*, 329–347. doi:10.1146/annurev.publhealth.012809.103538

Hodge, S., & Canter, D. (1998). Victims and perpetrators of male sexual assault. *Journal of Interpersonal Violence, 13*, 222–239.

Hollander, J. (2004). "I Can Take Care of Myself": The impact of self-defense training on women's lives. *Violence Against Women, 10*, 205–235.

Kessler, R., Berglund, P., Demler, O., Jin, R., Merikangas, K., & Walters, E. (2005). Lifetime prevalence and age-of-onset distributions of DSM-IV disorders in the national comorbidity survey replication. *Archives of General Psychiatry, 62*, 593–602.

Horn, J.L. (1982). The aging of human abilities. In B.B. Wolman (Ed.), *Handbook of developmental psychology* (pp. 847–870). Englewood Cliffs, NJ: Prentice-Hall.

Hotton, T. (2001). Spousal violence after marital separation (Cat. no. 85-002). *Juristat 21*(7), 2–18.

Housman, J., & Dorman, S. (2005). The Alameda County Study: A systematic, chronological review. *American Journal of Health Education, 36*, 302–308.

Hu, F., Li, T., Colditz, G., Willet, W., & Manson, J. (2003). Television watching and other sedentary behavior in relation to risk of obesity and type 2 diabetes mellitus in women. *Journal of the American Medical Association, 289*, 1785–1791.

Hunter, Z., & Francescutti, L.H. (2013). Facing the consequences of binge drinking. *Canadian Family Physician, 59*(10), 1041–1042.

Irwin, M., & Pike, J. (1993). Bereavement, depressive symptoms, and immune function. In M.S. Stroebe, W. Stroebe, & R.O. Hansson (Eds.), *Handbook of bereavement: Theory, research, and intervention* (pp. 160–171). Cambridge, England: Cambridge University Press.

Iverson, K.M., McLaughlin, K.A., Gerber, M.R., Dick, A., Smith, B.N., Bell, M.E., . . . Mitchell, K.S. (2013). Exposure to interpersonal violence and its associations with psychiatric morbidity in a U.S. national sample: a gender comparison. *Psychology of Violence, 3*(3), 273–287. doi:10.1037/a0030956

Jaremka, L.M., Fagundes, C.P., Glaser, R., Bennett, J.M., Malarkey, W.B., & Kiecolt-Glaser, J.K. (2013). Loneliness predicts pain, depression, and fatigue: Understanding the role of immune dysregulation. *Psychoneuroendocrinology, 38*(8), 1310–1317. doi:10.1016/j.psyneuen.2012.11.016

Johnson, J.A., & Tough, S. (2012). Delayed child-bearing. *Journal of Obstetrics and Gynaecology Canada, 34*(1), 80–93. Retrieved from http://www.jogc.com/abstracts/full/201201_SOGCClinical-PracticeGuidelines_1.pdf

Kallman, D.A., Plato, C.C., & Tobin, J.D. (1990). The role of muscle loss in the age-related decline of grip strength: Cross-sectional and longitudinal perspectives. *Journals of Gerontology: Medical Sciences, 45*, M82–88

Kalmuss, D. (2004). Nonviolational sex and sexual health. *Archives of Sexual Behavior, 33*, 197–209.

Kane, T., Staiger, P., & Ricciardelli, L. (2000). Male domestic violence: Attitudes, aggression and interpersonal dependency. *Journal of Interpersonal Violence, 15*, 16–29.

Kaplan, H., & Sadock, B. (1991). *Synopsis of psychiatry* (6th ed.). Baltimore, MD: Williams & Wilkins.

Kendler, K., Kessler, R., Walters, E., MacLean, C., Neale, M., Heath, A., & Eaves, L. (1995). Stressful life events, genetic liability, and onset of an episode of major depression in women. *American Journal of Psychiatry, 152*, 833–842.

Keon, W.J., & Pépin, L. (2009). *A healthy, productive Canada: A determinant of health approach. The standing senate committee on social affairs, science and technology final report of senate subcommittee on population health.* Ottawa, ON: Senate Subcommittee on Population Health. Retrieved from http://www.parl.gc.ca/content/sen/committee/402/popu/rep/rephealth1jun09-e.pdf

Kiecolt-Glaser, J.K., & Glaser, R. (1995). Measurement of immune response. In S. Cohen, R.C. Kessler, & L.U. Gordon (Eds.), *Measuring stress: A guide for health and social scientists* (pp. 213–229). New York, NY: Oxford University Press.

King, P.M., & Kitchener, K.S. (2004). Reflective judgment: Theory and research on the development of epistemic assumption through adulthood. *Educational Psychologist, 39*(1), 5–18.

Kline, D.W., & Scialfa, C.T. (1996). Visual and auditory aging. In J.E. Birren & K.W. Schaie (Eds.), *Handbook of the psychology of aging* (4th ed., pp. 181–203). San Diego, CA: Academic Press.

Kohlberg, L. (1969). Stage and sequence: The cognitive-developmental approach to socialization. In D. Goslin (Ed.), *Handbook of socialization theory and research* (pp. 347–480). Chicago, IL: Rand McNally.

Kondro, W. (2012). Health disparities among income groups becoming more pronounced. *Canadian Medical Association Journal, 184*(13), E695–6. doi:10.1503/cmaj.109-4269

Kong, A., Frigge, M.L., Masson, G., Besenbacher, S., Sulem, P., Magnusson, G., . . . Stefansson, K. (2012). Rate of de novo mutations and the importance of father's age to disease risk. *Nature, 488*(7412), 471–475. doi:10.1038/nature11396

Kong, R., Johnson, H., Beattie, S., & Cardillo, A. (2003). Sexual offences in Canada (Cat. no. 85-002-XPE). Ottawa, ON: Statistics Canada.

Kozma, A., Stones, M.J., & Hannah, T.E. (1991). Age, activity, and physical performance: An evaluation of performance models. *Psychology and Aging, 6*, 43–49.

Kyriacou, D., Anglin, D., Taliaferro, E., Stone, S., Tubb, T., Linden, J., . . . Kraus, J. (1999). Risk factors for injury to women from domestic violence. *New England Journal of Medicine, 341*, 1892–1898.

Labouvie-Vief, G. (2006). Emerging structures of adult thought. In J. Arnett & J. Tanner (Eds.), *Emerging adults in America: Coming of age in the 21st century* (pp. 59–84). Washington, DC: American Psychological Association.

Lakatta, E.G. (1990). Heart and circulation. In E.L. Schneider & J.W. Rowe (Eds.), *Handbook of the biology of aging* (3rd ed., pp. 181–217). San Diego, CA: Academic Press.

Landolt, M., & Dutton, D. (1997). Power and personality: An analysis of gay male intimate abuse. *Sex Roles, 37*, 335–359.

Lauriello, J., McEvoy, J., Rodriguez, S., Bossie, C., & Lasser, R. (2005). Long-acting risperidone vs. placebo in the treatment of hospital inpatients with schizophrenia. *Schizophrenia Research, 72*, 249–258.

Lebel, C., & Beaulieu, C. (2011). Longitudinal development of human brain wiring continues from childhood into adulthood. *The Journal of Neuroscience, 31*(30), 10937–10947. doi:10.1523/JNEUROSCI.5302-10.2011

Leuner, B., & Gould, E. (2010). Structural plasticity and hippocampal function. *Annual Review of Psychology, 61*, 111–140.

Lim, K.O., Zipursky, R.B., Watts, M.C., & Pfefferbaum, A. (1992). Decreased gray matter in normal aging: An in vivo magnetic resonance study. *Journal of Gerontology: Biological Sciences, 47*(1), B26–30.

Lissner, L., Bengtsson, C., Björkelund, C., & Wedel, H. (1996). Physical activity levels and changes in relation to longevity: A prospective study of Swedish women. *American Journal of Epidemiology, 143*, 54–62.

Low, C., Bower, J., Moskowitz, J., & Epel, E. (2011). Positive psychological states and biological processes. In K.M. Sheldon, T.B. Kashdan, & M.F. Steger, (Eds.), *Designing positive psychology: Taking stock and moving forward* (pp. 41–50). New York, NY: Oxford University Press.

Manson, J.E., Willett, W.C., Stampfer, M.J., Colditz, G.A., Hunter, D.J., Hankinson, S.E., . . . Speizer, F.E. (1995). Body weight and mortality among women. *New England Journal of Medicine, 333*, 677–685.

McFalls, J.A., Jr. (1990). The risks of reproductive impairment in the later years of childbearing. *Annual Review of Sociology, 16*, 491–519.

McHugh, M. (2005). Understanding gender and intimate partner abuse. *Sex Roles: A Journal of Research, 52*, 717–724.

McIntosh, C.N., Finès, P., Wilkins, R., & Wolfson, M.C. (2009). Income disparities in health adjusted life expectancy for Canadian adults, 1991 to 2001. *Health Reports, 20*(4), 1–10.

McNeal, C., & Amato, P. (1998). Parents' marital violence: Long-term consequences for children. *Journal of Family Issues, 19*, 123–139.

Mikkonen, J., & Raphael, D. (2010). *Social determinants of health: The Canadian facts.* Toronto, ON: York University School of Health Policy and Management. Retrieved from http://www.thecanadianfacts.org/

Miller, R.A. (1996). Aging and the immune response. In E.L. Schneider & J.W. Rowe (Eds.), *Handbook of the biology of aging* (4th ed., pp. 355–392). San Diego, CA: Academic Press.

Monarch, E., Saykin, A., & Flashman, L. (2004). Neuropsychological impairment in borderline personality disorder. *Psychiatric Clinics of North America, 27*, 67–82.

Morissette, R., Garnett, P., & Lu, Y. (2013). *The evolution of Canadian wages over the last three decades* (Cat. no. 11F0019MWE). Retrieved from Statistics Canada Website http://www.statcan.gc.ca/pub/11f0019m/11f0019m2013347-eng.pdf

Mundy, G.R. (1994). Osteoporosis: Boning up on genes. *Nature, 367*(216), 216–217. doi:10.1038/367216a0

National Institute of Mental Health. (2016). *Schizophrenia's strongest known genetic risk deconstructed.* Retrieved from http://www.nimh.nih.gov/news/science-news/2016/schizophrenias-strongest-known-genetic-risk-deconstructed.shtml

Nikolich-Žugich, J. (2005). T cell aging: Naive but not young. *The Journal of Experimental Medicine, 201*(6), 837–840. doi.org/10.1084/jem.20050341

Organisation for Economic Co-operation and Development. (2015). *Education at a Glance 2015 OECD indicators.* Retrieved from http://www.oecd-ilibrary.org/

Perkins, H.W. (2002). Surveying the damage: A review of research on consequences of alcohol misuse in college populations. *Journal of Studies on Alcohol. Supplement. 14*, 91–100.

Perkins, H.W. (2007). Misperceptions of peer drinking norms in Canada: Another look at the "reign of error" and its consequences among college students. *Addictive behaviors, 32*(11), 2645–2656. doi:10.1016/j.addbeh.2007.07.007

Perry, W. (1968). *Forms of intellectual and ethical development in the college years.* New York, NY: Holt, Rinehart & Winston.

Peterson, C., Seligman, M.E.P., & Vaillant, G.E. (1988). Pessimistic explanatory style is a risk factor for physical illness: A thirty-five-year longitudinal study. *Journal of Personality and Social Psychology, 55*, 23–27.

Phillips, S.K., Bruce, S.A., Newton, D., & Woledge, R.C. (1992). The weakness of old age is not due to failure of muscle activation. *Journals of Gerontology: Medical Sciences, 47*, M45–49.

Pickett, K., & Wilkinson, R. (2010). *The spirit level: Why greater equality makes societies stronger.* Toronto, ON: Penguin Group (Canada).

Public Health Agency of Canada (2010c). *Population-specific HIV/AIDS status report: Aboriginal peoples.* Retrieved from http://www.phac-aspc.gc.ca/aids-sida/publication/ps-pd/aboriginalautochtones/pdf/pshasrap-revspda-eng.pdf

Public Health Agency of Canada (2011a). *STI & hepatitis C statistics.* Retrieved from http://www.phac-aspc.gc.ca/sti-its-surv-epi/surveillance-eng.php

Public Health Agency of Canada. (2012d). *Health-adjusted life expectancy in Canada: 2012.* Retrieved from http://www.phac-aspc.gc.ca/cd-mc/index-eng.php

Public Health Agency of Canada (2012e). *Summary: Estimates of HIV prevalence and incidence in Canada, 2011, Surveillance and Epidemiology Division.* Retrieved from http://www.phac-aspc.gc.ca/aids-sida/publication/survreport/estimat2011-eng.php

Public Health Agency of Canada. (2013b). *Canadian guidelines on sexually transmitted infections: Section 2 - primary care and sexually transmitted infections.* Retrieved from http://www.phac-aspc.gc.ca/std-mts/sti-its/cgsti-ldcits/section-2-eng.php

Raphael, D. (2016). Social determinants of health: An overview of key issues and themes. In D. Raphael (ed.) *Social determinants of health: Canadian perspectives* (3rd ed.). Toronto, ON: Canadian Scholars' Press.

Rhodes, J., van Praag, H., Jeffrey, S., Girard, I., Mitchell, G., Garland, T., & Gage, F. (2003). Exercise increases hippocampal neurogenesis to high levels but does not improve spatial learning in mice bred for increased voluntary wheel running. *Behavioral Neuroscience, 117*, 1006–1016.

Rodgers, W.M., Murray, T.C., Selzler, A., & Norman, P. (2013). Development and impact of exercise self-efficacy types during and after cardiac rehabilitation. *Rehabilitation Psychology, 58*(2), 178–184. doi.org/10.1037/a0032018

Ross, N.A., Wolfson, M.C., Dunn, J.R., Berthelot, J-M., Kaplan, G.A., & Lynch, J.W. (2000). Relation between income inequality and mortality in Canada and in the United States. *British Medical Journal, 320*(7239), 898–902.

Rotter, J. (1990). Internal versus external control of reinforcement: A case history of a variable. *American Psychologist, 45*(4), 489–493.

Salthouse, T.A. (2010). Selective review of cognitive aging. *Journal of the International Neuropsychological Society. 16*(5), 754–760. doi:10.1017/S1355617710000706

Salthouse, T.A. (2012a). Are individual differences in rates of aging greater at older ages? *Neurobiology of Aging, 33*(10), 2373–2381. doi:10.1016/j.neurobiolaging.2011.10.018

Sands, L.P., Terry, H., & Meredith, W. (1989). Change and stability in adult intellectual functioning assessed by Wechsler item responses. *Psychology and Aging, 4*, 79–87.

Sax, L., & Bryant, A. (2006). The impact of college on sex-atypical career choices of men and women. *Journal of Vocational Behavior, 68*, 52–63.

Schaie, K. (2009). "When does age-related cognitive decline begin?" Salthouse again reifies the "cross-sectional fallacy." *Neurobiology of Aging, 30*, 528–529.

Schaie, K. (2013). *Developmental influences on adult intelligence: The Seattle Longitudinal Study* (2nd ed.). New York, NY: Oxford University Press.

Schaie, K.W. (1983). The Seattle longitudinal study: A 21-year exploration of psychometric intelligence in adulthood. In K.W. Schaie (Ed.), *Longitudinal studies of adult psychological development* (pp. 64–135). New York, NY: Guilford Press.

Schaie, K.W., & Hertzog, C. (1983). Fourteen-year cohort-sequential analyses of adult intellectual development. *Developmental Psychology, 19*, 531–543.

Scheibel, A.B. (1992). Structural changes in the aging brain. In J.E. Birren, R.B. Sloane, & G.D. Cohen (Eds.), *Handbook of mental health and aging* (2nd ed., pp. 147–174). San Diego, CA: Academic Press.

Scheibel, A.B. (1996). Structural and functional changes in the aging brain. In J.E. Birren & K.W. Schaie (Eds.), *Handbook of the psychology of aging* (4th ed., pp. 105–128). San Diego, CA: Academic Press.

Scholle, S., Buranosky, R., Hanusa, B., Ranieri, L., Dowd, K., & Valappil, B. (2003). Routine screening for intimate partner violence in an obstetrics and gynecology clinic. *American Journal of Public Health, 93*, 1070–1072.

Schroeder, D., & Salthouse, T. (2004). Age-related effects on cognition between 20 and 50 years of age. *Personality & Individual Differences, 36*, 393–404.

Sekar, A., Biala, A.R., de Rivera, H., Davis, A., Hammond, T.R., Kamitaki, N., . . . McCarroll, S.A. (2016). Schizophrenia risk from complex variation of complement component 4. *Nature. 530*(7589), 177–183. doi:10.1038/nature16549

Seligman, M. (2006). *Learned optimism: How to change your mind and your life*. New York, NY: Vintage Books.

Shock, N.W., Greulich, R.C., Andres, R., Arenberg, D., Costa, P.T., Jr., Lakatta, E.G., & Tobin, J.D. (1984). *Normal human aging: The Baltimore Longitudinal Study of Aging*. NIH Publication No. 84–2450, U.S. Department of Health and Human Services, National Institute on Aging. Washington, DC: U.S. Government Printing Office.

Siddiqi, A., Kawachi, I., Keating, D.P., & Hertzman, C. (2013). A comparative study of population health in the United States and Canada during the neoliberal era, 1980–2008. *International Journal of Health Services, 43*(2), 193–216. doi:10.2190/HS.43.2.b

Siegler, I.C. (1983). Psychological aspects of the Duke Longitudinal Studies. In K.W. Schaie (Ed.), *Longitudinal studies of adult psychological development* (pp. 136–190). New York, NY: Guilford Press.

Silveri, M.M. (2012). Adolescent brain development and underage drinking in the United States: Identifying risks of alcohol use in college populations. *Harvard Review of Psychiatry, 20*(4), 189–200. doi:10.3109/10673229.2012.714642

Sinha, M. (2012). *Family violence in Canada: A statistical profile, 2010* (Cat. no. 85-002-XWE). Retrieved from Statistics Canada website http://www.statcan.gc.ca/pub/85-002-x/2012001/article/11643-eng.pdf

Sinha, M. (2013). *Measuring violence against women: Statistical trends* (Cat. no. 85-002-X). Retrieved from Statistics Canada website http://www.statcan.gc.ca/pub/85-002-x/2013001/article/11766-eng.pdf

Smith, P., White, J., & Holland, L. (2003). A longitudinal perspective on dating violence among adolescent and college-age women. *American Journal of Public Health, 93*, 1104–1109.

Sowell, E.R., Peterson, B.S., Thompson, P.M., Welcome, S.E., Henkenius, A.L., & Toga, A.W. (2003). Mapping cortical change across the human life span. *Nature Neuroscience, 6*(3), 309–315.

Sowell, E.R., Thompson, P.M., Tessner, K.D., & Toga, A.W. (2001). Mapping continued brain growth and gray matter density reduction in dorsal frontal cortex: Inverse relationships during post-adolescent brain maturation. *The Journal of Neuroscience, 21*(22), 8819–8829.

Statistics Canada. (2001b). *Family violence in Canada: A statistical profile* (Cat. no. 85-224-XIE). Ottawa, ON: Author. Retrieved from www.statcan.ca/english/freepub/85-224-XIE/0100085-224-XIE.pdf

Statistics Canada. (2012k). *Economic downturn and educational attainment: Canada in an international context. Fact sheet.* (Cat. no. 81-599-X — Issue no. 009). Retrieved from http://www.statcan.gc.ca/pub/81-599-x/81-599-x2012009-eng.pdf

Statistics Canada. (2013e). *Education in Canada: Attainment, field of study and location of study* (Cat. no. 99-012-X2011001). Retrieved from http://www12.statcan.gc.ca/nhs-enm/2011/as-sa/99-012-x/99-012-x2011001-eng.pdf

Statistics Canada. (2015d). *Leading causes of death, total population, by age group and sex, Canada, annual* (CANSIM Table 102-0561). Retrieved from http://www5.statcan.gc.ca/cansim/a26?lang=eng&id=1020561

Statistics Canada. (2015g). *Career decision-making patterns of Canadian youth and associated postsecondary educational outcomes* (Cat. no. 81-599-X — No. 10). Retrieved from http://www.statcan.gc.ca/pub/81-599-x/81-599-x2015010-eng.pdf

Statistics Canada. (2016f). *Health indicator profile, annual estimates, by age group and sex, Canada, provinces, territories, health regions (2013 boundaries) and peer groups* (CANSIM Table 105-0501). Retrieved from http://www5.statcan.gc.ca/cansim/a26?lang=eng&id=1050501

Statistics Canada. (2016g). *Education indicators in Canada: An international perspective, 2015* (Cat. no. 81-604-X). Retrieved from http://www.statcan.gc.ca/pub/81-604-x/81-604-x2015001-eng.pdf

Strawbridge, W.J., Camacho, T.C., Cohen, R.D., & Kaplan, G.A. (1993). Gender differences in factors associated with change in physical functioning in old age: A 6-year longitudinal study. *The Gerontologist, 33*, 603–609.

Suderman, M., Borghol, N., Pappas, J.J., McArdle, W., Racine, A., Hallett, M.T., . . . Szyf, M. (2013). Epigenomic socioeconomic studies are more similar than different, *Proceedings of the National Academy of Sciences of the United States of America, 110*(4), E1246; Advanced online publication, doi:10.1073/pnas.1221019110

Symister, P., & Friend, R. (2003). The influence of social support and problematic support on optimism and depression in chronic illness: A prospective study evaluating self-esteem as a mediator. *Health Psychology, 22*, 123–129.

Thompson, W., & Lande, R. (2007). *Alcoholism*. Retrieved from eMedicine website: www.emedicine.com/med/topic98.htm

United Nations Development Programme (2009). *Human development report 2009*. New York, NY: Author. Retrieved from http://hdr.undp.org/en/statistics/indices/hdi/

Uppal, S., & LaRochelle-Côté, S. (2014a). Overqualification among recent university graduates in Canada. *Insights on Canadian Society* (Cat. no. 75-006-X). Ottawa, ON: Statistics Canada.

Uppal, S., & LaRochelle-Côté, S. (2014b). Changes in the occupational profile of young men and women in Canada. *Insights on Canadian Society* (Cat. no. 75-006-X). Ottawa, ON: Statistics Canada.

Walker, D.M., Cates, H.M., Heller, E.A., & Nestler, E.J. (2015). Regulation of chromatin states by drugs of abuse. *Current Opinion in Neurobiology, 30*(Feb), 112–121. http://doi.org/10.1016/j.conb.2014.11.002

Weisse, C.S. (1992). Depression and immunocompetence: A review of the literature. *Psychological Bulletin, 111*, 475–489.

Welford, A.T. (1993). The gerontological balance sheet. In J. Cerella, J. Rybash, W. Hoyer, & M.L. Commons (Eds.), *Adult information processing: Limits on loss* (pp. 3–10). San Diego, CA: Academic Press.

Wellman, R.J., Contreras, G.A., Dugas, E.N., O'Loughlin, E.K., & O'Loughlin, J.L. (2014). Determinants of sustained binge drinking in young adults. *Alcoholism, Clinical and Experimental Research, 38*(5), 1409–1415. doi:10.1111/acer.12365

Wilmore, J., Stanforth, P., Gagnon, J., Rice, T., Mandel, S., Leon, A., . . . Bouchard, C. (2001). Cardiac output and stroke volume changes with endurance training: The HERITAGE Family Study. *Medicine and Science in Sports and Exercise, 33*(1), 99–106.

Yang, H., Youm, Y, Sun, Y., Rim, J., Galban, C., Vandanmagsar, B., & Dixit, V. (2009). Axin expression in thymic stromal cells contributes to an age-related increase in thymic adiposity and is associated with reduced thymopoiesis independently of ghrelin signaling. *Journal of Leukocyte Biology, 85*, 928–938. http://www.pbo-dpb.gc.ca/en/blog/news/Labour_Market_Assessment_2015

Chapter 14

Abma, J., & Martinez, G. (2006). Childlessness among older women in the United States: Trends and profiles. *Journal of Marriage and Family, 68*, 1045–1056.

Ambert, A. (2003). *Cohabitation and marriage: Are they equivalent?* Ottawa, ON: The Vanier Institute of the Family. Retrieved from the York University Faculty of Arts website: www.arts.yorku.ca/soci/ambert/writings/cohabitation.html

Ambert, A. (2005). Cohabitation and marriage: How are they related? Ottawa, ON: The Vanier Institute of the Family. Retrieved from www.vifamily.ca/library/cft/cohabitation.pdf

Ambert, A. (2009). *Divorce: Facts, causes & consequences*. Retrieved from www.vanierinstitute.ca/include/get.php?nodeid=190

American Psychological Association. (2016). *Managing stress for a healthy family*. Retrieved from http://www.apa.org/helpcenter/managing-stress.aspx

Arnett, J. (1998). Risk behavior and family role transitions during the twenties. *Journal of Youth & Adolescence, 27*, 301–320.

Arnett, J.J. (2000). Emerging adulthood. A theory of development from the late teens through the twenties. *American Psychologist, 55*(5), 469–480.

Arnett, J.J. (2004). *Emerging adulthood: The winding road from the late teens through the twenties.* Toronto, ON: Oxford University Press.

Baker, L., & McNulty, J. (2010). Shyness and marriage: Does shyness shape even established relationships? *Personality and Social Psychology Bulletin, 36*, 665–676.

Beaujot, R. (2004). *Delayed life transitions: Trends and implications.* Ottawa, ON: The Vanier Institute of the Family. Retrieved from www.vifamily.ca/library/cft/delayed_life.pdf

Belsky, J., Jaffee, S., Caspi, A., Moffitt, T., & Silva, P. (2003). Intergenerational relationships in young adulthood and their life course, mental health, and personality correlates. *Journal of Family Psychology, 17*, 460–471.

Belsky, J., Lang, M.E., & Rovine, M. (1985). Stability and change in marriage across the transition to parenthood: A second study. *Journal of Marriage and the Family, 47*, 855–865.

Beyers, W., & Seiffge-Krenke, I. (2010). Does identity precede intimacy? Testing Erikson's theory on romantic development in emerging adults of the 21st century. *Journal of Adolescent Research, 25*, 387–415.

Blackwell, D., & Lichter, D. (2000). Mate selection among married and cohabiting couples. *Journal of Family Issues, 21*, 275–302.

Bonello, K., & Cross, M. (2010). Gay monogamy: I love you but I can't have sex with only you. *Journal of Homosexuality, 57*, 117–139.

Bouchard, G. (2014). The quality of the parenting alliance during the transition to parenthood. *Canadian Journal of Behavioural Science, 46*(1), 20–28. http://dx.doi.org/10.1037/a0031259

Brown, S. (2003). Relationship quality dynamics of cohabiting unions. *Journal of Family Issues, 24*(5), 583–601.

Buss, D. (2011). *Evolutionary psychology. The new science of the mind* (4th ed.). Boston, MA: Allyn & Bacon.

Buss, D., Abbott, M., Algleitner, A., Ahserian, A., Biaggio, A., Blanco-Villasenor, A. . . . Yang, K. (1990). International preferences in selecting mates: A study of 37 cultures. *Journal of Cross-Cultural Psychology, 21*, 5–47.

Buss, D.M. (1999). *Evolutionary psychology: The new science of the mind.* Boston, MA: Allyn & Bacon.

Castle, N., Engberg, J., & Anderson, R. (2007). Job satisfaction of nursing home administrators and turnover. *Medical Care Research and Review, 64*, 191–211.

Ciabattari, T. (2004). Cohabitation and housework: The effects of marital intentions. *Journal of Marriage & the Family, 66*(1), 118–125.

Clark, W., & Crompton, S. (2006). Till death do us part? The risk of first and second marriage dissolution (Cat. No. 11-008). *Social Trends, 81*, 24–34.

Cooke-Reynolds, M., & Zukewich, N. (2004). The feminization of work (Cat. no. 11-008). *Canadian Social Trends, 72*, 24–29.

Copeland, D.B., & Harbaugh, B.L. (2010). Psychosocial differences related to parenting infants among single and married mothers. *Issues in Comprehensive Pediatric Nursing, 33*(3), 129–148. doi:10.3109/01460862.2010.498330

Cotton, L., Bynum, D., & Madhere, S. (1997). Socialization forces and the stability of work values from late adolescence to early adulthood. *Psychological Reports, 80*, 115–124.

Crompton, S. (2005). Always the bridesmaid: People who don't expect to marry (Cat. no. 11-008). *Canadian Social Trends, 77*, 2–8.

Crompton, S. (2011). What's stressing the stressed? Main sources of stress among workers (Cat. no. 11-008). *Canadian Social Trends, 92*, 44–51. Retrieved from http://www.statcan.gc.ca/pub/11-008-x/2011002/article/11562-eng.pdf

Crone, E.A., Wendelken, C., Donohue, S., van Leijenhorst, L., & Bunge, S.A. (2006). Neurocognitive development of the ability to manipulate information in working memory. *Proceeding for the National Academy of Sciences, 103*, 9315–9320.

Daly, K. (2000). *It keeps getting faster: Changing patterns of time in families.* Ottawa, ON: The Vanier Institute of the Family. Retrieved from www.vifamily.ca/cft/daly/dalye.htm

Davies, L. (2003). Singlehood: Transitions within a gendered world. *Canadian Journal on Aging, 22*, 343–352.

Dindia, K., & Allen, M. (1992). Sex differences in self-disclosure: A meta-analysis. *Psychological Bulletin, 112*, 106–124.

Dinera, R., Conger, R., Shaver, P., Widaman, K., & Larsen-Rife, D. (2008). Influence of family of origin and adult romantic partners on romantic attachment security. *Journal of Family Psychology, 22*, 622–632.

Doss, B.D., Rhoades, G.K., Stanley, S.M., & Markman, H.J. (2009). The effect of the transition to parenthood on relationship quality: An eight-year prospective study. *Journal of Personality and Social Psychology, 96*(3), 601–619. http://doi.org/10.1037/a0013969

Drolet, M. (2003). Motherhood and paycheques (Cat. no. 11-008). *Canadian Social Trends, 68*, 7–10.

Drolet, M. (2011). Why has the gender wage gap narrowed? *Perspectives on Labour and Income, 23*(1), 3–13.

Dush, C., Cohan, C., & Amato, P. (2003). The relationship between cohabitation and marital quality and stability: Change across cohorts? *Journal of Marriage & the Family, 65*, 539–549.

Eagly, A.H., & Wood, W. (2012). Social role theory. In P. Van Lange, A. Kruglanski, & E. Higgins (Eds.), *Handbook of theories of social psychology* (Vol. 2, pp. 458–476). Thousand Oaks, CA: Sage Publications.

Eagly, A.H., & Wood, W. (2013). The nature—nurture debates: 25 years of challenges in understanding the psychology of gender. *Perspectives on Psychological Science, 8*(3), 340–357. doi:10.1177/1745691613484767

Findly, L.C., & Kohen, D.E. (2012). Leave practices of parents after the birth or adoption of young children (Cat. no. 11-008). *Canadian Social Trends, 94*, 3–12. Retrieved from http://www.statcan.gc.ca/pub/11-008-x/2012002/article/11697-eng.pdf

Finnie, R., Mueller, R., Sweetman, A., & Usher, A. (2010). *New perspectives on access to postsecondary education* (81-004-X). Ottawa, ON: Statistics Canada. Retrieved from www.statcan.gc.ca/pub/81-004-x/2010001/article/11152-eng.htm

Fisher, J., Feekery, C., & Rowe-Murray, H. (2002). Nature, severity and correlates of psychological distress in women admitted to a private mother-baby unit. *Journal of Paediatrics & Child Health, 38*, 140–145.

Flouri, E., & Hawkes, D. (2008). Ambitious mothers—successful daughters: Mothers' early expectations for children's education and children's earnings and sense of control in adult life. *British Journal of Educational Psychology, 78*, 411–433.

Fraley, R.C., Roisman, G.I., Booth-LaForce, C., Owen, M.T., & Holland, A.S. (2013). Interpersonal and genetic origins of adult attachment styles: A longitudinal study from infancy to early adulthood. *Journal of Personality and Social Psychology, 104*(5), 817–838. doi:10.1037/a0031435

Frederick, D., Reynolds, T.A., & Fisher, M.L. (2013). The importance of female choice: Evolutionary perspectives on constraints, expressions, and variations in female mating strategies. In M. Fisher, J. Garcia, & R. Sokol Chang (Eds.), *Evolution's empress: Darwinian perspectives on the nature of women* (pp. 304–329). New York, NY: Oxford University Press.

Fullerton, A., & Wallace, M. (2007). Traversing the flexible turn: US workers' perceptions of job security, 1977–2002. *Social Science Research, 36*, 201–221.

Galambos, N.L., Fang, S., Krahn, H.J., Johnson, M.D., Lachman, M.E. (2015). Up, not down: The age curve in happiness from early adulthood to midlife in two longitudinal studies. *Developmental Psychology, 51*(11), 1664–1671. doi:10.1037/dev0000052

Galambos, N.L., Turner, P.K., & Tilton-Weaver, L.C. (2005). Chronological and subjective age in emerging adulthood: The crossover effect. *Journal of Adolescent Research, 20*, 538–556.

Garza-Mercer, F., Christensen, A., & Doss, B. (2006). Sex and affection in heterosexual and homosexual couples: An evolutionary perspective. *Electronic Journal of Human Sexuality, 9*, Retrieved from http://ejhs.org/volume9/Garza.htm

Goldberg, A.E., Smith, J.Z., & Perry-Jenkins, M. (2012). The division of labor in lesbian, gay, and heterosexual new adoptive parents. *Journal of Marriage and Family, 74*(4), 812–828. doi:10.1111/j.1741-3737.2012.00992.x

Goodwin, P., Mosher, W., & Chandra, A. (2010). Marriage and cohabitation in the United States: A statistical portrait based on Cycle 6 (2002) of the National Survey of Family Growth. *Vital Health Statistics, 23*, 1–55.

Gotay, N., Giedd, J., Lusk, L., Hayashi, K., Greenstien, D., Vaituzis, A., . . . Thompson, P. (2004). Dyanmic mapping of human cortical development during childhood through early adulthood. *Proceeding for the National Academy of Sciences, 101*, 8174–8179.

Gottman, J.M. (1994). *Why marriages succeed or fail*. New York, NY: Simon & Schuster.

Gwartney-Gibbs, P.A. (1988). Women's work experience and the "rusty skills" hypothesis: A reconceptualization and reevaluation of the evidence. In B.A. Gutek, A.H. Stromberg, & L. Larwood (Eds.), *Women and work: An annual review: Vol. 3* (pp. 169–188). Newbury Park, CA: Sage.

Harzer, C., & Ruch, W. (2013). The application of signature character strengths and positive experiences. *Journal of Happiness Studies, 14*(June), 965–983. doi:10.1007/s10902-012-9364-0

Hazan, C., Hutt, M., Sturgeon, J., & Bricker, T. (1991, April). *The process of relinquishing parents as attachment figures*. Paper presented at the biennial meetings of the Society for Research in Child Development, Seattle, WA.

Hoffman, J. (2010). The new face of fatherhood. *Today's Parent, June*. Retrieved from http://www.todaysparent.com/parenting/home/new-face-fatherhood

Hoffnung, M. (2004). Wanting it all: Career, marriage, and motherhood during college-educated women's 20s. *Sex Roles, 50*, 711–723.

Holland, J.L. (1973). *Making vocational choices: A theory of careers*. Englewood Cliffs, NJ: Prentice-Hall.

Holland, J.L. (1992). *Making vocational choices: A theory of vocational personalities and work environments* (2nd ed.). Odessa, FL: Psychological Assessment Resources.

Horowitz, A., McLaughlin, J., & White, H. (1998). How the negative and positive aspects of partner relationships affect the mental health of young married people. *Journal of Health & Social Behavior, 39*, 124–136.

Howard, A.L., Galambos, N.L., & Krahn, H.J. (2014). Forecasting life and career satisfaction in midlife from young adult depressive symptoms. *Journal of Applied Developmental Psychology, 35*(1), 51–57. doi:10.1016/j.appdev.2013.10.003

Human Resources and Skills Development Canada [HRSDC]. (2011a). *Indicators of well-being in Canada: Family life-marriage*. Retrieved from http://www4.hrsdc.gc.ca/.3ndic.1t.4r@-eng.jsp?iid=78

Ipsos-Reid/Globe and Mail. (2003). *What are Canadians' top indicators of career success?* Toronto, ON: Author. Retrieved from www.ipsos-na.com/news/pressrelease.cfm?id=1803#

Jacobs, J., Chin, C., & Bleeker, M. (2006). Enduring links: Parents' expectations and their young adult children's gender-typed occupational choices. *Educational Research and Evaluation, 12*, 395–407.

Jensen, L.A., & Arnett, J.J. (2012). Going global: New pathways for adolescents and emerging adults in a changing world. *Journal of Social Issues, 68*(3), 473–492. doi:10.1111/j.1540-4560.2012.01759.x

Joeng, J., Turner, S.L., & Lee, K. (2013). South Korean college students' Holland types and career compromise processes. *The Career Development Quarterly, 61*(1), 64–73. doi:10.1002/j.2161-0045.2013.00036.x

Johnson, M.D., Galambos, N.L., & Anderson, J.R. (2016). Skip the dishes? Not so fast! Sex and housework revisited. *Journal of Family Psychology, 30*(2), 203–213. doi:10.1037/fam0000161

Jose, O., & Alfons, V. (2007). Do demographics affect marital satisfaction? *Journal of Sex & Marital Therapy, 33*, 73–85.

Joy, S., Templeton, H.B., & Mattingly, P.J. (2016). *Postpartum depression*. Retrieved from http://reference.medscape.com/article/271662-overview#a1

Keizer, R., & Schenk, N. (2012). Becoming a parent and relationship satisfaction: A longitudinal dyadic perspective. *Journal of Marriage and Family, 74*(4), 759–773. doi:10.1111/j.1741-3737.2012.00991.x

Kins, E., & Beyers, W. (2010). Failure to launch, failure to achieve criteria for adulthood? *Journal of Adolescent Research, 25*, 743–777.

Kline, G., Stanley, S., Markman, H., & Olmos-Gallo, P. (2004). Timing is everything: Pre-engagement cohabitation and increased risk for poor marital outcomes. *Journal of Family Psychology, 18*(2), 311–318.

Korobov, N., & Thorne, A. (2006). Intimacy and distancing: Young men's conversations about romantic relationships. *Journal of Adolescent Research, 21*, 27–55.

Lachman, M.E., Teshale, S., & Agrigoroaei, S. (2015). Midlife as a pivotal period in the life course: Balancing growth and decline at the crossroads of youth and old age. *International Journal of Behavioral Development, 39*(1), 20–31. doi:10.1177/0165025414533223

Larson, L.M. (2012). Worklife across the lifespan. In E. Altmaier, & J. Hansen (Eds.), *The Oxford handbook of counseling psychology*. Oxford library of psychology (pp. 128–178). New York, NY: Oxford University Press.

Leemann, R. (2002). Transitions into research careers in Switzerland. *Education & Training, 44*, 185–198.

Levinson, D.J. (1978). *The seasons of a man's life*. New York, NY: Knopf.

Levinson, D.J. (1990). A theory of life structure development in adulthood. In C.N. Alexander & E.J. Langer (Eds.), *Higher stages of human development* (pp. 35–54). New York, NY: Oxford University Press.

Lindsay, J. (2000). An ambiguous commitment: Moving in to a cohabiting relationship. *Journal of Family Studies, 6*, 120–134.

Liossis, P., Shochet, I., Millear, P., & Biggs, H. (2009). The Promoting Adult Resilience (PAR) program: The effectiveness of the second, shorter pilot of a workplace prevention program. *Behaviour Change, 26*, 97–112.

Maccoby, E.E. (1990). Gender and relationships: A developmental account. *American Psychologist, 45*, 513–520.

Mackey, R.A., Diemer, M.A., & O'Brien, B.A. (2004). Relational factors in understanding satisfaction in the lasting relationships of same sex and heterosexual couples. *Journal of Homosexuality, 47*(1), 111–136.

Mäenpää, E., & Jalovaara, M. (2013). The effects of homogamy in socio-economic background and education on the transition from cohabitation to marriage. *Acta Sociologica, 56*(3), 247–263. doi:10.1177/0001699312474385

Maheux, H. (2014). *Mixed unions in Canada (National Household Survey [NHS], 2011)* (Cat. no. 99-010-X2011003). Ottawa, ON: Minister of Industry. Retrieved from http://www12.statcan.gc.ca/nhs-enm/2011/as-sa/99-010-x/99-010-x2011003_3-eng.pdf

Marks, N., & Lamberg, J. (1998). Marital status continuity and change among young and midlife adults. *Journal of Family Issues, 19*, 652–686.

Marshall, K. (2006). Converging gender roles (75-001-XPE). *Perspectives on Labour and Income, 18*(2), 14–22.

Marshall, K. (2011). Generational change in paid and unpaid work (Cat. no. 11-008). *Canadian Social Trends, 92*, 13–24. Ottawa, ON: Statistics Canada. Retrieved from http://www.statcan.gc.ca/pub/11-008-x/2011002/article/11520-eng.pdf

Martinez-Schallmoser, L., Telleen, S., & MacMullen, N. (2003). Effect of social support and acculturation on postpartum depression in Mexican American women. *Journal of Transcultural Nursing, 14*, 329–338.

McMullen, K., Gilmore, J., & Le Petit, C. (2010). *Women in nontraditional occupations and fields of study*. (81-004-X). Ottawa, ON: Statistics Canada. Retrieved from www.statcan.gc.ca/pub/81-004-x/2010001/article/11151-eng.htm

Milan, A. (2003). Would you live common-law? (Cat. no. 11-008). *Canadian Social Trends, 70*, 2–6.

Milan, A., Maheux, H., & Chui, T. (2010). A portrait of couples in mixed unions (Cat. no.11-008). *Canadian Social Trends, 89*, 70–80.

Moen, P. (1996). Gender, age, and the life course. In R.H. Binstock & L.K. George (Eds.), *Handbook of aging and the social sciences* (4th ed., pp. 171–187). San Diego, CA: Academic Press.

Moen, P. (2005). Beyond the career mystique: "Time in," "time out," and "second acts." *Sociological Forum, 20*, 187–208.

Mohr, J.J., Selterman, D., & Fassinger, R.E. (2013). Romantic attachment and relationship functioning in same-sex couples. *Journal of Counseling Psychology, 60*(1), 72–82. doi:10.1037/a0030994

Morgan, C.V. (2012). Toward a more nuanced understanding of intercoupling: Second-generation mixed couples in Southern California. *Journal of Family Issues, 33*(11), 1423–1449. doi:10.1177/0192513X11433693

Muzi, M. (2000). *The experience of parenting.* Upper Saddle River, NJ: Prentice Hall.

Neff, L., & Karney, B. (2009). Stress and reactivity to daily relationship experiences: How stress hinders adaptive processes in marriage. *Journal of Personality and Social Psychology, 97*, 435–450.

O'Rourke, N., Claxton, A., Chou, P.H., Smith, J.Z., & Hadjistavropoulos, T. (2011). Personality trait levels within older couples and between-spouse trait differences as predictors of marital satisfaction. *Aging and Mental Health, 15*(3), 344–53. doi:10.1080/13607863.2010.519324

Oldershaw, L. (2002). *A national survey of parents of young children.* Toronto, ON: Invest in Kids. Retrieved from www.investinkids.ca/content/documents/parent_poll_10_29_02.pdf

Parsons, G. & McMullen, K. (2009). *Trends in university graduation, 1992 to 2007* (81-004-X). Ottawa, ON: Statistics Canada. Retrieved from www.statcan.gc.ca/pub/81-004-x/2009005/article/11050-eng.htm

Parsons, J.T., Starks, T.J., Garnarel, K.E., & Grov, C. (2012). Non-monogamy and sexual relationship quality among same-sex male couples. *Journal of Family Psychology, 26*(5), 669–677. doi:10.1037/a0029561

Quam, J.K., Whitford, G.S., Dziengel, L.E., & Knochel, K.A. (2010). Exploring the nature of same-sex relationships. *Journal of Gerontological Social Work, 53*(8), 702–722. doi:10.1080/01634372.2010.518664

Radmacher, K., & Azmitia, M. (2006). Are there gendered pathways to intimacy in early adolescents' and emerging adults' friendships? *Journal of Adolescent Research, 21*, 415–448.

Ravanera, Z., & Roderic, B. (2009). Life course and structural factors in childlessness: The waiting game and constrained choices in the second demographic transition. *PSC Discussion Papers Series, 23*(6, Article 1). Retrieved from http://ir.lib.uwo.ca/pscpapers/vol23/iss6/1

Robards, J., Evandrou, M., Falkingham, J., & Vlachantoni, A. (2012). Marital status, health and mortality. *Maturitas, 73*(4), 295–299. doi:10.1016/j.maturitas.2012.08.007

Roisman, G., Masten, A., Coatsworth, J., & Tellegen, A. (2004). Salient and emerging developmental task in the transition to adulthood. *Child Development, 75*, 123–133.

Rollins, B.C., & Feldman, H. (1970). Marital satisfaction over the family life cycle. *Journal of Marriage and the Family, 32*, 20–27.

Rotermann, M. (2007). Marital breakdown and subsequent depression (82–033). *Health Reports, 18*(2), 33–44.

Salari, S., & Zhang, W. (2006). Kin keepers and good providers: Influence of gender socialization on well-being among USA birth cohorts. *Aging and Mental Health, 10*(5), 485–496.

Schlosser, L., Safran, D., & Sbaratta, C. (2010). Reasons for choosing a correction officer career. *Psychological Services, 7*, 34–43.

Schmitt, D., Shackelford, T., & Buss, D. (2001). Are men really more "oriented" toward short-term mating than women? A critical review of theory and research. *Psychology, Evolution, & Gender, 3*, 211–239.

Sherman, A., Lansford, J., & Volling, B. (2006). Sibling relationships and best friendships in young adulthood: Warmth, conflict, and well-being. *Personal Relationships, 13*, 151–165.

Shockley, K.M., & Allen, T.D. (2012). Motives for flexible work arrangement use. *Community, Work, & Family, 15*(2), 217–231. doi:10.1080/13668803.2011.609661

Simpson, J., Collins, W., Tran, S., & Haydon, K. (2008). Developmental antecedents of emotion in romantic relationships. In J. Forgas & J. Fitness (Eds.), *Social relationships: Cognitive, affective, and motivational processes* (pp. 185–202). New York, NY: Psychology Press.

Smith, S., Maas, I., & van Tubergen, F. (2012). Irreconcilable differences? Ethnic intermarriage and divorce in the Netherlands, 1995–2008. *Social Science Research, 41*(5), 1126–1137. doi:10.1016/j.ssresearch.2012.02.004

Solomon, S., Rothblum, E., & Balsam, K. (2004). Pioneers in partnership: Lesbian and gay male couples in civil unions compared with those not in civil unions and married heterosexual siblings. *Journal of Family Psychology, 18*, 275–286.

Spokane, A., & Cruza-Guet, M. (2005). Holland's theory of vocational personalities in work environments. In S. Brown & R. Lent (Eds.), *Career development and counseling: Putting theory and research to work* (pp. 24–41). Hoboken, NJ: John Wiley & Sons.

Statistics Canada (2008d). *30 and 50 year total divorce rates per 1,000 marriages, Canada, provinces and territories (year-to-date) (averages)* (Cat. no. 84F0213XWE). Retrieved from http://www.statcan.gc.ca/pub/84f0213x/2005000/6500117-eng.htm

Statistics Canada (2012l). *Living arrangements of young adults aged 20 to 29* (Cat. no. 98-312-X2011003). Retrieved from http://www12.statcan.gc.ca/census-recensement/2011/as-sa/98-312-x/98-312-x2011003_3-eng.pdf

Statistics Canada. (2004). *Women in Canada: Work chapters updates, 2003* (Cat. no. 89F0133XIE), March 25. Ottawa, ON: Author. Retrieved from www.statcan.ca/english/freepub/89F0133XIE/89F0133XIE2003000.pdf

Statistics Canada. (2012m). *Father's Day . . . by the numbers 2012.* Retrieved from http://www42.statcan.gc.ca/smr08/2012/smr08_165_2012-eng.htm

Statistics Canada. (2015h). *Same-sex couples and sexual orientation... by the numbers. 2015.* Retrieved from http://www.statcan.gc.ca/eng/dai/smr08/2015/smr08_203_2015#a1

Statistics Canada. (2016h). *Labour force survey estimates (LFS), wages of employees by type of work, North American Industry Classification System (NAICS), sex and age group* (CANSIM Table 282-0072). Retrieved from http://www5.statcan.gc.ca/cansim/pick-choisir?lang=eng&p2=33&id=2820072

Statistics Canada. (2016i). The rise of the dual-earner family with children. *The Daily, Canadian Megatrends.* Ottawa, ON: Statistics Canada. Retrieved from http://www.statcan.gc.ca/pub/11-630-x/11-630-x2016005-eng.htm

Statistics Canada. (2016j). *Satisfaction with work-life balance: Fact sheet* (Cat. no. 89-652-X2016003). Ottawa, ON: Minister of Industry. Retrieved from http://www.statcan.gc.ca/pub/89-652-x/89-652-x2016003-eng.pdf

Sternberg, R.J. (1987). Liking versus loving: A comparative evaluation of theories. *Psychological Bulletin, 102*, 331–345.

Stobert, S. & Kemeny, A. (2003). Childfree by choice (Cat. no. 11-008). *Canadian Social Trends, 69*, 7–10.

Super, D. (1990). A life-span, life-space approach to career development. In D. Brown & L. Brooks (Eds.), *Applying contemporary theories to practice.* (2nd ed.) (pp. 197–261). The Jossey-Bass management series and the Jossey-Bass social and behavioral science series. San Francisco, CA: Jossey-Bass.

Swendsen, J., & Mazure, C. (2000). Life stress as a risk factor for postpartum depression: Current research and methodological issues. *Clinical Psychology, 7*, 17–31.

Taylor, P., Funk, C., & Clark, A. (2007). *Generation gap in values, behaviors: As marriage and parenthood drift apart, public is concerned about social impact.* Pew Research Center. Retrieved from http://pewresearch.org/assets/social/pdf/Marriage.pdf

Teachman, J. (2003). Premarital sex, premarital cohabitation and the risk of subsequent marital dissolution among women. *Journal of Marriage & the Family, 65*(2), 444–455.

Thiessen, V., & Nickerson, C. (2001). *Canadian gender trends in education and work* (Cat. no. MP32-30/00-4E). Ottawa, ON: Human Resources Development Canada. Retrieved from www.hrdc-drhc.gc.ca/arb/publications/research/2000docs/t-00-4e.pdf

Thompson, B., Brough, P., & Schmidt, H. (2006). Supervisor and subordinate work-family values: Does similarity make a difference? *International Journal of Stress Management, 13*, 45–63.

Trivers, R. (1972). Parental investment and sexual selection. In B. Campbell (Ed.), *Sexual selection and the descent of man: 1871–1971* (pp. 136–179). Chicago, IL: Aldine.

Turcotte, M. (2007). Time spent with family during a typical workday, 1986 to 2005 (Cat. no. 11–008). *Canadian Social Trends, 83*, 2–11.

Turcotte, M. (2013b). *Living apart together* (Cat. no. 75-006-x). Retrieved from Statistics Canada Website http://www.statcan.gc.ca/pub/75-006-x/2013001/article/11771-eng.pdf

Umberson, D., Pudrovska, T., & Reczek, C. (2010). Parenthood, childlessness, and well-being: A life course perspective. *Journal of Marriage and the Family, 72*(3), 612–629. doi:10.1111/j.1741-3737.2010.00721.x

Vézina, M. (2011). Quality of personal networks: Does living alone make a difference (Cat. no. 11-008)? *Canadian Social Trends, 92*, 62–69. Retrieved from http://www.statcan.gc.ca/pub/11-008-x/2011002/article/11591-eng.pdf

Wiederman, M., & Allgeier, E. (1992). Gender differences in mate selection criteria: Sociobiological or socioeconomic explanation? *Ethology and Sociobiology, 13*, 115–124.

Wood, W., & Eagly, A. (2007). Social structure origins of sex differences in human mating. In Gangestad, S., & Simpson, J. (Eds.), *The evolution of mind: Fundamental questions and controversies* (pp. 383–390). New York, NY: Guilford Press.

Wright, T., & Bonett, D. (2007). Job satisfaction and psychological well-being as nonadditive predictors of workplace turnover. *Journal of Management, 33*, 141–160.

Yerkes, M. (2010). Diversity in work: The heterogeneity of women's employment patterns. *Gender, Work and Organization, 17*(6), 696–720. doi:10.1111/j.1468-0432.2009.00462.x

Zhang, X. (2009). Earnings of women with and without children. In *Perspectives*. Ottawa, ON: Statistics Canada. Retrieved from www.statcan.gc.ca/cgi-bin/af-fdr.cgi?l=eng&loc=../pdf/10823-eng.pdf

Chapter 15

Addis, M., & Mahalik, J. (2003). Men, masculinity, and the contexts of help seeking. *American Psychologist, 58*, 5–14.

Amenedo, E., & Diaz, F. (1998). Aging-related changes in processing of non-target and target stimuli during an auditory oddball task. *Biological Psychology, 48*, 235–267.

Amenedo, E., & Diaz, F. (1999). Aging-related changes in the processing of attended and unattended standard stimuli. *Neuroreport: For Rapid Communication of Neuroscience Research, 10*, 2383–2388.

Anderson, K.M., Castelli, W.P., & Levy, D. (1987). Cholesterol and mortality: 30 years of follow-up from the Framingham study. *Journal of the American Medical Association, 257*, 2176–2180.

Andreasen, N.C., Liu, D., Ziebell, S., Vora, A., & Ho, B.C. (2013). Relapse duration, treatment intensity, and brain tissue loss in schizophrenia: A prospective longitudinal MRI study. *The American Journal of Psychiatry, 170*, 609–615. doi:10.1176/appi.ajp.2013.12050674

Andrews, M., Dowling, W., Bartlett, J., & Halpern, A. (1998). Identification of speeded and slowed familiar melodies by younger, middle-aged, and older musicians and nonmusicians. *Psychology & Aging, 13*, 462–471.

Antonsson, A., Wilson, L.F., Kendall, B.J., Bain, C.J., Whiteman, D.C., & Neale, R.E. (2015). Cancers in Australia in 2010 attributable to infectious agents. *Australian and New Zealand Journal of Public Health, 39*(5), 446–451. doi:10.1111/1753-6405.12445

Baltes, P.B., & Baltes, M.M. (1990). Psychological perspectives on successful aging: The model of selective optimization with compensation. In P.B. Baltes & M.M. Baltes (Eds.), *Successful aging* (pp. 1–34). Cambridge, England: Cambridge University Press.

Barrett-Connor, E., & Bush, T.L. (1991). Estrogen and coronary heart disease in women. *Journal of the American Medical Association, 265*, 1861–1867.

Bassior, J-N., Graff, G., Dumas, J., Tyndall, K., Dreifus, C., Pierce, P., & Kinosian, J. (2000, March/April). The creators: How they keep going and going. *Modern Maturity, 43*(2), 38–44.

Basson, R. (2005). Women's sexual dysfunction: Revised and expanded definitions. *Canadian Medical Association Journal, 172*(10), 1327–1333. doi:10.1503/cmaj.1020174

Basson, R., & Bronner, G. (2015). Management and rehabilitation of neurologic patients with sexual dysfunction. *Handbook of Clinical Neurology, 130*, 415–434. doi:10.1016/B978-0-444-63247-0.00024-9

Basson, R., Rees, P., Wang, R., Montejo, A.L., & Incrocci, L. (2010). Sexual function in chronic illness. *The Journal of Sexual Medicine, 7*(1 Pt 2), 374–388. doi:10.1111/j.1743-6109.2009.01621.x

Bibbins-Domingo, K., Coxson, P., Pletcher, M.J., Lightwood, J., & Goldman, L. (2007). Adolescent overweight and future adult coronary heart disease. *New England Journal of Medicine, 357*, 2371–2379.

Bosworth, H., Siegler, I., Brummett, B., Barefoot, J., Williams, R., Clapp-Channing, N., & Mark, D. (2000, August). *Health-related quality of life in a coronary artery sample.* Paper presented at the annual meeting of the American Psychological Association. Washington, DC.

Bromberger, J., Schott, L., Kravitz, H., Sowers, M., Avis, N., Gold, E., Randolph, J., & Matthews, K. (2010). Longitudinal change in reproductive hormones and depressive symptoms across the menopausal transition: Results from the Women's Health across the Nation (SWAN). *Archives of General Psychiatry, 67*, 598–607.

Brotto, L., Atallah, S., Johnson-Agbakwu, C., Rosenbaum, T., Abdo, C., Byers, E.S., . . . Wylie, K. (2016). Psychological and interpersonal dimensions of sexual function and dysfunction. *The Journal of Sexual Medicine, 13*(4), 538–571. doi:10.1016/j.jsxm.2016.01.019

Brown, L.M. (2000). *Helicobacter pylori: Epidemiology and routes of transmission. Epidemiology Review, 22*(2), 283–297.

Byberg, L., Melhus, H., Gedeborg, R., Sundstrom, J., Ahlbom, A., Zethelius, B., Berglund, L., Wolk, A., & Michaelsson, K. (2009). Total mortality after changes in leisure time physical activity in 50 year old men: 35 year follow up of population based cohort. *British Medical Journal, Mar 5*, 338:b688. doi:10.1136/bmj.b688

Canadian Cancer Society. (2007). *The human papillomavirus (HPV) and the HPV vaccine.* Toronto, ON: Author. Retrieved from www.cancer.ca/ccs/internet/standardpf/0,3182,3172_1242735771_1242735798_langId-en,00.html

Canadian Cancer Society's Advisory Committee on Cancer Statistics. (2015). *Canadian Cancer Statistics 2015.* Toronto, ON: Canadian Cancer Society.

Canadian Heart Health Strategy and Action Plan. (2009). *Building a heart healthy Canada.* Retrieved from www.chhs.ca/en/reports

Castellsagué, X., Bosch, X., Muñoz, N., Meijer, C., Shah, K., Sanjosé, S., . . . Franceschi, S. (2002). Male circumcision, penile human papillomavirus infection, and cervical cancer in female partners. *New England Journal of Medicine, 346*, 1105–1112.

Cauley, J.A., Seeley, D.G., Ensrud, K., Ettinger, B., Black, D., & Cummings, S.R. (1995). Estrogen replacement therapy and fractures in older women. *Annals of Internal Medicine, 122*, 9–16.

Centers for Disease Control. (1994). Prevalence of adults with no known major risk factors for coronary heart disease—behavioral risk factor surveillance system, 1992. *Morbidity and Mortality Weekly Report, 43*, 61–69.

Cheitlin, M. (2003). Cardiovascular physiology: Changes with aging. *American Journal of Geriatric Cardiology, 12*, 9–13.

Cheng, C.H., & Lin, Y.Y. (2012). The effects of aging on lifetime of auditory sensory memory in humans. *Biological Psychology, 89*(2), 307–312. doi:10.1016/j.biopsycho.2011.11.003

Cohen, H., Hailpern, S., & Alderman, M. (2004). Glucose-cholesterol interaction magnifies coronary disease risk for hypertensive patients. *Hypertension, 43*, 983.

Colditz, G.A., Hankinson, S.E., Hunter, D.J., Willett, W.C., Manson, J.E., Stampfer, M.J., . . . Speizer, F.E. (1995). The use of estrogens and progestins and the risk of breast cancer in postmenopausal women. *New England Journal of Medicine, 332*, 1589–1593.

Coney, P. (2013). *Menopause.* Retrieved from http://emedicine.medscape.com/article/264088-overview#aw2aab6b2

Corona, G., Lee, D.M., Forti, G., O'Connor, D.B., Maggi, M., O'Neill, T.W., . . . EMAS Study Group. (2010). Age-related changes in general and sexual health in middle-aged and older men: Results from the European Male Ageing Study (EMAS). *The Journal of Sexual Medicine, 7*(4 Pt 1), 1362-1380. doi:10.1111/j.1743-6109.2009.01601.x

Courtney, K.E., & Polich, J. (2010). Binge drinking effects on EEG in young adult humans. *International Journal of Environmental Research and Public Health, 7*(5), 2325–2336. doi:10.3390/ijerph7052325

Cramer, D. (1991). Type A behavior pattern, extraversion, neuroticism and psychological distress. *British Journal of Medical Psychology, 64,* 73–83.

Crompton, S. (2000). Health (Cat. no. 11-008-XPE). *Canadian Social Trends, Winter*(59), 12–17.

Daurignac, E., Toga, A., Jones, D., Aronen, H., Hommer, D., Jernigan, T., . . . Mathalon, D. (2005). Applications of morphometric and diffusion tensor magnetic resonance imaging to the study of brain abnormalities in the alcoholism spectrum. *Alcoholism: Clinical and Experimental Research, 29*(1), 159–166. doi:10.1097/01.ALC.0000150891.72900.62

Dawber, T.R., Kannel, W.B., & Lyell, L.P. (1963). An approach to longitudinal studies in a community: The Framingham study. *Annals of the New York Academy of Science, 107,* 539–556.

Dennerstein, L., Lehert, P., & Guthrie, J. (2002). The effects of the menopausal transition and biopsychosocial factors on well-being. *Archives of Women's Mental Health, 5,* 15–22.

Denney, N.W. (1982). Aging and cognitive changes. In B.B. Wolman (Ed.), *Handbook of developmental psychology* (pp. 807–827). Englewood Cliffs, NJ: Prentice-Hall.

Denney, N.W. (1984). Model of cognitive development across the life span. *Developmental Review, 4,* 171–191.

Denollet, J. (1997). Personality, emotional distress and coronary heart disease. *European Journal of Personality, 11,* 343–357.

Desjardins-Crépeau, L., & Bherer, L. (2016). Hypertension and age-related cognitive decline. In H. Girouard (Ed.), *Hypertension and the brain as an end-organ target* (pp. 21–38). Switzerland: Springer International Publishing.

Dobson, A., Brown, W., Ball, J., Powers, J., & McFadden, M. (1999). Women drivers' behaviour, socio-demographic characteristics and accidents. *Accident Analysis & Prevention, 31,* 525–535.

Duursma, S.A., Raymakers, J.A., Boereboom, F.T.J., & Scheven, B.A.A. (1991). Estrogen and bone metabolism. *Obstetrical and Gynecological Survey, 47,* 38–44.

Dwyer, J.H., Allayee, H., Dwyer, K.M., Fan, J., Wu, H., Mar, R., . . . Mehrabian, M. (2004). Arachidonate 5-lipoxygenase promoter genotype, dietary arachidonic acid, and atherosclerosis. *New England Journal of Medicine, 350*(1), 29–37. doi:10.1056/NEJMoa025079

Erickson, K.I., & Liu-Ambrose, T. (2016). Exercise, cognition, and health. In K.W. Schaie, & S.L. Willis (Eds.), *Handbook of the psychology of aging* (8th ed., pp. 187–201). London, UK: Elsevier Inc.

Esposito, K., Giugliano, F., Di Palo, C., Giugliano, G., Marfella, R., D'Andrea, F., . . . Giugliano, D. (2004). Effect of lifestyle changes on erectile dysfunction in obese men: A randomized controlled trial. *Journal of the American Medical Association, 291,* 2978–2984.

Ewald, P. (2000). *Plague time.* New York, NY: Free Press.

Friedman, M., & Rosenman, R.H. (1974). *Type A behavior and your heart.* New York, NY: Knopf.

Frisch, M., Glimelius, B., van den Brule, A., Wohlfahrt, J., Meijer, C., Walboomers, J., . . . Melbye, M. (1997). Sexually transmitted infection as a cause of anal cancer. *New England Journal of Medicine, 337,* 1350–1358.

Gallo, D.A., & Wheeler, M.E. (2013). Episodic memory. In D. Reisberg, D. (Ed.), *The Oxford handbook of cognitive psychology* (pp. 189–205). New York, NY: Oxford University Press.

Gambert, S.R., Schultz, B.M., & Hamdy, R.C. (1995). Osteoporosis: Clinical features, prevention, and treatment. *Endocrinology and Metabolism Clinics of North America, 24,* 317–371.

Garrison, R.J., Gold, R.S., Wilson, P.W.F., & Kannel, W.B. (1993). Educational attainment and coronary heart disease risk: The Framingham offspring study. *Preventive Medicine, 22,* 54–64.

Gaziano, J.M., & Hennekens, C.H. (1995). Dietary fat and risk of prostate cancer. *Journal of the National Cancer Institute, 87,* 1427–1428.

Gingras, Y. (2015). Drifts and pernicious effects of the quantitative evaluation of research: The misuse of bibliometrics [Article in French]. *Recherche en Soins Infirmiers, 2*(121), 72–78. doi:10.3917/rsi.121.0072

Goldberg, A.P., & Hagberg, J.M. (1990). Physical exercise in the elderly. In E.R. Schneider & J.W. Rowe (Eds.), *Handbook of the biology of aging* (3rd ed., pp. 407–428). San Diego, CA: Academic Press.

Goleman, D.D., Kaufman, P., & Ray, M. (1992). *The creative spirit.* New York, NY: Dutton.

Gordon, G.S., & Vaughan, C. (1986). Calcium and osteoporosis. *Journal of Nutrition, 116,* 319–322.

Guilford, J. (1967). *The nature of human intelligence.* New York, NY: McGraw-Hill.

Guralnik, J.M., Land, K.C., Blazer, D., Fillenbaum, G.G., & Branch, L.G. (1993). Educational status and active life expectancy among older blacks and whites. *New England Journal of Medicine, 329,* 110–116.

Hackett, G., Krychman, M., Baldwin, D., Bennett, N., El-Zawahry, A., Graziottin, A., . . . Incrocci, L. (2016). Coronary heart disease, diabetes, and sexuality in men. *The Journal of Sexual Medicine, 13*(6), 887–904. doi:10.1016/j.jsxm.2016.01.023

Health Canada. (2002c). *Cardiovascular disease surveillance on-line: Mortality by age group.* Ottawa, ON: Author. Retrieved from http://dsol-smed.hc-sc.gc.ca/dsol-smed/cvd/c_age_e.html

Heart & Stroke Foundation (2010). *Statistics.* Ottawa, ON: Author. Retrieved from www.heartandstroke.com/site/c.ikIQLcMWJtE/b.3483991/k.34A8/Statistics.htm

Heiss, G., Wallace, R., Anderson, G.L., Aragaki, A., Beresford, S.A.A., Brzyski, R., . . . Stefanick, M.L. (2008). Health risks and benefits 3 years after stopping randomized treatment with estrogen and progestin. *Journal of the American Medical Association, 299*(9), 1036–1045.

Helme, R.D., & Gibson, S.J. (2001). The epidemiology of pain in elderly people. *Clinics in Geriatric Medicine, 17*(3), 417–431.

Holloway, V., & Wylie, K. (2015). Sex drive and sexual desire. *Current Opinion in Psychiatry, 28*(6), 424–429. doi:10.1097/YCO.0000000000000199

Howieson, D.B. (2015). Cognitive skills and the aging brain: What to expect. *Cerebrum,* (Dec). Retrieved from http://www.dana.org/Cerebrum/2015/Cognitive_Skills_and_the_Aging_Brain__What_to_Expect/

Hunter, D.J., Spiegelman, D., Adami, H., Beeson, L., van den Brandt, P.A., Folsom, A.R., . . . Willett, W. (1996). Cohort studies of fat intake and the risk of breast cancer—a pooled analysis. *New England Journal of Medicine, 334,* 356–361.

Ide, J.S., Zhang, S., Hu, S., Matuskey, D., Bednarski, S.R., Erdman, E., . . . Li, C.S. (2014). Gray matter volume correlates of global positive alcohol expectancy in non-dependent adult drinkers. *Addiction Biology, 19*(5), 895–906. doi:10.1111/adb.12046

Jacobs-Kosmin, D. (2013). *Osteoporosis.* Retrieved from http://emedicine.medscape.com/article/264088-overview#aw2aab6b2

Jaglal, S., Weller, I., Mamdani, M., Hawker, G., Kreder, H., Jaakkimainen, L., & Adachi, J. (2005). Population trends in BMD testing, treatment, and hip and wrist fracture rates: Are the hip fracture projections wrong? *Journal of Bone and Mineral Research, 20,* 898–905.

Judd, F.K., Hickey, M., & Bryant, C. (2012). Depression and midlife: Are we overpathologising the menopause? *Journal of Affective Disorders, 136*(3), 199–211. doi:10.1016/j.jad.2010.12.010

Kannel, W.B., & Gordon, T. (1980). Cardiovascular risk factors in the aged: The Framingham study. In S.G. Haynes & M. Feinleib (Eds.), *Second conference on the epidemiology of aging.* NIH Publication No. 80–969 (pp. 65–89). U.S. Department of Health and Human Services. Washington, DC: U.S. Government Printing Office.

Kensinger, E., Clarke, R., & Corkin, S. (2003). What neural correlates underlie successful encoding and retrieval? A functional magnetic resonance imaging study using a divided attention paradigm. *Journal of Neuroscience, 23,* 2407–2415.

Kim, E.D. (2013). *Erectile dysfunction.* Retrieved from http://emedicine.medscape.com/article/444220-overview

Kristenson, H., Österling, A., Nilsson, J., & Lindgärde, F. (2002). Alcoholism: Clinical and experimental research. *Alcoholism: Clinical and Experimental Research, 26,* 478–484.

Kronenberg, F. (1994). Hot flashes: Phenomenology, quality of life, and search for treatment options. *Experimental Gerontology, 29*, 319–336.

Kubzansky, L., Cole, S., Kawachi, I., Vokonas, P., & Sparrow, D. (2006). Shared and unique contributions of anger, anxiety, and depression to coronary heart disease: A prospective study in the normative aging study. *Annals of Behavioral Medicine, 31*, 21–29.

Kunkel, S.R., & Applebaum, R.A. (1992). Estimating the prevalence of long-term disability for an aging society. *Journals of Gerontology: Social Sciences, 47*, S253–260.

Kushi, L., & Giovannucci, E. (2002). Dietary fat and cancer. *The American Journal of Medicine, 113*(9), 63–70.

Lee, D.M., Nazroo, J., O'Connor, D.B., Blake, M., & Pendleton, N. (2016). Sexual health and well-being among older men and women in England: Findings from the English Longitudinal Study of Ageing. *Archives of Sexual Behavior, 45*(1), 133–144. doi:10.1007/s10508-014-0465-1

Lee, D.S., Chiu, M., Manuel, D.G., Tu, K., Wang, X., Austin, P.C., . . . Tu, J. (2009). Trends in risk factors for cardiovascular disease in Canada: Temporal, socio-demographic and geographic factors. *Canadian Medical Association Journal, 181*(3–4), E55–E65.

Lee, I., Manson, J.E., Hennekens, C.H., & Paffenbarger, R.S., Jr. (1993). Body weight and mortality: A 27-year follow-up of middle-aged men. *Journal of the American Medical Association, 270*, 2823–2828.

Lee, I.-M., Hsieh, C., & Paffenbarger, R.S. (1995). Exercise intensity and longevity in men. *Journal of the American Medical Association, 273*, 1179–1184.

Lincourt, A., Rybash, J., & Hoyer, W. (1998). Aging, working memory, and the development of instance-based retrieval. *Brain & Cognition, 37*, 100–102.

Lindsay, R. (1985). The aging skeleton. In M.R. Haug, A.B. Ford, & M. Sheafor (Eds.), *The physical and mental health of aged women* (pp. 65–82). New York, NY: Springer.

Lindwall, M., Cimino, C.R., Gibbons, L.E., Mitchell, M.B., Benitez, A., Brown, C.L., . . . Piccinin, A.M. (2012). Dynamic associations of change in physical activity and change in cognitive function: Coordinated analyses of four longitudinal studies. *Journal of Aging Research, 2012*, 1–12. doi:10.1155/2012/493598

Lineweaver, T., & Hertzog, C. (1998). Adults' efficacy and control beliefs regarding memory and aging: Separating general from personal beliefs. *Aging, Neuropsychology, & Cognition, 5*, 264–296.

Lineweaver, T.T., Berger, A.K., & Hertzog, C. (2009). Expectations about memory change across the life span are impacted by aging stereotypes. *Psychology and Aging, 24*(1), 169–176.

Lissner, L., Bengtsson, C., Björkelund, C., & Wedel, H. (1996). Physical activity levels and changes in relation to longevity: A prospective study of Swedish women. *American Journal of Epidemiology, 143*, 54–62.

Lorenzo-López, L., Maseda, A., Buján, A., de Labra, C., Amenedo, E., & Millán-Calenti, J.C. (2016). Preserved Suppression of salient irrelevant stimuli during visual search in age-associated memory impairment. *Frontiers in Psychology, 6*, 2033. doi:10.3389/fpsyg.2015.02033

Manson, J.E., Willett, W.C., Stampfer, M.J., Colditz, G.A., Hunter, D.J., Hankinson, S.E., . . . Speizer, F.E. (1995). Body weight and mortality among women. *New England Journal of Medicine, 333*, 677–685.

Marques, P., Moreira, P., Magalhães, R., Costa, P., Santos, N., Zihl, J., . . . Sousa, N. (2016). The functional connectome of cognitive reserve. *Human Brain Mapping*, (May 4). doi:10.1002/hbm.23242 [Epub ahead of print]

Marques, P., Soares, J.M., Magalhães, R., Santos, N.C., & Sousa, N. (2015). The bounds of education in the human brain connectome. *Scientific Reports, 5*(12812). doi:10.1038/srep12812

Mason, B., Goodman, A., Chabac, S., & Lehert, P. (2006). Effect of oral acamprosate on abstinence in patients with alcohol dependence in a double-blind, placebo-controlled trial: The role of patient motivation. *Journal of Psychiatric Research, 40*, 383–393.

Matzen, L.E., & Benjamin, A.S. (2013). Older and wiser: Older adults' episodic word memory benefits from sentence study contexts. *Psychology and Aging, 28*(3), 754–767. doi:10.1037/a0032945

McNulty, J.K., Wenner, C.A., & Fisher, T.D. (2016). Longitudinal associations among relationship satisfaction, sexual satisfaction, and frequency of sex in early marriage. *Archives of Sexual Behavior, 45*(1), 85–97. doi:10.1007/s10508-014-0444-6

Meeks, S. (1997). Illnesses in late life: Short-term course of mental illness in middle age and late life. *International Psychogeriatrics, 9*, 343–358.

Miller, T.Q., Turner, C.W., Tindale, R.S., Posavac, E.J., & Dugoni, B.L. (1991). Reasons for the trend toward null findings in research on Type A behavior. *Psychological Bulletin, 110*, 469–495.

Mitchell, M.B, Cimino, C.R., Benitez, A., Brown, C.L., Gibbons, L.E., Kennison, R.F., . . . Piccinin, A.M. (2012). Cognitively stimulating activities: Effects on cognition across four studies with up to 21 years of longitudinal data. *Journal of Aging Research, 2012*, doi:10.1155/2012/461592

Mohan, J. (2006). Cardiac psychology. *Journal of the Indian Academy of Applied Psychology, 32*, 214–220.

Mork, J., Lie, K., Glattre, E., Clark, S., Hallmans, G., Jellum, E., . . . Dillner, J. (2001). Human papillomavirus infection as a risk factor for squamous-cell carcinoma of the head and neck. *New England Journal of Medicine, 344*, 1125–1131.

Morris, D.L., Kritchevsky, S.B., & Davis, C.E. (1994). Serum carotenoids and coronary heart disease. The Lipid Research Clinics Coronary Primary Prevention Trial and Follow-up Study. *Journal of the American Medical Association, 272*, 1439–1441.

Morrison, N.A., Qi, J.C., Tokita, A., Kelly, P.J., Crofts, L., Nguyen, T.V., . . . Eisman, J.A. (1994). Prediction of bone density from vitamin D receptor alleles. *Nature, 367*, 284–287.

Morrow, D., Menard, W., Ridolfo, H., Stine-Morrow, E., Teller, T., & Bryant, D. (2003). Expertise, cognitive ability, and age effects on pilot communication. *International Journal of Aviation Psychology, 13*, 345–371.

Nathanson, C.A., & Lorenz, G. (1982). Women and health: The social dimensions of biomedical data. In J.Z. Giele (Ed.), *Women in the middle years* (pp. 37–88). New York, NY: Wiley.

National Institute of Health (2005). *Menopausal hormone therapy* (NIH Publication No. 05-5200). Bethesda, MD: Author. Retrieved from www.nhlbi.nih.gov/health/women/pht_facts.pdf

National Institute on Aging (NIA). (2010). *Age page: Hearing loss.* Retrieved from http://www.nia.nih.gov/healthinformation/publications/hearing.htm

Nelson, M.E., Fiatarone, M.A., Morganti, C.M., Trice, I., Greenberg, R.A., & Evans, W.J. (1994). Effects of high-intensity strength training on multiple risk factors for osteoporotic fractures. *Journal of the American Medical Association, 272*, 1909–1914.

O'Connor, N.J., Manson, J.E., O'Connor, G.T., & Buring, J.E. (1995). Psychosocial risk factors and nonfatal myocardial infarction. *Circulation, 92*, 1458–1464.

Olshansky, S.J., Passaro, D.J., Hershow, R.C., Layden, J., Carnes, B.A., Brody, J., . . . Ludwig, D. (2005). A potential decline in life expectancy in the United States in the 21st century. *New England Journal of Medicine, 352*, 1138–1145.

Olson, M., Krantz, D., Kelsey, S., Pepine, C., Sopko, G., Handberg, E., . . . Merz, N. (2005). Hostility scores are associated with increased risk of cardiovascular events in women undergoing coronary angiography: A report from the NHLBI-sponsored WISE study. *Psychosomatic Medicine, 67*, 546–552.

Orpana, H.M., Ross, N., Feeny, D., McFarland, B., Bernier, J., & Kaplan, M. (2009). The natural history of health-related quality of life: A10-year cohort study. *Health Reports, 20*(1), 29–35. Retrieved from http://www.statcan.gc.ca/pub/82-003-x/2009001/article/10794-eng.htm

Orth, U., Trzesniewski, K.H., & Robins, R.W. (2010). Self-esteem development from young adulthood to old age: A cohort-sequential longitudinal study. *Journal of Personality and Social Psychology, 98*(4), 645–658. doi:10.1037/a0018769

Philip, P., Sagaspe, P., Prague, M., Tassi, P., Capelli, A., Bioulac, B., . . . Taillard, J. (2012). Acute versus chronic partial sleep deprivation in middle-aged people: Differential effect on performance and sleepiness. *Sleep: Journal of Sleep and Sleep Disorders Research, 35*(7), 997–1002. doi:10.5665/sleep

Porjesz, B., & Begleiter, H. (2003). Alcoholism and human electrophysiology. *Alcohol Research and Health, 27*(2), 153–160.

Posthuma, W.F.M., Westendorp, R.G.J., & Vandenbroucke, J.P. (1994). Cardioprotective effect of hormone replacement therapy in postmenopausal women: Is the evidence biased? *British Medical Journal, 308,* 1268–1269.

Public Health Agency of Canada. (2009b). *Tracking heart disease and stroke in Canada 2009* (HP32-3/2009E). Ottawa, ON: Ministry of Health. Retrieved from www.phac-aspc.gc.ca/publicat/2009/cvdavc/pdf/cvd-avs-2009-eng.pdf

Rabinowitz, P. (2000). Noise-induced hearing loss. *American Family Physician, 61,* 1053.

Raz, N., & Rodrigue, K. (2006). Differential aging of the brain: Patterns, cognitive correlates and modifiers. *Neuroscience and Biobehavioral Reviews, 30,* 730–748.

Raz, N., Rodrigue, K., Kennedy, K., & Acker, J. (2007). Vascular health and longitudinal changes in brain and cognition in middle-aged and older adults. *Neuropsychology, 21,* 149–157.

Reid, R., Abramson, B.L., Blake, J., Desindes, S., Dodin, S., Johnston, S., . . . Menopause and Osteoporosis Working Group (SOGC). (2014). Managing menopause. *Journal of Obstetrics and Gynaecology Canada, 36*(9), 830–838.

Reuter-Lorenz, P.A., & Park, D.C. (2014). How does it STAC up? Revisiting the scaffolding theory of aging and cognition. *Neuropsychology Review, 24*(3), 355–370. doi:10.1007/s11065-014-9270-9

Rich-Edwards, J.W., Manson, J.E., Hennekens, C.H., & Buring, J.E. (1995). The primary prevention of coronary heart disease in women. *New England Journal of Medicine, 332,* 1758–1766.

Risch, H.A., Jain, M., Marrett, L.D., & Howe, G.R. (1994). Dietary fat intake and risk of epithelial ovarian cancer. *Journal of the National Cancer Institute, 86,* 1409–1415.

Rodriguez, C., Calle, E.E., Coates, R.J., Miracle-McMahil, H.L., Thun, M.J., & Heath, C.W., Jr. (1995). Estrogen replacement therapy and fatal ovarian cancer. *American Journal of Epidemiology, 141,* 828–835.

Rose, D.P. (1993). Diet, hormones, and cancer. *Annual Review of Public Health, 14,* 1–17.

Rosenman, R.H., & Friedman, M. (1983). Relationship of type A behavior pattern to coronary heart disease. In H. Selye (Ed.), *Selye's guide to stress research: Vol. 2* (pp. 47–106). New York, NY: Scientific and Academic Editions.

Ross, R.K., Paganini-Hill, A., Mack, T.M., & Henderson, B.E. (1987). Estrogen use and cardiovascular disease. In D.R. Mishell, Jr. (Ed.), *Menopause: Physiology and pharmacology* (pp. 209–224). Chicago, IL: Year Book Medical Publishers.

Rossouw, J., Anderson, G., Prentice, R., LaCroix, A., Kooperberg, C., Stefanick, M., . . . Ockene, J. (2002). Risks and benefits of estrogen plus progestin in healthy postmenopausal women: Principal results from the Women's Health Initiative randomized controlled trial. *Journal of the American Medical Association, 288,* 321–333.

Rossow, I., & Amundsen, A. (1997). Alcohol abuse and mortality: A 40-year prospective study of Norwegian conscripts. *Social Science & Medicine, 44,* 261–267.

Rowland, D., & Tai, W. (2003). A review of plant-derived and herbal approaches to the treatment of sexual dysfunctions. *Journal of Sex & Marital Therapy, 29,* 185–205.

Salthouse, T. (2004). What and when of cognitive aging. *Current Directions in Psychological Science, 13,* 140–144.

Salthouse, T. (2012b). Consequences of age-related cognitive declines. *Annual Review of Psychology, 63*(July), 201–226. doi:10.1146/annurev-psych-120710-100328

Schachar, R. (2010). *Presbyopia—Cause and treatment.* Retrieved from http://emedicine.medscape.com/article/1219573-overview

Schaie, K. (2013). *Developmental influences on adult intelligence: The Seattle Longitudinal Study* (2nd ed.). New York, NY: Oxford University Press.

Schaie, K.W., & Willis, S.L. (2010). The Seattle longitudinal study of adult cognitive development. *ISSBD bulletin, 57*(1), 24–29.

Scheibner, G.B., & Leathem, J. (2012). Memory control beliefs and everyday forgetfulness in adulthood: The effects of selection, optimization, and compensation strategies. *Aging, Neuropsychology, and Cognition, 19*(3), 362–379. doi:10.1080/13825585.2011.615905

Schmiedeberg, C., & Schröder, J. (2016). Does sexual satisfaction change with relationship duration? *Archives of Sexual Behavior, 45*(1), 99–107. doi:10.1007/s10508-015-0587-0

Sher, L. (2004). Type D personality, cortisol and cardiac disease. *Australian and New Zealand Journal of Psychiatry, 38,* 652–653.

Simonton, D. (2000). Creativity: Cognitive, personal, developmental, and social aspects. *American Psychologist, 55,* 151–158.

Simonton, D.K. (1988). Age and outstanding achievement: What do we know after a century of research? *Psychological Bulletin, 104,* 251–267.

Simonton, D.K. (1991). Career landmarks in science: Individual differences and interdisciplinary contrasts. *Developmental Psychology, 27,* 119–130.

Simonton, D.K. (2013). Age and creative productivity. In E.G. Carayannis (Ed.), *Encyclopedia of creativity, invention, innovation and entrepreneurship* (pp. 40–44). New York, NY: Springer. doi:10.1007/978-1-4614-3858-8_345

Simonton, D.K. (in press). Creative productivity across the lifespan. In J.A. Plucker (Ed.), *Creativity and innovation: Current understandings and debates.* Waco, TX: Prufrock Press.

Smith, E.L. (1982). Exercise for prevention of osteoporosis: A review. *Physician and Sportsmedicine, 10,* 72–83.

Society of Obstetricians and Gynaecologists of Canada. (n.d.). *Menopause.* Retrieved from http://sogc.org/publications/menopause/

Sowell, E.R., Peterson, B.S., Thompson, P.M., Welcome, S.E., Henkenius, A.L., & Toga, A.W. (2003). Mapping cortical change across the human life span. *Nature Neuroscience, 6*(3), 309–315.

Sowell, E.R., Thompson, P.M., & Toga, A.W. (2004). Mapping changes in the human cortex throughout the span of life. *Neuroscientist, 10*(4), 372–392.

Stadel, B.V., & Weiss, N.S. (1975). Characteristics of menopausal women: A survey of King and Pierce Counties in Washington, 1973–74. *American Journal of Epidemiology, 102*(3), 209–216.

Stampfer, M.J., Colditz, G.A., Willett, W.C., Manson, J.E., Rosner, B., Speizer, F.E., & Hennekens, C.H. (1991). Postmenopausal estrogen therapy and cardiovascular disease: Ten-year follow-up from the Nurses' Health Study. *New England Journal of Medicine, 325,* 756–762.

Stampfer, M.J., Hennekins, C.H., Manson, J.E., Colditz, G.A., Rosner, B., & Willett, W.C. (1993). Vitamin E consumption and the risk of coronary disease in women. *New England Journal of Medicine, 328,* 1444–1449.

Statistics Canada. (2015d). *Leading causes of death, total population, by age group and sex, Canada, annual* (CANSIM Table 102-0561). Retrieved from http://www5.statcan.gc.ca/cansim/a26?lang=eng&id=1020561

Statistics Canada. (2015i). *Population by sex and age group* (CANSIM Table 051-0001). Retrieved from http://www.statcan.gc.ca/tables-tableaux/sum-som/l01/cst01/demo10a-eng.htm

Statistics Canada. (2015j). *Heavy drinking, 2014* (Cat. no. 82-625-x). Retrieved from http://www.statcan.gc.ca/pub/82-625-x/2015001/article/14183-eng.htm

Steptoe, A., Jackson, S.E., & Wardle, J. (2016). Sexual activity and concerns in people with coronary heart disease from a population-based study. *Heart,* (Apr 28). doi:10.1136/heartjnl-2015-308993

Terashima, K., Mikami, A., Tachibana, N., Kumano-Go, T., Teshima, Y., Sugita, & Takeda, M. (2004). Sleep characteristics of menopausal insomnia: A polysomnographic study. *Psychiatry & Clinical Neurosciences, 58,* 179–185.

Thompson, W. (2013). *Alcoholism.* Retrieved from http://emedicine.medscape.com/article/285913-overview

Thompson, W., Lande, R., & Kalapatapu, R. (2010). *Alcoholism*. Retrieved from http://emedicine.medscape.com/article/285913-overview

Toh, S., Hernández-Díaz, S., Logan, R., Rossouw, J.E., & Hernán, M.A. (2010). Coronary heart disease in postmenopausal recipients of estrogen plus progestin therapy: Does the increased risk ever disappear? *Annals of Internal Medicine, 152*(4), 211–217.

Tolomio, S., Ermolao, A., Lalli, A., & Zaccaria, M. (2010). The effect of a multicomponent dual-modality exercise program targeting osteoporosis on bone health status and physical function capacity of postmenopausal women. *Journal of Women & Aging, 22*(4), 241–254. doi:10.1080/08952841.2010.518866

Tsang, P. (1998). Age, attention, expertise, and time-sharing performance. *Psychology & Aging, 13*, 323–347.

Tu, J.V., Nardi, L., Fang, J., Liu, J., Khalid, L., & Johansen, H. (2009). National trends in rates of death and hospital admissions related to acute myocardial infarction, heart failure and stroke, 1994–2004. *Canadian Medical Association Journal, 180*(13), 188–125. doi:10.1503/cmaj.081197

Tulving, E. (1972). Episodic and semantic memory. In E. Tulving & W. Donaldson (Eds.), *Organization of memory* (pp. 381–403). New York, NY: Academic Press.

Tulving, E. (1999). *What is episodic memory and why is it unique?* Bauer Colloquium Series. Toronto, ON: University of Toronto. Retrieved from www.bio.brandeis.edu/news/bauer/1999/tulving.html

Tulving, E. (2004). Episodic memory: From mind to brain. *Revue Neurologique (Paris), 160*(4), 9–23.

Uemura, N., Okamoto, S., Yamamoto, S., Matsumura, N., Yamaguchi, S., Yamakido, M., . . . Schlemper, R. (2001). *Helicobacter pylori infection and the development of gastric cancer. New England Journal of Medicine, 345*, 784–789.

van Doornen, L., Snieder, H., & Boomsma, D. (1998). Serum lipids and cardiovascular reactivity to stress. *Biological Psychology, 47*, 279–297.

Verbrugge, L.M. (1989). Gender, aging, and health. In K.S. Markides (Ed.), *Aging and health* (pp. 23–78). Newbury Park, CA: Sage.

Voelcker-Rehage, C., & Niemann, C. (2013). Structural and functional brain changes related to different types of physical activity across the life span. *Neuroscience and Biobehavioral Reviews, 37*(9 Pt B), 2268–2295. doi:10.1016/j.neubiorev.2013.01.028

Women's Health Initiative Steering Committee (2004). Effects of conjugated equine estrogen in postmenopausal women with hysterectomy. The Women's Health Initiative randomized controlled trial. *Journal of the American Medical Association, 291*(14), 1701–1712.

Wong, B., Iam, S., Wong, W., Chen, J., Zheng, T., Feng, R., . . . & Chen, J. (2004). Helicobacter pylori eradication to prevent gastric cancer in a high-risk region of China: A randomized controlled trial. *Journal of the American Medical Association, 127*, 344–346.

Woodward, M., & Tunstall-Pedoe, H. (1995). Alcohol consumption, diet, coronary risk factors, and prevalent coronary heart disease in men and women in the Scottish heart health study. *Journal of Epidemiology and Community Health, 49*, 354–362.

Working Group for the PEPI Trial, The (1995). Effects of estrogen or estrogen/progestin regimens on heart disease risk factors in postmenopausal women: The Postmenopausal Estrogen/Progestin Interventions (PEPI) Trial. *Journal of the American Medical Association, 273*, 199–208.

Wylie, K., & Kenney, G. (2010). Sexual dysfunction and the ageing male. *Maturitas, 65*(1), 23–27. doi:10.1016/j.maturitas.2009.10.018

Yordanova, J., Kolev, V., & Basar, E. (1998). EEG theta and frontal alpha oscillations during auditory processing change with aging. *Electroencephalography & Clinical Neurophysiology: Evoked Potentials, 108*, 497–505.

Zannas, A.S., McQuoid, D.R., Payne, M.E., Steffens, D.C., Macfall, J.R., Ashley-Koch, A., & Taylor, W.D. (2013). Negative life stress and longitudinal hippocampal volume changes in older adults with and without depression. *Journal of Psychiatric Research, 47*(6), 829–834. doi:10.1016/j.jpsychires

Zelinski, E., & Burnight, K. (1997). Sixteen-year longitudinal and time lag changes in memory and cognition in older adults. *Psychology & Aging, 12*, 503–513.

Zerbe, K., & Domnitei, D. (2004). Eating disorders at middle age. *Eating Disorders Review, 15*(2). Retrieved from http://www.eatingdisordersreview.com/nl/nl_edr_15_2_1.html

Zysset, S., Schroeter, M., Neumann, J., & von Cramon, D. (2007). Stroop interference, hemodynamic response and aging: An event-related fMRI study. *Neurobiology of Aging, 28*, 937–946.

Chapter 16

Ackerman, S., Zuroff, D., & Moskowitz, D. (2000). Generativity in midlife and young adults: Links to agency, communion and subjective well-being. *Aging and Human Development, 50*, 17–41.

Adcox, S. (2016). Grandparents' visitation rights in Canada. *About Parenting*. Retrieved from http://grandparents.about.com/od/Grandparents-Rights/tp/Grandparents-Visitation-Rights-In-Canada.htm

Ahituv, A., & Lehman, R. (2004). *Job turnover, wage rates, and marital stability*. Retrieved from Urban Institute website: www.urban.org

Anrig, G., & Parekh, M. (2010). *The Century Foundation issue brief: The impact of housing and investment market declines on the wealth of baby boomers*. Retrieved from http://www.tcf.org/publications/economicsinequality/parekh_brief.pdf

Atkins, H.L., Bowman, M., Allan, D., Anstee, G., Arnold, D.L., Bar-Or, A., . . . Freedman, M.S. (2016). Immunoablation and autologous haemopoietic stem-cell transplantation for aggressive multiple sclerosis: A multicentre single-group phase 2 trial. *Lancet*, Jun 8. pii: S0140-6736(16)30169-6. doi:10.1016/S0140-6736(16)30169-6. [Epub ahead of print]

Attar-Schwartz, S., Tan, J.P. & Buchanan, A. (2009). Adolescents' perspectives on relationships with grandparents: The contribution of adolescent, grandparent, and parent-grandparent relationship variables. *Children and Youth Services Review, 31*(9), 1057–1066. doi:10.1016/j.childyouth.2009.05.007

Attar-Schwartz, S., Tan, J.P., Buchanan, A., Flouri, E., & Griggs, J. (2009). Grandparenting and adolescent adjustment in two-parent biological, lone-parent, and step-families. *Journal of family psychology, 23*(1), 67–75. doi:10.1037/a0014383

Baltes, B., & Heydens-Gahir, H. (2003). Reduction of work-family conflict through the use of selection, optimization, and compensation behaviors. *Journal of Applied Psychology, 88*, 1005–1018.

Baltes, P.B., & Baltes, M.M. (1990). Psychological perspectives on successful aging: The model of selective optimization with compensation. In P.B. Baltes & M.M. Baltes (Eds.), *Successful aging* (pp. 1–34). Cambridge, England: Cambridge University Press.

Beaujot, R., & Ravanera, Z. (2008). Family change and implications for family solidarity and social cohesion. *Canadian Studies in Population, 35*(1), 73–101.

Beaujot, R., & Ravanera, Z.R. (2001, January). *An interpretation of family change, with implications for social cohesion*. Paper presented at a conference "Have the Factors of Social Inclusiveness Changed?" organized by the Centre de recherche interuniversitaire sur les transformations et les régulations économiques et sociales (CRITERES) and the Policy Research Secretariat, Montreal, PQ.

Blanchard-Fields, F., Chen, Y., Schocke, M., & Hertzog, C. (1998). Evidence for content-specificity of causal attributions across the adult life span. *Aging, Neuropsychology, & Cognition, 5*, 241–263.

Bonikowska, A., & Schellenberg, G. (2013). *An overview of the working lives of older baby boomers* (Cat. no. 11F0019M). Analytical Studies Branch Research Paper Series, no. 352. Ottawa, ON: Statistics Canada.

Bonikowska, A., & Schellenberg, G. (2014). *Employment transitions among older workers leaving long-term jobs: Evidence from administrative data* (Cat. no. 11F0019M). Analytical Studies Branch Research Paper Series, no 355. Ottawa, ON: Statistics Canada.

Boswell, W., Shipp, A., Payne, S., & Culbertson, S. (2009). Changes in newcomer job satisfaction over time: Examining the pattern of honeymoons and hangover. *Journal of Applied Psychology, 94*, 844–858.

Brucker, E., & Leppel, K. (2013). Retirement plans: Planners and nonplanners. *Educational Gerontology*, 39(1), 1–11. doi:10.1080/0360 1277.2012.660859

Buchanan, A. (2014). Risk and protective factors in child development and the development of resilience. *Open Journal of Social Sciences*, 2(4), 244–249. doi:10.4236/jss.2014.24025

Burn, K., & Szoeke, C. (2016). Boomerang families and failure-to-launch: Commentary on adult children living at home. *Maturitas*, 83(1), 9–12. doi:10.1016/j.maturitas.2015.09.004

Buyens, D., Hans, V. D., Dewilde, T., & De Vos, A. (2009). The aging workforce: Perceptions of career ending. *Journal of Managerial Psychology*, 24(2), 102–117. doi:http://dx.doi.org/10.1108/02683940910928838

Cable, N., Bartley, M., Chandola, T., & Sacker, A. (2013). Friends are equally important to men and women, but family matters more for men's well-being. *Journal of Epidemiology and Community Health*, 67(2), 166–171. doi:10.1136/jech-2012-201113

Campbell, P.A., & Rudnicki, M.A. (2013). Oct4 interaction with Hmgb2 regulates Akt signaling and pluripotency. *Stem Cells*, 31(6), 1107–20. doi:10.1002/stem.13

Campbell, P.A., Perez-Iratxeta, C., Andrade-Navarro, M.A., & Rudnicki, M.A. (2007, June 20). Oct4 targets regulatory nodes to modulate stem cell function. *PLoS ONE*, 2(6), e553. http://dx.doi.org/10.1371/journal.pone.0000553

Canadian Institutes of Health Research. (2007, June 29). *Updated guidelines for human pluripotent stem cell research*. Ottawa, ON: Author. Retrieved from www.cihr-irsc.gc.ca/e/34460.html

Carstensen, L.L. (1992). Social and emotional patterns in adulthood: Support for socioemotional selectivity theory. *Psychology and Aging*, 7, 331–338.

Cate, R., & John, O. (2007). Testing models of the structure and development of future time perspective: Maintaining a focus on opportunities in middle age. *Psychology and Aging*, 22, 186–201.

Cherlin, A., & Furstenberg, F.F. (1986). *The new American grandparent*. New York, NY: Basic Books.

Cook, S., & Heppner, P. (1997). Coping control, problem-solving appraisal, and depressive symptoms during a farm crisis. *Journal of Mental Health Counseling*, 19, 64–77.

Costa, P.T., Jr., & McCrae, R.R. (1980). Still stable after all these years: Personality as a key to some issues in adulthood and old age. In P.B. Baltes & O.G. Brim, Jr. (Eds.), *Life-span development and behavior* (pp. 65–102). New York, NY: Academic Press.

Daire, A. (2004). Investigating caregiver distress with the Parental Bonding Instrument (PBI). *Dementia: The International Journal of Social Research & Practice*, 3, 83–94.

Deakin, J., Aitken, M., Robbins, T., & Sahakian, B. (2004). Risk taking during decision-making in normal volunteers changes with age. *Journal of the International Neuropsychological Society*, 10, 590–598.

Dennerstein, L., Dudley, E., & Guthrie, J. (2002). Empty nest or revolving door? A prospective study of women's quality of life in midlife during the phase of children leaving and re-entering the home. *Psychological Medicine*, 32, 545–550.

Dietz, B., Carrozza, M., & Ritchey, P. (2003). Does financial self-efficacy explain gender differences in retirement saving strategies? *Journal of Women & Aging*, 15, 83–96.

Drolet, M., & Morissette, R. (2014). New facts on pension coverage in Canada. *Insights on Canadian Society* (Cat. no. 75-006-X). Ottawa, ON: Statistics Canada. Retrieved from http://www.statcan.gc.ca/pub/75-006-x/2014001/article/14120-eng.pdf

Due, P., Holstein, B., Lund, R., Modvig, J., & Avlund, K. (1999). Social relations: Network, support and relational strain. *Social Science & Medicine*, 48, 661–673.

Dunifon, R., & Bajracharya, A. (2012). The role of grandparents in the lives of youth. *Journal of Family Issues*, 33(9), 1168–1194. doi:10.1177/0192513X12444271

Dykstra, P., van den Broek, T., Muresan, C., Haragus, M., Haragus, P.T., Abramowska-Kmon, A., & Kotowska, I. (2014). State-of-the-art report: Intergenerational linkages in families. *Families and Societies Working Papers Series*. Retrieved from http://www.familiesandsocieties.eu/wp-content/uploads/2014/12/WP01DykstraEtal2013.pdf

Ebner, N.C., Freund, A.M., & Baltes, P.B. (2006). Developmental changes in personal goal orientation from young to late adulthood: From striving for gains to maintenance and prevention of losses. *Psychology and Aging*, 21(4), 664–678. doi:10.1037/0882-7974.21.4.664

Enright, E. (2004). A house divided. *AARP Magazine*. Retrieved from www.aarpmagazine.org/family/Articles/a2004-05-26-mag-divorce.html

Erikson, E.H. (1963). *Childhood and society* (2nd ed.). New York, NY: Norton.

Evans, S., Huxley, R., Gately, C., Webber, M., Mears, A., Pajak, S., . . . Katona, C. (2006). Mental health, burnout and job satisfaction among mental health social workers in England and Wales. *The British Journal of Psychiatry*, 188, 75–78.

Farrow, J.A.H. (2012). The adult years. In O.J. Sahler, J.E. Carr, J.B. Frank, & J. Nunes, (Eds.), *The behavioral sciences and health care* (3rd ed. pp. 112–120). Cambridge, MA: Hogrefe Publishing.

Freudenberger, H.J., & Richelson, G. (1980). *Burn-out: The high cost of high achievement*. Garden City, NY: Anchor Press.

Freund, A.M. (2008). Successful aging as management of resources: The role of selection, optimization, and compensation. *Research in Human Development*, 5(2), 94–106. doi:10.1080/15427600802034827

Gobeski, K., & Beehr, T. (2009). How retirees work: Predictors of different types of bridge employment. *Journal of Organizational Behavior*, 30, 401–425.

Goyer, A. (2012). *AARP survey: Grandparents providing more care, money, and advice*. Retrieved from http://blog.aarp.org/2012/03/28/grandparent-roles-survey-amy-goyer/

Graham, E.K., & Lachman, M.E. (2012). Personality stability is associated with better cognitive performance in adulthood: Are the stable more able? *The Journals of Gerontology. Series B*, 67(5), 545–554. doi:10.1093/geronb/gbr149

Grant, S., & Langan-Fox, J. (2007). Personality and the occupational stressor-strain relationship: The role of the Big Five. *Journal of Occupational Health Psychology*, 112, 20–33.

Hampson, S., & Goldberg, L. (2006). A first large cohort study of personality trait stability over the 40 years between elementary school and midlife. *Journal of Personality and Social Psychology*, 91, 763–779.

He, Y., Colantonio, A., & Marshall, V. (2003). Later-life career disruption and self-rated health: An analysis of General Social Survey data. *Canadian Journal on Aging*, 22, 45–57.

Health Reports. (2001). Death-shifting trends (Cat. no. 82-003-XPE). *Health Reports*, 12(3), 41–47.

Heppner, M., Fuller, B., & Multon, K. (1998). Adults in involuntary career transition: An analysis of the relationship between the psychological and career domains. *Journal of Career Assessment*, 6, 329–346.

Hess, T., Bolstad, C., Woodburn, S., & Auman, C. (1999). Trait diagnosticity versus behavioral consistency as determinants of impression change in adulthood. *Psychology & Aging*, 14, 77–89.

Hofer, J., Busch, H., Au, A., Poláčková Šolcová, I., Tave, P., & Wong, T.T. (2016). Generativity does not necessarily satisfy all your needs: Associations among cultural demand for generativity, generative concern, generative action, and need satisfaction in the elderly in four cultures. *Developmental Psychology*, 52(3), 509–519. doi:10.1037/dev0000078

Hom, P.W., Mitchell, T.R., Lee, T.W., & Griffeth, R.W. (2012). Reviewing employee turn-over: Focusing on proximal withdrawal states and an expanded criterion. *Psychological Bulletin*, 138(5), 831–58. doi:10.1037/a0027983

Huber, C., Navarro, R., Wombie, M., & Mumme, F. (2010). Family resilience and midlife marital satisfaction. *The Family Journal*, 18, 136–145.

Human, L. J., Biesanz, J. C., Miller, G. E., Chen, E., Lachman, M. E. & Seeman, T. E. (2013). Is change bad? Personality change is associated with poorer psychological health and greater metabolic syndrome in midlife. *Journal of Personality*, 81(3), 249–60. doi:10.1111/jopy.12002

Insured Retirement Institute. (2013). *The great divide: Financial comparison of early and late Boomers' retirement preparedness*. Retrieved from https://avectra.myirionline.org/eweb/uploads/2013%20 JUNE%20Research%20-%20Early%20v%20Late%20Boomers.pdf

Jacques, E. (1965). Death and the mid-life crisis. *International Journal of Psychoanalysis, 46*(4), 502–514.

James, J.B., McKechnie, S., & Swanberg, J. (2011). Predicting employee engagement in an age-diverse retail workforce. *Journal of Organizational Behavior, 32*(2), 173–196.

Jones, B.K., & McAdams, D.P. (2013). Becoming generative: Socializing influences recalled in life stories in late midlife. *Journal of Adult Development, 20*(3), 158–172. doi:10.1007/s10804-013-9168-4

Kalmijn, M. (2003). Shared friendship networks and the life course: An analysis of survey data on married and cohabiting couples. *Social Networks, 25*, 231–249.

Kalmijn, M. (2003). Shared friendship networks and the life course: An analysis of survey data on married and cohabiting couples. *Social Networks, 25*, 231–249.

Kandler, C., Bleidorn, W., Riemann, R., Spinath, F., Thiel, W., & Angleitner, A. (2010). Source of cumulative continuity in personality: A longitudinal multiple-rater twin study. *Journal of Personality and Social Psychology, 98*, 995–1008.

Kelly, M.B. (2012). *Divorce cases in civil court, 2010/2011*. (Catalogue no. 85-002-X). Retrieved from Statistics Canada website http://www.statcan.gc.ca/pub/85-002-x/2012001/article/11634-eng.pdf

Kerr, M. (2006, March 13). *Menstrual blood shows good potential as stem cell source*. Reuter's Health Information. Retrieved from www.medscape.com/viewarticle/527401

Kimmelman, J., Hyun, I., Benvenisty, N., Caulfield, T., Heslop, H.E., Murry, C.E., ... Daley, G.Q. (2016). Policy: Global standards for stem-cell research. *Nature, 533*(7603), 311–313. doi:10.1038/533311a

Kooij, D.T.A.M., De Lange, A.H., Jansen, P.G.W., Kanfer, R., & Dikkers, J.S.E. (2011). Age and work-related motives: Results of a meta-analysis. *Journal of Organizational Behavior, 32*(2), 197–225. doi:10.1002/job.665

Kopala-Sibley, D.C., Mongrain, M., & Zuroff, D.C. (2013). A lifespan perspective on dependency and self-criticism: Age-related differences from 18 to 59. *Journal of Adult Development, 20*(3), 126–141. doi:10.1007/s10804-013-9163-9

Lachman, M. (2004). Development in midlife. *Annual Review of Psychology, 55*, 305–331.

Lachman, M., & Weaver, S. (1998). Sociodemographic variations in the sense of control by domain: Findings from the MacArthur studies of midlife. *Psychology & Aging, 13*, 553–562.

Lachman, M.E. (2015). Mind the gap in the middle: A call to study midlife. *Research in Human Development, 12*(3–4), 327–334. doi:10.1080/15427609.2015.1068048

Lachman, M.E., Teshale, S., & Agrigoroaei, S. (2015). Midlife as a pivotal period in the life course: Balancing growth and decline at the crossroads of youth and old age. *International Journal of Behavioral Development, 39*(1), 20–31. doi:10.1177/0165025414533223

Laird, P.W. (2005). Cancer epigenetics. *Human Molecular Genetics, 14*(Review Issue 1), R65–R76.

Levy, B.R. (2003). Mind matters: Cognitive and physical effects of aging self-stereotypes. *The Journals of Gerontology. Series B, 58*(4), 203–211. doi:10.1093/geronb/58.4.P203

Levy, B.R., & Leifheit-Limson, E. (2009). The stereotype-matching effect: Greater influence on functioning when age stereotypes correspond to outcomes. *Psychology and Aging, 24*(1), 230–233. doi:10.1037/a0014563

Levy, B.R., Zonderman, A.B., Slade, M.D., & Ferrucci, L. (2010). Age stereotypes held earlier in life predict cardiovascular events in later life. *Psychological Science, 20*(3), 296–298. doi:10.1111/j.1467-9280.2009.02298.x

Levy, B.R., Zonderman, A.B., Slade, M.D., & Ferrucci, L. (2012). Memory shaped by age stereotypes over time. *The Journals of Gerontology. Series B, 67*(4), 432–436. doi:10.1093/geronb/gbr120

Li, W.D., Zhang, Z., Song, Z., & Arvey, R.D. (2016). It is also in our nature: Genetic influences on work characteristics and in

explaining their relationships with well-being. *Journal of Organizational Behavior*. doi:10.1002/job.2079 [Epub ahead of print]

Luarte, A., Bátiz, L.F., Wyneken, U., & Lafourcade, C. (2016). Potential therapies by stem cell-derived exosomes in cns diseases: Focusing on the neurogenic niche. *Stem Cells International, 2016*, Article ID 5736059, e1–16. http://dx.doi.org/10.1155/2016/5736059

Lucas, R.E., & Donnellan, M.B. (2011). Personality development across the life span: Longitudinal analyses with a national sample from Germany. *Journal of Personality and Social Psychology, 101*(4), 847–861. doi:10.1037/a0024298

Mandal, B., & Roe, B. (2008). Job loss, retirement and the mental health of older Americans. *Journal of Mental Health Policy and Economics, 11*(4), 167–176. doi:10.2139/ssrn.991134

Mandal, B., Ayyagari, P., & Gallo, W.T. (2011). Job loss and depression: The role of subjective expectations. *Social Science & Medicine, 72*(4), 576–583. doi:10.1016/j.socscimed.2010.11.014

Mao, H. (2003). The relationship between voluntary employer changes and perceived job stress in Taiwan. International Journal of Stress Management, 10, 75–85.

Marks, N., & Lamberg, J. (1998). Marital status continuity and change among young and midlife adults. *Journal of Family Issues, 19*, 652–686.

Martin-Matthews, A.E. (2001). *The ties that bind aging families: Caregiving roles and relationships*. Ottawa, ON: Vanier Institute of the Family. Retrieved December 23, 2001 from www.vifamily.ca/cft/aging/caregiving.htm

Mauldin, J. (2005). *The new retirement model*. Retrieved from Age-Wave website: www.agewave.com/media_files/ota.htm

Maurer, T.J., Barbeite, F.G., Weiss, E.M., & Lippstreu, M. (2008). New measures of stereotypical beliefs about older workers ability and desire for development. *Journal of Managerial Psychology, 23*(4), 395–418. doi:http://dx.doi.org/10.1108/02683940810869024

McCrae, R.R., & Costa, P.T., Jr. (1984). *Emerging lives, enduring dispositions: Personality in adulthood*. Boston, MA: Little, Brown.

Meisner, B.A. (2012). A meta-analysis of positive and negative age stereotype priming effects on behavior among older adults. *The Journals of Gerontology. Series B, 67*(1), 13–17. doi:10.1093/geronb/gbr062

Milan, A. (2016). Diversity of young adults living with their parents. *Statistics Canada* (Cat. no. 75-006-X). Ottawa, ON: Minister of Industry.

Milan, A., Laflamme, N., & Wong, I. (2015). Diversity of grandparents living with their grandchildren. *Insights on Canadian Society* (Cat. no. 75-006-X, no. 2015001). Ottawa, ON: Minister of Industry.

Milan, A., Wong, I., & Vézina, M. (2014). Emerging trends in living arrangements and conjugal unions for current and future seniors. *Insights on Canadian Society* (Cat. no. 75-006-X). Ottawa, ON: Minister of Industry.

Mitchell, B.A. (2000). The refilled "nest": Debunking the myth of families-in-crisis. In E.M. Gee & G. Gutman (Eds.), *The overselling of population aging: Apocalyptic demography and intergenerational challenges* (pp. 80–99). Toronto, ON: Oxford University Press.

Mitchell, B.A. (2006). *The boomerang age: Transitions to adulthood in families*. New Jersey: Aldine-Transaction.

Mitchell, B.A., & Lovegreen, L.D. (2009). The empty nest syndrome in midlife families: A multi-method exploration of parental gender differences and cultural dynamics. *Journal of Family Issues, 30*(12), 1654–1670.

Mitchell, B.A., & Wister, A.V. (2015). Midlife challenge or welcome departure? Cultural and family-related expectations of empty nest transitions. *The International Journal of Aging and Human Development, 81*(4), 260–280. doi:10.1177/0091415015622790

Monroy, T. (2000, March 15). Boomers alter economics. *Interactive Week*. Retrieved from ZDNet website: www.ZDNet.com

Muzi, M. (2000). *The experience of parenting*. Upper Saddle River, NJ: Prentice Hall.

National Institute of Health. (2009). *Stem cell basics*. Retrieved from http://stemcells.nih.gov/info/basics/defaultpage.asp

Ng, T.W.H., & Feldman, D.C. (2012). Evaluating six common stereotypes about older workers with meta-analytical data. *Personnel Psychology, 65*(4), 821–858. doi:10.1111/peps.12003

Perho, H., & Korhonen, M. (1999). Coping in work and marriage at the onset of middle age. *Psykologia, 34*, 115–127.

Phanse, R., & Kaur, R. (2015). An exploratory study on "self-renewal" in mid-life voluntary career changes for managers. *Journal of Management Research and Analysis, 2*(3), 204–213.

Phillipson, C. (2013). Commentary: The future of work and retirement. *Human Relations, 66*(1), 143–153. doi:10.1177/0018726712465453

Pinquart, M., & Sorensen, S. (2006a). Gender differences in caregiver stressors, social resources, and health: An updated meta-analysis. *Journals of Gerontology: Series B: Psychological Sciences and Social Sciences, 61B*, P33–P45.

Pinquart, M., & Sorensen, S. (2006b). Helping caregivers of persons with dementia: Which interventions work and how large are their effects? *International Geriatrics, 18*, 577–595.

Poeschla, B., Strachan, E., Dansie, E., Buchwald, D.S., & Afari, N. (2013). Chronic fatigue and personality: A twin study of causal pathways and shared liabilities. *Annals of Behavioral Medicine, 45*(3), 289–298. doi:10.1007/s12160-012-9463-5

Randall, K. (2007). Examining the relationship between burnout and age among Anglican clergy in England and Wales. *Mental Health, Religion, & Culture, 10*, 39–46.

Ravanera, Z.R., & Rajulton, F. (1998, April 2–4). *Variations in the length of male parenting: Evidence from the 1995 GSS Canada* (Discussion Paper No. 98-6). Paper presented at the Annual Meeting of the Population Association of America, Chicago, IL. Retrieved from The University of Western Ontario, Faculty of Social Science website: www.ssc.uwo.ca/sociology/popstudies/dp/dp98-6.pdf

Rosenthal, C.J., & Gladstone, J. (2000). *Grandparenthood in Canada*. Ottawa, ON: The Vanier Institute of the Family. Retrieved from www.vifamily.ca/cft/grandpt/CONTEXT.HTM

Roth, M. (2003). Validation of the Arnett Inventory of Sensation Seeking (AISS): Efficiency to predict the willingness towards occupational change, and affection by social desirability. *Personality & Individual Differences, 35*, 1307–1314.

Russo, F. (2010). *They're your parents too! How siblings can survive their parents' aging without driving each other crazy*. Mississauga, ON: Random House of Canada.

Saad, L. (2008). *U.S. workers' job satisfaction is relatively high: Older employees are more upbeat than younger workers. (Gallop Poll, August 21).* Retrieved from http://www.gallup.com/poll/109738/us-workers-job-satisfaction-relatively-high.aspx

Santos, M.J., & Ventura-Juncá, P. (2012). Bioethical aspects of basic research and medical applications of human stem cells. *Biological Research, 45*(3), 317–326. doi:10.4067/S0716-97602012000300013

Scudellari, M. (2016). How iPS cells changed the world. *Nature, 534*(7607), 310–312. doi:10.1038/534310a

Shannon, T. (2004). *Stem cell research: How Catholic ethics guides us*. Catholic Update. Retrieved from www.usccb.org/prolife/issues/bioethic/stemcelltest71801.htm

Shiner, R.L., & Caspi, A. (2012). Temperament and the development of personality traits, adaptations, and narratives. In M. Zentner, M., & R. Shiner, R.L. (Eds.), *Handbook of temperament* (pp. 497–516). New York, NY: Guilford Press.

Sinha, M. (2013). Portrait of caregivers, 2012. *Statistics Canada* (Cat. no. 89-652-X — no. 001). Ottawa, ON: Minister of Industry.

Sneed, J.R., Whitbourne, S.K., Schwartz, S.J., & Huang, S. (2012). The relationship between identity, intimacy, and midlife wellbeing: Findings from the Rochester adult longitudinal study. *Psychology and Aging, 27*(2), 318–323. doi:http://dx.doi.org/10.1037/a0026378

Spencer, C. (2008). *Grandparent rights*. Retrieved from www.canadianelderlaw.ca/GrandparentsRights.htm

Srivastava, S., John, O.P., Gosling, S.D., & Potter, J. (2003). Development of personality in early and middle adulthood: Set like plaster or persistent change? *Journal of Personality and Social Psychology, 84*(5), 1041–1053.

Stengård, J., Bernhard-Oettel, C., Berntson, E., Leineweber, C., & Aronsson, G. (2016). Stuck in a job: Being "locked-in" or at risk of becoming locked-in at the workplace and well-being over time. *Work and Stress, 30*(2), 152–172. doi:10.1080/02678373.2016.1163804

Stewart, C. (2004). The physiology of stem cells: Potential for the elderly patient. *Journal of Musculoskeletal Neuron Interaction, 4*, 179–183.

Tabuchi, M., Nakagawa, T., Miura, A., & Gondo, Y. (2015). Generativity and interaction between the old and young: The role of perceived respect and perceived rejection. *Gerontologist, 55*(4), 537–547. doi:10.1093/geront/gnt135

Tai, M.H., Chang, C.C., Kiupel, M., Webster, J.D., Olson, L.K., & Trosko, J.E. (2005). Oct4 expression in adult human stem cells: Evidence in support of the stem cell theory of carcinogenesis. *Carcinogenesis 26*(2), 495–502.

Takahashi, K., & Yamanaka, S. (2006). Induction of pluripotent stem cells from mouse embryonic and adult fibroblast cultures by defined factors. *Cell, 126*(4), 663–676. doi:10.1016/j.cell.2006.07.024

Thiele, D.M., & Whelan, T.A. (2008). The relationship between grandparent satisfaction, meaning, and generativity. *International Journal of Aging & Human Development, 66*(1), 21–48. doi:10.2190/AG.66.1.b

Tomasetti, C., & Vogelstein, B. (2015). Variation in cancer risk among tissues can be explained by the number of stem cell divisions. *Science, 347*(6217), 78–81. doi:10.1126/science.1260825

Turcotte, M. (2006). Parents with adult children living at home (11–008). *Canadian Social Trends, 80*, 2–9.

Turcotte, M. (2013a). Family caregiving: What are the consequences? (Cat. no. 75-006-X). *Insights on Canadian Society*. Ottawa, ON: Minister of Industry.

Turcotte, M., & Sawaya, C. (2015). Senior care: Differences by type of housing (Cat. no. 75-006-X). *Insights on Canadian Society*. Ottawa, ON: Statistics Canada. Retrieved from http://www.statcan.gc.ca/pub/75-006-x/2015001/article/14142-eng.pdf

Turner, A., & Findlay, L. (2012). Informal caregiving for seniors. *Health Reports, 23*(3), 1–4.

Uppal, S. (2016). Financial literacy and retirement planning (Cat. no. 75-006-X). *Insights on Canadian Society*. Ottawa, ON: Statistics Canada. Retrieved from http://www.statcan.gc.ca/pub/75-006-x/2016001/article/14360-eng.pdf

Vaillant, G. (2002). *Aging well: Surprising guideposts to a happier life from the landmark Harvard Study of Adult Development*. New York, NY: Little, Brown & Company.

Vaillant, G.E. (2012). *Triumphs of experience: The men of the Harvard Grant Study*. Cambridge, MA: Belknap Press of Harvard University Press.

Vézina, M., & Turcotte, M. (2010). Caring for a parent who lives far away: The consequences. *Canadian Social Trends, 89*, 3–13.

Vinokur, A.D., & van Ryn, M. (1993). Social support and undermining in close relationships: Their independent effects on the mental health of unemployed persons. *Journal of Personality and Social Psychology, 65*, 350–359.

Westermeyer, J.F. (2004). Predictors and characteristics of Erikson's life cycle model among men: A 32-year longitudinal study. *International Journal of Aging & Human Development, 58*(1), 29–48.

Westermeyer, J.F. (2013). Predictors and Characteristics of Successful Aging among Men: A 48-Year Longitudinal Study. *International Journal of Aging & Human Development, 76*(4), 323–345. doi:10.2190/AG.76.4.c

Whitbourne, S.K. (2009). *The search for fulfillment: Revolutionary new research reveals the secret to long-term happiness*. New York, NY: Ballantine Books.

Whitbourne, S.K., Sneed, J.R., & Sayer, A. (2009). Psychosocial development from college through midlife: A 34-year sequential study. *Developmental Psychology, 45*(5), 1328–1340. doi:10.1037/a0016550

Wortman, J., Lucas, R.E., & Donnellan, M.B. (2012). Stability and change in the Big Five personality domains: Evidence from a longitudinal study of Australians. *Psychology and Aging, 27*(4), 867–874. doi:10.1037/a0029322

Wrenn, K., & Maurer, T. (2004). Beliefs about older workers' learning and development behavior in relation to beliefs about malleability of skills, age-related decline, and control. *Journal of Applied Social Psychology, 34,* 223–242.

Young, L.M., Baltes, B.B., & Pratt, A. (2007). Using selection, optimization, and compensation to reduce job/family stressors: Effective when it matters. *Journal of Business and Psychology, 18,* 1–29.

Zacher, H., & Frese, M. (2011). Maintaining a focus on opportunities at work: The interplay between age, job complexity, and the use of selection, optimization, and compensation strategies. *Journal of Organizational Behavior, 32*(2), 291–318. doi:10.1002/job.683

Zucker, A., Ostrove, J., & Stewart A. (2002). College-educated women's personality development in adulthood: Perceptions and age differences. *Psychology & Aging, 17,* 236–244.

Zunker, V.G. (2016). *Career counseling: A holistic approach* (9th ed.). Boston, MA: Cengage Learning.

Chapter 17

Alzheimer Society of Canada (2010). *Rising tide: The impact of dementia on Canadian society.* Toronto, ON: Author. Retrieved from www.alzheimer.ca/docs/RisingTide/Rising%20Tide_Full%20Report_Eng_FINAL_Secured%20version.pdf

American Psychiatric Association. (2013). *Diagnostic and Statistical Manual of Mental Disorder: DSM-5* (5th ed.). Washington, DC: American Psychiatric Publishing.

Anderson, H. (2013). *Alzheimer disease.* Retrieved from http://emedicine.medscape.com/article/1134817-overview

Aneshensel, C.S., Pearlin, L.I., Levy-Storms, L., & Schuler, R.H. (2000). The transition from home to nursing home mortality among people with dementia. *The Journals of Gerontology. Series B, Psychological Sciences and Social Sciences, 55*(3), S152–162. doi:10.1093/geronb/55.3.S152

Anthony, J.C., & Aboraya, A. (1992). The epidemiology of selected mental disorders in later life. In J.E. Birren, R.B. Sloane, & G.D. Cohen (Eds.), *Handbook of mental health and aging* (2nd ed., pp. 28–73). San Diego, CA: Academic Press.

Ardelt, M., & Edwards, C.A. (2015). Wisdom at the end of life: An analysis of mediating and moderating relations between wisdom and subjective well-being. *The Journals of Gerontology. Series B, Psychological Sciences and Social Sciences, 71*(3), 502–513. doi:10.1093/geronb/gbv051

Areán, P.A., Mackin, S., Vargas-Dwyer, E., Raue, P., Sirey, J.A., Kanellopoulos, D., & Alexopoulos, G.S. (2013). Treating depression in disabled, low-income elderly: A conceptual model and recommendations for care. *International Journal of Geriatric Psychiatry, 25*(8), 765–769. doi:10.1002/gps.2556

Arganini, C., & Sinesio, F. (2015). Chemosensory impairment does not diminish eating pleasure and appetite in independently living older adults. *Maturitas, 82*(2), 241–244. doi:10.1016/j.maturitas.2015.07.015

Artuso, C., Cavallini, E., Bottiroli, S., & Palladino, P. (2016). Updating working memory: Memory load matters with aging. *Aging Clinical and Experimental Research,* (May 6). [Epub ahead of print]

Atalayer, D., & Astbury, N.M. (2013). Anorexia of aging and gut hormones. *Aging and Disease, 4*(5), 264–275. doi:10.14336/AD.2013.0400264

Babiloni, C., Babiloni, F., Carducci, F., Cappa, S., Cincotti, F., Del Percio, C., ... Rossini, P.M. (2004). Human cortical rhythms during visual delayed choice reaction time tasks: A high–resolution EEG study on normal aging. *Behavioural Brain Research, 153,* 261–271.

Ballard, J. (2010). Forgetfulness and older adults: Concept analysis. *Journal of Advanced Nursing, 66*(6), 1409–1419. doi:10.1111/j.1365-2648.2010.05279

Baltes, P., & Kunzmann, U. (2004). The two faces of wisdom: Wisdom as a general theory of knowledge and judgment about excellence in mind and virtue vs. wisdom as everyday realization in people and products. *Human Development, 47,* 290–299.

Baltes, P., & Staudinger, U. (2000). Wisdom: A metaheuristic (pragmatic) to orchestrate mind and virtue toward excellence. *American Psychologist, 55,* 122–136.

Baltes, P.B., & Kliegl, R. (1992). Further testing of limits of cognitive plasticity: Negative age differences in a mnemonic skill are robust. *Developmental Psychology, 28,* 121–125.

Bannon, G., Boswell, L., & Schneider, R. (2010). *Alzheimer disease.* Retrieved from http://emedicine.medscape.com/article/295558-overview

Basson, R. (2010). Sexual function of women with chronic illness and cancer. *Women's Health, 6*(3), 407–429. doi:10.2217/whe.10.23

Bauman, A., Merom, D., Bull, F.C., Buchner, D.M., Fiatarone, Singh. M.A. (2016). Updating the evidence for physical activity: Summative reviews of the epidemiological evidence, prevalence, and interventions to promote "active aging." *Gerontologist, 56*(Suppl 2), S268–S280. doi:10.1093/geront/gnw031

Beeri, M.S., & Middleton, L. (2012). Being physically active may protect the brain from Alzheimer disease. *Neurology, 78*(17), 1290–1291. doi:10.1212/WNL.0b013e3182535f0e

Benelam, B. (2009). Satiety and the anorexia of ageing. *British Journal of Community Nursing, 14*(8), 332–335. doi:10.12968/bjcn.2009.14.8.43512

Berdasco, M, & Esteller, M. (2012) Hot topics in epigenetic mechanisms of aging: 2011. *Aging Cell, 11,* 181–186. doi:10.1111/j.1474-9726.2012.00806.x

Bherer, L. (2015). Cognitive plasticity in older adults: Effects of cognitive training and physical exercise. *Annals of the New York Academy of Sciences, 1337*(Mar), 1–6. doi:10.1111/nyas.12682

Billette, J-M., & Janz, T. (2011). *Injuries in Canada: Insights from the Canadian Community Health Survey.* (Cat. No. 82-624-X). Ottawa, ON: Statistics Canada. Retrieved from http://www.statcan.gc.ca/pub/82-624-x/2011001/article/11506-eng.pdf

Blackburn, E.H. (2012, March). *Telomere, telomerase dysfunction triggers disease.* Presented at the Summer Academy Meeting: American Academy of Dermatology, Boston, MA. Retrieved from http://www.aadmeetingnews.org/highlight.aspx?id=4313&p=355

Blackburn, E.H., & Gall, J.G. (1978). A tandemly repeated sequence at the termini of the extrachromosomal ribosomal RNA genes in Tetrahymena. *Journal of Molecular Biology, 120*(1), 33–53.

Blumenthal, J.A., Babyak, M.A., Moore, K.A., Craighead, W.E., Herman, S., Khatri, P., . . . Krishnan, K.R. (1999). Effects of exercise training on older patients with major depression. *Archives of Internal Medicine, 159*(19), 2349–2356.

Blumenthal, J.A., Sherwood, A., Babyak, M.A., Watkins, L.L., Smith, P.J., Hoffman, B.M., . . . Hinderliter, A.L. (2012). Exercise and pharmacological treatment of depressive symptoms in patients with coronary heart disease: Results from the UPBEAT (understanding the prognostic benefits of exercise and antidepressant therapy) study. *Journal of the American College of Cardiology, 60*(12), 1053–1063. doi.org/10.1016/j.jacc.2012.04.040

Bocklandt, S., Lin, W., Sehl, M.E., Sánchez, F.J., Sinsheimer, J.S., Horvath, S., & Vilain, E. (2011). Epigenetic predictor of age. *PLoS ONE 6*(6), e14821. doi:10.1371/journal.pone.0014821

Bonelli, R., Dew, R.E., Koenig, H.G., Rosmarin, D.H., & Vasegh, S. (2012). Religious and spiritual factors in depression: Review and integration of the research. *Depression Research and Treatment, 2012,* doi:10.1155/2012/962860

Bornstein, M.H. (1992). Perception across the life span. In M.H. Bornstein & M.E. Lamb (Eds.), *Developmental psychology: An advanced textbook* (3rd ed., pp. 155–210). Hillsdale, NJ: Erlbaum.

Broemeling, A., Watson, D.E., & Prebtani, F. (2008). Population patterns of chronic health conditions, co-morbidity and healthcare use in Canada: Implications for policy and practice. *Healthcare Quarterly, 11*(3), 70–76.

Buchman, A.S., Boyle, P.A., Yu, L., Shah, R.C., Wilson, R.S., & Bennett, D.A. (2012). Total daily physical activity and the risk of AD and cognitive decline in older adults. *Neurology, 78*(17), 1323–1329. doi:10.1212/WNL.0b013e3182535d35

Burnham, H., & Hogervorst, E. (2004). Recognition of facial expressions of emotion by patients with dementia of the Alzheimer type. *Dementia & Geriatric Cognitive Disorders, 18,* 75–79.

Butters, M., Whyte, E., Nebes, R., Begley, A., Dew, M., Mulsant, B., . . . Becker, J. (2004). Nature and determinants of neuropsychological functioning in late-life depression. *Archives of General Psychiatry, 61,* 587–595.

Byrne, G., & Raphael, B. (1999). Depressive symptoms and depressive episodes in recently widowed older men. *International Psychogeriatrics, 11,* 67–74.

Canadian Coalition for Seniors' Mental Health. (2009). Depression in older adults: A guide for seniors and their families. Retrieved from http://www.ccsmh.ca/pdf/ccsmh_depressionBooklet.pdf

Canadian Coalition for Seniors' Mental Health. (2009). Depression in older adults: A guide for seniors and their families. Retrieved from http://www.ccsmh.ca/pdf/ccsmh_depressionBooklet.pdf

Canadian Hearing Society. (2013). *Tinnitus and hyperacusis.* Retrieved from https://www.chs.ca/tinnitus-and-hyperacusis

Canadian Institute for Health Information. (2010). *Depression among seniors in residential care.* Retrieved from https://secure.cihi.ca/estore/productFamily.htm?locale=en&pf=PFC1432

Canadian Longitudinal Study on Aging. (2016). *History.* Retrieved from https://www.clsa-elcv.ca/about-us/history

Canadian Society for Exercise Physiology (2012). *Canadian physical activity guidelines for older adults 65 years and older.* [Brochure]. Retrieved from http://www.csep.ca/CMFiles/Guidelines/CSEPInfoSheets-older%20adults-ENG.pdf

Canadian Society for Exercise Physiology (2012). *Canadian physical activity guidelines for older adults 65 years and older.* [Brochure]. Retrieved from http://www.csep.ca/CMFiles/Guidelines/CSEPInfoSheets-older%20adults-ENG.pdf

Cappeliez, P. (2009). *Depression among seniors.* Retrieved from http://www.cpa.ca/psychologyfactsheets/depressionamongseniors/

Cardin, V. (2016). Effects of aging and adult-onset hearing loss on cortical auditory regions. *Frontiers in Neuroscience, 10*(May), 199. doi:10.3389/fnins.2016.00199

Carlsson, P.I., Hjaldahl, J., Magnuson, A., Ternevall, E., Edén, M., Skagerstrand, Å., & Jönsson, R. (2015). Severe to profound hearing impairment: Quality of life, psychosocial consequences and audiological rehabilitation. *Disability and Rehabilitation, 37*(20), 1849–1856. doi:10.3109/09638288.2014.982833

Cheah, Y.S., Lee, S., Ashoor, G., Nathan, Y., Reed, L.J., Zelaya, F.O., . . . Amiel, S.A. (2014). Ageing diminishes the modulation of human brain responses to visual food cues by meal ingestion. *International Journal of Obesity, 38*(9), 1186–1192. doi:10.1038/ijo.2013.237

Chen, J., Bierhals, A., Prigerson, H., Kasl, S., Mazure, C., & Jacobs, S. (1999). Gender differences in the effects of bereavement-related psychological distress in health outcomes. *Psychological Medicine, 29,* 367–380.

Childs, B.G., Durik, M., Baker, D.J., & van Deursen, J.M. (2015). Cellular senescence in aging and age-related disease: From mechanisms to therapy. *Nature Medicine, 21*(12), 1424–1435. doi:10.1038/nm.4000

Cohen, A.-L., Dixon, R.A., Lindsay, D.S., & Masson, M.E.J. (2003). The effect of perceptual distinctiveness on the prospective and retrospective. *Canadian Journal of Experimental Psychology, 57*(4), 274–289.

Cohen, G. (2000). *The creative age: Awakening human potential in the second half of life.* New York, NY: Avon Books.

Cohen, P. (2012, January 19). A sharper mind, middle age and beyond. *The New York Times, Educational Life.* Retrieved from www.nytimes.com/2012/01/22/education/edlife/a-sharper-mindmiddle-age-and-beyond.html?pagewanted=all

Craik, F. (2002). Human memory and aging. In L. Backman & C. von Hofsten (Eds.), *Psychology at the turn of the millennium, Volume 1: Cognitive, biological, and health perspectives* (pp. 261–280). Hove, UK: Psychology Press/Taylor & Francis (UK).

de Graaf, C., Polet, P., & van Staveren, W.A. (1994). Sensory perception and pleasantness of food flavors in elderly subjects. *Journals of Gerontology: Psychological Sciences, 49,* P93–99.

De Vadder, F., & Mithieux, G. (2015). Glucose homeostasis and gut-brain connection [Article in French]. *Médecine Sciences, 31*(2), 168–173. doi:10.1051/medsci/20153102013

Deal, J.A., Betz, J., Yaffe, K., Harris, T., Purchase-Helzner, E., Satterfield, S., . . . Health ABC Study Group. (2016). Hearing impairment and incident dementia and cognitive decline in older adults: The Health ABC Study. *The Journals of Gerontology. Series A, Biological Sciences and Medical Sciences,* (Apr 12), pii: glw069. [Epub ahead of print]

Decaria, J.E., Sharp, C., & Petrella, R.J. (2012). Scoping review report: Obesity in older adults. *International Journal of Obesity, 36*(9). doi:10.1038/ijo.2012.29

Delprado, J., Kinsella, G., Ong, B., & Pike, K. (2013). Naturalistic measures of prospective memory in amnestic mild cognitive impairment. *Psychology and Aging, 28*(2), 322–332. doi:10.1037/a0029785

Diamond, J. (2011). *Alzheimer's disease: What's it all about? Where do we stand in the search for a cure?* Retrieved from http://www.alzheimer.ca/en/Research/~/media/Files/national/Research/Research_Lay_Report_2011_e.ashx

Dixon, R.A., Rust, T.B., Feltmate, S.E., & Kwong See, S. (2007). Memory and aging: Selected research directions and application issues. *Canadian Psychology, 48*(2), 67–76. doi:10.1037/cp2007008

Do, M.T., Chang, V.C., Kuran, N., & Thompson, W. (2015). Fall-related injuries among Canadian seniors, 2005–2013: An analysis of the Canadian Community Health Survey. *Health Promotion and Chronic Disease Prevention in Canada, 35*(7), 99–108.

Doty, R.L., Shaman, P., Appelbaum, S.L., Bigerson, R., Sikorski, L., & Rosenberg, L. (1984). Smell identification ability: Changes with age. *Science, 226,* 1441–1443.

Edwards, J.D., Ruva, C.L., O'Brien, J.L., Haley, C.B., & Lister, J.J. (2013). An examination of mediators of the transfer of cognitive speed of processing training to everyday functional performance. *Psychology and Aging, 28*(2), 314–321. doi:10.1037/a0030474

Elias-Sonnenschein, L.S., Bertram, L., & Visser, P.J. (2012). Relationship between genetic risk factors and markers for Alzheimer's disease pathology. *Biomarkers in Medicine, 6*(4), 477–495. doi:10.2217/bmm.12.56

Erickson, K.I., & Liu-Ambrose, T. (2016). Exercise, cognition, and health. In K.W. Schaie, & S.L. Willis (Eds.), *Handbook of the psychology of aging* (8th ed., pp. 187–201). London, UK: Elsevier Inc.

Farfel, J.M., Nitrini, R., Suemoto, C.K., Grinberg, L.T., Ferretti, R.E., Leite, R.E., . . . Brazilian Aging Brain Study Group. (2013). Very low levels of education and cognitive reserve: A clinicopathologic study. *Neurology, 81*(7), 650–657. doi:10.1212/WNL.0b013e3182a08f1b

Federal Interagency Forum on Aging-Related Statistics (FIFARS). (2012). *Older Americans 2010: Key indicators of well-being.* Washington, DC: Author. Retrieved from http://www.agingstats.gov/agingstatsdotnet/main_site/default.aspx

Finlayson, M.L., & Peterson, E.W. (2010). Falls, aging, and disability. *Physical Medicine and Rehabilitation Clinics of North America, 21*(2), 357–373. doi:10.1016/j.pmr.2009.12.003

Flores, E.K. (2012). Falls risk assessment and modification. *Home Healthcare Management & Practice, 24*(4), 198–204.

Fozard, J.L. (1990). Vision and hearing in aging. In J.E. Birren & K.W. Schaie (Eds.), *Handbook of the psychology of aging* (3rd ed., pp. 150–171). San Diego, CA: Academic Press.

Fraga, M.F. (2009). Genetic and epigenetic regulation of aging. *Current Opinion in Immunology, 21*(4), 446–453.

Gallagher-Thompson, D., Tazeau, Y., & Basilio L. (1997). The relationships of dimensions of acculturation to self-reported depression in older Mexican-American women. *Journal of Clinical Geropsychology, 3,* 123–137.

Gavrilov, L.A., & Gavrilova, N.S. (2011). Mortality measurement at advanced ages: A study of the social security administration death master file. *North American Actuarial Journal, 15*(3), 432–447. Retrieved from http://www.ncbi.nlm.nih.gov/pmc/articles/PMC3269912/pdf/nihms329478.pdf

Gavrilova, N.S., & Gavrilov, L.A. (2009). Genetic influences, later in life. In D.S. Carr (Ed.), *Encyclopedia of the Life course and human development* (Vol. 3., pp. 165–170). Detroit, MI: Macmillan Reference USA.

Gilmour, H., & Park, J. (2006). Dependency, chronic conditions and pain in seniors (Catalogue No. 82-003). *Health Reports, 16*(Supplement), 21–31.

Goldsmith, T.C. (2011). *Aging by design: How new thinking on aging will change your life*. Crownsville, MD: Azinet Press.

Govindaraju, D.R. (2015). Evolutionary genetic bases of longevity and senescence. *Advances in Experimental Medicine and Biology, 847*(Apr), 1–44. doi:10.1007/978-1-4939-2404-2_1

Greider, C.W. & Blackburn, E.H. (1985). Identification of a specific telomere terminal transferase activity in tetrahymena extracts. *Cell, 43*(2 Pt. 1), 405–413.

Guo, Z., Liu, X., Hou, H., Wei, F., Liu, J., & Chen, X. (2016). Abnormal degree centrality in Alzheimer's disease patients with depression: A resting-state functional magnetic resonance imaging study. *Experimental Gerontology, 79*(June), 61–66. doi:10.1016/j.exger.2016.03.017

Hagovská, M., Takáč, P., & Dzvoník, O. (2016). Effect of a combining cognitive and balanced training on the cognitive, postural and functional status of seniors with a mild cognitive deficit in a randomized, controlled trial. *European Journal of Physical and Rehabilitation Medicine, 52*(1), 101–109.

Havens, B., & Finlayson, M. (1999). *Analysis of Canada's oldest old: From the survey of ageing and independence*. Ottawa, ON: Health Canada. Retrieved from www.hc-sc.gc.ca/seniors-aines/pubs/havens/index_e.htm

Hayflick, L. (1977). The cellular basis for biological aging. In C.E. Finch & L. Hayflick (Eds.), *Handbook of the biology of aging* (pp. 159–186). New York, NY: Van Nostrand Reinhold.

Hayflick, L. (1987). Origins of longevity. In H.R. Warner, R.N. Butler, R.L. Sprott, & E.L. Schneider (Eds.), *Aging: Vol. 31. Modern biological theories of aging* (pp. 21–34). New York, NY: Raven Press.

Hayflick, L. (2000). The illusion of immortality. *British Journal of Cancer, 83*(7), 841–846. doi:10.1054/bjoc.2000.1296

Hayflick, L. (2007). Biological aging is no longer an unsolved problem. *Annals of the New York Academy of Sciences, 1100*, 1–13. doi:10.1196/annals.1395.001

Hayflick, L., & Moorhead, P.S. (1961). The serial cultivation of human diploid cell strains. *Experimental Cell Research 25*(3), 585–621. doi:10.1016/0014-4827(61)90192-6

Health Canada. (2011). *Eating well with Canada's food guide*. Retrieved from http://www.hc-sc.gc.ca/fn-an/food-guide-aliment/order-commander/index-eng.php

Health Canada. (2012b). *Canadian guidelines for body weight classification in adults*. Retrieved from http://www.hc-sc.gc.ca/fn-an/alt_formats/hpfb-dgpsa/pdf/nutrition/weight_book-livres_des_poids-eng.pdf

Heerema, E. (2016). *Benefits of interacting with young children for people with dementia: How intergenerational care benefits young children and adults*. Retrieved from https://www.verywell.com/therapeutic-benefits-children-dementia-98690

Henry, J.D., MacLeod, M.S., Phillips, L.H., & Crawford, J.R. (2004). A meta-analytic review of prospective memory and aging. *Psychology & Aging, 19*(1), 27–39. doi:10.1037/0882-7974.19.1.27. 27

Herring, M.P., Puetz, T.W., O'Connor, P.J., & Dishman, R.K. (2012). Effect of exercise training on depressive symptoms among patients with a chronic illness: A systematic review and meta-analysis of randomized controlled trials. *Archives of Internal Medicine, 172*(2), 101–111. doi:10.1001/archinternmed.2011.696

Hester, R., Kinsella, G., & Ong, B. (2004). Effect of age on forward and backward span tasks. *Journal of the International Neuropsychological Society, 10*, 475–481.

Hillen, T., Davies, S., Rudd, A., Kieselbach, T., & Wolfe, C. (2003). Self ratings of health predict functional outcome and recurrence free survival after stroke. *Journal of Epidemiology & Community Health, 57*, 960–966.

Hirsch, C.H., Diehr, P., Newman, A.B., Gerrior, S.A., Pratt, C., Lebowitz, M.D., & Jackson, S.A. (2010). Physical activity and years of healthy life in older adults: Results from the cardiovascular health study. *Journal of Aging and Physical Activity, 18*(3), 313–334.

Hjelmborg, J., Iachine, I., Skytthe, A., Vaupel, J.W., McGue, M., Koskenvuo, M., . . . Christensen, K. (2006). Genetic influence on human lifespan and longevity. *Human Genetics, 119*(3), 312–321. doi:10.1007/s00439-006-0144-y

Horswill, M.S., Sullivan, K., Luri-Beck, J.K., & Smith, S. (2013). How realistic are older drivers' ratings of their driving ability? *Accident Analysis and Prevention, 50*(Jan), 130–137. doi:10.1016/j.aap.2012.04.001

Hunsley, J., Elliot, K., & Therrien, Z. (2013). *The efficacy and effectiveness of psychological treatments*. Ottawa, ON: Canadian Psychological Association. Retrieved from http://www.cpa.ca/docs/File/Practice/TheEfficacyAndEffectivenessOfPsychologicalTreatments_web.pdf

Jedrziewski, M.K., Ewbank, D.C., Wang, H., & Trojanowski, J.Q. (2010). Exercise and cognition: Results from the National Long Term Care Survey. *Alzheimer's & Dementia: The Journal of the Alzheimer's Association, 6*(6), 448–455. doi:10.1016/j.jalz.2010.02.004

Jedrziewski, M.K., Ewbank, D.C., Wang, H., & Trojanowski, J.Q. (2014). The impact of exercise, cognitive activities, and socialization on cognitive function: Results from the National Long-Term Care Survey. *American Journal of Alzheimer's Disease and Other Dementias, 29*(4), 372–378. doi:10.1177/1533317513518646

Jin, K. (2010). Modern biological theories of aging. *Aging and Disease, 1*(2), 72–74.

Johnson, J.M., Minson, C.T., & Kellogg, D.L. (2014). Cutaneous vasodilator and vasoconstrictor mechanisms in temperature regulation. *Comprehensive Physiology, 4*(1), 33–89. doi:10.1002/cphy.c130015

Jung, Y., & Brack, A.S. (2014). Cellular mechanisms of somatic stem cell aging. *Current Topics in Developmental Biology, 107*, 405–438. doi:10.1016/B978-0-12-416022-4.00014-7

Kahn, A., & Fraga, M.F. (2009). Epigenetics and aging: Status, challenges, and needs for the future. *Journals of Gerontology. Series A, Biological Sciences and Medical Sciences, 64*(2), 195–198. doi:10.1093/gerona/gln064

Kannayiram, A. (2012). *Vascular dementia*. Retrieved from http://emedicine.medscape.com/article/292105-overview

Kasen, S., Wickramaratne, P., Gameroff, M.J., & Weissman, M.M. (2012). Religiosity and resilience in persons at high risk for major depression. *Psychological Medicine, 42*(3), 509–519. doi: http://dx.doi.org/10.1017/S0033291711001516

Kenyon, C.J. (2010). The genetics of ageing. *Nature, 464*(7288), 504–512. doi:10.1038/nature08980

Kingma, B.R.M., Frijns, A.J.H., Saris, W.H.M., van Steenhoven, A.A., & van Marken Lichtenbelt, W.D. (2010). Cold-induced vasoconstriction at forearm and hand skin sites: The effect of age. *European Journal of Applied Physiology, 109*(5), 915–921. doi.org/10.1007/s00421-010-1414-x

Kirkland, S.A., Griffith, L.E., Menec, V., Wister, A., Payette, H., Wolfson, C., & Raina, P.S. (2015). Mining a unique Canadian resource: The Canadian Longitudinal Study on Aging. *Canadian Journal on Aging, 34*(3), 366–377. doi:10.1017/S071498081500029X

Kirk-Sanchez, N.J., & McGough, E.L. (2014). Physical exercise and cognitive performance in the elderly: Current perspectives. *Clinical Interventions in Aging, 9*, 51–62. doi:10.2147/CIA.S39506

Kliegl, R., Smith, J., & Baltes, P.B. (1990). On the locus and process of magnification of age differences during mnemonic training. *Developmental Psychology, 26*, 894–904.

Kline, D.W., & Scialfa, C.T. (1996). Visual and auditory aging. In J.E. Birren & K.W. Schaie (Eds.), *Handbook of the psychology of aging* (4th ed., pp. 181–203). San Diego, CA: Academic Press.

Kmieć, Z., Pétervári, E., Balaskó, M., & Székely, M. (2013). Anorexia of aging. *Vitamins and Hormones, 92*, 319–355. doi:10.1016/B978-0-12-410473-0.00013-1

Kocsis, J. (1998). Geriatric dysthymia. *Journal of Clinical Psychiatry, 59*, 13–15.

Koliada, A.K., Krasnenkov, D.S., & Vaiserman, A.M. (2015). Telomeric aging: Mitotic clock or stress indicator? *Frontiers in Genetics*, 6(Mar), 82. doi:10.3389/fgene.2015.00082

Kramer, J.H., Mungas, D., Reed, B.R., Wetzel, M.E., Burnett, M.M., Miller, B.L., . . . Chui, H.C. (2007). Longitudinal MRI and cognitive change in healthy elderly. *Neuropsychology*, 21(4), 412–418.

Krampe, R. (2002). Aging, expertise and fine motor movement. *Neuroscience & Biobehavioral Reviews*, 26(7), 769–776.

Lee, D.M., Nazroo, J., O'Connor, D.B., Blake, M., & Pendleton, N. (2016). Sexual health and well-being among older men and women in England: Findings from the English Longitudinal Study of Ageing. *Archives of Sexual Behavior*, 45(1), 133–144. doi:10.1007/s10508-014-0465-1

Li, Y., Daniel, M., & Tollefsbol, T.O. (2012). Epigenetic regulation of caloric restriction in aging. *BMC Medicine*, 9, 98. doi:10.1186/1741-7015-9-98

Lindau, S., Schumm, P., Laumann, E., Levinson, W., Muircheartaigh, C., & Waite, L. (2007). A study of sexuality and health among older adults in the United States. *New England Journal of Medicine*, 357, 762–774. doi:10.1056/NEJMoa067423

Lindo, G., & Nordholm, L. (1999). Adaptation strategies, well-being, and activities of daily living among people with low vision. *Journal of Visual Impairment & Blindness*, 93, 434–446.

Lindsay, J., Sykes, E., McDowell, I., Verreault, R., & Laurin, D. (2004). More than the epidemiology of Alzheimer's disease: Contributions of the Canadian study of health and aging. *Canadian Journal of Psychiatry*, 49(2), 83–91.

Liu, J., Cao, L., & Finkel, T. (2011). Oxidants, metabolism, and stem cell biology. *Free radical Biology & Medicine*, 51(12), 2158–2162. doi:http://dx.doi.org/10.1016/j.freeradbiomed.2011.10.434

Liu, W., Galik, E., Boltz, M., Nahm, E.S., & Resnick, B. (2015). Optimizing eating performance for older adults with dementia living in long-term care: A systematic review. *Worldviews on Evidence-based Nursing*, 12(4), 228–235. doi:10.1111/wvn.12100

Liu, W., Galik, E., Boltz, M., Nahm, E.S., Lerner, N., & Resnick, B. (2016). Factors associated with eating performance for long-term care residents with moderate-to-severe cognitive impairment. *Journal of Advanced Nursing*, 72(2), 348–360. doi:10.1111/jan.12846

Lowenstein, D., Acevedo, A., Czaja, S., & Duara, R. (2004). Cognitive rehabilitation of mildly impaired Alzheimer disease patients on cholinesterase inhibitors. *American Journal of Geriatric Psychiatry*, 12, 395–402.

Maglione, J.E., & Ancoli-Israel, S. (2012). Sleep disorders in the elderly. In C.M. Morin, & C.A. Espie (Eds.), *The Oxford handbook of sleep and sleep disorders* (pp. 769–786). New York, NY: Oxford University Press.

Malchiodi, C.A. (2012). Creativity and aging: An art therapy perspective. In C.A. Malchiodi (Ed.), *Handbook of art therapy* (2nd ed., pp. 275–287). New York, NY: Guilford Press.

Manini, T.M., Everhart, J.E., Patel, K.V., Schoeller, D.A., Colbert, L.H., Visser, M., . . . Harris, T.B. (2006). Daily activity energy expenditure and mortality among older adults. *Journal of the American Medical Association*, 296(2), 171–179. doi:10.1001/jama.296.2.171

Market Wire. (2003). *Research from Quality Planning Corporation shows elderly drivers involved in more accidents, fewer violations than younger drivers*. Retrieved from http://findarticles.com/p/articles

Marques, P., Moreira, P., Magalhães, R., Costa, P., Santos, N., Zihl, J., . . . Sousa, N. (2016). The functional connectome of cognitive reserve. *Human Brain Mapping*, (May 4). doi:10.1002/hbm.23242 [Epub ahead of print]

Marques, P., Soares, J.M., Magalhães, R., Santos, N.C., & Sousa, N. (2015). The bounds of education in the human brain connectome. *Scientific Reports*, 5(12812). doi:10.1038/srep12812

Mast, B., Azar, A., MacNeill, S., & Lichtenberg, P. (2004). Depression and activities of daily living predict rehospitalization within 6 months of discharge from geriatric rehabilitation. *Rehabilitation Psychology*, 49, 219–223.

McCormack, A., Edmondson-Jones, M., Somerset, S., & Hall, D. (2016). A systematic review of the reporting of tinnitus prevalence and severity. *Hearing Research*, 337(July), 70–79. doi:10.1016/j.heares.2016.05.009

McCurry, S.M., Pike, K.C., Logsdon, R.G., Vitiello, M.V., Larson, E.B., & Teri, L. (2010). Predictors of short- and long-term adherence to a daily walking program in persons with Alzheimer's disease. *American Journal of Alzheimer's Disease and Other Dementias*, 25(6), 505–512. doi:10.1177/1533317510376173

McGregor, M.J., & Ronald, L.A. (2011). Residential care for long-term care for Canadian seniors: Nonprofit, for-profit or does it matter? *Institute for Research on Public Policy*, (no. 14, Jan), 1–50. Retrieved from http://archive.irpp.org/pubs/IRPPstudy/2011/IRPP_Study_no1.pdf.

McLaughlin, T., Feldman, H., Fillit, H., Sano, M., Schmitt, F., Aisen, P., . . . Stern, Y. (2010). Dependence as a unifying construct in defining Alzheimer's disease severity. *Alzheimer's & Dementia: The Journal of the Alzheimer's Association*, 6(6), 482–493. doi:10.1016/j.jalz.2009.09.004.

Menna, L.F., Fontanella, M., Santaniello, A., Ammendola, E., Travaglino, M., Mugnai, F., . . . Fioretti, A. (2012). Evaluation of social relationships in elderly by animal-assisted activity. *International Psychogeriatrics*, 24(6), 1019–1020. doi:10.1017/S1041610211002742

Miech, R., & Shanahan, M. (2000). Socioeconomic status and depression over the life course. *Journal of Health & Social Behavior*, 41, 162–176.

Millar, W.J. (2004). Vision problems among seniors (Catalogue No. 82-003). *Health Reports*, 16(1), 45–49.

Miller, L., Wickramaratne, P., Gameroff, M.J., Sage, M., Tenke, C.E., & Weissman, M.M. (2012). Religiosity and major depression in adults at high risk: A ten-year prospective study. *The American Journal of Psychiatry*, 169(1), 89–94. doi:10.1176/appi.ajp.2011.10121823

Mooney, L., Knox, D., & Schacht, C. (2013). *Understanding social problems* (8th ed.). Belmont, CA: Wadsworth.

Morgan, C., Covington, J., Geisler, M., Polich, J., & Murphy, C. (1997). Olfactory event-related potentials: Older males demonstrate the greatest deficits. *Electroencephalography & Clinical Neurophysiology*, 104, 351–358.

Morita, K., & Kobayashi, M. (2013). Interactive programs with preschool children bring smiles and conversation to older adults: Time-sampling study. *BMC Geriatrics*, 13, 111. doi.org/10.1186/1471-2318-13-111

Mudar, R.A., & Husain, F.T. (2016). Neural alterations in acquired age-related hearing loss. *Frontiers in Psychology*, 7, 828. http://doi.org/10.3389/fpsyg.2016.00828

National Institute on Aging. (2000) *Depression: A serious but treatable illness* [Online "Age Page"]. Retrieved from www.nih.gov/nia

National Seniors Council. (2014). *Report on the social isolation of seniors* (Cat. no. Em12-6/2014E-PDF). Ottawa, ON: Government of Canada.

Navaneelan, T. (2012). *Suicide rates: An overview* (Cat. no. 82-624-X). Retrieved from http://www.statcan.gc.ca/pub/82-624-x/2012001/article/11696-eng.htm

Negrila-Mezei, A., Enache, R., & Sarafoleanu, C. (2011). Tinnitus in elderly population: Clinic correlations and impact upon QoL. *Journal of Medicine and Life*, 4(4), 412–416.

Nichols, D., & Melov, S. (2004). The aging cell. *Aging*, 3, 1474–1497.

Norwood, T.H., Smith, J.R., & Stein, G.H. (1990). Aging at the cellular level: The human fibroblast-like cell model. In E.R. Schneider & J.W. Rowe (Eds.), *Handbook of the biology of aging* (3rd ed., pp. 131–154). San Diego, CA: Academic Press.

Nusselder, W.J., Franco, O.H., Peeters, A., & Mackenbach, J.P. (2009). Living healthier for longer: Comparative effects of three heart-healthy behaviors on life expectancy with and without cardiovascular disease. *BMC Public Health*, 9, 487. doi:10.1186/1471-2458-9-487

Oh, J., Lee, Y.D., & Wagers, A.J. (2014). Stem cell aging: Mechanisms, regulators and therapeutic opportunities. *Nature Medicine, 20*(8), 870–880. doi.org/10.1038/nm.3651

Olin, J., & Zelinski, E. (1997). Age differences in calibration of comprehension. *Educational Gerontology, 23,* 67–77.

Olovnikov, A.M. (1971). "Принцип маргинотомии в матричном синтезе полинуклеотидов [Principle of marginotomy in template synthesis of polynucleotides]. *Doklady Akademii nauk SSSR, 201*(6), 1496–1499.

Olovnikov, A.M. (1996). Telomeres, telomerase and aging: Origin of the theory. *Experimental Gerontology, 31*(4), 443–448.

Østbye, T., Kristjansson, B., Hill, G., Newman, S.C., Brouwer, R.N., & McDowell, I. (2005). Prevalence and predictors of depression in elderly Canadians: The Canadian study of health and aging. *Chronic Diseases in Canada, 26*(4), 93–99. Retrieved from http://www.phac-aspc.gc.ca/publicat/cdic-mcbc/pdf/cdic264e.pdf

Patten, S.B., Wang, J.L., Williams, J.V., Currie, S., Beck, C.A., Maxwell, C.J., & El-Guebaly, N. (2006). Descriptive epidemiology of major depression in Canada. *Canadian Journal of Psychiatry, 51*(2), 84–90. Retrieved from https://ww1.cpa-apc.org/Publications/Archives/CJP/2006/february/cjp-feb-06-patten-OR.pdf

Patten, S.B., Wang, J.L., Williams, J.V., Lavorato, D.H., Khaled, S.M., & Bulloch, A.G. (2010). Predictors of the longitudinal course of major depression in a Canadian population sample. *Canadian Journal of Psychiatry, 55*(10), 669–676. Retrieved from http://publications.cpa-apc.org/media.php?mid=1052

Peigneux, P., & van der Linden, M. (1999). Influence of ageing and educational level on the prevalence of body-part-as-objects in normal subjects. *Journal of Clinical & Experimental Neuropsychology, 21,* 547–552.

Pitkala, K.H. (2016). Loneliness in nursing homes. *Journal of the American Medical Directors Association,* May 20. pii: S1525-8610(16)30092-5. doi:10.1016/j.jamda.2016.04.007. [Epub ahead of print]

Plomin, R., & McClearn, G.E. (1990). Human behavioral genetics of aging. In J.E. Birren & K.W. Schaie (Eds.), *Handbook of the psychology of aging* (3rd ed., pp. 67–79). San Diego, CA: Academic Press.

Pollina, E.A., & Brunet, A. (2011). Epigenetic regulation of aging stem cells. *Oncogene, 30*(28), 3105–3126. doi:10.1038/onc.2011.45

Public Health Agency of Canada. (2010d). *Annual Report on the State of Public Health in Canada, 2010. Growing Older – Adding Life to Years* (Chapter 3: The Health and Well-being of Canadian Seniors). Retrieved from http://www.phac-aspc.gc.ca/cphorsphcresp-cacsp/2010/fr-rc/pdf/cpho_report_2010_e.pdf

Public Health Agency of Canada. (2012d). *Health-adjusted life expectancy in Canada: 2012.* Retrieved from http://www.phac-aspc.gc.ca/cd-mc/index-eng.php

Public Health Agency of Canada. (2012f). *Physical activity tips for older adults (65 years and older).* Retrieved from http://www.phac-aspc.gc.ca/hp-ps/hl-mvs/pa-ap/assets/pdfs/08paap-eng.pdf

Public Health Agency of Canada. (2014a). *Seniors' falls in Canada second report.* Retrieved from http://www.phac-aspc.gc.ca/seniors-aines/publications/public/injury-blessure/seniors_falls-chutes_aines/index-eng.php

Public Health Agency of Canada. (2016b). *If you fall or witness a fall, do you know what to do?* Retrieved from http://www.phac-aspc.gc.ca/seniors-aines/publications/public/injury-blessure/falls-chutes/index-eng.php

Ramage-Morin, P.L. (2006). Successful aging in health care institutions (Statistics Canada, Catalogue 82-003). *Health Reports, 19*(1), 37–52.

Ramage-Morin, P.L., Shields, M., & Martel, L. (2010). Health-promoting factors and good health among Canadians in mid-to-late life (82-003-X). *Health Reports, 21*(3), 1–9.

Rattan, S.I. (2006). Theories of biological aging: Genes, proteins, and free radicals. *Free Radical Research, 40*(12), 1230–1238.

Reiman, E. E., Webster, J., Myers, A., Hardy, J., Dunckley, T., Zismann, V., . . . Stephan, D. (2007). *GAB2* alleles modify Alzheimer's risk in *ApoE* 4 carriers. *Neuron, 54,* 713–720.

Reimers, C.D., Knapp, G., & Reimers, A.K. (2012). Does physical activity increase life expectancy? A review of the literature. *Journal of Aging Research, 2012,* 1–9. doi:10.1155/2012/243958

Rendell, P., & Thomson, D. (1999). Aging and prospective memory: Differences between naturalistic and laboratory tasks. *Journals of Gerontology, 54B,* P256–P269.

Rodríguez-Rodero, S., Fernández-Morera, J.L., Menéndez-Torre, E., Calvanese, V., Fernández, A.F., & Fraga. M.F. (2011). Aging genetics and aging. *Aging and Disease, 2*(3), 186–195.

Roland, P.S., & Kutz, J.W. (2015). *Inner ear, presbycusis.* Retrieved from http://emedicine.medscape.com/article/855989-overview

Ronald, L.A., McGregor, M.J., Harrington, C., Pollock, A., & Lexchin, J. (2016) observational evidence of for-profit delivery and inferior nursing home care: When is there enough evidence for policy change? *PLoS Med, 13*(4), e1001995. doi:10.1371/journal.pmed.1001995

Sakurai, R., Yasunaga, M., Murayama, Y., Ohba, H., Nonaka, K., Suzuki, H., . . . Fujiwara, Y. (2016). Long-term effects of an intergenerational program on functional capacity in older adults: Results from a seven-year follow-up of the REPRINTS study. *Archives of Gerontology and Geriatrics, 64*(May–Jun), 13–20. doi:10.1016/j.archger.2015.12.005

Salthouse, T. (2004). What and when of cognitive aging. *Current Directions in Psychological Science, 13,* 140–144.

Salthouse, T.A. (2011). What cognitive abilities are involved in trail-making performance? *Intelligence, 39*(4), 222–232. doi:10.1016/j.intell.2011.03.001

Schaie, K.W., & Willis, S.L. (2005). *Mind alert: Intellectual functioning in adulthood: Growth, maintenance, decline, and modifiability.* Lecture presented at the Joint Conference of the American Society on Aging and the National Council on Aging as part of the Mind-Alert Program. Retrieved from http://geron.psu.edu/sls/publications/MindAlert.pdf

Schieber, F. (1992). Aging and the senses. In J.E. Birren, R.B. Sloane, & G.D. Cohen (Eds.), *Handbook of mental health and aging* (2nd ed., pp. 252–306). San Diego, CA: Academic Press.

Schlee, W., Kleinjung, T., Hiller, W., Goebel, G., Kolassa, I.T., & Langguth, B. (2011). Does tinnitus distress depend on age of onset? *PLoS ONE, 6*(11), e27379. doi.org/10.1371/journal.pone.0027379

Schultz, M.B., & Sinclair, D.A. (2016). When stem cells grow old: Phenotypes and mechanisms of stem cell aging. *Development, 143*(1), 3–14. doi:10.1242/dev.130633

Scott, V., Wagar, L., & Elliott, S. (2010). *Falls and related injuries among older Canadians: Fall related hospitalizations and prevention initiatives.* Retrieved from http://www.hiphealth.ca/media/research_cem-fia_phac_epi_and_inventor_20100610.pdf

Shahar, D.R, Yu, B., Houston, D.K., Kritchevsky, S.B., Lee, J.S., Rubin, S.M., . . . Harris, T.B. (2009). Dietary factors in relation to daily activity energy expenditure and mortality among older adults. *Journal of Nutrition, Health, and Aging, 13*(5), 414–420.

Silverman, J., Ciresi, G., Smith, C., Marin, D., & Schnaider-Beeri, M. (2005). Variability of familial risk of Alzheimer's disease across the late life span. *Archives of General Psychiatry, 62,* 565–573.

Simpson, P., Horne, M., Brown, L. J., Dickinson, T., & Wilson, C. B. (2016). Sexuality and intimacy among care home residents. *Nursing times, 112*(10), 14–16.

Smith, J.A., & Daniel, R. (2012). Stem cells and aging: A chicken-or the-egg issue? *Aging and Disease, 3*(3), 260–268.

Somani, S., Hoskin-Mott, A., Mishra, A., Bois, A., Book, B.H., Chute, M., et al. (2009). Managing patients at risk for age-related macular degeneration: A Canadian strategy. *Canadian Journal of Optometry, 71* (2), 14–20.

Sowell, E.R., Peterson, B.S., Thompson, P.M., Welcome, S.E., Henkenius, A.L., & Toga, A.W. (2003). Mapping cortical change across the human life span. *Nature Neuroscience, 6*(3), 309–315.

Speechley, M. (2011). Unintentional falls in older adults: A methodological historical review. *Canadian Journal on Aging, 30*(1), 21–32. doi.org/10.1017/S0714980810000735

Statistics Canada (2012n). *The Canadian population in 2011: Age and sex* (Cat. no. 98-311-X2011001). Retrieved from http://www12.statcan.gc.ca/census-recensement/2011/as-sa/98-311-x/98-311-x2011001-eng.pdf

Statistics Canada (2012o). *Centenarians in Canada—age and sex, 2011 census* (Cat. no. 98-311-XWE2011003). Retrieved from http://www12.statcan.gc.ca/census-recensement/2011/assa/98-311-x/98-311-x2011003_1-eng.pdf

Statistics Canada (2012q). Chart 2—Percentage reporting very good or excellent health, by age group and sex, household population aged 12 or older, Canada, 2011 – description. Retrieved from http://www.statcan.gc.ca/pub/82-625-x/2012001/article/c-g/desc/11665-02-desc-eng.htm

Statistics Canada (2012r). Health indicator profile, annual estimates, by age group and sex, Canada, provinces, territories, health regions (2011 boundaries) and peer groups (CANSIM Table 105-0501). Retrieved from http://www5.statcan.gc.ca/cansim/pick-choisir?lang=eng&id=1050501&pattern=1050501&searchTypeByValue=1

Statistics Canada. (2001c). Deaths, 1998. *The Daily* (May 23). Ottawa, ON: Author. Retrieved from www.statcan.ca/Daily/English/010523/d010523e.htm

Statistics Canada. (2002b). *Risk of depression, by age group and sex, household population aged 12 and over, Canada, 2000/01* (Health indicators Cat. no. 82-221). Ottawa, ON: Author. Retrieved from www.statcan.ca/english/freepub/82-221-XIE/00604/tables/pdf/1295.pdf

Statistics Canada. (2012s). *Deaths and mortality rate, by selected grouped causes, age group and sex, Canada* (CANSIM Table 102-0551). Retrieved from http://www5.statcan.gc.ca/cansim/a26

Statistics Canada. (2015k). *Population aged 0 to 14 years and 65 years and over, 1995 to 2035, Canada* (Cat. no. 91-215-X). Retrieved from http://www.statcan.gc.ca/pub/91-215-x/2015000/longdesc-ct001-eng.htm

Statistics Canada. (2016k). *Elements of the life table, Canada, provinces and territories* (CANSI Table 053-0003). Retrieved from http://www5.statcan.gc.ca/cansim/a26?lang=eng&id=530003

Statistics Canada. (2016l). *Health indicator profile, annual estimates, by age group and sex, Canada, provinces, territories, health regions (2013 boundaries) and peer groups* (CANSIM Table 105-0501). Retrieved from http://www5.statcan.gc.ca/cansim/pick-choisir?lang=eng&id=1050501&pattern=1050501&searchTypeByValue=1

Steptoe, A., Jackson, S.E., & Wardle, J. (2016). Sexual activity and concerns in people with coronary heart disease from a population-based study. *Heart*, (Apr 28). doi:10.1136/heartjnl-2015-308993

Streiner, D.L., Cairney, J., & Veldhuizen, S. (2006). The epidemiology of psychological problems in the elderly. *Canadian Journal of Psychiatry*, 51(3), 185–191.

Stroebe, M.S., & Stroebe, W. (1993). The mortality of bereavement: A review. In M.S. Stroebe, W. Stroebe, & R.O. Hansson (Eds.), *Handbook of bereavement: Theory, research, and intervention* (pp. 175–195). Cambridge, England: Cambridge University Press.

Stuart-Hamilton, I. (2012, July 9). Does it matter or doesn't it? What importance do we place on measures of aging intelligence? [Web log post]. Retrieved from http://www.psychologytoday.com/blog/the-gift-aging/201207/does-it-matter-or-doesnt-it

Suryadevara, V., Storey, S., Aronow, W., & Ahn, C. (2003). Association of abnormal serum lipids in elderly persons with atherosclerotic vascular disease and dementia, atherosclerotic vascular disease without dementia, dementia without atherosclerotic vascular disease, and no dementia or atherosclerotic vascular disease. *Journals of Gerontology, Series A: Biological Sciences & Medical Sciences*, 58A, 859–861.

Tani, Y., Kondo, N., Takagi, D., Saito, M., Hikichi, H., Ojima, T., & Kondo, K. (2015). Combined effects of eating alone and living alone on unhealthy dietary behaviors, obesity and underweight in older Japanese adults: Results of the JAGES. *Appetite*, 95(Dec), 1–8. doi:10.1016/j.appet.2015.06.005

Tani, Y., Sasaki, Y., Haseda, M., Kondo, K., & Kondo, N. (2015). Eating alone and depression in older men and women by cohabitation status: The JAGES longitudinal survey. *Age and Ageing*, 44(6), 1019–1026. doi.org/10.1093/ageing/afv145

Tanuseputro, P., Chalifoux, M., Bennett, C., Gruneir, A., Bronskill, S.E., Walker, P., & Manuel, D. (2015). Hospitalization and mortality rates in long-term care facilities: Does for-profit status matter? *Journal of the American Medical Directors Association*, 16(10), 874–883. doi:10.1016/j.jamda.2015.06.004. pmid:26433862

Thomas, H.N., Hess, R., & Thurston, R.C. (2015). Correlates of sexual activity and satisfaction in midlife and older women. *Annals of Family Medicine*, 13(4), 336–342. doi.org/10.1370/afm.1820

Tice, R.R., & Setlow, R.B. (1985). DNA repair and replication in aging organisms and cells. In C.E. Finch & E.L. Schneider (Eds.), *Handbook of the biology of aging* (2nd ed., pp. 173–224). New York, NY: Van Nostrand Reinhold.

Tom, S.E., Hubbard, R.A., Crane, P.K., Haneuse, S.J., Bowen, J., McCormick, W.C., . . . Larson, E.B. (2015). Characterization of dementia and Alzheimer's disease in an older population: Updated incidence and life expectancy with and without dementia. *American Journal of Public Health*, 105(2), 408–413. doi.org/10.2105/AJPH.2014.301935

Tremblay, K.R., & Barber, C.E. (2013). *Preventing falls in the elderly*. Colorado State University Cooperative Extension. http://www.ext.colostate.edu/pubs/consumer/10242.html

Turcotte, M. & Schellenberg, G. (2007). *A portrait of seniors in Canada 2006* (89-519-XIE). Ottawa, ON: Statistics Canada. Retrieved from www.statcan.gc.ca/pub/89-519-x/89-519-x2006001-eng.pdf

Turner, G.R., & Spreng, R.N. (2012). Executive functions and neuro-cognitive aging: Dissociable patterns of brain activity. *Neurobiology of Aging*, 33(4), 826.e1–13. doi:10.1016/j.neurobiolaging.2011.06.005

Turner, G.R., & Spreng, R.N. (2015). Prefrontal engagement and reduced default network suppression co-occur and are dynamically coupled in older adults: The default-executive coupling hypothesis of aging. *Journal of Cognitive Neuroscience*, 27(12), 2462–2476. doi:10.1162/jocn_a_00869

Verhaegen, P. (2013). Cognitive aging. In D. Reisberg (Ed.), *The Oxford handbook of cognitive psychology*. (pp. 1014–1035). New York, NY: Oxford University Press.

Voelcker-Rehage, C. (2008) Motor-skill learning in older adults: A review of studies on age-related differences. *European Review of Aging and Physical Activity*, 5, 5–16. doi:10.1007/s11556-008-0030-9

Voelcker-Rehage, C., & Niemann, C. (2013). Structural and functional brain changes related to different types of physical activity across the life span. *Neuroscience and Biobehavioral Reviews*, 37 (9 Pt B), 2268–2295. doi:10.1016/j.neubiorev.2013.01.028

Volkert, D. (2013). Malnutrition in older adults – urgent need for action: A plea for improving the nutritional situation of older adults. *Gerontology*, 59(4), 328–333. doi:10.1159/000346142

Voss, M.W., Heo, S., Prakash, R.S., Erickson, K.I., Alves, H., Chaddock, L., . . . Kramer, A.F. (2013). The influence of aerobic fitness on cerebral white matter integrity and cognitive function in older adults: Results of a one-year exercise intervention. *Human Brain Mapping*, 34(11), 2972–2985. doi:10.1002/hbm.22119

West, R.L., & Crook, T.H. (1990). Age differences in everyday memory: Laboratory analogues of telephone number recall. *Psychology and Aging*, 5, 520–529.

Wiskerke, E., & Manthorpe, J. (2016). Intimacy between care home residents with dementia: Findings from a review of the literature. *Dementia*, (Jul 13). doi:10.1177/1471301216659771 [Epub ahead of print]

Wong, T.Y., Solis, M.A., Chen, Y.H., & Huang, L.L.H. (2015). Molecular mechanism of extrinsic factors affecting anti-aging of stem cells. *World Journal of Stem Cells*, 7(2), 512–520. http://doi.org/10.4252/wjsc.v7.i2.512

World Health Organization. (2011). *Mental health: Country reports and charts available*. Retrieved from: http://www.who.int/mental_health/prevention/suicide/country_reports/en/

Xiao, F.H., He, Y.H., Li, Q.G., Wu, H., Luo, L.H., & Kong, Q.P. (2015). A genome-wide scan reveals important roles of DNA methylation in human longevity by regulating age-related disease genes. *PLoS ONE, 10*(3), e0120388. doi:10.1371/journal.pone.0120388

Yasunaga, M., Murayama, Y., Takahashi, T., Ohba, H., Suzuki, H., Nonaka, K., . . . Fujiwara, Y. (2016). Multiple impacts of an intergenerational program in Japan: Evidence from the Research on Productivity through Intergenerational Sympathy Project. *Geriatrics & Gerontology International, 16*(Mar Suppl 1), 98–109. doi:10.1111/ggi.12770

Chapter 18

Abu-Bader, S.H., Rogers, A., & Barusch, A.S. (2002). Predictors of life satisfaction in frail elderly. *Journal of Gerontological Social Work, 38*(3), 3–17. doi:10.1300/J083v38n03_02

Akiyama, H., Antonucci, T., Takahashi, K., & Langfahl, E. (2003). Negative interactions in close relationships across the life span. *Journals of Gerontology, Series B: Psychological Sciences & Social Sciences, 58B*, P70–P79.

Anderson, J.R., Van Ryzin, M.J., & Doherty, W.J. (2010). Developmental trajectories of marital happiness in continuously married individuals: A group-based modeling approach. *Journal of Family Psychology, 24*(5), 587–596. doi:10.1037/a0020928

Antonucci, T., Lansford, J., & Akiyama, H. (2001). Impact of positive and negative aspects of marital relationships and friendships on well-being of older adults. *Applied Developmental Science, 5*, 68–75.

Atchley, R. (1989). A continuity theory of normal aging. *The Gerontologist, 29*, 183–190.

Baker, J., Meisner, B.A., Logan, A.J., Kungl, A.M., & Weir, P. (2009). Physical activity and successful aging in Canadian older adults. *Journal of Aging and Physical Activity, 17*(2), 223–235.

Barer, B. (2001). The "grands and greats" of very old black grandmothers. *Journal of Aging Studies, 15*, 1–11.

Bengtson, V., Rosenthal, C., & Burton, L. (1996). Paradoxes of families and aging. In R. H. Binstock & L. K. George (Eds.), *Handbook of aging and the social sciences* (4th ed., pp. 253–282). San Diego, CA: Academic Press.

Bibby, R.W. (2001). *Canada's teens: Today, yesterday and tomorrow.* Toronto, ON: Stoddart Publishing Co. Limited.

Bohn, A., & Berntsen, D. (2011). The reminiscence bump reconsidered: Children's prospective life stories show a bump in young adulthood. *Psychological Science, 22*(2), 197–202. doi:10.1177/0956797610395394

Bowling, A., Fleissig, A., Gabriel, Z., Banister, D., Dyjes, J., Dowding, L., . . . Sutton, S. (2003). Let's ask them: A national survey of definitions of quality of life and its enhancement among people aged 65 and over. *International Journal of Aging & Human Development, 56*, 269–306.

Brennon, S. (2012). *Victimization of older Canadians, 2009: Juristat article.* Retrieved from http://www.statcan.gc.ca/pub/85-002-x/2012001/article/11627-eng.pdf

Brown, R.L. (2011). Economic security in an aging Canadian population. *Canadian Journal on Aging, 30*(3), 391–399. doi:10.1353/cja.2011.0034

Butler, R. (1963). The life review: An interpretation of reminiscence in the aged. *Psychiatry: Interpersonal & Biological Processes, 26*, 65–76.

Butler, R. (2002). The life review. *Journal of Geriatric Psychiatry, 35*, 7–10.

Calero, M., & Navarro, E. (2007). Cognitive plasticity as a modulating variable on the effects of memory training in elderly persons. *Archives of Clinical Neuropsychology, 22*, 63–72.

Canadian Anti-Fraud Centre (2015). *Canadian anti-fraud centre annual statistical report 2014.* Retrieved from http://www.antifraudcentre-centreantifraude.ca/reports-rapports/2014/ann-ann-eng.htm

Carrière, Y., & Galaneau, D. (2011). Delayed retirement: A new trend (Cat. no. 75-001-X). *Perspectives on Labour and Income, 23*(4), 4–16. Retrieved from: http://www.statcan.gc.ca/pub/75-001-x/2011004/article/11578-eng.pdf

CBC News (2009, Aug 20). *Mandatory retirement fades in Canada.* Author. Retrieved from www.cbc.ca/canada/story/2009/08/20/mandatory-retirement-explainer523.html

Chappell, N. (1999). *Volunteering and healthy aging: What we know.* Retrieved from Volunteer Canada website: www.volunteer.ca/volunteer/canada_adults_report_printable.htm

Cheng, S.T. (2009b). Generativity in later life: Perceived respect from younger generations as a determinant of goal disengagement and psychological well-being. *The Journals of Gerontology Series B: Psychological Sciences and Social Sciences, 64B*(1), 45–54. http://doi.org/10.1093/geronb/gbn027

Choi, N. (2003). Nonmarried aging parents' and their adult children's characteristics associated with transitions into and out of intergenerational coresidence. *Journal of Gerontological Social Work, 40*, 7–29.

CIBC. (2012a). *CIBC poll: Canada's baby boomers not interested in a modest retirement.* Retrieved from: http://micro.newswire.ca/release.cgi?rkey=2009218096&view=14730-0&Start=&htm=0

CIBC. (2012b). *CIBC poll: Short on savings, Canada's 50-somethings plan to retire at age 63 - and keep working.* Retrieved from: http://micro.news-wire.ca/release.cgi?rkey=2008208163&view=14730-0&Start=&htm=0

Clark, W. (1998). Religious observance: Marriage and family (Cat. no. 11-008-XPE). *Canadian Social Trends, 50*, 2–7.

Clark, W. (2000). Patterns of religious attendance (Cat. no. 11-008-XPE). *Canadian Social Trends, 59*, 23–27.

Clark, W., & Schellenberg, G. (2006). Who's religious? *Canadian Social Trends* (11-008). Ottawa, ON: Statistics Canada. Retrieved from www.statcan.gc.ca/pub/11-008-x/2006001/pdf/9181-eng.pdf

Conference Board of Canada. (2012). *Canadian income inequality: Is Canada becoming more unequal?* Retrieved from http://www.conferenceboard.ca/hcp/hot-topics/caninequality.aspx

Connidis, I.A. (1989). *Family Ties Later in Life.* Toronto, ON, & Vancouver, BC: Butterworths.

Connidis, I.A. (1994). Sibling support in older age. *Journals of Gerontology: Social Sciences, 49*, S309–317.

Crawford-Achour, E., Castro-Lionard, K., Tardy, M., Trombert-Paviot, B., Barthélémy, J.C., & Gonthier, R. (2012). La promotion du bien vieillir et sa représentation par la personne âgée: quels axes de prévention privilégier ? [Successful aging: How to improve its occurrence in the elderly?] *Gériatrie et Psychologie Neuropsychiatrie du Vieillissement, 10*(2), 207–214. doi:10.1684/pnv.2012.0318

Cress, C. (2007). *Geriatric care management.* Sudbury, MA: Jones & Bartlett Learning.

Cumming, E. (1975). Engagement with an old theory. *International Journal of Aging and Human Development, 6*, 187–191.

Cumming, E., & Henry, W.E. (1961). *Growing old.* New York, NY: Basic Books.

Dickson, R.A., Pillemer, D.B., & Bruehl, E.C. (2011). The reminiscence bump for salient personal memories: Is a cultural life script required? *Memory & Cognition, 39*(6), 977–991. doi:10.3758/s13421-011-0082-3

Dillaway, H., & Byrnes, M. (2009). Reconsidering successful aging: A call for renewed and expanded academic critiques and conceptualizations. *Journal of Applied Gerontology, 28*, 702–722.

Doyle, P.J., Rubinstein, R.L., & de Medeiros, K. (2015). Generative acts of people with dementia in a long-term care setting. *Dementia, 14*(4), 409–417. doi:10.1177/1471301213498246

Draper, B., Gething, L., Fethney, J., & Winfield, S. (1999). The Senior Psychiatrist Survey III: Attitudes towards personal ageing, life experiences and psychiatric practice. *Australian & New Zealand Journal of Psychiatry, 33*, 717–722.

Duchesne, D. (2004). More seniors at work (Cat. no. 75-001). *Perspectives on Labour and Income, 5*(2). Retrieved from Statistics Canada website: www.statcan.ca/english/studies/75-001/10204/high-1.htm

EKOS. (2011). *Follow-up and final awareness and perceptions of elder abuse survey 2010.* Retrieved from http://www.ekos.com/admin/articles/09610.pdf

Ennis, G.E., Hess, T.M., & Smith, B.T. (2013). The impact of age and motivation on cognitive effort: Implications for cognitive engagement in older adulthood. *Psychology and Aging, 28*(2), 495–504. doi:10.1037/a0031255

Fiocco, A., & Yaffe, K. (2010). Defining successful aging: The importance of including cognitive function over time. *Archives of Neurology, 67,* 876–880.

Fisher, B., & Specht, D. (1999). Successful aging and creativity in later life. *Journal of Aging Studies, 13,* 457–472.

Flood, M. (2007). Exploring the relationship between creativity, depression, and successful aging. *Activities, Adaptation, & Aging, 31,* 55–71.

Foos, P., & Goolkasian, P. (2010) Age differences and format effects in working memory. *Experimental Aging Research, 36,* 273–286.

Foreign Affairs and International Trade (2008). *Retirement abroad: Seeing the sunsets.* Retrieved from http://publications.gc.ca/pub?id=80112&sl=0

Fouquereau, E., & Baudoin, C. (2002). The marital satisfaction questionnaire for older persons: Factor structure in a French sample. *Social Behavior & Personality, 30,* 95–104.

Frieswijk, N., Buunk, B., Steverink, N., & Slaets, J. (2004). The effect of social comparison information on the life satisfaction of frail older persons. *Psychology & Aging, 19,* 183–190.

Gaggioli, A., Morganti, L., Bonfiglio, S., Scaratti, C., Cipresso, P., Serino, S., & Riva, G. (2014b). Intergenerational group reminiscence: A potentially effective intervention to enhance elderly psychosocial wellbeing and to improve children's perception of aging. *Educational Gerontology, 40*(7), 486–498. doi:10.1080/03601277.2013.844042

Gaggioli, A., Scaratti, C., Morganti, L., Stramba-Badiale, M., Agostoni, M., Spatola, C. A., . . . Riva, G. (2014a). Effectiveness of group reminiscence for improving wellbeing of institutionalized elderly adults: Study protocol for a randomized controlled trial. *Trials, 15,* 408. http://doi.org/10.1186/1745-6215-15-408

Gana, K., Alaphilippe, D., & Bailly, N. (2004). Positive illusions and mental and physical health in later life. *Aging & Mental Health, 8,* 58–64.

Gerwood, J., LeBlanc, M., & Piazza, N. (1998). The Purpose-in-Life Test and religious denomination: Protestant and Catholic scores in an elderly population. *Journal of Clinical Psychology, 54,* 49–53.

Gillum, R.F., King, D.E., Obisesan, T.O., & Koenig, H.G. (2008). Frequency of attendance at religious services and mortality in a U.S. national cohort. *Annals of Epidemiology, 18*(2), 124–129. http://doi.org/10.1016/j.annepidem.2007.10.015

Globe and Mail. (n.d.). *How much money will I need when I retire?* Retrieved from http://www.theglobeandmail.com/globe-investor/investor-education/investor-education-fund/ief-retirement/howmuch-money-will-i-need-when-i-retire/article4203603/

Godbout, E., Filiatrault, J., & Plante, M. (2012). The participation of seniors in volunteer activities: a systematic review. *Canadian Journal of Occupational Therapy, 79*(1), 23–32.

Government of Alberta. (2010). *What works? Career-building strategies for people from diverse groups* (Older workers). Edmonton, AB: Alberta Employment and Immigration. Retrieved from http://alis.alberta.ca/pdf/cshop/whatworks/ww_older.pdf

Government of Canada. (2008). *Care facilities.* Ottawa, ON: Author. Retrieved from www.seniors.gc.ca/s.2.1rchcat@.jsp?lang=eng&cat=712

Government of Canada. (2015a). *Elder abuse: It's time to face the reality.* Retrieved from http://www.seniors.gc.ca/eng/pie/eaa/elderabuse.shtml

Government of Canada. (2015b). *Crime and abuse against seniors: A review of the research literature with special reference to the Canadian situation.* Retrieved from http://www.justice.gc.ca/eng/rp-pr/cj-jp/fv-vf/crim/sum-som.html

Greenfield, E., & Marks, N. (2007). Continuous participation in voluntary groups as a protective factor for the psychological wellbeing of adults who develop functional limitations: Evidence from the National Survey of Families and Households. *The Journals of Gerontology Series B: Psychological Sciences and Social Sciences, 62,* S60–S68.

Grossman, A.H., Daugelli, A.R., & Hershberger, S.L. (2000). Social support networks of lesbian, gay, and bisexual adults 60 years of age and older. *Journals of Gerontology, Series B: Psychological Sciences & Social Sciences, 55*(3), 171–179.

Guse, L., & Masesar, M. (1999). Quality of life and successful aging in long-term care: Perceptions of residents. *Issues in Mental Health Nursing, 20,* 527–539.

Hahn, C., Yang, M-S., Yang, M-J., Shih, C., & Lo, H. (2004). Religious attendance and depressive symptoms among community dwelling elderly in Taiwan. *International Journal of Geriatric Psychiatry, 19,* 1148–1154.

Hall, M., Havens, B., & Sylvestre, G. (2003). The experience of social isolation and loneliness in among older men in Manitoba. *Aging in Manitoba Study Dept of Community Health Sciences University of Manitoba report prepared for Veterans Affairs Canada.* Retrieved from http://www.veterans.gc.ca/pdf/about-us/research-directorate/social-isol-loneliness-vac-report.pdf

Halleröd, B., Örestig, J., & Stattin, M. (2013). Leaving the labour market: The impact of exit routes from employment to retirement on health and wellbeing in old age. *European Journal of Ageing, 10*(1), 25–35. doi:10.1007/s10433-012-0250-8

Hardy, M.A., & Quadagno, J. (1995). Satisfaction with early retirement: Making choices in the auto industry. *Journals of Gerontology: Social Sciences, 50B,* S217-228.

Havens, B., & Finlayson, M. (1999). *Analysis of Canada's oldest old: From the survey of ageing and independence.* Ottawa, ON: Health Canada. Retrieved from www.hc-sc.gc.ca/seniors-aines/pubs/havens/index_e.htm

Hayman, S. (2011). Older people in Canada: their victimization and fear of crime. *Canadian Journal on Aging, 30*(3), 423–436. doi:10.1017/S0714980811000225

Hayward, M.D., & Hardy, M.A. (1985). Early retirement processes among older men: Occupational differences. *Research on Aging, 7,* 491–518.

Hayward, M.D., Friedman, S., & Chen, H. (1996). Race inequities in men's retirement. *Journals of Gerontology: Social Sciences, 51B,* S1–10.

Health Canada. (2003b). *Canada's seniors: No. 19—Private retirement pensions largest source of income.* Ottawa, ON: Author, Division of Aging and Seniors. Retrieved from www.hc-sc.gc.ca/seniors-aines/pubs/factoids/2001/no19_e.htm

Health Canada. (2003c). *Canada's seniors: No. 13—Gender differences in income.* Ottawa, ON: Author, Division of Aging and Seniors. Retrieved from www.hc-sc.gc.ca/seniors-aines/pubs/factoids/2001/no13_e.htm

Heckhausen, J., & Brim, O. (1997). Perceived problems for self and others: Self-protection by social downgrading throughout adulthood. *Psychology & Aging, 12,* 610–619.

Herzog, A.R., House, J.S., & Morgan, J.N. (1991). Relation of work and retirement to health and well-being in older age. *Psychology and Aging, 6,* 202–211.

Holstein, M., & Minkler, M. (2003). Self, society, and the "new gerontology." *Gerontologist, 43,* 787–796.

Huang, C.Y., Hsu, M.C., & Chen, T.J. (2012). An exploratory study of religious involvement as a moderator between anxiety, depressive symptoms and quality of life outcomes of older adults. *Journal of Clinical Nursing, 21*(5–6), 609–619. doi:10.1111/j.1365-2702.2010.03412.x

Hudon, T., & Milan, A. (2016). Senior women. *Women in Canada: A gender-based statistical report* (Cat. no. 89-503-X). Ottawa, ON: Statistics Canada. Retrieved from http://www.statcan.gc.ca/pub/89-503-x/89-503-x2010001-eng.htm

Hughes, S., & Hayman, L. (2007). Cardiovascular risk reduction: The fountain of youth. *Journal of Cardiovascular Nursing, 22,* 84–85.

Human Resources and Skills Development Canada. (2011b). *HRSDC Consultations with Older Workers and Employers* (Cat. no.: HS4-109/2011E-PDF). Retrieved from: http://publications.gc.ca/collections/collection_2011/rhdcc-hrsdc/HS4-109-2011-eng.pdf

Hutchinson, S.L., & Nimrod, G. (2012). Leisure as a resource for successful aging by older adults with chronic health conditions.

International Journal of Aging & Human Development, 74(1), 41–65. doi:http://dx.doi.org/10.2190/AG.74.1.c

Huxhold, O., Fiori, K.L., & Windsor, T.D. (2013). The dynamic interplay of social network characteristics, subjective well-being, and health: The costs and benefits of socio-emotional selectivity. *Psychology and Aging*, 28(1), 3–16. doi:10.1037/a0030170

Ibrahim, D. (2016a). Section 5: Police-reported family violence against seniors. *Family violence in Canada: A statistical profile*, 2014 (Juristat Cat. no. 85-002-x). Ottawa, ON: Ministry of Industry. Retrieved from http://www.statcan.gc.ca/pub/85-002-x/2016001/article/14303-eng.htm

Ibrahim, D. (2016b). Section 3: Police-reported intimate partner violence. *Family violence in Canada: A statistical profile*, 2014 (Juristat Cat. no. 85-002-x). Ottawa, ON: Ministry of Industry. Retrieved from http://www.statcan.gc.ca/pub/85-002-x/2016001/article/14303-eng.htm

Idler, E., & Kasl, S. (1997). Religion among disabled and nondisabled persons II: Attendance at religious services as a predictor of the course of disability. *Journals of Gerontology: Series B: Psychological Sciences & Social Sciences*, 52B, S306–S316.

Idler, E.L., Boulifard, D.A., Labouvie, E., Chen, Y.Y., Krause, T.J., & Contrada, R.J. (2009). Looking inside the black box of "attendance at services": New measures for exploring an old dimension in religion and health research. *International Journal for the Psychology of Religion*, 19(1):1–20. doi:10.1080/10508610802471096

Idler, E.L., McLaughlin, J., Kasl, S. (2009). Religion and the quality of life in the last year of life. *Journal of Gerontology B: Psychological Sciences and Social Sciences* 64(4), 528–537. doi:10.1093/geronb/gbp028

Ito, Y. & Sagara, J. (2012). [Reliability and validity of marital love scale in middle-aged and elderly couples]. *Shinrigaku Kenkyu*, 83(3). 211–6.

Iwashyna, T., & Christakis, N. (2003). Marriage, widowhood, and health-care use. *Social Science & Medicine*, 57, 2137–2147.

Kamp Dush, C.M., & Taylor, M.G. (2012). Trajectories of martial conflict across the life course: Predictors and interactions with marital happiness trajectories. *Journal of Family Issues*, 33(3), 341–386. doi:10.1177/0192513X11409684

Ko, H., Mehta, K.K., & Meng, K.S. (2006). *Understanding and counselling older persons: A handbook*. Singapore: Sage Counselling Centre.

Koenig, H.G. (2009). Research on religion, spirituality, and mental health: A review. *Canadian Journal of Psychiatry*, 54(5), 283–291.

Koenig, H.G. (2012). Religion, spirituality, and health: The research and clinical implications. *ISRN Psychiatry*, 2012 (Article ID 278730), 33. doi:10.5402/2012/278730

Korte, J., Westerhof, G.J., & Bohlmeijer, E.T. (2012). Mediating processes in an effective life-review intervention. *Psychology and Aging*, 27(4), 1172–1181. doi:10.1037/a0029273

Krause, N., Ingersoll-Dayton, B., Liang, J., & Sugisawa, H. (1999). Religion, social support, and health among the Japanese elderly. *Journal of Health Behavior & Health Education*, 40, 405–421.

la Cour, P., Avlund, K., & Schultz-Larsen, K. (2006). Religion and survival in a secular region. A twenty year follow-up of 734 Danish adults born in 1914. *Social Science & Medicine*, 62, 157–164.

Landis, M., Peter-Wight, M., Martin, M., & Bodenmann, G. (2013). Dyadic coping and marital satisfaction of older spouses in long-term marriage. *GeroPsych: The Journal of Gerontopsychology and Geriatric Psychiatry*, 26(1), 39–47. doi:10.1024/1662-9647/a000077

Langlois, A. (2004, May). Retiring on the instalment plan. *CAmagazine.com*. Retrieved from www.camagazine.com/index.cfm/ci_id/20901/la_id/1/camagazine/1/print/true.htm

Lawrence, R.H., Bennett, J.M., & Markides, K.S. (1992). Perceived intergenerational solidarity and psychological distress among older Mexican Americans. *Journals of Gerontology: Social Sciences*, 47, S55–65.

Leung, Y.W., Grewal, K., Gravely-Witte, S., Suskin, N., Stewart, D.E., & Grace, S.L. (2011). Quality of life following participation in cardiac rehabilitation programs of longer or shorter than 6 months: Does duration matter? *Population Health Management*, 14(4), 181–188. doi:10.1089/pop.2010.0048

Li, S., Stampfer, M.J., Williams, D.R., & VanderWeele, T.J. (2016). Association of religious service attendance with mortality among women. *JAMA Internal Medicine*, 176(6), 777–785. doi:10.1001/jamainternmed.2016.1615

Lindsay, C. (2008). *Canadians attend weekly religious services less than 20 years ago* (89-630-X). Ottawa, ON: Statistics Canada. Retrieved from www.statcan.gc.ca/pub/89-630-x/2008001/article/10705-eng.pdf

Liu, J.L., & Richardson, P.K. (2012). Successful aging in older adults with disability. *OTJR: Occupation, Participation and Health*, 32(4), 126–134. doi:10.3928/15394492-20120203-02

Longino, C. (2003). A first look at retirement migration trends in 2000. *The Gerontologist*, 43, 904–907.

Longino, C., Bradley, D., Stoller, E., & Haas, W. (2008). Predictors of non-local moves among older adults: A prospective study. *The Journals of Gerontology: Series B*, 63, S7–S14.

Lorant, V., Kunst, A., Huisman, M., Bopp, M., & Mackenbach, J. (2005). A European comparative study of marital status and socio-economic inequalities in suicide. *Social Science & Medicine*, 60, 2431–2441.

Maas, H.S., & Kuypers, J.A. (1974). *From thirty to seventy*. San Francisco, CA: Jossey-Bass.

Malchiodi, C.A. (2012). Creativity and aging: An art therapy perspective. In C.A. Malchiodi (Ed.), *Handbook of art therapy* (2nd ed., pp. 275–287). New York, NY: Guilford Press.

Maniecka-Bryla, I., Gajewska, O., Burzynska, M., & Bryla, M. (2013). Factors associated with self-rated health (SRH) of a University of the Third Age (U3A) class participants. *Archives of Gerontology and Geriatrics*, 57(2), 156–161. doi:10.1016/j.archger.2013.03.006

Manzoli, L., Villari, P., Pironec, G., & Boccia, A. (2007). Marital status and mortality in the elderly: A systematic review and meta-analysis. *Social Science & Medicine*, 64, 77–94.

Marques, P., Moreira, P., Magalhães, R., Costa, P., Santos, N., Zihl, J., . . . Sousa, N. (2016). The functional connectome of cognitive reserve. *Human Brain Mapping*, (May 4). doi:10.1002/hbm.23242 [Epub ahead of print]

Marques, P., Soares, J.M., Magalhães, R., Santos, N.C., & Sousa, N. (2015). The bounds of education in the human brain connectome. *Scientific Reports*, 5(12812). doi:10.1038/srep12812

McDaniel, S. (1994). *Family and friends: General Social Survey analysis series* (Cat. no. 11-612E—No. 9). Ottawa, ON: Statistics Canada.

McDonald, L., & Donahue, P. (2011). Retirement lost? *Canadian Journal on Aging*, 30(3), 401–422. doi:10.1017/S0714980811000298

McDonald, P.L., & Wanner, R.A. (1990). *Retirement in Canada*. Toronto, ON: Butterworths.

McIntosh, B.R., & Danigelis, N.L. (1995). Race, gender, and the relevance of productive activity for elders' affect. *Journals of Gerontology: Social Sciences*, 50B, S229–239.

Mehta, K. (1997). The impact of religious beliefs and practices on aging: A cross-cultural comparison. *Journal of Aging Studies*, 11, 101–114.

Meisenhelder, J., & Chandler, E. (2000). Faith, prayer, and health outcomes in elderly Native Americans. *Clinical Nursing Research*, 9, 191–203.

Meisner, B.A., Dogra, S., Logan, A.J., Baker, J., & Weir, P.L. (2010). Do or decline?: Comparing the effects of physical inactivity on biopsychosocial components of successful aging. *Journal of Health Psychology*, 15(5), 688–696. doi:10.1177/1359105310368184

Menec, V., Bell, S., Novek, S., Minnigaleeva, G.A., Morales, E., Ouma, T., . . . Winterton, R. (2015). Making rural and remote communities more age-friendly: Experts' perspectives on issues, challenges, and priorities. *Journal of Aging and Social Policy*, 27(2), 173–191. doi:10.1080/08959420.2014.995044

Menec, V.H., & Nowicki, S. (2014). Examining the relationship between communities' 'age-friendliness' and life satisfaction and self-perceived health in rural Manitoba, *Canada. Rural and remote health [electronic resource]*, 14(Jan), 2594.

Menec, V.H., Newall, N.E., & Nowicki, S. (2016). Assessing communities' age-friendliness: How congruent are subjective versus objective assessments? *Journal of Applied Gerontology, 35*(5), 549–565. doi:10.1177/0733464814542612

Milan, A., & Hamm, B. (2003). Across the generations: Grandparents and grandchildren (Cat. No. 11-008). *Canadian Social Trends, Winter*(71), 2–7.

Milan, A., Wong, I., & Vézina, M. (2014). Emerging trends in living arrangements and conjugal unions for current and future seniors. *Insights on Canadian Society* (Cat. no. 75-006-X). Ottawa, ON: Minister of Industry.

Milkie, M.A., Bierman, A., & Schieman, S. (2008). How adult children influence older parents' mental health: Integrating stress-process and life-course perspectives. *Social Psychology Quarterly, 71*(1), 86–105. doi:10.1177/019027250807100109

Minkler, M., & Fadem, P. (2012). Successful aging: A disability perspective. In I. Marini, & M. Stebnicki (Eds.), *The psychological and social impact of illness and disability* (6th ed., pp. 395–404). New York, NY: Springer Publishing Co.

Morganti, L., Scaratti, C., Cipresso, P., Gaggioli, A., Bonfiglio, S., & Riva, G. (2016). How can technology help intergenerational reminiscence? A pilot study. *International Journal of Web Based Communities, 12*(1), 35–54. doi:10.1504/IJWBC.2016.074275

Mullins, L.C., & Mushel, M. (1992). The existence and emotional closeness of relationships with children, friends, and spouses. The effect on loneliness among older persons. *Research on Aging, 14,* 448–470.

Murphy, B., Zhang, X., & Dionne, C. (2015). *Low income in Canada - A multi-line and multi-index perspective* (Income Research Paper Series - 75F0002M). Ottawa, ON: Statistics Canada. Retrieved from http://www.statcan.gc.ca/pub/75f0002m/75f0002m2012001-eng.htm

National Seniors Council. (2010). *Report of the national seniors council on volunteering among seniors and positive and active aging.* Retrieved from http://www.seniorscouncil.gc.ca/eng/research_publications/volunteering.pdf

Northcott, H.C., & Petruik, C.R. (2011). The geographic mobility of elderly Canadians. *Canadian Journal on Aging, 30*(3), 311–322. doi:10.1353/cja.2011.0045

O'Rourke, N., Cappeliez, P., & Claxton, A. (2011). Functions of reminiscence and the psychological well-being of young-old and older adults over time. *Aging and Mental Health, 15*(2), 272–281. doi:10.1080/13607861003713281

Onen, S., Onen, F., Mangeon, J., Abidi, H., Courpron, P., & Schmidt, J. (2005). Alcohol abuse and dependence in elderly emergency department patients. *Archives of Gerontology and Geriatrics, 41,* 191–200.

O'Rourke, N., Bachner, Y.G., Cappeliez, P., Chaudhury, H., & Carmel, S. (2015). Reminiscence functions and the health of Israeli Holocaust survivors as compared to other older Israelis and older Canadians. *Aging & Mental Health, 19*(4), 335–346. doi:10.1080/13607863.2014.938607

Palmore, E.B. (2016). Auto-gerontology: A personal odyssey. *Journal of Applied Gerontology,* (May 12), pii: 0733464816648140. [Epub ahead of print]

Park, C., Edmondson, D., & Mills, M. (2010). Religious worldviews and stressful encounters: Reciprocal influence from a meaning-making perspective. In T. Miller (Ed.), *Handbook of stressful transitions across the lifespan* (pp. 485–501). New York, NY: Springer Science+Business Media.

Park, J. (2011). Retirement, health, and employment among those 55 plus (Cat. no. 75-001-X). *Perspectives on Labour and Income, 23*(1), 5–13. Retrieved from http://www.statcan.gc.ca/pub/75-001-x/2011001/pdf/11402-eng.pdf

Park, N.S. (2009). The relationship of social engagement to psychological well-being of older adults in assisted living facilities. *Journal of Applied Gerontology, 28*(4), 461–481. doi:10.1177/0733464808328606

Pillemer, K., & Suitor, J.J. (1990). Prevention of elder abuse. In R. Ammerman & M. Hersen (Eds.), *Treatment of family violence: A sourcebook* (pp. 406–422). New York, NY: Wiley.

Pillemer, K., & Suitor, J.J. (1992). Violence and violent feelings: What causes them among family caregivers? *Journals of Gerontology: Social Sciences, 47,* S165–172.

Pinquart, M., & Forstmeier, S. (2012). Effects of reminiscence interventions on psychosocial outcomes: A metaanalysis. *Aging and Mental Health, 16*(5), 541–558. doi:10.1080/13607863.2011.651434

Pinquart, M., & Soerensen, S. (2000). Influences of socioeconomic status, social network, and competence on subjective well-being in later life: A meta-analysis. *Psychology & Aging, 15,* 187–224.

Podnieks, E., Rietschlin, J., & Walsh, C.A. (2012). Introduction: Elder abuse in Canada—Reports from a national roundtable discussion. *Journal of Elder Abuse and Neglect, 24*(2), 85–87. doi:10.1080/08946566.2011.646500

Powell, R. (May 31, 2006). The $400 billion income shortfall: Baby-boomer women have tougher road to retirement. *Market Watch.* Retrieved from www.marketwatch.com/News/Story/Story.aspx?guid=%7B107BAF88-C68D-473E-B022-6C3533D216AD%7D

Public Health Agency of Canada. (2016c). *Age-friendly communities.* Retrieved from http://www.phac-aspc.gc.ca/seniors-aines/afc-caa-eng.php

Reker, G.T., Birren, J., & Svensson, C. (2012). Restoring, maintaining, and enhancing personal meaning in life through autobiographical methods. In P.T. P. Wong (Ed.), *The human quest for meaning* (2nd ed., pp. 383–408). London, England: Routledge.

Riggs, A. (1997). Men, friends, and widowhood: Towards successful aging. *Australian Journal on Ageing, 16,* 182–185.

Riva, G., Villani, D., Cipresso, P., Repetto, C., Triberti, S., Di Lernia, D., . . . Gaggioli, A. (2016). Positive and transformative technologies for active ageing. In J.D. Westwood., S.W., Westwood, L., Felländer-Tsai, C.M., Fidopiastis, A., Liu, S., Senger, & K.G. Vosburgh, (Eds.) *Medicine meets virtual reality 22.* Amsterdam, The Netherlands: IOS Press.

Rivera-Nivar, M., & Pomales-García, C. (2010). E-training: Can young and older users be accommodated with the same interface? *Computers & Education, 55,* 949–960.

Robinson-Whelen, S., & Kiecolt-Glaser, N. (1997). The importance of social versus temporal comparison appraisals among older adults. *Journal of Applied Social Psychology, 27,* 959–966.

Rowe, J., & Kahn, R. (1998). *Successful aging.* New York, NY: Pantheon.

Rowe, J.W., & Kahn, R.L. (1987). Human aging: Usual and successful. *Science, 237*(4811), 143–149.

Rubinstein, R.L. (1986). *Singular paths: Old men living alone.* New York, NY: Columbia University Press.

Sarma, S., Hawley. G., & Basu, K. (2009). Transitions in living arrangements of Canadian seniors: Findings from the NPHS longitudinal data. *Social Science and Medicine. 68*(6), 1106–1113.

Schellenberg, G. & Ostrovsky, Y. (2008). The retirement plans and expectations of older workers. In *2007 General Social Survey Report* (11-008-X). Ottawa, ON: Statistics Canada. Retrieved from www.statcan.gc.ca/pub/11-008-x/2008002/article/10666-eng.pdf

Schoebi, D., Karney, B.R., & Bradbury, T.N. (2012). Stability and change in the first 10 years of marriage: Does commitment confer benefits beyond the effects of satisfaction? *Journal of Personality and Social Psychology, 102,* 729–742. doi:10.1037/a0026290

Service Canada. (2016). *Canadian retirement income calculator.* Retrieved from: http://www.esdc.gc.ca/en/cpp/cric.page

Sherrod, A., (2012). Learning resources book review [Review of the book *Total engagement: An arts-based guide to providing meaningful activities* (2nd ed.), by P. Atwood & T. Atwood]. *Educational Gerontology, 38,* 824–825. doi:10.1080/03601277.2011.595352

Silverstein, M., & Long, J. (1998). Trajectories of grandparents' perceived solidarity with adult grandchildren: A growth curve analysis over 23 years. *Journal of Marriage & the Family, 60,* 912–923.

Sinha, M. (2012). *Family violence in Canada: A statistical profile, 2010* (Cat. no. 85-002-XWE). Retrieved from Statistics Canada website http://www.statcan.gc.ca/pub/85-002-x/2012001/article/11643-eng.pdf

Smith, D., & Moen, P. (2004). Retirement satisfaction for retirees and their spouses: Do gender and the retirement decision-making process matter? *Journal of Family Issues, 25,* 262–285.

Social Data Research/Pollara (2005). *Searchable database of supportive housing for seniors in Canada final report*. Retrieved from http://www.hc-sc.gc.ca/hcs-sss/alt_formats/hpb-dgps/pdf/pubs/2005-seniors-aines/2005-seniors-aines-eng.pdf

Soldo, B.J., Wolf, D.A., & Agree, E.M. (1990). Family, households, and care arrangements of frail older women: A structural analysis. *Journals of Gerontology: Social Sciences, 45*, S238–249.

Sørensen, T., Lien, L., Holmen, J., & Danbolt, L.J. (2012). Distribution and understanding of items of religiousness in the Nord-Trøndelag Health Study, Norway. *Mental Health, Religion, & Culture, 15*(6), 571–585. doi:10.1080/13674676.2011.604868

Spina, J., & Menec, V.H. (2015). What community characteristics help or hinder rural communities in becoming age-friendly? Perspectives from a Canadian prairie province. *Journal of Applied Gerontology, 34*(4), 444–464. doi:10.1177/0733464813496164

Stanford, E.P., Happersett, C.J., Morton, D.J., Molgaard, C.A., & Peddecord, K.M. (1991). Early retirement and functional impairment from a multiethnic perspective. *Research on Aging, 13*, 5–38.

Statistics Canada. (2001d). Retirement by sex, class of worker, Canada, annual average (File No. CDIT28AN). *Labour Force Survey, 2000–2001* (CD-ROM, Cat. no. 71F0004XCB). Ottawa, ON: Author.

Statistics Canada. (2010b). *Religious attendance rates, by sex, 1985 to 2008* (11-008-X). Ottawa, ON: Author. Retrieved from www.statcan.gc.ca/pub/11-008-x/2010001/c-g/11132/desc/desc001-eng.htm

Statistics Canada. (2012t). *Table 2 volunteer rate, average and median annual volunteer hours, by personal and economic characteristics, population aged 15 and over, 2004, 2007 and 2010*. Retrieved from http://www.statcan.gc.ca/pub/11-008-x/2012001/t/11638/tbl02-eng.htm

Statistics Canada. (2012u). *Living arrangements of seniors* (Cat. no. 98-312-X2011003). Retrieved from: http://www12.statcan.gc.ca/census-recensement/2011/as-sa/98-312-x/98-312-x2011003_4-eng.pdf

Statistics Canada. (2012v). *Labour force characteristics by sex and age group* (CANSIM Table 282-0002). Retrieved from http://www.statcan.gc.ca/tables-tableaux/sum-som/l01/cst01/labor05-eng.htm

Statistics Canada. (2012w). *Persons in low income families-annual* (CANSIM Table 202-0802). Retrieved from http://www5.statcan.gc.ca/cansim/a01?lang=eng

Statistics Canada. (2013c). *Figure 1 Population pyramid by living arrangement and sex for the population aged 65 and over, Canada, 2011*. Retrieved from http://www12.statcan.ca/censusrecensement/2011/as-sa/98-312-x/2011003/fig/desc/desc3_4-1-eng.cfm

Statistics Canada. (2016m). *Labour force survey estimates (LFS), retirement age by class of worker and sex* (CANSIM Table 282-0051). Retrieved from http://www5.statcan.gc.ca/cansim/a26?lang=eng&id=2820051

Stones, M., Kozma, A., McNeil, K., & Worobetz, S. (2011). Subjective well-being in later life: 20 years after the Butterworths monograph series on individual and population aging. *Canadian Journal on Aging, 30*(3), 467–477. doi:10.1017/S0714980811000365

Suri, G., & Gross, J.J. (2012). Emotion regulation and successful aging. *Trends in Cognitive Sciences, 16*(8), 409–410. doi:10.1016/j.tics.2012.06.007

Swanson, S.M. (1999). *Abuse and neglect of older adults*. Ottawa, ON: Health Canada, The National Clearinghouse on Family Violence. Retrieved from www.hc-sc.gc.ca/hppb/familyviolence/pdfs/abuseneg98en.pdf

Tabuchi, M., Nakagawa, T., Miura, A., & Gondo, Y. (2015). Generativity and interaction between the old and young: The role of perceived respect and perceived rejection. *Gerontologist, 55*(4), 537–547. doi:10.1093/geront/gnt135

Takahashi, K., Tamura, J., & Tokoro, M. (1997). Patterns of social relationships and psychological well-being among the elderly. *International Journal of Behavioral Development, 21*, 417–430.

Tapanya, S., Nicki, R., & Jarusawad, O. (1997). Worry and intrinsic/extrinsic religious orientation among Buddhist (Thai) and Christian (Canadian) elderly persons. *International Journal of Aging and Human Development, 44*, 73–83.

Taylor, P., Funk, C., Craighill, P., & Kennedy, C. (2006). *Families drawn together by communication revolution*. Retrieved from http://pewsocialtrends.org/assets/pdf/FamilyBonds.pdf

Tomassini, C., Kalogirou, S., Grundy, E., Fokkema, T., Martikainen, P., van Groenou, M., . . . Karisto, A. (2004). Contacts between elderly parents and their children in four European countries: Current patterns and future prospects. *European Journal of Ageing, 1*, 54–63.

Turcotte, M. & Schellenberg, G. (2007). *A portrait of seniors in Canada 2006* (89-519-XIE). Ottawa, ON: Statistics Canada. Retrieved from www.statcan.gc.ca/pub/89-519-x/89-519-x2006001-eng.pdf

Uppal, S. (2011). Seniors' self-employment (Cat. no. 75-001-X). *Perspectives on Labour and Income, 23*(1), 3–14. Retrieved from http://www.statcan.gc.ca/pub/75-001-x/2011001/pdf/11400-eng.pdf

Uriarte-Landa, J., & Hebert, B. (2009). Work-life balance of older workers. In *Perspectives* (75-001-X). Ottawa, ON: Statistics Canada. Retrieved from www.statcan.gc.ca/pub/75-001-x/2009110/pdf/10944-eng.pdf

van Dyk, S. (2014). The appraisal of difference: Critical gerontology and the active-ageing-paradigm. *Journal of Aging Studies, 31*(Dec), 93–103. doi:10.1016/j.jaging.2014.08.008

van Solinge, H. (2007). Health change in retirement: A longitudinal study among older workers in the Netherlands. *Research on Aging, 29*, 225–256.

Veenhof, B., & Timusk, P. (2009). Online activities of Canadian boomers and seniors (Chart 1) (Cat. no. 11-008-X). *Canadian Social Trends, 88*, 25–32.

Venkatraman, M.M. (1995). A cross-cultural study of the subjective well-being of married elderly persons in the United States and India. *Journals of Gerontology: Social Sciences, 50B*, S35–44.

Volz, J. (2000). Successful aging: The second 50. *Monitor, 31*, 24–28.

Waldinger, R., & Schulz, M. (2010). What's love got to do with it? Social functioning, perceived health, and daily happiness in married octogenarians. *Psychology and Aging, 25*, 422–431.

Walsh, C.A., & Yon, Y. (2012). Developing an empirical profile for elder abuse research in Canada. *Journal of Elder Abuse and Neglect, 24*(2), 104–119. doi:10.1080/08946566.2011.644088

Weir, P.L., Meisner, B.A., & Baker, J. (2010). Successful aging across the years: Does one model fit everyone? *Journal of Health Psychology, 15*(5), 680–687. doi:10.1177/1359105309353648

Wink, P., & Staudinger, U.M. (2016). Wisdom and psychosocial functioning in later life. *Journal of Personality, 84*(3), 306–318. doi:10.1111/jopy.12160

Winstead, V., Yost, E.A., Cotton, S.R., Berkowsky, R.W., & Anderson, W.A. (2015). The impact of activity interventions on the well-being of older adults in continuing care communities. *Journal of Applied Gerontology, 33*(7), 888–911. doi:10.1177/0733464814537701

World Health Organization. (2014). *Age-friendly world: Adding years to life*. Retrieved from https://extranet.who.int/agefriendlyworld/

Yon, Y., Wister, A.V., Mitchell, B., & Gutman, G. (2014). A national comparison of spousal abuse in mid- and old age. *Journal of Elder Abuse & Neglect, 26*(1), 80–105. doi:10.1080/08946566.2013.784085

Zhou, M., Yao, L., & Xu, J. (2002). Studied the influence of Taoist education on the subjective well-being of the elderly. *Chinese Mental Health Journal, 16*, 175–176.

Zunzunegui, M., Alvarado, B., Del Ser, T., & Otero, A. (2003). Social networks, social integration, and social engagement determine cognitive decline in community-dwelling Spanish older adults. *Journals of Gerontology, Series B: Psychological Sciences & Social Sciences, 58B*, S93–S100.

Chapter 19

Alsop, S. (1973). *Stay of execution*. New York, NY: Lippincott.

American Psychiatric Association. (2013). *Diagnostic and Statistical Manual of Mental Disorder: DSM-5* (5th ed.). Washington, DC: American Psychiatric Publishing.

Ardelt, M., & Koenig, C.S. (2006). The role of religion for hospice patients and relatively healthy older adults. *Research on Aging, 28*(2), 184–215.

Auman, M. (2007). Bereavement support for children. *The Journal of School Nursing*, 23(1), 34–39.

Bacon, J. (2008). *Hospice palliative home care in Canada: A progress report*. Ottawa, ON: Quality End-of-Life Care Coalition of Canada.

Bailley, S., Kral, M., & Dunham, K. (1999). Survivors of suicide do grieve differently: Empirical support for a common sense proposition. *Suicide and Life-Threatening Behavior*, 29, 256–271.

Barrett, H., & Behne, T. (2005). Children's understanding of death as the cessation of agency: A test using sleep versus death. *Cognition*, 96(2), 93–108.

Batten, M., & Oltjenbruns, K. (1999). Adolescent sibling bereavement as a catalyst for spiritual development: A model for understanding. *Death Studies*, 23, 529–546.

Beem, E., Hooijkaas, H., Cleriren, M., Schut, H., Garssen, B., Croon, M., . . . de Vries, M. (1999). The immunological and psychological effects of bereavement: Does grief counseling really make a difference? A pilot study. *Psychiatry Research*, 85, 81–93.

Bibby, R.W. (2001). *Canada's teens: Today, yesterday and tomorrow*. Toronto, ON: Stoddart Publishing Co. Limited.

Blau, G. (1996). Adolescent depression and suicide. In G. Blau & T. Gullotta (Eds.), *Adolescent dysfunctional behavior: Causes, interventions, and prevention* (pp. 187–205). Newbury Park, CA: Sage.

Bonoti, F., Leondari, A., & Mastora, A. (2013). Exploring children's understanding of death: Through drawings and the Death Concept Questionnaire. *Death Studies*, 37(1), 47–60. doi:10.1080/07481187.2011.623216

Boyle, P.J., Feng, Z., & Raab, G.M. (2011). Does widowhood increase mortality risk? Testing for selection effects by comparing causes of spousal death. *Epidemiology*, 22(1), 1–5. doi:10.1097/EDE.0b013e3181fdcc0b

Braun, K., & Nichols, R. (1997). Death and dying in four Asian American cultures: A descriptive study. *Death Studies*, 21, 327–359.

Brent, D., Melhem, N., Donohoe, M., & Walker, M. (2009). The incidence and course of depression in bereaved youth 21 months after the loss of a parent to suicide, accident, or sudden natural death. *The American Journal of Psychiatry*, 166, 786–794.

British Columbia Ministry of Health (2006). *A provincial framework for end-of-life care*. Victoria, BC: Author. Retrieved from www.health.gov.bc.ca/library/publications/year/2006/framework.pdf

Bryden, J. (2016). *Indigenous parliamentarians brought unique perspective to C-14 debate*. Ottawa, ON: iPolitics Canadian Press. Retrieved from https://ipolitics.ca/2016/07/03/indigenous-parliamentarians-brought-unique-perspective-to-c-14-debate/

Callaway, E. (2010). How bereavement stress can cause "widowhood effect". *New Scientist*, 206(2766),13. doi.org/10.1016/S0262-4079(10)61531-X

Canadian Hospice Palliative Care Association. (2013). *A model to guide hospice palliative care: Based on National Principles and Norms of Practice*. Ottawa, ON: Author. Retrieved from http://www.chpca.net/media/319547/norms-of-practice-eng-web.pdf

Canadian Hospice Palliative Care Association. (2016a). *The Canadian Hospice Palliative Care Association ... A History*. Ottawa, ON: Author. Retrieved from http://www.chpca.net/about-us/history.aspx

Canadian Hospice Palliative Care Association. (2016b). *Canadian directory of hospice Palliative care services*. Ottawa, ON: Author. Retrieved from http://www.chpca.net/family-caregivers/directory-of-services.aspx

Canadian Institute for Health Information (2007b). Health care use at the end of life in Western Canada. Ottawa, ON: Author. Retrieved from http://secure.cihi.ca/cihiweb/products/end_of_life_report_aug07_e.pdf

Canadian Institute for Health Information. (2007a). HSMR: A new approach for measuring hospital mortality trends in Canada. Ottawa, ON: Author. Retrieved from http://secure.cihi.ca/cihiweb/products/HSMR_hospital_mortality_trends_in_canada.pdf

Canadian Virtual Hospice. (2015a). *About us*. Winnipeg, MB: Canadian Virtual Hospice. Retrieved from http://www.virtualhospice.ca/en_US/Main+Site+Navigation/Home+Navigation/About+Us/The+Story+of+the+Virtual+Hospice.aspx

Canadian Virtual Hospice. (2015b). *Health care directives*. Winnipeg, MB: Canadian Virtual Hospice. Retrieved from http://www.virtualhospice.ca/en_US/Main+Site+Navigation/Home/Topics/Topics/Decisions/Health+Care+Directives.aspx

Carnelley, K., Wortman, C., & Kessler, R. (1999). The impact of widowhood on depression: Findings from a prospective survey. *Psychological Medicine*, 29, 1111–1123.

Carnelley, K., Wortman, C., Bolger, N., & Burke, C. (2006). The time course of grief reactions to spousal loss: Evidence from a national probability sample. *Journal of Personality and Social Psychology*, 91(3), 476–492.

Chochinov, H.M. (2006). Dying, dignity, and new horizons in palliative end-of-life care. *A Cancer Journal for Clinicians*, 56(2), 84–103.

Chochinov, H.M. (2007). Dignity and the essence of medicine: The A, B, C and D of Dignity Conserving Care. *British Medical Journal*, 335(7612), 184–187.

Chochinov, H.M., Hack, T., Hassard, T., Kristjanson, L.J., McClement, S., & Harlos, M. (2005). Dignity therapy: A novel psychotherapeutic intervention for patients near the end of life. *Journal of Clinical Oncology*, 23(24), 5520–5525.

Chochinov, H.M., Hassard, T., McClement, S., Hack, T., Kristjanson, L.J., Harlos, M., . . . Murray, A. (2009). The landscape of distress in the terminally ill. *Journal of Pain and Symptom Management*, 38(5), 641–649.

Chochinov, H.M., Hassard, T., McClement, S., Hack, T., Kristjanson, L.J., Harlos, M. . . . Murray, A. (2008). The Patient Dignity Inventory: A Novel Way of Measuring Dignity-Related Distress. *Palliative Care Journal of Pain and Symptom Management*, 36(6), 559–571.

Chochinov, H.M., Johnston, W., McClement, S.E., Hack, T.F., Dufault, B., Enns, M., . . . Kredentser, M.S. (2016). Dignity and distress towards the end of life across four non-cancer populations. *PLoS ONE*, 11(1), e0147607. doi:10.1371/journal.pone.0147607

Chochinov, H.M., Kristjanson, L.J., Hack, T., Hassard, T., McClement, S., & Harlos, M. (2006). Dignity in the terminally ill: Revisited. *Journal of Palliative Medicine*, 9(3), 666–672.

Chochinov, H.M., McClement, S.E., Hack, T.F., McKeen, N.A., Rach, A.M., Gagnon, P., . . . Taylor-Brown, J. (2012). The patient dignity inventory: Applications in the oncology setting. *Journal of Palliative Medicine*, 15(9), 998–1005. doi:10.1089/jpm.2012.0066

Chochinov, H.M., McClement, S.E., Hack, T.F., McKeen, N.A., Rach, A.M., Gagnon, P., . . . Taylor-Brown, J. (2013). Health care provider communication: An empirical model of therapeutic effectiveness. *Cancer*, 119(9), 1706–1713. doi:10.1002/cncr.27949

Cicirelli, V. (2006). Fear of death in mid-old age. *Journals of Gerontology: Series B: Psychological Sciences and Social Sciences*, 61(B), 75–81.

Cicirelli, V.G. (2011). Elders' attitudes toward extending the healthy life span. *Journal of Aging Studies*, 25(Paper 20), 84–93. doi:10.1016/j.jaging.2010.08.011

Ciocco, A. (1940). On the mortality in husbands and wives. *Human Biology*, 12(4), 508–531.

Coelho, A., & Barbosa, A. (2016). Family anticipatory grief: An integrative literature review. *The American Journal of Hospice & Palliative Care*, (May 5), pii. doi:10.1177/1049909116647960. [Epub ahead of print]

Corr, C.A. (1991/1992). A task-based approach to coping with dying. *Omega*, 24, 81–94.

Cox, M., Garrett, E., & Graham, J. (2004–2005). Death in Disney films: Implications for children's understanding of death. *Omega: Journal of Death and Dying*, 50(4), 267–280.

Crehan, G. (2004). The surviving sibling: The effects of sibling death in childhood. *Psychoanalytic Psychotherapy*, 18, 202–219.

Cunningham, A. J. (2008). The healing journey: Incorporating psychological and spiritual dimensions into the care of cancer patients. *Current Oncology*, 15(Suppl 2), 37–41.

Cunningham, A.J. & Watson, K. (2004). How psychological therapy may prolong survival in cancer patients: New evidence and a simple theory. *Integrative Cancer Therapies*, 3(3), 214–229.

Cunningham, A.J. (2004). *Healing journey level I workbook*. Toronto, ON: Ontario Cancer Institute/The Princess Margaret Hospital. Retrieved from http://individual.utoronto.ca/hayman/HJPlev1.pdf

Cunningham, A.J. (2005). Can the mind heal cancer? A clinician-scientist examines the evidence. Toronto, ON: Hushion House.

Cunningham, A.J., Phillips, C., Lockwood, G.A., Hedley, D., & Edmonds, C.V.I. (2000). Association of involvement in psychological self-regulation with longer survival in patients with metastatic cancer: An exploratory study. *Advances in Mind-Body Medicine*, 16(4), 276–287.

Cunningham, A.J., Phillips, C., Stephen, J., and Edmonds, C. (2002). Fighting for life: A qualitative analysis of the process of psychotherapy-assisted self-help in patients with metastatic cancer. *Integrative Cancer Therapies* 1(2), 146–161.

Cunningham, L. (1996). *Grief and the adolescent*. Newhall, CA: Teen-Age Grief, Inc.

Currier, J., Holland, J., & Neimeyer, R. (2006). Sense-making, grief, and the experience of violent loss: Toward a mediational model. *Death Studies*, 30(5), 403–428.

Daniels, K. (2014). Implications of brain death as a criterion for legal death. *McGill Journal of Law and Health, MJLH Online* (Mar 16). Retrieved from http://mjlh.mcgill.ca/blog.php?blog_id=115#_ftn2

Dionne-Odom, J.N., Azuero, A., Lyons, K.D., Hull, J.G., Prescott, A.T., Tosteson, T., . . . Bakitas, M.A. (2016). Family caregiver depressive symptom and grief outcomes from the ENABLE III Randomized Controlled Trial. *Journal of Pain and Symptom Management*, (Jun 2), pii. S0885-3924(16)30147-6. doi:10.1016/j.jpainsymman.2016.03.014. [Epub ahead of print]

Doka, K.J. (2013). Grief and the DSM: A brief Q&A. *The Huffington Post*, (July 29). Retrieved from http://www.huffingtonpost.com/kenneth-j-doka/grief-and-the-dsm_b_3340216.html%20%20

Downe-Wamboldt, B., & Tamlyn, D. (1997). An international survey of death education trends in faculties of nursing and medicine. *Death Studies*, 21, 177–188.

Dyregrov, A., Gjestad, R., Bie Wikander, A., & Vigerust, S. (1999). Reactions following the sudden death of a classmate. *Scandinavian Journal of Psychology*, 40, 167–176.

Dysvik, E., & Furnes, B. (2010). Dealing with grief related to loss by death and chronic pain: Suggestions for practice. Part 2. *Patient Preference and Adherence*, 24(4), 163–170.

Elwert, F., & Christakis, N. (2006). Widowhood and race. *American Sociological Review*, 71(1), 16–41. doi:10.1177/000312240607100102

Elwert, F., & Christakis, N.A. (2008a). The effect of widowhood on mortality by the causes of death of both spouses. *American Journal of Public Health*, 98(11), 2092–2098. doi:10.2105/AJPH.2007.114348

Elwert, F., & Christakis, N.A. (2008b). Wives and ex-wives: A new test for homogamy bias in the widowhood effect. *Demography*, 45(4), 851–873.

Eyetsemitan, F. (1998). Stifled grief in the workplace. *Death Studies*, 22, 469–479.

Federal Interagency Forum on Aging-Related Statistics (FIFARS). (2012). *Older Americans 2010: Key indicators of well-being*. Washington, DC: Author. Retrieved from http://www.agingstats.gov/agingstatsdotnet/main_site/default.aspx

Fischoff, B., de Bruin, W., Parker, A.M., Millstein, S.G., & Halpern-Felsher, B.L. (2010). Adolescents' perceived risk of dying. *Journal of Adolescent Health*, 46(3), 265–269. doi:10.1016/j.jadohealth.2009.06.026

Fowler, R., & Hammer, M. (2013). End-of-life care in Canada. *Clinical & Investigative Medicine*, 36(3), e127–e132.

Francis, L. (1997). Ideology and interpersonal emotion management: Redefining identity in two support groups. *Social Psychology Quarterly*, 60, 153–171.

Gallagher, R. (2015). *Physician-assisted suicide and euthanasia: The issues*. Winnipeg, MB: Canadian Virtual Hospice. Retrieved from http://www.virtualhospice.ca/en_US/Main+Site+Navigation/Home/Topics/Topics/Decisions/Physician_Assisted+Suicide+and+Euthanasia_+The+Issues.aspx

Gerstorf, D., Ram, N., Estabrook, R., Schupp, J., Wagner, G.G., & Lindenberger, U. (2008). Life satisfaction shows terminal decline in old age: Longitudinal evidence from the German Socio-Economic Panel Study (SOEP). *Developmental Psychology*, 44(4), 1148–1159.

Gibson, M. (2007a). Death and mourning in technologically mediated culture. *Health Sociology Review*, 16 (5), 415–424. doi:10.5172/hesr.2007.16.5.415

Gibson, M. (2007b). Some thoughts on celebrity deaths: Steve Irwin and the issue of public mourning. *Mortality*, 12(1), 1–3. doi:10.1080/13576270601089663

Gibson, M. (2011a). Real-life death: Between public and private, interior and exterior, the real and the fictional. *South Atlantic Quarterly*, 110(4), 917–932. doi:10.1215/00382876-1382321

Gibson, M. (2011b). Death and grief in the landscape: Private memorials in public space, *Cultural Studies Review*, 17(1), 146–161.

Goodman, L.M. (1981). *Death and the creative life: Conversations with eminent artists and scientists as they reflect on life and death*. New York, NY: Springer Publishing Company.

Goodrum, S. (2005). The interaction between thoughts and emotions following the news of a loved one's murder. *Omega: Journal of Death and Dying*, 51(2), 143–160.

Gothelf, D., Apter, A., Brand-Gothelf, A., Offer, N., Ofek, H., Tyano, S., & Pfeffer, C. (1998). Death concepts in suicidal adolescents. *Journal of the American Academy of Child & Adolescent Psychiatry*, 37, 1279–1286.

Government of Canada. (2016c). *Medical assistance in dying*. Retrieved from http://healthycanadians.gc.ca/health-system-systeme-sante/services/palliative-pallatifs/medical-assistance-dying-aide-medicale-mourir-eng.php

Greer, S. (1991). Psychological response to cancer and survival. *Psychological Medicine*, 21, 43–49.

Greer, S. (1999). Mind-body research in psychooncology. *Advances in Mind-Body Medicine*, 15(4), 236–244. doi:10.1054/ambm.1999.0096

Greer, S. (2000). Fighting spirit in patients with cancer. *The Lancet*, 355(9206), 847–848.

Greer, S. (2002). Psychological intervention. The gap between research and practice. *Acta Oncologica*, 41(3), 238–243.

Greer, S. (2008). CBT for emotional distress of people with cancer: Some personal observations. *Psycho-oncology*, 17(2), 170–173. doi:10.1002/pon.1205

Greer, S., Morris, T., & Pettingale, K.W. (1979). Psychological response to breast cancer: Effect on outcome. *Lancet*, 2(8146), 785–787.

Haase, T.J., & Johnston, N. (2012). Making meaning out of loss: A story and study of young widowhood. *Journal of Creativity in Mental Health*, 7(3), 204–221. doi:10.1080/15401383.2012.710170

Ho, A.H., Chan, C.L., Leung, P.P., Chochinov, H.M., Neimeyer, R.A., Pang, S.M., & Tse, D.M. (2013). Living and dying with dignity in Chinese society: Perspectives of older palliative care patients in Hong Kong. *Age and Ageing*, 42(4), 455–61. doi:10.1093/ageing/aft003

Hospice Friendly Hospitals Programme. (2013). *End-of-life care & supporting staff: A literature review*. Retrieved from http://hospice-foundation.ie/wp-content/uploads/2013/04/End-of-Life-Care-Supporting-Staff-a-literature-review.pdf

Jarolmen, J. (1998). A comparison of the grief reaction of children and adults: Focusing on pet loss and bereavement. *Omega: Journal of Death & Dying*, 37, 133–150.

Johansson, B., Hofer, S., Allaire, J., Maldonado-Molina, M., Piccinin, A., . . . McClearn, G. (2004). Change in cognitive capabilities in the oldest old: The effects of proximity to death in genetically related individuals over a 6-year period. *Psychology & Aging*, 19, 145–156.

Kalish, R.A. (1985). The social context of death and dying. In R.H. Binstock & E. Shanas (Eds.), *Handbook of aging and the social sciences* (2nd ed., pp. 149–170). New York, NY: Van Nostrand Reinhold.

Kalish, R.A., & Reynolds, D.K. (1976). *Death and ethnicity: A psychocultural study*. Los Angeles, CA: University of Southern California Press (reprinted 1981, Baywood Publishing Co, Farmingdale, NJ).

Karlsson, M., Kasén, A., & Wärnå-Furu, C. (2016). Reflecting on one's own death: The existential questions that nurses face during end-of-life care. *Palliative and Supportive Care*, (Jun 27), 1–10. doi:10.1017/S1478951516000468 [Epub ahead of print]

Kaslow, F. (2004). Death of one's partner: The anticipation and the reality. *Professional Psychology: Research & Practice, 35,* 227–233.

Katz, P., & Bartone, P. (1998). Mourning, ritual and recovery after an airline tragedy. *Omega: Journal of Death & Dying, 36,* 193–200.

Keith, P.M. (1981/1982). Perception of time remaining and distance from death. *Omega, 12,* 307–318.

Kristjanson, L.J., & Aoun, S. (2004). Palliative care for families: Remembering the hidden patients. *Canadian Journal of Psychiatry, 49*(6), 359–365.

Kübler-Ross, E. (1969). *On death and dying.* New York, NY: Macmillan.

Kübler-Ross, E. (1974). *Questions and answers on death and dying.* New York, NY: Macmillan.

Kumabe, C. (2006). Factors influencing contemporary Japanese attitudes regarding life and death. *Japanese Journal of Health Psychology, 19*(1), 10–24.

Landes, S.D., & Ardelt, M. (2011). The relationship between spirituality and death fear in aging adults. *Counselling and Spirituality, 30*(2) 87–111.

Lenhardt, A., & McCourt, B. (2000). Adolescent unresolved grief in response to the death of a mother. *Professional School Counseling, 3,* 189–196.

Lester, D. (1990). The Collett-Lester fear of death scale: The original version and a revision. *Death Studies, 14,* 451–468.

Ley, D.C.H., & van Bommel, H. (1994). *The heart of hospice.* Toronto, ON: NC Press Limited.

Lichtenthal, W.G., Neimeyer, R.A., Currier, J.M., Roberts, K., & Jordan, N. (2013). Cause of death and the quest for meaning after the loss of a child. *Death Studies, 37*(4), 311–342. doi: 10.1080/07481187.2012.673533

Lieberman, M.A. (1965). Psychological correlates of impending death: Some preliminary observations. *Journal of Gerontology, 20,* 182–190.

Lieberman, M.A., & Coplan, A.S. (1970). Distance from death as a variable in the study of aging. *Developmental Psychology, 2,* 71–84.

Lindstrom, T. (1997). Immunity and somatic health in bereavement. A prospective study of 39 Norwegian widows. *Omega: Journal of Death & Dying, 35,* 231–241.

Liu, W., & Aaker, J. (2007). Do you look to the future or focus on today? The impact of life experience on intertemporal decisions. *Organizational Behavior and Human Decision Processes, 102,* 212–225.

Lohan, J., & Murphy, S. (2001/2002). Parents' perceptions of adolescent sibling grief responses after an adolescent or young adult child's sudden, violent death. *Omega, 44,* 195–213.

MacDonald, S.W. S., Hultsch, D.F., & Dixon, R.A. (2011). Aging and the shape of cognitive change before death: Terminal decline or terminal drop? *The Journals of Gerontology. Series B, 66*(3), 292–301. doi:10.1093/geronb/gbr001

Malkinson, R., & Bar-Tur, L., (1999). The aging of grief in Israel: A perspective of bereaved parents. *Death Studies, 23,* 413–431.

Marshall, V.W. (1975). Age and awareness of finitude in developmental gerontology. *Omega, 6,* 113–129.

Marshall, V.W., & Levy, J.A. (1990). Aging and dying. In R.H. Binstock & L.K. George (Eds.), *Handbook of aging and the social sciences* (3rd ed., pp. 245–260). San Diego, CA: Academic Press.

McBurney, K. (Spring, 2008). *Leading the Integration of Compassion: Winnipeg's palliative care program.* Winnipeg, MB: Aspire. Retrieved from Winnipeg Regional Health Authority website: www.wrha.mb.ca/media/files/Aspire_Spring08_E.pdf

Moon, J.R., Kondo, N., Glymou, M.M., & Subramanian, S.V. (2011) Widowhood and mortality: A meta-analysis. *PLoS ONE 6*(8), e23465. doi:10.1371/journal.pone.0023465

Moore, J., & Moore, C. (2010). Talking to children about death-related issues. In C. Corr & D. Balk (Eds.), *Children's encounters with death, bereavement, and coping* (pp. 277–291). New York, NY: Springer Publishing.

Moorman, S.M., & Inoue, M. (2013). Persistent problems in end-of-life planning among young- and middle-aged American couples. *The Journals of Gerontology Series B: Psychological Sciences and Social Sciences, 68*(1), 97–106. doi:10.1093/geronb/gbs103

Muniz-Terrera, G., van den Hout, A., Piccinin, A.M., Matthews, F.E., & Hofer, S.M. (2013). Investigating terminal decline: Results from a UK population-based study of aging. *Psychology and Aging, 28*(2), 377–385. doi:10.1037/a0031000

Neimeyer, R., Prigerson, H., & Davies, B. (2002). Mourning and meaning. *American Behavioral Scientist, 46*(2), 235–251.

Neimeyer, R.A., Wittkowski, J., & Moser, R.P. (2004). Psychological research on death attitudes: An overview and evaluation. *Death Studies, 28*(4), 309–340.

O'Connor, M.F., Shear, M.K., Fox, R., Skritskaya, N., Campbell, B., Ghesquiere, A., & Glickman, K. (2013). Catecholamine predictors of complicated grief treatment outcomes. *International Journal of Psychophysiology, 88*(3), 349–352. doi:10.1016/j.ijpsycho.2012.09.014

Oatley, K., & Jenkins, J. (1996). *Understanding emotions.* Cambridge, MA: Blackwell Publishers.

Onrust, S., & Cuijpers, P. (2006). Mood and anxiety disorders in widowhood: A systematic review. *Aging & Mental Health, 10*(4), 327–334.

Onrust, S., Cuijpers, P., Smit, F., & Bohlmeijer, E. (2007). Predictors of psychological adjustment after bereavement. *International Psychogeriatrics, 19*(5), 921–934.

Ottawa Citizen (April 25, 2005). *A moral force: The story of Dr. Balfour Mount.* Winnipeg, MB: Canwest Global Communications Corp. Retrieved from www.canada.com/ottawacitizen/story.html?id=896d005a-fedd-4f50-a2d9-83a95fc56464

Pang, T., & Lam, C. (2002). The widowers' bereavement process and death rituals: Hong Kong experiences. *Illness, Crisis, & Loss, 10,* 294–303.

Pettingale, K.W., Morris, T., Greer, S., & Haybittle, J.L. (1985). Mental attitudes to cancer: An additional prognostic factor. *Lancet, 1*(8431), 750.

Pollack, J.M. (1979/1980). Correlates of death anxiety: A review of empirical studies. *Omega, 10,* 97–121.

Popham, L.E., Kennison, S.M., & Bradley, K.I. (2011). Ageism and risk-taking in young adults: Evidence for a link between death anxiety and ageism. *Death Studies, 35*(8), 751–763. doi:10.1080/07481187.2011.573176

Prigerson, H., Bierhals, A., Kasl, S., Reynolds, C., Shear, M.K., Day, N. . . . Jacobs, S. (1997). Traumatic grief as a risk factor for mental and physical morbidity. *American Journal of Psychiatry, 154,* 616–623.

Prigerson, H., Bridge, J., Maciejewski, P., Beery, L., Rosenheck, R., Jacobs, S., . . . Brent, D. (1999). Influence of traumatic grief on suicidal ideation among young adults. *American Journal of Psychiatry, 156,* 1994–1995.

Pyne, D. (2008). *A Model of Religion and Death.* Papers on Economics of Religion 08/06, Department of Economic Theory and Economic History of the University of Granada. Retrieved from www.ugr.es/~teoriahe/RePEc/gra/paoner/per08_06.pdf

Radford, S.K., & Bloch, P. (2013). Consumers' online responses to the death of a celebrity. *Marketing Letters, 24*(1), 43–55. doi:10.1007/s11002-012-9202-5

Rajkumar, A.P., Mohan, T.S., & Tharyan, P. (2013). Lessons from the 2004 Asian tsunami: Epidemiological and nosological debates in the diagnosis of post-traumatic stress disorder in non-Western post-disaster communities. *International Journal of Social Psychiatry, 59*(2), 123–129. doi:10.1177/0020764011423468

Roos, S. (2013). The Kübler-Ross Model: An esteemed relic. *Gestalt Review, 17,* 312–315.

Rubin, S., & Schechter, N. (1997). Exploring the social construction of bereavement: Perceptions of adjustment and recovery in bereaved men. *American Journal of Orthopsychiatry, 67,* 279–289.

Rumpold, T., Schur, S., Amering, M., Ebert-Vogel, A., Kirchheiner, K., Masel, E.K., . . . Schrank, B. (2016a). Hope as determinant for psychiatric morbidity in family caregivers of advanced cancer patients. *Psycho-oncology,* (Jun 30). doi:10.1002/pon.4205. [Epub ahead of print]

Rumpold, T., Schur, S., Amering, M., Kirchheiner, K., Masel, E.K., Watzke, H., & Schrank, B. (2016b). Informal caregivers of advanced-stage cancer patients: Every second is at risk for psychiatric morbidity. *Supportive Care in Cancer, 24*(5), 1975–1982. doi:10.1007/s00520-015-2987-z

Schaan, B. (2013). Widowhood and depression among older Europeans—The role of gender, caregiving, marital quality, and regional context. *The Journals of Gerontology Series B: Psychological Sciences and Social Sciences, 68*(3), 431–442. doi:10.1093/geronb/gbt015

Schneider, R.M. (2006). Group bereavement support for spouses who are grieving the loss of a partner to cancer. *Social Work with Groups: A Journal of Community and Clinical Practice, 29*(2–3), 259–278. doi:10.1300/J009v29n02_17

Schulz, R., Hebert, R., & Boerner, K. (2008). Bereavement after Caregiving. *Geriatrics, 63*(1), 20–22.

Shaw, J. (2014). Of mitochondria and men: Why brain death is not the death of the human "organism as a whole". *McGill Journal of Law and Health, 7*(2), 235–312. doi:10.2139/ssrn.2414051

Shneidman, E.S. (1980). *Voices of death.* New York, NY: Harper & Row.

Shneidman, E.S. (1983). *Deaths of man.* New York, NY: Jason Aronson.

Sinclair, S. (2011). Impact of death and dying on the personal lives and practices of palliative and hospice care professionals. *Canadian Medical Association Journal, 183*(2), 180–187. doi.org/10.1503/cmaj.100511

Sinclair, S., McClement, S., Raffin-Bouchal, S., Hack, T.F., Hagen, N.A., McConnell, S., & Chochinov, H.M. (2016a). Compassion in health care: An empirical model. *Journal of Pain and Symptom Management, 51*(2), 193–203. doi:10.1016/j.jpainsymman.2015.10.009

Sinclair, S., Norris, J.M., McConnell, S.J., Chochinov, H.M., Hack, T.F., Hagen, N.A., . . . Bouchal, S.R. (2016b). Compassion: A scoping review of the healthcare literature. *BMC Palliative Care, 15,* 6. doi:10.1186/s12904-016-0080-0

Slaughter, V. (2005). Young children's understanding of death. *Australian Psychologist, 40*(3), 179–186.

Slaughter, V., & Lyons, M. (2003). Learning about life and death in early childhood. *Cognitive Psychology, 46,* 1–30.

Song, J., Floyd, F.J., Seltzer, M.M., Greenberg, J.S., & Hong, J. (2010). Long-term effects of child death on parents' health related quality of life: A dyadic analysis. *Family Relations, 59*(3), 269–282.

Statistics Canada. (2014). *End-of-life care, 2012* (Cat. no. 89-652-X). Ottawa, ON: Minister of Industry. Retrieved from http://www.statcan.gc.ca/pub/89-652-x/89-652-x2014004-eng.htm

Statistics Canada. (2015l). *Deaths in hospital and elsewhere, Canada, provinces and territories* (CANSIM Table 102-0509). Retrieved from http://www5.statcan.gc.ca/cansim/a26?lang=eng&id=1020509

Stenekes, S., & Streeter, L. (2015). *Considerations for a home death.* Winnipeg, MB: Canadian Virtual Hospice. Retrieved from http://www.virtualhospice.ca/en_US/Main+Site+Navigation/Home/Topics/Topics/Decisions/Considerations+for+a+Home+Death.aspx

Stephen, J.E., Rahn, M., Verhoef, M., & Leis, A. (2007). What is the state of the evidence on the mind–cancer survival question, and where do we go from here? A point of view. *Supportive Care in Cancer, 15*(8), 903–1010.

Stetson, B. (2002). *Living victims, stolen lives: Parents of murdered children speak to American about death value, and meaning.* New York, NY: Baywood Publishing Company.

Sullivan, M., Ormel, J., Kempen, G., & Tymstra, T. (1998). Beliefs concerning death, dying, and hastening death among older,

functionally impaired Dutch adults: A one-year longitudinal study. *Journal of the American Geriatrics Society, 46,* 1251–1257.

Tam, K. (2013). Existential motive underlying cosmetic surgery: A terror management analysis. *Journal of Applied Social Psychology, 43*(5), 947–955. doi:10.1111/jasp.12059

Thompson, G.N., Chochinov, H.M., Wilson, K.G., McPherson, C.J., Chary, S., O'Shea, F.M. . . . Macmillan, K. (2009). Prognostic acceptance and the well-being of patients receiving palliative care for cancer. *Journal of Clinical Oncology, 27*(34), 5757–5762.

Thorson, J.A., & Powell, F.C. (1992). A revised death anxiety scale. *Death Studies, 16,* 507–521.

Thorvaldsson, V., Macdonald, S.W., Fratiglioni, L., Winblad, B., Kivipelto, M., Laukka, E.J., . . . Bäckman, L. (2011). Onset and rate of cognitive change before dementia diagnosis: Findings from two Swedish population-based longitudinal studies. *Journal of the International Neuropsychological Society, 17*(1), 154–162. doi:10.1017/S1355617710001372

Utz, R.L., Caserta, M., & Lund, D. (2012). Grief, depressive symptoms, and physical health among recently bereaved spouses. *The Gerontologist, 52*(4), 460–471. doi:10.1093/geront/gnr110

van Bommel, H. (1992). *Dying for care: Hospice care or euthanasia.* Toronto, ON: NC Press Limited.

van Bommel, H. (2002). *Family hospice care: Pre-planning and care guide* (16th Anniversary Edition). Scarborough, ON: Resources Supporting Family and Community Legacies Inc. Retrieved from www.legacies.ca/Family_Hospice_Care%20Index.htm

Vig, E.K., & Pearlman, R.A.. (2003). Quality of life while dying: A qualitative study of terminally ill older men. *Journal of the American Geriatrics Society, 51*(11), 1595–601.

Watt, N. (2009). *Disabled peer pleads against legalising assisted suicide.* Retrieved from http://www.guardian.co.uk/society/2009/jul/07/disabled-peer-against-assisted-suicide

Wilson, R.S., Segawa, E., Buchman, A.S., Boyle, P.A., Hizel, L.P., & Bennett, D.A. (2012). Terminal decline in motor function. *Psychology and Aging, 27*(4), 998–1007. doi:10.1037/a0028182

Winter, R. (1999). A Biblical and theological view of grief and bereavement. *Journal of Psychology & Christianity, 18,* 367–379.

Wong, P.T.P. (2000). Meaning in life and meaning in death in successful aging. In A. Tomer (Ed.), *Death attitudes and the older adult: Theories, concepts, and applications* (pp. 23–36). Philadelphia, PA: Brunner/Mazel.

Wong, P.T.P. (2003). *From death anxiety to death acceptance: A meaning management model.* Langley, BC: International Network on Personal Meaning. Retrieved from www.meaning.ca/articles/death_acceptance.htm

Zick, C., & Holden, K. (2000). An assessment of the wealth holdings of recent widows. *Journal of Gerontology, 55B,* S90–S97.

Zisook, S., Chentsova-Dutton, Y., & Shuchter, S. (1998). PTSD following bereavement. *Annals of Clinical Psychiatry, 10,* 157–163.

Zisook, S., Iglewicz, A., Avanzino, J., Maglione, J., Glorioso, D., Zetumer, S., . . . Shear, M.K. (2014). Bereavement: Course, consequences, and care. *Current Psychiatry Reports, 16*(10), 482. doi:10.1007/s11920-014-0482-8

Zisook, S., Paulus, M., Shuchter, S., & Judd, L. (1997). The many faces of depression following spousal bereavement. *Journal of Affective Disorders, 45,* 85–94.

Name Index

A

Aaker, J., 507
Abbott, R., 255
Abecassis, M., 280
Abma, J., 300, 391
Abonyi, S., 32
Aboraya, A., 465
Abraham, E., 146
Abu-Bader, S.H., 482
Accardo, P., 67
Acevedo, A., 464
Acker, J., 405
Ackerman, S., 428
Adams, G.R., 345
Adams, P., 203
Adamson, K., 146
Adcox, S., 435
Addis, M., 417
Addy, R., 300
Adelman, W., 295, 296
Adi-Japha, E., 163
Adlaf, E.M., 306
Adolph, E., 94
Adolph, K.E., 5, 96, 98
Adomako, P., 104
Adres, R., 356
Afari, N., 437
Afifi, T.O., 209
Agree, E.M., 488
Agrigoroaei, S., 390
Ahadi, S.A., 270
Aharon-Peretz, J., 242
Ahituv, A., 439, 440
Ahlberg, C., 233
Ahmed, R., 305
Ahn, C., 465
Ahnert, L, 162
Ahola, S., 113
Ainsworth, M.D., 150
Ainsworth, M.D.S., 147, 148, 150
Aitken, M., 436
Aitken Harris, J., 57
Akai, C.E., 211
Akers, J., 343
Akiyama, H., 490, 491
Aknin, L.B., 223
Aksu-Koc, A.A., 139
Al Otaiba, S., 254
Alam, S., 339
Alaphilippe, D., 482
Albareda-Castellot, B., 134
Albersheim, L., 149
Alberts, A., 313
Alderman, M., 416
Alessandri, G., 340
Alfons, V., 390
Ali, J., 309
Allami, Y., 348, 349
Allen, I.E., 95
Allen, J., 367
Allen, M., 257, 391
Allen, M.K., 339

Allen, T.D., 396
Allen, W., 288
Allesandri, S.M., 157
Allgeier, E., 383
Alloway, T.P., 250
Al-Sahab, B., 295
Alsop, S., 502
Alspaugh, J., 316
Alvarado, B., 479
Alzheimer Society of Canada, 462, 463, 465
Amato, P., 364, 386
Amato, P.R., 217
Amato, S., 68
Ambert, A., 215, 216, 217, 385, 386, 387
Ambridge, B., 315
Amenedo, E., 405
American Psychiatric Association, 27, 73, 144, 149, 261, 262, 263, 264, 307, 339, 340, 348, 367, 368, 462, 466, 521
American Psychological Association, 399
Ames, E.W., 144
Amit, M., 106
Amundsen, A., 418
Anastasia, M.L., 85
Ancoli-Israel, S., 460
Anderman, E., 316, 317
Anderman, L., 316, 317
Anderson, C.A., 246
Anderson, C.M., 48
Anderson, D., 155
Anderson, D.R., 288
Anderson, E., 216
Anderson, H., 463, 464
Anderson, J., 172
Anderson, J.R., 399, 489
Anderson, K.G., 146
Anderson, K.M., 415
Anderson, L.M., 172
Anderson, R., 396
Anderson, R.T, 138
Anderson, W.A., 478
Andonotopo, W., 64
Andrade-Navarro, M.A., 444
Andreasen, N.C., 404
Andreou, E., 284
Andrews, M., 421
Aneshensel, C.S., 463
Ang, R., 338
Angleitner, A., 225
Anglin, J.M., 187, 253
Angst, J., 309
Anisfeld, M., 124
Anrig, G., 441
Anteunis, L., 116
Anthony, J.C., 465
Antonsson, A., 414
Antonucci, T., 490, 491
Antrop, I., 263
Anway, M.D., 28
Aoun, S., 505
APA Task Force On Violent Media, 246
Apgar, V.A., 84

Apostolidis, T., 328
Appelbaum, S.L., 458
Applebaum, R.A., 416
Apter-Levi, Y., 146
Aque, C., 211
Arabin, B., 66
Aranha, M., 285
Archer, J., 97
Archibald, L., 135
Arcidiacono, F., 179
Arcus, D., 155
Ardelt, M., 473, 510, 511
Ardern, C.I., 295
Areán, P.A., 466
Arganini, C., 460
Arikan, D., 126
Armbruster, B., 254
Armer, M., 228
Armstrong, T.A., 340
Armstrong-Stassen, M., 438
Arnedt, C., 302
Arnett, J., 390
Arnett, J.J., 380
Arning, L., 171
Arnold, D.H., 190, 191
Arnold, M., 336
Arnold, M.L., 336
Aronen, E.T., 264
Aronow, W., 465
Aronson, J., 130
Aronson, S., 151
Aronsson, G., 440
Arriagada, P., 318, 319
Arterberry, M., 109
Artuso, C., 469
Arvey, R.D., 440
Asbjornsen, A., 101
Aschersleben, G, 127
Asendorpf, J.B., 157
Ashenhurst, J.R., 369
Asher, S.R., 280, 287
Ashkar, P., 338
Ashkenazi, S., 251
Aslam, M., 101
Aslin, R., 106, 114
Aslin, R.N., 132
Astbury, N.M., 460
Astington, J., 182
Astington, J.W., 182, 185
Astor, R., 283
Atalayer, D., 460
Atasoy, S., 243
Atchley, R., 479
Atkins, H.L., 444
Atkinson, L., 205
Attar-Schwartz, S., 435
Atterberry, M., 111
Atwood, S., 246
Atzil, S., 146
Audet, K., 144
Audet, K.N., 144
Auerback, S., 4

Human Resources Development Canada, 15, 159, 216, 319
Humphrey, N., 259
Humphreys, A., 97
Hunsley, J., 468
Hunt, J., 309
Hunter, D.J., 414
Hunter, J., 346
Hunter, Z., 369
Huntington Society of Canada, 68
Husain, F.T., 458
Huston, A., 151
Huston, A.C., 237, 288
Hutchinson, S.L., 480
Huth-Bocks, A., 152
Huth-Bocks, A.C., 149
Hutt, M., 391
Huxhold, O., 481
Hyatt, D., 160
Hyde, J., 328
Hyde, J.S., 97, 338

I

Iacono, W.G., 306
Ibrahim, D., 486
Ide, J.S., 404
Idler, E., 485
Idler, E.L., 484
Ierardi-Curto, L., 68
Incrocci, L, 409
Ingersoll-Dayton, B., 481
Ingoldsby, E., 215
Inhelder, B., 40, 312, 313
Inoue, M., 511
Insured Retirement Institute, 441
International Cancer Genome Consortium, 31
International Human Epigenome Consortium, 31
Ippolito, M., 309
Ipsos-Reid/*Globe And Mail*, 396
Ireson, J., 189
Irwin, M., 358
Isaacowitz, D. M., 13
Isabella, R.A., 151
Isles, A.R., 28
Issanchou, S., 108
Ito, Y, 488
Ivanova, K., 345
Iverson, K.M., 364
Iverson, T., 10
Ivorra, C., 72
Ivy, G.O., 356
Iwashyna, T., 489
Izard, C.E., 157

J

Jablonka, E., 28, 31
Jackson, A., 238, 319
Jackson, L., 273
Jackson, S.E., 409
Jacobs, J., 393
Jacobs-Kosmin, D., 409
Jacques, E., 428
Jacques, S., 184, 252
Jacquet, A., 168
Jadack, R.A., 338
Jaffee, S., 391
Jaglal, S., 410
Jain, M., 414

Jalovaara, M., 387
Jambon, M., 204
James, A., 101
James, J.B., 437
Jampol, N., 277
Jang, K.L., 57
Jang, S.J., 343
Jankowski, J., 130
Jansen, P.G.W., 438
Janson, L.J., 505
Janssen, I., 288, 299
Janssens, J., 279
Jansz, J., 343
Janz, T., 309, 461
Japal, C., 296
Japel, C., 160
Jarolmen, J., 518
Jarrold, C., 252
Jarusawad, O., 484
Jarvenpaa, A., 152
Jasik, C., 296
Jawahar, M.C., 175
Jedrziewski, M.K., 455
Jefferies, A.L., 101
Jeffery, L., 113
Jelínek, M., 155
Jenkins, J., 182, 212, 518
Jenkins, J.M., 182, 212
Jennen-Steinmetz, C., 85
Jensen, F.E., 305
Jensen, L.A., 380
Jensen, P., 28
Jernigan, T.L., 169
Jeschonek, S., 127
Jewell, J., 69
Jeynes, W., 216
Jiang, D., 345
Jilek, W.G., 307
Jimenez, M.E., 175
Jin, K., 450
Joanisse, M., 135
Joels, T., 162
Joeng, J., 393
Johansson, B., 512
John, O., 430
John, O.P., 270, 436
John P. Robarts Research Institute, 32
Johnson, A., 445
Johnson, B., 211
Johnson, B.R., 343
Johnson, B.T., 301
Johnson, C., 150
Johnson, E., 85
Johnson, H., 365
Johnson, J.A., 56, 74, 358
Johnson, J.M., 459
Johnson, M., 64, 92, 154
Johnson, M.D., 392, 399
Johnson, M.H., 93
Johnson, P., 262
Johnson, P.A, 24
Johnson, S., 130
Johnston, A.M., 255
Johnston, C., 103
Johnston, C.C., 103
Johnston, N., 521
Jones, B.K., 428
Jones, J.M., 308
Jones, L.E., 265
Jones, R., 343

Jordan, N., 518
Jordan, N.C., 192
Jorgensen, G., 337
Jose, O., 390
Joseph, R., 63
Josephson, W.L., 123
Jospe, N., 27
Joy, S., 390
Judd, F.K., 408
Judd, L., 520
Juffer, F., 144
Júlvez, J., 131
Jung, Y., 451
Jusczyk, P., 134

K

Kaciroti, N., 182
Kagan, J., 153, 155
Kahana-Kalman, R., 157, 177
Kahle, L.R., 248, 249
Kahn, A., 449
Kahn, R.L., 480
Kahn, R.S., 123
Kail, R., 185, 242, 250, 314
Kaiser, A.P., 237
Kalapatapu, R., 418
Kalish, R.A., 508
Kallman, D.A., 356, 357
Kalmijn, M., 431, 436
Kalmuss, D., 366
Kalter, H., 76
Kaminsky, Z., 28
Kaminsky, Z.A., 57
Kamp Dush, C.M., 489
Kamphuis, J.H., 284
Kandhadai, P., 114
Kandler, C., 436
Kane, A., 173
Kane, T., 364
Kanfer, R., 438
Kaniuk, J., 152
Kann, L., 302
Kannayiram, A., 465
Kannel, W.B., 415
Kanouse, D., 301
Kao, K., 153
Kaplan, D., 192
Kaplan, G.A., 360
Kaplan, H., 364, 366
Kaplowitz, P., 296
Kapoor, S., 295
Karasik, L.B., 96
Karlsson, M., 505
Karney, B., 384
Karney, B.R., 488
Karp, J., 212
Karreman, A., 225
Karrison, T., 83
Kasén, A., 505
Kasen, S., 468
Kasl, S., 485
Kaslow, F., 519
Kato, M., 343
Kattimani, S., 310, 311
Katz, P., 517
Katz, P.A., 328
Kaufman, M., 146
Kaufman, P., 423
Kaur, R., 440
Kavšek, M., 130

Subject Index